| | GROSS REAL DOMESTIC PRODUCT | | PRICES AND INFLATION | | | |
| | | | GDP DEFLATOR | | CONSUMER PRICE INDEX | |
YEAR	BILLIONS OF 1987 DOLLARS	ANNUAL RATE OF CHANGE	INDEX (1987 = 100)	ANNUAL PERCENTAGE CHANGE	INDEX (1982–84 = 100)	PERCENTAGE CHANGE (DEC. TO DEC.)
1929	821.8	—	12.5	—	17.1	0.0
1939	840.7	7.9	10.8	−0.9	13.9	1.4
1949	1,305.5	0.4	19.9	−0.5	23.8	−1.8
1956	1,803.6	2.0	23.6	3.1	27.2	2.9
1957	1,838.2	1.9	24.4	3.4	28.1	3.0
1958	1,829.1	−0.5	24.9	2.0	28.9	1.8
1959	1,928.8	5.5	25.6	2.8	29.1	1.7
1960	1,970.8	2.2	26.0	1.6	29.6	1.4
1961	2,023.8	2.7	26.3	1.2	29.9	0.7
1962	2,128.1	5.2	26.9	2.3	30.2	1.3
1963	2,251.6	4.1	27.2	1.1	30.6	1.6
1964	2,340.6	5.6	27.7	1.8	31.0	1.0
1965	2,470.5	5.5	28.4	2.5	31.5	1.9
1966	2,617.2	5.9	29.4	3.5	32.4	3.5
1967	2,685.2	2.6	30.3	3.1	33.4	3.0
1968	2,796.9	4.2	31.8	5.0	34.8	4.7
1969	2,873.0	2.7	33.4	5.0	36.7	6.2
1970	2,873.9	0.0	35.2	5.4	38.8	5.6
1971	2,955.9	2.9	37.1	5.4	40.5	3.3
1972	3,107.1	5.1	38.8	4.6	41.8	3.4
1973	3,268.6	5.2	41.3	6.4	44.4	8.7
1974	3,248.1	−0.6	44.9	8.7	49.3	12.3
1975	3,221.7	−0.8	49.2	9.6	53.8	6.9
1976	3,380.8	4.9	52.3	6.3	56.9	4.9
1977	3,533.9	4.5	55.9	6.9	60.6	6.7
1978	3,703.5	4.8	60.3	7.9	65.2	9.0
1979	3,796.8	2.5	65.5	8.6	72.6	13.3
1980	3,776.3	−0.5	71.7	9.5	82.4	12.5
1981	3,843.1	1.8	78.9	10.0	90.9	8.9
1982	3,760.3	−2.2	83.8	6.2	96.5	3.8
1983	3,906.3	3.9	87.2	4.1	99.6	3.8
1984	4,148.5	6.2	91.0	4.4	103.9	3.9
1985	4,279.8	3.2	94.4	3.7	107.6	3.8
1986	4,404.5	2.9	96.9	2.6	109.6	1.1
1987	4,539.9	3.1	100.0	3.2	113.6	4.4
1988	4,718.6	3.9	103.9	3.9	118.3	4.4
1989	4,838.0	2.5	108.5	4.4	124.0	4.6
1990	4,897.3	1.2	113.3	4.4	130.7	6.1
1991	4,861.4	−0.7	117.7	3.9	136.2	3.1
1992	4,986.3	2.6	121.1	2.9	140.3	2.9
1993	5,132.7	2.9	124.2	2.5	144.5	2.7

Source: *Economic Report of the President*, (1970 and 1994).

ECONOMICS
PRIVATE AND PUBLIC CHOICE

SEVENTH EDITION

JAMES D. GWARTNEY
Florida State University

RICHARD L. STROUP
Montana State University

with the assistance of
A. H. STUDENMUND
Occidental College

THE DRYDEN PRESS
Harcourt Brace College Publishers

Fort Worth   Philadelphia   San Diego   New York   Orlando   Austin   San Antonio
Toronto   Montreal   London   Sydney   Tokyo

Acquisitions Editor	Rick Hammonds
Developmental Editor	Jeanie Anirudhan
Project Editor	Sheila M. Spahn
Art Director	Melinda Huff
Production Manager	Mandy Manzano
Permissions and Photo Research Editor	Elizabeth Banks
Editorial Assistant	Virginia Warren
Product Manager	Craig Johnson
Marketing Assistant	Kathleen Sharp
Director of Editing, Design, and Production	Diane Southworth
Publisher	Elizabeth Widdicombe
Copyeditor	Maggie Jarpey
Indexer	Michael Ferriera
Compositor	Monotype Composition Company, Inc.
Text Type	10/12 Palatino
Cover Photo	© Eva Rubenstein/Photonica

Address for orders:
The Dryden Press
6277 Sea Harbor Drive
Orlando, FL 32887
1-800-782-4479 or 1-800-433-0001 (in Florida)

Address for editorial correspondence:
The Dryden Press
301 Commerce Street, Suite 3700
Fort Worth, TX 76102

ISBN: 0-03-098345-2

Library of Congress Catalog Card Number: 94-77470

Photo Credits appear on pages 1041-1042,
which constitute a continuation of the copyright page.

Printed in the United States of America

5 6 7 8 9 0 1 2 3 048 10 9 8 7 6 5 4 3 2

The Dryden Press
Harcourt Brace College Publishers

THE DRYDEN PRESS SERIES
IN ECONOMICS

Nicholson
INTERMEDIATE MICROECONOMICS
AND ITS APPLICATION
Sixth Edition

Nicholson
MICROECONOMIC THEORY: BASIC
PRINCIPLES AND EXTENSIONS
Sixth Edition

Puth
AMERICAN ECONOMIC HISTORY
Third Edition

Ragan and Thomas
PRINCIPLES OF ECONOMICS
*Second Edition (also available in micro
and macro paperbacks)*

Ramanathan
INTRODUCTORY ECONOMETRICS WITH
APPLICATIONS
Third Edition

Rukstad
CORPORATE DECISION MAKING IN THE
WORLD ECONOMY: COMPANY CASE
STUDIES

Rukstad
MACROECONOMIC DECISION MAKING IN
THE WORLD ECONOMY: TEXT AND CASES
Fourth Edition

Samuelson and Marks
MANAGERIAL ECONOMICS
Second Edition

Scarth
MACROECONOMICS: AN INTRODUCTION
TO ADVANCED METHODS
Third Edition

Thomas
ECONOMICS: PRINCIPLES AND
APPLICATIONS
*(also available in micro and macro
paperbacks)*

Wachtel
LABOR AND THE ECONOMY
Third Edition

Walton and Rockoff
HISTORY OF THE AMERICAN
ECONOMY
Seventh Edition

Welch and Welch
ECONOMICS: THEORY AND PRACTICE
Fifth Edition

Yarbrough and Yarbrough
THE WORLD ECONOMY: TRADE AND
FINANCE
Third Edition

PREFACE

This is an exciting time to study economics. While the former socialist countries of Eastern Europe and the former Soviet Union search for an alternative form of economic organization more consistent with economic prosperity, several countries of Latin America, Asia, and Africa are in the midst of economic and political change that will influence the future shape of the world. As Europe moves toward political and economic unification, North America is now committed to the development of a common economic market. Basic economic analysis enhances our understanding of these forces, helping to clarify their impact on our lives.

Perhaps more than any other science, economics is about people and how change influences their lives. Why do some people prosper, while others live on the edge of starvation? Why are people in some countries generally more successful than seemingly similar people in other countries? Will the adoption of democratic political institutions improve economic conditions? Is economic activity destroying the environment of planet Earth and, if so, what can be done about it? As we proceed, we will use the tools of economics to address these and many other important issues that affect our lives.

SEVENTH EDITION

As in previous editions, our central objective is to help the reader develop the economic way of thinking. While this method of thinking is in many ways simply common sense, it is a powerful tool of analysis when woven together in a logical manner. The material of this textbook is designed to stimulate students, challenge their reasoning ability, and teach them to think like economists. We use examples to illustrate the power and relevance of economic analysis, and real-world data to analyze and illustrate the implications of economic theory. We think this approach will enliven the study of economics for both the student and the teacher.

Our experience writing about and teaching economics for over two decades has made us aware of a challenging fact: many things that seem so obvious to professional economists are extremely complex for even the best students of economics. Thus, we must not take it for granted that students will necessarily grasp points that are straightforward to us. The key concepts of economics must be reinforced. We have incorporated a number of features into this edition in order to make the textbook more accessible for students. First, selective use of pictures and cartoons designed to illuminate various concepts appear throughout the textbook. These visual aids add meaning to the concepts. Second, we have expanded the Myths of Economics series. Several users have informed us that this is their students' favorite feature. In our own teaching, we have found that casting a fallacious economic idea in the form of a myth (and explaining why the view is incorrect) is a useful teaching device. Finally, we have expanded the use of tables and graphics presenting empirical evidence on the validity of various theories. Comparisons across countries are often used to enrich this material.

Even more than in the past, the Seventh Edition highlights the linkage between the basic principles of economics and of economic progress. In our effort to cover an abundance of material, we sometimes fail to describe the importance of a relatively small number of factors that are central to the understanding of economic progress. Division of labor, mass-production methods, specialization and comparative advantage, capital formation, and improvements in technology provide the foundation of our modern living standards. This edition analyzes how the realization of gains from these sources is influenced by various economic policies and institutions. In addition, many of the exercises at the end of each chapter are designed to clarify the relationship between the basic concepts of economics and prosperity of nations.

While economists do not have a complete theory of growth and development, we do know several of the ingredients that are principal to the economic success of nations. Chapter 33 focuses on development and growth, considers these ingredients, and analyzes how the policies of the high- and low-growth countries differ. This chapter will help students assimilate some of the most important lessons of economics and simultaneously enhance their understanding of the wealth and poverty of nations.

The textual material in Chapter 34 is almost entirely new, focusing on the transitional economies of Eastern Europe and the former Soviet Union. The reasons for the failure of central planning and the problems confronting these countries are analyzed in detail. People sometimes tend to think that these countries confront similar problems and that they have followed similar transitional strategies. This is not the case. Chapter 34 is substantially enriched by Professor Gwartney's recent teaching experience at Central European University in the Czech Republic, and his work with some of the brightest students from almost all of the former socialist countries.

CHANGES IN THE CORE MACROECONOMICS

Modern macroeconomics stresses the importance of (a) expectations and decision-making in an uncertain world, (b) microeconomic elements (for example, search theory and the incentive effects of relative price changes) that influence outcomes in aggregated markets, (c) whether a change is anticipated or unanticipated, (d) interrelations among aggregate markets, (e) whether a change is expected to be temporary or permanent, and (f) differences between the long-run and short-run effects of a macroeconomic change. Our approach reflects this modern view.

While the organization of the core macroeconomics is basically the same as for the previous edition, almost every chapter has been extensively revised. The following list highlights some of the specific changes.

- Reflecting the recent shift to gross domestic product (GDP) as the primary measure of output, the GDP data are featured throughout the core macro. Chapter 6 indicates the difference between GDP and GNP and explains how both are derived. Data on the differences between the two measures are presented for several countries.

■ Chapters 8 and 9 present the basic aggregate-demand/aggregate-supply model used throughout the core macro. We strived to make this material both more interesting and more easily understandable for the student.

■ Students are increasingly interested in the economies of other countries—their performance record and how their economic organization and policies differ from those of the United States. The core macro of this edition focuses on this issue at length and presents data on macro policy indicators (for example, money growth, budget deficits, and taxes) and economic performance (price stability, employment, and growth of output) across countries.

■ Given the global nature of modern economies, international financial markets are of increasing importance. This edition explains in more detail how these markets work and presents data on how currency controls and other financial trade restrictions influence the growth and prosperity of nations.

■ The Myths of Economics series is expanded in the core macro. For example, the myths that trade restrictions benefit domestic economies (Chapter 31), that inflation systematically helps borrowers (Chapter 8), and that inflation is caused by greedy business and labor leaders (Chapter 13) have been added in this edition.

CHANGES IN THE CORE MICROECONOMICS

■ Our discussion of the size and importance of brand name capital has been expanded in Chapter 17. Estimates of the value of that capital for some major firms have been included to illustrate the size and importance of this marketing factor.

■ Our explanation (in Chapter 18) of the discipline placed by stock market price changes on corporate executives and boards of directors is enlarged in this edition. The discussion incorporates the example of changes at Eastman Kodak in August 1993, that led to a surge in Eastman's stock price.

■ Data on lobbying groups' spending, and on lobbyists' salaries has been incorporated into our discussion of rent-seeking costs in Chapter 20, underscoring for students the magnitude and importance of these activities.

■ Business failure is often in the news. We have added a box feature on the positive role played by business failure in a market economy, and the need for such failure in any economy experiencing progress (Chapter 21).

DISTINGUISHING FEATURES OF OUR APPROACH

Difficult language and new terminology often hinder successful learning. Without sacrificing accuracy, we employ simple and readable language and use examples and illustrations to reinforce basic concepts. Simplicity, however, is not substituted for depth. Rather, our aim is to highlight the power, accessibility, and relevance of economic concepts. We believe that the economics required for the 1990s can be comprehensible to the student as well as challenging and applicable to the real world.

Economic reasoning is central to our approach. Although models, theories, and exercises are important, they are only tools with which to develop the economic way of thinking. We have avoided abstractions and mechanical exercises that obscure basic concepts. Instead, we have integrated applications and real-world data in an effort to make the basic concepts come alive for the reader.

The tools of economics are relevant to both the market and political processes. Most textbooks tell students how an ideal market economy would operate, how real-world markets differ from the hypothetical ideal, and how ideal public policy can correct the shortcomings of the market. In addition to discussing these three basic issues, we apply the tools of economics to the collective decision-making process and consider the types of policies that are likely to emerge from this process. We believe that this approach enlivens the study of economics.

ORGANIZATIONAL FEATURES

We have engaged several organizational features designed to make the presentation both more interesting and more understandable.

1. *Myths of Economics*   In a series of boxed articles, commonly held fallacies of economic reasoning are dispelled. Each myth is followed by a concise explanation of why it is incorrect and each appears within a chapter containing closely related material.

2. *Applications in Economics*   These boxed features apply economic theory to real-world issues and controversies. They add breadth on topics of special interest and illustrate the relevance of basic principles to the world in which we live.

3. *Measures of Economic Activity*   Measurement is an important element of economics. These features explain how important economic indicators such as the Consumer Price Index, unemployment rate, and index of leading indicators are assembled.

4. *Chapter Focus Questions and Closing Summaries*   Each chapter begins with several questions that summarize the focus of the chapter. A summary, which provides the student with a concise statement of the material (chapter learning objectives), appears at the end of each chapter. Reviewing the focus questions and chapter summaries will help the student better understand the material and integrate it into the broader economic picture.

5. *Key Terms*   The terminology of economics is often confusing to introductory students. Key terms are introduced in the text in bold-faced type; simultaneously, each term is defined in the margin opposite the first reference to the term. A glossary containing the key terms also appears at the end of the book.

6. *Critical-Analysis Questions*   Each chapter concludes with a set of discussion questions designed to test the student's ability to analyze an economic problem and to apply economic theory to real-world events. Appendix C at the end of the textbook contains suggested answers for approximately half of the critical-analysis questions. We

think these answers, illustrating the power of economics, will interest students, encouraging them to develop the economic way of thinking.

SUPPLEMENTARY MATERIALS

COURSEBOOK

Prepared by Professor A. H. Studenmund of Occidental College, the Coursebook is more than a study guide. It includes numerous multiple-choice, true-false, and discussion questions permitting students to self-test their knowledge of each chapter. Answers and short explanations for most questions are provided in the back of the Coursebook. Each chapter also contains problem and project exercises designed to improve the student's knowledge of the mechanics. A set of short readings chosen to supplement the classroom teaching of important topics is also included in the Coursebook. Several of the readings are arranged in a debate format and cover areas of controversy in economics. Discussion questions follow each article, challenging students to demonstrate their understanding of the material and their ability to distinguish a sound argument from economic nonsense. Like the textbook, the Coursebook is designed to help students develop the economic way of thinking.

TESTBANK

The Testbanks for the Seventh Edition of *Macroeconomics* and *Microeconomics* were prepared by Russell Sobel, Edward Bierhanzl, and J. J. Bethune. They contain approximately 7,500 questions—multiple choice and short answer—most of which have been extensively tested in the classroom. Within each chapter, the questions correspond to the major subheadings of the text. The Testbank is available on computer disk for IBM and Macintosh users. The ExaMaster system accompanying the Computerized Testbank makes it easy to create tests, print scrambled versions of the same test, modify questions, and reproduce any of the large number of graphic questions.

INSTRUCTOR'S MANUAL/TRANSPARENCY MASTERS

The Instructor's Manual/TM was prepared by Professor Gary Galles of Pepperdine University. It is divided into three parts. The first part, which is also available on computer disk, is a detailed outline of each chapter in lecture-note form. It is designed to help instructors organize and structure their current lecture notes according to the format of the Seventh Edition of *Economics: Private and Public Choice*. Instructors can easily prepare a detailed, personalized set of notes by revising the computerized form of the notes. The second part of the Instructor's Manual contains teaching tips, sources of supplementary materials, and other helpful information. The third part provides instructors with several games designed to illustrate and enliven important economic concepts. Suggested answers to most of the critical-analysis questions that were not answered in Appendix C of the textbook are also provided in the Instructor's Manual. Transparency Masters of some major exhibits are also available.

COLOR TRANSPARENCIES

Color transparencies of the major exhibits of the Seventh Edition have been especially prepared for overhead projectors. They are available to adopters upon request for Macroeconomics and Microeconomics.

TUTORIAL, ANALYTICAL, AND GRAPHICAL (TAG) SOFTWARE

This award-winning software by Todd Porter and Teresa Riley of Youngstown State University has been significantly enhanced to contain an extensive chapter-by-chapter tutorial, a hands-on graphic section where students are actually required to draw curves (with key strokes or a mouse) and a practice exam for each section. Students receive feedback on their answers. Available in IBM versions.

VIDEO PACKAGES

The *Economics in Focus* video series facilitates multi-level learning and critical thinking through its up-to-date coverage of current events in our society, while focusing on the economic issues important to students and their understanding of the economy. Recent segments from *MacNeil/Lehrer News Hour* are updated quarterly.

These videos look at three major themes:

- International Economic Scene covers free trade, foreign policy, and other issues.
- Economic Challenges and Problems explores topics such as declining incomes, the budget deficit, and inflation.
- The Political Economy looks at the role of the government, free enterprise, and economic stabilization.

Each segment of *Economics in Focus* closes with a special feature story or one-to-one interview with a noted economist.

Milton Friedman's *Free to Choose* video series is available in 10 half-hour videotapes. These videos update the earlier series, *Milton Friedman Speaks*, by including introductions by Arnold Schwarzenegger, George Schultz, Steve Allen, David Friedman, and Ronald Reagan.

LASER DISCS

These discs focus on the core principles of macro and micro economics and present the information interactively. A brief 5 to 7 minute video from CBS begins each learning section. Related animated graphics follow. Once students understand the concepts, they are then challenged with critical-thinking questions. A printed Media Instructor's Manual explains how the laser disc coordinates with the text.

ACKNOWLEDGMENTS

Creating a project of this caliber is a team effort. Several people contributed substantially to the development of this edition. Once again, Woody Studenmund of Occidental College prepared the Coursebook and provided valuable direction and insightful comments. As in the prior edition, Gary Galles of Pepperdine University authored the Instructor's Manual. The teaching tips and special games (and projects) contained in the manual reflect his creativity, communication skills, and talent for the teaching of economics.

We would also like to express our appreciation to J. J. Bethune, Edward Bierhanzl, and Russell Sobel for their preparation of the Testbank accompanying the textbook, and the generous encouragement they have provided. Barbara Morgan provided us with excellent assistance and helped us update several empirical sections.

We also owe a special debt to the faculty and students in the Economics Department of Central European University. During Professor Gwartney's tenure on the CEU faculty during 1993–94, they provided both helpful comments and an academic environment that enhanced the quality of this edition, particularly those chapters related to economic growth and transitional economies. The contributions of Professors John S. Earle and Christof Ruehl were particularly significant.

We have often revised material in light of suggestions made by reviewers, users, friends, and even a few competitors. In this regard, we would like to express our appreciation to the following people for their contributions to the Seventh Edition: Donald Alexander, Western Michigan University; John Erkklia, Lake Superior State University; Robert Puth, University of New Hampshire; Howard Wall, West Virginia University; Shyam L. Bhatia, Indiana University—Northwest; John Lajauine, Nicholls State University; Thaxter Dickey, Florida College; Richard Coffman, University of Idaho.

Valuable comments were made in previous editions by Paul Azrak, Queensborough Community College; Jacqueline Kasun, Humboldt State University; Norlin Masih, St. Cloud State University; Richard Torz, SUNY—Queens College; Lucinda Coulter-Burbach, Seminole Community College; Sue Hayes, Sonoma State; Fred Goddard, University of Florida; Larry Lichtenstein, Canisius College; Jeffrey Herbener, Washington and Jefferson College; Lawrence Martin, Michigan State University; J. P. Egan, University of Wisconsin, Eau Claire; Michael White, St. Cloud State University; Dona A. Derr, Rutgers College; Don Millman, Itasca Community College; Nathan Eric Hampton, St. Cloud State University; D. E. Morris, University of New Hampshire; James T. Bennett, George Mason University; Jeffrey Young, St. Lawrence University; Sam Osemene, Prairie View A&M University; Harold Katz, United States Merchant Marine Academy; James Wible, University of New Hampshire; Frank Scott, University of Kentucky; John Neal, Lake Sumter Community College; Wilson Mixon, Berry College; James Long, Auburn University; Denise Rogers, Arizona Western College; Patrick McMurry, Missouri Western State College; William Jahn, American Institute of Business; David Emery, St. Olaf College; Joseph M. Lammert, Raymond Walters College; Abdalla Gergis, Framingham State College; Darrell Irvin, Spokane Community College; Ken Somppi, Auburn University; Seren Burg, Eastern Michigan University; James A. Dunlevy, Miami University; Michael Loewy, George Washington University; John C. McCarthy, Armstrong State College; Eric N. Baklanoff, University of Alabama; William Steiden, Bellarmine College; Julia Lee, University of Louisville; Marshall Edwards, Armstrong State College; John Leevries, Brainerd Community College; Pati Crabb, Bellarmine College; Terry R. Ridgway, University of Nevada, Las Vegas; Dale Bails, Memphis State; Luther D. Lawson, University of North Carolina—Wilmington; Jack Morgan, University of North Carolina—Wilmington; William Sher, Duquesne University; Kevin C. Sontheimer, University of Pittsburgh; Kurt Rethwisch, Duquesne University; Marsha Goldfarb, University of Maryland—Baltimore County; Arthur Janssa, Emporia State University; Chas C. Milliken, Siena Heights College; Thomas Wyrick, Southwest Missouri State University; Jim Scheib, Red Rocks Community College; Alan Sleeman, Western Washington University; Robert E. Williams, The School of the Ozarks; Anthony Yezer, George Washington University; L. Aubrey Drewery, Birmingham Southern College; Ernest M. Buchholz, Santa Monica College; Shirley Svorny, California State University—Northridge; Henry Demmert, Santa Clara University; C. Fred DeKay, Seattle University; David O.

Whitten, Auburn University; Randall G. Holcombe, Florida State University; Ralph Bristol, University of New Hampshire—Durham.

We are also indebted to the excellent team of professionals at The Dryden Press. Rick Hammonds, senior acquisitions editor; Jeanie Anirudhan, developmental editor; and Sheila M. Spahn, senior project editor provided us with editorial assistance and encouragement. We would also like to thank Mandy Manzano, senior production manager; Elizabeth Banks, picture developmental editor; Melinda Huff, art director; and Craig Johnson, product manager, who have worked together to create the finest edition of this textbook yet. Finally, we would like to acknowledge the assistance of Valerie Colvin, Amy Gwartney, and Jane Shaw Stroup, all of whom contributed in numerous ways to the success of this project. Without their assistance and encouragement, we would have been unable to meet the demands and deadlines of this project.

A NOTE TO STUDENTS

This textbook contains several features that we think will help you maximize (a good economics term) the returns derived from your study effort. Our past experience indicates that awareness of the following points will help you use the book more effectively.

Each chapter begins with a series of focus questions which communicate the central issues of the chapter. Before you read the chapter, briefly think about the focus questions, why they are important, and how they relate to the material of prior chapters.

The textbook is organized in the form of an outline. The headings within the text are the major points of the outline. Minor headings are subpoints under the major headings. In addition, important subpoints within sections are often set off and numbered. Sometimes thumbnail sketches are used to help the reader better organize important points. Careful use of the headings and thumbnail sketches will help you better visualize the organization of the material.

A summary appears at the end of each chapter. Use the summary as a check-list to determine whether or not you understand the major points of the chapter.

Review of the exhibits will also provide you with a summary of each chapter. The accompanying legend briefly describes the content and analysis of each exhibit. After studying the chapter, briefly review the exhibits to ensure that you have mastered the central points.

The key terms introduced in each chapter are in boldfaced type and defined in the margins. As you study the chapter, go over the marginal definition of each key term as it is introduced. Later, you may also find it useful to review the marginal definitions. If you have forgotten the meaning of a term introduced earlier, consult the glossary at the end of the book.

The boxed features provide additional depth on various topics without disrupting the flow of the text. In general, the boxed feature topics were chosen because of their relevance as an application of the theory or because of past student interest in the topic. Reading the boxed features will supplement the text and enhance your understanding of important economic concepts.

The critical-analysis questions at the end of each chapter are intended to test your understanding of the economic way of thinking. They provide you with another opportunity to review each chapter. Working these questions and problems will greatly enhance your knowledge of the material. Answers to approximately half of these questions are provided in Appendix C.

If you would like more practice, be sure to obtain a Coursebook and work the questions and problems for each chapter. The Coursebook also contains the answers to the multiple-choice questions and a brief explanation of why an answer is correct (and why other choices are incorrect). In most cases, if you master the concepts of the test items in the Coursebook, you will do well on your instructor's quizzes and examinations.

APPLICATIONS IN ECONOMICS

MEASURES OF

ECONOMIC ACTIVITY

MYTHS OF ECONOMICS

CONTENTS IN BRIEF

CONTENTS

PART ONE

THE ECONOMIC WAY OF THINKING – AN INTRODUCTION

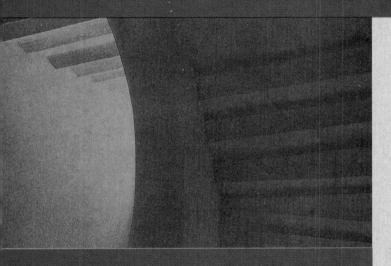

CHAPTER ONE

THE ECONOMIC APPROACH

[Economics] is not a body of concrete truth, but an engine for the discovery of concrete truth.

ALFRED MARSHALL[1]

CHAPTER FOCUS

■ *Why is scarcity a key economic concept, even in an affluent economy?*
■ *How does scarcity differ from poverty?*
■ *What are the basics underlying the economic way of thinking? What is different about the way economists look at choices and human decision-making?*
■ *What is the difference between positive and normative economics?*

[1]Alfred Marshall, *The Present Position of Economics*, 1885, p. 25.

his is an exciting time to study economics. Recent political campaigns in the United States have centered on economic issues such as budget deficits, the structure and level of taxes, and policies toward international trade. Economic issues also occupy center stage in other countries. The market economies of Western Europe are struggling to develop a single integrated economy with a common currency and legal structure. The countries of Eastern Europe and the former Soviet Union are trying to figure out how to convert from socialist central planning to market-directed economies. In both Latin America and Africa, people are searching for an economic prescription that will generate prosperity and upgrade living standards.

Simultaneously, the economies around the world are becoming more and more interrelated. Many of the goods at your favorite shopping mall are produced, at least in part, by people who speak a different language and live in a country far from your own. Similarly, many Americans work for companies that market their products in Europe, Japan, Latin America, or Africa. Ownership shares of American companies are traded not only in New York, but also on stock exchanges in London, Tokyo, and throughout the world.

How will our current economic policies and rapidly changing world affect the economic status of Americans? What impact will the globalization of our economy have on our living standards, lifestyles, and future opportunities? This book will help you better understand the world in which you live. This is not to imply that economics provides easy answers for problems. As Alfred Marshall stated more than a century ago, economics is a discovery process—a way of thinking—rather than "a body of concrete truth" (see chapter opening quote). In fact, economics is more likely to reveal the limitations of "grand design" proposals than it is to offer one. Nonetheless, "economic thinking" is a powerful tool that can help you understand a broad range of real-world events. Our goals are to communicate the basics of economics and to illustrate their relevance to a changing world.

WHAT IS ECONOMICS ABOUT?

[Economics is] the science which studies human behavior as a relationship between ends and scarce means which have alternative uses.

LIONEL ROBBINS [2]

Economics is about people and the choices they make. The unit of analysis in economics is the individual. Of course, individuals group together to form collective organizations such as corporations, labor unions, and governments. Individual choices, however, still underlie and direct these organizations. Thus, even when we study collective organizations, we will focus on the ways in which their operation is affected by the choices of individuals.

---

[2]Lionel Robbins, *An Essay on the Nature and Significance of Economic Science,* 1932.

SCARCITY AND CHOICE

Would you like some new clothes, a nicer car, and a larger apartment? How about better grades and more time to watch television, go skiing, and travel abroad? Most of us would like more of all of these goods. The human desire for goods is virtually unlimited. We cannot, however, have more of everything. Both individually and collectively we face a constraint called **scarcity,** the most basic concept in economics, meaning that people's desire for things is far greater than what is freely available from nature. Since scarcity prevents us from having as much as we would like of **economic goods,** or goods that are scarce, we are forced to choose among a restricted set of potential alternatives. **Choice,** therefore, the act of selecting among alternatives, is the logical consequence of scarcity. These two—scarcity and choice—are the basic ingredients of an economic topic.

Resources are inputs that we use to produce goods. In essence, they are tools that we can use to battle scarcity. There are three general categories of resources. First, there are human resources, the productive knowledge, skill, and strength of human beings. Second, there are physical resources, things like tools, machines, and buildings that enhance our ability to produce goods. Economists often use the term *capital* when referring to these man-made resources. Third, there are natural resources—things like land, mineral deposits, oceans, and rivers. The ingenuity of humans is often required in order to transform these natural resources into useful productive inputs.

With the passage of time, investment activities can increase the availability of resources; but more investment requires the sacrifice of additional current consumption. If we use more of today's resources to produce education and skill enhancement, or tools, machines, and factories, then fewer resources will be available to produce goods for consumption now. Economics is about trade-offs. **Exhibit 1–1** lists some desired goods and limited resources.

During the last 250 years, we have loosened the grip of scarcity a little. Think for a moment what life was like in 1750. People all over the world struggled 50, 60, and 70 hours a week to obtain the basic necessities of life—food, clothing, and shelter. Manual labor was the major source of energy. Animals provided the means of transportation. Tools and machines were primitive by today's standards. As the English philosopher Thomas Hobbes put it, life was "solitary, poor, nasty, brutish, and short."

Throughout much of South America, Africa, and Asia, economic conditions continue to be exceedingly difficult. In North America, Western Europe, Oceania, and some parts of Asia however, substantial economic progress has been made. Of course, scarcity is still a fact of life in these areas, too; the desire for goods and services still far outstrips the ability of people to produce them. But from a material standpoint, life is now far less grueling. Modern energy sources and means of transportation are available there. Subsistence levels of food, shelter, and clothing are taken for granted, and the typical family there can worry instead about financing summer vacations, obtaining videocassette recorders, and providing for the children's college education.

It is important to note that scarcity and poverty are not the same thing. Poverty implies some basic level of need, either in absolute or relative terms. Absence of poverty means that the basic level has been attained. In contrast, the absence of scarcity would imply that we have as much of all goods as we would like. Both individuals and countries may win the battle against poverty—people may achieve income levels that allow them to satisfy a basic level of need. But it is

Scarcity
Fundamental concept of economics which indicates that less of a good is freely available than consumers would like.

Economic good
A good that is scarce. The desire for economic goods exceeds the amount that is freely available from nature.

Choice
The act of selecting among alternatives.

Resource
An input used to produce economic goods. Land, labor, skills, natural resources, and capital are examples.

Our history is a record of our struggle to transform available, but limited, resources into things that we would like to have—economic goods.

EXHIBIT 1–1

A GENERAL LISTING OF DESIRED ECONOMIC GOODS AND LIMITED RESOURCES

ECONOMIC GOODS	LIMITED RESOURCES
Food (bread, milk, meat, eggs, vegetables, coffee, etc.)	Land (various degrees of fertility)
Clothing (shirts, pants, blouses, shoes, socks, coats, sweaters, etc.)	Natural resources (rivers, trees, minerals, oceans, etc.)
Household goods (tables, chairs, rugs, beds, dressers, television sets, etc.)	Machines and other man-made physical resources
Space exploration	Nonhuman animal resources
Education	Technology (physical and scientific "recipes" of history)
National defense	Human resources (the knowledge, skill, and talent of individual human beings)
Recreation	
Leisure time	
Entertainment	
Clean air	
Pleasant environment (trees, lakes, rivers, open spaces, etc.)	
Pleasant working conditions	
More productive resources	

painfully obvious that we will not triumph over scarcity. Even in the wealthiest of countries, productive capabilities cannot keep pace with material desires. People always want more goods and services than they have.

THE ECONOMIC WAY OF THINKING

It [economics] is a method rather than a doctrine, an apparatus of the mind, a technique of thinking which helps its possessor to draw correct conclusions.

JOHN MAYNARD KEYNES [3]

One does not have to spend much time around economists to recognize that there is an "economic way of thinking." Admittedly, economists, like others, differ

---

[3]John Maynard Keynes (1883–1946) was an English economist whose writings during the 1920s and the 1930s exerted an enormous impact on both economic theory and policy. Keynes established the terminology and the economic framework that are still widely used today when economists study problems of unemployment and inflation.

widely in their ideological views. A news commentator once remarked that "any half-dozen economists will normally come up with about six different policy prescriptions." Yet, in spite of their philosophical differences, there is a common ground in the approach of economists.

That common ground is **economic theory,** developed from basic postulates of human behavior. Economic theory, like a road map or a guidebook, establishes reference points indicating what to look for, and how economic issues are interrelated. To a large degree, the basic economic principles are merely common sense. When applied consistently, however, these commonsense concepts can provide interesting and powerful insights.

Economic theory
A set of definitions, postulates, and principles assembled in a manner that makes clear the "cause-and-effect" relationships of economic data.

EIGHT GUIDEPOSTS
TO ECONOMIC THINKING

The economic way of thinking requires the incorporation of certain guidelines—some would say the building blocks of basic economic theory—into one's thought process. Once these guidelines are incorporated, we believe that economics can be a relatively easy subject to master. Students who have difficulty with economics have almost always failed to assimilate these principles. We will outline and discuss eight principles that characterize the economic way of thinking and that are essential to the understanding of the economic approach.

1. THE USE OF SCARCE RESOURCES TO PRODUCE A GOOD IS ALWAYS COSTLY.

The use of resources to produce one good diverts the resources away from the production of other goods that are also desired. The highest valued alternative that must be sacrificed is the **opportunity cost** of an option. For example, if you use one hour of your scarce time to study economics, you will have one hour less time to watch television, read magazines, sleep, work at a job, or study other subjects. Time spent working at a job, or even time spent sleeping, might be viewed as your highest valued option forgone. The cost of an action is always the highest valued option that must now be sacrificed because you chose the action.

If the residents of a community choose to build a new civic auditorium, the opportunity cost of the building is the highest valued option—perhaps a new hospital—that must now be forgone because the resources used to produce the auditorium are now unavailable for other uses. It is important to recognize that the "scarce resources have a cost" concept is true regardless of who pays for the good

Opportunity cost
The highest valued alternative that must be sacrificed as a result of choosing among alternatives.

Reprinted by permission: Tribune Media Services.

or service produced. In many countries, various kinds of schooling are provided free of charge to students. However, provision of the schooling is not free to the community. Buildings, books, and teachers' salaries must be paid for from tax revenues, which the taxpayer could have used for other goods and services. The scarce resources used to produce the schooling could have been used instead to produce more recreation, entertainment, housing, or other goods. The cost of the schooling is the highest valued option that must now be given up because the resources required for its production were instead used to produce the schooling.

By now the central point should be obvious. Economic thinking recognizes that the use of a scarce resource always involves a cost. The use of more resources to do one thing implies fewer resources with which to achieve other objectives.

2. DECISION MAKERS CHOOSE PURPOSEFULLY; THEREFORE THEY WILL ECONO-MIZE.

Since resources are scarce, decision makers seek to choose wisely and avoid wasting their valuable resources. Recognizing the restrictions imposed by the limited resources available to them (income, time, talent, and so on), they try to select the options that best advance their own personal objectives. In turn, the objectives or preferences of individuals are revealed by the choices they make. **Economizing behavior** results directly from purposeful decision making. Economizing individuals will seek to accomplish an objective at the least possible cost to themselves. When choosing among things that yield equal benefit, an economizer will select the cheapest option. For example, if a pizza, lobster dinner, and a prime sirloin steak are expected to yield identical benefits, economizing behavior implies that the cheapest of the three alternatives, probably the pizza, will be chosen. Correspondingly, when choosing among alternatives of equal cost, economizing decision makers will select the option that yields the greatest benefit. Purposeful decision makers will not deliberately pay more for something than is necessary.

Purposeful choosing implies that decision makers have some basis for their evaluation of alternatives. Economists refer to this evaluation as **utility,** the benefit or satisfaction that an individual expects from the choice of a specific alternative. The utility of an alternative is highly subjective, often differing widely from person to person.

Economizing behavior
Choosing with the objective of gaining a specific benefit at the least possible cost. A corollary of economizing behavior implies that when choosing among items of equal cost, individuals will choose the option that yields the greatest benefit.

Utility
The benefit or satisfaction expected from a choice or course of action.

3. INCENTIVES MATTER—CHOICE IS INFLUENCED IN A PREDICTABLE WAY BY CHANGES IN ECONOMIC INCENTIVES.

This guidepost to clear economic thinking might be called the basic postulate of all economics. As the personal benefits from choosing an option increase, other things constant, a person will be more likely to choose that option. In contrast, as the personal costs associated with the choice of an item increase, the individual will be less likely to choose that option. For a group, this basic economic postulate suggests that making an option more attractive will influence more people to choose it. In contrast, as the cost of a selection to the members of a group increases, fewer of them will make this selection.

This basic postulate of economics is a powerful tool because its application is so widespread. Incentives affect behavior in virtually all aspects of our lives, ranging from market decisions about what to buy to political choices on whom to elect.

According to this basic postulate, how will consumers react if the price of beef increases (relative to other goods)? Since the higher beef prices make beef

THE FAMILY CIRCUS®   By Bil Keane

3-25
Copyright 1988
Cowles Syndicate, Inc.

"Everybody wants to be sick.
I'm using M&M's for pills."

Reprinted with special permission of King Features Syndicate.

consumption more expensive, the basic postulate indicates that consumers will be less likely to choose it. The predicted result is a decline in the amount of beef consumed as the result of the increase in its price.

To show its broad application, let us apply this basic postulate of economics to the examination process. If a classroom instructor makes it more costly to cheat, students will be less likely to do so. There will be little cheating on a closely monitored, individualized, essay examination. Why? Because it is difficult (that is, costly) to cheat on such an exam. Suppose, however, that an instructor gives an objective "take-home" exam, basing students' course grades entirely on the results. Among the same group of students, more will be likely to cheat because the benefits of doing so will be great and the risk (cost) minimal.

The "incentives matter" postulate is just as applicable to human behavior under socialism as under capitalism. For example, at one time in the former Soviet Union, the managers of glass plants were rewarded according to the tons of sheet glass produced. Not surprisingly, most plants produced sheet glass so thick that one could hardly see through it. The rules were changed so that the managers were rewarded according to the square meters of glass produced. Under the new rules, Soviet firms stretched their resources, producing very thin glass that was easily broken. Incentives matter in both capitalist and socialist countries. (The boxed feature "Do Incentives Matter?" gives yet another application of this principle.)

4. ECONOMIC THINKING IS MARGINAL THINKING.   Fundamental to economic reasoning and economizing behavior are the effects of decisions made to change the status quo. Economists refer to such decisions as **marginal.** Marginal choices always involve the effects of net additions to or subtractions from the current conditions. In fact, the word "additional" is often used as a substitute for marginal.

Marginal
Term used to describe the effects of a change in the current situation. For example, the marginal cost is the cost of producing an additional unit of a product, given the producer's current facility and production rate.

For example, we might ask, "What is the marginal (or additional) cost of producing one more automobile?"

Marginal decisions may involve large or small changes. The "one more unit" could be a new plant or a new stapler. It is marginal because it involves additional costs and additional benefits. Given the current situation, what marginal benefits (additional sales revenues, for example) can be expected from the plant, and what will be the marginal cost of constructing the facility? The answers to these questions will determine whether or not building the new plant is a good decision.

It is important to distinguish between *average* and *marginal*. A manufacturer's current average cost of producing automobiles (total cost divided by total number of cars produced) may be $20,000, but the marginal cost of producing an additional automobile (or an additional 1,000 automobiles) might be much lower, say, $5,000 per car. Costs associated with research, testing, design, molds, heavy equipment, and similar factors of production must be incurred whether the manufacturer is going to produce 1,000 units, 10,000 units, or 100,000 units. Such costs will clearly contribute to the average cost of an automobile. However, since these activities have already been undertaken to produce the manufacturer's current output level, they may add little to the cost of producing additional units. Thus, the manufacturer's marginal cost may be substantially less than the average cost. When determining whether to expand or reduce the production of a good, the choice should be based on marginal costs, not the current average cost.

We often confront decisions involving a possible change from the current situation. The marginal benefits and marginal costs associated with the choice will determine the wisdom of our decisions. What happens at the margin is therefore an important element of the economic way of thinking.

APPLICATIONS IN ECONOMICS

DO INCENTIVES MATTER?

How generally can we apply the "incentives matter" principle? Does it apply, for example, to drinking and driving? Will changing the incentives with regard to drinking and driving change behavior? Consider the case of Norway, the country that has the toughest drunk-driving laws in the Western world.[1] Drinking a single can of beer before driving can put a first offender in jail for a minimum sentence of three weeks. These drivers generally lose their licenses for up to two years and often get stiff fines as well. Repeat offenders are treated even more harshly. These laws are far more draconian than those of the United States. And the results?

1. One out of three Norwegians arrives at parties in a taxi, while nearly all Americans drive their own cars.

2. One out of ten Norwegian partygoers spends the night at the host's home; Americans seldom do.

3. In Norway, 78 percent of drivers totally avoid drinking at parties, compared to only 17 percent of American drivers.

Norwegians do like to drink, though they consume only half as much alcohol as Americans. The strong incentives built into Norwegian law, however, clearly make a difference in the incidence of drunken driving in that country. Once again, incentives do matter, and matter in a big way.

[1]The information in this feature is taken from L. Erik Calonius, "Just a Bottle of Beer Can Land a Motorist in Prison in Norway," *The Wall Street Journal,* August 16, 1985, p.1.

5. WHILE INFORMATION CAN HELP US MAKE BETTER CHOICES, ITS ACQUISITION IS COSTLY.

Thus we will almost always make choices based on limited knowledge. Information that will help us make better choices is valuable. Like other resources, however, it is also scarce and therefore costly to acquire. As a result, individuals will economize on their search for information just as they economize on the use of other scarce resources. For example, when purchasing a pair of jeans, you may check price and evaluate quality at several different stores. At some point, though, you will decide that additional shopping—that is, acquisition of additional information—is simply not worth the trouble. You will make a choice based on the limited knowledge that you already possess.

The process is similar when individuals search for a place to eat, a new car, or a roommate. They will seek to acquire some information, but at some point, they will perceive that the expected benefit derived from still more information is simply not worth the cost. When individual choice is likely to make an important difference to the decision maker, more time and effort will be spent to make a better individual decision. Even then, limited knowledge and resulting uncertainty about the outcome characterize the decision-making process.

6. ECONOMIC ACTIONS OFTEN GENERATE SECONDARY EFFECTS IN ADDITION TO THEIR IMMEDIATE EFFECTS.

Failure to consider these secondary effects is the most common source of economic error. Frederic Bastiat, a nineteenth-century French economist, stated that the difference between a good and a bad economist is that the bad economist considers only the immediate, visible effects, whereas the good economist is also aware of the **secondary effects,** effects that are indirectly related to the initial policy and can be seen or felt only with the passage of time.

Perhaps consideration of both immediate and secondary effects in areas outside economics will help us grasp this point. For example, the immediate effect of an aspirin is a bitter taste in one's mouth. The secondary effect, which is not immediately observable, is relief from a headache. The immediate effect of drinking six quarts of beer might be a warm, jolly feeling. The secondary effect, for many, would be a pounding headache the next morning.

In economics, the immediate, short-term effects that are highly visible are often quite different from the long-term effects. Changes in economic policy often alter the structure of incentives, which indirectly affect things like how much people work, earn, and invest, and care for things in the future. But the impact of the secondary effects is often observable only after the passage of time—and then only to those who know what to look for.

Secondary effects
Economic consequences of an economic change that are not immediately identifiable but are felt only with the passage of time.

Reprinted with special permission of King Features Syndicate.

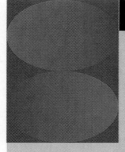

MYTHS OF ECONOMICS

"ECONOMIC ANALYSIS ASSUMES PEOPLE ACT ONLY OUT OF SELFISH MOTIVES. IT REJECTS THE HUMANITARIAN SIDE OF HUMANKIND."

Probably because economics focuses on the efforts of individuals to satisfy material desires, many casual observers of the subject argue that its relevance hinges on the selfish nature of humankind. But economists recognize that people act for a variety of reasons, some selfish and some humanitarian. The point is that actions of whichever type will be influenced by costs and benefits, as viewed by the decision maker. As an activity becomes more costly, it is less likely to be chosen. As it becomes more attractive, it is more likely to be chosen.

The choices of both the humanitarian and the egocentric individual will be influenced by changes in personal costs and benefits. For example, both will be more likely to try to save the life of a small child in a three-foot swimming pool than in the rapid currents approaching Niagara Falls. Both will be more likely to give a needy person their hand-me-downs rather than their best clothes. Similarly, both will be more likely to support a policy that generates benefits for others (farmers, the poor, the elderly) when the personal cost of doing so is low. Incentives matter for both the humanitarian and the egocentric person.

Observation would suggest that the right to control one's destiny is an "economic good" for most persons. Most of us would prefer to make our own choices rather than have someone else decide for us. But, is this attitude necessarily greedy and selfish? If so, why do people often make choices in a way that is charitable toward others? After all, many people freely choose to give a portion of their wealth to the sick, the needy, the less fortunate, and to religious and charitable institutions. Economics does not imply that these choices are irrational. It does imply that if you make it more (less) costly to act charitably, fewer (more) persons will do so.

Economics deals with people as they are—not as we would like to remake them. Should people act more charitably? Perhaps so. But this is not the subject matter of economics.

Consider tariffs, quotas, and other restrictions that limit imports. Proponents of such restrictions argue that they will increase employment; and, indeed, at first they do. If, for example, the supply of foreign-produced automobiles to the U.S. market were restricted, Americans would buy more American-made automobiles, increasing output and employment in the domestic auto industry. These would be the immediate, easily identified effects. But consider the secondary effects. The restrictions would also reduce supply to the domestic market and increase the price of both foreign- and American-made automobiles. As a result of the higher prices, many auto consumers would pay more for automobiles and thus be forced to curtail their purchases of food, clothing, recreation, and literally thousands of other items. These reductions in spending would mean less output and employment in those areas. There would also be a secondary effect on sales to foreigners. Since foreigners would be selling fewer automobiles to Americans, they would acquire fewer dollars with which to buy American-made goods. U.S. exports, therefore, would fall as a result of the restrictions on automobile imports.

Once the secondary effects are considered, the net impact on employment of the import restrictions is no longer obvious. The restrictions will increase employment in the auto industry, but they will also reduce employment in other industries, particularly export industries. Primarily, they will reshuffle employment rather than increase it. As this example illustrates, consideration of secondary effects is an important ingredient of the economic way of thinking.

7. THE VALUE OF A GOOD OR SERVICE IS SUBJECTIVE. Preferences differ, sometimes dramatically, between individuals. How much is a ticket to see tonight's performance of the Bolshoi Ballet worth? Some would be willing to pay a very high price, while others might even be willing to pay to avoid the ballet if attendance were mandatory. Even for a given individual, circumstances can change from day to day. Alice, who usually would value the ballet ticket at $20, is invited to a party, and suddenly becomes uninterested in the ballet tonight. Now what is the ticket worth? If she knows a friend who would give her $5 for the ticket, it is worth at least that much. If she advertises on a bulletin board and gets $10 for it, a higher value is created. One thing is certain: the value of the ticket depends on several things, among them, who uses it and when.

Seldom will one individual know how others value an item. Consider how difficult it often is to know what would make a good gift, even for a close friend or family member! So, arranging trades, or otherwise moving items to higher-valued users and uses, is not a simple task. In fact, how society promotes such coordination in the behavior of individuals is a key subject in many of the chapters that follow.

8. THE TEST OF A THEORY IS ITS ABILITY TO PREDICT. Economic thinking is **scientific thinking.** The proof of the pudding is in the eating. The usefulness of an economic theory is proved by its ability to predict the future consequences of economic action. Economists develop economic theory from scientific thinking, in which basic postulates are used to analyze how incentives will affect decision makers, and the analysis is then compared against events in the real world. If the events in the real world are consistent with a theory, we say that the theory has *predictive value* and is therefore valid.

If it is impossible to test the theoretical relationships of a discipline, the discipline does not qualify as a science. So, since economics deals with human beings, who can think and respond in a variety of ways, can economic theories really be tested? The answer to this question is yes, if, on average, human beings respond in predictable and consistent ways to certain changes in economic conditions. The economist believes that this is the case. Note that the economist is not saying that all individuals will respond in a specified manner. Economics usually does not seek to predict the behavior of a specific individual; instead, it focuses on the general behavior of a large number of individuals.

How can we test economic theory when controlled experiments with all the interactions of real life are not feasible? This is a problem, but economics is no different from astronomy in this respect. Astronomers must also deal with the world as it is. They cannot change the course of the stars or planets to see what impact the change would have on the gravitational pull of the earth. And so it is with economists, who cannot arbitrarily change the price of cars or unskilled labor services just to observe the effect on quantity purchased or level of employment. However, economic conditions (for example, prices, production costs, technology, transportation costs, and so on), like the location of the planets, do change from time to time. As actual conditions change, economic theory can be tested by comparing its predictions with real-world outcomes. Just as the universe is the laboratory of the astronomer, the real economic world is the laboratory of the economist.

Scientific thinking
Development of theory from basic postulates and the testing of the implications of that theory as to their consistency with events in the real world. Good theories are consistent with and help explain real-world events. Theories that are inconsistent with the real world are invalid and must be rejected.

POSITIVE AND NORMATIVE ECONOMICS

A positive science may be defined as a body of systematized knowledge concerning what is; a normative or regulative science is a body of systematized knowledge relating to criteria of what ought to be, and concerned therefore with the ideal as distinguished from the actual.

JOHN NEVILLE KEYNES[4]

Positive economics
The scientific study of "what is" among economic relationships.

Economics as a social science is concerned with predicting or determining the impact of changes in economic variables on the actions of human beings. Scientific economics, commonly referred to as **positive economics,** attempts to determine "what is." Positive economic statements postulate a relationship that is potentially verifiable or refutable. For example: "If the price of butter were higher, people would buy less." Or, "As the money supply increases, the price level will go up." We can statistically investigate (and estimate) the relationship between butter prices and sales, or between the supply of money and the general price level. We can analyze the facts to determine the correctness of a statement about positive economics.

Normative economics
Judgments about "what ought to be" in economic matters. Normative economic views cannot be proved false, because they are based on value judgments.

Normative economics involves the advocacy of specific policy alternatives, because it uses ethical or value judgments as well as knowledge of positive economics. Normative economic statements concern "what ought to be," given the preferences and philosophical views of the advocate. Value judgments may be the source of disagreement about normative economic matters. Two persons may differ on a policy matter because one is a socialist and the other a libertarian, because one wants cheaper food while the other favors organic farming, or even because one values wilderness highly while the other wants more improved campsites that can be easily reached by roads. They may agree as to the expected outcome of altering an economic variable (that is, the positive economics of an issue), but disagree as to whether that outcome is "good" or "bad."

In contrast with positive economic statements, normative economic statements cannot be tested and proved false (or confirmed to be correct). "Business firms should not maximize profits." "The use of pesticides on food to be sold in stores should not be allowed." "More of our National Forests should be set aside for wilderness." These normative statements cannot be scientifically tested, since their validity rests on value judgments.

Positive economics does not tell us which policy is best. The purpose of positive economics is to increase our knowledge of all policy alternatives, thereby eliminating one source of disagreement about policy matters. The knowledge that we gain from positive economics also serves to reduce a potential source of disappointment with policy. Those who do not understand how the economy operates may advocate policies that are actually inconsistent with their philosophical views. Sometimes what one thinks will happen if a policy is instituted may be a very unlikely result in the real world.

Our normative economic views can sometimes influence our attitude toward positive economic analysis. When we agree with the objectives of a policy, it is

---

[4]John Neville Keynes, *The Scope and Method of Political Economy*, 4th ed., 1917, pp. 34–35.

easy to overlook its potential liabilities. Desired objectives, though, are not the same as workable solutions. The actual effects of policy alternatives often differ dramatically from the objectives of their proponents. A new law forcing employers to pay all employees at least $15 per hour might be intended to help workers, but the resulting decline in the number of workers employed (and increase in the number unemployed) would be disastrous despite the good intentions. Proponents of such a law, of course, would not want to believe the economic analysis that predicted the unfortunate outcome.

Sound positive economics will help us evaluate more accurately whether or not a policy alternative will, in fact, accomplish a desired objective. The task of the professional economist is to expand our knowledge of how the real world operates. If we do not fully understand the implications, including the secondary effects, of alternative policies, we will not be able to choose intelligently. Yet, it is not always easy to isolate the impact of a change in an economic variable or policy. Let us consider some of the potential pitfalls to avoid in economic thinking.

PITFALLS TO AVOID IN ECONOMIC THINKING

VIOLATION OF THE *Ceteris Paribus* CONDITION

Economists often preface their statements with the words *ceteris paribus,* meaning "other things constant." "Other things constant, an increase in the price of housing will cause buyers to reduce their purchases." Unfortunately for the economic researcher, we live in a dynamic world. Other things seldom remain constant. For example, as the price of housing rises, the income of consumers may simultaneously be increasing. Both of these factors—higher housing prices and an expansion in consumer income—will have an impact on housing purchases. In fact, we would generally expect them to exert opposite effects: higher prices retarding housing purchases but the rise in consumer income stimulating the demand for housing. The task of sorting out the specific effects of interrelated variables thus becomes more complex when several changes take place simultaneously.

Economic theory acts as a guide, suggesting the probable linkages among economic variables. However, the relationships suggested by economic theory must be tested for consistency with events in the real world. Statistical procedures are often used by economists to correctly identify and more accurately measure relationships among economic variables. In fact, the major portion of the day-to-day work of many professional economists consists of statistical research.

ASSOCIATION IS NOT CAUSATION

In economics, causation is very important, and statistical association alone cannot establish causation. Perhaps an extreme example will illustrate the point. Suppose that each November a witch doctor performs a voodoo dance designed to arouse the cold-weather gods of winter, and that soon after the dance is performed the weather in fact begins to turn cold. The witch doctor's dance is associated with the arrival of winter, but does it cause the arrival of winter? Most of us would answer in the negative, even though the two are linked statistically.

Unfortunately, cause-and-effect relationships in economics are not always self-evident. For example, it is sometimes difficult to know whether a rise in income has caused people to buy more or, conversely, whether an increase in people's willingness to buy more has created more business and caused incomes to rise. Similarly, economists sometimes argue whether rising money wages are a cause or an effect of inflation. Economic theory, if rooted to the basic postulates, can often help to determine the source of causation, even though competitive theories may sometimes suggest differing directions of causation.

FALLACY OF COMPOSITION

What is true for the individual (or subcomponent) may not be true for the group (or the whole). If you stand up for an exciting play during a football game, you will be better able to see. But what happens if everyone stands up at the same time? What benefits the individual does not necessarily benefit the group as a whole. When everyone stands up, the view for individual spectators fails to improve; in fact, it probably becomes even worse.

Fallacy of composition
Erroneous view that what is true for the individual (or the part) will also be true for the group (or the whole).

People who argue that what is true for the part is also true for the whole may err because of the **fallacy of composition.** Consider an example from economics. If you have an extra $10,000 in your bank account, you will be better off. But, what if everyone suddenly has an additional $10,000? This increase in the money supply will result in higher prices, as people with more money bid against each other for the existing supply of goods. Without an increase in the availability (or production) of scarce economic goods, the additional money will not make anyone better off. What is true for the individual is misleading and often fallacious when applied to the entire economy.

Potential error associated with the fallacy of composition highlights the importance of considering both a micro- and a macroview in the study of economics. Since individual decision makers are the moving force behind all economic action, the foundations of economics are clearly rooted in a microview. Analysis that focuses on a single consumer, producer, product, or productive resource is referred to as **microeconomics.** As Professor Abba Lerner put it, "Microeconomics consists of looking at the economy through a microscope, as it were, to see how the millions of cells in the body economic—the individuals or households as consumers, and the individuals or firms as producers—play their part in the working of the whole organisms."[5]

Microeconomics
The branch of economics that focuses on how human behavior affects the conduct of affairs within narrowly defined units, such as individual households or business firms.

As we have seen, however, what is true for a small unit may not be true in the aggregate. **Macroeconomics** focuses on how the aggregation of individual microunits affects our analysis. Macroeconomics, like microeconomics, is concerned with incentives, prices, and output. In macroeconomics, however, the markets

Macroeconomics
The branch of economics that focuses on how human behavior affects outcomes in highly aggregated markets, such as the markets for labor or consumer products.

---

[5]Abba P. Lerner, "Microeconomy Theory" in *Perspectives in Economics,* edited by A. A. Brown, E. Neuberger, and M. Palmatier (New York: McGraw-Hill, 1968), p. 29.

THE IMPORTANCE OF ADAM SMITH: THE FATHER OF ECONOMICS

The foundation of economics was laid in 1776, when Adam Smith (1723–1790) published *An Inquiry Into the Nature and Causes of the Wealth of Nations*, perhaps the most influential book since the Bible. Smith put forth the revolutionary view that the wealth of a nation did not lie in gold and silver, but rather in the goods and services—whether produced at home or abroad—available to the people. He argued that free exchange in a market economy would harness self-interest as a creative force. In the course of seeking their own gain, people would provide valuable goods and services to others. The "invisible hand" of market prices would direct individuals and resources into those areas where their production was valued most. Coordination, order, and efficiency would result, without a central authority being necessary to plan and direct the economy.

Adam Smith was a lecturer at the University of Glasgow, in his native Scotland. Morals and ethics actually were his concern before economics. His student Thomas Millar reported that Smith's favorite lecture subjects, in order of preference, were natural theology, ethics, jurisprudence, and economics. His first book, in fact, was *The Theory of Moral Sentiments*. For Smith, self-interest and sympathy for others were complementary. He believed that charity alone cannot provide the essentials for a good life. The possibilities for mutual gain from exchange, however, can improve life for all involved, according to Smith, by encouraging each person to produce more of what others want. In a market setting, those who have sympathy for others, or act as if they do by producing for others and economizing on what they consume for themselves, prosper. Smith, the moral philosopher, pointed out that free exchange harnesses self-interest and yokes together desire for personal gain with a consideration of the benefits and costs to others.

Ideas have consequences. Smith's ideas greatly influenced not only Europeans, but also those who mapped out the structure of the U.S. government. Since then, the effectiveness of the "invisible hand" of the market has become accepted as critical to the prosperity of nations.[6]

---

[6]For an excellent biographical sketch of Adam Smith, used to prepare this feature, see David Henderson, ed., *The Fortune Encyclopedia of Economics* (New York: Warner Books, 1993), pp. 836–838.

are highly aggregated. In our study of macroeconomics, the 90 million households in this country will be lumped together when we consider such topics as the importance of consumption spending, saving, and employment. Similarly, the nation's 18 million firms will be lumped together into something we call "the business sector."

What factors determine the level of aggregate output, the rate of inflation, the amount of unemployment, and interest rates? These are macroeconomic questions. In short, macroeconomics examines the forest rather than the individual trees. As we move from the microcomponents to a macroview of the whole, it is important that we beware of the fallacy of composition.

WHAT ECONOMISTS DO

The primary functions of economists are to teach, conduct research, and formulate policies. Approximately one half of all professional economists are affiliated with academic institutions. Many of these academicians are involved both in teaching and in scientific research.

The job of the research economist is to increase our understanding of economic matters. The tools of statistics and mathematics help the researcher carry out this task. Government agencies and private business firms generate a vast array of economic statistics on such matters as income, employment, prices, and expenditure patterns. A two-way street exists between statistical data and economic theory. Statistics can be used to test the consistency of economic theory and measure the responsiveness of economic variables to changes in policy. At the same time, economic theory helps to explain which economic variables are likely to be related and why they are linked. Statistics do not tell their own story. We must utilize economic theory to properly interpret and better understand the actual statistical relationships among economic variables.

Economics is a social science. The fields of political science, sociology, psychology, and economics often overlap. Because of the abundance of economic data and the ample opportunity for scientific research in the real world, economics has sometimes been called the "queen of the social sciences." Reflecting the scientific nature of economics, the Swedish Academy of Science in 1969 instituted the Nobel Prize in economic science. The men and women of genius in economics now take their place alongside those in physics, chemistry, physiology and medicine, peace, and literature.

A knowledge of economics is essential for wise policy-making. Policy-makers who do not understand the consequences of their actions will not likely reach their goals. Recognizing the link between economic analysis and policy, Congress in 1946 established the Council of Economic Advisers. The purpose of the council is to provide the president with analyses of how the activities of the federal government influence the economy. The chairmanship of the Council of Economic Advisers is a cabinet-level position.

LOOKING AHEAD

The primary purpose of this book is to encourage you to develop the economic way of thinking so that you can differentiate sound reasoning from economic nonsense. Once you have developed the economic way of thinking, economics will be relatively easy. Using the economic way of thinking can also be fun. Moreover, it will help you become a better citizen. It will give you a different and fascinating perspective on what motivates people, why they act the way they do, and why their actions are sometimes in conflict with the best interest of the community or nation. It will also give you

some valuable insight into how people's actions can be rechanneled for the benefit of the community at large.

Economics is a relatively young science. Current-day economists owe an enormous debt to their predecessors. The feature on "The Importance of Adam Smith: the Father of Economics" spotlights the pivotal role played by that great economist.

CHAPTER SUMMARY

1. Scarcity and choice are the two essential ingredients of an economic topic. Goods are scarce because desire

for them far outstrips their availability from nature. Since scarcity prevents us from having as much of everything as we would like, we must choose among the alternatives available to us. Any choice involving the use of scarce resources requires an economic decision.

2. Scarcity and poverty are not the same thing. Absence of poverty implies that some basic level of need has been met. Absence of scarcity would mean that all of our desires for goods have been met. We may someday be able to eliminate poverty, but scarcity will always be with us.

3. Economics is a method of approach, a way of thinking. The economic way of thinking emphasizes the following:

    a. Among economic goods, there are no free lunches. Someone must give up something if we are to have more scarce goods.

    b. Individuals make decisions purposefully, always seeking to choose the option they expect to be most consistent with their personal goals. Purposeful decision making leads to economizing behavior.

    c. Incentives matter. People will be more likely to choose an option as the benefits expected from that option increase. In contrast, higher costs will make an alternative less attractive, reducing the likelihood that it will be chosen.

    d. Marginal costs and marginal benefits (utility) are fundamental to economizing behavior. Economic reasoning focuses on the impact of marginal changes.

    e. Since information is scarce, uncertainty will be present when decisions are made.

    f. In addition to their initial impact, economic events often alter personal incentives in a manner that leads to important secondary effects that may be felt only with the passage of time.

    g. The value of a good or service is subjective and will differ among individuals.

    h. The test of an economic theory is its ability to predict and to explain events in the real world.

4. Economic science is positive. It attempts to explain the actual consequences of economic actions and alternative policies. Positive economics alone does not state that one policy is superior to another. Normative economics is advocative; using value judgments, it makes suggestions about "what ought to be."

5. Testing economic theory is not an easy task. When several economic variables change simultaneously, it is often difficult to determine the relative importance of each. The direction of economic causation is sometimes difficult to ascertain. Economists consult economic theory as a guide and use statistical techniques as tools to improve our knowledge of positive economics.

6. Microeconomics focuses on narrowly defined units, such as individual consumers or business firms. Macroeconomics is concerned with highly aggregated units, such as the markets for labor or goods and services. When shifting focus from micro- to macro-units, one must beware of the fallacy of composition. Both micro- and macroeconomics use the same postulates and tools. The level of aggregation is the distinction between the two.

7. The origin of economics as a systematic method of analysis dates back to the publication of *The Wealth of Nations* by Adam Smith in 1776. Smith argued that production and wealth would increase if individuals were left free to work, produce, and exchange goods and services. He believed that individuals pursuing their own interests would be led by the "invisible hand" of market incentives (prices) to employ their productive talents in a manner "most advantageous to the society." Smith's central message is that when markets are free—when there are no legal restraints limiting the entry of producer-sellers—individual self-interest and the public interest are brought into harmony.

CRITICAL-ANALYSIS QUESTIONS

1. Indicate how each of the following changes would influence the incentive of a decision maker to undertake the action described.

    a. A reduction in the temperature from 80 degrees to 50 degrees on one's decision to go swimming.

    b. A change in the meeting time of the introductory economics course from 11:00 A.M. to 7:30 A.M. on one's decision to attend the lectures.

    c. A reduction in the number of exam questions that relate to the text on the student's decision to read the text.

    d. An increase in the price of beef on one's decision to have steak.

    e. An increase in the rental price of apartments on one's decision to build additional housing units.

*2. "The government should provide goods such as health care, education, and highways because it can provide them free." Is this statement true or false? Explain your answer.

3. "Reasonable rental housing could be brought within the economic means of all if the government would prevent landlords from charging more than $200 per month rent for a quality three-bedroom house." Use the

---

*Asterisk denotes questions for which answers are given in Appendix C.

economic way of thinking to evaluate this view.

*4. Legislation has been introduced which would require airlines to provide and parents to purchase a special safety seat for small children. Proponents of this legislation argue that it would save lives. Do you agree? Can you think of any "secondary effects" that might actually increase injuries and fatalities?

5. Is the following disagreement between Senator Dogooder and Senator Donothing positive or normative? Explain.

SENATOR DOGOODER: I favor an increase in the minimum wage because it would help the unskilled worker.

SENATOR DONOTHING: I oppose an increase in the minimum wage because it would cause the unemployment rate among the young and unskilled to rise.

*6. The United States has raised the personal income tax exemption from $1,080 to $2,350 and thereby increased the tax saving provided to parents of dependent children. According to the basic postulate of economics, how will this change affect the birth rate?

*7. "The economic way of thinking stresses that good intentions lead to sound policy." Is this statement true or false? Explain your answer.

8. Economic theory postulates that self-interest is a powerful motivation for action. Does this imply that people are selfish and greedy? Do self-interest and selfishness mean the same thing?

*9. Congress and government agencies often make laws to help protect the safety of product consumers. New cars, for example, are required to have many safety features before they can be sold in the United States. These rules do indeed provide added safety for buyers, although they also add to the cost and price of the new vehicles. But can you think of secondary effects of the laws that tend to undercut or reduce the intended effect of increasing auto safety?

*10. "Individuals who economize are missing the point of life. Money is not so important that it should rule the way we live." Evaluate this statement.

11. "Positive economics cannot tell us which agricultural policy is better, so it is useless to policy-makers." Evaluate this statement.

12. "I examined the statistics for our basketball team's wins last year and found that when the third team played more, the winning margin increased. If the coach played the third team more, we would win by a bigger margin." Evaluate this statement.

---

*Asterisk denotes questions for which answers are given in Appendix C.

ADDENDUM: UNDERSTANDING GRAPHS

Economists often use graphs to illustrate economic relations. Graphs are like pictures. They are visual aids that can communicate valuable information in a small amount of space. It has been said that a good picture is worth a thousand words. But, one must understand the picture (and the graph) if it is to be enlightening.

This addendum is designed to illustrate the use of simple graphs as an instrument of communication. Many students, particularly those with an elementary mathematics background, are already familiar with this material, and they may safely ignore it. This addendum is for those who need to be assured that they have the ability to understand graphic economic illustrations.

THE SIMPLE BAR GRAPH

A simple bar graph helps one to visualize comparative relationships and thus understand them better. It is particularly useful for illustrating how an economic indicator varies among countries, time periods, or under alternative economic conditions.

Exhibit 1A-1 shows how a bar graph can be used to illustrate economic data. Part "a" presents tabular data on the income per person in 1991 for several countries. Part "b" uses a bar graph to illustrate the same data. The horizontal scale of the graph indicates the total income per person in 1991. A bar is constructed indicating the income level of each country. The length of each bar is in proportion to the per person income of the country. Thus, the length of the bars is a visual aid to understanding how the per capita income varies across the countries. For example, the extremely short bar for Rwanda makes it immediately apparent that income per person there is only a small fraction of the comparable figure for the United States, Switzerland, Canada, and several other countries.

LINEAR GRAPHIC PRESENTATION

Economists are often interested in illustrating variations in economic variables with the passage of time. A linear graph with time on the horizontal axis and an economic variable on the vertical axis is a useful tool to indicate variations over time. **Exhibit 1A–2** illustrates a simple linear graph of changes in consumer prices (the inflation rate) in the United States between 1960 and 1993. The table of the exhibit presents data on the percent change in consumer prices for each year. Beginning with 1960, the horizontal axis indicates the time period (year). The inflation rate for a country is plotted vertically above each year. Of course, the height of the plot (line) indicates the inflation rate during that year. For example, in 1975 the inflation rate was 6.9 percent. This point is plotted at the 6.9 percent vertical distance directly above the year 1975. In 1976 the inflation rate fell to 4.9 percent. Thus, the vertical plot of the 1976 inflation rate is lower than for 1975. The inflation rate for each year (part "a") is plotted at the corresponding height directly above the year. The linear graph is simply a line connecting the points plotted for each of the years 1960 through 1993.

Source: Robert Summers and Alan
Heston, "The Penn World Tables
(Mark 5): An Expanded Set of
International Comparisons,
1950–1988," *Quarterly Journal of
Economics*, May 1991; updated data
supplied by Summers and Heston.

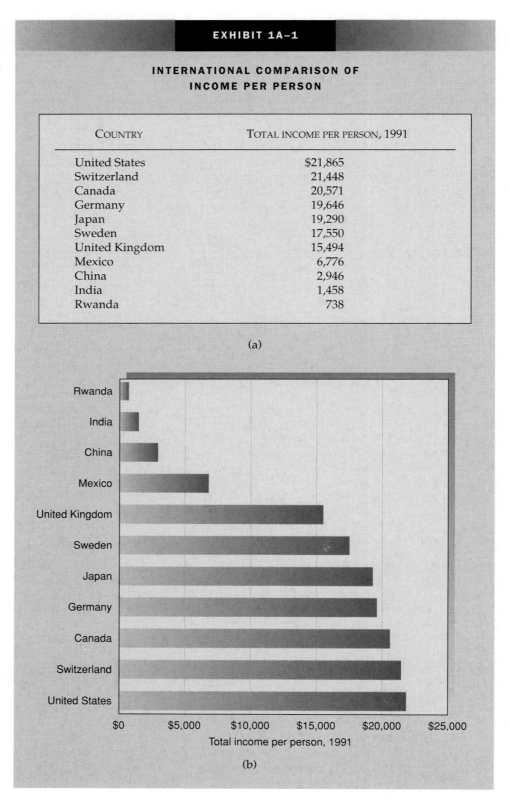

EXHIBIT 1A–1

INTERNATIONAL COMPARISON OF
INCOME PER PERSON

COUNTRY	TOTAL INCOME PER PERSON, 1991
United States	$21,865
Switzerland	21,448
Canada	20,571
Germany	19,646
Japan	19,290
Sweden	17,550
United Kingdom	15,494
Mexico	6,776
China	2,946
India	1,458
Rwanda	738

(a)

Total income per person, 1991

(b)

EXHIBIT 1A–2

CHANGES IN LEVEL OF PRICES IN UNITED STATES, 1960–1993

YEAR	PERCENT CHANGE IN CONSUMER PRICES	YEAR	PERCENT CHANGE IN CONSUMER PRICES
1960	1.4	1977	6.7
1961	0.7	1978	9.0
1962	1.3	1979	13.3
1963	1.6	1980	12.5
1964	1.0	1981	8.9
1965	1.9	1982	3.8
1966	3.5	1983	3.8
1967	3.0	1984	3.9
1968	4.7	1985	3.8
1969	6.2	1986	1.1
1970	5.6	1987	4.4
1971	3.3	1988	4.4
1972	3.4	1989	4.6
1973	8.7	1990	6.1
1974	12.3	1991	3.1
1975	6.9	1992	2.9
1976	4.9	1993	2.7

(a)

The tabular data (a) of the inflation rate is presented in graphic form in (b).

Source: *Economic Report of the President, 1991*, Table B-61; and *Economic Report of the President, 1994*, Table B-62.

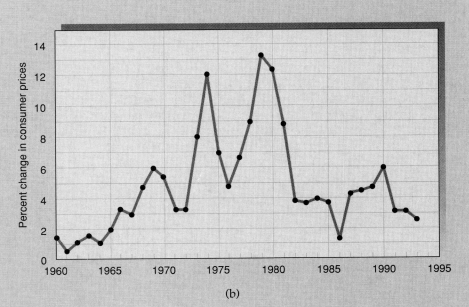

(b)

The linear graph is a visual aid to understanding what happens to the inflation rate during the period. As the graph shows, the inflation rate rose sharply between 1967 and 1969, in 1973–1974, and again in 1977–1979. It was substantially higher during the 1970s than it was in the early 1960s or the mid-1980s. While the linear graph does not communicate any information not in the table, it does make it easier to see the pattern of the data. Thus, economists often use simple graphics rather than tables to communicate information.

DIRECT AND INVERSE RELATIONSHIPS

Economic logic often suggests that two variables are linked in a specific way. Suppose an investigation reveals that, other things constant, farmers supply more wheat as the price of wheat increases. **Exhibit 1A–3** presents hypothetical data on the relationship between the price of wheat and the quantity supplied by farmers, first in tabular form (part "a") and then as a simple two-dimensional graph (part "b"). Suppose we measure the quantity of wheat supplied by farmers on the x-axis (the horizontal axis) and the price of wheat on the y-axis (the vertical axis). Points indicating the value of x (quantity supplied) at alternative values of y (price of wheat) can then be plotted. The line (or curve) linking the points together illustrates the relationship between the price of wheat and amount supplied by farmers.

In the case of price and quantity supplied of wheat, the two variables are directly related. When the y-variable increases, so does the x-variable. When two variables are directly related, the graph illustrating the linkage between the two will slope upward to the right (as in the case of *SS* in part "b").

Sometimes the x-variable and the y-variable are inversely related. A decline in the y-variable is associated with an increase in the x-variable. Therefore, a curve picturing the inverse relationship between x and y slopes downward to the right.

Exhibit 1A–4 illustrates this case. As the data of the table indicate, consumers purchase less as the price of wheat increases. Measuring the price of wheat on the y-axis (by convention, economists always place price on the y-axis) and the quantity of wheat purchased on the x-axis, the relationship between these two variables can also be illustrated graphically. If the price of wheat was $5 per bushel, only 60 million bushels would be purchased by consumers. As the price declines to $4 per bushel, annual consumption increases to 75 million bushels. At still lower prices, the quantity purchased by consumers will expand to larger and larger amounts. As part "b" illustrates, the inverse relationship between price and quantity of wheat purchased generates a curve that slopes downward to the right.

COMPLEX RELATIONSHIPS

Sometimes the initial relationship between the x- and y-variables will change. **Exhibit 1A–5** illustrates more complex relations of this type. Part "a" shows the typical relationship between annual earnings and age. As a young person acquires work experience and develops skills, earnings usually expand. Thus, initially, age

EXHIBIT 1A-3

DIRECT RELATIONSHIP BETWEEN VARIABLES
(HYPOTHETICAL DATA)

PRICE	AMOUNT OF WHEAT SUPPLIED BY FARMERS PER YEAR (MILLIONS OF BUSHELS)
$1	45
2	75
3	100
4	120
5	140

(a)

As the table (a) indicates, farmers are willing to supply more wheat at a higher price. Thus, there is a direct relation between the price of wheat and the quantity supplied. When the x- and y-variables are directly related, a curve mapping the relationship between the two will slope upward to the right like SS.

Q = 140, P = $5
S
Q = 120, P = $4
Q = 100, P = $3
Q = 75, P = $2
S
Q = 45, P = $1

Price

0   50   100   150   200

Quantity/year

(b)

and annual earnings are directly related; annual earnings increase with age. However, beyond a certain age (approximately age 55), annual earnings generally decline as workers approach retirement. As a result, the inital direct relationship between age and earnings changes to an inverse relation. When this is the case, annual income expands to a maximum (at age 55) and then begins to decline with years of age.

As the table (a) shows, consumers will demand (purchase) more wheat as the price declines. Thus, there is an inverse relationship between the price of wheat and the quantity demanded. When the x- and y-variables are inversely related, a curve showing the relationship between the two will slope downward to the right like DD.

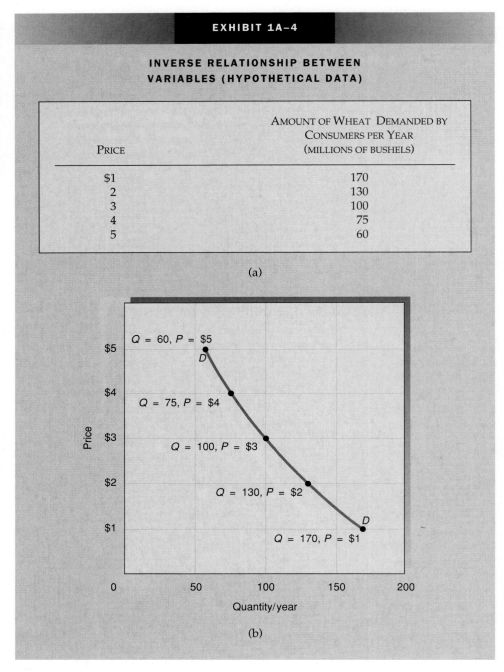

EXHIBIT 1A–4

INVERSE RELATIONSHIP BETWEEN VARIABLES (HYPOTHETICAL DATA)

PRICE	AMOUNT OF WHEAT DEMANDED BY CONSUMERS PER YEAR (MILLIONS OF BUSHELS)
$1	170
2	130
3	100
4	75
5	60

(a)

(b)

Part "b" illustrates an initial inverse relation that later changes to a direct relationship. Consider the impact of travel speed on gasoline consumption per mile. At low speeds, the automobile engine will not be used efficiently. As speed increases from 5 mph to 10 mph and on to a speed of 40 mph, gasoline consumption per mile declines. In this range, there is an inverse relationship between speed of travel (x) and gasoline consumption per mile (y). However, as speed increases

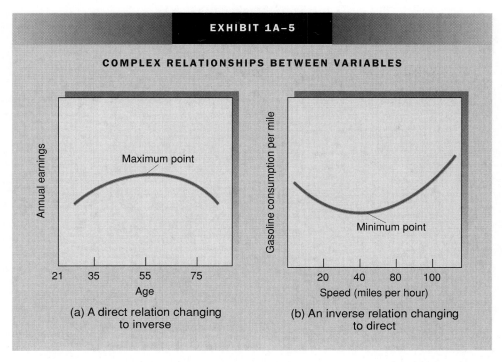

EXHIBIT 1A–5

COMPLEX RELATIONSHIPS BETWEEN VARIABLES

(a) A direct relation changing
to inverse

(b) An inverse relation changing
to direct

At first, an increase in age (and work experience) leads to a higher income, but later earnings decline as the worker approaches retirement (a). Thus, age and annual income are initially directly related but at approximately age 55 an inverse relation emerges. Part (b) illustrates the relationship between travel speed and gasoline consumption per mile. Initially, gasoline consumption per mile declines as speed increases (an inverse relation), but as speed increases above 40 mph, gasoline consumption per mile increases with the speed of travel (direct relation).

beyond 40 mph, more gasoline per mile is required to achieve the additional acceleration. At very high speeds, gasoline consumption per mile increases substantially with speed of travel. Thus, gasoline consumption per mile reaches a minimum and a direct relationship between the *x*- and *y*-variables emerges beyond the minimum point (40 mph).

SLOPE OF A STRAIGHT LINE

In economics, we are often interested in how much the *y*-variable changes in response to a change in the *x*-variable. The *slope* of the line or curve reveals this information. Mathematically, the slope of a line or curve is equal to the change in the *y*-variable divided by the change in the *x*-variable.

Exhibit 1A–6 illustrates the calculation of the slope for a straight line. The exhibit shows how the daily earnings (*y*-variable) of a worker change with hours worked (the *x*-variable). The wage rate of the worker is $5 per hour. Thus, when 1 hour is worked, earnings are equal to $5; for 2 hours of work, earnings jump to $10, and so on. A one-hour change in hours worked leads to a $5 change in earnings. Thus, the slope of the line ($\Delta Y/\Delta X$) is equal to 5. (The symbol Δ means "change in".) In the case of a straight line, the change in *y*, per unit change in *x*, is equal for all points on the line. Thus, the slope of a straight line is constant for all points along the line.

Exhibit 1A–6 illustrates a case in which there is a direct relation between the *x*- and *y*-variable. For an inverse relation, the *y*-variable decreases as the *x*-variable increases. So, when *x* and *y* are inversely related, the slope of the line will be negative.

The slope of a line is equal to change in y divided by the change in x. The line above illustrates the case in which daily earnings increase by $5 per hour worked. Thus, the slope of the earnings function is 5 ($5 ÷ by 1 hr). For a straight line, the slope is constant at each point on the line.

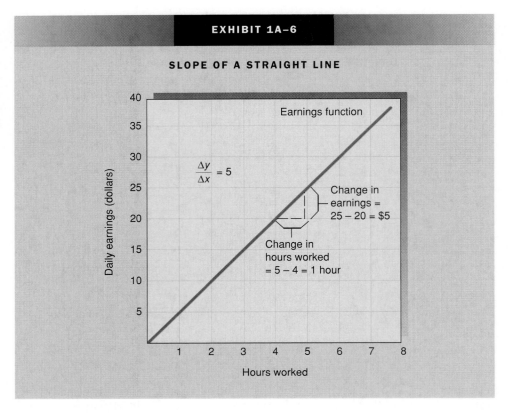

EXHIBIT 1A–6

SLOPE OF A STRAIGHT LINE

SLOPE OF A CURVE

In contrast with a straight line, the slope of a curve is different at each point along the curve. The slope of a curve at a specific point is equal to the slope of a line *tangent* to the curve at the point, meaning a line that just touches the curve.

Exhibit 1A–7 illustrates how the slope of a curve at a specific point is determined. First, let us consider the slope of the curve at point *A*. A line tangent to the curve at point *A* indicates that *y* changes by one unit when *x* changes by two units at point *A*. Thus, the slope ($\Delta Y/\Delta X$) of the curve at *A* is equal to one-half unit.

Now consider the slope of the curve at point *B*. The line tangent to the curve at *B* indicates that *y* changes by two units for each one unit change in *x* at point *B*. Thus, at *B* the slope ($\Delta Y/\Delta X$) is equal to 2. At point *B*, a change in the *x*-variable leads to a much larger change in *y* than was true at point *A*. The greater slope of the curve at *B* reflects this greater change in *y* per unit change in *x* at *B* relative to *A*.

GRAPHS ARE NOT A SUBSTITUTE FOR ECONOMIC THINKING

By now you should have a fairly good understanding of how to read a graph. If you still feel uncomfortable with graphs, try drawing (graphing) the relationship between several things with which you are familiar. If you work, try graphing the relationship between your hours worked (*x*-axis) and your weekly earnings

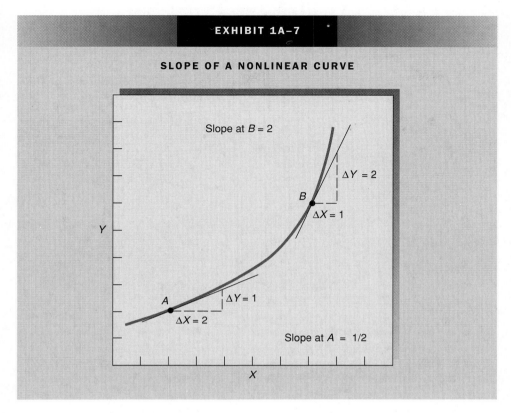

EXHIBIT 1A–7

SLOPE OF A NONLINEAR CURVE

Slope at B = 2

ΔY = 2

B

ΔX = 1

Y

A

ΔY = 1

ΔX = 2

Slope at A = 1/2

X

The slope of a curve at any point is equal to the slope of the straight line tangent to the curve at the point. As the lines tangent to the above curve at point A and B illustrate, the slope of a curve will change from point to point along the curve.

(y-axis). If need be, refer to Exhibit 1A–6 to help guide you with this exercise. Can you graph the relationship between the price of gasoline and your expenditures on gasoline? Graphing these simple relationships will give you greater confidence in your ability to grasp more complex economic relationships presented in graphs.

This text uses only simple graphs. Thus, there is no reason for you to be intimidated. Graphs look much more complex than they really are. In fact, they are nothing more than a simple device to communicate information quickly and concisely. One cannot communicate anything with a graph that cannot be communicated verbally.

Most important, graphs are not a substitute for economic thinking. While a graph may illustrate that two variables are related, it tells us nothing about the cause-and-effect relationship between the variables. To determine probable cause and effect, we must rely on economic theory. Thus, the economic way of thinking, not graphs, is the power station of economic analysis.

CHAPTER TWO

SOME TOOLS OF THE ECONOMIST

The goods people sell usually are made by processes using a high proportion of the skills they are gifted in, whereas the goods people buy usually are made by processes they are comparatively ungifted in.

ROBERT A. MUNDELL[1]

CHAPTER FOCUS

■ *What is opportunity cost? Why do economists place so much emphasis on it?*
■ *What does a production-possibilities frontier demonstrate?*
■ *How do specialization and exchange create value?*
■ *What three economic decisions are faced by every nation?*
■ *What are the two major methods of economic organization? How do they differ?*

[1]Robert A. Mundell, *Man and Economics: The Science of Choice* (New York: McGraw-Hill, 1968), p. 19.

In the last chapter, you were introduced to the economic approach. In this chapter, we discuss a few important tools that will help you develop the economic way of thinking.

WHAT SHALL WE GIVE UP?

Scarcity calls the tune in economics. We cannot have as much of everything as we would like. Most of us would like to have more time for leisure, recreation, vacations, hobbies, education, and skill development. We would also like to have more wealth, a larger savings account, and more consumable goods. However, all of these things are scarce, in the sense that they are limited. Our efforts to get more of one will conflict with our efforts to get more of the others. We can have more leisure time if we sacrifice some wealth. We can increase our current consumption if we reduce our rate of saving. Choosing more of one alternative requires us to give up something of the other.

OPPORTUNITY COST

An unpleasant fact of economics is that the choice to do one thing is, at the same time, a choice not to do something else. Your choice to spend time reading this book is a choice not to play tennis, go out on a date, listen to a math lecture, or attend a party. These things must be given up because of your decision to read. As we indicated in Chapter 1, the highest valued alternative that must be sacrificed because one chooses an option is the opportunity cost of the choice.[2]

Costs are subjective. (So are benefits. After all, a cost is a sacrificed benefit!) A cost exists in the mind of the decision maker. It is based on expectation—the expected value of the forgone alternative. Cost can never be directly measured by someone other than the decision maker because only the decision maker can place a value on what is given up.[3] In fact, this is one reason that voluntary trade is so critical in the creation of value, as we discussed in the last chapter. Only individuals are in a position to evaluate options for themselves, and to decide whether a possible trade is personally a good thing.

Cost, however, often has a monetary component that enables us to approximate its value. For example, the cost of attending a ballet is the highest valued opportunity lost as a result of (1) the time necessary to attend and (2) the purchasing power (that is, money) necessary to obtain a ticket. The monetary component is, of course, objective and can be measured. So long as individuals are paying the money price in voluntary exchange, and the good is available to others at that price, it represents for them a true opportunity cost. When nonmonetary considerations are relatively unimportant, the monetary component will approximate the total cost of an option.

---

[2]See also David Henderson, "Opportunity Cost," in *The Fortune Encyclopedia of Economics,* edited by David Henderson (New York: Warner Books, Inc., 1993), pp. 44–45.

[3]See James M. Buchanan, *Cost and Choice* (Chicago: Markham, 1969), for an analysis of the relationship between cost and choice.

OPPORTUNITY COST AND THE REAL WORLD

Is real-world decision making influenced by opportunity cost? Remember, the basic economic postulate states that an option is more likely to be chosen when its cost to the decision maker is less. So economic theory does imply that differences (or changes) in opportunity cost will influence how decisions are made.

Some examples will demonstrate the real-world application of the opportunity-cost concept. Poor people are more likely to travel long distances by bus, whereas the wealthy are more likely to travel by airplane. Why? A simple answer would be that the bus is cheaper; therefore, the poor will be more likely to purchase the cheaper good. But is the bus cheaper for a relatively well-off individual whose opportunity cost of travel time is high? Suppose that a round-trip airline ticket from Kansas City to Denver costs $150, whereas a bus ticket costs only $110. The bus requires ten hours of travel time, however, and the airplane only two hours. Which would be cheaper? It depends on the opportunity cost of time. The money cost of air travel is $40 more, but the time cost is eight hours less. For someone whose opportunity cost is evaluated at less than $5 per hour, the bus is cheaper. But for the person whose time is valued at more than $5 per hour, the airplane is clearly the cheaper option. Since the opportunity cost of the travel time will usually be greater for the wealthy than for the poor, the airplane is likely to be much cheaper for those with high incomes.

The concept of opportunity cost also helps us understand labor allocation and wage differences. Setting aside the nonmonetary aspects of a job for the moment, workers whose skills make them valuable to other employers will have to be paid enough to compensate them for what they could be making elsewhere—their highest valued employment alternatives. Thus, a filling station owner is unlikely to hire a physician to pump gas because the physician would have to be paid at least his or her opportunity cost—perhaps $100 per hour or more that could be earned for delivering babies or performing surgery. Similarly, since the job opportunities forgone on other jobs will be greater for a skilled carpenter than for an unskilled worker, an employer must pay the skilled carpenter a higher wage. Skills and abilities, if they create more valuable alternatives, increase an individual's earning capability.

Elderly retirees watch considerably more television than high-income lawyers, accountants, and other professionals. Why? Is it because the elderly can better afford the money cost of a television? Clearly, this is not the case. The time cost, though, is another matter. Consider the difference in the opportunity cost of time between the retirees and the professionals. In terms of lost earnings, watching television will generally cost the professional a lot more than it costs the elderly. The professional watches less television because it is an expensive good in terms of time.

Why do students watch less television and spend less time at the movies or on the beach during final exam week? Recreation is more costly then, that's why. Using valuable study time to go to the beach might well mean lower grades in several classes, although a student's grade in economics might be unaffected if he or she kept up during the semester and developed the economic way of thinking!

By now you should have the idea. Choosing one thing means giving up others that might have been chosen. Opportunity cost is the highest-valued option sacrificed as the result of choosing an alternative.

Failure to consider opportunity cost often leads to unwise decision making. Suppose that your community builds a beautiful new civic center. The mayor, speaking at the dedication ceremony, tells the world that the center will improve the quality of life in your community. Persons who understand the concept of opportunity cost may question this view. If the center had not been built, the resources could have been used to build a new hospital, improve the educational system, or perhaps provide better housing for low-income families. Will the civic center contribute more to the well-being of the people in your community than these other facilities? If so, it was a wise investment. If not, however, your community will be worse off than it might have been had a higher valued project (that must now be forgone) been built instead.

TRADE CREATES VALUE

We learned in the last chapter that preferences are subjective, are known only to the individual, and differ among individuals. This means that mere trading—rearranging goods and services among people—can create value. In our Chapter 1 example, the value to Alice of a ticket to attend the Bolshoi ballet performance was zero once she received the party invitation, but the value to other individuals was greater. Suppose the value of the ticket to Jim, who bought it at the advertised price of $10, was $11. An unforeseen change in Alice's schedule had destroyed the value of the performance that evening for her, but trading (selling) the ticket to Jim created $10 in value for her, and it netted $1 in value for Jim—the $11 value he placed on the performance minus the $10 he gave to Alice. The performance remained the same, and the seats available remained the same, but value had been created just as surely as if an additional seat had been made available. It is wrong to assume that a particular good or service has value just because it exists, independent of the circumstances and who uses it.[4] As the example of the ballet ticket illustrates, the value of goods and services depends on who uses them, when they are used, and where they are used, as well as on their own physical characteristics.

TRANSACTION COSTS— A BARRIER TO TRADE

Unfortunately, Alice did not know about Andrew, another ballet fan, who would have been willing to pay $15 for the ticket. Andrew lives off campus and failed to see the bulletin board ad, so the potential for another $4 increase in value failed to materialize. If, however, Jim and Andrew happen to meet and talk about the ballet before the show, the additional $4 in value for the ticket might be created by another transaction: Jim trading the ticket to Andrew. Such a transaction is unlikely, because getting together requires either good luck or costly measures such as searching bulletin boards. Of course new and cheaper marketing methods, such as electronic bulletin boards, can reduce the cost and increase the frequency

---

[4]An illuminating discussion of this subject, termed the "physical fallacy," is found in Thomas Sowell, *Knowledge and Decisions* (New York: Basic Books, 1980), pp. 67–72.

of value-creating trades. Still, not every trade that could potentially create value will be discovered and made.

While exchange creates value, it is also costly. The costs of the time, effort, and other resources necessary to search out, negotiate, and conclude an exchange are called **transaction costs.** Transaction costs reduce our ability to gain from mutually advantageous potential trades.

Because of transaction costs, we should not expect all potentially valuable trades to take place, any more than we expect all useful knowledge to be learned, all safety measures to be taken, or all potential "A" grades to be earned. Frequent fliers know that if they never miss a flight, they are probably spending too much time waiting in airports. Similarly, the seller of a car, a house, or a ballet ticket knows that to find that single person in the world who would be willing to pay the most money is not worth the enormous effort required to locate that buyer. The cost of perfection in exchange, as in most other endeavors, is just too high.

Transaction costs
The time, effort, and other resources needed to search out, negotiate, and consummate an exchange.

MIDDLEMAN AS COST REDUCER

Since there are gains from exchange, some people, called **middlemen,** specialize in providing information and arranging trades. Often thought to be unnecessary, middlemen are perceived as adding to the buyer's expense without benefiting the buyer. Now that we recognize transaction costs, however, we can see the fallacy of this view. The auto dealer, for example, can help both the makers and the buyers of cars. By keeping an inventory of autos, and by hiring knowledgeable salespeople, the dealer helps the car shopper learn about the many cars offered, and how each car looks, performs, and "feels." (Don't forget that since preferences are subjective, they are not objectively known to others.) Car buyers also like to know that the local dealer will honor the warranty and provide parts and service for the car when they are needed. The car maker, by using the dealer as a middleman, is able to concentrate on designing and making cars, leaving to middlemen—that is, dealers—the task of marketing and servicing them in each community.

Grocers are another provider of middleman services. Each of us could deal with food producers directly, buying in large quantities, perhaps shopping through catalogs to choose what we want. If we did, though, we wouldn't be able to squeeze the tomatoes! Besides, we would all need giant refrigerators, freezers, and storerooms at home to hold huge quantities of food. Or, perhaps we could

Middleman
A person who buys and sells, or who arranges trades. A middleman reduces transaction costs, usually for a fee or a markup in price.

OUTSTANDING ECONOMIST

THOMAS SOWELL (1930–)

Thomas Sowell, a senior fellow at the Hoover Institution, recognizes the critical importance of the institutions—the "rules of the game"—that shape human interactions. His book, *Knowledge and Decisions,* stresses the difficulty of obtaining knowledge and explores the way different institutional arrangements provide different kinds and amounts of scarce information.

form consumer cooperatives, banding together to eliminate the middleman, using our own warehouses and our own volunteer labor to order, receive, display, redistribute, and collect payment for the food. In fact, some cooperatives like this do exist, but most people prefer instead to hire the space and do the planning, record keeping, and labor through the grocer, paying markup for middleman services.

Stockbrokers, publishers of the Yellow Pages, and merchants of all sorts are middlemen—specialists in selling, guaranteeing, and servicing the items traded. For a fee, they reduce transaction costs both for the shopper and for the seller. By making exchange cheaper and more convenient, middlemen cause more efficient trades to happen. In so doing, they themselves create value.

PROPERTY RIGHTS

Property rights
The right to use, control, and obtain the benefits from a good or service.

The buyer of an automobile or an apple may take the item home. The buyer of a steamship or an office building, though, might never touch it. When exchange occurs, it is really the rights—the **property rights**—to the item that change hands. It is ownership and control that count, rather than physical possession. In a market system with voluntary trade, it is property rights and the signals from market prices that cause individuals to take into account how others are affected by the owner's use of property.

Powerful incentive effects follow from private ownership of the rights to a good. The owner has the right to control the good's use, and must accept responsibility for the outcomes of that control. As we will be discussing, private ownership provides a strong incentive for the owner-controller to bear in mind both the costs and the benefits of decisions about how the good is used.

Private-property rights
Property rights that are exclusively held by an owner, or group of owners, and that can be transferred to others at the owner's discretion.

Private-property rights exist when property rights are (1) exclusively controlled by one owner (or jointly by a group of owners) and (2) transferable to others. Private property rights give owners a chance to act selfishly. However, since they link responsibility to the authority to control, they also make owners accountable for their actions. The incentives that arise from private ownership are strong and automatic.

1. Private owners can gain by employing their resources in ways that are beneficial to others. On the other hand, owners bear the opportunity cost of ignoring the wishes of others. If someone values an asset more than its current owner, the current owner can gain by paying heed to the wishes of others. For example, suppose Ed owns a car that others would also like to have. What incentive is there for Ed to pay attention to the desires of the others? If someone else values the car at $2,000, while Ed values it at only $1,500, then Ed can gain by selling the car at any price higher than $1,500. Turning down the offer of $2,000 costs Ed $500. In fact, if transaction costs are low (if search is cheap and easy), Ed might gain by searching for people (potential buyers) who want the car more than he does. If he fails to yield to the desires of others, Ed "pays" the opportunity cost for continued ownership of the car by not receiving the $2,000. Failing to consider the wishes of others may penalize the potential buyer, but it would also hurt Ed. When potential buyers and sellers know that cars are privately owned and thus easily transferable, each has every incentive to search out mutually advantageous trades. After all, if they find such a trade, only the buyer and seller have to approve the deal, and both will gain.

As a second example, suppose Ed owns a house and will be out of town all summer. Will the house stay vacant, or will Ed let someone else use it during those months? We don't know, but we do know that Ed can rent the house to someone else if he chooses, and that if he does not, he will pay the opportunity cost—the rental payments he could get, minus any damages, added upkeep, and transaction costs. Ownership of the private property rights has again faced Ed with the opportunity costs of his actions, and provided him with a strong incentive to consider the wishes of others regarding the use of his property.

"Their house looks so nice. They must be getting ready to sell it."

Pepper . . . and Salt © *The Wall Street Journal.*

2. The private owner has a strong incentive to properly care for the item he or she owns. Will Ed change the oil in his car? Will he take care to see that the seats do not get torn? Probably so, since being careless about these things would reduce the car's value, both to him and to any future owner. The car and its value—the sale price if he sells it—belong just to Ed, so he would bear the burden of a decline in the car's value if the oil ran low and ruined the engine, or if the seats were torn. Similarly, he would capture the value of an investment that improves the car, such as providing a new paint job to make the car more attractive. As the owner, Ed has both the authority and the incentive to protect the car against harm or neglect, and even to enhance its value. Private-property rights give the owner a strong incentive for good stewardship.

3. The private owner has an incentive to conserve for the future if the item is expected to be worth more then. Suppose our man Ed owns a case of very good red wine, which is only two years old. Age will improve it substantially if he puts it in his cellar for another five years. Will he do so? Well, if he does not, he will personally bear the consequences. He (and presumably his friends) will drink wine sooner, but they will sacrifice quality. Also, Ed will forgo the chance to sell the wine later for much more than its current worth. The opportunity cost of drinking the wine now is its unavailability later, for drinking or for sale. Ed bears that cost. Private-property rights assure that Ed has the authority to preserve the wine, and that he gains the benefits if he does so. If the greater quality is expected to be worth the wait, then Ed can capture the benefits of not having the wine "before its time."

In a similar way, if Ed owns land, or a house, or a factory, he has a strong incentive to bear costs now, if necessary, to preserve the asset's value. His wealth is tied up in its value, which reflects nothing more than the net benefits that will be available to the owner in the future. So Ed's wealth depends on his ability to look ahead, maintain, and conserve those things that will be highly valued in the future.

4. With private-property rights, the property owner is accountable for damage to others through misuse of the property. Ed, the car owner, has a right to drive his car, but he has no right to drive in a drunken or reckless way that injures Alice. A chemical company has control over its products, but exactly for that reason, it is legally liable for damages if it mishandles the chemicals. Courts of law recognize and enforce the authority granted by ownership, but they also enforce the responsibility that goes with that authority. Once again, property rights hold accountable the person (owner) with authority over property.

These incentives provided by private ownership of property rights are very useful, and in fact are critical for market coordination of an economy. When private-property rights are not present or are not enforced, other methods must be found to provide the incentives for good stewardship of property, and for proper concern for others by the users of property. For example, when the owner of an automobile or a factory pollutes the air and is not made to pay for damage done to the property of others, property rights are not being enforced. Without effective property rights, other measures may be needed to control polluting behavior. We will return to this problem in Chapter 4.

PRODUCTION-POSSIBILITIES CURVE

Production-possibilities curve
A curve that outlines all possible combinations of total output that could be produced, assuming (1) the utilization of a fixed amount of productive resources, (2) full and efficient use of those resources, and (3) a specific state of technical knowledge. The slope of the curve indicates the rate at which one product can be traded off to produce more of the other.

The resources of every individual are limited. Purposeful decision making and economizing behavior imply that individuals seek to get the most from their limited resources. They do not deliberately waste resources.

The nature of the economizing problem can be made more clear by the use of a conceptual tool, the production-possibilities diagram. A **production-possibilities curve** from this diagram reveals the maximum amount of any two products that can be produced from a fixed set of resources, and the possible trade-offs in production between them.

Exhibit 2–1 illustrates the production-possibilities curve for Susan, an intelligent economics major. This curve indicates the combinations of grades possible for two alternative amounts of study time—six hours and eight hours. If Susan uses her six hours of study time efficiently, she can choose any grade combination

The production possibilities for Susan, in terms of grades, are illustrated for two alternative quantities of total study time. If Susan studied six hours per week, she could attain (1) an F in English and an A in economics, (2) a D in English and a B in economics, (3) a C in both, (4) a B in English and a D in economics, or (5) an F in economics and an A in English.

Could she make higher grades in both? Yes, if she were willing to apply more resources, thereby giving up some leisure. The colored line indicates her production-possibilities curve if she studied eight hours per week.

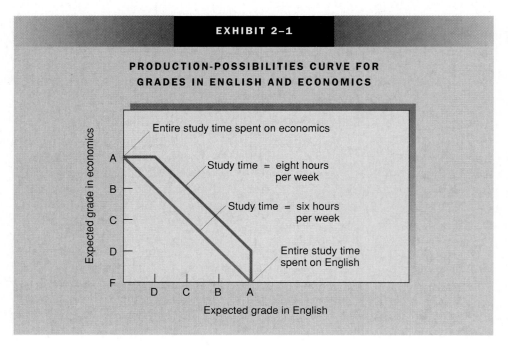

EXHIBIT 2–1

PRODUCTION-POSSIBILITIES CURVE FOR GRADES IN ENGLISH AND ECONOMICS

Entire study time spent on economics

Study time = eight hours per week

Study time = six hours per week

Entire study time spent on English

Expected grade in economics

Expected grade in English

along the six-hour production-possibilities curve. When her study time is limited to six hours per week, though, Susan is able to raise her grade in one of the subjects only by accepting a lower grade in the other. If she wants to improve her overall performance (raise at least one grade without lowering the other), she will have to spend more time on academic endeavors. For example, she might increase her weekly study time from six to eight hours. Of course, this would require her to give up something else—leisure.

Can the production-possibilities concept be applied to the entire economy? The answer is yes. Having more guns means having less butter, as the old saying goes. Beefing up the military requires the use of resources that otherwise could be used to produce nonmilitary goods. If scarce resources are being used efficiently, more of one thing means the sacrifice of others.

Exhibit 2–2 shows a production-possibilities curve for an economy producing only two goods: food and clothing. The curve is concave, or bowed out from the origin. Why? Resources are not equally well suited to produce food and clothing. Consider an economy that is using all of its resources to produce clothing. At that point *(S)*, food production can be expanded by transferring those resources which are best suited for production of food (and least suitable for clothing production) from clothing to food production. Since the resources transferred are highly productive in food and not very productive in clothing, in this range the opportunity cost (clothing forgone) of producing additional food is low. However, as more and more resources are devoted to food production, and successively larger amounts of food are produced (moving from *S* to *A* to *B* and so on), the opportunity cost of food will rise. This results because as more and more food is produced, additional food output can be achieved only by using resources that are less and less suitable for the production of food relative to clothing. Thus, as food output is

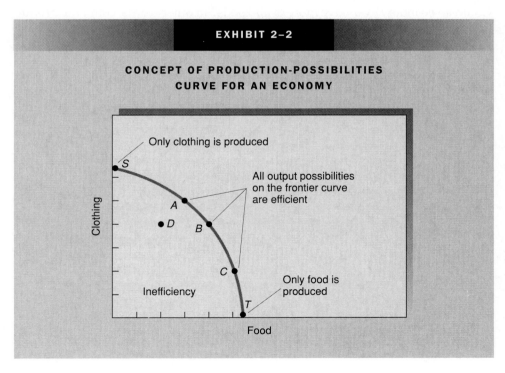

EXHIBIT 2–2

CONCEPT OF PRODUCTION-POSSIBILITIES CURVE FOR AN ECONOMY

Only clothing is produced

All output possibilities on the frontier curve are efficient

Clothing

Inefficiency

Only food is produced

Food

When an economy is using its limited resources efficiently, production of more clothing requires the economy to give up some other goods—food in this simple example. With time, *a technological discovery, expansion of the economy's resource base, or improvement in its economic organization could make it possible to produce more of both, shifting the production-possibilities curve outward. Or the citizens of the economy might decide to give up some leisure for more of both goods. These factors aside, limited resources will constrain the production possibilities of an economy.*

expanded, successively larger amounts of clothing must be forgone per unit of additional food.

What restricts the ability of an economy, once resources are fully utilized, from producing more of everything? The same thing that kept Susan from making a higher grade in both English and economics—lack of resources. There will be various maximum combinations of goods that an economy will be able to produce when

1. It uses some fixed quantity of resources.
2. The resources are not unemployed or used inefficiently.
3. The level of technology (discussed later in this chapter) is constant.

When these three conditions are met, the economy will be at the perimeter of its production-possibilities frontier (points such as *A, B,* and *C* on Exhibit 2–2). Producing more of one good, such as clothing, will necessitate less production of other goods (for example, food).

When the resources of an economy are unemployed or used inefficiently, the economy is operating at a point inside the production-possibilities curve—point *D,* for example. Why might this happen? It happens because the economy is not properly solving the economizing problem. A major function of economic decision making is to help us get the most out of available resources, to move us out to the production-possibilities frontier. We will return to this problem again and again.

SHIFTING THE PRODUCTION-POSSIBILITIES CURVE OUTWARD

Could an economy ever have more of all goods? In other words, could the production-possibilities curve be shifted outward? The answer is yes, under certain circumstances. There are four major methods.

Capital formation
The production of buildings, machinery, tools, and other equipment that will enhance the ability of future economic participants to produce. The term can also be applied to efforts to upgrade the knowledge and skill of workers and thereby increase their ability to produce in the future.

1. An increase in the economy's resource base would expand our ability to produce goods and services. If we had more and better resources, we could produce a greater amount of all goods. Many resources are human-made. If we were willing to give up some current consumption, we could invest more of today's resources into the production of long-lasting physical structures, machines, education, and the development of human skills. This **capital formation** would provide us with better tools and skills in the future and thereby increase our ability to produce goods and services. **Exhibit 2–3** illustrates the link between capital formation and the future production possibilities of an economy. The two economies illustrated start with the same production possibilities curve *(RS)*. However, since Economy A (part "a") allocates more of its resources to investment than does Economy B, A's production-possibilities curve shifts outward with the passage of time by a greater amount. The growth rate of A—the expansion rate of the economy's ability to produce goods—is enhanced because the economy allocates a larger share of its output to investment. Of course, more investment in machines and human skills requires a reduction in current consumption.

Technology
The body of skills and technological knowledge available at any given time. The level of technology establishes the relationship between inputs and the maximum output they can generate.

2. Advancements in Technology Can Expand the Economy's Production Possibilities. **Technology** determines the maximum physical output obtainable from any par-

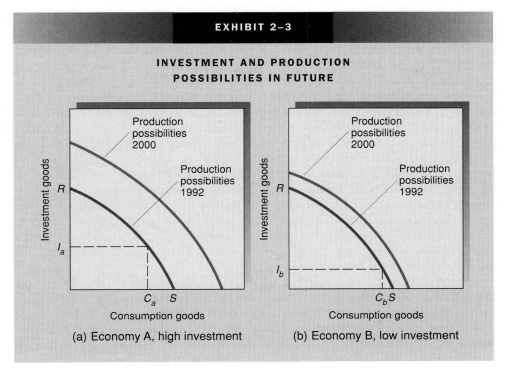

EXHIBIT 2–3

INVESTMENT AND PRODUCTION POSSIBILITIES IN FUTURE

(a) Economy A, high investment

(b) Economy B, low investment

Here we illustrate two economies that initially confront identical production-possibilities curves (RS). The economy illustrated on the left allocates a larger share of its output to investment (I_a, compared to I_b for the economy on the right). As a result, the production possibilities of the high-investment economy will tend to shift outward by a larger amount than will be true for the low-investment economy.

ticular set of resource inputs. New technology can make it possible to get more from our given base of resources.[5] An important form of technological change is **invention,** the use of science and engineering to create new products or processes. Sending information instantly and cheaply by satellite, getting more oil from a well, and growing more corn from newly developed hybrid seed are all examples of technological advances resulting from inventions. Each one has pushed our production-possibilities curve outward.

An economy can also benefit from technology change through **innovation,** the practical and effective adoption of new techniques. Such innovation is commonly carried out by an **entrepreneur**—one who seeks profit by introducing new products or improved techniques to satisfy consumers at a lower cost.[6] To prosper, an entrepreneur must undertake projects that convert and rearrange resources in a manner that will increase their value, thus expanding our production possibilities. Some examples will help us explain.

Invention
The creation of a new product or process, often facilitated by the knowledge of engineering and scientific relationships.

Innovation
The successful introduction and adoption of a new product or process; the economic application of inventions and marketing techniques.

Entrepreneur
A profit-seeking decision maker who decides which projects to undertake and how they should be undertaken. A successful entrepreneur's actions will increase the value of resources.

---

[5]Without modern technical knowledge, it would be impossible to produce the vast array of goods and services responsible for our standard of living. Thomas Sowell makes this point clear when he notes:

The cavemen had the same natural resources at their disposal as we have today, and the difference between their standard of living and ours is a difference between the knowledge they could bring to bear on those resources and the knowledge used today.

See Thomas Sowell, *Knowledge and Decisions* (New York: Basic Books, 1980), p. 47.

[6]This French-origin word literally means "one who undertakes." The entrepreneur is the person who is ultimately responsible. Of course, this responsibility may be shared with others (partners or stockholders, for example) or it may be partially delegated to technical experts. Nevertheless, the success or failure of the entrepreneur is dependent on the outcome of the choices he or she makes.

One entrepreneur, Henry Ford, changed car-making technology by pioneering the assembly line for making cars. With the same amount of labor and materials, Ford made more cars, more cheaply. Another entrepreneur, the late Ray Kroc, founded the McDonald's hamburger chain. In addition to a popular restaurant menu, he provided information to potential customers. By carefully designing a limited menu that could be prepared according to strict formulas, setting up a training school (Hamburger University, outside Chicago) for managers, and providing a program for regular inspection of restaurants, he could guarantee uniformity (known products and quality level) to each customer. Once the McDonald's reputation spread, hungry people knew what to expect at the "golden arches" without even having to enter the restaurant. Trying McDonald's in one location provides information on thousands of others. Nationwide franchises and quality control make it easy for McDonald's fans to find these quick, cheap meals. The same information makes it easy for those who dislike the formula to avoid it. There is no need to sample each restaurant's offerings. In both cases, we benefit from Mr. Kroc's entrepreneurship—an innovative way to guarantee quality and to transmit instant information cheaply.

Another type of entrepreneur takes inventions produced by others and applies them more effectively. Steven Jobs, co-founder of the Apple Computer Corporation, is an example. He and his firm used the new computer technology to create personal and small-business computers, and pioneered the "user-friendly" software needed by most of us to use such machines. Selling the combination helped make computers useful to millions of people, both at home and on the job, and brought the new technology within their financial reach. Once again, entrepreneurship expanded our production possibilities.

3. An improvement in the rules under which the economy functions can increase output. The legal system of a country influences the ability of people to cooperate with each other and produce desired goods. Changes in legal institutions that promote social cooperation and enhance the incentive of people to produce will shift the production-possibilities curve outward.

Historically, legal innovations have been an important source of economic progress. During the eighteenth century, a system of patents provided investors with a private-property right to their ideas. At about the same time, the recognition of the corporation as a legal entity reduced the cost of forming large firms that were often required for the mass production of manufactured goods. Both of these legal changes improved economic organization and thereby accelerated the growth of output (that is, shifted the production-possibilities curve outward) in Europe and North America.

Sometimes countries may, perhaps as the result of ignorance or prejudice, adopt legal institutions that will reduce production possibilities. Laws that restrict or prohibit trade among various groups provide an illustration. For example, the laws of several southern states prohibited the employment of African Americans in certain occupations, and restricted other economic exchanges between blacks and whites for almost 100 years following the Civil War. This legislation was not only harmful to African Americans, it retarded progress and reduced the production possibilities of these states.

4. By working harder and giving up current leisure, we could increase our production of goods and services. Strictly speaking, this is not an expansion in the production frontier because leisure is also a good. We are giving up some of that good to have more of other things.

The work effort of individuals depends not only on their personal preferences but also on public policy. For example, high tax rates may induce individuals to reduce their work time. The basic economic postulate implies that as high tax rates reduce the personal payoff from working (and earning taxable income), individuals will shift more of their time to other, untaxed activities, including the consumption of leisure, moving the production-possibilities curve for market goods inward. (Recall, from Exhibit 2–1, how Susan's production possibilities for grades shifted inward if she changed from eight hours of study per week to only six hours.) Any reduction in market work time not only reduces output directly, but it is likely also to reduce the gains from the division of labor. We turn now to look at why this is important.

DIVISION OF LABOR AND PRODUCTION POSSIBILITIES

In a modern economy, individuals do not produce most of the items we consume. Instead, we sell our labor services (usually agreeing to do specified productive work) and use the income we get in exchange to buy what we want. We do this because the **division of labor,** together with exchange, allow us to produce far more goods and services through cooperative effort than we could if each household produced its own food, clothing, shelter, transportation, and other desired goods.

Division of labor
A method that breaks down the production of a commodity into a series of specific tasks, each performed by a different worker.

Observing the operation of a pin manufacturer more than 200 years ago, Adam Smith noted that specialization and division of labor permitted far more output. When each worker specialized in a productive function, ten workers were able to produce 48,000 pins per day, or 4,800 pins per worker. Without specialization and division of labor, Smith doubted an individual worker could produce even 20 pins per day.[7]

The division of labor separates production tasks into a series of related operations. Each worker performs a single task, only one of perhaps hundreds of tasks necessary to produce a commodity. There are several reasons why the division of labor often leads to enormous gains in output per worker. First, specialization permits individuals to take advantage of their existing abilities and skills. (Put another way, specialization permits an economy to take advantage of the fact that individuals have different skills.) Different types of work can be assigned to those individuals who are able to accomplish them most efficiently. Second, a worker who specializes in just one task (or one narrow area) becomes more experienced and more skilled in that task with the passage of time. Most importantly, the division of labor lets us adopt complex, large-scale production techniques unthinkable for an individual household. As our knowledge of technology and the potential of machinery expand, capital-intensive production procedures and the division of labor permit us to attain living standards undreamed of just a few decades ago.

---

[7]See Adam Smith, *An Inquiry into the Nature and Causes of the Wealth of Nations* (1776; Cannan's ed., Chicago: University of Chicago Press, 1976), pp. 7–16, for additional detail on the importance of the division of labor.

TRADE AND COMPARATIVE ADVANTAGE

Economizing means getting the most out of our available resources. How can this be accomplished? How can we reach our production-possibilities frontier and get more value from our productive activities? To answer these questions, we must understand several important principles.

First, let us consider the economizing problem of Woodward and Mason, individuals in the construction business. **Exhibit 2–4** presents certain facts about the abilities of Woodward and Mason. Woodward is highly skilled, fast, and reliable. During one month, he can build either four frame houses or two brick houses. Mason is less skilled, and is slower than Woodward at building both kinds of houses. It takes Mason an entire month to build either a frame or a brick house.

Last year, Woodward spent 8 months producing 16 brick houses and the other 4 months producing 16 frame houses. Mason was able to produce only 6 frame and 6 brick houses during the year. Their joint output was 22 frame and 22 brick houses.

Since Woodward has an absolute advantage (he can build both frame and brick houses more rapidly than Mason) it might appear that he could not gain from specialization and trade of products with Mason. Potential gain, though, is clearly present. Suppose Mason specializes in the production of brick houses, while Woodward spends 6 months producing both types of house. Woodward can produce 24 frame houses (4 per month) in those 6 months, and 12 brick houses (2 per month) in another 6 months. After they became more specialized, Mason and Woodward can produce 24 frame houses (all by Woodward) and 24 brick houses (12 each) in the same 12-month period. Together, the builders are better off. If 5 of Mason's 12 brick houses are traded to Woodward for 7 frame houses, then Mason will have 7 frame and 7 brick houses to show for his efforts, compared to last year's individual output rate of 6 frame and 6 brick. Similarly, upon receipt of the 5 brick houses from Mason in exchange for 7 frame ones, Woodward is also left with 17 frame and 17 brick houses, definitely an improvement over last year's output of 16 frame and 16 brick houses. Thus, specialization and exchange allow both Woodward and Mason to surpass last year's production rate.

Despite the fact that Woodward is better than Mason at producing both frame and brick houses, the two are able to gain from trade and specialization.[8] Is it magic? What is happening here? Our old friend, opportunity cost, will help us unravel this seemingly paradoxical result. In what sense is Woodward better at producing brick houses than Mason? True, in one month, Woodward can produce twice as many brick houses as Mason, but what is Woodward's opportunity cost of producing a brick house? Two frame ones, right? In the same time required to produce a single brick house, Woodward can produce two frame houses.

Consider Mason's opportunity cost of producing a brick house. It is only one frame house. So who is the cheaper producer of brick houses? Mason is, because

---

[8]Throughout this section we will assume that individuals are equally content to produce either product. Dropping this assumption would add to the complexity of the analysis, but it would not change the basic principle.

EXHIBIT 2-4

COMPARATIVE ADVANTAGE
AND INCREASING OUTPUT

THE MONTHLY POSSIBILITIES OF WOODWARD AND MASON ARE:

FRAME HOUSES PER MONTH		BRICK HOUSES PER MONTH	
WOODWARD	MASON	WOODWARD	MASON
4	1	2	1

Initially each produced an equal quantity of both frame and brick houses. Annually, Woodward could produce 16 of each, and Mason only 6 of each. Thus, their total output could reach 22 frame and 22 brick units.

After each specialized in the area of their comparative advantage, Mason produced only brick houses, building 12 of them (one each month). Woodward spent 6 months building frame houses, and 6 months building brick houses, producing 24 frame (4 per month) and 12 brick units (2 per month). As the chart shows, after specialization, their total output of both frame houses and brick houses increased from 22 to 24.

If Mason trades 5 brick houses to Woodward for 7 frame houses, Woodward would end up with 17 brick and 17 frame houses, one more of each than he could achieve without specialization and trade. Similarly, Mason would be left with 7 brick and 7 frame (received in the trade with Woodward). Specialization and exchange permit both parties to gain.

	ANNUAL OUTPUT BEFORE SPECIALIZATION		ANNUAL OUTPUT AFTER SPECIALIZATION	
	FRAME HOUSES	BRICK HOUSES	FRAME HOUSES	BRICK HOUSES
Woodward	16	16	24	12
Mason	6	6	0	12
Total	22	22	24	24

Mason's opportunity cost of producing a brick house is one frame house, compared to Woodward's opportunity cost of two frame houses.

The reason that Woodward and Mason can both gain is that their exchange allows each of them to specialize in the production of the product that, comparatively speaking, they can produce most cheaply. Mason is the cheaper producer of brick houses. Woodward is the cheaper producer of the frame ones. They are able to economize—get more out of their resources—by trading and specializing in the thing that each does better, comparatively speaking.

Law of comparative advantage

A principle that states that individuals, firms, regions, or nations can gain by specializing in the production of goods that they produce cheaply (that is, at a low-opportunity-cost) and exchanging those goods for other desired goods for which they are a high-opportunity-cost producer.

This simple example demonstrates a basic truth known as the **law of comparative advantage,** which lies at the heart of economizing behavior for any economy. Initially developed in the early 1800s by the great English economist David Ricardo, this law states that the total output of a group of individuals, an entire economy, or a group of nations will be greatest when the output of each good is produced by the person (or firm) with the lowest opportunity cost.

If a product, any product made in the economy, can be produced by someone else with a lower opportunity cost, the economy is giving up more than necessary. It is not economizing. Economizing, or economic efficiency, requires that output always be generated by the producer who has the lowest opportunity cost.

Perhaps one additional example will help to drive home the implications of the law of comparative advantage. Consider the situation of an attorney who can type 120 words per minute. The attorney is trying to decide whether to hire a secretary, who types only 60 words per minute, to complete some legal documents. If the lawyer does the typing job, it will take four hours; if a secretary is hired, the typing job will take eight hours. Thus, the lawyer has an absolute advantage in typing compared to the prospective employee. The attorney's time, though, is worth $50 per hour when working as a lawyer, whereas the typist's time is worth $5 per hour as a typist. Although a fast typist, the attorney is also a high-opportunity-cost producer of typing service. If the lawyer types the documents, the job will cost $200, the opportunity cost of four hours of lost time as a lawyer. Alternatively, the cost of having the documents typed by the typist is only $40 (eight hours of typing service at $5 per hour). The lawyer's comparative advantage thus lies in practicing law. He or she will gain by hiring the typist and spending the additional time specializing in the practice of law.

DIVISION OF LABOR, SPECIALIZATION, AND EXCHANGE

It is difficult to exaggerate the gains derived from specialization , division of labor, and exchange in accordance with the law of comparative advantage. These factors are the primary source of our modern standard of living. Can you imagine the difficulty involved in producing one's own housing, clothing, and food, to say nothing of radios, television sets, dishwashers, automobiles, and telephone services? Yet, most families in North America, Western Europe, Japan, and Australia enjoy these conveniences. They are able to do so largely because their economies are organized in such a way that individuals can cooperate, specialize, and trade, thereby reaping the benefits of the enormous increases in output—both in quantity and diversity—thus produced. An economy not realizing the gains from specialization and division of labor is ignoring the law of comparative advantage. It is operating inside its production-possibilities curve, at a point such as D in Exhibit 2–2. This is the case for most of the less developed economies. For various reasons, production in these economies is centered primarily in the individual household. Therefore, the output level per worker of these economies falls well below the attainable level.

Once we have thought about it, the law of comparative advantage is almost common sense. Stated in layman's terms, it simply means that if we want to accomplish a task with the least effort, each of us should specialize in that component of the task that we do best, comparatively speaking.

The principle of comparative advantage is universal. It is just as valid in socialist countries as it is in capitalist countries. Socialist planners, to get the most out of available resources, must also apply the principle of comparative advantage.

MUTUAL DEPENDENCE, SPECIALIZATION, AND EXCHANGE

Specialization and mutual dependence are directly related. If the United States specializes in the production of agricultural products and Middle East countries specialize in the production of oil, the two countries become interdependent. Similarly, if Texas specializes in the production of cotton and Kansas specializes in the production of wheat, interdependence results. In some cases, this interdependence can have serious consequences for one or both of the parties—for example, vulnerability to economic pressure applied by a trading partner. Potential benefits include increased international understanding with reduced likelihood of war. The potential costs and benefits should be weighed along with the mutual consumption gains when one is evaluating the merits of specialization.

SPECIALIZATION AND JOB SATISFACTION

Specialization clearly makes it possible to produce more goods, but it may also cause a job to become boring. Our friend Woodward may get tired of building frame houses, and Mason's life may lose a certain zest because he produces only brick ones. Carried further, specialization often results in assembly-line production techniques. Workers may become quite skilled because they perform identical tasks over and over again, but some of the gains associated with the expansion of physical output may result in worker dissatisfaction with monotonous, unchallenging work.

Our initial approach to the topic of specialization considered only material goods in the interest of making the principle simpler to communicate. However, specialization can also be considered from the viewpoint of utility, in which both output and job satisfaction are economic goods.

An individual's opportunity cost of producing a good (or performing a service) includes the sacrifice of both physical production of other goods and any change in the desirability of working conditions. The consideration of working conditions and job preferences does not invalidate the basic concept. It is still true that maximum economic efficiency, in the utility sense, requires that each productive activity be performed by those persons with the lowest opportunity cost, including satisfaction given up by turning down other jobs. Individuals could still gain by producing and selling those things for which they have a comparatively low opportunity cost, including the job-satisfaction component, while buying other things for which their opportunity cost is high. They would tend to specialize in the provision of those things they both do well and enjoy most. People with a strong aversion to monotonous work would be less likely to choose such work even though they might be skilled at it. Those with a smaller comparative advantage,

Trade makes it possible for individuals, regions, and nations to gain from specialization, division of labor, and adoption of mass production techniques.

measured strictly in terms of physical goods, might have a lower opportunity cost because they find the work more rewarding.

PERSONAL MOTIVATION, SPECIALIZATION, AND EXCHANGE

Economic thinking implies that people will choose an option only if they expect the benefits (utility) of the choice to exceed its opportunity cost. Purposeful decision makers will be motivated by the pursuit of personal gain. They will never knowingly choose an alternative when they expect the opportunity cost to exceed the benefits. To do so would be to make a choice with the full awareness that it meant the sacrifice of another, preferred course of action. That simply would not make sense. To say that people are motivated by personal gain does not, of course, mean that they are inconsiderate of others. Other people's feelings will often affect the personal benefit received by a decision maker.

When an individual's interest, aptitudes, abilities, and skills make it possible to gain by exchanging low-opportunity-cost goods for those things that he or she could produce only at a high opportunity cost, pursuit of the potential gain will motivate the individual to trade precisely in this manner. If free exchange is allowed, it will not be necessary for people to be assigned the "right" job or to be told that, comparatively speaking, they should trade A for B because they are good at producing A but not so good at producing B. In a market setting, individuals will voluntarily specialize because they will gain by doing so. People following their own interests will produce and sell items for which they have a comparative advantage—items they can produce cheaply—and will buy those things that others can produce more cheaply. (See "Myths of Economics" box.)

THREE ECONOMIC QUESTIONS

We have outlined several basic concepts that are important if one is to understand the economizing problem. In this section, we outline three general economic questions that every nation, regardless of its institutions, must answer.

1. What will be produced?   We cannot produce as many goods as we desire. So what goods should we produce and in what quantities? Should we produce more food and less clothing, more consumer durables and less clean air, more national

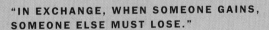

MYTHS OF ECONOMICS

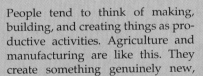

"IN EXCHANGE, WHEN SOMEONE GAINS, SOMEONE ELSE MUST LOSE."

People tend to think of making, building, and creating things as productive activities. Agriculture and manufacturing are like this. They create something genuinely new, something that was not there before. Trade, on the other hand, which is merely the exchange of one thing for another without creating anything new, may be perceived as a zero-sum game in which one person's gain is necessarily a loss to another. A closer look at the motivation for trade helps one see through this popular myth. Mutual gain is the motivation for voluntary exchange. If the parties to the exchange do not anticipate that the trade will improve their well-being, they will not agree to it. Trade is therefore productive because it increases the well-being of each trading partner.

There are three major reasons why trade is a positive-sum activity. First, it channels goods and services to those who value them most. People have fallen into the habit of thinking of material things as wealth, but material things are not wealth until they are in the hands of someone who values them. A highly technical mathematics book is not wealth to a dock laborer with a sixth-grade education. It becomes wealth only after if it is in the hands of a mathematician. A master painting may be wealth to the collector of art, but it is of little value to someone uninterested in art. Wealth is created by the act of channeling goods to persons who value them highly.

Second, exchange can be advantageous to trading partners because it permits each to specialize in areas in which he or she has a comparative advantage. For example, exchange permits a skilled carpenter to concentrate on building house frames, while contracting for electrical and plumbing services from others who have comparative advantages in those areas. Similarly, trade permits a country such as Canada to specialize in the production of wheat, while Brazil specializes in coffee. Such specialization enlarges joint output and permits both countries to gain from the exchange of Canadian wheat for Brazilian coffee.

Third, voluntary exchange makes it possible for individuals to produce more goods through cooperative effort. In the absence of exchange, productive activity would be limited to the individual household. Self-provision and small-scale production would be the rule. Voluntary exchange permits us to realize gains derived from the division of labor and the adoption of large-scale production methods. Production can be broken down into a series of specific operations, each performed by those most suitable. This procedure often leads to a more efficient application of both labor and machinery. Without voluntary exchanges, these gains would be lost.

defense and less leisure? Or, should we use up some of our productive resources, producing more consumer goods today even though it will mean fewer goods in the future? If our economy is operating efficiently (that is, on its production-possibilities curve), the choice to produce more of one commodity will reduce our ability to produce others. Sometimes the impact may be more indirect. Production of some goods will not only require productive resources but may, as a by-product, reduce the actual availability of other goods. For example, production of warmer houses and more automobile travel may, as a by-product, increase air pollution, and thus reduce the availability of clean air (another desired good). Use of natural resources (water, minerals, trees, and so on) to produce some goods may simultaneously reduce the availability of wildlife habitat. Every economy must answer these and similar questions concerning what should be produced.

2. How will goods be produced?   Usually, different combinations of productive resources can be used to produce a good. Education could be produced with less labor by the use of more television lectures, recording devices, and books. Wheat could be raised with less land and more fertilizer. Chairs could be constructed with more labor and fewer machines. Thus, decisions must be made as to which combinations of alternative productive resources will be used to produce the goods of an economy.

After the decision to produce, resources must be organized and people must be motivated. How can the resources of an economy be transformed into the final output of goods and services? Economies may differ as to the combination of economic incentives, threats of force, and types of competitive behavior that are permissible, but all still face the problem of how their limited resources can be used to produce desired goods.

3. For whom will goods be produced?   Who will actually consume the available products? This economic question is often referred to as the *distribution* problem. Property rights for resources, including labor skills, might be established and resource owners permitted to sell their services to the highest bidder. Income from the sale of resource services then would be used to bid for goods. In this case, prices and resource ownership would be the determining factors of distribution. Alternatively, goods might be split on a strict per capita basis, with each person getting an equal share of the pie. Or they might be divided according to the relative political influence of citizens, with larger shares going to those who are more persuasive and skillful than others at organizing and obtaining political power. They could also be distributed according to need, with a dictator or even an all-powerful, democratically elected legislature deciding which citizens had which needs.

INTERRELATEDNESS OF THE ECONOMIC QUESTIONS

One thing is clear—these three questions are highly interrelated. How goods are distributed will exert considerable influence on the "voluntary" availability of productive resources, including human resources. The choice of what to produce will influence how resources are used. In reality, these three basic economic questions must be resolved simultaneously, and all economies, whatever their other differences, must somehow answer them. There are many ways to set up the institutions—the "rules of the game"—by which an economy makes these decisions. Each will result in a different set of answers to the universal questions.

TWO METHODS OF MAKING DECISIONS— THE MARKET OR GOVERNMENT PLANNING

Two prominent ways to organize economic activity are through the market mechanism and collective decision making. Let us briefly consider each of these methods.

Private ownership, voluntary contracts (often these contracts are verbal), and reliance upon market prices are the distinguishing characteristics of the **market mechanism,** or of *capitalist economies,* as they are often called. Under market **capitalism,** people have private ownership rights to consumption goods, their labor, and productive assets.[9] Private parties are permitted to buy and sell ownership rights at mutually agreeable prices in unregulated markets. The role of government is limited to that of a referee—a neutral party enforcing the rules of the game. The government defines and protects private ownership rights, enforces contracts, and protects people from fraud. But the government is not an active player; the political process will not be used to modify market outcomes or favor some at the expense of others. For example, the government will not prevent a seller from using price reductions and quality improvements to compete with other sellers. Nor will the government prevent a buyer from using a higher price to bid a product or productive resource away from another potential buyer. Legal restraints (for example, government licensing) will not be used to limit potential buyers or sellers from producing, selling, or buying in the marketplace. Under market organization, planning by a central authority is absent. The three basic economic questions are answered through the market coordination of the decentralized choices of buyers and sellers.

The major alternative to market organization is **collective decision making,** the use of political organization and government planning to allocate resources. In some cases, the government may own the income-producing assets (machines, buildings, and land) and directly determine what goods they will produce. This form of economic organization is referred to as **socialism.** Alternatively, the government may maintain private ownership in name, but use taxes, subsidies, and regulations to answer the basic economic questions. In both instances, political powers rather than market forces are used to direct the economy. In both cases, the decision to expand or contract the output of education, medical services, automobiles, electricity, steel, consumer durables, and thousands of other commodities is made by government officials and planning boards. This is not to say that the preferences of individuals are of no importance. If the government officials and central planners are influenced by the democratic process, they have to consider how their actions will influence their election prospects. Otherwise, like the firm that produces a product in a market economy that consumers do not want, their tenure of service is likely to be a short one.

Market mechanism
A method of organization that allows unregulated prices and the decentralized decisions of private-property owners to resolve the basic economic problems of consumption, production, and distribution.

Capitalism
An economic system based on private ownership of productive resources and allocation of goods according to the signals provided by free markets.

Collective decision making
The method of organization that relies on public-sector decision making (voting, political bargaining, lobbying, and so on). It can be used to resolve the basic economic problems of an economy.

Socialism
A system of economic organization in which (1) the ownership and control of the basic means of production rest with the state and (2) resource allocation is determined by centralized planning rather than by market forces.

---

[9]*Capitalism* is a term coined by Karl Marx.

In most economies, including that of the United States, a large number of decisions are made both through the decentralized pricing system and through public-sector decision making. Both exert considerable influence on how we solve fundamental economic problems. Although the two arrangements are different, in each case the choices of individuals acting as decision makers are important. Economics is about how people make decisions; and the tools of economics can be applied to both market- and public-sector action. Constraints on the individual and incentives to pursue various types of activities will differ according to whether decisions are made in the public sector or in the marketplace. Still, people are people; changes in personal costs and benefits will influence their choices. In turn, the acts of political participants—voters, lobbyists, and politicians—will influence public policy and its economic consequences.

LOOKING AHEAD

The next chapter presents an overview of the market sector. Chapter 4 focuses on how the public sector, the democratic collective decision-making process, functions. It is not enough merely to study how the pricing system works. To understand the forces influencing the allocation of economic resources in a country such as the United States, we must apply the tools of economics of both market- and public-sector choices.

We think this approach is important, fruitful, and exciting. How does the market sector really work? What does economics say about which activities should be handled by government? What types of economic policies are politically attractive to democratically elected officials? Is sound economic policy sometimes in conflict with good politics? We will tackle all these questions.

CHAPTER SUMMARY

1. Because of scarcity, when an individual chooses to do, to make, or to buy something, that individual must simultaneously give up something else that might otherwise have been chosen. The highest valued activity sacrificed is the opportunity cost of the choice.

2. Trade is productive. Voluntary exchange creates value by channeling goods into the hands of people who value them most. Recognition of this fact exposes the physical fallacy, which incorrectly assumes that a good or a service has a given value, regardless of who uses it and how it is used. Trade is a positive-sum game that improves the economic well-being of each voluntary participant.

3. The production-possibilities curve reveals the maximum combination of any two products that can be produced with a fixed quantity of resources, assuming that the level of technology is constant. When an individual or an economy is operating at maximum efficiency, the combination of output chosen will be on the production-possibilities curve. In such cases, greater production of one good will necessitate a reduction in the output of other goods.

4. The production-possibilities curve of an economy can be shifted outward by (1) current investment that expands the future resource base of the economy, (2) technological advancement, (3) improved institutions, and (4) the forgoing of leisure and an increase in work effort. The last factor indicates that the production-possibilities constraint is not strictly fixed, even during the current time period. It is partly a matter of preference.

5. Production can often be expanded through division of labor and cooperative effort among individuals. With division of labor, production of a commodity can be broken down into a series of specific tasks. Specialization and division of labor often lead to an expansion in output per worker because they (1) permit productive tasks to be undertaken by the individuals who can accomplish those tasks most efficiently, (2) lead to improvement in worker efficiency as specific tasks are performed numerous times, and (3) facilitate the efficient applications of machinery and advanced technology to the production process.

6. Joint output of individuals, regions, or nations will be maximized when goods are exchanged between parties in accordance with the law of comparative advantage. This law states that total output is maximized when parties specialize in the production of goods for which they are low-opportunity-cost producers and exchange these for goods for which they are high-opportunity-cost producers. Pursuit of personal gain will motivate people to specialize in those things they do best (that is, for which they are low-opportunity-cost producers).

7. Every economy must answer three basic questions: (1) What will be produced? (2) How will goods be produced?

(3) How will the goods be distributed? These three questions are highly interrelated.

8. There are two basic methods of making economic decisions: The market mechanism and public-sector decision making. The decisions of individuals will influence the result in both cases. The tools of economics are general. They are applicable to choices that influence both market- and public-sector decisions.

CRITICAL-ANALYSIS QUESTIONS

1. "If Jones trades $2,000 to Smith for a used car, the items exchanged must be of equal value." Is this statement true, false, or uncertain?

*2. Economists often argue that wage rates reflect productivity. Yet, the wages of housepainters have increased nearly as rapidly as the national average, even though these workers use approximately the same methods that were applied 50 years ago. Can you explain why the wages of painters have risen substantially even though their productivity has changed so little?

3. It takes one hour to travel from New York City to Washington, D.C., by air, but it takes five hours by bus. If the air fare is $55 and the bus fare is $35, which would be cheaper for someone whose opportunity cost of travel time is $3 per hour? For someone whose opportunity cost is $5 per hour? $7 per hour?

4. Explain why the percentage of college-educated women employed outside the home exceeds the percentage of women with eight years of schooling who are engaged in outside employment.

5. Explain why parking lots in downtown areas of large cities often have several decks, whereas many of equal size in suburban areas cover only the ground level.

*6. "People in business get ahead by exploiting the needs of their consumers. The gains of business are at the expense of suffering imposed on their customers." Evaluate this statement from the producer of a prime-time television program.

7. Consider the questions below:
a. Do you think that your work effort is influenced by whether there is a close link between personal output and personal compensation (reward)? Explain.
b. Suppose the grades in your class were going to be determined by a random draw at the end of the course. How would this influence your study habits?

c. How would your study habits be influenced if everyone in the class were going to be given an A grade? How about if grades were based entirely on examinations composed of the multiple-choice questions in the coursebook for this textbook?
d. Do you think the total output of goods in the United States is affected by the close link between productive contribution and individual reward? Why or why not?

8. In many states, the resale of tickets to sporting events at prices above the original purchase price ("ticket scalping") is prohibited. Who is helped and who is hurt by such prohibitions? Can you think of ways ticket owners who want to sell might get around the prohibition? Do you think it would be a good idea to extend the resale prohibition to other things—automobiles, books, works of art, or stock shares, for example? Why or why not?

*9. Does a 60-year-old tree farmer have an incentive to plant and care for Douglas fir trees that will not reach optimal cutting size for another 50 years?

*10. What forms of competition does a private-property, market-directed economy authorize? What forms does it prohibit?

11. With regard to the use of resources, what is the objective of the entrepreneur? What is the major function of the middleman? Is the middleman an entrepreneur?

12. Do private-property rights permit owners to use their property selfishly to the detriment of others? Do private-property rights protect owners against the selfishness of others? Explain your answers.

13. "The rancher, who owns his grazing land, may overgraze it [let the cattle eat so much of the grass that erosion ruins the land] if he is desperate to make money now. Private ownership of land is dangerous." Evaluate this statement.

*14. "Really good agricultural land should not be developed for housing. Food is far more important." Evaluate this statement.

15. The United States imposes tariffs (taxes) on textiles, automobiles, computer chips, and many other import products. Other trade restraints prohibit the importation of sugar and cheese products. How do these trade restraints affect the economic well-being of Americans?

*16. "When you're dealing with questions related to human life, economic costs are irrelevant." Evaluate this statement made by a congressman.

---

*Asterisk denotes questions for which answers are given in Appendix C.

CHAPTER THREE

SUPPLY, DEMAND, AND THE MARKET PROCESS

I am convinced that if it [the market system] were the result of deliberate human design, and if the people guided by the price changes understood that their decisions have significance far beyond their immediate aim, this mechanism would have been acclaimed as one of the greatest triumphs of the human mind.

NOBEL LAUREATE FRIEDRICH HAYEK[1]

From the point of view of physics, it is a miracle that [seven million New Yorkers are fed each day] without any control mechanism other than sheer capitalism.

SCIENTIST JOHN H. HOLLAND AT THE SANTA FE INSTITUTE

CHAPTER FOCUS

■ *What do economists mean when they talk about the laws of supply and demand?*
■ *How do market prices respond to changes in supply and demand?*
■ *As buyers and sellers respond to changes in supply and demand, what role does time play in the adjustment process?*
■ *Why are waiting lines, "sold out" signs, and huge inventories seldom observed in market economies? What is the "invisible hand?"*
■ *What happens when prices are fixed above or below the market level?*
■ *Are rent controls an effective means of increasing the availability of rental housing?*

---

[1]Friedrich Hayek, "The Use of Knowledge in Society," *American Economic Review* 35, September 1945, pp. 519–530.

omputer scientist John H. Holland, quoted on the previous page, and other scientists are using *chaos theory* and other computerized mathematical techniques to study how complex systems develop and operate without central direction. They focus on biological questions such as, how do many kinds of specialized cells in a tree organize themselves into leaves, and, how do forests comprised of many species develop? But they also consider economic questions such as, how are the millions of people of New York City fed day after day with very few shortages or surpluses despite a lack of central planning of food supply and distribution? These studies in recent years have added emphasis to Professor Hayek's statement, made in 1945, and quoted on the previous page, about the effectiveness of the market system. The signals and incentives in a working market perform so well that the scientists who study complex systems are amazed by them.

The point made by Hayek was also underscored by the poor performance of the centrally planned economies of Eastern Europe and the former Soviet Union, which was revealed in detail after the fall of the Berlin Wall in 1989. Millions of citizens in those economies desperately want the prosperity enjoyed by their Western European neighbors and others with market-directed economic systems.

The difficulty of coordinating the components of a national economy is enormous. Although the sophisticated central planning in the Soviet Union and Eastern European economies could not do the job in an acceptable fashion, in Western European nations and the United States, where economic activity is directed primarily by the market mechanism, productivity and output have continued to grow.

To appreciate these results, consider the awesome task of coordinating the economic activity of the United States, with 260,000,000 people, 67,000,000 families, and 130,000,000 workers, each having various skills and job preferences. In the market sector, roughly 7,000,000 businesses produce a vast array of products ranging from toothpicks to supercomputers.

How can the actions of these economic participants be coordinated in a sensible manner? How do producers know how much of each good to produce? What keeps them from producing too many ballpoint pens and too few bicycles with reflector lights? Who directs each labor-force participant to the job that best fits his or her skills and preferences? How can we be sure that business firms will choose the correct production methods? In this chapter, we analyze how a market-directed pricing system answers these questions.

In the ideal market economy, no individual or planning board tells the participants what to do. Markets are free and competitive, in the sense that there are no legal restrictions limiting the entry of either buyers or sellers. The economic role of government is limited to defining property rights, enforcing contracts, protecting people from fraud, and similar activities that establish the rules of the game. Although centralized planning is absent, the participants are not without direction. As we shall see, the decentralized decision making of market participants provides direction and leads to economic order.

In the real world, even economies that are strongly market-oriented, such as the U.S. economy, use a combination of market- and public-sector answers to the basic economic questions. In all economies, the institutions provide a mixture of market-sector and government allocation. Nevertheless, it is still quite useful to understand how a free-market pricing system functions, how it motivates people, and how it allocates goods and resources.

SCARCITY NECESSITATES RATIONING

When a good (or resource) is scarce, some criterion must be set up for deciding who will receive the good (or resource) and who will do without it. Scarcity makes **rationing** a necessity.

There are several possible criteria that could be used in rationing a limited amount of a good among citizens who would like to have more of it. If the criterion were first-come, first-served, goods would be allocated to those who were fastest at getting in line or to those who were most willing to wait in line. If beauty were used, goods would be allocated to those who were thought to be most beautiful. The political process might be used, and goods would be allocated on the basis of political status and ability to manipulate the political process to personal advantage. One thing is certain: Scarcity means that methods must be established to decide who gets the limited amount of available goods and resources.

Rationing
An allocation of a limited supply of a good or resource to users who would like to have more of it. Various criteria, including charging a price, can be utilized to allocate the limited supply. When price performs the rationing function, the good or resource is allocated to those willing to give up the most "other things" in order to obtain ownership rights.

COMPETITION RESULTS FROM SCARCITY

Competition is not unique to a market system. Rather, it is a natural outgrowth of scarcity and the desire of human beings to improve their conditions. Competition exists both in capitalist and in socialist societies. It exists both when goods are allocated by price and when they are allocated by other means—collective decision making, for example.

Certainly, though, the rationing criterion will influence which competitive techniques will be used. When the rationing criterion is price, individuals will engage in income-generating activities that enhance their ability to pay the price. The market system encourages individuals to provide services to others in exchange for income. In turn, the income will permit them to procure more scarce goods.

A different rationing criterion will encourage other types of behavior. When the appearance of sincerity, broad knowledge, fairness, good judgment, and a positive television image are important, as they are in the rationing of elected political positions, people will use resources to project these qualities. They will hire makeup artists, public relations experts, and advertising agencies to help them compete. We can change the form of competition, but no society has been able to eliminate it, because no society has been able to eliminate scarcity and the resulting necessity of rationing. When people who want more scarce goods seek to meet the criteria established to ration those goods, competition occurs.

The market is one method of producing and rationing scarce goods and resources. Let us investigate how it works.

CONSUMER CHOICE AND LAW OF DEMAND

Our desire for goods is far greater than the purchasing power of our income. Even rich consumers cannot purchase everything that they would like. Thus, all of us are forced to make choices.

Since we want to get as much satisfaction (value) as possible out of our limited income, we will make such choices purposefully. Predictably, we will choose those alternatives that we expect to enhance our welfare the most, relative to their cost. Prices will therefore influence our decisions. If the price of a desired good increases relative to the price of other goods, we must give up more of other goods if we want to buy the now higher-priced commodity.

According to the basic postulate of economics, an increase in the cost of an alternative reduces the likelihood that it will be chosen. This basic postulate implies that higher prices will discourage consumption. In contrast, lower prices, by reducing the opportunity cost of choosing a good, will stimulate the consumption of it. The inverse relationship between the price of a good and the amount of it that consumers are willing to buy is called the **law of demand.**

The availability of *substitutes*—goods that perform similar functions—is the main reason that consumers buy less of a product as its price increases. No single good is absolutely essential. To some extent, each good can be replaced by other goods. Margarine can be substituted for butter. Wood, aluminum, bricks, and glass can take the place of steel. Car pools, slower driving, bicycling, and smaller cars are substitutes for gasoline, allowing households to reduce their gas consumption. When the price (and therefore the consumer's opportunity cost) of a good increases, people turn to substitute products that serve almost as well and economize on their use of the more expensive good. Prices really do matter.

Law of demand

A principle that states there is an inverse relationship between the price of a good and the amount of it buyers are willing to purchase.

MARKET DEMAND SCHEDULE

Exhibit 3–1 is a graphic presentation of the law of demand. We will assume that the price reductions that occurred in videocassette recorders (VCRs) resulted from decreasing costs facing suppliers, and that consumer desires for the product, along with their incomes and other prices, did not change significantly during this period. This important assumption allows us to estimate the influence of price on quantity demanded by constructing a demand curve from the three quantity observations, one at each price. To do so, economists measure price on the vertical axis, the *y*-axis, and the amount demanded on the horizontal axis, the *x*-axis. The demand curve will slope downward to the right, indicating in this case that the number of VCRs demanded will increase as price declines. During 1979–1987 the price of VCRs fell sharply. Consumers happily responded by purchasing more of them. In 1979, when the average price of a VCR was $1,413 (in 1987 dollars), manufacturers sold less than half a million (478,000) of them. But costs dropped, and the price fell steadily. By 1983 the average VCR sold for only $652. In fact, this reduction in average price understates the price drop, since quality and features also were improving at the same time. Sales climbed and by 1983 reached 4,020,000 units. The downward fall of price continued, and at the 1987 price of $389, people were watching a lot of movies at home! VCR sales in 1987 were 12,304,000, even though by that time 49 percent of all households with television sets already had VCRs. After 1987 VCR prices fell only very slowly, and annual sales fell somewhat. But by 1991, 72 percent of all households with television sets also had VCRs.

Some commodities are much more responsive to change in price than others.[2] Consider a good for which there are several viable substitutes—a Florida

---

[2]The technical term for price responsiveness is *elasticity*. For those in a microeconomics course, this concept will be explored in the chapter on demand and consumer choice.

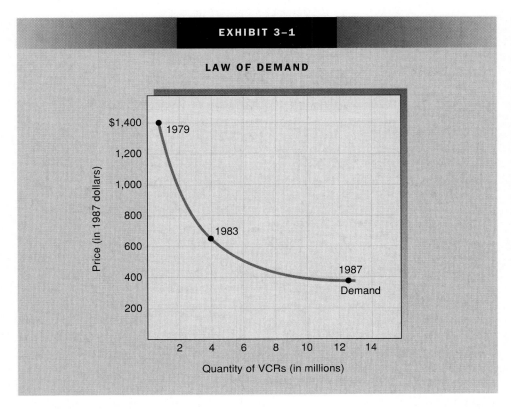

EXHIBIT 3–1

LAW OF DEMAND

As the price of VCRs fell during 1979–1987, consumers purchased more of them. The consumption level of VCRs (and other products) is inversely related to their price, as consumers substitute the good with the falling price for more costly alternative ways to satisfy their wants.

(AUTHORS' NOTE: When we interpret these points as part of a single demand curve, the reader is cautioned that we are assuming that consumer incomes and other demand shifters did not change significantly.)

vacation. If the price of a Florida vacation increases, perhaps because of higher air fares, consumers will substitute more movies, local camping trips, baseball games, television programs, and other recreational activities for the Florida vacation. **Exhibit 3–2** illustrates that, since good substitutes are available, an increase in the price of Florida vacations will cause a sharp reduction in quantity demanded. The quantity of Florida vacations demanded is quite responsive to a change in price.

Other goods may be much less responsive to a change in price. Suppose the price of dentists' services were to rise 15 percent, as indicated in Exhibit 3–2. What impact would this price increase have on the quantity demanded? The higher price would cause some people to prescribe their own medications for toothaches. A few might turn to painkillers, magic potions, and faith healers for even major dental problems. Most consumers, though, would consider these to be poor substitutes for the services of a dentist. Thus, the higher price for dentists' services would cause a relatively small reduction in the quantity demanded. The amount of dentist services demanded is relatively unresponsive to a change in price.

However, despite differences in the degree of responsiveness, the fundamental law of demand holds for all goods. A price increase will induce consumers to turn to substitutes, leading to a reduction in the amount purchased. In contrast, a price reduction will make a commodity relatively cheaper, inducing consumers to purchase more of it as they substitute it for other goods.

The entire market demand schedule is not something that can be observed directly by government planners or decision makers of a business firm. At any point in time, only the amount purchased at the current price is observed. Nonetheless, the choices of consumers reveal important information about their preferences—their valuation of goods. The height of the unseen demand curve

A 15 percent increase in the price of Florida vacations (D₁) caused the quantity demanded to decline from Q₀ to Q₁, a 50 percent reduction. In contrast, a 15 percent increase in the price of dentists' services (D₂) resulted in only a 5 percent reduction in quantity demanded (from Q₀ to Q₂). Florida vacations have more good substitutes than do dentists' services.

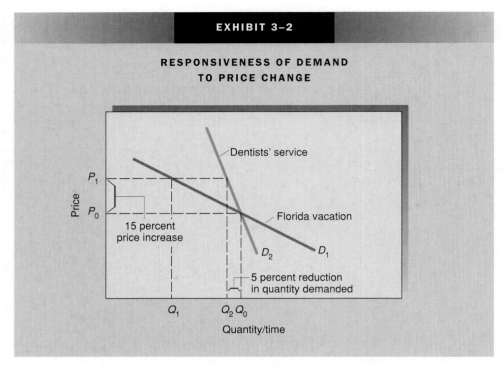

EXHIBIT 3–2

RESPONSIVENESS OF DEMAND TO PRICE CHANGE

indicates the maximum price that consumers are willing to pay for an additional unit of a product. If consumers value an additional unit of a product highly, they will be willing to pay a large amount (a high price) for it. Conversely, if their valuation of an additional unit of the good is low, they will be willing to pay only a small amount for it.

PRODUCER CHOICE AND LAW OF SUPPLY

How does the market process determine the amount of each good that will be produced? We cannot answer this question unless we understand the factors that influence the choices of those who supply goods. Producers of goods and services, often using the business firm,

1. organize productive inputs, such as labor, land, natural resources, and intermediate goods,
2. transform and combine these factors of production into goods desired by households,
3. sell the final products to consumers for a price.

Production involves the conversion of resources into commodities and services. Producers have to pay the owners of scarce resources a price that is at least equal to what the resources could earn elsewhere. Stated another way, each

"THE DEMAND CURVE FOR SOME GOODS IS VERTICAL, SINCE FIXED AMOUNTS OF THEM ARE NEEDED FOR CONSUMPTION."

Noneconomists often ignore the impact of price and make statements implying that, for some goods, there is a fixed amount that must be available for consumption. "During the next five years the United States will need 30 million barrels of oil." "Next year the United States will need 20,000 more physicians." Have you ever heard popular commentators make statements like these, implying that the demand for some commodity is vertical—that some fixed quantity is absolutely required, regardless of the price or cost of the good?

Two points should be recognized when evaluating such statements. *First, we live in a world of substitutes.* There are alternative ways of satisfying needs. The amount of each good that it makes sense for an individual to consume is influenced by the price and availability of other goods. Often the substitutes are seemingly unrelated. For example, reading, staying home and watching television, and backyard picnics are substitutes for gasoline (going some place). In varying degrees, there are substitutes for everything. Thus, there is not a critical amount or minimum requirement of any commodity in the sense that some fixed amount of it is an absolute necessity, regardless of its price.

Second, since scarcity and limited income restricts our options, each of us will have to forgo many things that we "need"—or at least think that we need. Given our limited income, purchasing them would mean that we would have to give up other things that we value more highly and therefore apparently need more urgently.

Even the concept of need or the minimal amount required is ambiguous and changes with cultural differences, fluctuations in wealth, and individual perceptions. In affluent countries such as the United States, families are thought to need at least one bathroom with hot and cold running water, sink, toilet, and bath or shower. Yet the typical family in many other countries would perceive that it was luxurious to have such conveniences in one's home. Outdoor or communal facilities can be substituted, and things other than a modern bathroom have higher priority in

their limited budgets. They would purchase modern facilities only at a very low price (or if they became much richer!). Wealthier people may be willing to pay more for the same item, but their demands too, will depend on the cost. For them, patience in waiting for an available shower is a substitute for a second or a third bathroom.

What about a good like water? Don't people need water to live? Of course that is true but it doesn't negate the point that there are substitutes for water and people buy varying amounts depending on its price. When water is cheap and abundantly available, people will use it for not only drinking, cleaning, and cooking, but also washing cars, watering lawns, and irrigating crops. On the other hand, when it is expensive, consumers will use water constrictors for their showers, substitute cactus gardens for lush green lawns, wash their car less often, and employ numerous other methods to conserve on its usage. The quantity of water demanded, like the quantity demanded of other goods, is inversely related to its price.

Price (and cost) influence our actions in numerous areas. Consider how badly you need an A grade in your economics class. We suspect that if it would take you 30 hours per week to earn an A, while a B would only cost you 3 hours per week, you would choose the cheaper B grade. At least a great many students would do so. Time, like other goods and resources, is scarce. However, if the cost of an A were only 5 hours per week, while a B grade still required 3 hours, then a great many students would choose to work the extra 2 hours per week for the A.

Demand is important precisely because it provides information about the preferences of people—how much they value alternative scarce goods and how much they are willing to give up in order to have additional units. After all, the choice to purchase a good reveals that the consumer values ("needs") that good more than the other goods that could have been purchased instead with the resources. Since there are substitutes for everything and our incomes are limited, the amount of each good that each of us will choose to purchase will be dependent upon its price. The vertical demand curve, like the unicorn, is a myth.

resource employed has to be bid away from all other uses; its owner will have to be paid its opportunity cost. The sum of the amounts paid by the producer for each productive resource, including the cost of production coordination and management, will equal the product's opportunity cost. That cost represents the value of those things given up by society to produce the product.

All economic participants have a strong incentive to undertake activities that generate **profit,** which can be viewed as a residual "income reward" earned by decision makers who produce a good or service that is valued more highly than the resources that were required for its production. It is what is left over after all costs have been paid. If an activity is to be profitable, the revenue derived from the sale of the product must exceed the cost of employing the resources that have been diverted from other uses to make the product. Sometimes decision makers use resources unwisely. They divert resources to production of an output that consumers value less than the opportunity cost of the resources used. **Losses** result, since the sales revenue derived from the project is insufficient to pay the opportunity cost of the resources.

Losses discipline even the largest of firms. For example in 1985 the Coca-Cola Company announced its carefully planned multimillion-dollar strategy to replace its main product, Coca-Cola, with "New Coke," which had a slightly different taste. There was a lukewarm reception to the new product, consumers missed the old Coke, and investors were sufficiently worried about the decision that the firm's stock quickly fell in value by $500 million. Most of that loss was regained when the company reintroduced the original Coke, calling it "Coke Classic," to be sold alongside New Coke (later renamed "Coke II.") The market had disciplined the giant company, despite its huge advertising campaign to sell what it had thought would be a more popular product. The company had made a mistake, but was smart enough to correct it quickly in the face of strong consumer demand.

In 1987 General Motors launched the Cadillac Allanté as a $54,700 coupe that would appeal to car buyers shifting their demands to European cars in that price range. But the car did not have the qualities consumers wanted at that price. It never sold even half of the 7,000 cars per year that General Motors planned. In April of 1993 the Allanté went out of production. Once again, a giant corporation had been taken to the woodshed and forced to learn a costly lesson.

The Allanté had been on the market for six years at the time of its demise. That is longer than many new products last. Marketing studies have found that only about 55 to 65 percent of new products introduced are still on the market five years later.[3]

As we learned in the last chapter, entrepreneurs undertake production organization, deciding what to produce and how to produce it. The business of the entrepreneur is to figure out which projects will, in fact, be profitable. Since the profitability of a project is affected by the price consumers are willing to pay for a product, the price of resources required to produce it, and the cost of alternative production processes, successful entrepreneurs must either be knowledgeable in each of these areas or obtain the advice of others who have such knowledge.

Profit

An excess of sales revenue relative to the cost of production. The cost component includes the opportunity cost of all resources, including those owned by the firm. Therefore, profit accrues only when the value of the good produced is greater than the sum of the values of the individual resources utilized.

Loss

Deficit of sales revenue relative to the cost of production, once all the resources used have received their opportunity cost. Losses are a penalty imposed on those who use resources in lower, rather than higher, valued uses as judged by buyers in the market.

---

[3]See "Flops," the *Business Week* cover story, August 16, 1993 (pages 76–82), for a recent history and explanation of new-product failures in the United States.

To prosper, entrepreneurs must convert and rearrange resources in a manner that will increase their value. An individual who purchases 100 acres of raw land, puts in a street and a sewage-disposal system, divides the plot into one-acre lots, and sells them for 50 percent more than the opportunity cost of all resources used is clearly an entrepreneur. This entrepreneur "profits" because the value of the resources has been increased. Sometimes entrepreneurial activity is less complex. For example, a 15-year-old who purchases a power mower and sells lawn service to the neighbors is also an entrepreneur seeking to profit by increasing the value of resources. In a market economy, profit is the reward to the entrepreneur who discovers and acts upon an opportunity to produce a good or service that is valued more highly than the resources required for its production. It also provides an incentive for rival entrepreneurs to enter the market.

How will producer-entrepreneurs respond to a change in product price? Other things constant, a higher price will increase the producer's incentive to supply the good. New entrepreneurs, seeking personal gain, will enter the market and begin supplying the product. Established producers will expand the scale of their operations, leading to an additional expansion in output. Higher prices will induce producers to supply a greater amount. The direct relationship between the price of a product and the amount of it that will be supplied is termed the **law of supply.**

Exhibit 3–3 presents a graphic picture of this law. The *supply curve* summarizes information about production conditions. Unless the profit-seeking producer receives a price that is at least equal to the opportunity cost of the resources employed, the producer will not continue to supply the good. The height of the supply curve indicates both (1) the minimum price necessary to induce producers to supply a specific quantity and (2) the valuation of the resources used in the production of the marginal unit of the good. This minimum supply price will be high (low) if the opportunity cost of supplying the marginal unit is high (low).

Law of supply
A principle that states there is a direct relationship between the price of a good and the amount of it offered for sale.

As the price of a product increases, other things constant, producers will increase the amount of the product supplied to the market.

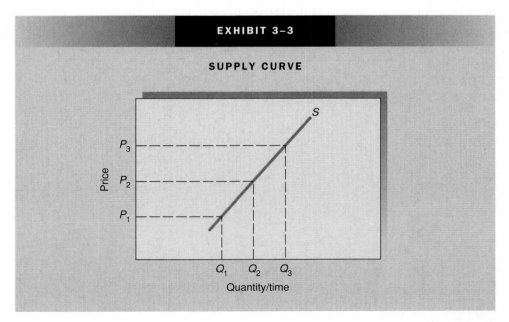

EXHIBIT 3–3

SUPPLY CURVE

MARKETS: SUPPLY AND DEMAND

Market
An abstract concept that encompasses the trading arrangements of buyers and sellers that underlie the forces of supply and demand.

Consumer-buyers and producer-sellers make decisions independent of each other, but markets coordinate their choices and influence their actions. To the economist, a **market** is not a physical location, but an abstract concept that encompasses the forces generated by the buying and selling decisions of economic participants. A market may be quite narrow (for example, the market for razor blades), or it may be quite large when it is useful to aggregate diverse goods into a single market, such as the market for "consumer goods." There is also a broad range of sophistication among markets. The New York Stock Exchange is a highly computerized market in which each weekday buyers and sellers, who never formally meet, exchange shares of corporate ownership worth billions of dollars. In contrast, the neighborhood market for lawn-mowing services may be highly informal, since it brings together buyers and sellers primarily by word of mouth.

Equilibrium
A state of balance between conflicting forces, such as supply and demand.

Equilibrium is a state in which conflicting forces are in perfect balance. When there is a balance—an equilibrium—the tendency for change is absent. Before a market equilibrium can be attained, the decisions of consumers and producers must be coordinated. Their buying and selling activities must be brought into harmony with one another.

SHORT-RUN MARKET EQUILIBRIUM

Short run
A time period of insufficient length to permit decision makers to adjust fully to a change in market conditions. For example, in the short run, producers will have time to increase output by using more labor and raw materials, but they will not have time to expand the size of their plants or to install additional heavy equipment.

The great English economist Alfred Marshall pioneered the development of supply and demand analysis. From the beginning, Marshall recognized that time plays a role in the market process. He introduced the concept of the **short run,** a time period of such short duration that decision makers do not have time to adjust fully to a change in market conditions. During the short run, producers are able to alter the amount of a good supplied only by using more (or less) labor and raw materials with their existing plant and heavy equipment. There is insufficient time to build a new plant or to obtain new "made-to-order" heavy equipment for the producer's current facility. (For more information on Alfred Marshall, see the "Outstanding Economist" box.)

As Exhibit 3–1 illustrates, the amount of a good demanded by consumers will be inversely related to its price. On the other hand, a higher price will induce producers to use their existing facilities more intensively in the short run. As

OUTSTANDING ECONOMIST

ALFRED MARSHALL (1842–1924)

The most influential economist of his era, Marshall introduced many of the concepts and tools that form the core of modern microeconomics including the short run, the long run, and equilibrium.

Exhibit 3–3 depicts, the amount of a good supplied will be directly related to its market price.

The market price of a commodity will tend to change in a direction that will bring the rate at which consumers want to buy into balance with the rate at which producers want to sell. If the price is too high, the quantity supplied will exceed the quantity demanded. Producers will be unable to sell as much as they would like unless they reduce their price. Alternatively, if price is too low, the quantity demanded will exceed the quantity supplied. Some consumers will be unable to get as much as they would like, unless they are willing to pay a higher price. Thus, there will be a tendency for price to move toward equilibrium—toward the single price that will bring the quantity demanded by consumers into balance with the quantity supplied by producers.

Exhibit 3–4 illustrates short-run supply and demand curves in the market for oversize playing cards. At a high price—$12, for example—card producers will

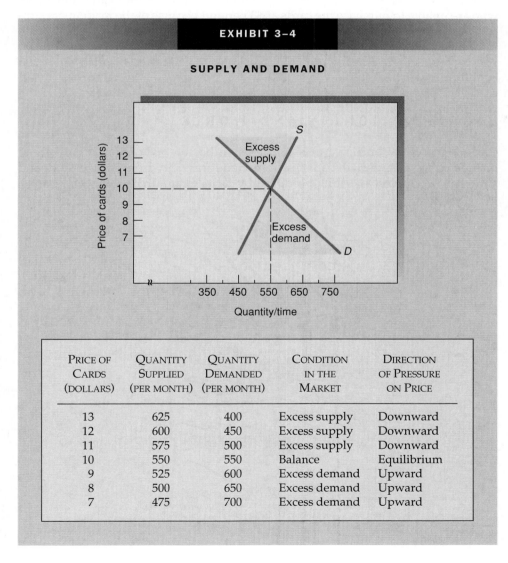

EXHIBIT 3–4

SUPPLY AND DEMAND

PRICE OF CARDS (DOLLARS)	QUANTITY SUPPLIED (PER MONTH)	QUANTITY DEMANDED (PER MONTH)	CONDITION IN THE MARKET	DIRECTION OF PRESSURE ON PRICE
13	625	400	Excess supply	Downward
12	600	450	Excess supply	Downward
11	575	500	Excess supply	Downward
10	550	550	Balance	Equilibrium
9	525	600	Excess demand	Upward
8	500	650	Excess demand	Upward
7	475	700	Excess demand	Upward

The table indicates the supply and demand conditions for oversize playing cards. These conditions are also illustrated by the graph. When the price exceeds $10, an excess supply is present, which places downward pressure on price. In contrast, when the price is less than $10, an excess demand results, which causes the price to rise. Thus, the market price will tend toward $10, at which point supply and demand will be in balance.

plan to supply 600 decks of the cards per month, whereas consumers will choose to purchase only 450. An excess supply of 150 decks will result. Production exceeds sales, so inventories of producers will rise. To reduce undesired inventories, some of the oversize card producers will increase their sales by cutting their price. Other firms will have to lower their price also, or sell even fewer decks. The lower price will make production of the cards less attractive to producers. Some of the marginal producers will go out of business, and others will reduce their current output. How low will the price go? When it has declined to $10, the quantity supplied by producers and the quantity demanded by consumers will be in balance at 550 decks per month. At this price ($10), coordination of buyer and seller is achieved. The production plans of producers are in harmony with the purchasing plans of consumers.

What will happen if the price per deck is low—$8, for example? The amount demanded by consumers (650 units) will exceed the amount supplied by producers (500 units). An excess demand of 150 units will be present. Some consumers who are unable to purchase the cards at $8 per unit because of the inadequate supply would be willing to pay a higher price. Recognizing this fact, producers will raise their price. As the price increases to $10, producers will expand their output and consumers will cut down on their consumption. At the $10 price, short-run equilibrium will be restored.

LOCAL, NATIONAL, AND WORLD MARKETS

Consider a typical breakfast of a consumer in Boston or London. It is likely to include coffee from Brazil, bananas from Honduras, jelly from Switzerland, and strawberries, apples, and milk produced by farmers hundreds, if not thousands,

"GIVEN THE DOWNWARD SLOPE OF OUR DEMAND CURVE, AND THE EASE WITH WHICH OTHER FIRMS CAN ENTER THE INDUSTRY, WE CAN STRENGTHEN OUR PROFIT POSITION ONLY BY EQUATING MARGINAL COST AND MARGINAL REVENUE. ORDER MORE JELLY BEANS."

©1995 Sydney Harris.

of miles away. This remarkable diversity is a reflection of low transportation costs, which expand the opportunity gains from specialization and exchange. During the last 200 years, dramatic reductions in the cost of transporting goods have changed our lives and linked markets around the world.

When there are no trade barriers (legal restrictions limiting exchange), transportable goods will tend to trade for the same price in all markets, except for price differences caused by transportation costs and taxes. This **price equalization principle** reflects the fact that any inequality in the price of a good, for reasons other than taxes and transport costs, creates a profit opportunity for entrepreneurs. One could profit by buying the good in the market where its price is low and selling it in the high-price market. But the additional buying will push the good's price upward in the low-price market, and the additional supply will drive its price down in the high-price market. Therefore, as entrepreneurs act on the opportunity for profit, they tend to equalize the price of each good across all markets, except for price differences reflecting transport costs and taxation among markets.

The price equalization principle explains why if it costs 5 cents to transport oranges from Florida to Wisconsin, oranges will not sell for 25 cents in Florida and 50 cents in Wisconsin. If those prices were present, entrepreneurs would buy the oranges at the cheap Florida price and ship them to Wisconsin, driving the price up in Florida while decreasing the Wisconsin price. This continues to be profitable until the price differential between the two locations is reduced to only the cost of transportation (assuming similar tax treatment between the two states).

The principle is just as applicable to international markets as to a regional or national market. It explains why the price of a good transportable at a relatively low cost will not be cheap in one market and expensive in another if free trade is present. In fact, when the costs of transportation are low, the presence of substantial price differences between two markets is evidence that there are either substantial trade barriers or differences in the taxation of the good in the markets.

Price equalization principle
The tendency for markets, when trade restrictions are absent, to establish a uniform price for each good throughout the world (except for price differences due to transport costs and differential tax treatment of the good).

LONG-RUN MARKET EQUILIBRIUM

In the **long run,** decision makers have time to adjust fully to a change in market conditions. Thus, they can alter their output not only by using their current plant more intensively, but by changing its size and/or its equipment. In other words, the long run is a time period long enough to permit producers to expand the size of their *capital stock* (the physical structure and heavy equipment of their plant).

A balance between amount supplied and amount demanded will bring about market equilibrium in the short run. However, if the current market price is going to persist in the future, that is, in the long run, an additional condition must be present: the opportunity cost of producing the product must also be equal to the market price.

If the market price of a good is greater than the opportunity cost of producing it, suppliers will gain from an expansion in production. Profit-seeking entrepreneurs will be attracted to the industry. Investment capital will flow into the industry, and output (supply) will expand until the additional supply lowers the

Long run
A time period of sufficient length to enable decision makers to adjust fully to a market change. For example, in the long run, producers will have time to alter their utilization of all productive factors, including the heavy equipment and physical structure of their plants.

market price sufficiently to eliminate the profits. In contrast, if the market price is less than the good's opportunity cost of production, suppliers will lose money if they continue to produce the good.[4] The losses will drive producers from the market and capital will flow away from the industry. Eventually the decline in supply and shrinkage in the *capital base* (durable productive assets) of the industry will push prices upward and eliminate the losses.

In a market economy, characterized by freedom of entry and exit, there will be a tendency for the after-tax rate of return on investment to move toward a uniform rate, the competitive or normal-profit return. Neither abnormally high nor abnormally low after-tax returns will persist for long periods of time. This tendency for returns on investment capital to move toward a uniform, normal rate is sometimes referred to as the **rate-of-return equalization principle.**

Rate-of-return equalization principle

The tendency for capital investment in each market to move toward a uniform, or normal, rate of return. An abnormally high return in a market will attract additional investment, which will drive returns down. Conversely, an abnormally low return will result in investment flight from the market, which will eventually lead to the restoration of normal returns.

It is easy to see why there is a tendency for abnormal investment returns—that is, both profits and losses—to be eliminated with the passage of time in a competitive environment. Suppose the after-tax investment return on capital was abnormally high in the retail clothing industry and abnormally low in the publishing industry. The high return in retail clothing would attract additional investors (rival suppliers). Supply in the clothing industry would expand, causing both prices and returns on investment to decline. Eventually, normal returns would be restored in the clothing industry. Conversely, the abnormally low return in the publishing industry would cause investment flight and a reduction in supply. This shrinkage of the capital base and decline in supply in the publishing industry would lead to higher prices until eventually the remaining firms in the industry could once again earn normal returns.

The rate-of-return equalization principle enhances our understanding of supply changes and capital movements when the market price of a good differs from its opportunity cost of production. However, the principle also explains why it will be very difficult for public policy to alter the market returns to any activity over the long term. Suppose the government tries to enhance the returns of farmers (or small business operators, or any other group). For example, it might provide low-cost loans, tax breaks, and subsidies in other forms. Such a policy might initially increase the returns in farming, but it will fail to do so in the long run. If the subsidies increase the returns in farming, capital will flow into the industry, driving commodity prices down (or land and other production costs up) until normal returns are restored. In the long run, the subsidies do not enhance the profitability of investment in farming.

Conversely, consider what will happen if the government imposes higher taxes or discriminatory regulations on an industry. Returns in the industry may temporarily fall below normal. But if they do, capital flight and reductions in supply will push prices upward and eventually restore normal returns.

---

[4]Bear in mind that economists use the opportunity-cost concept for *all* factors of production, including those owned by the producers. Therefore, the owners are receiving a return equal to the opportunity cost of their investment capital even when profits are zero. Zero profits therefore mean that the capital owners are being paid precisely their opportunity cost, precisely what they could earn if their resources were employed in the highest-valued alternative that must be forgone as the result of current use. Far from indicating that a firm is about to go out of business, zero economic profits imply that each factor of production, including the capital owned by the firm and the managerial skills of the owner-entrepreneur, is earning the market rate of return.

In a market economy, prices are determined and economic activity is coordinated by the forces of demand and supply.

SHIFTS IN DEMAND *VS.* CHANGES IN QUANTITY DEMANDED

A *demand curve* isolates the impact that price has on the amount of a product purchased. Of course, factors other than price—for example, consumer income, tastes, prices of related goods, and expectations as to the future of a product—also influence the decisions of consumers. Until now, we have assumed that these factors stay the same. If one of them changes, though, the entire demand curve will shift. Economists refer to such shifts in the demand curve as a change in *demand.*

Let us take a closer look at some of the factors that would cause the demand for a product to change. Expansion in income makes it possible for consumers to purchase more goods at current prices. They usually respond by increasing their spending on a wide cross section of products. Changes in prices of closely related products also influence the choices of consumers. If the price of butter were to fall, many consumers would substitute it for margarine. The demand for margarine would decline (shift to the left) as a result. If coffee and cream are frequently used together, a rise in the price of coffee may decrease the demand for cream, since less coffee will be consumed at the higher price.

Our expectations about the future price of a product also influence our current decisions. For example, if you think that the price of automobiles is going to rise by 20 percent next month, this will increase your incentive to buy now, before the price rises. In contrast, if you think that the price of a product is going to decline, you will demand less now, as you attempt to extend your purchasing decision into the future, when prices are expected to be lower.

Failure to distinguish between a change in *demand* and a change in *quantity demanded* is one of the most common mistakes made by beginning economics students.[5] A change in demand is a shift in the entire demand curve. A change in quantity demanded is a movement along the same demand curve.

Exhibit 3–5 clearly demonstrates the difference between the two. The demand curve D_1 indicates the initial demand (the entire curve) for doorknobs. At a price of $3, consumers would purchase Q_1. If the price declined to $1, there would be an increase in quantity demanded from Q_1 to Q_3. Arrow *A* indicates the change in quantity demanded—a movement along demand curve D_1. Now, suppose that there is a 20 percent increase in income that causes a housing boom. The demand for doorknobs would increase from D_1 to D_2. As indicated by the *B* arrows, the entire demand curve would shift. At the higher income level, consumers would be willing to purchase more doorknobs at $3, at $2, at $1, and at every other price than was previously true. The increase in income leads to an increase in demand—a shift in the entire curve.

How will a market adjust to a change in demand conditions? Using bicycles as an example, **Exhibit 3–6** illustrates how the market for a product will react to an increase in demand. Initially, the market for bicycles reflected the demand D_1 and supply *S*. Given the initial market conditions, the equilibrium price of bicycles was P_1. Now suppose that consumer incomes increase or that people suddenly decide that they want to exercise more or engage in more recreational activities. As a result, the demand for bicycles increases from D_1 to D_2. This increase in demand will disrupt the initial equilibrium. After the increase in demand, consumers will want to purchase a larger quantity of bicycles than producers are willing to supply at the initial price (P_1). The excess demand will push the price of bicycles up to P_2. At the higher price, producers are willing to supply a larger quantity (Q_2 rather than Q_1). The higher price will also moderate the increase in purchases by consumers. At the price of P_2, the quantity demanded by consumers will again be brought into balance with the quantity supplied by producers. The pricing system responds to the increase in demand by providing (1) producers with a stronger incentive to supply more bicycles and (2) consumers with more incentive to search for substitutes and moderate their additional purchases.

When the demand for a product declines, the adjustment process will provide buyers and sellers with just the opposite signals. A decline in demand (a shift to the left) will lead to lower prices. In turn, the lower prices will reduce the incentive of producers to supply the goods and moderate the decline in purchases by consumers.

SHIFTS IN SUPPLY

The decisions of producers lie behind the supply curve. Other things constant, the supply curve summarizes the willingness of producers to offer a product at alternative prices. As with demand, it is important to note the difference between (1) a

[5]Questions designed to test the ability of students to make this distinction are favorites of many economics instructors. A word to the wise should be sufficient.

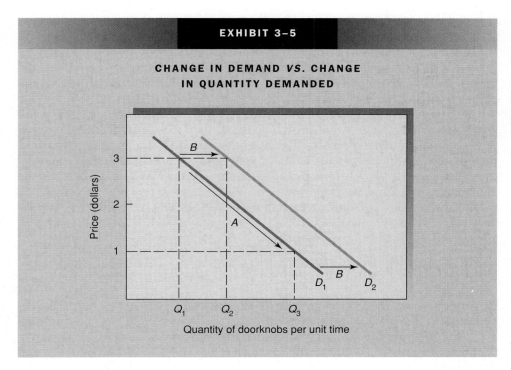

EXHIBIT 3–5

CHANGE IN DEMAND *VS*. CHANGE IN QUANTITY DEMANDED

Quantity of doorknobs per unit time

Arrow A *indicates a change in* quantity demanded, *a movement along the demand curve* D_1, *in response to a change in the price of doorknobs. The* B *arrows illustrate a change in* demand, *a shift of the entire curve, in this case due to a housing boom.*

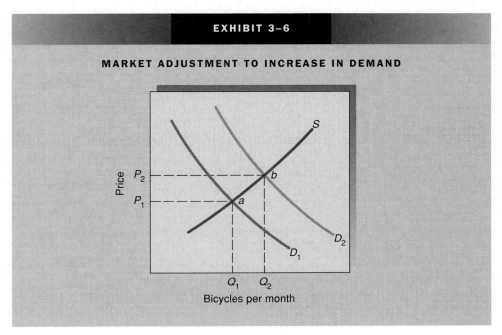

EXHIBIT 3–6

MARKET ADJUSTMENT TO INCREASE IN DEMAND

Bicycles per month

Initially the market for bicycles reflected demand D_1 *and supply S. Suppose that there is an increase in demand for bicycles (shift from* D_1 *to* D_2*), perhaps as the result of an increase in income or an exercise craze. The higher level of demand would increase both the equilibrium price (from* P_1 *to* P_2*) and the quantity supplied (from* Q_1 *to* Q_2*) in the market for bicycles.*

change in quantity supplied and (2) a change in supply. A change in *quantity supplied* is a movement along the same curve in response to a change in price. A change in *supply* indicates a shift in the entire supply curve.

What factors would cause a shift in the entire supply curve? How does the market for consumer goods adjust to a shift in supply? We now turn to an analysis of these two questions.

We previously indicated that a profit-seeking entrepreneur will produce a good only if the sales price of the good exceeds its opportunity cost. Factors that increase the opportunity cost of producers will discourage production and thereby decrease supply (shift the entire curve to the left). Conversely, changes that decrease the opportunity cost of producers will increase supply (shift the entire curve to the right).

Let us consider a number of important factors that will shift the supply curve.

CHANGES IN RESOURCE PRICES

Resource and product markets are closely linked. Firms demand labor, machines, and other resources because they contribute to the production of goods and services. In turn, individuals supply resources in order to earn income.

In resource markets, the demand curve is typically downward-sloping and the supply curve upward-sloping, just as it is in product markets. An inverse relationship will exist between the amount of a resource demanded and its price because businesses will substitute away from a resource as its price rises. Less of the resource will be used at higher prices. In contrast, there will be a direct relationship between the amount of a specific resource supplied and its price. An increase in the price of a resource—for example, the labor services of an automotive mechanic—will make the prospect of supplying the resource more attractive. Some people who would choose to do other things when the wage (price) of automotive mechanics is low will be willing to supply the resource (or more of the resource) when the payoff from doing so improves.

Just as in markets for consumer goods, prices will coordinate the choices of business firms and households in resource markets. There will be a tendency for the price of each resource to move toward an equilibrium, where the amount of the resource supplied by households is in balance with the amount demanded by businesses.

How will an increase in the price of a resource affect product markets? Higher resource prices will increase the opportunity cost of producing consumer goods that use the resource. The higher costs will reduce supply and increase price in the product market. **Exhibit 3–7** illustrates this point. Many economists are forecasting that the wages of low-skill workers will increase substantially in the next few years, primarily because there will be fewer youthful workers (teenagers and persons in their early twenties). As part "a" illustrates, a reduction in the supply of low-skill workers will push their wage rates upward (from $4.55 to $5.45). The higher price of this resource will increase the opportunity cost of hamburgers at fast-food restaurants such as McDonald's and Wendy's. In turn, the higher opportunity cost will reduce supply (from S_1 to S_2) and increase hamburger prices at fast-food establishments (part "b").

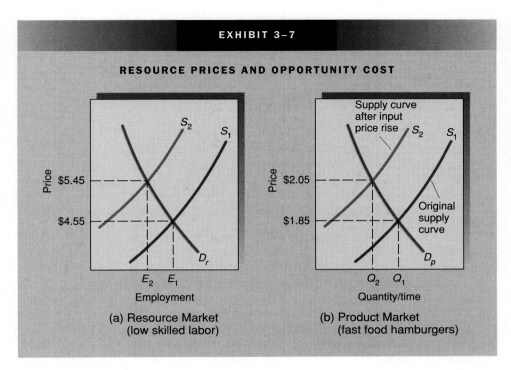

EXHIBIT 3-7

RESOURCE PRICES AND OPPORTUNITY COST

Price

$5.45

$4.55

S_2 S_1

D_r

E_2 E_1

Employment

(a) Resource Market
(low skilled labor)

Price

$2.05

$1.85

Supply curve
after input
price rise S_2 S_1

Original
supply
curve

D_p

Q_2 Q_1

Quantity/time

(b) Product Market
(fast food hamburgers)

Suppose a reduction in the supply of low-skill labor pushes the wage rates of workers hired by fast-food restaurants upward (a). In the product market (b), the higher wage rates will increase the restaurant's opportunity cost, causing a reduction in supply (shift from S_1 to S_2), leading to higher hamburger prices.

Of course, lower resource prices would exert the opposite effect in the product market. A reduction in resource prices will reduce costs and expand the supply (a shift to the right) of consumer goods using the lower-priced resources. The increase in supply will lead to a lower price in the product market.

CHANGES IN TECHNOLOGY

Technological improvements—the discovery of new, lower-cost production techniques—will reduce the opportunity cost of production and increase supply (shift the supply curve to the right) in the product market. Previously we showed how consumers increased their purchases of VCRs as prices for those items declined between 1979 and 1987 (see Exhibit 3–1). **Exhibit 3–8** illustrates why VCR prices fell. Technological improvements substantially reduced the opportunity cost of producing VCRs between 1979 and 1987. The reduction in cost made the prospect of producing VCRs more attractive for entrepreneurs. Established firms expanded output. New firms began production, further contributing to the expansion of supply. The supply curve shifted to the right (from S_{79} to S_{87}). At the old $1,413 price (an average for VCRs sold in 1979, adjusted to 1987 dollars), consumers would not buy the larger supply of VCRs. A reduction in price was necessary to bring the desires of producers to expand production into line with consumers' willingness to purchase the output. By 1987 the average VCR was not only a much better machine, but its price had fallen to $389. At that price, coordination of buyer and seller decisions was achieved.

In 1979 VCRs were selling for $1,413 (in 1987 dollars). Improved technology and manufacturing substantially reduced their production cost, shifting the supply curve to the right (from S_{79} to S_{87}). Prices declined, inducing consumers to purchase a larger quantity of VCRs.

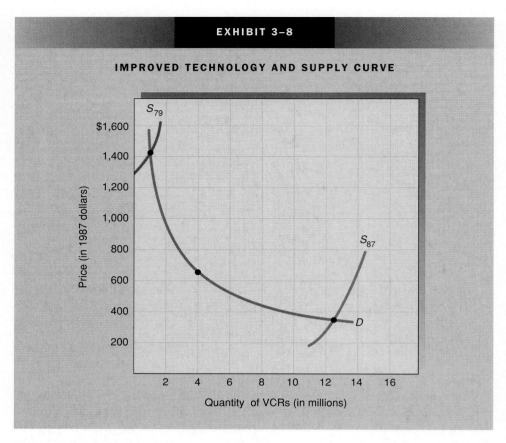

EXHIBIT 3–8

IMPROVED TECHNOLOGY AND SUPPLY CURVE

NATURAL DISASTERS AND POLITICAL DISRUPTIONS

Natural disasters and changing political conditions may also alter supply, sometimes dramatically. For example, in 1986 a drought hit Brazil, destroying a substantial portion of that year's coffee crop. War and political unrest in Iran exerted a major impact on the supply of oil in the late 1970s, as did the invasion of Kuwait by Iraq in 1990.

In the early 1980s there was substantial overfishing in the Atlantic haddock fishery of Georges Bank, off the coasts of New England and Canada. No one owned the fishery; no one controlled access. As a result, too many fishing boats took too many fish. The breeding stock fell, and by 1986 the catch was much smaller than it had been. At the 1981 price, there would have been an excess demand for haddock. In response to the reduction in supply (shift from S_1 to S_2), price rose sharply (**Exhibit 3–9**). Consumers cut back on their consumption of the more expensive good. Some switched to substitutes—in this case probably other fish. By 1986 the price of haddock had risen to more than twice its 1981 level, rationing the smaller supply of haddock to those most willing to pay the higher price. Balance was maintained in the market, despite the sharp drop in the supply of haddock. The accompanying "Thumbnail Sketch" summarizes the major factors causing shifts in demand and supply.

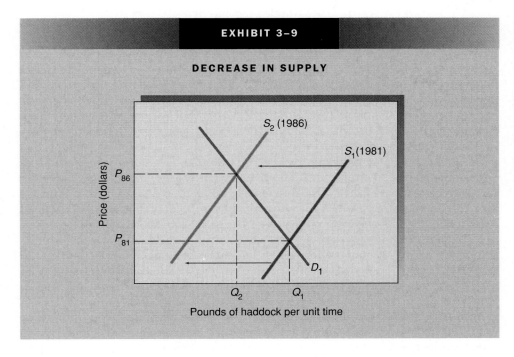

EXHIBIT 3-9

DECREASE IN SUPPLY

Pounds of haddock per unit time

Overfishing of the Atlantic haddock fishery off Georges Bank in the early 1980s caused the number of haddock to decline dramatically. Supply was reduced (the supply curve shifted upwards) so that 1986 prices were more than double those of 1981. The smaller supply was rationed to buyers willing to pay the higher prices. Other buyers shifted to cheaper substitutes.

TIME AND THE ADJUSTMENT PROCESS

The signals that the pricing system sends to consumers and producers will change with market conditions. The market-adjustment process will not be completed instantaneously, though. Sometimes various signals are sent out and acted upon only gradually, with the passage of time.

Using gasoline as an example, **Exhibit 3–10** illustrates the role of time as market participants adjust to a decline in supply. During the late 1970s, political turmoil in Iran—an important oil producer—caused a reduction in supply,

THUMBNAIL SKETCH

These factors increase (decrease) the demand for a good:

1. A rise (fall) in consumer income
2. A rise (fall) in the price of a good used as a substitute
3. A fall (rise) in the price of a complementary good often used with the original good
4. A rise (fall) in the expected future price of the good

These factors increase (decrease) the supply of a good:

1. A fall (rise) in the price of a resource used in producing the good
2. A technological change allowing cheaper production of the good
3. Favorable weather (bad weather or a disruption in supply due to political factors, or war)

represented by the shift from S_1 to S_2. This led to sharply higher prices for gasoline. Adjusted for inflation, gasoline prices rose from $.70 in 1978 to $1.20 in 1980. Initially, consumers responded to rising prices by cutting out some unnecessary trips and leisure driving, and by driving more slowly in order to get better gasoline mileage. Adjustments like these allowed consumers to reduce their consumption of gasoline, but only by a small amount (from 7.4 million to 7.0 million barrels per day), moving them up D_{sr} from point a to point b. The quantity demanded for gasoline in the short run was not very responsive to the change in price.

Given time, however, consumers were able to make additional adjustments that influenced their consumption of gasoline. For example, as larger cars that used a lot of gasoline became old and worn out, new car purchases shifted toward smaller cars with better gas mileage. Adjustments like this caused a more price-responsive long-run demand for gasoline. By late 1981, consumption of gasoline had declined to 6.6 million barrels per day, and there was downward pressure on prices.

This adjustment process for gasoline was a typical one. The consumption response to a price change will usually be smaller in the short run than over a longer period of time. As a result, an unexpected reduction in the supply of a product will generally push the price up more in the short run than in the long run.

Similarly, the adjustments of producers to changing market conditions take time. Suppose that specialized new computer software is developed which causes an increase in demand for notebook computers. How will this change be reflected in the market? **Exhibit 3–11** provides an overview. The increase in demand is shown by the shift from D_1 to D_2. Initially, suppliers of notebooks see a decline in their inventories as the computers move off their shelves more rapidly. Discounts will be more difficult to find, deliveries to buyers will be slower, and

Here we illustrate the adjustment of a market to an unanticipated reduction in supply, such as occurred in the market for gasoline during 1978–1982. Initially, the price of gasoline was 70 cents (equilibrium a). Supply declined (shifted from S_1 to S_2) as the result of military conflict and political unrest in the Middle East. In the short run, prices rose sharply to $1.20, and consumption declined by only a small amount (equilibrium moved from a to b). In the long run, however, the demand for gasoline was more responsive to the price change. As a result, in the long run the price increase was more moderate (equilibrium moved from b to c).

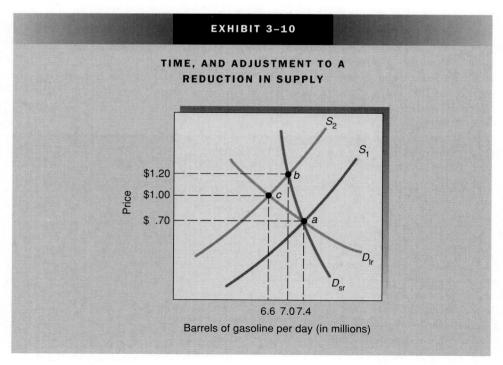

EXHIBIT 3–10

TIME, AND ADJUSTMENT TO A REDUCTION IN SUPPLY

prices will begin to rise as sellers ration their limited supplies among the increased number of buyers. The market price rises from P_1 to P_2.

A few aggressive entrepreneurs in the computer producing business may quickly expand their production of notebooks. They increase the quantity supplied quickly, by rush orders of new materials, having employees work overtime, and so on. But since it is costly to expand output quickly, the higher market price (P_2) will lead to only a modest increase in output from Q_1 to Q_2 in the short run. The higher prices and improved profitability, however, will encourage other, more deliberate efforts to supply more notebooks. With the passage of time, more resources will be brought into notebook computer production. Some resource prices will have to be bid higher in order to obtain larger quantities. This raises costs, but over time relatively efficient expansion will take place. In the long run the quantity supplied will be more responsive (S_{lr} rather than S_{sr}) and the price increase will be more moderate (P_3 rather than P_2). All of these responses will take time, however, even though economists sometimes talk as if the process were instantaneous.

REPEALING THE LAWS OF SUPPLY AND DEMAND

Buyers often believe that prices are too high, while sellers complain that they are too low. Unhappy with prices established by market forces, individuals may seek to

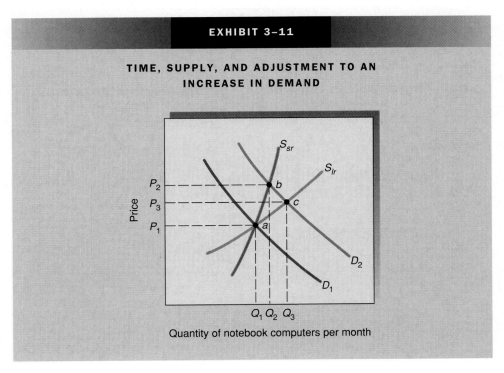

EXHIBIT 3–11

TIME, SUPPLY, AND ADJUSTMENT TO AN INCREASE IN DEMAND

Quantity of notebook computers per month

It takes time for producers to respond to an increase in price. Therefore, supply is generally more responsive to a price change in the long run than in the short run. If the market for notebook computers was initially in equilibrium at P_1 and Q_1, an unexpected increase in demand would push the price of the notebooks up sharply to price P_2 (moved from a to b). Given more time, however, producers will expand output by a larger amount in response to higher prices. The long-run supply curve will be more responsive to a price change than the short-run curve (S_{lr} rather than S_{sr}). The more responsive supply will place downward pressure on price (moved from b to c) with the passage of time.

Price ceiling

A legally established maximum price that sellers may charge.

have prices set by legislative action. Fixing prices seems like a simple, straightforward solution. However, do not forget the phenomenon of secondary effects.

Price ceilings are often popular during a period of inflation, a situation in which prices of most products are continually rising. Many people mistakenly believe that the rising prices are the cause of the inflation rather than just one of its effects. **Exhibit 3–12,** part "a," illustrates the impact of fixing a price of a product below its equilibrium level. Of course, the price ceiling does result in a lower price than market forces would produce, at least in the short run. However, that is not the end of the story. At the below-equilibrium price, producers will be unwilling to supply as much as consumers would like to purchase. A **shortage** ($Q_D - Q_S$ in part "a") of the goods will result, a situation in which the quantity demanded by consumers exceeds the quantity supplied by producers *at the existing price*. Normally, competing buyers would bid up the price. Fixing the price will prevent that, but it will not eliminate the rationing problem. Nonprice factors will now become more important in the rationing process. Producers must discriminate on some basis other than willingness to pay as they ration their sales to eager buyers. Sellers will be partial to friends, to buyers who do them favors, and even to buyers who are willing to make illegal black-market payments.

Shortage

A condition in which the amount of a good offered by sellers is less than the amount demanded by buyers at the existing price. An increase in price would eliminate the shortage.

In addition, the below-equilibrium price reduces the incentive of sellers to expand the future supply of the good. Fewer resources will flow into the production of this good, because higher profits will be available elsewhere. With the passage of time, the shortage conditions will worsen as suppliers direct resources away from production of this commodity and into other areas.

When price is fixed below the equilibrium level by a price ceiling, shortages will develop (a). The quantity demanded at the ceiling price is greater than the quantity supplied. If price is fixed above its equilibrium level by a price floor, then a surplus will result (b). The quantity supplied at the floor price exceeds the quantity demanded. When ceilings and floors prevent prices from bringing about a market equilibrium, nonprice factors will play a more important role in the rationing process.

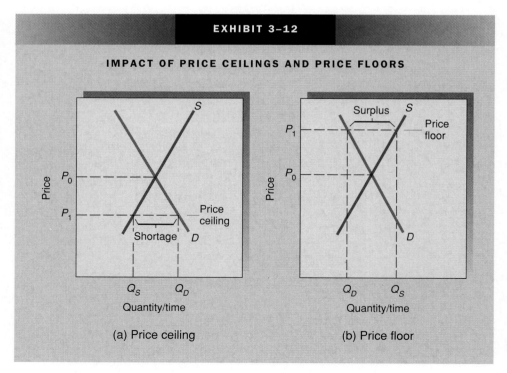

EXHIBIT 3–12

IMPACT OF PRICE CEILINGS AND PRICE FLOORS

(a) Price ceiling

(b) Price floor

What other secondary effects can we expect? In the real world, there are two ways that sellers can raise prices. First, they can raise their money price, holding quality constant. Or, second, they can hold the money price constant while reducing the quality of the good. (The latter could include the amount of each individual purchase, as in the reduced size of a candy bar.) Confronting a price ceiling, sellers will rely on the latter method of raising prices. Rather than do without the good, some buyers will accept the lower-quality product. It is not easy to repeal the laws of supply and demand. (See the following "Myths of Economics" box.)

It is important to note that a shortage is not the same as scarcity. *Scarcity is inescapable.* Scarcity exists whenever people want more of a good than nature has provided. This means, of course, that almost everything of value is scarce. *Shortages, on the other hand, are avoidable if prices are permitted to rise.* A higher, unfixed price (P_0 rather than P_1 in part "a" of Exhibit 3–12) would (1) stimulate additional production, (2) discourage consumption, and (3) ration the available supply to those willing to give up the most in exchange; that is, to pay the highest prices. These forces, an expansion in output and a reduction in consumption, would eliminate the shortage.

Part "b" of Exhibit 3–12 illustrates the case of a **price floor,** which fixes the price of a good or resource above its equilibrium level. At the higher price, sellers will want to bring a larger amount to the market, while buyers will choose to buy less of the good. A **surplus** ($Q_S - Q_D$) will result. Agricultural price supports and minimum wage legislation are examples of price floors. Predictably, nonprice factors will again play a larger role in the rationing process than would be true without a price floor. Buyers can now be more selective, since sellers want to sell more than buyers, in aggregate, desire to purchase. Buyers can be expected to seek out sellers willing to offer them favors (discounts on other products, easier credit, or better service, for example). Some sellers may be unable to market their product or service.[6] Unsold merchandise and underutilized resources will result.

Note that a surplus does not mean the good is no longer scarce. People still want more of the good than is freely available from nature, even though they desire less, *at the current price,* than sellers desire to bring to the market. A decline in price would eliminate the surplus but not the scarcity of the item.

Price floor
A legally established minimum price that buyers must pay for a good or resource.

Surplus
A condition in which the amount of a good that sellers are willing to offer is greater than the amount that buyers will purchase at the existing price. A decline in price would eliminate the surplus.

THE MARKET ANSWERS THE THREE BASIC ECONOMIC QUESTIONS

How does the market's pricing mechanism resolve the three basic economic questions introduced in Chapter 2—what goods will be produced, how will they be produced, and for whom will they be produced?

In a market economy, what will be produced is determined by the consumer's evaluation of a good (demand) relative to its opportunity cost (supply). If consumers value a good (in terms of money) more than its opportunity cost, they

---

[6]Our theory indicates that minimum wage legislation (a price floor for unskilled labor) will generate an excess supply of inexperienced, low-skilled workers. The extremely high unemployment rate of teenagers—a group with little work experience—supports this view.

"RENT CONTROLS ARE AN EFFECTIVE METHOD OF ENSURING ADEQUATE HOUSING AT A PRICE THE POOR CAN AFFORD."

Over 200 American cities have rent controls, intended to protect residents from high housing prices. However, economic theory suggests that when rents (a price for a good) are set below the equilibrium level, the amount of rental housing demanded by consumers will exceed the amount landlords will make available. Initially, if the mandated price is not set too much below equilibrium, the impact of rent controls may be barely noticeable. With the passage of time, however, their effects will grow. Inevitably, controls will lead to the following results.

1. The future supply of rental houses will decline. The below-equilibrium price will discourage entrepreneurs from constructing new rental housing units. Private investment will flow elsewhere, since the controls have depressed the rate of return in the rental housing market. The current owners of such housing may be forced to accept the lower price. However, potential future suppliers of rental housing have other alternatives. Many of them will opt to use their knowledge and resources in other areas. In the city of Berkeley, rental units available to students of the University of California reportedly dropped 31 percent in the first five years after the city adopted rent controls in 1978.[1]

2. Shortages and black markets will develop. Since the quantity of housing supplied will fail to keep pace with the quantity demanded, some persons who value rental housing highly will be unable to find it. Frustrated by the shortage, they will seek methods by which they may induce landlords to rent to them. Some will agree to prepay their rent, including a substantial damage deposit. Others will resort to *tie-in agreements* (for example, they might also agree to rent or buy the landlords' furniture at an exorbitant price) in their efforts to evade the controls. Still others will make under-the-table payments to secure the cheap housing.

3. The quality of rental housing will deteriorate. Economic thinking suggests that there are two ways to raise prices. The nominal price can be increased, quality being held constant. Alternatively, quality can be reduced, while the nominal price is maintained. When landlords are prohibited from adopting the former, they will use the latter. They will paint rental units less often. Normal maintenance and repair service will deteriorate. Tenant parking lots will be eliminated (or rented). Cleaning and maintenance of the general surroundings will be neglected. Eventually, the quality of the rental housing will reflect the controlled price. Cheap housing will be of cheap quality.

4. Nonprice methods of rationing will increase in importance. Since price no longer plays its normal role, other forms of competition will develop. Prohibited from price rationing, landlords will have to rely more heavily on nonmonetary discriminating devices. They will favor friends, persons of influence, and those with lifestyles similar to their own. In contrast, applicants with many children, unconventional lifestyles, or perhaps dark skin will find fewer landlords who cater to their personal requirements. Since the cost to landlords of discriminating against those with characteristics they do not like has been reduced, such discrimination will become more prevalent in the rationing process.

5. Inefficient use of housing space will result. The tenant in a rent-controlled apartment will think twice before moving. Why? Even though the tenant might want a larger or smaller space, or might want to move closer to work, he or she will be less likely to move because it is much more difficult to find a vacancy if rent control ordinances are in effect. As a result, turnover will be lower, and even many who gain financially from living in rent-controlled units will find themselves in apartments not well suited to their needs.

6. Long-term renters will benefit at the expense of newcomers. People who stay for lengthy time periods in the same apartment often pay rents substantially below market value (because the controls restrict rent increases), while newcomers are forced to pay exorbitant prices for units sublet from tenants, or for the limited supply of unrestricted units—typically newly constructed and thus temporarily exempted. Distortions and inequities result. A recent book on housing and the homeless by William Tucker reports several examples, such as "actress Ann Turkel, who paid $2,350 per month for a seven-room, four-and-a-half bathroom duplex on the East Side (of New York City). . . . Identical apartments in the building were subletting for $6,500."[2] Turkel had been spending only two months each year in New York. "Former mayor Edward Koch . . . pays $441.49 a month for a large, one-bedroom apartment . . . that would probably be worth $1,200 in an unregulated market. Koch kept the apartment the entire twelve years he lived in Gracie Mansion (the official mayor's residence)." Tucker reports on many other such cases, involving celebrities with other housing in addition to their rent-controlled units, to illustrate the distortions brought on by the control of rental prices. Although rent controls may appear to be a simple solution, the truth of the matter is that a decline in the supply of rental housing, poor maintenance, and shortages are the inevitable results. Controls may initially lead to lower housing prices for some, but in the long run the

potential for the deterioration of urban life is almost unlimited. In the words of Swedish economist Assar Lindbeck: "In many cases rent control appears to be the most efficient technique presently known to destroy a city—except for bombing."[3] Though this may overstate the case somewhat, economic analysis suggests that the point is well taken.

_____

[1]William Tucker, *The Excluded Americans* (Washington, DC: Regnery Gateway, 1990), p. 162. For a more detailed exposition on rent controls, see Walter Block, "Rent Controls," in *Fortune Encyclopedia of Economics,* edited by David Henderson (New York: Warner Books, 1993).

[2]Tucker, *The Excluded Americans,* p. 248.

[3]Assar Lindbeck, *The Political Economy of the New Left, 1970* (New York: Harper & Row, 1972), p. 39.

will choose to purchase it. Simultaneously, profit-seeking producers will supply a good as long as consumers are willing to pay a price that is sufficient to cover the opportunity cost of producing it. The result: There is an incentive to produce those goods, and only those goods, to which consumers attach a value at least as high as the production costs of the goods.

How goods will be produced is determined by the economizing behavior of suppliers. Suppliers have a strong incentive to use production methods that minimize costs, because lower costs will mean larger profits. Thus, producers can be expected to organize production efficiently—to use division of labor, to invent and adapt new technologies, and to choose labor-capital combinations that will result in lower production costs.

What assurances are there that producers will not waste resources or exploit consumers by charging high prices? Competition provides the answer. Inefficient producers will have higher costs. They will find it difficult to meet the price competition of sellers who use resources wisely. Similarly, in a market with many sellers, competition among firms will, on the whole, keep prices from straying much above production costs. When prices are above the opportunity costs of a good, profits for the producers will result. As we have discussed, the profits will attract additional suppliers into the market, driving the price down.

To whom will the goods be distributed? Goods will be allocated to consumers willing and able to pay the market price. Of course, some consumers will be better able to pay the market price—they have larger incomes (more "dollar votes") than others. The unequal distribution of income among consumers is directly related to what is produced and how. The income of individuals reflects the extent of their provision of resources to others. Those who supply large amounts of highly valued resources—resources for which market participants are willing to pay a high price—will have high incomes. In contrast,

When price controls, such as those imposed on gasoline in the 1970s, push the price of a good or service below the market equilibrium, waiting lines and shortages will result.

those who supply few resources or resources that are not valued by others will have low incomes.

As long as the preferences and productive abilities of individuals differ, a market solution will lead to unequal incomes. Many people are critical of the pricing system because of the income inequality that results. But, unequal incomes are not unique to a market economy. In virtually all systems, unequal income shares exist and provide at least some of the incentive for individuals to undertake productive activities. Since efforts to alter the allocation of income will also affect supply conditions, this issue is highly complex. As we proceed, we will investigate it in more detail.

INVISIBLE HAND PRINCIPLE

The market system is a mechanism for social cooperation. As Adam Smith, the father of economics (see page 17) noted more than 200 years ago, the remarkable thing about a market economy—an economy based on private property and free-dom of exchange—is that market prices will bring the actions of self-interested indi-viduals into harmony with the general welfare. Emphasizing his point, Smith stated:

Every individual is continually exerting himself to find out the most advantageous employment for whatever capital he can command. It is his own advantage, indeed, and not that of the society which he has in view. But the study of his own advantage naturally, or rather necessarily, leads him to prefer that employment which is most advantageous to society. . . . He intends only his own gain, and he is in this, as in many other cases, led by an invisible hand to promote an end which was not part of his intention. By pursuing his own interest he frequently promotes that of the society more effectually than when he really intends to promote it.[7]

Economists refer to the tendency of market prices to *communicate* information, *coordinate* the actions of self-interested individuals, and *motivate* them into engaging in activities that promote the general welfare as the **invisible hand principle.** An efficiently operating economy must communicate, coordinate, and motivate the actions of decision makers. Let us take a closer look at how the invisible hand of market prices performs these functions.

Invisible hand principle
The tendency of market prices to direct individuals pursuing their own interests into productive activities that also promote the economic well-being of the society.

COMMUNICATING INFORMATION TO DECISION MAKERS

Communication of information is one of the most important functions of a market price. We cannot directly observe the preferences of consumers. How highly do consumers value tricycles relative to attic fans, television sets relative to trampolines, or automobiles relative to swimming pools? Product prices and quantities sold communicate up-to-date information about consumers' valuation of additional units of these and numerous other commodities. Similarly, we cannot turn to an engineering equation in order to calculate the opportunity cost of alternative commodities. But resource prices tell the business decision maker the relative importance others place on production factors (skill categories of labor, natural resources, and machinery, for example). With this information, in addition to knowledge of the relationship between potential input combinations and the output of a product, producers can make reliable estimates of their opportunity costs.

Without the information provided by market prices, it would be impossible for decision makers to determine how intensively a good was desired relative to its opportunity costs—that is, relative to other things that might be produced with the resources required to produce the good. Markets collect and register bits and pieces of information reflecting the choices of consumers, producers, and resource suppliers. This vast body of information, which is almost always well beyond the comprehension of any single individual, is tabulated into a summary statistic called the *market price.* This summary statistic provides market participants with information on the relative scarcity of products.

When weather conditions, consumer preferences, technology, political revolution, or natural disasters alter the relative scarcity of a product or resource, market prices communicate this information to decision makers. Knowing why conditions were altered is not necessary for making the appropriate adjustments. It is enough to know, through the market price, that an item has become more or less scarce.

---

[7]Adam Smith, *An Inquiry into the Nature and Causes of the Wealth of Nations* (New York: Modern Library, 1937), p. 423.

COORDINATING ACTIONS OF MARKET PARTICIPANTS

Market prices coordinate the choices of buyers and sellers, bringing their decisions into line with each other. If producers are currently supplying a larger amount than consumers are willing to purchase at the current price, then the excess supply will lead to falling prices, which discourage production and encourage consumption and thereby eliminate the excess supply. Alternatively, if consumers want to buy more than producers are willing to supply at the current price, then the excess demand will lead to price increases. The price rise will encourage consumers to economize on their uses of the good and encourage suppliers to produce more of it. Eventually, these forces will eliminate the excess demand and bring the choices of market participants into harmony.

Prices also direct entrepreneurs to undertake the production projects that are demanded most intensely (relative to their cost) by consumers. Entrepreneurial activity is guided by the signal lights of profits and losses. If consumers really want more of a good—for example, luxury apartments—the intensity of their demand will lead to a market price that exceeds the opportunity cost of constructing the apartments. A profitable opportunity will be created. Entrepreneurs will soon discover this opportunity for gain, undertake construction, and thereby expand the availability of the apartments. In contrast, if consumers want less of a good—very large cars, for example—the opportunity cost of supplying such cars will exceed the sales revenue from their production. Entrepreneurs who undertake such unprofitable production will be penalized by losses.

An understanding of the importance of the entrepreneur also sheds light on the market-adjustment process. Since entrepreneurs, like the rest of us, have imperfect knowledge, they will not be able to instantaneously identify profitable opportunities and the disequilibrium conditions that accompany them. With the passage of time, however, information about a profitable opportunity will become more widely disseminated. More and more producers will move to supply a good that is intensely desired by consumers relative to its cost. Of course, as entrepreneurs expand supply, they will eventually eliminate the profit.

The move toward equilibrium will typically be a groping process. With time, successful entrepreneurial activity will be more clearly identified. Successful methods will be copied by other producers. Learning-by-doing and trial-and-error will help producers sort out attractive projects from "losers." The process, though, will never quite be complete. By the time entrepreneurs discover one intensely desired product (or a new, more efficient production technique), change will have occurred elsewhere, creating other unrealized profitable opportunities. The wheels of dynamic change never stop.

MOTIVATING ECONOMIC PLAYERS

As many leaders of centrally planned economies have discovered, people must be motivated to act before production plans can be realized. One of the major advantages of the pricing system is its ability to motivate people. Market prices establish a reward-penalty (profit-loss) structure that induces the participants to work, cooperate with others, use efficient production methods, supply goods that are intensely desired by others, and invest for the future.

No government agency needs to tell business decision makers to use resources wisely and thereby minimize the cost of producing their product. The pursuit of profit will encourage them to economize. If they do not, they will be unable to compete successfully with more cost-effective rivals. No control authority has to force the farmer to raise wheat, the construction firm to build houses, or the furniture manufacturer to produce chairs. When the market prices of these and literally millions of other products indicate that consumers value them as much or more than their production costs, producers seeking personal gain will supply them.

Similarly, no one has to tell resource suppliers to invest and develop productive resources. Why are many young people willing to undertake the necessary work, stress, late hours of study, and financial cost to acquire a medical or law degree, an advanced degree in economics, physics, or business administration? Why do others seek to master a skill requiring an apprentice program? Why do individuals save to buy businesses, machines, and other capital assets? Although many factors undoubtedly influence one's decision to acquire skills and capital assets, the expectation of financial reward is an important stimulus. Without this stimulus, the motivation to work, create, develop skills, and supply capital assets to those productive activities most desired by others would be weakened.

PRICES AND MARKET ORDER

How is it that grocery stores in thousands of different locations have approximately the right amount of milk, bread, vegetables, and other goods—an amount sufficiently large that the goods are nearly always available but not so large that spoilage and waste are a problem? How is it that refrigerators, automobiles, and VCRs, produced at diverse places around the world, are supplied in the U.S. market in approximately the same amount that they are demanded by consumers? Why are long waiting lines and "sold out until next week" signs that are commonplace in centrally planned economies almost completely absent in market economies? In each case, the answer is that the invisible hand of market prices directs self-interested individuals into cooperative action and brings their choices into harmony.

The market process works so automatically that most people fail to grasp the concept—they fail to understand the source of the social coordination. Perhaps an illustration will help the reader grasp the concept. Visualize a busy limited-access highway with four lanes of traffic moving in each direction. No central planning agency assigns lanes and directs traffic. No one tells drivers when to shift to the right, middle, or left lane. Drivers are left to choose for themselves. Nonetheless, they do not all try to drive in the same lane. Drivers are alert for adjustment opportunities that offer personal gain. When traffic in a lane slows due to congestion, some drivers will shift to other lanes and thereby smooth out the flow of traffic among the lanes. Even though central planning is absent, this process of mutual adjustments by the individual drivers results in order and social cooperation. In fact, the degree of social cooperation is generally well beyond what could be achieved if central coordination was attempted; if, for example, each vehicle were assigned a lane.

Market participation is a lot like driving on the freeway. It is often necessary to alter one's actions in light of the choices made by others. Success is dependent upon one's ability to act upon opportunities. Like the degree of traffic in a lane, profits and losses provide market participants with information concerning the advantages and disadvantages of alternative economic activities. Losses indicate that an economic activity is congested, and as a result, producers are unable to cover their costs. Successful market participants will shift away from such activities. The most mobile resources will be moved to other, more valuable uses. Conversely, profits are indicative of an open lane, the opportunity to experience gain if one shifts into an activity where price is currently high relative to per-unit cost. As producers and resource suppliers shift away from activities characterized by congestion and into those characterized by the opportunity for gain (profit), they smooth out economic activity and enhance its flow. Order is the result, even though central authority is absent. This order in the absence of central planning is precisely what Adam Smith was referring to more than 200 years ago when he spoke of the "invisible hand" of market coordination.

QUALIFICATIONS

In this chapter, we have focused on the operation of a market economy. The efficiency of market organization is dependent on (1) competitive markets and (2) well-defined private property rights. Competition, the great regulator, can protect both buyer and seller. The presence (or possible entry) of independent alternative suppliers protects the consumer against a seller who seeks to charge prices substantially above the cost of production. The existence of alternative resource suppliers protects the producer against a supplier who might otherwise be tempted to withhold a vital resource unless granted exorbitant compensation. The existence of alternative employment opportunities protects the employee from the power of any single employer. Competition can equalize the bargaining power between buyers and sellers.

Understanding the information, coordination, and motivation results of the market mechanism helps us see all the more clearly the importance of property rights, the things actually traded in markets. Although property rights are often thought to increase selfish behavior, they are actually an arrangement to (1) force resource users—including those who own them—to bear fully the opportunity cost of their actions and (2) prohibit persons from engaging in destructive forms of competition. When property rights are well-defined, secure, and tradeable, suppliers of goods and services will be required to pay resource owners the opportunity cost of each resource employed. They will not be permitted to seize and use scarce resources without compensating the owners—that is, without bidding the resources away from alternative users.

Similarly, secure property rights eliminate the use of violence as a competitive weapon. A producer you do not buy from (or work for) will not be permitted to burn down your house. Nor will a competitive resource supplier whose prices you undercut be permitted to slash your automobile tires or threaten you with bodily injury.

Lack of competition and poorly defined property rights will alter the operation of a market economy. As we proceed, we will investigate each of these problems in detail.

CHAPTER SUMMARY

1. Because people want more of scarce goods than nature has made freely available, a rationing mechanism is necessary. Competition is the natural outgrowth of the necessity for rationing scarce goods. A change in the rationing mechanism used will alter the form of competition, but it will not eliminate competitive tactics.

2. The law of demand holds that there is an inverse relationship between price and the amount of a good purchased. A rise in price will cause consumers to purchase less because they now have a greater incentive to use substitutes. On the other hand, a reduction in price will induce consumers to buy more, since they will substitute the cheaper good for other commodities.

3. The law of supply states that there is a direct relationship between the price of a product and the amount supplied. Other things constant, an increase in the price of a product will induce established firms to expand their output and new firms to enter the market. The quantity supplied will then expand.

4. Market prices will bring the conflicting forces of supply and demand into balance. If the quantity supplied to the market by producers exceeds the quantity demanded by consumers, price will decline until the excess supply is eliminated. On the other hand, if the quantity demanded by consumers exceeds the quantity supplied by producers, price will rise until the excess demand is eliminated.

5. If there are no restrictions on the movement of a good, the good will tend to sell for the same price in all markets, except for variations resulting from differences in transport costs and taxes. This price-equalization principle applies to regional, national, and global markets.

6. When a market is in long-run equilibrium, supply and demand will be in balance and the producer's opportunity cost will equal the market price. If the opportunity cost of supplying the good is less than the market price, profits will accrue. The profits will attract additional suppliers, which will expand supply and reduce price until profit is eroded. On the other hand, if the opportunity cost of producing a good exceeds the market price, suppliers will experience losses. The losses will induce producers to leave the market, causing price to rise until long-run equilibrium is restored.

7. Changes in consumer income, prices of closely related goods, preferences, and expectations as to future prices will cause the entire demand curve to shift. An increase (decrease) in demand will cause prices to rise (fall) and quantity supplied to increase (decline).

8. Changes in input prices, technology, and other factors that influence the producer's cost of production will cause the entire supply curve to shift. An increase (decrease) in supply will cause prices to fall (rise) and quantity demanded to expand (decline).

9. The constraint of time temporarily limits the ability of consumers to adjust to changes in prices. With the passage of time, a price increase will usually elicit a larger reduction in quantity demanded. Similarly, the market supply curve shows more responsiveness to a change in price in the long run than during the short-term time period.

10. When a price is fixed below the market equilibrium, buyers will want to purchase more than sellers are willing to supply. A shortage will result. Nonprice factors such as waiting lines, quality deterioration, and illegal transactions will play a more important role in the rationing process. When a price is fixed above the market equilibrium level, sellers will want to supply a larger amount than buyers are willing to purchase at the current price. A surplus will result.

11. The pricing system answers the three basic allocation questions in the following manner.

a. What goods will be produced? Additional units of goods will be produced only if consumers value them more highly than the opportunity cost of the resources necessary to produce them.

b. How will goods be produced? The methods that result in the lowest opportunity cost will be chosen. Since lower costs mean larger profits, markets reward producers who discover and utilize efficient (low-cost) production methods.

c. To whom will the goods be distributed? Goods will be distributed to individuals according to the quantity and price of the productive resources they supply in the marketplace. A large quantity of goods will be allocated to persons who are able to sell a large quantity of highly valued productive resources; few goods will be allocated to persons who supply only a small quantity of low-valued resources.

12. Market prices communicate information, coordinate the actions of buyers and sellers, and provide the incentive structure that motivates decision makers to act. The information provided by prices instructs entrepreneurs as to (1) how to use scarce resources and (2) which products are intensely desired (relative to their opportunity cost) by consumers. Market prices establish a reward-penalty system, which induces individuals to cooperate with each other and motivates them to work efficiently, invest for the future, supply intensely desired goods, economize on the use of scarce resources, and use efficient production methods. Even though decentralized individual planning is a characteristic of the market system, there is a harmony between personal self-interest and the general welfare, as Adam Smith noted long ago. The efficiency of the system is dependent on (1) competitive market conditions and (2) securely defined private-property rights.

CRITICAL-ANALYSIS QUESTIONS

*1. Which of the following do you think would lead to an increase in the current demand for beef: (a) higher pork

---

*Asterisk denotes questions for which answers are given in Appendix C.

prices, (b) higher incomes, (c) higher feed grain prices, (d) a banner-year corn crop, (e) an increase in the price of beef?

2. How many of the following "goods" do you think conform to the general law of supply: (a) gasoline, (b) cheating on exams, (c) political favors from legislators, (d) the services of heart specialists, (e) children, (f) legal divorces, (g) the services of a minister? Explain your answer in each case.

3. **What's Wrong with This Way of Thinking?** "Economists argue that lower prices will necessarily result in less supply. However, there are exceptions to this rule. For example, in 1970, ten-digit electronic calculators sold for $100. By 1985 the price of the same type of calculator had declined to less than $15. Yet business firms produced and sold five times as many calculators in 1985 as in 1970. Lower prices did not result in less production or in a decline in the number of calculators supplied."

*4. A drought during the summer of 1988 sharply reduced the 1988 output of wheat, corn, soybeans, and hay. Indicate the expected impact of the drought on the following:
  a. Prices of feed grains and hay during the summer of 1988.
  b. Price of cattle during the summer and fall of 1988.
  c. Price of cattle during the summer and fall of 1989.

5. The county commission recently voted $15 million for the construction of a new civic center. The chairperson of the commission stated, "We are undertaking this project because the community needs a civic center and the 500 new jobs the project will create." Answer the following questions about this news item:
  a. Does a "need" for a project mean it should be undertaken?
  b. What is the opportunity cost of the project?
  c. Will the project expand employment by 500 workers?

*6. To be meaningful, a price ceiling must be below the market price. Conversely, a meaningful price floor must be above the market price. What impact will a meaningful price ceiling have on the quantity exchanged? What impact will a meaningful price floor have on the quantity exchanged? Explain.

7. Which of the following statements are true? Explain your answers.
  a. The high excise tax on cigarettes reduces the profitability of cigarette manufacturers.
  b. Government-subsidized, low-interest loans to farmers increase the profitability of farming.
  c. A tariff (tax) that restricts the supply of textile products to the domestic market pushes up domestic prices and increases the profitability of domestic textile manufacturers.

*8. "The future of our industrial strength cannot be left to chance. Somebody has to develop notions about which industries are winners and which are losers." Is this statement by a newspaper columnist true? Who is the "somebody"?

9. What is the invisible hand principle? Does it indicate that "good intentions" are necessary if one's actions are going to be beneficial to others?

*10. "Production should be for people and not for profit." Answer the following questions concerning this statement:
  a. If production is profitable, are people helped or hurt? Explain.
  b. Are people helped more if production results in a loss than if it leads to profit?
  c. Is there a conflict between production for people and production for profit?

11. Suppose a disease destroys half of the cattle herds in Kansas and Missouri. Should we expect shortages and sky-high beef prices in these states as the result of the disease?

*12. Suppose a drought destroyed half of the wheat crop in France. What is the expected impact on the market price of wheat in France?

13. If there is a surplus of a good, does this mean that the good is not scarce? Indicate what the supply and demand curves would look like for a good that was not scarce.

*14. When the price of a commodity (for example, rental housing or campus parking) is below equilibrium, then waiting in line rather than monetary payments will play a greater role in the allocation of the good. What is a major disadvantage of rationing by having consumers wait in line rather than by raising prices. (Hint: How do the alternative methods affect future supply?)

15. "Economists claim that when the price of something goes up, producers bring more of it to the market. But the last year in which the price was really high for oranges, there were not nearly as many oranges as usual. The economists are wrong!" How would an economist respond to this statement?

*16. A popular California winery, and the restaurant on its grounds, can be reached only by a tram with gondola cars, similar to those used at ski resorts. Suppose the owners are charging $3 to winery visitors and restaurant diners alike, but are thinking about providing "free rides" to diners. Explain how this change would affect the following:
  a. The demand for dining at the restaurant.

---

*Asterisk denotes questions for which answers are given in Appendix C.

b. The price and quantity of meals served at the restaurant.

17. If everyone had an income above the current poverty level, would substandard, shoddy housing disappear?

18. Trina's Cakes, owned and operated by Trina Mendoza, specializes in making wedding and birthday cakes. Trina employs four workers in her business, which produces and sells 800 cakes per month. If Trina were not running this cake shop, she would be doing similar work managing a bakery for a larger firm. The table below lists the monthly expenses for Trina's Cakes.

INPUTS	COST PER MONTH
Employee compensation	$6,000
Ovens and equipment	3,000
Flour, sugar, supplies	1,500
Rent for space	700
Utilities and business taxes	1,000
Compensation for Trina	2,000

a. Is the $2,000 received by Trina really a cost of making and selling the cakes? Why or why not?

b. What is the cost of producing the 800 cakes per month?

c. The cakes are sold each month for $20 each. What are the monthly sales revenues?

d. Is Trina making a profit or a loss? How large? Would you say that this business is productive? Explain.

CHAPTER FOUR

SUPPLY AND DEMAND FOR THE PUBLIC SECTOR

A century ago there was little federal regulation of private economic activity: today, federal nonmarket control of the private sector is very nearly ubiquitous.

JONATHAN HUGHES[1]

[Public choice] analyzes the motives and activities of politicians, civil servants and government officials as people with personal interests that may or may not coincide with the interest of the general public they are supposed to serve. It is an analysis of how people behave in the world as it is.

ARTHUR SELDON[2]

CHAPTER FOCUS

■ *What does the economic way of thinking have to say about economic efficiency?*

■ *When do markets fall short of the ideal of economic efficiency?*

■ *Can government action improve on the efficiency of the market? When is it most likely to do so?*

■ *What is public-choice analysis? What does it reveal about how the political process works?*

■ *Is there sometimes a conflict between good economics and good politics? Why?*

---

[1]Jonathan Hughes, "Do Americans Want Big Government?" in *Second Thoughts*, edited by Donald N. McCloskey (New York: Oxford University Press, 1993), p. 115.

[2]Preface to Gordon Tullock, *The Vote Motive* (London: Institute of Economic Affairs, 1976), p. x.

T he economic role of government is pivotal. The government sets the rules of the game. It establishes and defines property rights, which are necessary for the smooth operation of markets. It can also be an important determinant of economic stability. The government sometimes uses subsidies to encourage the production of some goods while it applies special taxes to reduce the availability of others. In a few cases—education, the mail service, and local electric power, for example—the government becomes directly involved in the production process. As the quote from economic historian Jonathan Hughes suggests, the economic involvement of government has been growing for many decades in the United States. The rest of the world has had a similar experience.

Because of government's broad economic role and its increasing size, it is vital that we understand how it works and the circumstances under which it contributes to the efficient allocation of resources. In this chapter, we examine the shortcomings of the market and the potential of government policy as an alternate means for resolving economic problems. Issues involving market- and public-sector organization will be discussed repeatedly throughout this book. Public-choice analysis, as suggested in the quotation from British economist Arthur Seldon, is an important way of using economics to better understand the workings of the political sector. Political economy—how the public sector works, and how its workings compare with those of the market—is an integral and exciting aspect of economic analysis.

IDEAL ECONOMIC EFFICIENCY

Economic efficiency
Economizing behavior. When applied to a community, it implies that (1) an activity should be undertaken if the sum of the benefits to the individuals exceeds the sum of their costs and (2) no activity should be undertaken if the costs borne by the individuals exceed the benefits.

We need a criterion by which to judge alternative institutional arrangements—that is, market- and public-sector policies. Economists often use the standard of **economic efficiency.** The central idea is straightforward. It simply means that for any given level of effort (cost), we want to obtain the largest possible benefit. A corollary to this is that we want to obtain any specific level of benefits with the least possible effort. Economic efficiency simply means getting the most value from the available resources—making the largest pie from the available set of ingredients, so to speak.

Why efficiency? Economists acknowledge that people generally do not have the efficiency of the economy as a primary goal. Rather, each person wants the largest possible "piece of the pie." All might agree that a bigger pie is preferred, however, particularly if they are allowed a larger slice as a result. Thus, efficiency can be in everyone's interest because it makes that larger pie possible.

What does efficiency mean when applied to the entire economy? Individuals are the final decision makers of an economy, and individuals will bear the costs and reap the benefits of economic activity. When applied to the entire economy, two conditions are necessary for ideal economic efficiency to exist:

Rule 1. Undertaking an economic action will be efficient if it produces more benefits than costs for the individuals of the economy. Such actions result in gain—improvement in the well-being of at least some individuals without creating reductions in the welfare of others. Failure to undertake such activities means that potential gain has been forgone.

Rule 2. *Undertaking an economic action will be inefficient of it produces more costs than benefits to the individuals.*   When an action results in greater total costs than benefits, somebody must be harmed. The benefits that accrue to those who gain are insufficient to compensate for the losses imposed on others. Therefore, when all persons are considered, the net impact of such an action is counterproductive.

When either Rule 1 or Rule 2 is violated, economic inefficiency results. The concept of economic efficiency applies to each and every possible income distribution, although a change in income distribution may alter the precise combination of goods and services that is most efficient.[3] Positive economics does not tell us how income should be distributed. Of course, we all have ideas on the subject. Most of us would like to see more income distributed our way. Agreement on what is the best distribution of income is unlikely, but for any particular income distribution, there will be an ideal resource allocation that will be most efficient.

MARKETS, INCENTIVES, AND EFFICIENCY

A closer look at the way in which markets work can help us to understand the concept of efficiency and the role markets play in providing incentives for individuals to make efficient production and consumption decisions. When property rights are privately owned, competitive market forces represented by supply and demand provide both the signals needed for decision makers to use resources efficiently and the incentive to do so.

The supply curve reflects producers' opportunity costs. Each point along the supply curve indicates the minimum price for which the units of a good could be produced without a loss to the seller. It is cost that pushes producers to economize on the use of valuable inputs. Each point along the demand curve indicates the consumer's valuation of an extra unit of the good—the maximum amount the consumer of each unit is willing to pay for the unit. Consumer willingness to pay urges producers to add to output. The necessity for payment restrains consumer demands. Any time the consumer's valuation exceeds the producer's opportunity cost—the producer's minimum supply price—producing and selling more units of the good can generate mutual gain.

When only the buyer and seller are affected by production and exchange, and the options are known to each, they are directed by the market forces of supply and demand to be efficient in the use of marketed goods. **Exhibit 4–1** illustrates why this is true. Suppliers of a good, bicycles in this example, will produce additional units as long as the market price exceeds the production cost. Similarly, consumers will gain from the purchase of additional units as long as their benefits, revealed by the height of the demand curve, exceed the market price. Market

---

[3]Note to students who may pursue advanced study in economics: Using the concept of efficiency to compare alternative policies typically requires that the analyst estimate costs and benefits that are difficult or impossible to measure. Costs and benefits are the values of opportunities forgone or accepted by individuals, *as evaluated by those individuals.* Then, these costs and benefits must be added up across all individuals, and compared. But does a dollar's gain for one individual really compensate for a dollar's sacrifice by another? Some economists simply reject the validity of making such comparisons. They say that neither the estimates by the economic analyst of subjectively determined costs and benefits nor the adding up of these costs and benefits across individuals is meaningful. Their case may be valid, but most economists today nevertheless use the concept of efficiency as we present it. No other way to use economic analysis to compare policy alternatives has been found.

When competitive forces are present, price will tend toward the supply-demand intersection P. At that price, the seller's opportunity cost of producing the last unit will just equal the buyer's evaluation of that unit. All potential mutual gains from production and exchange are realized. If producers and users are paying the full cost of their actions and receiving the benefit of the value they produce, then such trading is efficient.

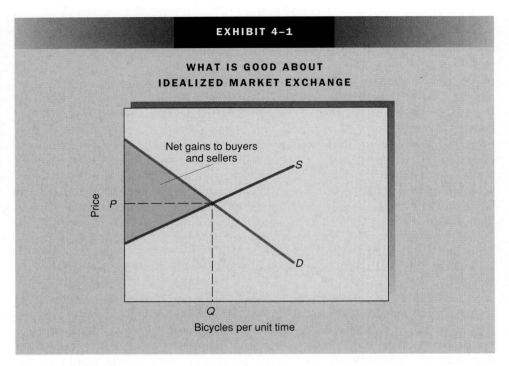

EXHIBIT 4–1

WHAT IS GOOD ABOUT IDEALIZED MARKET EXCHANGE

forces will result in an equilibrium output level of *Q:* All units for which the benefits to consumers exceed the costs to suppliers will be produced. Rule 1 is met; all potential gains from exchange (the shaded area) between consumers and producers are fully realized. Production beyond *Q*, however, would prove inefficient. If more than *Q* bicycles were produced, Rule 2 would be violated; consumers value the additional units less than their cost. With competitive markets, suppliers will find it unprofitable to produce units beyond *Q* because the cost of the additional units will exceed revenues.

Consumers and producers alike will thus be guided by the pricing system to output level *Q*, just the right amount. The market works beautifully. Individuals, pursuing their own interests, are guided as if by an invisible hand to promote the general welfare. This was the message of Adam Smith, more than 200 years ago.

WHY MIGHT THE INVISIBLE HAND FAIL?

Is the invisible hand still working today? Why might it fail? There are four important factors that can limit the ability of the invisible hand to perform its magic.

LACK OF COMPETITION

Competition is vital to the proper operation of the pricing mechanism. It is competition that drives the prices for consumer goods down to the level of their cost. Similiarly, competition in markets for productive resources prevents (1) sellers from charging exorbitant prices to producers and (2) buyers from taking advantage of the owners of productive resources. The existence of competitors reduces the power of buyers and sellers alike to rig the market in their own favor.

Modern mass-production techniques, marketing, and distributing networks often make it possible for a large-scale producer to gain a cost advantage over smaller competitors. In several industries—automobiles, aircraft, and aluminum, for example—a few large firms produce the entire output. Because an enormous amount of capital investment is required to enter these industries, existing large-scale producers may be partially insulated from the competitive pressure of new rivals.

Since competition is the enemy of prices higher than costs, sellers have a strong incentive to escape from its pressures by colluding rather than competing. Competition is something that is good when the other guy faces it. Individually, each of us would prefer to be loosened from its grip. Students do not like stiff competitors at exam time, when seeking entry to graduate school, or in their social or romantic lives. Similarly, sellers prefer few real competitors.

Exhibit 4–2 illustrates how sellers can gain from collusive action. If a group of sellers could eliminate the competition from new entrants to the market, they would be able to raise their prices. The total revenue of sellers is simply the market price multiplied by the quantity sold. The sellers' revenues may well be greater, and their total costs would surely be lower, if the smaller, restricted output Q_2 were sold rather than the competitive output Q_1. The artificially high price P_2 reflects not only resource scarcity, but also the reduction in output brought on by collusion among sellers.

It is in the interest of consumers and the community that output be expanded to Q_1, the output consistent with economic efficiency. It is in the interest of sellers, though, to make the good artificially scarce and raise its price. If sellers can use

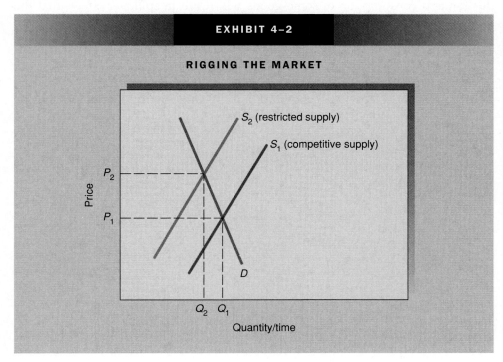

EXHIBIT 4–2

RIGGING THE MARKET

S_2 (restricted supply)

S_1 (competitive supply)

P_2

P_1

Price

D

Q_2 Q_1

Quantity/time

If a group of sellers can restrict the entry of competitors and connive to reduce their own output, they can sometimes obtain more total revenue by selling fewer units. Note that the total sales revenue P_2Q_2 for the restricted supply exceeds the sales revenue P_1Q_1 for the competitive supply, in this case. Such restriction on trade reduces the gains from trade, making the market less efficient as a result.

collusion, government action, or other means of restricting supply, they can gain. However, the restricted output level would violate Rule 2. Inefficiency would result. There is a conflict between the interests of sellers and what is best for the entire community.

When there are only a few firms in the industry, and competition from new entrants can be restrained, sellers may be able to rig the market in their favor. Through collusion, either tacit or overt, suppliers may be able to escape competitive pressures. What can the government do to preserve competition? Congress has enacted a series of antitrust laws, most notably the Sherman Antitrust Act and the Clayton Act, making it illegal for firms to collude or attempt to monopolize a product market. Congress also established the Federal Trade Commission, which prohibits "unfair methods of competition in commerce," such as false advertising, improper grading of materials, and deceptive business practices.

For the most part, economists favor the principle of government action to ensure and promote competitive markets. There is considerable debate, however, about the effectiveness of past public policy in this area. Many economists believe that, by and large, antitrust policy has been ineffective. Others stress that government regulatory policies have often restricted entry, protected existing producers, and limited price competition. These critics charge that the government has thus reduced the competitiveness of markets.

EXTERNALITIES—FAILURE TO SOLVE THE INCENTIVE PROBLEM

Externalities

The side effects, or spillover effects, of an action that influence the well-being of nonconsenting parties. The nonconsenting parties may be either helped (by external benefits) or harmed (by external costs).

When property rights are not fully enforced, the actions of a producer or consumer might harm the property (or the person) of another. In this situation, production and consumption of some goods will result in spillover effects that the market prices fail to register. These spillover effects, called **externalities,** are present when the actions of one individual or group harm the property of others without their consent. The presence of externalities means that the incentive problem has not been solved, that decision makers do not have the proper cost and price incentives.

Examples of externalities abound. If you live in an apartment house and the noisy stereo of your next-door neighbors keeps you from studying economics, your neighbors are creating an externality. Their actions are imposing an unwanted cost on you. Driving your car during rush hour increases the level of congestion, thereby imposing a cost on other motorists.

The existence of externalities implies the lack of property rights, or of enforcement of those rights. The apartment dweller who is bothered by a neighbor's noise either does not have a right to quiet, or is unable to enforce the right. In either case, the maker of the noise need not take into account the resulting discomfort of neighbors. Similarly, each motorist adding his or her car to heavy traffic will not be forced to consider the effects on others, unless there is a highway access fee reflecting the costs of congestion. When enforceable property rights are not present, externalities are a normal result.

Not all externalities result in the imposition of a cost. Sometimes human actions generate benefits for nonparticipating parties. The homeowner who keeps a house in good condition and maintains a neat lawn improves the beauty of the entire community, thereby benefiting community members. A flood-control dam project built by upstream residents for their benefit may also generate gains for those who live downstream. Scientific theories benefit their authors, but the knowledge gained also contributes to the welfare of others who do not help to pay for the benefits. Again, a lack of enforceable property rights keeps the producers of the goods or services that provide the positively valued externalities from reaping fully the benefits of them.

Why do externalities create problems for the market mechanism? **Exhibit 4–3** can help answer this question. With competitive markets in equilibrium, the cost of a good (including the opportunity cost borne by the producer) will be paid by consumers. Unless consumer benefits exceed the opportunity cost of production, the goods will not be produced. What happens, though, when externalities are present?

Suppose that a business firm discharges unwanted smoke into the air or sewage into a river. Valuable resources, clean air and pure water, are used essentially for garbage disposal. When those downwind or downstream who are harmed cannot successfully sue for damages, neither the firm nor the consumers of its products will pay for these costs. As part "a" of Exhibit 4–3 shows, the supply curve will understate the opportunity cost of production when these external costs are present. Since the producer has to consider only the cost to the firm, and can ignore the cost imposed on secondary parties, supply curve S_1 will result. If the producer had to pay all costs, supply would be S_2. The actual supply curve S_1 will not reflect the full opportunity cost of producing the good. For the producer, the opportunity cost paid is low enough to merit an increase in supply. Output will be expanded beyond Q_2 (to Q_1), even though the buyer's valuation of the additional units is less than their full opportunity cost. The second efficiency condition, Rule 2, is violated. Inefficiency in the form of excessive air and water

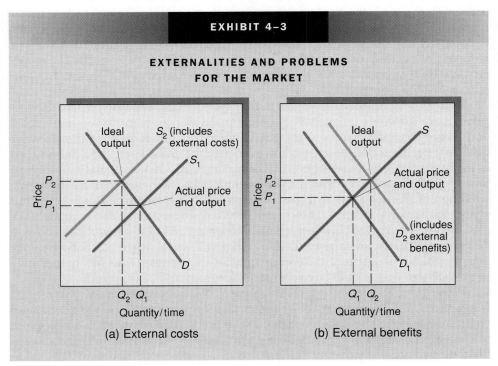

EXHIBIT 4–3

EXTERNALITIES AND PROBLEMS FOR THE MARKET

(a) External costs

(b) External benefits

When external costs are present (a), the output level of a product will exceed the desired amount. Some units (beyond Q_2) will be produced even though their costs exceed the benefits they generate, causing reduced efficiency. In contrast, market output of goods that generate external benefits (b) will be less than the ideal level. Production that could generate more benefits than costs is not undertaken, and a lack of efficiency results.

pollution results. In the total picture, the harm caused by the added pollution outweighs the net benefits derived by buyers and sellers from the production of units beyond Q_1.

As part "b" of Exhibit 4–3 shows, external benefits often result in opportunities forgone. When they are present, the market demand curve D_1 will not fully reflect the total benefits, which include those going to parties who receive the benefits without payment. They may be unwilling to pay, since they already receive benefits without payment. Output Q_1 will result. Could the community gain from a greater output of the product? Yes. The demand curve D_2 reflects both the direct benefits to paying consumers and the benefits bestowed on secondary, nonpaying parties. Expansion of output beyond Q_1 to Q_2 would result in net gain to the community. But since neither producers nor paying consumers can capture the secondary benefits, consumption level Q_1 will result. The potential net gain from the greater output level Q_2 will be lost. Rule 1 of our ideal efficiency criterion is violated.

Competitive markets will fail to give consumers and producers the correct signals and incentives when property rights are not fully defined and enforced, creating externalities. The market will tend to underallocate resources to the production of goods with external benefits and overallocate resources to the production of goods that impose external costs on nonconsenting parties.

PUBLIC GOODS—MORE PROBLEMS FOR THE MARKET

Public goods
Jointly consumed goods. When consumed by one person, they are also made available to others. National defense, poetry, and scientific theories are all public goods.

Some goods are difficult to provide commercially through the marketplace because there is no way to exclude nonpaying customers. Goods that must be consumed jointly by all are called **public goods.** National defense, the judicial and legal systems, and the monetary system are examples of public goods. The national defense that protects you also protects others. Unlike candy bars, national defense cannot just be provided to the citizens who pay and not to others. Similarly, the actions of a central monetary authority are a public good. The monetary system that provides price stability (or instability) for you also provides it for others.

Why are public goods troublesome for the market? Typically, in the marketplace, there is a direct link between consumption and payment. If you do not pay, you do not consume. Similarly, the payments of consumers provide the incentive to supply products. Public goods, however, are consumed jointly. If a public good is made available to one person, it is simultaneously made available to others. Since people cannot be excluded, their incentive to pay, or even to reveal their true valuation of the good, is destroyed. Why would you voluntarily pay your "fair share" for national defense, the courts, or police protection if these goods were provided in the market? If others contribute a large amount, the public good will be provided pretty much regardless of what you do. If others do not pay, your actions will not make much difference anyway. Each person thus has an incentive to opt out, to refuse to help pay voluntarily for the public good.

When everybody opts out, what happens? Not very much of the public good is produced. This is precisely why the market cannot handle public goods very well. Resources will be underallocated to the production of public goods because self-interested consumers, recognizing that there is little relationship between their specific contribution and the quantity of a public good supplied, will fail to contribute to its costs. But when many people follow this course, too little of the public good is produced. Thus, the nature of public goods causes a conflict between self-interest and the public interest of economic efficiency.

ECONOMIC INSTABILITY

If markets are to function well, individuals need to know the value to others of what they are buying or selling. For market prices to convey this information, a stable monetary exchange system must be provided. This is especially true for the many market exchanges that involve a time dimension. Houses, cars, consumer durables, land, buildings, equipment, and many other items are often paid for over a period of months or even years. If the purchasing power of the monetary unit, the dollar in the United States, gyrated wildly, previously determined prices would not represent their intended values. Few would want to make transactions involving long-term commitments because of the uncertainty. The smooth functioning of the market would be retarded. Many economists believe that without the help of government, the economy would be less stable than it is.

The government's spending and monetary policies exert a powerful influence on economic stability. If properly conducted, these policies contribute to economic stability, full and efficient utilization of resources, and stable prices. Improper stabilization policies, though, can cause massive unemployment, rapidly rising prices, or both.

Economists are not in complete agreement on the extent to which public policy can stabilize the economy and promote full employment. They often debate the impact of various policy tools. All agree, however, that a stable economic environment is vital to a market economy. Those pursuing a course in macroeconomics will find both the potential and the limitations of government action as a stabilizing force in the economy discussed further in Part Two.

THE ECONOMICS OF COLLECTIVE ACTION

The pricing system will fail to meet our ideal efficiency standards if (1) markets are not competitive, (2) externalities are present, (3) public goods necessitate joint consumption, or (4) the aggregate economy is characterized by instability and the resultant uncertainty. If public-sector action can correct these deficiencies, net gains for the community are possible. Public policy does not have to be a zero-sum game.

Just because it is possible to visualize that public-sector action will promote economic welfare, it does not follow that real-world governments, including those organized democratically, will necessarily institute sound policies. Government is *not* a supraindividual that will always make decisions in the "public interest," however that nebulous term might be defined. Neither is it a corrective device available for use when market organization fails to achieve a desired outcome. It is instead an alternative method of social organization—an institutional process through which individuals collectively make choices and carry out activities. The information and incentive structure facing decision makers in the public sector are typically imperfect, just as they are in the private sector.

Public-choice analysis
The study of decision making as it affects the formation and operation of collective organizations, such as governments. The discipline bridges the gap between economics and political science. In general, the principles and methodology of economics are applied to political science topics.

If we are going to make meaningful comparisons between market allocation and collective action, we need to develop a sound theory that will help us understand both forms of economic organization. **Public-choice analysis** has significantly advanced our understanding of the collective decision-making process in recent years. Something of a cross between economics and political science, public-choice theory applies the principles and methodology of economics to collective choices.

In a democratic setting, individual beliefs and preferences will influence the outcome of collective decisions, just as they influence outcomes in the market. Public-choice theory postulates that individual behavior in the political arena will be motivated by considerations similar to those that influence market behavior. If self-interest is a powerful motivator in the marketplace, there is every reason to believe it will also be a motivating factor when choices are made collectively. If market choices are influenced by changes in projected personal costs relative to benefits, we can expect that such changes will also influence political choices. Public-choice theory, in other words, suggests that the number of saints and sinners in the two sectors will be comparable.

In analyzing the behavior of people in the marketplace, economists develop a logically consistent theory of behavior that can be tested against reality. Through theory and empirical testing, we seek to explain various economic actions of decision makers and, in general, how the market operates.

In the public sphere, our purpose should be the same: to explain how the collective decision-making process really operates. This means developing a logically consistent theory linking individual behavior to collective action, analyzing the implications of that theory, and testing these implications against events in the real world.

Since the theory of collective decision making is not as well developed as our theory of market behavior, our conclusions will, of course, be less definitive. In the last 30 years, however, social scientists have made great strides in our understanding of resource allocation by the public sector.[4] Currently, this subject is often dealt with at a more advanced academic level. Even on an introductory level, though, economic tools can be used to shed light on how the public sector handles economic activities.

DIFFERENCES AND SIMILARITIES BETWEEN MARKET AND COLLECTIVE ACTION

There are some basic characteristics that influence outcomes in both the market and the public sectors.[5] As we have noted, there is reason to believe that the motivations of individuals present in both sectors are similar. There are, however, basic structural differences. Voluntary exchange coordinated by prices is the dominant characteristic of a market economy (although, of course, when externalities are present, involuntary exchange may also result). In a democratic setting, the

---

[4]The contributions of Kenneth Arrow, James Buchanan, Duncan Black, Anthony Downs, Mancur Olson, Robert Tollison, and Gordon Tullock have been particularly important.

[5]The "Public Choice" section of this book analyzes the topics of alternative forms of economic organization—market versus collective action—in more detail.

JAMES BUCHANAN (1919–)

James Buchanan is a key figure in the "public choice revolution." His most famous work, *The Calculus of Consent* (1962), coauthored with Gordon Tullock,[1] argues that unless rules bring the self-interest of the political players into harmony with the wise use of resources, government will go awry. This and related contributions won him the 1986 Nobel Prize in economics.

[1]J.M. Buchanan and G. Tullock, *The Calculus of Consent* (Ann Arbor: University of Michigan Press, 1962).

dominant characteristic of collective action is majority rule, effective either directly or through legislative procedures. Let us take a look at both the differences and similarities between the two sectors.

1. COMPETITIVE BEHAVIOR IS PRESENT IN BOTH THE MARKET AND PUBLIC SECTORS. Although the market sector is sometimes referred to as the "competitive sector," it is clear that competitive behavior is present in both sectors. Politicians compete with each other for elective office. Bureau chiefs and agency heads compete for additional taxpayer dollars. Public-sector employees, like their counterparts in the private sector, compete for promotions, higher incomes, and additional power. Lobbyists compete to secure funds, to receive favorable rulings, and to secure legislation for the interest groups they represent—including both private and government clients. (See the "Applications in Economics" box.) The nature of the competition and the criteria for success do differ between the two sectors. Nonetheless, competitive behavior is present in both sectors.

2. PUBLIC-SECTOR ORGANIZATION CAN BREAK THE INDIVIDUAL CONSUMPTION-PAYMENT LINK. In the market, a consumer who wants to obtain a commodity must be willing to pay the price. For each person, there is a one-to-one correspondence between consuming the commodity and paying the purchase price. In this respect, there is a fundamental difference between market and collective action. The government usually does not establish a one-to-one relationship between the individual's payment and receipt of a good.

Your tax bill will be the same whether you like or dislike the national defense, agriculture, or antipoverty policies of the government. You will be taxed for subsidies to higher education, sugarbeet growers, food stamps, cultural centers, and many other **political goods** regardless of whether or not you consume or use them. In some cases, you may receive very large benefits (either monetary or subjective) from a government action without any significant impact on your tax bill. The direct link between individual consumption of the good and individual payment for the good is not required in the public sector. Without individual payment to discipline individual consumption, rationing of the good must be accomplished by other means.

Political good
Any good (or policy), whether a public good or a private good, supplied through the political process.

PERSPECTIVES ON THE COST OF POLITICAL COMPETITION

We all have our own ideas concerning how government should be run. Since government is such an extremely important force in our economy and in our lives, individuals and groups try to influence election outcomes by voting, by contributing to political campaigns, and by ringing doorbells, among other activities. In addition, legislative and executive branch decisions can be influenced directly, by lobbying.

Competition for elective office is fierce, and campaigns are expensive. In preparation for the 1992 elections, for example, candidates for House and Senate positions spent $678 million. Unlike bidders in a market auction, winners and losers alike pay the full costs of the election bid. It is common for lobbying groups to donate to opposing candidates in a close race.

During and after the election, lobbying groups compete for the attention—the ear—of elected officials. In fact, the greatest portion of campaign funds raised by incumbents is not raised at election time; rather, it accrues over their entire term in office. A large campaign contribution may not be able to "buy" a vote, but it certainly enhances the lobbyist's chance to sit down with the elected official to explain the power and the beauty of the contributor's position. In the competitive world of politics, the politician who does not at least listen to helpful "friends of the campaign" is less likely to survive.

Campaign contributions are only the tip of the lobbying iceberg. In Washington, D.C., alone, thousands of offices and tens of thousands of individuals, many of them extremely talented, hard-working, and well-paid, are dedicated to lobbying Congress and the executive branch of the federal government. Trade associations, for example, have more than 3,000 offices and 80,000 employees in Washington.[1] Another indicator of the enormous amount of time and effort allocated to influencing government is that 65 percent of *Fortune* 200 chief executive officers travel to Washington at least every two weeks, on average. Billions of dollars in budgets, in taxes, and in expenditures required by regulation are at stake, in addition to such emotional issues as gun control and abortion. The natural result is huge expenditures designed to influence government policy.

_____

[1]More details on campaign finance can be found in Michael Barone and Grant Ujifusa, *The Almanac of American Politics: 1994* (Washington, D.C.: National Journal, 1993). See also David Boaz, "Spend Money to Make Money," *The Wall Street Journal,* November 13, 1983.

3. SCARCITY IMPOSES THE AGGREGATE CONSUMPTION-PAYMENT LINK IN BOTH SECTORS. Although the government can break the link between an individual's payment for a good and the right to consume the good, the reality of the *aggregate consumption-aggregate payment* link will remain. Provision of scarce goods requires sacrificing alternatives. Someone must cover the cost of providing scarce goods, regardless of the sector used to produce (or distribute) them. There are no free lunches in either the private or the public sector. Free goods provided in the public sector are "free" only to individuals. They are most certainly not free from the viewpoint of society.

An increase in the amount of goods provided by the public sector will mean an increase in the total costs of government. Given the fact of scarcity, the link between aggregate consumption and aggregate costs of production cannot be broken by public-sector action.

4. THE ELEMENT OF COMPULSION IS PRESENT IN THE PUBLIC SECTOR. As we have already discussed, voluntary exchange is the dominant characteristic of market organization. Except when externalities are present, involuntary exchange is absent. In the marketplace, a minority need not yield to the majority. For example, the views of the majority, even an overwhelming majority, do not prevent minority consumers from purchasing desired goods.

Governments possess an exclusive right to the use of coercion. Large corporations like Exxon and General Motors are economically powerful, but they cannot require you to buy their products. In contrast, in the political arena, if a legislative majority decides on a particular policy, the minority must accept the policy and help pay for its cost, even if that minority strongly disagrees. If representative legislative policy allocates $10 billion for the development of a superweapon system, the dissenting minority is required to pay taxes that will help finance the project. Other dissenting minorities will be compelled to pay taxes for the support of welfare programs, farm subsidies, foreign aid, or hundreds of other projects on which reasonable people will surely differ. When issues are decided in the public sector, dissidents must, at least temporarily, yield to the current dominant view.

5. WHEN COLLECTIVE DECISIONS ARE MADE LEGISLATIVELY, VOTERS MUST CHOOSE AMONG CANDIDATES WHO REPRESENT A BUNDLE OF POSITIONS ON ISSUES.

On election day, the voter cannot choose the views of Representative Free Lunch on poverty and business welfare and simultaneously choose the views of challenger Ms. Austerity on national defense and tariffs. Inability to support a candidate's views on one issue while rejecting his or her views on another greatly reduces the voter's power to register preferences on specific issues. Since the average representative is asked to vote on roughly 2,000 different issues during a two-year term, the enormity of the problem is obvious.

To the average individual, choosing a representative is a bit like choosing an agent who will control a substantial portion of one's income and also regulate one's activites. Even if this individual voter could personally elect the agent, it would be impossible for the voter to select one agent's views on issue X and another agent's views on issue Y. Looked at another way, deciding to vote for (or against) a candidate on the basis of one issue essentially means being disenfranchised on all others. As a result of the "bundle-purchase" nature of the political process, the ability of each voter to express his or her preference at the ballot box, on each issue, is severely limited.

6. INCOME AND POWER ARE DISTRIBUTED DIFFERENTLY IN THE TWO SECTORS.

Individuals who supply more highly valued resources in the marketplace have larger incomes. The number of dollar votes available to an individual reflect her or his abilities, ambitions, skills, perceptiveness, past savings, inheritance, and good fortune, among other things. An unequal distribution of consumer power is the result.

In the public sector, ballots call the tune when decisions are made democratically. One citizen, one vote is the rule. This does not mean, however, that political goods and services—those resources that make up political power or political income—are allocated equally to all citizens by the collective decision-making process. Some individuals are much more astute than others at using the political process to personal advantage. The political process rewards those who are most capable of delivering votes—not only their own individual votes but those of others as well. Persuasive skills (that is, lobbying, public speaking, public relations), organizational abilities, financial contributions, and knowledge are vital to success in politics. Persons who have more of these resources—and are willing to spend them in the political arena—can expect to benefit more handsomely, in terms of both money and power, from the political process than individuals who lack these personal resources.

SUPPLY OF AND DEMAND FOR PUBLIC-SECTOR ACTION

Consumers use their dollar votes to demand goods in the marketplace. Producers supply goods. The actions of both are influenced by self-interest. In a democratic political system, voters and legislators are counterparts to consumers and producers. Voters demand political goods using their political resources—votes, lobbying, contributions, and organizational abilities. Vote-conscious legislators are suppliers of political goods.

How does a voter decide which political supplier to support? Since there is no evidence that entrance into a voting booth or participation in the political process causes a personality transformation, there is sound reason to believe that the motivation of participants in the market and political processes is similar. The voter who selects among political alternatives is the same person who selects among market alternatives. If Jones is influenced by expected personal benefits and costs when he makes choices in the department store, it makes sense that he will be similarly influenced by personal benefits and costs when he makes choices in the voting booth.

Other things constant, voters will support those candidates whom they expect to provide them with the most benefits, net of cost. The greater the expected gains from a candidate's election, the more voters will do to ensure the candidate's success. A voter, like the consumer in the marketplace, will ask the supplier, "What can you do for me and how much will I pay?"

SUPPLY OF PUBLIC-SECTOR ACTION

The goal of the political supplier is to put together a majority coalition—to win the election. Vote-seeking politicians, like profit-seeking business decision makers, will have a strong incentive to cater to the views of politically active constituents. The easiest way to win votes, both politically and financially, is to give the constituents—or at least appear to give them—what they want. A politician who pays no heed to the views of his or her constituents is as rare as a businessperson selling swimsuits in the Arctic.

DEMAND FOR PUBLIC-SECTOR ACTION

There are two major reasons that voters are likely to turn to public-sector economic organization: (1) to reduce waste and inefficiency stemming from noncompetitive markets, externalities, public goods, and economic instability and (2) to redistribute income. Public-sector action that corrects, or appears to correct, the shortcomings of the market will be attractive. If properly conducted, it will generate more benefits than costs to the community. Much real-world public policy is motivated by a desire to correct the shortcomings of the market. Antitrust action is designed to promote competition. Government provision of national defense, crime prevention, a legal system, and flood-control projects is related to the public-good nature of these activities. Similarly, externalities help justify public-sector action in such areas as pollution control, education, pure research, and disease control. Furthermore, the tax, spending, and monetary policies of the government are generally used to influence the level and stability of economic activity in most Western nations.

Demand for public-sector action may also stem from a desire to change the income distribution. There is no reason to presume that the unhampered market will lead to the most desirable distribution of income. In fact, the ideal distribution of income is largely a matter of personal preference. There is nothing in positive economics that tells us that one distribution of income is better than another. Some people may desire to see more income allocated to low-income citizens. The most common scientific argument for redistribution to the poor is based on the "public-good" nature of adequate income for all. Alleviation of poverty may help not only the poor but also those who are well-off. Middle- and upper-income recipients, for example, may benefit if the less fortunate members of the community enjoy better food, clothing, housing, and health care. If the rich would gain, why will they not voluntarily give to the poor? In fact they do give, but they may give too little for the same reason that individuals will do little to provide national defense voluntarily. The antipoverty efforts of any single individual will exert little impact on the total amount of poverty in the community. Because individual action is so insignificant, each person has an incentive to opt out. When everyone opts out, the market provides less than the desired amount of antipoverty action.

Others may desire public-sector redistribution for less altruistic reasons—they may seek to enhance their own personal incomes. This poses a problem: How can government engage in income redistribution based on the "public-good" nature of antipoverty transfers and at the same time restrain income transfers based on the political clout of various interest groups? This is an important question because there is reason to believe that economic waste is a side effect of substantial government involvement in the determination of income shares. There are three major reasons why large-scale redistribution is likely to reduce the size of the economic pie.

First, such redistribution weakens the link between productive activity and reward. When taxes take a larger share of one's income, tax revenues are spread among all beneficiaries, so the benefits derived from hard work and productive service are reduced. The basic economic postulate suggests that when benefits allocated to producers are reduced (and benefits of nonproducers are raised), less productive effort will be supplied.

Second, as public policy redistributes a larger share of income, individuals will allocate more resources to **rent seeking**.[6] Rent seeking is a term used by economists to denote those actions designed to change public policy—tax structure, composition of spending, or regulation—in a manner that will redistribute income toward themselves. Resources used for lobbying and other means of rent seeking

Rent seeking
Actions by individuals and interest groups designed to restructure public policy in a manner that will either directly or indirectly redistribute more income to themselves.

[6]See Charles K. Rowley, Robert D. Tollison, and Gordon Tullock, *The Political Economy of Rent-Seeking* (Boston: Kluewer Academic Publishers, 1988), for additional details on rent seeking.

(perhaps "favor seeking" would be more descriptive) will not be available to increase the size of the economic pie.

Third, higher taxes to finance income redistribution and an expansion in rent-seeking activities will induce taxpayers to engage in protective action. Taxpayers will be encouraged to take steps to protect their income. More accountants, lawyers, and tax-shelter experts will be retained as people seek to limit the amount of their income that is redistributed to others. Like the resources allocated to rent seeking, resources allocated to protecting one's wealth from public policy will also be wasted. They will not be available for productive activity. Therefore, given the incentive structure generated by large-scale redistribution policies, there is good reason to expect that such policies will reduce the size of the economic pie.

CONFLICTS BETWEEN GOOD ECONOMICS AND GOOD POLITICS

When collective decision making has the potential to improve economic efficiency, current economic and political research reveals factors that limit our ability to use government to correct shortcomings of the market. We deal with these factors in more detail in a later chapter, but three important characteristics of the political process are introduced here.

THE RATIONALLY IGNORANT VOTER

Less than one half of the American electorate can correctly identify the names of their representatives to Congress, much less state where those representatives stand on various issues. Why are so many people ignorant of the simplest facts regarding the political process? The explanation does not lie with a lack of intelligence on the part of the average American. The phenomenon is explained by the incentives confronting the voter. Most citizens recognize that their vote is unlikely to determine the outcome of an election. Consequently, they have little incentive to spend much effort to seek the information needed to cast an informed ballot. Economists refer to this lack of incentive as the **rational ignorance effect.**

Rational ignorance effect
Voter ignorance resulting from the fact that people perceive their individual votes as unlikely to be decisive. Therefore, they rationally have little incentive to seek the information needed to cast an informed vote.

The rationally ignorant voter is exercising good judgment as to how his or her time and effort will yield the most personal benefits. There is a parallel between the voter's failure to acquire political knowledge and the farmer's inattention to the factors that determine the weather. Weather is probably the most important factor determining the income of an individual farmer, yet it makes no sense for the farmer to invest time and resources attempting to understand atmospheric science. An improved knowledge of how weather systems work will seldom enable the farmer to avoid their adverse effects. So it is with the average voter. The voter stands to gain little from acquiring more information about a wide range of issues that are decided in the political arena.

Because of this fact, most voters simply rely on information that is supplied to them freely by candidates (via political advertising) and the mass media, as well as conversations with friends and coworkers. It is not surprising, then, that few voters are able to accurately describe the consequences of raising tariffs on automobiles or of abolishing the farm price support program. In using their time and efforts in ways other than studying these policy issues, voters are merely responding to economic incentives.

THE PROBLEM OF SPECIAL INTEREST

A **special interest issue** is one that generates substantial personal benefits for a small number of constituents while imposing a small individual cost on a large number of other votes. A few gain a great deal individually, whereas a large number lose a little individually.

Special interest issues are very attractive to vote-conscious politicians (that is, to those most eager and most likely to win elections). Voters who have a small cost imposed on them by a policy favoring a special interest will not care enough about the issue to examine it, particularly if it is complex enough that the imposition of the cost is difficult to identify. Because information is costly, most of those harmed will not even be aware of the legislator's views on such an issue. On the other hand, those most directly affected by such an issue will let the candidate (or legislator) know that it is important to them. Because they are a small group, they may be able to organize and to give financial and other help to politicians receptive to their ideas, while opposing those who are not.

What would you do if you wanted to win an election? You might support the special interest groups, milk them for financial resources, and use those resources to promote your candidacy among the uninformed majority of voters. You would have an incentive to follow this path even if the total community benefits from the support of the special interest were less than the cost. The policy might cause economic inefficiency, but it could still be a political winner.

Why stand up for a large majority? Even though the total cost may be large, each person bears only a small cost. Most voters are uninformed on the issue and do not care much about it. They would do little to help you get elected even if you supported their best interests on this issue. Astute politicians will support the special interest group if they plan to be around for very long.

The political process tends to work in favor of special interest groups, even when their programs are inefficient. This means that sometimes there is a conflict between good politics (winning elections) and ideal public policy. Throughout, as we consider public-policy alternatives, we will remind you to consider how public policy is likely to operate when special interest influence is strong.

Special interest issue
An issue that generates substantial individual benefits to a small minority while imposing a small individual cost on many other voters. In total, the net cost to the majority might either exceed or fall short of the net benefits to the special interest group.

POLITICAL GAINS FROM SHORTSIGHTED POLICIES

The complexity of many issues makes it difficult for voters to identify the future benefits and costs. Can a change in tax rates lead to a greater rate of economic growth? Will a change in environmental policy now lead to a healthier environment for our grandchildren, or to slower economic growth? What impact will a rise in the national debt have on future prosperity? These questions are complex. The difficulty of predicting the future results of current policies acts to reinforce the rational ignorance effect. Few voters will analyze the long-run implications of complex policy alternatives having impacts mainly in the future. Unlike the choice to purchase or sell a private good or investment, the voter's individual ballot choice will almost never determine the election outcome, so for the individual, a mistaken vote seldom makes a difference in the outcome. Voters judging the performance of incumbents will have a tendency to rely simply on current conditions.[7] To the voter, the most easily seen indicator of the success of a policy is, "How are things now?"

Accordingly, politicians seeking reelection have a strong incentive to support policies that generate current benefits in exchange for future costs, particularly if the future costs will be difficult to identify on election day. Public-sector action will therefore be biased in favor of legislation that offers immediate (and easily identifiable) current benefits in exchange for future costs that are complicated and difficult to identify. Simultaneously, there is a bias against legislation that involves immediate and easily identifiable costs (for example, higher taxes) while yielding future benefits that are complex and difficult to identify. Economists refer to this bias inherent in the collective decision-making process as the **shortsightedness effect.**

The nature of democratic institutions restricts the planning horizon of elected officials. Positive results must be observable by the next election, or the incumbent is likely to be replaced by someone who promises more rapid results. Policies that will eventually pay off in the future (after the next election) will have little appeal to vote-seeking politicians. As we shall subsequently see, the shortsighted nature of the political process reduces the likelihood that it will be able to promote economic stability and a noninflationary environment.

What if shortsighted policies lead to serious problems after an election? This can be sticky for politicians, but is it not better to be an officeholder explaining why things are in a mess than a defeated candidate trying to convince people who will not listen why you were right all the time? The political entrepreneur has a strong incentive to win the next election and worry about the problems later, as they arise.

Shortsightedness effect
Misallocation of resources that results because public-sector action is biased (1) in favor of proposals yielding clearly defined current benefits in exchange for difficult-to-identify future costs and (2) against proposals with clearly identifiable current costs but yielding less concrete and less obvious future benefits.

IMPLICATIONS OF PUBLIC CHOICE

It is important to distinguish between ordinary politics and constitutional rules. Constitutions establish the procedures that will be utilized to make decisions. They also may limit the boundary of ordinary politics, placing certain matters (for example, the taking of private property without compensation, restrictions on freedom of speech or worship, and various restrictions on voting) beyond the reach of majority rule or normal legislative procedures.

---

[7]As we will see in more detail in the later chapter on public choice, the public sector lacks a market in stock ownership. It is the ability to buy or sell stock which gives stockholders the incentive to monitor current corporate decisions that affect future corporate costs and benefits, so that they can individually sell their corporate stock if they think bad decisions are currently being made, or buy more stock if they think current decisions will produce net future benefits for the corporation. Their buying and selling activities cause the stock price to rise or fall, sending an instant signal and incentive to corporate management to avoid decisions which are shortsighted, in order to avoid falling prices for their corporate stock. Such market signals cannot be generated in the public sector.

Both bad news and good news flow from public-choice analysis. The bad news is that for certain classes of economic activity, unconstrained democratic government will predictably be a source of economic waste and inefficiency. Not only does the invisible hand of the market sometimes fail to meet our ideal efficiency criteria, so too, does political decision making. That makes the growth of government (noted by Jonathan Hughes in the chapter-opening quote) rather worrisome. But there is also some good news arising from public-choice theory: properly structured constitutional rules can improve the expected result from government. So the study of how people behave in the government process "in the world as it really is" (noted by Arthur Seldon in the other chapter-opening quote) suggests constructive alternatives for improving the government process.

Whether political organization leads to desirable or undesirable economic outcomes is critically dependent upon the structure of the political (constitutional) rules. In government as elsewhere, proper incentives are critical to good decision making. When the structure of the political rules brings the self-interest of individual voters, politicians, and bureaucrats into harmony with the general welfare, government will promote economic prosperity. On the other hand, if the rules fail to bring about this harmony, politically determined outcomes will often conflict with economic efficiency. The challenge before us is to develop political-economy institutions that are more consistent with economic prosperity. As we proceed, we will discuss several modifications of the political rules that public-choice theory indicates would improve the economic effectiveness of the political process. Needless to say, this general topic is one of the most exciting and potentially fruitful areas of study in economics.

LOOKING AHEAD

In the next chapter, we will examine the government's actual spending and tax policies. In subsequent chapters, the significance of economic organization and issues of political economy will be highlighted. The tools of economics are used with a dual objective. We will point out what government ideally might do, but we will also focus on what government can be expected to do. Not surprisingly, the two are not always identical. *Political economy*—the use of economic tools to explain how both the market and the public sectors actually work—is a fascinating subject. It helps us to understand the "why" behind many of today's current events. Who said economics is the dismal science?

CHAPTER SUMMARY

1. Economic efficiency—creating as much value as possible from a given set of resources—is a goal by which alternative institutions and policies can be judged. Two conditions must be met to achieve economic efficiency: (1) all activities that produce more benefits than costs for the individuals within an economy must be undertaken and (2) activities that generate more costs than benefits to the individuals must not be undertaken. If only the buyer and the seller are affected and competition is present, the incentives built into market production and exchange are consistent with the ideal efficiency criteria.

2. Lack of competition may make it possible for a group of sellers to gain by restricting output and raising prices. There is a conflict between (1) the self-interest of sellers that leads them to collude, restrict output, and raise product prices above their production costs and (2) economic efficiency. Public-sector action—promoting competition or regulating private firms—may be able to improve economic efficiency in industries in which competitive pressures are lacking.

3. When property rights are imperfectly defined or enforced market exchange will tend to underallocate resources to the production of goods with external benefits and overallocate resources to those products that generate external costs.

4. Public goods are troublesome for the market to handle because nonpaying customers cannot easily be

excluded. Since the amount of a public good that each individual receives is largely unaffected by whether he or she helps pay for it, many individuals will contribute little. The market will thus tend to undersupply public goods.

5. The public sector will improve the operation of markets if it provides a stable economic environment.

6. The public sector is an alternative means of organizing economic activity. Public-sector decision making will reflect the choices of individuals acting as voters, politicians, financial contributors, lobbyists, and bureaucrats. Public-choice analysis applies the principles and methodology of economics to group decision making to help us understand collective organizations.

7. Successful political candidates will seek to offer programs that appeal to voters. Voters, in turn, will be attracted to candidates who reflect the voters' own views and interests. In a democratic setting, there are two major reasons why voters will turn to collective organization: (1) to reduce waste and inefficiency stemming from noncompetitive markets, externalities, public goods, and economic instability and (2) to alter the income distribution.

8. Public-sector action may sometimes improve the market's efficiency and lead to an increase in the community's welfare, all individuals considered. However, the political process is likely to conflict with ideal economic efficiency criteria when (1) voters have little knowledge of an issue, (2) special interests are strong, and/or (3) political figures can gain from following shortsighted policies.

CRITICAL-ANALYSIS QUESTIONS

1. Explain in your own words what is meant by external costs and external benefits. Why may market allocations be less than ideal when externalities are present?

*2. If producers are to be provided with an incentive to produce a good, why is it important for them to be able to prevent nonpaying customers from receiving the good?

3. Do you think real-world politicians adopt political positions to help their election prospects? Can you name a current political figure who consistently puts "principles above politics"? If so, check with three of your classmates to see if they agree.

4. Do you think special interest groups exert much influence on local government? Why or why not? As a test, check the composition of the local zoning board in your community. How many real-estate agents, contractors, developers, and landlords are on the board? Are there any citizens without real-estate interests on the board?

*5. "Economics is a positive science. Government by its very nature is influenced by philosophical considerations.

Therefore, the tools of economics cannot tell us much about how the public sector works." Do you agree or disagree with this statement. Why?

*6. Which of the following are public goods: (a) an antimissile system surrounding Washington, D.C.; (b) a fire department; (c) tennis courts; (d) Yellowstone National Park; (e) elementary schools? Explain, using the definition of a public good.

7. "A democratic government is a corrective device used to remedy inefficiencies that arise when market allocation is not working well." Is this statement true or false? Explain.

8. Incentives are important in both the market and political sectors. Discuss the similarities and differences in the incentives of the following pairs of people to use resources efficiently and provide value to others.

   a. The president of General Motors and the president of a large state university.

   b. A member of the board of directors of IBM and a congressional representative.

   c. The general manager of Walt Disney World and the superintendent of Yellowstone National Park.

   d. The president of a textbook-publishing company and the superintendent of public schools in your state.

*9. How can you determine if a market action is efficient? How can you determine if a government action is efficient? If the majority of the citizens favor a project, does this indicate it is productive?

10. English philosopher John Locke argued that the protection of each individual's person and property was the primary function of government. Why is the secure protection of each individual's person and property (that is, property acquired without the use of violence, theft, or fraud) important to the efficient operation of an economy?

*11. Does the democratic political process incorporate the invisible hand principle? Is the presence or absence of the invisible hand principle important? Why or why not?

*12. "The average person is more likely to make an informed choice when he or she purchases a personal computer than when he or she votes for a congressional candidate." Evaluate this statement.

13. Suppose that Abel builds a factory next to Baker's farm, and air pollution from the factory harms Baker's crops. Is Baker's property right to the land being violated? Is an externality present? What if the pollution invades Baker's home and harms her health. Are her property rights violated? Is an externality present? Explain.

*14. Jack, who holds stock in General Motors Corporation, lives in an apartment in Los Angeles. In two years he expects to sell the stock and retire in Florida.

---

*Asterisk denotes questions for which answers are given in Appendix C.

General Motors announces that profits will not be paid out to stockholders this year, but will be used to finance a new auto design that is expected to return more than enough money in ten years to compensate stockholders for this year's lack of dividend payments. On the same day, the Los Angeles mayor announces that a city sales tax will be imposed to finance better streets. Over the next ten years, by coincidence, the benefits to Jack would be exactly the same as the General Motors benefits (just as the costs paid this year would be the same), *if he holds the stock and stays in Los Angeles*. Explain why Jack is not bothered by the GM announcement, but is very unhappy about the mayor's announcement. (Hint: he will sell the stock, but can't sell his right to future benefits in Los Angeles.)

CHAPTER FIVE

GOVERNMENT SPENDING
AND TAXATION

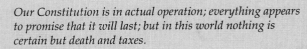

Our Constitution is in actual operation; everything appears to promise that it will last; but in this world nothing is certain but death and taxes.

BENJAMIN FRANKLIN, 1789

CHAPTER FOCUS

■ *How big is government? What goods and services do we provide through government? How are they financed?*
■ *Why has the size of government grown more rapidly than our economy during the last several decades? Does government now provide more goods and services than it did in the past? Does it redistribute more income?*
■ *How do taxes influence the behavior of people? If a tax rate is increased by 10 percent, will revenue from the tax increase by 10 percent?*
■ *How did tax legislation passed during the 1980s affect the taxes paid by the rich?*
■ *How does the size of government in the United States compare with the size of government in other countries?*

T he activities of government have an enormous impact on our lives. Governments levy taxes and organize the production of many goods and services. Sometimes governments tax income away from some people and transfer it to others. Governments also provide the legal infrastructure for economic activity. Laws against theft, fraud, and the private use of violence greatly influence how markets work and the degree of cooperation and conflict among economic participants. Similarly, the monetary framework and regulatory activities of government are vitally important. In fact, in its role as rule-maker and referee, government probably exerts more influence on the economic prosperity of a nation than it does as a producer of goods and services.

Nevertheless, taxation and government expenditures are the most direct means by which the government influences the economy. Analysis of the government's spending policies and methods of finance will reveal a great deal about the size and economic character of government.

THE GROWTH OF GOVERNMENT

Prior to the 1930s, government expenditures generally amounted to less than 10 percent of our gross domestic product (GDP).[1] Except during times of war, federal government expenditures were quite small in the early part of this century. As **Exhibit 5–1** illustrates, the expenditures of the federal government were only 3.0 percent of GDP in 1929, compared with 7.1 percent for state and local expenditures.

During the 1930–1970 period, both the size and composition of government changed dramatically. By 1970 total government expenditures comprised 30.8 percent of our economy, more than triple the level of 1929. Most of this growth of government took place at the federal level. As a share of our economy, federal expenditures tripled during the 1930s, while state and local expenditures increased by only a small amount. Between 1940 and 1970, federal expenditures more than doubled in size (from 9.5 percent to 20.6 percent) as a share of our economy. State and local spending grew more slowly, advancing from 9.0 percent of GDP in 1940 to 10.2 percent in 1970. In contrast with 1929, when government expenditures were small and mostly at the local level, by 1970 government spending summed to nearly one-third of our total output, and most of this spending was undertaken by the federal government.

Since 1970 the growth of government as a proportion of our economy has continued, albeit at a slower rate. In 1993 total government expenditures comprised 34.4 percent of GDP, up from 30.8 percent in 1970. More than two-thirds of the government spending in 1993 was undertaken at the federal level.

FEDERALISM AND GOVERNMENT EXPENDITURES

The economic functions of government in the United States vary among the different levels. The United States has a federalist system of government. While many

---

[1]GDP is discussed in Chapter 6. For now, it can be thought of as a measure of total output produced during a period.

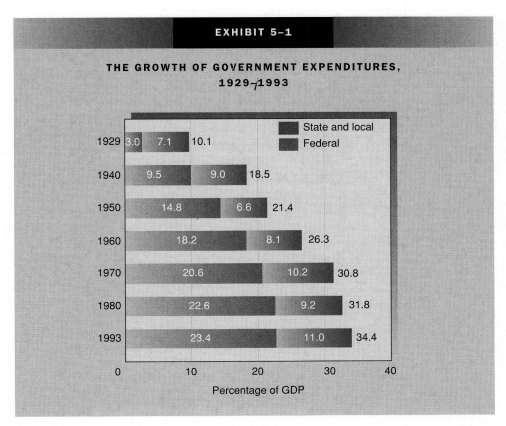

EXHIBIT 5-1

THE GROWTH OF GOVERNMENT EXPENDITURES, 1929–1993

Legend: State and local / Federal

Year	State and local	Federal	Total
1929	3.0	7.1	10.1
1940	9.5	9.0	18.5
1950	14.8	6.6	21.4
1960	18.2	8.1	26.3
1970	20.6	10.2	30.8
1980	22.6	9.2	31.8
1993	23.4	11.0	34.4

Percentage of GDP (0, 10, 20, 30, 40)

In 1929 total government spending summed to 10.1 percent of total output. During the 1930–1970 period, the size of government as a share of the U.S. economy rose substantially, reaching 30.8 percent of GDP in 1970. In 1993 total government spending was 34.4 percent of GDP.

Source: *Economic Report of the President* various issues. Grants to state and local governments are included in federal expenditures.

economic activities are conducted at the federal level, the primary responsibility for other functions remains with state and local governments. A breakdown of expenditures and revenues, as shown in **Exhibit 5–2**, helps to highlight the functional differences among the levels of government.

This exhibit shows the broad categories of federal expenditures for fiscal year 1993. The federal government is solely responsible for national defense. A little less than one-quarter of federal expenditures went for defense and related areas (space, veterans' benefits, and foreign affairs) in 1993. The largest item in the federal budget was cash-income maintenance—social security, unemployment payments, and public assistance to the poor and the disabled. These income transfers accounted for 36.1 percent of the total federal budget. Programs to help people buy essentials (medical care, housing, food, and so on) made up 17.2 percent of all federal spending in 1993. This category differs from cash-income maintenance in that people must purchase specific goods in order to qualify for the assistance. Thus, spending in these two categories—cash-income transfers and subsidies for specific goods purchased by some people—accounted for more than half of the federal expenditures.

Expenditures on education, manpower development, agriculture, energy, and transportation also constitute major items in the federal budget from year to year. Interest payments on the national debt for 1993 constituted 13.7 percent of total federal outlays.

Exhibit 5–3 is a graphic presentation of state and local government expenditures. In the United States, public education has traditionally been the responsibility

The breakdown of the 1993 fiscal year federal budget is presented here. Defense accounted for 23.9 percent of federal spending. More than half of the federal tax dollar was spent on cash-income maintenance and helping people buy essentials.

[a]*Spending on veterans' benefits and services are included in this category.*

Source: *Economic Report of the President, 1994*, Table B-78.

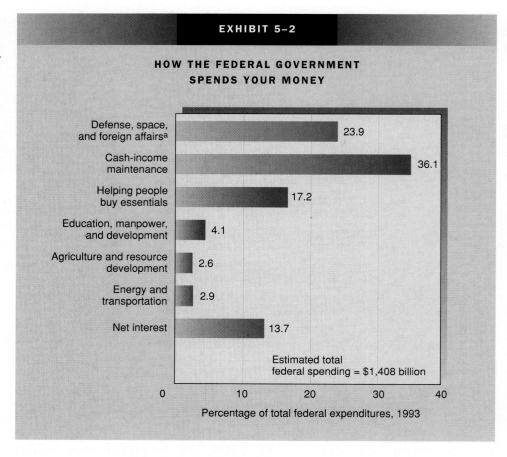

EXHIBIT 5–2

HOW THE FEDERAL GOVERNMENT SPENDS YOUR MONEY

Defense, space, and foreign affairs[a] — 23.9
Cash-income maintenance — 36.1
Helping people buy essentials — 17.2
Education, manpower, and development — 4.1
Agriculture and resource development — 2.6
Energy and transportation — 2.9
Net interest — 13.7

Estimated total federal spending = $1,408 billion

Percentage of total federal expenditures, 1993

of state and local governments. Thirty-four percent of state and local government expenditures were allocated to education during the fiscal year 1991. State governments supplement federal allocations in the areas of social welfare, public welfare, and health. These social welfare expenditures comprised 23 percent of the total spending of state governments during 1991. Highways, utilities, insurance trust funds, law enforcement, and fire protection are other major areas of expenditure for state and local government.

GOVERNMENT PURCHASES AND TRANSFER PAYMENTS

Government purchases
Current expenditures on goods and services provided by federal, state, and local governments; they exclude transfer payments.

It is important to distinguish between (1) government purchases of goods and services and (2) transfer payments. **Government purchases** are expenditures incurred when goods and services are supplied through the public sector. They include items such as jet planes, missiles, highway construction and maintenance, police and fire protection, and computer equipment. Governments also purchase the labor services of teachers, clerks, lawyers, accountants, and public relations experts to produce goods ranging from public education to administrative services. Since

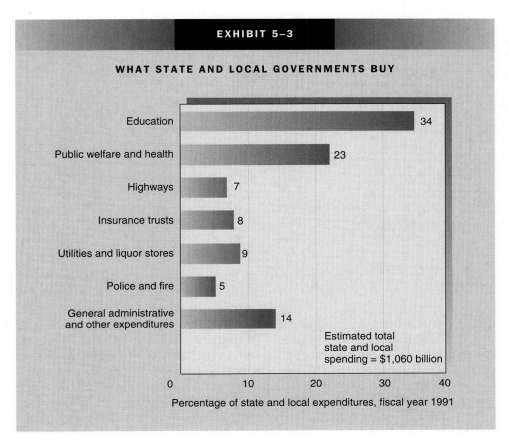

EXHIBIT 5-3

WHAT STATE AND LOCAL GOVERNMENTS BUY

Education   34

Public welfare and health   23

Highways   7

Insurance trusts   8

Utilities and liquor stores   9

Police and fire   5

General administrative
and other expenditures   14

Estimated total
state and local
spending = $1,060 billion

0   10   20   30   40

Percentage of state and local expenditures, fiscal year 1991

Education, public welfare, and general administrative expenditures comprise the major budget items of state and local governments.

Source: U.S. Department of Commerce.

they consume resources with alternative uses, government purchases directly reduce the supply of resources available to produce private goods and services.

Transfer payments are transfers of income from taxpayers to recipients who do not provide current goods and services in exchange for these payments. Simply put, transfer payments take income from some to provide additional income to others. Social security benefits, pensions of retired government employees, and Aid to Families with Dependent Children (AFDC) are examples of transfer payments.

Unlike government purchases, transfer payments do not directly reduce the resources available to the private sector. They do, however, alter the incentive structure of the economy and almost certainly exert an indirect impact on the size of the economic pie. The taxes necessary to finance transfer payments reduce the personal payoff from saving, investing, and working. If receipt of transfer payments is inversely related to income level, they will also reduce the recipient's incentive to earn taxable income. As we proceed, we will investigate the link between aggregate output and the incentive structure in more detail.

Transfer payments
Payments to individuals or institutions that are not linked to the current supply of a good or service by the recipient.

ALTERNATIVE MEASURES OF GOVERNMENT'S SIZE

Exhibit 5-4 presents four alternative measures of government size. In 1992 the purchases of federal, state, and local governments amounted to $1,132 billion, or

Source: *Economic Report of the President, 1994* (Washington, DC: U.S. Government Printing Office, 1994), and *Monthly Labor Review,* October 1993. Intergovernmental transfer payments (i.e., federal grants to state and local governments) are not counted twice.

EXHIBIT 5-4

FOUR MEASURES OF SIZE OF GOVERNMENT: FEDERAL, STATE, AND LOCAL, 1992

1.	Government purchases of goods and services	(a) Billions of dollars	1,132
		(b) Percentage of GDP	18.7
2.	Government employment	(a) Millions of employees	18.7
		(b) Percentage of total employment	17.2
3.	Total government expenditures including transfer payments	(a) Billions of dollars	2,119
		(b) Percentage of GDP	35.1
4.	Total taxes and other revenues	(a) Billions of dollars	1,849
		(b) Percentage of GDP	30.6

18.7 percent of total U.S. output. Government purchases thus consumed a little less than one-fifth of our resources. Government employment offers a second gauge by which we can measure the size of government. In 1992 a little more than one out of every six workers (17.2 percent) was employed by a government unit.

As we have already pointed out, government purchases fail to tell the whole story. Governments not only employ people and provide goods and services, they also tax the income of some and transfer it to others. Once transfer payments are included, total government expenditures (the third measure of size) in 1992 summed to $2,119 billion, or 35.1 percent of GDP.[2] The total tax bill (the fourth measure of size) was slightly less, accounting for 30.6 percent of GDP. Therefore, during 1992 approximately one-third of the national output was channeled through the public sector.

On a per capita basis, government expenditures were equal to $8,290 in 1992. If government expenditures in 1992 had been divided equally among the 94 million households in the United States, each household would have received $22,500.

CHANGING COMPOSITION OF GOVERNMENT

For many years, government has been involved in the providing of national defense, police and fire protection, roads, education, and other jointly consumed goods and services. Since defense is a classic example of a public good, it is not surprising that this good is supplied through the public rather than through the private sector. Police and fire protection, road maintenance, and education have traditionally been financed and distributed by state and local governments. Each

---

[2]The public administration costs associated with income-transfer programs do involve the direct use of resources, and they therefore are counted as government purchases. Only the redistribution portion is counted as a transfer payment.

of these goods either generates external *spillover effects* or exhibits public-good characteristics.

Interestingly, these traditional public-sector functions are not responsible for the growth of government in recent years. As **Exhibit 5–5** shows, the growth of government during the last four decades is almost exclusively the result of increased government involvement in income-transfer activities. Perhaps surprisingly to some, government *purchases* of goods and services have fluctuated within a narrow band, around 20 percent of GDP during the last 40 years. Defense expenditures have declined from 10 percent of GDP in the mid-1950s to approximately 5 percent in the early 1990s. In contrast, income transfers grew from less than 5 percent of GDP in the mid-1950s to approximately 15 percent in the mid-1970s. Currently, the government taxes approximately 16 percent of total output away from producers and channels it to the elderly, the unemployed, farmers, children in single-parent families, persons with disabilities, and other transfer recipients.

FINANCING GOVERNMENT EXPENDITURES

If the government is going to supply goods, services, or income transfers, then these activities must be financed. Governments use three major sources of funds to pay

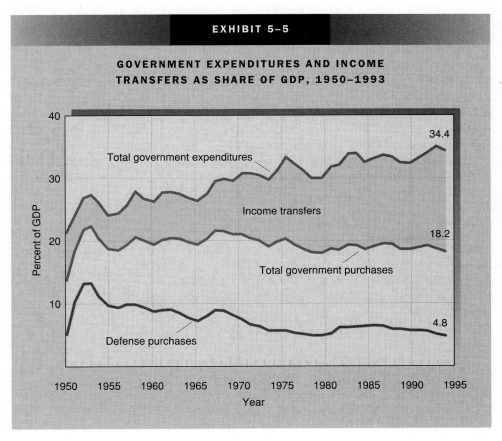

EXHIBIT 5–5

GOVERNMENT EXPENDITURES AND INCOME TRANSFERS AS SHARE OF GDP, 1950–1993

As a percent of GDP, total government expenditures have grown from approximately 25 percent in the mid-1950s to 34.4 percent in 1993. As shown here, growth of income transfers has been the primary source of the increasing size of government. During the last four decades, government purchases of goods and services have been approximately constant at about 20 percent of GDP, while defense expenditures have actually declined relative to the size of the economy.

for their expenditures: (1) taxes, (2) user charges, and (3) borrowing.[3] In the United States, taxes are by far the largest source of government revenue. The power to tax sets governments apart from private businesses. Of course, a private business can put whatever price tag it wishes on its products; but no private business can force you to buy. With its power to tax, a government can force citizens to pay, regardless of whether they receive a "good" of equal or greater value in return.

Let's take a closer look at the taxes levied by governments and at the other sources of revenues available for the finance of government activities.

PERSONAL INCOME TAXES

The largest single source of revenue for governments is the personal income tax. This tax is particularly important at the federal level, where it accounts for 44 percent of federal budget receipts (see **Exhibit 5–6**). Since the Second World War, the income tax has also become an important source of revenue at the state level, where it now accounts for 10 percent of the tax receipts collected by the states. Only six states (Florida, Nevada, South Dakota, Texas, Washington, and Wyoming) now fail to levy a state income tax.

Progressive tax
A tax that requires those with higher taxable incomes to pay a larger percentage of their incomes to the government than those with lower taxable incomes.

The rate structure of the federal income tax is progressive, although less so than in the past. A **progressive tax** takes a larger percentage from high-income recipients. For example, using the rate structure applicable to income in 1993, the tax liability of a single person with $20,000 of taxable income is $3,004. The **average tax rate (ATR)** can be expressed as follows:

$$ATR = \frac{\text{tax liability}}{\text{taxable income}}$$

Average tax rate (ATR)
One's tax liability divided by one's taxable income.

The single person's ATR on $20,000 of income is 15.0 percent ($3,004/$20,000). Since the federal income tax structure is progressive, the ATR will increase with taxable income. For example, the tax liability (1993) of a single person with a taxable income of $40,000 is $8,334, resulting in an ATR of 20.8 percent, higher than the ATR for $20,000 of taxable income.

Marginal tax rate (MTR)
Additional tax liability divided by additional income. Thus, if $100 of additional earnings increases one's tax liability by $30, the marginal tax rate would be 30 percent.

The economic way of thinking stresses that what happens at the margin is of crucial importance in personal decision making. The **marginal tax rate (MTR)** can be expressed as follows:

$$MTR = \frac{\text{change in tax liability}}{\text{change in income}}$$

The MTR reveals both how much of one's additional income can be retained and how much must be turned over to the tax collector. For example, when the MTR is 25 percent, $25 of every $100 of additional earnings must be paid to the taxing authority. The individual is permitted to keep $75 of his or her additional income.

---

[3]In addition to borrowing from private sources, the federal government also may borrow from its central bank. As we will see later, borrowing from a central bank is equivalent to the finance of government via the creation of money.

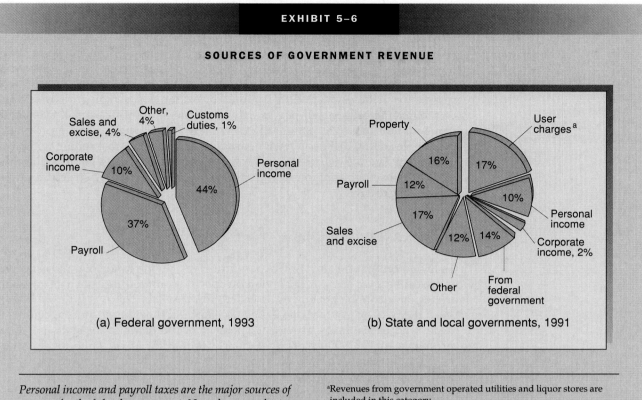

EXHIBIT 5-6

SOURCES OF GOVERNMENT REVENUE

(a) Federal government, 1993

Other, 4%
Sales and excise, 4%
Customs duties, 1%
Corporate income 10%
Personal income 44%
Payroll 37%

(b) State and local governments, 1991

Property 16%
User charges[a] 17%
Payroll 12%
10%
17%
Personal income
Sales and excise 12% 14% Corporate income, 2%
Other
From federal government

Personal income and payroll taxes are the major sources of revenue for the federal government. User charges, sales taxes, property taxes, and grants from the federal government provide the major revenue sources for state and local governments.

[a]Revenues from government operated utilities and liquor stores are included in this category.

Source: *Statistical Abstract of the United States, 1993* and *Economic Report of the President, 1994.*

PAYROLL TAXES

Although income from all sources is covered by the income tax, only earnings derived from labor are subject to the payroll tax. Interest, dividends, rents, and other income derived from capital are not subject to payroll taxes. Payroll taxes on the earnings of employees and self-employed workers are used to finance social security (including Medicare) and unemployment-compensation benefits. Payroll taxes constitute the second largest and most rapidly expanding source of tax revenue. In 1993 payroll taxes comprised 37 percent of all federal revenues, compared to only 16 percent in 1960. Payroll taxes are often criticized because of their regressive structure, but actually, the payroll tax encompasses both proportional and regressive features.

A **proportional tax** is one that takes the same percentage of income from all taxpayers, regardless of income level. Until the maximum taxable income ceiling is reached, the payroll tax is proportional. For example, in 1993, both employees and their employers paid a tax rate of 7.65 percent on all employee earnings up to $57,600. (Self-employed workers paid a 15.3 percent rate.) Beyond that taxable income ceiling, no additional payroll tax is levied. So a worker earning $10,000

Proportional tax
A tax for which individuals pay the same percentage of their income (or other tax base) in taxes, regardless of income level.

incurs a payroll tax of $765, whereas one earning $20,000 is taxed twice that amount, or $1,530. Until the taxable income ceiling is met, all workers (and their employers) pay exactly the same tax rate.

Regressive tax
A tax that takes a smaller percentage of one's income as one's income level increases. Thus, the proportion of income allocated to the tax would be greater for the poor than for the rich.

A **regressive tax** takes a smaller percentage of income from those in high-earnings brackets than it does from low-income recipients. Since the social security payroll tax does not apply beyond the maximum income ceiling, it is regressive for incomes beyond that point. For example, a person with an income twice the taxable ceiling will pay exactly the same amount of payroll taxes (and only one-half the average tax rate) as another individual whose earnings are equal to the taxable ceiling. All people with earnings above the taxable ceiling will pay a lower average tax rate than people with earnings below the ceiling. Thus, since the payroll tax does not apply to earnings above the ceiling, its basic structure can be considered regressive.

SALES AND EXCISE TAXES

Taxes levied on the consumption expenditures for a wide range of goods and services are called *sales taxes*. A tax levied on specific commodities, such as gasoline, cigarettes, or alcoholic beverages, is called an *excise tax*. There is little difference between the two, except that one is a general tax and the other is quite specific.

Sales and excise taxes provide 17 percent of the revenue for state and local governments in 1991. They are particularly important at the state level, where they account for almost a third of the revenue raised by state governments.

PROPERTY TAXES

Despite their unpopularity, property taxes still constitute the bulk of local tax revenues. In 1991, 75 percent of the tax revenue raised by local governments was generated from this source. Property taxes are often criticized because they are cumbersome. The assessor must set a value on taxable property. This generally involves a certain amount of judgment and arbitrariness. During a period of rising prices, property that has recently been exchanged is likely to command a higher valuation than similar property without an easily identifiable indicator of current value. High administration costs and problems in providing equal treatment for similarly situated taxpayers are associated with property taxes.

CORPORATE INCOME TAX

The corporate income tax is levied on the net income—that is, the income after deductions for the business expenses accompanying the provisions of goods or services. It might also be properly thought of as a tax on the accounting profit of corporate firms.

Many public finance economists are critical of the corporate income tax because it discriminates against the corporate business structure. The owners of business firms organized as proprietorships or partnerships pay only personal income taxes on their business earnings. In contrast, the income generated through the corporate business structure is taxed twice—once as net income of the business firm and again when it accrues to shareholders as dividends or appreciation in the value of the stock.

The structure of the corporate income tax is relatively simple. In 1993 the first $50,000 of corporate profit was taxed at a rate of 15 percent. Corporate earnings in the range from $50,000 to $75,000 were taxed at a rate of 25 percent, and earnings above $75,000 but less than $10 million were taxed at a 34 percent rate. For earnings above $10 million, the rate was 35 percent.[4]

The double-taxation feature of the corporate tax can result in very high marginal rates of taxation. For example, if a corporation earns $1,000 for a shareholder, only $660 will remain after a 34 percent corporate tax is paid. If the individual is in the 36 percent personal income tax bracket, payment of the $660 in dividends would only generate $422.40 in after-tax earnings for the shareholder. Thus, taxes take almost 58 percent of the original business earnings.

Corporate incomes in the United States have been taxed since 1909.[5] The tax currently generates approximately 10 percent of all federal tax receipts and 2 percent of the revenue of state and local governments (see Exhibit 5–6 again).

Since federal tax procedures do not allow businesses to take the opportunity cost of equity as an expense, the corporate income tax encourages corporate firms to use debt financing rather than equity ownership. A corporation that uses debt to finance a capital expenditure will incur an interest cost, which will reduce its accounting profits and tax liability. In contrast, if the same firm uses equity financing (that is, raises financial capital by issuing additional stock), the interest cost will not appear on the firm's accounting statement. Therefore, even though there is an opportunity cost of capital, regardless of whether it is raised by equity financing or by debt, only the latter will reduce the firm's tax liability.

USER CHARGES

Not all government revenue comes from taxes. For some services, governments charge consumers a price, just as private businesses do. **User charges** differ from taxes in that one's payment is directly linked to the consumption of a good or service. Citizens who do not consume the government-provided good or service do not have to pay for it. User charges are particularly important at the state and local level, where they account for 17 percent of government revenue. Local governments often provide utility services, garbage pickup, hospital care, and bus transportation. These government-operated businesses—many of which are in competition with private firms—are often partially or entirely financed by prices charged to the users of these services. In general, when the nature of the good permits, economists favor the user of charges rather than taxes, since the former

User charge
A payment that users (consumers) are required to make if they want to receive certain services provided by the government.

---

[4]Since the benefits of paying a 34 percent (rather than 35 percent) rate are phased out for corporations with taxable income of more than $15 million, in effect, corporations with taxable incomes between $15 million and $18.3 million pay a top marginal rate of 38 percent.

[5]For a short, readable summary of the history and impact of the corporate income tax, see Rob Norton, "Corporate Taxation" in *The Fortune Encyclopedia of Economics,* edited by David R. Henderson (New York: Warner Books, 1993).

provide better information on whether consumers value the good or service produced more than its cost of production.

Sometimes taxes can be used to approximate the effects of a user charge. For example, an excise tax on gasoline used to finance roads imposes the cost of the roads on individuals roughly in proportion to their consumption (use). Similarly, if a civic auditorium is operated by the government, a ticket tax used to finance the arena's cost approximates a user charge.

BORROWING

In addition to taxes and user charges, government has one other method of financing expenditures: borrowing. When the total spending exceeds revenue from taxes and user charges, the government will have to borrow to cover its budget deficit. Governments generally borrow by issuing interest-bearing bonds. With borrowing, governments can affect the *timing* of taxation, but the burden cannot be escaped. In essence, borrowing commits the government to higher future taxes in order to meet the interest obligations on the outstanding debt.

In recent years, the federal government has borrowed funds to cover a major proportion—approximately 20 percent during the last decade—of its expenditures. Constitutional provisions often limit the borrowing powers of state governments. Thus, state and local governments borrow much less than the federal government. In fact, state and local governments in aggregate have generally run a budget surplus in recent years.

ISSUES OF EFFICIENCY AND EQUITY

There are two major factors to consider when choosing among taxation alternatives. First, taxes should be consistent with economic efficiency. Taxes should not encourage people to use scarce resources wastefully. A tax system is inconsistent with economic efficiency if it encourages individuals (1) to buy goods costing more than their value to consumers and/or (2) to channel time into tax-avoidance activities. We will examine these issues in detail later in this section.

Second, a tax system should be equitable; that is, it should be consistent with widely accepted principles of fairness. Economists often speak of "horizontal" and "vertical" equity. Horizontal equity means equal treatment of equals. If two parties earn equal incomes, for example, horizontal equity implies that the two should be taxed equally. The corollary concept of vertical equity requires that persons who are situated differently should be taxed differently. It encompasses what economists refer to as the **ability-to-pay principle,** the seemingly straightforward idea that taxes should be levied according to the ability of the taxpayer to pay. Deciding exactly what this means, however, is at least partially subjective. Most people find it reasonable that the rich should pay more taxes than the poor. This would be the case under a proportional tax system since high-income taxpayers would pay the flat (constant) rate on a larger tax base. Many would also find it reasonable that the rich should pay a *higher proportion* of their income (or wealth or

Ability-to-pay principle
The equity concept that people with larger incomes (or more consumption or more wealth) should be taxed at a higher rate because their ability to pay is presumably greater. The concept is subjective and fails to reveal how much higher the rate of taxation should be as income increases.

consumption) in taxes than the poor. Of course, progressive taxation incorporates this concept. But how much higher should the rate be for those with higher incomes? At this point, the consensus breaks down. There is little agreement among either the general public or economists about the proper degree of tax progressivity.

Moreover, the ability-to-pay principle—particularly the view that some should be forced to pay a larger proportion of their income for government—often conflicts another broad notion of fairness, the **benefit principle.** According to the benefit principle, those benefiting from government services should be the ones to pay for them. In this case, taxes are thought of as a payment for government services. People who use more government-supplied services like garbage collection, highways, schools, retirement benefits, agricultural programs—should pay more, because after all, they are the beneficiaries. Why should they expect others to pay for things that they do not consume. Of course, the benefit principle suggests that whenever possible, the government should finance services that it provides with the aforementioned user charges.

While the concept of equity, or fairness, is ambiguous and subject to different interpretations, it cannot be ignored. People will have a more positive view toward their government and be more likely to comply voluntarily with tax and regulatory policies if they believe that the policies are reasonable and equitable. In contrast, the enforcement costs of a tax system that is widely perceived as unreasonable or unfair is certain to be extremely high.

Equity, though, must be balanced with efficiency. A tax system that ignores economic efficiency will also be extremely costly to an economy. But what exactly is economic efficiency? As we touched on earlier, it has to do with using scarce resources wisely. In other words, a tax system that encourages a wasteful use of resources is inefficient. It might, for example, encourage individuals to spend more of their income on business travel, housing, medical service, or professional-association publications and less of their income on food and clothing, because the former are tax-deductible and the latter are not. Similarly, it might encourage an individual to allocate more time and money to investments that reduce the tax burden (depreciable assets, municipal bonds, tax-free retirement plans, and so on), and less time and money to savings and work activities that generate taxable income.

An ideal tax system will avoid these inefficiencies; it will not retard the incentive of individuals to allocate their time and income into those areas that yield them the most satisfaction. A tax of this kind is called a **neutral tax.** Probably the only tax that would meet the hypothetical ideal of neutrality, however, is a **head tax,** a tax imposing an equal lump-sum tax on all individuals, poor or rich (or the same liability on those who consume few goods as on those who consume many goods). Since a head tax conflicts with the concept of vertical equity—the view that persons who are situated differently should be taxed differently—it fails to pass our test of fairness.

Thus, we generally tax things such as income, consumption, and property. However, taxes on these items distort pricing signals and thereby cause individuals to forgo productive activities. Economists refer to this inefficiency and the accompanying reduction in private-sector output over and above the tax revenue collected as the **excess burden of taxation.** It is easy to think of cases that illustrate the excess burden of taxation. For example, if two individuals decide to forgo a

Benefit principle
The principle that those who receive government services should pay taxes or user charges for their provision according to the amount of the service or benefit derived from the government activity.

Neutral tax
A tax that does not (1) distort consumer buying patterns or producer production methods or (2) induce individuals to engage in tax-avoidance activities. There will be no excess burden if a tax is neutral.

Head tax
A lump-sum tax levied on all individuals, regardless of their income, consumption, wealth, or other indicators of economic well-being.

Excess burden of taxation
A burden of taxation over and above the burden associated with the transfer of revenues to the government. An excess burden usually reflects losses that occur when beneficial activities are forgone because they are taxed.

mutually advantageous exchange because a tax makes the transaction unprofitable, they incur a burden from the taxation even though they do not pay a tax, because the transaction did not take place. Similarly, if a taxpayer decides to allocate more time to leisure or to household production and less time to market work—because the tax system limits the individual's ability to retain income generated by market work—a burden over and above tax revenues collected from the individual is imposed. Income from market work is lost to the individual, and whatever benefits for others that might have resulted from the work are sacrificed. Excess burdens reflect economic inefficiency, relative to our hypothetical ideal. They impose a **deadweight loss** on an economy, because they reflect a cost imposed on some individuals without any offsetting benefit to others.

Exhibit 5–7 illustrates the distinction between the tax burden associated with the transfer of purchasing power and the excess burden of taxation. Here we show the impact of a 50-cent tax imposed on each pack of cigarettes. Prior to the imposition of the tax, 35 billion packs of cigarettes were produced and sold to consumers at a market price of $1.00 per pack. The cigarette tax increases the cost of supplying and marketing cigarettes by 50 cents per pack. Thus, the supply curve of cigarettes shifts vertically by the amount of the tax. Consumers, however, would not continue to purchase as many cigarettes if the full burden of the tax were passed on to them in the form of a 50-cent increase in the per-pack price. So when the supply curve shifts vertically, the market price of cigarettes rises by less than the amount of the tax. Since the number of cigarettes demanded is thus responsive to the higher price, some of the tax burden will fall on cigarette producers. In our

Deadweight loss
A net loss associated with the forgoing of an economic action. The loss does not lead to an offsetting gain for other participants. It thus reflects economic inefficiency.

Here we illustrate the impact of a 50-cent tax (per pack) on cigarettes. Since the tax increases the cost of supplying cigarettes for consumption, the supply curve is shifted vertically by the amount of the tax. At the higher price, however, consumers reduce their consumption. The equilibrium price increases from $1.00 to $1.25 per pack. Consumers pay 25 cents more per pack and sellers receive 25 cents less as the result of the 50-cent tax. In addition, consumers and producers lose the mutual gains from exchange (triangle ABC) that would be realized if the tax did not reduce the volume of trade between cigarette producers and consumers.

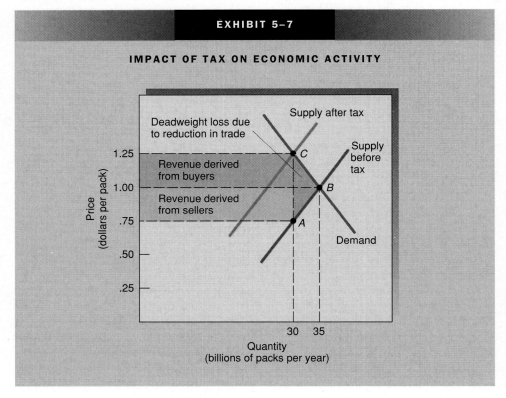

EXHIBIT 5–7

IMPACT OF TAX ON ECONOMIC ACTIVITY

hypothetical example, the new equilibrium price for cigarettes will become $1.25 per pack, with an annual output rate of 30 billion packs of cigarettes. The tax will raise $15 billion (50 cents times 30 billion packs) of revenue. Buyers will pay 25 cents more per pack for the 30 billion packs of cigarettes purchased after the tax is imposed. Simultaneously, sellers will receive 25 cents less per pack. The tax thus transfers $15 billion of revenue from cigarette buyers and sellers to the government.

Note, though, that the quantity of cigarettes produced and consumed has fallen by 5 billion packs. The mutually advantageous gains that would have accrued to producers and consumers from these unrealized trades (the triangle *ABC*) are lost. (Remember that trade is a positive-sum game, so a reduction in the volume of trade will result in economic loss.) This loss of welfare (triangle *ABC*) associated with the unrealized exchanges imposes an *excess burden* on buyers and sellers over and above the burden accompanying the transfer of revenue to the government. Clearly, the triangle *ABC* is a deadweight loss, since it is not accompanied by an offsetting gain in the form of additional tax revenue for the government.

In our example, the burden of the tax was divided equally between sellers and buyers. This will not always be the case. If the demand curve were steeper (and the supply curve flatter), the price of the taxed good would rise by a larger amount, imposing more of the burden on buyers. In contrast, if the demand curve were flatter (and the supply curve steeper), the market price would rise by a smaller amount, and a larger share of the tax burden would fall on sellers.

The burden of taxes is not always borne by the person who writes a check to the Internal Revenue Service. Economists use the term **tax incidence** when discussing the question of how the burden of a tax is distributed among parties. Since the distribution of the tax burden is dependent on the slope of the supply and demand curves for the activity being taxed, it is not easy to determine how it is distributed among parties.

Tax incidence
The manner in which the burden of the tax is distributed among economic units (consumers, employees, employers, and so on). The tax burden does not always fall on those who pay the tax.

TAX RATES, TAX REVENUES, AND LAFFER CURVE

Tax rate
The per unit or percentage rate at which an economic activity is taxed.

Governments generally levy taxes in order to raise revenues. The basic postulate of economics indicates that when an activity is taxed more heavily, people will choose less of it because the tax will make it more expensive. Thus, it is important to distinguish between a change in tax rates and a change in tax revenues. A higher **tax rate** will lead to a shrinkage in the size of the **tax base**—the quantity or level of the activity that is being taxed. If there are attractive substitutes for the activity that is taxed, the decline in the tax base due to the higher tax may be substantial.

Perhaps a real-world example will help clarify the importance of this point. In 1981 the District of Columbia increased the tax rate on gasoline from 10 cents to 13 cents per gallon, a 30 percent increase. Tax revenues, however, increased not by 30 percent, but by only 12 percent. Why? The higher tax rate discouraged motorists from purchasing gasoline in the District of Columbia. There was a

Tax base
The level of the activity that is taxed. For example, if an excise tax is levied on each gallon of gasoline, the tax base is the number of gallons of gasoline sold. Since higher tax rates generally make the taxed activity less attractive, the size of the tax base is inversely related to the rate at which the activity is taxed.

pretty good alternative to the purchase of the more highly taxed (and therefore higher-priced) gasoline—the purchase of gasoline in Virginia and Maryland, where the tax rates (and therefore prices) were slightly lower.

The revenue the government derives from a tax is equal to the tax base multiplied by the tax rate. When taxpayers can easily shift to substitutes or escape the tax by altering their behavior, the tax base will shrink significantly as rates are increased. As the result of this erosion of the tax base, an increase in tax rates will generally lead to a less than proportional increase in tax revenues.

Economist Arthur Laffer has popularized the idea that, *beyond some point, higher tax rates will shrink the tax base so much that tax revenues will decline when tax rates are increased.* The curve illustrating the relationship between tax rates and tax revenues is called the **Laffer curve. Exhibit 5–8** illustrates the concept of the Laffer curve as it applies to income-generating activities. Obviously, tax revenues would be zero if the income tax rate were zero. What is not so obvious is that tax revenues would also be zero (or at least very close to zero) if the tax rate were 100 percent. Confronting a 100 percent tax rate, most individuals would go fishing—or find something else to do rather than engage in taxable productive activity, since the 100 percent tax rate would completely remove the material reward derived from earning taxable income.

As tax rates are reduced from 100 percent, the incentive to work and earn taxable income increases, income expands, and tax revenues rise. Similarly, as tax rates increase from zero, tax revenues expand. Clearly, at some rate greater than

Laffer curve

A curve illustrating the relationship between tax rates and tax revenues. The curve reflects the fact that tax revenues are low for both very high and very low tax rates.

Since taxation affects the amount of the activity being taxed, a change in tax rates will not lead to a proportional change in tax revenues. As the Laffer curve indicates, beyond some point (B), an increase in tax rates may actually cause tax revenues to fall. Since large tax rate increases will lead to only a small expansion in tax revenue as B is approached, there is no presumption that point B is an ideal rate of taxation.

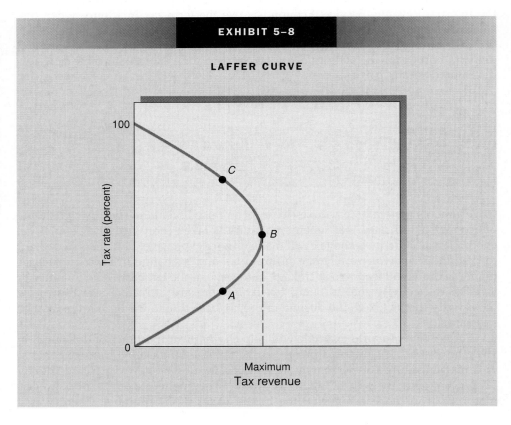

EXHIBIT 5–8

LAFFER CURVE

zero but less than 100 percent, tax revenues will be maximized (point *B* in Exhibit 5–8). This is not to imply that the tax rate that maximizes revenue is ideal. In fact, as rates are increased and the maximum revenue point (*B*) approached, relatively large tax rate increases will be necessary to expand tax revenue by even a small amount. In this range, the excess burden of taxation in the form of reductions in gains from trade will be substantial.

The Laffer curve suggests that under a progressive income tax system, the impact of a change in tax rates on tax revenues will vary across tax brackets (and income groupings). When people confront a low tax rate (for example, the 25 percent rate associated with point *A* in Exhibit 5–8), a rate reduction will reduce revenues. Similarly, a rate increase from, say, 25 percent to 30 percent, will increase tax revenues. On the other hand, for high-income taxpayers confronting extremely high rates (for example, the 75 percent rate associated with point *C* in the exhibit), a rate reduction would actually increase the revenues collected from this group. Similarly, an increase in the high tax rate would reduce the revenues the government would collect from high-income groups.[6]

When the rates of some taxpayers are above and others are below the revenue maximum point (*B* in the exhibit), the implications of the Laffer curve are significant. Under these circumstances, a general reduction in tax rates would reduce the revenues collected from low-income taxpayers, while increasing the revenues deriving from high-income taxpayers. A general tax increase would have just the opposite effect—more revenue would be collected from those in lower income brackets, while less would be collected from the rich.

LAFFER CURVE AND TAX CHANGES IN THE 1980S

It is interesting to view the tax changes instituted in the United States during the last 15 years within the framework of the Laffer curve. During the 1980s the top marginal tax rates—the rates confronted by high-income taxpayers—were reduced sharply by major legislation passed in 1981 and 1986. At the beginning of the decade, the United States had fourteen different marginal tax brackets ranging from a beginning rate of 14 percent to a top rate of 70 percent. By 1988 the number of brackets had been reduced to only three, with marginal rates of 15, 28, and 33 percent. The personal-exemption allowance for each taxpayer, spouse, and dependent and the standard deduction (the amount of tax-free income granted

---

[6]Similar *percentage* reductions in income tax rates will generally increase the incentive to earn taxable income in the upper tax brackets more than it will in the lower brackets. Consider how a reduction in a marginal tax rate from 70 percent to 50 percent would influence the incentive of a high-income professional or business executive to earn taxable income. When confronting a 70 percent marginal tax rate, the taxpayer gets to keep only 30 cents of each additional dollar earned by cutting costs, producing more, or investing more wisely. However, after the tax cut, take-home pay from each dollar of taxable income jumps to 50 cents—a whopping 67 percent increase in the incentive to earn. In contrast, consider the incentive effects of an identical percentage rate reduction in lower tax brackets. Suppose the 14 percent marginal rate were cut to 10 percent. Take-home pay, per dollar of additional earnings, would expand from 86 cents to 90 cents, only a 5 percent increase. Since the incentive effects are greater in the upper brackets, changes in the tax base (taxable income) will tend to, at least partially if not entirely, offset changes in revenues resulting from increases (and decreases) in high marginal tax rates.

each taxpayer) were also increased. In effect, these latter changes reduced the tax rates of low-income taxpayers. In many cases, the tax liabilities of low-income recipients were completely eliminated.

Focusing on the sharp reduction in the top rates (from 70 percent to 33 percent during the decade), critics charged that the 1980s' tax policies were a bonanza for the rich. In analyzing the position of the critics, once again it is important to distinguish between changes in tax rates and changes in tax revenues. As the Laffer curve indicates, reduction in high marginal tax rates can sometimes increase the tax revenue collected from high-income taxpayers. This is true because the incentive to earn additional income as the rates are reduced will be particularly strong in the upper tax brackets. Both additional work effort and a decline in tax-avoidance activities will contribute to the expansion in the tax base as the rates are reduced. In some cases, taxpayers will work more hours; perhaps they will take fewer and less lengthy vacations. In other instances, spouses may choose to enter the labor force because they are now permitted to keep more of what they earn.[7] Still others may work more intensely, accepting higher paying positions involving more responsibility and fewer nonpecuniary benefits. Simultaneously, tax avoidance will decline. Given time, many taxpayers will opt out of business ventures designed to show an accounting loss that would shelter income from the tax collector. Less money will now be spent on tax-deductible items like plush offices, Hawaiian business conferences, and various fringe benefits (for example, a company luxury automobile, business entertainment, and a company retirement plan), since the *personal* cost of these things is now higher. As taxpayers make adjustments like these, their "true" income will become more visible and their taxable income base will expand as they adjust to the lower rates. In turn, the expansion in the tax base will, at least partially, replace revenues lost as a result of the rate cuts.[8]

Exhibit 5–9 presents data on the real tax revenue collected from various income categories for 1980, 1985, and 1990. Measured in 1982–1984 dollars, the income tax revenue collected from high-income taxpayers rose throughout the decade. Even though their marginal rates were cut sharply, the real tax revenue collected from the top 1 percent of earners rose a whopping 51.4 percent between 1980 and 1990. *Per tax return*, the real taxes paid by this top group increased 24.1 percent. During the decade, the real revenues collected from the top 5 percent and top 10 percent of returns rose by 35.9 percent and 28.8 percent, respectively. The real revenues per return in these categories also increased.

The picture was quite different for other taxpayers. While the real revenues for those between the 50th and 90th percentile changed little, the bottom 50 percent of taxpayers paid less in 1990 than in 1980. Per return, the average real tax liability of the bottom 90 percent of taxpayers declined between 1980 and 1990. Perhaps surprising

---

[7]According to a Brookings Institution study by Barry Bosworth and Gary Burtless, in 1988 men between the ages of 25 and 64 worked 5.2 percent more hours than they would have under the tax rate structure of 1980; women ages 25 to 64 worked 5.8 percent more; and married women worked 8.8 percent more. See Bosworth and Burtless, *Effects of Tax Reform on Labor Supply, Investment, and Savings* (Washington, DC: Brookings Institution, 1990).

[8]See Joel B. Slemrod, ed., *Do Taxes Matter: The Impact of the Tax Reform Act of 1986* (Cambridge, MA: MIT Press, 1990) for an excellent set of readings on the impact of the tax changes adopted during the 1980s.

EXHIBIT 5-9

CHANGE IN FEDERAL INCOME TAX REVENUE DERIVED
FROM VARIOUS INCOME GROUPS, 1980–1990

	TAX REVENUE COLLECTED FROM GROUP (IN BILLIONS OF 1982–1984 DOLLARS)			PERCENT CHANGE 1980–1990	
INCOME GROUP	1980	1985	1990	GROUP	PER RETURN[a]
TOP 10 PERCENT OF EARNERS	149.0	154.0	191.9	+28.8	+5.6
TOP 1 PERCENT	57.6	65.3	87.2	+51.4	+24.1
TOP 5 PERCENT	111.4	116.0	151.4	+35.9	+11.4
NEXT 40 PERCENT	132.0	123.8	133.5	+1.1	−17.1
BOTTOM 50 PERCENT	21.3	21.4	19.5	−8.5	−25.0
TOTAL	302.3	299.2	344.9	+14.1	−6.5

[a]The number of returns in each category increased by 22 percent between 1980 and 1990.

Source: U.S. Department of Treasury, Internal Revenue Service.

to some, the real (inflation-adjusted) income tax revenues collected from high-income Americans actually rose during the 1980s, while the revenues derived from all other taxpayers (the bottom 90 percent of income recipients) declined.

Overall, the real revenue on the average return declined by 6.5 percent during the 1980s. Failing to understand the implications of the Laffer curve, some suggested that across-the-board lower rates would increase tax revenues. Clearly, this is not the case. As the Laffer curve shows, a reduction in low marginal rates—say, rates of 30 percent or less—will reduce revenues. The decline in revenues per return for the bottom 90 percent of taxpayers indicates that most taxpayers fall into this category. However, when marginal rates are high—say, 45 percent or more—lower rates may indeed lead to an increase in revenues derived from (those facing the high rates).[9] The increase in revenues collected from a small group of high-income taxpayers indicates that these taxpayers may well have been on the backward-bending portion of the Laffer curve in 1980.

---

[9]Harvard economist Lawrence Lindsey, now a governor of the Federal Reserve System, estimates that in the United States, marginal personal income rates above 43 percent reduce tax revenues. See Lawrence Lindsey, *Estimating the Revenue-Maximizing Top Personal Tax Rate*, Working Paper 1761 (New York: National Bureau of Economic Research, 1985) and *The Growth Experiment: How the New Tax Policy Is Transforming the U.S. Economy* (New York: Basic Books, 1989). Also see James E. Long and James D. Gwartney, "Income Tax Avoidance: Evidence from Individual Tax Returns," *National Tax Journal*, December 1987, for additional evidence on this topic.

APPLICATIONS IN ECONOMICS

INDEXING, INFLATION, AND THE TAXES PEOPLE PAY

The 1970s were a period of substantial inflation in the United States. Prices and wages rose rapidly and, as a result, *nominal* incomes also rose rapidly. Under a progressive tax rate structure, as nominal incomes grow during a period of inflation, taxpayers will be pushed into higher and higher tax brackets *even if the growth of their income is just keeping up with the price increases*. This is precisely what happened during the 1970s. Congress did not pass any significant legislation increasing personal income tax rates, yet, average and marginal tax rates of most households increased substantially as the result of the inflation.

In order to prevent such unlegislated tax increases, Congress provided for the indexing of the personal income tax rate structure beginning in 1985. **Indexing** increases the nominal income tax brackets (and the personal-exemption allowance) in proportion to the general increase in prices. This widening of the tax brackets each year in order to compensate for the impact of inflation on nominal incomes reduces the increase in taxes resulting from inflation.

Perhaps an example will help clarify how indexing of the rate structure works. Suppose a marginal tax rate of 10 percent is applied to the initial income bracket of $0 to $10,000, and also suppose that a 20 percent marginal tax rate is applicable for incomes between $10,000 and $25,000. Still higher rates may be applicable at still higher levels of income.

In the absence of indexing, taxpayers whose incomes merely keep pace with inflation are pushed into higher tax brackets. For example, suppose that prices and wages double (perhaps over a period of several years) and, as a result of this inflation, the taxable income of a worker expands from $10,000 to $20,000. If the tax structure is not indexed, this worker's tax liability will increase from $1,000 (10 percent of the $10,000 income) to $3,000 (10 percent of $10,000 plus 20 percent of the next $10,000 of taxable income). Even though his nominal income, like the general level of prices, merely doubled, his tax liability more than doubled since the inflation pushed him into a higher tax bracket. As the result of the inflation, both his average and marginal tax rates are increased.

Indexing widens the tax brackets for the effects of inflation and thereby keeps inflation from pushing taxpayers with incomes of constant purchasing power into higher tax brackets. With indexing, the $0–$10,000 income bracket would be expanded to $0–$20,000 when prices increase by 100 percent. So when inflation increases the income of a taxpayer by 100 percent, the taxpayer's average and marginal tax rates remain constant.

The objective of indexing is to protect taxpayers from unlegislated tax increases that, under a progressive tax system, would otherwise be automatically imposed by inflation. However, when only the rate structure is indexed, this objective is not fully achieved. There are two major reasons why this will be the case. First, inflation will still result in the taxation of "phantom" capital gains. Between 1979 and 1993 the general level of prices approximately doubled in the United States. Suppose that Marcia bought 100 shares of stock for $5,000 in 1979 and sold the stock in 1993 for $10,000. Her true capital gain is zero. The $10,000 sale price of the stock will not buy any more goods and services than the original $5,000 purchase. Nonetheless, under current tax law, if Marcia is in the 28 percent marginal tax bracket, her tax liability will increase by $1,400 (28 percent of the $5,000 nominal capital gain) as a result of the transaction.

Second, the same problem arises with the current treatment of interest income. Persistent inflation will push up nominal interest rates. In essence, the higher nominal rates merely reflect compensation for the decline in the purchasing power of proceeds during the period the loan is outstanding. For example, when the inflation rate is 5 percent, nominal interest earnings of 9 percent will not provide the lender with any additional purchasing power relative to what would have been earned from a 4 percent interest return during a period of stable prices. The Internal Revenue Service, however, will tax the entire 9 percent as earnings. Even though less than half of the nominal interest earnings represents real income to the lender, all of it will be subject to taxation.

Of course, indexing the rate structure does reduce the size of the unlegislated tax increases that result from inflation. Most economists, however, would like to see the concept of indexing applied more comprehensively so it would also reduce the taxation of nominal income components that do not represent real, or true, gains to the recipient.

The tax policy of the United States during the 1980s was not unusual. Of 86 countries with an income tax, 55 reduced their top marginal tax rate during the 1985–1990 period, while only two (Luxembourg and Lebanon) increased their top rate. Australia, Brazil, Italy, Japan, New Zealand, Sweden, and the United Kingdom substantially reduced their top marginal rates during the latter half of the 1980s.

Beginning with the Omnibus Budget Reconciliation Act of 1990, the United States began to reverse the tax policy adopted during the 1980s. The 1990 legislation—which reflected a budget agreement between Congress and the Bush administration—increased the top marginal rate in 1991 from 28 percent to 31 percent and subjected additional income of top-earners to taxation. In 1993 legislation was adopted providing for two additional tax brackets—a 36 percent rate that would take effect at $140,000 for a married couple filing jointly and a 39.6 percent rate that would apply at still a higher level of income ($250,000 for married couples). Counting a recently adopted 2.9 percent Medicare payroll tax, the top marginal tax rate imposed by the *federal* government has now been pushed back up to 42.5 percent (the 39.6 percent rate plus the 2.9 percent Medicare rate).

The Clinton administration estimates that these higher rates will raise an additional $126 billion from high-income taxpayers during the 1993–1998 period and result in a reduction in the size of the budget deficit. It will be interesting to track the future revenues collected from high-income Americans and see how close these projections are to the mark. The data from the 1980s indicate that the higher rates are unlikely to generate much additional revenue from high-income Americans. The early evidence is consistent with this view. Measured in 1982–1984 dollars, the personal income tax revenue collected in 1991 from the top 1 percent of taxpayers *declined* by 8.3 percent following the increase in the top rates during that year.[10]

WHO PAYS THE TAX BILL?

How is the overall burden of taxation distributed among income groupings? This is not an easy question to answer. As we have discussed, several different types of taxes are levied, and it is difficult to identify who actually bears the burden of many taxes. In some cases, taxes are designed to act as a proxy for a user charge for public services. Motor fuel taxes to finance roads provide an example. Taxes of this type allocate costs to users, independent of income.

Indexing
The automatic increasing of money values as the general level of prices increases. Economic variables that are often indexed include wage rates and tax brackets.

---

[10]Of course, the recession of 1990–1991 contributed to the decline in the tax revenues paid by high-income Americans. Overall, the inflation-adjusted personal income tax revenues declined by 4.9 percent in 1991. However, the larger decline in revenues derived from those with high incomes indicates that the 1991 tax rate increases in the highest tax brackets generated little, if any, additional revenue during that year.

[11]Joseph Pechman, *Who Paid the Taxes, 1966–85?* (Washington, DC: The Brookings Institute, 1985).

[12]E Browning and William R. Johnson, *The Distribution of the Tax Burden* (Washington, DC: American Enterprise Institute, 1979).

THE TAXATION OF CAPITAL GAINS

A capital gain (or loss) is experienced when individuals sell an asset such as land or real estate for more (or less) than they paid for it.

In the United States, *nominal* capital gains are fully taxable as personal income, while capital losses are deductible against one's income subject to a maximum deduction of $3,000 during any one year (excess losses can be carried forward to future years). Prior to 1987, capital gains were taxed at a lower rate than other forms of income.

Since capital gains take place over a time period—and sometimes the period is lengthy—the real gains of taxpayers can be substantially distorted by inflation. For example, suppose that Susan Brown bought a plot of land for $10,000 in 1979 and sold the land for $20,000 in 1993. Since prices doubled during this period, the investor's real rate of return is zero. Nonetheless, she will be subject to a capital gains tax on the *nominal* gain. If she is in the 28 percent tax bracket, Susan will owe an additional tax bill of $2,800, *even though she reaped no real gain from the transaction.*

Alternatively, suppose the land was sold for $25,000. In this case, *measured in 1993 dollars,* the investor's inflation-adjusted capital gain would be $5,000 ($25,000 minus a $20,000 purchase price in terms of 1993 dollars) and her additional tax liability $4,200 (28 percent of the $15,000 nominal gain). She is liable for $4,200 in additional taxes even though her real capital gain in current dollars is only $5,000. In fact, her marginal tax rate is 84 percent, not 28 percent. Clearly, when the initial purchase price is not indexed (see the "Applications in Economics" feature on indexing), taxation of nominal capital gains can confront taxpayers with exceedingly high marginal rates of taxation.

Paradoxically, the more successful the investment, the *lower* the real rate of taxation. For example, if the land were sold for $50,000, the individual's real capital gain would be $30,000 (the $50,000 sale price minus the $20,000 purchase price in terms of 1993 dollars) and she would be subject to an additional tax liability of $11,200 (28 percent of the $40,000 nominal gain). In this case, the rate of taxation on the real gain would be 37 percent, less than the rate of taxation when the real gain was smaller.

The problem that arises under the current system is that it reduces the funding available for venture capital investment projects and encourages people to continue holding assets (until death or retirement) that they otherwise would like to sell. As a result, most economists favor either the indexing of capital gains or a return of the imposition of lower rates.

One thing is certain, the realization of capital gains is highly sensitive to changes in the tax rate. The accompanying indicates the capital gains tax rate, the realization of capital gains, and the tax revenue derived from the realization for the 1985–1992 period.

	TAX RATE	REALIZATION OF GAINS (IN BILLIONS OF 1991 DOLLARS)	TAX REVENUES FROM CAPITAL GAINS (IN BILLIONS OF 1991 DOLLARS)
1985	20	$212	$33
1986	20	394	60
1987	28	169	41
1988	28	185	44
1989	28	166	40
1990	28	125	30
1991	28	108	26

These data indicate that when the 1986 legislation increased the capital gains tax rate beginning in 1987, many taxpayers responded by taking their capital gains prior to the rate increase. Thus, the realized capital gains in 1986 were almost twice the level of 1985. Once the higher rate took effect, the realization of capital gains plummeted. Futhermore, despite the 40 percent rate increase (from 20 percent to 28 percent), the revenues derived from capital gains taxes were only modestly higher during 1987–1989, and they were *lower* in 1990–1991, than the revenues derived in 1985 (prior to the rate increase and the response to the legislation increasing the rate).

Economists are not in full agreement with regard to the precise revenue impact of a reduction in the current capital gains rate. For example, in 1990 the Office of Tax Analysis of the Department of Treasury estimated that a 30 percent reduction (from 28 percent to 19.6 percent) in the capital gains tax rate would *increase* tax revenues by approximately 6 percent over the five-year period following the reduction. At the same time, the Congressional Joint Committee on Taxation estimated that the same rate reduction would *reduce* revenues by about the same amount during the same period.[1] While these two studies differ with regard to the direction of the change, both indicate that the revenue impact of lower rates would be substantially smaller than the rate reductions. In a 1987 study, Lawrence Lindsey, then of Harvard University and now a member of the Board of Governors of the Federal Reserve Board, estimated that the revenue-maximizing capital gains rate was only about 15 percent.[2] Taken together, all of these studies indicate that there is substantial agreement that lower rates would result in more realized capital gains and only modest (if any) reductions in revenue.

The United States taxes capital gains much more heavily than other countries. Belgium, Italy, and the Netherlands totally exempt capital gains from taxation, and Germany exempts capital gains on assets held for six months or more. Canada, Japan, and France impose much lower rates of taxation on capital gains than the United States. Many economists think the United States should reconsider the merits of the current policy in this area.

---

[1]Ronald A. Pearlman, Chief of Staff, Joint Committee on Taxation, *Testimony before the Senate Finance Committee*, March 28, 1990.

[2]Lawrence Lindsey, "Capital Gains Taxes Under the Tax Reform Act of 1986: Revenue Estimates Under Various Assumptions," *National Tax Journal*, September 1987.

The late Joseph Pechman of the Brookings Institution conducted a detailed study on the U.S. tax structure that found it to be within the proportional-to-mildly-progressive range.[11] Even Pechman's assumptions that yielded his most progressive estimates project that high-income recipients pay only slightly higher average tax rates—27.3 percent compared with 20.6 percent—than households with much lower incomes.

Edgar Browning of Texas A&M and William Johnson of the University of Virginia dispute the findings of the Pechman study.[12] They claim that the U.S. tax structure is highly progressive, with high income groups paying approximately three times the average rate of low-income groups.

A recent study by the Congressional Budget Office (CBO) also indicates that federal taxes are quite progressive, though somewhat less so than during the 1970s.[13] The CBO study estimated that personal income, corporate income, payroll, and excise taxes account for 93 percent of federal tax revenue. According to CBO projections, these four federal taxes consumed between 25 percent and 26.6 percent of the income of the top 20 percent of wage earners in 1988, compared with slightly less than 10 percent for the bottom decile of earners. Taxpayers in middle-income groupings paid average rates ranging from 13 percent (the third decile) to 24 percent (the ninth decile). The CBO study indicates that the progressivity of federal taxes had declined during the 1980s, though. For example, in 1977 federal taxes took between 26.7 percent and 29.5 percent of the income of the top decile of earners, compared to approximately 8 percent for the bottom decile.

With regard to the burden of taxation, two additional points should be noted. First, middle- and upper-middle-income taxpayers earn the bulk of income and pay the bulk of the tax bill. In 1990, 55 percent of households in the United States

---

[13]Congressional Budget Office, *The Changing Distribution of Federal Taxes: 1975–1990* (Washington, DC: U.S. Government Printing Office), October 1987.

All taxes are paid by people in their roles as consumers, earners, or owners of assets.

"THIS NEW TAX PLAN SOUNDS PRETTY GOOD... WE GET A 9% CUT AND BUSINESS PICKS UP THE BURDEN...."

By John Trever, *Albuquerque Journal* © by and Permission of News America Syndicate.

had incomes between $25,000 and $75,000. These households earned approximately 70 percent of the total income, and they shouldered slightly more than 70 percent of the tax burden. The findings of both Pechman and Browning-Johnson are consistent with this view.

Second, although politicians sometimes speak of imposing taxes on businesses, as if part of the tax burden could be transferred from individuals to nonpersons (business firms), people pay all taxes. Like all other taxes, business taxes are paid by individuals. A corporation or business firm may write the tax check to the government, but it does not pay the taxes; it merely collects the money from people—customers, employees, or stockholders—and transfers it to the government. It makes good political rhetoric to talk about "businesses" paying taxes, but the hard facts are that individuals provide all tax revenues.

THE COST OF GOVERNMENT

Do taxes measure the cost of government? One might think so, but the answer to this question is, in fact, "Not entirely." Our old friend—the opportunity-cost concept—will help us understand why. There are three types of costs incurred when governments provide goods and services.

First, there is the opportunity cost of the resources used to produce goods supplied through the public sector. When governments purchase missiles, education, highways, health care, and other goods, resources to provide these goods must be bid away from private-sector activities. If these resources were not tied up producing goods supplied through the public sector, they would be available to produce private-sector goods. Note that this cost is incurred regardless of whether the provision of the public-sector goods is financed by current taxes, an increase in government debt, or money creation. This cost can be diminished only by reducing the size of government purchases.

Second, there is the cost of resources expended in the collection of the tax. Tax laws must be enforced. Tax returns must be prepared and monitored. Resources used to prepare, monitor, and enforce tax legislation are unavailable for the production of either private- or public-sector goods. In the United States, studies indicate that these compliance costs amount to between 5 percent and 7 percent of the tax revenue raised.

Finally, there is the excess burden cost due to price distortions emanating from the levying of taxes (and the provision of transfers). Less output will result because

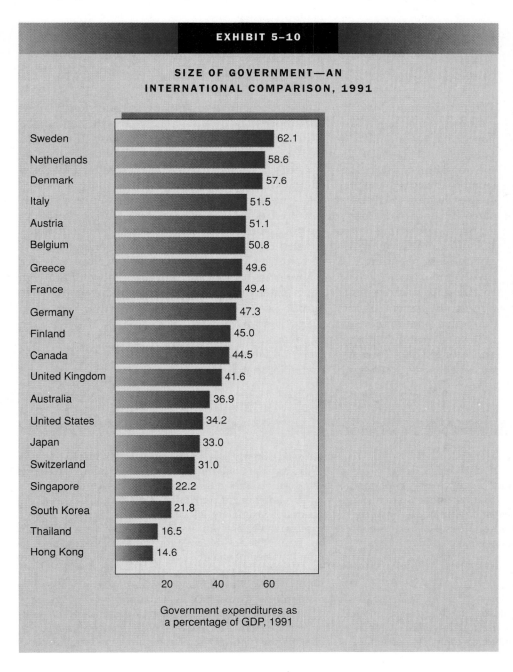

EXHIBIT 5-10

SIZE OF GOVERNMENT—AN INTERNATIONAL COMPARISON, 1991

Country	
Sweden	62.1
Netherlands	58.6
Denmark	57.6
Italy	51.5
Austria	51.1
Belgium	50.8
Greece	49.6
France	49.4
Germany	47.3
Finland	45.0
Canada	44.5
United Kingdom	41.6
Australia	36.9
United States	34.2
Japan	33.0
Switzerland	31.0
Singapore	22.2
South Korea	21.8
Thailand	16.5
Hong Kong	14.6

Government expenditures as a percentage of GDP, 1991

The size of government varies substantially across countries. Government expenditures comprise approximately 60 percent of GDP in Denmark, Sweden, and the Netherlands. In contrast, government spending amounts to only about one third of GDP in the United States, Australia, Japan, and Switzerland. In Singapore, Thailand, South Korea, and Hong Kong, four rapidly growing Asian countries, the size of government is still smaller.

Source: Government Information Services: Hong Kong, *Hong Kong 1992,* and International Monetary Fund, *Government Finance Statistics, Yearbook,* 1992.

the tax-transfer structure will cause individuals to forgo productive activities and engage in counterproductive action (for example, tax-avoidance activities).

In essence, the cost of government activities is the sum of (1) the opportunity cost of resources used to produce government supplied goods and services, (2) the cost of tax compliance, and (3) the excess-burden cost of taxation. Thus, government purchases of goods and services generally cost the economy a good bit more than either the size of the tax bill or the level of budget expenditures imply.

SIZE OF GOVERNMENT IN UNITED STATES VERSUS OTHER COUNTRIES

There is substantial variation in the size of government across countries. In a few countries, government does little more than provide a legal structure and a few goods like roads and national defense that are difficult to provide through the private sector. In other countries, it is involved in all sorts of activities, including the operation of businesses like hotels, theaters, mining, airlines, radio and television broadcasting, and steel manufacturing.

As **Exhibit 5–10** illustrates, government spending sums to approximately three-fifths of the total output in Denmark, Sweden, and the Netherlands. Approximately one-half of the total income of Italy, Austria, Greece, France, Belgium, and Germany is channeled through the public sector. The high level of government spending in these countries primarily reflects greater public-sector involvement in the provision of housing, health care, retirement benefits, and aid to the poor and unemployed. In Canada, public-sector spending summed to almost 45 percent of total output in 1991. The size of the public sectors in Australia, Japan, and Switzerland is approximately the same as in the United States. Interestingly, the size of government in South Korea, Singapore, Thailand, and Hong Kong, four Asian nations where income has grown very rapidly in recent decades, is substantially smaller than for the United States.

LOOKING AHEAD

Government expenditures and tax rates are important determinants of an economy's output and employment. They also influence the price and output of consumer goods and income of resource suppliers. As we proceed, we will investigate these topics in greater detail.

CHAPTER SUMMARY

1. Government expenditures have grown more rapidly than the U.S. economy during this century. In 1929 government spending accounted for only 10 percent of GDP; since then, it has expanded every decade. In the early 1990s more than one-third of the total output of the United States was channeled through the public sector.

2. Government purchases of goods and services constitute approximately 20 percent of the national output. Approximately one out of every six Americans works for the local, state, or federal government. Taking into account transfer payments, total government expenditures amounted to 34.4 percent of the GDP in 1993.

3. During the last four decades, government spending in traditional areas such as national defense, highways, police and fire protection, and the provision of other goods and services has changed very little relative to the size of the economy. The growth of government in recent decades

is almost exclusively the result of increased government involvement in the redistribution of income.

4. Personal income taxes, payroll taxes, and corporate income taxes are the major sources of federal tax revenues. Sales taxes provide the major tax base for state governments, whereas local governments still rely primarily on property taxes for their revenue.

5. Payroll taxes constitute the most rapidly expanding source of tax revenues. In 1993 payroll taxes comprised 37 percent of the total tax revenue at the federal level. The social security payroll tax is a regressive tax because it is not levied on income beyond a designated maximum.

6. As the marginal tax rates increase, the proportion of income individuals are permitted to keep for private use declines. Since it determines the share of earnings available for private expenditures, the marginal tax rate exerts a major impact on the incentive of individuals to earn taxable income.

7. Both efficiency and equity should be considered when choosing among taxation alternatives. A tax system that induces inefficient behavior will be costly to a society. Similarly, it will be costly to induce compliance with a tax system that is perceived as unreasonable or unfair.

8. Ideally, we would all prefer a neutral tax system—one that does not distort prices or induce individuals to channel scarce resources into tax-avoidance activities. However, a tax on productive activity will always alter some prices. Our goal should be to adopt an equitable system that will minimize the inefficiency effects.

9. It is important to distinguish between a change in tax rates and a change in tax revenues. The size of the tax base will generally be inversely related to the rate of taxation. Therefore, an increase in tax rates will lead to a less than proportional increase in tax revenues, particularly if there are viable substitutes for those things that are taxed.

10. At very high rates of taxation, it is possible that an increase in tax rates will cause a reduction in tax revenues, because people will make substantial shifts away from the activity that is being taxed. The Laffer curve illustrates this possibility.

11. The cost of government activities encompasses the following components: (a) the opportunity cost of resources used to produce public-sector goods and services, (b) the compliance costs of taxation, and (c) the excess burden costs associated with price distortions and inefficiencies emanating from taxation. Generally, these costs will exceed both the size of the government budget and the dollar amount of the tax revenue collected.

12. The size of government as a share of the economy in the United States is approximately the same as for Japan and Switzerland, but significantly smaller than for Canada and most Western European nations. As a share of GDP, government expenditures are smallest in the high growth countries of Asia (Hong Kong, Thailand, Singapore, and South Korea).

CRITICAL-ANALYSIS QUESTIONS

1. Major categories of government spending include (a) national defense, (b) education, and (c) income transfers and antipoverty expenditures. Why do you think the public sector has become involved in these activities? Why not leave them to the market?

*2. People can avoid local taxes and, to a lesser degree, state taxes by moving. In comparison with the federal government, how does this characteristic influence people's ability to achieve value for their tax dollar at these levels of government?

*3. "User charges are simply another name for taxes. It makes no difference whether a government activity is financed by taxes or user charges." Evaluate this statement.

4. "Transfer payments exert no influence on our economy because they merely transfer income from one group of individuals to another." Evaluate this statement.

5. Do you think your college should cover the cost of providing campus parking through user charges, higher tuition for all students, or taxation? Should waiting in line (that is, time spent hunting for a parking space) play a substantial role in the allocation of parking spaces? Discuss this issue.

*6. "A government project financed by taxation should be undertaken only if the expected value of the project is somewhat greater than the outlay necessary for its finance." Evaluate this statement.

*7. How would a reduction in marginal tax rates influence the incentive of a taxpayer to incur a tax deduction expenditure?

8. As of 1990, capital gains (income from assets that were sold for more than they were purchased during an earlier time period) were taxed at the same rate as other income. From an equity viewpoint, is this policy sound?

9. How would each of the following affect the ability of the "invisible hand" to bring self-interest and helping others into harmony?

   a. A tax transfer system that equalized incomes.
   b. High tax rates and a large public sector that allocated most goods and services.

*10. A popular sticker on trucks reads, "This truck pays $6,775 (or some other figure) in annual road-use taxes." Is this statement true?

11. Under current tax law, the interest income on

---

*Asterisk denotes questions for which answers are given in Appendix C.

municipal bonds (bonds issued by cities and other local governments) is not taxable. How does this tax exemption influence the attractiveness of these bonds to potential investors? How does it affect the interest yield of the bonds? Who is the major beneficiary of this tax exemption? Explain.

12. Both the initial tax structure and the tax structure after a 20 percent rate reduction are indicated in the accompanying table.
   a. Fill in the missing blanks.
   b. By what percent did the tax cut increase the amount of additional earnings that people making less than $10,000 were allowed to keep?
   c. By what percent did the tax cut increase the amount of additional earnings that people making more than $70,000 were allowed to keep?
   d. How will the tax cut affect the revenues derived from people making less than $10,000 per year? Be specific. How will the rate cut affect the revenues derived from those making more than $70,000 per year? Explain.

13. Smith purchased 500 shares of stock in 1982 and sold them in 1994. The nominal purchase and sales prices are indicated in the table below.

   a. If Smith is liable for a 28 percent tax on the nominal capital gain derived from the stock, calculate her capital gain tax liability as the result of the stock sale.
   b. Fill in the blanks in the last column of the table. What was Smith's real capital gain measured in 1994 dollars?
   c. What was Smith's marginal tax rate on the real capital gain?
   d. If the inflation rate and the increase in the nominal price of the stock had both been 20 percent greater during the 1982–1994 period, what would have happened to Smith's marginal tax rate on her real capital gain?

	PRICE OF 500 SHARES OF STOCK	PRICE INDEX (1982 = 100)	REAL PRICE OF STOCK (1994 DOLLARS)
Bought in 1982	$2,500	100	———
Sold in 1994	$4,950	180	———

	INITIAL TAX STRUCTURE		TAX STRUCTURE AFTER A 20% RATE CUT	
ANNUAL TAXABLE INCOME (IN DOLLARS)	MARGINAL TAX RATE	PERCENT OF ADDITIONAL EARNINGS TAXPAYERS KEEP	MARGINAL TAX RATE	PERCENT OF ADDITIONAL EARNINGS TAXPAYERS KEEP
Less than 10,000	10	———	8	———
10,000 to 20,000	20	———	16	———
20,000 to 30,000	30	———	———	———
30,000 to 50,000	50	———	———	———
50,000 to 70,000	70	———	———	———
More than 70,000	90	———	———	———

PART TWO

MACROECONOMICS

CHAPTER SIX

TAKING THE NATION'S
ECONOMIC PULSE

*It has been said that figures rule the world; maybe. I am quite
sure that it is figures which show us whether it is being ruled
well or badly.*

JOHANN WOLFGANG GOETHE, 1830

*Measurement is the making of distinction; precise
measurement is making sharp distinctions.*

ENRICO FERMI[1]

CHAPTER FOCUS

- *What is GDP? How is it calculated?*
- *What is the difference between GDP and GNP?*
- *What is the difference between real and nominal GDP?*
- *How are changes in the price level measured? How
much have prices increased in recent years?*
- *Is GDP a good measure of output? What are the
strengths and weaknesses?*

---

[1]As quoted by Milton Friedman in Walter Block, ed., *Economic
Freedom: Toward a Theory of Measurement* (Vancouver: B.C.,
The Fraser Institute, 1991), p. 11.

Our society likes to keep score. The sports pages supply us with the win-loss records that reveal how well the various teams are doing. We also keep score on the performance of our economy. The scoreboard for economic performance is the *national-income accounting system.*

Simon Kuznets, the winner of the 1971 Nobel Prize in economics, developed the basic concepts and outlined the measurement procedures for national-income accounting during the 1920s and 1930s. Through the years, these procedures have been modified and improved. Kuznets's contribution in this area is so great that he is often referred to as the "father of national-income accounting."

Just as the accounting statement of a firm is designed to provide information relevant to the assessment of a firm's performance, national-income accounts are designed to supply similar information for the entire economy. They provide a comprehensive overview of how the economy is doing.

Without a measuring rod for national output, it would be difficult to determine the health of the economy. In this chapter, we will explain how the flow of an economy's output is measured. We will also explain how changes in national income that reflect changes in production are separated from those that reflect merely inflation (changes in prices). Finally, we will analyze the strengths and weaknesses of the measurement tools used to assess the performance of our national economy.

GDP—A MEASURE OF OUTPUT

Gross domestic product (GDP)

The total market value of all final goods and services produced domestically during a specific period, usually a year.

The **gross domestic product (GDP)** is the most widely used measure of economic performance. It is the market value of goods and services produced *domestically* during a specific time period, usually a year. GDP estimates in the United States are prepared quarterly and released a few weeks subsequent to the end of each quarter. The numbers are widely reported and closely watched, particularly in the business and financial communities.

GDP is a "flow" concept. By analogy, a water gauge is a device designed to measure the amount of water that flows through a pipe each hour. Similarly, GDP is a device designed to measure the market value of production that "flows" through the economy's factories and shops each year.

OUTSTANDING ECONOMIST

SIMON KUZNETS (1901–1985)

Simon Kuznets provided the methodology for modern national income accounting and developed the first reliable national income measures for the United States. A native Russian, he immigrated to the U.S. at the age of 21 and spent his academic career teaching at the University of Pennsylvania, Johns Hopkins, and Harvard University.

WHAT COUNTS TOWARD GDP?

Since GDP seeks to measure only current production, it cannot be arrived at merely by summing the totals on all of the nation's cash registers. Many transactions have to be excluded. GDP counts (1) only the goods and services purchased by their ultimate, or final, users; (2) only the goods and services produced during the specified period; and (3) it excludes financial transactions and income transfers.

FINAL GOODS AND SERVICES.   If output is going to be measured accurately, all goods and services produced during the year must be counted once, but only once. Most goods go through several stages of production before they end up in the hands of their ultimate users. To avoid double-counting, care must be taken to differentiate between **intermediate goods**—goods in intermediate stages of production—and **final goods and services,** which are those purchased for final use rather than for resale or further processing.

Intermediate goods
Goods purchased for resale or for use in producing another good or service.

Final goods and services
Goods and services purchased by their ultimate user.

Sales at intermediate stages of production are not counted by GDP because the value of an intermediate good is embodied within the final-user good. Counting both the intermediate good and the final-user good would exaggerate GDP. For example, when a wholesale distributor sells steak to a restaurant, the final purchase price paid by the patron of the restaurant for the steak dinner will reflect the cost of the meat. Double-counting would result if we included both the sale price of the intermediate good (the steak sold by the wholesaler to the restaurant) *and* the final purchase price of the steak dinner.

Exhibit 6–1 will help clarify the accounting method for GDP. Before the final good, bread, is in the hands of the consumer, it will go through several intermediate stages of production. The farmer produces a pound of wheat and sells it to the miller for 30 cents. The miller grinds the wheat into flour and sells it to the baker for 65 cents. The miller's actions have added 35 cents to the value of the wheat. The baker combines the flour with other ingredients, makes a loaf of bread, and sells it to the grocer for 90 cents. The baker has added 25 cents to the value of the bread. The grocer stocks the bread on the grocery shelves and provides a convenient location for consumers to shop. The grocer sells the loaf of bread for $1, adding 10 cents to the value of the final product. Only the market value of the final product—the $1 for the loaf of bread—is counted by GDP. This price reflects the value added at each stage of production. The 30 cents added by the farmer, the 35 cents by the miller, the 25 cents by the baker, and the 10 cents by the grocer sum to the $1 purchase price.

GDP PERIOD OF PRODUCTION.   Keep in mind that GDP is a measurement of current production. Therefore, transactions that merely involve the exchange of goods or assets produced during an earlier period or the transfer of ownership rights are excluded since they do not contribute to current production. Thus, secondhand sales are excluded. The purchase of a used car produced last year will not enhance current GDP, nor will the sale of a "used" home, constructed five years ago. Production of these goods was counted at the time they were produced and initially purchased. Resale of such items produced during earlier years merely changes the ownership of the goods or assets. It does not add to current production. (Note: If a sales commission is involved in the exchange of a used car or home, the commission would add to current GDP since it involves a *service* during the current period.)

Since GDP counts long-lasting goods such as automobiles and houses when they are produced, it is not always an accurate gauge of what is currently being

Most goods go through several stages of production. This chart illustrates both the market value of a loaf of bread as it passes through the various stages of production (column 1) and the amount added to the bread by each intermediate producer (column 2). GDP counts only the market value of the final product. Of course, the amount added by each intermediate producer (column 2) sums to the market value of the final product.

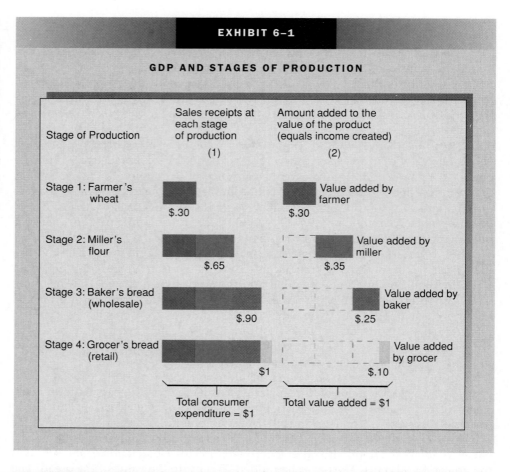

EXHIBIT 6–1

GDP AND STAGES OF PRODUCTION

Stage of Production	Sales receipts at each stage of production (1)	Amount added to the value of the product (equals income created) (2)
Stage 1: Farmer's wheat	$.30	Value added by farmer $.30
Stage 2: Miller's flour	$.65	Value added by miller $.35
Stage 3: Baker's bread (wholesale)	$.90	Value added by baker $.25
Stage 4: Grocer's bread (retail)	$1	Value added by grocer $.10
	Total consumer expenditure = $1	Total value added = $1

GDP is a measure of current production. It counts only goods and services produced during the year. Exchanges involving ownership rights to previously produced goods and assets are not included in GDP.

consumed. During an economic slowdown, few new durable assets will be produced. However, the consumption of durable goods that were produced and counted during an earlier period will continue. During good times, there will be a rapid expansion in the production of durable assets, which will generally provide consumption benefits for several years in the future. Because of this cycle, GDP tends to understate consumption during an economic decline and overstate it during a rapid expansion in economic activity.

FINANCIAL TRANSACTIONS AND INCOME TRANSFERS.   GDP does not count purely financial transactions, since they do not involve current production. For example, the purchases and sales of stocks, bonds, and U.S. securities are not counted as part of GDP because such transactions merely transfer ownership rights; they do not add to current production. Similarly, both private- and public-sector income transfers are excluded since they do not enhance current production. If your aunt sends you $100 to help pay for your college expenses, your aunt has less wealth and you have more, but the transaction adds nothing to current production. Thus, it is not included in GDP. Neither are government income transfer payments like social security, welfare, and veterans' payments. The recipients of these transfers are not producing goods in return for the transfers. Therefore, it would be inappropriate to add them to GDP.

DOLLARS—THE COMMON DENOMINATOR FOR GDP

In elementary school, each of us was instructed about the difficulties of adding apples and oranges. Yet, this is precisely the nature of the aggregate measurement problem. Literally millions of different commodities and services are produced each year. How can the production of apples, oranges, shoes, movies, roast beef sandwiches, automobiles, dresses, legal services education, heart transplants, astrological services, and many other items be added together?

The vastly different goods and services produced in our modern world have only one thing in common: someone pays a price for them. Therefore, when measuring output, units of each good are weighted according to their purchase price. If a consumer pays $10,000 for a new automobile and $10 for a nice meal, production of the automobile adds 1,000 times as much to output as production of the meal. Similarly, production of a television set that is purchased for $500 will add $\frac{1}{20}$ as much to output as the new automobile and 50 times the amount of the meal. Each good produced increases output by the amount the consumer pays for the good. The total spending on all goods produced during the year is then summed, in dollar terms, to obtain the annual GDP.

GNP—A CLOSELY RELATED MEASURE TO GDP

Prior to 1991 the United States used **gross national product (GNP)** as its primary measure of output. GDP and GNP are very closely related. GDP is a measure of the output that is produced domestically, while GNP measures the output that is produced by the "nationals" of a country. Put another way, GDP is a measure of

Gross national product (GNP)
The total market value of all final goods and services produced by the citizens of a country. It is equal to GDP plus the income the nationals earned abroad minus the income foreigners earned domestically.

the output that is produced by labor and capital *within the borders of a country,* regardless of whether the laborer or owner of capital is a citizen of the country or a foreigner. On the other hand. GNP measures the output generated by the labor and capital *owned by the citizens of the country,* regardless of whether that output is produced domestically or abroad.

Written in equation form,

$$
\text{GNP} = \text{GDP} + \begin{array}{c}\text{Income received by citizens}\\ \text{for factors of production}\\ \text{supplied abroad}\end{array} - \begin{array}{c}\text{Income paid to foreigners}\\ \text{for their contribution}\\ \text{to domestic output}\end{array}
$$

The two measures differ only in their handling of (1) income earned by citizens from their work and investments abroad and (2) income earned by foreigners from their work and investments domestically. GDP includes the income payments to foreigners for their contribution to domestic production, but excludes the income earned abroad by domestic citizens. GNP does just the opposite.

TWO WAYS OF MEASURING GDP

There are two ways of looking at and measuring GDP. First, the GDP of an economy can be reached by totaling the expenditures on goods and services produced during the year. National-income accountants refer to this method as the *expenditure approach.* Alternatively, GDP can be calculated by summing the cost of supplying those goods and services. Production of goods and services is costly because the resources required for their production must be bid away from their alternative uses. These costs generate incomes for resource suppliers. Thus, this method of calculating GDP is referred to as the *resource cost-income approach.*

GDP derived by the resource cost-income approach will equal GDP derived by the expenditure approach. It is easy to see why this will be the case. From an accounting viewpoint, total payments to the factors of production, including the producer's profit or loss, must be equal to the sales price generated by the good.[2] This is true for each good or service produced, and it is also true for the aggregate economy. This is a fundamental accounting identity.

$$
\begin{array}{c}\text{Dollar flow of}\\ \text{expenditures}\\ \text{on final goods}\end{array} = \text{GDP} = \begin{array}{c}\text{Dollar flow of}\\ \text{producer's cost}\\ \text{on final goods}\end{array}
$$

This relationship highlights two important characteristics of GDP. First, GDP is a measure of the value of the goods and services that were purchased by households, investors, governments, and foreigners. These purchasers valued the goods and services more than the purchase price; otherwise they would not have purchased them. At the same time, however, production of the goods involved human toil, wear and tear on machines, use of natural resources, risk, managerial responsibilities, and other of life's unpleasantries. Resource owners had to be

---

[2]In the national-income accounts, the terms "profit" and "corporate profit" are used in the accounting sense. Thus, they reflect *both* the rate of return on assets owned by a business firm (which is sometimes referred to as normal profit) *and* the firm's economic profit and loss which was discussed in Chapter 3.

compensated with income payments in order to induce them to supply these resources. Thus, GDP is a measure of both aggregate output and aggregate income.

Exhibit 6–2 summarizes the components of GDP for both the expenditure and resource cost-income approaches. When calculated by the expenditure approach, there are four components of GDP: (1) consumption purchases, (2) gross investment, (3) government purchases, and (4) net exports to foreigners. Except for a few complicating elements that we will discuss in a moment, the revenues derived from the sale of goods and services are paid directly to resource suppliers in the form of wages, self-employment income, rents, profits, and interest. We now turn to an examination of these components.

EXPENDITURE APPROACH

The left side of **Exhibit 6–3** presents the values in 1993 for the four components of GDP when it is derived by the expenditure approach. Later we will discuss the right side, which deals with the resource cost-income approach. **Exhibit 6–4** presents the components in graphic form.

CONSUMPTION PURCHASES. Personal **consumption** purchases are the largest component of GDP; in 1993 they amounted to $4,391 billion. Most consumption expenditures are for nondurable goods or services. Food, clothing, recreation, medical and legal services, education, and fuel are included in this category. These items are used up or consumed in a relatively short time. Durable goods, such as appliances and automobiles, comprise approximately one-seventh of all consumer purchases. These products are enjoyed over a longer period of time even though they are fully counted at the time they are purchased.

Consumption
Household spending on consumer goods and services during the current period. Consumption is a flow concept.

There are two methods of calculating GDP. It can be calculated either by summing the expenditures on the "final-user" goods and services purchased in each sector of the economy or by summing the income payments and direct cost items (plus the GNP-GDP adjustment) that accompany the production of goods and services.

EXHIBIT 6–2

TWO WAYS OF MEASURING GDP

EXPENDITURE APPROACH	RESOURCE COST-INCOME APPROACH
Consumption purchases of households	Income payments of resource owners (at factor cost)
+	Wages
Gross investment expenditures of businesses	Self-employment income
	Rents
+	Profits
Government purchases of goods and services	Interest
+	+
Net exports of goods and services	Nonincome cost items
	Indirect business taxes
	Depreciation
	+
	GNP-GDP adjustment

EXHIBIT 6-3

**TWO WAYS OF MEASURING GDP—
1993 DATA (BILLIONS OF DOLLARS)**[a]

EXPENDITURE APPROACH			RESOURCE COST-INCOME APPROACH	
Personal consumption		$4,391	Employee compensation	$3,772
Durable goods	$ 538		Proprietors' income	442
Nondurable goods	1,350			
Services	2,503		Rents	13
			Corporate profits	459
Gross private investment		892		
Fixed investment	875		Interest income	448
Inventories	17			
Government purchases		1,157	Indirect business taxes	572
Federal	443			
State and local	714		Depreciation	
			(capital consumption)	671
Net exports		−66	GNP-GDP adjustment	
			(minus net income earned abroad)	−3
Gross domestic product		$6,374	Gross domestic product	$6,374

[a]The left side shows the flow of expenditure and the right side the flow of income payments and indirect costs (plus the GNP-GDP adjustment). Both procedures yield GDP.

Source: U.S. Department of Commerce. These data are also available in the *Federal Reserve Bulletin*, which is published monthly.

Investment
The flow of expenditures on durable assets (fixed investment) plus the addition to inventories (inventory investment) during a period. These expenditures enhance our ability to provide consumer benefits in the future.

GROSS INVESTMENT PURCHASES.   The next item in the expenditure approach, **investment,** is the construction or manufacture of capital goods that provide a "flow" of future consumption or production service. Unlike food or medical services, they are not immediately "used." A house, for example, is an investment good because it will provide a stream of services long into the future. Business plants and equipment are investment goods because they, too, will provide productive services in the future. Changes in business inventories are also classed as investment goods, since they measure goods that will provide future consumer benefits.

Gross investment includes expenditures for both (1) the replacement of machinery, equipment, and buildings worn out during the year and (2) net additions to the stock of capital assets. Net investment is simply gross investment minus an allowance for depreciation and obsolescence of machinery and other physical assets during the year.

Net investment is an important indicator of the economy's future productive capability. Substantial net investment indicates that the capital stock of the economy is growing, thereby enhancing the economy's future productive potential

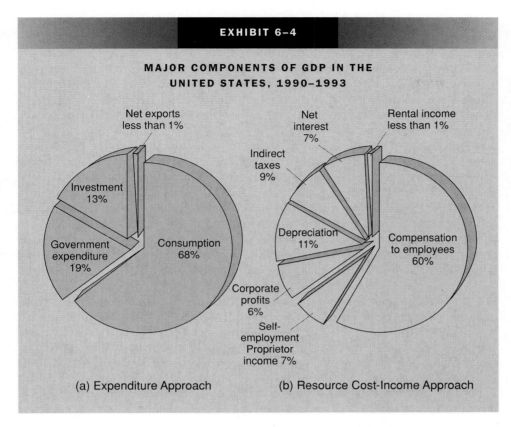

EXHIBIT 6–4

MAJOR COMPONENTS OF GDP IN THE UNITED STATES, 1990–1993

Net exports less than 1%

Investment 13%

Government expenditure 19%

Consumption 68%

(a) Expenditure Approach

Net interest 7%

Rental income less than 1%

Indirect taxes 9%

Depreciation 11%

Compensation to employees 60%

Corporate profits 6%

Self-employment Proprietor income 7%

(b) Resource Cost-Income Approach

The relative sizes of the major components of GDP usually fluctuate within a fairly narrow range. The average proportion of each component during 1990–1993 is demonstrated here for both (a) the expenditure approach and (b) the resource cost-income approach.

Source: *Economic Report of the President, 1994.*

(shifting the economy's production-possibilities frontier outward). In contrast, a low rate of net investment, or, even worse, negative net investment, implies a stagnating or even contracting economy. Of course, the impact of investment on future income will also be affected by the productivity of investment—whether the funds invested are channeled into wealth-creating projects. Other things the same, however, countries with a large net investment rate will tend to grow more rapidly. Income levels in countries with a low or negative net investment rate will tend to stagnate or even regress. In 1993 gross investment expenditures in the United States were $892 billion, including $671 billion for the replacement of assets worn out during the year. Thus, net investment was $221 billion, only about 3 percent of GDP.

Since GDP is designed to measure current production, allowance must be made for goods produced but not sold during the year—that is, for **inventory investment,** changes during the year in the market value of unsold goods on shelves and in warehouses. If business firms have more goods on hand at the end of the year than they had at the beginning of the year, inventory investment will be positive. This inventory investment must be added to GDP. On the other hand, a decline in the market value of inventories would indicate that the purchases of goods and services exceeded current production. In this case, inventory *disinvestment* would be a subtraction from GDP. In 1993 the United States invested $17 billion in additions to inventories.

The inventory component of investment varies substantially. At the beginning of an unexpected recession, inventories often rise as the result of weak demand.

Inventory investment
Changes in the stock of unsold goods and raw materials held during a period.

Later in the recession, businesses reduce their inventories in response to weak sales. In contrast, businesses generally rebuild their inventories during prosperous times when strong future sales are anticipated.

Many goods possess both consumer- and investment-good characteristics. There is not always a clear distinction between the two. National accounting procedures have rather arbitrarily classified business purchases of final goods as investment and considered household purchases, except housing, as consumption.

GOVERNMENT PURCHASES.   In 1993 federal, state, and local government purchases were $1,157 billion, approximately 18 percent of total GDP. The purchases of state and local governments exceeded those of the federal government by a wide margin. The government component includes both investment and consumption services. Thus, current public-sector expenditures on missiles, highways, and dams for flood control, as well as the operation of veterans' hospitals, public schools, and law enforcement agencies, are all included in the government component. Since transfer payments are excluded, the total expenditures of the public sector are substantially greater than government purchases of goods and services.

Net exports
Exports minus imports.

Exports
Goods and services produced domestically but sold to foreigners.

Imports
Goods and services produced by foreigners but purchased by domestic consumers, investors, and governments.

NET EXPORTS.   The final item in the expenditure approach is **net exports,** or total exports minus imports. **Exports** are domestically-produced goods and services sold to foreigners. **Imports** are foreign-produced goods and services purchased domestically. We want GDP to measure only the domestic production of a nation. Therefore, when measuring GDP by the expenditure approach, we must (1) add exports (goods produced domestically that were sold to foreigners) and (2) subtract imports (goods produced abroad that were purchased by Americans). For national-income accounting purposes, we can combine these two factors into a single entry:

$$\text{Net exports} = \text{Total exports} - \text{Total imports}$$

Net exports may be either positive or negative. When we sell more to foreigners than they buy from us, net exports are positive. In recent years, net exports have been negative, indicating we were buying more goods and services from foreigners than we were selling to them. In 1993 net exports were −$66 billion.

RESOURCE COST-INCOME APPROACH

Exhibit 6–3 illustrates how, rather than summing the flow of expenditures on final goods and services, we could reach GDP by summing the flow of costs incurred and income generated. Labor services play a very important role in the production process. It is therefore not surprising that employee compensation, $3,772 billion in 1993, provides the largest source of income generated by the production of goods and services.

Self-employed proprietors undertake the risks of owning their own businesses and simultaneously provide their own labor services to the firm. Their earnings in 1993 contributed $442 billion to GDP, 7 percent of the total. Together, employees and self-employed proprietors accounted for approximately two-thirds of GDP.

Machines, buildings, land, and other physical assets also contribute to the production process. Rents, corporate profits, and interest are payments to persons who provide either physical resources or the financial resources with which to purchase physical assets. *Rents* are returns to resource owners who permit others to use their assets during a time period. *Corporate profits* are compensation earned by stockholders, who bear the risk of the business undertaking and who provide financial capital with which the firm purchases resources. *Interest* is a payment to parties who extend loans to producers.

Not all cost components of GDP result in an income payment to a resource supplier. There are two major indirect costs: indirect business taxes and the cost of depreciation.

INDIRECT BUSINESS TAXES.   Taxes imposed on the sale of many goods, which are passed on to the consumer, are **indirect business taxes.** The sales tax is a clear example. When you make a $1 purchase in a state with a 5 percent sales tax, the purchase actually costs you $1.05. The $1 goes to the seller to pay wages, rent, interest, and managerial costs. The 5 cents goes to the government. Indirect business taxes boost the market price of goods when GDP is calculated by the expenditure approach. Similarly, when looked at from the factor-cost viewpoint, taxes are an indirect cost of supplying the goods to the purchasers.

Indirect business taxes
Taxes that increase the business firm's costs of production and therefore the prices charged to consumers. Examples would be sales, excise, and property taxes.

DEPRECIATION.   Using machines to produce goods causes the machines to wear out. **Depreciation** of capital goods is a cost of producing current goods, but it is not a direct cost because it reflects what is lost to the producer when machines and facilities become less valuable. Depreciation does not involve a direct payment to a resource owner. It is an estimate, based on the expected life of the asset, of the decline in the asset's value during the year. In 1993 depreciation (sometimes called *capital consumption allowance*) amounted to $671 billion, a little less than 11 percent of GDP.

Depreciation
The estimated amount of physical capital (for example, machines and buildings) that is worn out or used up producing goods during the period.

GNP-GDP ADJUSTMENT.   Last, adjustment has to be made for the difference between GNP and GDP. The sum of employee compensation, proprietors' income, rents, corporate profits, and interest yields the income of Americans, regardless of whether that income was earned domestically or abroad. This aggregated figure is referred to as **national income.** If depreciation and indirect business taxes—the two indirect cost components—are added to national income, the result will be gross national product (GNP) rather than GDP. As we previously discussed, GDP and GNP are slightly different. GDP includes the domestic income of foreigners and omits the income that Americans earn abroad, while GNP does just the opposite. GNP counts the income that Americans earn abroad, but it omits the income foreigners earn in the United States. Therefore, when deriving GDP by the resource cost-income approach, we must subtract the *net* income Americans earned abroad. This *net* income figure is equal to the income Americans earned abroad minus the income that foreigners earned in the United States. Since it is *net* income, it may be either positive or negative.

National income
The total income payments to owners of human (labor) and physical capital during a period. It is also equal to NDP minus indirect business taxes plus net income earned abroad by the citizens of the country.

If Americans earned more income abroad than foreigners earned in the United States, the net income of Americans would be positive. Since this net income adds to GNP but not GDP, it must be subtracted when GDP is derived by the resource cost-income method. When the citizens of a country earn *net* income abroad, GDP will be less than GNP. In 1993 the GNP of the United States was $6,377 billion, but Americans earned $3 billion *more* abroad than foreigners earned in the United States. This $3 billion of net income is part of GNP, but not GDP. In order to convert to GDP, this $3 billion that Americans earned abroad must be subtracted from the GNP figure, which results in the 1993 GDP of $6,374 billion.

Of course, the domestic earnings of foreigners may exceed the earnings of the domestic nationals abroad. If this is the case, the figure for net earnings abroad will be negative. When net income earned abroad is negative, it should be added (subtraction of a negative number yields a plus) when GDP is derived by the resource cost-income approach. Whenever the net income earned abroad of a country is negative, the country's GDP will exceed its GNP.

RELATIVE SIZE OF GDP COMPONENTS

Of course, the relative importance of the components of GDP changes from time to time. Exhibit 6–4 shows the average proportion of GDP accounted for by each of the components during 1990–1993. When the expenditure approach is used, personal consumption is by far the largest and most stable component of GDP. Consumption accounted for 68 percent of GDP during 1990–1993, compared to only 13 percent for investment and 19 percent for government expenditures. When GDP is measured by the resource cost-income approach, compensation to employees is the dominant component (60 percent of GDP). During 1990–1993, rents, corporate profits, and interest combined to account for 13 percent of GDP.

DEPRECIATION AND NET DOMESTIC PRODUCT

Net domestic product (NDP)
Gross domestic product minus a depreciation allowance for the wearing out of machines and buildings during the period.

The inclusion of depreciation costs in GDP points out that it is indeed a "gross" rather than a "net" measure of economic production. Since GDP fails to allow for the wearing out of capital goods, it overstates the net output of an economy. The **net domestic product (NDP)** is a concept designed to correct this deficiency. It is the total market value of the goods and services produced domestically and purchased by consumers, governments, and foreigners, plus any net additions to the nation's capital stock. In accounting terms, net domestic product is simply GDP minus depreciation.

Since NDP counts only net additions to the nation's capital stock, it is less than GDP. Net investment—the additions to capital stock—is always equal to gross investment minus depreciation. NDP counts only net investment.

WHEN WILL GDP AND GNP DIFFER?

In most cases, the overwhelming bulk of output is produced domestically, and it is produced with resources owned by the nationals of the country. Thus, the difference between the GDP and the GNP of a country is usually quite small. As **Exhibit 6–5** illustrates, the difference is less than 1 percent for the United States, Germany, Japan, United Kingdom, France, Netherlands, and Spain.

The two output measures, however, will differ significantly when there is a substantial difference between the income citizens earn abroad and the domestic income generated by foreigners. This will generally be true if the country has attracted either a relatively large number of foreign workers or a large amount of foreign investment. Under these circumstances, the incomes of foreigners within a country will tend to be large relative to the earnings of domestic citizens abroad. As a result, the country's GDP will exceed its GNP. In recent years, foreign investment in Indonesia, Malaysia, Australia, and Canada has been quite large. Therefore, foreigners earn more in these countries than domestic nationals earn abroad. This investment income of foreigners contributes to GDP, but not GNP. Thus, the GDP of these countries is somewhat larger than their GNP (refer again to Exhibit 6–5).

In contrast, when the citizens of a country have made substantial investments abroad, or if a relatively large number of them work abroad, the earnings from these activities will add to GNP, but not GDP. Under these circumstances, a country's GDP will tend to be less than its GNP. Kuwait and Switzerland are examples of countries where substantial income from investments abroad results in GNP that is significantly greater than GDP.

REAL AND NOMINAL GDP

It is important to distinguish between real and nominal economic values. **Nominal values** (or *money values,* as they are often called) are expressed in current dollars. Over time, nominal values reflect both (1) changes in the real size of an

Nominal values
Values expressed in current dollars.

[a]Year of data in parentheses
Source: Derived from the International Monetary Fund, *International Financial Statistics,* August 1993.

EXHIBIT 6–5

RELATIONSHIP BETWEEN GDP AND GNP FOR SELECTED COUNTRIES

Country[a]	GDP as a Percent of GNP
United States (1992)	99.8
Germany (1992)	100.0
Japan (1992)	99.1
United Kingdom (1992)	99.5
France (1992)	100.6
Netherlands (1992)	100.2
Spain (1991)	100.9
Indonesia (1991)	105.0
Malaysia (1990)	104.5
Australia (1992)	104.1
Canada (1992)	103.6
Kuwait (1992)	86.2
Switzerland (1992)	96.0

Real values

Values that have been adjusted for the effects of inflation.

Nominal GDP

GDP expressed at current prices. It is often called money GDP.

Real GDP

Gross domestic product adjusted for changes in the price level. Mathematically, real GDP_2 is equal to nominal GDP_2 multiplied by (GDP $Deflator_1$/GDP $Deflator_2$). Thus, if prices have risen between Periods 1 and 2, the ratio of the GDP deflator in Period 1 to the deflator in Period 2 will be less than 1. This ratio will therefore deflate the nominal GDP for the rising prices.

GDP deflator

A price index that reveals the cost of purchasing the items included in GDP during the period relative to the cost of purchasing these same items during a base year (currently, 1987). Since the base year is assigned a value of 100, as the GDP deflator takes on values greater than 100, it indicates that prices have risen.

Consumer price index CPI

An indicator of the general level of prices. It attempts to compare the cost of purchasing the market basket bought by a typical consumer during a specific period with the cost of purchasing the same market basket during an earlier period.

economic variable and (2) inflation—a change in the general level of prices. In contrast, **real values** eliminate the impact of changes in the price level, leaving only the real changes in the size of an economic variable. Whenever economists use the term "real" (for example, "real GDP" and "real income"), this means that the data have been adjusted for the effects of inflation. When comparing data at different points in time, it is nearly always the real changes that are of most interest.

Perhaps an example will help clarify the difference between real and nominal values. In 1992 per capita **nominal GDP**—that is, GDP expressed at current prices—in the United States was $23,645, compared to only $2,840 in 1960. Does this mean we produced more than eight times as much output per person in 1992 as we did in 1960? No; in 1992 the general level of prices was 4.66 times the level of 1960. Measured in terms of the price level in 1960, **real GDP**—that is, GDP adjusted for the effects of inflation—per person in 1992 was $5,074, only about 79 percent more than GDP per person in 1960.

Nominal GDP will increase if either (1) more goods and services are produced or (2) prices rise. Often, both factors will contribute to an increase in GDP. Since we are usually interested in comparing only the output or actual production during two different time intervals, GDP must be adjusted for the change in prices.

How can we determine how much the prices of items included in GDP have risen during a specific period? We answer this question by constructing a price index called the **GDP deflator.** The Department of Commerce estimates how much of each item included in GDP has been produced during a year. This *bundle of goods* will include automobiles, houses, office buildings, medical services, bread, milk, entertainment, and all other goods included in the GDP, in the quantities actually produced during the current year. The Department of Commerce then calculates the ratio of (1) the cost of purchasing this representative bundle of goods at current prices divided by (2) the cost of purchasing the same bundle at the prices that were present during a designated earlier *base year.* The base year chosen (currently 1987 for the GDP deflator) is assigned the value 100. The GDP deflator is equal to the calculated ratio multiplied by 100. If prices are, on average, higher during the current period than they were during the base year, the GDP deflator will exceed 100. The relative size of the GDP deflator is thus a measure of the current price level compared to the price level during the base year. (See the boxed feature on p. 158, "Measures of Economic Activity," for additional detail on how the GDP deflator and another important price index, the **consumer price index,** are constructed.)

We can use the GDP deflator together with nominal GDP to measure real GDP: GDP in dollars of constant purchasing power. If prices are rising, we simply deflate the nominal GDP during the latter period to account for the effects of inflation.

Exhibit 6–6 illustrates how real GDP is measured and why it is important to adjust for price changes. Between 1987 and 1993, the nominal GDP of the United States increased from $4,540 billion to $6,374 billion, an increase of 40.4 percent. However, a large portion of this increase in nominal GDP reflected inflation rather than an increase in real output. The GDP deflator, the price index that measures changes in the cost of all goods included in GDP, increased from 100 in the 1987 base year to 124.2 in 1993. This indicates that prices rose by 24.2 percent between 1987 and 1993. To determine the real GDP for 1993 in terms of 1987 dollars, we deflate the 1993 nominal GDP for the rise in prices:

$$\text{Real GDP}_{93} = \text{Nominal GDP}_{93} \times \frac{\text{GDP deflator}_{87}}{\text{GDP deflator}_{93}}$$

EXHIBIT 6–6

CHANGES IN PRICES AND REAL GDP OF UNITED STATES, 1987–1993

	NOMINAL GDP (BILLIONS OF DOLLARS)	PRICE INDEX (GDP DEFLATOR, 1987 = 100)	REAL GDP (BILLIONS OF 1987 DOLLARS)
1987	$4,540	100.0	$4,540
1993	6,374	124.2	5,132
Percent Increase	40.4	24.2	13.0

Between 1987 and 1993, nominal GDP increased by 40.4 percent. But, when the 1993 GDP is deflated to account for price increases, we see that real GDP increased by only 13.0 percent.

Source: U.S. Department of Commerce.

Because prices were rising, the latter ratio is less than 1. In terms of 1987 dollars, the real GDP in 1993 was $5,132 billion, only 13.0 percent more than in 1987. So although money GDP (nominal GDP) expanded by 40.4 percent, real GDP increased by only 13.0 percent.

A change in money GDP tells us nothing about what is happening to the rate of real production unless we also know what is happening to prices. Money income could double while production actually declines if prices more than double. On the other hand, money income could remain constant while real GDP increases if prices fall. Data on both money GDP and price changes are essential for a meaningful comparison of real income between two time periods.

PROBLEMS WITH GDP AS A MEASURING ROD

GDP is not a perfect device for measuring current production and income. Some items that involve current production are excluded because their value is difficult to determine. The introduction of new products complicate the use of GDP as a measuring rod. Also, when production involves harmful "side effects" that are not fully registered in the market price of inputs, GDP will fail to accurately measure the level of output. These limitations are particularly important when GDP is used as an indicator of economic well-being, rather than simply a measure of the rate of *market* output over time or across countries. Let us consider some of the major limitations of GDP.

MEASURES OF ECONOMIC ACTIVITY

DERIVING THE GDP DEFLATOR AND THE CONSUMER PRICE INDEX

When making comparisons of output and expenditures between periods, it is important to adjust for price changes. Economists measure changes in prices by constructing a *price index*, which, as explained earlier, measures the cost (or value) of a given "bundle of goods" at a point in time relative to the cost of the same bundle of goods during a prior base year. The base year is assigned a value of 100. If prices are higher during the current period (that is, if the cost of purchasing the given bundle of goods has risen), the value of the price index during the current period will exceed 100.

A simple example can be used to illustrate the concept of a price index. Imagine that students at your college purchase only four items: hamburgers, T-shirts, blue jeans, and compact disks (CDs). In recent years, the prices of some of these goods have risen. Suppose we want to determine the degree to which prices rose between 1985 (the base year) and 1994. A careful sampling of prices is used to determine the average price of each item in the students' budget for both 1985 and 1994. These data are presented in **Exhibit 1.** Note that price changes varied among the goods. The price of hamburgers doubled between 1985 and 1994, while the price of jeans remained unchanged. T-shirt prices rose by 80 percent (from $10 to $18), but the price of CDs declined between 1985 and 1994. How can the price data for 1985 and 1994 be used to determine the difference in the level of prices between the two years?

EXHIBIT 1

THE 1994 PRICE INDEX (1985 = 100) BASED ON TYPICAL MARKET BASKET CONSUMED BY COLLEGE STUDENTS IN 1985 (HYPOTHETICAL DATA)

	Average Price		Cost of 1985 Market Basket	
Monthly Purchases, 1985	1985	1994	1985 Prices	1994 Prices
60 hamburgers	$ 1.60	$ 3.20	$ 96.00	$192.00
4 T-shirts	10.00	18.00	40.00	72.00
2 jeans	24.00	24.00	48.00	48.00
1 compact disc	16.00	12.00	16.00	12.00
		Total	$200.00	$324.00

Price index in 1994

$$(1985 = 100) = \frac{324}{200} \times 100 = 162$$

Method I: Using the base-year market basket. A price index reveals the cost of purchasing a *market basket* (or "bundle") of goods at a point in time compared to the cost of purchasing the identical market basket during an earlier base period. What market basket should be used? One obvious possibility would be the market basket

NONMARKET PRODUCTION

The GDP fails to count household production because such production does not involve a market transaction. Because of this, the household services of millions of people are excluded. If you mow the yard, repair your car, paint your house, pick up relatives from school, or perform similar productive household activities, your labor services add nothing to GDP, since no market transaction is involved. Such nonmarket productive activities are sizable—10 or 15 percent of total GDP, perhaps more. Their exclusion results in some oddities in national-income accounting.

For example, if a woman marries her gardener, and, if after the marriage the spouse-gardener works for love rather than for money, GDP will decline because the services of the spouse-gardener will now be excluded: there is no longer a market transaction. If a family member decides to enter the labor force and hire

MEASURES OF ECONOMIC ACTIVITY (continued)

consumed by students during the base period. Suppose a survey of the student population indicates that, on average, students purchased 60 hamburgers, 4 T-shirts, 2 pairs of blue jeans and 1 compact disk monthly during the 1985 base year. This information permits us to determine the cost of the market basket purchased by the typical student in 1985 at both 1985 and 1994 prices. Exhibit 1 presents these calculations. The market basket consumed by the typical student in 1985 costs $200 at 1985 prices. At 1994 prices, the identical market basket costs $324. We can now calculate the 1994 college student price index (CSPI) based on the 1985 market basket:

$$\frac{\text{Cost of base-year market basket at current (1994) prices}}{\text{Cost of base-year market basket at base-year (1985) prices}} \times 100$$

The cost of the base-year market basket in 1994 was $324, compared to a cost of $200 in 1985. Thus, the 1994 CSPI using the base-year market basket is equal to 162:

$$\frac{324}{200} \times 100$$

Method II: Using the current-year market basket. Rather than using the base-year market basket, we might use the current-year quantity of each good purchased to weight the 1985 and 1994 prices. In this case, the formula for the CSPI would be

$$\frac{\text{Cost of current-year market basket at current (1994) prices}}{\text{Cost of current-year market basket at base-year (1985) prices}} \times 100$$

A 1994 survey of students indicates the quantity of each commodity purchased monthly during the year. These data can be used to calculate the cost of purchasing the 1994 typical market basket at both 1985 and 1994 prices. As **Exhibit 2** shows, the typical market basket actually purchased in 1994 would have cost $196 at 1985 prices. The same market basket cost $280 at 1994 prices. Based on the current-year market basket, then, the 1994 CSPI is equal to 142.9:

$$\frac{280}{196} \times 100$$

EXHIBIT 2

THE 1994 PRICE INDEX (1985 = 100) BASED ON TYPICAL MARKET BASKET CONSUMED BY COLLEGE STUDENTS IN 1994 (HYPOTHETICAL DATA)

Monthly Purchases, 1994	Average Price 1985	Average Price 1994	Cost of 1985 Market Basket 1985 Prices	Cost of 1985 Market Basket 1994 Prices
50 hamburgers	$ 1.60	$ 3.20	$ 80.00	$160.00
2 T-shirts	10.00	18.00	20.00	36.00
2 jeans	24.00	24.00	48.00	48.00
3 compact disks	16.00	12.00	48.00	36.00
Total			$196.00	$280.00

Price index in 1994

$$(1985 = 100) = \frac{280}{196} \times 100 = 142.9$$

Why do the two alternative methods yield different values for the price index? The differences reflect the weights applied to 1985–1994 price changes. Method I uses the quantity purchased of each good during 1985 to weight the price changes; Method II uses the quantities of the current period (1994).

If the changes in purchases of goods were random, the two alternative methods would tend toward equality. However, changes in the pattern of purchases will not be random. Customers will systematically reduce their purchases of those items that increase the most in price. Similarly, they will tend to expand their consumption of commodities that become relatively cheaper. The consumption patterns of Exhibits 1 and 2 illustrate this point. As the prices of hamburgers and T-shirts rose sharply between 1985 and 1994, the quantity purchased of these items declined. In contrast, the quantity of jeans and compact disks purchased increased as their relative prices declined between 1985 and 1994.

Since Method I assumes that consumers will purchase the base-year bundle, it makes no allowance for substitution away from those goods (hamburgers and T-shirts in our hypothetical case) that increase most in price. So, it overstates the "true" increase in prices (and the inflation rate).

In contrast, Method II imposes the current-year bundle on consumers during the base year. In reality, they would substitute away from the goods that were relatively more expensive during the earlier base year. Thus, the imposition of the current-year market basket on consumers overstates the level of prices during the base year and understates the change in prices between periods.

It was therefore no coincidence that our Method I price index (using the base-year market basket) was greater than our Method II price index (based on the current-year market basket). Method I systematically overstates the increase in prices (and the inflation rate), while Method II systematically understates it.

CONSUMER PRICE INDEX   The consumer price index (CPI) is the most widely used index of price changes over time. It is prepared monthly by the Bureau of Labor Statistics of the Department of Labor. The methodology underlying the CPI is much like our Method I calculations of Exhibit 1, except that the market basket for the CPI is much broader. The composition (quantities) of that market basket is based on the *Consumer Expenditure Survey* of urban consumers conducted during 1982–1984. This survey identified 364 items that comprised the typical bundle purchased by urban consumers during 1982–1984.[1]

Each month, some 250 survey workers call or visit approximately 21,000 stores in urban areas selected to represent all urban places in the United States. All together, the CPI each month uses approximately 125,000 prices in order to derive the average price for each of the 364 food items, consumer goods and services, housing, and property taxes included in the CPI. Just as we illustrated for the four-item market basket of Exhibit 1, the cost of purchasing the 364-item market basket at current prices is then compared with the cost of purchasing the same market basket at base-year prices. The result is a measure of current prices compared to base-year prices.

Like Method I, the CPI measures the percent change in the cost of purchasing a fixed basket of goods consumed during an earlier period (1982–1984). However, consumers will tend to substitute away from the goods that increase most in price, while consuming more of goods that have become relatively cheaper. For example, if the price of beef doubles and the price of

turkey falls (or increases by only a small amount), consumers will substitute turkey for the more expensive beef. Since the CPI is based on the fixed market basket of the earlier period and therefore fails to adjust for consumer substitution away from the goods that increase most in price, it tends to overstate the rate of inflation.

In 1993 the value of the CPI was 144.5, compared to the 100 during the 1982–1984 base period. This indicates the price level in 1993 was 44.5 percent higher than the price level of 1982–1984.

GDP DEFLATOR   The most general price index is the GDP deflator. It differs from the CPI in two important respects. First, the GDP inflator is based on the typical market basket that goes into GDP—that is, all final goods and services produced. In addition to consumer goods, it includes prices for goods and services purchased by businesses and governments. Thus, items such as computers, airplanes, welding equipment, and office space are included in the GDP deflator. Second, it is calculated by Method II procedures. Prices during each period are weighted by the current-year market basket rather than the base-year market basket as for the CPI.

COMPARISON OF THE CPI AND GDP DEFLATOR   **Exhibit 3** presents data for both the CPI and GDP deflator during the 1967–1993 period. Even though they are based on different market baskets and procedures, the two measures of the inflation rate are quite similar for most years. There were three exceptions: 1974, 1979, and 1980—years during which the change in the CPI was quite a bit larger than the change in the GDP deflator. Since the CPI is based on the market basket of the earlier period (Method I procedure), it tends to overstate the inflation rate. The upward bias is more important when there is substantial substitution away from items for which prices have increased sharply. Many economists believe this was the case during the 1970s, a period of sharply higher oil prices. This may well account for the differences between the CPI and GDP deflator during 1974, 1979, and 1980.

---

[1]Actually, the Bureau of Labor Statistics now publishes two indexes of consumer prices—one for "all urban households" and the other for "urban wage earners and clerical workers." The two differ slightly because the typical bundles of goods purchased by the two groups are not identical.

MEASURES OF ECONOMIC ACTIVITY *(continued)*

The CPI and GDP deflator were designed for different purposes. Choosing between the two depends on what we are trying to measure. If we want to determine how rising prices affect the money income of consumers, the CPI would be most appropriate since it includes only consumer goods. However, if we want an economy-wide measure of inflation with which to adjust GDP or national income data, clearly the GDP deflator is the appropriate index since it includes the price of every good and service produced.

EXHIBIT 3

CONSUMER PRICE INDEX AND GDP DEFLATOR, 1967–1993

YEAR	CPI (1982–84 = 100)	INFLATION RATE (PERCENT)	GDP DEFLATOR (1987 = 100)	INFLATION RATE (PERCENT)
1967	33.4	—	30.3	—
1968	34.8	4.2	31.8	5.0
1969	36.7	5.5	33.4	5.0
1970	38.8	5.7	35.2	5.4
1971	40.5	4.4	37.1	5.4
1972	41.8	3.2	38.8	4.6
1973	44.4	6.2	41.3	6.4
1974	49.3	11.0	44.9	8.7

CONSUMER PRICE INDEX AND GDP DEFLATOR, 1967–1993 *(continued)*

YEAR	CPI (1982–84 = 100)	INFLATION RATE (PERCENT)	GDP DEFLATOR (1987 = 100)	INFLATION RATE (PERCENT)
1975	53.8	9.1	49.2	8.7
1976	56.9	5.8	52.3	6.3
1977	60.6	6.5	55.9	6.9
1978	65.2	7.6	60.3	7.9
1979	72.6	11.3	65.5	8.6
1980	82.4	13.5	71.7	9.5
1981	90.9	10.3	78.9	10.0
1982	96.5	6.2	83.8	6.2
1983	99.6	3.2	87.2	4.1
1984	103.9	4.3	91.0	4.4
1985	107.6	3.6	94.4	3.7
1986	109.6	1.9	96.9	2.6
1987	113.6	3.6	100.0	3.2
1988	118.3	4.1	103.9	3.9
1989	124.0	4.8	108.5	4.4
1990	130.7	5.4	113.2	4.3
1991	136.2	4.2	117.8	8.1
1992	140.2	2.9	120.9	2.6
1993	144.5	3.0	124.2	2.7

Source: *Economic Report of the President, 1993.*

someone to perform services previously provided by household members, there will be a double-barreled impact on GDP. It will rise as a result of (1) the market earnings of the new labor-force entrant plus (2) the amount paid to the person hired to perform the services that were previously supplied within the household.

The omission of many nonmarket productive activities makes comparisons over time and across countries at various stages of market development less meaningful. For example, more women are currently involved in market work than was true 30 years ago. There is widespread use of appliances today to perform functions previously performed by women at home. Remember that the initial purchase of the appliance contributes to GDP while the unpaid household labor is not counted. Thus, a larger share of total production was previously excluded. This implies that the current GDP, even in real dollars, is overstated relative to the earlier period.

Similarly, GDP comparisons overstate the output of developed countries when compared to underdeveloped countries. A larger share of the total production of underdeveloped countries originates in the household sector. For example,

Mexican families are more likely than their U.S. counterparts to make their own clothing, raise and prepare their own food, provide their own child-rearing services, and even build their own homes. These productive labor services, originating in the household sector, are excluded from GDP. Therefore GDP understates total output in Mexico even more than it does in the United States.

THE UNDERGROUND ECONOMY

Underground economy

Unreported barter and cash transactions that take place outside recorded market channels. Some are otherwise legal activities undertaken to evade taxes. Others involve illegal activities such as trafficking in drugs and prostitution.

Some people attempt to conceal various economic activities in order to evade taxes or because the activities themselves are illegal. Economists refer to these unreported and therefore difficult to measure activities as the **underground economy.**

Since cash transactions are more difficult for government authorities to trace, they provide the lifeblood of the underground economy. This is why drug trafficking, smuggling, prostitution, and other illegal activities are generally conducted in cash. However, a large portion of this underground economy encompasses unreported transactions involving legal goods and services. The participants in this legal-if-reported portion of the underground are quite diverse. Taxicab drivers and waitresses may pocket fees and tips. Small-business proprietors may fail to ring up and report various cash sales. Craft and professional workers may fail to report cash income. Employees ranging from laborers to bartenders may work "off books" and accept payment in cash in order to qualify for income-transfer benefits or evade taxes (or allow their employers to evade taxes).

Many of these "underground" activities produce goods and services that are valued by purchasers. Nevertheless, since the activities are unreported, they do not contribute to GDP. Estimates of the size of the underground economy in the United States range from 10 to 15 percent of total output. The available evidence indicates that the size of the underground economy is even larger in Western Europe (where tax rates are higher) and South America (where regulations often make it more costly to operate a business). Most researchers in this area believe that since the 1960s these unrecorded transactions have grown more rapidly than measured output. If this is true, it implies that the published GDP figures are actually understating the recent growth rate of output, since an expanding proportion of total output is being excluded.

LEISURE AND HUMAN COSTS

GDP excludes leisure, a good that is valuable to each of us, and the human cost associated with the production of goods and services. Simon Kuznets, the "inventor" of GDP, believed that this omission substantially reduced the accuracy of GDP as a measure of economic well-being. One country might attain a $20,000 per capita GDP with an average workweek of 30 hours. Another might attain the same per capita GDP with a 50-hour workweek. The market output per person of the two countries would be identical. In terms of economic well-being, however, the first country would be better off because it "produces" more leisure, or sacrifices less human cost. GDP, though, does not reflect this fact.

The average number of hours worked per week in the United States has declined steadily over the years. The average nonagricultural production worker spent only 34.5 hours per week on the job in 1993, compared to more than 40 hours in 1947—a 14 percent reduction in weekly hours worked. Clearly, this reduction in the length of the workweek raised the American standard of living, even though it did not enhance GDP.

GDP also fails to take into account human costs. On average, jobs today are less physically strenuous and are generally performed in a safer, more comfortable environment than was true a generation ago. To the extent that working conditions have improved through the years, GDP figures understate the growth of real income.

QUALITY VARIATION AND INTRODUCTION OF NEW GOODS

In a dynamic world, changes in quality and the introduction of new goods make income comparisons over time more difficult. During the last 10 or 20 years, there have been substantial changes in the quality and availability of products. Today, new automobiles are more fuel-efficient and generally safer than were new automobiles 20 years ago. Dental services are generally much less unpleasant than was true 20 years ago. Some commodities—compact disc players, video recorders, personal computers, and fax machines, to name a few—simply were unavailable. Statisticians devising price indexes attempt to make some allowance for quality improvements. Many economists believe, however, that failure to fully adjust for quality improvements and the introduction of new products results in an overestimation of the inflation rate by as much as 1 or 2 percent annually.

When the bundle of goods available differs substantially between years, the significance of income comparisons is reduced. As **Exhibit 6–7** shows, per capita real GDP in 1930 was less than one-third the figure for 1992. Does this mean that, on average, Americans produced and consumed three times more goods in 1992 than in 1930? Caution should be exercised before arriving at this conclusion. In the 1930s there were no jet planes, television programs, automatic dishwashers, personal computers, videocassette players, or fax machines. In 1930 even a millionaire could not have purchased the typical bundle consumed by Americans in 1992.[3] On the other hand, in 1930 there were plenty of open spaces, trees, uncongested (but rough) roads, pure-water rivers, hiking trails, and areas with low crime rates. Thus, many goods were available in 1992 that were not available in 1930, and vice versa. Under such circumstances, comparative GDP statistics lose much of their relevance.

HARMFUL SIDE EFFECTS AND ECONOMIC "BADS"

GDP makes no adjustment for harmful side effects that sometimes arise from production, consumption, and the events of nature. If they do not involve market

---

[3]The following quotation from Mancur Olson, Professor of Economics at the University of Maryland, illustrates this point:

The price level has risen about eight times since 1932, so a $25,000 income then would be the "equivalent" of an income of $200,000 today—one could readily afford a Rolls-Royce, the best seats in the theater, and the care of the best physicians in the country. But the 1932 Rolls-Royce, for all its many virtues, does not embody some desirable technologies available today in the humblest Ford. Nor would the imposing dollar of 1932 buy a TV set or a home videocassette recorder. And if one got an infection, the best physicians in 1932 would not be able to prescribe an antibiotic.

Source: Derived from U.S.
Department of Commerce data.

*In 1992 per capita real GDP
was a little more than twice the
1950 level, 2.8 times the 1940
level, and 3.2 times the 1930
value. How meaningful are
these numbers?*

EXHIBIT 6–7

PER CAPITA REAL GDP, 1930–1992

YEAR	PER CAPITA REAL GDP (IN 1987 DOLLARS)	YEAR	PER CAPITA REAL GDP (IN 1987 DOLLARS)
1930	$ 6,079	1970	$14,013
1940	6,857	1980	16,584
1950	9,352	1990	19,595
1960	10,903	1992	19,523

transactions, economic "bads" are ignored. Yet, in a modern industrial economy, production and consumption sometimes generate side effects that either detract from current consumption or reduce our future production possibilities. When property rights are defined imperfectly, air and water pollution are sometimes side effects of economic activity. For example, an industrial plant may pollute the air or water while producing goods. Automobiles may put harmful chemicals into the atmosphere while providing us with transportation. GDP makes no allowance for these negative side effects. In fact, expenditures on the cleanup of air and water pollution, should they be undertaken, will add to GDP.

Similarly, GDP makes no allowance for destructive acts of nature. Consider the impact of Hurricane Andrew, which left a path of destruction as it roared through South Florida during the fall of 1992. Numerous buildings, bridges, and homes were destroyed or damaged. Yet nothing was subtracted from GDP, because it makes no allowance for losses that operate outside of market channels. In fact, Andrew probably increased GDP in late 1992 and throughout 1993. Several hundred million dollars were poured into the reconstruction efforts that went on for more than a year. The cleanup and replacement of items lost undoubtedly caused people to work longer and purchase more goods and services than otherwise would have been the case. Since GDP ignored the destruction, but counted the rebuilding activities, it tended to overstate the change in living standards during the period.

THE GREAT CONTRIBUTION OF GDP

When considering the function of the GDP data, it is important to keep in mind what the data are intended to measure. GDP is not a measure of economic welfare or happiness of the citizenry. It is not even primarily a measure of economic well-being. Indeed, a number of things like leisure and household production that obviously influence the well-being of people are omitted.

GDP was designed to measure the value of the goods and services produced in the market (or business) sector. In spite of its shortcomings and limitations, real GDP is a reasonably precise measure of the rate of output in the market sector and how that output rate is changing.

Adjusted for changes in prices, annual and quarterly GDP data provide the information required to track the performance level of the economy. These data allow us to compare the current output of goods and services relative to the rate of output in the recent past. This is a vitally important contribution. Without this information, policy-makers would be less likely to adopt productive policies and many business decision makers would be less able to determine the future direction of demand for their product. In the words of Kenneth Boulding, this contribution is significant enough to rank GDP as "one of the great inventions of the twentieth century, probably almost as significant as the automobile and not quite as significant as TV."[4]

RELATED INCOME MEASURES

Exhibit 6–8 illustrates the relationship among five alternative measures of aggregate income. GDP, of course, is the broadest and most frequently quoted index of economic performance. As we previously discussed, the net domestic product (NDP) is simply GDP minus depreciation. NDP measures the total purchases of consumers, governments and foreigners, plus the net additions to the capital stock. It values the production of goods and services of the economy at market prices. These prices, however, include indirect business taxes, which boost market prices but do not represent the cost of using a factor of production. When these indirect taxes are subtracted from NDP and the net income earned abroad added (or subtracted if the net earnings abroad are negative), the resulting figure is the *national income*. National income thus represents net output valued at factor cost. It includes the income that domestic citizens (*nationals*) earn domestically as well as abroad. As Exhibit 6–8 shows, the sum of employee compensation, interest, self-employment income, rents, and corporate profits also yields national income.

Although national income represents the earnings of all resource owners, it is not the same as **personal income,** which is the total of all income received by individuals. This is the income with which they consume goods, add to savings, and pay taxes. It differs from national income in two respects. First, some income is earned but not directly received. Stockholders, for example, do not receive all the income generated by corporations. Corporate taxes take a share. Additional profits are channeled back into the business, remaining undistributed to the stockholder. Social security taxes, as another example, are deducted from the employee's paycheck, forming a component of income earned but not directly received. These factors must be subtracted when calculating personal income.

Second, some income is received even though it was not earned during the current period. Government transfer payments, including social security and interest payments, are included in this category. By the same token, dividends received add to personal income, regardless of when they were earned. These components must be added to yield personal income.

As anyone who has ever worked on a job knows, the amount shown on your paycheck does not equal your salary. Personal taxes must be deducted.

Personal income
The total income received by individuals that is available for consumption, saving, and payment of personal taxes.

[4]Kenneth Boulding, "Fun and Games with the Gross National Product—The Role of Misleading Indicators in Social Policy" in *The Environment Crisis*, edited by Harold W. Helfrich, Jr. (New Haven, Connecticut: Yale University Press, 1970), p. 157.

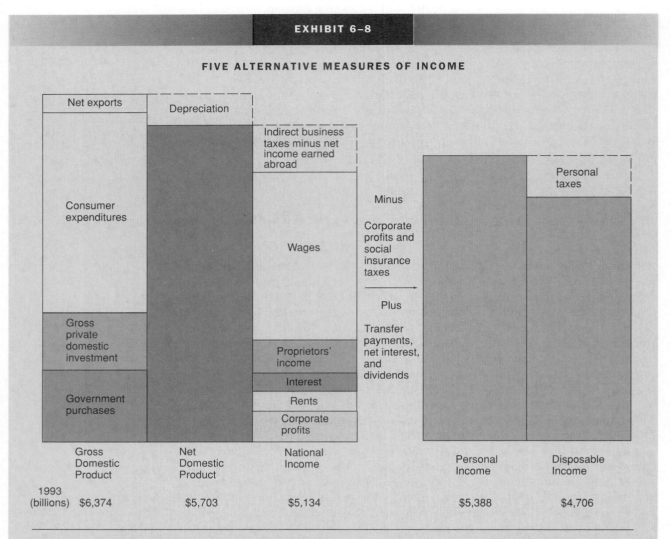

EXHIBIT 6–8

FIVE ALTERNATIVE MEASURES OF INCOME

	Gross Domestic Product	Net Domestic Product	National Income	Personal Income	Disposable Income
1993 (billions)	$6,374	$5,703	$5,134	$5,388	$4,706

The bars illustrate the relationship among five alternative measures of national income. The alternatives range from the gross domestic product, which is the broadest measure of output, to disposable income, which indicates the funds available to households for either personal consumption or saving.

Disposable income

The income available to individuals after personal taxes. It can either be spent on consumption or saved.

Disposable income is the income that is yours to do with as you please. It is simply personal income minus personal taxes.

There are thus five alternative measures of domestic product and income:

1. Gross domestic product
2. Net domestic product
3. National income
4. Personal income
5. Disposable income

Each of the five alternatives measures something different, but they are all closely related. Movement of one nearly always parallels movement of the other indicators. Since the five measures move together, economists often use only GDP or the terms *income, output,* or *aggregate production* when referring to the general movement of all five of the indicators of productive activity.

LOOKING AHEAD

GDP and the related income concepts provide us with a measure of economic performance. In the next chapter, we will take a closer look at the movements of prices and real output in the United States and in other countries. As we proceed, we will investigate the factors that underlie these movements. Models that rely heavily on the interrelationships among household consumption, business investment, and government expenditures will be central to our analysis. As we compare the implications of our analysis with the real world, measurement of GDP and related indicators of income will help us sort out sound theories from economic nonsense.

CHAPTER SUMMARY

1. Gross domestic product (GDP) is a measure of the market value of final goods and services produced domestically during a specific time period, usually a year.

2. Since GDP is designed to measure output, only the production of final-user goods and services produced during the period are counted. Dollars act as a common denominator for GDP. Production of each final product is weighted according to its selling price. GDP excludes income transfers, exchanges involving purely financial transactions, and goods produced during earlier periods because they do not represent current production.

3. GDP can be calculated by either adding up the market value of the final-user goods and services purchased during the period or by summing the income payments to the resource owners who contributed to the production. The two methods sum to an identical result. They also highlight the linkage between output and income. The value of the goods and services produced is also equal to the income payments—broadly defined to include both the accounting profits of producers and indirect business costs—to the resource owners who supplied the factors of production. Thus, GDP is a measure of both aggregate output and aggregate income.

4. Gross national product (GNP) is closely related to gross domestic product. While GDP measures the output produced domestically, (including that produced with resources supplied by foreigners), GNP measures the output produced by the nationals (domestic citizens) of a country. Since the overwhelming bulk of output is usually produced domestically by the nationals of a country, in most cases, GDP and GNP are similar.

5. When GDP is measured by the expenditure approach, it has four major components: consumption, investment, government, and net exports.

6. When GDP is calculated by the resource cost-income approach, it is equal to (a) the direct income components (wages and salaries, self-employment income, rents, interest, corporate profits), plus (b) the indirect business costs (depreciation and indirect business taxes), minus (c) the net income earned abroad by the nationals of the country.

7. When comparing income and output data over time, it is important to distinguish between real and nominal values. Changes in nominal values reflect changes in the general level of prices, as well as changes in the economic variable. In contrast, data measured in real terms have been adjusted to eliminate the impact to changes in the price level. Since economics focuses primarily on real changes, economists generally use real data to measure income, output, and other variables influenced by the level of prices.

8. In effect, price indexes compare the cost of purchasing a typical bundle of goods during a time period relative to the cost of the same bundle during an earlier base year. The base-year price level is assigned a value of 100. Thus, if prices have risen relative to the base year, the price index will exceed 100. The two most widely used price indexes in the United States are the GDP deflator and the consumer price index (CPI).

9. GDP may increase because of an increase in either output or prices. The GDP deflator can be used to convert nominal GDP to real GDP. Measured in Period 1 dollars,

$$\text{Real GDP}_2 = \text{nominal GDP}_2 \times \frac{\text{GDP deflator}_1}{\text{GDP deflator}_2}$$

10. GDP is an imperfect measure of current production. It excludes household production and the underground (unreported) economy. It fails to take leisure and human costs into account. It adjusts imperfectly for quality changes and it fails to account for the negative side effects of current production, such as air and water pollution, depletion of natural resources, and other factors that do not flow through markets. GDP comparisons are less meaningful when the typical bundle of available goods and services differs widely between two time periods (or between two nations).

11. Despite all its limitations, GDP is vitally important because it is an accurate tool in enabling us to identify short-term fluctuations in the output of goods and services supplied in the market sector. Without such an indicator, our understanding of business fluctuations and their underlying causes would be substantially limited.

12. Economists frequently refer to four other income measures that are related to GDP: net domestic product (NDP), national income, personal income, and disposable income. All of these measures of income tend to move together.

CRITICAL-ANALYSIS QUESTIONS

*1. Indicate how each of the following actvities will affect this year's GDP:
  a. The sale of a used economics textbook to the college bookstore.
  b. Smith's $500 doctor bill for the setting of his son's broken arm.
  c. Family lawn services provided by Smith's 16-year-old child.
  d. Lawn services purchased by Smith from the neighbor's 16-year-old child who has a lawn-mowing business.
  e. A $5,250 purchase of 100 shares of stock at $50 per share plus the sales commission of $250.
  f. A multibillion dollar discovery of natural gas in Oklahoma.
  g. A hurricane that causes $10 billion of damage in Florida.
  h. $50,000 of income earned by an American college professor teaching in England.

2. Explain why the rate of growth in GDP in current dollars can sometimes be a misleading statistic.

*3. A large furniture retailer sells $100,000 of household furnishings from inventories built up last year. How does this sale influence GDP? How are the components of GDP affected?

4. If a nation's gross investment exceeds its depreciation (capital consumption allowance) during the year, what has happened to the nation's stock of capital during the year? How will this affect future output? Is it possible for the net investment of a nation to be negative? Explain. What would negative net investment during a year imply about the nation's capital stock and future production potential?

*5. Why might the GDP be a misleading index of changes in output between 1900 and 1994 in the United States? Of differences in output between the United States and Mexico?

6. "GDP counts the product of steel but not the disproduct of air pollution. It counts the product of automobiles but not the disproduct of 'blight' due to junkyards. It counts the product of cigarettes but not the disproduct of a shorter life expectancy due to cancer. Until we can come up with a more reliable index, we cannot tell whether economic welfare is progressing or regressing." Explain why you either agree or disagree with this view.

*7. In 1982 the average earnings of private nonagricultural workers was $267.26 per week. By 1992 the average earnings of private nonagricultural workers had risen to $364.30. In 1992 the CPI was 140.2, compared to 96.5 in 1982. What were the real earnings of private nonagricultural workers in 1992 measured in 1982 dollars?

8. Consider an economy with the following data:

	NOMINAL GDP (IN TRILLIONS)	GDP DEFLATOR
1993	6.0	120
1994	6.2	125

  a. What was the 1994 GDP in constant 1993 dollars?
  b. What was the growth rate of real GDP between 1993 and 1994?
  c. What was the inflation rate between 1993 and 1994?

*9. How much do each of the following contribute to GDP?
  a. Jones pays a repair shop $1,000 to have the engine of her automobile rebuilt.
  b. Jones spends $200 on parts and pays a mechanic $400 to rebuild the engine of her automobile.
  c. Jones spends $200 on parts and rebuilds the engine of her automobile herself.
  d. Jones sells her four-year-old automobile for $5,000 and buys Smith's two-year-old model for $10,000.
  e. Jones sells her four-year-old automobile for $5,000 and buys a new car for $10,000.

10. What is the distinction between all market transactions and final-good transactions? Which is a better measure of the economy's rate of production? Why? What is the relationship between final-good transactions and the sum of the value added of producers?

*Asterisk denotes questions for which answers are given in Appendix C.

*11. Indicate whether the following statements are true or false:

   a. "For the economy as a whole, inventory investment can never be negative."
   b. "The net investment of an economy must always be positive."
   c. "An increase in GDP indicates that the standard of living of people has risen."

*12. How do the receipts and expenditures of a state-operated lottery affect GDP?

13. Distinguish between the consumer price index (CPI) and the GDP deflator. Which is the better measure of price increases?

*14. Indicate how each of the following will affect this year's GDP:

   a. You suffer $10,000 of damage when you wreck your automobile.
   b. You win $10,000 in a state lottery.
   c. You spend $5,200 in January for 100 shares of stock ($5,000 for the stock and $200 for the sales commission) and sell the stock in August for $8,300 ($8,000 for the stock and $300 for the sales commission).
   d. You pay $300 for this month's rental of your apartment.
   e. You are paid $300 for computer services provided to a client.
   f. You receive $300 from your parents.
   g. You get a raise from $4 to $5 per hour and simultaneously decide to reduce your hours worked from 20 to 16 per week.
   h. You earn $2,000 working in Spain as an English instructor.

15. GDP does not count productive services such as child care, food preparation, cleaning, and laundry provided within the household. Why are these things excluded? Is GDP a sexist measure? Does it understate the productive contributions of women relative to men? Discuss.

16. Suppose a group of British investors finances the construction of a plant to manufacture skateboards in St. Louis, Missouri. How will the construction of the plant affect GDP? Suppose the plant generates $100,000 in corporate profits this year. Will these profits contribute to GDP?

*17. Would you rather have a $40,000 income in 1929 or in 1994, assuming you could buy only the goods that were available during each of those years? Explain your answer.

18. What does GNP measure? How does it differ from GDP? Under what circumstances would the GDP of a country be substantially greater than GNP. When would GDP be less than GNP? In the case of the United States, is there much difference between GDP and GNP? Why or why not?

19. The accompanying chart presents 1991 data from the national income accounts of the United States.

NATIONAL INCOME (IN BILLIONS)	
Personal consumption	$3,906
Employee compensation	3,402
Rents	−13
Government purchases	1,099
Imports	621
Depreciation	626
Corporate profits	370
Interest income	463
Exports	602
Gross private investment	737
Indirect business taxes	516
Self-employment income	376
Net income of Americans abroad	17

   a. Indicate the various components of GDP when it is derived by the expenditure approach. Calculate GDP using the expenditure approach.
   b. Indicate the various components of GDP when it is derived by the resource cost-income approach. Calculate GDP using the resource cost-income approach.

20. Fill in the blanks in the following table:

YEAR	NOMINAL GDP (IN BILLIONS)	GDP DEFLATOR (1987 = 100)	REAL GDP (BILLIONS OF 1987 DOLLARS)
1940	$ 100.0	11.0	a. _____
1955	$ 404.3	22.9	b. _____
1965	$ 702.7	c. _____	$2,470.5
1975	d. _____	49.2	$3,221.7
1985	$4,038.7	e. _____	$4,279.8
1991	$5,723.9	117.7	f. _____

---

*Asterisk denotes questions for which answers are given in Appendix C.

CHAPTER SEVEN

ECONOMIC FLUCTUATIONS, UNEMPLOYMENT, AND INFLATION

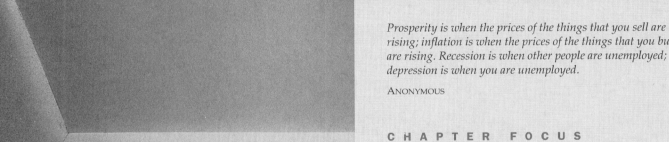

Prosperity is when the prices of the things that you sell are rising; inflation is when the prices of the things that you buy are rising. Recession is when other people are unemployed; depression is when you are unemployed.

ANONYMOUS

CHAPTER FOCUS

- *What is a business cycle? How much economic instability has the United States experienced?*
- *Why do we experience unemployment? Are some types of unemployment worse than others?*
- *What do economists mean by full employment? How is full employment related to the natural rate of unemployment?*
- *How is the rate of inflation measured? What is the difference between anticipated and unanticipated inflation? What are some of the dangers that accompany inflation?*
- *How does the economic performance of the United States stack up with other major industrial countries?*

M easures of output, employment, and the level of prices are widely used to assess the health of an economy. Key indicators of performance in these areas, such as growth of real GDP, the rate of unemployment, and the inflation rate, are closely watched by investors, politicians, and the media. Most governments are committed to the achievement of rapid growth in output, a high level of employment, and relatively stable prices. There is, however, substantial disagreement about what governments can do to accomplish these objectives. In subsequent chapters, this issue will be analyzed in detail.

What happens to output, employment, and prices is closely related to the *economic stability* of a nation. It is crucial to economic efficiency. In this chapter, we will analyze the historical record and discuss some of the measurement problems in regard to the stability of real output, employment, and prices. We will also analyze the side effects of inflation and consider how buyers and sellers adjust their choices when they anticipate rising prices in the future.

Our goal in this chapter is to provide the reader with basic knowledge about the causes of economic instability and how it influences our lives. As we proceed, we will develop a model of our economy that will help us in this endeavor. Then we can better understand the potential for using government policy as a stabilizing force.

SWINGS IN THE ECONOMIC PENDULUM

During this century, the growth rate of real GDP in the United States has averaged approximately 3 percent. The rate of growth, however, has not been steady. **Exhibit 7–1** illustrates the fluctuation of real GDP, beginning with the Great Depression of the 1930s. On several occasions, the annual growth rate of real GDP has exceeded 6 percent for brief periods of time. In other instances, output as

Note that although fluctuations are present, the periods of positive growth outweigh the periods of declining real income. The long-run, real GDP in the United States has grown approximately 3.0 percent annually.

Source: *Economic Report of the President: 1993,* Tables B-2 and B-111.

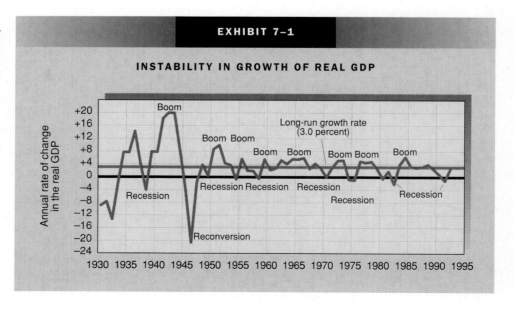

EXHIBIT 7–1

INSTABILITY IN GROWTH OF REAL GDP

measured by real GDP actually declined. During the Great Depression, economic growth plunged. Real GDP declined by 7.5 percent or more each year between 1930 and 1932. In 1933 it was almost 30 percent less than it was in 1929. The 1929 level of real GDP was not reached again until 1939. The Second World War was characterized by a rapid expansion of GDP, which was followed by a decline after the war. Real GDP did not reach its 1944 level again until 1953, although the output of consumer goods did increase significantly in the years immediately following the war as the conversion was made to a peacetime economy.

Since 1950, growth has been more stable. Economic booms and serious declines in the rate of output, though, continue to occur. The years 1954, 1958, 1960, 1974, 1979–1982, and 1991 were characterized by downswings in economic activity. Upswings in real GDP came in 1950, 1955, most of the 1960s, 1972–1973, 1976–1977, and 1983–1988. During the last four decades, however, annual fluctuations in real GDP have fallen within the range of −2 percent to +6 percent. Compared to prior periods, this is a definite improvement.

A HYPOTHETICAL BUSINESS CYCLE

Historically, the United States and all other modern economies have experienced swings in the rate of economic activity. Even economies that have grown significantly over extended time periods have experienced periods of economic expansion followed by economic slowdown and contraction. During the slowdown, real GDP grows at a slower rate, if at all. During the expansion phase, real GDP grows rapidly. Economists refer to these changes in economic conditions as constituting a **business cycle,** meaning a period of increase followed by a decline in aggregate measures of current economic output and income.

Business cycle
Characterized by fluctuations in the general level of economic activity as measured by such variables as the rate of unemployment and changes in real GDP.

Exhibit 7–2 illustrates a hypothetical business cycle. When most businesses are operating at capacity level and real GDP is growing rapidly, a business *peak,* or *boom,* is present. As aggregate business conditions slow, the economy begins the *contraction,* or *recessionary,* phase of a business cycle. During the contraction, the sales of most businesses fall, real GDP grows at a slow rate or perhaps declines, and unemployment in the aggregate labor market increases.

The bottom of the contraction phase is referred to as the *recessionary trough.* After the downturn reaches bottom, and economic conditions begin to improve, the economy enters an *expansionary* stage. Here business sales rise, GDP grows rapidly, and the rate of unemployment declines. The expansion eventually blossoms into another business peak. The peak, however, peters out and turns into a contraction, beginning the cycle anew.

Recession
A downturn in economic activity characterized by declining real GDP and rising unemployment. In an effort to be more precise, many economists define a recession as two consecutive quarters in which there is a decline in real GDP.

The term **recession** is widely used to describe conditions during the contraction and recessionary trough phases of the business cycle—that is, a period during which real GDP declines. Many economists specify that a recession means a decline in real GDP for two or more successive quarters.[1] When a recession is prolonged and characterized by a sharp decline in economic activity, it is called a **depression.**

Depression
A prolonged and very severe recession.

---

[1]See Geoffrey H. Moore, "Recessions" in *The Fortune Encyclopedia of Economics,* edited by David R. Henderson (New York: Time Warner Inc., 1993), for additional information on the timing and length of recessions in the United States.

In the past, ups and downs have often characterized aggregate business activity. Despite these fluctuations there has been an upward trend in real GDP in the United States and other industrial nations.

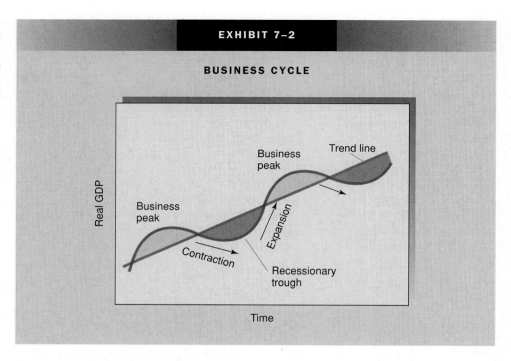

EXHIBIT 7–2

BUSINESS CYCLE

In one important respect, the term *business cycle* is misleading. *Cycle* generally implies that there is some regularity—like that indicated by the hypothetical business cycle of Exhibit 7–2—in the timing and duration of the activity. In the real world, as Exhibit 7–1 illustrates, this is not the case. The observed fluctuations in real output are irregular and unpredictable. The expansions and contractions last varying lengths of time, and the swings differ in terms of their magnitudes. For example, the U.S. economy experienced recessions in 1961, 1970, 1974–1975, 1980, 1982, and again in 1991. The expansion following the recession of 1980 lasted only two years. In contrast, the recessions of 1961 and 1982 were followed by approximately eight years of uninterrupted growth of output. The expansionary phase following the recessions of 1970 and 1974–1975 fell between these two extremes.[2]

ECONOMIC FLUCTUATIONS AND THE LABOR MARKET

Labor force
The portion of the population 16 years of age and over who are either employed or unemployed, according to the official definition of "unemployed."

Fluctuations in real GDP influence the demand for labor and employment. In our modern world, people are busy with jobs, household work, school, and other activities. **Exhibit 7–3** illustrates how economists classify these activities in relation to the **labor force,** defined as that portion of the population 16 years and over

---

[2]See Robert J. Gordon, ed., *The American Business Cycle: Continuity and Change,* (Chicago: University of Chicago Press, 1986), for an excellent set of readings on the topic of business cycles.

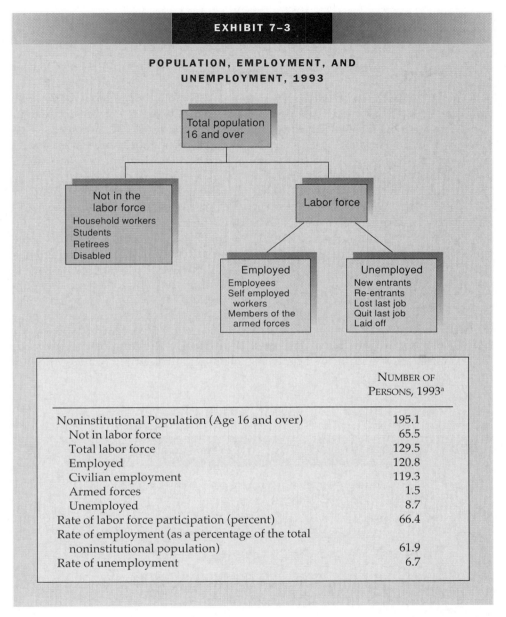

EXHIBIT 7–3

POPULATION, EMPLOYMENT, AND
UNEMPLOYMENT, 1993

Total population
16 and over

Not in the
labor force
Household workers
Students
Retirees
Disabled

Labor force

Employed
Employees
Self employed
workers
Members of the
armed forces

Unemployed
New entrants
Re-entrants
Lost last job
Quit last job
Laid off

	NUMBER OF PERSONS, 1993[a]
Noninstitutional Population (Age 16 and over)	195.1
Not in labor force	65.5
Total labor force	129.5
Employed	120.8
Civilian employment	119.3
Armed forces	1.5
Unemployed	8.7
Rate of labor force participation (percent)	66.4
Rate of employment (as a percentage of the total noninstitutional population)	61.9
Rate of unemployment	6.7

The accompanying diagram illustrates the alternative participation-status categories for the adult population.

[a]Data are measured in millions, except those expressed as percentages. U.S. Department of Labor, *Monthly Labor Review,* March 1994.

who are either working or seeking work. The noninstitutional adult population is grouped into the two broad categories of (1) persons not in the labor force and (2) persons in the labor force. There are a variety of reasons why individuals may not currently be in the labor force. Some are retired. Others may be working in their own household or attending school. Still others may not be working as a result of illness or disability. While many of these people are quite busy, their activities are outside the market labor force.

As Exhibit 7–3 illustrates, unemployed workers who are seeking work are included in the labor force along with employed workers. The **rate of labor-force participation** is the number of persons in the labor force (including both the

Rate of labor-force participation
The number of persons 16 years of age or over who are either employed or actively seeking employment as a percentage of the total noninstitutional population 16 years of age and over.

employed and the unemployed) as a percentage of the total population 16 years of age and over. In 1993, the population (16 years of age and over) of the United States was 195.1 million, 129.5 million of whom were in the labor force. Thus, the U.S. rate of labor-force participation was 66.4 percent (129.5 million divided by 195.1 million).

The rate of labor-force participation varies substantially across countries. For example, in 1990 the rate of labor-force participation was 67 percent in Canada and 66 percent in the United States, but only 55 percent in Germany and 47 percent in Italy. The percent of married women in the labor force is generally smaller in countries like Italy and Germany that have a low rate of labor-force participation.

In the United States, one of the most interesting labor-force developments of the post-Second World War era is the dramatic increase in the labor-force participation rate of women. **Exhibit 7–4** visually illustrates this point. In 1948 the labor-force participation rate of women was 32.7 percent, compared to 87 percent for men. Since then, the market work-participation rate of women has steadily increased while the rate for men has fallen. By 1993, 57.9 percent of adult women worked outside the home. Married women accounted for most of this increase. More than half of all married women now are in the labor force, compared to only 20 percent immediately following the Second World War. In contrast, the labor-force participation rate for men fell to 75 percent in 1993, down from 83 percent in 1960 and 87 percent in 1948. Clearly, the composition of workforce participation within the family has changed substantially during the last four decades.

As the chart illustrates, the labor-force participation rate for women has been steadily increasing for several decades, while the rate for men has been declining.

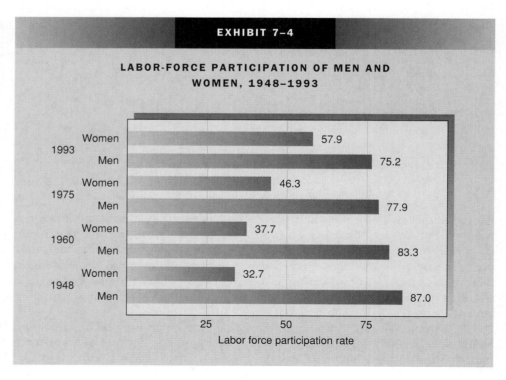

EXHIBIT 7–4

LABOR-FORCE PARTICIPATION OF MEN AND WOMEN, 1948–1993

Year		Labor force participation rate
1993	Women	57.9
	Men	75.2
1975	Women	46.3
	Men	77.9
1960	Women	37.7
	Men	83.3
1948	Women	32.7
	Men	87.0

The **rate of unemployment** is a key barometer of conditions in the aggregate labor market. This notwithstanding, the term is often misunderstood. At the most basic level, it is important to note that unemployment is different from not working. As we have already indicated, there are several reasons—including household work, school attendance, retirement, and illness or disability—why a person may be neither employed nor looking for a job. These people, though not employed, are not counted in the unemployment tally.

Moreover, persons must either be employed or **unemployed** before they are counted as part of the labor force. The rate of unemployment is the number of persons unemployed expressed as a percentage of the labor force. In 1993 the rate of unemployment in the United States was 6.7 percent (8.7 million out of a labor force of 129.5 million). (See the "Measures of Economic Activity" boxed feature for information on how the Bureau of Labor Statistics derives the unemployment rate.)

Rate of unemployment
The percent of persons in the labor force who are unemployed, according to the official definition of "unemployed." Mathematically, it is equal to

$$\frac{\text{Number of persons unemployed}}{\text{Number in the labor force}} \times 100$$

Unemployed
The term used to describe a person not currently employed who is either (1) actively seeking employment or (2) waiting to begin or return to a job.

MEASURES OF ECONOMIC ACTIVITY

DERIVING THE UNEMPLOYMENT RATE

Each month, the Bureau of Labor Statistics (BLS) of the U.S. Department of Labor calculates the number of people employed, unemployed, and not in the labor force. Because it would be too burdensome, the BLS does not contact each person in the United States to determine his or her employment status. Instead, it randomly samples 59,500 households drawn from 729 different locations in the United States. The survey is conducted during the week containing the twelfth day of each month and is designed to reflect geographic and demographic groups in proportion to their representation in the nation as a whole.

Specially trained interviewers pose identical questions in the same order to each of the 59,500 households (which include approximately 100,000 adults). People are classified as employed, unemployed, or not in the labor force on the basis of their responses to questions designed to elicit this information. People are considered *employed* if they (1) worked at all (even as little as one hour) for pay or profit during the survey week, (2) worked 15 hours or more without pay in a family-operated enterprise during the week, or (3) have a job at which they did not work during the survey week because of illness, vacation, industrial disputes, bad weather, time off, or personal reasons.

People are considered *unemployed* if they (1) do not have a job, (2) are available for work, and (3) have actively looked for work during the past four weeks. Looking for work may involve any of the following activities: (1) registration at a public or private employment office, (2) meeting with prospective employers, (3) checking with friends or relatives, (4) placing or answering advertisements, (5) writing letters of application, or (6) being on a union or professional register. In addition, those not working are classified as unemployed if they are either waiting to start a new job within 30 days or waiting to be recalled from a layoff.

Only people in the labor force—that is, only those classified as either employed or unemployed—enter into the calculation of the *unemployment rate*, which is the number of people unemployed divided by the number of people in the labor force. Based on its survey data, the BLS publishes the unemployment rate and other employment-related statistics monthly. Since employment and unemployment patterns vary during the year due to holidays, vacations, shifts in production schedules, and other seasonally related reasons, the unemployment data are seasonally adjusted. In addition, states use the BLS survey data and employment data from industries covered by unemployment insurance to construct state and area unemployment estimates based on BLS guidelines. The major sources of employment data are the *Monthly Labor Review* and *Employment and Earnings*, monthly publications of the U.S. Department of Labor.

REASONS FOR UNEMPLOYMENT

Not all people who are unemployed lost their last job. A dynamic economy will be characterized by considerable labor mobility as workers move (1) from contracting to expanding industries and (2) into and out of the labor force. Spells of unemployment often accompany such changes.

The Department of Labor indicates five reasons why workers may experience unemployment. **Exhibit 7–5** indicates the share of unemployed workers in each of these five categories in 1993. Interestingly, 10.0 percent of the unemployed workers were first-time entrants into the work force. Another 24.6 percent were reentering after exiting for additional schooling, household work, or other reasons. Thus, more than one-third of the unemployed workers were experiencing unemployment as the result of entry or reentry into the labor force. Approximately 11 percent of the unemployed quit their last job. People laid off and waiting to return to their previous positions contributed 12.6 percent to the total. Workers terminated from their last job accounted for 42 percent of the unemployed workers.

In a dynamic world where information is imperfect and people are free to choose among jobs, some unemployment is inevitable. As new products are introduced and new technologies developed, some firms are expanding while others are contracting. Still other firms may be going out of business. This process results in the creation of new jobs and the disappearance of old ones. Similarly, at any point in time potential workers are switching from school (or nonwork) into the labor force, while others are retiring or taking a leave from the labor force. As long as workers are mobile—as long as they can voluntarily quit and search for better

This chart indicates the various reasons why persons were unemployed in 1993. More than two-fifths (42 percent) of the persons unemployed were terminated from their last job. More than one-third of the unemployed workers were new entrants and re-entrants to the labor force.

Source: *Monthly Labor Review, March 1994.*

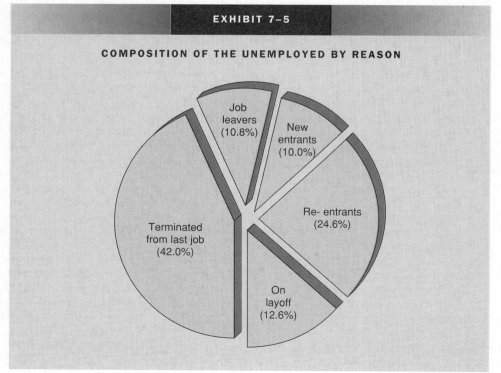

EXHIBIT 7–5

COMPOSITION OF THE UNEMPLOYED BY REASON

Job leavers (10.8%)

New entrants (10.0%)

Re- entrants (24.6%)

On layoff (12.6%)

Terminated from last job (42.0%)

opportunities in a changing world, switching from one job to another and reallocating work responsibilities within the family—some unemployment will be present.

There is a positive side to job search and unemployment: it generally permits individuals to better match their skills and preferences with the requirements of a job. Such job moves enhance both employee productivity and earnings.

Young workers often switch jobs and move between schooling and the labor force as they search for a career path that best fits their abilities and preferences. As the result of this job switching, the unemployment rate of younger workers is substantially higher than for more established workers. As **Exhibit 7–6** shows, in 1993 the unemployment rate of young men was more than double the rate for men age 25 years and over. Similarly, the unemployment rate of young women was well above the rate for older women.

THREE TYPES OF UNEMPLOYMENT

While some unemployment is perfectly consistent with economic efficiency, this is not always the case. Abnormally high rates of unemployment generally reflect weak demand conditions for labor, counterproductive policies, and/or the inability or lack of incentive on the part of potential workers and potential employers to arrive at mutually advantageous agreements. To clarify matters, economists divide unemployment into three categories: frictional, structural, and cyclical. Let us take a closer look at each of these three classifications.

FRICTIONAL UNEMPLOYMENT.   Unemployment that is caused by constant changes in the labor market is called **frictional unemployment.** It occurs because (1) employers are not fully aware of all available workers and their job qualifications and (2) available workers are not fully aware of the jobs being offered by employers. In other words, the basic cause of frictional unemployment is

Frictional unemployment
Unemployment due to constant changes in the economy that prevent qualified *unemployed workers from being immediately matched up with existing job openings. It results from lack of complete information on the part of both job seekers and employers and from the amount of unemployed time spent by job seekers in job searches (pursuit of costly information).*

Source: *Monthly Labor Review,* March 1994.

EXHIBIT 7–6

UNEMPLOYMENT RATE BY AGE AND SEX, 1993

Group	Civilian Rate of Unemployment, 1993 (Percent)
Total, all workers	6.8
Men, Total	7.1
Ages 16–19	20.4
Ages 20–24	11.3
Ages 25 and over	5.8
Women, Total	6.5
Ages 16–19	17.4
Ages 20–24	9.6
Ages 25 and over	5.4

imperfect information. The number of job vacancies may match up with the number of persons seeking employment. The qualifications of the job seekers may even meet those required by firms seeking employees. Frictional unemployment will still occur, however, because persons seeking jobs and firms hiring employees with the qualifications of the job seekers do not know about each other. In the real world, information is scarce. Both employers and employees will search for information that will help them make better choices.

Employers looking for a new worker seldom hire the first applicant who walks into their employment office. They want to find the "best available" worker to fill their opening. It is costly to hire workers who perform poorly. It is sometimes even costly to terminate their employment. So, employers search—they expend time and resources screening applicants in an effort to find the best qualified workers willing to accept their wage and employment conditions.

Similarly, unemployed workers seeking a job usually do not accept the first one offered. They, too, search among potential alternatives, seeking their best option. They make telephone calls, respond to newspaper ads, submit to job interviews, use employment services, and so on. Pursuit of personal gain—the landing of a job that is more attractive than the current options of which they are aware— motivates job seekers to engage in job search activities.

Additional search leads to the discovery of higher paying, preferable alternatives. However, as a job searcher finds out about more potential job opportunities, it becomes less likely that additional search will uncover a more preferable option. Therefore, as **Exhibit 7–7** illustrates, the marginal gain from job search declines with time spent searching. The primary cost of job search is generally the opportunity cost of wages forgone as the result of failure to accept one's best current alternative. This cost will increase as additional search leads to the discovery of better alternatives not accepted. Thus, the marginal cost of job search will rise with time spent searching.

The marginal gain from job search generally declines with time spent searching for a job, because it becomes less likely that additional search will lead to a better position. Conversely, the marginal cost of additional search rises with search time, primarily because still more search means forgoing wages on more attractive jobs discovered by prior search. When the job seeker perceives that the marginal gain from additional search no longer exceeds the marginal cost, the best option discovered by the search process will be accepted.

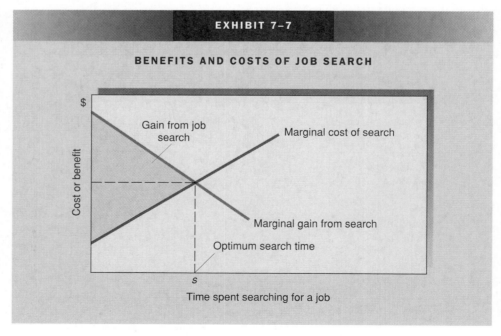

EXHIBIT 7–7

BENEFITS AND COSTS OF JOB SEARCH

The rational job seeker will search for employment as long as the expected marginal gain from the search exceeds the expected marginal cost of the search. Eventually, as the marginal gains decline and marginal costs rise, the job seekers will conclude that additional search is not worth the cost. The best alternative resulting from the search process will be accepted. However, this process takes time, and during this time the job seeker is contributing to the frictional unemployment of the economy.

It is important to note that even though frictional unemployment is a side effect, the job search process typically leads to improved economic efficiency and a higher real income for employees (see "Myths of Economics"). If a job seeker were to search less than the optimal amount (search time S in Exhibit 7–7), potential gains (from the achievement of a better job) in excess of the marginal search costs would be forgone. Similarly, job search beyond the optimal level is simply not worth the cost.

Policies that influence the costs and benefits of searching will influence the level of unemployment. If the job seeker's search costs are reduced, he or she will spend more time searching. For example, higher unemployment benefits make it less costly to continue looking for a preferred job. This decline in the marginal cost of job search (a shift of the marginal cost curve to the right in Exhibit 7–7) will induce job seekers to expand their search time beyond the optimal level. A higher level of unemployment will result.

STRUCTURAL UNEMPLOYMENT. In the case of **structural unemployment,** changes in the basic characteristics of the economy prevent the "matching up" of available jobs with available workers. It is not always easy to distinguish between frictional and structural unemployment. In each case, job openings and potential workers searching for jobs are present. The crucial difference between the two is that with frictional unemployment, workers possess the requisite skills to fill the job openings; with structural unemployment, they do not. Essentially, the skills of a structurally unemployed worker have been rendered obsolete by changing market conditions and technology. Realistically, the structurally unemployed worker faces the prospect of either a career change or prolonged unemployment. For older workers in particular, these are bleak alternatives.

There are many causes of structural unemployment. Dynamic change is of course at the top of the list. The introduction of new products or productive methods can substantially alter the employment and earnings opportunities of even highly skilled workers, particularly if the skills are not easily transferable to other industries. Many automobile workers experienced this reality in the early 1980s, as increased competition from foreign producers and changing technology reduced employment in the U.S. automobile industry.

Shifts in public-sector priorities can also cause structural unemployment. As changing international conditions permitted the United States to significantly reduce national defense expenditures in the early 1990s, these expenditure cuts resulted in substantial increases in unemployment in several regions. Southern California and New England were particularly hard hit since they were heavily dependent on the defense industry. Since the skills of many workers who lost their jobs in defense-related industries were not well suited for employment in expanding sectors of the economy, structural unemployment was a result.

Institutional factors that reduce the ability of employees to obtain skills necessary to fill existing job openings also increase structural unemployment. For

Structural unemployment
Unemployment due to structural changes in the economy that eliminate some jobs while generating job openings for which the unemployed workers are not well suited.

MYTHS OF ECONOMICS

"UNEMPLOYED RESOURCES WOULD NOT EXIST IF THE ECONOMY WERE OPERATING EFFICIENTLY."

Nobody likes unemployment. Certainly, extended unemployment can be a very painful experience. Not all unemployment, however, reflects waste and inefficiency. If the resources of an economy are going to be used effectively, the skills of workers must be matched with the jobs of employers. People must end up working on jobs that fit their knowledge, skills, and preferences. Similarly, firms must employ workers that are well suited for their jobs. Waste will result if, for example, a person with high-level computer skills ends up working as a janitor while someone else with minimal computer skills is employed as a computer programmer.

Prospective employees searching for the right job need information on job requirements and availability, wage rates, work environment, and so on. This information is scarce and is generally acquired by "shopping"—by searching for employment. Thus, job seekers usually do not take just any available job. They shop for jobs in order to acquire valuable information that will help them find employment that fits their skills, earning capabilities, and preferences.

Similarly, employers shop when they are seeking labor services. They, too, acquire information about available workers that will help them select employees whose skills and preferences match with the demands of the job. The shopping of job seekers and employers results in some unemployment, but it also communicates information that leads to a better match between the characteristics of job seekers and job requirements. Improvement in the match between employees and

jobs will lead to an expansion in real output and higher wage rates. Thus, job search can yield a return (in excess of its cost) to both the individual and the society. Such job search, even though it often involves unemployment, is a natural part of an efficiently operating labor market.

Perhaps thinking about the housing market will help the reader better understand why search time can be both beneficial and productive. As with the employment market, the housing market is characterized by dynamic change. New housing structures are brought into the market; older structures depreciate and wear out. Families move from one community to another. In this dynamic world, it makes sense for renters from time to time to shop among the available accommodations, seeking the housing quality, price, and location that best fits their preferences and budget. Similarly, landlords search among renters, seeking to rent their accommodations to those who value them most highly. "Frictional unemployment" of houses is inevitable, but does it indicate inefficiency? No. It results from people's attempts to acquire information that will eventually promote an efficient match between housing units and renters.

Of course, some types of unemployment, particularly cyclical unemployment, are indicative of inefficiency. However, the frictional unemployment that results from the shopping of job seekers and employers helps decision makers make better choices and results in a more efficient match of applicants with job openings than would otherwise be possible. It is perfectly consistent with economic efficiency.

example, minimum wage legislation may reduce the incentive of business firms to offer on-the-job training to low-skill workers, thereby contributing to structural unemployment.

CYCLICAL UNEMPLOYMENT. When there is a general downturn in business activity, **cyclical unemployment** arises. Since fewer goods are being produced, fewer workers are required to produce them. Employers lay off workers and cut back employment.

Cyclical unemployment
Unemployment due to recessionary business conditions and inadequate aggregate demand for labor.

Unexpected reductions in the general level of demand for goods and services are the major cause of cyclical unemployment. In a world of imperfect information, adjustments to unexpected declines in demand will be painful. When the demand for labor declines generally, workers will at first not know whether they are being laid off because of a specific shift in demand away from their previous employer or because of a general decline in aggregate demand. Similarly, they will not be sure whether their current bleak employment prospects are temporary or long-term. Workers will search for employment, hoping to find a job at or near their old wage rate. If their situation was merely the result of shifts among employers in demand, or if the downturn is brief, terminated workers will soon find new employment similar to their old jobs. When there is a general decline in demand, however, most workers' search efforts will be fruitless. Their duration of unemployment will be abnormally long.

With time, unemployed workers will lower their expectations and be willing to take some cut in wages. However, when the reduction in aggregate demand is substantial, the adjustment process may be lengthy and a substantial increase in the unemployment rate is the expected result. As we proceed, we will investigate potential sources of cyclical unemployment and consider policy alternatives to reduce it.

EMPLOYMENT FLUCTUATIONS— THE HISTORICAL RECORD

Employment and output are closely linked over the business cycle. If we are going to produce more goods and services, we must either increase the number of workers or increase the output per worker. While *output*, or productivity per worker, is an important source of long-term economic growth, it changes slowly from year to year.

Thus, rapid increases in output, such as those that occur during a strong business expansion, generally require an increase in employment. As a result, output and employment tend to be positively related. Thus, the unemployment rate generally increases when the economy dips into a recession.

The empirical evidence of **Exhibit 7–8** illustrates the inverse relationship between output and rate of unemployment. When output declines during a recession, the unemployment rate generally rises. During the recessions of 1958 and 1960–1961, unemployment rose to approximately 7 percent. In contrast, it declined throughout the economic boom of the 1960s, only to rise again during the recession of 1970. During the recession of 1974–1975, the unemployment rate jumped to more than 9 percent. Similarly, it soared to nearly 11 percent during the severe, but relatively brief, recession of 1982 and to 7.6 percent during the 1991 recession. Conversely, it declined substantially during the economic boom of the 1960s and the expansions of 1976–1978 and 1982–1989.

THE CONCEPT OF FULL EMPLOYMENT

Full employment, a term widely used by economists and public officials alike, does not mean zero unemployment. In the United States, it means that 94 to 95 percent of the labor force is employed. In a world of imperfect information, employers and employees will "shop" before they buy and sell, and much of this shopping is efficient, since it leads to a better match between the skills of employees and the skills necessary to carry out productive tasks. Some unemployment is thus entirely consistent with the efficient operation of a dynamic labor market.

Full employment
The level of employment that results from the efficient use of the labor force after allowance is made for the normal (natural) rate of unemployment due to information cost, dynamic changes, and the structural conditions of the economy. For the United States, full employment is thought to exist when between 94 and 95 percent of the labor force is employed.

The unemployment rate increases during recessions (such as those experienced in 1974–1975, 1982, and 1991) and declines during economic expansions (for example, the 1960s boom and 1983–1989 expansion). The estimated natural rate of unemployment is also indicated. Note that the actual unemployment rate is substantially greater than the natural rate during recessions.

Source: *Economic Report of the President: 1994;* and Robert J. Gordon, *Macroeconomics* (Boston: Little, Brown, 1990).

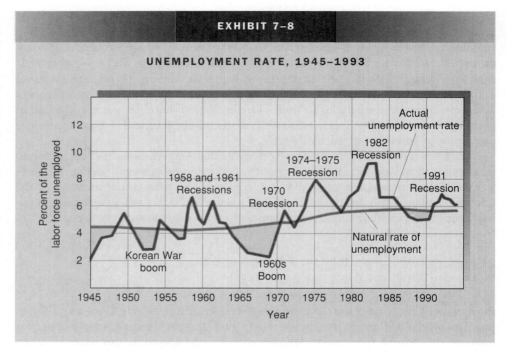

EXHIBIT 7–8

UNEMPLOYMENT RATE, 1945–1993

Natural rate of unemployment

The long-run average unemployment rate due to frictional and structural conditions of labor markets. This rate is affected both by dynamic change and by public policy. It is sustainable into the future.

Consequently, economists define full employment as the level of employment that results when the rate of unemployment is normal, considering both frictional and structural factors. As mentioned, most economists put this figure at 94 to 95 percent of the labor force.

This **natural rate of unemployment** that is incorporated in the concept of full employment arises from employees and employers shopping in a world characterized by both (1) dynamic change and (2) imperfect (scarce) information concerning job opportunities and the availability of potential workers. Both frictional and structural factors are involved. The natural rate of unemployment is not a temporary high or low, it is sustainable into the future. Economists sometimes refer to it as the unemployment rate accompanying the economy's "maximum sustainable rate of output."

The natural rate of unemployment, though, is not immutably fixed. It is influenced both by the structure of the labor force and by changes in public policy. For example, since youthful workers experience more unemployment because they change jobs and move in and out of the labor force often (refer again to Exhibit 7–6), the natural rate of unemployment increases when youthful workers comprise a larger proportion of the work force. This is precisely what happened during the 1960s and 1970s. In 1958 youthful workers (ages 16 to 24) constituted only 15.6 percent of the labor force. As the postwar "baby boom" generation entered the labor market, youthful workers as a share of the labor force rose dramatically. By 1980 one out of every four workers was in the youthful-worker grouping. In contrast, prime-age workers (over age 25) declined from 84.4 percent of the U.S. work force in 1958 to only 75.3 percent in 1980. Studies indicate that this increased representation of youthful workers pushed the natural rate of unemployment up by approximately 1.5 percent during the 1958–1980 period. (See the estimated natural rate of unemployment in Exhibit 7–8.)

Public policies also affect the natural rate of unemployment. Policies that (1) encourage workers to reject job offers and continue to search for employment, (2) prohibit employers from offering wage rates that would induce them to employ (and train) low-skill workers, and (3) reduce the employer's opportunity cost of using layoffs to adjust rates of production will increase the natural rate of unemployment. With regard to these points, most economists believe that increases in the legislated minimum wage and higher unemployment benefits push the natural rate of unemployment upward.

Exhibit 7–8 illustrates the relationship between the actual unemployment rate and the natural unemployment rate during the last five decades. The actual unemployment rate fluctuates around the natural rate, in response to cyclical economic conditions. The actual rate generally rises above the natural rate during a recession and falls below the natural rate when the economy is in the midst of an economic boom. For example, the actual rate of unemployment was substantially above the natural rate during the recessions of 1974–1975 and 1982, while the reverse was the case during the economic boom of the 1960s. As we proceed, we will often compare the actual and natural rates of unemployment. In a very real sense, macroeconomics studies why the actual and natural rates differ and attempts to discern the factors that cause the natural rate to change with the passage of time.

Without detracting from the importance of full employment—in the sense of maximum sustainable employment—we must not overlook another vital point. Employment is a means to an end. We use employment to produce desired goods and services. Full employment is an empty concept if it means employment at unproductive jobs. It is a meaningful concept only if it refers to productive employment that will generate goods and services desired by consumers at the lowest possible cost.

RATES OF UNEMPLOYMENT AND EMPLOYMENT—SOME MEASUREMENT PROBLEMS

The definition of *unemployment* is not without ambiguity. Remember that persons are counted as unemployed only if they are (1) available for and seeking work or (2) awaiting recall from a layoff. These criteria can lead to some paradoxical outcomes. For example, a person who quits looking for work because his or her job-seeking efforts have been discouraging is not counted as unemployed. On the other hand, a welder vacationing in Florida, receiving unemployment compensation while awaiting recall to a $50,000-per-year job in the automobile industry, is considered to be among the ranks of the unemployed.

One can argue that the statistical definition of unemployment results both in (1) people being excluded even though they would prefer to be working (or working more) and (2) people being included who are not seriously seeking employment. **Discouraged workers** are those whose employment prospects are so bleak that they no longer consider it worthwhile to search for employment. Though not counted as unemployed, many of them would be willing to accept employment were it available. When the economy turns down, the number of workers in the

Discouraged workers
Persons who have given up searching for employment because they believe additional job search would be fruitless. Since they are not currently searching for work, they are not counted among the unemployed.

discouraged category rises substantially. For example, during the 1991 recession, the Department of Labor estimated that there were one million discouraged workers (approximately 0.8 percent of the labor force) in the United States, up from 715,000 prior to the recession.

The method of classifying part-time workers may also result in an understatement of the number of unemployed workers. Part-time workers who desire full-time employment are classified as employed rather than unemployed if they work as much as a single hour per week. Yet these people are certainly underemployed, if not unemployed.

On the other hand, some people who claim to be searching for work, and are thus classified as unemployed are not seriously seeking employment. For example, an individual who rejects available employment because it is less attractive than the current combination of household work, continued job search, unemployment benefits, food stamps, and other government welfare programs is numbered among the unemployed. The work-registration requirement that accompanies several government income-assistance programs, including food stamps and Aid to Families with Dependent Children (AFDC), further adds to the ambiguity of the unemployment statistics. Many recipients of income-transfer programs register for work in order to qualify for the assistance even though they have no plans to search for and accept employment. According to a study by Lawrence Summers and Kim Clark of Harvard University, the work-registration requirements accompanying government assistance programs increases the number of people who are counted as unemployed by 600,000 to 1 million people, approximately 0.5 to 0.8 percent of the labor force.[3] In addition, unemployment insurance benefits push up the measured unemployment rate by reducing the incentive of recipients to accept available jobs while inducing them to indicate that they are job hunting in order to qualify for the benefits.

If they are not otherwise gainfully employed, people engaged in criminal activities (for example, drug pushers, gamblers, and prostitutes) or working "off the books" in the underground economy may also be numbered among the unemployed. Although estimates are difficult to project, some researchers believe that as many as 1 million people classified as unemployed are active participants in the underground economy.

Rate of employment
The number of persons 16 years of age and over who are employed as a percentage of the total noninstitutional population 16 years of age and over. One can calculate either (1) a civilian rate of employment, in which only civilian employees are included in the numerator, or (2) a total rate of employment, in which both civilian and military employees are included in the numerator.

As a result of these ambiguities, some economists argue that the **rate of employment**—the number of persons employed (over the age of 16) as a percentage of the total population over 16 years of age—is a more objective and meaningful indicator of job availability than is the rate of unemployment. Both variables involved in calculating the rate of employment (the level of employment and the adult population) can be readily measured. In addition, they are relatively clear. Their measurement does not require a subjective judgment as to whether a person is actually "available for work" or "actively seeking employment."

The rate of employment is relatively free of several defects that may distort the unemployment figures. For example, when a large number of discouraged

---

[3]Lawrence H. Summers and Kim B. Clark. "Labor Market Dynamics and Unemployment: A Reconsideration," *Brookings Papers on Economic Activity* 1 (1979): 99. 13–60. Also see Lawrence H. Summers, *Understanding Unemployment* (Cambridge, Mass., MIT Press, 1990).

job seekers stop looking for work, the rate of unemployment drops. The rate of employment, however, does not follow such a misleading course.

Which of the two figures should the wise observer follow? The answer is both. Our economy has been undergoing several structural changes that affect both the rate of unemployment and the rate of employment. The increased incidence of working wives, changes in the proportion of youthful workers as a percentage of the labor force, and changes in eligibility requirements for various income transfer programs—all of these factors contribute to the diversity of the unemployed population. Clearly, "the unemployed" is not a homogeneous category.

ACTUAL AND POTENTIAL GDP

If an economy is going to realize its potential, full employment is essential. When the actual rate of unemployment exceeds the natural rate, the actual output of the economy will fall below its potential. Some resources that could be productively employed will be underutilized.

The Council of Economic Advisers defines the **potential output** as: "the amount of output that could be expected at full employment. . . . It does not represent the absolute maximum level of production that could be generated by wartime or other abnormal levels of aggregate demand, but rather that which would be expected from high utilization rates obtainable under more normal circumstances."

The concept of potential output encompasses two important ideas: (1) full utilization of resources, including labor, and (2) an output constraint. Potential output might properly be thought of as the maximum sustainable output level consistent with the economy's resource base, given its institutional arrangements.

Estimates of the potential output level involve three major elements: the size of the labor force, the quality (productivity) of labor, and the natural rate of unemployment. Since these factors cannot be estimated with certainty, there is some variation in the estimated values of the potential rate of output for the U.S. economy. Relying on the projections of potential output developed by the Council of Economic Advisers, **Exhibit 7–9** illustrates the record of the U.S. economy since 1965. During the latter half of the 1960s, output expanded and even temporarily exceeded the sustainable potential output rate of the economy. However, during the recessions of 1969–1970, 1974–1975, 1982, and 1991, output fell well below the economy's potential.

Note the similarity in the pattern of the actual real GDP data of Exhibit 7–9 and the hypothetical data of an idealized business cycle of Exhibit 7–2. While the actual data of Exhibit 7–9 are irregular compared to the hypothetical data, nonetheless periods of expansion and economic boom followed by contraction and recession are clearly observable. During the boom phase, actual output expands rapidly and may temporarily exceed the economy's long-run potential. In contrast, recessions are characterized by an actual real GDP that is less than potential. As we proceed, we will focus on how we can achieve the maximum potential output while minimizing economic instability.

Potential output
The level of output that can be achieved and sustained into the future, given the size of the labor force, expected productivity of labor, and natural rate of unemployment consistent with the efficient operation of the labor market. For periods of time, the actual output may differ from the economy's potential.

The graph indicates the gap between the actual and potential GDP for the period from 1965 to 1993. Note the gap between the actual and potential GDP during the recessions of 1969–1970, 1974–1975, 1982 and 1991.

Source: U.S. Department of Commerce, Bureau of Economic Analysis.

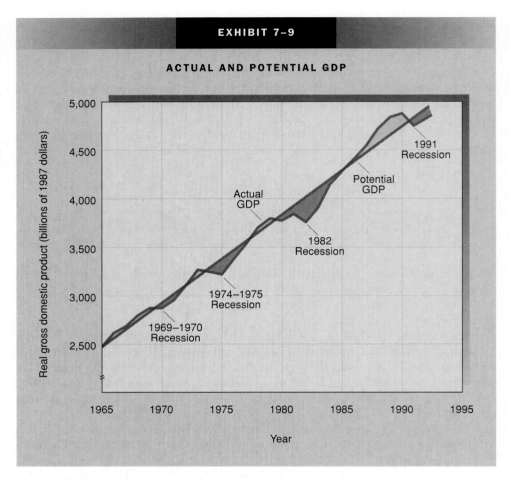

EXHIBIT 7–9

ACTUAL AND POTENTIAL GDP

EFFECTS OF INFLATION: AN OVERVIEW

Inflation

A continuing rise in the general level of prices of goods and services. The purchasing power of the monetary unit, such as the dollar, declines when inflation is present.

Inflation is a continuing rise in the level of prices, such that it costs more to purchase the typical bundle of goods and services that is produced and/or consumed. Of course, even when the general level of prices is stable, some prices will be rising and others will be falling. During a period of inflation, however, the impact of the rising prices will outweigh that of falling prices. Because of the higher prices (on average), a dollar will purchase less than it did previously. Inflation, therefore, might also be defined as a decline in the value (the purchasing power) of the monetary unit.

How do we determine whether prices, in general, are rising or falling? Essentially, we answered that question in the last chapter when we indicated how a price index is constructed. When prices are rising, on average, the price index will also rise. The annual inflation rate is simply the percent change in the price index (PI) from one year to the next. Mathematically, the inflation rate (i) can be written as:

$$i = \frac{\text{This year's PI} - \text{last year's PI}}{\text{last year's PI}} \times 100$$

So if the price index this year was 220, compared to 200 last year, the inflation rate would equal 10 percent:

$$\frac{220 - 200}{200} \times 100$$

The consumer price index (CPI) and the GDP deflator are the price indexes most widely used to measure the inflation rate in the United States. Since the CPI and the GDP deflator are calculated monthly and quarterly, respectively, we often compare their value during a specific month (or quarter) with their value during the same month (or quarter) one year earlier to calculate the inflation rate during the most recent 12 months.

How rapidly have prices risen in the United States? **Exhibit 7-10** illustrates the record since 1930. Prices declined sharply during the early years of the Great Depression. In contrast, the Second World War was characterized by a double-digit inflation rate. During the 1950s and into the mid-1960s, the annual inflation rate was generally low. The average inflation rate during the 1952–1966 period was 1.5 percent. Beginning in the latter half of the 1960s, inflation began to accelerate upward, jumping to 12 percent or more during 1974, 1979, and 1980. During the 1967–1982

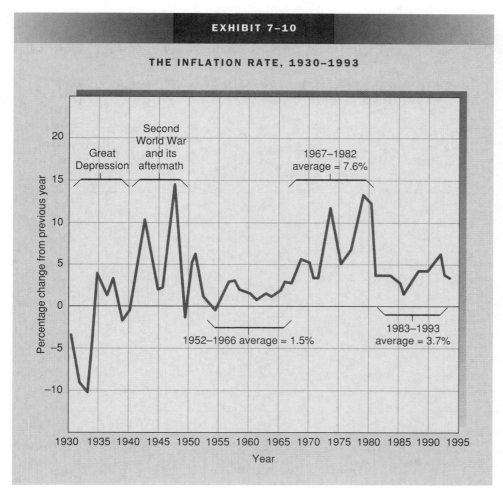

EXHIBIT 7-10

THE INFLATION RATE, 1930–1993

Great Depression

Second World War and its aftermath

1967–1982 average = 7.6%

1952–1966 average = 1.5%

1983–1993 average = 3.7%

Percentage change from previous year

Year

Prices fell as the economy plunged into the Great Depression during the 1930s. The Second World War was characterized by high rates of inflation. During the 1952–1966 period, prices increased at an annual rate of only 1.5 percent. In contrast, the inflation rate averaged 7.6 percent during the 1967–1982 era, reaching double-digit rates during several years. During 1983–1993 the rate of inflation averaged 3.7 percent annually.

period, the inflation rate averaged 7.6 percent. Price increases moderated again in the mid-1980s, as the inflation rate averaged 3.7 percent during 1983–1993.

The rate of inflation varies widely among countries. **Exhibit 7–11** provides data on the annual inflation rates during 1986–1992 for Japan, Singapore, United States, Germany, Canada, and Thailand—six countries with low rates of inflation. The annual inflation rate of these countries was generally less than 5 percent during this period, and moreover, the year-to-year variation was relatively small. The inflation rate of these countries seldom changed by more than 1 or 2 percent from one year to the next.

Exhibit 7–11 also presents parallel inflation rate data for six high-inflation countries: Venezuela, Turkey, Mexico, Brazil, Argentina, and Zaire. In contrast with the low-inflation countries, the inflation rate of the high-inflation countries was not only higher, it varied substantially more from one year to another. For example, consider the data for Venezuela. The inflation rate of Venezuela jumped from 11.5 percent in 1986 to 28.4 percent in 1987 and 84.3 percent in 1989, before receding to 40.8 percent in 1990 and 34.2 percent in 1991 and 1992. In Brazil the inflation rose from 145 percent in 1986 to 682.8 percent in 1988 and 2928.4 percent in 1990. This latter figure indicates that the general level of prices in Brazil in 1990

EXHIBIT 7–11

VARIATION IN ANNUAL INFLATION RATE OF SELECTED COUNTRIES, 1986–1992

	RATE OF INFLATION						
COUNTRY	1986	1987	1988	1989	1990	1991	1992
LOW INFLATION							
Japan	0.6	0.1	0.7	2.3	3.1	3.3	1.7
Singapore	−1.4	0.5	1.5	2.4	3.5	3.4	2.3
United States	1.9	3.7	4.0	4.3	5.4	4.5	3.6
Germany	−0.1	0.2	1.3	2.8	2.7	3.5	4.0
Canada	4.2	4.4	4.0	5.0	4.8	5.6	1.5
Thailand	1.8	2.6	3.8	5.4	5.9	5.7	4.1
HIGH INFLATION							
Venezuela	11.5	28.4	29.5	84.3	40.8	34.2	34.2
Turkey	34.6	38.8	75.4	63.3	60.3	66.0	70.1
Mexico	86.2	131.8	114.2	20.0	26.7	22.7	15.5
Brazil	145.0	229.8	682.8	1,286.9	2,928.4	440.7	1,008.7
Argentina	90.0	131.6	342.7	3,079.2	2,311.3	171.7	29.9
Zaire	46.7	90.4	82.7	104.1	81.3	2,154.7	4,129.7

Source: International Monetary Fund, *International Financial Statistics,* August 1993. The consumer price index was used to measure the inflation rate of each country.

was more than 29 times the level of just one year earlier! The data of Exhibit 7–11 reflect a general pattern. High rates of inflation are almost always associated with wide year-to-year swings in the inflation rate.

ANTICIPATED AND UNANTICIPATED INFLATION

Before examining the effects of inflation, it is important that we distinguish between unanticipated and anticipated inflation. **Unanticipated inflation** is an increase in the price level that comes as a surprise, at least to most individuals. It may either exceed or fall short of the inflation rate expected by most people. For example, suppose that based on the recent past, most people anticipate an inflation rate of 4 percent. If the actual inflation rate turns out to be 10 percent, it will catch people off-guard. A rate of zero will do the same.

When the rate of inflation is high and variable, like the rates for the high-inflation countries of Exhibit 7–11, it will be virtually impossible for decision makers to anticipate future rates accurately, and long-range planning will be extremely difficult.

Anticipated inflation is a change in the price level that is widely expected. Decision makers are generally able to anticipate slow steady rates of inflation—such as those present in Japan, Singapore, United States, Germany, Canada, and Thailand during 1986–1992—with a high degree of accuracy.

Contrary to the satirical statement at the beginning of the chapter, inflation will affect the prices of things we sell as well as the prices of goods we buy. Both resource and product prices are influenced by inflation. Before we become too upset about inflation "robbing us of the purchasing power of our paychecks," we should recognize that inflation influences the size of those paychecks. The weekly earnings of employees would not have risen at an annual rate of 7 percent during the 1970s if the rate of inflation had not increased rapidly during that period. Wages are a price, also. Inflation raises both wages and prices.

Unanticipated inflation
Increase in the general level of prices that was not expected by most decision makers.

Anticipated inflation
An increase in the general level of prices that is expected by economic decision makers based on their evaluation of past experience and current conditions.

DANGERS OF INFLATION

Simply because money income initially tends to rise with prices, it does not follow that there is no need to be concerned about inflation, particularly high rates of inflation. Two negative aspects of inflation are particularly important.

First, inflation can frustrate the intent of long-term contracts. Since the rate of inflation varies, it cannot be predicted with certainty. Most market exchanges, including long-term contracts, are made in money terms. If unanticipated inflation takes place, it can change the result of long-term contracts, such as mortgages, life insurance policies, pensions, bonds, and other arrangements that involve a debtor-lender relationship.

As we previously indicated, higher rates of inflation are generally associated with greater year-to-year-variability in the price level. This variability adds to the risks of time dimension contracts. If price level changes are unpredictable (for example, if price level rises 10 percent one year, 5 percent the next year, and then increases again by 10 or 15 percent the following year), no one knows what to expect. Long-term money exchanges must take into account the uncertainty created by high and variable rates of inflation. Given this additional uncertainty, many decision makers will forgo exchanges involving long-term contracts. Because of this, mutually advantageous gains will be lost and the efficiency of markets is thus reduced.[4]

A second negative effect of inflation is that real resources are used up as decision makers seek to protect themselves from it. Since the failure to accurately anticipate the rate of inflation can have a substantial effect on one's wealth, individuals will divert scarce resources from the production of desired goods and services to the acquisition of information on the future rate of inflation. The ability of business decision makers to forecast changes in prices becomes more valuable relative to their ability as managers and organizers of production. Speculative practices are encouraged as people try to outguess each other with regard to the future direction of prices. Funds flow into speculative investments such as gold, silver, and art objects rather than into productive investments (buildings, machines, and technological research) that expand the investor's ability to produce goods and services. Such practices are socially counterproductive. They reduce our production possibilities.

STAGFLATION

Stagflation
A period during which an economy is experiencing both substantial inflation and a slow growth in output.

For a time, inflation may lead to temporary prosperity and economic growth. But as high rates of inflation persist, real output inevitably stagnates. The two inflationary recessions of the United States during the 1970s illustrate this point. Economists have coined the term **stagflation** to describe the phenomenon of rapid inflation and sluggish economic growth. One of the challenges of modern economic policy is to develop a solution to the problem of stagflation—to develop economic policies that will lead to stable prices, efficient utilization of resources, and expansion in the future production possibilities available to economic participants. Again and again, we will return to this issue as we probe more deeply into macroeconomics.

ADJUSTING TO INFLATION

Escalator clause
A contractural agreement that periodically and automatically adjusts the wage rates of a collective-bargaining agreement upward by an amount determined by the rate of inflation.

When inflation is commonplace, people will adopt a variety of economic arrangements designed to protect their wealth and income against erosion by inflation. For example, collective-bargaining agreements will incorporate **escalator clauses** that provide for automatic wage adjustments to anticipated inflation or contain a premium to compensate for it. Variable-rate home mortgages will be more widely used. Life and home insurance policies will be updated more often. Many long-term contracts will provide for *indexing*—adjustments in the nominal terms that are tied to the rate of inflation. Such arrangements may help to offset some of the most dangerous side effects of inflation. Their application, however, is often costly. Moreover, it will not be possible to adjust all agreements for the effects of inflation. Therefore, while indexing and similar arrangements designed to adjust

---

[4]See Robert Higgs, "Inflation and the Destruction of the Free Market Economy," *The Intercollegiate Review* (Spring 1979), for an excellent discussion of this point.

agreements for the effects of inflation may help to minimize its negative effects, they are not a substitute for price stability.

WHAT CAUSES INFLATION?

We must acquire some additional tools before we can answer the question of what causes inflation in detail, but at this point we can outline a couple of theories. First, economists emphasize the link between aggregate demand and supply. If aggregate demand rises more rapidly than supply, prices will rise. Second, nearly all economists believe that a rapid expansion in a nation's stock of money causes inflation. The old saying is that prices will rise because "there is too much money chasing too few goods." The hyperinflation experienced by South American countries and, more recently, the countries of the former Soviet Union, has mainly been the result of monetary expansion. Once we develop additional knowledge about the operation of our economy, we will consider this issue in more detail.

ECONOMIC PERFORMANCE OF INDUSTRIAL COUNTRIES COMPARED

How does the economic performance of the United States compare with the other major industrial countries? **Exhibit 7–12** presents data on the economic record of the United States, Canada, Europe, and Japan during 1970–1982 and 1983–1991. The top frame provides data on the unemployment rate, the middle frame the inflation rate, and the lower frame the growth rate of real GDP.

The unemployment rate in Japan has been persistently lower than for other major industrial countries in recent years. During 1983–1991 the rate of unemployment in Japan averaged 2.5 percent, less than half the comparable rate for the United States and less than a third of the rate for Canada and Europe. Compared to other countries, Japanese employers are far more reluctant to lay off workers and bid employees away from other employers. In addition, during times of economic difficulty, Japanese employees are more likely to accept wage cuts from their current employer than workers in other countries. Thus, there is less job switching and more long-term employment relationships in Japan. No doubt, these factors contribute to Japan's low unemployment.

After experiencing high rates of inflation in the 1970s, the major industrial countries saw a substantial decline during 1983–1991. During the more recent period the inflation rate has been lowest in Japan, followed in order by the United States, Canada, and Europe.

During the 1950s and 1960s, the growth of real GDP in Japan averaged approximately 10 percent annually, well above the rates of other industrial nations. In recent years, the growth rate of Japan has slowed. Nonetheless, it continues to be impressive. During the 1983–1991 period, the growth of real GDP of Japan averaged 4.5 percent annually, compared to 3.3 percent for Canada, 2.9 percent for the United States, and 2.6 percent for Europe.

Compared with other countries, clearly the economic performance of Japan has been outstanding. The recent Japanese record is one of low unemployment,

Source: *Economic Report of the President: 1993,* and *Monthly Labor Review,* various issues.

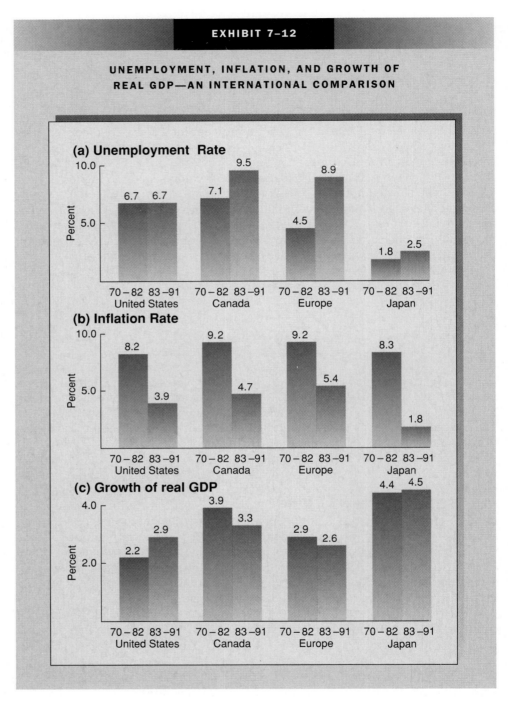

EXHIBIT 7–12

UNEMPLOYMENT, INFLATION, AND GROWTH OF REAL GDP—AN INTERNATIONAL COMPARISON

relatively stable prices, and rapid economic growth. In contrast, the European economy has been characterized by a high rate of unemployment and a slower growth rate. As we proceed, we will analyze important economic factors that contribute to the variation in economic performance among countries.

LOOKING AHEAD

In this chapter, we have examined the historical record for real income, employment, and prices. Measurement problems and the side effects of economic instability were discussed. In the next chapter, we will begin to develop a macroeconomic model that will help us better understand both the sources of and potential remedies for economic instability.

CHAPTER SUMMARY

1. Historically, real GDP in the United States has grown unevenly. Periods of rapid real growth have been followed by economic slowdowns. Nevertheless, the long-term trend has been upward. During the last 80 years, real GDP in the United States has grown at an average annual rate of approximately 3 percent.

2. *Business peak, contraction, recessionary trough,* and *expansion* are terms used by economists to describe the four phases of the business cycle. During an expansion, output increases rapidly and unemployment declines. The highest output rate of an expansion is referred to as a business peak or economic boom. Contraction is characterized by increasing unemployment, declining business conditions, and a low rate of growth. The bottom of the contraction is referred to as the recessionary trough.

3. Officially, the Commerce Department defines a recession as two successive quarters of declining real GDP. If a recession is quite severe, it is called a depression.

4. Even an efficient exchange economy will experience some unemployment. Frictional unemployment results because of imperfect information about available job openings and qualified applicants. Structural unemployment stems from the presence of factors that prevent the "matching up" of available applicants with available jobs. Currently, frictional and structural unemployment in the United States are thought to involve between 5 and 6 percent of the labor force.

5. Cyclical unemployment results when aggregate demand for labor is insufficient to maintain full employment. A primary concern of macroeconomics is how cyclical unemployment can be minimized.

6. Full employment is the employment level consistent with the economy's natural rate of unemployment, which reflects both frictional and structural factors. The natural rate is neither a temporary high nor low, but rather the rate of unemployment associated with the economy's maximum sustainable rate of output. It is not immutable, but rather, can be affected by public policies and changes in the composition of the labor force.

7. Employment is a means to an end. The meaningful goal of full employment is productive employment that produces desired goods and services.

8. The statistical definition of *unemployed* is imperfect. Some persons are not counted as unemployed because they are currently too discouraged to actively seek employment. Others are counted even though they may be employed in the underground economy or only casually seeking employment, perhaps because of an incentive structure that makes unemployment more attractive. Because of these ambiguities, some observers believe that the rate of employment (the percentage of the noninstitutional population, age 16 and over, who are employed) may be a more objective and accurate indicator of current employment opportunities. A prudent observer will consider both measures.

9. The concept of potential output encompasses two important ideas: (a) full utilization of resources and (b) a supply constraint that limits our ability to produce desired goods and services. When the resources of the economy are not fully and efficiently used, output will fall below its potential rate.

10. Inflation is a general rise in the level of prices. Alternatively, we might say that it is a decline in the purchasing power of the monetary unit—the dollar, in the case of the United States. The inflation rate accelerated upward in the United States during the 1970s. Since 1982 it has been more moderate.

11. It is important to distinguish between anticipated and unanticipated inflation. Anticipated inflation involves increases in the general level of prices that are expected by most people. Unanticipated inflation catches decision makers by surprise. When a rate of inflation is anticipated, people will plan for it and adjust their behavior accordingly, prior to the occurrence of the inflation. When it is unanticipated, it will often alter the intended terms of long-term agreements and cause people to make choices that they will later regret.

12. Inflation has a harmful effect on an economy because it (a) increases the uncertainty of exchanges involving time, and (b) consumes valuable resources as individuals use their skills and talents to protect themselves from it.

13. When the inflation rate is high, the year-to-year variability in the rate will generally be large. Since it will be impossible for decision makers to anticipate high and variable rates of inflation, such rates inhibit the willingness of individuals to invest. Thus, high and variable rates of inflation are particularly destructive to an economy.

14. During the last two decades Japan has achieved a more rapid growth rate of real output, less inflation, and a lower rate of unemployment than the United States, Canada, and Western Europe.

CRITICAL-ANALYSIS QUESTIONS

1. List the major phases of the business cycle and indicate how real GDP, employment, and unemployment change during these phases. Are the time periods of business cycles and the duration of the various phases relatively similar and therefore highly predictable? Are the magnitudes of the changes in the key variables influenced by the business cycle similar?

*2. Explain why even an efficiently functioning economic system will have some unemployed resources.

3. Classify each of the following as employed, unemployed, or not in the labor force:

   a. Brown, who is not working but is available for work, applied for a job at XYZ Company and is awaiting the result of her application.

   b. Smith is vacationing in Florida during a layoff at a General Motors plant due to a model changeover, but he expects to be recalled in a couple of weeks.

   c. Green was laid off as a carpenter when a construction project was completed. He is looking for work but has been unable to find anything except an $8-per-hour job, which he turned down.

   d. West works 50 to 60 hours per week as a home-maker for her family of nine.

   e. Carson, a 17-year-old, works six hours per week as a route person for the local newspaper.

   f. Johnson works three hours in the mornings at a clinic and for the last two weeks has spent the afternoons looking for a full-time job.

4. What is full employment? How are full employment and the natural rate of unemployment related? Indicate several factors that would cause the natural rate of unemployment to change. Is the actual rate of unemployment currently greater than or less than the natural rate of unemployment? Why?

5. How does the rate of employment differ from the rate of unemployment? Which is the better indicator of employment opportunity? Why?

*6. "As the inflation proceeds and the real value of the currency fluctuates widely from month to month, all permanent relations between debtors and lenders, which form the ultimate foundation of capitalism, become so utterly disordered as to be almost meaningless; and the process of wealth-getting degenerates into a gamble and a lottery." Do you agree with this well-known economist's view? Why or why not? How high do you think the inflation rate would have to climb before these effects would become pronounced? How does the inflation rate, particularly high rates of inflation influence the operation of a market economy? Discuss.

*7. How are the following related to each other?
   a. Actual rate of unemployment.
   b. Natural rate of unemployment.
   c. Cyclical unemployment.
   d. Potential GDP.

*8. Use the following data to calculate the (a) labor-force participation rate, (b) rate of unemployment, and (c) rate of employment:

Population	10,000
Labor force	6,000
Not currently working	4,500
Employed full time	4,000
Employed part time	1,500
Unemployed	500

*9. Persons are classified as unemployed if they are not currently working at a job and if they made an effort to find a job during the past four weeks. Does this mean that there were no jobs available? Does it mean that there were no jobs available that unemployed workers were qualified to perform? What does it mean?

*10. Indicate how an unanticipated 5 percent jump in the inflation rate will influence the wealth of the following:

   a. A person whose major asset is a house with a 30-year mortgage at a fixed interest rate.

   b. A family holding most of its wealth in long-term fixed yield bonds.

   c. A retiree drawing a monthly pension.

   d. A heavily indebted small-business owner.

   e. The owner of an apartment complex with substantial outstanding debt at a fixed interest rate.

   f. A worker whose wages are determined by a three-year union contract ratified three months ago.

11. Is the natural rate of unemployment fixed? Why or why not?

12. If a group of employees has a relatively low opportunity cost of job search, how will this affect their unemployment rate? How do you think the opportunity cost of job search of teenagers living with their parents compares with that of a prime earner with several dependents? How will this affect the unemployment rate of teenagers?

*13. How will each of the following affect a job seeker's decision to reject an available job offer and continue searching for a superior alternative?

   a. The rumor that a major firm in the area is going to expand employment next month.

   b. The availability of food stamps.

   c. Optimism about the future of the economy.

*14. *What's wrong with this way of thinking?* "My money wage rose by 6 percent last year, but inflation completely

---

*Asterisk denotes questions for which answers are given in Appendix C.

erased these gains. How can I get ahead when inflation continues to wipe out my increases in earnings?"

15. Suppose that the consumer price index at year-end 1991 was 140 and by year-end 1992 had risen to 150. What was the inflation rate during 1992?

16. Data for the nominal GDP and the GDP deflator (1985 = 100) in 1991 and 1992 for seven major industrial countries are presented in the accompanying Table A.

   a. Use the data provided to calculate the 1991 and 1992 real GDP of each country measured in 1985 prices. Place in the blanks provided.
   b. Use the data for the GDP deflator to calculate the 1992 inflation rate of each country. Place in the blanks provided.
   c. Which country had the highest growth rate of real GDP during 1992? Which had the lowest growth rate?

   d. Indicate the countries that had the highest and the lowest inflation rates in 1992.
   e. Which one of the countries had the most inflation during the 1985–1992 period?

17. The accompanying Table B presents the 1990 population and labor-force data for several countries.

   a. Calculate the number of people in the labor-force for the United States, Canada, and Japan in 1990.
   b. Calculate the 1990 rate of labor-force participation for each country and place in the blanks provided. Which country had the highest rate of labor-force participation? Which country had the lowest?
   c. Calculate the rate of unemployment in 1990 for each country, and place in the blanks provided. Which country had the highest rate of unemployment? Which had the lowest?

Table A

	NOMINAL GDP (BILLIONS OF LOCAL CURRENCY UNITS)[a]		GDP DEFLATOR (1985 = 100)		REAL GDP (IN 1985 CURRENCY UNITS)		INFLATION RATE
COUNTRY	1991	1992	1991	1992	1991	1992	1992
United States	5,722.9	6,038.5	124.7	128.3	_____	_____	_____
Canada	675.9	688.5	124.9	125.9	_____	_____	_____
Japan	450.8	464.8	108.6	110.5	_____	_____	_____
Germany	2,631.2	2,772.8	118.2	123.5	_____	_____	_____
France	6,746.9	6,993.0	121.7	124.5	_____	_____	_____
United Kingdom	573.3	595.2	140.3	146.6	_____	_____	_____
Italy	1,426.6	1,507.2	147.7	156.7	_____	_____	_____

[a]The data for Japan are in trillions of yen.

Table B

COUNTRY	POPULATION 16 YEARS AND OVER (IN MILLIONS)	NUMBER EMPLOYED (IN MILLIONS)	NUMBER UNEMPLOYED (IN MILLIONS)	RATE OF LABOR-FORCE PARTICIPATION (PERCENT)	RATE OF UNEMPLOYMENT (PERCENT)
United States	188.0	117.9	6.87	_____	_____
Canada	20.4	12.6	1.11	_____	_____
Japan	101.9	62.4	1.34	_____	_____
Germany	54.6	28.5	1.53	_____	_____
France	44.1	22.2	2.22	_____	_____
United Kingdom	45.0	26.8	1.99	_____	_____
Italy	50.1	21.4	2.35	_____	_____

CHAPTER EIGHT

AN INTRODUCTION TO BASIC
MACROECONOMIC MARKETS

*Macroeconomics is interesting . . . because it is
challenging to reduce the complicated details of the
economy to manageable essentials. Those essentials
lie in the interactions among the goods, labor, and
assets [loanable funds] markets of the economy.*

RUDIGER DORNBUSCH AND STANLEY FISCHER[1]

CHAPTER FOCUS

■ *What are the major markets that coordinate
macroeconomic activities?*
■ *Why is the aggregate demand for goods and services
inversely related to the price level?*
■ *Why is an increase in the price level likely to expand
output in the short run, but not in the long run?*
■ *What determines the equilibrium level of GDP of
an economy?*
■ *How is the natural rate of unemployment related to
the concept of long-term aggregate supply?*
■ *What is the difference between the real interest
rate and the money interest rate? Does inflation help
borrowers relative to lenders?*

---

[1]Rudiger Dornbusch and Stanley Fischer, *Macroeconomics*
(New York: McGraw-Hill, 1978).

I n Chapter 6 we explained how output is measured and how price indexes are developed and utilized to transform nominal data on output and income into real measures of output—that is, output adjusted for changes in the general level of prices. In Chapter 7 we presented historical data on fluctuations in real output, employment, and the price level and considered several important implications of these fluctuations. We are now ready to shift from the description of the performance of an economy to an analysis of that performance and the factors that influence it.

UNDERSTANDING MACROECONOMICS: OUR GAME PLAN

Let us develop a simple macroeconomic model—a road map, if you like—that will help us better understand macroeconomic relationships. This model will enhance our understanding of both how our macroeconomy works and the potential of policy to alter its performance.

Fiscal policy

The use of government taxation and expenditure policies for the purpose of achieving macroeconomic goals.

Monetary policy

The deliberate control of the money supply, and, in some cases, credit conditions, for the purpose of achieving macroeconomic goals.

Money supply

The supply of currency, checking account funds, and traveler's checks. These items are counted as money since they are used as the means of payment for purchases.

Macroeconomic policy is usually divided into two components: fiscal policy and monetary policy. **Fiscal policy** entails the use of the government's taxation, spending, and debt-management policies. In the United States, fiscal policy is conducted by Congress and the president. It is thus a reflection of the collective decision-making process. **Monetary policy** encompasses actions that alter the money supply. The direction of monetary policy is determined by a nation's central bank, the Federal Reserve System in the United States. Ideally, both monetary and fiscal policy are used to promote business stability, high employment, the growth of output, and a stable price level.

Initially, as we develop our basic macroeconomic model, we will assume that monetary and fiscal policy are unchanging. Stated another way, we will proceed as if the government's tax and spending policies are unaffected by economic circumstances. Similarly, we will assume that policy-makers maintain a constant **money supply**—that they follow policies that keep the amount of cash in our billfolds and deposits in our checking accounts constant. Of course, changes in government expenditures, taxes, and the money supply are potentially important. We will investigate their impact in detail in subsequent chapters. For now, though, things will go more smoothly if we simply assume that policy-makers are holding government expenditures, taxes, and the supply of money constant.

THREE KEY MARKETS: RESOURCES, LOANABLE FUNDS, AND GOODS AND SERVICES

Businesses generally purchase resources from households and use them to produce goods and services. In turn, households generally use a substantial portion of the income they earn from the sale of their productive services to purchase

As we noted in Chapter 6, there are two ways of measuring gross domestic product (GDP), the aggregate domestic output of an economy. First, GDP can be measured by adding up the expenditures of consumers, investors, governments, and foreigners (net exports) on goods and services produced during the year. This method is equivalent to measuring the flow of output as it moves through the top loop—the goods and services market—of the circular-flow diagram. Alternatively, GDP can be measured by summing the income payments, both direct and indirect, received by the resource suppliers who produced the goods and services. This method uses the bottom loop—the resource market—to measure the flow of output.

AGGREGATE DEMAND FOR GOODS AND SERVICES

What goes on in the aggregate goods and services market is vital to the health of an economy. Indeed, if we could keep our eye on just one market in an economy, we would choose the goods and services market since it exerts a vital impact on our economic opportunity and standard of living. It is important to note that the "quantity" and "price" variables in this highly aggregated market differ from their counterparts in the market for a specific good.

In the goods and services market, the "quantity" variable is real GDP; it is the flow of domestically produced goods and services during a period. The "price" variable in the goods and services market represents the average price of goods and services purchased during the period. In essence, it is the economy's price level, as measured by a general price index (for example, the GDP deflator).

Just as the concepts of demand and supply enhance our understanding of markets for specific goods, they also contribute to our understanding of a highly aggregated market such as the goods and services market. The demand in the goods and services market is comprised of the purchases of domestically produced goods and services by consumers, investors, governments, and foreigners. The aggregate demand curve indicates the various quantities of domestically produced goods and services that purchasers are willing to buy at different price levels. As **Exhibit 8–2** illustrates, the **aggregate-demand curve** slopes downward to the right, indicating an inverse relationship between the amount of goods and services demanded and the price level.

The explanation of the downward slope of the aggregate-demand (*AD*) schedule differs from that for a specific commodity, which we discussed previously in Chapter 3. The inverse relationship between price and the amount demanded of a specific commodity, television sets, for example, reflects the fact that consumers will substitute the good for other commodities when a price reduction makes the good less expensive relative to other goods. A price reduction in the aggregate goods and services market indicates that the *level* of prices has declined. On average, the prices of all goods are lower. When the price level declines—when the prices of all goods decline—there will be no incentive to substitute one for the other.

The aggregate-demand curve also differs from the demand curve for a specific commodity in another important respect. When the demand curve for a specific commodity is derived, the income of consumers is held constant. That will

Aggregate-demand curve
A downward-sloping curve indicating an inverse relationship between the price level and the quantity of domestically produced goods and services that households, business firms, governments, and foreigners (net exports) are willing to purchase during a period.

As illustrated here, the quantity of goods and services purchased will increase (to Y_2) as the price level declines (to P_2). Other things constant, the lower price level will increase the wealth of people holding the fixed quantity of money, lead to lower interest rates, and make domestically produced goods cheaper relative to foreign goods. All of these factors will tend to increase the quantity of goods and services purchased at the lower price level.

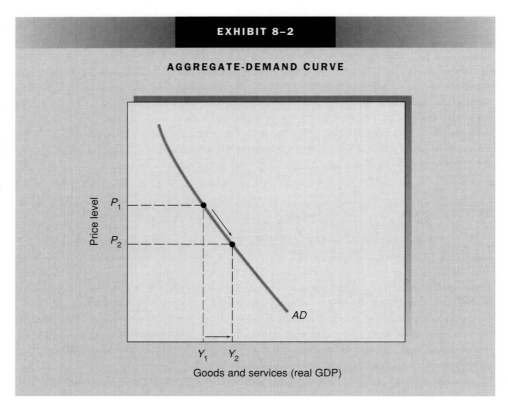

EXHIBIT 8–2

AGGREGATE-DEMAND CURVE

not be the case for the aggregate-demand curve. If there is an increase in the quantity of goods and services purchased, the circular flow of income indicates that the payments to resource suppliers must also increase. Therefore, movements along the aggregate-demand curve will be associated with changes in real income.

Clearly, both the nature of the aggregate-demand curve and the explanation for its downward slope differ substantially from that of the demand for a specific commodity. Why is there reason to expect that, other things constant, a reduction in the price level will lead to an increase in the aggregate quantity of goods and services demanded by purchasers? Three major factors contribute to the downward-sloping aggregate-demand curve: changes in the purchasing power of money balances, changes in the interest rate, and the effect of international substitution.

REAL-BALANCE EFFECT

As the *level* of prices declines, the purchasing power of the fixed quantity of money increases. For example, suppose that you have $2,000 in your bank account. Consider how a 20 percent reduction in the level of prices will influence your wealth and spending. At the lower price level, your $2,000 will buy more goods and services. In fact, your $2,000 will buy as much as $2,500 would have purchased at the previous higher level of prices. Other people are in an identical position. As the price level declines, the purchasing power of their money balances also increases.

Economists refer to this inverse relationship between the price level and the wealth of households and businesses holding a fixed supply of money as the **real-balance effect.** It helps to explain the downward slope of the aggregate-demand curve. When the price level declines, the purchasing power of money and the real wealth of people holding fixed money balances increases. As their wealth increases, people will increase their purchases. Therefore, a negative relationship between the price level and the quantity of goods and services purchased emerges from the real-balance effect.

Real-balance effect
The increase in wealth emanating from an increase in the purchasing power of a constant money supply as the price level decreases. This wealth effect leads to an inverse relationship between price (level) and quantity demanded in the goods and services market.

INTEREST-RATE EFFECT

Remember, when we construct an aggregate-demand curve, the supply of money is fixed all along the curve. A reduction in the price level increases the real money supply—the nominal supply of money relative to the level of prices. When the average price of goods and services declines, consumers and businesses will be able to conduct their normal activities with smaller average money balances. Households will be able to get by just fine with a smaller amount of cash and checking account funds since, at the lower price level, they will be spending a smaller nominal amount on food, clothing, and other items regularly purchased. Similarly, businesses will want to reduce their money balances since less funds will now be required to pay employee wages, taxes, and other business expenses at the lower price level. As both consumers and businesses attempt to reduce their money balances, they will channel some of these funds into savings—the loanable funds market. Thus, this decline in the demand for money relative to the fixed supply of money will place downward pressure on interest rates.[2]

What impact will a lower interest rate have on the demand for goods and services? A reduction in the interest rate will make it less costly to purchase goods and services during the current period, particularly those that are financed. Thus, households can be expected to increase their purchases of interest-sensitive consumption goods such as automobiles and consumer durables. Similarly, firms will expand their current investment expenditures on business expansion and new construction. Thus, a reduction in the price level leads to a lower interest rate that encourages both consumption and investment spending. This *interest-rate effect* also contributes to the downward slope of the aggregate-demand curve.

INTERNATIONAL-SUBSTITUTION EFFECT

A lower price level will make domestically produced goods less expensive relative to foreign goods. Imports will decline as Americans find that many domestically produced goods are now cheaper than products produced abroad. At the lower price level, Americans will tend to purchase fewer Japanese automobiles, Korean textiles, Italian shoes, and other imports since these products are now more expensive relative to domestically produced goods. At the same time, foreigners will increase their purchases of American-made goods which are now

---

[2]We will provide additional detail on this topic when we analyze the demand for money in Chapter 13.

relatively cheaper. Therefore, net exports will tend to rise (or net imports decline).[3] This increase in net exports at the lower U.S. price level will directly increase the quantity demanded of domestically produced goods. Thus, the *inter-national-substitution effect* provides a third reason for the downward slope of the aggregate-demand curve.

THE DOWNWARD SLOPING AGGREGATE-DEMAND CURVE: A SUMMARY

The accompanying "Thumbnail Sketch" indicates why the price level is inversely related to the amount demanded in the aggregate goods and services market. A lower price level will (1) increase the purchasing power of the fixed money supply, (2) lower interest rates, and (3) reduce the price of domestically produced goods relative to goods produced abroad. Each of these factors will tend to increase the quantity demanded of domestically produced goods and services.

When considering the aggregate-demand schedule, it is important to keep in mind the distinction between the price level and *changes* in the price level. The aggregate-demand schedule indicates the aggregate quantity of domestically produced goods and services that will be demanded at alternative price levels. When the schedule is derived, expectations concerning the level of prices and the inflation rate that accompanies a changing price level are held constant. If these expectations change as the result of new information—for example, a change in the price level (the rate of inflation) that is either higher or lower than what people had expected—the entire demand schedule will shift. We will consider this issue in the following chapter.

While we have considered the impact of a lower price level on the quantity purchased, the effects would be just the opposite for a higher price level. At a higher price level, (1) the wealth of people holding the fixed supply of money would be less, (2) the demand for money would be greater, which would lead to higher interest rates, and (3) domestic goods would be more expensive relative to

---

THUMBNAIL SKETCH

WHY IS THE AGGREGATE QUANTITY DEMANDED INVERSELY RELATED TO THE PRICE LEVEL?

A *decrease* in the price level will *raise* aggregate quantity demanded because

1. The real wealth of persons holding money balances will increase when prices fall; this will encourage additional consumption.

2. A reduction in the demand for money balances at the lower price level will reduce interest rates, which will encourage current investment and consumption.

3. Net exports will expand (since the prices of domestic goods have fallen relative to foreign goods).

---

[3]An increase in exports and decline in imports may cause a nation's currency to appreciate, which will partially offset the international-substitution effect.

those produced abroad. Each of these factors would tend to reduce the quantity of domestically produced goods demanded at the higher price level. Therefore, even though the explanation differs, the quantity demanded in the aggregate goods and services market, like the quantity demanded for a specific product, will be inversely related to price.

AGGREGATE SUPPLY OF GOODS AND SERVICES

In light of our discussion of aggregate demand, it should come as no great surprise that the explanation of the general shape of the **aggregate-supply curve** differs from that of the supply curve for a specific good. As we have already noted, an increase in price in the goods and services market indicates that the general level of prices has risen, rather than the price of one good relative to all other goods. Thus, the general shape of the aggregate-supply (*AS*) curve is not a reflection of changes in the relative prices of goods.

When considering aggregate supply, it is particularly important to distinguish between the short run and the long run. In this context, the short run is the time period during which some prices, particularly those in labor markets, are set by prior contracts and agreements. Therefore, in the short run, households and businesses are unable to adjust these prices when unexpected changes occur, including unexpected changes in the price level. In contrast, the long run is a time period of sufficient duration that people have the opportunity to modify their behavior in response to price changes. We now consider both the short-run and long-run aggregate-supply curves.

Aggregate-supply curve
A curve indicating the relationship between the nation's price level and quantity of goods supplied by its producers. In the short run, it is probably an upward-sloping curve, but in the long run most economists believe the aggregate-supply curve is vertical (or nearly so).

AGGREGATE SUPPLY IN THE SHORT RUN

The *short-run aggregate-supply (SRAS) curve* indicates the various quantities of goods and services that domestic firms will supply in response to changing demand conditions that alter the level of prices in the goods and services market. As **Exhibit 8–3** illustrates, the *SRAS* curve in the goods and services market slopes upward to the right. The upward slope reflects the fact that in the short run an unanticipated increase in the price level will, on average, improve the profitability of firms. They will respond with an expansion in output.

The *SRAS* curve is based on a specific expected price level, P_{100}, in the case of Exhibit 8–3, and rate of inflation that generates that price level. When the expected price level is actually achieved, firms will earn normal profits and supply output Y_0. Why will an increase in the price level (to P_{105}, for example) enhance profitability, at least in the short run? Profit per unit equals price minus the producer's per-unit costs. Important components of producers' costs will be determined by long-term contracts. Interest rates on loans, collective-bargaining agreements with employees, lease agreements on buildings and machines, and other contracts with resource suppliers will influence production costs during the current period. The prices incorporated into these long-term contracts at the time of the agreement are based on the expectation of price level (P_{100}) for the current period. These resource

The short-run aggregate-supply (SRAS) curve shows the relationship between the price level and the production of goods and services by domestic suppliers during the period immediately following the change in aggregate demand leading to the change in the price level. In the short run, firms will generally expand output as the price level increases because the higher prices will improve profit margins since many components of costs will be temporarily fixed as the result of prior long-term commitments.

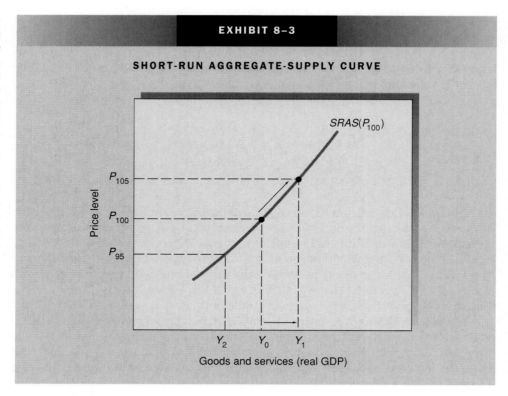

EXHIBIT 8–3

SHORT-RUN AGGREGATE-SUPPLY CURVE

costs tend to be temporarily fixed. If an increase in demand causes the price level to rise unexpectedly during the current period, prices of goods and services will increase relative to the temporarily fixed components of costs. Profit margins will improve, and business firms will happily respond with an expansion in output (to Y_1).[4]

---

[4]The short-run aggregate-supply schedule concerns the output that business firms will supply in response to a change in aggregate demand. Viewed from this perspective, there are other reasons why an increase in aggregate demand will cause firms to produce a larger output in the short run. For the representative firm, an increase in aggregate demand will lead to strong sales for a few weeks or months. Consider how a typical business firm will respond to the strong demand for their product. Initially, the manager of the firm will not know whether the increased sales are temporary or permanent. If the strong sales are only temporary, the firm will be fearful that a large price increase might drive their regular customers to rival suppliers. Therefore, until it is convinced that the temporary increase in sales reflects a genuine long-term increase in demand for its product, the typical business firm will increase its price only moderately, if at all. In the short run, firms will generally supply the larger output that their customers are demanding without much increase in price.

In addition, some firms may be confused by the general increase in demand for products. Mistakenly, they may believe that the demand for their product has increased *relative* to other products. If this were the case, the firm would be able to purchase the resources required to expand long-term output without much increase in costs. Fooled by the general increase in demand, many firms will hire resources, make investments, and expand output in the short run. Since many other firms are also expanding output, with the passage of time the outcome is going to be higher resource prices and increases in costs. Initially, however, the firms undertaking the expansions in output will be unaware that this will be the case. This factor may also contribute to the positive relationship between the price level and output as firms respond to an increase in aggregate demand in the short run.

An unexpected reduction in the price level to P_{95} would exert just the opposite effect. It would decrease product prices relative to costs and thereby reduce profitability. In response, firms would reduce output to Y_2. Therefore, in the short run, there will be a direct relationship between amount supplied and the price level in the goods and services market.

AGGREGATE SUPPLY IN THE LONG RUN

The *long-run aggregate supply (LRAS) curve* indicates the relationship between the price level and quantity of output after decision makers have had sufficient time to adjust their prior commitments where possible, or take steps to counterbalance them, in the light of any unexpected changes in market prices. A higher price level in the goods and services market will fail to alter the relationship between product and resource prices in the long run. Once people have time to fully adjust their prior commitments, competitive forces will restore the usual relationship between product prices and costs. Profit rates will return to normal, removing the incentive for firms to supply a larger rate of output. Therefore, as **Exhibit 8–4** illustrates, the *LRAS* curve is vertical.

The forces that provided for an upward-sloping *SRAS* curve are absent in the long run. Costs that are temporarily fixed due to long-run contracts will eventually rise. With time, the long-term contracts will expire and be renegotiated. Once the contracts are renegotiated, resource prices will increase in the same proportion as product prices. A proportional increase in costs and product prices will leave the incentive to produce unchanged. Consider how a firm with a selling price of $20 and per-unit costs of $20 will be affected by the doubling of both product and resource prices. After the price increase, the firm's sales price will be $40, but so,

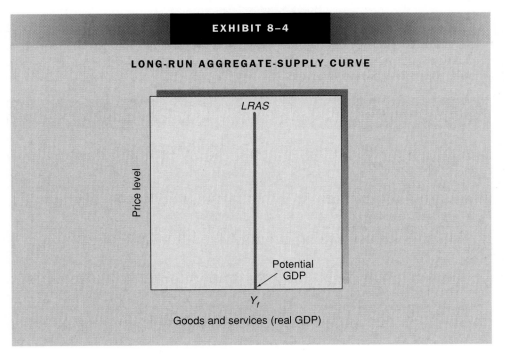

EXHIBIT 8–4

LONG-RUN AGGREGATE-SUPPLY CURVE

LRAS

Price level

Potential GDP

Y_f

Goods and services (real GDP)

In the long run, a higher price level will not expand an economy's rate of output. Once people have time to adjust their prior long-term commitments, resource markets (and costs) will adjust to the higher level of prices and thereby remove the incentive of firms to supply a larger output at the higher price level. An economy's sustainable potential output rate is determined by the supply of resources, level of technology, and structure of institutions, factors that are insensitive to changes in the price level. The vertical LRAS curve illustrates this point.

too, will its per-unit costs. Thus, neither the firm's profit rate nor the incentive to produce is changed. Therefore, in the long run an increase in the nominal value of the price level will fail to exert a lasting impact on aggregate output.

Reflecting on the production possibilities of an economy also sheds light on why the *LRAS* curve is vertical. As we discussed in Chapter 2, at a point in time, the production possibilities of a nation are constrained by the supply of resources, level of technology, and institutional arrangements that influence the efficiency of resource use. A higher price level does not loosen these constraints. For example, a doubling of prices will not improve technology. Neither will it expand the availability of productive resources, nor improve the efficiency of our economic institutions. Thus, there is no reason for a higher price level to increase our ability to produce goods and services. This is precisely what the vertical *LRAS* curve implies. The accompanying "Thumbnail Sketch" summarizes the factors that underlie both the short-run and long-run aggregate-supply curves.

EQUILIBRIUM IN GOODS AND SERVICES MARKET

We are now ready to combine our analysis of aggregate demand and aggregate supply and consider how they act to determine the price level and rate of output. When a market is in **equilibrium,** there is a balance of forces such that the actions of buyers and sellers are consistent with one another.

Equilibrium
A balance of forces permitting the simultaneous fulfillment of plans by buyers and sellers.

EQUILIBRIUM IN SHORT RUN

As **Exhibit 8–5** illustrates, short-run equilibrium is present in the goods and services market at the price level (P) where the aggregate quantity demanded is equal to the aggregate quantity supplied. This occurs at the output rate (Y) where the *AD* and *SRAS* curves intersect.

THUMBNAIL SKETCH

WHY IS THE SHORT-RUN AGGREGATE QUANTITY SUPPLIED DIRECTLY RELATED TO THE PRICE LEVEL?

• As the price level increases, profit margins of firms also increase, because firms will initially increase their product prices relative to costs (important components of which are fixed by long-term contracts).

WHY IS THE LONG-RUN AGGREGATE-SUPPLY CURVE VERTICAL?

• Once people have the time to adjust fully to a new price level, the normal relationship between product prices and resource costs is restored.

• The sustainable potential output of a national economy is determined by its quantity of resources, technology, and the efficiency of its institutional structures, *not* by the price level.

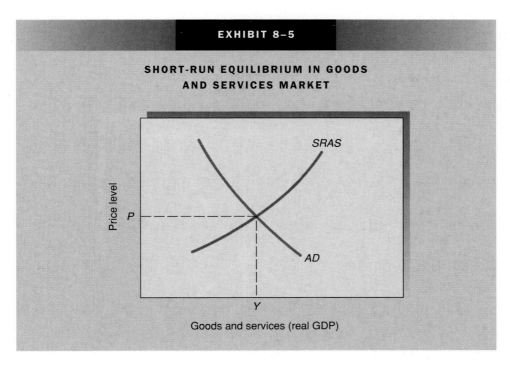

EXHIBIT 8-5

SHORT-RUN EQUILIBRIUM IN GOODS AND SERVICES MARKET

Short-run equilibrium in the goods and services market occurs at the price level (P) where AD and SRAS intersect. If the price level were lower than P, general excess demand in goods and services markets would push prices upward. Conversely, if the price level were higher than P, excess supply would result in falling prices.

If a price level of less than P were present, the aggregate quantity demanded would exceed the aggregate quantity supplied. Purchasers would be seeking to buy more goods and services than producers were willing to produce. This excess demand would place upward pressure on prices, causing the price level to rise toward P. On the other hand, at a price level greater than P, the aggregate quantity supplied would exceed the aggregate quantity demanded. Producers would be unable to sell all the goods produced. This would result in downward pressure (toward P) on prices. Only at the price level P would there be a balance of forces between the amount of goods demanded by consumers, investors, governments, and foreigners, and the amount supplied by domestic firms.

EQUILIBRIUM IN LONG RUN

The price level in the economy-wide goods and services market will tend to bring quantity demanded and quantity supplied into balance. However, a second condition is required for long-run equilibrium: the buyers and sellers must be happy with the results of their choices. If they are not satisfied, they will want to change their actions in the future. Thus, long-run equilibrium requires that decision makers who agreed to long-term contracts influencing current prices and costs must have correctly anticipated the current price level *at the time they arrived at the agreements*. If this is not the case, buyers and sellers will want to modify the agreements when the long-term contracts expire. In turn, their modifications will affect costs, profit margins, and output.

Exhibit 8–6 illustrates a long-run equilibrium in the goods and services market. As in Exhibit 8–3, the subscripts attached to the *SRAS* and *AD* curves indicate the price level (an index of prices) that was anticipated by decision makers at the

When the goods and services market is in long-run equilibrium, two conditions must be present. First, the quantity demanded must equal the quantity supplied at the current price level. Second, the price level anticipated by decision makers must equal the actual price level. The subscripts on the SRAS *and* AD *curves indicate that buyers and sellers alike anticipated the price level* P_{100}, *where the 100 represents an index of prices during an earlier base year. When the anticipated price level is actually attained, current output* (Y_f) *will equal the economy's potential GDP and full employment will be present.*

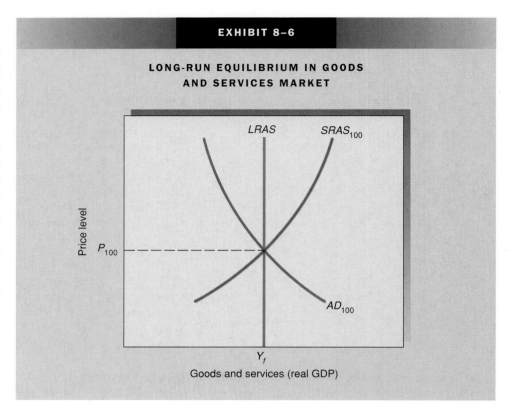

EXHIBIT 8–6

LONG-RUN EQUILIBRIUM IN GOODS AND SERVICES MARKET

time they made decisions affecting the schedules. In this case, when buyers and sellers made their purchasing and production choices, they anticipated that the price level during the current period would be P_{100} where the 100 refers to an index of prices during an earlier base year. As the intersection of the *AD* and *SRAS* curves reveals, the P_{100} was actually attained.

When the price level expectations imbedded in the long-term contracts turn out to be correct, there is no reason for buyers and sellers in resource markets to modify resource prices when their contracts come up for renegotiation. Therefore, the resource prices, costs, and profits will continue into the future. Since the price-cost relationship is unchanged, firms have no incentive to alter either their product prices or rate of output. Thus, the equilibrium price level and output (Y_f) will *persist* into the future—until changes in other factors alter *AD* or *SRAS*. It is a long-run equilibrium.

LONG-RUN EQUILIBRIUM, POTENTIAL OUTPUT, AND FULL EMPLOYMENT

When long-run equilibrium is present, the actual output achieved is equal to the economy's potential GDP. In other words, when a short-run equilibrium (*AD* intersects with *SRAS*) occurs along the economy's vertical aggregate-supply curve (*LRAS*), long-run equilibrium will also be present. Exhibit 8–6 illustrates this case.

As we discussed in Chapter 7, *potential GDP* is equal to the economy's maximum sustainable output consistent with its resource base, current technology, and institutional structure. Potential GDP is neither a temporary high nor an abnormal low. Rather, it reflects the normal operation of markets, the situation when decision makers (including those involved in long-term agreements) neither systematically underestimate nor overestimate the current price level.

The long-run equilibrium output rate (Y_f in Exhibit 8–6) also corresponds with the full employment of resources. When full-employment output is present, the job-search time of unemployed workers will be normal, given the characteristics of the labor force and the institutional structure of the economy. Only frictional and structural unemployment will be present; cyclical unemployment will be absent.

When an economy is in long-run equilibrium, the actual rate of unemployment will be equal to the natural rate. Remember, the natural rate of unemployment reflects the normal job-search process of employees and employers, given the structure of the economy and the laws and regulations that affect the operation of markets. It is a rate that is neither abnormally high nor abnormally low; it can be sustained into the future. When an economy is in long-run equilibrium, this will be the case. Decision makers will have correctly anticipated the inflation rate and the current price level that it generates. Thus, they will have no reason to undertake changes that will affect costs relative to prices. On average, the profitability of firms will be normal. This situation is sustainable into the future.

Therefore, in long-run equilibrium, output will be equal to its potential, full employment will be achieved, and the rate of unemployment will be equivalent to the natural rate of unemployment. (See boxed feature, "Measures of Economic Activity.")

What happens when changes in the price level catch buyers and sellers by surprise? When the actual price level differs from the level forecast by buyers and sellers, some decision makers will enter into agreements that they will later regret—agreements that they will want to change as soon as they have an opportunity to do so.

Consider the situation when the price level increases more than was anticipated. Failing to foresee the price increase, lenders in the loanable funds market agree to interest rates that are lower than they are willing to accept once the general increase in prices (inflation) is taken into account. Similarly, anticipating a lower current price level, union officials and employees accept money-wage increases that end up creating lower real wages than were initially perceived. In the short run, the atypically low interest rates and real wages reduce costs relative to product prices. Profit margins are abnormally high, and firms respond with a larger output. Employment expands. Unemployment falls below its natural rate.

But this abnormally large output and high level of employment is not sustainable. The "mistakes," based on a failure to predict the strength of current demand, will be recognized and corrected when contracts expire. Real wages and interest rates will increase and eventually reflect the higher price level and rate of inflation. Profit margins will return to normal. When these adjustments are completed, the temporarily large output rate and high employment level will decline and return to normal.

What will happen if product prices decline or increase less rapidly than decision makers anticipate? Anticipating a higher price level (a higher inflation rate than actually occurs), borrowers agree to interest rates that later prove to be unacceptably

MEASURES OF ECONOMIC ACTIVITY

NATURAL RATE OF UNEMPLOYMENT

Since the natural rate of unemployment is a theoretical concept, it cannot be directly observed. The theory, however, indicates how it can be estimated. The natural rate of unemployment will be present when decision makers correctly anticipate the inflation rate. When the inflation rate of an economy is relatively constant—when it is neither increasing nor decreasing—buyers and sellers will be able to accurately anticipate it and adjust nominal prices, wages, and interest rates accordingly. Thus, the actual unemployment rate will tend to gravitate toward the economy's natural rate of unemployment when the inflation rate is steady (when the change in the inflation rate is zero). As a result, the natural rate of unemployment is sometimes called the "nonaccelerating inflation rate of unemployment."

A statistical equation that links the unemployment rate to the rate of inflation can be used to estimate the natural rate of unemployment. When the change in the inflation rate is set equal to zero within this equation, the results will provide an estimate for the natural rate of unemployment.

The natural rate is also influenced by changes in the demographic composition of the labor force. Since younger workers are more likely than their older counterparts both to switch jobs and enter (and reenter) the labor force, the natural unemployment rate increases when youthful workers grow as a proportion of the labor force. Thus, some researchers have also used historical data on the relative size of various demographic groups in an effort to derive more accurate estimates.

Perhaps the most widely cited estimates of the natural rate of unemployment are those derived by Robert Gordon of Northwestern University. The accompanying chart presents the estimates of Gordon, along with the low and high estimates of other researchers for 1955, 1970, 1980, and 1990. In the mid-1950s, the natural rate of unemployment was estimated at between 4 percent and 5.5 percent. Gordon's estimate for the natural rate in 1955 was 5.1 percent. Researchers agree that the natural rate increased during the 1960s and 1970s, primarily as the result of a large influx of youthful workers into the labor force. By 1980 the estimated natural rate had risen to between 5 percent and 7 percent. As the baby-boom generation matured and the growth of the labor force slowed during the 1980s, the natural rate declined. In the early 1990s researchers placed the natural rate of unemployment between 4.5 percent and 6.5 percent.

ESTIMATED NATURAL RATE OF UNEMPLOYMENT

YEAR	LOW ESTIMATE	ROBERT GORDON	HIGH ESTIMATE
1955	4.0	5.1	5.5
1970	4.5	5.6	6.0
1980	5.0	5.9	7.0
1990	4.5	6.0	6.5

Sources: Robert Gordon, *Macroeconomics,* 5th ed. (Glenview, IL: Scott Foresman Company, 1990); Stuart E. Weiner, "The Natural Rate of Unemployment: Concepts and Issues," *Economic Review—Federal Reserve Bank of Kansas City,* January 1986, pp. 11–24; Keith M. Carlson, "How Much Lower Can the Unemployment Rate Go?" *Review—Federal Reserve Bank of St. Louis,* July/August 1988, pp. 44–57; and Lowell E. Gallaway and Richard K. Vedder, *The Natural Rate of Unemployment,* Joint Economic Committee, Congress of the United States (Washington, DC: Government Printing Office, 1982).

high in terms of the current price level. Similarly, employers agree to wage increases that result in higher *real* wages than expected, since the price level rises more slowly than people thought it would. The abnormally high interest and wage rates increase costs relative to product prices. As profit margins are squeezed, producers reduce output and lay off employees. Unemployment rises above the natural rate of unemployment. Current output falls short of the economy's potential GDP.

Many economists think this is precisely what happened during 1982. After inflation rates of 13 percent in 1979 and 12 percent in 1980, price increases plummeted to 4 percent in 1982. This sharp reduction in the inflation rate caught many decision makers by surprise. Unable to pass along to consumers the large increases in money wages agreed to in 1980 and 1981, employers cut back production and laid off workers. The unemployment rate soared to 10.8 percent in late 1982, up from 7.6 percent in 1981. Eventually, new agreements provided for smaller money wage increases, or even wage reductions, in 1983 and 1984. Unemployment fell. Nevertheless, in 1982 unemployment was well above its natural rate. The necessary adjustments could not be made instantaneously.

In summary, a current output rate will be sustained into the future only when the price agreements of buyers and sellers were based on an accurate forecast of the current price level. If the decision makers were able to accurately forecast the current price level when they arrived at their agreements, then the current resource prices and real interest rates will tend to persist into the future. Profit rates will be normal. The choices of buyers and sellers will harmonize, and neither will have reason to alter their choices. When this is the case, long-run equilibrium will be present and the economy's sustainable potential rate of output (Y_f in Exhibit 8–6) will be achieved. It is the long-run maximum sustainable output that economists are referring to when they speak of "full employment output" or "potential GDP."

RESOURCE MARKET

Until now in this chapter, we have discussed only the aggregate goods and services market, but there are two other basic macroeconomic markets that are quite important. These two markets are the resource market and the loanable funds market. After we discuss the resource market in this section and the loanable funds market in the section that follows, we will be ready to link all three markets together and analyze general macroeconomic equilibrium.

It is not hard to guess that the resource market is a market for resources, but what does that mean? Resources are factors of production such as labor, natural resources, and machines, so the resource market is nothing more than a place where such items are bought and sold. The resource market thus coordinates the choices of business firms that demand resources and resource owners who supply them. When you hunt for a summer job, for instance, you are participating in the resource market.

Why do business firms demand resources? In a market economy, the demand for resources is merely a reflection of the contribution of the resources to the production of goods and services. Business firms employ labor and other resources because they contribute to the production of goods the firm believes it can sell at a profit. For example, a builder purchases resources such as lumber, cement, and windows, and hires the labor services of carpenters, bricklayers, and roofers, because they are required in order to produce the houses that the contractor hopes to sell for a profit. The demand for a resource such as labor reflects the law of demand, which says that the higher the price of something, the less the quantity demanded. If the wages that firms must pay for workers increase, the firms will choose to hire fewer workers. In contrast, a lower wage rate will increase the quantity of labor demanded by firms. Therefore, the demand for resources, like the demand for goods and services, slopes downward to the right.

Why are labor and other resources supplied? Most people work and supply resources to earn income. Working, though, requires us to give up something else that is valuable: leisure—time to do nonmarket work and other things. So a tradeoff must be made between working for income and spending leisure time on nonmarket activities. Higher real wages increase the opportunity cost of leisure.

Because of this, as real wages increase, individuals generally make substitutions that permit them to supply more market work time. Therefore, the quantity of labor and other resources supplied expands as resource prices increase.

Exhibit 8–7 illustrates equilibrium in the aggregate-resource market. Price coordinates the actions of buyers and sellers. In equilibrium, the market price of resources will bring the amount demanded by business firms into balance with the amount supplied by resource owners. An above-equilibrium price will result in an excess supply of resources. The excess supply will push resource prices downward toward equilibrium. In contrast, if resource prices are below equilibrium, excess demand will place upward pressure on the price of resources. Market forces will thus tend to move resource prices toward equilibrium.

As we discussed in Chapter 3, the markets for resources and products are highly interrelated. The cost of producing goods and services is influenced directly by the price of resources. Other things remaining constant, an increase in resource prices will increase costs and squeeze profit margins in the goods and services market. Aggregate supply will decline (*SRAS* will shift to the left). Conversely, a reduction in resource prices will lower costs and improve profit margins in the goods and services market. An increase in aggregate supply (a shift to the right in *SRAS*) will result.

The demand for resources is directly linked to the demand for goods and services. In fact, the demand for resources is a derived demand—it emanates from the demand for goods and services. An increase in aggregate demand will increase the demand for resources. Similarly, a reduction in aggregate demand will reduce the demand for resources.

Since the resource and goods and services markets are highly interrelated, obviously changes in either one of these markets will have repercussions in the

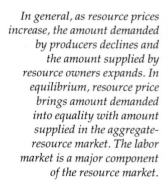

In general, as resource prices increase, the amount demanded by producers declines and the amount supplied by resource owners expands. In equilibrium, resource price brings amount demanded into equality with amount supplied in the aggregate-resource market. The labor market is a major component of the resource market.

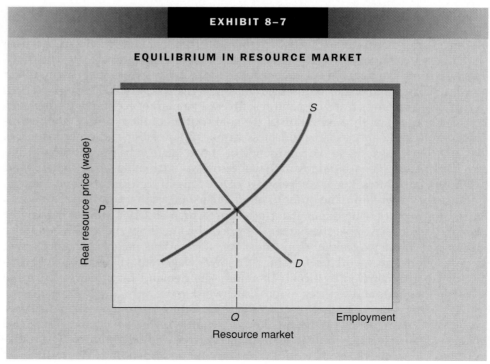

EXHIBIT 8–7

EQUILIBRIUM IN RESOURCE MARKET

other. Much of macroeconomics concerns these repercussions. As we proceed, we will consider these two important markets in more depth.

While we have lumped all resources together into a single aggregated market, it is important to recognize that the market for labor services is the dominant resource market. In the United States, wage costs make up approximately 70 percent of production costs. Since the labor market is both large and very important, we will often concentrate on it rather than the general resource market.

LOANABLE FUNDS MARKET

The loanable funds market coordinates the actions of borrowers and lenders. This market permits households, businesses, and governments to borrow against their assets or against future expected income. As the circular flow of income implies, households are generally net suppliers of loanable funds (see Exhibit 8–1). Businesses and governments often demand loanable funds to finance capital investment projects and other expenditures. Financial institutions, such as savings and loan associations, commercial banks, insurance companies, pension funds, and the stock and bond markets, form the core of this market.

In essence, borrowers are exchanging future income for purchasing power now. The interest rate is the price they must pay to do so. Most of us are impatient, wanting things now rather than in the future, and interest is the cost we pay for impatience. From the lender's viewpoint, interest is a premium received for waiting, for delaying possible expenditures into the future.

The interest rate can also be thought of as the price of credit. Lenders are supplying credit and borrowers are demanding credit. The interest rate brings the choices of borrowers and lenders into harmony.

It is helpful to think of the interest rate in two ways. First, there is the **money interest rate,** the percentage of the amount borrowed that must be paid to the lender in the future, in addition to the principal amount borrowed. Money interest rates are those typically quoted in newspapers and business publications. When there is inflation, the money rate of interest may be a misleading indicator of real borrowing costs, since rising prices shrink the purchasing power of the loan's principal. When the principal is repaid in the future, it will not purchase as much as when the funds were initially loaned. Recognizing this fact, borrowers and lenders implicitly agree on an interest premium when they expect inflation. So the inflation leads to a higher money interest rate, which is necessary to compensate the lender for the decline in the purchasing power of money during the lifetime of the loan.

Second, there is the **real interest rate,** which reflects the real burden to borrowers and the payoff to lenders in terms of command over goods and services. The real interest rate is simply the money rate of interest adjusted for the expected rate of inflation.

Perhaps an example will clarify the distinction between the two. Suppose a person borrows $1,000 for one year at an 8 percent interest rate. After a year, the borrower must pay the lender $1,080—the $1,000 principal plus the 8 percent interest. Now, suppose during the year prices rose 8 percent as the result of inflation. Because of this, the $1,080 repayment after a year commands exactly the same purchasing power as the original $1,000 did when it was loaned. In effect,

Money interest rate
The interest rate measured in monetary units. It overstates the real cost of borrowing during an inflationary period. When inflation is anticipated, an inflationary premium will be incorporated into the nominal value of this rate. The money interest rate is often referred to as the nominal interest rate.

Real interest rate
The interest rate adjusted for expected inflation; it indicates the real cost to the borrower (and yield to the lender) in terms of goods and services.

the borrower pays back exactly the same amount of purchasing power as was borrowed. The lender receives nothing for making the purchasing power available to the borrower. In this case, the effective real interest rate was zero.

Lenders are unlikely to continue making funds available at such bargain rates. When the 8 percent inflation rate is anticipated, they will demand (and borrowers will agree to pay) a higher money interest rate to compensate for the decline in the purchasing power of the dollar. This premium for the expected decline in purchasing power of the dollar is called the **inflation premium.** Once borrowers and lenders anticipate 8 percent inflation, for example, they might agree to a 16 percent money interest rate, 8 percent of which reflects an inflationary premium and 8 percent a real interest return. (See the boxed feature, "Myths of Economics" for further explanation.) We can illustrate the relationship between the real interest rate and the money interest rate as follows:

Inflation premium
A component of the money interest rate that reflects compensation to the lender for the expected decrease, due to inflation, in the purchasing power of the principal and interest during the course of the loan. It is determined by the expected rate of future inflation.

$$\text{Real interest rate} = \text{Money interest rate} - \text{Inflation premium}$$

The size of the inflation premium, of course, varies directly with the expected rate of future inflation. When inflation is correctly anticipated, it is the real interest rate, not the money rate, that indicates the true burden of borrowers and the true yield to lenders derived from a loan.

An increase in the real interest rate makes borrowing more costly. Households, investors, and governments will reduce the amount of funds demanded as the real interest rate rises. On the other hand, a higher interest rate increases the payoff derived from waiting. Lenders will therefore supply more funds as the real interest rate increases. So, as **Exhibit 8–8** illustrates, the supply curve for loanable funds slopes upward to the right, while the demand curve has the usual downward slope. Equilibrium is present in the loanable funds market at the real interest rate that

As illustrated, the quantity of loanable funds demanded is inversely related to the real interest rate. The quantity of funds lenders are willing to supply is directly related to the real interest rate. In equilibrium, the real interest rate (r) will bring the quantity demanded and quantity supplied into balance.

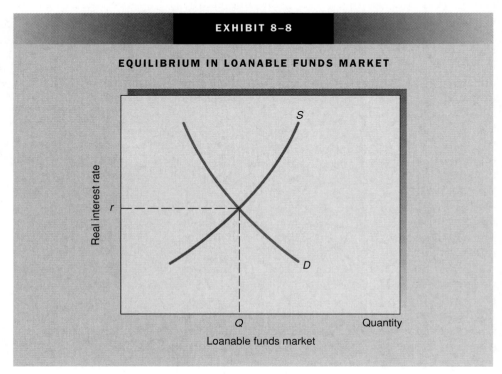

EXHIBIT 8–8

EQUILIBRIUM IN LOANABLE FUNDS MARKET

MYTHS OF ECONOMICS

"SINCE INFLATION ERODES THE BURDEN OF OUTSTANDING DEBT, IT SYSTEMATICALLY HELPS BORROWERS AT THE EXPENSE OF LENDERS."

Like most myths, this one has a grain of truth in it. Inflation does reduce the purchasing power of the proceeds paid by borrowers and received by lenders during the period while a loan is outstanding. But this is only part of the story. Inflation also influences money interest rates and therefore the amount paid by borrowers and received by lenders when funds are borrowed.

When higher rates of inflation are anticipated by decision makers, lenders will demand and borrowers will grant higher interest rates on loans because both parties will expect the value of the dollar to depreciate during the period that the loan is outstanding. If borrowers and lenders accurately anticipate a rate of inflation, they will agree to a money interest rate that will be just high enough to compensate lenders for the decline in the purchasing power of the loan proceeds due to inflation during the period while the loan is outstanding. For example, suppose a borrower and a lender would agree to a 5 percent interest rate if they anticipated a stable price level in the future. Instead, if both expected prices to rise 10 percent annually, they would agree to a 15 percent interest rate. If their expectations are realized, the real interest rate will be 5 percent in both cases.

Of course, decision makers will not always be able to forecast the future rate of inflation accurately. Sometimes the actual rate of inflation may prove to be higher than expected, while in other instances it may be lower. There is no reason, however, to expect that these errors will be systematic.

If the actual rate of inflation is higher than was expected, borrowers will tend to gain relative to lenders. For example, suppose borrowers and lenders expect a 3 percent future rate of inflation and therefore agree to an 8 percent interest rate on a loan—5 percent representing the real interest rate and 3 percent the inflation premium. If the actual rate of inflation turns out to be higher than 3 percent—6 percent for example—the real amount paid by the borrower and received by the lender will decline. When the actual rate of inflation is greater than was anticipated, borrowers gain relative to lenders.

But, the converse is true when the actual rate of inflation is less than expected. Suppose that after the borrower and lender agree to the 8 percent loan, the price level is stable while the loan is outstanding. In this case, the borrower ends up paying an 8 percent real interest rate, rather than the 5 percent that was anticipated. When the actual rate of inflation is less than anticipated, lenders gain at the expense of borrowers.

Thus, it is not inflation per se that produces any redistributional effects, but rather the actual rate of inflation relative to the expected rate. Since there is no reason to believe that borrowers and lenders will systematically either underestimate or overestimate the future rate of inflation, there is no reason to believe that it will systematically help one relative to the other.

brings the amount of funds demanded by borrowers into equality with the amount supplied by lenders.

Businesses and governments often borrow funds by issuing bonds that yield an interest rate. Issuing bonds is simply a method of demanding loanable funds. In turn, the purchasers of bonds are supplying loanable funds. It is important to note that there is an inverse relationship between bond prices and interest rates. Higher bond prices are the same thing as lower interest rates. (See the boxed feature, "Applications in Economics," for further explanation.)

As was true for the resource market, the loanable funds and the goods and services markets are closely interrelated. We previously indicated that the reduction in the interest rate that generally accompanies a lower price level when the supply of money is constant helps explain why the *AD* curve slopes downward to the right. In addition, the real interest rate may change for other reasons. When it does, it will affect the aggregate-demand schedule. The real interest rate influences aggregate demand because people who borrow money generally do so in order to

BONDS, INTEREST RATES, AND BOND PRICES

Bonds are simply IOUs issued by firms and governments. Issuing bonds is a method of borrowing money to finance economic activity. The entity issuing the bond promises to pay the bondholder the amount borrowed (called *principal*) at a designated future date plus a fixed amount of interest. Some bonds pay the interest at designated intervals (that is, on a specific date each year). Others pay both principal and interest when the bonds mature at a specified date in the future. The bond shown here is a typical government bond. Its face value is $10,000, and it will pay the owner 9¼ percent interest paid annually (half in August and half in February) over a 30-year period. The bond matures on February 15, 2016. At that time, the owner of the bond will receive from the Treasury Department the $10,000 principal plus the interest for the final six months.

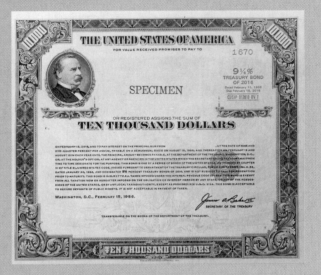

Even though most bonds are issued for long periods of time, they can be sold to another party prior to their maturity. Each day, sales of previously issued bonds comprise the majority of bonds bought and sold on the bond market. Like most stocks traded on the stock market, new issues of bonds account for only a small portion of all bond sales.

So how does a change in the market interest rate affect bond prices? Suppose you have just bought a newly issued $1,000 bond that pays 8 percent per year *in perpetuity* (forever) on the $1,000 principal.[1] As long as you own the bond, you are entitled to a fixed return of $80 per year. Let us also assume that after you have held the bond for one year and have collected your $80 interest for that year, the market interest rate increases to 10 percent.[2] How will the increase in the interest rate affect the market price on your bond? Since bond purchasers can now earn 10 percent interest if they buy newly issued bonds, they will be unwilling to pay more than $800 for your bond, which pays only $80 interest per year. After all, why would anyone pay $1,000 for a bond that yields only $80 interest per year when the same $1,000 will now purchase a bond that yields $100 (10 percent) per year? Once the interest rate has risen to

10 percent, your 8 percent, $1,000 bond will no longer sell for its original value. If potential buyers expect the new 10 percent rate to continue, the market value of your bond will fall to $800. You have experienced a $200 capital loss on the bond during the year. In this manner, rising market interest rates cause bond prices to decline.

On the other hand, falling interest rates will cause bond prices to rise. If the market interest rate had fallen to 6 percent, what would have happened to the market value of your bond? (Hint: $80 is 6 percent of $1,333.) Bond prices and interest rates are inversely linked to each other.

---

[1] Undated securities of this sort are available in the United Kingdom. They are called *consols*.

[2] The astute reader will recognize an oversimplification in this discussion. In reality, the economy supports a variety of interest rates, which usually tend to move together.

Note: Bonds like the one shown above are no longer distributed to buyers. Instead, a buyer receives a letter certifying that a bond is held in the buyer's name on a database at the institution of purchase.

---

buy things. Since a higher real interest rate would discourage borrowing, it would also discourage spending. As we proceed, we will analyze in more detail the interrelationship between the loanable funds market and the goods and services market.

EQUILIBRIUM IN OUR THREE-MARKET MACROECONOMY

We have now discussed all three basic macroeconomic markets: the goods and services market, the resource market, and the loanable funds market. From these discussions it would be easy to get the impression that each market exists more or less independently. Nothing could be further from the truth. Instead, the three basic macroeconomic markets are as dependent on one another in the way that they work as the legs of a three-legged stool.

Exhibit 8–9 illustrates equilibrium conditions in the three basic macroeconomic markets of our circular flow model of Exhibit 8–1. Aggregate demand and aggregate supply are in equilibrium at the price level P_1 and output rate Y_f (part "a"). Since the P_1 price level was anticipated both by buyers and by sellers, the economy is operating at its long-run (full-employment) capacity. In the resource market, price also equates amount demanded and amount supplied (part "b"). Since the economy is at long-run capacity, only normal unemployment is present in the labor market, an important subcomponent of the resource market. Finally, the real interest rate (r) has brought the amount demanded and amount supplied into balance in the loanable funds market (part "c").

Before an economy can achieve macroeconomic equilibrium, equilibrium must be achieved in each of the three basic macromarkets. Changes in any one of these markets will influence the equilibrium price and quantity in other markets. In fact, macroeconomics largely concerns tracing the impact of a change in one market through to other markets, particularly the goods and services market.

When an economy is in long-run macroeconomic equilibrium, interrelationships among the three basic markets—goods and services, resources, and loanable funds—will be in harmony. The price of resources relative to the price of goods and services will be such that business firms, on average, will be just able to cover their cost of production, including a competitive return on their investment. If this were not the case, producers would seek to either contract or expand output. For example, if the prices of resources were so high (relative to producers' prices) that firms were unable to cover their costs, many producers would cut back output or perhaps even discontinue production. Aggregate output would thereby be altered. Conversely, if resource prices were so low that firms were able to earn an above-market return, profit-seeking firms would expand output. New firms would begin production. Again, these forces would alter conditions in the goods and services market.

Similarly, the relationship between interest rates in the loanable funds market and product prices must be such that the typical firm is just able to earn normal returns on its investments. In other words, the typical producer's return to capital must equal the interest rate—that is, the opportunity cost of capital. Higher returns would induce producers to expand output, while lower returns would cause them to cut back on production. Therefore, when macroeconomic equilibrium is present, prices in these three markets will be such that buyers and sellers in each of the markets are willing to continue with the current arrangements.

Here we indicate equilibrium conditions in the three basic markets that coordinate macroeconomic activity. These markets are highly interrelated. Changes in one influence equilibrium conditions in the other two.

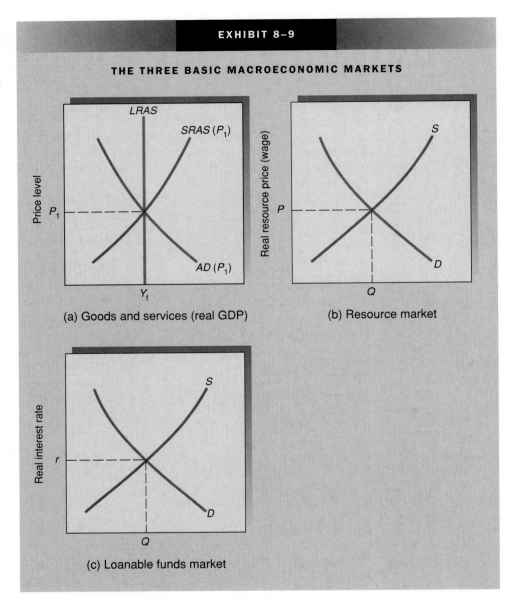

EXHIBIT 8-9

THE THREE BASIC MACROECONOMIC MARKETS

(a) Goods and services (real GDP)

(b) Resource market

(c) Loanable funds market

LOOKING AHEAD

In the next chapter, we will consider how our simple aggregate-demand/aggregate-supply model adjusts to changing conditions. Factors that shift demand and supply in one or more of the markets will be analyzed. The interrelationships among the basic macroeconomic markets will be discussed in more detail. As we proceed, we will use our model of basic macroeconomic markets to address these questions.

CHAPTER SUMMARY

1. The circular flow of income illustrates the significance of three highly aggregated markets: (a) goods and

services, (b) resources, and (c) loanable funds. The resource market coordinates the exchange of labor and other productive inputs between the household and business sectors. In the goods and services market, the demand of households, business investors, governments, and foreigners for products is coordinated with the current supply of commodities produced. The loanable funds market coordinates the actions of borrowers and lenders, and thereby channels the net savings of households back into the flow of income as investment or government expenditures.

2. The willingness of consumers, investors, governments, and foreigners (net exports) to purchase goods and services determines aggregate demand. The aggregate-demand curve indicates the various quantities of domestically produced goods and services that purchasers are willing to buy at different price levels.

3. Assuming the money supply is constant, there are three reasons why the aggregate quantity demanded of goods and services will be greater at a lower price level than at a higher level. First, a lower price level will increase the wealth of persons holding the fixed money balances. This increase in wealth will stimulate additional spending on goods and services. Second, at the lower price level, the demand for money will decline relative to the fixed supply, pushing interest rates downward, which will stimulate expenditures on interest-sensitive goods such as automobiles, homes, and investment projects. Third, a lower price level makes domestic goods less expensive relative to foreign goods, which will lead to an increase in net exports (or a decline in net imports). Each of these factors will increase the quantity of domestically produced goods and services purchased at the lower price level.

4. The aggregate-supply (AS) curve indicates the various quantities of goods and services domestic suppliers will produce at different price levels. In the short run, the aggregate-supply curve will generally slope upward to the right. This is because a higher price level improves profit margins, since the prices of important cost components are temporarily fixed in the short run.

5. Once decision makers adjust fully to a higher price level, the factors that justified the upward-sloping SRAS (short-run aggregate-supply) curve are no longer present. Output is constrained by factors such as technology and resource supply. A higher price level does not loosen these constraints. Thus, the LRAS (long-run aggregate-supply) curve is vertical.

6. Two conditions are necessary for long-run equilibrium in the goods and services market: (a) quantity demanded must equal quantity supplied, and (b) the actual price level must equal the price level decision makers anticipated when they made buying and selling decisions for the current period.

7. When the economy is in long-run equilibrium, output will be at its maximum sustainable level. Similarly, the actual rate of unemployment will equal the natural rate (the lowest rate of unemployment that can be sustained over a long period of time). Economists would say that the economy is operating at full employment in this case.

8. The aggregate-demand/aggregate-supply model tells us where the nation's price level and real output will be moving toward. In the short run, price and output will move toward an intersection of the aggregate-demand (AD) and short-run aggregate-supply (SRAS) curves. In the long run, price and output will gravitate to the levels represented by the intersection of AD, SRAS, and LRAS.

9. When the current price level differs from what was expected, output will differ from the economy's long-run capacity. When the current price level is higher than anticipated, real wages and interest rates will be abnormally low. Unemployment will temporarily fall below its natural rate. Current output will temporarily exceed the economy's long-run capacity. In contrast, when the current price level is lower than was anticipated, real wages and interest rates will be abnormally high. Unemployment will exceed its natural rate. Under such circumstances, current output will be lower than the economy's long-run capacity.

10. Business firms demand labor and other resources because they contribute to the production of goods and services that the firms hope to sell at a profit. Individuals supply resources in order to earn income. Price in the resource market coordinates the actions of buyers and sellers. The labor market is the largest component of the general resource market.

11. The interest rate in the loanable funds market is the price borrowers pay to obtain purchasing power now rather than in the future. From the lender's viewpoint, interest is a premium one receives for delaying expenditures into the future. It is the price of credit.

12. It is important to distinguish between real and money interest rates. The real interest rate reflects the real burden to borrowers and the payoff to lenders in terms of command over goods and services. In addition to this real burden, the money rate of interest also reflects the expected rate of inflation during the period the loan is outstanding. The real rate of interest is equal to the money rate of interest minus the inflation premium. The latter depends on the expected rate of inflation.

13. Inflation results in higher nominal interest rates. It only helps debtors when it is underestimated. Since there is no reason to expect decision makers to systematically underestimate the inflation rate, there is no reason to expect that it will systematically be advantageous to debtors.

14. The presence of macroeconomic equilibrium requires that equilibrium be achieved in all three key macroeconomic markets: (a) goods and services, (b) resources, and (c) loanable funds. Changes in any one of these markets

will influence price and quantity in the other markets. Macroeconomics is primarily about how these key markets adjust to various changes in economic conditions and alternative policies.

CRITICAL-ANALYSIS QUESTIONS

1. In your own words, explain why aggregate demand is inversely related to the price level. Why isn't the slope of the aggregate-demand curve determined in the same way as the slope of the demand curve for an individual good?

2. What are the major factors influencing aggregate supply in the long run? Why doesn't the long-run aggregate-supply (*LRAS*) curve slope upward to the right like *SRAS*?

3. What is the natural rate of unemployment? Why might the actual rate of unemployment differ from the natural rate of unemployment? If the actual rate of unemployment is less than the natural rate, can this situation be sustained over a long period of time? Why or why not?

*4. Suppose prices had been rising at a 3 percent annual rate in recent years. A major union signs a three-year contract calling for increases in money wage rates of 6 percent annually. What will happen to the real wages of the union members if the price level is constant (unchanged) during the next three years? If other unions signed similar contracts, what will probably happen to the unemployment rate? Why? Answer the same questions under conditions in which the price level increases at an annual rate of 8 percent during the next three years.

5. What is the current money interest rate on 30-year government bonds? Is this also the real interest rate? Why or why not?

6. What conditions are required for a short-run equilibrium in the goods and services market? For a long-run equilibrium?

*7. In Chapter 3, we indicated the other things that are held constant when the supply and demand schedules for a specific good are constructed. What were they? What are the key "other things" held constant when the *AS, LRAS,* and *SRAS* schedules are constructed?

8. If the price level in the current period is higher than what buyers and sellers anticipated, what will tend to happen to real wages, real interest rates, and the level of employment? How will the actual rate of unemployment compare with the natural rate of unemployment? Will the current rate of output be sustainable in the future? Why or why not?

9. Suppose that you saved and purchased a $5,000 bond which pays 6 percent interest and matures in three years. If the inflation rate in recent years has been steady at 3 per cent annually, what is the estimated real rate of interest? If the inflation rate during the next three years remains steady at 3 percent, by how much will the purchasing power of your bond increase each year? If the inflation rate during the next three years is 6 percent, what will happen to the purchasing power of the interest and principal derived from your bond?

*10. How are the following related to each other?
   a. The long-run equilibrium rate of output.
   b. The potential real GDP of the economy.
   c. The output rate resulting in the equality of the actual and natural rates of unemployment.

*11. Can the real interest rate ever be negative? Can you cite any examples of a negative real interest rate? If the interest rate is determined by market forces, is a negative real interest likely to persist over a long period of time? Why or why not?

*12. If a bond pays $1,000 per year in perpetuity (each year in the future), what will be the market price of the bond when the long-term interest rate is 10 percent? What would it be if the interest rate were 5 percent?

*13. How are bond prices related to interest rates? Why are they related?

14. The following chart indicates the aggregate demand (*AD*) and short-run aggregate supply (*SRAS*) schedules of decision makers for the current period. Both buyers and sellers previously anticipated that the price level during the current period would be P_{105}.

AD_{105}	PRICE LEVEL	$SRAS_{105}$
6,300	90	4,500
6,000	95	4,800
5,700	100	5,100
5,400	105	5,400
5,100	110	5,700
4,800	115	6,000

   a. Indicate the quantity of GDP that will be produced during this period.
   b. Will it be a long-run equilibrium level of GDP? Why or why not?
   c. What will be the relationship between the actual and natural rates of unemployment during the period? Explain your answer.

15. Consider an economy with the following aggregate-demand (*AD*) and aggregate-supply (*AS*) schedules.

---

*Asterisk denotes questions for which answers are given in Appendix C.

Decision makers have previously made decisions anticipating that the price level during the current period would be P_{105}.

AD_{105}	PRICE LEVEL	$SRAS_{105}$
6,900	90	4,500
6,600	95	4,800
6,300	100	5,100
6,000	105	5,400
5,700	110	5,700
5,400	115	6,000

a. Indicate the quantity of GDP that will be produced during the period.

b. Is it a long-run equilibrium level of GDP? Why or why not?

c. How will the unemployment rate during the current period compare with this economy's natural rate of unemployment?

d. Will the current rate of GDP be sustainable into the future? Why or why not?

16. Does inflation help debtors relative to lenders? Why or why not? Do you think that inflation will help people with low incomes relative to those with higher incomes? Explain. How will an unanticipated increase in the inflation rate influence the government's liability for the national debt? Is the government helped by inflation? Discuss.

CHAPTER NINE

WORKING WITH OUR
BASIC AGGREGATE-DEMAND/
AGGREGATE-SUPPLY MODEL

We might as well reasonably dispute whether it is the upper or under blade of a pair of scissors that cuts a piece of paper, as whether value is governed by [demand] or [supply].

ALFRED MARSHALL[1]

CHAPTER FOCUS

■ What factors will cause shifts in aggregate demand? What factors will shift aggregate supply?
■ How will the goods and services market adjust to changes in aggregate demand?
■ How does the economy adjust to changes in aggregate supply?
■ What causes fluctuations in output and employment?
■ Does a market economy have a self-correcting mechanism that will lead it to full employment?

---

[1]Alfred Marshall, *Principles of Economics*, 8th ed. (London: Macmillan, 1920), p. 348.

I n Chapter 8, we focused on the equilibrium conditions in the three basic macroeconomic markets. Equilibrium is important, but we live in a dynamic world that continually wars against it. Markets are always being affected by unexpected changes such as the discovery of a vastly improved computer chip, shifts in consumer confidence, a drought in midwestern agricultural states, or changes in defense expenditures as the result of national security conditions. Consequently, equilibrium is continually disrupted. Thus, if we want to understand how the real world works, analysis of how macroeconomic markets adjust to dynamic change is of crucial importance.

We are now ready to consider how macroeconomic markets adjust to changes in aggregate demand and aggregate supply. As in the last chapter, we will continue to assume that the government's tax, spending, and monetary policies are unchanged. For now, we want to help the reader understand how macroeconomic markets work. Once this objective is achieved, we will be better able to understand both the potential and the limitations of macroeconomic policy.

ANTICIPATED AND UNANTICIPATED CHANGES

Anticipated change
A change that is foreseen by decision makers in time for them to adjust.

It is important to distinguish between anticipated and unanticipated changes in markets. **Anticipated changes** are foreseen by economic participants. Decision makers have time to adjust to them before they occur. For example, suppose that under normal weather conditions, a new drought-resistant hybrid seed can be expected to expand the production of feed grain in the Midwest by 10 percent next year. As a result, buyers and sellers will plan for a larger supply and lower prices in the future. They will adjust their decision-making behavior accordingly.

Unanticipated change
A change that decision makers could not reasonably foresee. Thus, choices made prior to the event did not take the event into account.

In contrast, **unanticipated changes** catch people by surprise. Our world is characterized by dynamic change—new products are introduced, technological discoveries alter production costs, droughts reduce crop yields, demand expands for some goods and contracts for others. It is impossible for decision makers to foresee many of these changes.

Economics largely concerns how people respond and markets adjust to changing circumstances. As we will explain in a moment, there is good reason to expect that the adjustment process will differ depending on whether a change is anticipated or not.

FACTORS THAT SHIFT AGGREGATE DEMAND

The aggregate-demand curve isolates the impact of the price level on the quantity demanded of goods and services. However, the price level is not the only factor that influences the demand for goods and services. When we constructed the aggregate-demand curve, we assumed that several other factors affecting the choices of buyers in the goods and services market were constant. Changes in these "other factors" will shift the entire aggregate-demand schedule, altering the amount purchased at each price level. Let us take a closer look at the major factors capable of doing this.

CHANGES IN REAL WEALTH

In Chapter 8 we indicated that changes in the price level will alter the real value of money balances and therefore the real wealth of people. But the wealth of individuals—the value of their assets—may change for reasons other than a change in the price level. For example, during the 1982–1987 period, stock prices in the United States nearly tripled. This stock-market boom increased the real wealth of stock-holders. In contrast, both stock prices and housing prices declined during 1990, reducing the wealth of households.

How will changes in the wealth of households affect the demand for goods and services? As the real wealth of households increases—perhaps as the result of higher prices in stock, housing, and/or real estate markets—people will demand more goods and services. As **Exhibit 9–1** illustrates, the increase in wealth will shift the entire aggregate-demand *(AD)* schedule to the right (from AD_0 to AD_1). More goods and services are purchased at each price level. Conversely, a reduction in wealth will reduce the demand for goods and services, shifting the *AD* curve to the left (to AD_2) as the result of a decline in the wealth of households.

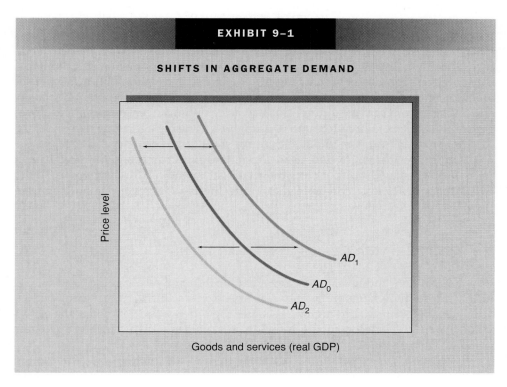

EXHIBIT 9–1

SHIFTS IN AGGREGATE DEMAND

Price level

AD_1

AD_0

AD_2

Goods and services (real GDP)

An increase in real wealth, such as would result from a stock-market boom, for example, will increase aggregate demand, shifting the entire curve to the right (from AD_0 to AD_1). In contrast, a reduction in real wealth decreases the demand for goods and services, causing AD to shift to the left (from AD_0 to AD_2).

CHANGES IN REAL INTEREST RATE

As we discussed previously, the major macroeconomic markets are closely related. A change in the real interest rate in the loanable funds market will influence the choices of consumers and investors in the goods and services market. A lower real interest rate makes it cheaper for consumers to buy major appliances, automobiles, and houses now rather than in the future. Simultaneously, a lower interest rate will also stimulate business spending on *capital goods* (investment). The interest rate influences the opportunity cost of all investment projects. If the firm must borrow, the real interest rate will contribute directly to the cost of an investment project. If the firm uses its own funds, it sacrifices real interest that could have been earned by loaning the funds to someone else had it not undertaken the investment project. Therefore, a lower real interest rate reduces the opportunity cost of a project, regardless of whether it is financed with internal funds or by borrowing.

Predictably, both households and investors will increase their current expenditures on goods and services in response to a reduction in the real interest rate. A lower real interest rate will increase aggregate demand, shifting the entire schedule to the right. In contrast, a higher real interest rate makes current consumption and investment goods more expensive and therefore tends to reduce aggregate demand, shifting the *AD* curve to the left.

BUSINESS AND HOUSEHOLD EXPECTATIONS ABOUT THE ECONOMY

What people think will happen in the future influences current purchasing decisions. Optimism concerning the future direction of the economy will stimulate current investment. Business decision makers know that an expanding economy will mean strong sales and improved profit margins. Investment today may be necessary if business firms are going to benefit fully from these opportunities. Similarly, consumers are more likely to buy big-ticket items such as automobiles and houses when they expect an expanding economy to provide them with both job security and rising income in the future. So increased optimism encourages additional expenditures by both investors and consumers, increasing aggregate demand.

Of course, pessimism about the future state of the economy exerts just the opposite impact. When investors and consumers expect an economic downturn (a recession), they will cut back on their current spending for fear of becoming overextended. This pessimism leads to a decline in aggregate demand, shifting the *AD* schedule to the left.

EXPECTED RATE OF INFLATION

When consumers and investors believe that the inflation rate is going to accelerate in the future, they have an incentive to spend more during the current period. "Buy now before prices go higher" becomes the order of the day. Thus, the expectation of an acceleration in the inflation rate will stimulate current aggregate demand, shifting the *AD* curve to the right.

In contrast, the expectation of a deceleration in the inflation rate will tend to discourage current spending. When prices are expected to stabilize (or at least increase less rapidly), the gain obtained by moving expenditures forward in time is reduced. The expectation of a deceleration in the inflation rate will thus reduce current aggregate demand, shifting the *AD* curve to the left.

CHANGES IN INCOME ABROAD

Changes in the income of a nation's trading partners will influence the demand for the nation's exports. If the income of a nation's trading partners is increasing rapidly, the demand for exports will expand. In turn, the strong demand for exports will stimulate aggregate demand. For example, rapid growth of income in Europe and Japan increases the demand of European and Japanese consumers for U.S.–produced goods. As U.S. exports expand, aggregate demand increases (the *AD* schedule shifts to the right).

Conversely, when a nation's trading partners are experiencing recessionary conditions, they reduce their purchases, including their purchases abroad. Thus, a decline in the income of a nation's trading partners tends to reduce both exports and aggregate demand.

Currently, approximately 10 percent of the goods and services produced in the United States are sold to purchasers abroad. The export sector is still larger for Canada, Mexico, and most Western European countries. The larger the size of the trade sector is, the greater the potential importance of fluctuations in income abroad as a source of instability in aggregate demand. If the demand of foreign buyers does not rise and fall at the same time as domestic demand, however, the diversity of markets will reduce the impact of fluctuations in domestic demand.

CHANGES IN EXCHANGE RATES

As we previously explained, a change in a nation's price level relative to that of its trading partners will influence both net exports and the quantity of goods and services demanded at home. So will a change in the *exchange rate*, the value of a nation's currency in terms of the curency of another country. Changes in the value of the dollar on the foreign exchange rate market will alter the prices of imports to U.S. consumers and the prices of U.S. exports to foreign consumers.

Consider the impact of an increase in the exchange rate value of the U.S. dollar relative to the British pound. The increase in the exchange rate value of the dollar will make the dollar price of British goods cheaper to U.S. consumers because each dollar will now buy more pounds. In turn, this reduction in the dollar price of British goods will stimulate U.S. imports. Simultaneously, the increase in the exchange rate value of the dollar will make the price tag on U.S. goods (in terms of pounds) more expensive to British consumers, since it will take more pounds to purchase a dollar than was previously the case. Predictably, British consumers will reduce their purchases of American-made goods. Thus, the increase in the exchange rate value of the dollar will stimulate imports and retard exports to the United States. Net exports will decline, which will retard aggregate demand (that is, shift the *AD* schedule to the left).

A decline in the exchange rate value of the dollar will have just the opposite effect. When there is a decline in the value of the dollar on the foreign exchange market, foreign-produced goods become more expensive for U.S. consumers, while U.S.–produced goods become cheaper for foreigners. As a result, net exports will increase and thereby stimulate aggregate demand (shifting *AD* to the right).[2]

SUMMARY OF FACTORS THAT SHIFT AGGREGATE DEMAND

The accompanying "Thumbnail Sketch" summarizes the major factors causing shifts in aggregate demand. Shortly, we will analyze how the goods and services market adjusts to changes in demand. The government's spending, taxing, and monetary policies also influence aggregate demand. Knowledge of how the goods and services market works will help us better understand how fiscal and monetary policies work.

UNANTICIPATED CHANGES IN AGGREGATE DEMAND

How will unanticipated changes in aggregate demand influence price and output in the goods and services market? It will take time for decision makers to respond fully to unexpected changes. Initially, it may be unclear to decision makers whether a change—an increase in sales, for example—reflects a random occurrence or a real change in demand conditions. It will also take businesses some time to differentiate between temporary fluctuations and more permanent changes. Even after decision makers are convinced that market conditions have changed, time will be required for them to make new decisions and carry them out. In some cases, complete adjustment will also be delayed by the presence of

---

THUMBNAIL SKETCH

WHAT FACTORS WILL INFLUENCE AGGREGATE DEMAND?

These factors will increase (decrease) aggregate demand (*AD*).[a]

1. An increase (decrease) in real wealth.
2. A decrease (increase) in the real rate of interest.
3. An increase in the optimism (pessimism) of businesses and consumers about future economic conditions.

4. An increase (decrease) in the expected rate of inflation.
5. Higher (lower) real incomes abroad.
6. A reduction (increase) in the exchange rate value of the nation's currency.

---

[a]The important factors of macroeconomic policy will be considered later.

---

[2]Later, when we consider the topic of international finance, we will analyze in more detail the determinants of the exchange rate and consider more fully the impact of changes in the exchange rate value of a nation's currency.

long-term contracts. All of these factors will reduce the speed of market adjustments to changing demand conditions.

INCREASES IN AGGREGATE DEMAND

Part "a" of **Exhibit 9–2** illustrates how an economy that is initially in long-run equilibrium will adjust to an unanticipated increase in aggregate demand. Initially the economy is in long-run equilibrium at output Y_f and price level P_{100} (point E_1). Aggregate demand and aggregate supply are in balance. Decision makers have correctly anticipated the current price level, and the economy is operating at its full-employment level of output.

Consider what would happen if this equilibrium were disrupted by a stock-market boom or burst of business optimism that caused an unanticipated increase in aggregate demand (shift from AD_1 to AD_2). An excess demand for goods and services would result at the initial price level, (P_{100}). Responding to the strong sales and excess demand, businesses would increase their prices. Their profit margins would improve (since product prices increase relative to the cost of resources), and they would expand output along the *SRAS*. The economy would move to a short-run equilibrium (e_2), at a larger output (Y_2) and higher price level (P_{105}). (Note: a short-run equilibrium is indicated with a small e, while a capital E is used to designate a long-run equilibrium.)

For a time, many wage rates, interest payments, rents, and other resource prices would still reflect the initial price level (P_{100}) and the previously weaker demand. Since markets do not adjust instantaneously, these resource prices, and therefore costs, would lag behind prices in the goods and services market. Thus, the higher price level temporarily would improve profit margins, which, in turn, would provide the incentive for business firms to expand both output and employment in the short run. As a result, the unemployment rate would drop below its natural rate, and output would temporarily exceed the economy's long-run potential output level.[3]

This is not the end of the story, however. The strong demand accompanying this high level of output will place upward pressure on prices in resource and loanable funds markets. With time, the strong demand conditions will push wages, other resource prices, and real interest rates upward. As part "b" of

---

[3]Thoughtful students may wonder how output (and by implication, the quantity of resources) can be increased, even temporarily, when *real* wages and resource prices more generally are declining. There are two reasons why this may be the case. First, in an inflationary environment workers (and other resource suppliers) may be fooled, at least temporarily, by an increase in *money* wages (and resource prices) that is *less rapid than the inflation rate*. Responding to the higher money wages, workers may supply more labor even though their real wages have fallen. While we have presented the analysis within the framework of a noninflationary environment, the basic linkage between real wages (costs) and *SRAS* still holds. A reduction in the real wage rate, even when it takes the form of a nominal wage increase that is less than the inflation rate, will reduce real costs, and thereby increase *SRAS*. Second, the resource base may temporarily expand in response to strong demand conditions because the *cost of entering* the labor force will decline during this boom phase of the business cycle. Potential new labor-force entrants will be able to find jobs quickly at this time. Thus, the size of the labor force will tend to grow rapidly during an economic expansion. Conversely, the labor force will tend to shrink (or grow less rapidly) during a business contraction, when the cost of entering the labor force will be high.

In response to an unanticipated increase in aggregate demand for goods and services (shift from AD_1 to AD_2), prices will rise (to P_{105}) in the short run and output will temporarily exceed full-employment capacity (a). However, with the passage of time, prices in resource markets, including the labor market, will rise as the result of the strong demand. The higher resource prices will mean higher costs, which will reduce aggregate supply to $SRAS_2$ (b). In the long run, a new equilibrium at a higher price level (P_{110}) and an output consistent with the economy's sustainable potential will result. Thus, the increase in demand will expand output only temporarily.

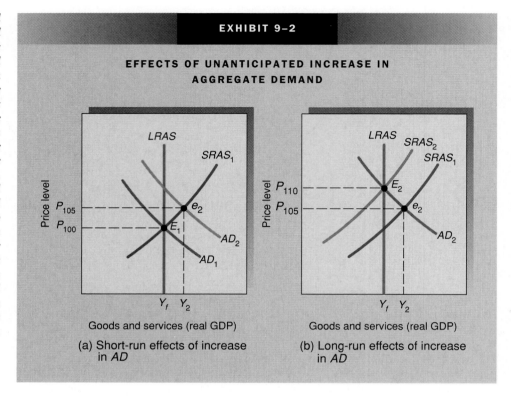

EXHIBIT 9–2

EFFECTS OF UNANTICIPATED INCREASE IN AGGREGATE DEMAND

(a) Short-run effects of increase in *AD*

(b) Long-run effects of increase in *AD*

Exhibit 9–2 illustrates, the rising resource prices and costs will shift the short-run aggregate supply to the left (to $SRAS_2$). Eventually, a new long-run equilibrium (E_2) will be established at a higher price level (P_{110}) that is correctly anticipated by decision makers.

Thus, the increase in real GDP above the economy's long-run potential is only temporary. It will last only until there is an opportunity to alter the temporarily fixed resource prices (and interest rates) upward in light of the new stronger demand conditions. As this happens, profit margins return to their normal level, output recedes to the economy's long-run potential, and unemployment returns to its natural rate.

Since an increase in aggregate demand does not alter the economy's productive capacity, it cannot permanently expand output (beyond Y_f). The expansion in demand temporarily expands output, but over the long term its major effect will be higher prices (inflation).

REDUCTIONS IN AGGREGATE DEMAND

How would the goods and services market adjust to an unanticipated reduction in aggregate demand? For example, suppose decision makers become more pessimistic about the future or that an unexpected decline in income abroad reduces the demand for exports. **Exhibit 9–3** will help us analyze this issue.

Once again, we consider an economy that is in long-run equilibrium (E_1) at output Y_1 and price level P_{100} (part "a"). Long-run equilibrium is disturbed by the

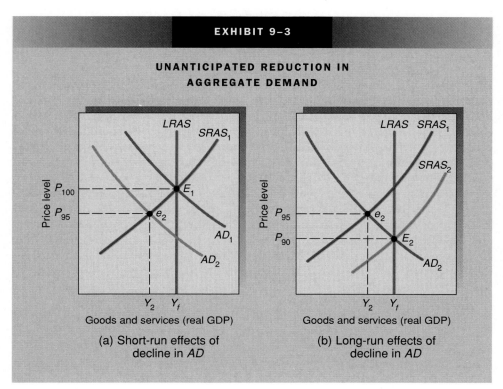

EXHIBIT 9–3

UNANTICIPATED REDUCTION IN AGGREGATE DEMAND

(a) Short-run effects of decline in AD

(b) Long-run effects of decline in AD

The short-run impact of an unanticipated reduction in aggregate demand (shift from AD_1 to AD_2) will be a decline in output to Y_2 and a lower price level, P_{95} (a). Temporarily, profit margins will decline, output will fall, and unemployment will rise above its natural rate. In the long run, weak demand and excess supply in the resource market will lead to lower wage rates and resource prices. This will reduce costs, leading to an expansion in short-run aggregate supply (shift to $SRAS_2$ (b). However, this method of restoring equilibrium (E_2) may be both highly painful and quite lengthy.

reduction in aggregate demand: the shift from AD_1 to AD_2. As the result of the decline in demand, businesses will be unable to sell Y_f units of output at the initial price level of P_{100}. In the short run, business firms will both reduce output (to Y_2) and cut prices (to P_{95}) in response to the weak demand conditions. Since many costs of business firms are temporarily fixed, profit margins will decline. Predictably, firms will cut back on output and lay off workers, causing the unemployment rate to rise. The actual rate of unemployment will rise above the economy's natural rate of unemployment. Weak demand and excess supply will be widespread in resource markets. These forces will place downward pressure on resource prices.

If resource prices quickly adjust downward in response to weak demand and rising unemployment, then the decline in output to Y_2 will be brief. Lower resource prices will reduce costs and thereby increase aggregate supply (shift to $SRAS_2$). As part "b" of Exhibit 9–3 illustrates, the result will be a new equilibrium (E_2) at the economy's full-employment output rate (Y_f) and a lower price level (P_{90}).

Resource prices, though, may not adjust quickly. Long-term contracts and uncertainty as to whether the weak demand conditions are merely temporary will slow the adjustment process. In addition, individual workers and union officials may be highly reluctant to be the first to accept lower nominal wages.

If resource prices are inflexible in a downward direction, as many economists believe, the adjustment to a reduction in aggregate demand will be both lengthy and painful. Prolonged periods of economic recession—below-capacity output rates and abnormally high unemployment—may occur before long-run equilibrium is restored.

SHIFTS IN AGGREGATE SUPPLY

What happens if aggregate demand stays the same but aggregate supply changes? The answer to this question depends on whether the aggregate supply change is long run or short run. By a long-run change in aggregate supply, we mean a change in the economy's long-run production possibilities (sustainable potential output). For example, the invention of a more efficient source of energy would cause a long-run change in aggregate supply. In such a situation, both long-run *(LRAS)* and short-run *(SRAS)* aggregate supply would change.

In contrast, changes that *temporarily* alter the productive capability of an economy will shift the *SRAS* curve, but not the *LRAS*. A drought in California would be an example of such a short-run change. The drought will hurt in the short run, but it will eventually end, and output will return to the long-run normal rate. Changes that are temporary in nature will shift only *SRAS*. Let us now consider the major factors capable of shifting the *LRAS* and *SRAS* schedules.

CHANGES IN LONG-RUN AGGREGATE SUPPLY

When constructing the *LRAS* curve, the quantity of resources, level of technology, and institutional arrangements that influence the productivity and efficiency of resource use are held constant. Changes in any of these three determinants of output would cause the *LRAS* curve to shift.

As part "a" of **Exhibit 9–4** illustrates, changes that increase the economy's productive capacity—its maximum sustainable output at full employment—will shift the *LRAS* curve to the right. With the passage of time, net investment can expand the supply of physical capital, natural resources, and labor (human resources). Investment in physical capital can expand the supply of buildings, machines, and other physical assets. Search and discovery can increase the supply of natural resources. With the passage of time, changes in population and labor-force participation may affect the supply of labor. Similarly, education, training, and skill-enhancing experience can improve the quality of the labor force, and thereby expand the supply of human resources.

Such increases in the economy's resource base will make it possible to produce and sustain a larger rate of output. Both the *LRAS* and *SRAS* curves will increase (shift to the right). On the other hand, a lasting reduction in the quantity (or quality) of resources will reduce both the current and long-term production capacity of the economy, shifting both *LRAS* and *SRAS* curves to the left.

Improvements in technology—the discovery of economical new products or less costly ways of producing goods and services—also permit us to squeeze a larger output from a specific resource supply. The enormous improvement in our living standards during the last 250 years is, to a large degree, the result of the discovery and adoption of technologically superior ways of transforming resources into goods and services. The discovery of the steam engine, and later the internal combustion engine, electricity, and nuclear power has vastly altered our energy sources. The development of the railroad, the automobile, and the airplane dramatically changed both the cost and speed of transportation. More recently,

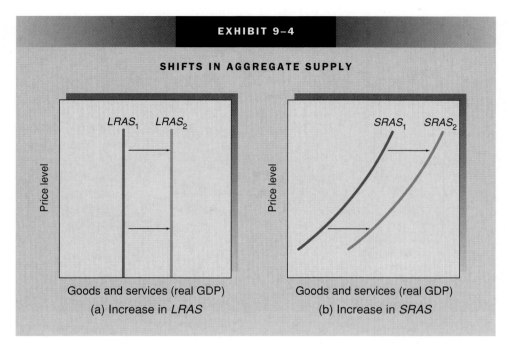

EXHIBIT 9–4

SHIFTS IN AGGREGATE SUPPLY

(a) Increase in *LRAS*

(b) Increase in *SRAS*

Such factors as an increase in the stock of capital or an improvement in technology will expand the economy's potential output and shift the LRAS to the right (a). Such factors as a reduction in resource prices, favorable weather, or a temporary decrease in the world price of an important imported resource would shift the SRAS to the right (b). Of course, changes that resulted in a decrease in either LRAS or SRAS would shift the respective schedules to the left.

the development of the microcomputers, compact disc players, microwave ovens, video cameras and cassette players, and fax machines has vastly expanded our productive capacity and the ways in which we work and play. Improvements in technology enhance our **productivity** and thereby shift the *LRAS* curve to the right.

Finally, institutional changes may also influence the efficiency of resource use and thereby alter the *LRAS* schedule. Public policy increases aggregate supply when it enhances economic efficiency by providing, for example, public goods at a low cost, or police and legal protection against invasions by others, including polluters, who would use resources without the permission of their owners. In contrast, institutional arrangements sometimes promote waste and increase production costs. For example, studies indicate that minimum wage legislation reduces employment and restricts the opportunity for training, particularly in the case of youthful workers. Output restrictions accompanying agricultural price supports generally result in inefficient production methods and reductions in output. Such arrangements reduce aggregate supply.

The long-run growth trend of real GDP in the United States has been approximately 3 percent per year. This indicates that increases in the supply of resources and improvements in productivity have gradually expanded potential real output. Hence, the *LRAS* and *SRAS* curves have gradually drifted to the right at about a 3 percent annual rate, sometimes a little faster and sometimes a little slower.

Productivity
The average output produced per worker during a specific time period. It is usually measured in terms of output per hour worked.

CHANGES IN SHORT-RUN AGGREGATE SUPPLY

Changes can sometimes influence current output without altering the economy's long-run capacity. When this is the case, the *SRAS* curve will shift even though *LRAS*

Improvements in technology enhance our production possibilities and thereby shift the long-run aggregate supply to the right.

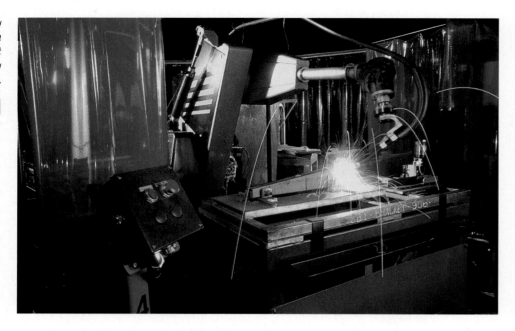

is unchanged. What types of changes would do this? When we derived the *SRAS* schedule in Chapter 8, we noted explicitly that resource prices and the expected price level (and therefore the inflation rate in the immediate future) were being held constant. Changes in either of these factors will alter *SRAS* but not necessarily *LRAS*.

A reduction in resource prices will lower costs and therefore shift the *SRAS* curve to the right, as illustrated in part "b" of Exhibit 9–4. However, unless the lower prices of resources reflect a long-term increase in the supply of resources, they will not alter *LRAS*. Conversely, an increase in the price of resources will increase costs, shifting the *SRAS* curve to the left. But unless the higher prices are the result of a long-term reduction in the size of the economy's resource base, they will not reduce *LRAS*.[4]

Supply shock
An unexpected event that temporarily either increases or decreases aggregate supply.

In addition, various supply shocks may also alter current output without directly affecting the productive capacity of the economy. **Supply shocks** are surprise occurrences that temporarily increase or decrease current output. For example, adverse weather conditions, a natural disaster, or a temporary increase in the price of imported resources (for example, oil in the case of the United States) will reduce current supply, even though they do not alter the economy's long-term production capacity. They will thus decrease short-run aggregate supply (shift *SRAS* to the left) without directly affecting *LRAS*. On the other hand, favorable weather conditions or temporary reductions in the world price of imported

---

[4]The definition of long-run aggregate supply helps clarify why a change in resource prices will affect short-run aggregate supply, but not long-run aggregate supply. When an economy is operating on its *LRAS* curve, the relationship between resource prices (costs) and product prices will reflect normal competitive market conditions. Since both profit and unemployment rates are at their normal levels, there is no tendency for resource prices to change *relative* to product prices when current output is equal to the economy's long-run potential. Therefore, *when an economy is operating on its LRAS schedule,* any change in resource prices will be matched by a proportional change in product prices, leaving the incentive to supply resources (and output) unchanged.

resources will increase current output, even though the economy's long-run capacity remains unchanged.

The accompanying "Thumbnail Sketch" summarizes the major factors influencing both long-run and short-run aggregate supply. Of course, macroeconomic policy may also influence aggregate supply. As in the case of aggregate demand, we will consider the impact of macroeconomic policy on supply in subsequent chapters.

IMPACT OF CHANGES IN AGGREGATE SUPPLY

As we have previously stressed, the impact of changes in market conditions will be influenced by whether the changes are anticipated or unanticipated. When a change takes place slowly and predictably, decision makers will make choices based on the anticipation of the event. Such changes do not generally disrupt equilibrium conditions in markets.

ECONOMIC GROWTH AND SHIFTS IN LONG-RUN AGGREGATE SUPPLY

Increases in net investment, improvements in technology, and growth in the labor force will result in economic growth, which will shift the economy's *LRAS* curve to the right. When expansions in the productive capacity of an economy take place gradually, they will be anticipated by decision makers. Thus, they need not disrupt macroeconomic equilibrium.

THUMBNAIL SKETCH

WHAT FACTORS WILL INFLUENCE SHORT-RUN AND LONG-RUN AGGREGATE SUPPLY?

These factors will increase (decrease) long-run aggregate supply (*LRAS*).[a]

1. An increase (decrease) in the supply resources.
2. An improvement (deterioration) in technology and productivity.
3. Institutional changes that increase (reduce) the efficiency of resource use.

These factors will increase (decrease) short-run aggregate supply (*SRAS*).[a]

1. A decrease (increase) in resource prices, that is, production costs.
2. Favorable (unfavorable) supply shocks such as good (bad) weather.
3. A decrease (increase) in the world price of imported resources.

---

[a]The important factors of macroeconomic policy will be considered later.

Here we illustrate the impact of economic growth due to capital formation or a technological advancement, for example. The full-employment output of the economy expands from Y_{f_1} to Y_{f_2}. Thus, both LRAS and SRAS increase (to LRAS$_2$ and SRAS$_2$). A sustainable, higher level of real output and real income is the result. If the money supply is held constant, a new long-run equilibrium will emerge at a larger output rate (Y_{f_2}) and lower price level (P_2).

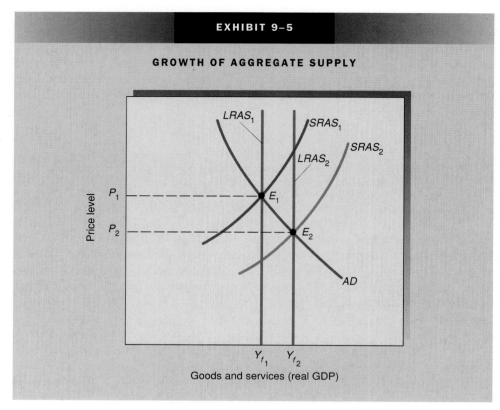

EXHIBIT 9–5

GROWTH OF AGGREGATE SUPPLY

Exhibit 9–5 illustrates the impact of economic growth on the goods and services market. Initially, the economy is in long-run equilibrium at price level P_1 and output Y_{f_1}. The growth expands the economy's potential output, shifting both the *LRAS* and *SRAS* curves to the right (to *LRAS$_2$* and *SRAS$_2$*). Since these changes are gradual, decision makers have time to anticipate the changing market conditions and adjust their behavior accordingly.

When economic growth expands the economy's production possibilities, it will be possible to both produce and sustain a higher rate of real output (Y_{f_2}). The larger output rate can be achieved even while unemployment remains at its natural rate. If the money supply is held constant, the increase in aggregate supply will lead to a lower price level (P_2).

During the last 50 years, real output has expanded significantly in the United States and other countries. However, contrary to the presentation of Exhibit 9–5, the price level has generally not declined. This is because the monetary authorities have expanded the supply of money. As we will see later, an increase in the money supply stimulates aggregate demand (shifts *AD* to the right) and thereby pushes the price level upward.[5]

---

[5]In subsequent chapters, we will explain how stable prices can be achieved as real output increases.

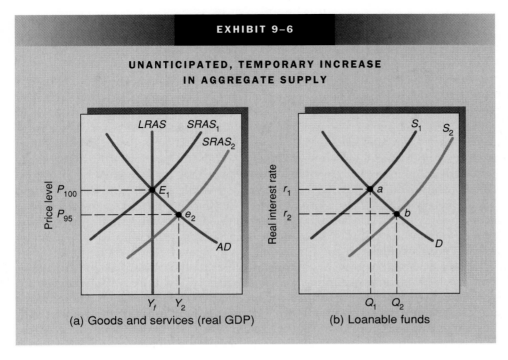

EXHIBIT 9–6

UNANTICIPATED, TEMPORARY INCREASE
IN AGGREGATE SUPPLY

(a) Goods and services (real GDP)

(b) Loanable funds

Here we illustrate the impact of an unanticipated, but temporary increase in aggregate supply such as might result from a bumper crop due to highly favorable weather conditions. The increase in aggregate supply (shift to $SRAS_2$) would lead to a lower price level (P_{95}) and an increase in current GDP to Y_2. Since the favorable supply conditions cannot be counted on in the future, the economy's long-run aggregate supply will not increase. Predictably, decision makers will save a large proportion of their temporarily higher real income, spreading the benefits into the future. Thus, the supply of loanable funds will increase. The real interest rate will fall to r_2, encouraging expenditures on interest-sensitive capital goods and consumer durables.

UNANTICIPATED CHANGES IN AGGREGATE SUPPLY

In addition to changes that can be anticipated, unanticipated disturbances will often influence the level of prices and output in the aggregate goods and services market. Changes in the factors that influence the *SRAS* curve are particularly likely to be unanticipated. By their nature, supply shocks are unpredictable. We now turn to an analysis of unexpected changes in aggregate supply.

UNANTICIPATED INCREASES IN SRAS.   What would happen if highly favorable weather conditions or a temporary decline in the world market price of a critical imported resource increased the current output and income of a nation? **Exhibit 9–6** addresses this issue. Since the temporarily favorable supply conditions cannot be counted on in the future, they will not directly alter the economy's long-term production capacity. Given that the favorable supply conditions are temporary, short-run aggregate supply will increase (to $SRAS_2$), while *LRAS* will remain constant. Output (and income) will temporarily expand beyond the economy's full-employment constraints. The increase in current supply will place downward pressure on the price level.

How will households respond to their temporarily higher incomes? The **permanent income hypothesis,** developed by Nobel Prize–winning economist Milton Friedman, will help us answer this question. According to the permanent income hypothesis, the consumption of households is determined largely by their long-range expected, or permanent, income. Since temporary changes in income generally do not exert much impact on long-term expected income, transitory

Permanent income hypothesis
The hypothesis that consumption depends on some measure of long-run expected (permanent) income rather than on current income.

increases or decreases in income do not exert a large impact on current consumption. Thus, a large proportion of a temporary income gain usually flows into saving and debt reduction. (Note: Remember "saving"—without an "s" on the end—is income that is not spent on current consumption.)

Perhaps a personal application will help explain why it is important to distinguish between temporary and long-term changes in income. Think for a moment how you would adjust your current spending on goods and services if an aunt left you $10,000 next month. No doubt you would spend some of the money almost immediately. Perhaps you would buy a new stereo or take a nice vacation. However, you would probably also use a significant portion of this temporary (one-time only) increase in income to pay bills or save for future education. Now, consider how you would alter your current spending if your aunt indicated you were to receive $10,000 per year for the next 20 years. In this case, you are likely to spend most of this year's $10,000 almost immediately. You might even borrow money to buy an automobile or make some major expenditures, and thereby expand your spending on goods and services this year by more than $10,000.

The permanent income hypothesis indicates that a substantial share of a temporarily high income resulting from unexpectedly favorable supply conditions will flow into saving as individuals seek to spread the benefits over a longer time period. The increased saving will expand the supply of loanable funds (shift to S_2 in part "b" of Exhibit 9–6), causing the real interest rate to decline. The lower real interest rate will stimulate investment and encourage the purchase of consumer durables such as automobiles and appliances.

An increase in aggregate supply that is expected to be temporary will expand output and place downward pressure on prices in the goods and services market. It will also lead to an increase in the supply of loanable funds and place downward pressure on the real rate of interest. In turn, the lower interest rate will encourage capital formation that will expand the resource base, permitting individuals to spread some of the benefits of the current high level of income into the future.

What would happen if the favorable conditions increasing supply reflected long-term factors? For example, suppose that adoption of a new oil production technology resulted in a decline in the price of oil that was expected to be permanent rather than temporary. In this case, both the *LRAS* and the *SRAS* would increase (shift to the right). This case would parallel the analysis of Exhibit 9–3. A new long-run equilibrium at a higher output would result. In contrast with a temporary increase in income, there is no reason to expect that a disproportional amount of a permanent increase in income will flow into savings. Thus, there is no reason to expect that a permanent increase in income will reduce interest rates.

UNANTICIPATED DECREASES IN SRAS.   In recent decades, the U.S. economy has been jolted by several unfavorable supply-side factors. In 1973, and again in 1979, the United States and other oil-importing countries were hit with sharply higher oil prices as the result of unstable conditions in the Middle East. During the summer of 1988, the most severe drought conditions in 50 years resulted in an extremely poor harvest in the U.S. agricultural belt. In August of 1990, Iraq

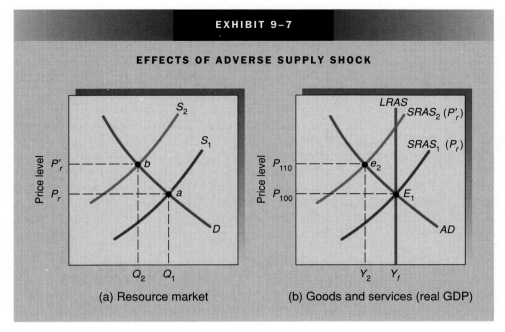

EXHIBIT 9-7

EFFECTS OF ADVERSE SUPPLY SHOCK

(a) Resource market

(b) Goods and services (real GDP)

Suppose there is an unanticipated reduction in the supply of resources, perhaps as the result of a crop failure or sharp increase in the world price of a major imported resource such as oil. Resource prices would rise from P_r to P'_r (a). The higher resource prices would shift the SRAS curve to the left. In the short run, the price level would rise to P_{110} (b), and output would decline to Y_2. What happens in the long run depends on whether the reduction in the supply of resources is temporary or permanent. If it is temporary, resource prices will fall in the future, permitting the economy to return to its initial equilibrium (E_1). Conversely, if the reduced supply of resources is permanent, the productive potential of the economy will shrink (LRAS will shift to the left) and e_2 will become a long-run equilibrium.

suddenly invaded Kuwait and threatened the oil fields of Saudi Arabia. Once again the world price of oil shot up, sharply increasing the cost of energy in the United States and other oil importing countries.

How do such supply-side shocks influence macroeconomic markets? **Exhibit 9–7** illustrates the answer. Both an unfavorable harvest due to adverse weather conditions and a higher world price of oil will reduce the supply of resources (from S_1 to S_2 in part "a") in the domestic market. Resource prices will rise to P'_r. In turn, the higher resource prices will reduce short-run aggregate supply (the shift from $SRAS_1$ to $SRAS_2$ in part "b") in the goods and services market. Since supply shocks of this type are generally unanticipated, initially they will reduce output and place upward pressure on prices (the rate of inflation) in the goods and services market.

If an unfavorable supply shock is expected to be temporary, as will generally be the case for a bad harvest, long-run aggregate supply will be unaffected. After all, unfavorable growing conditions for a year or two do not represent a permanent change in climate. Therefore, as normal weather patterns return with the passage of time, both supply and price conditions in the resource market will return to normal, permitting the economy to return to long-run equilibrium at output Y_f.

As in the case of the temporary increase in output depicted in Exhibit 9–6, people will use the loanable funds market to smooth consumption in response to a temporary reduction in income. Believing that their lower incomes are temporary, households will reduce their current saving level (and dip into past savings) to maintain a current consumption level more consistent with their longer-term perceived opportunities. But when each household reduces its saving level, the supply of loanable funds decreases, causing an increase in the real interest rate. The higher real interest rate rations funds to those willing to pay the most to maintain their current spending during the economic hard times. Of course, a higher real interest rate will also retard capital investment. A reduction in net investment and an accompanying decline in near-term economic growth are predictable side effects of a temporary reduction in aggregate supply.

When an adverse supply-side factor is more permanent, as in the case of a long-term increase in the price of oil imports, the long-run supply curve would also shift to the left. Under these circumstances, the economy would have to adjust to a lower level of real output.

Regardless of whether the decline in aggregate supply is temporary or permanent, other things constant, the price level will rise. Similarly, output will decline, at least temporarily. Theory thus indicates that the adverse supply shocks of recent years contributed to the sluggish growth and inflation of the era.

DOES A MARKET ECONOMY HAVE A SELF-CORRECTING MECHANISM?

In a dynamic world of changing demand conditions and supply shocks, economic ups and downs are inevitable. Sometimes (during periods of economic boom) output will exceed the economy's long-run capacity, while at other times (during periods of recession) output will fall short of its potential. Are there market forces that will help stabilize an economy and cushion the effects of economic shocks? Does a market economy have a built-in mechanism that will prevent an economic downturn from plunging into a depression? There are three reasons to believe that the answer to both of these questions is yes.

1. Consumption demand is relatively stable over the business cycle. By far, consumption is the largest component of aggregate demand. The permanent income hypothesis indicates that the consumption component of aggregate demand will be substantially more stable than income. When income falls during a recession, households will reduce their current saving (and draw on their prior savings) in order to maintain a high level of current consumption. Thus, consumer demand will decline by a smaller amount than income during a recession. This relative stability of consumer demand will help stabilize aggregate demand and reverse an economic downturn.

Similarly, during an economic expansion, a substantial amount of the above-normal gains in income enjoyed by most households will be allocated to saving. So consumption demand will increase less rapidly than income during a business expansion. Thus, during an economic boom, the stability of consumption will dampen the growth of aggregate demand and the accompanying inflationary forces. In this manner, the stability of consumption will help keep a market economy on track.

2. Changes in real interest rates will help to stabilize aggregate demand and redirect economic fluctuations. Previously, we noted that sudden changes in the confidence of consumers and investors were a potential source of instability. However, interest-rate adjustments will, at least partially, offset disturbances arising from this source. Suppose consumers and investors, motivated by a burst of optimism, suddenly decide to spend more of their current income on goods and services. In order to do so, they will either have to reduce their saving or increase their borrowing. But these actions will reduce the supply of loanable funds relative to the demand. Predictably, the real rate of interest will rise. But the higher real interest rate will make current consumption and investment spending more expensive. Thus, the rising real interest rate will limit the increases in spending of consumers and investors, and thereby help to stabilize aggregate demand.

Interest-rate changes will also help to offset reductions in aggregate demand stemming from business pessimism. If consumers and investors suddenly reduce their spending of current income, other things being constant, an increase in saving is implied. The supply of loanable funds will increase relative to the demand. Real interest rates will fall, which will stimulate additional current spending. When changes in aggregate demand arise from business pessimism, adjustments in the loanable funds market will exert a stabilizing effect.

Perhaps even more important, changes in the real interest rate tend to redirect both recessions and booms. During an economic downturn, business demand for new investment projects and therefore loanable funds is generally quite weak. The weak demand, however, leads to a lower real interest rate. In turn, the lower interest rate both encourages current consumption and reduces the opportunity cost of investment projects, dampening the decline in aggregate demand. On the other hand, the real interest rate increases as many businesses borrow in order to undertake investment projects during an economic expansion. The higher real interest rate discourages both consumption and investment and thereby minimizes the increase in aggregate demand during a business expansion. Thus, the interest rate acts as a shock absorber helping both to stabilize aggregate demand and redirect economic fluctuations.

3. Changes in real resource prices will redirect economic fluctuations. Price adjustments in the resource market will also help to keep the economy on an even keel. **Exhibits 9–8** and **9–9** illustrate this point. Exhibit 9–8 depicts the response of resource prices to business cycles. When the current output of an economy is less than its full-employment potential (Y_f), weak demand and slack employment in resource markets will place downward pressure on real resource prices. Under these conditions, real wages and other resource prices will decline (or increase at a very slow rate). In contrast, when an economy is operating beyond its full-employment capacity—that is, when unemployment is less than the natural unemployment rate—strong demand will push the real price of resources up rapidly.

Exhibit 9–9 indicates the significance of this pattern of dynamic change in resource prices in response to business conditions. Part "a" illustrates the supply and demand conditions that might result in the goods and services market from an unanticipated increase in aggregate demand. Current output exceeds the economy's full-employment capacity. A high level of employment will be required to achieve the output (Y_1 in part "a") beyond the economy's potential sustainable rate. Initially, unemployment is less than the natural rate of unemployment. When these conditions are present, however, real resource prices will increase rapidly, pushing costs upward. The higher resource prices will reduce short-run aggregate supply (shift to $SRAS_2$ in part "a"). As resource prices and costs rise, profit margins will decline to normal competitive rates, and output

When aggregate output is less than the economy's full employment potential (Y_f), the weak demand and slack employment in resource markets place downward pressure on wages and other resource prices (P_r). Conversely, when output exceeds Y_f, strong demand and tight market conditions result in rising real prices in resource markets.

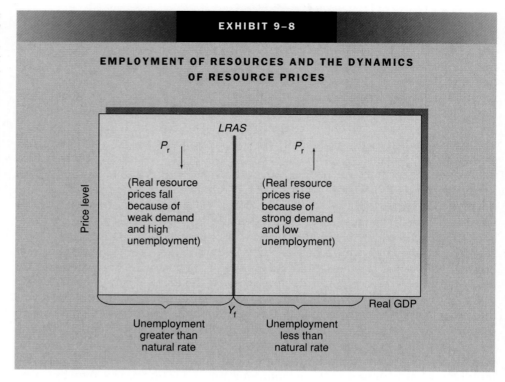

EXHIBIT 9-8

EMPLOYMENT OF RESOURCES AND THE DYNAMICS OF RESOURCE PRICES

will recede to its long-run potential. In this way, market forces will help direct the over-employed economy back to long-run equilibrium.

Part "b" of Exhibit 9–9 illustrates an economy initially operating at less than full-employment capacity. When current output is less than an economy's long-run potential, resource prices will decline relative to product prices. An abnormally high unemployment rate (in excess of the natural rate) in resource markets will eventually induce suppliers to accept lower wage rates and prices for other resources. The declining real cost of labor and other resources will shift *SRAS* to the right. With time, the lower resource prices will restore long-run equilibrium (E_2) at the full-employment rate of output.

THE BUSINESS CYCLE REVISITED

Our aggregate-demand/aggregate-supply *(AD/AS)* model enhances our understanding of economic instability. In a dynamic world of changing demand conditions and supply-side shocks, the model indicates that economic ups and downs will be present. Macroeconomic markets do not adjust instantaneously, and decision makers do not always accurately anticipate changes in the price level. Therefore, in the short run, output sometimes exceeds and sometimes falls short

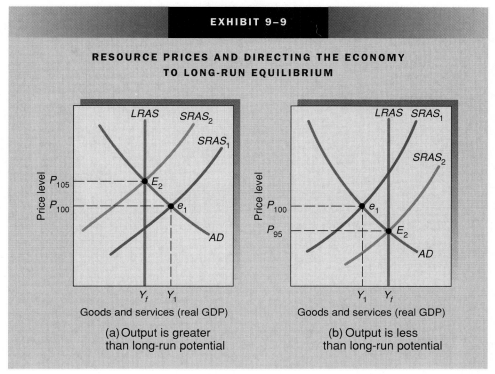

EXHIBIT 9-9

RESOURCE PRICES AND DIRECTING THE ECONOMY TO LONG-RUN EQUILIBRIUM

(a) Output is greater than long-run potential

(b) Output is less than long-run potential

In the short run, output may either exceed or fall short of the economy's full employment capacity (Y_f). If output is temporarily greater than the economy's potential (a), resource prices and production costs will rise. The higher production costs will decrease aggregate supply to $SRAS_2$ (a), restoring equilibrium at full-employment capacity and a higher price level (P_{105}). When an economy is temporarily operating at less than capacity (b), abnormally high unemployment and an excess supply in the resource market may lead to lower resource prices and production costs. The lower cost would increase aggregate supply to $SRAS_2$ (b). Thus, the output of a market economy will tend to move toward full-employment capacity. However, this self-correction process may require considerable time. As we proceed, we will consider alternative methods of attaining full-employment equilibrium more rapidly.

of its long-run potential. This is precisely what periods of economic boom and recession imply.

Exhibit 9–10 presents a picture of the economic fluctuations during the last 25 years. It is interesting to reflect on these cycles within the framework of our model. Periods of economic boom, such as were present in the late 1960s, 1973, 1978, and 1986–1989, imply that the *AD* and *SRAS* curves look something like the initial conditions (associated with e_1) of Exhibit 9–9 (part "a"). The intersection of the *AD* and *SRAS* curves would be at an output rate beyond the economy's full-employment potential.

Conversely, when an economy is in a recession, such as was experienced in the United States during 1970, 1974–1975, 1979–1982, and 1990–1991, conditions similar to the initial situation (associated with e_1) depicted by part "b" of Exhibit 9–9 are implied. During a recession, the intersection of the *AD* and *SRAS* curves will be at an output rate that is less than full employment. Therefore, as part "b" of Exhibit 9–10 illustrates, the unemployment rate will fall below the natural rate during a period of economic boom and rise above the natural rate during recessions. (Note: Since the natural rate of unemployment is not directly observable, a range of estimates is provided in part "b" of Exhibit 9–10.)

However, our *AD/AS* model also indicates that market forces will redirect both an expansionary boom and a recessionary contraction. A boom will not continue to spiral upward. Neither will a contraction continue to plunge downward.

Recent periods of economic expansion and contraction are illustrated here. Our analysis indicates that real interest rates and wages will rise during expansions and fall during recessions, and thereby help to stabilize the economy. Exhibit 9–11 presents data on this topic.

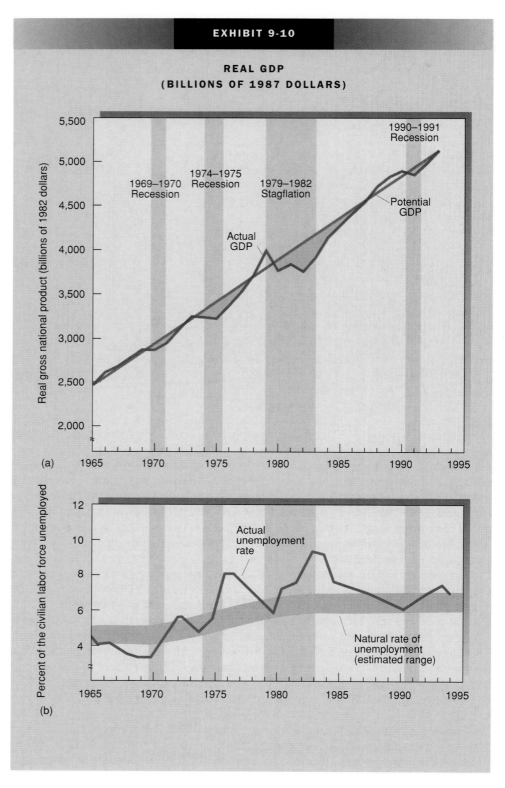

EXHIBIT 9-10

**REAL GDP
(BILLIONS OF 1987 DOLLARS)**

(a)

(b)

During periods of weak resource demand, high unemployment, and output less than the economy's potential GDP, our analysis indicates that real interest rates and real wages will eventually decline (or increase at a sluggish rate.) Conversely, they will rise during periods of economic boom.

Exhibit 9–11 presents data on the estimated real interest rate and annual rate of change in the real hourly compensation of nonfarm employees for the 1966–1987 period. Real interest rates did tend to increase during economic expansions and recede during recessionary periods. The estimated real interest rate declined to less than 1 percent during the recession of 1970 and, for a time, it was actually negative during the severe 1974–1975 recession. It also declined sharply (from 3.5 percent to zero) during the 1979–1982 period.[6] Similarly, real wages increased less rapidly during each of the three recessions than during the preceding and subsequent periods of economic expansion. In fact, real compensation actually declined during the 1974–1975, 1979–1982, and 1990–1991 recessions. Clearly, this pattern of change in real interest rates and real wages is consistent with our analysis of macroeconomic markets.

Source: The real interest rate data are from the Board of Governors of the Federal Reserve System and the University of Michigan Household Survey. The real compensation data are from the Department of Labor, Bureau of Labor Statistics.

EXHIBIT 9–11

BUSINESS CYCLE CONDITIONS AND REAL WAGES, 1966–1991

EXPANSIONS AND RECESSIONS	ESTIMATED REAL INTEREST RATE (AT PEAK FOR EXPANSION AND AT TROUGH FOR RECESSION)	ANNUAL PERCENT RATE OF CHANGE IN REAL COMPENSATION PER HOUR (NONFARM BUSINESS SECTOR)
1966–1968 Expansion	1.5	2.9
1969–1970 Recession	0.5	1.0
1971–1973 Expansion	1.0	2.2
1974–1975 Recession	−2.0	−0.4
1976–1978 Expansion	3.5	1.5
1979–1982 Recessions	0.0	−1.0
1983–1989 Expansion	5.4	0.5
1990–1991 Recession	4.4	−1.1

[6]Officially, there were two recessions during the 1979–1982 stagnation: one of approximately 6 months duration in 1980 and a second lasting approximately 18 months during 1981–1982. In the 1980 recession, the short-term real interest rate fell from 3.5 percent to zero. During the sharp deceleration of the inflation rate and more severe recession of 1981–1982, the real interest rate tumbled from nearly 10 percent to approximately 3 percent.

THE GREAT DEBATE: HOW RAPIDLY DOES THE SELF-CORRECTIVE MECHANISM WORK?

Following the Great Depression, many economists thought that market economies were inherently unstable. They argued that unless monetary and fiscal policy were used to stimulate and guide the macroeconomy, prolonged recessions would result. Influenced by both a reevaluation of the 1930s and the experience of the last 50 years, most modern economists reject this stagnation view of market economies.[7] Today, there is a widespread consensus that market economies possess stabilizing forces.

What divides economists is disagreement about how rapidly the self-correcting forces work. This is a key issue. If the self-corrective process works quite slowly, then market economies will still experience prolonged periods of abnormally high unemployment and below-capacity output. Many economists believe this is the case. As a result, they have a good deal of confidence that discretionary monetary and fiscal policy will promote stability and prosperity.

Conversely, other economists believe that the self-corrective mechanism of a market economy works reasonably well when monetary and fiscal policy follow a stable course. This latter group argues that macroeconomic policy mistakes are a major source of economic instability. Because of this, they call for the use of policy rules, such as a constant growth rate in the supply of money and balanced budgets, rather than discretionary use of macroeconomic policy. We will return to this debate when we consider the impact of monetary and fiscal policy.

LOOKING AHEAD

Modern macroeconomics reflects an evolutionary process. The Great Depression and the accompanying prolonged unemployment exerted an enormous impact on macroeconomics. John Maynard Keynes, the brilliant English economist, developed a theory that sheds light on the operation of an economy experiencing high rates of unemployment. The next chapter focuses on the Keynesian theory.

CHAPTER SUMMARY

1. It is important to distinguish between anticipated and unanticipated changes. Anticipated changes are foreseen by decision makers, who can therefore adjust their choices accordingly. In contrast, unanticipated events catch people by surprise, not allowing them to make such adjustments until after the fact.

2. An increase in aggregate demand involves a shift of the entire *AD* schedule to the right. Other than policy, major factors causing an increase in aggregate demand are (a) an increase in real wealth, (b) a lower real interest rate, (c) increased optimism on the part of businesses and consumers, (d) an increase in the expected rate of inflation, (e) higher real income abroad, and (f) a reduction in a nation's exchange rate. Conversely, if these factors change in the opposite direction, a decrease in aggregate demand will result.

3. When the long-run equilibrium of an economy is disrupted by an unanticipated increase in aggregate

---

[7]A detailed analysis of the forces causing and prolonging the Great Depression is presented in Chapter 13.

demand, output will temporarily increase beyond the economy's long-run capacity and unemployment will fall below its natural rate. However, as decision makers adjust to the increase in demand, resource prices will rise and output will recede to long-run capacity. In the long run, the major impact of the increase in aggregate demand will be a higher price level (inflation).

4. An unanticipated reduction in aggregate demand will temporarily reduce output below capacity and push unemployment above its natural rate. Eventually, unemployment and excess supply in resource markets will reduce wage rates and resource prices. Costs will decline, and output will return to its long-run potential. However, if wages and prices are inflexible downward, less-than-capacity output and abnormally high unemployment may persist for a substantial period of time.

5. Changes that alter the economy's maximum sustainable output will shift the LRAS curve. The following factors will increase LRAS: (a) increases in the supply of labor and capital resources, (b) improvements in technology and productivity and (c) institutional changes improving the efficiency of resource use.

6. In the short run, output may change as the result of temporary factors that do not directly alter the economy's long-run capacity. The major factors leading to an increase in the short-run aggregate supply (a shift of the SRAS curve to the right) are (a) a reduction in resource prices, (b) favorable weather conditions, and (c) a decline in the world price of imported resources. Conversely, if these factors changed in the opposite direction, SRAS would decline (shift to the left).

7. An increase in output due to economic growth (an increase in the economy's production capacity) will increase both short-run and long-run aggregate supply. The economy will now be able to produce and sustain a larger output level. If the supply of money is constant, a lower price level will result.

8. When an economy in long-run equilibrium experiences an unanticipated favorable supply shock, output (and income) will temporarily rise above capacity and prices will decline. A lower real interest rate is also a predicted result, since a large amount of a temporary increase in income will flow into saving. The lower real interest rate will stimulate capital formation and, other things constant, will lead to more rapid short-run economic growth.

9. An adverse supply shock (decrease in SRAS) will reduce output and increase the price level. If the reduction in income is expected to be temporary, people will increase their borrowing (and reduce their saving) to maintain a consumption level more consistent with their longer-term income. As a result, the real interest rate will rise. Many economists think adverse supply shocks, particularly the

sharp increase in the price of imported oil, contributed to the slow rate of growth and rapid increase in the price level during the 1970s.

10. When output and employment exceed the rates associated with an economy's long-run equilibrium, real interest rates and resource prices (including real wages) will rise, increasing costs and thereby shifting the SRAS to the left until long-run equilibrium is restored at full-employment output and a higher price level. Similarly, when current output is less than the economy's potential GDP, lower real interest rates and falling real resource prices (and wages) will reduce costs and thereby shift SRAS to the right until long-run equilibrium is restored. These forces provide the economy with a self-corrective mechanism, directing it toward the full-employment rate of output.

11. Many economists believe the economy's self-corrective mechanism works quite slowly and that discretionary monetary and fiscal policy changes are necessary to minimize economic instability. Others believe that the self-corrective mechanism works reasonably well and that discretionary policy is likely to do more harm than good.

CRITICAL-ANALYSIS QUESTIONS

*1. Explain how and why each of the following factors would influence current aggregate demand in the United States:
   a. Increased fear of recession.
   b. Increased fear of inflation.
   c. Rapid growth of real income in Japan and Western Europe.
   d. A reduction in the real interest rate.
   e. A higher price level (be careful).
*2. Indicate how each of the following would influence U.S. aggregate supply in the short run:
   a. An increase in real wage rates.
   b. A severe freeze that destroys half of the orange trees in Florida.
   c. A drought in the midwestern agricultural states.
   d. An increase in the world price of oil, a major import.
   e. Abundant rainfall during the growing season of agricultural states.
3. Suppose that the key macroeconomic markets are initially in long-run equilibrium. How will an unanticipated reduction in aggregate demand affect real output, employment, and the price level in the short run? In the long run?
*4. When an economy is at a short-run equilibrium below the full-employment output rate, explain how the

*Asterisk denotes questions for which answers are given in Appendix C.

self-correcting mechanism will direct the economy back to its long-run potential rate of output. Can you think of any reason why this mechanism might not work? Discuss.

5. What is the difference between an anticipated and an unanticipated increase in aggregate demand? Provide an example of each. Which is most likely to result in a temporary spurt in the growth of real output?

*6. Assume that both union and management representatives agree to wage increases because of their expectation that prices will rise 10 percent during the next year. Explain why the unemployment rate will probably increase if the actual rate of inflation next year is only 3 percent.

7. During 1980–1985, the exchange-rate value of the dollar increased sharply. How did this change influence aggregate demand, output, and the inflation rate during the 1980–1985 period? During 1986–1988, the exchange-rate value of the dollar fell. What impact did this decline have on aggregate demand, output, and inflation?

*8. When the actual output exceeds the long-run potential of the economy, how will the self-correcting mechanism direct the economy to long-run equilibrium? Why can't the above-normal output be maintained?

*9. Are the real wages of workers likely to increase more rapidly when the unemployment rate is high or when it is low? Why?

10. Suppose consumers and investors suddenly become more pessimistic about the future and therefore decide to reduce their consumption and investment spending. How will a market economy adjust to this increase in pessimism?

11. "Unemployment benefits should replace 100 percent of an employee's earnings from his or her previous job when the employee is terminated or laid off through no fault of his or her own." Evaluate this statement. Do you think the idea expressed is a good one? How would such a practice affect the search time of the unemployed workers? What impact would it have on the unemployment rate?

*12. An unexpectedly rapid growth in real income abroad leads to a sharp increase in demand for U.S. exports.

What impact will this change have on the price level, output, and employment in the short run? In the long run?

13. If the real interest rate increases, how will this affect the incentive of consumers and investors to purchase goods and services? How will it affect the AD curve? How will a higher real interest rate affect the cost of producing goods? How will it affect the $SRAS$ curve?

14. Construct the AD, $SRAS$, and $LRAS$ curves for an economy experiencing (a) full employment and (b) an economic boom.

15. As the result of changing international conditions, there was a decline in real national defense expenditures of approximately 15 percent between 1989 and 1991. What is the expected short-run impact of this decline in defense expenditures on aggregate demand and output? If the United States is able to spend less on national defense in the future, how will this factor influence the standard of living of Americans? Discuss.

16. Consider an economy with the following aggregate-demand (AD) and aggregate-supply (AS) schedules. These schedules reflect the fact that prior to the period in question, decision makers entered into contracts and made choices anticipating that the price level would be P_{105}.

AD_{105} (IN TRILLIONS)	PRICE LEVEL	$SRAS_{105}$ (IN TRILLIONS)
$5.1	95	$3.5
4.9	100	3.8
4.7	105	4.2
4.5	110	4.5
4.3	115	4.8

a. Indicate the quantity of GDP that will be produced and the price level that will emerge during this period.

b. Is the economy in long-run equilibrium? Why or why not?

c. How will the unemployment rate during the current period compare with this economy's natural rate of unemployment?

---

*Asterisk denotes questions for which answers are given in Appendix C.

d. What will tend to happen to resource prices in the future? How will this effect the equilibrium rate of output?

e. Will the rate of GDP produced during this period be sustainable into the future? Why or why not?

17. Suppose that the price level that emerges from aggregate-demand and aggregate-supply conditions during the current period is lower than decision makers had anticipated.

a. Construct *AD, SRAS,* and *LRAS* schedules that reflect these conditions.

b. During the current period, how will the actual rate of unemployment compare with the natural rate? How will actual output compare with the economy's potential?

c. As the result of the current conditions, what will tend to happen to resource prices and interest rates? Why?

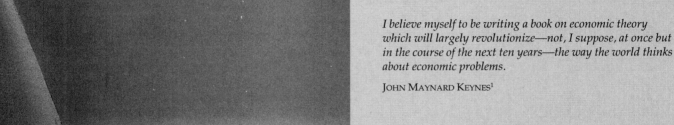

CHAPTER TEN

KEYNESIAN FOUNDATIONS OF
MODERN MACROECONOMICS

*I believe myself to be writing a book on economic theory
which will largely revolutionize—not, I suppose, at once but
in the course of the next ten years—the way the world thinks
about economic problems.*

JOHN MAYNARD KEYNES[1]

CHAPTER FOCUS

■ *What are the major components of the Keynesian
model? What is the major factor that causes the level of
output and employment to change?*
■ *What was Keynes's explanation for the high rates of
unemployment that persisted during the Great
Depression?*
■ *What determines the equilibrium level of output in the
Keynesian model?*
■ *What is the multiplier principle? Why is it important?*
■ *Why do Keynesians believe market economies
experience business instability?*

---

[1]Letter from John Maynard Keynes to George Bernard Shaw,
New Year's Day, 1935.

T he best test of an economic theory is how well it works in the real world. If a theory is inconsistent with real-world events, it should be discarded (or modified) and replaced with a theory that has more predictive power. Modern macroeconomics is the product of just such an evolutionary process. In particular, Keynesian economics emerged because the prevailing macroeconomic theory of the early 1930s was unable to explain the Great Depression of that decade.

Prior to the Great Depression of the 1930s, most economists thought market adjustments would automatically guide an economy to full employment within a relatively brief time. A decade of double-digit unemployment rates during the 1930s undermined the credibility of this view. The experience of the Great Depression also provided the background for the development of a new theory, one capable of explaining the prolonged unemployment of the period.

The new theory, developed by the English economist John Maynard Keynes (pronounced "canes") has exerted enormous influence on modern macroeconomics.[2] For three decades following the Second World War, Keynesian economics represented the core of macroeconomics. Several basic concepts and much of the terminology we use today can be traced to Keynes. Modern macroeconomics is built on the foundation of Keynesian analysis. This chapter presents the Keynesian view and illuminates its influence on modern macroeconomic theory.

KEYNESIAN EXPLANATION OF THE GREAT DEPRESSION

Classical economists
Economists from Adam Smith to the time of Keynes who focused their analyses on economic efficiency and production. With regard to business instability, they thought market prices and wages would decline during a recession quickly enough to bring the economy back to full employment within a short period of time.

Say's Law
The view that production creates its own demand. Thus, there cannot be a general oversupply, because the total value of goods and services produced (income) will always be available for purchasing them.

Mainstream economists prior to the time of Keynes (often called **classical economists**) emphasized the importance of aggregate supply and paid little heed to aggregate demand. The lack of interest in demand issues by classical economists stemmed from their adherence to **Say's Law,** named for nineteenth-century French economist, J. B. Say, and stating that a general overproduction of goods relative to total demand is impossible, since supply (production) creates its own demand. The reasoning here is that the purchasing power necessary to buy (demand) desired products is generated by production. A farmer's supply of wheat generates income to meet the farmer's demand for shoes, clothes, automobiles, and other desired goods. Similarly, the supply of shoes generates the purchasing power with which shoemakers (and their employees) demand the farmer's wheat and other desired goods.

Classical economists granted the possibility of producing too much of some goods and not enough of others. But they maintained that at such times, the prices of goods in excess supply would fall, and the prices of products in excess demand would rise. The pricing system would thus correct any imbalances that might temporarily exist. Consequently, a general overproduction of goods would be impossible, because, in aggregate, demand would always be sufficient to purchase the goods produced.

---

[2]See the classic book, John Maynard Keynes, *The General Theory of Employment, Interest, and Money* (London: Macmillan, 1936), for the presentation of this theory.

Prior to the Great Depression, the classical view seemed reasonable. But the depth and the prolonged duration of the decline during the 1930s challenged the validity of the classical view and provided the foundation for what we now refer to as Keynesian economics. The extent of the economic decline during the 1930s is difficult to comprehend, particularly for those who are familiar only with the relative stability of the last four decades. In 1933, 25 percent of the U.S. labor force was unemployed. International trade came to a virtual standstill. Real GDP in the United States declined by more than 30 percent between 1930 and 1933.

In 1939, a decade after the plunge began, the unemployment rate still stood at 17 percent of the work force. Per capita income in 1939 was nearly 10 percent less than 1929, and the depressed conditions were worldwide; other industrial countries experienced similar conditions.

KEYNESIAN VIEW OF SPENDING AND OUTPUT

Against this background of the 1930s, Keynes developed a theory that provided an explanation for the prolonged depressed conditions of the era. Keynes rejected the classical view and offered a completely new concept of output determination. He believed that spending induced business firms to supply goods and services. From this, he argued that if total spending fell (as it might, for example, if consumers and investors became pessimistic about the future or tried to save more of their current income), then business firms would respond by cutting back production. Less spending would thus lead to less output.

Of course, classical economists were aware of this possibility, but they believed the labor surplus would drive down wages, reducing costs and lowering prices until the surplus was eliminated and the economy was directed to full employment within a reasonable time. Keynes and his followers disagreed. They argued that wages and prices are highly inflexible, particularly in a downward direction, in modern economies characterized by large business firms and powerful trade unions. Because of this, they did not believe in the scenario of flexible wages and prices directing the economy to equilibrium at full employment.

Keynes also introduced a different concept of equilibrium and a different mechanism for its achievement. In the Keynesian view, equilibrium takes place when the level of total spending is equal to current output. When this is the case, producers will have no reason to either expand or contract output. In the Keynesian view, *changes in output* rather than *changes in prices* direct the economy to equilibrium. If total spending is less than full-employment output, output will be cut back to the level of spending and, most significantly, it will remain there until the level of spending changes. Therefore, if total spending is deficient, equilibrium output will be less than full-employment output, and high rates of unemployment will continue. This is precisely what Keynes believed was happening during the 1930s.

The message of Keynes can be summarized as follows: Businesses will produce only the quantity of goods and services they believe consumers, investors, governments, and foreigners will plan to buy. If these planned aggregate expenditures are less than the economy's full-employment output, output will fall short of its potential. When aggregate expenditures are deficient, there are no automatic forces capable of assuring full employment. Prolonged unemployment will persist. Against the background of the Great Depression, this was a compelling argument.

BASIC KEYNESIAN MODEL

As we will show, the Keynesian analysis could be presented within the framework of our aggregate-demand/aggregate-supply (*AD/AS*) model. However, an alternative framework, an aggregate-expenditure model, is generally used to present the Keynesian view. Equality between aggregate expenditures and output is central to this view, and the aggregate-expenditure model helps us visualize that point. The model will also help us better understand why Keynesians believe that changes in aggregate spending exert a powerful influence on equilibrium output and employment.

The key to the basic Keynesian model is the concept of planned aggregate expenditures. As with aggregate demand, the four components of planned aggregate expenditures are consumption, investment, government purchases, and net exports. Before we develop the Keynesian model, however, it's useful to make a few assumptions in order to simplify the analysis. First, as with our *AD/AS* model, we will assume there is a specific full-employment level of output. Only the natural rate of unemployment is present when full-employment capacity is attained. Second, following in the Keynesian tradition, we will assume that wages and prices are completely inflexible until full employment is reached. Once full employment is achieved, though, additional demand will lead only to higher prices. Strictly speaking, these polar assumptions will not hold in the real world. They may, however, approximate conditions in the short run. Finally, we will continue to assume that the government's taxing, spending, and monetary policies are constant.

PLANNED CONSUMPTION EXPENDITURES

The most important component of planned aggregate expenditures is planned aggregate consumption. Keynes believed that current income is the primary determinant of consumption expenditures. As he stated:

Consumption function
A fundamental relationship between disposable income and consumption, in which as disposable income increases, current consumption expenditures rise, but by a smaller amount than the increase in income.

> *Men are disposed, as a rule and on the average, to increase their consumption as their income increases, but not by as much as the increase in their income.*[3]

According to Keynes, disposable income is by far the major determinant of current consumption. If disposable income increases, consumers will increase their planned expenditures.

This positive relationship between consumption spending and disposable income is called the **consumption function**. **Exhibit 10–1** illustrates this

---

[3]John Maynard Keynes, *The General Theory of Employment, Interest, and Money* (London: Macmillan, 1936), p. 96

JOHN MAYNARD KEYNES (1883–1946)

Keynes's ideas and writings were so powerful that an entire school of modern economics bears his name. He might properly be referred to as the "father of macroeconomics." The son of a prominent nineteenth-century economist (John Neville Keynes), he earned a degree in mathematics from King's College, Cambridge, where he would later return and spend most of his career as an economist. During the 1920s, his work on finance and monetary economics was widely read and respected. Later, he was an influential participant in the 1944 Bretton Woods Conference that led to the adoption of an international system of fixed exchange rates following the Second World War. Keynes is widely referred to as the architect of that system.

He is best known, however, for his work in macroeconomics, where his *General Theory of Employment, Interest, and Money*, published in 1936, revolutionized the way that economists think about macroeconomics. This work, written in the midst of the Great Depression, provided both a plausible explanation for the massive unemployment and a strategy for ending it. Keynes's message married an idea with a moment in time.

Keynes's work was both path-breaking and controversial. He was the first to introduce the concept of aggregate demand as the sum of consumption, investment, and government spending (and also net exports in an open economy). His concept of macroequilibrium as the income level where planned aggregate demand was equal to output was novel. Perhaps most significantly, his view that governments should run budget deficits during a recession in order to stimulate demand and direct the economy back to full employment challenged the entrenched views of both policy-makers and classical economists. Debate concerning the impact of budget deficits continues to this day.

Keynes correctly anticipated that his ideas would, with the passage of time, exert a powerful influence (see the chapter's opening quote). By the 1950s the Keynesian analysis was dominant in academic circles throughout the Western world. By the 1960s the Keynesian view formed the foundation for the macroeconomic policy of the United States and most other Western nations. Keynes died rather suddenly in 1946, so he did not live to observe the enormous impact of his ideas on public policy, though he had indeed predicted it.

The economic events of the 1970s tempered the confidence of macroeconomists in the basic analysis of Keynes. Nevertheless, his imprint is sure to endure. He revolutionized our way of thinking about macroeconomic issues.

relationship for an economy. At low levels of aggregate income (less than $2 trillion), the consumption expenditures of households will exceed their disposable income. When income is low, households dissave—they either borrow or draw from their past savings to purchase consumption goods. Since consumption does not increase as rapidly as income, the slope of the consumption function will be less than 1. So the consumption schedule is flatter than the 45-degree line of Exhibit 10–1. As income increases, household aggregate income eventually equals and exceeds current consumption. For aggregate incomes above $2 trillion, saving increases as income rises.

The Keynesian model assumes that there is a positive relationship between consumption and income. However, as income increases, consumption expands by a smaller amount. Thus, the slope of the consumption function (line C) is less than 1 (less than the slope of the 45-degree line).

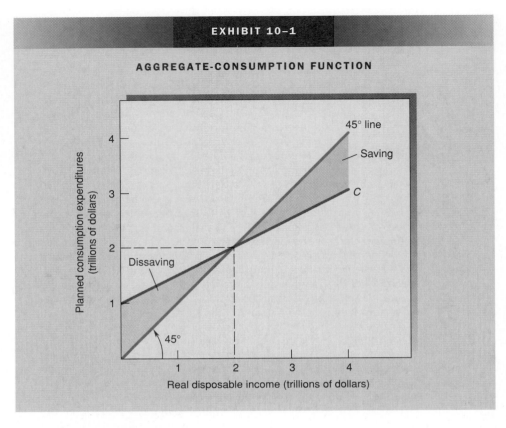

EXHIBIT 10–1

AGGREGATE-CONSUMPTION FUNCTION

PLANNED INVESTMENT EXPENDITURES

Investment encompasses (1) expenditures on fixed assets such as buildings and machines and (2) changes in the inventories of raw materials and final products not yet sold. Keynes argued that in the short run, investment was best viewed as an **autonomous expenditure,** one independent of income.

Autonomous expenditures
Expenditures that do not vary with the level of income. They are determined by factors (such as business expectations and economic policy) that are outside the basic income-expenditure model.

Exhibit 10–2 illustrates an autonomous investment schedule. The flat investment schedule indicates that businesses plan to spend $700 billion on investment, regardless of current income. Planned investment is thus independent of income. In the Keynesian model, investment is primarily a function of current sales relative to plant capacity, expected future sales, and the interest rate. Changes in these latter factors would alter investment—they would cause the entire schedule to shift either upward or downward. But when focusing on the forces pushing an economy toward an equilibrium level of output, the basic Keynesian model postulates a constant level of planned investment expenditures.

PLANNED GOVERNMENT EXPENDITURES

As with investment, planned government expenditures in the basic Keynesian model are assumed to be independent of income. Exhibit 10–2 illustrates an

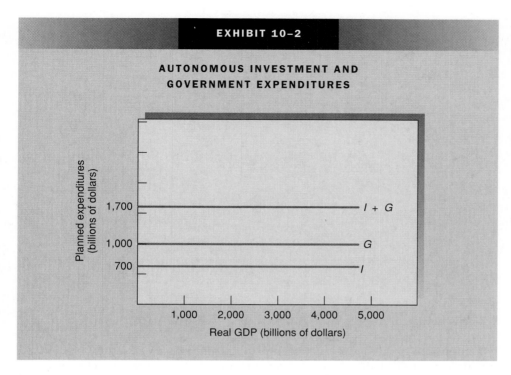

EXHIBIT 10–2

**AUTONOMOUS INVESTMENT AND
GOVERNMENT EXPENDITURES**

Within the basic Keynesian model, planned investment (line I) is autonomous of income. Investment may shift either up or down in response to changes in factors such as business optimism or the real interest rate, but it is independent of the income level. Similarly, the level of government expenditures (line G) is a policy variable, independent of income. Thus, as income changes, planned investment and government expenditures (I + G) remain constant.

autonomous government expenditure function of $1,000 billion. The combined investment and government expenditures sum to $1,700 billion.

The forces underlying government expenditures differ from those influencing private consumption and investment. Government expenditures need not be constrained by income (tax revenues) or the pursuit of profit. Governments can, and often do, spend more than they receive in taxes. Planned government expenditures are best viewed as a policy variable, subject to alteration by the political process. Perceiving them as autonomous of income allows us to focus more clearly on the stability characteristics of a private economy. Later, we will analyze how changes in government expenditures influence output and employment within the framework of the Keynesian aggregate-expenditures model.

PLANNED NET EXPORTS

Exports are dependent on spending choices and income levels abroad. These decisions are, by and large, unaffected by changes in a nation's domestic income level. Therefore, as **Exhibit 10–3** illustrates, exports remain constant when income changes. In contrast, increases in domestic income will induce consumers to purchase more foreign as well as domestic goods. So the level of imports increases as income rises.

Since exports remain constant and imports increase as aggregate income expands, net exports will decline as income expands (see Exhibit 10–3). Accordingly, the Keynesian model postulates a negative relationship between income and net exports.

Since exports are determined by income abroad, they are constant at $350 billion. Imports increase as domestic income expands. Thus, planned net exports fall as domestic income increases.

EXHIBIT 10–3

INCOME AND NET EXPORTS

TOTAL OUTPUT (REAL GDP IN BILLIONS)	PLANNED EXPORTS (BILLIONS)	PLANNED IMPORTS (BILLIONS)	PLANNED NET EXPORTS (BILLIONS)
$5,600	$350	$150	$200
5,900	350	200	150
6,200	350	250	100
6,500	350	300	50
6,800	350	350	0

PLANNED VERSUS ACTUAL EXPENDITURES

It is important to distinguish between planned and actual expenditures. Planned expenditures reflect the choices of consumers, investors, governments and foreigners, *given their expectations as to the choices of other decision makers.* Planned expenditures, though, need not equal actual expenditures. If purchasers spend a different amount on goods and services than business firms anticipate, the firms will experience unplanned changes in inventories. When this is the case, actual investment will differ from planned investment because inventories are a component of investment in our national-income accounts.

Consider what would happen if the planned expenditures of consumers, investors, governments, and foreigners on goods and services were less than what business firms thought they would be. If this were the case, business firms would be unable to sell as much of their current output as they had anticipated. Their *actual* inventories would increase as they unintentionally made larger inventory investments than they planned. On the other hand, consider what would happen if purchasers bought more goods and services than business expected. The unexpected brisk sales would draw down inventories and result in less inventory investment than business firms planned. In this case, *actual* inventory investment would be less than they *planned.*

Actual and planned expenditures are equal only when purchasers buy the quantity of goods and services business decision makers anticipate. Only then will the plans of buyers and sellers in the goods and services market harmonize.

KEYNESIAN EQUILIBRIUM

Equilibrium is present in the Keynesian model when planned aggregate expenditures equal the value of current output. When this is the case, businesses are able to sell the total amount of goods and services that they produce. There are no unexpected changes in inventories. Thus, producers have no incentive to either expand or contract their output during the next period. In equation form, Keynesian macroequilibrium is attained when:

$$\underbrace{\text{Total output}}_{\text{Real GDP}} = \underbrace{\text{Planned } C + I + G + X}_{\text{Planned aggregate expenditures}}$$

KEYNESIAN EQUILIBRIUM— A NUMERIC EXAMPLE

As an example of Keynesian macroeconomic equilibrium, let's take a look at the hypothetical economy described by **Exhibit 10–4.** To begin with, let's focus on columns 1 and 2. At what level of total output is this economy in Keynesian macroeconomic equilibrium? The answer is $6,200 billion, because only there is total output exactly equal to planned aggregate expenditures. When real GDP is equal to $6,200 billion, the planned expenditures of consumers, investors, governments, and foreigners (net exports) are precisely equal to the value of the output produced by business firms. To see this, note that only at $6,200 billion do columns 3 + 4 + 5 equal column 1. Because of this equality, the spending plans of purchasers mesh with the production plans of business decision makers. Given this balance, there is no reason for producers to change their plans.

What happens at other output levels? At any output other than equilibrium, the plans of producers and purchasers will conflict. If output is $5,900 billion, for example, planned aggregate expenditures will be $6,050 billion, and the economy will have a tendency to expand because planned aggregate expenditures are greater than output, decreasing inventories, and stimulating firms to expand their output, moving the economy toward equilibrium.

Note: All figures are in trillions of dollars. Column 2 equals the sum of columns 3 + 4 + 5.

EXHIBIT 10–4

EXAMPLE OF KEYNESIAN MACROECONOMIC EQUILIBRIUM

TOTAL OUTPUT (REAL (GDP) (1)	PLANNED AGGREGATE EXPENDITURES (2)	PLANNED CONSUMPTION (3)	PLANNED INVESTMENT + GOVERNMENT EXPENDITURES (4)	PLANNED NET EXPORTS (5)	TENDENCY OF OUTPUT (6)
$5,600	$5,900	$4,000	$1,700	$200	Expand
5,900	6,050	4,200	1,700	150	Expand
6,200	6,200	4,400	1,700	100	Equilibrium
6,500	6,350	4,600	1,700	50	Contract
6,800	6,500	4,800	1,700	0	Contract

At $6,500 billion, output will be greater than planned aggregate expenditures, and unwanted inventories will accumulate. Of course, business firms will not continue to produce goods they cannot sell, so they will reduce production during the subsequent period, moving the economy toward equilibrium.

EQUILIBRIUM AT LESS THAN FULL EMPLOYMENT

Since Keynesian equilibrium is dependent on equality between planned aggregate expenditures and output, it need not take place at full employment. If an economy is in Keynesian equilibrium, there will be no tendency for output to change even if output is well below full-employment capacity.

To see this in our example, assume that full employment is at an output of $6,500 billion, in Exhibit 10–4. Given the current planned spending, the economy will not reach its full-employment level, and significant unemployment will exist. In the Keynesian model, neither wages nor other resource prices will decline in the face of abnormally high unemployment and excess capacity. Therefore, output will remain at less than the full-employment rate as long as insufficient spending prevents the economy from reaching its full potential.

This is precisely what Keynes thought was happening during the Great Depression. He believed that Western economies were in equilibrium at an employment rate substantially below capacity. Unless aggregate expenditures increased, therefore, the prolonged unemployment had to continue—as it did throughout that period.

KEYNESIAN EQUILIBRIUM— A GRAPHIC PRESENTATION

The Keynesian analysis is presented graphically in **Exhibit 10–5,** where planned aggregate consumption, investment, government, and net export expenditures are measured on the *Y*-axis and total output is measured on the *X*-axis. The 45-degree line that extends from the origin maps out all the points where aggregate expenditures (*AE*) are equal to total output (*GDP*).

Since aggregate expenditures equal total output for all points along the 45-degree line, the line maps out all possible equilibrium income levels. As long as the economy is operating at less than its full-employment capacity, producers will produce any output along the 45-degree line they believe purchasers will buy. Producers, though, will supply a level of output only if they believe planned expenditures will be large enough to purchase it. Depending on the level of aggregate expenditures, each point along the 45-degree line is a potential equilibrium.

Using the data of Exhibit 10–4, **Exhibit 10–6** graphically depicts the Keynesian equilibrium. The *C + I + G + X* line indicates the total planned expenditures of consumers, investors, governments, and foreigners (net exports) at each income level. Reflecting the consumption function, the aggregate expenditure (*AE*) line is flatter than the 45-degree line. Remember, as income rises, consumption also increases, but by less than the increase in income. Therefore, as income expands, total expenditures increase by less than the expansion in income.

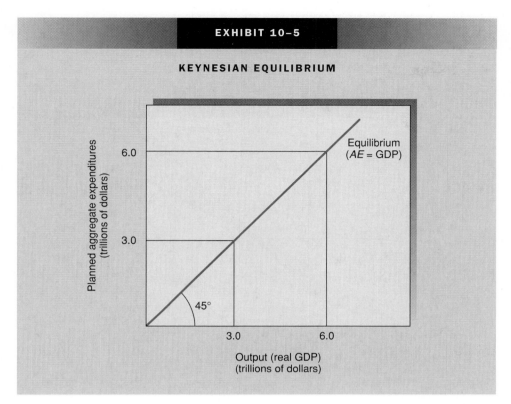

EXHIBIT 10–5

KEYNESIAN EQUILIBRIUM

Planned aggregate expenditures (trillions of dollars)

6.0

3.0

Equilibrium
(AE = GDP)

45°

3.0   6.0

Output (real GDP)
(trillions of dollars)

Aggregate expenditures will be equal to total output for all points along a 45-degree line from the origin. The 45-degree line thus maps out potential equilibrium levels of output for the Keynesian model.

The equilibrium level of output will be $6.2 trillion, the point at which the total expenditures (measured vertically) are just equal to total output (measured horizontally). Of course, the aggregate-expenditures function $C + I + G + X$ will cross the 45-degree line at the $6.2 trillion equilibrium level of output.

As long as the aggregate-expenditures function remains unchanged, no other level of output can be sustained. When total output exceeds $6.2 trillion (for example, $6.5 trillion), the aggregate expenditure line lies below the 45-degree line. Remember that when the $C + I + G + X$ line is less than the 45-degree line, total spending is less than total output. Unwanted inventories will then accumulate, leading businesses to reduce their future production. Employment will decline. Output will fall back from $6.5 trillion to the equilibrium level of $6.2 trillion. Note that it is changes in output and employment, not price changes, that restore equilibrium in the Keynesian model.

In contrast, if total output is temporarily below equilibrium, there is a tendency for income to rise. Suppose output is temporarily at $5.9 trillion. At that output level, the $C + I + G + X$ function lies above the 45-degree line. Aggregate expenditures exceed aggregate output. Businesses are selling more than they currently produce. Their inventories are falling. Excess demand is present. They will react to this state of affairs by hiring more workers and expanding producton. Income will rise to the $6.2 trillion equilibrium level. Only at the equilibrium level, the point at which the $C + I + G + X$ function crosses the 45-degree line, will the spending plans of consumers, investors, and governments sustain the existing output level into the future.

Here the data of Exhibit 10–4 are presented within the Keynesian graphic framework. The equilibrium level of output is $6.2 trillion since planned expenditures (C + I + G + X) are just equal to output at that level of income. At a lower level of income, $5.9 trillion, for example, unplanned inventory reduction would cause business firms to expand output (right-pointing arrow). Conversely, at a higher income level, such as $6.5 trillion, accumulation of inventories would lead to a reduction in future output (left-pointing arrow). Given current aggregate expenditures, only the $6.2 trillion output could be sustained. Note the $6.2 trillion equilibrium income level is less than the economy's potential of $6.5 trillion.

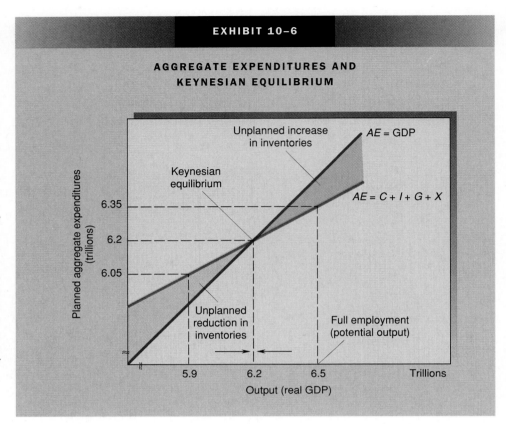

EXHIBIT 10–6

AGGREGATE EXPENDITURES AND KEYNESIAN EQUILIBRIUM

As Exhibit 10–6 illustrates, the economy's full-employment potential income level is $6.5 trillion. At this income level, though, aggregate expenditures are insufficient to purchase the output produced. Given the aggregate-expenditures function, output will remain below its potential. Unemployment will persist. Within the Keynesian model, equilibrium need not coincide with full employment.

AGGREGATE EXPENDITURES, OUTPUT, AND EMPLOYMENT

How could the economy reach its full-employment capacity? According to the Keynesian model, it will not do so unless there is a change in the aggregate-expenditures schedule. Since the Keynesian model assumes that prices are fixed until potential capacity is reached, wage and price reductions are ruled out as a feasible mechanism for directing the economy to full employment.

If consumers, investors, governments, and foreigners could be induced to expand their expenditures, output would expand to full-employment capacity. **Exhibit 10–7** illustrates this point. If additional spending shifted the aggregate-expenditures schedule (AE) upward to AE_2, equilibrium output would expand to its potential capacity. At the higher level of expenditures, AE_2, total spending would equal output at $6.5 trillion.

EXHIBIT 10–7

SHIFTS IN AGGREGATE EXPENDITURES AND CHANGES IN EQUILIBRIUM OUTPUT

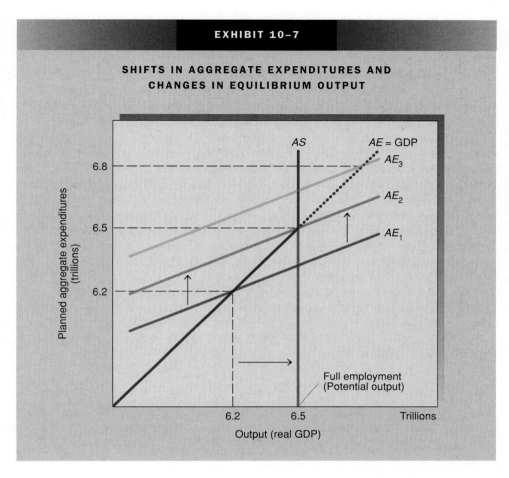

When equilibrium output is less than the economy's capacity, only an increase in expenditures (a shift in AE) will lead to full employment. If consumers, investors, governments, or foreigners would spend more and thereby shift the aggregate-expenditures schedule to AE_2, output would reach its full- employment potential ($6.5 trillion). Once full-employment is reached, further increases in aggregate expenditures, such as indicated by the shift to AE_3, would lead only to higher prices. Nominal output will expand (the dotted segment of the AE = GDP schedule), but real output will not.

What would happen if aggregate expenditures exceeded the economy's production capacity? For example, suppose aggregate expenditures rose to AE_3. Within the basic Keynesian model, aggregate expenditures in excess of output lead to a higher price level once the economy reaches full employment. Nominal output will increase, but it merely reflects higher prices, rather than additional real output. Total spending in excess of full-employment capacity is inflationary within the Keynesian model.

Aggregate expenditures are the catalyst of the Keynesian model. Changes in expenditures make things happen. Until full employment is attained, supply is always accommodative. An increase in aggregate expenditures will thus lead to an increase in real output and employment. Once full employment is reached, however, additional aggregate expenditures lead merely to higher prices.

The Keynesian model implies that regulation of aggregate expenditures is the crux of sound macroeconomic policy. If we could assure aggregate expenditures large enough to achieve capacity output, but not so large as to result in inflation, the Keynesian view implies that maximum output, full employment, and price stability could be attained.

KEYNESIAN MODEL WITHIN AD/AS FRAMEWORK

The Keynesian model can also be presented within the now familiar aggregate-demand/aggregate-supply (*AD/AS*) framework of the previous two chapters. The only difference in the graphic analysis is that the short-run aggregate-supply curve (*SRAS*) has a different shape than in previous chapters because of the assumptions of the Keynesian model. Take a look at **Exhibit 10–8.** Note that the *SRAS* is completely flat at the existing price level until full-employment capacity is reached. This is because the Keynesian model assumes that at less than full employment output levels, prices (and wages) are fixed since they are inflexible in a downward direction. In essence, firms have a horizontal supply curve when operating below normal capacity, so any change in aggregate demand will lead to a corresponding change in output. Economists refer to this horizontal segment as the *Keynesian range* of the aggregate-supply curve.

What happens to the *SRAS* in Exhibit 10–8 when capacity is reached? In this situation, firms raise their prices to ration the capacity output to those willing to pay the highest prices. Thus, the economy's *SRAS* is vertical at full-employment capacity. So both *SRAS* and *LRAS* are vertical at the full-employment rate of output (Y_f in Exhibit 10–8).

The Keynesian model implies a 90-degree angle-shaped aggregate-supply curve. Since the model postulates downward wage and price inflexibility, the SRAS curve is flat for outputs less than potential GDP (Y_f). In this range, often referred to as the Keynesian range, output is entirely dependent on the level of aggregate demand. The Keynesian model implies that real output rates beyond full employment are unattainable. Thus, both SRAS and LRAS are vertical at the economy's full-employment potential output.

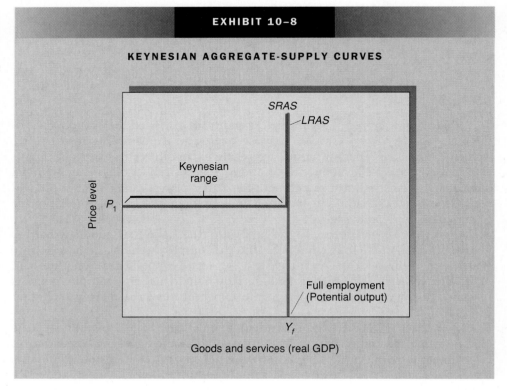

EXHIBIT 10–8

KEYNESIAN AGGREGATE-SUPPLY CURVES

Part "a" of **Exhibit 10–9** illustrates the impact of a change in aggregate demand within the polar assumptions of the Keynesian model. When aggregate demand is less than AD_2 (for example, AD_1), the economy will languish below potential capacity. Since prices and wages are inflexible downward, below-capacity output rates (Y_1, for example) and abnormally high unemployment will persist unless there is an increase in aggregate demand. When output is below its potential, any increase in aggregate demand (for example, the shift from AD_1 to AD_2) brings previously idle resources into the productive process at an unchanged price level. In this range, the Keynesian analysis essentially turns Say's Law (supply creates an equivalent amount of demand) on its head. In the Keynesian range, an increase in demand creates its own supply.

Of course, once the economy's potential output constraint (Y_f) is reached, additional demand would merely lead to higher prices rather than to more output. Since both the *SRAS* and *LRAS* curves are vertical at capacity output, an increase in aggregate demand to AD_3 fails to expand real output.

When constructing models, we often make polar assumptions to illustrate various points. The Keynesian model is no exception. In the real world, prices will not be completely inflexible. Similarly, in the short run, unanticipated increases in demand will not lead solely to higher prices. Nevertheless, the Keynesian model implies an important point that is illustrated more realistically by part "b" of Exhibit 10–9. The horizontal segment of the *SRAS* curve is an oversimplification intended to reinforce the idea that changes in aggregate demand exert little impact on prices and substantial impact on output when an economy is operating well

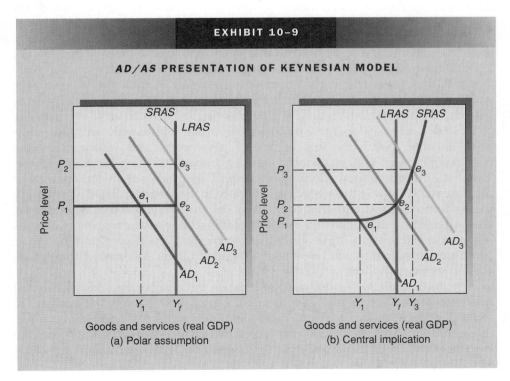

EXHIBIT 10–9

AD/AS PRESENTATION OF KEYNESIAN MODEL

(a) Polar assumption

(b) Central implication

Part "a" illustrates the polar implications of the Keynesian model. When output is less than capacity (for example, Y_1), an increase in aggregate demand such as illustrated by the shift from AD_1 to AD_2 will expand output without increasing prices. But, increases in demand beyond AD_2, such as a shift to AD_3, lead only to a higher price level (P_2). Part "b" relaxes the assumption of complete price inflexibility and short-run output inflexibility beyond Y_f. The SRAS therefore turns from horizontal to vertical more gradually. This would imply that unanticipated increases in aggregate demand would lead (1) primarily to increases in output when output is below capacity (for example, (Y_1), and (2) primarily to increases in the price level when output is greater than capacity (for example, Y_3).

below capacity. Therefore, under conditions like those of the 1930s—when idle factories and widespread unemployment are present—an increase in aggregate demand will exert its primary impact on output.

On the other hand, the vertical segment of the aggregate-supply curve is a simplifying assumption meant to illustrate the concept that there is an attainable output rate beyond which increases in demand will lead almost exclusively to price increases (and only small increases in real output). So when aggregate demand is already quite strong (for example, AD_3), increases in aggregate demand will predictably exert their primary impact on prices rather than output.

THE MULTIPLIER

Expenditure multiplier
The ratio of the change in equilibrium output to the independent change in investment, consumption, or government spending that brings about the change. Numerically, the multiplier is equal to 1/(1 − MPC) when the price level is constant.

The multiplier occupies a central position in the Keynesian model. A change in autonomous expenditures—investment, for example—generally leads to an even larger change in aggregate income. The **expenditure multiplier** is defined as the change in total income (equilibrium output) divided by the autonomous expenditure change that brought about the enlarged income.

The multiplier principle builds on the point that one individual's expenditure becomes the income of another. As we previously discussed, consumption expenditures are directly related to income—an increase in income (or wealth) will lead to an increase in consumption. Predictably, income recipients will spend a portion of their additional earnings on consumption. In turn, their consumption expenditures will generate additional income for others who will also spend a portion of it.

Perhaps an example will illuminate the multiplier concept. Suppose that there were idle unemployed resources and that an entrepreneur decided to undertake a $1 million investment project. Since investment is a component of aggregate demand, the project will increase demand directly by $1 million. This is not the entire story, however. The investment project will require plumbers, carpenters, masons, lumber, cement, and many other resources. The incomes of the suppliers of these resources will increase by $1 million. What will they do with this additional income? Given the link between one's income and consumption, the resource suppliers will predictably spend a fraction of the additional income. They will buy more food, clothing, recreation, medical care, and thousands of other items. How will this spending influence the incomes of those who supply these additional consumption products and services? Their incomes will increase, also. After setting aside (saving) a portion of this additional income, these persons will also spend some of their additional income on current consumption. Their consumption spending will result in still more additional income for other product and service suppliers.

The term *multiplier* is also used to indicate the number by which the initial investment would be multiplied to obtain the total summation of the increases in income. If the $1 million investment resulted in $4 million of additional income, the multiplier would be 4. The total increase in income would be four times the amount of the initial increase in spending. Similarly, if total income increased by $3 million, the multiplier would be 3.

THE SIZE OF THE MULTIPLIER

The size of the multiplier is dependent on the proportion of the additional income that households choose to spend on consumption.[4] Keynes referred to this fraction as the **marginal propensity to consume (MPC).** Mathematically:

$$MPC = \frac{\text{Additional consumption}}{\text{Additional income}}$$

For example, if your income increases by $100 and you therefore increase your current consumption expenditures by $75, your marginal propensity to consume is ¾, or .75.

Exhibit 10–10 illustrates why the size of the multiplier is dependent on MPC. Suppose the MPC is equal to ¾, indicating that consumers spend 75 cents of each additional dollar earned. Continuing with our previous example, we know that a $1 million investment would initially result in $1 million of additional income in round 1. Since the MPC is ¾, consumption would increase by $750,000 (the other $250,000 would flow into saving), contributing that amount to income in round 2. The recipients of the round-2 income of $750,000 would spend three-fourths of it on current consumption. Hence, their spending would increase income by $562,500 in round 3. Exhibit 10–10 illustrates the additions to income through other rounds. In total, income would increase by $4 million, given an MPC of ¾. The multiplier is 4.

If the MPC had been greater, income recipients would have spent a larger share of their additional income on current consumption during each round. Thus, the additional income generated in each round would have been greater, increasing the size of the multiplier. There is a precise relationship between the expenditure multiplier and the MPC. The *expenditure multiplier, M,* is

$$M = \frac{1}{1 - MPC}$$

Exhibit 10–11 indicates the size of the multiplier for several different values of MPC.

REAL-WORLD SIGNIFICANCE OF THE MULTIPLIER

Within the framework of the Keynesian model, the multiplier is important because it explains why even small changes in investment, government, or consumption spending can trigger much larger changes in output. The multiplier magnifies the fluctuations in output and employment that emanate from autonomous changes in spending.

There are both positive and negative sides to the amplified effects. On the negative side, the multiplier principle indicates that a small reduction in expenditures on investment and consumption durables, perhaps due to a decline in business

Marginal propensity to consume (MPC)
Additional current consumption divided by additional current disposable income.

---

[4]For the purposes of simplicity when calculating the size of the multiplier, we will assume that all additions to income are either (1) spent on domestically produced goods or (2) saved. This assumption means that we are ignoring the impact of taxes and spending on imports as income expands via the multiplier process. At the conclusion of our analysis, we will indicate the significance of this assumption.

EXHIBIT 10–10

THE MULTIPLIER PRINCIPLE

EXPENDITURE STAGE	ADDITIONAL INCOME (DOLLARS)		ADDITIONAL CONSUMPTION (DOLLARS)	MARGINAL PROPENSITY TO CONSUME
Round 1	1,000,000	→	750,000	3/4
Round 2	750,000	⇄	562,500	3/4
Round 3	562,500	⇄	421,875	3/4
Round 4	421,875	⇄	316,406	3/4
Round 5	316,406	⇄	237,305	3/4
Round 6	237,305	⇄	177,979	3/4
Round 7	177,979	⇄	133,484	3/4
Round 8	133,484	⇄	100,113	3/4
Round 9	100,113	⇄	75,085	3/4
Round 10	75,085	⇄	56,314	3/4
All Others	225,253	⇄	168,939	3/4
Total	4,000,000		3,000,000	

and consumer optimism about the future, can be an important source of economic instability. As a result, most Keynesian economists believe that the stability of a market economy is quite fragile and constantly susceptible to even modest disruptions. On the positive side, the multiplier principle illustrates the potential of macroeconomic policy to stimulate output even if it is able to exert only a small impact on autonomous expenditures.

In evaluating the significance of the multiplier, it is important to keep three points in mind. First, in addition to saving, leakages in the form of taxes and

EXHIBIT 10–11

A HIGHER MPC MEANS A LARGER MULTIPLIER

MPC	SIZE OF MULTIPLIER
9/10	10
4/5	5
3/4	4
2/3	3
1/2	2
1/3	1.5

spending on imports will also reduce the size of the multiplier. In order to keep things simple, we assumed that all income was either saved or spent on domestically produced goods throughout our analysis. Like saving, taxes and imports will siphon some of the additional income away from spending on *domestic* goods and services. These leakages from the flow of spending will dampen the effects of the multiplier. Therefore, the actual multiplier will be somewhat smaller than the simple expenditure multiplier of our analysis.

Second, it takes time for the multiplier to work. In the real world, several weeks or perhaps even months will be required for each successive round of spending. Only a fraction of the multiplier effect will be observed quickly. Most researchers believe that only about one-half of the total multiplier effect will be felt during the first six months following a change in expenditures.

Third, the multiplier implies that the additional spending brings idle resources into production, leading to additional real output rather than to increased prices. When unemployment is widespread, this is a realistic assumption. However, when there is an absence of abundant idle resources, the multiplier effect will be dampened by an increase in the price level.

MAJOR INSIGHTS OF KEYNESIAN ECONOMICS

Keynesian economics dominated the thinking of macroeconomists for three decades following the Second World War. What are its major insights? Three points stand out.

1. Changes in output, as well as changes in prices, play a role in the macroeconomic adjustment process, particularly in the short run. The classical model emphasized the role of prices in directing an economy to macroeconomic equilibrium. Keynesian analysis highlights the importance of changes in output. Modern analysis incorporates both. Market prices do not adjust instantaneously to economic change. In the short run, changes in output and employment often signal economic change to decision makers and provide the impetus for price adjustments. Hence, modern economists believe that both price and output conditions play a role in the adjustment process.

2. The responsiveness of aggregate supply to changes in demand will be directly related to the availability of unemployed resources. Keynesian analysis emphasizes that when idle resources are present, output will be highly responsive to changes in aggregate demand. Conversely, when an economy is operating at or near its capacity, output will be much less sensitive to changes in demand. So the *SRAS* curve is relatively flat when an economy is well below capacity and relatively steep when the economy is operating near and beyond capacity (see Exhibit 10–9).

3. Fluctuations in aggregate demand are an important potential source of business instability. Abrupt changes in demand are a potential source of both recession and inflation. Policies that effectively stabilize aggregate demand—that minimize abrupt changes in demand—will substantially reduce economic instability.

For more on the Keynesian view on economic instability, see the "Applications in Economics" boxed feature on the Keynesian view of the business cycle.

EVOLUTION OF MODERN MACROECONOMICS

As we previously discussed, the prolonged unemployment of the Great Depression undermined the classical view that markets will quickly restore full employment. Keynesian analysis provides an explanation for what happened during the 1930s. However, other explanations are also possible. As we will discuss in Chapter 13, many economists believe that misguided economic policies, particularly monetary policy, contributed to the depth and duration of the Great Depression. According to this view, markets were unable to restore full employment within a reasonable length of time during the 1930s because policies were inadvertently adopted that not only hampered recovery, but actually depressed economic conditions.

What emerges as the modern view is a hybrid, reflecting elements of both classical and Keynesian analysis, as well as some unique insights drawn from other areas of economics. As we discussed in the previous chapter, various shocks (unanticipated changes in *AD* or *AS*) can disrupt full-employment equilibrium and lead either to recessionary unemployment or to an inflationary boom in the short run. Furthermore, since macroeconomic markets do not adjust immediately, the short-run disequilibrium conditions may persist for a significant time period, perhaps a year or two. On this point, modern analysis is highly consistent with the Keynesian view.

However, the long-run implications of modern analysis are more consistent with the classical view. In the long run, modern analysis indicates that changes in real wages and interest rates will act as a stabilizing force. When an economy is operating below its potential during a recession, falling real wages and interest rates will help restore full employment. Similarly, rising real wages and interest rates will tend to retard an economic boom.

Economic conditions during the last several decades are consistent with the modern view. We continue to experience economic ups and downs, short-run disequilibrium conditions resulting from various shocks. But economic downturns do not spiral downward and result in prolonged periods of stagnation. Rather, market forces respond and redirect the economy. For example, during the 1991–1992 recession, real wages even in several highly unionized industries declined. Similarly, real interest rates fell. Both of these forces helped to reverse the recessionary forces and direct the economy to a recovery.

Market adjustments also helped keep the economy on track following the 1987 stock-market crash. Some commentators predicted dire consequences ahead, after the crash of 1987 eroded approximately one-third of the market value of stocks around the world. But markets handled the shock quite well. Real interest rates fell and thereby encouraged current spending on interest-sensitive goods and investment projects. In contrast with 1929, the disruptions in the financial sector did not spill over and disrupt economic activity in the production and employment sectors of the economy. In spite of the shock, the expansion of the 1980s continued.

KEYNESIAN VIEW OF THE BUSINESS CYCLE

Keynesian economists believe that a market economy, if left to its own devices, will fluctuate between economic recession and inflationary boom.

The Keynesian view emphasizes the destabilizing potential of changes in expenditures powered by changes in optimism and the multiplier. Suppose there is an increase in income triggered by what appears to be a relatively minor disruption—a new innovation, an increase in consumer optimism, or a reduction in taxes, for example. The process of increased expansion will have a tendency to feed on itself. Higher incomes will lead to additional consumption and strong business sales. Inventories will decline, and business will expand output (to rebuild inventories) and move investment projects forward as they become more optimistic about the future. The additional investment, magnified by the multiplier, will lead to an expansion in employment and a rapid growth of income and consumption. Unemployment will decline to a low level. Stock prices will rise as the future begins to look rosy.

Can this expansionary phase continue indefinitely? The answer is no. Eventually, full employment of both manpower and machines will result. The economy will reach its sustainable capacity. Constrained by the short supply of resources, the growth rate of the economy will have to slow. As the growth rate decelerates, business investors will become less optimistic about the future and will cut back fixed investment. The combination of a reduction in investment and increased pessimism about the future will cause consumers to spend less, further reducing aggregate expenditures. The decline in aggregate expenditures, again magnified by the multiplier, will reduce the equilibrium level of income. As the economy plunges into a recession, inventories will rise as businesses are unable to sell their goods because of the low level of demand. Workers will be laid off. The ranks of unemployed workers will grow. Bankruptcies will become more common.

This is what Keynes perceived was happening in the 1930s. Consumers were not spending because their incomes had fallen and they were extremely pessimistic about the future. Similarly, businesses were not producing because there was little demand for their products. Investment had come to a complete standstill because underutilized resources and capacity were abundantly available. Lack of aggregate demand, the moving force of the Keynesian model, paralyzed Western economies during the 1930s. Keynes believed that his underemployment equilibrium model explained why.

Could an economy caught in the web of a depression ever turn upward? The answer is yes. Eventually, machines will wear out, and capital stock will decline to a level consistent with current income and consumption. At that point, some investment will be necessary for replacement purposes. With time, inventories will be depleted, and businesses will begin placing new orders, which will stimulate production. The gradual upturn in investment and production will generate additional income, which will stimulate consumption and start the cycle anew.

INVESTMENT INSTABILITY AND THE BUSINESS CYCLE

Private investment is the villain in the Keynesian theory of the busines cycle. An economic expansion accelerates into a boom because investment, amplified by the multiplier, stimulates other sectors of the economy. At the first sign of a slowdown, though, investment plans are sharply curtailed. The Keynesian theory implies that the investment component, responsive to even small shifts in other economic sectors, acts as the moving force behind the business cycle.

The inventory component of investment is particularly likely to fluctuate throughout the business cycle. During the expansionary phase, inventories will be reduced, since producers will be unable to keep up with the rapid expansion in demand. In contrast, during a downturn, inventories will rise sharply, reflecting the unexpectedly slow growth of aggregate demand.

Is the empirical evidence consistent with the Keynesian view? Clearly, investment is more volatile than aggregate income. Similarly, inventories tend to rise during the early phase of an economic downturn and decline to a low level during the early phase of a business expansion, just as Keynesian theory predicts. Association, however, is not the same thing as causation. The fact that investment fluctuates substantially over the business cycle does not prove that changes in investment cause business instability. Many economists believe that economic fluctuations originate from other sources, particularly fluctuation in the supply of money. We will analyze alternative theories of the business cycle in Chapters 13 and 14.

While modern macroeconomics contains elements of both classical and Keynesian analysis, it also indicates that the impact of economic change is more complex than either view indicated. When analyzing the impact of a change, it makes a difference whether the change is anticipated or unanticipated. It is also important whether people expect the change to be temporary or permanent. In addition, the impact may differ depending on whether long-run equilibrium, underemployment, or overemployment is initially present. As we proceed, we will stress the importance of these factors continually as we use modern macroeconomic theory to enhance our understanding of the real-world economy.

AD/AS OR *AE*—WHICH MODEL SHOULD WE USE?

Our three-market basic macroeconomic model featuring *AD* and *AS* and the aggregate-expenditures (*AE*) model developed in this chapter offer alternative tools with which to analyze macroeconomic change. Which model should we use? Prior to the 1980s, the aggregate-expenditures model was a central focus of macroeconomics. We have shown that it continues to provide valuable insight in various areas. Nevertheless, we believe that reliance upon the multimarket macroeconomic model offers several advantages.

First, the simultaneous occurrence of high unemployment and inflation is easier to visualize within the *AD/AS* framework. The aggregate-expenditure (*AE*) model makes it easy to see why an economy might experience unemployment (demand is deficient). It also offers a straightforward explanation for inflation (excess demand). But it does not readily explain the simultaneous occurrence of the two. Given the reliance on this model in the 1960s and 1970s, it is no coincidence that the simultaneous occurrence of inflation and unemployment during the 1970s took many macroeconomists by surprise.

Second, recent developments in macroeconomics place much more emphasis on price changes in aggregate markets, expectations, and interrelationships among macroeconomic markets. These factors are more easily visualized within the framework of the multimarket *AD/AS* model, which emphasizes *both* price and quantity (output) changes. Similarly, the *AD/AS* model enables us to see why it makes a difference whether an event is anticipated or unanticipated. These factors are the heart of modern macroeconomics.

Finally, the *AD/AS* model makes it easier to understand and make a distinction between long-run and short-run conditions. In essence, the *AE* model is a short-run excess-capacity model. Since it assumes that prices are inflexible downward, price adjustments fail to direct the economy toward full employment. For short periods of time, the Keynesian assumption of price inflexibility may be a reasonable approximation of real-world macroeconomic markets. In the long run, however, this will not be the case. With the passage of time, weak demand will result in downward real price adjustments. The *AE* model conceals the significance of factors that are important in the long run. In contrast, the *AD/AS* model emphasizes the importance of both "sticky prices" in the short run and price adjustments in the long run. Thus, it sheds light on the likely impact of macroeconomic changes during both the immediate time period and the longer time period as markets adjust.

We believe the *AD/AS* model is more flexible and will help us better understand a broader range of economic issues. Thus, it will be our primary tool as we seek to develop more depth in our understanding of macroeconomic issues.

LOOKING AHEAD

Although Keynes emphasized that a market economy might fail to automatically reach its potential capacity, he argued that governments could use their tax and expenditure policies to stabilize aggregate demand and assure full employment. Keynes and his followers forced a reluctant economics profession to think seriously about macroeconomic policy. We turn next to this issue. We will begin by considering the potential of fiscal policy as a tool with which to promote full employment, stable prices, and the growth of real output.

CHAPTER SUMMARY

1. Classical economists emphasized the importance of supply because they believed that production created an equivalent amount of current demand (Say's Law) and that flexible wages and prices would assure full employment. The Great Depression undermined the credibility of the classical view.

2. The concept of planned aggregate expenditures is central to the Keynesian analysis. Aggregate expenditures are the sum of spending on consumption, investment, government purchases, and net exports.

3. In the Keynesian model, planned consumption expenditures are positively related to income. As income expands, though, consumption increases by a lesser amount. Both planned investment and government expenditures are independent of income in the Keynesian model. Planned *net* exports decline as income increases. The Keynesian model postulates that business firms will produce the amount of goods and services they believe consumers, investors, governments, and foreigners (net exports) plan to buy.

4. In the Keynesian model, equilibrium is present when planned total expenditures are equal to output. The equilibrium output level may take place at less than full employment. When it does, the high rate of unemployment will persist into the future. Since the Keynesian model assumes that wages and prices are inflexible downward, reductions in real wages are ruled out as a mechanism to restore full employment. Unless aggregate spending (demand) increases, there is no mechanism for the restoration of full employment.

5. Planned expenditures need not equal actual expenditures. If purchasers spend less than business firms anticipate, unplanned additions to inventories will result. Rather than continuing to accumulate undesired inventories, businesses will cut back output. Income will recede to the equilibrium level.

6. If planned total expenditures temporarily exceed output, businesses will sell more of their products than they anticipate. An unplanned decline in inventories will result. In an effort to restore their abnormally low inventories, businesses will expand future output, and income will rise toward the equilibrium level.

7. Aggregate expenditures are the catalyst of the Keynesian model. Until full employment is attained, supply (real GDP) is always accommodative. Increases in aggregate expenditures thus lead to an expansion in both output and employment as long as the economy is operating below potential capacity. Once capacity is reached, further expansions in expenditures lead only to higher prices, without expanding real output. The Keynesian model implies that maintaining aggregate expenditures at the level consistent with full employment and stable prices is the primary function of sound macroeconomic policy.

8. The expenditure multiplier indicates that independent changes in planned investment, government expenditures, and consumption have a magnified impact on income. Income will increase by some multiple of the initial increase in spending. The multiplier is the number by which the initial change in spending is multiplied to obtain the total amplified increase in income. The size of the multiplier increases with the marginal propensity to consume.

9. In evaluating the importance of the multiplier, it is important to remember that (a) taxes and spending on imports will dampen the size of the multiplier; (b) it takes time for the multiplier to work; and (c) the amplified effect on real output will only be valid when the additional spending brings idle resources into production without price changes.

10. The Keynesian view of the business cycle emphasizes that market forces, once begun, tend to move together, reinforcing either expansion or contraction. Upswings and downswings feed on themselves. During a downturn, business pessimism, declining investment, and the multiplier principle combine to plunge the economy further toward recession. During an economic upswing, business and consumer optimism and expanding investment interact with the multiplier principle to propel the economy further upward. Keynesian theory suggests that a market-directed economy, left to its own devices, will be inherently unstable and fluctuate between economic recession and inflationary boom.

11. Modern macroeconomic analysis incorporates elements of both Keynesian and classical economics. In the short run, market adjustments will not quickly restore full employment. Thus, a less-than-capacity output rate may exist for a period of time, much as the Keynesian model implies. However, in the long run, modern analysis indicates that the changes in real wages and interest rates cushion economic shocks and direct the economy toward full employment, much as the classical model implies.

CRITICAL-ANALYSIS QUESTIONS

1. You have just been appointed to the president's Council of Economic Advisers. Write a short essay explaining to the president the Keynesian view concerning why a market economy may be unable to generate the full-employment level of income. Be sure to explain why equilibrium may result at less than full employment.

*2. How will each of the following factors influence the consumption schedule?
   a. The expectation that consumer prices will rise more rapidly in the future.
   b. Pessimism about future employment conditions.
   c. A reduction in income taxes.
   d. An increase in the interest rate.
   e. A decline in stock prices.
   f. A redistribution of income from older workers (age 45 and over) to younger workers (under 35).
   g. A redistribution of income from the wealthy to the poor.

3. Why does output change in the Keynesian model? Can the Keynesian model explain prolonged unemployment such as was present during the 1930s? How?

*4. What is the multiplier principle? What determines the size of the multiplier? Does the multiplier principle make it more or less difficult to stabilize the economy? Explain.

5. "How can the Keynesian model be correct? According to Keynes, falling income, unemployment, and bad times result because people have so much income that they fail to spend enough to buy all of the goods produced. Paradoxically, rising income and good times result because people are reducing their savings, and spending more than they are making. This doesn't make sense." Explain why you either agree or disagree with this view.

6. Widespread acceptance of the Keynesian aggregate-expenditures (AE) model took place during and immediately following the Great Depression. Can you explain why? The aggregate-expenditures model declined in popularity when many economies experienced both high rates of unemployment and inflation during the 1970s. Was this surprising? Explain.

*7. According to the Keynesian AE model, if people suddenly decide they want to spend more of their current income on consumption, where do they get the funds for the additional spending? What does the model assume with regard to this source of funds?

8. Suppose that individuals suddenly decided to spend less and save more of their current income. Compare and contrast this change within the framework of the Keynesian AE and the AS/AD models.

*9. "Historically, interest rates have generally been higher during periods of economic boom than during recessions. This indicates that higher interest rates stimulate additional investment." Evaluate this view.

10. How would an increase in income abroad influence the equilibrium level of output at home within the framework of the Keynesian AE model? Would the results differ within the framework of the AD/AS model?

*11. When is a change in expenditures most likely to cause a corresponding change in production and employment *in a specific industry*?

12. Economists often state that the Keynesian AE model has its greatest relevance in the short run, while the classical model is most relevant to the long run. In what sense is this true?

*13. What role do declining real wages and resource prices play in the restoration of full employment in the Keynesian model? If output is currently below the full-employment rate, what will direct the economy to full employment in the Keynesian model?

14. In the Keynesian AE model, why does an increase in aggregate spending lead to an equal increase in real GDP as long as output is at less than full-employment capacity? What does this imply about the shape of the aggregate-supply curve?

---

*Asterisk denotes questions for which answers are given in Appendix C.

*15. Within the framework of the Keynesian model, what is the expected impact of a stock-market crash such as the one experienced in October 1987? What adjustments would take place within the framework of the *AD/AS* model?

16. In recent years, approximately 25 percent of the income of Canadians has been spent on imports. In the United States, spending on imports constitutes about 10 percent of income. Would you expect the size of the multiplier to be larger or smaller in Canada than in the United States? Explain.

17. The rate of output and planned expenditures for an economy is indicated in the accompanying table.

TOTAL OUTPUT (REAL GDP IN BILLIONS)	PLANNED AGGREGATE EXPENDITURES (IN BILLIONS)
$500	$525
550	550
600	575
650	600
700	625

a. If the current output rate were $500 billion, what would tend to happen to business inventories, future output, and employment?
b. If the current output rate were $650 billion, what would tend to happen to inventories, future output, and employment?
c. What is the equilibrium rate of income of this economy?
d. If the economy's full-employment rate of output were $600 billion, would the rate of unemployment be high, low, or normal, assuming the current planned demand persisted into the future?
e. What would happen if there was an autonomous increase in investment of $25 billion?

*Asterisk denotes questions for which answers are given in Appendix C.

CHAPTER ELEVEN

MODERN MACROECONOMICS:
FISCAL POLICY

Fiscal policy has come almost full cycle in the past 50 years. From a position of no status in the classical model that dominated economic thinking until 1935, contracyclical fiscal policy reached its pinnacle in the 1960s—the heyday of Keynesian macroeconomics. It may now be on the wane as the "new macroeconomics". . . replaces the Keynesian model.

J. Ernest Tanner, Tulane University[1]

CHAPTER FOCUS

- *How does fiscal policy affect aggregate demand? How does it affect aggregate supply?*
- *What is the Keynesian view of fiscal policy? How do the crowding-out and new classical models modify the basic Keynesian analysis?*
- *How difficult is it to time fiscal policy properly? Why is proper timing important?*
- *Is there a synthesis view of fiscal policy? What does it state?*
- *Are there supply-side effects of fiscal policy?*
- *Do budget deficits cause inflation? Do they cause high interest rates?*

---

[1]J. Ernest Tanner, "Fiscal Policy: An Ineffective Stabilizer?" *Economic Review: Federal Reserve Bank of Atlanta,* August 1982.

A s we indicated in Chapter 8, fiscal policy involves the use of the government's spending and taxing authority. We are now ready to use our basic macroeconomic model to investigate the impact of fiscal policy on output, prices, and employment.

Previously, we assumed that the government's taxing and spending policies remained unchanged. We will now relax that assumption. However, we want to isolate the impact of changes in fiscal policy from changes in monetary policy. Because of this, we will continue to assume that the monetary authorities maintain a constant supply of money. The impact of monetary policy will be considered beginning in Chapter 12.

BUDGET DEFICITS AND SURPLUSES

Balanced budget
A situation in which current government revenue from taxes, fees, and other sources is just equal to current expenditures.

Budget deficit
A situation in which total government spending exceeds total government revenue during a specific time period, usually one year.

Budget surplus
A situation in which total government spending is less than total government revenue during a time period, usually a year.

Discretionary fiscal policy
A change in laws or appropriation levels that alters government revenues and/or expenditures.

Active budget deficits
Deficits that reflect planned increases in government spending or reductions in taxes designed purposely to generate a budget deficit.

Passive budget deficits
Deficits that merely reflect reduced tax revenues or increased spending due to a decline in economic activity during a recession.

Since fiscal policy encompasses both government spending and revenues, it is reflected in the government's budget. When government revenues from all sources are equal to government expenditures (including both purchases of goods and services and transfer payments), the government has a **balanced budget.** The budget need not be in balance, however. A **budget deficit** is present when total government spending exceeds total revenue from taxes, user charges, and other sources. When the government runs a budget deficit, where does it get the money to finance the excess of its spending relative to revenue? It borrows by issuing interest-bearing bonds that become part of what we call the *national debt.* A **budget surplus** is present when the government's revenues exceed the government's spending, reducing the national debt.

The federal budget is much more than a mere revenue and expenditure statement of a large organization. Of course, its sheer size means that it exerts a substantial influence on the economy. Its importance, though, emanates from its position as a policy variable. The federal budget is the primary tool of fiscal policy. In contrast with private organizations that are directed by the pursuit of income and profit, the federal government can alter its budget with an eye toward influencing the future direction of the economy.

Changes in the size of the federal deficit or surplus are often used to gauge whether fiscal policy is adding additional demand stimulus or imposing additional demand restraint. When using it as such a gauge, however, it is important to note that changes in the size of the deficit may arise from two different sources. First, the deficit may reflect **discretionary fiscal policy.** Policy-makers may institute deliberate changes in tax laws or spending on government programs that are designed to generate a budget deficit. Economists often refer to deficits emanating from this source as **active budget deficits.** Second, changes in the size of the deficit may merely reflect the state of the economy. During a recession, tax revenues often fall substantially as the result of reductions in personal income and business profits. Therefore, even if government expenditures are not increased or tax rates cut, an economic recession will tend to increase the size of the budget deficit. Deficits arising from recessionary conditions are often termed **passive budget deficits.** When we speak of "changes in fiscal policy," we are referring to active budget deficits—deliberate changes in government expenditures and/or tax policy that are designed to affect aggregate demand.

KEYNESIAN VIEW OF FISCAL POLICY

Prior to the 1960s, the desirability of a balanced federal budget was widely accepted among business and political leaders. Keynesian economists, though, were highly critical of this view. They argued that the federal budget should be used to promote a level of aggregate demand consistent with full-employment output.

How does the government budget influence the level of aggregate demand? First, the government will directly stimulate aggregate demand if it increases its purchases of goods and services while holding its taxes constant. As the government spends more on highways, flood control projects, education, and national defense, for example, it will increase aggregate demand. Second, changes in tax policy will also influence aggregate demand. A reduction in personal taxes (or an increase in spending on income-transfer programs) increases the disposable income of households. As their after-tax income rises, individuals spend more on consumption. In turn, this increase in consumption will stimulate aggregate demand. Similarly, a reduction in business taxes increases after-tax profitability, which will stimulate both business investment and aggregate demand.

According to the Keynesian view, fluctuations in aggregate demand are the major source of economic disturbances. If demand could therefore be stabilized and maintained at a level consistent with the economy's full-employment productive capacity, the major source of economic instability would be eliminated.

Keynesian theory highlights the potential of fiscal policy as a tool capable of reducing fluctuations in demand. When an economy is operating below its potential output, the Keynesian model suggests that government should institute **expansionary fiscal policy.** In other words, the government should either increase its purchases of goods and services and/or cut taxes. The enlargement of the government's budget deficit stemming from this policy should be financed by borrowing. The budget deficit can be covered by borrowing from private sources: individuals, business firms, and other sources of loanable funds.[2]

Exhibit 11–1 illustrates the case for expansionary fiscal policy when an economy is experiencing abnormally high unemployment due to deficient aggregate demand. Initially, the economy is operating at e_1. Output is below potential capacity, Y_f, and unemployment is above its natural rate. As we have previously discussed, if there is no change in policy, abnormally high unemployment and excess supply in the resource market would eventually reduce real wages and other resource prices. The accompanying lower costs would increase supply (shift to $SRAS_3$) and guide the economy to a full-employment equilibrium (E_3) at a lower price level (P_3). In addition, lower real interest rates resulting from weak business demand for investment funds may help stimulate aggregate demand and restore full employment.

Expansionary fiscal policy
An increase in government expenditures and/or a reduction in tax rates such that the expected size of the budget deficit expands.

---

[2]Alternatively, the government could borrow from its central bank, the Federal Reserve Bank in the United States. However, as we will see in the following chapter, this method of financing a budget deficit would expand the money supply. Since we want to differentiate between fiscal and monetary effects, we must hold the supply of money constant. So for now, we assume that the government deficit must be financed by borrowing from private sources.

Here we illustrate an economy operating in the short run at Y_1, below its potential capacity of Y_f. There are two routes to a long-run full-employment equilibrium. First, policy-makers could wait for lower wages and resource prices to reduce costs, increase supply to $SRAS_3$, and restore equilibrium at E_3. Keynesians believe this market-adjustment method will be slow and uncertain. Alternatively, expansionary fiscal policy could stimulate aggregate demand (shift to AD_2) and guide the economy to E_2.

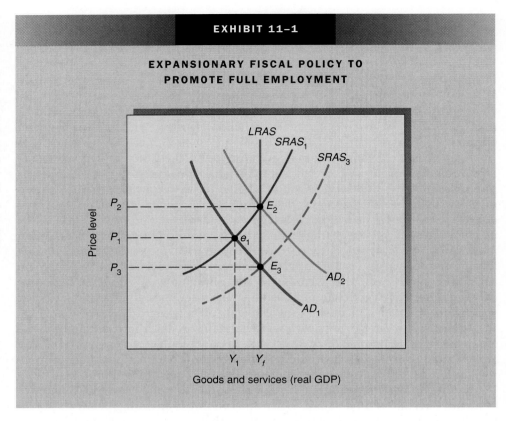

EXHIBIT 11-1

EXPANSIONARY FISCAL POLICY TO PROMOTE FULL EMPLOYMENT

Most Keynesian economists, however, do not believe that this self-corrective mechanism will work very rapidly. Thus, they recommend that policy-makers shift to a more expansionary fiscal policy and thereby speed up the recovery process. An increase in government purchases would stimulate aggregate demand directly. Alternatively, taxes could be reduced. A reduction in income taxes would expand the after-tax income of households, stimulating consumption. Similarly, business taxes could be reduced, which would help stimulate private investment. Furthermore, both an increase in government purchases and a reduction in taxes would be magnified by the multiplier process. Thus, the total increase in aggregate demand would be substantially greater than the increase in government purchases and/or the cut in taxes. An appropriate dose of fiscal policy, if timed properly, would stimulate aggregate demand (shift the curve to AD_2) and guide the economy to full-employment equilibrium (E_2). So when an economy is operating below its potential capacity, the Keynesian prescription calls for an active budget deficit.

The Keynesian view also provides a fiscal policy remedy for inflation. Suppose that an economy is experiencing an inflationary economic boom as the result of excessive aggregate demand. As **Exhibit 11–2** illustrates, in the absence of a change in policy, the strong demand (AD_1) would push up wages and other resource prices. In time, the higher resource prices would increase costs, reduce aggregate supply (from $SRAS_1$ to $SRAS_3$), and lead to a higher price level (P_3). The basic Keynesian model, however, indicates that **restrictive fiscal policy** could be used to reduce aggregate demand (shift to AD_2) and guide the economy to a

Restrictive fiscal policy
A reduction in government expenditures and/or an increase in tax rates such that the expected size of the budget deficit declines (or the budget surplus increases).

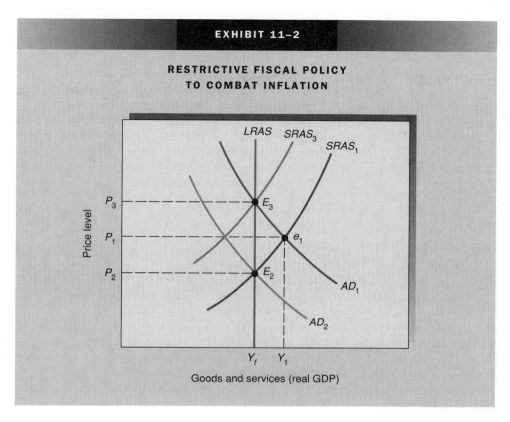

EXHIBIT 11–2

**RESTRICTIVE FISCAL POLICY
TO COMBAT INFLATION**

Strong demand such as AD_1 will temporarily lead to an output rate beyond the economy's long-run potential (Y_f). If maintained, the high level of demand will lead to long-run equilibrium (E_3) at a higher price level. However, restrictive fiscal policy could restrain demand to AD_2 (or better still, prevent demand from expanding to AD_1 in the first place) and thereby guide the economy to a noninflationary equilibrium (E_2).

noninflationary equilibrium (E_2). A reduced level of government purchases would diminish aggregate demand directly. Alternatively, higher taxes on households and businesses could be used to dampen consumption and private investment. The restrictive fiscal policy—a spending reduction and/or increase in taxes—would tend to shift the government budget toward a surplus (or smaller deficit). The Keynesian analysis suggests that this is precisely the proper policy prescription with which to combat inflation generated by excessive aggregate demand.

Prior to the Keynesian revolution, it was widely believed that a responsible government would constrain spending within the bounds of its revenues. The Keynesian revolution drastically altered this view, proposing that general economic conditions, rather than the concept of the annually balanced budget, determine the appropriateness of budget policy.

The Keynesian view stresses the importance of **countercyclical policy,** meaning that the government should adopt policies that will shift its budget toward a deficit when the economy is threatened by a recession. In contrast, fiscal policy should shift the budget toward a surplus in response to the threat of inflation. The Keynesian model indicates that fiscal policy can help stabilize aggregate demand at a level consistent with full employment and price stability, and thereby offset the major source of economic instability.

When judging whether fiscal policy is expansionary or restrictive, economists generally focus on *changes* in the size of the budget deficit (or surplus). A change in policy is generally described as restrictive if it reduces the size of the budget deficit. For example, a fiscal policy change that reduced the size of the annual budget deficit

Countercyclical policy
A policy that tends to move the economy in an opposite direction from the forces of the business cycle. Such a policy would stimulate demand during the contraction phase of the business cycle and restrain demand during the expansionary phase.

from $200 billion to $100 billion would be reflective of restrictive fiscal policy, even though the budget remains in a deficit position. Correspondingly, changes in fiscal policy that increase the size of the budget deficit (or reduce the size of the budget surplus) would be reflective of a more expansionary fiscal policy.

By the early 1960s, the Keynesian view was widely accepted by both economists and policy-makers. The early Keynesian view stressed the potency of fiscal policy—how changes in the budget would exert a powerful impact on aggregate demand and output. More recently, however, economists have noted that budget deficits and surpluses often generate important secondary effects in other markets—particularly the loanable funds market—that tend to weaken their impact on aggregate demand. We turn now to an analysis of these secondary effects.

FISCAL POLICY AND CROWDING-OUT EFFECT

Holding the supply of money constant, when the government runs a deficit, it must borrow from private lenders. Typically, the government will finance its deficit by issuing bonds. As we previously discussed, issuing bonds is simply a means of demanding loanable funds. The total demand for loanable funds will increase as government borrowing competes with private borrowing for the available supply of funds. If the supply of loanable funds does not increase, government borrowing to finance a larger deficit will drive up the real rate of interest.

What impact will a higher real interest rate have on private spending? Consumers will reduce their purchases of interest-sensitive goods such as automobiles and consumer durables in response to a higher real interest rate. More importantly, a higher interest rate will increase the opportunity cost of investment projects. Businesses will postpone spending on plant expansions, heavy equipment, and capital improvements. Residential housing construction and sales will also be hurt. Thus, the higher real interest rates emanating from the larger deficit

OUTSTANDING ECONOMIST

PAUL SAMUELSON (1915–)

The first American to win the Nobel Prize, Paul Samuelson's writings (including his best-selling introductory textbook), played a central role in the development and acceptance of Keynesian economics in the 1950s and 1960s. A professor of Economics at MIT for more than four decades, his *Collected Scientific Papers* encompass five lengthy volumes.[1]

[1]Paul Samuelson, *Collected Scientific Papers of Paul Samuelson* (Cambridge: MIT Press, 1966).

will retard private spending. Economists refer to this squeezing out of private spending by a deficit-induced increase in the real interest rate as the **crowding-out effect.**

The crowding-out effect suggests that budget deficits will exert less impact on aggregate demand than the basic Keynesian model implies. Since financing the deficit pushes up interest rates, budget deficits will tend to retard private spending, particularly spending on investment. This reduction in private spending as the result of higher interest rates will at least partially offset additional spending emanating from the deficit. Thus, a budget deficit may not exert a very powerful impact on demand, output, and employment.

Furthermore, the crowding-out effect implies that the budget deficit will change the composition of aggregate demand. As the higher interest rates accompanying the deficits crowd out private investment, the output of capital goods will decline. As a result, the future stock of capital (for example, heavy equipment, other machines, and buildings) will be smaller than would otherwise have been the case. To the extent that budget deficits push up interest rates and crowd out private investment, they will reduce the supply of capital available to future workers and thereby reduce their productivity and income.[3]

While most modern economists accept the logic of the crowding-out effect, many would argue that it is unlikely to be very important during a recession. If expansionary fiscal policy is applied when an economy is operating at less than capacity, then the accompanying demand stimulus will lead to an increase in both real output and income. At the higher income level, households will save more, which will permit the government to finance its enlarged deficit without much upward pressure on interest rates. In addition, when applied during a recession, the demand stimulus may improve business profit expectations and thereby stimulate additional private investment. Therefore, *if applied during a recession,* an active budget deficit may not crowd out much private investment.

The implications of the crowding out analysis are symmetrical. Restrictive fiscal policy will "crowd in" private spending. If the government increases taxes and/or cuts back on expenditures and thereby reduces its demand for loanable funds, the real interest rate will decline. The lower real interest rate will stimulate additional private investment and consumption. So the fiscal policy restraint will be at least partially offset by an expansion in private spending. As the result of this crowding in, restrictive fiscal policy may not be very effective as a weapon against inflation.

Crowding-out effect
A reduction in private spending as a result of higher interest rates generated by budget deficits that are financed by borrowing in the private loanable funds market.

INTERNATIONAL LOANABLE FUNDS MARKET

In Chapter 3, we explained that when legal restraints on trade are absent, there will be a tendency for goods to exchange for the same price in all markets, except for price differences due to taxes and transportation costs. This *price equalization principle* reflects the incentive of producers to expand supply in markets when prices are high relative to costs (and reduce supply in markets when prices are low relative to costs).

---

[3]The impact of budget deficits on the welfare of future generations is dealt with in detail in Chapter 16.

The price equalization principle also applies to the loanable funds market. People with funds available for loan (or the purchase of bonds) can supply them to markets in London, New York, Toronto, Tokyo, Hong Kong, Sydney, and elsewhere around the world. Adjusted for taxes and transaction costs (including those of a political nature), the real interest rate in one location will be approximately the same as the real interest rate in other locations (and countries).[4]

Suppose the United States cuts taxes and therefore runs a larger budget deficit. The financing of the deficit increases the demand for loanable funds and pushes up the real interest rate as the crowding-out effect implies. How will foreigners respond to this situation? The higher after-tax real interest yield will attract funds from abroad. In turn, this inflow of loanable funds will moderate the rise in real interest rates in the United States.

But how does the inflow of foreign credit influence the crowding-out effect? Since the inflow of loanable funds from abroad moderates the upward pressure on domestic interest rates, it looks, at first glance, as if this factor will tend to minimize the crowding out of private spending. Closer inspection, though, reveals this will not be the case. Foreigners must acquire dollars before they can make financial investments in the United States. Therefore, the higher real interest rates in the United States will not only attract foreign investors, they also will result in an increase in the demand for the U.S. dollar in the **foreign exchange market**—the market that coordinates exchanges of the various national currencies. As foreigners demand more dollars in order to increase their financial investments in the United States, they will bid up the price of the dollar in the foreign exchange rate market. Thus, the dollar will appreciate relative to other currencies.

Foreign exchange market
A highly organized market where the currencies of different countries are bought and sold.

Consider how this increase in the foreign exchange value of the dollar relative to other currencies will influence the net exports of the United States. The appreciation of the dollar will make imports cheaper for Americans. Simultaneously, it will make U.S. exports more expensive for foreigners. Predictably, the United States will import more and export less. Thus, net exports will decline (or net imports increase), causing a reduction in aggregate demand. Therefore, while the inflow of capital from abroad will moderate the increase in the interest rate and the crowding out of private domestic investment, it will reduce net exports and thereby retard aggregate demand.

In summary, the inflow of capital from abroad changes the form of the crowding-out effect, but not its magnitude. Rather than increased real interest rates crowding out domestic investment and interest-sensitive consumer goods, the appreciation in the foreign exchange value of the dollar crowds out net exports (and stimulates imports). Just as a reduction in private investment tends to offset the demand stimulus emanating from budget deficits, so, too, will the decline in net exports.

Furthermore, our analysis indicates that budget deficits and trade deficits—an excess of imports relative to exports—will tend to be linked. When budget deficits push up interest rates and thereby attract an inflow of foreign capital, they will simultaneously cause a nation's currency to appreciate and its imports to rise relative to its exports.

---

[4]Differences in risk associated with loaning funds in another currency will also contribute to differences in real interest rates across countries. Since the rate of return on a loan extended in foreign currency is also influenced by changes in exchange rates, the risk accompanying such loans is greater. Therefore, foreigners will generally be unwilling to extend such loans unless they receive a somewhat higher interest rate in order to compensate them for the additional risk.

NEW CLASSICAL VIEW OF FISCAL POLICY

Some economists stress still another possible secondary effect of budget deficits—the impact of the deficits on saving. When the government runs a budget deficit and increases its outstanding debt, higher future taxes have to be levied to meet the interest obligations of the larger debt. Until now, we have implicitly assumed that the current saving decisions of taxpayers are unaffected by the higher future taxes implied by budget deficits. Some economists argue that this is an unrealistic view. Robert Lucas (University of Chicago), Thomas Sargent (University of Minnesota), and Robert Barro (Harvard University) have been leaders among a group of economists arguing that taxpayers will reduce their current consumption and increase their saving in anticipation of the higher future taxes implied by the debt financing. Since this position has its foundation in classical economics, these economists and their followers are referred to as **new classical economists.**

In the basic Keynesian model, a reduction in current taxes financed by borrowing increases the current disposable income of households. Given their additional disposable income, households increase their current consumption. New classical economists argue that this analysis is incorrect because it ignores the impact of the higher future tax liability implied by the budget deficit and the interest payments required to service the additional debt. New classical economists stress that debt financing merely affects the timing of taxes, not their magnitude. It merely substitutes higher future taxes for lower current taxes.

According to the new classical view, households will reduce their current consumption in response to additional government debt (and the higher taxes that the debt implies) just as surely as would be the case if an equivalent amount of current taxes were levied. If this is true, the current consumption of households will be unaffected when current taxes are cut and government debt and future taxes increased by an equivalent amount. In essence, households will simply save the reduction in their current taxes so they will have the income with which to pay the higher future taxes implied by the additional government debt. Since current consumption declines as the result of the additional debt—just as it would have declined had the equivalent amount of taxes been levied—new classical economists do not believe that the substitution of debt for taxes will stimulate either private consumption or aggregate demand. According to this view, taxes and debt financing are essentially equivalent.

Perhaps an illustration will help explain the underlying logic of the new classical view. Consider the following alternative methods of paying a $1,000 tax liability: (1) a one-time payment of $1,000, or (2) payments of $100 each year in the future. When the interest rate is 10 percent, a $100 liability each year imposes a current cost of $1,000. Therefore, just as the first option reduces current wealth by $1,000, so, too, does the second.

Now let us consider the impact of the two options on future income. If you dip into your savings to make a one-time $1,000 payment, your future interest income will be reduced by $100 each year in the future (assuming a 10 percent interest rate). Just as the second option reduces your future net income by $100 each year, so, too, does the first. In both cases, current wealth is reduced by $1,000. Similarly, in both cases the flow of future net income is reduced by $100 each year. Because of this, the new classical economists believe the two options are essentially the same.

New classical economists
Modern economists who believe there are strong forces pushing a market economy toward full-employment equilibrium and that macroeconomic policy is an ineffective tool with which to reduce economic instability.

Exhibit 11–3 illustrates the implications of the new classical view as to the potency of fiscal policy. Suppose the fiscal authorities issue $50 billion of additional debt in order to cut taxes by an equal amount. The government borrowing increases the demand for loanable funds (D_1 shifts to D_2 in part "b" of Exhibit 11–3) by $50 billion. If the taxpayers did not recognize the higher future taxes implied by the debt, they would expand consumption in response to the lower taxes and the increase in their current disposable income. Under such circumstances, aggregate demand in the goods and services market would expand to AD_2. In the new classical model, though, this will not be the case. Recognizing the higher future taxes, taxpayers will cut back their spending and increase their savings by $50 billion— the amount of saving necessary to generate the income required to pay the higher future taxes implied by the additional debt. This additional saving will allow the government to finance its deficit without an increase in the real interest rate. Since debt financing, like tax financing, causes taxpayers to reduce their expenditures, aggregate demand in the goods and services market is unchanged (at AD_1). In this polar case, fiscal policy exerts no demand stimulus. Output, employment, and the price level are all unchanged.

The new classical view might be summarized as follows: Higher current taxes and an equivalent increase in government debt reduce the wealth (and permanent income) of taxpayers by identical amounts. Substituting government debt for current taxation does not change anything. Taxpayers will recognize the higher future taxes implied by the debt and reduce their current expenditures just as if the equivalent taxes had been levied now. Thus, budget deficits do not stimulate aggregate demand. Similarly, the real interest rate is unaffected by deficits since people will save more in order to pay the higher future taxes. According to the new classical view, fiscal policy is completely impotent.

New classical economists emphasize that budget deficits merely substitute future taxes for current taxes. If households did not anticipate the higher future taxes, aggregate demand would increase to AD₂ (a). However, demand remains unchanged at AD₁ when households fully anticipate the future increase in taxes. Simultaneously, the additional saving to meet the higher future taxes will increase the supply of loanable funds to S₂ (b) and permit the government to borrow the funds to finance its deficit without pushing up the real interest rate. In this model, fiscal policy exerts no effect. The real interest rate, real GDP, and level of employment all remain unchanged.

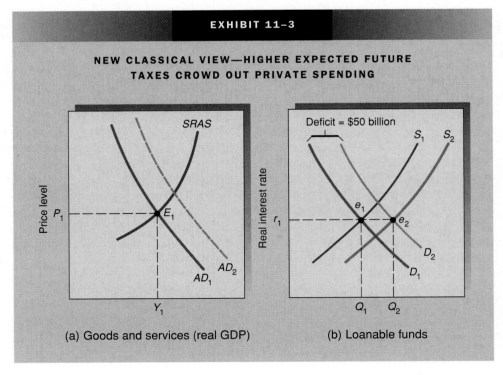

EXHIBIT 11–3

NEW CLASSICAL VIEW—HIGHER EXPECTED FUTURE TAXES CROWD OUT PRIVATE SPENDING

(a) Goods and services (real GDP)

(b) Loanable funds

This new classical theory of fiscal policy is controversial.[5] Critics argue that it is unrealistic to expect that taxpayers will anticipate all or even most of the increase in future taxes implied by additional government debt. In addition, even if people did anticipate the higher future taxes, in our world of limited life spans, many would recognize that they will not be around to pay, at least not in full, the future tax liability implied by debt financing. Thus, many economists reject the new classical view of fiscal policy, at least in its pure form. Nonetheless, the significance of the new classical theory and its implications with regard to fiscal policy continue to provide one of the lively topics of debate in modern macroeconomics.

THE TIMING OF CHANGES IN FISCAL POLICY

If fiscal policy is going to reduce economic instability, changes in policy must inject stimulus during a recession and restraint during an inflationary boom. But proper timing of fiscal policy is not an easy task. Since forecasting a forthcoming recession or boom is a highly imperfect science, there is usually a time lag between when a change in policy is needed and when its need is widely recognized by policy-makers.

In addition, there is generally a lag between the time when the need for a fiscal policy change is recognized and the time when it is actually instituted. Discretionary fiscal policy requires changes in tax laws and government expenditure programs. Before such changes can be instituted, Congress must act. Experts must study the problem. Congressional committees must meet, hear testimony, and draft legislation. And key legislators may choose to delay action if they can use their positions to obtain special favors for their constituencies. A majority of the lawmakers must be convinced that a proposed action is in the interest of the country, and the details of the policy must be arranged such that they will also believe that their own districts and supporters will not be disadvantaged. All of these things take time.

Finally, there is still another factor that adds to the complexity of fiscal policy-making: even after a policy is adopted, it may be six to twelve months before its major impact is felt. If government expenditures are going to be increased, time will be required for competitive bids to be submitted and new contracts granted. Contractors may be unable to begin work right away. While a tax reduction will generally exert demand stimulus more quickly, it will take time for these effects to work their way through the economy.

Macroeconomic policy-making is a little bit like lobbing a ball at a moving target that sometimes changes directions in an unpredictable manner. In order to

---

[5]See Robert J. Barro, "Are Government Bonds Net Wealth?", *Journal of Political Economy*, November–December 1974, pp. 1095–1117; Robert J. Barro, "The Ricardian Approach to Budget Deficits," *Journal of Economic Perspectives*, Spring 1989, pp. 37–44; Alan S. Blinder, "Keynes after Lucas," *American Economic Review*, May 1987, pp. 130–136; James M. Buchanan, "Barro on the Ricardian Equivalence Theorem," *Journal of Political Economy*, April 1976, pp. 337–342; and Gerald P. O'Driscoll, Jr., "The Ricardian Nonequivalence Theorem, *Journal of Political Economy*, February 1977, pp. 207–210.

institute fiscal policy in a manner that will help stabilize the economy, policy-makers need to know what economic conditions are going to be like six, twelve, or eighteen months in the future. Unfortunately, our ability to forecast future economic conditions is limited. Therefore, in a world characterized by dynamic change and unpredictable events, some policy errors are inevitable.

Exhibit 11–4 illustrates the implications of the difficulties involved in the proper timing of fiscal policy. Suppose that policy-makers attempt to use expansionary fiscal policy to stimulate aggregate demand during an economic downturn. If inability to forecast a recession and delays accompanying the adoption of a

EXHIBIT 11–4

WHY PROPER TIMING OF FISCAL POLICY IS DIFFICULT

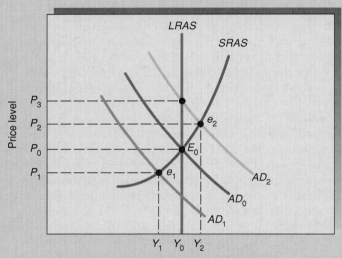

Here we consider an economy that experiences shifts in AD that are not easy to forecast. Initially, the economy is in long-run equilibrium (E_0) at price level P_0 and output Y_0. At this output, only the natural rate of unemployment is present. However, an investment slump and business pessimism result in an unanticipated decline in aggregate demand (to AD_1). Output falls and unemployment increases. After a time, policy-makers institute expansionary fiscal policy seeking to shift aggregate demand back to AD_0. By the time fiscal policy begins to exert its primary effect, though, private investment has recovered and decision makers have become increasingly optimistic about the future. So AD_1 is already, on its own accord, shifting back to AD_0. Thus, the expansionary fiscal policy over-shifts aggregate demand to AD_2, rather than AD_0. Prices rise as the economy is now overheated. Unless the expansionary fiscal policy is reversed, wages and other resource prices will eventually increase, shifting SRAS to the left, thus pushing the price level still higher (to P_3). Alternatively, suppose an investment boom disrupts the initial equilibrium. The increase in investment shifts aggregate demand to AD_2, placing upward pressure on prices. Policy-makers respond by increasing taxes and cutting government expenditures. By the time the restrictive fiscal policy exerts its primary impact, though, investment returns to its normal rate. As a result, the restrictive fiscal policy over-shifts aggregate demand to AD_1 and throws the economy into a recession. Since fiscal policy does not work instantaneously, and since dynamic factors are constantly influencing private demand, proper timing of fiscal policy is not an easy task.

policy change take a substantial period of time, the economy's self-corrective mechanism may already have restored full employment by the time the fiscal stimulus begins to exert its primary impact. If so, the fiscal stimulus will cause excessive demand and inflation. Similarly, restrictive fiscal policy to cool an over-heated economy may cause a recession if aggregate demand declines prior to the fiscal restraint.

In the real world, a fiscal policy change is like a two-edged sword; it can both harm and help. If timed correctly, it will reduce economic instability. If timed incorrectly, however, the fiscal change will increase rather than reduce economic instability.

AUTOMATIC STABILIZERS

Fortunately, there are a few fiscal programs that tend automatically to apply demand stimulus during a recession and demand restraint during an economic boom. Programs of this type are called **automatic stabilizers.** They are automatic in that, without any new legislative action, they tend to increase the budget deficit (or reduce the surplus) during a recession and increase the surplus (or reduce the deficit) during an economic boom.

Automatic stabilizers
Built-in features that tend automatically to promote a budget deficit during a recession and a budget surplus during an inflationary boom, even without a change in policy.

The major advantage of automatic stabilizers is that they institute counter-cyclical fiscal policy without the delays that inevitably accompany legislation. Thus, they minimize the problem of proper timing. When unemployment is rising and business conditions are slow, these stabilizers automatically reduce taxes and increase government expenditures, giving the economy a shot in the arm. On the other hand, automatic stabilizers help to apply the brakes to an economic boom, increasing tax revenues and decreasing government spending. Three of these built-in stabilizers deserve specific mention: unemployment compensation, corporate profit tax, and progressive income tax.

UNEMPLOYMENT COMPENSATION.   When an economy begins to dip into a recession, government payments for unemployment benefits will increase as the number of laid off and unemployed workers expands. Simultaneously, the receipts from the unemployment compensation tax will decline because of the reduction in employment during a recession. Therefore, this program will auto-matically run a deficit during a business slowdown. In contrast, during an eco-nomic boom, the tax receipts from the program will increase because more people are now working, and the amount paid out in benefits will decline since fewer people are unemployed. Thus, the program will automatically tend to run a sur-plus during good times. So without any change in policy, the unemployment compensation program has the desired countercyclical effect on aggregate demand.[6]

CORPORATE PROFIT TAX.   Tax studies show that the corporate profit tax is the most countercyclical of all the automatic stabilizers. This results because corporate

---

[6]Although unemployment compensation has the desired countercyclical effects on demand, it also reduces the incentive to accept available employment opportunities. As a result, researchers have found that the existing unemployment compensation system actually increases the long-run normal unemployment rate. This issue is discussed in more detail in Chapter 14.

profits are highly sensitive to cyclical conditions. Under recessionary conditions, corporate profits will decline sharply, and so will corporate tax payments. This sharp decline in tax revenues will tend to enlarge the size of the government deficit. During economic expansion, corporate profits typically increase much more rapidly than wages, income, or consumption. This increase in corporate profits will result in a rapid increase in the "tax take" from the business sector during an expansion. Thus, corporate tax payments will go up during an expansion and fall rapidly during a contraction if there is no change in tax policy.

PROGRESSIVE INCOME TAX   When income grows rapidly, the average, personal-income-tax liability of individuals and families increases. With rising incomes, more people will find their income above the "no tax due" cutoff. Others will be pushed into a higher tax bracket. Therefore, during an economic expansion, revenue from the personal income tax increases more rapidly than income. Other things constant, the budget moves toward a surplus (or smaller deficit), even though the economy's tax rate structure is unchanged. On the other hand, when income declines, many individuals will be taxed at a lower rate or not at all. Income tax revenues will fall more rapidly than income, automatically enlarging the size of the budget deficit during a recession.

FISCAL POLICY AS A STABILIZATION TOOL: A MODERN SYNTHESIS

During the 1960s the basic Keynesian view was widely accepted. Fiscal policy was thought to be highly potent. Furthermore, it was widely believed that policy-makers, with the assistance of their economic advisors, would adopt fiscal changes in a manner that would help stabilize the economy. During the 1970s and 1980s both the operation of fiscal policy and its efficacy as a stabilization tool were analyzed and hotly debated among professional economists. A synthesis view has emerged from that debate. Most macroeconomists—both Keynesian and non-Keynesian—now accept the following three elements of the modern synthesis view.

1. When substantial unused capacity is present during a recession, expansionary fiscal policy is able to stimulate aggregate demand and real output. Since both unemployed workers and unused production capacity are present during a recession—particularly if the recession is severe—the primary impact of demand-stimulus policies during this phase of the business cycle will be on output and employment rather than prices and interest rates. If timed properly so that its effects are present during a recession, the impacts of demand-stimulus policies will be much like those implied by the basic Keynesian model. Fiscal policy can help prevent a recurrence of the problems experienced in the 1930s. This is a major accomplishment that those who grew up during the relatively stable post–Second World War era often fail to appreciate.

2. During more normal times, the ability of fiscal policy to influence real output is far more limited than the early Keynesian view implied. The current debate among macroeconomists concerning the impact of fiscal policy during normal times is not whether crowding out takes place, but rather how it takes place. The interest-rate crowding-out and new classical models highlight this point. Both models indicate that there are side effects of budget deficits that will substantially, if not entirely, offset their impact on aggregate demand. In the crowding-out model, higher real interest rates and a decline in net exports as the result of currency appreciation reduce private demand and offset the expansionary effects of budget deficits. In the new classical model, higher anticipated future taxes lead to the same result. Both models indicate that fiscal policy will exert little, if any, impact on current aggregate demand, employment, and real output during normal economic times.

3. Proper timing of discretionary fiscal policy is both difficult to achieve and of crucial importance. Given our limited ability to forecast turns in the business cycle and the various delays that accompany the execution of fiscal policy, the likelihood of improper timing of a discretionary change reduces its effectiveness as a stabilization weapon. Rather than smoothing the business cycle, an ill-timed fiscal policy change will add to economic instability. Therefore, most macroeconomists now favor the use of active discretionary fiscal policy only in response to major economic disturbances. It is widely recognized now that in a world of dynamic change and imperfect information concerning the future, active changes in fiscal policy in response to minor economic ups and downs can themselves become a source of economic instability.

SUPPLY-SIDE EFFECTS OF FISCAL POLICY

Thus far, we have focused on the potential demand-side effects of fiscal policy. However, when fiscal changes alter tax rates, they influence the incentive of people to work, invest, and use resources efficiently. Thus, tax changes may also influence aggregate supply. In the past, macroeconomists have often ignored the impact of changes in tax rates, thinking they were of little importance. In recent years, **supply-side economists** have challenged this view.[7] The supply-side argument provided the foundation for the substantial reduction in marginal tax rates in the United States and several other countries that took place during the 1980s.

Supply-side economists
Modern economists who believe that changes in marginal tax rates exert important effects on aggregate supply.

From a supply-side viewpoint, the marginal tax rate is of crucial importance. As we discussed in Chapter 5, the marginal tax rate determines the breakdown of one's additional income between tax payments on the one hand and personal income on the other. A reduction in marginal tax rates increases the reward derived from added work, investment, saving, and other activities that become less heavily taxed. People shift into these activities away from leisure (and leisure-intensive activities), tax shelters, consumption of tax-deductible goods, and other forms of tax avoidance. Supply-side economists believe that these substitutions both enlarge the effective resource base and improve the efficiency with which the resources are applied.

---

[7]See Dwight Lee, ed., *Taxation and the Deficit Economy* (San Francisco: Pacific Institute, 1986), and Lawrence Lindsey, *The Growth Experiment: How the New Tax Policy Is Transforming the U.S. Economy* (New York: Basic Books, 1989), for additional information on supply-side economics. Also see Michael J. Boskin, "Tax Policy and Economic Growth: Lessons from the 1980s," *Journal of Economic Perspectives,* Fall 1988, pp. 71–97, for an evaluation of U.S. tax policy during the 1980s.

The source of the supply-side effects accompanying a change in tax rates is fundamentally different than the source of the demand-side effects. A change in tax rates affects aggregate demand through its impact on disposable income and the flow of expenditures. In contrast, it affects aggregate supply through changes in marginal tax rates, which influence the relative attractiveness of productive activity in comparison to leisure and tax avoidance.

Exhibit 11–5 graphically depicts the impact of a supply-side tax cut, one that reduces marginal tax rates. The lower marginal tax rates increase aggregate supply as the new incentive structure encourages taxpayers to earn additional income and use resources more efficiently. If the tax change is perceived as long-term, both long- and short-term aggregate supply (*LRAS* and *SRAS*) will increase. Real output and income expand.

Of course, the increase in real income will also increase demand (shift to AD_2). If the lower marginal rates are financed by a budget deficit, depending on the strength of the crowding-out effect and the anticipation of higher future taxes (new classical theory), aggregate demand may increase by more than aggregate supply. If this is the case, the price level will rise.

Supply-side economics should not be viewed as a short-run countercyclical tool. It will take time for changing market incentives to move resources out of tax-motivated investments and into higher-yield activities. The full positive effects of lower marginal tax rates will not be observed until labor and capital markets have time to adjust fully to the new incentive structure. Clearly, supply-side economics is a long-run growth-oriented strategy.

Here we illustrate the supply-side effects of a reduction in marginal tax rates. The lower marginal tax rates increase the incentive to earn and use resources efficiently. Since these effects are long-run as well as short-run, both LRAS and SRAS increase (shift to the right). Real output expands. If the lower tax rates are financed by a budget deficit, aggregate demand may expand by a larger amount than aggregate supply, leading to an increase in the price level.

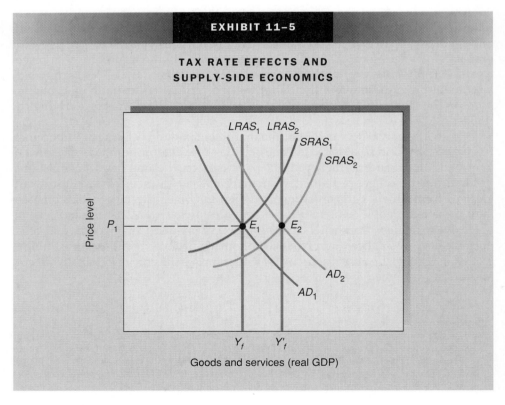

EXHIBIT 11–5

TAX RATE EFFECTS AND SUPPLY-SIDE ECONOMICS

WHY HIGH TAX RATES
TEND TO RETARD OUTPUT

There are three major reasons why high tax rates are likely to retard the growth of output. *First, high marginal tax rates discourage work effort and reduce the productive efficiency of labor.* When marginal tax rates soar to 55 percent or 60 percent, individuals get to keep less than half of what they earn—and when the payoff from working declines, people tend to work less. Some (for example, those with a working spouse) will drop out of the labor force. Others will simply work fewer hours. Still others will decide to take more lengthy vacations, forgo overtime opportunities, retire earlier, be more particular about accepting jobs when unemployed, or forget about pursuing that promising but risky business venture. In some cases, high tax rates will even drive highly productive citizens to other countries where taxes are lower. High tax rates will also result in inefficient utilization of labor. Some individuals will substitute less-productive activities that are not taxed (for example, do-it-yourself projects) for work opportunities yielding taxable income.

Second, high tax rates will adversely affect the rate of capital formation and the efficiency of its use. When tax rates are high, foreign investment will be repelled and domestic investors will search for investment projects abroad where taxes are lower. In addition, domestic investors will direct more of their time and effort into hobby businesses (for example, collecting antiques, raising horses, or providing golf lessons) that provide both enjoyable activities and tax-shelter benefits. This process will divert investment resources away from projects with a higher rate of return but fewer tax-avoidance benefits. As the result of the tax-shelter benefits, individuals will often be able to gain even though the "investments" reduce the value of resources. Scarce capital is wasted and resources are channeled away from their most productive uses.

Third, high marginal tax rates encourage individuals to substitute less desired tax-deductible goods for more desired, nondeductible goods. Here the inefficiency stems from the fact that individuals do not bear the full cost of tax-deductible purchases. High marginal tax rates make tax-deductible expenditures cheap for persons in high tax brackets. Since the personal cost, but not the cost of society, is cheap, taxpayers confronting high marginal tax rates will spend more money on pleasurable, tax-deductible items, such as plush offices, Hawaiian business conferences, and various fringe benefits (for example, a company luxury automobile, business entertainment, and a company retirement plan). Since such tax-deductible purchases reduce their taxes, people will often buy such goods even though they do not value them as much as the cost of producing them.

How important are the supply-side effects accompanying changes in marginal tax rates? As was the case with regard to the demand-side potency of fiscal policy during the 1970s and 1980s, the economics profession is currently divided with regard to the importance of the supply-side factors accompanying changes in fiscal policy. Critics of supply-side economics stress that the rate reductions of the 1980s were associated with a modest growth rate of output, a significant reduction in the real tax revenue of the federal government, and large budget deficits. These outcomes do not indicate that the supply-side effects are highly potent. Defenders of the supply-side position respond by noting that the rate reductions of both the 1960s and the 1980s resulted in lengthy, sustained economic expansions. Among the major industrial countries, only Japan was able to achieve a growth rate similar to that of the United States during the 1980s. Furthermore, supply-side economists stress that the real tax revenues derived from high-income taxpayers in the top brackets—precisely the area where lower rates have the largest incentive effects—actually increased as the highest rates were reduced during the 1980s. (See Exhibit 5–9, page 131 for evidence on this point.)

The top marginal tax rates were increased in 1990 by the Bush administration and again in 1993 by the Clinton administration. The impact of these rate increases on output and tax revenue will provide additional evidence on the importance of supply-side effects. Clearly, this is a topic of important ongoing research, as economists attempt to isolate and measure the supply-side effects of fiscal policy more precisely.

FISCAL POLICY: A CLOSER LOOK AT THE EMPIRICAL EVIDENCE

The accompanying "Thumbnail Sketch" summarizes the major implications of the alternative theories with regard to the impact of expansionary fiscal policy. In general, the effects of restrictive fiscal policy would be just the opposite. As we previously mentioned, economists use *changes* in the size of the deficit, rather than on the absolute amount of a deficit or surplus, to determine whether fiscal policy is shifting toward expansion or restriction. An increase in the size of the deficit relative to the size of the GDP indicates that fiscal policy is becoming more

THUMBNAIL SKETCH

IMPACT OF EXPANSIONARY FISCAL POLICY—A SUMMARY

1. *Basic Keynesian model:* An increase in government spending and/or reduction in taxes will be magnified by the multiplier process and lead to a substantial increase in aggregate demand. When an economy is operating below capacity, real output and employment will also increase substantially.

2. *Crowding-out model:* The potency of expansionary fiscal policy will be dampened because borrowing to finance the budget deficit will push up interest rates and crowd out private spending, particularly investment. In an open economy, the higher interest rates will lead to an inflow of capital, currency appreciation, and a decline in net exports.

3. *New classical model:* The potency of expansionary fiscal policy will be dampened because households will anticipate the higher future taxes implied by the debt and reduce their spending (and increase their saving) in order to pay them. Like current taxes, debt (future taxes) will crowd out private spending.

4. *Supply-side model:* A reduction in marginal tax rates will increase the incentive to earn (produce) and improve the efficiency of resource use, leading to an increase in aggregate supply (real output) in the long run.

expansionary. Conversely, a reduction in the size of the deficit relative to GDP would imply a more restrictive fiscal policy.

We are now prepared to take a closer look at the fiscal policy record and consider the actual effects of policy changes more closely. **Exhibit 11–6** provides data on the federal expenditures and revenues for the United States during the last three decades. In general, the data indicate that the budget deficits as a percentage of GDP expanded during recessions (shaded in blue in Exhibit 11–6) and contracted during business expansions. For example, revenues declined sharply, leading to a substantial increase in the size of the deficit, during the recession of 1970. In contrast, even though a budget surplus was not achieved, the budget deficit declined as a share of GDP during the 1971–1973 expansion. The deficit also increased sharply during the recessions of 1974–1975, 1980–1982, and 1990–1991. Correspondingly, it shrank during the periods of growth following each of these recessions. This pattern of deficits and surpluses indicates that fiscal policy was countercyclical—that it added stimulus during recessions and moved toward restraints during periods of expansion.

However, closer inspection of the 1960–1993 period indicates that the general countercyclical pattern of fiscal policy was primarily the result of automatic stabilizers, rather than active discretionary changes in fiscal policy. Judged from the viewpoint of stabilization policy, the timing of discretionary changes in fiscal policy is clearly mixed.

Perhaps the most effective discretionary fiscal change of recent decades was the 1964 tax cut. Persuaded by his economic advisors, President John F. Kennedy

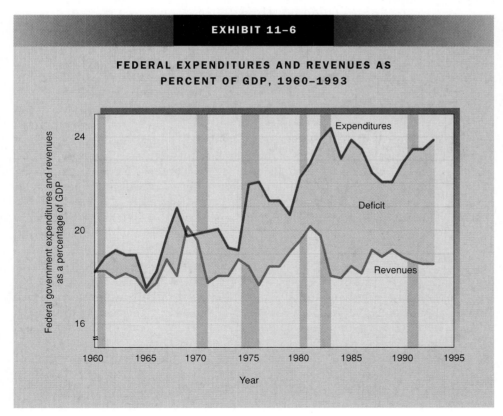

EXHIBIT 11–6

FEDERAL EXPENDITURES AND REVENUES AS PERCENT OF GDP, 1960–1993

Expenditures

Deficit

Revenues

Federal government expenditures and revenues as a percentage of GDP

Year

Since 1960 the federal budget deficit as a percent of GDP has generally increased during recessions and declined during periods of economic expansion. (The blue areas indicate periods of recession.)

Source: *Economic Report of the President*, 1994, tables B–1 and B–77.

recommended legislation cutting personal income tax rates by almost 20 percent over a two-year period. After President Kennedy's assassination in 1963, the legislation was passed by Congress and signed into law by President Lyndon B. Johnson in early 1964. The 1964 tax cut worked marvelously. Output increased, and unemployment, which had been hovering near 6 percent, fell below 4 percent in 1966. Fiscal policy had worked just as the president's economic advisors had predicted. It was a golden era for economists, particularly Keynesian economists.

Unfortunately, it did not last very long. As Exhibit 11–6 shows, federal expenditures expanded rapidly during 1966–1968, and the budget deficits were quite large during both 1967 and 1968. Even though the economy was operating at a high level of employment, fiscal policy was nonetheless highly expansionary. What is the predicted result of fiscal stimulus when an economy is already operating at capacity? Answer: an increase in the price level. Pushed along by the demand stimulus of both the Vietnam War and Great Society programs, the inflation rate began to accelerate in 1966. In early 1966, many economists—including close advisors of President Johnson—called for a tax increase to reduce the fiscal stimulus and retard the rising inflationary pressure. Both President Johnson and Congress failed to heed these early warnings. Finally, after months of delay, President Johnson recommended and Congress passed a temporary (one-year only) 10 percent "surcharge" on personal income tax payments. The tax increase was a case of too little, too late. Since the surtax was for only one year, households did not reduce their spending very much. In fact, personal savings declined as individuals borrowed to pay their temporarily higher tax bill. Since the tax increase was not instituted until the deficit was expanding and the inflation rate accelerating, the modest policy shift was unable to turn the tide against the rising prices of the late 1960s.

In 1975 the United States had a similar experience with discretionary fiscal policy—this time in the case of a tax cut. With the economy already in the midst of serious recession, President Gerald Ford and Congress agreed to a tax-rebate package. The legislation granted taxpayers a partial rebate of their 1974 tax payments and reduced rates for the balance of 1975. The change did little to minimize the effects of the 1974–1975 recession. It came too late—the economy was already beginning to recover when it was instituted. Since the tax cut was temporary and partially in the form of an unanticipated rebate, consumers saved a large portion of the tax cut. This reduced its demand-stimulus effects. In addition, since it failed to reduce marginal tax rates, supply-side effects were absent.

While the discretionary fiscal policy changes of 1964, 1968, and 1975 were motivated by cyclical conditions, the tax changes of the 1980s were overtly tied to the supply-side view that high tax rates retarded long-term economic growth. Nonetheless, the 1982–1984 rate reductions did coincide with the sharp deceleration in the inflation rate and a severe recession in 1982. Thus, fiscal policy during and immediately following the 1982 recession was highly expansionary (see Exhibit 11–6). Later, the Tax Reform Act of 1986 further reduced marginal tax rates, while reducing tax deductions and thus broadening the tax base. Economists who stress the supply-side effects of lower marginal tax rates believe that the rate reductions in the 1980s provided the foundation for the longest peacetime expansion in the history of the United States.

In 1989 and 1990, the U.S. economy was hit with several shocks. First, changing world conditions permitted the United States to reduce substantially expenditures on national defense. With the passage of time, a lowered level of defense expenditures will release resources that can be used to expand output in other areas. During the transition period, however, there will be some dislocation of resources and upward pressure on the unemployment rate. Thus, the cut in defense expenditures placed a drag on the economy in the early 1990s. In addition, several European economies were in the midst of recessions that reduced the demand for U.S. exports. Finally, strong German demand for investment funds to update and modernize manufacturing and other facilities in what was previously East Germany was placing substantial upward pressure on interest rates in international financial markets. All of these factors contributed to the 1990–1991 recession in the United States.

The situation was further complicated by the 1990 budget accord between Congress and the Bush administration. This agreement, designed to reduce the budget deficit, increased tax rates and shifted discretionary fiscal policy toward restriction. Many economists—particularly those of Keynesian and supply-side persuasions—believe that this shift toward a more restrictive fiscal policy actually prolonged the recession and contributed to the sluggishness of the recovery during the early 1990s. Clearly, the policy failed to accomplish its objective. As Exhibit 11–6 illustrates, the higher tax rates failed to raise additional revenue, and both federal expenditures and the budget deficit rose substantially during the recession and sluggish recovery.

BUDGET DEFICITS AND INTEREST RATES

Do budget deficits cause higher interest rates? The implications of the major fiscal policy models provide different answers to this question. The crowding-out model indicates that deficits will increase the demand for loanable funds and thereby place upward pressure on the real rate of interest. In an open economy, however, the increase in domestic interest rates will be moderated by an inflow of financial capital from abroad. The new classical model implies that the higher expected future taxes will stimulate additional saving and thereby permit the government to expand its borrowing at an unchanged interest rate.

What does the empirical evidence indicate with regard to the relationship between budget deficits and the interest rate? Several studies have addressed this issue. Thus far, the results are mixed. A Congressional Budget Office survey of 24 studies found that only a few indicated that there was a significant positive link between budget deficits and real interest rates. The majority of the studies found no statistically significant relationship.[8] Seemingly, these findings would buttress the new classical view that deficits exert little impact on interest rates. They must, however, be interpreted with caution. Most of the studies cover the post–Second World War period. During most of that period, budget deficits were relatively small as a percent of GDP. Persistent budget deficits running 4 or 5 percent of GDP during prosperous peacetime periods

---

[8]Congressional Budget Office, "Deficits and Interest Rates: Empirical Findings and Selected Biography," Appendix A in *The Economic Outlook*, February 1984, pp. 99–102. Also see Charles Plosser, "The Effects of Government Financing Decisions on Asset Returns," *Journal of Monetary Economics*, May 1982, and Paul Evans, "Do Large Deficits Produce High Interest Rates?," *American Economic Review*, March 1985.

are a recent occurrence. The impact of relatively small, generally temporary deficits, such as those experienced by the United States throughout most of the postwar period, may be a misleading indicator of the interest rate impact of large, long-term deficits.

In addition, it is important to distinguish between budget deficits that merely reflect the state of the economy and those that reflect discretionary changes in fiscal policy. When an economy dips into a recession, the budget deficit will tend to rise as the result of the weak state of the economy. In a depressed economy, however, the demand for investment funds is generally weak, which will tend to reduce interest rates. Thus, recessionary business conditions tend to generate both larger budget deficits and lower interest rates. Clearly, this phenomenon makes it more difficult to determine the *independent* impact of budget deficits on interest rates.

Exhibit 11–7 presents data on both the size of the deficit as a share of GDP and the real interest rate during the last three decades. While the year-to-year linkage between the size of the deficit and the real interest rate is weak, there is some evidence that the generally rising and persistently large deficits of the 1980–1986

While the real interest rate is not closely associated with year-to-year changes in the budget deficit, the persistent large deficits of the 1980–1985 period were associated with high real interest rates.

aWe use the average quarterly interest rate on 3-month Treasury bills minus the quarterly change in the GDP implicit price deflator to approximate the real interest rate.

Source: *Board of Governors, Federal Reserve System and the Office of Management and Budget.*

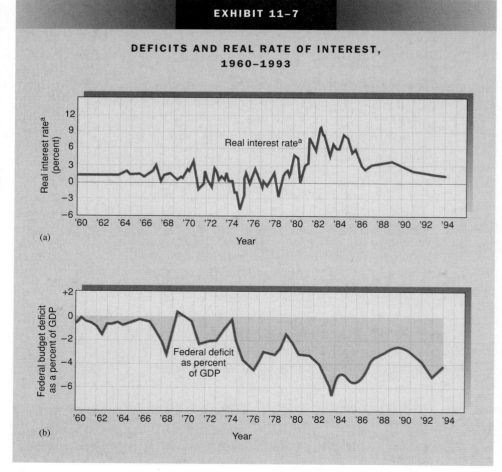

EXHIBIT 11–7

DEFICITS AND REAL RATE OF INTEREST, 1960–1993

period did push the real interest rate upward.[9] Prior to the late 1970s, the real interest rate was generally less than 2 percent. In fact, it hovered in the 2 percent range for three decades following the Second World War. In contrast, during 1981–1986, it fluctuated between 4 and 9 percent. In the latter half of the 1980s and in the early 1990s, however, real interest rates were only slightly higher than during the 1960–1980 period, even though the budget deficits were quite large by historical standards. As a sluggish economy contributed to the larger deficits of the early 1990s, the real interest rate continued to decline. Clearly, the evidence indicates that the relationship between budget deficits and real interest rates is weak, at best.

Given both the implications of our analysis and the difficulty of isolating the *independent* impact of the deficit, the weak relationship between budget deficits and real interest rates is not particularly surprising. After all, even the crowding-out theory indicates that, in an open economy, the upward pressure on interest rates resulting from budget deficits will be moderated by an inflow of capital from abroad.

BUDGET DEFICITS, CAPITAL INFLOW, AND NET EXPORTS

What does the evidence say about the inflow of capital during the 1981–1986 period of increasing and persistently large budget deficits? In 1980 the financial investments of Americans abroad exceeded the investments of foreigners in the United States. Thus, there was an outflow of capital. The situation had changed dramatically by the mid-1980s. By 1984 the United States was experiencing an inflow of capital from abroad equal to 2.1 percent of GDP. During the 1985–1987 period, the capital inflow increased to 2.5 percent of GDP. And, just as our theory predicts, this large inflow of capital pushed up the foreign exchange value of the dollar. Between 1980 and 1985, the U.S. dollar appreciated by more than 50 percent (relative to the currencies of our major trading partners) on the foreign exchange market.

As we explained earlier, an appreciation of the dollar will make imports cheaper for Americans, while making American goods more expensive for foreigners. Therefore, appreciation of a currency will depress net exports (or increase net imports). In 1980 the merchandise net imports of the United States were $25 billion—less than 1 percent of GDP. By 1984 the excess of imports relative to exports had jumped to $112 billion, 3 percent of GDP. During 1985–1987, the net imports of the United States averaged approximately 3.5 percent of GDP.

An inflow of capital, appreciation in currency, and increase in net imports—these are precisely the predicted side effects of large deficits and high real interest rates within the framework of the crowding-out model and an open economy. They indicate that the sharp decline in net exports (increase in net imports) accompanying the inflow of capital and appreciation in the dollar

---

[9]Of course, the real interest rate is the money interest rate minus the expected rate of inflation. Since the expected rate of inflation cannot be directly observed, it must be approximated. Exhibit 11–7 uses the actual change in the GDP deflator as a proxy for the expected rate of inflation.

provided the primary source of the crowding out associated with the persistently large deficits of 1980–1986.

DO BUDGET DEFICITS CAUSE INFLATION?

Despite the continued popularity of the "budget-deficits-cause-inflation" view, macroeconomic analysis provides little support for the theory. The crowding-out model indicates that, when the supply of money is constant, budget deficits will simply lead to higher real interest rates and a fall in net exports, which will crowd out private spending and thereby dampen the stimulus effect of the deficit. In the new classical model, the expectation of higher future taxes crowds out private spending and thereby retards the inflationary effects of deficits.

The Keynesian model does indicate that an increase in the size of the deficit will shift the aggregate demand schedule to the right and lead to a higher price level. This adjustment to a higher price level will take place over time, and during the transition period, the inflation rate will accelerate. However, *once the adjustment to the higher price level occurs*, the impact of the deficit on the inflation rate will cease. Thus, while a larger deficit may permanently increase the level of prices, it will not exert a lasting impact on the inflation rate. Accordingly, none of the major macroeconomic models indicates that budget deficits financed by borrowing from the general public will cause sustained inflation.[10]

The major statistical analysis in this area is supportive of this view. *Independent of monetary expansion*, the major empirical studies have failed to find a significant relationship between budget deficits and the rate of inflation.[11] Recent economic events in the United States also illustrate the uncertainty of the frequently alleged relationship between deficits and inflation. Since 1960 the federal government has run a budget surplus during only one year, 1969. This surplus was associated with an acceleration in the inflation rate from 4.7 percent in 1968 to 6.2 percent in 1969. Perhaps the 1980s offer the strongest evidence against the deficits-cause-inflation view. As we have already noted, the budget deficits were both large and increasing during the early 1980s. Did these deficits cause inflation? Hardly. The inflation rate decelerated from 11.6 percent in 1979–1981 to 3.8 percent during the 1983–1985 period. Of course, other factors, including a deceleration in the growth rate of the money supply, contributed to the decline in the inflation rate during the early 1980s. Nevertheless, the point is that even highly expansionary fiscal policy failed to offset the other factors placing downward pressure on the inflation rate. This is exactly what modern macroeconomic theory would predict.

---

[10]Some economists argue that large budget deficits will induce the monetary authorities to expand the supply of money more rapidly and thereby promote inflation. According to this theory, budget deficits are an indirect cause of inflation.

[11]For evidence on this point, see Gerald P. Dwyer, Jr., "Inflation and Government Deficits," *Economy Inquiry*, July 1982; and Scott E. Hein, "Deficits and Inflation," *Review—Federal Reserve Bank of St. Louis*, March 1981.

LOOKING AHEAD

As we proceed, we will use our knowledge of fiscal policy to investigate several other issues. Later, in Chapter 16, we will consider a related topic—the impact of the national debt on the future health of the economy. We are now ready, though, to integrate the monetary system into our analysis. Chapter 12 will focus on the operation of the banking system and the factors that determine the supply of money. In Chapter 13, we will analyze the impact of monetary policy on real output, interest rates, and the price level. Once we understand how both fiscal and monetary policy work, we will be better able to comprehend the potential of policy as a tool for the promotion of high employment, stable prices, and the growth of income.

CHAPTER SUMMARY

1. The federal budget is the primary tool of fiscal policy. Discretionary fiscal policy encompasses deliberate changes in the government's spending and tax policies designed to alter the size of the budget deficit and thereby influence the overall level of economic activity.

2. According to the Keynesian view, fluctuations in aggregate demand are the major source of economic instability. Policies that help to maintain aggregate demand at a level consistent with the economy's full-employment capacity will reduce economic instability.

3. Rather than balancing the budget annually, Keynesian analysis indicates that policy-makers should use general economic conditions to determine the appropriateness of a budget deficit or surplus. During a recession, Keynesian analysis indicates that expansionary fiscal policy that enlarged the budget deficit would stimulate aggregate demand and help direct the economy to its full-employment capacity. Conversely, restrictive fiscal policy—higher taxes and/or a reduction in government expenditures—would be most appropriate during an inflationary boom.

4. Modern macroeconomists stress the potential importance of secondary effects that modify the basic Keynesian analysis. The crowding-out model highlights one of these effects, showing how budget deficits increase the demand for loanable funds and thereby increase the real interest rate. In turn, the higher real interest rate crowds out private spending, particularly investment, and thereby dampens the stimulus effects of expansionary fiscal policy. Similarly, restrictive fiscal policy will reduce the demand for loanable funds and lower the real interest rate. The decline in the interest rate will stimulate private spending and thereby

retard the effectiveness of restrictive policy as an anti-inflation weapon.

5. To the extent that budget deficits lead to higher interest rates, they will encourage an inflow of foreign capital, which will cause the nation's currency to appreciate. While the inflow of foreign capital will moderate interest-rate increases and the reduction in private investment, the currency appreciation will reduce net exports. Thus, the capital inflow changes the nature of the crowding out rather than its magnitude.

6. The new classical model introduces another secondary effect—the impact of debt on future taxes. New classical economists argue that substitution of debt for tax financing merely changes the timing, not the level, of taxes. According to this view, taxpayers will anticipate the higher future taxes implied by additional government debt, save more to pay the high future taxes, and as a result, reduce their current consumption just as if the equivalent taxes had been levied during the current period. The expansion in saving will permit the government to finance its deficit without an increase in the real interest rate. According to the new classical view, substitution of debt for tax financing will leave real interest rates, aggregate demand, output, and employment unchanged.

7. Changes in fiscal policy must be timed properly if they are going to exert a stabilizing influence on an economy. In a world of dynamic change, the effectiveness of fiscal policy as a stabilization tool is reduced because of (a) our limited ability to forecast future macroeconomic conditions, (b) predictable delays that will accompany the institution of a policy change, and (c) a time lag between when a policy change is instituted and when it will exert its primary impact.

8. The problem of proper timing is reduced in the case of automatic stabilizers—programs that apply stimulus during a recession and restraint during a boom even though no legislative action has been taken. Unemployment compensation, corporate profit taxes, and the progressive income tax are examples of automatic stabilizers.

9. With the passage of time, a modern synthesis concerning the impact of fiscal policy as a stabilization tool has emerged. The major points of the synthesis view are: (a) During a recession, expansionary fiscal policy is able to stimulate aggregate demand, real output, and employment much as the basic Keynesian model implies; (b) during normal times, higher real interest rates and/or higher expected future taxes substantially dampen the stimulative effects of expansionary fiscal policy; and (c) the difficulties involved in the proper timing of discretionary changes in fiscal policy limit our ability to use it effectively to smooth the economic ups and downs of the business cycle.

10. When fiscal policy changes marginal tax rates, it influences aggregate supply by altering the relative attractiveness of productive activity compared to leisure and tax avoidance. Other things constant, lower marginal tax rates will increase aggregate supply. Most economists believe that the demand-side effects of changes in taxes will dominate the supply-side effects in the short run. Consequently, supply-side economics should be viewed as a long-run strategy, not a countercyclical tool.

11. During the last several decades, the budget deficit has generally expanded as a percentage of GDP during recessions and declined during periods of expansion. This countercyclical pattern of fiscal policy primarily reflects automatic stabilizers rather than discretionary changes in fiscal policy.

12. The year-to-year relationship between budget deficits and the real interest rate is weak. However, the large and increasing deficits of the 1980–1986 period were associated with high real interest rates, an inflow of capital, appreciation in the dollar, and a decline in net exports (increase in net imports). These outcomes are highly consistent with the crowding-out view in open economy.

13. Independent of monetary expansion, neither economic theory nor the empirical evidence indicates that budget deficits are a major cause of inflation.

CRITICAL-ANALYSIS QUESTIONS

1. Suppose that you are a member of the Council of Economic Advisers. The president has asked you to prepare a statement of "What is the proper fiscal policy for the next 12 months?" Prepare such a statement, indicating (a) the current state of the economy (that is, unemployment rate, growth in real income, and rate of inflation) and (b) your fiscal policy suggestions. Should the budget be in balance? Explain the reasoning behind your suggestions.

*2. What is the crowding-out effect? How does it modify the implications of the basic Keynesian model with regard to fiscal policy? How does the new classical theory of fiscal policy differ from the crowding-out model?

3. Why is it difficult to properly time discretionary changes in fiscal policy? Do you think political factors, as well as economic factors, limit the use of fiscal policy as a stabilization tool? Why or why not?

*4. What are automatic stabilizers? Explain their major advantage.

5. Which of the following changes in the personal income tax would a supply-side economist be most likely to favor? Explain why.
   a. An increase in the personal-exemption allowance.
   b. A flat-rate tax.
   c. Lower tax rates financed by elimination of various tax-deductible items (interest expense, medical expenditures, and state and local taxes, for example).

6. *What's wrong with this way of thinking?* "Keynesians argue that a budget deficit will stimulate the economy. The historical evidence is highly inconsistent with this view. A $53 billion budget deficit in 1975 was associated with a serious recession, not expansion. We experienced recessions in 1961, 1970, 1982, and 1991 despite budget deficits. The federal budget ran a deficit every year from 1931 through 1939. Yet the economy continued to wallow in the Depression. Obviously, budget deficits do not stimulate GDP and employment."

7. "The economic stimulus of deficit spending is based on money illusion. When the government issues bonds to finance its deficit, it is promising to levy future taxes so that bondholders can be paid back with interest. Bond financing is merely a substitution of future taxation for current taxation. If there are any stimulus effects, they result because taxpayers fail to recognize fully their greater future tax liability and thus they are deceived into thinking that their wealth has increased." Is this view correct? Why or why not?

*8. "If we set aside our reluctance to use fiscal policy as a stabilization force, it is quite easy to achieve full employment and price stability. When output is at less than full employment, we run a budget deficit. If inflation is a problem, we run a budget surplus. Quick implementation of proper fiscal policy will stabilize the economy." Evaluate this view.

9. "Budget deficits may stimulate aggregate demand and output in the short run, but since they divert funds away from capital formation and toward current consumption, they will retard the growth of output in the long run."
   a. Explain why you either agree or disagree with the statement.
   b. Would a proponent of the crowding-out theory agree with this view? Why or why not?
   c. Would a new classical economist agree with it? Why or why not?

*10. Some people argue that the growth of output and employment in the 1980s was the result of the large budget deficits. As one politician put it, "Anyone could create prosperity if he wrote $200 billion of hot checks every year." Evaluate this view.

11. Suppose the federal government decided to systematically reduce the budget deficit by $25 billion each year and eventually run a budget surplus that would be used to reduce its outstanding debt. What would be the consequences of this policy?

12. If deficits tend to be larger during a recession, how will this affect the relationship between budget deficits and real interest rates?

*13. "If the MPC is .75, a $10 billion increase in government expenditures will stimulate $40 billion of additional expenditures ($10 billion times the multiplier of 4), while a $10 billion tax increase will reduce spending by only $30 billion ($7.5 billion times the multiplier of 4). Thus, a $10 billion increase in both government expenditures and taxes will stimulate aggregate output by $10 billion." Evaluate this statement.

*14. If the impact on tax revenues is the same, does it make any difference whether the government cuts taxes by (a) reducing marginal tax rates or (b) increasing the personal exemption allowance? Explain.

15. The "Thumbnail Sketch" on page 298 summarizes the Keynesian, crowding-out, new classical, and supply-side models concerning the impact of expansionary fiscal policy. As an exercise, summarize the implications of the four models with regard to the impact of restrictive fiscal policy.

---

*Asterisk denotes questions for which answers are given in Appendix C.

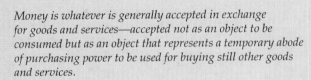

CHAPTER TWELVE

MONEY AND THE
BANKING SYSTEM

*Money is whatever is generally accepted in exchange
for goods and services—accepted not as an object to be
consumed but as an object that represents a temporary abode
of purchasing power to be used for buying still other goods
and services.*

MILTON FRIEDMAN[1]

CHAPTER FOCUS

■ *What is money? How is the money supply defined?*
■ *What is a fractional reserve banking system? How does
it influence the ability of banks to create money?*
■ *What are the major functions of the Federal Reserve
System?*
■ *What are the major tools with which the Federal
Reserve controls the supply of money?*
■ *Why has the United States experienced so many bank
failures in the 1980s?*

[1]Milton Friedman, *Money Mischief: Episodes in Monetary History*
(New York: Harcourt Brace Jovanovich, 1992), p. 16.

T he simple model we have developed thus far in this text has three major markets: (1) goods and services, (2) resources, and (3) loanable funds. However, when people make exchanges in any of these markets, they generally use money. Money is used to purchase commodities, resource services (labor, for example), and all types of goods and services, as well as bonds and other savings instruments. Money and monetary policy thus play an important role in the operation of an economy. Some economists believe that money plays a role similar to that of the quarterback in football—it is the central moving force that makes things happen. While the majority of economists would assign a somewhat lesser role to money, almost all recognize that money matters a great deal.

This chapter focuses on money and the related issue of how the operation of the banking system and the actions of the central monetary authorities influence the supply of money. In the next chapter, we will analyze how monetary policy affects the level of prices, output, employment, and other important economic variables. But before we are able to deal with this latter topic, we need to know something about the nature of money, how it is measured, and the factors that influence its availability.

WHAT IS MONEY?

Money makes the world go around. Yet, paradoxically, most modern money has no intrinsic worth. Nonetheless, most of us would like to have more of it. Why? Because money is an asset that performs three basic functions: it serves as a medium of exchange, a measuring rod for value, and a store of value.

MEDIUM OF EXCHANGE

Medium of exchange
An asset that is used to buy and sell goods or services.

Money is one of the most important inventions in human history because of its role as a **medium of exchange.** Money simplifies and reduces the costs of transactions. This reduction in transaction cost permits us to realize the enormous gains from specialization, division of labor, and mass-production techniques that underlie our modern standard of living. Without money, exchange would be complicated, time-consuming, and enormously costly. Think what it would be like to live in a barter economy—one without money, where goods were traded for goods. If you wanted to buy a pair of jeans, for example, you would have to first find someone willing to sell you the jeans who also wanted to purchase something you were willing to supply. Such an economy would be highly inefficient.

Money oils the wheels of trade and makes it possible for each of us to specialize in the supply of those things that we do best and to purchase (and consume) a broad cross section of goods and services consistent with our individual preferences. People simply sell their productive services or assets for money and, in turn, use the money to buy the goods and services they want. For example, if a farmer wants to exchange a cow for electricity and medical services, the cow is sold for money, which is then used to buy the electricity and the medical services. Money permits a society to escape the cumbersome procedures of a barter economy.

MEASURING ROD FOR VALUE

Since money is widely used in exchange, it also serves as a unit of measurement—some would say an accounting unit—that can be used to compare the value and cost of things. Just as we use yards or meters to measure distance, units of money are used to measure to the exchange value and costs of goods, services, assets, and resources.

Money serves as a common denominator into which the current value of all goods and services can be expressed. If consumers are going to spend their income wisely, they must be able to compare the costs of a vast array of goods and services. Prices measured in units of money help them make such comparisons. Similarly, sound business decision making will require cost and productivity comparisons among vastly different productive services. Resource prices and accounting procedures measured in money units facilitate this task.

STORE OF VALUE

Money is a financial asset—a method of storing value and moving purchasing power from one time period to another. There are some disadvantages to using money as a vehicle for storing value (wealth), though. Many methods of holding money do not yield an interest return. During a time of inflation, the purchasing power of money will decline, imposing a cost on those who are holding wealth in the form of money. Money does, however, have the advantage of being a perfectly **liquid asset.** It can be easily and quickly transformed into other goods at a low transaction cost and without an appreciable loss in its nominal value. Because of this, most people hold some of their wealth in the form of money because it provides readily available purchasing power for dealing with an uncertain future.

Liquid asset
An asset that can be easily and quickly converted to purchasing power without loss of value.

WHY IS MONEY VALUABLE?

At various times in the past, societies have used gold, silver, beads, sea shells, cigarettes, precious stones, and other commodities as money. When commodities are used as money, people use valuable resources to expand the supply of those commodities. Because of this, the opportunity cost of commodity-based money is high.

If a society uses something as money that costs little or nothing to produce, more scarce resources are available for the production of desired goods and services. Thus, most modern nations use **fiat money,** money that has little or no intrinsic value. A dollar bill is just a piece of paper. Checkable deposits are nothing more than accounting numbers. Coins have some intrinsic value as metal, but in most cases this value is considerably less than their value as money.

How can fiat money be valuable? To a degree, its value is based on the confidence of the people who use it. People are willing to accept fiat money because they know it can be used to purchase real goods and services. This is partly a matter of law. The government designates fiat money as "legal tender," meaning it is acceptable for payment of debts.

Fiat money
Money that has neither intrinsic value nor the backing of a commodity with intrinsic value; paper currency is an example.

Money's main source of value, however, is the same as for other commodities; it is determined by demand relative to supply. People demand money because it reduces the cost of exchange. When the supply of money is limited relative to the demand, money will be valuable.

The value of a unit of money—a dollar, for example—is measured in terms of what it will buy. Its value, therefore, is inversely related to the level of prices. An increase in the level of prices and a decline in the purchasing power of a unit of money are the same thing. If the purchasing power of money is to remain stable over time, the supply of money must be controlled. Assuming a constant rate of use, if the supply of money grows more rapidly than the real output of goods and services, prices will rise. In layman's terms, there is "too much money chasing too few goods."

When government authorities rapidly expand the supply of money, it becomes less valuable in exchange and is virtually useless as a store of value. The rapid growth in the supply of money in Germany following the First World War provides a dramatic illustration of this point. During 1922–1923, the supply of German marks increased by 250 percent per month for a time. The German government was printing money almost as fast as the printing presses would run. Since money became substantially more plentiful in relation to goods and services, it quickly lost its value. As a result, an egg cost 80 billion marks and a loaf of bread 200 billion. Workers picked up their wages in suitcases. Shops closed at lunch hour to change price tags. The value of money had eroded. More recently, Yugoslavia, Russia, Ukraine, and several other countries of the former Soviet Union have experienced this same cycle of rapid growth in the money supply (to pay for government expenditures) and hyperinflation.

THE SUPPLY OF MONEY

How is the supply of money defined? There is no straightforward, single answer to this question. Economists and policy-makers have developed three alternative measures of the supply of money, termed M1, M2, and M3.

THE M1 MONEY SUPPLY

M1 (money supply)
The sum of (1) currency in circulation (including coins), (2) demand deposits, (3) other checkable deposits of depository institutions, and (4) traveler's checks.

Transaction accounts
Accounts including demand deposits, NOW accounts, and other checkable deposits against which the account holder is permitted to transfer funds for the purpose of making payment to a third party.

Demand deposits
Non-interest-earning deposits in a bank that either can be withdrawn or made payable on demand to a third party via check. In essence, they are "checkbook money" because they permit transactions to be paid for by check rather than by currency.

Other checkable deposits
Interest-earning deposits that are also available for checking.

Above all else, money is a medium of exchange. The narrowest definition of the money supply, **M1,** focuses on this function. Based on its role as a medium of exchange, it is clear that currency (including both coins and paper bills) and checkable deposits should be included in the supply of money. Deposits that can be drawn from by writing a check are called **transaction accounts.** There are two general categories of transaction accounts. First, there are **demand deposits,** non-interest-earning deposits with banking institutions that are available for withdrawal ("on demand") at any time without restrictions. Demand deposits are usually withdrawn by writing a check. Second, there are **other checkable deposits** that earn interest but carry some restrictions on their transferability. Interest-earning checkable deposits generally either limit the number of checks written each month or require the depositor to maintain a substantial minimum balance ($1,000, for example). Like currency and demand deposits, interest-earning checkable deposits are available for use as a medium of exchange. Traveler's checks are also a means

As the Yugoslavian (Serbian) government financed the military and other expenditures in Bosnia with money creation, inflation soared. Just prior to the introduction of a new currency in 1994, this 1 billion dinara bill was required to purchase a single egg and the price of a "Big Mac" at McDonald's in Belgrade was 10 billion dinara.

of payment. They can be freely converted to cash at *parity* (equal value).

The money supply termed M1 reflects the function of money as a medium of exchange in that it includes only assets that are directly used that way: (1) currency in circulation, (2) demand deposits, (3) other (interest-earning) checkable deposits, and (4) traveler's checks.

As **Exhibit 12–1** shows, the total M1 money supply in the United States was $1,128 billion at year-end 1993. Demand and other checkable deposits accounted for 71 percent of the M1 money supply. This percentage reflects the fact that most of the nation's business—more than 70 percent—is conducted by check.

BROADER DEFINITIONS OF MONEY: M2 AND M3

Since in modern economies, several financial assets can easily be converted into checking deposits or currency, the line between money and "near monies" is often blurred. Broader definitions of the money supply include various assets that can be easily converted to checking account funds and cash. The most common broad definition of the money supply is **M2.** It includes M1 plus (1) savings and small-denomination time deposits at all **depository institutions,** (2) money market mutual fund shares, (3) money market deposit accounts, (4) overnight loans from customers to commercial banks (called *repurchase agreements*), and (5) overnight Eurodollar deposits of U.S. residents. **Money market mutual funds** are interest-earning accounts offered by brokerage firms that pool depositors' funds and invest them in highly liquid short-term securities. Since these securities can be quickly converted to cash, depositors are permitted to write checks (which reduce their share holdings) against their accounts. **Eurodollar deposits** are deposits of U.S. residents denominated in U.S. dollars at banks and other institutions outside the United States. The owners of these financial assets may perceive of them as funds available for use as payment, and in some cases, the assets may even be directly used as a means of exchange. Therefore, many economists—particularly those that stress the store-of-value function of money—prefer the broader M2 definition of the money supply to the narrower M1 concept. As Exhibit 12–1 shows, at year-end 1993 the M2 money supply was $3,566 billion, more than three times the M1 money supply.

M2 (money supply)
Equal to M1, plus (1) savings and time deposits (accounts of less than $100,000) of all depository institutions, (2) money market mutual fund shares, (3) money market deposit accounts, (4) overnight loans from customers to commercial banks, and (5) overnight Eurodollar deposits held by U.S. residents.

Depository institutions
Businesses that accept checking and saving deposits and use a portion of them to extend loans and make investments. Banks, savings and loan associations, and credit unions are examples.

Money market mutual funds
Interest-earning accounts offered by brokerage firms that pool depositors' funds and invest them in highly liquid short-term securities. Since these securities can be quickly converted to cash, depositors are permitted to write checks (which reduce their share holdings) against their accounts.

Eurodollar deposits
Deposits of U.S. residents denominated in U.S. dollars at banks and other financial institutions outside the United States. Although this name originated because of the large amounts of such deposits held at banks in Western Europe, similar deposits in other parts of the world are also called Eurodollars.

The size (as of December 1993) of three alternative measures of the money supply is shown. M1 is the narrowest and most commonly used definition of the money supply. M2, which contains M1 plus the various savings components indicated, is a little more than three times the size of M1. The broadest measure, M3, contains less liquid forms of savings. M3 is nearly four times the size of M1.

^aIncluding money market deposit accounts.

Source: *Federal Reserve Bulletin,* April 1994.

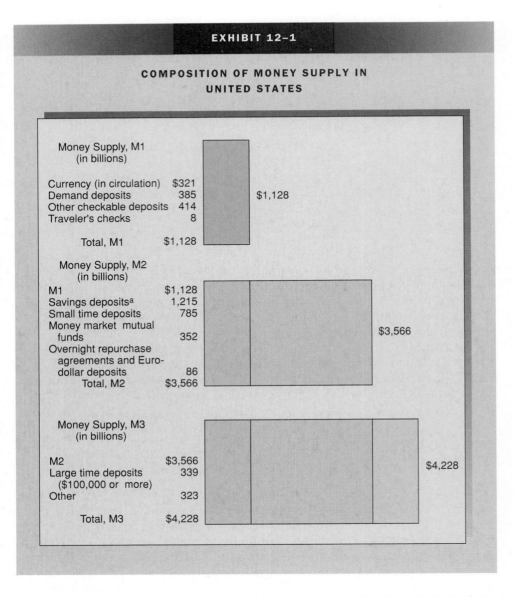

EXHIBIT 12–1

COMPOSITION OF MONEY SUPPLY IN UNITED STATES

Money Supply, M1 (in billions)

Currency (in circulation)	$321
Demand deposits	385
Other checkable deposits	414
Traveler's checks	8
Total, M1	$1,128

$1,128

Money Supply, M2 (in billions)

M1	$1,128
Savings deposits^a	1,215
Small time deposits	785
Money market mutual funds	352
Overnight repurchase agreements and Euro-dollar deposits	86
Total, M2	$3,566

$3,566

Money Supply, M3 (in billions)

M2	$3,566
Large time deposits ($100,000 or more)	339
Other	323
Total, M3	$4,228

$4,228

M3 (money supply)
Equal to M2, plus (1) time deposits (accounts of more than $100,000) at all depository institutions and (2) longer-term (more than overnight) loans of customers to commercial banks and savings and loan associations.

There is a third method of measuring the money supply, **M3,** which includes (1) large-denomination (more than $100,000) time deposits at all depository institutions and (2) longer-term (more than overnight) loans from customers to commercial banks and savings and loan associations. The additional assets included in M3 are not quite as liquid as the items that comprise M2. The M3 money supply in December of 1993 was $4,228, almost four times the M1 figure.

CHANGES IN THE NATURE OF M1 AND A NEW EMPHASIS ON M2

Recent developments in financial markets have, to some extent, changed the nature of the M1 money supply. As **Exhibit 12–2** illustrates, during the 1970s M1

EXHIBIT 12-2

THE CHANGING NATURE OF THE M1 MONEY SUPPLY

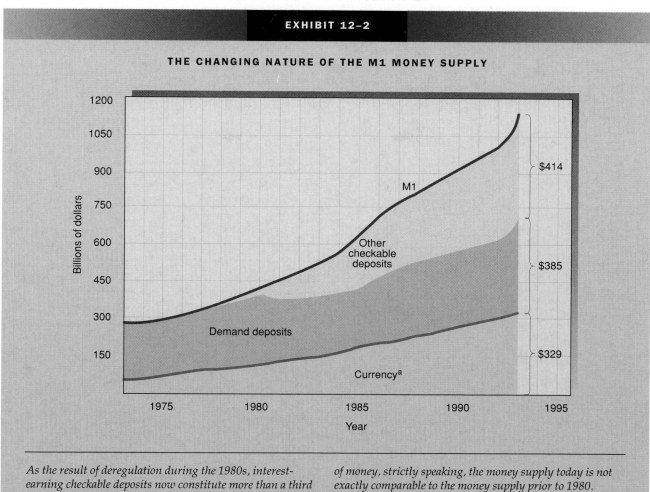

As the result of deregulation during the 1980s, interest-earning checkable deposits now constitute more than a third of the M1 money supply. Since the opportunity cost of holding these other checkable deposits is less than for other forms of money, strictly speaking, the money supply today is not exactly comparable to the money supply prior to 1980.

[a]Travelers checks are included in this category.
Source: *Federal Reserve Bulletin,* April 1994.

was almost entirely composed of currency and demand deposits, neither of which earned interest. The situation changed substantially during the 1980s. Responding to the availability of interest-earning checking accounts, many depositors held some of their savings in these accounts. By 1990 these interest-earning other checkable deposits exceeded demand deposits, and they now comprise more than one-third of the M1 money supply.

Since they earn interest, interest-earning checking accounts are less costly to hold than currency and demand deposits. In essence, interest-earning checking accounts are partly medium-of-exchange money and partly savings. The rapid growth of interest-earning checking accounts during the mid-1980s accelerated the growth rate of the M1 money supply. But they also reduced its comparability with earlier data. Today the M1 money supply has a larger savings component and a smaller medium-of-exchange component than was true during the 1970s.

The changes in the nature of M1 during the 1980s caused economists and monetary planners to pay more attention to M2. Since both savings and interest-earning checking accounts are components of M2, the financial innovations of the 1980s exerted less impact on M2 than on M1. Most analysts now rely more extensively on M2 (rather than M1) when making comparisons of the money supply (and its growth rate) across time periods that include the 1980s. Reflecting these views, when we use money supply data over the last several decades to assess the impact of monetary policy, we will generally use the M2 definition of money.

CREDIT CARDS VERSUS MONEY

Credit
Funds acquired by borrowing.

It is important to distinguish between money and credit. Money is a financial asset that provides the holder with future purchasing power. **Credit** is liability acquired when one borrows funds. This distinction sheds light on a question students frequently ask, "Since credit cards are often used to make purchases, why aren't credit card expenditures part of the money supply?" In contrast with money, credit cards are not purchasing power. They are merely a convenient means of arranging a loan. When you use your Visa or MasterCard to buy a compact disk player, for example, you are not really paying for the player. Instead, you are taking out a loan from the institution issuing your card, and that institution is paying for the player. Payment is not made by you until you write a check to settle your credit card bill and thereby reduce your money balances. Thus, credit card purchases are not money; they are not an asset representing future purchasing power.

THE BUSINESS OF BANKING

Federal reserve system
The central bank of the United States; it carries out banking regulatory policies and is responsible for the conduct of monetary policy.

We must understand a few things about the business of banking before we can explain the factors that influence the supply of money. The banking industry in the United States operates under the jurisdiction of the **Federal Reserve System,** the nation's central bank. Not all banks belong to the Federal Reserve, but under legislation enacted in 1980 only a nominal difference exists between member and nonmember banks. We will discuss the Fed, as it is often called, in detail later in this chapter.

The banking system is an important component of the capital market. Like other private businesses, banks are profit-seeking operations. Banks provide services (for example, safekeeping of funds and checking-account services) and pay interest in order to attract depositors. Most of these depositors are then used to extend loans and undertake investments, which are the primary sources of income for banks.

Banking plays an important role in bringing together people who want to save for the future with those who want to borrow in order to undertake investment projects. The profitability of a bank is very much linked to its ability to invest in and extend loans to financially successful projects. When the investment projects backed by a bank are profitable, borrowers will be able to consistently repay their loans, which generate income for the bank. Therefore, when making loans, banks have a strong incentive to judge both the expected profitability of the project and the creditworthiness of the borrower.

In the United States, the banking system consists of savings and loan institutions, credit unions, and commercial banks. **Savings and loan associations** accept deposits in exchange for shares that pay dividends. **Credit unions** are cooperative financial organizations of individuals with a common affiliation (such as an employer) that accept deposits, pay interest (or dividends) on them out of earnings, and channel funds primarily into loans to members. **Commercial banks** offer a wide range of services—including checking and saving accounts and extension of loans—and are owned by stockholders. Under legislation passed in 1980, all of these depository institutions are authorized to offer both checking and savings accounts and to extend a wide variety of loans to customers. Similar regulations apply to each of them. Therefore, when we speak of the banking industry, we are referring to not only commercial banks, but savings and loan associations and credit unions as well.

The consolidated balance sheet of commercial banking institutions (**Exhibit 12–3**) illustrates the major banking functions. It shows that the major liabilities of banks are transactions, savings, and time deposits. *From the viewpoint of a bank,* these are liabilities because they represent an obligation of the bank to its depositors. Outstanding interest-earning loans comprise the major class of banking assets. In addition, most banks own sizable amounts of interest-earning securities, bonds issued by either governments or private corporations.

Banking differs from most businesses in that a large portion of its liabilities are payable on demand. However, even though it would be possible for all depositors to demand the money in their checking accounts on the same day, the probability of this occurring is quite remote. Typically, while some individuals are making withdrawals, other are making deposits. These transactions tend to balance out, eliminating sudden changes in demand deposits.

Thus, banks maintain only a fraction of their assets in reserves to meet the requirements of depositors. As Exhibit 12–3 illustrates, **bank reserves**—vault cash plus reserve deposits with the Federal Reserve—were only $63 billion at year-end 1993, compared to transaction (checking) deposits of $852 billion. Thus, on average, banks were maintaining less than 10 percent of their assets in reserve against the checking deposits of their customers.

FRACTIONAL RESERVE GOLDSMITHING

Economists often like to draw an analogy between the goldsmith of the past and our current banking system. In the past, gold was used as the means of making payments. It was money. People would store their money with a goldsmith for safekeeping, just as many of us open a checking account for safety reasons. Gold owners received a certificate granting them the right to withdraw their gold anytime they wished. If they wanted to buy something, they would go to the goldsmith, withdraw gold, and use it as a means of making a payment. Thus, the money supply was equal to the amount of gold in circulation plus the gold deposited with goldsmiths.

The day-to-day deposits of and requests for gold were always only a fraction of the total amount of gold deposited. A major portion of the gold simply "lay idle in the goldsmiths' vaults." Taking notice of this fact, goldsmiths soon began loaning gold to local merchants. After a time, the merchants would pay back the gold, plus pay interest for its use. What happened to the money supply when a

Savings and loan associations
Financial institutions that accept deposits in exchange for shares that pay dividends. Historically, these funds have been channeled into residential mortgage loans. Under banking legislation adopted in 1980, S&Ls are now permitted to offer a broad range of services similar to those of commercial banks.

Credit unions
Financial cooperative organizations of individuals with a common affiliation (such as an employer or labor union). They accept deposits, including checkable deposits, pay interest (or dividends) on them out of earnings, and channel funds primarily into loans to members.

Commercial banks
Financial institutions that offer a wide range of services (for example, checking accounts, savings accounts, and extension of loans) to their customers. Commercial banks are owned by stockholders and seek to operate at a profit.

Bank reserves
Vault cash plus deposits of the bank with Federal Reserve Banks.

Banks provide services and pay interest to attract transaction, savings, and time deposits (liabilities). A portion of their assets is held as reserves (either cash or deposits with the Fed) to meet their daily obligations toward their depositors. Most of the rest is invested and loaned out, providing interest income for the bank.

[a]This figure includes deposits of the U.S. government and other depository institutions.

Source: *Federal Reserve Bulletin,* April 1994.

EXHIBIT 12–3

FUNCTIONS OF COMMERCIAL BANKING INSTITUTIONS

CONSOLIDATED BALANCE SHEET OF COMMERCIAL BANKING INSTITUTIONS, YEAR-END 1993 (BILLIONS OF DOLLARS)

ASSETS		LIABILITIES	
Vault cash	$ 34	Transaction deposits	$ 852[a]
Reserves at the Fed	29	Savings and time deposits	1,699
Loans outstanding	2,357	Borrowings	539
U.S. government securities	700	Other liabilities	383
Other securities	166	Net worth	300
Other assets	487		
Total	$3,773	Total	$3,773

---

goldsmith extended loans to local merchants? The deposits of persons who initially brought their gold to the goldsmith were not reduced. Depositors could still withdraw their gold anytime they wished (as long as they did not all try to do so at once). In addition, the merchants were now able to use the gold they borrowed from the goldsmith as a means of payment. As goldsmiths lent gold, they increased the amount of gold in circulation, thereby increasing the money supply.

It was inconvenient to make a trip to the goldsmith every time one wanted to buy something. Since people knew that the certificates were redeemable in gold, certificates began circulating as a means of payment. The depositors were pleased with this arrangement because it eliminated the need for a trip to the goldsmith every time something was exchanged for gold. As long as they had confidence in the goldsmith, sellers were glad to accept the certificates as payment.

Since depositors were now able to use the gold certificates as money, the daily withdrawals and deposits with goldsmiths declined even more. Local goldsmiths would keep about 20 percent of the total gold deposited with them so they could meet the current requests to redeem the gold certificates in circulation. The remaining 80 percent of their gold deposits would be loaned out to business merchants, traders, and other citizens. Therefore, 100 percent of the gold certificates was circulating as money; and that portion of gold that had been loaned out, 80 percent of the total deposits, was also circulating as money. The total money supply, gold certificates plus gold, was now 1.8 times the amount of gold that had been originally deposited with the goldsmith. Since the goldsmiths issued loans and kept only a fraction of the total gold deposited with them, they were able to increase the money supply.

As long as the goldsmiths held enough reserves to meet the current requests of the depositors, everything went along smoothly. Most gold depositors probably did not even realize that the goldsmiths did not have their actual gold and that of other depositors, precisely designated as such, sitting in the "vaults."

Goldsmiths derived income from loaning gold. The more gold they loaned, the greater their total income. Some goldsmiths, trying to increase their income by extending more and more interest-earning loans, depleted the gold in their vaults to imprudently low levels. If an unexpectedly large number of depositors wanted their gold, these greedy goldsmiths would have been unable to meet their requests. They would have lost the confidence of their depositors, and the system of fractional reserve goldsmithing would have begun to break down.

FRACTIONAL RESERVE BANKING

In principle, our modern banking system is very similar to goldsmithing. The United States has a **fractional reserve banking** system. Banks are required to maintain only a fraction of their deposits in the form of cash and other reserves. Just as the early goldsmiths did not have enough gold to pay all their depositors simultaneously, neither do our banks have enough reserves (vault cash and deposits with Federal Reserve banks) to pay all their depositors simultaneously (see Exhibit 12–3). The early goldsmiths expanded the money supply by issuing loans. So do present-day bankers. The amount of gold held in reserve to meet the requirements of depositors limited the ability of the goldsmiths to expand the money supply. The amount of cash and other **required reserves** limits the ability of present-day banks to expand the money supply.

However, there are also important differences between modern banking and early goldsmithing. Today, the actions of individual banks are regulated by a central bank. The central bank is supposed to follow policies designed to promote a healthy economy. It also acts as a lender of last resort. If all depositors in a specific bank suddenly attempted to withdraw their funds simultaneously, the central bank would intervene and supply the bank with enough funds to meet the demand.

Fractional reserve banking
A system that permits banks to hold reserves of less than 100 percent against their deposits.

Required reserves
The minimum amount of reserves that a bank is required by law to keep on hand to back up its deposits. Thus, if reserve requirements were 15 percent, banks would be required to keep $150,000 in reserves against each $1 million of deposits.

FEDERAL DEPOSIT INSURANCE CORPORATION

There is another reason for today's customers having greater confidence in today's banks than yesterday's customers had in early "goldsmith banks": the **Federal Deposit Insurance Corporation (FDIC).** Television ads often boast that a given bank is "a member of the FDIC." Why should a depositor care? The FDIC guarantees the deposits of almost all banks—both state and national—up to a $100,000 limit per account. Even if the bank should fail, the depositors will be able to get their money (up to the $100,000 limit). Individual member banks pay a small insurance premium to the FDIC for each dollar on deposit, and the FDIC uses these premiums to reimburse depositors with funds in a bank that fails. Thus, deposit insurance assures people that their deposits are safe.

The confidence emanating from deposit insurance, however, does more than just give depositors peace of mind. It also reduces the level of risk for those making deposits, thus helping to avoid "runs" on banks. Before the FDIC was created in 1933, a rumor (true or false) that a bank was running short on funds often caused a panic withdrawal of funds by many depositors fearing that the bank would fail. Remember, under a fractional reserve system, banks do not have a

Federal Deposit Insurance Corporation (FDIC)
A federally chartered corporation that insures the deposits held by commercial banks and thrift institutions.

sufficient amount of reserves to redeem the funds of all (or even most) depositors seeking to withdraw their funds at the same time. Prior to the establishment of the FDIC in 1933, more than 10,000 banks (one-third of the total) failed between 1922 and 1933. Most of these failures were the result of "bank runs," panic withdrawals as people lost confidence in the banking system. Since the advent of the FDIC, bank failures stemming from such runs are virtually nonexistent.[2]

HOW BANKS CREATE MONEY BY EXTENDING LOANS

Under a fractional reserve system, an increase in reserves will permit banks to extend additional loans and thereby create additional transaction (checking) deposits. Since transaction deposits are money, the extension of the additional loans expands the supply of money.

To enhance our understanding of this process, let us consider a banking system without a central bank, one in which only currency acts as a reserve against deposits. Initially, we will assume that all banks are required by law to maintain vault currency equal to at least 20 percent of the checking accounts of their depositors. Suppose you found $1,000 that your long-deceased uncle had apparently hidden in the basement of his house. How much would this newly found $1,000 of currency expand the money supply? You take the bills to the First National Bank, open a checking account of $1,000, and deposit the cash with the banker. First National is now required to keep an additional $200 in vault cash, 20 percent of your deposit. However, it received $1,000 of additional cash, so after placing $200 in the bank vault, First National has $800 of **excess reserves,** reserves over and above the amount it is required by law to maintain. Given its current excess reserves, First National can now extend an $800 loan. Suppose it loans $800 to a local citizen to help pay for a car. At the time the loan is extended, the money supply will increase by $800 as the bank adds the funds to the checking account of the borrower. No one else has less money. You still have your $1,000 checking account, and the borrower has $800 for a new car.

When the borrower buys a new car, the seller accepts a check and deposits the $800 in a bank, Citizen's State Bank. What happens when the check clears? The temporary excess reserves of the First National Bank will be eliminated when it pays $800 to the Citizen's State Bank. But when Citizen's State Bank receives $800 in currency (or as a deposit in its account with a Federal Reserve bank), it will now have excess reserves. It must keep 20 percent, an additional $160, in the reserve against the $800 checking account deposit of the automobile seller. This is the **required reserve ratio**—the percentage of a specified liability category (in this case, transaction accounts) that banking institutions are required to hold as reserves against that type of liability.

Excess reserves
Actual reserves that exceed the legal requirement.

Required reserve ratio
A percentage of a specified liability category (for example, transaction accounts) that banking institutions are required to hold as reserves against that type of liability.

[2]There was a substantial increase in bank failures during the 1980s. However, these failures were fundamentally different than the bank failures of the 1920s and 1930s. The underlying causes of the recent bank failures are analyzed later in this chapter. Many economists believe that the FDIC's practice of charging all banks the same deposit insurance premium, regardless of the riskiness of the bank's asset portfolio, contributed to the recent bank failures. This issue is also discussed later in this chapter.

The remaining $640 could be loaned out. Since Citizen's State, like other banks, is in business to make money, it will be quite happy to "extend a helping hand" to a borrower. When the second bank loans out its excess reserves, the deposits of the persons borrowing the money will increase by $640. Another $640 has now been added to the money supply. You still have your $1,000, the automobile seller has an additional $800, and the new borrower has just received an additional $640. Because you found the $1,000 that had been stashed away by your uncle, the money supply has increased by $2,440.

Of course, the process can continue. **Exhibit 12–4** follows the potential creation of money resulting from the initial $1,000 through several additional stages. When the reserve requirement is 20 percent, the money supply can increase by a maximum of $5,000, the initial $1,000 plus an additional $4,000 in demand deposits that can be created by extending new loans.

The multiple by which new reserves increase the stock of money is referred to as the **deposit expansion multiplier.** The amount by which additional reserves can increase the supply of money is determined by the ratio of required reserves to demand deposits. In fact, the potential deposit expansion multiplier is merely the reciprocal of the required reserve ratio. In our example, the required reserves are 20 percent, or one-fifth of the total deposits. So the potential deposit expansion multiplier is 5. If only 10 percent reserves were required, the potential deposit expansion multiplier would be 10, the reciprocal of one-tenth. The lower the percentage of the reserve requirement, the greater is the potential expansion in the money supply resulting from the creation of new reserves. The fractional reserve requirement places a ceiling on potential money creation from new reserves.

Deposit expansion multiplier
The multiple by which an increase (decrease) in reserves will increase (decrease) the money supply. It is inversely related to the required reserve ratio.

EXHIBIT 12–4

CREATING MONEY FROM NEW RESERVES

BANK	NEW CASH DEPOSITS: ACTUAL RESERVES	NEW REQUIRED RESERVES	POTENTIAL DEMAND DEPOSITS CREATED BY EXTENDING NEW LOANS
Initial deposit (Bank A)	$1,000.00	$ 200.00	$ 800.00
Second stage (Bank B)	800.00	160.00	640.00
Third stage (Bank C)	640.00	128.00	512.00
Fourth stage (Bank D)	512.00	102.40	409.60
Fifth stage (Bank E)	409.60	81.92	327.68
Sixth stage (Bank F)	327.68	65.54	262.14
Seventh stage (Bank G)	262.14	52.43	209.71
All others (other banks)	1,048.58	209.71	838.87
Total	$5,000.00	$1,000.00	$4,000.00

When banks are required to maintain 20 percent reserves against demand deposits, the creation of $1,000 of new reserves will potentially increase the supply of money by $5,000.

THE ACTUAL DEPOSIT MULTIPLIER

Will the introduction of the new currency reserves necessarily have a full deposit expansion multiplier effect? The answer is no. The actual deposit multiplier will generally be less than the potential for two reasons.

First, the deposit expansion multiplier will be reduced if some persons decide to hold the currency rather than deposit it in a bank. For example, suppose the person who borrowed the $800 in the preceding example spends only $700 and stashes the remaining $100 away for a possible emergency. Only $700 can then end up as a deposit in the second stage and contribute to the excess reserves necessary for expansion. The potential of new loans in the second stage and in all subsequent stages will be reduced proportionally. When currency remains in circulation, outside the banks, it reduces the size of the deposit expansion multiplier.

Second, the actual deposit multiplier will be less than its maximum potential when banks fail to use all the new excess reserves to extend loans. Banks, though, have a strong incentive to loan out most of their new excess reserves. Idle excess reserves do not draw interest. Banks want to use most of these excess reserves so they can generate interest income. **Exhibit 12–5** shows that this is indeed the case. In recent years, excess reserves have accounted for only 1 or 2 percent of the total reserves of banks.

Currency leakages and idle excess bank reserves will result in a deposit expansion multiplier that is less than its potential maximum. However, since people generally keep most of their money in bank deposits rather than as currency, and since banks typically eliminate most of their excess reserves by extending loans, strong forces are present that will lead to multiple expansion.

FEDERAL RESERVE SYSTEM

Most countries have a central banking authority that controls the money supply and conducts monetary policy. As we previously noted, the central bank of the

Profit-maximizing banks use their excess reserves to extend loans and other forms of credit. Thus, excess reserves are very small, between 1 and 2 percent of the total reserves in recent years.

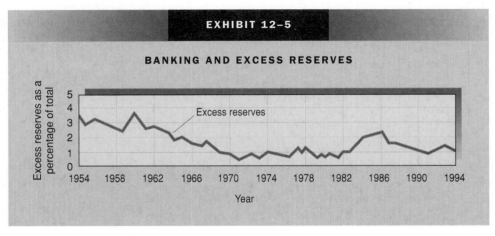

EXHIBIT 12–5

BANKING AND EXCESS RESERVES

United States is the Federal Reserve System. In the United Kingdom, the central bank is the Bank of England; in Germany, it is the Bundesbank.

Central banks are charged with the responsibility of carrying out monetary policy. The major purpose of the Federal Reserve System (and other central banks) is to regulate the money supply and provide a monetary climate that is in the best interest of the entire economy. In some countries, the central bank is largely independent of the political authorities. The German Bundesbank provides an example. In other instances, central banks are directly beholden to political officials. The central banks of most Latin American countries fit into this category.

STRUCTURE OF THE FED

In the United States, the Federal Reserve System, or the Fed, as it is often called, operates with considerable independence of both Congress and the executive branch of government. **Exhibit 12–6** illustrates the structure of the Federal Reserve System. While there are 12 Federal Reserve District banks with 25 regional branches spread throughout the nation, the Board of Governors is the decision-making center of the Fed. This powerful board consists of seven members, each appointed to a staggered 14-year term by the president of the United States with the advice and consent of the Senate. The president designates one of the seven members as chair for a four-year term. However, since a new member of the governing board is appointed only every other year, each president has only limited power over the Fed. This enhances the independence of the Fed and makes monetary policy less subject to political manipulation.

The Board of Governors and the Fed in general have the responsibility of monitoring the health of the banking industry, supervising its procedures, and enforcing Fed regulations. Thus, the country looks to the Fed to act to keep the

The Board of Governors of the Federal Reserve System conducts monetary policy in the United States.

bankruptcy of a few banks or savings and loan institutions from having a "domino effect" and threatening the integrity and safety of the system as a whole. The Board of Governors establishes rules and regulations applicable to all depository institutions. It sets the reserve requirements and regulates the composition of the asset holdings of depository institutions. The board is the rule-maker, and often the umpire, of the banking industry.

The Federal Advisory Council provides the Board of Governors with input from the banking industry. The Federal Advisory Council is composed of 12 commercial bankers, one from each of the 12 Federal Reserve districts. As the name implies, this council is purely advisory.

In addition to the Board of Governors, the Federal Open Market Committee (FOMC) exerts an important influence on monetary policy. This powerful policy-making arm of the Fed is made up of (1) the seven members of the Board of Governors, (2) the president of the New York District Bank, and (3) four (of the remaining eleven) additional presidents of the Fed's District Banks, who rotate on the committee. While they do not always have a vote, all 12 presidents of the Federal Reserve regional banks attend the FOMC meetings, held every five to

The Board of Governors of the Federal Reserve System is at the center of the banking system in the United States. The board sets the rules and regulations for all depository institutions. The seven members of the Board of Governors also serve on the Federal Open Market Committee, a 12-member board that establishes Fed policy with regard to the buying and selling of government securities, the primary mechanism used to control the money supply in the United States.

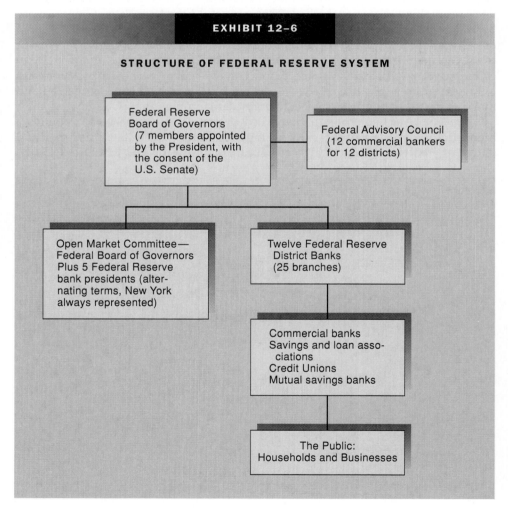

EXHIBIT 12–6

STRUCTURE OF FEDERAL RESERVE SYSTEM

Federal Reserve Board of Governors (7 members appointed by the President, with the consent of the U.S. Senate)

Federal Advisory Council (12 commercial bankers for 12 districts)

Open Market Committee—Federal Board of Governors Plus 5 Federal Reserve bank presidents (alternating terms, New York always represented)

Twelve Federal Reserve District Banks (25 branches)

Commercial banks
Savings and loan associations
Credit Unions
Mutual savings banks

The Public: Households and Businesses

eight weeks. The FOMC determines the Fed's policy with respect to the purchase and sale of government bonds. As we shall soon see, this is the Fed's most frequently used method of controlling the money supply in the United States.

The 12 Federal Reserve District Banks operate under the control of the Board of Governors.[3] These district banks handle approximately 85 percent of all check-clearing services of the banking system. Federal Reserve District Banks differ from commercial banks in several important respects.

1. Federal Reserve Banks are not profit-making institutions. Instead, they are an arm of the government. All of their earnings, above minimum expenses, belong to the Treasury.

2. Unlike other banks, Federal Reserve Banks can actually issue money. Approximately 90 percent of the currency in circulation was issued by the Fed. Look at the dollar bill in your pocket. Chances are that it has "Federal Reserve Note" engraved on it, indicating that it was issued by the Federal Reserve System. The Fed is the only bank that can issue money.

3. Federal Reserve Banks act as bankers' banks. Private citizens and corporations do not bank with Federal Reserve Banks. Commercial depository institutions and the federal government are the only banking customers of the Fed. Most depository institutions, regardless of their membership status with the Fed, usually maintain some deposits with the Federal Reserve System. Of course, deposits with the Fed count as reserves. The Fed audits the books of depository institutions regularly to assure regulatory compliance and the protection of depositors against fraud. The Fed also plays an important role in the clearing of checks through the banking system. Since most banks maintain deposits with the Fed, the clearing of checks becomes merely an accounting transaction.

The primary function of the Fed is to conduct monetary policy and regulate the banking system in a manner that will promote full employment, steady economic growth, and a stable level of prices. Initially, the Fed was made independent of the executive branch so that the Treasury would not use it for political purposes. The policies of the Treasury and the Fed, though, are usually closely coordinated. For example, the chair of the Board of Governors of the Federal Reserve, the Secretary of the Treasury, and the chair of the President's Council of Economic Advisers meet weekly to discuss and plan macroeconomic policy. In reality, it would be more accurate to think of the Fed and the executive branch as equal partners in the determination of policies designed to promote economic stability.

HOW THE FED CONTROLS THE MONEY SUPPLY

The Fed has three major means of controlling the money stock: (1) establishing reserve requirements for depository institutions, (2) buying and selling U.S. government securities in the open market, and (3) setting the interest rate at which it will loan funds to commercial banks and other depository institutions. We will analyze in detail how each of these tools can be used to regulate the amount of money in circulation.

---

[3]Federal Reserve District Banks are located in Boston, New York, Philadelphia, Cleveland, Richmond, Atlanta, Chicago, St. Louis, Minneapolis, Kansas City, Dallas, and San Francisco. There are also 25 district "branch banks."

RESERVE REQUIREMENTS.   The Federal Reserve System requires banking institutions (including credit unions and savings and loan associations) to maintain reserves against the demand deposits of their customers. The reserves of banking institutions are composed of (1) currency held by the bank (vault cash) and (2) deposits of the bank with the Federal Reserve System. A bank can always obtain additional currency by drawing on its deposits with the Federal Reserve. So both cash-on-hand and the bank's deposits with the Fed can be used to meet the demands of depositors. Both therefore count as reserves.

Exhibit 12–7 indicates the required reserve ratio—the percentage of each deposit category that banks are required to keep in reserve (that is, their cash plus deposits with the Fed). As of December 1993 the reserve requirement for transactions accounts was set at 3 percent for amounts under $51.9 million and 10 percent for amounts in excess of $51.9 million.[4] Currently, banks are not required to keep additional reserves against their savings and time deposits.

Why are commercial banks required to maintain assets in the form of reserves? One reason is to prevent imprudent bankers from overextending loans and thereby placing themselves in a poor position to deal with any sudden increase in withdrawals by depositors. The quantity of reserves needed to meet such emergencies is not left totally to the judgment of individual bankers. The Fed sets the rules.

The Fed's control over reserve requirements, however, is important for another reason. By altering reserve requirements, the Fed can alter the money supply. The law does not prevent commercial banks from holding reserves over and above those required by the Fed, but, as we have noted, profit-seeking banking institutions prefer to hold interest-bearing assets such as loans rather than large amounts of excess reserves. **Exhibit 12–8** illustrates this point—the actual reserves maintained by commercial banks are only slightly greater than the reserve level required by the Fed (see also Exhibit 12–5). Since reserves draw no interest, banks will shave their excess reserve to a low level.

When the Fed reduces the reserve requirements, it creates additional excess reserves for banks. Predictably, profit-seeking banks will use a large portion of

Banking institutions are required to maintain 3 percent reserves against transaction-account deposits of less than $51.9 million and 10 percent reserves for transaction deposits over $51.9 million (in effect January 1994).

Source: *Federal Reserve Bulletin,* April 1994.

EXHIBIT 12–7

REQUIRED RESERVE RATIO OF BANKING INSTITUTIONS

	TRANSACTION ACCOUNTS	
	$0–$51.9 MILLION	OVER $51.9 MILLION
Required reserves as a percent of deposits	3%	10%

[4]The $51.9 million dividing point is adjusted each year by 80 percent of the change in total transaction-account deposits in all banking institutions.

EXHIBIT 12-8

RESERVES OF BANKING INSTITUTIONS

	TOTAL—BANKING INSTITUTIONS (DECEMBER 1993) (BILLIONS OF DOLLARS)
Total transaction deposits	$ 799.2
Total time deposits	2000.2
Actual reserves	62.9
Required reserves	61.8
Excess reserves	1.1

The actual and required reserves of banking institutions (December 1993) are indicated in the accompanying chart. The required reserves average approximately 8 percent against transaction deposits and 3 percent against total time deposits. Note that excess reserves of banking institutions are exceedingly small.

Source: *Federal Reserve Bulletin,* April 1994.

these newly created excess reserves to extend additional loans. As they do so, their actions will expand the supply of money. Thus, lower requirements increase the capacity of banks to lend and, as they extend additional loans, the money supply increases.

An increase in the reserve requirements mandated by the Fed will exert just the opposite impact. Since banks typically have very small excess reserves, an increase in reserve requirements will force banks to extend fewer loans. As the volume of loans extended by banks declines, so too will the money supply. Thus, an increase in the reserve requirements will reduce the supply of money.

In recent years, the Fed has seldom used its regulatory power over reserve requirements to alter the supply of money. Changes in reserve requirement are a blunt instrument—small changes in reserve requirements can sometimes lead to large changes in the money supply. The magnitude and timing of a change in the money stock resulting from a change in reserve requirements are difficult to predict with precision. For these reasons, the Fed has usually preferred to use other monetary tools: open market operations and the discount rate.

OPEN MARKET OPERATIONS.   Unlike individuals, businesses, and even other government agencies, the Fed can write a check without funds in its account. When the Fed buys things, it creates money. The primary thing that the Fed buys is the national debt, bonds that were originally issued by the U.S. Treasury and sold to private parties in order to finance budget deficits.

As we indicated earlier, the Federal Open Market Committee (FOMC), a special committee of the Fed, decides when and how **open market operations**—that is, the buying and selling of U.S. securities by the Fed on the open market—will be used. The members meet every five or six weeks to map out the Fed's policy concerning these operations, which are by far the most important tool that the Fed uses to control the money supply.

Open market operations affect both the supply of money directly and the reserves available to the banking system. When the Fed purchases U.S. securities, it injects "new money" into the economy in the form of an increase in either the currency in circulation or the deposits with commercial banks. The sellers of the

Open market operations
The buying and selling of U.S. government securities (national debt) by the Federal Reserve.

securities receive checks drawn on a Federal Reserve Bank. If a seller cashes the check, the amount of currency in circulation expands. If, as is more likely to be the case, the seller deposits the check with a commercial bank, the supply of checking-account money increases *and* new bank reserves are created. When the check is deposited in a bank, the receiving bank acquires a deposit or credit with the Federal Reserve as the check clears. This increases the reserves of the bank, placing it in a position to extend additional loans. As the new loans are extended, the money supply expands by a still larger amount.

Let us consider a hypothetical case. Suppose the Fed purchases $10,000 of U.S. securities from Mary Jones. The Fed receives the securities and Jones receives a check for $10,000, which she deposits in her checking account at City Bank. Her deposit increases the money supply by $10,000, only a fraction of which must be held as required reserves against the new deposits of Jones. Assuming a 10 percent required reserve ratio, City Bank can now extend new loans of up to $9,000 while maintaining its initial reserve position. As the new loans are extended, they too will contribute to a further expansion in the money supply. Part of the new loans will eventually be deposited in other banks, and they also will be able to extend additional loans. As the process continues, the money supply expands by a multiple of the securities purchased by the Fed.

Open market operations can also be used to reduce the money stock, or reduce its rate of increase. If the Fed wants to reduce the money stock, it sells some of its current holdings of government securities. When the Fed sells securities, the buyer pays for them with a check drawn on a commercial bank. As the check clears, both the buyer's checking deposits and the reserves of the bank on which the check was written will decline. Thus, the action will reduce the money supply both directly (by reducing checking deposits) and indirectly (by reducing the quantity of reserves available to the banking system).

Monetary base

The sum of currency in circulation plus bank reserves (vault cash and reserves with the Fed). It reflects the stock of U.S. securities held by the Fed.

The Fed's purchase and sale of U.S. securities determines the size of the **monetary base,** which provides the foundation for the supply of money in the United States. The monetary base is equal to the reserves of commercial banks (vault cash and reserve deposits with the Fed) *plus* the currency in circulation. Fed purchases of U.S. securities increase the monetary base. Since some of this increase in the monetary base will come in the form of additions to bank reserves, every dollar of securities that the Fed buys will eventually increase the money supply by several dollars. Conversely, every dollar of securities that the Fed sells will reduce the money supply by several dollars.

By how much will the money supply change as the Fed injects and withdraws reserves through open market operations? With time, the money supply will be altered by an amount equal to the change in the size of the monetary base multiplied by the actual deposit expansion multiplier. Given the reserve requirements present in the early 1990s (see Exhibit 12–7), potentially an increase in the monetary base could expand the money supply (M1) by a multiple of 10 or more. However, as new reserves are injected into the banking system, there is some leakage either because of potential currency reserves circulating as cash or because some banks may be accumulating excess reserves. Thus, the actual size of the deposit expansion multiplier will be substantially less than its potential. As **Exhibit 12–9** shows, since 1970, the money supply (M1) has been between 3.32 and 2.74 times as large as the monetary base, suggesting that the actual deposit expansion multiplier is generally about 3. Therefore, when the Fed's open market operations change the size of the monetary base, the money supply, on average,

EXHIBIT 12–9

HOW BIG IS THE ACTUAL MONEY DEPOSIT MULTIPLIER?

YEAR (DECEMBER)	MONEY SUPPLY (M1) (BILLIONS OF DOLLARS)	MONETARY BASE (BILLIONS OF DOLLARS)	ACTUAL MONEY DEPOSIT EXPANSION MULTIPLIER
1970	214.5	65.0	3.30
1972	249.3	75.2	3.32
1974	274.4	87.5	3.14
1976	306.4	101.5	3.02
1978	358.4	120.4	2.98
1980	408.8	142.0	2.88
1982	474.6	160.1	2.96
1984	552.5	187.2	2.96
1985	620.2	203.6	3.05
1986	724.6	223.7	3.24
1987	750.0	239.9	3.13
1988	786.9	256.9	3.04
1989	794.1	267.7	2.97
1990	826.4	293.1	2.82
1991	897.7	317.1	2.74
1992	1,024.8	350.6	2.92
1993	1,128.5	385.9	2.92

In recent years, the actual deposit expansion multiplier has been between 2.74 and 3.32. Of course, if the reserve requirements were lowered (raised), the deposit expansion multiplier would rise (fall).

Source: Board of Governors of the Federal Reserve System and *Economic Report of the President, 1994* (Table B-70).

will tend to change by approximately $3 for each dollar of securities that the Fed either purchases or sells.

DISCOUNT RATE—THE COST OF BORROWING FROM THE FED. When banking institutions borrow from the Federal Reserve, they must pay interest on the loan. The interest rate that banks pay on loans from the Federal Reserve is called the **discount rate.** Borrowing from the Fed is a privilege, not a right. The Fed does not have to loan funds to banking institutions. Banks borrow from the Fed primarily to meet temporary shortages of reserves. They are most likely to borrow from the Fed for a brief period of time while they are making other adjustments in their loan and investment portfolios that will permit them to meet their reserve requirement.

An increase in the discount rate makes it more expensive for banking institutions to borrow from the Fed. Borrowing is discouraged, and banks are more likely to build up their reserves to ensure that they will not have to borrow from

Discount rate
The interest rate the Federal Reserve charges banking institutions for borrowing funds.

FRANK AND ERNEST® by Bob Thaves

Frank and Ernest reprinted by permission of NEA, Inc.

the Fed. An increase in the discount rate is thus restrictive. It tends to discourage banks from shaving their excess reserves to a low level.

In contrast, a reduction in the discount rate is expansionary. At the lower interest rate, it costs banks less if they have to turn to the Fed to meet a temporary emergency. Therefore, as the cost of borrowing from the Fed declines, banks are more likely to reduce their excess reserves to a minimum, extending more loans and increasing the money supply.

The general public has a tendency to overestimate the importance of a change in the discount rate. Many people think an increase in the discount rate means their local banker will (or must) charge them a higher interest rate for a loan.[5] This is not necessarily so. Reserves acquired through transaction and time deposits are the major source of loanable funds for commercial banks. Borrowing from the Fed amounts to less than one-tenth of 1 percent of the available loanable funds of commercial banks. Since borrowing from the Fed is such a negligible source of funds, a 0.5 percent change in the discount rate has something less than a profound impact on the availability of credit and the supply of money. Certainly, it does not necessarily mean that your local bank will alter the rate at which it will lend to you.

Federal funds market
A loanable funds market in which banks seeking additional reserves borrow short-term (generally for seven days or less) funds from banks with excess reserves. The interest rate in this market is called the federal funds rate.

If a bank has to borrow to meet its reserve requirements, it need not turn to the Fed. Instead, it can go to the **federal funds market.** In this market, banks with excess reserves extend short-term (sometimes for as little as a day) loans to other banks seeking additional reserves. If the *federal funds rate* (the interest rate in the federal funds market) is less than the discount rate, banks seeking additional reserves will tap this source rather than borrow from the Fed. In recent years, the Fed has kept its loans to banking institutions at a low level by altering the discount rate to match the federal funds rate more closely. As a result, the federal funds rate and the discount rate tend to move together. If the federal funds rate is significantly higher than the discount rate, banks will attempt to borrow heavily from the Fed. Typically, when this happens, the Fed will raise its discount rate, removing the incentive for banks to borrow from it rather than from the federal funds market.

---

[5]The discount rate is also sometimes confused with the prime interest rate, the rate at which banks loan money to low-risk customers. The two rates are different. A change in the discount rate will not necessarily affect the prime interest rate.

CONTROLLING THE MONEY SUPPLY— A SUMMARY

As **Exhibit 12–10** illustrates, the foundation of the M1 money supply is the monetary base, primarily composed of the Fed's holdings of U.S. securities. The monetary base can be decomposed into (1) currency in circulation and (2) bank reserves. Of course, the currency in circulation ($329 billion in December 1993) contributes directly to the money supply. In turn, the bank reserves ($63 billion in December 1993) underpin the checking deposits ($799 billion).

The Fed can determine the size of the monetary base through its buying and selling of securities and its discount-rate policy. It can also use adjustments in the reserve requirements to influence the size of checking deposits relative to bank reserves. If the Fed wants to follow an expansionary policy, it can decrease reserve requirements, purchase additional U.S. securities, and/or lower the discount rate. If it wants to reduce the money stock, it can increase the reserve requirements, sell U.S. securities, and/or raise the discount rate. Since the Fed typically seeks only small changes in the money stock (or its rate of increase), it typically uses only one or two of these tools at a time to accomplish a desired objective. **Exhibit 12–11** summarizes the monetary tools of the Federal Reserve.

CHANGES IN THE MONEY SUPPLY

As the economy grows, the money supply is generally expanded also. In a dynamic setting, therefore, the direction of monetary policy is best gauged by the rate of change in the money supply. When economists say that monetary policy is expansionary, they mean that the rate of growth of the money stock is rapid.

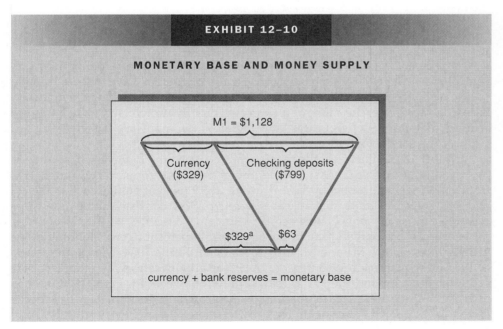

EXHIBIT 12–10

MONETARY BASE AND MONEY SUPPLY

M1 = $1,128

Currency ($329)

Checking deposits ($799)

$329[a] $63

currency + bank reserves = monetary base

The monetary base (currency plus bank reserves) provides the foundation for the money supply. The currency in circulation contributes directly to the money supply, while the bank reserves provide the underpinnings for checking deposits. Fed actions that alter the monetary base will affect the money supply.

[a]Travelers checks are included in this category.

EXHIBIT 12–11

SUMMARY OF MONETARY TOOLS OF THE FEDERAL RESERVE

FEDERAL RESERVE POLICY	EXPANSIONARY MONETARY POLICY	RESTRICTIVE MONETARY POLICY
1. Reserve requirements	*Reduce reserve requirements,* because this will create additional excess reserves and induce banks to extend additional loans, which will expand the money supply	*Raise reserve requirements,* because this will reduce the excess reserves of banks, causing them to make fewer loans; as the outstanding loans of banks decline, the money stock will be reduced
2. Open market operations	*Purchase additional U.S. securities,* which will expand the money stock directly, and increase the reserves of banks, inducing bankers in turn to extend more loans; this will expand the money stock indirectly	*Sell previously purchased U.S. securities,* which will reduce both the money stock and excess reserves; the decline in excess reserves will indirectly lead to an additional reduction in the money supply
3. Discount rate	*Lower the discount rate,* which will encourage more borrowing from the Fed; banks will tend to reduce their reserves and extend more loans because of the lower cost of borrowing from the Fed if they temporarily run short on reserves	*Raise the discount rate,* thereby discouraging borrowing from the Fed; banks will tend to extend fewer loans and build up their reserves so they will not have to borrow from the Fed

Similarly, restrictive monetary policy implies a slow rate of growth, or a decline, in the money stock.

Since open market operations have been the Fed's primary tool of monetary control in recent years, the monetary base and money stock have followed similar paths. When the Fed purchases U.S. securities and thereby expands the monetary base at a rapid rate, the money stock grows rapidly. Conversely, when the Fed reduces its holdings of securities (and therefore the monetary base), the money supply grows less rapidly.

Exhibit 12–12 illustrates the relationship between the monetary base and the money supply during the last decade. From 1981 (fourth quarter) through 1983 (fourth quarter), the monetary base grew at an 8.9 percent annual rate, while M1 and M2 grew at slightly higher rates. During 1984, the Fed shifted to a more restrictive monetary policy. Between 1984 (first quarter) and 1984 (fourth quarter), the monetary base grew at an annual rate of 5.8 percent. Correspondingly, the growth rates of both M1 and M2 also decelerated during 1984. During the period of 1985 (first quarter) to 1988 (first quarter), the growth rate of the monetary base accelerated again, and the M1 money supply followed suit. From 1988 (second quarter) through 1992 (fourth quarter), as the growth of the monetary base decelerated to 7.2 percent, once again the growth rate of the money supply measures

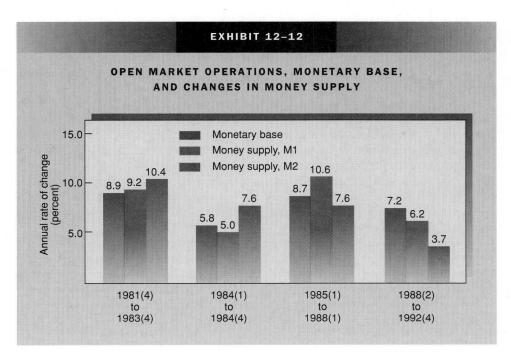

EXHIBIT 12–12

OPEN MARKET OPERATIONS, MONETARY BASE, AND CHANGES IN MONEY SUPPLY

Annual rate of change (percent)

- Monetary base
- Money supply, M1
- Money supply, M2

1981(4) to 1983(4): 8.9, 9.2, 10.4

1984(1) to 1984(4): 5.8, 5.0, 7.6

1985(1) to 1988(1): 8.7, 10.6, 7.6

1988(2) to 1992(4): 7.2, 6.2, 3.7

Here we show that changes in the growth rates of the monetary base and money supply are associated. This is what we would expect when open market operations are the primary tool of monetary policy. The numbers in parentheses indicate the quarter of the year.

slowed. There is a strong tendency for the monetary base and money supply measures to move together. This is precisely what we would expect when open market operations are the primary tool used by the Fed to control the money supply.

THE FED AND THE TREASURY

Many students have a tendency to confuse the Federal Reserve with the U.S. Treasury, probably because both sound like monetary agencies. The Treasury is a budgetary agency. If there is a budgetary deficit, the Treasury will issue U.S. securities as a method of financing the deficit. Newly issued U.S. securities are almost always sold to private investors (or invested in government trust funds). Bonds issued by the Treasury to finance a budget deficit are seldom purchased directly by the Fed. In any case, the Treasury is primarily interested in obtaining funds so it can pay Uncle Sam's bills. Except for nominal amounts, mostly coins, the Treasury does not issue money. Borrowing—the public sale of new U.S. securities—is the primary method used by the Treasury to cover any excess of expenditures in relation to revenues from taxes and other sources.

Whereas the Treasury is concerned with the revenues and expenditures of the government, the Fed is concerned primarily with the availability of money and credit for the entire economy. The Fed does not issue U.S. securities. It merely purchases and sells government securities issued by the Treasury as a means of controlling the economy's money supply. Unlike the Treasury, the Fed can purchase government bonds by writing a check on itself without having deposits, gold, or anything else to back it up. In doing so, the Fed creates money out of thin air. The Treasury does not have this power. The Fed does not have an obligation to meet the financial responsibilities of the U.S. government. That is the domain of the Treasury. The Fed's responsibility is to provide a stable monetary framework for the entire economy. So although the two agencies cooperate with each other, they are distinctly different institutions established for different purposes (see accompanying "Thumbnail Sketch").

It is important to recognize that the buying and selling of bonds by the Treasury and by the Fed exert different effects on the supply of money. The key point here is that the Treasury and the Fed handle revenues collected from the selling of bonds in a different manner. When the Treasury issues and sells bonds, it does so to pay for federal government expenditures. After all, the Treasury issues the bonds in order to generate the required revenue for its spending. The people who buy the bonds from the Treasury have less money, but when the Treasury spends, the recipients of its spending will have more money. Thus, there is no change in the supply of money.

In contrast, when the Fed sells bonds, it, in effect, takes the revenues and holds them, keeping them out of circulation. Because this money is out of circulation and can no longer be used for the purchase of goods and services, the money supply shrinks. On the other hand, if the Fed later wishes to increase the money supply, it can buy bonds, which will increase the availability of bank reserves and the money supply.

RECENT DEVELOPMENTS AND CURRENT PROBLEMS IN BANKING

During the 1940–1975 period, banking was a quiet industry. Checking accounts were available only at commercial banks. Regulations prevented banks from paying their customers interest on checking deposits. The interest-free checking deposits, along with savings accounts, provided commercial banks with a low-cost source of funds, which were invested and loaned to customers at market interest rates. The interest rate differential provided banks with a steady source of income. Simultaneously, savings and loan associations (S&Ls) were

THUMBNAIL SKETCH

WHAT ARE THE DIFFERENCES BETWEEN THE U.S. TREASURY AND THE FEDERAL RESERVE BANK?

U.S. Treasury	Federal Reserve
1. Concerned with the finance of the federal government.	1. Concerned with the monetary climate for the economy.
2. Issues bonds to the general public to finance the budget deficits of federal government.	2. Does *not* issue bonds.
3. Does *not* determine the money supply.	3. Determines the money supply—primarily through its buying and selling of bonds issued by the U.S. Treasury.

the primary source of mortgage funds for the housing industry; regulations protected S&Ls from competition with commercial banks in the home mortgage market. Generally, S&Ls attracted funds by paying savers a little higher interest rate than commercial banks, marking up the funds a few percentage points, and then loaning the funds to home buyers. In essence, both banks and S&Ls operated in protected markets; they were largely insulated from the rigors of competition.

INCREASED COMPETITION FOR FUNDS

This quiet life began to change in the mid-1970s. Merrill Lynch and other investment firms introduced the money market mutual fund. These funds were invested in a diverse portfolio of highly liquid assets, particularly Treasury bills and highly rated bonds. Shareholders could sell shares in their fund simply by writing a check. Thus, these funds were able to provide shareholders with checking privileges and a safe investment with a high interest yield.

In the 1970s a government-imposed interest rate ceiling limited the amount banks and S&Ls could pay on saving deposits. This interest-rate ceiling reduced the competition for deposits within the banking industry and helped provide banks with a low-cost source of funds. However, the newly introduced money market mutual funds undermined this anticompetitive practice.

When many depositors shifted funds from banking institutions to money market mutual funds, banks were forced to borrow from other sources at higher interest rates. Since most of the loans of commercial banks were short-term, they were well-positioned to pass the higher cost of funds onto their customers. However, the increase in the cost of funds was a much more serious problem for S&Ls. In the late 1970s long-term, fixed-interest-rate mortgages provided the primary source of income for S&Ls. Unsurprisingly, income from these assets failed to keep up with rising interest costs during the inflationary 1970s. Thus, the increased competitiveness, higher inflation rates, and the accompanying rise in the cost of funds really put the squeeze on S&Ls (see the "Applications in Economics" boxed feature).

MONETARY CONTROL ACT OF 1980

Responding to the pressures on the banking industry, Congress passed the Monetary Control Act of 1980. In effect, this act restructured the banking industry, eroding the prior distinctions between commercial banks, S&Ls, and credit unions. The legislation lifted most of the restrictions on the types of loans and investments that S&Ls and credit unions could make. Interest-rate ceilings on time and savings deposits were phased out. S&Ls and credit unions were permitted to offer checking-account deposits. All banking institutions were allowed to pay interest on checking accounts. Finally, all depository institutions were placed under the jurisdiction of the Federal Reserve System, which was instructed to apply uniform reserve requirements and to offer similar services (for example, check-clearing and access to borrowing from the Fed) to all banking institutions. In essence, the 1980 legislation transformed S&Ls and credit unions into banks and placed them under the control of the Fed.

THE SAVINGS AND LOAN CRISIS

Savings and loan associations (S&Ls) are institutions similar to commercial banks that have traditionally concentrated on the financing of home mortgages. During the 1980s, almost half of the S&Ls in the United States either failed or merged with other banking institutions. These S&L failures were so numerous that they resulted in the collapse of the Federal Savings and Loan Insurance Corporation (FSLIC), a government agency established to insure the accounts of S&L depositors. Congress intervened, eventually appropriating more than $400 billion to make the insured accounts of depositors good and to assist with the phasing out of troubled S&Ls.

ORIGIN OF THE S&L CRISIS   What caused the S&L crisis? Why have the S&L failures been far more numerous than commercial bank failures? In a few isolated cases that sometimes dominated the news, managers of S&Ls defrauded customers and used institutional funds for private purposes. In some of these cases, political contributions were used in an effort to get bank regulators to look the other way. The basic cause of the S&L crisis, however, was more fundamental, though perhaps less intriguing. Having specialized in the fixed-rate home mortgage market, the value of the primary asset of S&Ls was highly vulnerable to the inflation, high interest rates, and the competitive financial markets of the late 1970s and early 1980s.

In the 1970s, S&Ls were financing home mortgages (typically long-term, fixed-rate assets) with deposits that were generally short-term in nature. This financing of long-term fixed-rate loans with short-term deposits is extremely risky. To see why, consider a typical S&L with assets of 30-year mortgages paying 8 percent (for instance) and with liabilities of short-term (say, one year) deposits whose interest rates can rise or fall. If nominal interest rates rise, the S&L cannot change the interest rates on its outstanding mortgages, but it still has to pay a higher interest rate on the short-term deposits. If it does not, savers will take their funds elsewhere. As interest rates rose during the inflationary 1970s, many S&Ls found themselves, for example, paying 10 percent on deposits while they were earning only 8 percent on their mortgage loans. It was situations like this that resulted in industry-wide losses and the bankruptcy of many S&Ls during the 1980s.

The single-premium deposit insurance system added to the problem. The banking deregulation of the 1980s allowed S&Ls to acquire assets that were riskier but that paid higher interest rates than fixed-rate mortgages. Unfortunately, the deposit insurance premiums that the S&Ls paid were not adjusted for the additional risk the S&Ls undertook; all S&Ls paid the same premium rate regardless of whether thay purchased risky or conservative assets. This is similar to charging a race car driver (while racing) the same automobile insurance premium you would charge a Sunday-only driver!

The single-premium element of the deposit insurance system actually encouraged a type of "reverse bank run"—the movement of funds from low-risk to high-risk depository institutions—that plagued the S&L industry during the 1980s.[1] Why did this occur? Since their deposit insurance premium was not linked to the soundness of their investment practices, many troubled S&Ls turned to risky investments as they sought to escape the losses caused by the rising interest rates of the inflationary 1970s. In order to attract funds, these troubled S&Ls offered depositors higher interest rates than could be earned elsewhere. Recognizing that federal deposit insurance protected their funds, savers were encouraged to shift funds from more prudent to the riskier institutions paying higher interest rates. This shift of funds to shaky S&Ls, many of which eventually failed, substantially increased the federal government's deposit insurance liability (and eventually the size of the congressional bailout).

The large, fixed-rate mortgage portfolio of S&Ls in the 1970s made them far more vulnerable than commercial banks. This adverse situation was further aggravated by the single-premium deposit insurance system. Adoption of a deposit insurance system that will charge individual banks premiums that reflect the riskiness of their asset portfolios is one of the most urgent problems confronting policy-makers.

---

[1] For an additional analysis of the problems accompanying the current deposit insurance system, see Edward Kane, *The Gathering Crisis in Federal Deposit Insurance* (Cambridge: MIT Press, 1985); R. Dan Brumbaugh, Jr., Andrew S. Carron, and Robert E. Litan, "Cleaning Up the Depository Institutions Mess," *Brookings Papers on Economic Activity,* 1989, no. 1; and David O. Beim, "Beyond the Savings-and-Loan Crisis," *The Public Interest,* Spring 1989, pp. 88–99.

BANK FAILURES DURING THE 1980s

In a market economy, the investment loans of the banking industry play an important role in the allocation of resources. The financing of projects provides a reality check on the hopes and dreams of business entrepreneurs. If a business cannot find funding for a project, this is strong evidence that the viability (and profitability) of the project is highly questionable. Bankers and other financial investors such as stockholders and bondholders have a strong incentive to finance winners (profitable projects) and shun losers (business failures). Borrowers may be unable to repay their loans if the funds are channeled into unprofitable investments. In turn, lenders who finance business failures may lose all or part of their funds. Efficient allocation of investment funds is an important source of economic growth. Profitable business projects increase the value of resources and promote economic growth; unprofitable projects have the opposite effect. An efficient operating capital market, of which the banking system is an integral part, will be good at picking winners—providing funds for profitable rather than unprofitable projects.

There are two major reasons for bank failures. First, there are bank runs. If a large number of depositors lose confidence in a bank and, for whatever reason, seek to withdraw their funds at the same time, they will be unable to do so under a fractional reserve banking system. The numerous banking failures of the 1920s and 1930s emanated from this source. As we mentioned earlier, the Federal Deposit Insurance Corporation stemmed the tide against bank failures of this type. As **Exhibit 12–13** illustrates, the annual number of bank failures declined to a trickle, usually fewer than 15 per year, during the 1940–1980 period.

The second reason for bank failures is loan defaults. When banks finance investments that turn sour, borrowers are often unable to repay their loans. The bank loses funds when borrowers default. Banks that extend a high percentage of such bad loans will eventually fail.

As Exhibit 12–13 shows, commercial bank failures increased sharply during the 1980s, soaring to more than 200 per year during 1986–1988. In contrast with the earlier wave of bank failures during the 1920s and 1930s, the bank failures of the 1980s were generally the result of loan defaults (rather than bank runs).

Why were there so many commercial bank failures and loan defaults during the 1980s? There were at least four reasons.

1. Banks operated in a more competitive environment during the 1980s. In recent years, both financial innovations and deregulation increased the intensity of competition in financial markets. Increasingly, banks faced stiff competition from other financial institutions for both deposits and customers. Some banks, perhaps accustomed to the quiet world of a protected market, were ill-prepared to deal with the competitive environment of the 1980s.

2. Instability in regional markets and industries increased the number of bad loans. After rising rapidly during the 1970s, oil prices collapsed during 1981–1985. Many loans extended to oil industry interests in the late 1970s went into default in the 1980s. Banks in states such as Oklahoma, Texas, and Louisiana were particularly hard hit by these defaults. Similarly, agricultural land values in the Midwest, after rising sharply during the 1970s, declined in the early 1980s. Later, housing prices declined substantially throughout much of the Northeast. Many borrowers financing agricultural land and houses in these regions were unable to repay their loans. Since the assets declined in value, even foreclosure would not allow the banks extending the "bad loans" to fully

Following the establishment of the FDIC in 1933, bank failures in the United States numbered only 10 or 15 per year during the 1940–1980 period. In contrast, the number of bank failures jumped sharply during the 1980s, soaring to over 200 in 1986, 1987, and 1988. The number of bank failures in the early 1990s declined sharply from the high levels of the 1986–1988 period.

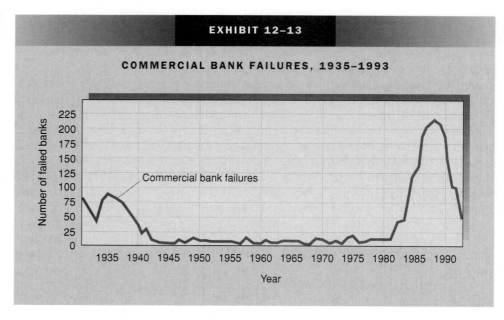

EXHIBIT 12–13

COMMERCIAL BANK FAILURES, 1935–1993

recoup their funds. During the mid-1980s, most of the bank failures were in states hard hit by recessionary conditions in important regional industries.

3. *The United States has many small banks holding poorly diversified asset portfolios.* In contrast with the United States, bank failures have not been a serious problem in other industrial countries. Why? In other countries there are fewer banks, and the existing banks tend to operate over a larger market area. There are more than 12,000 commercial banks in the United States. By comparison, there are approximately 150 banks in Japan, 65 in Canada, 550 in the United Kingdom, and 900 in Germany. Given their size and national scope, banks in these countries finance a more diverse portfolio of loans than U.S. banks. Thus, they are not as vulnerable to changing conditions in geographic regions and local markets.

4. *Deposit insurance premiums are not based on the financial strength of the bank.* Unlike the premiums for other forms of insurance, banks pay a single premium on deposits, regardless of the risk accompanying the loan portfolio of the bank. When insuring deposits, the FDIC does not consider the financial health of the bank. When banking institutions got into financial trouble during the 1980s, they often attracted funds by offering depositors higher interest rates and sought to restore their financial health by investing these funds in high-yield, risky areas (for example, junk bonds and businesses with low credit ratings). With time, these actions increased both the number of bank failures and the liability of the FDIC. (These forces were also present in the savings and loan industry.) If banks were charged premiums that reflected the riskiness of their portfolio, the incentive to pursue this strategy would be eliminated.

REDUCING FUTURE BANK FAILURES

What can be done to strengthen the banking system and reduce the likelihood of future bank failures? Given the nature of the problem, action on two fronts is quite important. First, restrictions on interstate banking should be repealed. As conditions in other countries indicate, large banks operating in a national market are less likely to get into trouble than small banks dependent on local market conditions. While several banks do operate across state lines, they have to use a bank holding company to obtain separate corporate charters in each state. These restrictions increase costs and reduce profitability.

Second, the deposit insurance system needs to be modified so that the premiums charged to commercial banks for the insurance will reflect the riskiness of their asset portfolio. Under legislation adopted in 1991, Congress instructed the FDIC to introduce risk-based premiums. To date, the FDIC has failed to do so. In essence, the current single-rate system provides an implicit subsidy to banks that make risky (or imprudent) investments at the expense of healthy institutions. Removal of this implicit subsidy would encourage banks to evaluate loan applications more carefully, extend fewer risky loans, and follow sounder banking practices. Reform in this area is essential to the long-term health of our banking system.

LOOKING AHEAD

In this chapter, we focused on the banking industry and the mechanics of monetary policy. We are now ready to analyze the impact of monetary policy on output, growth, and prices. What factors does the Fed consider when deciding whether to expand or contract the money supply? Have Fed policies exerted a stabilizing influence on the economy? These topics will be considered in subsequent chapters.

CHAPTER SUMMARY

1. Money is a financial asset that is widely accepted as a medium of exchange. It also provides a measuring rod for value and a means of storing purchasing power into the future. Without money, exchange would be both costly and tedious.

2. There is some debate among economists as to precisely how the money supply should be defined. The narrowest definition of the money supply (M1) includes only (a) currency in the hands of the public, (b) demand deposits, (c) other (interest-earning) checkable deposits in depository institutions, and (d) traveler's checks. None of these categories of money has significant intrinsic value. Money derives its value from its scarcity relative to its usefulness.

3. The broader M2 money supply includes M1 plus (a) savings and small-denomination time deposits, (b) money market mutual funds shares, (c) money market deposit accounts, (d) overnight loans of customers to commercial banks, and (e) Eurodollar deposits. The introduc-

tion of interest-earning checkable deposits has changed the nature of M1 and reduced the comparability of M1 data over time. As a result, most analysts now rely more extensively on M2 data when making comparisons of money supply growth rates across time periods that include the 1980s.

4. Banking is a business. Banks provide their depositors with safekeeping of money, check-clearing services on demand deposits, and interest payments on time deposits. Banks derive most of their income from the extension of loans and investments in interest-earning securities.

5. Under legislation adopted in 1980, savings and loan associations and credit unions are permitted to provide essentially the same services as commercial banks. The Federal Reserve System now regulates all of these depository institutions and is legally required to apply uniform reserve requirements to each. In essence, they are all part of an integrated banking system.

6. Under a fractional reserve banking system, banks are required to maintain only a fraction of their deposits in the form of reserves (vault cash or deposits with the Fed). Excess reserves may be invested or loaned to customers. When banks extend additional loans, they create additional deposits and thereby expand the money supply.

7. The Federal Reserve System is a central banking authority designed to provide a stable monetary framework for the entire economy. The policies and regulations of the Fed determine the supply of money. The Fed issues most of the currency in the United States. It is a banker's bank.

8. The Fed has three major tools with which to control the money supply.

a. *Establishment of the required reserve ratio.* Under a fractional reserve banking system, reserve requirements limit the ability of banking institutions to expand the money supply by extending more loans. When the Fed lowers the required reserve ratio, it creates excess reserves and allows banks to extend additional loans, expanding the money supply. Raising the reserve requirements has the opposite effect.

b. *Open market operations.* The open market operations of the Fed can directly influence both the money supply and available reserves. When the Fed buys U.S. securities, the money supply will expand because bond buyers will acquire money and the reserves of banks will increase as checks drawn on Federal Reserve Banks are cleared. When the Fed sells securities, the money supply will contract because bond buyers are giving up money in exchange for securities and the reserves available to banks will decline (causing them to extend fewer loans).

c. *The discount rate.* An increase in the discount rate is restrictive because it discourages banks from borrowing from the Fed to extend new loans. A reduction in the discount rate is expansionary because it makes borrowing from the Fed less costly.

9. For a dynamic, growing economy, monetary policy can best be judged by the rate of change in the money supply and the monetary base—its primary determinant. When open market operations are the primary tool of monetary policy, the monetary base and money supply measures will tend to follow similar paths. Rapid growth of the monetary base and the money supply is indicative of expansionary monetary policy. Conversely, slow growth (or a decline) in the size of the monetary base and the money supply is indicative of restrictive money policy.

10. The Federal Reserve and the U.S. Treasury are distinct agencies. The Fed is concerned primarily with the money supply and the establishment of a stable monetary climate. The Treasury focuses on budgetary matters—tax revenues, government expenditures, and the financing of government debt.

11. During the 1980s there was a sharp increase in the number of bank failures in the United States. The primary reasons for these bank failures were (a) an increase in the competitiveness of the financial industry; (b) bad loans resulting from instability in land values, regional housing markets, and the oil industry; (c) a large number of small, poorly diversified banks; and (d) deposit insurance premi-ums that failed to reflect the financial health of individual banks.

CRITICAL-ANALYSIS QUESTIONS

*1. What is meant by the statement, "This asset is illiquid"? List some things that you own, ranking them from most liquid to most illiquid.

2. What determines whether or not a financial asset is included in the M1 money supply? Why are interest-earning checkable deposits included in M1, while interest-earning savings accounts and Treasury bills are not?

*3. What makes money valuable? Does money perform an economic service? Explain. Could money perform its function better if there were twice as much of it? Why or why not?

4. "People are poor because they don't have very much money. Yet, central bankers keep money scarce. If people had more money, poverty could be eliminated." Explain the confused thinking this statement reflects, and why it is misleading.

5. Why can banks continue to hold reserves that are only a fraction of the demand deposits of their customers? Is your money safe in a bank? Why or why not?

*6. Suppose you withdraw $100 from your checking account. How does this transaction affect (a) the supply of money, (b) the reserves of your bank, and (c) the excess reserves of your bank?

7. Explain how the creation of new bank reserves would cause the money supply to increase by some multiple of the newly created reserves.

*8. How will the following actions affect the money supply?

a. A reduction in the discount rate.

b. An increase in the reserve requirements.

c. Purchase by the Fed of $10 million of U.S. securities from a commercial bank.

d. Sale by the U.S. Treasury of $10 million of newly issued bonds to a commercial bank.

e. An increase in the discount rate.

f. Sale by the Fed of $20 million of U.S. securities to a private investor.

9. *What's wrong with this way of thinking?* "When the government runs a budget deficit, it simply pays its bills by printing more money. As the newly printed money works its way through the economy, it waters down the value of paper money already in circulation. Thus, it takes more money to buy things. Budget deficits are the major cause of inflation."

---

*Asterisk denotes questions for which answers are given in Appendix C.

*10. If the Federal Reserve does not take any offsetting action, what would happen to the supply of money if the general public decided to increase its holdings of currency and decrease its checking deposits by an equal amount?

11. If market interest rates on short-term loans (including the federal funds rate) are declining, does a reduction in the discount rate indicate that the Fed is trying to increase the money supply? What will happen to the amount of reserves borrowed from the Fed if it does not reduce its discount rate? Explain.

*12. If the Fed wants to expand the money supply, why is it more likely to do so by purchasing bonds rather than by lowering reserve requirements?

*13. Are the following statements true or false?
a. "You can never have too much money."
b. "When you deposit currency in a commercial bank, cash goes out of circulation and the money supply declines."
c. "If the Fed would create more money, Americans would achieve a higher standard of living."

14. "The bank failures of the 1980s are a replay of the 1920s and 1930s." Evaluate this statement.

15. How has the nature of the M1 money supply changed in recent years? How have these changes influenced the usefulness of M1 as an indicator of monetary policy? Why do many analysts prefer to use M2 rather than M1 when comparing the monetary policy of the 1980s with earlier periods?

16. During the 1980s, the failure rate of savings and loan associations was considerably higher than the rate for commercial banks. Why was the failure rate of S&Ls so high during the 1980s?

*17. Suppose that the Federal Reserve purchases a bond for $100,000 from Donald Truck, who deposits the proceeds in the Manufacturer's National Bank.
a. What will be the impact of this transaction on the supply of money?
b. If the reserve requirement ratio is 20 percent, what is the maximum amount of additional loans that the Manufacturer's Bank will be able to extend as the result of Truck's deposit?
c. Given the 20 percent reserve requirement, what is the maximum increase in the quantity of checkable deposits that could result throughout the entire banking system as the result of the Fed's action?
d. Would you expect this to happen? Why or why not? Explain.

18. Suppose that the reserve requirements are 10 percent and the balance sheet of the People's National Bank looks like the accompanying example.

ASSETS		LIABILITIES	
Vault cash	$20,000	Checking deposits	$200,000
Deposits at Fed	30,000	Net worth	15,000
Securities	45,000		
Loans	120,000		

a. What are the required reserves of People's National Bank? Does the bank have any excess reserves?
b. What is the maximum loan that the bank could extend?
c. Indicate how the bank's balance sheet would be altered if it extended this loan.
d. Suppose that the required reserves were 20 percent. If this were the case, would the bank be in a position to extend any additional loans? Explain.

*19. Suppose that the reserve requirements are 10 percent and that the Federal Reserve purchases $2 billion of additional securities on a given day.
a. How will this transaction affect the M1 money supply?
b. If the brokerage firm that sold the bonds to the Fed deposits the proceeds of the sale into its account with City Bank, what is the maximum amount of additional loans that City Bank will be able to extend as the result of this deposit?
c. If, as additional loans are extended throughout the banking system and the proceeds are always redeposited back into a checking account, by how much will the M1 money supply increase if banks use all of their additional reserves to extend new loans?
d. Suppose that banks use all of their additional reserves to extend new loans but that 10 percent of the loan proceeds (and the additional funds of the brokerage firm) are held as currency rather than being redeposited back into a checking account. When this is the case, by how much will the Fed's action increase the money supply?
e. Finally, suppose that banks use 5 percent of their additional reserves to build up their excess reserves and that 10 percent of the proceeds of new loans (and the initial bond sale) end up circulating as currency rather than being redeposited back into a checking account. When this is the case, by how much will the Fed's action increase the money supply? Indicate the size of both the potential and actual money deposit multiplier in this case.
f. Why is the actual money deposit multiplier generally less than the potential multiplier?

---

*Asterisk denotes questions for which answers are given in Appendix C.

CHAPTER THIRTEEN

MODERN MACROECONOMICS:
MONETARY POLICY

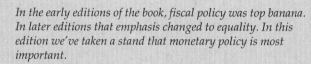

In the early editions of the book, fiscal policy was top banana. In later editions that emphasis changed to equality. In this edition we've taken a stand that monetary policy is most important.

PAUL SAMUELSON (1985 COMMENT ON THE TWELFTH EDITION OF HIS CLASSIC TEXT)[1]

CHAPTER FOCUS

■ *Why do individuals and businesses hold part of their wealth in the form of money?*

■ *How does monetary policy affect interest rates, output, and employment?*

■ *Can monetary policy stimulate real GDP in the short run? Can it do so in the long run?*

■ *Does it make any difference whether people quickly anticipate the effects of a change in monetary policy? Why?*

■ *Does an increase in the stock of money cause inflation?*

■ *What impact does monetary instability have on the economic health of a country?*

■ *Did macroeconomic policy cause the Great Depression?*

---

[1]Prior to the 1970s most economists thought that fiscal policy was far more important than monetary policy. As the statement of Nobel laureate Paul Samuelson implies, this is no longer true. Since Professor Samuelson is a long-time Keynesian economist, the change in his views concerning the importance of monetary policy is particularly revealing.

N ow that we have an understanding of the banking system and the determinants of the money supply, we can relax our prior assumption that the monetary authorities hold the supply of money constant. In this chapter, we will integrate the market for money balances into our basic macroeconomic model. As in the case of fiscal policy, modern views on the impact of monetary policy reflect an evolutionary process. We will consider briefly the historical roots of modern monetary theory. The primary focus of this chapter is an analysis of how monetary policy works—how shifts in monetary policy affect interest rates, output, and prices.

DEMAND FOR MONEY

Demand for money

At any given interest rate, the amount of wealth that people desire to hold in the form of money balances—that is, cash and checking-account deposits. The quantity demanded is inversely related to the interest rate.

The amount of wealth that households and businesses desire to hold in the form of money balances is called the **demand for money.** Why do individuals and businesses want to hold cash and checking-account money rather than stocks, automobiles, buildings, and consumer durables? When considering this question, it's important not to confuse (1) the demand for money balances with (2) the desire for more wealth (or income). Of course, all of us would like to have more wealth, but we may be perfectly satisfied with our holdings of money in relation to our holdings of other goods, *given our current level of wealth.* When we say people want to hold more (or less) money, we mean that they want to restructure their wealth toward larger (smaller) money balances.

REASONS FOR HOLDING MONEY

Economists emphasize three major reasons why people hold money: transaction demand, precautionary demand, and speculative demand.

TRANSACTION DEMAND.　　Money provides us with instant purchasing power. Therefore, at the most basic level, we hold money so we can conduct transactions for almost any commodity quickly and easily with numerous people. This is *transaction demand,* the principal motive for holding money balances. Households demand money so they can pay for the weekly groceries, the monthly house payment, gasoline for the car, lunch for the kids, and other items purchased regularly. Businesses demand money so they can meet the weekly payroll, pay the utility bill, purchase supplies, and conduct other transactions. Money balances are necessary for transaction purposes because we do not always receive our income at the time we want to buy things. So we keep a little cash or money in the bank to bridge the gap between everyday expenses and payday.

How much money will people desire in order to conduct their transactions? Other things constant, money balances for transaction purposes will increase with the nominal value of transactions. If prices remain constant, while the quantity of goods bought and sold increases, larger money balances will be required to conduct the larger volume of business. Similarly, if wages and prices increase, more money will be required by households to purchase the costlier weekly market basket and more money will be required by businesses to pay the larger wage bill. In essence, as money GDP increases as the result of either the growth of real output or higher prices, the demand for money balances will also increase.

PRECAUTIONARY DEMAND. Households and firms confront an uncertain future. Uncertainty produces two side effects that influence decisions: (1) risk and (2) opportunity for profit. Risk-averse households and firms, those that are uncertain about the amount and timing of the receipt of their income, will therefore hold additional cash, checking-account balances, and other highly liquid assets as a precaution against unforeseen circumstances. While transaction demand relates to the use of money for planned expenditures, this *precautionary demand* stems from the recognition that unplanned expenditures may be necessary as the result of unforeseen events—a medical emergency, an unexpected decline in income, an auto accident, or such. Generally, the amount of money people wish to hold as insurance against unforeseen circumstances rises with nominal income. The precautionary demand for money balances, like transaction demand, increases with nominal GDP.

SPECULATIVE DEMAND. Unforeseen changes may also present decision makers with an unexpected opportunity to purchase commodities or assets at bargain prices. Individuals and businesses may want to maintain part of their wealth in the form of money so they will be in a position to take ready advantage of opportunities to purchase desired items at low prices. Of course, money is the most liquid form of wealth. Unlike land or houses, money places an individual (or business) in a position to respond quickly to a profit-making opportunity. Money balances maintained for this purpose are termed the *speculative demand* for money.

OPPORTUNITY COST OF HOLDING MONEY

The motives for holding money indicate that the demand for money is linked to money income (nominal GDP). As nominal income expands, larger money balances are required to conduct transactions and respond effectively to unforeseen events. Money balances are like other goods, though, in that price influences the amount demanded. The price, or perhaps more accurately, the opportunity cost of holding money, is directly related to the nominal interest rate. Rather than maintaining $1,000 in cash or in a checking account that does not pay interest, you could earn interest by purchasing a $1,000 bond. Even if you are maintaining money balances in an interest-earning checking account, you could earn a higher rate of interest if you were willing to tie up the funds in a bond or some other less liquid form of savings.

As the nominal interest rate rises, the cost of continuing to hold money balances increases. Therefore, at the higher interest rate, individuals and businesses will try to manage their affairs with smaller money balances. As part "a" of **Exhibit 13–1** illustrates, there is an inverse relationship between the quantity of money demanded and the interest rate.

With the passage of time, changes in institutional factors will influence the demand schedule for money. Both evidence and logic indicate that changes in institutional arrangements have reduced the demand for money in recent years. The widespread use of general-purpose credit cards makes it easier for households to reconcile their bills with their receipt of income. Readily available short-term loans

The demand for money is inversely related to the money interest rate (a). The supply of money is determined by the monetary authorities (the Fed) through their open market operations, discount-rate policy, and reserve requirements (b).

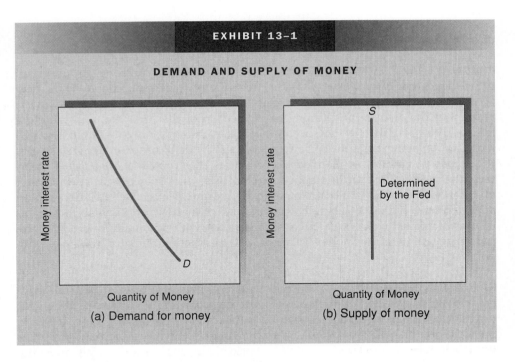

EXHIBIT 13–1

DEMAND AND SUPPLY OF MONEY

(a) Demand for money

(b) Supply of money

have reduced the need to maintain a substantial cash balance for emergencies. The movement away from agriculture means that more families have a steady income every two weeks or so, rather than an unpredictable income two or three times per year. This steady income makes planning easier. These factors have reduced the need for households to maintain large cash balances (shifting the demand for money schedule to the left).

SUPPLY OF MONEY

Part "b" of Exhibit 13–1 illustrates the supply schedule for money. Since the money supply is determined by the monetary authorities (the Fed in the United States), the supply curve is vertical. This implies that the supply of money is insensitive to the interest rate. It is whatever the Fed decides it should be, largely independent of the interest rate. In equilibrium, the quantity of money demanded must equal the quantity supplied at the economy's money interest rate.

What impact do changes in the money supply have on price and output? Like the modern view of fiscal policy, the modern view of monetary policy is the product of an evolutionary process. Let us consider prior views that have contributed to our modern outlook on the importance of money.

QUANTITY THEORY OF MONEY

For centuries, both laymen and economists recognized that increases in the money supply were a major determinant of changes in price level. Even prior to Adam

Smith, early social philosophers such as David Hume argued that rapid growth in the supply of money caused inflation. Nearly a hundred years ago, the great classical economists, Englishman Alfred Marshall and American Irving Fisher, formalized a theory in support of this view. According to this early **quantity theory of money,** an increase in the supply of money will lead to a proportional increase in the price level.

The quantity theory of money can be easily understood once we recognize that there are two ways of viewing GDP. As we previously discussed, nominal GDP is the sum of the price, P, times the output, Y, of each final-product good purchased during the period. In aggregate, P represents the economy's price level, while Y indicates real income or real GDP. There is also a second way of visualizing GDP. When the existing money stock, M, is multiplied by the number of times, V, that money is used to buy final products, this, too, yields the economy's nominal GDP. Therefore,

$$PY = GDP = MV$$

The **velocity of money** (V) is simply the average number of times a dollar is used to purchase a final product or service during a year. Velocity is equal to nominal GDP divided by the size of the money stock. For example, in 1993 GDP was equal to $6,374 billion while the M1 money supply was $1,128 billion. On average, each dollar in the M1 money supply was used 5.6 times to purchase final-product goods and services included in GDP. The velocity of the M1 money stock therefore was 5.6. The velocity of the M2 money stock can be derived in a similar manner. In 1993 the M2 money stock was $3,566 billion. Thus, the velocity of M2 was 1.79 ($6,374 billion ÷ $3,566 billion).

The concept of velocity is closely related to the demand for money. When decision makers conduct a specific amount of business with a smaller amount of money, their demand for money balances is reduced. Each dollar, though, is now being used more often. Therefore, the velocity of money is increasing. Thus, for a given income level, when the demand for money declines, the velocity of money increases.

When considering the behavior of prices, output, money, and velocity over time, we can write the quantity theory equation in terms of growth rates:

Growth of real output + Rate of inflation =
Growth rate of the money supply + Growth rate of velocity

The $MV = PY$ relationship is simply an identity, or a tautology. Economists refer to it as the **equation of exchange,** since it reflects both the monetary and real sides of each final-product exchange. The quantity theory of money, though, postulates that Y and V are determined by factors other than the amount of money in circulation. Classical economists believed that real output Y was determined by such factors as technology, the size of the economy's resource base, and the skill of the labor force. These factors were thought to be insensitive to changes in the money supply.

Similarly, classical economists thought the velocity of money was determined primarily by institutional factors such as the organization of banking and credit, the frequency of income payments, the rapidity of transportation, and the communication system. These factors would change quite slowly. Thus, classical economists thought that for all practical purposes, the velocity, or turnover rate, of money in the short run was constant.

Quantity theory of money
A theory that hypothesizes that a change in the money supply will cause a proportional change in the price level because velocity and real output are unaffected by the quantity of money.

Velocity of money
The average number of times a dollar is used to purchase final goods and services during a year. It is equal to GDP divided by the stock of money.

Equation of exchange
$MV = PY$, *where* M *is the money supply,* V *is the velocity of money,* P *is the price level, and* Y *is the output of goods and services produced.*

If both Y and V are constant, the $MV = PY$ relationship indicates that an increase in the money supply will lead to a proportional increase in the price level. Classical economists saw the link between the money supply and the price level as being quite mechanical. An increase in the quantity of money led to a proportional increase in the price level. Of course, they recognized that the link might not always be exact. For the purposes of theory, though, it was considered to be a reasonably close approximation to reality.

EARLY KEYNESIAN VIEWS ON MONEY

The Keynesian revolution emphasized the importance of aggregate demand. This notwithstanding, early Keynesians had little confidence in the ability of changes in the money supply to stimulate additional demand, particularly during an economic recession. During the 1950s, it was popular to draw an analogy between monetary policy and the workings of a string. Like a string, monetary policy could be used to pull (hold back) the economy and thereby control inflation. However, just as one cannot push with a string, according to this popular view, monetary policy could not be used to push (stimulate) aggregate demand.

In his *General Theory*, John Maynard Keynes offered a plausible explanation for why monetary policy might be an ineffective method of stimulating demand. What if the direction of changes in velocity were opposite to the direction of changes in the money stock? If a 5 percent increase in the supply of money led to a 5 percent reduction in velocity, monetary policy would directly influence neither real income nor the price level. Keynes himself recognized this was a highly atypical situation. He was not an advocate of the extreme position that held that changes in the money supply were of no consequence.[2] In the shadow of the Great Depression, though, many of his early followers took the unusual to be typical.

VIEWS OF THE MONETARISTS

Monetarists
A group of economists who believe that (1) monetary instability is the major cause of fluctuations in real GDP and (2) rapid growth of the money supply is the major cause of inflation.

Beginning in the late 1950s, economists hotly debated the potency of changes in the supply of money. Led by Milton Friedman, later a Nobel laureate, a group of economists, subsequently called **monetarists,** challenged the existing Keynesian view. In contrast with the early Keynesians, the monetarists argued that changes in the stock of money exerted a powerful influence on both nominal and real GDP, as well as on the level of prices. Indeed, the monetarists charged that erratic monetary policy was the primary source of both business instability and inflation. Milton Friedman proclaimed in his 1967 presidential address to the American Economic Association,

> *Every major contraction in this country has been either produced by monetary disorder or greatly exacerbated by monetary disorder. Every major inflation has been produced by monetary expansion.*[3]

---

[2]Keynes thought that money did matter, even during a recession. He stated, "So long as there is unemployment, employment will change in the same proportion as the quantity of money, and when there is full employment, prices will change in the same proportion as the quantity of money." *The General Theory of Employment, Interest, and Money* (New York: Harcourt, 1936), p. 296.

[3]Milton Friedman, "The Role of Monetary Policy," *American Economic Review*, March 1968, p. 12.

While monetarists believe that monetary policy exerts a powerful influence on the economy, they reject active use of **discretionary monetary policy** as an effective stabilization tool. According to the monetarist view, there are lengthy and unpredictable time lags between the implementation of a monetary policy change and the observation of its primary effects. When policy-makers change the direction of monetary policy, it may be between 6 and 18 months before the change exerts much effect on output. Correspondingly, the effects on the price level may not be felt for 12 to 36 months. During such lengthy time periods, market conditions may change dramatically. Thus, monetarists argue that it is a mistake for decision makers to alter monetary policy in light of current economic conditions. Monetarists believe that economic stability would be enhanced if the money supply were simply expanded at a rate equal to the economy's long-run rate of economic growth (approximately 3 percent).

Discretionary monetary policy
Changes in monetary policy instituted at the discretion of policy-makers. The policy is not predetermined by rules or formulas.

MODERN VIEW OF MONETARY POLICY

After nearly three decades of debate between Keynesians and monetarists concerning various aspects of monetary policy, a consensus view has emerged in some areas, while differences remain in others. Both modern Keynesians and monetarists, however, agree that monetary policy exerts an important impact on our economy.

TRANSMISSION OF MONETARY POLICY

The modern consensus view of monetary policy transmission has both Keynesian and monetarist roots. The modern view indicates that there are two channels through which changes in monetary policy are transmitted to the goods and services market. One of the channels, the interest rate, was previously stressed by Keynesians; the other, a more direct path, primarily by monetarists. First, let us consider the interest-rate path. Consider an economy initially experiencing equilibrium in the money, loanable funds, and goods and services markets. As **Exhibit 13–2** illustrates, the public is just willing to hold the existing money stock (S_1) provided by the Fed at the equilibrium money interest rate (i). Initially, the money interest is equal to the real interest rate (r_1), indicating that the expected rate of inflation is zero.

OUTSTANDING ECONOMIST

MILTON FRIEDMAN (1912–   )

Provocative and energetic, Friedman is perhaps the most influential spokesman for a free society in the twentieth century. The 1976 recipient of the Nobel Prize, Friedman maintains that business fluctuations are the result of short-run changes in the supply of money and that monetary stability is the key to a healthy, stable economy.

Here we illustrate the transmission of monetary policy via changes in interest rates. The monetary expansion creates an excess supply of money balances (part "a"), which induces individuals to purchase more bonds and thereby expand the supply of loanable funds (to S_2 in part "b"). The real interest rate falls (to r_2), which increases aggregate demand (to AD_2 in part "c"). Since the effects of the monetary expansion were unanticipated, the expansion in AD leads to both an increase in current output (to Y_2) and higher prices (inflation) in the short run.

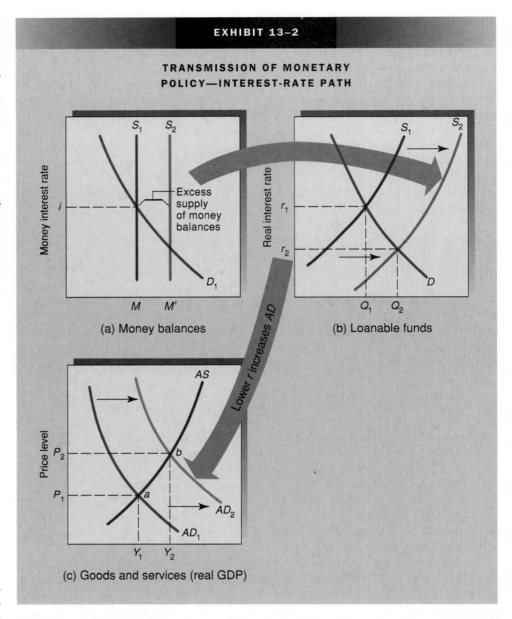

EXHIBIT 13–2

TRANSMISSION OF MONETARY POLICY—INTEREST-RATE PATH

(a) Money balances

(b) Loanable funds

(c) Goods and services (real GDP)

Expansionary monetary policy
An acceleration in the growth rate of the money supply.

Excess supply of money
Situation in which the actual money balances of individuals and business firms are in excess of their desired level. Thus, decision makers will increase their spending on other assets and goods until they reduce their actual balances to the desired level.

What will happen if the Fed shifts to **expansionary monetary policy**—if it unexpectedly increases the supply of money from S_1 to S_2? The increase in the money supply leaves decision makers with larger money balances than they desire to hold. The public will take steps to reduce its **excess supply of money.** Exhibit 13–2 shows how the public's response to an excess supply of money is transmitted through the interest rate to the goods and services market. To reduce their excess holdings of money balances, people will transfer funds from their checking accounts into savings accounts, bonds, stocks, and other financial assets. As they do, the supply of loanable funds will increase to S_2 (as shown in part "b" of Exhibit 13–2). In the short run, the real interest rate will fall to r_2.

The Fed generally pumps additional money into the economy via open market operations—the purchase of bonds in the open market. This method of increasing the money supply highlights the impact of expansionary monetary policy on the real interest rate. When the Fed purchases bonds, it bids up bond prices and supplies additional reserves to the banking system. The higher bond prices directly reduce the interest rate, and the additional reserves place banks in a position to extend additional loans. As banks increase the availability (supply) of credit, this too will place downward pressure on the real interest rates.

How will a lower real interest rate influence the demand for goods and services? The lower rate makes current investment and consumption cheaper relative to future spending. At the lower interest rate, entrepreneurs will undertake some investment projects they otherwise would have forgone. Spending by firms on plants and equipment will increase. Similarly, consumers will decide to expand their purchases of automobiles and consumer durables, which can now be enjoyed with smaller monthly payments. As part "c" of Exhibit 13–2 illustrates, aggregate demand increases to AD_2.

Many economists, particularly monetarists, believe that monetary policy also can be transmitted via a more direct path. **Exhibit 13–3** illustrates this point. Once again, an unanticipated increase in the money supply (shift from S_1 to S_2) leaves the public with an excess supply of money balances. Instead of increasing their spending exclusively or even primarily on bonds (and other saving instruments), suppose decision makers reduce their unexpected buildup of money balances by spending more on a broad cross section of goods and services. Households increase their spending on clothes, appliances, personal computers, automobiles, and recreational activities. Businesses purchase additional machinery or add to their fixed investments. To the extent this route is chosen, there will be a direct

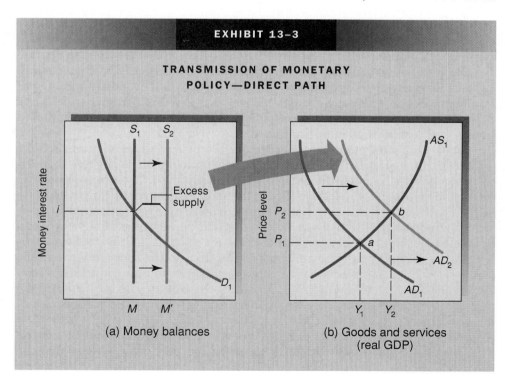

EXHIBIT 13–3

TRANSMISSION OF MONETARY
POLICY—DIRECT PATH

(a) Money balances

(b) Goods and services
(real GDP)

Here we illustrate the direct transmission of monetary policy to the goods and services market. An unanticipated increase in the supply of money (shift to S_2) generates an excess supply of money, which causes individuals to spend more, not just on bonds, but also on goods and services directly (a). Aggregate demand increases. As in the case of transmission via the real interest rate, the predicted results are higher prices (inflation) and an increase in real GDP in the short run (b).

increase in the aggregate demand for goods and services. Again, AD_1 shifts rightward to AD_2.

Aggregate demand (nominal spending on GDP) is closely linked to the money supply (M) and the velocity of money (V). As the equation of exchange highlights, in a sense, MV is the same thing as aggregate demand (AD). An increase in either M or V will increase spending and thereby shift the AD schedule to the right. In contrast, a decrease in either M or V will shift the AD schedule to the left.

UNANTICIPATED EXPANSIONARY MONETARY POLICY

As we have previously discussed, modern macroeconomic analysis stresses the importance of whether a change is anticipated or unanticipated. If people do not anticipate the increase in aggregate demand accompanying an expansionary monetary policy, costs will rise less than prices in the short run. Profit margins will improve. Businesses will respond with an expansion in the output of goods and services (as illustrated by the increase in real output from Y_1 to Y_2 in both Exhibits 13–2 and 13–3).

Modern analysis indicates that an unexpected increase in the supply of money will increase the demand for goods and services, either indirectly via a reduction in the real rate of interest or directly as people spend more in order to reduce their money balances. In turn, the increase in aggregate demand will expand real output and employment in the short run.

Part "a" of **Exhibit 13–4** illustrates the potential of expansionary monetary policy to direct a recessionary economy to full-employment capacity. Consider an economy initially at output Y_1, below full-employment capacity (Y_f). Expansionary monetary policy will increase aggregate demand (to AD_2). Real output will expand (to Y_f). In essence, the expansionary monetary policy provides an alternative to the economy's self-corrective mechanism. In the absence of demand stimulus, declining resource prices and real interest rates would eventually restore full employment. But many economists believe that this mechanism works quite slowly. If so, expansionary monetary policy may be able to restore long-run, full-employment equilibrium more rapidly.

How would a shift to expansionary monetary policy influence output and the price level if the economy were already at full employment? While this is generally not a desirable strategy, nonetheless, it is interesting to analyze the outcome. As part "b" of Exhibit 13–4 illustrates, in the short run, an unanticipated increase in aggregate demand resulting from a shift to a more expansionary monetary policy will temporarily push real output to Y_2, beyond the economy's long-run capacity of Y_f. Since important components of costs (for example, union wage contracts, fixed-interest loans, and lease agreements) are fixed in the short run, the strong demand for goods and services will temporarily increase product prices relative to costs. Profit margins will improve, providing the incentive for business firms to produce the larger output. Unemployment will fall below the natural rate of unemployment.

However, the high rate of output (Y_2) and employment will not be sustainable. Eventually, long-term contracts based on the previously weaker demand (AD_1) will expire. New agreements will reflect the stronger demand. Resource

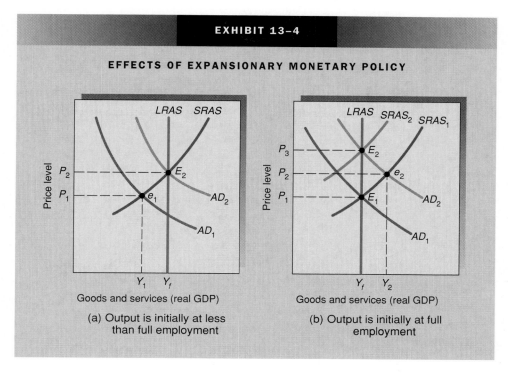

EXHIBIT 13–4

EFFECTS OF EXPANSIONARY MONETARY POLICY

(a) Output is initially at less than full employment

(b) Output is initially at full employment

If the impact of an increase in aggregate demand accompanying expansionary monetary policy is felt when the economy is operating below capacity, the policy will help direct the economy to a long-run full-employment equilibrium (a). In this case, the increase in output from Y_1 to Y_f will be long term. In contrast, if the demand-stimulus effects are imposed on an economy already at full employment (b), they will lead to excess demand and higher product prices. Output will temporarily increase (to Y_2). However, in the long run, the strong demand will push up resource prices, shifting short-run aggregate supply to $SRAS_2$. The price level will rise to P_3 and output will recede (to Y_f) from its temporary high.

prices will rise, shifting *SRAS* upward to the left. Eventually, long-run equilibrium (E_2) will result at a higher price level (P_3). Output will recede to Y_f. We can conclude that when an economy is already at full employment, an unexpected increase in the money supply will temporarily increase output, but in the long run it merely leads to higher prices. Hence, the wisdom of a shift to a more expansionary monetary policy is highly questionable when an economy is already operating at (or beyond) its full-employment capacity.

UNANTICIPATED RESTRICTIVE MONETARY POLICY

Suppose the Fed moves toward a more **restrictive monetary policy** and reduces the money supply (or in dynamic terms, reduces its rate of growth). How would a reduction in the money supply influence the economy? To stimulate your thoughts on this topic, consider what would happen if someone, perhaps a foreign agent, destroyed half of the U.S. money stock. We simply awake one morning and find that half of the cash in our billfolds and half of the checkable deposits in our banks are gone. Ignore, for the sake of analysis, the liability of bankers and the fact that the federal government would take corrective action. Just ask yourself, "What has changed because of the drastic reduction in the money supply?" The work force is the same. Our buildings, machines, land, and other productive resources are untouched. There are no consumer durables missing. Only the money, half of yesterday's money supply, is gone.

Exhibit 13–5 sheds some light on the situation. To make things simple, let us assume that before the calamity, the money balances of individuals and businesses

Restrictive monetary policy
A deceleration in the growth rate of the money supply.

A reduction in the money supply creates an excess demand for money balances. Economic agents will seek to restore their money balances by drawing on their savings, purchasing fewer bonds, and/or spending less on goods and services. As a result, aggregate demand will decline (shift to AD_2). When the reduction in aggregate demand is unanticipated, real output will decline (to Y_2) and downward pressure on prices will result.

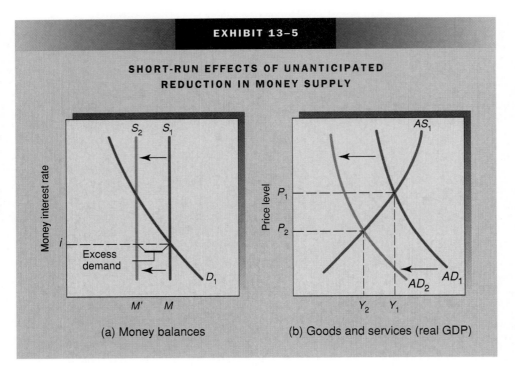

EXHIBIT 13–5

SHORT-RUN EFFECTS OF UNANTICIPATED REDUCTION IN MONEY SUPPLY

(a) Money balances

(b) Goods and services (real GDP)

were at the desired level, given current incomes and interest rates. Hence, the reduction in the supply of money (shift from S_1 to S_2) leaves people with less than the desired amount of money. People want to hold larger money balances, but the reduction in the money stock prevents them from doing so. Attempting to remedy the situation, people will try to restore at least part of their shrunken money balances.

How do people increase their money balances? Answer: they draw on their past savings, sell bonds and other liquid assets, and cut back on their current spending. As people reduce their savings and purchase fewer bonds, the supply of loanable funds will fall (relative to demand), causing the real rate of interest to increase. In turn, the higher real interest rate will induce both investors and consumers to cut back on their purchases of current goods and services. Simultaneously, others will seek to rebuild their money balances directly by spending less during the current period. Both the higher real interest rate and the direct reduction in current purchases will reduce aggregate demand (shift from AD_1 to AD_2 in part "b" of Exhibit 13–5).

In turn, the unexpected decline in the demand for goods and services will place downward pressures on prices, squeeze profit margins, and reduce output. As part "b" of Exhibit 13–5 illustrates, the price level will decline (to P_2) and output will fall (to Y_2) as the result of the restrictive monetary policy.

The appropriateness of a restrictive policy is dependent upon the initial state of the economy. **Exhibit 13–6** illustrates this point. When an economy is experiencing upward pressure on prices as the result of strong demand, restrictive policy is an effective weapon against inflation. Suppose that, as illustrated by part "a" of Exhibit 13–6, an economy is temporarily operating at e_1 and Y_1, beyond its full-employment real GDP of Y_f. Strong aggregate demand is placing upward pressure on prices. The problem is inflation, not recession. Under these circumstances,

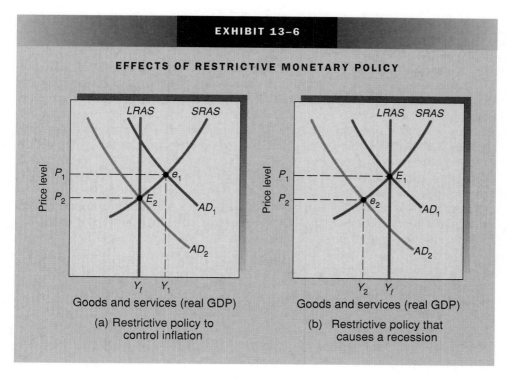

EXHIBIT 13–6

EFFECTS OF RESTRICTIVE MONETARY POLICY

(a) Restrictive policy to control inflation

(b) Restrictive policy that causes a recession

The stabilization effects of restrictive monetary policy are dependent upon the state of the economy when the policy exerts its primary impact. Restrictive monetary policy will reduce aggregate demand. If the demand restraint comes during a period of strong demand and an overheated economy, then it will limit or even prevent the occurrence of an inflationary boom (a). In contrast, if the reduction in aggregate demand takes place when the economy is at full employment, then it will disrupt long-run equilibrium, reduce output, and result in a recession (b).

restrictive policy makes good sense. It would help control the inflation. If the proper dosage is timed correctly, restrictive policy would retard aggregate demand (to AD_2) and direct the economy to a noninflationary, long-run equilibrium at P_2 and Y_f (that is, E_2).

As part "b" of Exhibit 13–6 illustrates, however, an unanticipated shift to restrictive policy would be damaging if applied to an economy in full-employment equilibrium. If the output of an economy is at full employment (or worse still, at less than full employment), a shift to restrictive policy would reduce aggregate demand (shift to AD_2) and throw the economy into a recession. Real GDP would decline from Y_f to Y_2. Output would fall below the economy's full-employment capacity, and unemployment would rise above the natural rate of unemployment.

PROPER TIMING

As with fiscal policy, monetary policy must be properly timed if it is to help stabilize an economy. Exhibits 13–4 and 13–6 emphasize this point. When an economy is operating below its long-run capacity, expansionary monetary policy can stimulate demand and push the output of the economy to its sustainable potential (part "a" of Exhibit 13–4). Similarly, if properly timed, restrictive monetary policy can help control (or prevent) inflation (part "a" of Exhibit 13–6).

If it is timed improperly, however, monetary policy can be destabilizing. Expansionary monetary policy is a source of inflation if the effects of the policy are felt when the economy is already at or beyond its capacity (part "b" of Exhibit 13–4). Similarly, if the effects of a restrictive policy come when an economy is operating at its potential GDP, recession is the likely outcome (part "b" of Exhibit 13–6). Worse still, the impact of restrictive policy may be disastrous if imposed on an economy already in the midst of a recession.

Proper timing of monetary policy is not an easy task. In contrast with fiscal policy changes requiring time-consuming congressional action, the Federal Reserve can institute a change in monetary policy quite rapidly. However, as an economy drifts toward a recession or an inflationary boom, policy-makers may not immediately recognize the need for a change. Therefore, there may be a time lag of several months between the change in economic conditions and the time that policy-makers at the Fed recognize that change. More importantly, there will be an additional time lag between the institution of a policy and when it begins to exert a significant impact on aggregate demand. Economists who have studied this issue estimate that this impact lag will be five or six months at a minimum. Some economists, particularly monetarists, estimate that the primary impact of a change in monetary policy on output and employment is often as much as 12 to 18 months after the change is instituted. In terms of its impact on the price level and rate of inflation, the estimated impact lag is even longer, perhaps as much as 36 months. Given our limited ability to forecast the future, such lengthy time lags clearly reduce the potential effectiveness of discretionary monetary policy as a stabilization tool.

MONETARY POLICY IN LONG RUN

Thus far, we have focused on the impact of monetary policy in a static framework. Of course, in a static framework, an increase in the price level implies inflation. However, inflation is a dynamic concept—a *rate of increase* in prices, not a once-and-for-all movement to a higher price level. It is also important to distinguish between the static and dynamic with regard to the money supply. Static analysis focuses on the change in the supply of money. In a dynamic setting, though, a change in the *growth rate* of the money supply is more indicative of the direction of monetary policy.

In this section, we want to recast our analysis slightly so we can better illustrate both dynamic factors and the long-run adjustment process. We will begin with a simple dynamic case. Suppose that the output of an economy is growing at a 3 percent annual rate and that the monetary authorities are expanding the money supply by 3 percent each year. In addition, let's assume that the velocity of money is constant. This would imply that the 3 percent annual increase in output would lead to a 3 percent annual increase in the demand for money. Under these circumstances, the 3 percent monetary growth would be consistent with stable prices (zero inflation). Initially, we will assume that the economy's real interest rate is 4 percent. Since the inflation rate is zero, the nominal rate of interest is also equal to 4 percent. **Exhibits 13–7** and **13–8** illustrate an economy initially (Period 1) characterized by these conditions.

What will happen if the monetary authorities permanently increase the growth rate of the money supply from 3 percent to 8 percent annually (see part "a" of Exhibit 13–7, beginning in Period 2)? In the short run, the expansionary monetary policy will reduce the real interest rate and stimulate aggregate demand

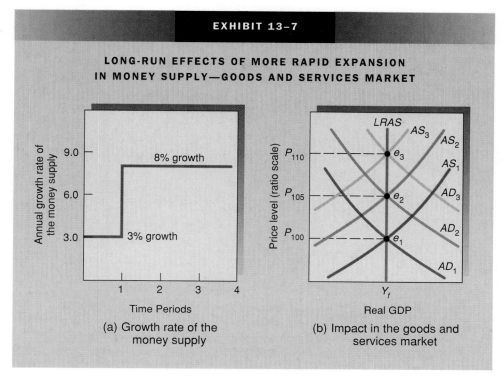

EXHIBIT 13–7

LONG-RUN EFFECTS OF MORE RAPID EXPANSION IN MONEY SUPPLY—GOODS AND SERVICES MARKET

(a) Growth rate of the money supply

(b) Impact in the goods and services market

Here we illustrate the long-term impact of an increase in the annual growth rate of the money supply from 3 to 8 percent. Initially, prices are stable (P_{100}) when the money supply is expanding 3 percent annually. The acceleration in the growth rate of the money supply increases aggregate demand (shift to AD_2). At first, real output may expand beyond the economy's potential (Y_f). However, abnormally low unemployment and strong demand conditions will create upward pressure on wages and other resource prices, shifting aggregate supply to AS_2. Output will return to its long-run potential, and the price level will increase to $P_{105}(e_2)$. If the more rapid monetary growth continues in subsequent periods, AD and AS will continue to shift upward, leading to still higher prices (e_3 and points beyond). The net result of this process is sustained inflation.

(shift to AD_2), just as we previously explained (Exhibits 13–2 and 13–3). For a time, real output may exceed the economy's potential. However, as they confront strong demand conditions, many resource suppliers (who previously committed to long-term agreements) will wish they had anticipated the strength of demand and driven harder bargains. With the passage of time, more and more resource suppliers (including labor represented by union officials) will have the opportunity to raise prices and wages in order to rectify past mistakes. As they do, costs will rise and profit margins will recede to normal levels. The higher costs will reduce aggregate supply (shift to AS_2). As the rapid monetary growth continues in subsequent periods (Period 3, 4, 5, and so on), both AD and AS will shift upward. The price level will rise to P_{105}, P_{110}, and on to still higher levels as the money supply continues to grow more rapidly than the monetary growth rate consistent with stable prices. The rapid monetary growth leads to a continual rise in the price level—that is, a sustained inflation.

Suppose an inflation rate of 5 percent eventually emerges from the more rapid growth rate (8 percent rather than 3 percent) of the money supply. With the passage of time, more and more people will adjust their decision making in light of the persistent 5 percent inflation. In the resource market, both buyers and sellers will eventually incorporate the expectation of the 5 percent inflation rate into long-term contracts such as collective-bargaining agreements. Once that happens, resource prices and costs will rise as rapidly as prices in the goods and services market. *When the inflation rate is anticipated fully, it will fail to either reduce real wages or improve profit margins.* Unemployment will return to its natural rate.

Exhibit 13–8 illustrates the adjustments in the loanable funds market once borrowers and lenders expect the 5 percent inflation rate. When lenders anticipate a

When prices are stable, supply and demand in the loanable funds market are in balance at a real and nominal interest rate of 4 percent. If more rapid monetary expansion leads to a long-term 5 percent inflation rate (see Exhibit 13–7), borrowers and lenders will build the higher inflation rate into their decision making. As a result, the nominal interest rate (i) will rise to 9 percent— the 4 percent real rate plus a 5 percent inflationary premium.

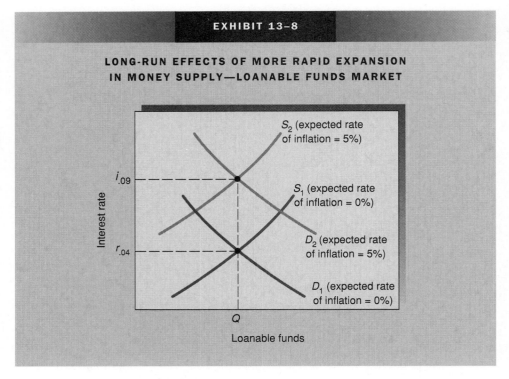

EXHIBIT 13–8

LONG-RUN EFFECTS OF MORE RAPID EXPANSION IN MONEY SUPPLY—LOANABLE FUNDS MARKET

S_2 (expected rate of inflation = 5%)

S_1 (expected rate of inflation = 0%)

D_2 (expected rate of inflation = 5%)

D_1 (expected rate of inflation = 0%)

$i_{.09}$

$r_{.04}$

Interest rate

Q

Loanable funds

5 percent annual increase in the price level, a 9 percent interest rate will be necessary to provide them with as much incentive to supply loanable funds as 4 percent interest provided when stable prices were expected. Thus, the supply of loanable funds will shift vertically by the 5 percent expected rate of inflation. Simultaneously, borrowers who were willing to pay 4 percent interest on loans when they expected stable prices will be willing to pay 9 percent when they expect prices to increase 5 percent annually. The demand for loanable funds will therefore also increase (shift vertically) by the expected rate of inflation. Once borrowers and lenders anticipate the higher (5 percent) inflation rate, the equilibrium money interest rate will rise to 9 percent. Of course, the real interest rate is equal to the money interest rate (9 percent) minus the expected rate of inflation (5 percent). In the long run, a 4 percent real interest rate will emerge with inflation, just as it did with stable prices.[4] Inflation, then, will fail to reduce the real interest rate in the long run.

Modern analysis indicates that the long-run effects of rapid monetary growth differ from the short-run effects of an unanticipated move to expansionary monetary policy. In the long run, the major consequences of rapid monetary growth are inflation and higher nominal interest rates. Rapid monetary growth will neither reduce unemployment nor stimulate real output in the long run.

[4]Higher rates of inflation are generally associated with an increase in the variability of the inflation rate. Thus, greater risk (the possibility of either a substantial gain or loss associated with a sharp change in the inflation rate) accompanies exchange in the loanable funds market when inflation rates are high. This additional risk may result in higher real interest rates than would prevail at lower rates of inflation. The text discussion does not introduce this consideration.

MONETARY POLICY WHEN EFFECTS ARE ANTICIPATED

Thus far, we have assumed that decision makers come to anticipate the effects of monetary policy only after they begin to occur. For example, we assumed that borrowers and lenders began to anticipate a higher inflation rate only after prices began to rise more rapidly. Similarly, resource suppliers anticipated the inflation only after it had begun.

What if enough decision makers in the market catch on to the link between expansionary monetary policy and an acceleration in the inflation rate? What if, in effect, they learn the model that you have learned? Suppose borrowers and lenders start paying attention to the money-supply figures. Observing substantial increases in the money supply, they revise upward their expectation of the future inflation rate. Lenders become more reluctant to supply loanable funds. Simultaneously, borrowers increase their demand for loanable funds at existing rates of interest because they also anticipate a higher rate of future inflation and they want to buy now before prices rise. Under these circumstances, a reduction in supply and an increase in demand for loanable funds will quickly push up the money interest rate. If borrowers and lenders quickly and accurately forecast the future rate of inflation accompanying the monetary expansion, the real interest rate will decline for only a short period of time, if at all.

If buyers and sellers in the goods and services market also watch the money-supply figures, they too may anticipate its inflationary consequences. As buyers anticipate the future price increases, many will buy now rather than later. Current aggregate demand will rise. Similarly, expecting an acceleration in the inflation rate, sellers will be reluctant to sell except at premium prices. Current aggregate supply will fall. This combination of factors will quickly push prices of goods and services upward.

Simultaneously, if buyers and sellers in the resource market believe that more rapid monetary growth will lead to a higher rate of inflation, they too will build this view into long-run contracts. Union officials will demand and employers will pay an inflationary premium for future money wages, based on their expectation of inflation. Alternatively, they may write an **escalator clause** into their collective-bargaining agreements that will automatically raise money wages when the inflation transpires (a cost-of-living adjustment, or COLA, raise). If decision makers in the resource market correctly anticipate the inflation, real resource prices will not decline once prices accelerate upward.

As **Exhibit 13–9** illustrates, when individuals correctly anticipate the effects of expansionary monetary policy *prior to their occurrence*, the short-run impact of monetary policy is much like its impact in the long run. The price level will increase, pushing up money income (P_2Y_1), but real income (Y_1) will be unchanged. Nominal interest rates will rise, but real interest rates will be unchanged. Thus, when the effects of expansionary monetary policy are fully anticipated, it exerts little impact on real economic activity.

Are people likely to anticipate the effects of monetary policy? This is a topic of hot debate among economists, and we will consider it in more detail in the next chapter. Since the effects of monetary policy differ substantially depending on whether they are anticipated, the question is clearly a very important one.

Escalator clause
A contractual agreement that periodically and automatically adjusts money wage rates upward as the price level rises. They are sometimes referred to as cost-of-living adjustments or COLAs.

When decision makers fully anticipate the effects of monetary expansion, it does not alter real output even in the short run. Suppliers, including resource suppliers, build the expected price rise into their decisions. The anticipated inflation leads to a rise in nominal costs (including wages), causing aggregate supply to decline (shift to AS_2). While nominal wages, prices, and interest rates rise, their real counterparts are unchanged. The result: inflation without any change in real output (Y_1).

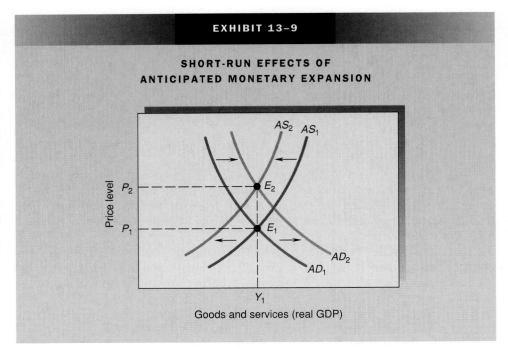

EXHIBIT 13-9

SHORT-RUN EFFECTS OF ANTICIPATED MONETARY EXPANSION

INTEREST RATES AND TIME LAG OF MONETARY POLICY

Can the Fed control interest rates? How do changes in nominal interest rates affect the velocity of money and, in turn, the impact of a shift in monetary policy? These two questions are interrelated and highly complex. Answering them provides insight into the workings of monetary policy.

Thus far, we have proceeded as if there were only a single interest rate. In the real world, of course, there are numerous interest rates reflecting loans of differing risk and time length. For example, there are short-term interest rates such as those present in the federal funds, Treasury bills, and savings deposit markets. In addition, there are longer-term rates such as those for home mortgages and long-term bonds.

When the Fed eases money and credit, it generally does so by purchasing additional securities, an action that tends to bid up bond prices and increase the availability of reserves to the banking system. As the result of this injection of additional reserves, fewer banks have reserve deficiencies and more banks have excess reserves. Rather quickly, these forces will place downward pressure on the interest rate in the federal funds market, a market where banks with excess reserves extend short-term loans to banks with insufficient reserves. As the federal funds rate declines, so too will other short-term interest rates—for example, the rates on savings deposits, three-month Treasury bills, and bank certificates of deposits (CDs).

The impact of the expansionary monetary policy on long-term interest rates, such as home mortgages and ten-year bonds, is likely to be substantially more modest. There are two reasons for this: First, the long-term rates are influenced more by real factors such as the demand for investment funds than by monetary factors. Second, to the extent that monetary factors influence long-term interest rates, they operate primarily through their impact on the expected rate of inflation. The expected long-term future rate of inflation is an important component of long-term nominal interest rates. If people expect a higher future rate of inflation as the result of the shift to a more expansionary policy, long-term rates may rise rather than fall. Thus, while a shift in Fed policy is able to exert a substantial impact on short-term interest rates rather quickly, its impact on longer term rates is far more modest and less predictable. Since it is the long-term rates that are most relevant when businesses and households undertake major investment projects, the ambiguity concerning the impact of monetary policy on these rates is particularly important.

Furthermore, the impact of the change in short-term nominal interest rates on the velocity of money adds an additional complication. A reduction in the short-term rates will reduce the opportunity cost of holding money balances. Predictably, the velocity of money will decline, which will tend to dampen the *initial* stimulus effects of the monetary expansion. Of course, if the more expansionary monetary policy persists, a combination of lower real interest rates—particularly short-term rates—and an excess supply of money balances will eventually stimulate aggregate demand (see Exhibits 13–2 and 13–3). With time, the additional demand will place upward pressure on prices, which will also serve to increase both the expected rate of inflation and nominal interest rates, including short-term nominal rates. When this happens—and several quarters may pass before it does—the higher short-term nominal interest rates will increase the velocity of money and amplify the demand-stimulus effects of the policy. It is at this point in time that the primary effects of the expansionary monetary policy will be most potent.

The same forces are also present in the case of a shift to a more restrictive monetary policy. When shifting toward restriction, the Fed generally sells bonds, which drains reserves from the banking system and places upward pressure on the federal funds rate and other short-term interest rates. The restrictive policy, however, will generally exert less impact on longer-term interest rates. If people perceive that inflation is less of a threat as the result of the more restrictive monetary policy, this will place downward pressure on long-term interest rates and act as an offset to the upward pressure arising from the decline in bank reserves. Thus, the more restrictive policy may fail to exert much impact on the longer-term interest rates that are an important determinant of investment.

At the same time, the higher short-term rates will increase the opportunity cost of holding money and, as a result, its velocity. This increase in the velocity of money will promote additional spending which will, *for a time*, tend to dampen the restrictive effects of the policy. Of course, the restrictive policy, if continued, will eventually begin to retard inflation and lower nominal interest rates, which will reduce the velocity of money. Once this happens, and many months may pass before it does, the restrictive policy will be highly potent—it will substantially reduce aggregate demand, output, and prices.

All of these factors suggest that the linkage between a change in monetary policy and a change in output and prices is likely to be a loose one. The short-run effects of a policy change are likely to differ from the effects over a longer period of time. In addition, the time lags between when a policy change is instituted and when it exerts its primary impact may be of varying length. Obviously, these factors will complicate the job of monetary policy-makers and make it more difficult for them to institute changes in a manner that will exert a stabilizing influence on the economy.

IMPORTANCE OF STABLE MONEY AND PRICES

As we have stressed throughout this text, our modern living standards are linked to the realization of gains from specialization, capital formation, and economies accompanying the adoption of mass-production methods. Money is productive because it reduces transaction costs and thereby enhances our ability to realize gains from specialization, production, and exchange.

The productive contribution of money, however, is directly related to the stability of its value. In this regard, money is to an economy what language is to communication. Without words that have clearly defined meanings to both the speaker and listener, communication is limited. So it is with money. If money does not have a stable and predictable value, it will be more costly for borrowers and lenders to conduct exchanges; saving and investing will involve additional risks; and time-dimension transactions (for example, the payment of the purchase price for a house or automobile over a given time period) will be fraught with additional danger. Therefore, rapid growth of the money supply and the high and variable rates of inflation that inevitably accompany such growth will reduce social cooperation and retard the realization of gains from trade.

There are three major reasons why inflation and monetary instability tend to retard economic progress.[5]

1. Inflation distorts the information delivered by prices and changes the results of long-term contracts from those that are intended, in unpredictable ways. Some prices will respond quickly to inflationary policies, while prices such as rental lease agreements, utility rates, and mortgage interest rates will change more slowly, since they generally reflect long-term contracts or regulatory policies. Thus, an unanticipated inflation will change relative prices, as well as the general price level. Producers and resource suppliers are often led astray by the unreliable price signals stemming from the inflation. This is particularly true in the case of capital-investment decisions. Unexpected changes in the inflation rate can quickly turn an otherwise profitable project into a personal economic disaster. Given the additional uncertainty, many decision makers will simply forgo capital investments and other transactions involving long-term commitments when the rate of inflation is highly variable and therefore unpredictable. As a result, potential gains from production and exchange will be lost.

2. People will respond to the inflation and monetary instability by spending less time producing and more time trying to protect their wealth. Since failure to anticipate accurately the rate of inflation can have a substantial effect on one's wealth, individuals will divert scarce resources away from the production of goods and services and put them into the acquisition of information on the future rate of inflation. Under these circumstances, the ability of business decision makers to forecast changes in prices increases in importance relative to their ability to manage and organize production. Speculative practices are encouraged while productive

---

[5]See Dennis W. Carlton, "The Disruptive Effect of Inflation on the Organization of Markets" in *Inflation Causes and Effects,* edited by Robert Hall (Chicago: University of Chicago Press, 1982), for additional details on how inflation adversely affects economic performance.

activities are discouraged. Predictably, more funds will flow into speculative investments (for example, gold, silver, and art objects), while the flow of funds into productive investments like buildings, machines, and technological research will decline. So, too, will the production possibilities of the country.

3. Inflation and monetary instability undermine the credibility of government. At the most basic level, people expect government to protect their person and property from intruders who would take what does not belong to them. When government becomes an intruder—when it cheats citizens by "watering down" the value of their currency—how can they have any confidence that the government will protect their property against other intrusions, or that it will enforce contracts and punish unethical and criminal behavior? When the government waters down its currency, it is in a weak position to punish, for example, an orange-juice producer that defrauds consumers by diluting juice sold to customers or a business that waters down its stock (by issuing additional stock without the permission of current stockholders).

EFFECTS OF MONETARY POLICY— A SUMMARY

The accompanying "Thumbnail Sketch" summarizes the theoretical implications of our analysis. The impact of monetary policy on major economic variables is indicated for three alternatives: (1) the short run when the effects are unanticipated, (2) the short run when the effects are anticipated, and (3) the long run. Note that the impact of monetary policy in the latter two cases is the same. When decision makers quickly anticipate the effects of monetary policy, the adjustment process speeds up, and therefore the short-run effects are identical to the long-run effects. Under these circumstances, only nominal variables (money interest rates and the inflation rate) are affected. Real variables (real GDP, employment, and the real interest rate) are unaffected.

Six major predictions flow from our analysis.

1. An unanticipated shift to a more expansionary (restrictive) monetary policy will temporarily stimulate (retard) output and employment. As Exhibits 13–2 and 13–3 illustrate, an increase in aggregate demand emanating from an unanticipated increase in the money supply will lead to a short-run expansion in real output and employment. Conversely, as Exhibit 13–5 shows, an unanticipated move toward more restrictive monetary policy reduces aggregate demand and retards real output.

2. The stabilizing effects of a change in monetary policy are dependent upon the state of the economy when the effects of the policy change are observed. If the effects of an expansionary policy come when the economy is operating at less than capacity, then the demand stimulus will push the economy toward full employment. However, if the demand stimulus comes when the economy is operating at or beyond capacity, it will contribute to an acceleration in the inflation rate. Correspondingly, restrictive policy will help to control inflation if the demand-restraining effects are felt when output is beyond the economy's long-run capacity. On the other hand, restrictive policy will result in recession if the reduction in demand comes when the economy is at or below long-run capacity.

THUMBNAIL SKETCH

WHAT IS THE IMPACT OF MONETARY POLICY?

	SHORT-RUN EFFECTS WHEN POLICY IS UNANTICIPATED (1)	SHORT-RUN EFFECTS WHEN POLICY IS ANTICIPATED[a] (2)	LONG-RUN EFFECTS (3)
IMPACT OF EXPANSIONARY MONETARY POLICY ON			
Inflation rate	Only a small increase, particularly if excess capacity is present.		Increase.
Real output and employment	Long-term increase if excess capacity is present; otherwise they increase temporarily.		No change.
Money interest rate	Short-term rates will probably decline.		Increase.
Real interest rate	Decrease.		No change.
IMPACT OF RESTRICTIVE MONETARY POLICY ON			
Inflation rate	Only a small decrease.		Decrease.
Real output and employment	Decrease, particularly if economy at less than capacity.		No change.
Money interest rate	Short-term rates will probably increase.		Decrease.
Real interest rate	Increase.		No change.

[a]Beginning from long-run equilibrium

3. Persistent growth of the money supply at a rapid rate will cause inflation. While the short-run effects of expansionary monetary policy may be primarily on output, particularly if excess capacity is present, a persistent expansion in the money supply at a rate greater than the growth of real output will cause inflation. The more rapid the sustained growth rate of the money supply (relative to real output) is, the higher the accompanying rate of inflation.

4. Money interest rates and the inflation rate will be directly related. As the inflation rate rises, money interest rates will eventually increase because both borrowers and lenders will begin to expect the higher rate of inflation and build it into their decision making. Conversely, as the inflation rate declines, a reduction in the expected rate of inflation will eventually lead to lower money interest rates.

Persistent increases in the quantity of money are the primary cause of inflation.

Therefore, when monetary expansion leads to an acceleration in the inflation rate, it will also result in an increase in nominal interest rates.

5. There will be only a loose year-to-year relationship between shifts in monetary policy and changes in output and prices. It takes time for markets to adjust to changing demand conditions. Some prices in both product and resource markets are set by long-term contracts. Obviously price responses in these markets will take time. In some cases, people may anticipate the effects of a policy change and adjust quickly; in others, the reaction to a policy change may take more time. Differences in this area will weaken the year-to-year relationship between monetary indicators and important economic variables.

In addition, a monetary policy shift will initially exert a far greater impact on short-term interest rates than longer-term rates. Movements in the short-term nominal rates are likely to cause changes in the velocity of money that will tend to dampen the initial effects of a monetary policy shift. This, too, will tend to weaken the year-to-year link between changes in monetary policy and changes in output and prices. Therefore, even though our analysis indicates that monetary policy does influence output and prices, the year-to-year relationships are likely to be weak.

6. Monetary and price level stability will reduce uncertainty and thereby promote the realization of gains from production, investment, and exchange. In contrast, monetary policies that lead to high and variable rates of inflation will retard economic progress. Such policies will reduce the ability of people to plan for the future, divert resources away from productive investments and toward speculation, and undermine the credibility of the government.

TESTING THE MAJOR IMPLICATIONS OF MONETARY THEORY

Is the real world consistent with our analysis? The next five exhibits provide evidence on this topic.

Our analysis indicates that a shift to more expansionary monetary policy will initially stimulate output, while a shift to monetary restriction will retard it. **Exhibit 13–10** shows the relationship between changes in the growth rate of the money supply and real output since the mid-1950s for the United States. Since the introduction of interest-earning checking accounts changed the nature of M1 (and affected its growth rate) during the 1980s, the M2 money-supply measure is used here. Of course, factors other than monetary policy (for example, supply shocks, fiscal policy, or changes in incomes abroad) will influence the growth of output. Thus, the relationship between changes in the money supply and the growth of real GDP will be fairly loose. However, close inspection of the data reveals that periods of sharp acceleration in the growth rate of the money supply were generally associated with an acceleration in the growth rate of real GDP. For example, an acceleration in the growth rate of the money supply during 1961–1964, 1971–1972, 1976, and 1983 was associated with an increase in the growth rate of real GDP during each of the periods. The converse was also true: periods of sharp

Periods of sharp acceleration in the growth rate of the money supply, such as 1961–1964, 1971–1972, and 1976 have generally been followed by a rapid growth of GDP. In contrast, sharp declines in the growth rate of the money supply such as those experienced in 1968–1969, 1973–1974, 1977–1979, and 1988–1991 have often been associated with (or closely followed by) reductions in real GDP and economic recession. The shaded years represent periods of recession.

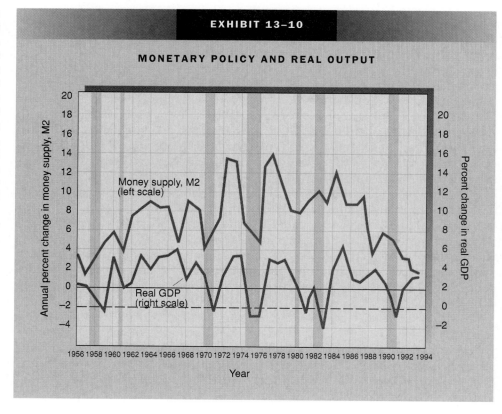

EXHIBIT 13–10

MONETARY POLICY AND REAL OUTPUT

deceleration in the growth rate of the money supply were generally associated with (or followed by) economic recession. A decline in the growth rate of the money supply preceded the recessions of 1958, 1960, 1970, and 1974–1975. Similarly, a sharp decline in the growth rate of the money stock from 13.7 percent in 1976 to 8 percent in 1978–1979 preceded the recession and sluggish growth of 1979–1982. Most recently, the recession and sluggish growth of 1989–1991 was preceded by a substantial deceleration in the growth rate of the money supply. Hence, just as our theory predicts, there does appear to be a relationship between shifts in monetary policy and changes in real GDP. (See the boxed feature, "What Caused the Great Depression" for further evidence on the impact of a decline in the money supply on real output and employment.)

Exhibit 13–11 presents a graphic picture of the relationship between monetary policy and the inflation rate for the United States. While our theory indicates that persistent, long-term growth of the money supply will be closely associated with inflation, it also indicates that it will take time for a monetary expansion (or contraction) to alter demand relationships and impact prices. Most economists believe that the time lag between shifts in monetary policy and observable changes in the level of prices is often two or three years. Reflecting these views, Exhibit 13–11 compares the current money supply (M2) data with the inflation rate three years in the future. Once again, while the linkage is far from tight, it definitely exists. Most noticeably, the rapid monetary acceleration during 1971–1973 was followed by a similar acceleration in the inflation rate during 1973–1975. Similarly, the sharp monetary contraction of 1974–1975 was accompanied by not only the recession of 1974–1975, but also a sharp deceleration in the inflation rate during 1976–1977. However, as monetary policy again shifted toward expansion in 1976–1977, the double-digit inflation rates of 1979–1980 were soon to follow.

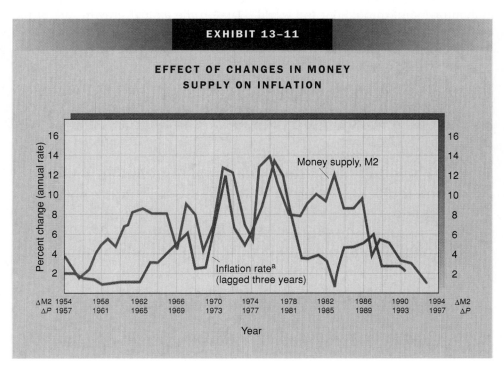

EXHIBIT 13–11

EFFECT OF CHANGES IN MONEY SUPPLY ON INFLATION

Money supply, M2

Inflation rate[a] (lagged three years)

Percent change (annual rate)

| ΔM2 | 1954 | 1958 | 1962 | 1966 | 1970 | 1974 | 1978 | 1982 | 1986 | 1990 | 1994 | ΔM2 |
| ΔP | 1957 | 1961 | 1965 | 1969 | 1973 | 1977 | 1981 | 1985 | 1989 | 1993 | 1997 | ΔP |

Year

Here we illustrate the relationship between the rate of growth in the money supply (M2) and the annual inflation rate three years later. While the two are not perfectly correlated, the data do indicate that periods of monetary acceleration (for example: 1971–1972 and 1975–1976) tend to be associated with an increase in the inflation rate about three years later.

[a]As measured by the consumer price index.

During the 1980–1986 period, the linkage between monetary growth and the inflation rate a few years later appeared to weaken. To some degree this may reflect the financial innovations and changing nature of money during this period. There is some evidence that the relationship is once again becoming more predictable now that the transition period to interest-earning checking accounts has been completed. During the 1989–1993 period, the annual growth rate of the money supply (M2) decelerated from approximately 6 percent to less than 2 percent. With a lag, the inflation rate followed a similar path during this period.

Exhibit 13–12 shows the relationship between the inflation rate (change in CPI) and the nominal interest rate. Since our measure of inflation is the annual rate of change in the price level, we will compare it with a short-term nominal interest rate—the three-month Treasury bill rate. Our theory implies that nominal interest rates will tend to rise with the rate of inflation. The empirical evidence indicates that is indeed the case. As the inflation rate rose significantly during the late 1960s, so also did the nominal rate of interest. During the 1970s, sharp increases in the inflation rate, particularly during 1977–1980, were accompanied by substantial increases in the nominal interest rate. Similarly, as the inflation rate decelerated from the double-digit levels of the late 1970s, the money interest rate also plunged during the 1980–1987 period. Later, a modest increase in the inflation rate during 1988–1990 resulted in a similar modest increase in short-term interest rates. Finally, as the inflation rate declined to its lowest level in 30 years in 1993, so did nominal interest rates. These data provide strong evidence that, just as our theory predicts, the choices of borrowers and lenders are strongly influenced by the inflation rate and expectations concerning its path in the future.

A major implication of our analysis is that rapid growth rates in the money supply *over long periods of time* will be associated with high rates of inflation. Exhibit 13–13 presents data on this issue for 54 countries (with a population of 6 million or more) throughout the world. Data on the annual growth rate of the money supply (adjusted for the growth rate of the nation's output) and the rate of

The expectation of inflation (a) reduces the supply and (b) increases the demand of loanable funds, causing money interest rates to rise (see Exhibit 13–8). Note how the short-term money rate of interest has tended to increase when the inflation rate accelerates (and decline as the inflation rate falls).

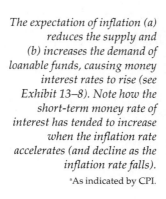

[a]As indicated by CPI.

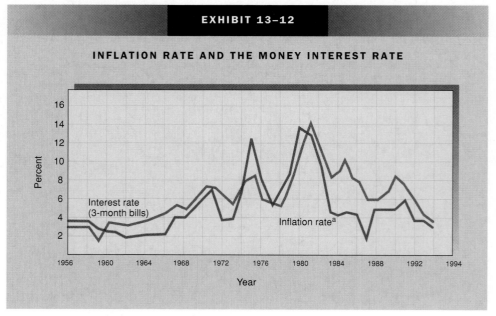

EXHIBIT 13–12

INFLATION RATE AND THE MONEY INTEREST RATE

MYTHS OF ECONOMICS

"INFLATION IS CAUSED BY GREEDY BUSINESSES AND UNION LEADERS."

Since businesses and union officials play a highly visible role in the setting of prices, it is often charged that greed on their part is a cause of inflation. Interestingly, political officials are frequently at the forefront of those making such charges.

When considering this topic, it is important to differentiate between *high* prices and *increasing* prices. Inflation is present when prices are *increasing* rapidly. Economic analysis indicates that businesses and labor unions that have monopoly power will often be able to charge *high* prices—prices that exceed competitive levels. But there is no reason to believe that they will be able to *increase* their prices (or wages) more rapidly than sellers operating in a more competitive environment.

Neither is there any reason to believe that a price or wage increase in one sector of the economy will trigger a general increase in the level of prices. Suppose that actions by the unionized workers and powerful automobile manufacturers push up the prices of autos. If, as the result of this price increase, Americans spend more of their income on automobiles, they will be forced to spend less on other goods and services. As expenditures are reduced for things other than automobiles, the demand for and price of goods in these sectors will tend to decline. Alternatively, if the demand for automobiles is such that Americans sharply curtail their purchases of autos and therefore spend less on automobiles as their price increases, then the employment of resources in the auto industry will decline. In turn, the resources released from their employment in the auto industry will expand the supply of resources in other industries.

This increase in supply will place downward pressure on resource prices and costs, which will tend to lower prices in other sectors of the economy. Thus, there is no reason to expect that price increases in an industry dominated by greedy business or union officials will be able to trigger a general increase in prices in all industries.

The greed-and-selfishness argument is unable to explain why prices rise more rapidly during some time periods and in some countries. For example, inflation in the United States was more rapid during the 1970s than during either the 1960s or 1980s. Were business and labor leaders more greedy during the 1970s? If so, what caused this increase in greed? Similarly, in recent years inflation has been very high in countries as diverse as Argentina, Israel, Zaire, and Poland. Are business and labor leaders in these countries greedier than in other countries with lower rates of inflation? These questions virtually answer themselves.

Inflation is not a mysterious occurrence. High, persistent rates of inflation are always associated with rapid growth in the money supply (see **Exhibit 13–13**). In turn, this monetary growth reflects the policies of political decision makers. Pure and simple, inflation is caused by political officials who are using money creation to finance government expenditures. Their actions dilute the purchasing power of the monetary unit and result in persistent increases in the level of prices.

Big businesses and unions—particularly those with monopoly power—have lots of faults, but causing inflation is not one of them. By and large, the efforts to blame them for inflation are designed to shift attention away from the real culprit—political officials financing government expenditures with printing-press money.

inflation during the 1980–1991 period are presented for each country. The results clearly illustrate the linkage between monetary policy and inflation. Just as our analysis implies, countries with low rates of monetary growth tend to experience low rates of inflation. The growth rate of the money supply was between 2.8 percent and 4.9 percent for seven of the countries (Senegal, Germany, Côte d'Ivoire, Netherlands, Switzerland, Japan, and Belgium) during 1980–1991; the accompanying inflation rate for each of these countries was between 1.5 percent and 5.9 percent.

As the growth rate of the money supply rose, so too did the rate of inflation. Of 12 countries that expanded the supply of money at annual rates between 5 percent and 10 percent during the 1980–1991 period, all but one (Malaysia, which had an inflation rate of 1.7 percent) experienced an average rate of inflation within the

EXHIBIT 13–13

MONEY AND INFLATION—AN INTERNATIONAL COMPARISON, 1980–1991

COUNTRY (RANKED ACCORDING TO LOW RATE OF MONEY GROWTH)	AVERAGE ANNUAL GROWTH RATE OF MONEY SUPPLY[a]	AVERAGE ANNUAL INFLATION RATE	COUNTRY (RANKED ACCORDING TO LOW RATE OF MONEY GROWTH)	AVERAGE ANNUAL GROWTH RATE OF MONEY SUPPLY[a]	AVERAGE ANNUAL INFLATION RATE
Senegal	2.8	5.9	Nigeria	13.8	18.2
Germany	4.1	2.8	Madagascar	14.9	16.8
Côte d'Ivoire	4.1	3.9	South Africa	15.3	14.4
Netherlands	4.2	1.8	Portugal	15.7	17.4
Switzerland	4.6	3.8	Philippines	15.7	14.6
Japan	4.7	1.5	Guatemala	16.1	15.9
Belgium	4.9	4.2	Syria	16.6	14.9
United Kingdom	5.1	5.8	Bangladesh	16.7	9.3
Canada	5.3	4.3	Egypt	17.0	12.6
United States	5.4	4.2	Indonesia	20.3	8.4
Cameroon	5.6	4.5	New Zealand	20.3	10.3
Malaysia	6.9	1.7	Greece	20.5	17.7
Sweden	7.2	7.4	Chile	26.2	20.5
Pakistan	7.2	7.0	Dominican Republic	26.3	24.5
France	7.6	5.7	Ecuador	33.4	38.1
Spain	7.6	8.9	Ghana	39.7	40.2
Australia	9.3	7.0	Zambia	44.3	46.5
Haiti	9.3	7.1	Turkey	47.7	44.7
Italy	9.6	9.5	Poland	57.4	63.1
Hungary	10.6	10.3	Mexico	60.8	66.5
Kenya	10.9	9.3	Uganda[b]	84.5	107.0
Thailand	11.0	3.7	Israel	95.5	89.0
India	11.4	8.2	Brazil[c]	179.5	163.0
Korea	11.7	5.7	Peru	224.4	287.4
Tunisia	11.8	7.3	Zaire	228.4	234.4[b]
Zimbabwe	12.3	13.5	Argentina	368.9	416.8
Iran	13.8	14.1	Bolivia	443.9	318.4

[a]The money-supply data are for the actual growth rate of the money supply minus the growth rate of real GDP. Thus, it is the actual supply of money adjusted to reflect the country's growth rate of real output.
[b]Data are for 1980–1990.
[c]Data are for 1980–1987.

Source: World Bank, *World Development Report: 1993* (Washington, DC: World Bank, 1993); and International Monetary Fund, *International Financial Statistics Yearbook* (Washington, DC: International Monetary Fund, 1993). Only countries with a population of more than 6 million in 1992 were included.

4.2 percent to 9.5 percent range. In contrast, of the 29 countries that expanded the supply of money at an annual rate in excess of 12 percent, all but two

EXHIBIT 13-14

PER CAPITA GROWTH OF GDP, 1980–1991 TEN COUNTRIES WITH THE MOST STABLE AND LEAST STABLE MONEY AND PRICES DURING THE 1980–1990 PERIOD

COUNTRIES	AVERAGE ANNUAL INFLATION RATE	AVERAGE ANNUAL GROWTH RATE OF MONEY SUPPLY	GROWTH OF GDP PER CAPITA
TEN MOST STABLE COUNTRIES[a]			
Japan	1.5	4.7	3.7
Netherlands	1.8	4.2	1.5
Malaysia	1.7	6.9	3.1
Singapore	1.9	6.9	4.9
Germany	2.8	4.1	2.2
Austria	3.6	5.1	2.1
Switzerland	3.8	4.6	1.6
United States	4.2	5.0	1.7
Belgium	4.2	4.9	2.0
Canada	4.3	5.3	1.9
AVERAGE GROWTH RATE (MOST STABLE COUNTRIES)			2.5
TEN LEAST STABLE COUNTRIES[a]			
Nicaragua	583.4	165.0[b]	−4.6
Argentina	416.8	368.9	−1.7
Brazil	327.7	179.5[b]	0.5
Bolivia	318.4	443.9	−2.2
Peru	287.4	224.4	−2.6
Zaire	234.4[c]	228.4	−2.3
Uganda	101.7[d]	84.5[d]	−0.5
Israel	89.0	95.5	1.5
Mexico	66.5	60.8	−0.8
Uruguay	63.6	69.1	0.0
AVERAGE GROWTH RATE (LEAST STABLE COUNTRIES)			−1.3

[a]The countries are rated on the basis of the stability of money and prices. However, countries with lower growth rates of the money supply and the price level also tend to have less variability in these variables. The money supply data are the actual growth rate of the money supply minus the growth rate of GDP.

[b]Data are for 1980–1987.

[c]Data are for 1980–1990.

[d]Data are for 1983–1991.

Source: Derived from International Monetary Fund, *International Financial Statistics Yearbook, 1993;* and World Bank, *World Development Report, 1993.*

WHAT CAUSED THE GREAT DEPRESSION?

As we previously discussed, the Great Depression exerted an enormous impact both on economic thought and on economic institutions. Other business recessions occurring before and since, both in the United States and in other countries, have reversed themselves after a year or two. The Great Depression was different. Exhibit 1 presents the economic record during the period. For four successive years (1930–1933), real output fell. Unemployment soared to nearly one-quarter of the work force in 1932 and 1933. Although recovery did take place during 1934–1937, the economy again fell into the depth of depression in 1938. Ten years after the catastrophe began, real GDP was virtually the same as it had been in 1929.[1]

Why did the economic system break down? Armed with knowledge of how monetary and fiscal policies work, we are now in a position to answer this question. Let us consider four important factors that contributed to the economic collapse of the 1930s.

1. A sharp reduction in the supply of money during 1930–1933 reduced aggregate demand and real output. The supply of money expanded slowly but steadily throughout the 1920s.[2] As Exhibit 1 shows, monetary policy suddenly shifted in 1930. The supply of money *declined* by 6.9 percent during 1930, by 10.9 percent in 1931, and by 4.7 percent in 1932. Banks failed, and the Fed also failed to act as a lender of last resort to head off the huge decline in the supply of money. From 1929 to 1933, the quantity of money in circulation *declined* by 27 percent!

What is the predicted impact of a sharp unexpected reduction in the money supply? Our analysis indicates it will lead to reductions both in prices and in real output (see Exhibit 13–5). This is precisely what happened. By 1933 prices were 24 percent below the level of 1929. Real output also plunged. By 1933 real GDP was 29 percent lower than the 1929 level. Changes

---

[1]See Robert J. Samuelson, "Great Depression" in *The Fortune Encyclopedia of Economics*, edited by David R. Henderson (New York: Warner Books, 1993), for an interesting and informative commentary on this time period.

[2]From 1921 through 1929, the money stock expanded at an annual rate of 2.7 percent, slightly less rapidly than the growth in the output of goods and services. Thus, the 1920s were a decade of price stability, even of slight deflation.

EXHIBIT 1

THE ECONOMIC RECORD OF THE GREAT DEPRESSION

YEAR	REAL GDP IN 1989 DOLLARS (BILLIONS)	IMPLICIT GDP DEFLATOR (1929 = 100)	UNEMPLOYMENT RATE	CHANGES IN THE MONEY SUPPLY (M1)
1929	821.8	100.0	3.2	+1.0
1930	748.9	96.8	8.7	−6.9
1931	691.3	88.0	15.9	−10.9
1932	599.7	77.6	23.6	−4.7
1933	587.1	76.0	24.9	−2.9
1934	632.6	82.4	21.7	+10.0
1935	681.3	84.8	20.1	+18.2
1936	777.9	84.8	16.9	+13.9
1937	811.4	89.6	14.3	+4.7
1938	778.9	87.2	19.0	−1.3
1939	840.7	86.4	17.2	+12.1

Source: Economic Report of the President: 1993; (Washington, D.C.: U.S. Government Printing Office, 1993); and Bureau of the Census, *The Statistical History of the United States from Colonial Times to Present* (New York: Basic Books, 1976).

in the purchasing power of money altered the terms of long-term contracts. During the 1930s farmers, business people, and others who had signed long-term contracts (for example, mortgages) in the 1920s were unable to meet their fixed-money commitments in an economy dominated by falling prices and wages. Bankruptcies resulted. Those trends bred fear and uncertainty, causing still more people to avoid investments involving long-term money commitments. Production and exchange dropped substantially. Gains previously derived from comparative advantage, specialization, and exchange were lost.[3]

2. A large tax increase in the midst of a severe recession made a bad situation worse. Prior to the Keynesian revolution, the dominant view was that the federal budget should be balanced. Reflecting the ongoing economic downturn, the federal budget ran a deficit in 1931, and an even larger deficit was shaping up for 1932. Assisted by the newly elected Democratic majority in the House of Representatives, the Republican Hoover administration passed the largest peacetime tax-rate increase in the history of the United States. At the bottom of the income scale, marginal tax rates were raised from 1.5 percent to 4 percent in 1932. At the top of the scale, tax rates were raised from 25 percent to 63 percent.

Our prior analysis of fiscal policy indicates the counterproductiveness of higher tax rates during a recession. Predictably, the tax increase reduced disposable income and placed still more downward pressure on aggregate demand, which had already fallen sharply in response to the monetary contraction. Simultaneously, the higher marginal tax rates reduced the incentive to earn taxable income. The restrictive fiscal policy further added to the severity of the economic decline. Exhibit 1 shows the degree to which this happened. As tax rates were increased in 1932, real GDP fell by 13.3 percent. Unemployment rose from 15.9 percent in 1931 to 23.6 percent in 1932.

3. Tariff increases retarded international exchange. Concern about low agricultural prices, an influx of

imports, rising unemployment, and declining tax revenues generated public sentiment for trade restraints. Responding to this pressure, the Hoover administration pushed for a substantial increase in tariffs on a wide range of products in early 1930. The tariff legislation took effect in June of 1930. Other countries promptly responded by increasing their tariffs, further slowing the flow of goods between nations. A tariff is, of course, nothing more than a tax on exchanges between parties residing in different countries. Since the increase in tariff rates made such transactions more costly and reduced their volume, additional gains from specialization and exchange were lost.

The high-tariff policy of the Hoover administration not only retarded the ability of the United States to generate output, it was also ineffective as a revenue measure. The tariff legislation increased the duty (tax) rate on imports into the United States by approximately 50 percent.[4] However, the value of the goods and services imported declined even more sharply. Thus, tariff revenues fell from $602 million in 1929 to $328 million in 1932.[5] Like the monetary and fiscal policies of the era, tariff policy retarded exchange and contributed to the uncertainty of the period.

4. The stock-market crash and the business pessimism that followed reduced both consumption and investment demand. Economists generally think of the stock market as an economic thermometer. Although it may register the temperature, it is not the major cause of the fever. While historians may exaggerate the importance of the stock-market crash of 1929, there is reason to believe that it was indeed significant. As the stock market rose substantially during the 1920s, business optimism soared. In contrast, as stock prices plummeted, beginning in October of 1929, aggregate demand fell. The falling stock prices reduced the wealth in the hands of consumers. This decline in wealth contributed to the sharp reduction in consumption expenditures in the early 1930s. In addition, the stock-market crash changed the expectations of consumers and investors.

---

[3]For a detailed analysis of the role of monetary policy during the 1930s, see Milton Friedman and Anna J. Schwartz, *A Monetary History of the United States, 1867–1960* (Princeton: Princeton University Press, 1963), particularly the chapter entitled "The Great Contraction."

[4]The ratio of duty revenue to the value of imports on which duties were levied rose from 40.1 percent in 1929 to 59.1 per-

cent in 1932. See U.S. Census Bureau, *The Statistical History of the United States from Colonial Times to the Present* (New York: Basic Books, 1979), p. 888.

[5]See Jude Wanniski, *The Way the World Works: How Economies Fail and Succeed* (New York: Basic Books, 1978), pp. 125–148, for additional information on the tariff policy of the period and its impact upon the economy.

Both reduced their expenditures as they became more pessimistic about the future. As spending continued to decline, unemployment rose, and the situation worsened. Given the impact of both the business pessimism and the perverse policies previously discussed, a minor recession was turned into an economic debacle.

COULD IT HAPPEN AGAIN?   The question on the minds of many people following the stock-market crash of October 1987 was, could it happen again? Numerous parallels were drawn between the crash of 1929 and the crash of 1987. In both cases, the stock market lost a third of its value in just a few days. But that is where the parallel ends. The Great Depression was the result of disastrous macroeconomic policy, not an inevitable consequence of a stock-market crash. The experience following the October 1987 crash illustrates

this point. In contrast with the crash of 1929, in 1987 the Fed moved quickly to supply reserves to the banking system. The money supply did not fall. Tax rates were not increased. And even though there was a lot of political rhetoric about "the need to protect American businesses," trade barriers were not raised. In short, sensible policies were followed subsequent to the crash of 1987. Continued growth and stability were the result. Inadvertently, perverse macroeconomic policies were followed subsequent to the crash of 1929. Economic disaster was the result.

There is no law able to guarantee that we will not pursue perverse policies again. However, given our current knowledge of macroeconomics, most economists believe that the likelihood of another Great Depression is remote.

(Bangladesh and Indonesia) experienced an average inflation rate in excess of 12 percent during 1980–1991. Five countries (Brazil, Peru, Zaire, Argentina, and Bolivia) expanded the money supply at annual rates of 150 percent or more; each of the five experienced similar average rates of inflation. Similarly, countries with monetary growth rates in the 25 percent to 100 percent range tended to experience rates of inflation in this same range. These data indicate that in the long run there is a relationship between monetary expansion and the rate of inflation.

Finally, our analysis indicates that monetary and price stability will help promote economic growth. **Exhibit 13–14** presents data on this topic.[6] Approximately 80 countries were rated on the basis of the stability of both their monetary growth rate and price level during the 1980–1991 period. Countries with the most stable growth rate of the money supply and rate of inflation are ranked the highest. Of course, countries with low rates of growth in the money supply and price level also tend to have greater monetary and price level stability. In contrast, countries that increase their supply of money rapidly and therefore experience high rates of inflation also tend to have more monetary and price level instability.

The ten countries with the most stable rates of inflation and monetary growth rate during the 1980–1991 period all experienced a positive growth rate in per capita GDP. On average, the output per person of these countries expanded at an annual rate of 2.5 percent. Data are also presented for the ten countries with the most unstable monetary policies during 1980–1991. Annual rates of inflation in these countries ranged from 63.6 percent in Uruguay to 583.4 percent in Nicaragua. The average growth of per capita GDP of these ten countries was –1.3 percent. Seven of the ten

---

[6]See Jose De Gregorio, "The Effects of Inflation on Economic Growth: Lessons from Latin America," *European Economic Review,* April 1992, pp. 417–425; and Mark A. Wynne, "Price Stability and Economic Growth," *The Southwest Economy: Federal Reserve Bank of Dallas,* May–June 1993, for additional empirical evidence that high rates of inflation retard economic growth.

countries experienced declines in per capita GDP. The per capita GDP of one other (Uruguay) was unchanged during the period. None of the ten countries with high and variable rates of inflation and money growth was able to achieve even the average growth rate of the countries following more stable policies. Just as the theory implies, these data indicate that monetary and price stability is an important source of economic prosperity. (Also see "Applications in Economics" boxed feature for additional evidence on the destructiveness of monetary instability.)

LOOKING AHEAD

As we discussed in this chapter, theory indicates that the impact of monetary policy will be influenced by whether economic agents anticipate its effects. Thus far, we have said little about how decision makers form expectations about the future. The next chapter will consider this important issue.

CHAPTER SUMMARY

1. There are three major reasons why households and businesses demand (hold) money balances. People demand money (a) in order to conduct planned transactions, (b) as a precaution against an uncertain future that may require unplanned expenditures, and (c) for speculative purposes so they can quickly respond to profit-making opportunities.

2. The quantity of money demanded is inversely related to the nominal interest rate and directly related to nominal income (GDP). The quantity of money supplied is determined by the central monetary authority (the Fed in the United States).

3. Classical economists developed the quantity theory of money that postulated that the velocity of money was constant (or approximately so) and that real output was independent of monetary factors. According to the quantity theory, therefore, an increase in the stock of money resulted in a proportional increase in prices, while output remained unchanged.

4. Modern economists stress that there are two channels through which monetary policy may influence the demand for goods and services: (a) an indirect path via the real interest rate and (b) a direct path through changes in spending on a broad cross section of goods resulting from an excess supply of (or demand for) money balances.

5. When monetary policy is transmitted by the interest rate, an unanticipated increase in the money supply will reduce the real interest rate and thereby cause investors and consumers to purchase more goods and services in the current period. In the short run, the unanticipated increase in aggregate demand will expand real output, although

with the passage of time, more and more of the demand stimulus will be transformed into price increases when output is pushed beyond long-run capacity. The analysis is symmetrical for an unanticipated reduction in the money supply. Restrictive policy will temporarily raise the real interest rate, reduce aggregate demand, and thereby cause a reduction in real output in the short run.

6. Expansionary monetary policy creates an excess supply of money. In addition to buying bonds (and thereby reducing the interest rate), people may reduce their money balances by increasing their spending in several markets, including the market for goods and services. This increased spending will directly increase aggregate demand. By parallel reasoning, a reduction in the supply of money will lead to a fall in aggregate demand.

7. Monetary policy is a potential tool of economic stabilization. If the effects of expansionary monetary policy are felt when aggregate output is at less than capacity, then the policy will stimulate demand, and push the economy toward full employment. Correspondingly, if restrictive monetary policy is properly timed, then it can help to control inflation.

8. In the long run, the primary impact of monetary policy will be on prices rather than on real output. When expansionary monetary policy leads to rising prices, decision makers eventually anticipate the higher inflation rate and build it into their choices. As this happens, money interest rates, wages, and incomes will reflect the expectation of inflation, so that real interest rates, wages, and output will return to their long-run normal levels.

9. When the effects of expansionary monetary policy are anticipated prior to their occurrence, the short-run impact of an increase in the money supply is similar to its impact in the long run. Nominal prices and interest rates rise, but real output remains unchanged. Thus, theory indicates that the short-run impact of monetary policy is dependent on whether the effects of the policy are anticipated.

10. Monetary instability and inflation create uncertainty, which makes exchange, capital investments, and long-term contracts more hazardous. Monetary instability

also tends to encourage speculation rather than production, and it tends to undermine the credibility of government. Thus, monetary instability tends to deter economic progress and the growth of income. In contrast, monetary stability reduces uncertainty and helps provide an environment conducive to economic growth.

11. The empirical evidence indicates that changes in monetary policy influence real GDP *in the short run*. Shifts toward monetary acceleration tend to be associated with a temporary increase in the growth rate of real GDP. Conversely, shifts toward monetary contraction have generally been associated with a slowdown in real output.

12. Both the U.S. experience and international comparisons strongly indicate that persistent, rapid growth in the money supply is closely linked with inflation. The U.S. data illustrate that shifts to rapid monetary growth for an extended period of time are generally followed by an acceleration in the inflation rate. Similarly, the international data show that countries with low (high) rates of growth in the money supply tend to experience low (high) rates of inflation.

13. Cross-country comparisons indicate that countries following more stable monetary policies tend to grow more rapidly than countries with high and variable rates of monetary growth and inflation.

14. Analysis of the Great Depression suggests that the depth of the economic plunge, if not its onset, was the result of perverse monetary and fiscal policies. The 27 percent reduction in the money supply between 1929 and 1933 is without parallel in United States history. It reduced aggregate demand, changed the intended real terms of the time dimension exchanges, and created enormous uncertainty. The substantial increase in tariffs (taxes on imports) in 1930 and the huge increases in tax rates in 1932 further reduced aggregate demand and the incentive to earn taxable income. Lacking understanding of monetary and fiscal tools, policy-makers followed precisely the wrong course during this period.

CRITICAL-ANALYSIS QUESTIONS

1. Why do people hold money? How will an increase in the interest rate influence the amount of money that people will want to hold? Are money balances a component of income? Are they a component of wealth?

*2. How would each of the following influence the quantity of money that you would like to hold?
   a. An increase in the interest rate on checking deposits.
   b. An increase in the expected rate of inflation.
   c. An increase in income.
   d. An increase in the differential interest rate between savings deposits and checking deposits.

*3. What is the opportunity cost of the following: (a) obtaining a $100,000 house, (b) holding the house during the next year, (c) obtaining $1,000, and (d) holding the $1,000 in your checking account during the next year?

4. What do economists mean when they say "the demand for money has increased?" How will an increase in the demand for money affect the velocity of money?

5. What impact will an unanticipated increase in the money supply have on the real interest rate, real output, and employment in the short run? How will expansionary monetary policy affect the economy when the effects are widely anticipated? Why does it make a difference whether the effects of monetary policy are anticipated?

6. How rapidly has the money supply (M1) grown during the last 12 months? How rapidly has M2 grown? Do you think the monetary authorities should increase or decrease the growth rate of the money supply during the next year? Why? (The data necessary to answer this question for the United States are available in the *Federal Reserve Bulletin*.)

7. Will a budget deficit be more expansionary if it is financed by borrowing from the Federal Reserve or from the general public? Explain.

8. "Inappropriate monetary and fiscal policy was the major cause of economic instability during the 1930s, and it was the major cause of inflation in the 1970s." Evaluate this view, presenting empirical evidence to defend your position.

9. Political officials often call on the monetary authorities to expand the money supply more rapidly so that interest rates can be reduced. Nonetheless, the highest interest rates in the world are found in countries that expand the supply of money rapidly. Can you explain these seemingly contradictory facts?

*10. Generally, monetarists argue that there is a "long and variable time lag" between when a change in monetary policy is instituted and when the change exerts its primary impact on output, employment, and prices. How does this long and variable time lag affect the case for discretionary monetary policy compared to the case for a monetary rule?

*11. Generally, Keynesians argue that the velocity of money is "variable and unpredictable." If velocity fluctuates substantially, how does this influence the case for discretionary monetary policy compared to the case for a monetary rule?

*12. "Historically, when interest rates are high, the inflation rate is high. High interest rates are a major cause of inflation." Evaluate this statement.

---

*Asterisk denotes questions for which answers are given in Appendix C.

*13. If the supply of money is constant, how will an increase in the demand for money influence aggregate demand?

14. Historically, shifts toward more expansionary monetary policy have often been associated with increases in real output. Why? Would a more expansionary policy increase the long-term growth rate of real GDP? Why or why not?

*15. Suppose that innovations in financial management during the 1990s permit individuals and business firms to conduct a given volume of transactions with an increasingly smaller average money balance. As a result, the velocity of money increases at a 3 percent annual rate during the decade. If the monetary authorities want to maintain stable prices, what growth rate of the money supply should they choose?

16. Politicians often blame inflation on greedy businesses, powerful labor unions, or foreigners that raise the prices of the goods or services they supply. Do you think that businesses, labor unions, or foreigners can cause inflation? Why or why not?

17. It is commonly held that the stock-market crash caused the Great Depression. Do you think this is true? Why or why not? Why has this belief been so widely accepted?

18. The accompanying chart presents data on the money supply, price level, and real GDP for three countries during the 1987–1990 period.
   a. Fill in the missing data.
   b. Which country followed the most expansionary monetary policy?
   c. Which country experienced the highest annual rate of inflation for the years 1988, 1989, and 1990?
   d. Which country experienced the most rapid increase in real output during the 1987–1990 period?

	MONEY SUPPLY (IN BILLIONS OF LOCAL CURRENCY)	GDP DEFLATOR (1987=100)	NOMINAL GDP (IN BILLIONS OF LOCAL CURRENCY)	REAL GDP (IN 1987 CURRENCY UNITS)	RATE OF CHANGE MONEY SUPPLY	RATE OF CHANGE PRICE LEVEL
UNITED STATES						
1987	2910.8	100.0	4539.9	_____	X	X
1988	3071.1	103.9	4900.4	_____	_____	_____
1989	3227.3	108.5	5250.8	_____	_____	_____
1990	3339.0	113.2	5522.2	_____	_____	_____
TURKEY						
1987	17992	100.0	56763	_____	X	X
1988	27881	166.7	97929	_____	_____	_____
1989	47958	273.0	164067	_____	_____	_____
1990	72618	423.4	277890	_____	_____	_____
ARGENTINA						
1987	48.4	100.0	163.5	_____	X	X
1988	259.9	490.0	773.0	_____	_____	_____
1989	5958.4	15919.0	22892.6	_____	_____	_____
1990	70000.0	322000.0	480000.0	_____	_____	_____

Source: World Bank, *World Tables*, 1992.

*Asterisk denotes questions for which answers are given in Appendix C.

CHAPTER FOURTEEN

EXPECTATIONS, INFLATION, AND UNEMPLOYMENT

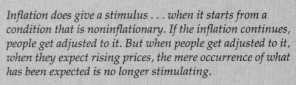

Inflation does give a stimulus . . . when it starts from a condition that is noninflationary. If the inflation continues, people get adjusted to it. But when people get adjusted to it, when they expect rising prices, the mere occurrence of what has been expected is no longer stimulating.

SIR JOHN R. HICKS[1]

CHAPTER FOCUS

■ *Why does it make a difference whether a change in macroeconomic policy is anticipated or unanticipated?*

■ *How do individuals form expectations about what will happen in the future?*

■ *Can a nation reduce its unemployment rate if it is willing to pay the price of a higher inflation rate?*

■ *How can one explain the simultaneous occurrence of inflation and a high rate of unemployment? Is this occurrence inconsistent with economic theory?*

■ *Can economic policy reduce the natural rate of unemployment? If so, how?*

■ *How has the natural rate of unemployment changed in recent years? How is it likely to change during the 1990s?*

---

[1]J. R. Hicks, "Monetary Theory and Keynesian Economics" in *Monetary Theory*, edited by R. W. Clower (Harmondsworth: Penguin, 1969), p. 260.

P eople make decisions on the basis of perceptions: the perceived costs and benefits associated with choices. What individuals think is going to happen in the future is important because it affects the choices they make in the present. Sometimes the results of those choices are different than expected. When this is true, people will often modify their future choices. In this chapter, we will explicitly incorporate the idea that expectations about the future influence the choices of individuals who think and learn from previous experience. We will consider alternative theories concerning how expectations are formed and investigate their implications.

What impact will a shift to a more expansionary macroeconomic policy have on output and employment? Can expansionary policies reduce the unemployment rate? If so, how long can the lower unemployment rate be maintained and at what cost? Expectations provide the key to answering these questions. Hence, we must more fully integrate expectations into our economic way of thinking about output, employment, and prices.

UNANTICIPATED AND ANTICIPATED DEMAND STIMULUS

Throughout this text, we have carefully differentiated between unanticipated and anticipated changes. **Exhibit 14–1** illustrates why this distinction is crucial. Beginning from a position of long-run equilibrium, the impact of expansionary macroeconomic policy is indicated under two alternative assumptions. Part "a" assumes that decision makers fail to anticipate the effects of the expansionary policies and therefore they do not expect the resulting cost and price increases. As we have previously discussed, unanticipated increases in aggregate demand will temporarily increase both output and employment. For a time, output will expand to a rate (Y_2) beyond the economy's long-run potential. Correspondingly, employment will expand and unemployment will recede below the economy's natural rate. When the effects of expansionary policy are unanticipated, both output and employment increase in the short run.

Part "b" of Exhibit 14–1 illustrates the impact of expansionary macroeconomic policy under the assumption that decision makers anticipate its effects prior to their occurrence. Recognizing that expansionary policies will strengthen demand and lead to inflation, market participants alter their choices accordingly. Agreements specifying future wage rates and resource prices immediately make allowance for an expected increase in the price level. These agreements may even include *escalator clauses* providing for automatic cost-of-living increases in nominal wages tied to the general price level. When buyers and sellers in the resource market fully anticipate and quickly adjust to the effects of the demand-stimulus policies, wage rates and resource prices will rise as rapidly as product prices. Profit margins will fail to improve. The rising nominal costs will decrease aggregate supply, offsetting the impact of the demand stimulus on output. The result: a higher price level, while real output is unchanged (see the shift from E_1 to E_2 in part "b" of Exhibit 14–1).

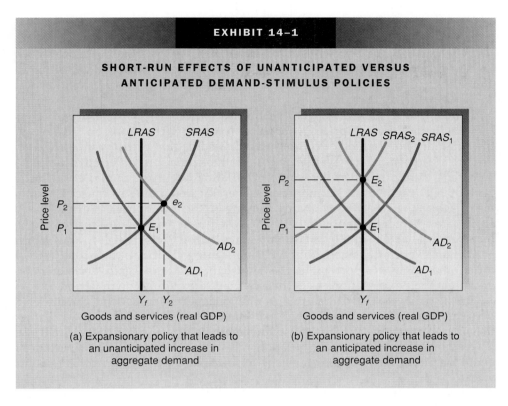

EXHIBIT 14-1

SHORT-RUN EFFECTS OF UNANTICIPATED VERSUS ANTICIPATED DEMAND-STIMULUS POLICIES

(a) Expansionary policy that leads to an unanticipated increase in aggregate demand

(b) Expansionary policy that leads to an anticipated increase in aggregate demand

When expansionary policies catch decision makers by surprise, the increase in aggregate demand will lead to an increase in real GDP (from Y_f to Y_2, in the short run (a). In contrast, when suppliers correctly anticipate the inflationary impact of demand-stimulus policies, nominal costs will rise, causing a decline in aggregate supply (shift to $SRAS_2$) (b). When the effects are anticipated, demand-stimulus policies merely increase prices without altering the rate of output.

Thus, the impact of expansionary macroeconomic policy is dependent on whether (and how quickly) decision makers anticipate the eventual effects. If decision makers fail to anticipate the strong demand and the increase in the price level that will eventually accompany the expansionary policy, the demand stimulus will temporarily increase output and reduce unemployment. In contrast, when the inflationary side effects of expansionary policies are anticipated quickly, the primary impact of the demand stimulus will be an increase in the price level (see this chapter's opening quote by Nobel laureate Sir John R. Hicks).

HOW EXPECTATIONS ARE FORMED

As Exhibit 14-1 illustrates, expectations concerning the future exert an important impact on the effectiveness of macroeconomic policy. Thus, it is vitally important that we understand how expectations are formed. There are two general theories in this area. Let us outline the essentials of each.

ADAPTIVE EXPECTATIONS

The simplest theory concerning the formation of expectations is that people rely on the past to predict future trends. According to this theory, which economists

Adaptive-expectations hypothesis

The hypothesis that economic decision makers base their future expectations on actual outcomes observed during recent periods. For example, according to this view, the rate of inflation actually experienced during the last two or three years would be the major determinant of the rate of inflation expected for next year.

call the **adaptive-expectations hypothesis,** decision makers believe that the best indicator of the future is what has happened in the recent past. For example, people would expect the price level to be stable next year if stable prices had been present during the last two or three years. Similarly, if prices had risen at an annual rate of 4 or 5 percent during the last several years, people would expect similar increases next year.

Exhibit 14–2 presents a graphic illustration of the adaptive-expectations hypothesis. In Period 1, prices were stable (part "a"). Therefore, on the basis of the experience of Period 1, decision makers assume that prices will be stable in Period 2 (part "b"). However, the actual rate of inflation in Period 2 jumps to 4 percent. Continuation of the 4 percent inflation rate throughout Period 2 (the periods may range from six months to several years in length) causes decision makers to change their expectations. Relying on the experience of Period 2, they anticipate 4 percent inflation in Period 3. When their expectations turn out to be incorrect (the actual rate of inflation during Period 3 is 8 percent), they again alter their expectations accordingly. Then, during Period 4, the actual rate of inflation declines to 4 percent, less than the expected rate. Again, decision makers adjust their expectations as to the expected rate of inflation in Period 5.

In the real world, of course, one would not expect the precise mechanical link between past occurrences and future expectations outlined in Exhibit 14–2. Rather than simply using the inflation rate of the immediate past period, people may use a weighted average of recent inflation rates when forming their expectations about the future. Nevertheless, the general point illustrated by the exhibit remains valid.

Under adaptive expectations, forecasts of the future rate of inflation will exhibit *systematic error,* that is, an error that is made over and over again in a regular methodical way. When the inflation rate is accelerating, decision makers will

According to the adaptive-expectations hypothesis, the actual occurrence during the most recent period (or set of periods) determines people's future expectations. Thus, the expected future rate of inflation (b) lags behind the actual rate of inflation (a) by one period as expectations are altered over time.

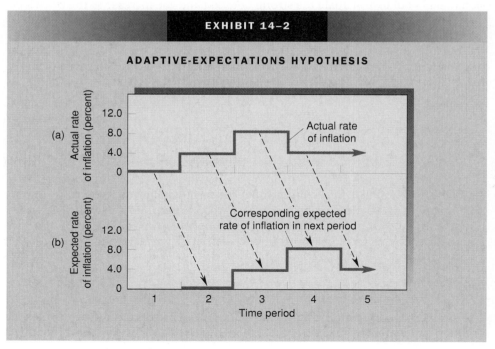

EXHIBIT 14–2

ADAPTIVE-EXPECTATIONS HYPOTHESIS

systematically tend to underestimate the future inflation rate. In contrast, when the rate of inflation is decelerating, individuals will tend systematically to overestimate its future rate. We will investigate the implication of this occurrence as we proceed.

RATIONAL EXPECTATIONS

The idea that people form their expectations concerning what will happen in the future on the basis of all available information, including information about how policy changes will affect the economy, is called the **rational-expectations hypothesis.** According to this view, rather than merely assuming the future will be pretty much like the immediate past, people also consider the expected effects of changes in policy. Based on their understanding of economic policy, people alter their expectations with regard to the future when the government, for example, runs a larger deficit, expands the supply of money more rapidly, or cuts the size of its expenditures.

Perhaps an example will help clarify the rational-expectations hypothesis. Suppose prices had increased at an annual rate of 6 percent during each of the last three years. In addition, assume that decision makers believe there is a relationship between the growth rate of the money supply and rising prices. They note that the money stock has expanded at a 12 percent annual rate during the last nine months, up from the 7 percent rate of the past several years. According to the rational-expectations hypothesis, they will then integrate the recent monetary acceleration into their forecast of the future inflation rate and will thus project an acceleration in the inflation rate, perhaps to the 10 to 12 percent range. In other words, they will expect the future inflation rate to respond to the more rapid growth of the money supply. In contrast, the adaptive-expectations hypothesis implies that people would expect the inflation rate for the next period to be the same as for the last period (or the last several periods).

Just as a football team alters its strategy in light of moves by an opponent, rational decision makers alter their expectations and strategies in light of policy developments. Although it has been accused of not accounting for the fact that people will make forecasting errors, the rational-expectations hypothesis does in fact account for such errors, but it assumes those errors will tend to be random.

Rational-expectations hypothesis
The hypothesis that economic decision makers weigh all available evidence, including information concerning the probable effects of current and future economic policy, when they form their expectations about future economic events (such as the probable future inflation rate).

OUTSTANDING ECONOMIST

ROBERT LUCAS (1937–   )

A long-time professor of economics at the University of Chicago, Lucas is generally given credit for the introduction of the rational-expectations theory into macroeconomics. His technical work integrating rational expectations into macroeconomic models, along with that of Robert Barro (Harvard University) and Thomas Sargent (University of Minnesota), has substantially altered the way economists think about macroeconomic policy.

For example, sometimes decision makers may overestimate the increase in the inflation rate caused by monetary expansion, and at other times they may underestimate it. But since they learn from prior experience, people will not continue to make the same kinds of systematic errors year after year.

PHILLIPS CURVE—THE DREAM AND THE REALITY

The integration of expectations into our analysis places us in a position to better understand the effects of inflation on unemployment. In an influential article published in 1958, the British economist A. W. Phillips noted that there had been an inverse relationship between the rate of change in wages and the unemployment rate for nearly a century in the United Kingdom.[2] When wages were rising rapidly, unemployment was low. Correspondingly, wage rates rose more slowly when the unemployment rate was high. Others noted that a similar inverse relationship was present between inflation and unemployment during the post–Second World War period in the United States. Since it is based on Phillip's earlier work, a curve indicating the relationship between the rate of inflation and the rate of unemployment is known as the **Phillips curve.**

Phillips curve
A curve that illustrates the relationship between the rate of change in prices (or money wages) and the rate of unemployment.

EARLY VIEWS ABOUT PHILLIPS CURVE

Phillips did not draw any policy implications from his analysis, but others did. During the 1960s many economists thought that demand-stimulus policies would permanently reduce the rate of unemployment. As early as 1959, Paul Samuelson and Robert Solow (each of whom would later win a Nobel Prize in economics) argued that we could trade a little more inflation for less unemployment. Samuelson and Solow told the American Economic Association,

> *In order to achieve the nonperfectionist's goal of high enough output to give us no more than 3 percent unemployment, the price index might have to rise by as much as 4 to 5 percent per year. That much price rise [inflation] would seem to be the necessary cost of high employment and production in the years immediately ahead.*[3]

During the 1960s many leading economists thought that expansionary macroeconomic policy—that is, budget deficits and rapid growth in the money supply—would stimulate output and reduce the rate of unemployment if we were willing to tolerate a little higher rate of inflation. As **Exhibit 14–3** indicates, even the prestigious annual *Economic Report of the President* argued

---

[2]A. W. Phillips, "The Relationship between Unemployment and the Rate of Change of Money Wages in the United Kingdom, 1861–1957," *Economica* 25 (1958), pp. 238–299.

[3]Paul A. Samuelson and Robert Solow, "Our Menu of Policy Changes," *American Economic Review*, May 1960.

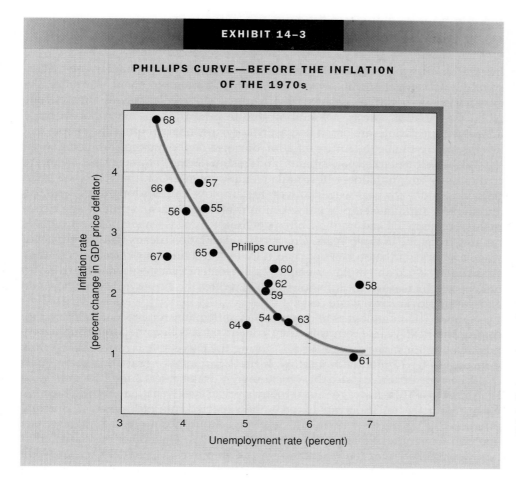

EXHIBIT 14–3

PHILLIPS CURVE—BEFORE THE INFLATION OF THE 1970s

Inflation rate (percent change in GDP price deflator)

Phillips curve

Unemployment rate (percent)

This exhibit is from the 1969 Economic Report of the President, *prepared by the President's Council of Economic Advisers. Each dot on the diagram indicates, as a coordinate point on the graph, the inflation rate and unemployment rate for the year. The report stated that the chart "reveals a fairly close association of more rapid price increases with lower rates of unemployment." Economists refer to this link as the Phillips curve. In the 1960s it was widely believed that policy-makers could pursue expansionary macroeconomic policies and thereby permanently reduce the unemployment rate. More recent experience has caused most economists to reject this view.*

Source: *Economic Report of the President, 1969,* p. 95. The Phillips curve is fitted to the points to illustrate the relationship.

that moderate inflation would reduce the unemployment rate.[4] At the time, most economists thought the inflation-unemployment relationship was stable. In other words, they thought that the short-run equilibrium presented in part "a" of Exhibit 14–1 was, in fact, a long-lasting relationship (a long-run equilibrium).

For a while, it did seem that demand-stimulus policies could reduce the unemployment rate. Both monetary and fiscal policy were more expansionary during the latter half of the 1960s. As Exhibit 14–3 illustrates, the unemployment rate declined while the inflation rate increased, just as the proponents of the inflation-unemployment trade-off theory had predicted.

[4]Not all economists accepted the view that there was a trade-off between inflation and unemployment. At the height of its popularity, the theoretical underpinning of the alleged trade-off was independently challenged by both Edmund Phelps and Milton Friedman. See Edmund S. Phelps, "Phillips Curves, Expectations of Inflation and Optimal Employment over Time," *Economica* 3 (1967), pp. 254–281; and Milton Friedman, "The Role of Monetary Policy," *American Economic Review,* May 1968, pp. 1–17.

ADAPTIVE EXPECTATIONS AND THE PHILLIPS CURVE

Integration of expectations into the Phillips-curve analysis enhances our understanding of the relationship between inflation and unemployment. The adaptive-expectations hypothesis explains why the unemployment rate will often decline when the inflation rate is accelerating due to expansionary macropolicy. Since adaptive expectations are based on past history, the theory implies the people will always *under*estimate the future inflation during a period of accelerating inflation.

When labor-market participants underestimate the inflation rate, there are two reasons why inflation will stimulate employment. First, unanticipated inflation will reduce the real wages of workers employed under long-term contracts and thereby stimulate employment. Union wage contracts and other wage agreements, both explicit and implicit, often determine money-wage rates over periods ranging from one to three years. Unanticipated inflation means that the impact of wage and price inflation has not been fully factored into long-term money-wage agreements. Once an employer-employee agreement establishes money rates, an unexpected increase in the inflation rate will reduce the employee's real wage rate and the employer's real wage costs.

Suppose that employees and employers anticipate an 8 percent inflation rate during the next year. From this, they concur on a collective-bargaining agreement calling for money wages of $10 during the current year and $10.80 for the year beginning 12 months from now. If the *actual* inflation rate this year equals the 8 percent expected rate, the $10.80 money-wage rate 12 months from now translates to a $10 real-wage rate at today's price level. What happens to the real-wage rate if the inflation rate exceeds the expected rate of 8 percent? If actual inflation during the next 12 months is 12 percent, for example, the *real-wage rate* one year from now will fall to $9.64 at current prices. The higher the actual inflation rate is, the lower the real wages of the employees. Unanticipated inflation tends to reduce the real-wage rates of employees whose money wages are fixed by long-term contracts. At the lower real-wage rate, firms will hire more workers and employment will expand.

There is a second reason why underestimation of the inflation rate will tend to expand employment. Misled by inflation, some job seekers will quickly accept job offers on the basis of a mistaken belief that the offers are particularly good ones *in relation to the market for their labor services.* As we discussed in Chapter 7, unemployed workers will search for job opportunities that fit their skills and preferences, expecting that additional search will pay off in the form of a better job. But in a world characterized by imperfect information, job search is costly, involving both personal costs and loss of potential earnings. Economizing behavior dictates that workers will continue searching for employment for only as long as their perceived benefits (finding a better job) exceed the cost of their search.

When people underestimate the extent to which inflation has increased both prices and money wages, many job seekers will fail to recognize how much nominal wages have increased in their skill category. Unaware of just how much their money-wage opportunities have improved, they will tend to accept offers that are not as good as they think they are (relative to jobs that could be found with additional search). Unemployed workers thus shorten their search time, which lowers the unemployment rate.

To summarize, unanticipated (or underestimated) inflation reduces the real-wage rate of workers whose money wages are determined by long-term contracts and reduces the search time of job seekers. Both of these factors will expand employment and reduce the unemployment rate below its natural rate.

With adaptive expectations, though, decision makers will eventually anticipate a higher inflation rate after it has been present for a period of time. They will build the higher expected inflation rate into their decision making. Eventually, workers and their union representatives will demand and employers will agree to money-wage increases that fully reflect the higher current and expected future inflation rate. Similarly, job seekers will become fully aware of the extent that inflation has increased (and continues to increase) their money-wage alternatives. As they do so, their search time will return to normal. Once decision makers fully anticipate the higher rate of inflation and reflect it in their choices, the inflation rate will neither depress real-wage rates nor reduce the search time of job seekers.[5] As this happens, employment and real output will return to their natural (long-run) rates.

Exhibit 14–4 uses our aggregate-demand/aggregate-supply (*AD/AS*) model to illustrate the implications of adaptive expectations with regard to the Phillips-curve analysis. Beginning from a position of stable prices and long-run equilibrium (point *A*), part "a" of Exhibit 14–4 illustrates the impact of an unanticipated increase in aggregate demand. As we previously discussed, initially the demand stimulus will increase output (to Y_2) and employment. The unemployment rate will recede below the economy's natural rate. The strong demand and tight resource markets will place upward pressure on resource prices. *For a time,* the economy will experience both rising prices and an output beyond its full-employment potential (point *B*). This high level of output, however, will not be long-lasting. With adaptive expectations, people will eventually anticipate the rising prices. When this happens, resource prices and costs will rise (from their temporary low levels) relative to product prices, causing the *SRAS* curve to shift to the left. As the previous relationship between resource prices and product prices is restored, output will recede to the economy's full-employment equilibrium level (point *C*).

Part "b" of Exhibit 14–4 illustrates the same case within the Phillips-curve framework. Since initially stable prices are present and the economy is in long-run equilibrium, unemployment is equal to its natural rate (point *A*). We assume that the economy's natural rate of unemployment is 5 percent. The condition of long-run equilibrium implies that the stable prices are both anticipated and observed. *Under adaptive expectations,* an unanticipated shift to a more expansionary policy will temporarily increase output and reduce unemployment. It will also place upward pressure on prices. Suppose that demand-stimulus policies lead to 4 percent inflation and a reduction in the unemployment rate from 5 percent to 3 percent (moving from *A* to *B* along the short-run Phillips curve PC_1). While point *B* is *attainable,* it will not be *sustainable.* After an extended period of 4 percent inflation, decision makers will begin to anticipate the higher rate of inflation. Workers and their union representatives will take the higher expected rate of inflation into

---

[5]For an analysis of how rapidly these adjustments take place, see Robert J. Gordon, "Price Inertia and Policy Ineffectiveness in the United States, 1890–1980," *Journal of Political Economy* 90, December 1982, pp. 1087–1117.

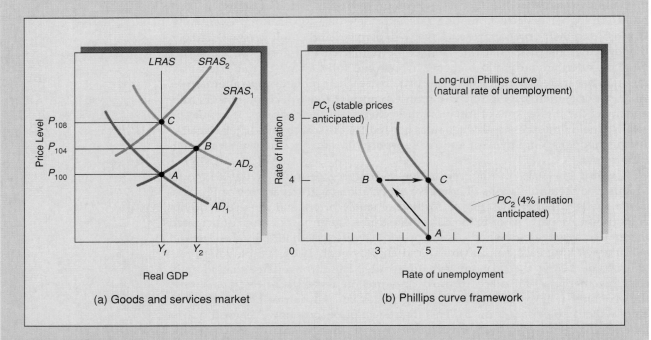

EXHIBIT 14–4

***AD/AS* MODEL, ADAPTIVE EXPECTATIONS, AND PHILLIPS CURVE**

(a) Goods and services market

(b) Phillips curve framework

When stable prices are observed and *anticipated, both full-employment output and the natural rate of unemployment will be present (A in both panels). With adaptive expectations, a shift to a more expansionary policy will increase prices, expand output beyond its full-employment potential, and reduce the unemployment rate below its natural level (move from A to B in both panels). Decision makers, though, will eventually anticipate the rising prices and incorporate them into their decision making. When this happens, the SRAS curve shifts to the left, output recedes to the economy's full-employment potential, and unemployment returns to the natural rate (move from B to C in both panels). Inflation fails to reduce the unemployment rate when it is anticipated by decision makers. Thus, the long-run Phillips curve is vertical at the natural rate of unemployment.*

account in their job search and collective-bargaining decision making. Once the 4 percent rate of inflation is fully anticipated, the economy will confront a new, higher short-run Phillips curve (PC_2). The rate of unemployment will return to the long-run natural rate of 5 percent, even though prices will continue to rise at an annual rate of 4 percent (point *C*).

The moves from point *A* to point *B* in both panels of Exhibit 14–4 are simply alternative ways of representing the same phenomenon—a temporary increase in output and reduction in unemployment as the result of an unanticipated increase in aggregate demand. Similarly, the moves from point *B* to point *C* in the two

EXHIBIT 14–5

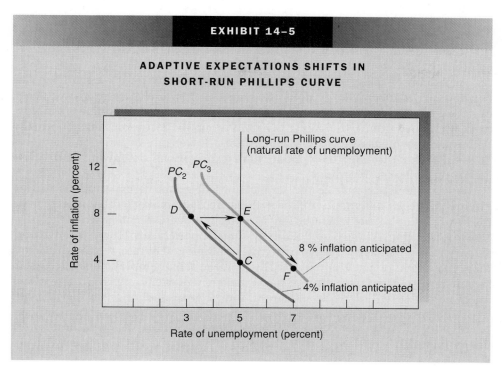

**ADAPTIVE EXPECTATIONS SHIFTS IN
SHORT-RUN PHILLIPS CURVE**

Continuing with the example of Exhibit 14–4, part "b," point C illustrates an economy experiencing 4 percent inflation that was anticipated by decision makers. Since the inflation was anticipated, the natural rate of unemployment is present. With adaptive expectations, demand-stimulus policies that result in a still higher rate of inflation (8 percent, for example) would once again temporarily reduce the unemployment rate below its long-run, normal level (move from C to D along PC_2). After a time, however, decision makers would come to anticipate the higher inflation rate, and the short-run Phillips curve would shift still further to the right to PC_3 (move from D to E). Once the higher rate is anticipated, if macroplanners try to decelerate the rate of inflation, unemployment will temporarily rise above its long-run natural rate (for example, move from E to F).

panels both represent the return of output to its long-run potential and unemployment to its natural rate, once decision makers fully anticipate the observed rate of inflation.

What would happen if the macroplanners attempted to keep the unemployment rate low (below its natural rate) by shifting to a still more expansionary policy? As **Exhibit 14–5** illustrates, this course of action would accelerate the inflation rate to still higher levels. Under adaptive expectations, once the 4 percent inflation rate is anticipated, the rate of unemployment can, for a time, be reduced to 3 percent only if the macroplanners are willing to tolerate 8 percent inflation (movement from C to D). Of course, once the 8 percent rate has persisted for a while, it, too, will be fully anticipated. The short-run Phillips curve will again shift to the right (to PC_3), unemployment will return to its long-run natural rate, and inflation will continue at a rate of 8 percent (point E).

Once decision makers anticipate a higher rate of inflation (for example, the 8 percent rate), what will happen if macroplanners shift to a more restrictive policy designed to reduce the rate of inflation? When the inflation rate is declining, decision makers will systematically overestimate the future inflation rate under the adaptive-expectations hypothesis. Suppose that wage rates are based on agreements that anticipated a continuation of the 8 percent inflation rate (point E of Exhibit 14–5). If the actual inflation rate falls to 4 percent when 8 percent inflation was expected, the real wages of workers will exceed the real wage present when the actual and expected rates of inflation were equal at 8 percent. The more the actual inflation rate falls short of the expected rate, the higher the real wages of workers will be. Similarly, the search time of job seekers will be longer when they overestimate the impact of inflation on money-wage rates. Unaware that the attractive money-wage offers they seek are unavailable, job hunters will lengthen their job search. In the short run, rising unemployment will be a side effect of the higher real wages and more lengthy job searches.

As Exhibit 14–5 illustrates, with adaptive expectations, once a high (8 percent) inflation rate is anticipated by decision makers, a shift to a more restrictive policy designed to decelerate the inflation rate will cause abnormally high unemployment (the move from E to F along PC_3) and economic recession. The abnormally high unemployment rate will continue until a lower rate of inflation convinces decision makers to alter their inflationary expectations downward and revise long-term contracts accordingly.

We can now summarize the implications of adaptive expectations for the Phillips curve. Under adaptive expectations, decision makers will underestimate the future inflation rate when the rate is rising and overestimate it when the inflation rate is falling. As the result of this systematic pattern, a shift to a more expansionary policy will temporarily reduce the unemployment rate, while a move to a more restrictive policy will temporarily increase the unemployment rate. As an inflation rate persists over time, decision makers will eventually anticipate it, and unemployment will return to its natural rate. There is no long-run (permanent) trade-off between inflation and unemployment under adaptive expectations. Like the *LRAS* curve, the long-run Phillips curve is vertical at the natural rate of unemployment.

RATIONAL EXPECTATIONS AND THE PHILLIPS CURVE

How would the Phillips-curve analysis be altered if the rational-expectations hypothesis is correct? In a world of rational expectations, people quickly anticipate the effects of policy changes and adjust their actions accordingly. For example, if people see a surge in the money supply or a tax cut coming, they will adjust their expectations in light of the shift toward expansionary policy. Anticipating the strong future demand, workers and union representatives immediately press for higher wages and/or inclusion of cost-of-living provisions to prevent the erosion of their real wages by inflation. Business firms, also anticipating the increase in demand, consent to the demands of labor, but they will also raise prices. By the time the demand stimulus arrives, it will have *already been counteracted* by higher money wages, costs, and product prices.[6] If decision makers accurately anticipate the inflationary effects of a more expansionary macroeconomic policy, then, the demand stimulus will merely increase the price level (inflation rate) without altering output or employment.

With regard to demand-stimulus policies, part "b" of Exhibit 14–1 illustrates the implications of rational expectations within the framework of our *AD/AS* model. **Exhibit 14–6** provides parallel analysis for the Phillips-curve framework. Suppose an economy is initially at point A, where a 4 percent inflation rate is both

---

[6]As we discussed in the last chapter, expansionary monetary policy will also increase the expected rate of inflation and lead to a higher money interest rate in the loanable funds market. The rational-expectations hypothesis also implies that money interest rates will rise quickly in response to expansionary monetary policy.

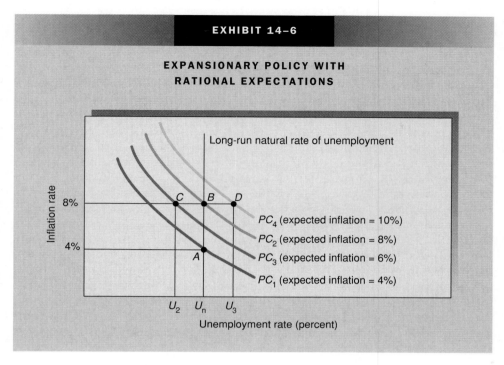

EXHIBIT 14–6

EXPANSIONARY POLICY WITH RATIONAL EXPECTATIONS

Long-run natural rate of unemployment

PC_4 (expected inflation = 10%)

PC_2 (expected inflation = 8%)

PC_3 (expected inflation = 6%)

PC_1 (expected inflation = 4%)

Inflation rate

8%

4%

U_2 U_n U_3

Unemployment rate (percent)

Initially, the actual and expected rates of inflation are equal at 4 percent and unemployment is equal to the economy's natural rate (point A). Policy-makers try to reduce unemployment by shifting to a more expansionary macropolicy consistent with an 8 percent inflationary rate. Proponents of rational explanations argue that the outcome is unpredictable. If people accurately anticipate the inflationary impact of the more expansionary course, the inflation rate will rise while unemployment remains unchanged (shift from A to B). On the other hand, if people underestimate the future inflation, unemployment will temporarily fall (as illustrated by the shift from A to C). In contrast, if individuals overestimate the actual increase in the inflation rate, unemployment will rise temporarily above its long-run natural rate (shift from A to D).

observed and expected. Since the actual and expected inflation rates are equal, the long-run natural rate of unemployment (U_n) is initially observed. Now, suppose policy-makers shift to a more expansionary policy—a demand-stimulus policy consistent with an 8 percent rate of inflation. With rational expectations, the Phillips curve will immediately shift upward as decision makers anticipate an acceleration in the inflation rate due to the more expansionary macropolicy. If decision makers correctly forecast the rise in the inflation rate (to 8 percent), a short-run Phillips curve PC_2 will result. Even though the inflation rate increases to 8 percent, unemployment remains at its long-run natural rate (shifting from A to B).

As explained earlier, the rational-expectations hypothesis does not imply that decision makers are always right. People may either underestimate or overestimate the inflationary effects of the demand stimulus. When they underestimate the inflationary effects, the actual inflation rate will temporarily exceed the expected rate. Suppose that even though the actual inflation rate rises to 8 percent, decision makers anticipate an increase to only 6 percent. In this case, the short-run Phillips curve (PC_3 in Exhibit 14–6) will shift outward by a lesser amount than if the increase in inflation had been accurately forecast. Since individuals do not fully build the higher (8 percent) inflation rate into their decision making, the current unemployment rate declines to U_2 in the short run (moving from point A to point C).

In contrast, when individuals overestimate the increase in inflation, the current unemployment rate will temporarily increase. For example, if decision makers expect the inflation rate to rise to 10 percent while the expansionary policies generate an increase to only 8 percent, the short-run Phillips curve will shift by a larger amount (PC_4 in Exhibit 14–6) than if the increase in inflation had been correctly forecast. In the short run, unemployment will rise above its long-run normal rate (moving from point A to point D).

How can policy-makers know whether rational decision makers will over- or underestimate the effects of a policy change? According to the proponents of rational expectations, they cannot. If the errors of decision makers are random, as the rational-expectations theory implies, people will be as likely to overestimate as to underestimate. Under the rational-expectations hypothesis, then, the impact of expansionary policy on real output and employment is unpredictable, even in the short run. If decision makers accurately anticipate the inflationary impact of expansionary policy, the unemployment rate will remain unchanged even though the inflation rate accelerates. However, if they underestimate the future inflation impact, the unemployment rate will temporarily decline. Conversely, the unemployment rate will temporarily rise if they overestimate the inflationary impact of the policy.

The rational-expectations hypothesis suggests it is extremely difficult for policy-makers to use demand-stimulus policies to reduce the unemployment rate. Such a strategy is effective only when it catches people by surprise, and then only temporarily. If policy-makers follow a systematic strategy, such as persistent demand stimulus or even countercyclical demand stimulus, rational human beings will catch on to the pattern, and the policy moves will fail to exert the intended effect.

RATIONAL EXPECTATIONS AND MACROECONOMIC POLICY

The policy implications of rational expectations are clear. The best policies are pre-announced, stable policies (for example, steady growth of the money supply and a balanced federal budget). Macroeconomic policy should be directed toward long-term objectives, and changes should be weighed very carefully. Policy should not attempt to fine-tune the economy. Efforts to do so will only contribute to economic uncertainty.

On the positive side, the rational-expectations hypothesis indicates that a move from inflation to stable prices can be achieved more easily than adaptive expectations imply. If policy-makers shift to a more restrictive course and convince the public they are going to stick to it until stable prices are achieved, the rational-expectations hypothesis implies that the expected rate of inflation will decline quickly (shifting the short-run Phillips curve down, and toward the origin). As the expectation of inflation declines, money-wage rates will be correspondingly scaled back. Money interest rates will fall.

If a restrictive policy is really credible, the rational-expectations hypothesis implies that the inflation rate can be reduced without the economy going through a prolonged period of recession and high unemployment—a situation that is implied by the adaptive-expectations hypothesis. Credibility that policy-makers will "stay the course" until inflation is brought under control, though, is absolutely essential.[7] If market participants lack confidence in the long-term

---

[7]For evidence that even hyperinflations can be brought under control quickly (with little loss of output) when credibility is present, see Thomas Sargent, "The Ends of Four Big Inflations" in *Inflation: Causes and Effects,* edited by Robert E. Hall (Chicago: University of Chicago Press for the National Bureau of Economic Research, 1982), pp. 41–98.

anti-inflationary commitment of policy-makers, they will reduce their expectations for the future rate of inflation slowly even if current policy is restrictive. When policy-makers have a past history of policy reversals and of saying one thing while doing another, it will be difficult for them to establish credibility. Proponents of rational expectations are thus not surprised that restrictive policies have often led to recession and abnormally high unemployment.

EXPECTATIONS AND MODERN VIEW OF PHILLIPS CURVE

Expectations substantially alter the naive Phillips curve view of the 1960s. Three major points of modern analysis follow:

1. Demand stimulus will lead to inflation without permanently reducing the unemployment rate. Once people fully anticipate the inflationary side effects of expansionary policies, resource prices will rise, profit margins will return to normal levels, and unemployment will return to its natural rate. Under adaptive expectations, this will happen only after the higher inflation rates have been observed for a period of time, say, a year or so. Under rational expectations, the adjustment process will occur more rapidly. If people accurately anticipate the inflationary effects, the demand-stimulus policies may fail to reduce, even temporarily, the unemployment rate when expectations are rational.

In the long run, though, the implications of adaptive and rational expectations are identical—persistent expansionary policy will lead to inflation without permanently reducing the unemployment rate. Neither the adaptive- nor the rational-expectations hypotheses indicate that expansionary policies can sustain unemployment below its natural rate.

2. When inflation is greater than anticipated, unemployment falls below the natural rate. When inflation is less than anticipated, unemployment will rise above the natural rate. It is the difference between the actual and expected rates of inflation that influences unemployment, not the magnitude of inflation, as some economists previously thought. **Exhibit 14–7** illustrates this point by recasting the Phillips curve within the expectations framework. When people underestimate the actual rate of inflation, abnormally low unemployment will occur. Conversely, when decision makers expect a higher rate of inflation than what actually occurs—when they overestimate the inflation rate—unemployment will rise above its natural rate. Equal changes in the actual and expected inflation rates, though, will fail to reduce the unemployment rate. If actual inflation rates of 5 percent, 10 percent, 20 percent, or even higher are accurately anticipated, they will fail to reduce unemployment below its natural rate.[8]

3. When the inflation rate is steady—when it is neither rising nor falling—the actual rate of unemployment will equal the economy's natural rate of unemployment. If the inflation rate of an economy is constant (or approximately so), decision makers

---

[8]Empirically, higher rates of inflation are generally associated with greater variability in the inflation rate. Erratic variability increases economic uncertainty. It is likely to inhibit business activity, reduce the volume of mutually advantageous exchange, and cause the level of employment to fall. Thus, higher, more variable inflation rates may actually increase the rate of unemployment.

It is the difference between the actual and expected rates of inflation that influences the unemployment rate, not merely the size of the inflation rate, as the earlier, naive Phillips-curve analysis implied. When inflation is greater than anticipated (people underestimate it), unemployment will fall below the natural rate. In contrast, when inflation is less than people anticipate, unemployment will rise above the natural rate. If the inflation rate is correctly anticipated by decision makers, the natural rate of unemployment will result.

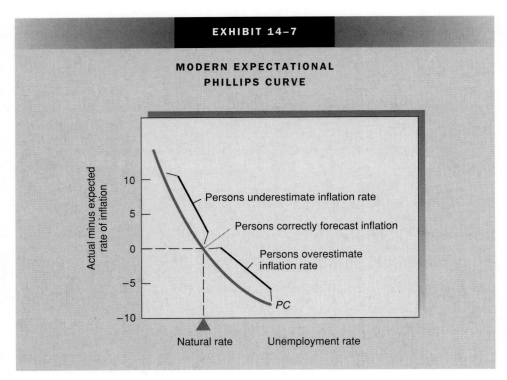

EXHIBIT 14–7

MODERN EXPECTATIONAL PHILLIPS CURVE

will come to anticipate the rate. This rate will be reflected in both long-term contracts and the job search of workers. Once this happens, unemployment will return to its natural rate. In fact, the natural rate of unemployment is sometimes defined as the unemployment rate present when the inflation rate is neither rising nor falling (see the accompanying boxed features, "Measures of Economic Activity" and "Applications in Economics" that follow).

PHILLIPS CURVE IN UNITED STATES, 1961–1993

Integration of expectations into our analysis helps clarify the U.S. data on inflation and unemployment during the last several decades. After nearly 20 years of low inflation (and moderate monetary and fiscal policy) following the Second World War, decision makers were accustomed to relative price stability. Against this background, the expected rate of inflation was low. As a result, the shift toward expansionary policies in the mid-1960s caught people by surprise.[9] Therefore, as Exhibit 14–3 shows, these policies initially reduced the unemployment rate.

---

[9]The following data are indicative of the shift toward more expansionary macroeconomic policies beginning in the mid-1960s. Between 1965 and 1980, the M1 money supply grew at an annual rate of 6.3 percent, compared to only 2.5 percent during the previous 15 years. Similarly, perpetual federal deficits replaced balanced budgets. During the 1950–1965 period, there were eight budget deficits and seven surpluses. On average, the federal budget was approximately in balance during the 15-year period. During the 1965–1980 period, however, there was only one year of budget surplus, and annual deficits averaged 1.5 percent of GDP.

MEASURES OF ECONOMIC ACTIVITY

NATURAL RATE OF UNEMPLOYMENT IN EUROPE, CANADA, JAPAN, AND THE UNITED STATES

Our analysis indicates that when the inflation rate of a country is steady (when it is neither rising nor falling) for an extended period of time, people will anticipate the rate, and unemployment will gravitate toward the economy's natural rate of unemployment. Interestingly, the inflation rates in the United States, Canada, Europe, and Japan were quite steady during 1986–1990. The inflation rate averaged approximately 4 percent during that period in the United States, Europe, and Canada. More importantly, in each of these areas it fluctuated within a narrow band (between 3 percent and 5 percent) during the five years. In Japan, the inflation rate was lower, and it was virtually constant at approximately 1.5 percent.

Given these steady rates of inflation, the actual unemployment rates during the latter part of the period should approximate the natural rate of unemployment for each of these economies. The unemployment rates in 1989 and 1990 follow:

	1989	1990
United States	5.3	5.5
Europe (11 EC Countries)	7.3	7.0
Canada	7.5	8.1
Japan	2.3	2.1

Thus, after an extended period of inflation at a steady rate, the unemployment rate during 1989–1990 was approximately 5.5 percent in the United States, approximately 7 percent in Europe, 8 percent in Canada, and 2 percent in Japan. These numbers imply that, compared to the United States, the natural rate of unemployment in the late 1980s was higher in Europe and Canada, but lower in Japan.

Compared to the United States, why might the natural rate of unemployment be higher in Europe and Canada but lower in Japan? There are two major reasons. First, wages tend to be more flexible in Japan as compared with the United States, but less flexible in Europe and Canada. Unions in Japan are almost exclusively of the "company union" variety. They seldom set wages for an entire industry, and they are much more likely than their U.S. counterparts to accept wage cuts during a period of declining demand for the products that they produce. Compared to the United States, therefore, a decline in demand in an industry in Japan is more likely to result in wage reductions and less likely to result in termination and worker layoffs.

In contrast, wages tend to be less flexible in Europe and Canada than in the United States because unionism is more prevalent there. For example, between 40 percent and 50 percent of the nonagricultural labor force is unionized in the United Kingdom, Italy, and Germany.[1] In Canada, 37 percent of the nonfarm workers belong to a union. By way of comparison, only 16 percent of the U.S. nonagricultural labor force is unionized. To the extent that strong unions in Europe and Canada push wages above the market level and reduce wage flexibility, they tend to increase the natural rate of unemployment. In addition, many of the governments in Europe set wages—often at or above equilibrium rates—in various occupations and industries. This, too, contributes to wage rigidity and tends to push the natural rate of unemployment up.

Second, the unemployment-compensation system is generally more lucrative (and less restrictive with regard to eligibility) in Europe and Canada than in the United States.[2] This encourages more lengthy periods of job search and thereby pushes up the natural rate of unemployment in Europe and Canada. In contrast, unemployment compensation and other income-transfer programs are less lucrative in Japan than in the United States. This, too, contributes to the low natural rate of unemployment in Japan.

Restrictions limiting the mobility of workers and businesses across national boundaries may also contribute to the high unemployment rate in Europe. Many of these barriers are declining with European unification. Thus, it will be interesting to follow the natural rate of unemployment in Europe during the 1990s as the unification process continues.

---

[1]Richard B. Freeman, "Contraction and Expansion: The Divergence of Private and Public Sector Unionism in the United States," *Journal of Economic Perspectives*, Spring 1988, pp. 63–88.

[2]See Vivek Moorthy, "Unemployment in Canada and the United States: The Role of Unemployment Insurance Benefits," *Federal Reserve Bank of New York: Quarterly Review*, Winter 1990, pp. 48–61.

APPLICATIONS IN ECONOMICS

WOULD INDEXED BONDS PROVIDE BETTER INFORMATION ABOUT THE PERFORMANCE OF THE FED AND LEAD TO BETTER MONETARY POLICY?

The U.S. Treasury currently issues only bonds that promise to pay interest in nominal terms. The interest rate on these bonds is unchanged regardless of the inflation rate during the period the bond is outstanding. Some economists argue that the conduct of monetary policy would improve if the Treasury issued an equal amount of *indexed bonds*. An indexed bond would pay a market-determined real interest rate plus a premium equal to the actual rate of inflation (measured by a price index like the GDP deflator or the CPI) that occurs *during the time period the bond is outstanding*. Since the variable component (the component tied to the inflation rate) would compensate financial investors for changes in the general level of prices, the fixed component of the interest rate on the indexed bonds would reflect only the real rate of interest.

If the Treasury issued such bonds, the interest-rate differential between the "regular bonds" paying a nominal interest rate and the interest rate on the indexed bonds would be equal to the expected rate of inflation. Bonds of differing maturing lengths would provide information on differences in the expected inflation rate for various future time periods. For example, the interest-rate differential between the regular and indexed 12-month Treasury bills would provide an estimate of the expected rate of inflation during the next 12 months. Similarly, the rate differentials for 5-year and 10-year bonds would provide estimates for the expected rate of inflation during the next five and ten years.

Expansionary monetary policy cannot—at least not for long—affect real variables. For example, it cannot reduce *real* interest rates, stimulate employment, or expand *real* output over any significant time period. As the 1970s illustrate, attempts to use it in this manner will merely lead to higher (and more variable) rates of inflation, additional uncertainty, and a lower rate of real output.

Monetary policy can—and this is a vitally important function—establish a stable and predictable price level that will allow people to produce and exchange with a minimal amount of uncertainty. When the price level is what people expected, the actual rate of unemployment will be equal to the natural rate, and the output level will be sustainable into the future. This will tend to be the case if the monetary authorities follow policies that keep the *expected* rate of inflation low (some would argue that it should be zero) and constant. When the expected rate of inflation is low and highly stable, decision makers—including those who enter into long-term contracts—will be able to easily and accurately predict what the price level will be in the future.

Since the expected rate of inflation is not currently observable, it is hard to tell how well the monetary authorities are doing. The presence of indexed bonds would allow us to monitor the Fed's performance regularly. A stable interest-rate differential would indicate that the Fed was doing a good job—that it was establishing a stable economic environment. For example, if the interest-rate differential between the nominal interest rate bonds and the indexed bonds was approximately 2 percent over a long period of time, this would indicate that the Fed was following policies that resulted in a rate of inflation (and a price level) that decision makers expected. In this case, long-term contracts would reflect the choices of the decision makers; the terms of trade implied by these contracts would not be altered by unexpected changes in monetary policy.

In contrast, if the expected rate of inflation was constantly jumping around—if it was 7 percent this year, 2 percent a year ago, and 5 percent the year before that, this would indicate that Fed policies were causing uncertainty because they were resulting in substantially different price levels than people expected to occur. Just as profitability indicates the degree of success of a business firm, a stable (and low) expected rate of inflation indicates how successful the Fed is in its efforts to establish a stable economic environment. The presence of indexed bonds would provide both the Fed and the "Fed watchers" with continuous feedback—week-to-week and month-to-month information. In turn, this information would help make the Fed more accountable for the quality of its performance.

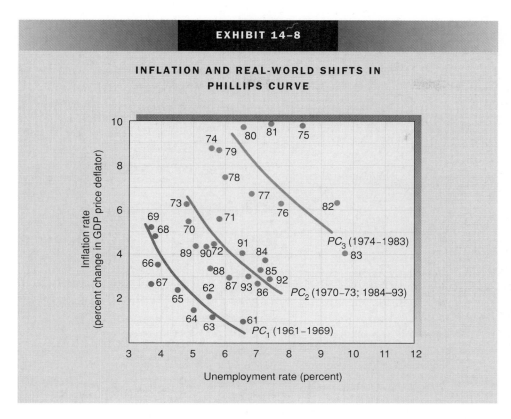

EXHIBIT 14–8

INFLATION AND REAL-WORLD SHIFTS IN PHILLIPS CURVE

The 1982 Economic Report of the President, prepared by the Council of Economic Advisers (CEA) contained this unemployment-inflation rate chart. While the 1961–1969 data mapped Phillips curve PC$_1$, as demand-stimulus policies led to higher inflation rates, the Phillips curve shifted outward to PC$_2$ (for the 1970–1973 period) and PC$_3$ (for the 1974–1983 period). In contrast with the 1969 CEA report (see Exhibit 14–3), the 1982 report stated:

(AUTHORS' NOTE: Nothing in Phillips' works or in subsequent studies showed that higher inflation was associated with sustainable lower unemployment, and nothing in economic theory gave reason to believe that the relationship uncovered by Phillips was a dependable basis for policies designed to accept more inflation or less unemployment.)

Source: *Economic Report of the President*, 1982, p. 51. The Phillips curves have been fitted and the 1982–1993 data added to the chart.

Contrary to the popular view of the 1960s, though, the abnormally low unemployment did not last. **Exhibit 14–8,** which is an updated version of Exhibit 14–3, makes this point clear. Just as our theory predicts, the inflation-unemployment conditions worsened substantially as the expansionary policy persisted. The Phillips curve consistent with the 1970–1973 data (PC$_2$) was well to the right of PC$_1$. During the 1974–1983 period, still higher rates of inflation were observed. As inflation rates in the 6 to 10 percent range became commonplace in the latter half of the 1970s, the Phillips curve once again shifted upward, to PC$_3$.

As monetary policy tightened in 1981–1983 and the Reagan administration promised to bring inflation under control, the inflation rate decelerated sharply. Just as our theory predicts, initially the unemployment rate soared, to 9.7 percent in 1982 and 9.6 percent in 1983 (see Exhibit 14–8) when macroeconomic policy shifted toward restraint. However, as the restraint continued, people scaled their expectations for the inflation rate downward, and the Phillips curve shifted inward. As Exhibit 14–8 indicates, during the 1984–1993 period, the inflation rate declined from the high rates of the late 1970s to the 2.5 percent to 4.5 percent range. Soon after the decline in inflation, people began to anticipate the lower rates, and the Phillips curve shifted inward (from PC$_3$ to PC$_2$).

Exhibit 14–9 presents the 1961–1993 inflation-unemployment data in a form that provides a still better test of our theory. Our analysis indicates that when the actual inflation rate is higher than people anticipate, unemployment will fall short of the natural rate. On the other hand, if the inflation rate is less than was antici-

Here we show the relationship between unanticipated inflation and actual unemployment compared to the natural rate for the period of 1961–1993. When the inflation rate is greater than anticipated, unemployment tends to fall below the natural rate. Conversely, when the inflation rate is less than anticipated, the unemployment rate is generally above the natural rate.

Source: *Economic Report of the President, 1994*; and Robert J. Gordon, *Macroeconomics* (Boston: Little Brown, 1993). The natural rate of unemployment data are from Gordon. The average inflation rate for the previous three years was used as a proxy for the anticipated inflation rate for each year.

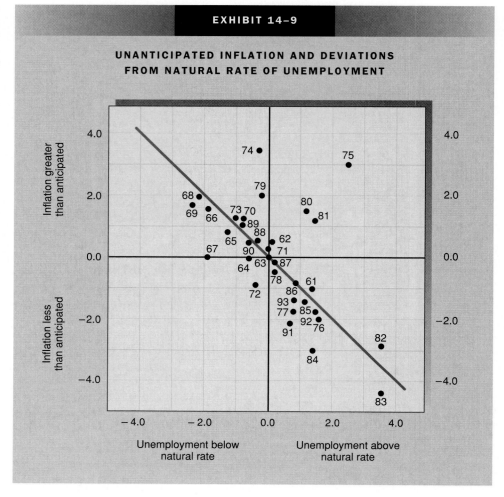

EXHIBIT 14–9

UNANTICIPATED INFLATION AND DEVIATIONS FROM NATURAL RATE OF UNEMPLOYMENT

pated, unemployment will exceed its natural rate. Of course, we cannot directly observe the expected inflation rate. However, we would expect that it will be influenced by recent experiences.

In Exhibit 14–9, for each year shown, the average inflation rate during the previous three years is used as a proxy for the expected rate of inflation. The exhibit illustrates that when the inflation rate was higher than anticipated (higher than the average of the last three years), the unemployment was generally less than the natural rate. For example, as the inflation rate rose in the late 1960s, the actual inflation rate was approximately 2 percent higher than anticipated during 1966, 1968, and 1969. Just as our theory implies, unemployment was well below the natural rate during each of these years.

Conversely, when the inflation rate was less than anticipated, unemployment rose above the natural rate. Look at the dots for the years 1976, 1977, 1982–1985, 1991, and 1992. During each of these years, the actual inflation rate was significantly less than the anticipated rate. And during each of these years, unemployment well above the natural rate was observed.

While the data of Exhibit 14–9 show an obvious negative relationship between unanticipated inflation and unemployment, the observations for five years (1974–1975 and 1979–1981) do not fit as well as the others. Interestingly, these five years encompass periods of soaring oil prices. Oil prices quadrupled (from $2.50 to $10.00 per barrel) between 1973 and 1975, and more than tripled (from $12.00 to $40.00 per barrel) between 1978 and 1981. As we previously discussed (see Chapter 9, Exhibit 9–7), supply shocks of this type tend to push the price level up. Predictably, they lead to dislocations and adjustments that weaken the normal relationship between inflation and unemployment.

ADAPTIVE- VERSUS RATIONAL-EXPECTATIONS DEBATE

Are expectations determined adaptively or rationally? The question is one of continuing debate among economists. Rational-expectations proponents charge that the adaptive-expectations hypothesis is naive. They find it difficult to accept the notion that individuals look only at past price changes while ignoring information on variables (for example, changes in the money supply, interest rates, and exchange rates) that play an important role in the actual generation of inflation.

The advocates of adaptive expectations reply that the rational-expectations theory implies that individuals possess an inordinate amount of information about highly complex issues. They note that the average person neither keeps up with the latest moves of the Fed nor forecasts changes in the federal budget. The proponents of adaptive expectations charge that it is unrealistic to assume that most people will (1) develop reliable theories about the operation of a highly complex economy, (2) monitor the necessary policy variables, and (3) consistently make the implied adjustments to changes in macroeconomic policy. They believe most people will find a simple rule of thumb such as "inflation next year will be about the same as the recent past" to be both sensible and "rational."

The proponents of rational expectations are unmoved by this argument. They believe that it overlooks several facts. After all, business firms and labor unions hire specialists to make forecasts about the future. Predictions made by prominent economists are often widely disseminated via television news and daily newspapers. Because of this, even relatively uninformed citizens, whether they realize it or not, develop a view on the expected rate of inflation.

The proponents of adaptive expectations also emphasize that long-term contracts constrain the responses of decision makers. For example, if long-term contracts specify nominal wages and prices over a longer time period than it takes the monetary authorities to alter the direction of monetary policy, the authorities are in a position to reduce real wages and thereby stimulate employment. Suppose that the wages of a group of workers are set by a three-year collective-bargaining agreement that calls for raises of 5 percent during each of the years. If the inflation rate accelerates upward to, say, 8 percent, the workers will still get only 5 percent annual pay increases during the period of their contract. Hence, even if decision makers anticipate the consequences of a shift toward monetary expansion, long-term contracts will limit their ability to respond quickly. To the extent that this is true, shifts in monetary policy will exert an impact on real wages, employment, and real GDP in the short run.

Advocates of rational expectations respond by pointing out that the nature of contracts is influenced by macroeconomic policy. If the monetary authorities seek to exploit long-term contracts, individuals will predictably respond by including cost-of-living provisions, choosing contracts of shorter duration, and permitting renegotiation at various time intervals. According to the proponents of rational expectations, then, if expansionary policies seek to reduce real wages and costs, they will only induce decision makers to alter the nature of long-term contracts. The growth of collective-bargaining agreements containing *escalator clauses* (provisions for automatic money wage increases as the price level rises) during the 1970s is consistent with this view. As inflation accelerated upward, the number of collective-bargaining agreements providing for cost-of-living wage adjustments rose from 20 percent in 1965 to nearly 70 percent in the late 1970s.

The proponents of adaptive expectations argue that the past performance of the economy is supportive of their view. For example, more rapid growth of the money supply has generally been associated with an expansion in real GDP, followed a year or two later by increases in the inflation rate. Similarly, deceleration in monetary growth has consistently led to a recession, prior to any significant reduction in the inflation rate (see Exhibits 13–11 and 13–12 in Chapter 13). These findings indicate that people alter their expectations slowly as the adaptive-expectations theory implies, not rapidly as suggested by the rational-expectations theory.

The proponents of rational expectations counter that a rapid change in the public's expectations in response to a policy change is dependent on confidence that the change is both real and long-term. In contrast, rational-expectations theory implies that people will respond cautiously to an apparent change when policy-makers have a past history of policy reversals. When the credibility of policy-makers is low, a gradual change in expectations in response to an apparent change in direction is the expected behavior. Thus, advocates of rational expectations do not believe that past evidence indicating expectations have often changed slowly is damaging to their theory.

Of course, the adaptive- versus rational-expectations controversy is important because the two theories have different implications for the short-run Phillips curve. We must not forget, however, that the implications of the two theories for the long-run Phillips curve are essentially the same. Both theories imply that expansionary macroeconomic policy that increases aggregate demand relative to aggregate supply will lead to inflation without permanently reducing unemployment below its normal, long-run rate.

MICROECONOMICS AND THE NATURAL RATE OF UNEMPLOYMENT

The integration of expectations into our analysis highlights the difficulties involved in the use of monetary and fiscal policy to promote high levels of employment. Can other methods be used to reduce the unemployment rate? In recent years, economists have turned to microeconomics as a means of addressing the traditional macroeconomic problem of high unemployment. The microeconomics approach to employment focuses on how the economy's natural rate of unemployment might be reduced and *LRAS* increased. Remember, the natural rate of unemployment is not immutable. Among other things, it reflects the incentive structure emanating from the economy's institutional arrangements. If changes in that incentive structure could improve the efficiency of job search and remove barriers to employment, the economy's natural rate of unemployment would decline. This implies that the long-run (vertical) Phillips curve would shift to the left.

What kinds of institutional changes would be most likely to reduce the natural rate of unemployment? We will consider three changes that have been widely discussed.

REVISING THE UNEMPLOYMENT-COMPENSATION SYSTEM

The unemployment-compensation system was designed to reduce the hardships of unemployment. As desirable as this program is from a humanitarian standpoint, it diminishes the opportunity cost of job search, leisure, nonproductive activities, and continued unemployment. The conflict between high benefit levels and low rates of unemployment should therefore not be surprising.

There are two major reasons why the current unemployment-compensation system increases the natural rate of unemployment. First, it reduces, and in some cases virtually eliminates, the personal cost of unemployment. The benefits in most states provide covered unemployed workers with payments of 50 to 60 percent of their previous *gross* earnings. Unemployment benefits are not subject to payroll taxes (and in some cases, income taxes). In addition, unemployed workers may also qualify for other transfer benefits such as food stamps and Medicaid. It is not unusual, then, for the benefit package of a covered unemployed worker to replace 75 percent or more of previous *net* earnings. Clearly, benefit levels in this range substantially reduce the incentive of individuals to search quickly and diligently for jobs and to accept employment at marginally lower wages prior to the exhaustion of their benefits.

Second, unemployment compensation acts as a subsidy to employers who offer unstable or seasonal employment opportunities. Employees would be more reluctant to work for such employers (for example, northern contractors who generally lay off workers in the winter) were it not for the fact that these employees can supplement their earnings with unemployment-compensation benefits during their layoffs. The system makes seasonal, temporary, and casual employment opportunities more attractive than would otherwise be the case. In essence, it encourages employers to adopt production methods and work rules that rely extensively on temporary employees and supplementary layoff benefits.

There is little doubt that the current unemployment-compensation system increases the natural rate of unemployment. Most researchers in the area believe that the long-run rate of unemployment is between 0.5 and 1.0 percent higher than it would be if the negative employment effects of the system could be eliminated.[10]

---

[10]See Ray Thorne, *The Unemployment Compensation System: Paying People Not to Work* (Dallas: National Center for Policy Analysis, 1988); and Bruce Meyer, *Unemployment Insurance and Unemployment Spells* (Cambridge: National Bureau of Economic Research, 1988) for additional detail on this topic.

In effect, unemployment benefits subsidize job search. There is one positive element accompanying this subsidy—the additional job search emanating from this subsidy may improve the match between the skills of unemployed workers and the requirements of potential jobs. To the extent this is true, the average productivity of workers is higher.

How can the unemployment-compensation system be reformed without undercutting its original humanitarian objectives? Several policy alternatives exist. Firms that regularly terminate and lay off a high percentage of their work force might be charged a payroll tax that more accurately reflects the cost of employment instability. (The current system performs this function imperfectly.) In addition, after a specified period of time, three months for example, unemployment-compensation recipients might be required to accept available jobs (including public-sector employment) that provide wage rates equal to their unemployment-compensation benefits. Alternatively, recipients' benefits might be gradually reduced as they engaged in more lengthy periods of job search and unemployment. This would reduce the incentive of individuals to wait until their benefits run out (generally 26 weeks) before accepting employment. Each of these proposals would increase the incentive of employers to offer stable employment and job searchers to seek out and accept employment more quickly.

REFORMING THE MINIMUM WAGE

Despite good intentions, minimum wage laws reduce the employment prospects of low-skilled, inexperienced workers. Many youthful workers fall into this category. As in the case of other price floors, the minimum wage leads to an excess supply. By mandating artificially high wage rates for jobs requiring few skills, the minimum wage reduces the employment opportunities available to low-skill workers.[11]

The adverse impact of the minimum wage on the on-the-job training opportunities available to low-skill workers is also important. The legislation often makes it unfeasible for an employer to (1) provide training to inexperienced workers and (2) pay the legal minimum wage at the same time. Thus, there are few low-paying jobs offering a combination of informal (or formal) training and skill-building experience. This makes it difficult for low-skill workers to acquire the training and experience necessary to move up to better, higher-paying jobs.

Several proposals have been suggested to minimize these negative effects. Some economists favor abolition of the minimum wage. Others would exempt teenagers from the legislation's coverage. Still others would exempt long-term unemployed workers from the legislation. In each case, the advocates argue that the wages of low-skill workers would settle at a market equilibrium, and the long-run employment and training opportunities available to such workers would improve.

---

[11]For additional information on this topic, see Charles Brown, Curtis Gilroy, and Andrew Cohen, "The Effect of Minimum Wage on Employment and Unemployment," *Journal of Economic Literature* 20, June 1982, pp. 487–528.

PROVIDING TRAINING OPPORTUNITIES

Unemployment may result from mismatches between the requirements of available jobs and the skills of potential workers. Many economists believe that programs designed to improve the basic skills of workers and facilitate the development of new skills could reduce the natural rate of unemployment. Of course, improvement in our elementary and secondary educational system would be a step in that direction. Others believe that a vocational-training-loan program, similar in design to present college-loan programs, would assist low- and middle-income youths in developing technical skills. Martin Feldstein, chairman of the Council of Economic Advisers under President Reagan, suggested that training subsidies (scholarships) be provided for youthful workers (for example, persons under 25 years of age) who maintain jobs, but do not attend college. These wage supplements might be limited to employment that provided the youthful workers significant amounts of on-the-job technical training. Such a plan would reward youthful workers for both continuous employment and the acquisition of craft, clerical, operative, and perhaps even managerial skills. The long-run goal of such training programs is to improve the quality and flexibility of the labor force. Accomplishment of this objective would lead to a lower natural rate of unemployment because it would reduce the frequency and duration of unemployment.

DEMOGRAPHICS AND THE NATURAL RATE OF UNEMPLOYMENT

Compared to their elders, youthful workers are more likely to switch back and forth between the labor force and school. And even after they permanently enter the labor force, they are more likely to switch jobs as they search for a career path. Because of this, younger workers historically experience higher unemployment rates. In fact, the unemployment rate of persons under age 25 has typically run three times or more the rate for workers age 35 and over. For people age 25–34, the unemployment rate has generally been at least one and one-half times the rate for their older counterparts (see **Exhibit 14–10,** part "b").

Given the less stable employment pattern of youthful workers, the natural rate of unemployment rises as they make up a larger share of the labor force. As Exhibit 14–10, part "a" shows, this is precisely what happened during the 1958–1980 period. As those born during the "baby boom" following the Second World War entered the work force during the 1960s and 1970s, the labor force grew rapidly and became progressively younger. In 1958 workers age 16–24 constituted only 15.6 percent of the labor force. By 1980 nearly one out of every four (23.7 percent) labor-force participants was in this age group. Similarly, young adults age 25–34 also increased as a proportion of the work force between 1958 and 1980. In contrast, workers over age 35 were a shrinking proportion of the labor force during the 1958–1980 period. As the youthful segments of the labor force grew rapidly, the natural rate of unemployment rose. Research in this area indicates that the natural rate of unemployment was between 0.5 percent and 1.5 percent

Since younger workers have less stable employment patterns (part "b"), the natural rate of unemployment rises when they comprise a larger share of the labor force. This was the case during the 1958–1980 period (part "a"). During the next decade, however, youthful workers will become a smaller proportion of the labor force. This will reduce the natural rate of unemployment during the 1990s.

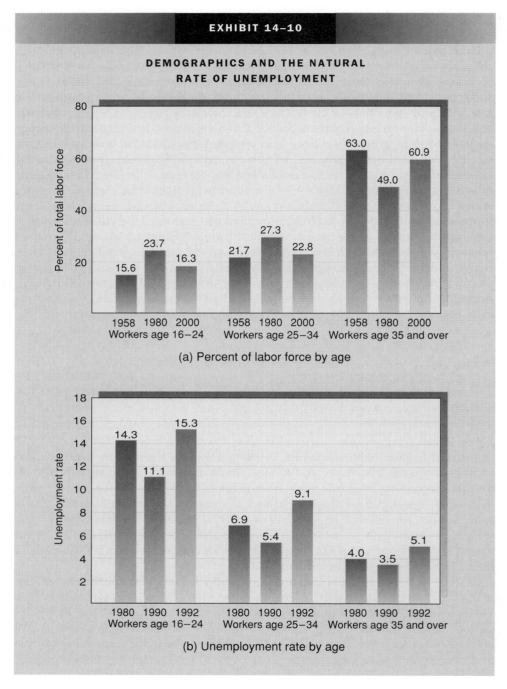

EXHIBIT 14–10

DEMOGRAPHICS AND THE NATURAL RATE OF UNEMPLOYMENT

(a) Percent of labor force by age

(b) Unemployment rate by age

higher in 1980 than in 1958 as a result of this factor. Obviously, it has contributed to the high unemployment rates of the 1970s and 1980s.

However, this adverse demographic factor has now reversed itself. By the year 2000 people age 16–24 are projected to comprise 16.3 percent of the work force, substantially lower than the 1980 figure. Conversely, projections indicate that workers age 35 and over will comprise 60.9 percent of the labor force in 2000, up from 49 percent in 1980 (see part "a" of Exhibit 14–10). Economic theory indicates that this maturing of the U.S. work force during the next decade will reduce the natural rate of unemployment.

LOOKING AHEAD

Now that we have integrated expectations into our analysis, we are prepared to take a closer look at the potential of macroeconomic policy as a stabilization tool. The next chapter focuses on stabilization policy and related issues.

CHAPTER SUMMARY

1. The impact of demand-stimulus policies is dependent on whether the effects are anticipated. When the effects are unanticipated, an increase in aggregate demand will temporarily expand real GDP beyond the economy's long-run output potential. In contrast, when decision makers correctly anticipate the effects of expansionary policy, real output will remain unchanged even though the price level increases.

2. There are two major theories as to how expectations are formed: the adaptive-expectations hypothesis and the rational-expectations hypothesis.

3. According to the adaptive-expectations hypothesis, individuals base their expectations for the future on observations of the recent past. Expectations for the future will lag behind observed changes.

4. The rational-expectations hypothesis assumes that people use all pertinent information, including data on the conduct of current policy, in forming their expectations about the future. While decision makers make forecasting errors under rational expectations, the errors are not systematic. They are as likely to overestimate as to underestimate the future change in an economic variable.

5. The Phillips curve indicates the relationship between the unemployment rate and inflation rate. Prior to the 1970s there was a widespread belief that higher inflation would lower the rate of unemployment.

6. Integrating expectations into macroeconomics makes it clear that any trade-off between unemployment and inflation is unstable. With adaptive expectations, expansionary policies will lead to a short-run trade-off of lower unemployment for an acceleration in the inflation rate. Individuals, though, will eventually come to expect the higher inflation rate and alter their decisions accordingly. This will cause unemployment to return to the natural rate.

7. With rational expectations, there is no consistent unemployment-inflation trade-off, not even in the short run. The impact of expansionary macropolicy is unpredictable. If decision makers accurately forecast the inflationary effects, expansionary policies will cause inflation while leaving the unemployment rate unchanged. However, if expansionary policy leads to an increase in inflation that exceeds (is less than) the expected increase, unemployment will temporarily fall below (rise above) its long-run normal level.

8. Contrary to the expectations of the 1960s, expansionary policy during the post-1965 period did not consistently reduce the unemployment rate. There is no evidence that in the long run inflationary policies can reduce the unemployment rate—that inflation can be "traded off" for unemployment. Both adaptive- and rational-expectations theories imply that the long-run Phillips curve is vertical at the natural rate of unemployment.

9. The modern view of the Phillips curve integrates the effect of expectations. When the inflation rate is greater than anticipated, unemployment will tend to fall below the natural rate. Conversely, when the inflation rate is less than anticipated, unemployment will rise above its natural rate. Even high rates of inflation will fail to reduce unemployment once they are anticipated by decision makers.

10. The validity of the adaptive- versus rational-expectations hypotheses is a topic of current debate among economists. Proponents of adaptive expectations believe that the expectations used in real-world decision making are typically based on a simple rule of thumb that the future rate of inflation will be similar to the recent past. They charge that the rational-expectations hypothesis implies that people possess an unrealistic amount of knowledge about how the economy works. Proponents of rational expectations counter that it is naive to believe that decision makers ignore information concerning how inflation is actually generated. They argue that relatively uninformed people will consult specialists. Choices made as a result will alter the nature of long-term contracts and thereby reduce the impact of inflation on real economic variables.

11. In recent years, economists have given increased attention to the importance of incentives in the determination of the natural rate of unemployment. Many

economists believe that the unemployment-compensation system, minimum wage legislation, and inadequate educational and training programs contribute to the high current rate of unemployment. Reform in these areas could lower the natural rate of unemployment.

12. During the 1960s and 1970s, rapid growth in the number of youthful labor-force participants increased the natural rate of unemployment. This demographic factor has now been reversed. As a share of the labor force, youthful workers will decline during the next decade. This will tend to reduce the natural rate of unemployment in the 1990s.

CRITICAL-ANALYSIS QUESTIONS

1. Suppose the monetary authorities accelerate the annual growth rate of the money supply from a long-term trend of 5 percent to 10 percent. If decision makers do not anticipate the effects of this policy change, how will it influence output, employment, and prices in the short run? If the effects are anticipated, how will the expansionary policy influence output, employment, and prices in the short run?

2. State in your own words the adaptive-expectations hypothesis. Explain why adaptive expectations imply that macroacceleration will only temporarily reduce the rate of unemployment.

3. Compare and contrast the rational-expectations hypothesis with the adaptive-expectations hypothesis. If expectations are formed "rationally" rather than "adaptively," will it be easier or more difficult to decelerate the inflation rate without causing an economic recession? Explain.

*4. How does the microeconomic approach to the problems of unemployment and economic growth differ from the traditional monetary and fiscal policy approach to these problems? Is the microeconomic approach a substitute for traditional monetary and fiscal policy? Explain.

5. After a period of persistent inflation, such as was experienced in the United States during the 1974–1981 period, most economists believe that a shift to restrictive monetary policy to reduce the inflation rate will cause a recession. Why? How could the monetary authorities minimize the danger of a severe, lengthy recession?

*6. Prior to the mid-1970s, many economists thought a higher rate of unemployment would reduce the inflation rate. Why? How does the modern view of the Phillips curve differ from the earlier view?

7. Why do most economists think the natural rate of unemployment rose during the 1960s and 1970s? Why do these same economists think the natural rate will fall during the next decade?

8. Throughout the 1960s, many economists believed that expansionary macroeconomic policy would result in both more inflation and less unemployment. How would acceptance of this theory influence policy-makers? Did the theory exert any impact on policy? Cite supportive evidence.

*9. Modern analysis rejects the view that inflationary policies reduce the long-term unemployment rate. How does this theory influence macroeconomic policy? Explain.

10. Suppose that a country were currently experiencing 10 percent inflation. Policy-makers want to achieve stable prices with a minimum reduction in output. What advice would you give them?

11. Evaluate each of the following statements:
   a. "The primary cause of inflation is excessive government spending."
   b. "The primary cause of inflation is large budget deficits."
   c. "The primary cause of inflation is the greed of business and labor leaders."

*12. Suppose that after 10 weeks of drawing unemployment compensation, the benefits were reduced weekly until they were phased out after 26 weeks. How might this policy influence the natural rate of unemployment? Discuss the pros and cons of such a policy.

13. How would you expect the actual unemployment rate to compare with the natural unemployment rate in the following cases?
   a. Prices are stable and have been stable for the last four years.
   b. The current inflation rate is 3 percent, and this rate was widely anticipated more than a year ago.
   c. Expansionary policies lead to an unexpected increase in the inflation rate from 3 percent to 7 percent.
   d. There is an unexpected reduction in the inflation rate from 7 percent to 2 percent.

*14. Explain what happens to real wages, the job-search time of workers, and the unemployment rate when there is unanticipated inflation. What happens when the inflation is anticipated?

15. The proponents of rational expectations argue that the cost of decelerating the inflation rate and moving to price stability will be reduced if people believe that the

---

*Asterisk denotes questions for which answers are given in Appendix C.

monetary authorities are really going to achieve and maintain stable prices. Why is this credibility important? How might the monetary authorities enhance the credibility of their policies?

16. Answer the following questions:
   a. What would cause the short-run Phillips curve to shift?
   b. What would cause the long-run Phillips curve to shift?

*17. Several European countries provide weekly unemployment benefits to persons for as long as they remain unemployed. Can you think of problems that are likely to accompany a program of this type? What impact will it have on the rate of unemployment?

18. If the Treasury issued indexed bonds, do you think this would result in a more stable monetary policy? Why or why not? How would the issuance of indexed bonds affect the ability of the federal government to gain at the expense of bondholders if a more expansionary monetary policy was followed? How would this influence the incentive of government officials to follow more inflationary policies? Do you think this is good or bad? Why?

*Asterisk denotes questions for which answers are given in Appendix C.

CHAPTER FIFTEEN

STABILIZATION POLICY, OUTPUT, AND EMPLOYMENT

Unfortunately, policymakers cannot act as if the economy is an automobile that can quickly be steered back and forth. Rather, the procedure of changing aggregate demand is much closer to that of a captain navigating a giant super-tanker. Even if he gives a signal for a hard turn, it takes a mile before he can see a change, and ten miles before the ship makes the turn.

ROBERT J. GORDON[1]

CHAPTER FOCUS

■ *Historically, how much has real output fluctuated? Are economic fluctuations becoming more or less severe?*
■ *Can macroeconomic policy moderate the business cycle?*
■ *Why is proper timing of changes in macroeconomic policy crucial to the effectiveness of stabilization policy? Why is proper timing difficult to achieve?*
■ *Would we have more or less instability if policy-makers simply expanded the money supply at a low, constant rate each year while balancing the federal budget?*
■ *Should policy-makers try to smooth minor ups and downs in the growth path of real GDP?*

---

[1]Robert J. Gordon, *Macroeconomics* (Boston: Little, Brown, 1978), p. 334.

D uring the 1960s, economists were highly confident that macroeconomic policy could neutralize the economic ups and downs of the business cycle. Some even thought that the business cycle, like polio, would soon be banished to the pages of history. In the 1973 edition of his all-time best-selling text, Nobel laureate Paul Samuelson reflected this general optimism when he forecast that we may have to redefine "the cycle so that stagnant growth below the trend potential of growth is to be called recession even though absolute growth has not vanished."[2]

Subsequent events have tempered this optimism. We now know that proper timing of macroeconomic policy is far more difficult than was perceived during the 1960s and 1970s. Although we have already discussed the effects of monetary and fiscal policy, we have generally glossed over the problem of proper timing. However, proper timing is crucial if macroeconomic policy is going to smooth the ups and downs of the business cycle. In this chapter, we will focus on the tools that enhance and the factors that limit our ability to time macropolicy properly. We will begin by taking a look at the historical record.

ECONOMIC FLUCTUATIONS— THE HISTORICAL RECORD

Wide fluctuations in the general level of business activity—in income, employment, and the price level—make personal economic planning extremely difficult. Such changes can cause even well-devised investment plans to go awry. The tragic stories of unemployed workers begging for food and newly impoverished investors jumping out of windows during the Great Depression vividly portray the enormous personal and social costs of economic instability and the uncertainty that it generates.

Historically, substantial fluctuations in real output have occurred. **Exhibit 15–1** illustrates the growth record of real GDP in the United States during the last 80 years. Prior to the Second World War, double-digit swings in real GDP during a single year were not uncommon. Real GDP rose by more than 10 percent annually during the First World War, during an economic boom in 1922, during a mid-1930s recovery, and again during the Second World War. In contrast, output fell at an annual rate of 5 percent or more during the 1920–1921 recession, in the Depression years 1930, 1931, 1932, and 1938, and again following the Second World War. During the last four decades, economic ups and downs have been more moderate. Nevertheless, substantial fluctuations are still observable.

ACTIVISM VERSUS NONACTIVISM— AN OVERVIEW

There is widespread agreement concerning the goals of macroeconomic policy. Economists of almost all persuasions believe that the performance of a market economy would be improved if economic fluctuations were minimal, prices were

---

[2]Paul Samuelson, *Economics*, 9th ed. (New York: McGraw-Hill, 1973), p. 266.

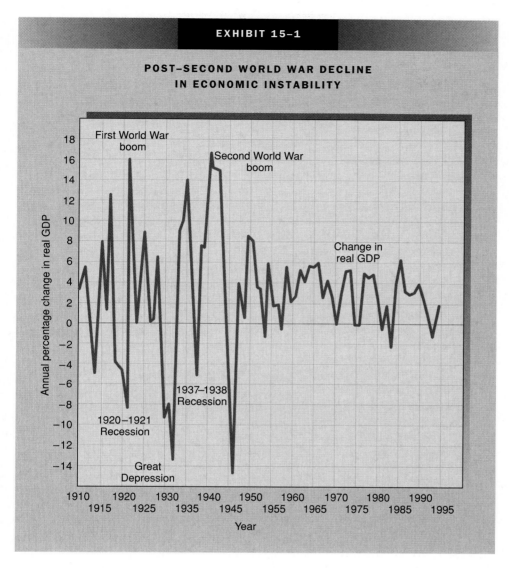

EXHIBIT 15–1

POST–SECOND WORLD WAR DECLINE
IN ECONOMIC INSTABILITY

First World War boom

Second World War boom

Change in real GDP

1937–1938 Recession

1920–1921 Recession

Great Depression

Annual percentage change in real GDP

Year

Prior to the conclusion of the Second World War, the United States experienced double-digit increases in real GDP (in 1918, 1922, 1935–1936, 1941–1943) and double-digit declines in real GDP (in 1930–1932 and 1946). In contrast, fluctuations in real GDP have moderated during the last four decades. Most economists believe that more appropriate macropolicy—particularly monetary policy—deserves much of the credit (see Exhibit 15–3).

Sources: *Historical Statistics of the United States,* p. 224; *Economic Report of the President,* 1994.

stable, and employment were at a high level (unemployment at the natural rate). How to achieve these goals is, however, a hot topic of debate among macroeconomists. In some respects, the current debate is an extension of earlier disagreements between Keynesians and monetarists. While consensus positions emerged from the Keynesian-monetarist debate in several areas—the potency of money and the transmission path of monetary policy, for example—this was not true with regard to the conduct of stabilization policy.

Most macroeconomists, particularly those of Keynesian persuasion, favor an **activist strategy.** According to the activist's view, it is reasonable to expect that discretionary macroeconomic policy will reduce economic instability. Not all activists are Keynesians. However activism generally reflects the Keynesian tradition. Activists have little confidence in the ability of a market economy to self-correct in response to inevitable economic shocks such as poor harvests, drastic changes in oil prices, or a strike in a major industry. Indeed, some activists charge

Activist strategy
Deliberate changes in monetary and fiscal policy in order to inject demand stimulus during a recession and apply restraint during an inflationary boom and thereby, it is hoped, minimize economic instability.

that market economies are inherently unstable—that both economic expansions and contractions tend to feed on themselves. According to this view, business expansion will induce additional investment and consumption that exert a *multiplier effect* and lead to an inflationary boom. Resources, though, constrain the economy. Rapid expansion in real output cannot proceed indefinitely. Growth of output will eventually slow. When this happens, optimism often turns to pessimism, which triggers a downturn. The multiplier effect also amplifies the downswing, creating unused industrial capacity and widespread unemployment. The proponents of the inherent-instability view generally point to the volatile behavior of expenditures on consumer durables and private investment as evidence for their position.

Other activists argue that although the self-corrective mechanism of a market economy works, the restoration of full employment via lower real-wage rates and interest rates is likely to be a lengthy process. They thus believe that prudent use of monetary and fiscal policy can speed the adjustment process and minimize the cost of economic instability.

Exhibit 15–2 illustrates the basic idea of the activists' strategy. Ideally, macroeconomic policy would apply demand restraint during an economic boom and demand stimulus during a recession. During an economic boom, then, proper macroeconomic policy would couple a deceleration in the growth rate of the money supply with movement toward a budget surplus (or smaller deficit). This would help restrain aggregate demand and thereby minimize the potential inflationary side effects of the boom. In contrast, when the economy dips into a recession, activist stabilization policy would shift toward stimulus. The money supply would be expanded more rapidly than normal, while budgetary policy would plan a budget deficit.

Activists believe it is feasible to apply macropolicy so that restraint will retard inflation during an economic boom and stimulus will minimize the decline in output during a recession. When macroeconomic policy is applied in this manner, it will reduce the swings in real GDP (as illustrated in part "a" of Exhibit 15–2) and employment.

Nonactivist strategy
The maintenance of the same monetary and fiscal policy—that is, no change in money growth, tax rates, or expenditures—during all phases of the business cycle.

In contrast with activist strategy, **nonactivist strategy** is based on the idea that we can best moderate the business cycle by adopting rules and guidelines (for example, a constant growth rate in the money supply and a balanced budget over the business cycle) that provide for stable monetary and fiscal policy, independent of current economic conditions. Furthermore, nonactivists argue that discretionary use of monetary and fiscal policy in response to changing economic conditions is likely to do more damage than good. They charge that erratic policy, particularly the instability of monetary policy, is a major source of economic fluctuations.

Clearly, the nonactivist view is reflective of the monetarists' tradition and the more recent developments in new classical economics. Nonactivists reject the view that minor disturbances, magnified by a multiplier effect, inevitably lead to either a recession or inflationary boom. They emphasize that consumption, the major component of spending, is relatively stable over the business cycle. Counter to the "instability feeds on itself" view, individuals cushion the effects of a downturn by dipping into their savings and maintaining a high level of consumer demand during a recession. Simultaneously, lower real wages will stimulate employment and lower real interest rates will encourage the purchase of both investment goods and consumer durables during a recession.

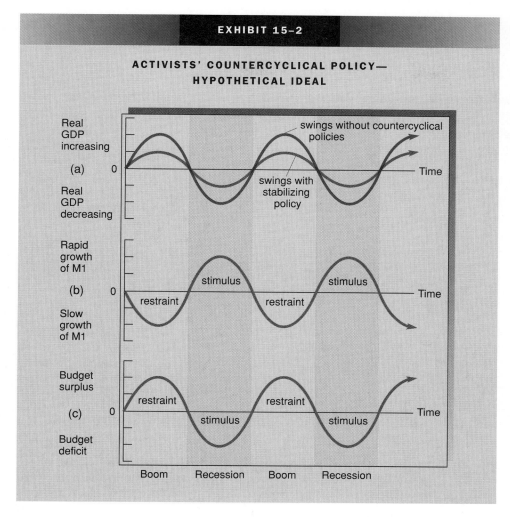

EXHIBIT 15–2

**ACTIVISTS' COUNTERCYCLICAL POLICY—
HYPOTHETICAL IDEAL**

Activists believe that macroeconomic policy based on current economic indicators can help stabilize the economy. Here we illustrate the hypothetical ideal in which both monetary and fiscal policy restrain demand during an inflationary boom and add stimulus during a recession.

According to the nonactivist view, the self-corrective mechanism of a market economy works quite well. If not stifled by perverse macroeconomic policy, nonactivists believe that the economy's self-correcting mechanism will prevent prolonged periods of economic decline and high unemployment. Nonactivists note that the really serious cases of economic instability, such as the Great Depression and the inflation of the 1970s, were primarily the result of policy errors, not an inherent instability of markets.

Activists and nonactivists agree that in the past, policy errors contributed to economic instability. Prior to the Keynesian revolution, governments often raised taxes to balance the budget as revenue declined during a recession. Of course, modern analysis implies that such a policy would add to the severity of the recession. Correspondingly, as **Exhibit 15–3** illustrates, extreme gyrations in the money supply characterized monetary policy prior to the Second World War. Prior to 1947, sharp contractions in the money supply often accompanied major recessions. For example, the M2 money supply declined at an annual rate of 6 percent during the 1920–1921 recession, and by 15 percent annually as the United States entered

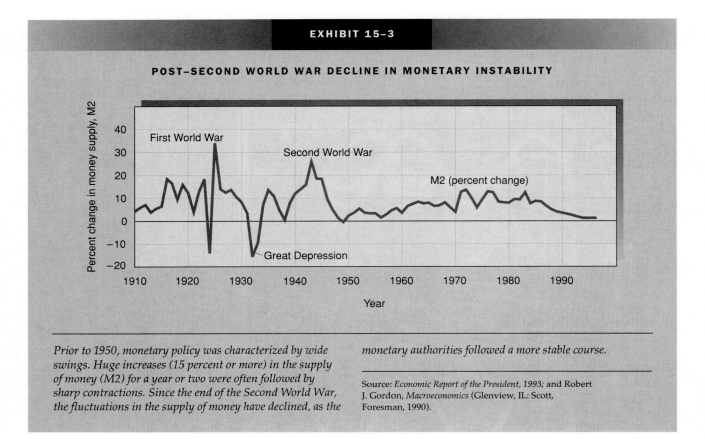

EXHIBIT 15–3

POST–SECOND WORLD WAR DECLINE IN MONETARY INSTABILITY

Prior to 1950, monetary policy was characterized by wide swings. Huge increases (15 percent or more) in the supply of money (M2) for a year or two were often followed by sharp contractions. Since the end of the Second World War, the fluctuations in the supply of money have declined, as the monetary authorities followed a more stable course.

Source: *Economic Report of the President, 1993*; and Robert J. Gordon, *Macroeconomics* (Glenview, IL: Scott, Foresman, 1990).

into the Great Depression; it dipped again during the 1937–1938 relapse of the economy. In contrast, double-digit growth rates in the money supply were observed during the inflationary periods of the First and Second World Wars. One need not be a monetarist (or nonactivist) to recognize that the erratic changes in the money supply contributed to instability prior to the Second World War.[3]

While monetary fluctuations have continued since the post-Second World War period, they have been much less erratic. As Exhibit 15–3 illustrates, during the last four decades, the annual growth rate of the M2 money supply has generally been within the 3 percent to 9 percent range. Correspondingly, modern governments seldom raise taxes during a business recession. As Exhibit 15–1 shows, more moderate swings in real output have accompanied the increased stability of monetary and fiscal policy during the postwar era.

---

[3]Macropolicy during the heyday of classical economic theory once again illustrates that ideas have consequences "both when they are right and when they are wrong" (to quote Keynes). Since classical economists thought the budget should be balanced annually, taxes were often raised during recessions prior to the Keynesian revolution. Similarly, classical economists, thinking price adjustments were both quick and painless, did not think that changes in the supply of money exerted much influence on real output. Thus, they paid little heed to monetary instability. For a detailed analysis of monetary instability, see Milton Friedman and Anna Schwartz, *A Monetary History of the United States, 1867–1960* (Princeton: Princeton University Press, 1963).

Activists and nonactivists agree that the link between the more stable macro-economic policy and moderation of the business cycle is no coincidence.

ACTIVIST STABILIZATION POLICY

Macroeconomic policy reduces instability only if it injects stimulus and applies restraint at the proper phase of the business cycle. Proper timing is the key to effective stabilization policy. But how can policy-makers know whether they should be stimulating aggregate demand or applying the economic brake?

Of course, economic indicators such as the unemployment rate, growth of real GDP, and the **industrial capacity-utilization rate** will provide policy-makers with information concerning the current state of the economy (see "Measures of Economic Activity" boxed feature). It takes time, though, for macroeconomic policy to work. Because of this, policy-makers really need to know about the future—where the economy is going to be 6 to 12 months from now. They need to know whether a business recession or an inflationary boom is around the corner. If they do not know where the economy is going, a policy change may fail to exert its primary impact quickly enough to offset a downturn or restrain future inflation.

How can policy-makers find out where the economy is going in the future and when a turn in the macroeconomic road is about to occur? The two most widely used sources of information on the future direction of the economy are the index of leading economic indicators and economic forecasting models.

Industrial capacity-utilization rate
An index designed to measure the extent to which the economy's existing plant and equipment capacity is being used.

MEASURES OF ECONOMIC ACTIVITY

CAPACITY-UTILIZATION RATE

The capacity-utilization rate is a ratio of actual output to capacity output, expressed as a percent. It is intended to measure the extent to which industrial facilities are being used to attain their potential output. The Bureau of Economic Analysis (BEA) conducts a quarterly survey that asks a random sample of industrial firms to report their capacity utilization as a percent of *practical capacity*, defined as the greatest level of output that the firm's existing plant and equipment could achieve, assuming (1) the availability of labor and other variable inputs and (2) normal, expected downtime for maintenance. The company utilization rates are weighted by asset size and then used to derive utilization rates for total industry and various subsectors (for example, manufacturing, mining, and utilities).

Just as one would not expect 100 percent employ-ment in a world of uncertainty and imperfect information, neither would one expect 100 percent utilization of plant capacity. Since the measure of capacity is based on the subjective views of firms' managers rather than actual experience, we cannot even be sure that it would be possible for a firm to achieve 100 percent capacity. It is not surprising, then, that broad capacity-utilization rates are generally well below 100 percent.

During the last three decades, the industrial capacity-utilization rate has averaged approximately 83 percent. Utilization rates as high as 90 percent have been achieved only during wartime. Most economists interpret the significance of current capacity-utilization rates by comparing them with past peaks and lows. A low rate compared to the rates of recent years indicates underutilization of industrial capacity, while a high rate indicates intensive use. Capacity-utilization rates are reported monthly in the *Federal Reserve Bulletin*.

INDEX OF LEADING INDICATORS

Index of leading indicators
An index of economic variables that historically has tended to turn down prior to the beginning of a recession and turn up prior to the beginning of a business expansion.

The **index of leading indicators** is a composite statistic based on 11 key variables that generally turn down prior to a recession and turn up before the beginning of a business expansion (see the "Measures of Economic Activity, Index of Leading Indicators" box). **Exhibit 15–4** illustrates the path of the index during the 1950–1993 period. This index has forecast each of the eight recessions since 1950. On four occasions, the turndown occurred eight to eleven months prior to a recession, providing policymakers with sufficient lead time to modify policy, particularly monetary policy. There has been significant variability, however, in the lead time of the index. Sometimes it is exceedingly short—the index declined just five months prior to the recession of 1954. In other instances it has been quite lengthy,

MEASURES OF ECONOMIC ACTIVITY

INDEX OF LEADING INDICATORS

History indicates that no single indicator is able to accurately forecast the future direction of the economy. However, several economic variables do tend to reach a high or low prior to the peak of a business expansion or the trough of an economic recession. Such variables are called *leading economic indicators*.

To provide more reliable information on the future direction of the economy, economists have devised an index of 11 such indicators:

1. Length of the average workweek in hours.
2. Initial weekly claims for unemployment compensation.
3. New orders placed with manufacturers.
4. Percent of companies receiving slower deliveries from suppliers.
5. Contracts and orders for new plants and equipment.
6. Permits for new housing starts.
7. Change in unfilled orders for durable goods.
8. Change in sensitive materials prices.
9. Change in the index of stock prices (500 common stocks).
10. Change in money supply (M2).
11. Index of consumer expectations.

Each component in the series is standardized and weighted according to its past performance as an indicator of macroeconomic turns. The variables included in the index were chosen both because of their tendency to lead (or predict) turns in the business cycle and because they are available frequently and promptly.

In some cases, it is easy to see why a change in an economic indicator precedes a change in general economic activity. Consider the indicator of "new orders placed with manufacturers" (measured in constant dollars). Manufacturers are usually quite willing to expand output in response to new orders. Thus, an expansion in the volume of orders is generally followed by an expansion in manufacturing output. Similarly, manufacturers will tend to scale back their future production when a decline in new orders signals the probability of weak future demand for their products.

The percentage change in the index is reported monthly. Two or three consecutive monthly declines in the index is considered a warning that the economy is about to dip into a recession. However, an up or down turn in the index for just a few months should be interpreted with caution. As Exhibit 15–4 indicates, brief downturns in the index are not always a reliable indicator that a recession is just around the corner. The components of the index of leading indicators often provide conflicting signals. One component may be signaling continued expansion while another indicates that a recession is imminent. It usually takes several months of continuous expansion or contraction in the index before all (or most all) of the components provide a consistent signal.

The index of leading indicators is calculated monthly by the Bureau of Economic Analysis of the Department of Commerce and published monthly in the *Survey of Current Business*.

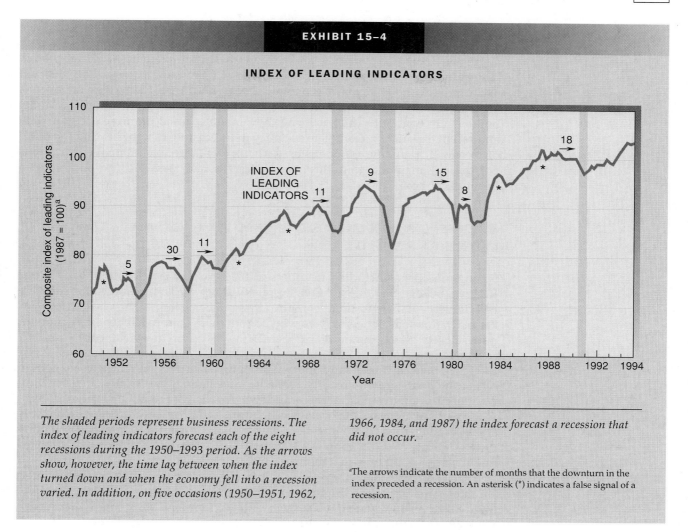

EXHIBIT 15-4

INDEX OF LEADING INDICATORS

The shaded periods represent business recessions. The index of leading indicators forecast each of the eight recessions during the 1950–1993 period. As the arrows show, however, the time lag between when the index turned down and when the economy fell into a recession varied. In addition, on five occasions (1950–1951, 1962, *1966, 1984, and 1987) the index forecast a recession that did not occur.*

^aThe arrows indicate the number of months that the downturn in the index preceded a recession. An asterisk (*) indicates a false signal of a recession.

as when it turned down 30 months prior to the recession of 1957–1958 and 18 months prior to the 1990–1991 recession.

Worse still, the index is not always an accurate indicator of the future. On five occasions (1950–1951, 1962, 1966, 1984, and 1987), a downturn in the index of leading indicators forecast a future recession that did not materialize. This has given rise to the quip that the index has accurately forecast thirteen of the last eight recessions.

FORECASTING MODELS

Economists have developed highly complex *econometric* (statistical) models to improve the accuracy of macroeconomic forecasts. In essence, these models use past data on economic interrelationships to project how currently observed changes will influence the future path of key economic variables such as real GDP, employment, and the price level. The most elaborate of these models use hundreds of variables and equations to simulate the various sectors and macroeconomic markets. Powerful, high-speed computers are employed to analyze the effects of various policy alternatives and attempt to predict the future.

To date, the record of computer forecasting models is mixed. When economic conditions are relatively stable, they generally provide accurate forecasts for both aggregate economic variables and important subcomponents of the economy. Unfortunately, they are much less effective at forecasting turns in the business cycle and the impact of major economic shocks. Of course, the models are only as accurate as the programmed relationships developed by their builders. Model builders are constantly restructuring their models, based on more accurate data and recent experience. Complete accuracy in forecasting may be beyond the reach of economics. Many economists, particularly those of rational-expectations persuasion, maintain that this is indeed the case (see the "Applications in Economics" box).

MARKETS AND DISCRETIONARY MONETARY POLICY

Some economists, including members of the Board of Governors of the Federal Reserve, believe that information supplied by key market relationships can help Fed decision makers formulate appropriate policy changes. There are three market indicators that policy-makers who adhere to this approach generally monitor quite closely: (1) commodity prices, (2) the slope of the yield curve, and (3) exchange rates.

Since they fluctuate daily and are determined in auction markets, changes in *commodity prices* provide readily available information that is often an early indicator of future movement in the price level. An increase in a broad index of commodity prices indicates that money is plentiful and provides the Fed with an early signal to shift toward a more restrictive policy. In contrast, falling commodity prices indicate that deflation is a potential future danger, in which case, the Fed might want to shift toward a more expansionary policy.

The *yield curve* maps the relationship between short-term and long-term interest rates. The longer the duration of a loan, the greater the possibility of change that will adversely affect the borrower's ability to repay. Thus, longer-term loans are more risky and consequently generally command a higher interest rate. As a result, the normal yield curve will slope upward, going from short-term to long-term interest rates. The further away the maturity date of the bond, the higher the interest rate will be. For example, a 30-year government security might have an interest rate of 9 percent, while a one-year security might have one of only 6 percent. However, when the demand for money is strong relative to the supply, short-term rates will rise relative to the long-term rates because short-term instruments, such as three-month Treasury bills and 90-day certificates of deposit (CDs), are a close substitute for money. Higher short-term interest rates relative to long-term rates imply that money is scarcer. This is a signal for the Fed to move toward a more expansionary policy. Alternatively, if long-term interest rates were abnormally high relative to short-term rates, this would imply that markets fear future inflation and think the current policy is too expansionary. This would be a signal to the Fed to shift to a more restrictive policy.

Finally, *exchange rates* provide additional information about what markets think of current monetary policy. A decline in the exchange-rate value of the dollar (the value of the dollar relative to other currencies) often implies a fear of higher inflation and a reluctance to hold dollars. This would signal the need to

APPLICATIONS IN ECONOMICS

HOW ACCURATE IS ECONOMIC FORECASTING?

Economic forecasting is the occupation that makes astrology respectable.

DAVID DREMAS[1]

Businesses and government units often pay thousands of dollars for the economic projections of highly complex computer forecasting models. Critical business and financial decisions are often based on the forecasts. It can be argued, however, that economic theory is sometimes oversold as a tool for predicting the future, for the following two reasons:

1. *Future changes in market conditions will primarily reflect events that cannot be foreseen.* Current market prices reflect both current conditions and future changes that are widely anticipated. For example, today's grain prices reflect not only current weather conditions in the grain belt but also the normal ones that are expected in the future. Any unanticipated future developments, such as abnormal rainfall, will change those prices. The same logic also applies to macroeconomic markets. Future market conditions will differ from the present, primarily as the result of economic changes that we cannot foresee—for example, an unexpected policy change, discovery of a new resource or technology, abnormal weather, or political upheaval in an important oil-exporting nation. There is no reason to believe that economists or anyone else will be able to predict such changes accurately and consistently. Thus, while economic theory helps to predict the *implications* of unforeseen events, it cannot foretell what those events will be.

2. *Decision makers will often make different choices in the future because of what they learn from the past.* The past is thus an imperfect indicator of the future. Almost all forecasters, including those who rely on complex computer models, use past relationships to project the future. In a world where people learn from experience, though, forecasts based on past relationships will never fully capture the future. The experience of the 1970s illustrates this point. Prior to 1970, the unemployment rate generally declined when prices rose more rapidly. Most forecasting models in the 1970s thus assumed that a higher inflation rate would reduce unemployment. Things did not turn out that way. The 1970s were different because people adjusted their decision making in light of past experience with inflation.

While macroeconomic forecasts are often quite accurate during normal times (when the growth of real GDP and the inflation rate are relatively steady), they usually miss major turns in the economic road. For example, none of the major computer models of the U.S. economy predicted the 1982 recession and the sharp deceleration of the inflation rate during 1982–1984. Neither were these models able to forecast the recession of 1990–1991. Unfortunately, it was precisely these turns that were most important from the viewpoint of economic policy-makers.

[1]David Dremas, "The Madness of Crowds," *Forbes*, September 27, 1982, p. 201.

shift to a more restrictive policy. Conversely, an increase in the exchange-rate value of the dollar is a strong vote of confidence in the future purchasing power of the dollar. This provides the Fed with some leeway to move toward a more expansionary policy.

If all three of these market indicators pointed in the same direction, then this would provide the Fed with a strong signal. For example, if commodity prices were falling, if short-term interest rates were abnormally high relative to long-term rates, and if the dollar were appreciating on the foreign exchange market, then these would provide strong evidence that current policy was restrictive. A shift toward a more expansionary policy would be in order. However, the world is generally not this simple, and the signals are often inconclusive or conflicting. In any case, most proponents of the validity of these signals currently believe that they should be used as a supplement to, rather than as a substitute for, other indicators monitored in the formulation of activist policy.

ACTIVIST VIEW OF DISCRETIONARY POLICY

Activists recognize that it is difficult to institute countercyclical macroeconomic policy. Nevertheless, they believe that discretionary action by policy-makers can help smooth business ups and downs.

The activist view stresses that the index of leading indicators, forecasting models, sensitive market variables, and other economic indicators provide policy-makers with an early warning system, alerting them to the need for a change in macroeconomic policy. Consequently, policy-makers have sufficient time to institute moderate changes in macroeconomic policy immediately and more substantial changes with the passage of time if additional information indicates they are needed.

The following scenario outlines the essentials of the activists' view. Suppose the economy were about to dip into a recession. Prior to the recession, the index of leading indicators would almost surely alert policy-makers to the possibility of a downturn. This would permit them to shift toward macroeconomic stimulus, expanding the money supply more rapidly. Initially, the shift toward macroeconomic stimulus could be applied in moderate doses. It could then be easily offset with future action. On the other hand, if the signs of a downturn became more pronounced and current business conditions actually weakened, additional stimulus could be injected. Perhaps a tax reduction or a speed-up in government expenditures might be used to supplement the more expansionary monetary policy.

Policy-makers can constantly monitor the situation as they inject additional stimulus. As economic indicators provide additional information with the passage of time, policy-makers can adjust their actions accordingly. If the weakness persists, the expansionary policy can be continued. Conversely, when the signs point to a strong recovery, policy-makers can move toward restraint and thereby head off potential inflationary pressure. According to the activist's view, the economy is more likely to stay on track when policy-makers are free to apply stimulus or restraint based on current information and economic conditions.

Activists point to the reduction in instability during the post–Second World War period as proof that discretionary policies enhance stability (see Exhibit 15–1). The United States has experienced five decades of economic growth without either a Great Depression or hyperinflation. Activists ask, "Who knows what disasters stabilization policies have prevented?" Even though minor mistakes have been made, activist policies have kept the economy on track. And activists believe that the future record will improve as better forecasting models are developed and data providing for early warnings of economic change are improved. They argue that now is not the time to discard a system that is working.

THE NONACTIVIST CASE

Nonactivists argue that economic and political factors undermine the potential effectiveness of discretionary macroeconomic policy. There are three major reasons why they believe discretionary policy will be ineffective as a stabilization tool.

LAGS AND THE PROBLEM OF TIMING

Discretionary changes in both monetary and fiscal policy must be timed properly if they are going to exert a stabilizing influence on the economy, and nonactivists believe that three time lags hinder proper timing. First, there is the **recognition lag,** the time period between a change in economic conditions and recognition by policy-makers of the change. It can take months to gather and tabulate reliable information on the performance of the economy in the recent past in order to determine whether it has dipped into a recession or whether the inflation rate has accelerated, and so forth.

Second, even after the need for a policy change is recognized, there is generally an additional time period before the policy change is instituted. Economists refer to this delay as **administrative lag.** In the case of monetary policy, the administrative lag is generally quite short. The Federal Open Market Committee meets monthly, and is at least potentially capable of instituting a change in monetary policy quickly. This is a major advantage of monetary policy. For discretionary fiscal policy, the administrative lag is likely to be much longer. Congressional committees must meet. Legislation must be proposed and debated. Congress must act, and the president must consent. Each of these steps takes time.

Finally, there is the **impact lag,** the time period between the implementation of a macropolicy change and when the change exerts its primary impact on the economy. While the impact of a change in tax rates is generally felt quickly, the expansionary effects of an increase in government expenditures are usually much less rapid. It will take time for the submission of competitive bids and the letting of new contracts. Several months may pass before work on a new project actually begins. The impact lag in the case of monetary policy is likely to be even longer. To the extent that monetary policy exerts stimulus via the interest rate, the time period between a shift in monetary policy, a change in interest rates, and in turn a change in the level of spending may be quite lengthy.

Economists who have studied this topic, including Milton Friedman and Robert Gordon, conclude that the combined duration of these time lags is generally 12 to 18 months in the case of monetary policy, and even longer in the case of fiscal policy. This means that if a policy is going to exert the desired effect at the proper time, policy-makers cannot wait until a problem develops before they act. Rather, they must act before an economic downturn or upturn in the inflation rate is observable. It will be necessary for them to correctly forecast turns in the economy if they are going to properly time changes in policy. Nonactivists argue this is highly unrealistic. Rhetoric aside, economic forecasters usually cannot predict such turns, nor can we expect them to do so in the foreseeable future (refer again to the Applications in Economics, "How Accurate is Economic Forecasting?" box). Moreover, even if they were able to forecast such events, the time lags accompanying changes in monetary and fiscal policies are so long and variable, it is highly unlikely that the primary effects of a policy change would come at the proper time. Therefore, nonactivists believe that discretionary policy is likely to be destabilizing rather than stabilizing.

Exhibit 15–5 shows the difference between the views of the activists and nonactivists graphically. When the economy begins to dip into a recession, activists argue that policy-makers can reasonably be expected to recognize the danger and shift to a more expansionary policy at point *B*. If the demand-stimulus effects are felt quickly (before the economy gets to point *C*), the shift to the more expansionary

Recognition lag
The time period between when a policy change is needed from a stabilization standpoint and when the need is recognized by policy-makers.

Administrative lag
The time period between when the need for a policy change is recognized and when the policy is actually implemented.

Impact lag
The time period between when a policy change is implemented and when the change begins to exert its primary effects.

Beginning with A, we illustrate the path of a hypothetical business cycle. If a forthcoming recession can be recognized quickly and a more expansionary policy instituted at point B, the policy may add stimulus at point C and help to minimize the magnitude of the downturn.

Activists believe that discretionary policy is likely to achieve this outcome. However, if delays result in the adoption of the expansionary policy at C and if it does not exert its major impact until D, the demand stimulus will exacerbate the inflationary boom. In turn, an anti-inflationary strategy instituted at E may exert its primary effects at F, just in time to increase the severity of a recession beyond F. Nonactivists fear that improper timing of discretionary macropolicy will exert such destabilizing effects.

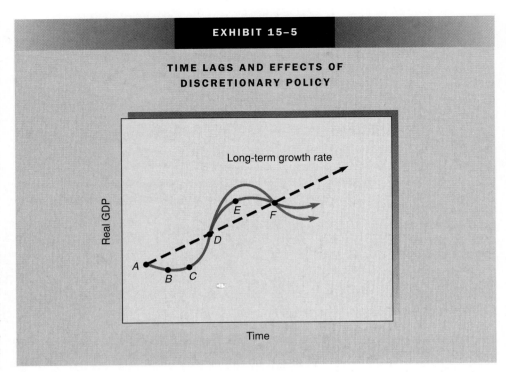

EXHIBIT 15-5

TIME LAGS AND EFFECTS OF DISCRETIONARY POLICY

macropolicy will help to minimize the decline in output accompanying the business downturn.

In contrast, nonactivists believe that policy-makers are unlikely to act so quickly, and even if they did, the time lags accompanying changes in monetary and fiscal policies are likely to make their actions ineffective. The shift to the more expansionary policy will not come until point *C*, according to this reasoning, and its effects will not be significant until point *D*. In this case, the expansionary policy will contribute to the severity of the inflationary boom (beyond point *D*). Similarly, a subsequent shift to an anti-inflationary policy may begin to exert its major impact at point *F*, just in time to make an oncoming recession worse (beyond point *F*). Therefore, nonactivists believe that discretionary policy shifts are likely to be destabilizing rather than stabilizing.

POLITICS AND THE TIMING OF POLICY CHANGES

Public-choice analysis has led to an increased awareness of an additional pitfall of discretionary policy-making—macropolicy might be used to pursue political objectives rather than stabilization. In a democracy, macropolicy will be designed by elected representatives, an elected president, and officials (such as the Board of Governors of the Federal Reserve) who are appointed by the elected president. Like other policy choices, macropolicy provides political entrepreneurs with a potential tool for furthering their political objectives. Predictably, discretionary macropolicy choices will be influenced by political considerations. It is naive to expect otherwise. (See the "Applications in Economics" box on the linkage between central bank independence and price stability.)

The nature of the political process, particularly the shortsightedness effect, provides politicians with little incentive to look beyond the next election. If the adaptive-expectations view is correct, expansionary policies 12 to 18 months prior to an election would stimulate output and employment, getting the economy in great shape by election day. Since demand-stimulus policies generally affect output before they begin to exert a major impact on the price level, the inflationary effects of such a policy would be most observable after the election.

Studies indicate that incumbents are far more successful at retaining their offices when real income grows rapidly, and the inflation rate is moderate.[4] Thus, political entrepreneurs have a strong incentive to stimulate the economy prior to a

APPLICATIONS IN ECONOMICS

RELATIONSHIP BETWEEN INDEPENDENT CENTRAL BANKING AND MONETARY STABILITY

The central bank of the United States has several built-in factors designed to insulate it from the ordinary political process. The seven members of the Board of Governors of the Federal Reserve System are each appointed to 14-year terms. Since these terms are staggered (only one member is appointed every two years), it would be near the end of the second term before even a two-term president would be able to appoint a majority of this powerful board. The Fed is prohibited from purchasing securities directly from the U.S. Treasury. Since it derives ample revenues from interest earned from its bond holdings (the excess revenues are turned over to the Treasury), the Fed is not dependent on congressional appropriations. All of these factors make the Fed less subject to political pressure and manipulation.

Is this independence wise? There is good reason to believe that it is. In many countries the governing officials of the central bank are highly dependent on political officials. In some cases, they serve at the discretion of the president (or equivalent), or simply a majority of the legislature. Under these circumstances, if the political officials do not like what the monetary policy-makers are doing, they simply replace them. When under the domination of political officials—even officials that are democratically elected—central banks have often been used to finance government expenditures with "printing-press" money. Monetary instability and inflation are the inevitable result.

While the degree of central-bank independence is difficult to measure precisely, it is widely believed that the monetary policy-makers of Germany, Switzerland, Japan, and the United States are the most independent in the world. Among the industrial countries, the central banks of Spain, Italy, and New Zealand are most clearly beholden to political forces.

The linkage between inflation and the dependence of monetary policy-makers on political pressures is clear. A 1990 study found that the industrial countries—Germany, Switzerland, Japan, and the United States—with the most independent central banks had the lowest average inflation rates during the 1973–1988 period, while the least independent central banks—those of Spain, Italy, and New Zealand—had the highest rates of inflation. This, coupled with the inflationary history of the politicized central banks of Latin America—and more recently, the politicized banks of the newly democratic countries of Eastern Europe and the former Soviet Union—indicates that subjecting monetary policy to the day-to-day pressures of politicians is not a good idea.

---

[4]For additional evidence on this point, see David Wyss and Jeanne Blondia, "The Economy and Presidential Elections," *Data Resources U.S. Review,* April 1988; Kevin B. Grier, "Presidential Elections and Federal Reserve Policy," *Southern Economic Journal,* October 1987, 475–486; and Ray C. Fair, "The Effect of Economic Conditions on Votes for the President," *Review of Economics and Statistics,* May 1978, 159–173.

major election. However, to the extent that politicians use macroeconomic policy for political purposes, they reduce its effectiveness as a stabilization weapon. There is some evidence that politicians have sought to use macropolicy for political gain.

Political scientist Edward Tufte has conducted extensive research on this issue. While reviewing evidence from 90 elections in 27 different countries, Tufte found that real disposable income accelerated in 77 percent of the election years compared to only 46 percent of the years without an election.[5] This suggests that there is at least a moderate tendency to follow more expansionary policies prior to major elections.

RATIONAL EXPECTATIONS AND POLICY INEFFECTIVENESS

The theory of rational expectations suggests that predictable changes in macropolicy will fail to promote economic stability. Unlike a machine, the moving parts of our economy are living, breathing human beings, capable of modifying their choices when the situation changes. As they learn from prior experience, their future response to a policy change may differ from their past responses.

As we have already discussed, the impact of macropolicy varies depending on whether it is anticipated by decision makers (see Chapter 14, Exhibit 14–1). The proponents of rational expectations believe that, sooner or later, the public will figure out any systematic policy, including countercyclical stabilization policy. And once a policy is widely anticipated and individuals adjust their decision making in light of its expected effects (for example, rising prices or higher interest rates), the policy no longer exerts its intended impact on real output and employment. Economists refer to this phenomenon as the **policy-ineffectiveness theorem.**

Policy-ineffectiveness theorem

The proposition that any systematic policy will be rendered ineffective once decision makers figure out the policy pattern and adjust their decision making in light of its expected effects. The theorem is a corollary of the theory of rational expectations.

Perhaps an example will illustrate why rational-expectations economists have little confidence that even properly timed macropolicy will be effective. Suppose it is widely anticipated that the government will employ expansionary macropolicy in response to a recession. As the signs of an economic slowdown appear, the public anticipates that policy-makers will increase the growth of the money supply and cut taxes (perhaps by allowing a more attractive depreciation allowance or an investment tax credit) to spur business investment. It makes sense, once this strategy is anticipated, for investors to delay investment projects and wait for the expected lower interest rates and investment tax incentives. This delay, though, only increases the severity of the current downturn and leads to pent-up investment demand. Then, once the anticipated expansionary policy is instituted, investment expenditures will tend to grow more rapidly than past experience indicated would be the case (and more rapidly than is desirable from a stabilization viewpoint). In essence, once decision makers adjust their choices in light of the anticipated countercyclical policy, the policy fails to exert the desired stabilizing effects.

The logic of the analysis applies symmetrically to an economic boom. If the public anticipates that slower money growth, higher interest rates, and higher taxes will be used to restrain an economic boom, they will spend and invest more

---

[5]Edward R. Tufte, *Political Control of the Economy* (Princeton: Princeton University Press, 1978).

prior to the expected restrictive policy. In turn, the increase in spending will contribute to the development of an economic boom.

The message of rational-expectations theory to stabilization policy-makers is clear. Human decision makers will foil your good intentions. Countercyclical macropolicy will fail because, once people expect your systematic response to recessions and booms, it will be in their personal interest to respond in a manner that will undermine the policy.

In the long run, of course, rational-expectations theory also suggests that the intentions of political entrepreneurs seeking to "hype" the economy prior to election time will be undermined. If the public expects expansionary policy during a preelection period, the primary impact of the policy will be on prices (inflation) and nominal interest rates, not real output and employment.

NONACTIVIST STABILIZATION POLICY

While the underlying logic of the monetarists, public-choice economists, and proponents of rational expectations differs, the three groups arrive at the same two conclusions: (1) discretionary policy is an important source of instability, and (2) greater stability would result if stable, predictable policies based on predetermined rules were followed.

Exhibit 15–6 illustrates empirical data that nonactivists cite in their criticism of discretionary policy. Since 1960 the U.S. economy has experienced six recessions (indicated by shaded areas), periods of at least two consecutive quarters of declining real GDP. If the effects of monetary policy are going to speed recovery, monetary policy must be expansionary prior to and during the recession. Nonactivists stress that discretionary policy has failed to achieve this outcome. In fact, the growth rate of the money supply has generally declined prior to and/or during the recent recessions. Far from offsetting recessionary forces, monetary policy has often contributed to the downturns and slowed the recovery process, according to the nonactivists.

Given the obstacles to the proper timing of policy changes, how can errors be minimized? Nonactivists recommend that policy-makers choose a long-run policy path (for example, 3 percent monetary growth and no change in tax rates or real government expenditures) and inform the public of this choice. This course should then be pursued regardless of cyclical ups and downs. As policy-makers stay on course, they will gain credibility. The public will develop confidence in the future stability of the policy. Uncertainty will be reduced, thereby increasing the efficiency of private decision making. Nonactivists are confident this strategy would result both in less instability and in more rapid growth than Western economies have experienced in the past.

NONACTIVIST MONETARY POLICY

Suppose we are going to adopt a nonactivist strategy. What rules or guidelines would we choose? Nonactivists believe that monetary policy should utilize one of

While monetary instability has declined in recent decades (see Exhibit 15–3), instability and poor timing persist. Here we show the annual growth rate of the M2 money supply for each year from 1960 to 1993. The graph also indicates the years of recession (shaded areas). The money supply was decelerating during or immediately prior to most of the recessions. If the effects of monetary policy are going to be stabilizing, this is the opposite of the desired pattern. According to nonactivists, a steady growth of the money supply or some other key aggregate variable (for example, nominal income) would result in more stability than discretionary monetary policy.

Source: *Economic Report of the President, 1994.*

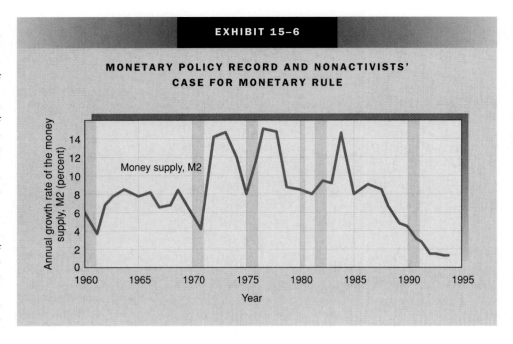

EXHIBIT 15–6

MONETARY POLICY RECORD AND NONACTIVISTS' CASE FOR MONETARY RULE

the following: (1) a monetary growth rule, (2) a nominal income growth rule, or (3) a price level rule.

MONETARY RULE. The most widely advocated nonactivist monetary policy is the constant-money-growth rate long championed by Milton Friedman. Under this plan, the money supply would be expanded continuously at an annual rate (3 percent, for example) that approximates the long-run growth of the U.S. economy. When real output is growing rapidly (for example, 5 percent annually), the supply of money would decline *relative to real GDP*. Thus, monetary policy would automatically exert a restraining influence during a period of rapid growth. In contrast, during a recession, the constant-money-growth rate would exceed the growth of real output, offsetting any tendency toward a downward spiral.

Nonactivists, particularly those with monetarist leanings, believe that steady growth of the money supply would eliminate instability arising from stop-go policies on the part of the Fed. They point out that monetary planners have often expanded the money supply more rapidly than the economy's long-term growth rate, and thereby caused inflation. Then, responding to an acceleration in the inflation rate, the monetary authorities have often stepped on the monetary brakes and thrown the economy into a recession (see Exhibit 15–6). Nonactivists see the fluctuations in the money supply accompanying discretionary monetary policies as, in fact, a major source of economic instability. Rather than responding to forecasts and current economic indicators, the Fed, they say, would be more of a stabilizing force if it simply increased the supply of money, month after month, at a low (noninflationary) constant annual rate.

If steady growth in the money supply is going to exert a stabilizing influence on aggregate demand, the velocity of money must be relatively stable. As we indicated when discussing the quantity theory of money in Chapter 13, one could think of aggregate demand (*PY*) as *MV*, the money supply (*M*) times velocity of circulation (*V*). However, the Fed controls only *M*. Therefore, unless *V* is relatively stable (or unless it changes at a steady rate), steady monetary growth will not stabilize aggregate demand. Thus, the case for a monetary rule is critically dependent upon the relative stability of the velocity of money.[6]

How stable is velocity? **Exhibit 15–7** illustrates the velocity of both M1 and M2 for the 1955–1993 period. During 1955–1980, the velocity of the M1 money supply increased at a fairly steady rate, approximately 3 percent annually. However, between 1982 and 1987, it declined sharply. Most nonactivists believe that this decline in the 1980s was a one-time occurrence, reflecting banking deregulation, the sharp deceleration in the inflation rate, and most importantly, the introduction of interest-earning checking accounts. Since the opportunity to earn interest on checking deposits reduces the opportunity cost of holding M1 money, the decline in M1 velocity during the 1982–1987 period is not really surprising. Nonetheless, the experience of the 1980s undermined the enthusiasm for a monetary rule based on M1.

In recent years, most proponents of a monetary rule have directed their attention toward the M2 money supply. The banking changes of the 1980s exerted much less impact on the M2 money supply. As Exhibit 15–7 illustrates, the velocity of M2 has been fairly constant at approximately 1.68 during the last several decades. As the result of this long-term stability in velocity, most nonactivists now prefer that the monetary rule be applied to the M2 money supply.

In 1975 Congress passed legislation requiring the Federal Reserve to adopt and announce target growth rates for the money supply during the next year. At the beginning of each year, the Fed announces its target range for the growth rates of various monetary aggregates. How does the steady growth rule differ from the monetary targets actually employed by the Fed? According to the nonactivists, the problem with the monetary targets is that the Fed does not take them very seriously. The Fed did not choose to adopt the targets. Rather, Congress imposed them. The Fed responded to the 1975 legislation by adopting target ranges that are wide enough to allow for substantial monetary variability. Finally, if the Fed wants to change policy course, it simply changes the targets. Nonactivists believe the targets are more cosmetic than real and thus fail to exert the stabilizing effects of a constant-money-growth rate rule.

NOMINAL INCOME RULE.   Nonactivists argue that even if the velocity of money sometimes changes unexpectedly, problems emanating from this source would be resolved if monetary authorities used monetary policy to provide for the steady growth of *nominal* income at a rate equal to the economy's long-run real growth of output (approximately 3 percent in the U.S. case). This rule would also provide long-run price stability because a stable price level is implied when nominal and real income expand at the same rate. In essence, this rule is a modified monetary rule, long advocated by Allan Meltzer of Carnegie Mellon University. Rather than expanding the supply of money by a constant amount, under this rule

---

[6]As we discussed in Chapter 13, initially any shifts to monetary acceleration tend to reduce short-term, nominal interest rates. Similarly, shifts to more restrictive monetary policy tend to increase short-term rates. Since the interest-rate fluctuations affect the opportunity cost of holding money, they also influence velocity. Monetarists believe that more stable monetary growth would also result in greater stability for both interest rates and the velocity of money than what we have observed under the stop-go policies of the Fed.

If steady growth in the money supply at a low rate is going to stabilize the economy, the velocity of money must be relatively stable (or grow at a stable rate). Between 1955 and 1980, the velocity of the M1 money supply grew at a relatively stable annual rate of approximately 3 percent. However, the velocity of M1 declined sharply with the introduction of interest-earning checking accounts during the 1980s. During the 1955–1993 period, the velocity of M2 has been relatively stable and at a value of approximately 1.68. As the result of this stability, most advocates of the monetary rule believe that the steady growth rule should be applied to the M2 money supply.

[a]Nominal GDP (*PY*) divided by the M2 money supply during the year.

[b]Nominal GDP (*PY*) divided by the M1 money supply during the year.

Source: *Economic Report of the President, 1994.*

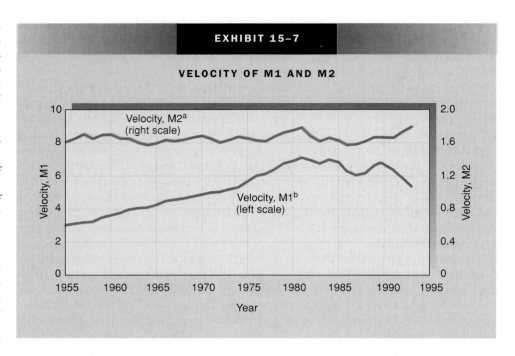

EXHIBIT 15–7

VELOCITY OF M1 AND M2

the supply of money would be increased by the economy's long-run growth rate (approximately 3 percent) minus the change in the velocity of money. If the velocity of money declined, as was the case for M1 during the 1980s, the money supply would grow more rapidly than real income. Alternatively, if velocity rose, the money supply would be slowed accordingly. In effect, the policy would adjust the monetary-growth rate to offset fluctuations in velocity (the demand for money).

PRICE LEVEL RULE. Some nonactivists argue that it would be better if the monetary authorities directly targeted a broad price index such as the GDP deflator or consumer price index. The advocates of this approach argue that, in the long run, monetary policy cannot determine real output, employment, interest rates, or other real variables. What it can and does determine is the level of prices. Therefore, why not target the price level directly? Under this plan, if the general price index were rising, monetary growth would be slowed. Conversely, if the price index were falling, the money supply would be expanded more rapidly. The proponents of this rule argue that it would reduce both instability arising from monetary sources and the uncertainty of time-dimension transactions (for example, loan agreements and other long-term contracts).

From the viewpoint of nonactivists, the important point is not the precise rule, but rather the removal of monetary policy from the hands of activist policy-makers. If left to their own discretion, policy-makers will inevitably make destabilizing errors, according to nonactivists.

NONACTIVIST FISCAL POLICY

In the area of fiscal policy, the simplest rule would require that the budget be balanced annually. Since revenues and expenditures fluctuate over the business cycle, however, a balanced budget rule would require tax increases and/or expenditure reductions during a recession. The opposite changes would be required during a period of rapid growth. Such changes are inconsistent with the nonactivist pursuit of stable (unchanged) policies.

In theory, the proper nonactivist fiscal strategy is a balanced budget over the business cycle. Under this plan, the same tax rates and expenditure policies would remain in effect during both booms and recessions. Surpluses would result during periods of prosperity, while deficits would accrue during recessions. The problem with this strategy is that it fails to provide a precise indicator revealing how well the policy-makers are adhering to the steady course. Thus, nonactivists, particularly those with a public-choice background, recognize that a "balance the budget over the business cycle" rule is unlikely to impose a steady course on policy-makers.

Some nonactivists believe that a constitutional amendment limiting both government spending and budget deficits is a necessary ingredient for stable fiscal policy. These nonactivists believe pressure from special interest groups and the short time horizon of political officials elected for limited terms bias the political process toward expansionary fiscal policy (expanding debt and spending increases). Because of this, they favor a constitutional amendment that would require supramajority (for example, 60 percent) congressional approval for either (1) deficit-financed government spending or (2) rapid increases (more rapid than the growth of national income) in federal spending.

It is one thing to favor a general strategy and another to develop a practical, workable policy to implement the strategy. Clearly, the nonactivists have not yet arrived at a detailed fiscal policy program that would command wide acceptance among even the proponents of nonactivism.

EMERGING CONSENSUS VIEW

The accompanying "Thumbnail Sketch" summarizes the differences between activists and nonactivists. From a policy viewpoint, the central focus of disagreement between the two groups centers on the merits of policy-making flexibility. Activists fear that if strictly followed, inflexible rules would prevent an appropriate response to uncertain future economic changes. In their view, failure to respond to a major shock, perhaps stemming from war, another oil-price run, or a collapse of investment, might well result in a major economic disaster.

On the other hand, the nonactivists fear that discretion will consistently be abused, that politicians will use policy to pursue either unattainable objectives or political goals. According to the nonactivists, unless you tie the hands of policy-makers, they will inevitably pursue an activist's strategy that will magnify instability and result in inflation.

While it is important to understand the fundamental differences between the activists' and nonactivists' viewpoints, we must not forget that most economists take a hybrid view, influenced by the analysis of alternative schools of thought. Also, activists and nonactivists actually share a great deal of common ground. Both recognize that the wrong use of policy is a potential source of economic instability. Both are sensitive to the potential destructiveness of policy swings like

THUMBNAIL SKETCH

WHAT ARE THE MAJOR DIFFERENCES BETWEEN ACTIVISTS AND NONACTIVISTS?

AREA OF DIFFERENCE	ACTIVISTS	NONACTIVISTS
1. Source of Instability	Economy is inherently unstable.	Perverse policies are the primary source of instability.
2. Speed of Self-Correcting Mechanism	Self-correcting mechanism works slowly and ineffectually.	Self-correcting mechanism works with reasonable speed if it is not stifled by perverse macroeconomic policy.
3. Proper Timing of Discretionary Policy	Even though timing is difficult, discretionary policy can promote stability and has done so.	Given time lags, forecasting deficiencies, and the political incentive structure, discretionary policy is an ineffective stabilization tool.
4. Impact of Monetary and Fiscal Rules	Inflexible rules would prevent policy-makers from responding to unanticipated shocks; thus, they would increase instability.	Rules providing for stable monetary and fiscal policy would reduce instability.

those that were followed during the 1930s. Similarly, both recognize the uncertainty and inflationary effects of rapid monetary growth.

Compared to their counterparts of the 1960s, economists in the 1990s are more aware of both the limitations and dangers of macroeconomic policy. Macroeconomic policy is a two-edged sword. If properly timed, it can help smooth business ups and downs, but proper timing is not easily achieved, and if the effects of a policy shift are improperly timed, they will be destabilizing. Consequently, the idea of fine-tuning, which implies that policy-makers can successfully promote stability by responding to each short-term bump in the economic road, has lost most of its luster. Today, most economists favor a policy response only in the case of major cyclical disturbances. Economists of all persuasions are more cautious than they were a couple of decades ago. More stable policies are likely to flow from this caution.

CONCLUDING THOUGHTS

Economists who pronounced the death of business instability during the 1960s clearly underestimated the difficulties involved in steering a stable economic course. Unfortunately, economic ups and downs are likely to continue in the foreseeable future. Recent economic instability must be placed in perspective, though. Just because macroeconomic stabilization policy has failed to achieve perfection, it does not follow that no progress has been made.

As Exhibit 15–1 clearly shows, economic fluctuations have been much less pronounced since the Second World War. Sensible macroeconomic policy deserves most of the credit for this increased stability (see Exhibit 15–3). The Keynesian revolution convinced economists and policy-makers alike that macroeconomic policy mattered—that it was too important to be left to fate. Since then, fiscal and monetary policy has been instituted in a manner that has prevented economic disturbances from becoming catastrophic depressions. This is an important achievement to which macroeconomists can point with a sense of pride.

CHAPTER SUMMARY

1. Historically, the United States has experienced substantial swings in real output. Prior to the Second World War, year-to-year changes in real GDP of 5 to 10 percent were experienced on several occasions. Since the Second World War, the fluctuations in real output have been more moderate.

2. Macropolicy activists believe that a market economy is inherently unstable, that is, that the market's self-corrective process works too slowly to be effective. They are confident that discretionary monetary and fiscal policy will promote economic stability.

3. Nonactivists believe that a market economy's self-correcting tendencies work quite well in a stable policy environment. They argue that policy-makers would make fewer errors if they merely instituted stable monetary and fiscal policies, rather than altering policy in response to current economic conditions.

4. The index of leading indicators and other forecasting devices warn policy-makers when a turn in the economic road is just ahead. While recognizing that forecasting devices sometimes give false signals, activists argue that policy-makers can initially respond cautiously to signals indicating the need for a policy change and then act more aggressively if the situation requires it. Activists thus believe that discretionary macroeconomic policy can effectively restrain the economy during an inflationary boom and stimulate output during a business recession.

5. Nonactivists stress that inability to accurately forecast the future and quickly modify macroeconomic policy, along with uncertainty as to when a policy change will exert its primary impact, substantially reduce the effectiveness of discretionary policy as a stabilization tool.

6. Public-choice theory suggests that politicians have a strong incentive to follow an expansionary course prior to major elections. Such political use of macropolicy reduces its effectiveness as a stabilization tool.

7. The theory of rational expectations argues that even properly timed countercyclical policy will fail to reduce instability once decision makers figure out the systematic pattern and adjust their choices in light of the expected effects.

8. Nonactivists believe that stability would be enhanced if, rather than attempting countercyclical policies, policy-makers simply pursued stable, predictable policies. In the area of monetary policy, nonactivists recommend that decision makers target one of the following: (a) slow, steady growth of the money supply, (b) growth of nominal GDP at a rate equal to the economy's long-run real growth rate, or (c) a constant price level. With regard to fiscal policy, nonactivists favor the maintenance of a stable tax and expenditure policy based on long-run considerations rather than current cyclical conditions.

9. The major disagreement between activists and nonactivists involves the merits of a policy response to changing circumstances. Activists fear that strict adherence to a policy such as the constant (fixed) money growth rule will prevent policy-makers from responding correctly to major recessions and inflations. Correspondingly, nonactivists fear that policy-maker discretion will result in destabilizing policies.

10. Despite their differences, activists and nonactivists agree that (a) it is more difficult to properly time stabilization policy than was generally perceived during the 1960s, (b) past errors have contributed to economic instability, and (c) it is a mistake for policy-makers to respond to minor changes in economic indicators.

11. While stabilization policy has not eliminated economic ups and downs, it has virtually eliminated the likelihood that an economic disturbance will become a catastrophic depression. This is an important achievement that is often overlooked today.

CRITICAL-ANALYSIS QUESTIONS

1. Compare the views of activists and nonactivists with regard to the following points:
   a. The self-stabilizing characteristics of a market economy.
   b. The ability of policy-makers to forecast the future.
   c. The validity of the rational-expectations hypothesis.
   d. The use of rules versus discretion in the institution of monetary and fiscal policy.

2. What is the index of leading indicators? Evaluate its potential usefulness to policy-makers.

3. Do you think more detailed computer models of the economy will enhance the ability of economists to forecast future economic changes more accurately? Why or why not?

*4. How does economic instability during the last four decades compare with instability prior to the Second World War? Is there any evidence that stabilization policy has either increased or decreased economic stability during the post–Second World War period?

*5. Why do most nonactivists favor a monetary rule such as expansion of the money supply at a constant annual rate? What are some of the potential problems with a monetary rule? How does the stability of the velocity of money affect the case for a monetary rule? Do you think a monetary rule could be devised that would reduce economic instability? Why or why not?

6. The chair of the Council of Economic Advisers has requested that you write a short paper indicating how economic policy can be used to stabilize the economy and achieve a high level of economic growth during the next five years. Be sure to make specific proposals. Indicate why your recommendations will work. You may submit your paper to your instructor.

7. Evaluate the effectiveness of monetary and fiscal policy during the last three years. Has it helped to promote stable prices, rapid growth, and high unemployment? Do you think policy-makers have made mistakes during this period? If so, indicate why.

8. "The Great Depression indicates that the self-correcting mechanism of a market economy is weak and unreliable." Evaluate this statement.

*9. Both activists and nonactivists point to the increased stability of the last four decades as evidence supportive of their view. Explain each of their positions.

10. What are some of the problems that would arise if the monetary authorities sought to maintain a constant price level?

*11. Suppose that the Fed tried to peg the real interest rate below the market level. How would it do so, and what would be the result of this policy?

12. In recent years, there has been less reliance on the use of discretionary fiscal policy changes as a stabilization tool. Why?

13. Suppose that presidents were limited to a single six-year term. Would this reform influence economic stability? Why or why not?

*14. What does the accuracy of the growth of real GDP and the inflation rate as a predictor of votes in presidential elections imply about the importance of candidate personalities, campaign strategies, choice of vice-presidential candidate, expenditures for television commercials, performance in television debates, and similar factors that most people believe determine the outcome in presidential elections?

---

*Asterisk denotes questions for which answers are given in Appendix C.

CHAPTER SIXTEEN

BUDGET DEFICITS
AND THE NATIONAL DEBT

The attractiveness of financing spending by debt issue to the elected politicians should be obvious. Borrowing allows spending to be made that will yield immediate political payoffs without the incurring of any immediate political cost.

JAMES BUCHANAN[1]

CHAPTER FOCUS

- *How large is the national debt? Will the debt have to be paid off?*
- *Are we mortgaging the future of our children and grandchildren? How do budget deficits affect future generations?*
- *Have the budget deficits of current years pushed the debt to a dangerous level?*
- *How does the budget deficit of the United States compare with deficits of other countries?*
- *Are the large budget deficits of recent years an aberration, or do they reflect a fundamental problem with the budget process?*

---

[1]James Buchanan, *The Deficit and American Democracy* (Memphis: P. K. Steidman Foundation, 1984).

Deficit spending and the national debt are enduring topics. They were hot topics during the 1940s and 1950s, as Keynesian economists challenged the reigning orthodoxy—the view that the federal budget should be balanced annually. By the 1960s the Keynesians had clearly won the debate in both the academic and political arenas. Thus, no one paid much attention as the federal government incurred a string of budget deficits during the 1960s and 1970s. These deficits were assumed to be temporary and the result of scientifically determined demand-management policies.

All of this changed during the last decade. Large and persistent deficits during a time of peace and prosperity brought the debt issue back to center stage. News commentators, business leaders, and others often told us that the "monstrous" deficits were the most critical problem facing America. Is this really true? If so, what is the nature of the problem? What can be done to deal with it? This chapter focuses on these topics and related issues.

EXPENDITURES, REVENUES, BUDGET DEFICITS, AND THE NATIONAL DEBT

Exhibit 16–1 illustrates the path of federal expenditures and revenues during the last four decades. During the last half of the 1950s, federal revenues averaged approximately 18 percent of GDP. Of course, revenues have fluctuated with economic conditions. Their trend, however, has been upward. During the last half of the 1980s, they averaged approximately 20 percent of GDP, before declining to 19 percent during the 1991 recession.

While revenues have increased modestly as a share of GDP, federal expenditures have risen more rapidly. During the mid-1980s, they averaged approximately 24 percent of GDP. In the early 1990s they were approximately 23.5 percent of GDP, up from 18 percent during the late 1950s. In recent years, there has been a persistent, sizable gap between federal expenditures and revenues. Thus, the government has had to borrow heavily in order to cover its expenditures.

When the federal government uses debt rather than taxes and user charges to pay for its expenditures, the U.S. Treasury issues interest-bearing bonds that are sold to private investors, government agencies, and the Federal Reserve Bank. These interest-bearing bonds comprise the **national debt.** In effect, the national debt consists of outstanding loans from financial investors to the general fund of the U.S. Treasury.

National debt

The sum of the indebtedness of the federal government in the form of outstanding interest-earning bonds. It reflects the cumulative impact of budget deficits and surpluses.

The federal budget deficit and the national debt are directly related. The deficit is a "flow" concept (like water running into a bathtub), while the national debt is a "stock" figure (like the amount of water in the tub at a point in time). In essence, the national debt represents the cumulative effect of all the prior budget deficits and surpluses. A budget deficit increases the size of the national debt by the amount of the deficit. Conversely, a budget surplus allows the federal government to pay off bondholders and thereby reduce the size of the national debt.

The creditworthiness of an organization is dependent upon the size of its debt *relative to its income base*. Therefore, when analyzing the significance of budget deficits and the national debt, it is important to consider their size relative to the

EXHIBIT 16-1

FEDERAL EXPENDITURES AND REVENUES AS A PERCENT OF GDP

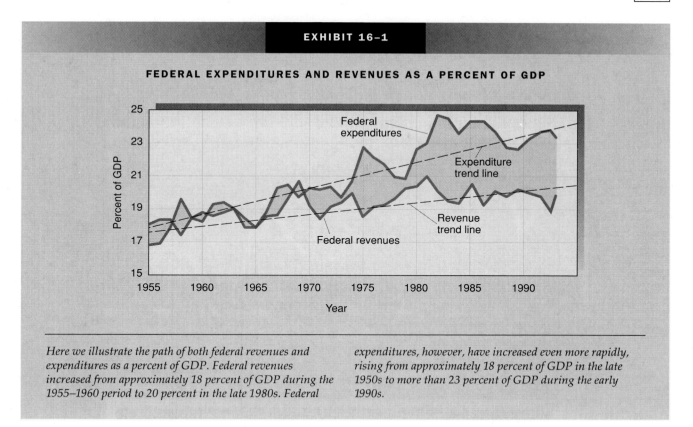

Here we illustrate the path of both federal revenues and expenditures as a percent of GDP. Federal revenues increased from approximately 18 percent of GDP during the 1955–1960 period to 20 percent in the late 1980s. Federal expenditures, however, have increased even more rapidly, rising from approximately 18 percent of GDP in the late 1950s to more than 23 percent of GDP during the early 1990s.

entire economy. **Exhibit 16–2** presents data during the last four decades for both the federal budget deficit and the national debt *as a percent of GDP*. Since the defense effort during the Second World War was financed substantially with debt rather than with taxes, the national debt was quite large at the end of the war. Following the war, the combination of economic growth and small budget deficits reduced the size of the national debt as a percent of GDP. During the 1950–1974 period, budget deficits averaged less than 1 percent of GDP. Historically, real output in the United States has grown at an annual rate of approximately 3 percent. As long as the budget deficit *as a percent of GDP* is less than the growth of real output, the federal debt will get smaller relative to the size of the economy. This is precisely what happened during the 1950–1974 period. Budget deficits were present, and they pushed up the nominal national debt (from $256.7 billion at year-end 1950 to $492.7 billion at the end of 1974). But GDP grew even more rapidly. By 1974 the national debt had fallen to 34 percent of GDP, down from 89 percent in 1950 (and 127 percent in 1946).

This situation was reversed in the mid-1970s. Since 1974 federal budget deficits have been much larger, averaging nearly 4 percent of GDP (part "a" of Exhibit 16–2). When the budget deficit as a percent of GDP exceeds the growth of real GDP, the national debt will increase relative to the size of the economy. As Exhibit 16–2 (part "b") illustrates, this has clearly been the case since 1980. Pushed along by the large budget deficits of the 1980s and early 1990s, the national debt expanded to 69 percent of GDP in 1993, up from 34 percent in 1974.

EXHIBIT 16–2

BUDGET DEFICITS AND THE NATIONAL DEBT AS A PERCENT OF GDP

(a) Federal budget deficit or surplus as a percent of GDP

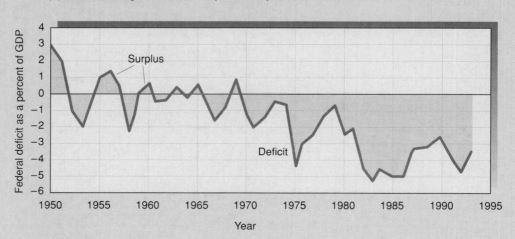

(b) Gross and net federal debt as a percent of GDP

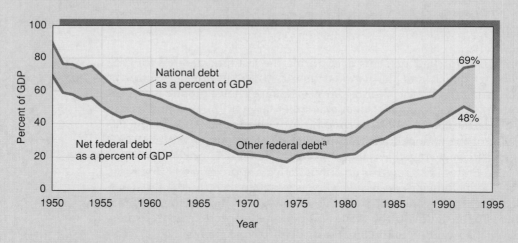

Throughout most of the 1950s and 1960s, federal budget deficits were small as a percent of GDP, and occasionally the government ran a budget surplus (a). During this period, the national debt declined as a proportion of GDP (b). Since 1974, however, the budget deficits have been quite large, *larger (as a percent of GDP) than the growth of real GDP. As a result, the national debt has increased as a percent of GDP in recent years.*

ᵃFederal debt held by U.S. government agencies and Federal Reserve banks.

A CLOSER LOOK AT THE NATIONAL DEBT

Who owns the national debt? As **Exhibit 16–3** illustrates, the biggest share of the national debt (53.9 percent in 1993) is held internally by U.S. citizens and private institutions, such as insurance companies and commercial banks. Foreigners hold slightly more than one-eighth of the total. The portion owned by foreigners is sometimes referred to as **external debt.** Approximately 25 percent of the debt is held by agencies of the federal government. For example, social security trust funds are often used to purchase U.S. bonds. When the debt is owned by the government agency, it is little more than an accounting transaction indicating that one government agency (for example, the Social Security Administration) is making a loan to another (the U.S. Treasury). Even the interest payments, in this case, represent little more than an internal government transfer.

Approximately 7 percent of the public debt is held by the Federal Reserve System. As we have previously discussed, when the Fed purchases U.S. securities, it creates money. The bonds held by the Fed, therefore, are indicative of prior government expenditures that have been paid for with "printing-press" money—money created by the central bank. As in the case of the securities held by government agencies, the interest on the bonds held by the Fed is returned to the Treasury after the Fed has covered its costs of operation.

Since the government both pays and receives the interest on the bonds held by government agencies and the Federal Reserve (minus Fed expenses), these bonds do not represent a net interest obligation. Only the bonds held by domestic and foreign investors will require additional taxes to meet future net interest payments. Thus, the portion of the debt owed to domestic and foreign investors is sometimes referred to as the **net federal debt** (or *net public debt*). As Exhibit 16–3

External debt
The portion of the national debt owed to foreign investors.

Net federal debt
The portion of the national debt owed to domestic and foreign investors. It does not *include bonds held by agencies of the federal government or the Federal Reserve.*

Source: *Federal Reserve Bulletin,* April 1994.

EXHIBIT 16–3

OWNERSHIP OF THE NATIONAL DEBT (1993.03)

OWNERSHIP OF U.S. SECURITIES	DOLLAR VALUE (BILLIONS)	PERCENT OF NATIONAL DEBT
Total national debt	4,411.5	100.0
U.S. government agencies	1,116.7	25.3
Federal Reserve Banks	325.7	7.4
Net federal debt	2,969.1	67.3
Domestic investors	2,376.8	53.9
Foreign investors	592.3	13.4

illustrates, the net public debt accounted for 67.3 percent of the national debt in 1993. Four-fifths of the net public debt is owned by domestic investors.

Part "b" of Exhibit 16–2 presents data on the size of the net federal debt as a percent of GDP for the 1950–1993 period. Like the overall national debt, the net federal debt as a share of GDP declined sharply during the 1950s and moderately during the 1960–1974 period. However, since 1974, it too has been rising as a percent of GDP. In 1993, the net federal debt stood at 48 percent of GDP, up from less than 20 percent in 1974.

CONCERNS ABOUT THE NATIONAL DEBT

Are large, persistent budget deficits harmful to the health of the U.S. economy? Persons who answer this question in the affirmative generally argue that the deficits (1) are harmful to the welfare of future generations, (2) result in a dangerous dependency on foreign capital, and (3) generate a large interest liability that threatens the financial stability of the federal government. Let us consider each of these concerns in some detail.

DEBT FINANCING AND FUTURE GENERATIONS

Laymen, politicians, and economists have debated about the burden of the national debt for many years.[2] One side argues that we are mortgaging the future of our children and grandchildren—that debt financing permits us to consume today, then send the bill to future generations. The other side, noting that most of the national debt is held by domestic citizens (see Exhibit 16–3), retorts, "We owe it to ourselves."

When considering our ability to shift the cost of government onto future generations, two points must be kept in mind. First, in the case of domestically held debt, our children and grandchildren will indeed pay the taxes to service the debt, but they will also receive the interest payments. Admittedly, those paying the taxes and receiving the interest payments will not always be the same people. Some will gain and others will lose. But both those who gain and those who lose will be members of the future generation.

Second, debt financing of a government activity cannot push the opportunity cost of the resources used by government onto future generations. If current GDP is $6 trillion and the federal government is spending $1.6 trillion, then $4.4 trillion will remain for private individuals, businesses, and state and local governments to spend or invest. This will be true regardless of whether the federal government finances its expenditures with taxes or debt. Debt financing cannot push the

---

[2]See Richard H. Fink and Jack High, eds., *A Nation in Debt: Economists Debate the Federal Budget Deficit* (Frederick: University Publications of America, 1987), for an excellent set of readings summarizing this debate.

opportunity cost of resources used by the government into the future. When the government builds a highway, constructs an anti-missile defense system, or provides police protection, it draws resources with alternative uses away from the private sector. *Current* output of goods for private consumption and investment will decline as the result of the government's employment of resources that otherwise would be available for use in the private sector. But this cost is incurred in the present; it cannot be avoided through debt financing.

That which debt can push into the future is the deadweight losses and disincentive effects of taxes. In some cases, these costs may be substantial. In most instances, however, they will be considerably smaller than the opportunity cost of the resources used by the government in the provision of goods and services.

If the opportunity cost of resources occurs during the current period, does this mean that there is little reason to be concerned about an adverse impact of deficits on future generations? Not necessarily. Debt financing influences future generations primarily through its potential impact on saving and capital formation. If lots of factories, machines, houses, technical knowledge, and other productive assets are available to future generations, then their productive potential will be high. Alternatively, if fewer productive assets are passed along to the next generation, then their productive capability will be less. Thus, the true measure of how government debt influences future generations involves knowledge of its impact on capital formation.

When excess capacity is present, a deficit can stimulate aggregate demand and bring otherwise idle resources into the production of houses and factories, as well as consumption goods. Under such circumstances, budget deficits enlarge the stock of capital available to future generations and thereby enhance their well-being.

The impact of budget deficits during normal times on capital formation and the welfare of future generations is a complex issue. Consider an economy that is operating at top productive capacity. Holding government expenditures constant, how would the substitution of debt financing for current taxation influence capital formation? As our discussion of fiscal-policy models implies, economists sometimes differ in their responses to this question. We will consider two alternative theories: the traditional view that budget deficits reduce future capital stock and the opposing new classical view that such deficits exert no significant future impact.

TRADITIONAL VIEW: BUDGET DEFICITS REDUCE FUTURE CAPITAL STOCK. Most economists embrace the traditional view that budget deficits will retard private investment and thereby reduce the welfare of future generations. The reasoning here is that people will tend to treat their additional holdings of government bonds (used to finance the debt) as wealth. After all, the bonds represent future income to their holders. In contrast, the proponents of the traditional view do not believe that taxpayers will fully recognize the future taxes implied by the outstanding debt. If bondholders recognize the asset value of the government bonds while taxpayers fail to recognize fully the accompanying tax liability, then the general populace will have an exaggerated view of its true wealth position. Wealth is an important determinant of consumption. When people think they are wealthier, they will consume more and save less than they would if they had fully recognized their future tax liability. Given the high consumption and low saving rates, the strong government demand for loanable funds to finance its deficit will push real interest rates upward.[3] In turn, the higher interest rates will crowd out private investment, and with the passage of time, reduce the capital stock available to future generations.

In addition, the higher interest rates will attract foreign investors. But investments in the United States will require dollars. As foreigners increase their investments in the United States, they will demand dollars in the international currency market. This strong demand will cause the dollar to appreciate. In turn, the appreciation in the exchange-rate value of the dollar will make foreign goods cheaper to Americans and American goods more expensive to foreigners. Thus, U.S. imports will rise relative to exports. A *balance-of-trade deficit* (an excess of imports over exports) follows directly from the inflow of foreign capital.

While the inflow of capital from abroad will dampen both the increase in interest rates and the reduction in domestic investment, it also implies that foreigners will receive larger future incomes from their asset holdings in the United States. Therefore, compared with the financing of government by current taxation, future generations of Americans will inherit both a smaller stock of physical capital and less income from that capital (since the share owned by foreigners has increased). Succeeding generations will be less well-off as a result.

In summary, the traditional view argues that the substitution of debt financing for current taxation will indirectly alter the composition of private domestic spending toward consumption and away from investment. Since households view government securities as wealth, they consume more and save (and invest) less than would be the case if government expenditures were financed by taxation. As a result, interest rates will increase and crowd out private investment. In turn, the growth rate of the capital stock will slow. Since future generations will be working with less capital (fewer productivity-enhancing tools and machines), their productivity and wages will be lower than would have been the case had the budget deficits not crowded out private investment. Thus, according to the traditional view, budget deficits will retard the growth rate of income and thereby reduce the living standard of future generations of Americans.

NEW CLASSICAL VIEW: BUDGET DEFICITS EXERT LITTLE IMPACT ON FUTURE CAPITAL STOCK. Not all economists accept the traditional view of budget deficits. An alternative view, most closely associated with Robert Barro of Harvard University, encompasses the new classical perspective of fiscal policy.[4] This new classical view stresses that additional debt implies an equivalent amount of future taxes. If, as the new classical model assumes, individuals fully anticipate the added future tax liability accompanying the debt, current consumption will be unaffected when the taxes are levied. According to this view, if future taxes (debt) are substituted for current taxes, then people will save the reduction in current taxes so that they will have the required income to pay the higher future taxes implied by the

---

[3]The substitution of debt for taxes will increase the disposable income of households, causing both consumption and saving to expand. But saving will increase by much less than the additional government demand for loanable funds to finance the deficit. Thus, real interest rates rise.

[4]See Robert Barro, "Are Government Bonds Net Wealth?" *Journal of Political Economy* 82 (November–December 1974), pp. 1095–1117; and "The Ricardian Approach to Budget Deficits," *Journal of Economic Perspectives* 2 (Spring 1989).

additional debt. As a result, the increase in the demand for loanable funds emanating from the budget deficit will be offset by an equivalent increase in private saving. Therefore, neither real interest rates nor private investment is altered. Since real interest yields are unaffected, neither is there an influx of foreign capital. Since neither capital formation nor wealth is altered, the substitution of debt for taxes does not affect the welfare of future generations in the new classical model.

EMPIRICAL EVIDENCE ON THE IMPACT OF THE DEFICIT. What does the empirical evidence indicate with regard to the validity of the two theories? Studies focusing on the period prior to the 1980s have found only a weak relationship, if any, between budget deficits and real interest rates. New classical economists argue that these findings are supportive of their theory. However, the experience with the big budget deficits of the 1980s would appear to be highly supportive of the traditional theory of deficit finance.

Exhibit 16–4 compares consumption, investment, and net exports as a share of GDP during the five years following the recession of 1982 with the five years subsequent to the recession of 1974–1975. Since the budget deficits averaged 5.1 percent of GDP during 1983–1987, compared with 2.9 percent during the 1976–1980 period, a comparison of the two periods sheds light on how larger budget deficits affect the economy. During the 1983–1987 period of larger budget deficits, personal consumption rose to 66.3 percent of GDP, compared with 64.2 percent during the earlier period. Gross investment as a percent of GDP declined from 18.1 percent in 1976–1980 to 17.2 percent during 1983–1987 even though there was a substantial inflow of foreign capital during the latter period.

EXHIBIT 16–4

RECENT CHANGES IN PERSONAL CONSUMPTION, INVESTMENT, AND NET EXPORTS AS A SHARE OF GDP

		COMPONENT AS A PERCENT OF GDP			
TIME PERIOD	FEDERAL DEFICIT	PERSONAL CONSUMPTION	GROSS PRIVATE INVESTMENT	GROSS INVESTMENT LESS NET FOREIGN INVESTMENT	NET EXPORTS
1976–1980	2.9	64.2	18.1	18.1	−0.8
1983–1987	5.1	66.3	17.2	14.5	−2.7
Differential (Later period minus earlier period)	+2.2	+2.1	−0.9	−3.6	−1.9

Source: *Economic Report of the President, 1993.*

But look what happened to the investment spending of Americans. The investment expenditures of Americans (gross investment less net foreign investment) fell from 18.1 percent of GDP in 1976–1980 to 14.5 percent in 1983–1987. Net exports decreased. Thus, during the period of larger sustained deficits, Americans cut their domestically financed capital formation, increased their imports (negative net exports), and expanded their current consumption. This pattern is precisely what the traditional theory predicts will happen when debt financing is substituted for current taxation.

Nominal data were used to derive the gross investment/GDP ratio presented in Exhibit 16–4. If the prices of investment goods and other components of GDP rose at approximately the same rate, it would not make any difference whether nominal or real numbers were used to calculate the ratio. However, this was not the case. While prices in general rose by 35 percent during 1982–1990, the price index for durable equipment, a large component of private investment, increased by only 13 percent during the same period. These extremely moderate price increases for investment equipment reflected the rapid technological change and cost reductions accompanying the computer revolution of the 1980s.

As Barro and other leading new classical economists have stressed, a different picture emerges when the investment/GDP ratio is calculated in real terms. As **Exhibit 16–5** illustrates, while nominal gross investment fell (from 18.1 percent to 17.2 percent) as a share of nominal GDP between 1976–1980 and 1983–1987, real investment as a percent of real GDP rose from 16.8 percent to 16.9 percent. Moreover, like investment, purchases of long-lasting consumer durables (such as appliances, furniture, and personally owned automobiles) also enhance our future welfare. Surprisingly, real spending on consumer durables and gross investment summed to 25.4 percent of real GDP during the 1983–1987 period, compared with only 24.4 percent during the earlier period of smaller deficits.

Exhibit 16–5 also presents data for 1988–1992 and 1965–1969, periods of sustained prosperity during which real gross investment averaged approximately 16 percent of real GDP. Thus, when measured in real terms, gross investment as a share of GDP during the 1983–1987 period is not out of line with the parallel figures for the 1960s and 1970s when budget deficits were much smaller.

Interestingly, expenditures on real gross investment and consumer durables were quite high during the 1980s. In fact, when measured in real terms, the spending on gross investment and consumer durables as a percent of GDP was at a post–Second World War high during the large deficit years of the 1980s. In contrast with the more widely cited nominal data, the real investment figures do not indicate that the budget deficits of the 1980s stimulated consumption and crowded out capital investment.

DEPENDENCE ON FOREIGN INVESTORS

While the real data indicate that gross investment was approximately constant as a share of GDP during the mid-1980s, a significant portion of the investment was financed by foreigners. Foreign investors supplied approximately one-seventh of the investment funds of the United States during this period. However, foreigners

EXHIBIT 16–5

HAVE THE DEFICITS REALLY REDUCED PRIVATE INVESTMENT?

	COMPONENT AS A SHARE OF GDP			
	GROSS INVESTMENT		GROSS INVESTMENT PLUS PURCHASES OF DURABLE GOODS	
PERIOD	NOMINAL	REAL	NOMINAL	REAL
1965–1969	16.2	16.2	25.1	22.6
1976–1980	18.1	16.8	26.8	24.4
1983–1987	17.2	16.9	25.9	25.4
1988–1992	14.4	15.4	22.8	24.4

Source: *Economic Report of the President, 1993*, Tables 1, 2, and 3.

still own only a small portion—approximately 5 percent—of the domestic capital assets of the United States. The view that foreigners are about to buy up the capital infrastructure of the United States is simply incorrect.

How does foreign investment affect the U.S. economy? When considering a possible burden emanating from foreign investment, it is important to keep an eye on both sides of the transaction. The inflow of foreign capital leads to lower interest rates and a higher level of investment than would take place in its absence. An increase in machines, structures, and other forms of capital formation from foreign investment will increase the productivity and income of American workers. Of course, the inflow of investment funds also enlarges the future profit and interest claims of foreigners. However, if the funds are invested wisely, the projects will generate returns (future income) that provide an offset against the future income claims of foreigners. On the other hand, if the funds are squandered on low-return projects, the wealth of investors will be reduced. But this would be equally true for projects financed solely with domestic funds.

Doesn't this inflow of capital from abroad make the United States more dependent on foreign creditors? When considering this issue, it is important to keep the nature of the foreign investment in mind. Substantial portions of the funds supplied by foreigners during the 1980s were in the form of risk capital—investments in stocks, land, physical structures, and business ventures. Such investments do not involve a contractual repayment commitment. Others are invested in bonds, both corporate and government. These investments are almost entirely fixed-interest-rate obligations. As long as the investment project is profitable, U.S. citizens as well as foreigners will gain as the result of undertaking the project.

What would happen if foreigners suddenly decided to take their "money" home and quit financing investments in the United States? It is not obvious why literally tens of thousands of foreign investors would be any more likely to suddenly "sell out" than tens of thousands of domestic investors. But, even if they did, market adjustments would exert a stabilizing effect. Remember, the "money" of foreigners is in the form of stocks, bonds, and physical assets. If foreigners suddenly tried to sell these assets, falling prices would create some real bargains for domestic investors. Domestic investors would gain and foreign investors would lose. Similarly, if foreigners cut back their financial investments in the United States, real interest rates would rise. But the higher real interest rates would make U.S. investments more attractive and thereby help deter any outflow of funds.

Finally, the vulnerability accompanying foreign investment almost certainly lies with the foreign investor rather than with the recipient country. It is much easier for a government to expropriate the property of a foreigner than it is for an investor to exercise much control over the policies of a foreign government. History illustrates the vulnerability of the foreign investor. The United States expropriated the property of Germans and Japanese during the Second World War. Several Middle Eastern countries expropriated the property of foreign investors when they nationalized their domestic oil industries in the 1950s and 1960s. Under Fidel Castro, the Cuban government expropriated the assets of foreigners. Foreign investment is a hostage to the domestic policies of the recipient country. A major reason why foreign investment is attracted to the United States is the confidence of foreigners that the U.S. government will not abuse its superior position.

COULD BUDGET DEFICITS CAUSE ECONOMIC COLLAPSE?

Some people fear that economic collapse is imminent if the size of the budget deficit is not reduced. When considering this issue, it is important to recognize that borrowing is a standard method of doing business. Many large and profitable corporations continually have debt outstanding. As long as the net income of a business firm is large relative to its interest liability, the outstanding debt poses little problem.

So it is with the federal government. As long as people have confidence that it can raise the tax revenue necessary to meet its debt obligations, the federal government will have no trouble financing and refinancing its outstanding debt. And it can do so in perpetuity. There is no date in the future at which the federal debt must be paid off.

Thus, the key to creditworthiness is expected future income relative to interest liability. This is true for individuals, private businesses, and governments. What is happening to the creditworthiness of the U.S. federal government? In the late 1940s approximately 10 percent of U.S. federal revenues went to pay the interest on the national debt. As **Exhibit 16–6** illustrates, net interest costs were approximately 7 percent of federal revenues throughout the 1951–1974 period. Since that time, interest costs as a share of federal revenues have risen, soaring to 10 percent in 1980, 14 percent in 1983, and 16.3 percent in 1992.

This is a trend that cannot continue, at least not without serious consequences. Why not? If the interest costs continue to rise relative to federal revenues, the growing interest costs will make it increasingly difficult to cut spending, and

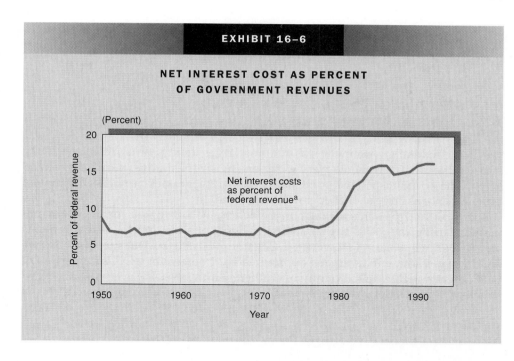

EXHIBIT 16-6

**NET INTEREST COST AS PERCENT
OF GOVERNMENT REVENUES**

During the period from 1950 to 1975, the net interest cost of the federal government consumed approximately 7 percent of federal revenues. By 1980 the ratio had jumped to 10 percent, and by 1992 it had risen to 16.3 percent. Obviously, interest costs cannot continue to increase as a share of federal revenue.

[a]The net interest costs include only the interest paid to private investors. The interest on debt held by federal government agencies and Federal Reserve banks is omitted.

Source: *Economic Report of the President,* various issues.

people will become more and more fearful that the government will resort to printing-press money in an effort to escape its loan obligations. This combination of forces—heavy government borrowing to finance and refinance its debt and the fear of rapid money growth and inflation—would push interest rates up and make it even more difficult for the government to meet its debt obligations. If sufficiently intense, the fear of inflation alone could seriously disrupt the long-term capital market, not only for the federal government, but for other borrowers as well. And if the government did resort to printing-press money in order to pay off its debt, hyperinflation and a breakdown in the exchange system would result. The economy would be severely crippled.

Excessive debt has led to financial crises elsewhere. The economies of several countries, including Bolivia, Argentina, Chile, Brazil, and Israel have been ravaged in recent years by excessive debt, money creation, and runaway inflation. Most economists are confident that in the United States constructive action will be taken well before such a crisis develops. However, the United States is not immune to the laws of economics. A continuation of the rising interest costs as a share of federal revenues will clearly bring severe economic consequences.

IS THE SIZE OF THE DEBT EXAGGERATED?

Some economists believe that the magnitude of the "deficit problem" has been exaggerated due to (1) lack of recognition that state and local governments ran sizable surpluses throughout much of the 1980s; (2) the failure of the federal accounting procedures to make the appropriate allowance for capital expenditures; and (3) the impact of inflation on the nominal budget deficit. Let us consider each of these points.

OFFSETTING EFFECT OF STATE AND LOCAL SURPLUSES

While the federal government was running larger deficits throughout the 1980s, state and local governments were experiencing sizable budget surpluses. Therefore, some economists have pointed out, the aggregate deficit of all government units was not as large as the federal data indicate.

Exhibit 16–7 presents the data on the deficit, including state and local governments. During the 1970s the combined budgets of state and local governments were roughly in balance. However, during the 1980s the budget surpluses of state and local governments averaged approximately 1 percent of GDP. As a percent of GDP, the aggregate deficit of all governments in the 1980s was almost one-third smaller than the federal deficit alone.

EXHIBIT 16–7

IMPACT OF STATE AND LOCAL FINANCE ON TOTAL GOVERNMENT DEFICIT

| | GOVERNMENT DEFICIT (–) OR SURPLUS (+) | | | DEFICIT AS A PERCENT OF GDP | |
YEAR	FEDERAL (BILLIONS)	STATE AND LOCAL (BILLIONS)	TOTAL (BILLIONS)	FEDERAL	TOTAL GOVERNMENT
1970	$– 12.4	$+ 1.8	$– 10.6	–1.2	–1.0
1975	– 69.4	+ 4.6	– 64.8	–4.4	–4.1
1980	– 60.1	+24.8	– 35.3	–2.2	–1.3
1982	–135.5	+26.9	–108.6	–4.3	–3.4
1983	–180.1	+40.3	–139.8	–5.2	–4.1
1985	–181.4	+56.1	–125.3	–4.5	–3.1
1986	–201.0	+54.3	–146.7	–4.7	–3.4
1987	–151.8	+40.1	–111.7	–3.3	–2.5
1988	–136.6	+38.4	– 98.2	–2.8	–2.0
1989	–122.3	+44.8	– 77.5	–2.3	–1.5
1990	–163.5	+25.1	–138.4	–2.9	–2.5
1991	–203.4	+ 7.3	–196.1	–3.6	–3.4
1992	–276.3	+ 7.2	–269.1	–4.6	–4.5
1993	–225.8	+ 2.1	–223.7	–3.5	–3.5

These data are for calendar years.   Source: *Economic Report of the President, 1994, Table B-1 amd B-80.*

For example, while the federal deficit was 4.7 percent of GDP ($201 billion) in 1986, the deficit for total government was only 3.4 percent of GDP ($146.7 billion). By 1989 the aggregate government deficit had fallen to 1.5 percent of GDP, a rate well below the long-term growth of income. Even during the recession years of 1982–1983 and 1991–1992, the overall deficit as a percent of GDP was not significantly larger than the deficit during the 1974–1975 recession. Thus, many economists argue that reliance on the federal data alone tends to exaggerate the growth of deficit financing.

ADJUSTMENT FOR CAPITAL EXPENDITURES

In private affairs, we recognize that it makes a difference whether borrowing is for long-lasting assets or current consumption. Borrowing to purchase a new home expected to last 30 years is one thing, borrowing to finance a weekend caper in Las Vegas is quite another. Businesses establish capital and current expense budgets in order to distinguish between expenditures for long-lasting assets and resources used during the current period. When undertaking a major capital expenditure, borrowing is a perfectly acceptable method of doing business.

In contrast, the federal government makes no distinction between expenditures for a new highway or aircraft and expenditures for current services or transfer payments. To the extent the budget deficit is used to finance long-lasting assets, future taxpayers will receive a stream of services as an offset to the tax liability. For example, suppose the federal government spends $100 million to provide office space that is currently rented for $12 million. If the expenditure is debt financed at an annual interest rate of 12 percent, then $100 million is added to the national debt. But there is no change in government's current expenditures; rent expense goes down by $12 million, and interest expense increases by $12 million.

Many economists believe that the government's inclusion of capital investment as a current expenditure exaggerates the magnitude of the deficit problem. While it is difficult to determine the precise magnitude of the federal government's net capital expenditures, it is clear that they are substantial. Recent research of the topic indicates that they were more than $20 billion in the mid-1980s.[5]

INFLATION DISTORTS THE BUDGET DEFICIT

By now you should be well aware that inflation affects nominal interest rates. Once people come to expect a given rate of inflation, it gets built into the nominal rate of interest.

When the rate of inflation accelerates to a higher level, the expected future inflation rate and nominal interest rates on *newly issued* bonds will also tend to rise. The interest rates applicable to previously issued bonds, however, will be unchanged until their maturity. Therefore, when there is an acceleration in the inflation rate, the government's interest costs will lag behind the general growth of revenues and expenditures. As a result, the current budget deficit will, *for a time*, understate the longer-term liability accompanying the government's outstanding debt. Eventually, the "old bonds" will have to be refinanced at the higher nominal interest rates. When this happens, both the government's interest costs

---

[5]Robert Eisner, "Which Budget Deficit? Some Issues of Measurement and Their Implications," *American Economic Review* 74 (May 1988), pp.138–143.

and its budget deficit will rise. Currently, the average maturity length on government debt is about six years. Thus, the time lag during which the relative size of the budget deficit is understated can be substantial.

The bias is in the opposite direction when there is a deceleration in the rate of inflation. While a lower actual and expected rate of inflation will reduce the nominal interest rate on *newly issued* bonds, the interest payments on the bonds that were previously issued at the higher nominal rates will be unchanged. Thus, the reduction in the nominal amount of the government's interest costs will decline more slowly than other expenditures and revenues due to the lower rate of inflation. Under these circumstances, the budget deficit will temporarily be larger than will be true in the future (if the government's real outstanding debt remains constant).

Inflation also distorts the size of the budget deficit for another reason. Once persistent inflation is in place and nominal interest rates rise as a result, the inflation both (1) increases the nominal cost of financing the debt and (2) erodes the real liability accompanying the bonds that are outstanding. These two items are offsetting, but only the higher interest costs will show up in the government's budget.

Consider the following situation. The government has a net public debt of $3 trillion and, as the result of a persistent inflation rate of 4 percent, nominal interest rates are 4 percent higher than would otherwise be the case. This 4 percent increase in nominal interest rates pushes the government's interest costs up by $120 billion (4 percent of $3 trillion). This increase in interest expense shows up in the budget. The 4 percent inflation also erodes the real burden of the $3 trillion of outstanding debt by $120 billion. This is a real capital gain (a decline in the liability of the government), but it does not appear in the budget. Therefore, even though the $120 billion of additional interest and $120 billion reduction in the government's real liability on outstanding debt are offsetting items resulting from the 4 percent inflation rate, only the additional nominal interest cost affects the budget.

What are the implications of this analysis for the U.S. budget deficit? First, it indicates that as the inflation rate accelerated upward during the 1970s and then decelerated during the early 1980s, these forces initially resulted in an understatement in the size of the deficit during the 1970s and overstatement during the early 1980s because the change in interest expense tends to lag behind the rate of inflation. Second, the increases in the budget deficit/GDP ratio (see Exhibit 16–2) and the interest cost as a percent of federal revenue (see Exhibit 16–6) during the last 25 years are at least partially the result of the higher inflation rates of the 1970s and 1980s compared to the 25-year period following the Second World War.

If we want to find out what is happening to the *real* debt outstanding, the nominal deficit figure needs to be reduced by the change in the real value of the outstanding bonds. In the early 1990s the inflation rate was approximately 4 percent, and the net public debt was in the $3 trillion range. This would imply that inflation reduced the real value of this outstanding debt by approximately $120 billion annually during the early 1990s. If this figure were included as an offset to the higher nominal interest payments emanating from inflation, then the federal budget deficit would be approximately 1.5 percent rather than 3.5 percent of GDP. The ratio is still larger than the comparable one during the relatively stable price era of the 1950s and early 1960s. However, it does not indicate that an impending catastrophe is right around the corner, as persons focusing on the nominal deficit figures have sometimes charged.

SOCIAL SECURITY SYSTEM AND NATIONAL DEBT

As conventionally measured, the budget deficit includes the revenues and expenditures of government trust funds, including the social security trust fund. Until recently, the net revenue (or expenditure) flowing into these funds was small relative to the size of the budget. Therefore, it really did not make much difference whether these funds were included in or excluded from budget deficit calculations.

All of this began to change during the latter half of the 1980s. Under legislation passed in 1983, the social security trust fund is scheduled to run huge budget surpluses throughout the 1990s and into the next century. Now the size of the federal budget deficit differs substantially depending on whether the social security trust funds are included or excluded in the deficit calculations. For example, if the social security trust fund surplus had been excluded from the 1992 deficit calculations, the fiscal-year federal deficit would have been $340 billion rather than $290 billion. By the late 1990s, inclusion of the social security trust fund surpluses will reduce the size of the perceived budget deficits by an estimated $100 billion *annually*.

More is at stake here than just a definitional issue. There is a reason for the planned social security surpluses. During the 15 years following the Second World War, there was a huge group of people born in the United States. When this "baby boom" generation is in the retirement phase of their life during 2020 to 2050, enormous strain will be placed on the social security system. Unless funds are set aside to finance the retirement benefits of the baby-boomers, the solvency of the social security system will be endangered. Hence the planned social security surpluses are intended to increase the national saving rate and stimulate additional investment, and thereby help to finance the retirement benefits of the baby-boom generation. Using the trust funds to finance current government expenditures completely undermines this strategy.

Given the future demands of the social security system, many economists argue that it will not be enough for the federal government to just balance its budget in the 1990s. They argue that the government should be running a budget surplus equal to the surplus in the social security trust fund.

DEBT FINANCING IN OTHER COUNTRIES

The United States has not been alone in its reliance on deficit financing. As **Exhibit 16–8** shows, most other industrial countries have also run substantial deficits in recent years. Among the G-7 countries, only Japan and the United Kingdom ran surpluses during the 1988–1992 period (when all levels of government are considered). The overall government deficits of France, Germany, and Canada averaged

Source: International Monetary Fund, *International Finance Statistics*, December 1993.

EXHIBIT 16–8

BUDGET DEFICITS OF SELECTED COUNTRIES

AVERAGE BUDGET DEFICIT AS A PERCENT OF GDP, 1988–1992

COUNTRY	ALL GOVERNMENT UNITS	CENTRAL GOVERNMENT ONLY	NET PUBLIC DEBT AS A PERCENT OF GDP, 1992
G–7 COUNTRIES			
Canada	−3.7	−3.3	54
United States	−2.4	−4.0	53
Japan	+2.7	−0.2	55
France	−1.4	−2.1	30
Germany	−2.4	−1.5	26
Italy	−10.1	−11.1	99
United Kingdom	+0.3	+0.1	32
OTHER COUNTRIES			
Belgium	—	−5.9	110
Netherlands	—	−3.9	64
Spain	—	−3.6	40
Australia	—	+0.5	15

between 1.4 percent and 3.7 percent of GDP, about the same as the average of the United States during the 1988–1992 period. Italy has consistently run larger budget deficits than the other G-7 countries. During the 1988–1992 period, the budget deficits of the Italian government summed to more than 10 percent of GDP. Belgium, Netherlands, and Spain have also run substantial deficits in recent years. Australia is atypical among the industrial democracies; the central government of Australia ran a surplus during the 1988–1992 period.

Exhibit 16–8 also provides data on the net public debt relative to the GDP. Among the G-7 nations, the net public debt/GDP ratio was lowest in Germany, France, and the United Kingdom at year-end 1992. This ratio was between 26 percent and 32 percent for these three countries. For Canada, Japan, and the United States, the size of the net public debt as a share of GDP was quite similar, ranging between 53 percent and 55 percent. In the case of Italy, the net public debt was 99 percent of GDP in 1992. The net public debt of Australia is the lowest of the industrial democracies—only 15 percent of GDP. In contrast, the net public debt of Belgium is the highest of any industrial country, 110 percent of GDP at year-end 1992.

The Belgium case sheds light on what is in store for countries that persistently run large budget deficits and expand their outstanding debt more rapidly than the growth of real GDP. The interest payments on the public debt now comprise approximately 30 percent of the government's budget and 15 percent of Belgian national income. Thus, the government of Belgium now has to tax away 15 percent of the income generated by its citizens just to make the interest payments on its outstanding debt. As a result, Belgium is one of the most highly taxed countries in the world. In turn, the disincentive effects of the high taxes retard economic growth, making it even more difficult to deal with the debt obligations. Concern about these issues coupled with a substantial decline in the value of the Belgian franc on the exchange-rate market more or less forced the government to reduce its 1994 spending on social programs—including social security, health care, and child benefits.

POLITICS AND BUDGET DEFICITS

Why has the federal government run a string of deficits during the last three decades? Why is deficit spending so popular around the world? Many public-choice economists, including the 1986 Nobel laureate James Buchanan, charge that politicians like to spend money in order to buy the favor of various interest groups and voting blocs, but they dislike taxes that impose visible costs on voting constituents.

However, government expenditures must be financed in some manner. Borrowing provides an alternative to current taxation. Since they push the taxes into the future, deficits are less visible to people than current taxation. Regardless of whether it is in fact true, political officials believe that the substitution of debt for taxes reduces the current visible cost of government programs and pushes some of the costs into the future. People imagine that government services cost less than is really the case. Thus, borrowing allows politicians to supply voters with immediate benefits without having to impose a parallel visible cost in the form of higher taxes or user charges.

Prior to the Keynesian analysis of the Great Depression, almost everyone—including the leading figures of both political parties—thought that the government should balance its budget except during times of war. In essence, until approximately 1960, there was widespread implicit agreement—much like a constitutional rule—that the federal budget should be balanced. The Keynesian revolution changed opinions, first among economists and later among others, including political officials. In essence, the Keynesian view eroded the discipline that emanated from the implicit balanced-budget concept. Released from that constraint, since the early 1960s politicians have consistently spent more than they have been willing to tax.[6]

Public-choice analysis explains why each representative has a strong incentive to fight hard for expenditures beneficial to his or her constituents and little incentive to oppose spending by others. A legislator who is a spending "watchdog"

---

[6]See James M. Buchanan and Richard Wagner, *Democracy in Deficit: The Political Legacy of Lord Keynes* (New York: Academic Press, 1977), for a detailed account of the changes wrought by the Keynesian revolution.

will incur the wrath of colleagues favoring special programs for their districts. More importantly, the benefits (for example, tax reductions and lower interest rates) of spending cuts and deficit reductions will be spread thinly among the voters in *all* districts. Thus, the legislator's constituents will reap only a small part of these benefits.

It is as if 535 families go out to dinner knowing that after the meal each will receive a bill for 1/535th of the cost. No family feels compelled to order less, because their restraint will exert little impact on the total bill. Why not order shrimp for an appetizer, entrees of steak and lobster, and a large piece of cheesecake for dessert? After all, the extra spending will add only a few pennies to each family's share of the total bill. However, when everybody follows this course of action, many items are purchased that are valued less than their cost.[7]

So it is with congressional decision making. Representatives have a strong incentive to push for "desserts" helpful to their own districts, particularly when each recognizes that other legislators are doing so. Then, after the spending decisions are made, Congress sums up the total and tries to figure out how to pay for it. Given this process, the presence of budget deficits should not come as a surprise.

STRUCTURAL CHANGE AND DEFICITS

Public-choice analysis indicates that budget deficits are an expected result of ordinary politics in the post-Keynesian era. Paradoxically, there is little reason to believe that a tax increase will do much to reduce the deficit—at least not for long. A 1991 study prepared by the Joint Economic Committee of Congress found that since 1947 every new dollar of tax revenue has generated spending increases of $1.59. On several occasions, most notably during 1982 and 1990, the president and congressional leaders have held a summit meeting and agreed to both raise taxes and cut spending. After tax rates were raised, though, the projected revenue increases proved to be disappointing and the spending cuts elusive. As a result, the deficit has continued to grow. Given the adjustments of people to higher tax rates and the spending inclinations built into the ordinary political process, these results, again, are not surprising.

According to the public-choice view, the budget deficits reflect the current rules of the game. If we want a different outcome, we will have to change the incentive structure confronted by legislators. Most public-choice economists believe that effective restraint on deficit spending would require constitutional action making it difficult for political officials to spend more than they are willing to tax. The simplest approach would be a constitutional amendment mandating that the federal government balance its budget. Proposed amendments of this type would allow only a supra-majority (for example, two-thirds or three-fourths)

---

[7]As E. C. Pasour, Jr., of North Carolina State University, has pointed out to the authors, the federal "dinner check" analogy can be carried one step further. Suppose the check is to be divided evenly among the large group, but the ordering will be done by committee so there will be separate committees for drinks, appetizers, entrees, salads, and desserts. Since each person can serve on the committee of his (or her) choice, lushes end up on the drinks committee, vegetarians on the salad committee, sweet-tooths on the dessert committee, and so on. This arrangement further exacerbates the tendency toward overordering and overspending. The arrangement just described closely resembles the committee structure of the U.S. Congress.

of Congress to override the restriction. In essence, this approach calls for an explicit constitutional restraint that its backers hope would reapply the kind of discipline that was present prior to the Keynesian revolution.

Is the balanced-budget requirement a good idea? Two criticisms are generally levied against it. First, some charge that it would reduce the effectiveness of fiscal policy as a stabilization tool. According to this view, Congress might feel compelled to raise taxes in the midst of a recession. Of course, the supra-majority override provision would reduce the likelihood of this occurrence. Nonetheless, some critics fear that limitations on budget deficits might reduce the effectiveness of fiscal policy and exert a destabilizing influence on the economy.

A second group of critics argues that a balanced-budget requirement would be easily evaded and largely ineffective. According to this view, Congress would use things like off-budget expenditures, mandated spending, and unrealistic budget projections in order to escape the proposed discipline.

There are other ways that fundamental rule changes might retard the deficit spending tendencies of Congress. Many believe that providing the president with a *line-item reduction veto* (the authority to reduce or eliminate spending on specific line items without having to veto an entire appropriations bill) would reduce pork-barrel spending and retard the power of special interests. William Niskanen, a member of the President's Council of Economic Advisers in the 1980s, has proposed that the Constitution be amended to require the approval of two-thirds of the members of both houses for an increase in either debt or taxes. Without eliminating the use of deficit financing, this proposal would stiffen the federal budget constraint. Others have proposed that Congress be required to adopt an aggregate spending constraint six months, for example, prior to the beginning of each fiscal year. Once the constraint was adopted, approval of any budget expenditure beyond the constraint would require a three-fourths majority.

Finally, Dwight Lee and Richard McKenzie have proposed that congressional salaries be inversely linked to the size of the deficit.[8] For example, congressional salaries might be reduced by 10 percent for each 1 percent increase in the deficit/GDP ratio. Therefore, if the budget deficit was 5 percent of GDP, as was the case in the mid-1980s, congressional salaries would be cut by 50 percent! The same pay scale could also be applied to the president and all cabinet officials. This proposal would not only let Congress and the president know that they were expected to balance the budget, it would provide them with an incentive to do so.

CONCLUDING THOUGHTS

The topic of the budget deficit is both interesting and complex. It encompasses both economic and political dimensions. It is a topic about which the popular media is constantly disseminating false information and half-truths, usually because so many do not understand the issue.

Our analysis indicates that the recent growth of the federal debt is troublesome, but not catastrophic. It is troublesome because debt financing may be misleading Americans in regard to their true wealth position and thereby causing them to save and invest less than would otherwise be the case. It is also troublesome because the deficit may be partially hiding the true cost of government

---

[8]Dwight R. Lee and Richard B. McKenzie, *Regulating Government: A Preface to Constitutional Economics* (Lexington: Lexington Books, 1987), p. 149–163.

and thereby contributing to the inefficient use of resources. But these effects imply a gradual slowdown in economic growth, not a future "day of reckoning."

If action is taken now to reduce the growth of the debt relative to GDP, there is no reason why a combination of expenditure cuts, revenue increases, and economic growth cannot return the ratio of debt to GDP to the downward path of the three decades following the Second World War. However, there is reason to doubt that this will happen in the current political environment. Given the political pressures, a quick resolution is unlikely. The "deficit issue" will almost surely be with us in the foreseeable future.

CHAPTER SUMMARY

1. The national debt is the sum of the outstanding bonds of the U.S. Treasury. Budget deficits increase the national debt. In fact, the national debt reflects the cumulative effect of all prior budget deficits and surpluses.

2. Approximately one-third of the national debt is owned by U.S. government agencies and Federal Reserve banks. For this portion of the debt, the government both pays and receives the interest (except for the expenses of the Fed). Therefore, only the net federal debt—the portion of the national debt owned by domestic and foreign investors —generates a net interest liability for the government. Most (80 percent in 1993) of the net federal debt is owed to domestic investors.

3. When considering the impact of the national debt on future generations, it is important to keep two points in mind. First, the future generations that pay the tax liability accompanying the debt will also receive the interest income implied by the debt. Second, the opportunity cost of using scarce resources to produce goods and services through the public sector is the decline in current private-sector output. This opportunity cost is incurred during the current period regardless of how the government activity is financed.

4. Budget deficits affect future generations through their impact on capital formation. When an economy is operating below capacity, a budget deficit may stimulate output and expand the stock of capital assets available to future generations.

5. According to the traditional view, the substitution of debt financing for taxes during normal times will indirectly alter the composition of private spending toward consumption and away from investment. From the standpoint of the entire nation, government securities do not represent wealth, since they imply a tax liability precisely equal to the future income the bond represents. However, since households are unlikely to recognize fully the implied future

taxes, they will tend to view the securities as wealth and therefore have an exaggerated view of their true wealth position. As a result, they will consume more and invest less than if government were fully financed by current taxation.

6. The traditional view of debt-financing also stresses that the strong demand for loanable funds will push real interest rates up and lead to an inflow of foreign capital. A persistent trade deficit will be required for the finance of the capital inflow.

7. In contrast with the traditional view, the new classical theory argues that households will anticipate fully the added future tax liability implied by debt financing and increase their savings in order to meet the higher future taxes. This increase in saving offsets the increase in demand for loanable funds emanating from the debt. In the new classical model, the substitution of debt for taxes leaves interest rates, consumption, and investment unaffected.

8. The high real interest rates, inflow of foreign capital, persistent trade deficits, and apparent reduction in domestically financed investment accompanying the large budget deficits of the 1980s were all highly consistent with the traditional view. However, the proponents of the new classical theory argue that *real* investment as a share of *real* GDP during the 1980s was similar to the real investment/GDP ratio of earlier decades. This suggests that the large deficits of the 1980s exerted little impact on capital formation, a finding consistent with the new classical view.

9. As long as the interest liability accompanying the debt grows less rapidly than national income, the relative burden imposed on the economy by the debt is declining. The increase in net interest cost relative to GDP during the last 15 years is a worrisome trend.

10. Since the increase in interest costs will tend to lag other expenditures and revenues, an acceleration in the rate of inflation will initially tend to result in a smaller deficit/GDP ratio than the ratio that will emerge in the long run. In contrast, a deceleration in inflation will initially increase the deficit/GDP ratio. Persistent inflation both increases the nominal interest payments on the debt and erodes the real value of the debt. Even though these two factors offset each other, only the higher nominal interest payments affect the budget. As a result, higher actual and expected rates of inflation will increase the size of the *nominal* debt/GDP ratio (relative to what it would be if the level of prices was stable) even if the *real* debt/GDP ratio is unchanged.

11. Many public-choice economists believe that the current budget process is structurally unsound. They argue that it encourages deficit financing and fails to confront Congress with a firm budget constraint. These economists believe that constitutional changes are necessary to deal with the "budget problem."

CRITICAL-ANALYSIS QUESTIONS

*1. Does the national debt have to be paid off at some-time in the future? What will happen if it is not?

2. Do we owe the national debt to ourselves? Does this mean the size of the national debt is of little concern? Why or why not?

3. "The national debt is a mortgage against the future of our children and grandchildren. We are forcing them to pay for our current consumption of goods and services." Evaluate this statement.

*4. When government bonds are held by foreigners, the interest income from the bonds goes to foreigners rather than to Americans. Would Americans be better off if we prohibited the sale of bonds to foreigners?

*5. If citizen-taxpayers fail to anticipate the future tax liability accompanying debt finance, what does this imply about their perception of the cost of government? How do you think this affects the political popularity of debt financing relative to taxes?

*6. Even if it were unable or unwilling to raise taxes in order to meet the interest payments on outstanding debt, the federal government would be unlikely to default on its outstanding bonds. Why? What would happen in the event of such a crisis?

7. Is the federal government more or less likely than state and local governments to default on outstanding bonds? Why?

*8. When there is a budget deficit, what happens to the nominal national debt? Could the real outstanding government debt decline even though a budget deficit is present?

9. "We must start paying for what we get from government. A government worth having is worth paying for!" Evaluate this statement. Can we get things from government without paying for them?

*10. Does an increase in the national debt increase the supply of money (M1)? Can the money supply increase when the U.S. Treasury is running a budget surplus?

11. "If the government is spending $20 billion to maintain and improve highways, these costs are incurred during the current period regardless of whether they are financed with taxes or debt." Evaluate this statement.

12. Will the $4.4 trillion debt of the United States impose a cost on future generations? When government expenditures are paid for with debt rather than with taxes, what is the likely impact on the growth of the U.S. economy? Explain.

13. Are the large deficits of the federal government a threat to our economy? Why or why not? Would our economy be healthier if taxes were raised sufficiently to generate a substantial budget surplus? Why or why not?

*14. Suppose that the Federal Reserve were a government agency under the direct control of Congress. Thus, the discount rate, open market policy, and growth rate of the money supply would be determined by Congress. How do you think this would affect the inflation rate and economic stability of the nation?

*15. Would you predict that government expenditures would be higher or lower if taxes (and user charges) were required for the finance of all expenditures? Why? Do you think the government would spend funds more or less efficiently if it could not issue debt? Why?

16. What are the implications of the shortsightedness effect with regard to the comparative attractiveness of tax and debt financing?

17. (a) Does it make any difference whether government debt is owed to foreign investors, rather than to domestic investors? Why? (b) Does it make any difference whether government debt is owed to private investors or held by a government agency or by the Fed? Why?

18. In most cases the credibility of governments in Eastern Europe and the former Soviet Union is very low with potential financial investors. Private investors are unwilling to purchase bonds issued by these governments. Under these circumstances, if the government runs a budget deficit how must that deficit be financed? How will this method of finance influence the inflation rate?

19. Consider the following hypothetical information (figures are in billions of dollars):

Budget receipts in 1993   1,150
Budget expenditures in 1993   1,300
Annual growth rate of GDP   6 percent

a. Complete the following table (some information has already been provided):

	BUDGET DEFICIT	NATIONAL DEBT (END OF PERIOD)	GDP	BUDGET DEFICIT AS SHARE OF GDP	NATIONAL DEBT AS SHARE OF GDP (END OF PERIOD)
1992	$145	$4,200	$6,000	——	——
1993	——	——	——	——	——

b. Why did the national debt fall as a share of GDP in 1993 even though the budget deficit rose?

---

*Asterisk denotes questions for which answers are given in Appendix B.

PART THREE

MICROECONOMICS

CHAPTER SEVENTEEN

DEMAND AND
CONSUMER CHOICE

The most famous law in economics, and the one economists are most sure of, is the law of demand. On this law is built almost the whole edifice of economics.

DAVID R. HENDERSON[1]

A thing is worth whatever a buyer will pay for it.

PUBLILIUS SYRUS, FIRST CENTURY B.C.[2]

CHAPTER FOCUS

■ *How do economists analyze consumer choice? What assumptions do they make?*
■ *What role does time play in the consumption of goods?*
■ *What factors will cause a demand curve to shift?*
■ *What determines the demand for a specific item? Is advertising effective? Is it useful to the consumer or just manipulative?*
■ *What is demand elasticity, and what factors determine its size? How is the elasticity concept used?*

[1]David R. Henderson, "Demand" in *The Fortune Encyclopedia of Economics,* edited by David R. Henderson (New York: Warner Books, Inc.), 1993, p. 7.

[2]Quoted in Michael Jackman, ed., *Macmillan Book of Business and Economic Quotations* (New York: Macmillan, 1984), p. 150.

T he quote from David Henderson highlights the fact that whether we are studying macroeconomics, which focuses on aggregate markets—the "big picture"—or the microeconomics of the individual decisions that make up the big picture, individual demand is a key concept. What exactly is demand? As Publilius Syrus, in our second quote, noted more than 2000 years ago, demand amounts to the willingness of individuals to pay for what is offered in the market. In this section, we begin our examination of microeconomic markets for specific products with an analysis of the demand side of those markets.

Microeconomics focuses on how changes in *relative* prices influence consumer decisions. As we stressed in Chapter 3, the price system guides individuals in their production and consumption decisions.[3] Prices coordinate the vast array of individual economic activities by signaling relative wants and needs, and by motivating market participants to bring their own activities into harmony with those of others. Changes in one market affect conditions in others. In this chapter, we take a closer look at (1) the interrelationships among markets and (2) the factors underlying the demand for specific products.

This chapter's topic, individual demand, or willingness to pay, is a critical determinant of the market price. In turn, the market price signals information about relative scarcity and value to all potential buyers and sellers of the item. The other critical element of market price—the cost of supplying the item into the market—will be examined in the next chapter.

CHOICE AND INDIVIDUAL DEMAND

The 98 million households in the United States spent $2.9 trillion in 1991. **Exhibit 17–1** shows how they allocated their spending in 1991. Data for 1986 are also provided for comparison. Income changed only a little during that five-year period. Consumers spent an average of $29,610 per household in 1991, down slightly from $29,640 (corrected for inflation) in 1986. But the composition of purchases changed significantly. For example, spending on transportation fell more than 14 percent, while spending on health care rose more than 10 percent. Furthermore, the broad categories of spending conceal some more dramatic changes, like the 27 percent drop in vehicle purchases (part of "transportation") and the 52 percent rise in property tax expenditures (part of "housing") that the exhibit does not show. Why did consumers make these changes? Economists can offer some partial explanations, and even predict consumer behavior to some extent, based on the following principles:

1. Limited income necessitates choice. Most of us are all too aware that our desire for goods far exceeds our limited income. People do not have enough resources to produce everything they would like. A limited income forces each of us to make choices. When more of one good or service is purchased, less of some others can be obtained. That is precisely the meaning of "cost."

2. Consumers make decisions purposefully. Consumption decisions are made with the desire to upgrade one's personal welfare in mind. A foolish purchase means giving up something more worthwhile. The goal behind a consumer decision can usually be met in many different ways, so careful consideration of alternatives is

---

[3]You may want to review Chapter 3 before proceeding with this chapter.

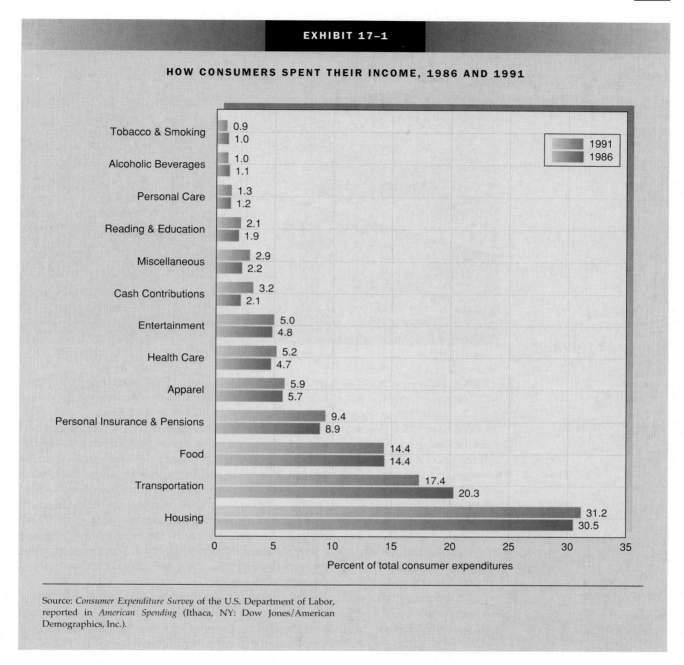

EXHIBIT 17–1

HOW CONSUMERS SPENT THEIR INCOME, 1986 AND 1991

Category	1991	1986
Tobacco & Smoking	0.9	1.0
Alcoholic Beverages	1.0	1.1
Personal Care	1.3	1.2
Reading & Education	2.1	1.9
Miscellaneous	2.9	2.2
Cash Contributions	3.2	2.1
Entertainment	5.0	4.8
Health Care	5.2	4.7
Apparel	5.9	5.7
Personal Insurance & Pensions	9.4	8.9
Food	14.4	14.4
Transportation	17.4	20.3
Housing	31.2	30.5

Percent of total consumer expenditures

Source: *Consumer Expenditure Survey* of the U.S. Department of Labor, reported in *American Spending* (Ithaca, NY: Dow Jones/American Demographics, Inc.).

useful. Consumers do not intentionally choose a lesser valued alternative when they know that another of equal cost but greater projected benefit is available.

3. *One good can be substituted for another.* Consumers have many goals, each with alternative means of satisfaction. No single good is so precious that some of it will not be given up in exchange for a large enough quantity of other goods. For example, consumers will give up some fried chicken to have more pizza, hamburgers, fish, ham sandwiches, or apple pie. Similarly, reading, watching movies and television, or playing cards can be substituted for playing football. Then, too, a recreational activity may partially substitute for food, as when a hamburger and

The purchasing choices of consumers underlie the demand for goods and service.

a movie replace a more elaborate four-course dinner. The buyer wants *utility*—satisfaction—from the substitute goods, not necessarily the same services. There are many alternative ways to satisfy the individual's wants and needs.

We have been discussing "wants," but how about our "need" for basic commodities such as water or energy? The need of a person for an item is closely related to its cost—what must be given up to obtain the item. Southern California residents need water from the north, but the individual resident, when faced with a high water bill, finds that cactus gardens or ivy can be substituted for lawns, a plumber's bill for water lost to a faucet drip, and flow constrictors for water used with full-force showers. The need for water thus depends on its cost. People living in Montana, where household electricity costs nearly twice as much as in nearby Washington, use about half as much electricity per household. Montanans reduce their "need" for electricity by substituting gas, fuel oil, insulation, and wool sweaters for the relatively more expensive electricity.

4. Consumers must make decisions without perfect information, but knowledge and past experience will help. No human being has perfect foresight. Napoleon did not anticipate Waterloo; Julius Caesar did not anticipate the actions of Brutus. Consumers will not always correctly anticipate the consequences of their choices. They will, however, have a good chance of doing so in areas of common knowledge and experience. Consumer choices are not made in a vacuum. You have a pretty good idea of what to expect when you buy a cup of coffee, five gallons of gasoline, or lunch at your favorite cafe. Why? Because you have learned from experience—your own and that of others—what to expect. Your expectations may not always be fulfilled precisely (for example, the coffee may be stronger than expected or the gasoline may make your car engine knock), but even then, you will gain valuable information that can be used to make better forecasts in the future.

5. The law of diminishing marginal utility applies: as the rate of consumption increases, the utility derived from consuming additional units of a good will decline. As explained earlier, *utility* is a term economists use to describe the subjective personal benefits that result from an action. The **law of diminishing marginal utility** states that the **marginal** (or additional) **utility** derived from consuming successive units of a product will eventually decline as the rate of utilization increases. For example, the law implies, even though you might like ice cream, your marginal satisfaction from additional ice cream will eventually decline. Ice cream at lunchtime might be great. An additional helping for dinner might be even better. However, after you have had it for evening dessert and a midnight snack, ice cream for breakfast will have lost some attraction. The law of diminishing marginal utility will have set in, and thus the marginal utility derived from the consumption of additional units of ice cream will decline.

MARGINAL UTILITY AND CONSUMER CHOICE

Consumer choices, like other decisions, are influenced by changes in benefits and costs. If a consumer wants to get the most out of his or her expenditures, these changes in benefits and costs will determine how much of a good should be purchased. As more of a good is consumed per unit of time, the law of diminishing marginal utility states that the consumer's marginal benefit per unit of time will decline. A consumer will gain by purchasing more of a product as long as the benefit, or marginal utility (*MU*), derived from the consumption of an additional unit exceeds the cost of the unit (the expected marginal utility from the highest valued consumption alternative that must now be given up).

Given a fixed income and specified prices for the commodities to be purchased, consumers will maximize their satisfaction (or total utility) by ensuring that the last dollar spent on each commodity purchased yields an equal degree of marginal utility. If consumers are to get the most for their money, the last dollar spent on Product A must yield the same utility as the last dollar spent on Product B (or any other product).[4] After all, if tickets for football games, for example, yielded less marginal utility *per dollar* than did opera tickets, the obvious thing for a consumer to do would be to cut back spending on football games and allocate more funds for opera tickets. If people really attempt to spend their money in a way that yields the greatest amount of satisfaction, the applicability of the consumer decision-making theory outlined here is difficult to question.

Law of diminishing marginal utility
The basic economic principle that as the consumption of a commodity increases, the marginal utility derived from consuming more of the commodity (per unit of time) will eventually decline. Marginal utility may decline even though total utility continues to increase, albeit at a reduced rate.

Marginal utility
The additional utility received by a person from the consumption of an additional unit of a good within a given time period.

---

[4]Mathematically, this implies that the consumer's total utility is at a maximum when limited income is spent on products such that

$$\frac{MU_a}{P_a} = \frac{MU_b}{P_b} = \ldots = \frac{MU_n}{P_n}$$

where *MU* represents the marginal utility derived from the last unit of a product, and *P* represents the price of the good. The subscripts *a, b, . . ., n* indicate the different products available to the consumer. In the continuous case, this expression implies that the consumer will get the most for his or her money when the consumption of each product is increased only to the point at which the marginal utility from one more unit of the good is equal to the marginal utility obtainable from the best alternative purchase that must now be foregone. For more advanced students, this proposition is developed in an alternative, more formal manner in the Addendum to this chapter on indifference curves.

PRICE CHANGES AND CONSUMER CHOICE

The *demand schedule* shows the amount of a product that consumers would be willing to purchase at alternative prices during a specific time period. The *first law of demand* states that the amount of a product purchased is inversely related to its price. Why? First, as the price of a product declines, the lower opportunity cost will induce consumers to buy more of it—and, the implication is, less of other, more highly priced products. Economists refer to this tendency to substitute a product that has become relatively cheaper for goods that are now more expensive as the **substitution effect.** What will happen to the marginal utility derived from the product, though, as the rate of consumption is increased? It will fall. Each additional unit consumed adds less to total utility. Thus, as more of the product is consumed, a point is reached where the benefits (marginal utility) derived from the consumption of still more units will again be less than the cost. Purposeful decision makers will not choose such units. A price reduction, then, will induce consumers to purchase more of a product, but the response will be limited because of the law of diminishing marginal utility.

Second, since the money income of consumers is constant, a reduction in the price of a product will increase real income—the amount of goods and services consumers are able to purchase. Typically, consumers will respond by purchasing more of the cheaper product (as well as other products) because they can now better afford to do so. This factor is referred to as the **income effect.** (Both the income and substitution effects are derived graphically in the addendum to this chapter, entitled "Consumer Choice and Indifference Curves.")

Of course, the substitution and income effects will generally induce consumers to purchase less of a good if its price rises. The rising opportunity cost of consuming the product makes it a less attractive buy. However, as consumption is reduced, remaining units have a higher marginal utility. If the price increase is not so great as to price the consumer out of the market completely, consumption of the item will fall until the product's marginal utility is high enough to again equal its new, higher opportunity cost. With moderate increases in price, the consumer's reduction in consumption will be limited. We must also bear in mind that if the consumer's money income is constant, and other prices have not fallen, the price increase reduces the individual's real income. A reduction in real income will tend to result in a reduction in the consumption of many goods, generally including the good that has increased in price.

Exhibit 17–2 illustrates the adjustment of consumers to a change in price. During 1985–1986, gasoline prices fell rapidly in the United States. As demand theory would predict, consumers increased their rate of consumption. As gasoline prices fell from $1.20 to $.80, Jones's average weekly consumption rose from 16 gallons to 20 gallons. The availability of less expensive fuel resulted in his postponement of a costly tuneup on his car, which would have saved some fuel. He went to the grocery store a little more often, rather than waiting as usual to combine shopping trips with other business near the shopping center. He and his family took a vacation by car, which would have been much more expensive at the 1985 gasoline price level. At the higher rate of use, the marginal utility of gasoline fell, bringing it into line with the lower price. Further price declines would have

Substitution effect

That part of an increase (decrease) in amount consumed that is the result of a good being cheaper (more expensive) in relation to other goods because of a reduction (increase) in price.

Income effect

That part of an increase (decrease) in amount consumed that is the result of the consumer's real income (the consumption possibilities available to the consumer) being expanded (contracted) by a reduction (rise) in the price of a good.

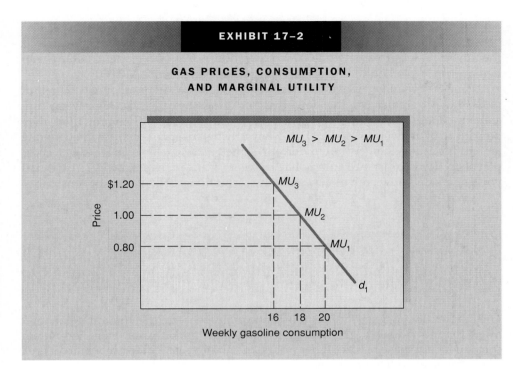

EXHIBIT 17–2

GAS PRICES, CONSUMPTION, AND MARGINAL UTILITY

$MU_3 > MU_2 > MU_1$

An individual, Jones in this case, will increase his rate of consumption of a product as long as his MU exceeds his opportunity cost (principally the price of the good). Lower prices will induce him to consume more, but the increase in consumption will be limited because the MU of the product will fall as consumption is expanded.

brought on even greater increases in consumption, but the price stabilized near its 1986 level for about four years. In late 1990 the price of gasoline jumped back up nearly to the 1985 level as a result of both higher gasoline taxes and Iraq's invasion of Kuwait. Responding to the higher price, consumers such as Jones once again began economizing more carefully on their use of the more expensive gasoline.

TIME COST AND CONSUMER CHOICE

The monetary price of a good is not always a complete measure of its cost to the consumer. Consumption of most goods requires time as well as money; and time, like money, is scarce to the consumer. Accordingly, a lower time cost, like a lower money price, will make a product more attractive.[5] Indeed, some commodities are demanded primarily because of their ability to save valuable time for consumers. People are often willing to pay relatively high money prices for such goods. The popularity of automatic dishwashers, prepared foods, air travel, and taxi service is based partly on their low time cost in comparison with substitutes.

---

[5]For a technical treatment of the importance of time as a component of cost from the vantage point of the consumer, see Gary Becker, "A Theory of the Allocation of Time," *Economic Journal* (September 1965), pp. 493–517.

What is the cost of a college education? Tuition payments and the price of books comprise only a small component. The major cost of a college education is the time cost—approximately 4,000 working hours. Even if a student's time is valued at only $5 per hour, the time cost of a college education is $20,000!

Time costs, unlike money prices, differ among individuals. They are higher for persons with greater earning power. Other things being equal, high-wage consumers choose fewer time-intensive (and more time-saving) commodities than persons with a lower time cost. High-wage consumers are overrepresented among air and taxicab passengers but underrepresented among television watchers, chess players, and long-distance automobile travelers. Can you explain why? You can, if you understand how both money and time cost influence the choices of consumers.

MARKET DEMAND AND CONSUMER CHOICE

The market demand schedule is the relationship between the amount demanded by all the individuals in the market area, and the market price. Since individual consumers purchase less at higher prices, the amount demanded in a market area is also inversely related to price.

Exhibit 17–3 illustrates the relationship between individual demand and market demand for a hypothetical two-person market. The individual demand curves

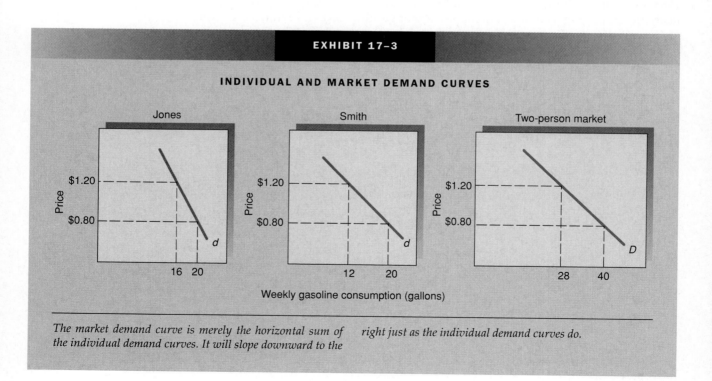

EXHIBIT 17–3

INDIVIDUAL AND MARKET DEMAND CURVES

The market demand curve is merely the horizontal sum of the individual demand curves. It will slope downward to the right just as the individual demand curves do.

for both Jones and Smith are shown. Jones and Smith each consume 20 gallons of gasoline weekly at 80 cents per gallon. The amount demanded in the two-person market is 40 gallons. If the price rises to $1.20 per gallon, the amount demanded in the market will fall to 28 gallons, 16 demanded by Jones and 12 by Smith. The market demand is simply the horizontal sum of the individual demand curves.

Market demand reflects individual demand. Individuals buy less as price increases. Therefore, the total amount demanded in the market declines as price increases.

CONSUMER SURPLUS

The demand curve reveals how many units consumers will purchase at various prices. In so doing, it reveals consumers' evaluation of units of a good. The height of the demand curve indicates how much consumers value an added unit. The difference between the amount that consumers would be willing to pay and the amount they actually pay for a good is called **consumer surplus.** As **Exhibit 17–4** illustrates, it is measured by the area under the demand curve but above the market price.

Consumer surplus
The difference between the maximum amount a consumer would be willing to pay for a unit of a good and the payment that is actually made.

Previously, we indicated that voluntary exchange is advantageous to buyer and seller alike. Consumer surplus is a measure of the net gain to the buyer/consumer. Consumer surplus also reflects the law of diminishing marginal utility. Consumers will continue to purchase additional units of a good, each yielding less marginal utility than the previous unit, until the marginal utility is just enough to justify paying the market price. Up to that point, however, consumption of each unit generates a surplus for the consumer, since the value of the unit exceeds the market price. In aggregate, the total value (utility) to consumers of a good may be far greater than its total cost.

The size of the consumer surplus is affected by the market price. A reduction in the market price will lead to an expansion in quantity purchased and a larger consumer surplus. Conversely, a higher market price will reduce the amount purchased and shrink the surplus (net gain) for consumers.

CONSUMER SURPLUS AND TOTAL VALUE

Nothing is more useful than water; but it will purchase scarce anything. . . . A diamond, on the contrary, has scarce any value in use; but a very great quantity of other goods may frequently be had in exchange for it.

ADAM SMITH[6]

The classical economists, including Adam Smith, were puzzled that water, which is necessary for life, sells so cheaply, while diamonds have a far greater price. A

---

[6]Adam Smith, *An Inquiry into the Nature and Causes of the Wealth of Nations*, 1776, (Cannan's edition Chicago: University of Chicago Press, 1976), p. 33.

As the shaded area indicates, the difference between the largest amount consumers would be willing to pay for each unit and the price they actually pay for the unit is the consumer surplus.

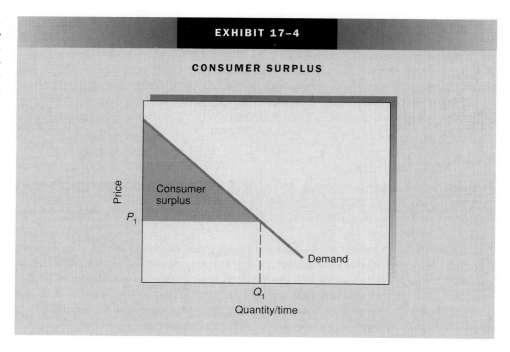

EXHIBIT 17–4

CONSUMER SURPLUS

century after Smith's time, economists discovered the importance of the marginal analysis we used in our discussions in the preceding sections. The willingness to pay for additional units depends on one's valuation of the *marginal* unit, not the value of all units taken together. When additional units are available at a low cost, they will be consumed until their marginal value is also low. Price is determined by the cost and value of marginal units, not average units. Thus, marginal value may be quite low, even though the total value is exceedingly high. This is the case for water and other commodities when they are plentiful. The total value (and average value) of a good includes consumer surplus; thus, the *total* value and the *average* value of goods like water can be quite large even though their price is low. These factors provide the explanation for why market price has so little to do with the total contribution that a good makes to the welfare of users.

WHAT CAUSES THE DEMAND CURVE TO SHIFT?

The demand schedule isolates the impact of price on the amount purchased, assuming other factors are held constant. What are these "other factors"? How do they influence demand? Since a market demand is the sum of individual demands, there are two kinds of factors, other than the price of the good, that can shift its demand.[7] First, the number or the characteristics of individuals in the market—the market's *demographics*—can change. All other factors shift market demands by influencing the demands of individuals.

CHANGES IN MARKET DEMOGRAPHICS

The demand for products in a market is directly related to the number and the characteristics of consumers in that market. Changes in population and its composition can have a large influence in markets. For example, young people age 15 to 24 are a major part of the U.S. market for jeans. When the population in that group fell by more than 5 million during the 1980s, fewer jeans were demanded. Sales had topped 500 million pairs in 1980, but fell to less than 400 million pairs in 1989.[8] An increase in the number of elderly people in the same time period increased the demand for medical care, retirement housing, and vacation travel.

CHANGES IN CONSUMER INCOME

The demand for most products is positively related to income. As their income expands, individuals normally spend more on consumption. Thus, the demand curve for most products shifts outward as the income of consumers increases. Conversely, a reduction in income generally causes the demand for a product to contract.

CHANGES IN DISTRIBUTION OF INCOME

Spending in the market for any product will vary both with the number of potential consumers in the market and with the income level of each consuming unit. When either of these two factors change, the distribution of income is altered among consumers, thus altering spending in various product markets. In other words, the demand curve for certain products shifts when there is a change in distribution of income.

For example, from 1986 to 1991, a rise in the number of households headed by individuals aged 35–44 pushed the total income of consumers in that group up so that their total spending rose by 31 percent.[9] Meanwhile, the number of households headed by individuals aged 25–34 fell, reducing that group's total income, so that spending by them fell by more than 9 percent. These changes were felt strongly in the markets for beer and wine. Beer purchases peak in the 25–34 age group, while wine purchases peak in the 35–44 group. The strong shift in income distribution between these two groups was a major reason why the demand for wine increased from 1986 to 1991, and sales rose 12 percent, while the demand for beer declined and sales fell 24 percent.

Many factors can change the distribution of income: a new tax may fall more heavily on one group than another, a new program may help some groups more than others, or market wages may shift to the advantage of some groups relative

---

[7]Do not forget that a change in *quantity demanded* is a movement along a demand curve in response to a change in price, but a change in *demand* is a shift in the entire demand curve. Review Chapter 3 if you find this point confusing.

[8]These figures are from Suzanne Tregarthen, "Market for Jeans Shrinks," *The Margin* 6, no. 3 (January–February 1991), p. 28.

[9]These data are from the *Consumer Expenditure Survey* of the U.S. Department of Labor, as reported in *American Spending* (Ithaca, NY: American Demographics, 1993), pp. 21–23.

to others. Whatever the reason for a change in income distribution, market demands are likely to shift as a result.

PRICES OF CLOSELY RELATED GOODS

Substitutes
Products that are related such that an increase in the price of one will cause an increase in demand for the other (for example, butter and margarine, Chevrolets and Fords).

Related goods may be either substitutes or complements. When two products perform similar functions or fulfill similar needs, they are **substitutes.** There is a direct relationship between the cost of a product and the demand for its close substitutes. For example, margarine is a substitute for butter. A supply problem that raises butter prices, or causes a butter shortage, will increase the demand for margarine. Consumers substitute margarine for the more expensive butter. Similarly, higher coffee prices will increase the demand for such substitutes as cocoa and tea. On the other hand, if technology, good weather, or some other factor reduces the price of a good, then the demand for its substitutes will decline. A substitute relationship exists between beef and pork, pencils and pens, apples and oranges, and so forth.

Complements
Products that are usually consumed jointly (for example, coffee and nondairy creamer). An increase in the price of one will cause the demand for the other to fall.

Other closely related products are consumed jointly. Goods that "go together," so to speak, are called **complements.** Ham and eggs are complementary items, as are tents and other camping equipment. With complements, there is an inverse relationship between the price of one and the demand for the other. For example, lower prices for videocassette players during the 1980s increased the demand for videocassette tapes. Similarly, declining prices for compact discs raised the demand for compact disc players.

CHANGES IN CONSUMER PREFERENCES

Why do preferences change? Preferences change because people change. New information, for example, might change their valuation of a good. Consider how consumers responded in the 1980s to new medical information linking certain fats and oils to heart disease. They purchased less of products such as whole milk and butter, which were thought to be dangerous, and increased their demand for such goods as olive oil and canola oil, thought to be much more "heart-healthy." Sales of olive oil doubled between 1984 and 1989, while canola oil sales doubled between 1988 and 1990. Consumption of butterfat fell at the same time. In 1987, for the first time, Americans bought more low-fat and skim milk than whole milk. As more consumers became aware of the health implications of their diet, their demand for various foods shifted.

PRICE EXPECTATIONS

When consumers expect the future price of a product to rise, their current demand for it will expand. "Buy now, before the price goes even higher" becomes the order of the day. When the price of coffee rose sharply in 1986, how did shoppers respond? Current sales increased as consumers hoarded the product because they expected its price to continue rising. The converse of this maxim would be consumers' delaying of a purchase if they expected the item to decrease in price. Current demand would be lower as a result of such expectations.

An economist constructing a demand schedule for a product assumes that factors other than the price of the product are held constant. As **Exhibit 17–5** shows, a

EXHIBIT 17–5

PRICE IS NOT ALL THAT MATTERS

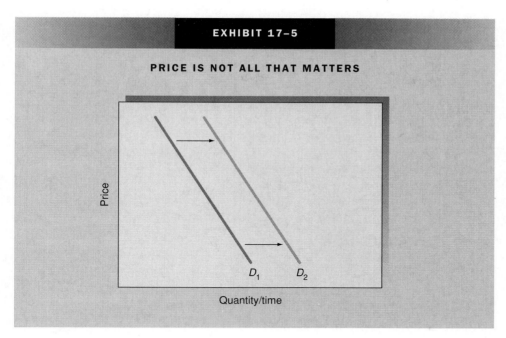

Other things constant, the demand schedule will slope downward to the right. However, changes in income and its distribution, in the prices of closely related products, in consumer preferences, in population (market demographics), and expectations about future prices will also influence consumer decisions. Changes in these factors will cause the entire demand curve to shift (for example, increase from D_1 to D_2).

change in any of these other factors that influence consumer decisions will cause the entire demand curve to shift. The accompanying "Thumbnail Sketch" points out that *quantity demanded* (but not demand) will change in response to a change in the price of a product. It also summarizes the major factors that cause a change in *demand* (a shift of the entire curve).

DETERMINANTS OF SPECIFIC PREFERENCES—WHY CONSUMERS BUY WHAT THEY BUY

Did you ever wonder why a friend spent hard-earned money on something that you would not want even if it were free? Tastes differ, and as we have already shown, they influence demand. What determines preferences? Why do people like one thing but not another? Economists have not been able to explain very much about how preferences are determined. The best strategy has generally been to take preferences as given, using price and other demand-related factors to explain and predict human behavior. Still, two observations about what influences consumer preferences have been made:

1. The determining factors in consumer preferences are frequently complex. People looking for a house want far more than just a shelter: they want an attractive setting, a convenient location, quality of public services, and a great many other things. Moreover, each person may evaluate the same housing attribute differently. For example, living near a school may be a high priority for a family with children but a nuisance to a retired couple.

THUMBNAIL SKETCH

WHAT FACTORS CAUSE A CHANGE IN QUANTITY DEMANDED, AND WHAT FACTORS CAUSE A CHANGE IN DEMAND?

A change in this factor will cause the *quantity demanded* (but not *demand*) to change.

1. The current price of the product.

Changes in these factors will cause the entire *demand* curve to shift.

1. Market demographics (population in the market.

2. Consumer income.

3. Distribution of consumer income.

4. Price of related products (substitutes and complements).

5. Consumer preferences.

6. Expectations about the future price of a product.

---

2. Advertising is a strong influence on consumer preferences. Advertisers would not spend tens of billions of dollars each year if they did not get results. But exactly how does advertising affect consumers? Does it simply provide valuable information about product quality, price, and availability? Or, does it use repetition and misleading information to manipulate consumers? Economists are not of one opinion. Let us take a closer look at this important issue.

ADVERTISING—HOW USEFUL IS IT?

One might ask, how did the $131 billion spent in the United States on advertising in 1992 benefit consumers? Advertising is often used as a sponsoring medium in that it reduces the purchase price of newspapers, magazines, and, most obviously, television viewing. But since the consumers of the advertised products indirectly pay for these benefits, advertising cannot be defended solely on the basis of its sponsorship role.

Advertising does convey information about product price, quality, and availability. New firms or those with new products, new hours, new locations, or new services can use advertising to keep consumers informed, thus facilitating trade and increasing efficiency. After all, people who do not know the advantages of the newly available product or service, or the details of its availability, are not likely to become customers. But what about those repetitious television commercials that offer little or no new information? Critics charge that this type of advertising is wasteful, misleading, and manipulative. Let us look at each of these charges.

IS ADVERTISING WASTEFUL? A great deal of media advertising simply seems to say, "We are better," without providing supportive evidence. An advertiser may wish to take customers from a competitor or establish a brand name for a product. A multimillion-dollar media campaign by a soap, cigarette, or automobile manufacturer may largely be offset by a similar campaign waged by a competitor. The consumers of these products end up paying the costs of these battles for their attention and their dollars. We must remember, though, that consumers are under no obligation to purchase advertised products. If advertising results in higher prices with no compensating benefits, consumers can turn to cheaper, unadvertised products. And this fact leads to another question: How can brand names, especially when they are created by competing advertising campaigns, possibly benefit consumers?

A brand name in which people have confidence, even if it has been established by advertising, has a function beyond gaining the attention of consumers. It is an asset at risk for the seller. People value buying from sellers in whom they have confidence, and will pay a premium to do so. That premium makes a brand name valuable. If something happens to damage a brand name, the willingness of consumers to purchase the product falls. In a very real sense, the brand name is hostage to consumer satisfaction.

When brand names are not allowed, as in the case of alcoholic beverages during the Prohibition era, consumers often suffer. For example, without brand names to protect, anonymous moonshiners sometimes were careless and allowed dangerous impurities into the brew. Some consumers were blinded, and others died. Today the situation is different. Those who buy Johnnie Walker scotch know that the distiller has an enormous sum of money tied up in the brand. In fact, *Financial World* magazine estimated that in 1992, the Johnnie Walker Red brand name was worth $2.6 billion.[10] The Guinness Corporation, owner of the brand, would spend a large amount of money to avoid even one death from an impure batch. And this brand's value is dwarfed by many others. The Marlboro brand had an estimated value of $31.2 billion at one time, and Coca-Cola's brand value has been estimated at $24.4 billion. Is a brand name, promoted by costly advertising, worthwhile to the customer? In a market, each customer decides whether to pay the premium for the brand name.

IS ADVERTISING MISLEADING?   Unfair and deceptive advertising—including false promises, whether spoken by a seller or packaged by an advertising agency—is illegal under the Federal Trade Commission Act. The fact that a publicly advertised false claim is easier to establish and prosecute than the same words spoken in private is an argument for freedom in advertising. But what about general, unsupported claims that a product is superior to the alternatives or that it will help a person enjoy life more? Some believe that such noninformational advertising should be prohibited. They would establish a government agency to evaluate the "informativeness" of advertising. But if consumers are mislead by slick advertisers to part with their money without good reason, might they not also be misled by a slick media campaign to support politicians and regulatory policies that are not in their interest? Yet, no one suggests outlawing "noninformational" political campaigns. Why should we expect consumers to make poor decisions when they make market choices, but wise decisions when they act in the

---

[10]This and forty-one additional *Financial World* estimates of brand-name values were reported in *USA Today*, August 12, 1992, p. 7B.

political (and regulatory) arena? Clearly, additional regulation is not a cure-all. Like freedom in advertising, it has some defects.

DOES ADVERTISING MANIPULATE CONSUMERS?   The demand for some products would surely be much lower without advertising. Some people's preferences may, in fact, be shaped by advertising. However, in evaluating the manipulative effect of advertising, we must keep two things in mind. First, business decision makers are likely to choose the simplest route to economic gain. Generally, it is easier for business firms to cater to the actual desires of consumers than to attempt to reshape their preferences or persuade them to purchase an undesired product. Second, even if advertising does influence preferences, does it follow that this is bad? College classes in music and art appreciation, for example, may also change preferences for various forms of art and music. Does this make them bad? Economic theory is neutral. It neither condemns nor defends advertising—or college classes—as they try to change the tastes of target audiences.

ELASTICITY OF DEMAND

How responsive will consumers be to a change in the price of a good? How many more units will producers supply if the price of a good increases? Economists have developed a concept called *elasticity* that they use when discussing the responsiveness of consumers and producers to changes in price. In fact, the term *elasticity* means "responsiveness." If consumers are highly responsive to a change in price—for example, if the amount purchased by consumers declines sharply in response to a price increase—demand is said to be elastic. In contrast, if a substantial increase in price results only in a small reduction in quantity demanded, the demand is inelastic.

Price elasticity of demand

The percent change in the quantity of a product demanded divided by the percent change in the price causing the change in quantity. Price elasticity of demand indicates the degree of consumer response to variation in price.

Price elasticity of demand is defined as

$$\frac{\text{Percent change in quantity demanded}}{\text{Percent change in price}}$$

This ratio is called the *elasticity coefficient*. (Although the sign of the coefficient for price elasticity of demand is often ignored, it is always negative, since a change in price causes the quantity demanded to change in the opposite direction.) To calculate the elasticity coefficient, we begin with a price change, say from P_0 to P_1, which causes a change in quantity demanded, from Q_0 to Q_1. The change in quantity demanded is $Q_0 - Q_1$. Therefore, the *percent* change in quantity demanded, using the average of the two quantities as a basis,[11] is

$$\frac{Q_0 - Q_1}{(Q_0 + Q_1)/2} \times 100.$$

Similarly, when the change in price is $P_0 - P_1$,

---

[11]This formula uses the average of the starting point and the ending point of the change so that it will give the same result whether we start from the lower or the higher price. This *arc* elasticity formula is not the only way to calculate elasticity, but it is the most frequently used.

the *percent* change in price is

$$\frac{P_0 - P_1}{(P_0 + P_1)/2} \times 100.$$

Dividing the percent change in quantity by the percent change in price gives us

$$\frac{(Q_0 - Q_1)/(Q_0 + Q_1)}{(P_0 - P_1)/(P_0 + P_1)}.$$

(Note that since each term within brackets is multiplied by 100 and the denominator of each term contains a 2, these factors offset each other and we can ignore them.)

A numerical example may help to illustrate the use of this formula to calculate price elasticity of demand. Suppose that Trina's Cakes can sell 50 specialty cakes per week at $7 each, or 70 of the cakes at $6 each. The elasticity coefficient for these cakes is

$$\frac{[(50 - 70)/(50 + 70)]}{[(7 - 6)/(7 + 6)]} =$$

$$\frac{-20/120}{1/13} = \frac{-1/6}{1/13} = \frac{-13}{6} = -2.17$$

indicating that the percentage change in quantity is more than twice the percentage change in price.

The elasticity coefficient permits us to make a precise distinction between elastic and inelastic. When the elasticity coefficient is greater than 1 (ignoring the sign), as it was for the demand for Trina's cakes, demand is elastic. When it is less than 1, demand is inelastic. *Unitary elasticity* is the term used to denote a price elasticity of 1.

GRAPHIC REPRESENTATION OF DEMAND ELASTICITY

Exhibit 17–6 presents demand curves of varying elasticity. A demand curve that is completely vertical is termed *perfectly inelastic*. The addict's demand for heroin or the diabetic's demand for insulin might *approximate* perfect inelasticity over a range of prices, although the income constraint alone is enough to ensure that no demand curve will be perfectly inelastic at all prices (see part "a" of Exhibit 17–6).

The more inelastic the demand, the steeper the demand curve *over any specific price range.* Inspection of the demand for cigarettes (part "b" of Exhibit 17–6), which is highly inelastic, and the demand for portable television sets (part "d"), which is relatively elastic, indicates that the inelastic curve tends to be steeper. When demand elasticity is unitary, as part "c" illustrates, a demand curve that is convex to the origin will result. When a demand curve is completely horizontal, an economist would say that it is *perfectly elastic.* Demand for the wheat of a single wheat farmer, for example, would approximate perfect elasticity (part "e").

Since elasticity is a relative concept, the elasticity of a straight-line demand curve will differ at each point along the line. As **Exhibit 17–7** illustrates, the elasticity of a straight-line demand curve (one with a constant slope) will range from highly elastic to highly inelastic. Here, when the price rises from $10 to $11, sales decline from 20 to 10. According to the *arc elasticity formula,* the price elasticity of demand is –7.0. Demand is very elastic in this region. In contrast, demand is quite

(a) **Perfectly inelastic**—
*Despite an increase in price,
consumers still purchase the
same amount. The price
elasticity of an addict's demand
for heroin or a diabetic's
demand for insulin in some
price ranges might be
approximated by this curve.*
(b) **Relatively inelastic**—*A
percent increase in price results
in a smaller percent reduction
in sales. The demand for
cigarettes has been estimated to
be highly inelastic.*
(c) **Unitary elasticity**—*The
percent change in quantity
demanded is equal to the
percent change in price. A
curve of decreasing slope
results. Sales revenue (price
times quantity sold)
is constant.*
(d) **Relatively elastic**—*A
percent increase in price leads
to a larger percent reduction in
purchases. Consumers
substitute other products for
the more expensive good.*
(e) **Perfectly elastic**—
*Consumers will buy all of
Farmer Jones's wheat at the
market price, but none will be
sold above the market price.*

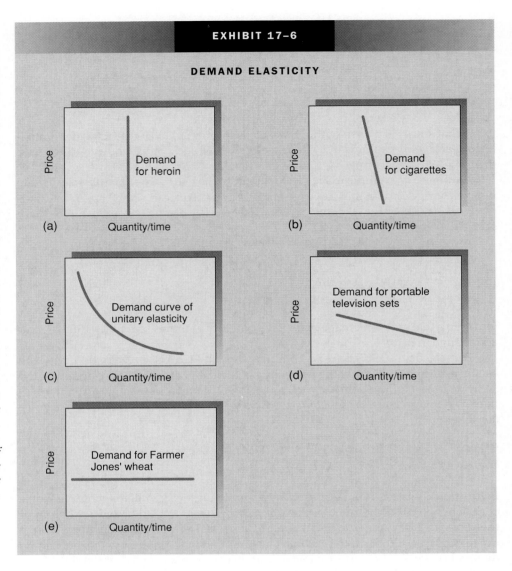

EXHIBIT 17–6

DEMAND ELASTICITY

(a) Demand for heroin — Price / Quantity/time

(b) Demand for cigarettes — Price / Quantity/time

(c) Demand curve of unitary elasticity — Price / Quantity/time

(d) Demand for portable television sets — Price / Quantity/time

(e) Demand for Farmer Jones' wheat — Price / Quantity/time

inelastic in the $1 to $2 price range. As the price increases from $1 to $2, the amount demanded declines from 110 to 100. The arc elasticity of demand in this range is only –0.14; demand is highly inelastic.

Why do we bother with elasticity? Why not talk only about the slope of a demand curve? We use elasticities because they are independent of the units of measure. Whether we talk about dollars per gallon or cents per liter, the elasticities, given in percentages, remain the same. This is appropriate because people do not care what units of measurement are used; their response depends on the actual terms of exchange.

DETERMINANTS OF DEMAND ELASTICITY

Economists have estimated the price elasticity of demand for many products. As the estimates of **Exhibit 17–8** illustrate the elasticity of demand among products varies substantially. The demand for several products—salt, toothpicks, matches,

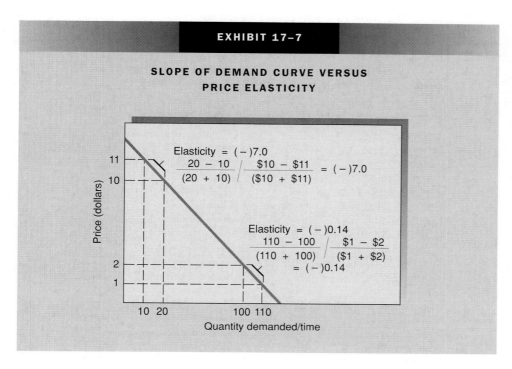

EXHIBIT 17–7

SLOPE OF DEMAND CURVE VERSUS PRICE ELASTICITY

Elasticity = (−)7.0

$$\frac{20 - 10}{(20 + 10)} \Big/ \frac{\$10 - \$11}{(\$10 + \$11)} = (-)7.0$$

Elasticity = (−)0.14

$$\frac{110 - 100}{(110 + 100)} \Big/ \frac{\$1 - \$2}{(\$1 + \$2)}$$

$$= (-)0.14$$

Price (dollars)

Quantity demanded/time

With this straight-line (constant-slope) demand curve, demand is more elastic in the high-price range. The formula for arc elasticity shows that when price rises from $1 to $2 and quantity falls from 110 to 100, demand is inelastic. A price rise of the same magnitude (but of a smaller percentage), from $10 to $11, leads to a decline in quantity of the same size (but of a larger percentage), so that elasticity is much greater. (Price elasticities are negative, but we typically ignore the sign and look only at the absolute value.)

light bulbs, and newspapers, for example—is highly inelastic. On the other hand, the demand curves for fresh tomatoes, Chevrolet automobiles, and fresh green peas are highly elastic. What factors explain this variation? Why is demand for some products, but not for others, highly responsive to changes in price? The answer lies primarily in the availability of good substitutes and also to some extent on the share of the typical consumer's total budget expended on a product.

AVAILABILITY OF SUBSTITUTES. The most important determinant of demand elasticity is the availability of substitutes. When good substitutes for a product are available, a price rise merely induces many consumers to switch to other products. Demand is elastic. For example, if the price of fountain pens increased, many consumers would simply switch to pencils, ballpoint pens, and felt-tip pens. If the price of Chevrolets increased, consumers would substitute Fords, Volkswagens, and other cars.

When good substitutes are unavailable, the demand for a product tends to be inelastic. Medical services are an example. When we are sick, most of us find witch doctors, faith healers, palm readers, and cod-liver oil to be highly imperfect substitutes for a physician. Not surprisingly, the demand for physician services is inelastic.

The availability of substitutes increases as the product class becomes more specific, thus enhancing price elasticity. For example, as Exhibit 17–8 shows, the price elasticity of Chevrolets, a narrow product class, exceeds that of the broad class of automobiles in general.

SHARE OF TOTAL BUDGET EXPENDED ON PRODUCT. If the expenditures on a product are quite small relative to the consumer's budget, demand tends to be more inelastic. Compared to one's total budget, expenditures on some commodities

Sources: Hendrick S. Houthakker and Lester D. Taylor, *Consumer Demand in the United States, 1929–1970* (Cambridge: Harvard University Press, 1966, 1970); Douglas R. Bohi, *Analyzing Demand Behavior* (Baltimore: Johns Hopkins University Press, 1981); Hsaing-tai Cheng and Oral Capps, Jr., "Demand for Fish," *American Journal of Agricultural Economics,* August 1988; and U.S. Department of Agriculture.

EXHIBIT 17–8

ESTIMATED PRICE ELASTICITY OF DEMAND FOR SELECTED PRODUCTS

Inelastic		Approximately unitary elasticity	
Salt	0.1	Movies	0.9
Matches	0.1	Housing, owner occupied, long-run	1.2
Toothpicks	0.1	Shellfish, consumed at home	0.9
Airline travel, short-run	0.1	Oysters, consumed at home	1.1
Gasoline, short-run	0.2	Private education	1.1
Gasoline, long-run	0.7	Tires, short-run	0.9
Residential natural gas, short-run	0.1	Tires, long-run	1.2
Residential natural gas, long-run	0.5	Radio and television receivers	1.2
Coffee	0.25	**Elastic**	
Fish (cod) consumed at home	0.5	Restaurant meals	2.3
Tobacco products, short-run	0.45	Foreign travel, long-run	4.0
Legal services, short-run	0.4	Airline travel, long-run	2.4
Physician services	0.6	Fresh green peas	2.8
Taxi, short-run	0.6	Automobiles, short-run	1.2–1.5
Automobiles, long-run	0.2	Chevrolet automobiles	4.0
		Fresh tomatoes	4.6

are almost inconsequential. Matches, toothpicks, and salt are good examples. Most consumers spend only $1 or $2 per year on each of these items. A doubling of their price would exert little influence on the family budget. Therefore, even if the price of such a product were to rise sharply, consumers would still not find it in their interest to spend much time and effort looking for substitutes.

TIME AND DEMAND ELASTICITY

As changing market conditions alter the price of a product, both consumers and producers will respond. However, their response will not be instantaneous, and it may change over time. In general, when the price of a product increases, consumers will reduce their consumption by a larger amount in the long run than in the short run. Thus, the demand for most products will be more elastic in the long run than in the short run. This relationship between the elasticity coefficient and the length of the adjustment time period is often referred to as the *second law of demand.*

Exhibit 17–9 provides a graphic illustration for both elastic and inelastic demand curves. In part "a" the demand curve for ballpoint pens is elastic, because there are good substitutes—for example, pencils and felt-tip pens—for ballpoint pens. Therefore, when the price of the pens increases by 50 percent (from $1.00 to $1.50), the quantity purchased declines sharply from 100,000 to only 25,000, a

EXHIBIT 17-9

INELASTIC AND ELASTIC DEMAND

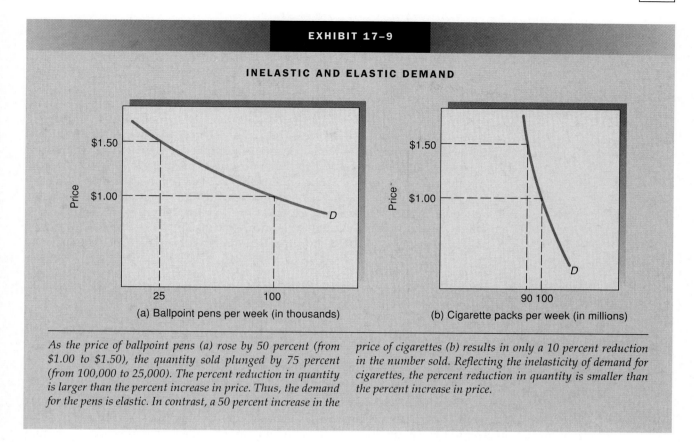

As the price of ballpoint pens (a) rose by 50 percent (from $1.00 to $1.50), the quantity sold plunged by 75 percent (from 100,000 to 25,000). The percent reduction in quantity is larger than the percent increase in price. Thus, the demand for the pens is elastic. In contrast, a 50 percent increase in the price of cigarettes (b) results in only a 10 percent reduction in the number sold. Reflecting the inelasticity of demand for cigarettes, the percent reduction in quantity is smaller than the percent increase in price.

75 percent reduction. The price elasticity coefficient will equal minus 3.0. The fact that the absolute value of the coefficient is greater than 1 also confirms that the demand for ballpoint pens is elastic over the price range illustrated. Part "b" of Exhibit 17–9 illustrates the demand curve for cigarettes. Since most consumers do not find other products to be a good substitute, the demand for cigarettes is highly inelastic. In the case of cigarettes, a 50 percent increase in price leads to only a 10 percent reduction in quantity demanded. The price elasticity coefficient is .26, substantially less than 1, confirming that the demand for cigarettes is inelastic.

TOTAL EXPENDITURES AND DEMAND ELASTICITY

Price elasticity shows us the relationship between a change in price and the resulting change in total expenditure on the product. When demand is inelastic, the percent change in unit sales is less than the percent change in price. Since quantity demanded changes by a smaller amount than price, the change in price will exert a larger impact on total expenditures than will the change in quantity demanded. Therefore, total expenditures will change in the same direction as price when demand is inelastic. For example, a higher product price will lead to an increase in expenditures on the product. Suppose that when the price of beef rises from $2 to $2.40 (a 20 percent increase), the quantity demanded by an average consumer falls from 100 pounds to 90 pounds (a 10 percent reduction) per year. Since the percent reduction in quantity demanded is less than the percent increase in price, we know that demand is inelastic.[12] At the $2 price, the average person spends $200 annually on beef. When the price rises to $2.40, the average annual expenditures rise to $216. The higher beef prices cause total expenditures to increase because demand is inelastic.

When demand is elastic, on the other hand, quantity demanded is more responsive to a change in price. The percent decline in quantity demanded will exceed the percent increase in price. The loss of sales will exert a greater influence on total expenditures than the rise in price. Therefore, a price increase will reduce total expenditures when the demand for a product is elastic.

Exhibit 17–10 summarizes the relationship between changes in price and total expenditures, for demand curves of varying elasticity. When demand is inelastic, a change in price will cause total expenditures to change in the same direction. If demand is elastic, price and total expenditures will change in opposite directions. For unitary elasticity, total expenditures will remain constant as price changes.

INCOME AND DEMAND

Income elasticity
The percent change in the quantity of a product demanded divided by the percent change in consumer income causing the change in quantity demanded. It measures the responsiveness of the demand for a good to a change in income.

As income expands, the demand for most goods will increase. **Income elasticity** indicates the responsiveness of the demand for a product to a change in income. It is defined as:

$$\frac{\text{Percent change in quantity demanded}}{\text{Percent change in income}}$$

As **Exhibit 17–11** shows, while the income elasticity coefficients for products vary, they are normally positive. In general, goods that people regard as "necessities" will have a low income elasticity of demand. As income increases, spending

[a] The sign of the elasticity coefficient is negative.

EXHIBIT 17–10

DEMAND ELASTICITY, CHANGE IN PRICE, AND CHANGE IN TOTAL EXPENDITURES

PRICE ELASTICITY OF DEMAND	NUMERICAL ELASTICITY COEFFICIENT[a]	IMPACT OF CHANGE IN PRICE ON TOTAL EXPENDITURES (AND SALES REVENUES)
Elastic	1 to ∞	Price and total expenditures change in opposite directions
Unitary	1	Total expenditures remain constant as price changes
Inelastic	0 to 1	Price and total expenditures change in the same direction

---

[12]Calculate the elasticity coefficient as an exercise. Is it less than 1?

EXHIBIT 17–11

ESTIMATED INCOME ELASTICITY OF DEMAND FOR SELECTED PRODUCTS

Low income elasticity		High income elasticity	
Margarine	−0.20	Private education	2.46
Fuel	0.38	New cars	2.45
Electricity	0.20	Recreation and amusements	1.57
Fish (Haddock)	0.46	Alcohol	1.54
Food	0.51		
Tobacco	0.64		
Hospital care	0.69		

Sources: Hendrik S. Houthakker and Lester D. Taylor, *Consumer Demand in the United States, 1929–1970* (Cambridge: Harvard University Press, 1966); L. Taylor, "The Demand for Electricity: A Survey," *Bell Journal of Economics* (Spring 1975); F. W. Bell, "The Pope and the Price of Fish," *American Economic Review* 58 (December 1968).

on these items will increase by a less than proportional amount. It is understandable that items such as fuel, electricity, bread, tobacco, economy clothing, and potatoes have a low income elasticity. Interestingly, jewelry falls into this category, at least in the United States. The *Consumer Expenditure Survey* of the U.S. Department of Labor reports that the poorest fifth of all households reporting income in 1991 spent $536 (4 percent) of their $13,464 total expenditures on jewelry, while jewelry purchases claimed only 2 percent ($1,133) of the $57,597 spent on average by the richest fifth. A few commodities, such as margarine, low-quality meat cuts, and bus travel actually have a negative income elasticity. Economists refer to goods with a negative income elasticity as **inferior goods.** As income expands, the demand for inferior goods will decline.

Goods that consumers regard as "luxuries" generally have a high (greater than 1) income elasticity. For example, private education, new automobiles, recreational activities, expensive foods, swimming pools, and air travel are all highly income-elastic. As income increases, the demand for these products thus expands even more rapidly.

Inferior goods
Goods for which the income elasticity is negative. An increase in consumer income causes the demand for such a good to decline.

USING THE CONCEPT OF ELASTICITY— THE BURDEN OF A TAX

When a tax is placed on the sale of a good, who pays it? How much does the price rise? How much is paid by the seller in the form of accepting a lower price, rather than being passed on to the customer through a price increase? When the price of a good rises, we have seen that the effect on revenue and sales depends on the price elasticity of demand. In determining the relative burden of a tax, price elasticity again plays a major role.

Sellers would like to pass the entire tax on to buyers, raising the price by the full amount of the tax, rather than paying any part of it themselves. However, as the price rises, customers respond by purchasing less. Sales decline, and sellers must then lower their price, accepting part of the tax burden themselves by receiving less revenue. In Chapter 5 we learned that when taxes raise the amount paid by consumers and reduce the *net* (after-tax) price received by sellers, both buyer and seller share in the tax burden. Using the concept of elasticity, we can now say more about how the burden is divided and the size of the deadweight loss associated with the tax. (Now would be a good time for the reader to review the "Issues of Efficiency and Equity" section, pages 124–127.)

Exhibits 17–12 through 17–14 illustrate the results of a new tax on gasoline. **Exhibit 17–12** shows the results in the short run, when the price elasticity of demand is only 0.2. **Exhibit 17–13** shows the result in the long run, when demand elasticity is 0.7. In order to demonstrate what happens when demand elasticity changes but supply is the same, in Exhibit 17–13 we temporarily assume the same supply curve applies in the long run as in the short run.

In Exhibit 17–12 the equilibrium price of gasoline before the new tax is $1 per gallon. The $.20 tax shifts the supply upward by the amount of the tax. Since they must turn over $.20 to the government for each gallon sold, sellers must receive

When a $.20 gasoline tax is imposed, the supply curve shifts vertically by the amount of the tax. Since consumers will buy less as the price increases, sellers will not be able to pass all of the tax along to consumers. The new short-run equilibrium will be at a price of $1.15. As the result of the tax, consumers pay $.15 more and sellers receive $.05 less.

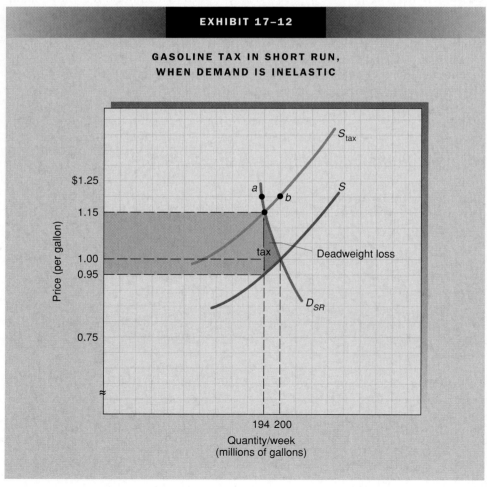

EXHIBIT 17–12

GASOLINE TAX IN SHORT RUN, WHEN DEMAND IS INELASTIC

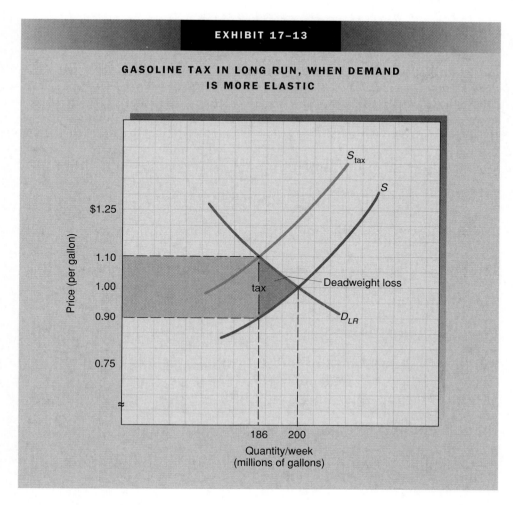

EXHIBIT 17-13

GASOLINE TAX IN LONG RUN, WHEN DEMAND IS MORE ELASTIC

Price (per gallon)

S_{tax}

S

$1.25

1.10

1.00 — tax — Deadweight loss

0.90 — D_{LR}

0.75

≈

186   200

Quantity/week
(millions of gallons)

When demand is more elastic, consumers reduce their purchases by greater amounts. As a result, sellers must reduce price further [to $1.10 in this case, compared with $1.15 in Exhibit 17–12], and the tax burden falls more heavily on sellers, due to the greater demand elasticity. Here we assume that supply is unchanged.

the old price plus $.20 per gallon in order to maintain their prior incentive to produce. This is precisely what happens when the pretax supply curve is shifted vertically by the $.20 tax.

Of course, sellers would like to raise prices to $1.20 and pass the entire amount of the tax onto motorists. However, they will be unable to do so, since motorists will reduce their purchases in response to higher prices. If the price of gasoline rose to $1.20, then an excess supply (*ab* in Exhibit 17–12) would result. Therefore, sellers are able to increase the price to only $1.15, where they are able to sell 194 million gallons, 6 million fewer than before the tax was imposed. *Short-run equilibrium* is present at that price ($1.15) and output (194 million). In the short run, the buyers pay $.15 more, and the seller receives $.05 less per gallon.

There are relatively few ways that buyers can substitute away from the more expensive gasoline in the short run. Since their responsiveness—the price elasticity of their demand—is relatively small in the short run, consumers shoulder most of the tax burden.

In the long-run, though, consumers will find more ways to economize on the more expensive gasoline (for example, they will shift to smaller cars). As consumer purchases decline by a larger amount, sellers must further decrease the price they will accept (reducing the quantity they will supply). As Exhibit 17–13 illustrates, in the long run the equilibrium price will decline to $1.10, and quantity exchanged will fall to 186 gallons per week. In this case, buyers and sellers divide the burden of the $.20 tax equally. Comparing Exhibit 17–12 with Exhibit 17–13 where supply is the same but the elasticities of demand differ, we can see that *when demand is more elastic, ceteris paribus, buyers pay a smaller share of the tax burden.* This makes good intuitive sense. When consumers find more ways to econo-mize—when they reduce their purchases more in response to the higher price—in the long run, they put more pressure on sellers to lower the price they will accept.

Exhibit 17–14 introduces the other factor determining the burden of a tax: the **elasticity of supply,** which is the percent change in quantity supplied, divided by the percent change in the price that causes the change. Since this measures the responsiveness of sellers to a change in price, it is analogous to the price elasticity of demand. In the next two chapters we will discuss the factors that determine supply elasticity. For now, it is important simply to recognize the concept of sup-ply elasticity and the fact that suppliers (like buyers) will be more responsive to price changes when they have more time to react to a change in price.

Earlier, in going from Exhibit 17–12 to Exhibit 17–13, we allowed demand to become more elastic, since Exhibit 17–13 represented the long run. However, we

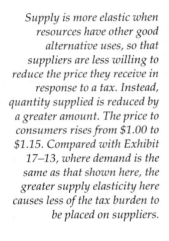

Elasticity of supply
The percent change in quantity supplied, divided by the percent change in the price causing that change in quantity supplied.

Supply is more elastic when resources have other good alternative uses, so that suppliers are less willing to reduce the price they receive in response to a tax. Instead, quantity supplied is reduced by a greater amount. The price to consumers rises from $1.00 to $1.15. Compared with Exhibit 17–13, where demand is the same as that shown here, the greater supply elasticity here causes less of the tax burden to be placed on suppliers.

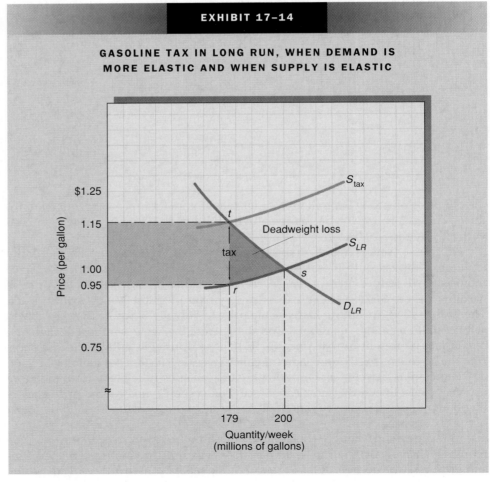

EXHIBIT 17–14

GASOLINE TAX IN LONG RUN, WHEN DEMAND IS MORE ELASTIC AND WHEN SUPPLY IS ELASTIC

unrealistically assumed that the elasticity of supply was the same in the long run as in the short run in order to isolate what would happen if only demand changed. Exhibit 17–14 shows the more realistic case in which supply, like demand, is more elastic in the long run. By comparing Exhibits 17–13 and 17–14, we can see that when supply elasticity is greater (and demand is the same), a smaller share of the tax burden is borne by suppliers. Here, supply is drawn so the gasoline price, tax included, happens to rise to $1.15, just as it did in the short-run case. That would not necessarily be the case in the real world. In general, however, *when supply is more elastic, ceteris paribus, suppliers will bear a smaller part of the tax burden.*

ELASTICITY AND THE DEADWEIGHT LOSS CAUSED BY A TAX

We have seen that elasticity of supply and demand plays an important part in determining how the burden of a tax is distributed between buyer and seller. Exhibits 17–12 through 17–14 also illustrate how these elasticities influence the size of the excess burden, or *deadweight loss* caused by the tax. As we saw in Chapter 5 (Exhibit 5–7), reducing trade by taxing it not only transfers revenue (amount of the tax per unit, multiplied by the number of units sold after the tax) from buyers and sellers to the government, but it also reduces the gains from trade for both buyers and sellers by the transferred amount, plus somewhat more. Trades that would have taken place in the absence of the tax are forestalled. When either demand or supply is inelastic, meaning that few trades are discouraged by imposition of the tax, the excess burden is smaller. Exhibit 17–12 illustrates this point in the case of a highly inelastic demand. Since demand is highly inelastic, the quantity of gasoline traded declines by only 6 million gallons as the result of the $.20 tax.

In contrast, when both demand and supply are elastic, as in Exhibit 17–14, more trades are prevented by the tax. Given the more elastic demand and supply curves of Exhibit 17–14, the quantity of gasoline produced and sold declines by 21 million gallons (from 200 million to 179 million). As the triangle *rst* illustrates, the excess burden of a tax increases as the higher tax cuts off more exchanges. Therefore, the burden of excise taxes will be less if they are levied on goods and services for which either demand or supply is highly inelastic.

LOOKING AHEAD

In this chapter, we outlined the mechanism by which consumers' wants and tastes are communicated to producers. Consumer choices underlie the market demand curve. Discovering the market demand for a product tells producers how strongly consumers desire each commodity relative to others. In the following chapter, we turn to costs of production that arise because resources have alternative uses. In fact, the cost of producing a good tells the producer how badly the resources are desired in other areas. An understanding of these two topics—consumer demand and cost of production—is essential if we are to understand how markets allocate goods and resources.

CHAPTER SUMMARY

1. The demand schedule indicates the amount of a good that consumers would be willing to buy at each potential price. The *first law of demand* states that the quantity of a product demanded is inversely related to its price.

A reduction in the price of a product reduces the opportunity cost of consuming it. At the lower price, many consumers will substitute the now cheaper good for other products. In contrast, higher prices will induce consumers to buy less as they turn to substitutes that are now *relatively* cheaper.

2. The market demand curve reflects the demand of individuals. It is simply the horizontal sum of the demand curves of individuals in that particular market. The market price is a marginal valuation, not an average valuation of the item.

3. Time, like money, is scarce for consumers. Consumers consider both time and money costs when they make decisions. Other things constant, a reduction in the time cost of consuming a good will induce consumers to purchase more of the good.

4. Consumers usually gain from the purchase of a good. The difference between the amount that consumers would be willing to pay for a good and the amount they actually pay is the consumer surplus. It is measured by the area under the demand curve but above the market price.

5. In addition to price, the demand for a product is influenced (shifted) by the (a) size and composition of the population in the market, (b) level of consumer income, (c) distribution of income among consumers, (d) cost of obtaining related products (substitutes and complements), (e) preferences of consumers, and (f) consumer expectations about the future price of the product. Changes in any of these six factors will cause the *demand* for the product to change (the entire curve to shift).

6. Both functional and subjective factors influence the demand for a product, including advertising. The effect of advertising on consumer decisions is difficult to quantify. The advertising budgets of profit-seeking business firms are strong evidence, though, that advertising significantly influences consumer decisions. Certainly, advertising can be useful by reducing consumers' search time and helping them make more informed choices. However, a sizable share of all advertising expenditures is for messages with little informational content. One explanation for this is the value to customers of brand name capital or reputation that could be lost by the seller if news spread about product problems. Although this is a controversial area, it is clearly much easier to point out the shortcomings of advertising than to devise an alternative that would not have similar imperfections.

7. Price elasticity reveals the responsiveness of the amount purchased to a change in price. When there are good substitutes available and the item forms a sizable component of the consumer's budget, its demand will tend to be more elastic. Typically, the price elasticity of a product will increase as more time is allowed for consumers to adjust to the price change. This direct relationship between size of the elasticity coefficient and the length of the adjustment time period is often referred to as the *second law of demand.*

8. The concept of elasticity is useful in explaining the effects of a policy change, such as the imposition of a sales tax. When demand is more elastic, buyers bear less of the tax burden; when supply is more elastic, sellers bear less of the burden. When either is inelastic, the excess burden, or deadweight loss, of the tax is smaller.

CRITICAL-ANALYSIS QUESTIONS

*1. What impact did the substantially lower gasoline prices of the mid-1980s have on the following?
   a. The demand for big cars.
   b. The demand for small cars.
   c. The incentive to experiment and to develop electric and other non-gas-powered cars.
   d. The demand for gasoline (*be careful*).
   e. The demand for vacations by automobile in Florida.

2. "As the price of beef rises, the demand of consumers will begin to decline. Economists estimate that a 5 percent rise in beef prices will cause demand to decline by 1 percent." Indicate the two errors in this statement.

*3. The accompanying chart presents data on the price of fuel oil, the amount of it demanded, and the demand for insulation.
   a. Calculate the price elasticity of demand for fuel oil as its price rises from 30 cents to 50 cents; from 50 cents to 70 cents.
   b. Are fuel oil and insulation substitutes or complements? How can you tell from the figures alone?

	FUEL OIL	INSULATION
PRICE PER GALLON (CENTS)	QUANTITY DEMANDED (MILLIONS OF GALLONS)	QUANTITY DEMANDED (MILLIONS OF TONS)
30	100	30
50	90	35
70	60	40

4. "Since the same price rise causes a reduction in the demand of each consumer, and since market demand is the sum of individual demands, the demand elasticity for the market must be much greater than for any individual. The same percent price change brings about a much larger quantity change in the market." Evaluate this statement.

---

*Asterisk denotes questions for which answers are given in Appendix C.

5. "As soon as they heard about the shortage of peaches in this year's crop, suppliers of canned peaches raised the price of peaches already on the shelf. This price increase serves no economic purpose, since those on the shelf now were from last year's plentiful crop." Explain why this statement is false.

6. "Economists recommend that taxes be levied on goods with inelastic demand. This means that consumers have no place to go. Their demand is inelastic, so no good substitutes exist for such goods. Taxing such goods hurts market participants, rather than helps them." Evaluate this statement.

7. Residential electricity in the state of Washington costs about half as much as in nearby Montana. A study showed that in Washington, the average household used about 1200 kilowatt-hours per month, whereas Montanans used about half that much per household. Do these data provide us with two points on the average household's demand curve for residential electricity in this region? Why or why not?

*8. *What's wrong with this way of thinking?* "Economics is unable to explain the value of goods in a sensible manner. A quart of water is much cheaper than a quart of oil. Yet water is essential to both animal and plant life. Without it, we could not survive. How can oil be more valuable than water? Yet economics says that it is."

*9. The wealthy are widely believed to have more leisure time than the poor. However, even though we are a good deal wealthier today than our great-grandparents were 100 years ago, we appear to live more hectic lives and have less free time. Can you explain why?

10. What are the major determinants of a product's price elasticity of demand? Studies indicate that the demand for Florida oranges, Bayer Aspirin, watermelons, and airfares to Europe are elastic. Why?

11. Most systems of medical insurance substantially reduce the costs to the consumer of using additional units of physician services and hospitalization. Some reduce these costs to zero. How does this method of payment affect the consumption levels of medical services? Might this method of organization result in "too much" consumption of medical services? Discuss.

*12. Are the following statements true or false? Explain your answers.
  a. A 10 percent reduction in price that leads to a 15 percent increase in amount purchased indicates a price elasticity of more than 1.
  b. A 10 percent reduction in price that leads to a 2 percent increase in total expenditures indicates a price elasticity of more than 1.
  c. If the percent change in price is less than the resul-

tant percent change in quantity demanded, demand is elastic.

*13. Respond to the following questions: If you really like pizza, should you try to consume as much pizza as possible? If you want to succeed, should you try to make the highest possible grade in your economics class?

*14. Sue loves ice cream but cannot stand frozen yogurt desserts. In contrast, Carole cannot tell the difference between ice cream and frozen yogurt desserts. Who will have the more elastic demand for yogurt?

*15. "If all the farmers reduced their output to one-half of the current rate, farm incomes would increase, the total utility derived from farm output would rise, and the nation would be better off." Is this statement true or false? Explain your answer.

16. Can you think of any circumstances under which an increase in price might temporarily lead to an *increase* in amount purchased?

17. Can you think of any reason why the prices of shares of stock of a specific company, gold, and other commodities for which the supply is (approximately) fixed will fluctuate more than the prices of goods that are reproduceable at a constant cost?

*18. "Market competition encourages deceitful advertising and dishonesty." Is this statement true or false? Explain your answer.

*19. What is the nature of the deadweight loss accompanying sales taxes? Why is it often referred to as an "excess burden" of the tax?

20. The demand and supply curves for unskilled labor are given in the accompanying table.

DEMAND		SUPPLY	
WAGE	QUANTITY DEMANDED	WAGE	QUANTITY SUPPLIED
$6.50	1,000	$6.50	1,900
$6.00	1,200	$6.00	1,800
$5.50	1,400	$5.50	1,700
$5.00	1,600	$5.00	1,600
$4.50	1,800	$4.50	1,500
$4.00	2,000	$4.00	1,400

  a. Find the equilibrium wage and number of workers hired.
  b. What is the elasticity of the demand for workers at wages between $6.00 and $6.50 per hour? Is this in the elastic or inelastic portion of the demand curve?
  c. What does this imply about what will happen to this firm's labor costs as wages increase from $6.00 to $6.50 per hour?

*Asterisk denotes questions for which answers are given in Appendix C.

d. What is the elasticity of demand for workers at wages between $4.00 and $4.50 per hour? Is this in the elastic or inelastic portion of the demand curve?

e. What does this imply about what will happen to this firm's labor costs as wages increase from $4.00 to $4.50 per hour?

f. What happens to the elasticity of demand for workers as wages increase?

Suppose that a new law is passed requiring employers to pay an unemployment insurance tax of $1.50 per hour for every employee.

g. What happens to the equilibrium wage rate and number of workers hired?

h. How is this tax burden distributed between employers and workers?

Now suppose that rather than being paid by the employers, the tax must be paid by workers. How does this affect the equilibrium wage rate and number of workers hired?

i. How is this tax burden distributed between employers and workers?

j. Does it matter who pays the tax?

ADDENDUM: CONSUMER CHOICE AND INDIFFERENCE CURVES

In the text of this chapter, we used marginal utility analysis to develop the demand curve of an individual. In developing the theory of consumer choice, economists usually rely on a more formal technique—**indifference curve** analysis. Since this technique is widely used at a more advanced level, many instructors like to include it in their introductory course. In this addendum, we use indifference curve analysis to develop the theory of demand in a more formal—some would say more elegant—manner.

WHAT ARE INDIFFERENCE CURVES?

There are two elements in every choice: (1) preferences (the desirability of various goods) and (2) opportunities (the attainability of various goods). The indifference curve relates to the former—preferences. It separates better (more preferred) bundles of goods from inferior (less preferred) bundles, providing a diagrammatic picture of how an individual ranks alternative consumption bundles.

In **Exhibit 17A–1,** we assume that Robinson Crusoe is initially consuming 8 fish and 8 breadfruit per week (point *A*). This initial bundle provides him with a certain level of satisfaction (utility). He would, however, be willing to trade this initial bundle for certain other consumption alternatives if the opportunity presented itself. Since he likes both fish and breadfruit, he would especially like to

Indifference curve
A curve, convex from below, that separates the consumption bundles that are more preferred by an individual from those that are less preferred. The points on the curve represent combinations of goods that are equally preferred by the individual.

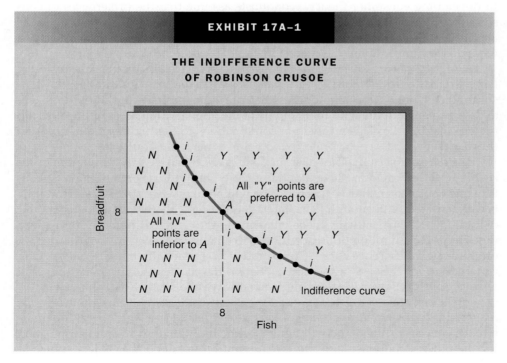

EXHIBIT 17A–1

THE INDIFFERENCE CURVE OF ROBINSON CRUSOE

The curve generated by connecting Crusoe's "I do not care" answers separates the combinations of fish and breadfruit that he prefers to the bundle A from those that he judges to be inferior to A. The i points map out an indifference curve.

obtain bundles to the northeast point of A, since they represent more of both goods. However, he would also be willing to give up some breadfruit if in return he received a compensatory amount of fish. Similarly, if the terms of trade were right, he would be willing to exchange fish for breadfruit. The trade-offs he is willing to make lie *along* the indifference curve. Of course, he is quite willing to move to any bundle on a higher indifference curve.

Starting from point A (8 fish and 8 breadfruit), we ask Crusoe if he is willing to trade that bundle for various other bundles. He answers "Yes" (Y), "No" (N), or "I do not care" (i). Exhibit 17A–1 illustrates the pattern of his response. Crusoe's "I do not care" answers indicate that the original bundle (point A) and each alternative indicated by an i are valued equally by Crusoe. These i points, when connected, form the indifference curve. This line separates the preferred bundles of fish and breadfruit from the less valued combinations. Note that such a curve is likely to be entirely different for any two people. The preferences of different individuals vary widely.

We can establish a new indifference curve by starting from any point not on the original curve and following the same procedure. If we start with a point (a consumption bundle) to the northeast of the original indifference curve, all points on the new curve will have a higher level of satisfaction for Crusoe than any on the old curve. The new curve will probably have about the same shape as the original.

CHARACTERISTICS OF INDIFFERENCE CURVES

In developing consumer theory, economists assume that the preferences of consumers exhibit certain properties. These properties enable us to make statements about the general pattern of indifference curves. What are these properties, and what do they imply about the characteristics of indifference curves?

1. More goods are preferable to fewer goods—thus, bundles on indifference curves lying farthest to the northeast of a diagram are always preferred. Assuming the consumption of only two commodities that are both desired, the individual will always prefer a bundle with more of one of the good (without loss of the other) to the original bundle. This means that combinations to the northeast of a point on the diagram will always be preferred to points lying to the southwest.

2. Goods are substitutable—therefore, indifference curves slope downward to the right. As we indicated in the text of this chapter, individuals are willing to substitute one good for another. Crusoe will be willing to give up some breadfruit if he is compensated with enough fish. Stated another way, there will be some amount of additional fish such that Crusoe will stay on the same indifference curve, even though his consumption of breadfruit has declined. However, in order to remain on the same indifference curve, Crusoe must always acquire more of one good to compensate for the loss of the other. The indifference curve for goods thus will always slope downward to the right (run northwest to southeast).

3. The valuation of a good declines as it is consumed more intensively—therefore, indifference curves are always convex when viewed from below. The slope of the indifference curve represents the willingness of the individual to substitute one good for the other. Economists refer to the amount of one good that is just sufficient to compensate the consumer for the loss of a unit of the other good as the **marginal rate of substitution.** It is equal to the slope of the indifference curve. Reflecting the principle of diminishing marginal utility, the marginal rate of substitution of a good will decline as the good is consumed more intensively relative to other goods. Suppose Crusoe remains on the same indifference curve while continuing to expand his consumption of fish relative to breadfruit. As his consumption of fish increases (and his consumption of breadfruit declines), his valuation of fish relative to breadfruit will decline. It will take more and more units of fish to compensate for the loss of still another unit of breadfruit. The indifference curve will become flatter, reflecting the decline in the marginal rate of substitution of fish for breadfruit as Crusoe consumes more fish relative to breadfruit.

Of course, just the opposite will happen if Crusoe's consumption of breadfruit increases relative to that of fish—if he moves northwest along the same indifference curve. In this case, as breadfruit is consumed more intensively, Crusoe's valuation of it will decline relative to that of fish, and the marginal rate of substitution of fish for breadfruit will rise (the indifference curve will become steeper and steeper). Therefore, since the valuation of each good declines as it is consumed more intensively, indifference curves must be convex when viewed from the origin.

4. Indifference curves are everywhere dense. We can draw an indifference curve through any point on the diagram. This simply means that any two bundles of goods can be compared by the individual.

5. Indifference curves cannot cross—if they did, rational ordering would be violated. If indifference curves crossed, our postulate that more goods are better than fewer goods would be violated. **Exhibit 17A–2** illustrates this point. The crossing of the indifference curves implies that points Y and Z are equally preferred, since they both are on the same indifference curve as X. Consumption bundle Y, though, represents more of both fish and breadfruit than bundle Z, so Y must be preferred to Z. Whenever indifference curves cross, this type of internal inconsistency (irrational ranking) will arise. So, the indifference curves of an individual must not cross.

Marginal rate of substitution

The change in the consumption level of one good that is just sufficient to offset a unit change in the consumption of another good without causing a shift to another indifference curve. At any point on an indifference curve, it will be equal to the slope of the curve at that point.

THE CONSUMER'S PREFERRED BUNDLE

Together with the opportunity constraint of the individual, indifference curves can be used to indicate the most preferred consumption alternatives available to an individual. The **consumption-opportunity constraint** separates consumption bundles that are attainable from those that are unattainable.

Assuming that Crusoe could produce only for himself, his consumption-opportunity constraint would look like the production-possibilities curves discussed in Chapter 2. What would happen if natives from another island visited Crusoe and offered to make exchanges with him? If a barter market existed that permitted Crusoe to exchange fish for breadfruit at a specified exchange rate, his options would resemble those of the market constraint illustrated by **Exhibit 17A–3.** First, let us consider the case where Crusoe inhabits a barter economy in which the current market exchange rate is 2 fish equal 1 breadfruit. Suppose as a result of his expertise as a fisherman, Crusoe specializes in this activity and is able to bring 16 fish to the market per week. What consumption alternatives

Consumption-opportunity constraint

The constraint that separates the consumption bundles that are attainable from those that are unattainable. In a money-income economy, this is usually a budget constraint.

If the indifference curves of an individual crossed, it would lead to the inconsistency pictured here. Points X and Y must be equally valued, since they are both on the same indifference curve (i_1). Similarly, points X and Z must be equally preferred, since they are both on the difference curve i_2. If this is true, Y and Z must also be equally preferred, since they are both equally preferred to X. However, point Y represents more of both goods than Z, so Y has to be preferred to Z. When indifference curves cross, this type of internal inconsistency always arises.

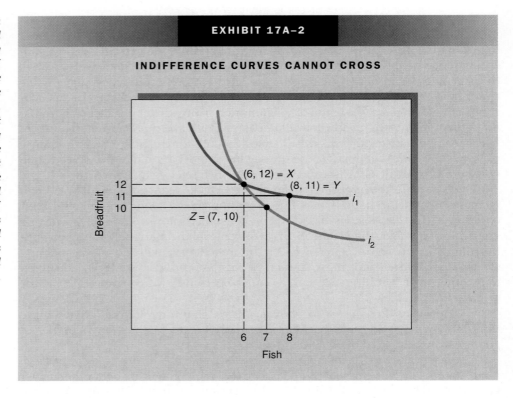

EXHIBIT 17A–2

INDIFFERENCE CURVES CANNOT CROSS

will be open to him? Since 2 fish can be bartered in the market for 1 breadfruit, Crusoe will be able to consume 16 fish, or 8 breadfruit, or any combination on the market constraint indicated by the line between these two points. For example, if he trades 2 of his 16 fish for 1 breadfruit, he will be able to consume a bundle consisting of 14 fish and 1 breadfruit. Assuming that the set of indifference curves of Exhibit 17A–3 outlines Crusoe's preferences, he will choose to consume 8 fish and 4 breadfruit. Of course, it will be possible for Crusoe to choose many other combinations of breadfruit and fish, but none of the other attainable combinations would enable him to reach as high a level of satisfaction. Since he is able to bring only 16 fish to the market, it would be impossible for him to attain an indifference curve higher than i_2.

Crusoe's indifference curve and the market-constraint curve will coincide (they will be tangent) at the point at which his attainable level of satisfaction is maximized. At that point (8 fish and 4 breadfruit), the rate at which Crusoe is willing to exchange fish for breadfruit (as indicated by the slope of the indifference curve) will be just equal to the rate at which the market will *permit* him to exchange the two (the slope of the market constraint).[13] If the two slopes differ at a point, Crusoe will always be able to find an attainable combination that will

---

[13]This actually is required only if the two goods are available in completely divisible amounts, not just as whole fish or whole breadfruit. For simplicity, we assume here that fractional availability is not a problem.

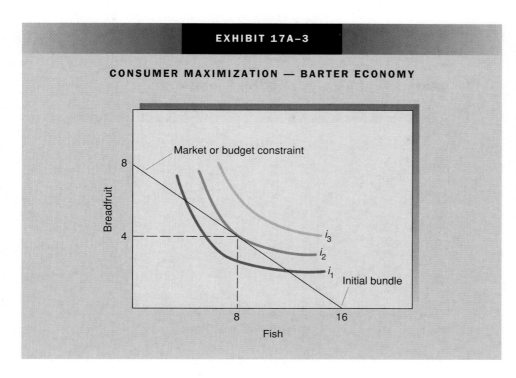

EXHIBIT 17A–3

CONSUMER MAXIMIZATION — BARTER ECONOMY

Market or budget constraint

*i*₃

*i*₂

*i*₁ Initial bundle

Breadfruit

Fish

Suppose that the set of indifference curves shown here outlines Crusoe's preferences. The slope of the market (or budget) constraint indicates that 2 fish trade for 1 breadfruit in this barter economy. If Crusoe produces 16 fish per week, he will trade 8 fish for 4 breadfruit in order to move to the consumption bundle (8 fish and 4 breadfruit) that maximizes his level of satisfaction.

permit him to reach a *higher* indifference curve. He will always move down the market constraint when it is flatter than his indifference curve, and up if the market constraint is steeper.[14]

CRUSOE IN A MONEY ECONOMY

As far as the condition for maximization of consumer satisfaction is concerned, moving from a barter economy to a money income economy changes little. **Exhibit 17A–4** illustrates this point. Initially, the price of fish is $1, and the price of breadfruit is $2. The market therefore permits an exchange of 2 fish for 1 breadfruit, just as was the case in Exhibit 17A–3. In Exhibit 17A–4, we assume Crusoe's money income is $16. At this level of income, he confronts the same market constraint (usually called a **budget constraint** in an economy with money) as for

Budget constraint
The constraint that separates the bundles of goods that the consumer can purchase from those that cannot be purchased, given a limited income and the prices of products.

---

[14]Mathematically, the satisfaction of the consumer is maximized when the marginal rate of substitution of fish for breadfruit is equal to the price ratio. In utility terms, the marginal rate of substitution of fish for breadfruit is equal to the *MU* of fish divided by the *MU* of breadfruit. Therefore, the following expression is a condition for maximum consumer satisfaction.

$$\frac{MU_f}{MU_b} = \frac{P_f}{P_b}$$

This can be rewritten as follows:

$$\frac{MU_f}{P_f} = \frac{MU_b}{P_b}$$

Note that this is precisely the condition of consumer maximization that we indicated earlier in this chapter (see footnote 4).

Suppose that Crusoe's income is $16 per day, the price of fish (P_f) is $1, and the price of breadfruit (P_b) is $2. Thus, Crusoe confronts exactly the same price ratio and budget constraint as in Exhibit 17A–3. Assuming that his preferences are unchanged, he will again maximize his satisfaction by choosing to consume 8 fish and 4 breadfruit. What will happen if the price of fish rises to $2? Crusoe's consumption opportunities will be reduced. His budget constraint will turn clockwise around point A, reflecting the higher price of fish. His fish consumption will decline to 5 units. (Note: since Crusoe's real income has been reduced, his consumption of breadfruit will also decline.

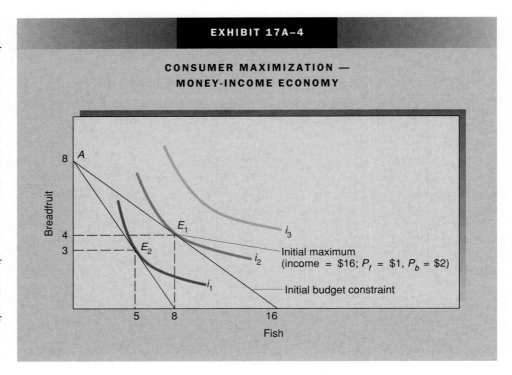

EXHIBIT 17A–4

CONSUMER MAXIMIZATION — MONEY-INCOME ECONOMY

Initial maximum (income = $16; P_f = $1, P_b = $2)

Initial budget constraint

Exhibit 17A–3. Given the product prices and his income, Crusoe can choose to consume 16 fish, or 8 breadfruit, or any combination indicated by a line (the budget constraint) connecting these two points. Given his preferences, Crusoe will again choose the combination of 8 fish and 4 breadfruit if he wishes to maximize his level of satisfaction. As was true for the barter economy, when Crusoe maximizes his satisfaction (moves to the highest attainable indifference curve), the rate at which he is willing to exchange fish for breadfruit will just equal the rate at which the market will permit him to exchange the two goods. Stated in more technical terms, when his level of satisfaction is at a maximum, Crusoe's marginal rate of substitution of fish for breadfruit, as indicated by the slope of the indifference curve at E_1, will just equal the price ratio (P_f/P_b, which is also the slope of the budget constraint).

What will happen if the price of fish increases? Exhibit 17A–4 also answers this question. Since the price of breadfruit and Crusoe's money income are constant, a higher fish price will have two effects. First, it will make Crusoe poorer, even though his *money* income will be unchanged. His budget constraint will turn clockwise around point *A*, illustrating that his consumption options are now more limited—that is, his real income has declined. Second, the budget line will be steeper, indicating that a larger number of breadfruit must now be sacrificed to obtain an additional unit of fish. It will no longer be possible for Crusoe to attain indifference curve i_2. The best he can do is indifference curve i_1, which he can attain by choosing the bundle of 5 fish and 3 breadfruit.

Using the information supplied by Exhibit 17A–4, we can now locate two points on Crusoe's demand curve for fish. When the price of fish was $1, Crusoe chose 8 fish; when the price rose to $2, Crusoe reduced his consumption to 5 (see

Exhibit 17A–5). Of course, other points on Crusoe's demand curve could also be located if we considered other prices for fish.

The demand curve of Exhibit 17A–5 is constructed on the assumption that the price of breadfruit remains $2 and that Crusoe's money income remains constant at $16. If either of these factors were to change, the entire demand curve for fish, illustrated by Exhibit 17A–5, would shift.

The indifference curve is a useful way to illustrate how a person with a fixed budget chooses between two goods. In the real world, of course, people have hundreds, or even thousands, of goods to choose from, and the doubling of only one price usually has a small impact on a person's overall consumption and satisfaction possibilities. In our simple example, the twofold increase in the price of fish makes Crusoe much worse off, since he spends a large portion of his budget on the item.

THE INCOME AND SUBSTITUTION EFFECTS

In the text, we indicated that when the price of a product rises, the amount consumed will change as a result of both an *income effect* and a *substitution effect*. Indifference curve analysis can be used to separate these two effects. **Exhibit 17A–6** is similar to Exhibit 17A–4. Both exhibits illustrate Crusoe's response to an increase in the price of fish from $1 to $2 when money income ($16) and the price of breadfruit ($2) are held constant. Exhibit 17A–6, however, breaks down his total response into the substitution effect and the income effect. The reduction in the consumption of fish solely because of the substitution (price) effect, holding

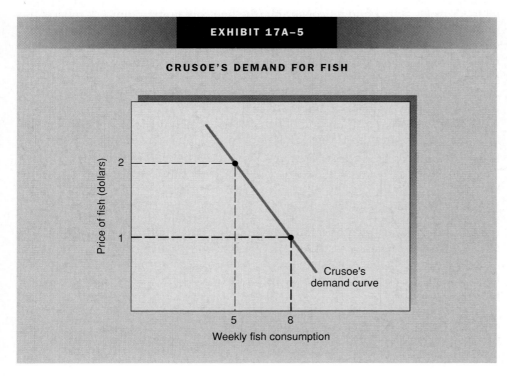

EXHIBIT 17A–5

CRUSOE'S DEMAND FOR FISH

Price of fish (dollars) / Weekly fish consumption

Crusoe's demand curve

As Exhibit 17A–4 illustrates, when the price of fish is $1, Crusoe chooses 8 units. When the price of fish increases to $2, he reduces his consumption to 5 units. This gives us two points on Crusoe's demand curve for fish. Other points on the demand curve could be derived by confronting Crusoe with still other prices of fish. [Note: Crusoe's money income ($16) and the price of breadfruit ($2) are unchanged in this analysis.]

Here we break down Crusoe's response to the rise in the price of fish from $1 to $2 (see Exhibit 17A-4) into the substitution and income effects. The move from E_1 to F illustrates the substitution effect, whereas the move fro F to E_2 reflects the income effect.

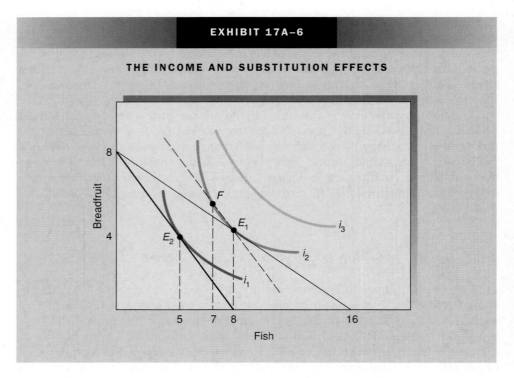

EXHIBIT 17A–6

THE INCOME AND SUBSTITUTION EFFECTS

Crusoe's real income (level of utility) constant, can be found by constructing a line tangent to Crusoe's original indifference curve (i_2), and having a slope indicating the higher price of fish. This line (the broken line in Exhibit 17A–6), which is parallel to Crusoe's actual budget constraint (the line containing point E_2), reflects the higher price of fish. It is tangent to the original difference curve i_2, so Crusoe's real income is held constant. As this line indicates, Crusoe's consumption of fish will fall from 8 to 7, due strictly to the fact that fish are now more expensive. This move from E_1 to F is a pure substitution effect.

Real income, though, has actually been reduced. As a result, Crusoe will be unable to attain point F on indifference curve i_2. The best he can attain is point E_2, which decreases his consumption of fish by another 2 units to 5. Since the broken line containing F and the budget constraint containing E_2 are parallel, the relative price of fish and breadfruit is held constant as Crusoe moves from F to E_2. This move from F to E_2 is thus a pure income effect. The reduction in the consumption of fish (and breadfruit) is due entirely to the decline in Crusoe's real income.

Indifference curve analysis highlights the assumptions and considerations that enter into consumer decisions. The logic of the proof that there is an inverse relationship between the price and the amount demanded is both elegant and reassuring. It is elegant because of the internal consistency of the logic and the precision of the analysis. It is reassuring because it conforms with our expectations, which are based on the central postulate of economics—that incentives matter in a predictable way.

CHAPTER EIGHTEEN

COSTS AND THE SUPPLY
OF GOODS

[A] supply curve traces out the quantity of a good that sellers will produce at various prices. As the price falls, so does the number of units supplied.

AL EHRBAR[1]

Opportunity cost is the value of the best alternative that must be sacrificed in order to engage in an activity. This is the only relevant cost in economic analysis. . . . The supply curve of any commodity or service consequently reflects opportunity costs which are determined indirectly by consumers clamoring for a myriad of goods.

MARSHALL COLBERG[2]

CHAPTER FOCUS

- *Why are business firms used by societies everywhere to organize production?*
- *How are firms organized in market economies?*
- *What are explicit and implicit costs, and how do they guide the behavior of the firm?*
- *How does economic profit differ from accounting profit, and what role does it play?*
- *How do short-run costs differ from long-run costs, and what factors shift the firm's cost curves?*

[1]Al Ehrbar, "Supply" in *The Fortune Encyclopedia of Economics* (New York: Warner Books, 1993), p. 87.

[2]Marshall R. Colberg, Dascomb R. Forbush, and Gilbert R. Whitaker, *Business Economics* (Homewood, IL: Irwin, 1980), p. 12.

Demand and supply interact to determine the market price of a product. In the last chapter, we illustrated that the demand for a product reflects the strength of consumer desire for that product. In this chapter, we focus on costs of producing such a product. The resources needed for production could be used to produce other goods instead. As Professor Colberg points out in the second quote opening this chapter, the cost of resources to produce one product reflects consumer demands for the other products that could be produced instead, with the same resources. We will deal with market firms, although the same basic principles of comparing cost with value produced will apply in any economy where rational economic decisions are made.

Costs are the major determinants of both the shape and the position of the supply curve for a good as described in the opening quote from Ehrbar. If the cost of producing a good exceeds its price, the market is signaling that while the good is desired, other goods that could be produced with the same resources are more urgently desired. In a market economy, producers who anticipate suffering a loss if they continue production are unlikely to continue production. This means that supply and cost of production must be closely linked. For example, a producer who faces a cost of $400 to produce a stereo set is unlikely to continue supplying the sets for very long if the market price is $200. In the long run, sets that cost $400 will be supplied only if they can command a price of at least $400.

In this chapter, we lay the foundation for a detailed investigation of the link between costs and market supply. The nature and function of costs are subjects central to economic analysis. The economist's use of the term *costs* differs sometimes from that of business decision makers and accountants. What do economists mean by costs? Why are costs so important? What is the function of costs in a market economy? We discuss these and related questions in this chapter.

ORGANIZATION OF THE BUSINESS FIRM

The business firm is an entity designed to organize raw materials, labor, and machines with the goal of producing goods and/or services. Firms (1) purchase productive resources from households and other firms, (2) transform them into a different commodity, and (3) sell the transformed product or service to consumers.

Economies differ in the amount of freedom they allow business decision makers. They differ also in the incentive structure used to stimulate and guide business activity. Nevertheless, every society relies on business firms to organize resources and transform them into products. In market economies, most business firms choose their own price, output level, and methods of production. They reap the benefits of sales revenues, but they are also fully responsible for their costs. In socialist countries, government policy often establishes the selling price and constrains the actions of business firms in various other ways. Firms typically are not expected to pay all their bills from their revenues, and they are often not allowed to keep the proceeds if revenues exceed costs. In any case, however, the central position of the business firm as the organized productive unit is universal to capitalist and socialist economies alike. In this chapter we focus on the organization and behavior of firms in a market economy.

INCENTIVES, COOPERATION, AND THE NATURE OF THE FIRM[3]

Most firms are privately owned in capitalist countries. The owners, who may or may not act as entrepreneurs, are the individuals who risk their wealth on the success of the business. If the firm is successful and makes profits, these financial gains go to the owners. Conversely, if the firm suffers losses, the owners must bear the consequences. Because the owners receive what remains after the revenue of the firm is used to pay the contractual costs, they are called **residual claimants.**

In a market economy, the property right of owners to the residual income of the firm plays a very important role: it provides owners with a strong incentive to organize and structure their business in a manner that will keep their cost of producing output low. The wealth of these residual claimants is directly influenced by the success or failure of the firm. Thus, they have a strong incentive to see that resources under their direction are used efficiently.

There are two ways of organizing productive activity: contracting and **team production,** in which workers are hired by a firm to work together under the supervision of the owner, or the owner's representative. Most business firms use both contracting and team production.

In principle, any production could be accomplished by contracts among individuals. For example, a builder might have a house built by contracting with one person to pour the concrete for the floor, another to construct the wooden part of the house, a third to install the roofing, a fourth to do the electrical wiring, and so on. No employees would have to be involved in such a project. More commonly though, goods and services are produced with some combination of contracting and the use of team production by employees of a firm.

Why do firms use team production? If contracting alone is used to produce something, the producer must, for each project, (1) determine what is required to produce the desired result in the best way, given the circumstances and the current technology and prices, (2) search out reliable suppliers, and (3) negotiate and enforce the contracts. The entrepreneur who wants to produce by this method must have specialized knowledge in a variety of areas and must devote a great deal of time and effort to the planning and contracting processes. Not many people have the expertise or the time to take care of all these tasks by themselves except on a small scale.

Accordingly, a builder is likely to hire knowledgeable, experienced workers to plan, to purchase materials, and to build structures such as houses and office buildings. The firm itself will then contract with others to obtain materials and specialized labor services.

A firm, then, is a business organization that may use team production to reduce many of the transaction costs associated with contracting. Team production, however, raises another set of problems. Team members—that is, the employees working for the firm—must be monitored and provided with an incentive system that discourages **shirking,** or working at less than a normal rate of

Residual claimants
Individuals who personally receive the excess, if any, of revenues over costs. Residual claimants gain if the firm's costs are reduced and if revenues are increased.

Team production
A process of production wherein employees work together under the supervision of the owner or the owner's representative.

Shirking
Working at less than a normal rate of productivity, thus reducing output. Shirking is more likely when workers are not monitored, so that the cost of lower output falls on others than themselves.

---

[3]A classic article on this topic is Ronald Coase, "The Nature of the Firm," *Economica* (1937), pp. 386–405. See also Armen Alchian and Harold Demsetz, "Production, Information Costs, and Economic Organization," *American Economic Review* (December 1972), pp. 777–795.

productivity. Taking long work breaks, paying more attention to their own convenience than to work results, and wasting time when diligence is called for are examples of shirking. A worker will shirk more when the costs of doing so are shifted to other team members, including the owners of the firm. Hired managers, even including those at the top, must be monitored and provided with the incentive to avoid shirking.

When team production is utilized, the problem of imperfect monitoring and imperfect incentives is always present. It is part of a larger class of problems called, in general, the **principal-agent problem** (see the "Applications in Economics" feature on this subject). Any person who has taken a car to an auto mechanic has experienced such a problem. The mechanic wants to get the job done quickly and to make as much money on it as possible. The car owner wants to get the job done quickly also, but in a way that permanently fixes the problem, at the lowest possible cost. Since the mechanic typically knows far more about the job than the customer, it is hard for the customer to monitor his work. There is a possibility, therefore, that the mechanic may charge a large amount for a "quick fix" that will not last.

The owner of a firm is in a similar situation. It is often difficult to monitor the performance of individual employees and provide them with an incentive structure that will encourage high productivity. Nonetheless, the success of the firm is crucially dependent upon how these problems are resolved. If a firm is going to keep costs low, it must discover and use an incentive structure that motivates workers and discourages shirking.

STRUCTURING THE FIRM

Business firms can be organized in one of three ways: as a proprietorship, a partnership, or a corporation. The structure chosen determines how the owners share the risks and liabilities of the firm and how they participate in the making of decisions.

A **proprietorship** is a business firm that is owned by a single individual who is fully liable for the debts of the firm. In addition to assuming the responsibilities of ownership, the proprietor often works directly for the firm, providing managerial and other labor services. Many small businesses, including neighborhood grocery stores, barbershops, and farms, are business proprietorships. As **Exhibit 18–1** shows, proprietorships comprised 73 percent of all business firms in 1989. Because most proprietorships are small, however, they generated only 6 percent of all business receipts for that year.

A **partnership** consists of two or more persons acting as co-owners of a business firm. The partners share risks and responsibilities in some pre-arranged manner. There is no difference between a proprietorship and a partnership in terms of owner liability. In both cases, the owners are fully liable for all business debts incurred by the firm. Many law, medical, and accounting firms are organized along partnership lines. This form of business structure accounts for only 8 percent of the total number of firms and 4 percent of all business receipts.

Even though **corporations** comprised less than 20 percent of all business firms in 1989, they accounted for 90 percent of all business receipts. One might ask, then, what accounts for the attractiveness of the corporate structure?

Principal-agent problem
The incentive problem arising when the purchaser of services (the principal) lacks full information about the circumstances faced by the seller (the agent) and thus cannot know how well the agent performs the purchased services. The agent may to some extent work toward objectives other than those sought by the principal paying for the service.

Proprietorship
A business firm owned by an individual who possesses the ownership right to the firm's profits and is personally liable for the firm's debts.

Partnership
A business firm owned by two or more individuals who possess ownership rights to the firm's profits and are personally liable for the debts of the firm.

Corporation
A business firm owned by shareholders who possess ownership rights to the firm's profits, but whose liability is limited to the amount of their investment in the firm.

APPLICATIONS IN ECONOMICS

THE PRINCIPAL-AGENT PROBLEM

In recent years, economists have focused a great deal of attention on a class of problems in which one individual is hired to act on behalf of another. This *principal-agent problem* arises when the purchaser of services (the principal) lacks full information about the circumstances faced by the seller (the agent), and thus cannot know how well the agent performs the purchased services. As a result, the agent may to some extent work toward objectives other than those sought by the principal, who is paying for the services. Because agents exercise their own judgment in performing the work and cannot be completely monitored, they have opportunities to shirk, and, in general, to serve their own ends rather than those of the principal.

We all run into the principal-agent problem when we pay a dentist, a mechanic, or a lawyer to perform services for us. These agents we hire know more than we do about their work and about the circumstances of the specific job we pay them to do. We cannot be sure that they are doing the best possible job for us. The owner of a business firm faces similar incentive problems with every employee hired. A large firm has many managers who spend a good deal of time monitoring the work of employees and providing them with the incentive to work efficiently. But they cannot monitor perfectly and, in any case, who will monitor the monitors?

Even top-level executives hired to manage a firm do not have the same objectives as owners—primarily profit maximization—unless, of course, the managers are the owners. So the judgments of executives, too, are influenced by what is in their personal best interests. They want perks, personal job security, and other benefits that may not be consistent with profit maximization for the firm. The problem is more serious as firms grow larger and acquire more managers and employees. Ultimately it is the job of the owners, as residual claimants, to develop an incentive structure that minimizes the principal-agent problem. For the owner, the saying "the buck stops here" always applies.

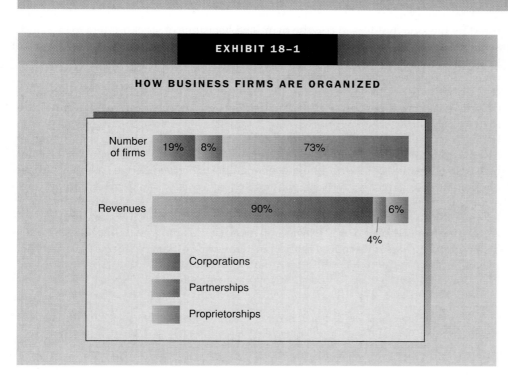

EXHIBIT 18–1

HOW BUSINESS FIRMS ARE ORGANIZED

Number of firms: 19% | 8% | 73%

Revenues: 90% | 6% | 4%

- Corporations
- Partnerships
- Proprietorships

Nearly three out of every four firms are proprietorships, but only 6 percent of all business revenue is generated by proprietorships. Corporations account for only one out of every five firms, but generate 90 percent of all revenues.

Source: *Statistical Abstract of the United States: 1993*, Table 848. (Data are for 1989.)

First, the stockholders of the corporation are the legal owners of the firm. Any profits of the firm belong to them. Their liability, however, is limited to the extent of their explicit investment. If a corporation owes you money, you cannot directly sue the stockholders. You can, of course, sue the corporation—but what if it goes bankrupt? You and others to whom the firm owes money will simply be out of luck.

This limited liability makes it possible for corporations to attract investment funds from a large number of "owners" who do not participate in the day-to-day management of the firm. The stockholders of many large corporations simply hire managers to operate the firm. Corporations are thus often characterized by a separation of ownership and operational management.

Another advantage of the corporate structure is that ownership can easily be transferred. The shares, or ownership rights, of an owner who dies can be sold by the heirs to another owner without disrupting the business firm. Because of this, the corporation is an ongoing concern. Similarly, stockholders who become unhappy with the way a corporation is run can bail out merely by selling their stock.

The corporate form of ownership is flexible enough to adjust easily to a different location or to many locations. Multinational corporations can do business wherever comparative advantage dictates, so many businesses operate in this way. In 1990 U.S. multinational firms had nearly $5 trillion in assets, while their foreign affiliates has assets of $1.6 trillion. They exported $108 billion worth of goods to their foreign affiliates, while importing $102 billion from them. IBM, for example, is an American corporation, but 55 percent of its employees were in foreign countries in 1990, and that percentage was growing. IBM Japan had more than 18,000 Japanese employees and annual sales of more than $6 billion, making it one of Japan's largest exporters of computers.[4] Corporations seeking lower production costs and higher-valued outputs are quite flexible in both hiring and location decisions.

The managers of a large corporation might be thought of as trained experts hired by the stockholders to run the firm. The decisions of stockholders to buy and sell shares of stock mirror the confidence of investors in the management of the firm. If enough current and prospective stockholders alike come to believe that the managers will do a good job, the demand for the firm's stock will increase. Rising stock prices will reflect this increase in demand. Conversely, when investors are dissatisfied with a corporation's management, the stock's price will tumble. In turn, falling stock prices will often lead to a shake-up in the management of the firm. A constructive management change can bring significant change in the price of a corporation's stock. Consider the case of Eastman Kodak Company's decision in August 1993 to search for a new chairman and chief executive, who would be allowed to bring in a new management team. Investors had been demanding stringent measures to cut costs, and the chief executive and chairman had not taken such measures. The announcement apparently made investors optimistic. According to *The Wall Street Journal* news story, "Kodak stock surged $3.25, or 5.9%, on the news."[5] The capital market provides one of several forms of discipline placed on corporate management in a market economy. (See the "Applications in Economics" boxed feature on modern corporate structure.)

---

[4]Aggregate figures are from the *Statistical Abstract of the U.S., 1993,* (Washington: U.S. Government Printing Office, 1993), Table 895, while the IBM data are from Robert Reich, "Does Corporate Nationality Matter?" *Issues in Science and Technology* (Winter 1990–1991), pp. 40–44.

[5]Joan E. Rigdon and Joann S. Lublin, "Kodak Seeks Outsider to Be Chairman, CEO," *The Wall Street Journal,* August 8, 1993, p. A3.

COSTS, SENSITIVITY TO CONSUMERS, AND STRUCTURE OF MODERN CORPORATIONS

How can we be sure that business firms will operate efficiently and respond to the interests of customers? In the case of owner-managed firms, clearly there is a strong incentive for efficient management, cost-effective production, and sensitivity to the interests of consumers. Offering consumers value at a low cost is the ticket to profitability. Since owner-managers are residual-income claimants, they have a strong incentive to manage firms wisely.

However, in the case of a large corporation with millions of stockholders, the situation is more complex. While the stockholders hold the legal claim to residual income, professional managers direct the operation of the firm. There is a separation between ownership and management. The objectives of managers may conflict with those of stockholders. For example, managers may prefer high salaries, large offices, and first-class travel. They may also prefer the power and prestige of business expansion, even if it reduces profitability.

Can the stockholders control the actions of managers and direct them toward the pursuit of profitability? For large corporations, *direct* control is unlikely. Most large corporations are owned by shareholders, none of whom owns more than a tiny fraction of the firm's outstanding stock. While they elect a board of directors, which in turn appoints high-level managers, individual stockholders have neither the incentive nor the information to exercise direct control. Most find it too expensive even to attend the annual shareholder's meeting. They can, of course, send a *proxy*—a designated person to vote their shares. But management generally solicits the proxies of shareholders prior to the annual meeting. If they do not throw their proxy vote in the wastebasket, most stockholders turn it over to the present management, and thereby provide management with the votes to reelect themselves.

Given this organizational structure, what keeps managers from using corporate resources as a personal feifdom? What prevents management from pursuing its own objectives at the expense of the stockholders and consumers? There are three major factors that promote cost efficiency and limit the power of corporate managers. Let us consider each.

COMPETITION FOR INVESTMENT FUNDS AND CUSTOMERS

Nobody forces stockholders to invest in corporations. Unless they are able to earn a competitive return, shareholders will invest their funds elsewhere—in other companies' stock or in bonds, real estate, or personal business activities for example. In fact, stockholders have an incentive to monitor management in order to anticipate problems or constructive innovations. Investors who are the first to spot a good, new management strategy can buy stock early, before others realize the opportunity and bid the price up. Stockholders who are the first to spot a problem can "bail out" by selling their stock before others see the problem and dump their stock, thus depressing the price. So managers get constant feedback via the stock price, which can be just as important as current profits to stockholders and boards of directors.

Similarly, consumers have an incentive to monitor the quality and price of the firm's output. No one forces them to buy the corporation's product; so if other firms supply superior products or offer a lower price, consumers can take their business to rival firms.

The corporation's need to meet the competition limits the ability of managers to pursue their personal objectives at the expense of either stockholders or customers.

COMPENSATION AND MANAGEMENT INCENTIVES

The compensation of managers can be structured in a manner that will bring the interests of managers into harmony with shareholders. Market determination of managerial salaries will help achieve this objective. Those managers who establish a track record of business profitability and rising stock prices will command higher-paying positions in the job market. The demand for managers associated with losing enterprises and business failures will be weak. And internally, corporate firms can, and generally do, tie the compensation of managers to the market success of the business. Salary increases and bonuses may be directly related to the firm's profitability. Senior managers may be paid in part with shares of corporate stock that will encourage them to follow policies that maximize the wealth holdings of all shareholders. Many firms have designed stock option-to-buy plans available to management that are extremely valuable if the market value of the firm's shares rise but worthless if they fall. All of these factors tend to reduce the conflict between the interests of managers and shareholders

THREAT OF CORPORATE TAKEOVER

Managers who do not serve the interests of their shareholders are vulnerable to a *takeover,* a move by an outside person or group to gain the control of the firm. As we previously noted, shareholders who lose confidence in management can "fire" management by selling their shares. When a significant number of shareholders follow this course of action, the market value of the firm's stock will decline. This will increase the attractiveness of the firm to takeover specialists shopping for a poorly run business, the value of which could be substantially increased by a new management team.[1]

Consider a firm currently earning $1.50 per share. Reflecting current earnings that are expected to continue, the market value of the firm's stock is $15 per share (assuming a 10 percent interest rate). If the earnings of the firm are reduced because the current management team is pursuing its own objectives at the expense of profitability, then a corporate takeover could lead to substantial gain. Suppose some outside persons believe that they could restructure the firm, improve the management, and thereby increase the firm's earnings to $3 per share. Therefore, they tender a takeover bid—an offer to buy shares of the firm's stock—for $20 per share. If the takeover team is correct, and if it is able to increase the firm's earnings to $3 per share, then the stock value of the firm will rise accordingly (to $30 per share).

Of course, the current management has an incentive to resist the takeover. After all, the current operating plans are their own, and the jobs they now hold are the best available to them. The outsiders who say that the current management is wrong and should be replaced will seldom be welcomed with open arms.

If the takeover specialists are right—if the new management is able to improve the cost efficiency and profitability of the firm—they will experience a handsome profit. Of course, they might be wrong and experience losses as a consequence. However, the important point is that the potential of a takeover acts as a check against managerial strategies that conflict with profit maximization. Managers who pursue their own interests at the expense of stockholders make themselves vulnerable to a takeover. The mere potential of the takeover reduces the likelihood that managers will stray too far from the profit-maximization strategy.

CONCLUDING THOUGHT

How efficient is the corporate business structure? Perhaps history provides the best answer. If the corporate structure were not an efficient form of business organization, it would not have continued to survive, nor would it be so prevalent. Rival forms of business organization, including proprietorships, partnerships, consumer cooperatives, employee ownership, and mutually owned companies can and do compete in the marketplace for investment funds. In certain industries, some of these alternative forms of business organization are dominant. Nonetheless, in most industries, the corporate structure is the dominant form of business organization (see Exhibit 18–1). This is strong evidence that, despite its defects, it is generally a cost-efficient, consumer-sensitive form of organization.

---

[1]For a discussion of corporate takeovers from various points of view, see Hal R. Varian et al., "Symposium on Takeovers," *The Journal of Economic Perspectives 2,* no. 1 (Winter 1988) pp. 3–81. See also John R. Coffee, Jr. et al., "Corporate Takeovers: Who Wins; Who Loses; Who Should Regulate?" *Regulation* 12, no. 1 (1988), p. 23.

ECONOMIC ROLE OF COSTS

Consumers would like to have more economic goods, but resources to produce them are scarce. We cannot produce as much of all goods as we would like, because the use of resources to make one commodity takes resources from the production of other desired goods. The desire for a given product must be balanced against the desire for other items that must be sacrificed to produce it. Every economic system must make these balancing judgments. When decisions are made in the political arena, the budget process performs this balancing function. Congress (or the central committee, or the king) decides which goods will be produced and which will be foregone. Taxes and budgets are set accordingly.

In a market economy, consumer demand and cost of production are central to the performance of this balancing function. The desire of consumers for a specific good must be balanced against the desire for other goods that could be produced with the resources. Production of one good necessitates a reduction in the output of other goods. The most highly valued of these foregone opportunities when a good is produced comprise the good's costs of production. The owner of a resource employed in the production of one good must be paid at least as much as the resource would be worth in alternative uses that must be foregone. The production cost of a good reveals the value of the resources used to produce it, in terms of other opportunities foregone.

The demand for a product can be thought of as the voice of consumers instructing firms to produce a good. On the other hand, costs of production represent the voice of consumers saying that other items that could be produced with the resources are also desired. The demand for a product indicates the intensity of consumers' desires for the item. The cost of producing a product indicates the desire of consumers for other goods that must now be foregone because the necessary resources have been employed in the production of the first item.

CALCULATING ECONOMIC COSTS AND PROFITS

Business firms, regardless of their size, are primarily concerned with profit. Profit, of course, is the firm's total revenue minus the sum of its costs. But to state profit correctly, it is imperative that costs be measured properly. Most people, including some who are in business, think of costs as amount paid for raw materials, labor, machines, and similar inputs. However, this concept of cost, which stems from accounting procedures, may exclude some of the firm's costs. When cost is miscalculated, profit is also misstated, and uneconomic decisions may result.

The key to understanding the economist's concept of profit is the oft-discussed *opportunity cost*. The firm incurs a cost whenever it uses a resource, thereby requiring the resource owner to forego the highest valued alternative. These costs may either be explicit or implicit. **Explicit costs** result when the firm makes a monetary payment to resource owners. Money wages, interest, and rental payments are a measure of what the firm gives up to employ the services of labor and capital resources. Firms may also incur **implicit costs**—those associated with the use of resources owned by the firm. Since implicit costs do not involve a direct money or contractual payment, they are sometimes excluded from accounting statements. For example, the owners of small proprietorships often supply labor services to their businesses. There is an opportunity cost associated with the use of this resource; other opportunities have to be given up because of the time spent by the owner in the operation of the business. The highest valued alternative foregone is the opportunity cost of the labor service provided by the owner. The **total cost** of production is the sum of the explicit and implicit costs incurred by the employment of all resources involved in the production process.

Accounting statements generally omit the implicit cost of equity capital—the cost of funds supplied by owners. If a firm borrows financial capital from a bank or other private source, it will have to pay interest. Accountants properly record this interest expense as a cost. In contrast, when the firm acquires financial capital

Explicit costs
Payments by a firm to purchase the services of productive resources.

Implicit costs
The opportunity costs associated with a firm's use of resources that it owns. These costs do not involve a direct money payment. Examples include wage income and interest foregone by the owner of a firm who also provides labor services and equity capital to the firm.

Total cost
The costs, both explicit and implicit, of all the resources used by the firm. Total cost includes an imputed normal rate of return for the firm's equity capital.

through the issuance of stock, accountants make no allowance for the cost of this financial capital. Regardless of whether it is acquired by borrowing or stock (equity capital), the use of financial capital involves an opportunity cost. Persons who supply equity capital to a firm expect to earn a normal rate of return—a return comparable to what they could earn if they chose other investment opportunities (including bonds). If they do not earn this normal rate of return, investors will not continue to supply financial capital to the business.

Opportunity cost of equity capital
The implicit rate of return that must be earned by investors to induce them to continue to supply financial capital to the firm.

When calculating costs, economists use the normal return on financial capital as a basis for determining the implicit **opportunity cost of equity capital.** If the normal rate of return on financial capital is 10 percent, equity investors will refuse funds to firms unable to earn a 10 percent rate of return on capital assets. As a result, earning the normal rate of return—that is, covering the opportunity cost of all of its capital—is vital to the survival of a business firm.

ACCOUNTING PROFIT AND ECONOMIC PROFIT

Economic profit
The difference between the firm's total revenues and total costs.

Since economists seek to measure the opportunities lost due to the production of a good or service, they include both explicit and implicit costs in total cost. **Economic profit** is equal to total revenues minus total costs, including both the explicit and implicit cost components. Economic profits will be present only if the earnings of a business are in excess of the opportunity cost of using the assets owned by the firm. Economic losses result when the earnings of the firm are insufficient to cover explicit and implicit costs. When the firm's revenues are just equal to its costs, both explicit and implicit, economic profits will be zero.

Remember that zero economic profits do not imply that the firm is about to go out of business. On the contrary, they indicate that the owners are receiving exactly the market (normal) rate of return on their investment (assets owned by the firms).

Accounting profits
The sales revenues minus the expenses of a firm over a designated time period, usually one year. Accounting profits typically make allowances for changes in the firm's inventories and depreciation of its assets. No allowance is made, however, for the opportunity cost of the equity capital of the firm's owners, or other implicit costs.

Since accounting procedures often omit implicit costs, such as those associated with owner-provided labor services or capital assets, the accounting costs of the firm generally understate the opportunity costs of production. This understatement of cost leads to an overstatement of economic profits. Therefore, the **accounting profits** of a firm are generally greater than the firm's economic profits (see the "Applications in Economics" boxed feature on accounting costs). When the omission of the costs of owner-provided services is unimportant, as is the case for most large corporations, accounting profits approximate the returns to the firm's equity capital. High accounting profits (measured as a rate of return on a firm's assets), relative to the average for other firms, suggest that a firm is earning an economic profit. Correspondingly, a low rate of accounting profit implies economic losses.

SHORT RUN AND LONG RUN

A firm cannot instantaneously adjust its output. Time plays an important role in the production process. All of a firm's resources can be expanded (contracted) over time, but for specialized or heavy equipment, expanding (contracting)

ECONOMIC AND ACCOUNTING COST—A HYPOTHETICAL EXAMPLE

The revenue-cost statement for a corner grocery store owned and operated by Terry Smith is presented here.

Terry works full-time as the manager, chief cashier, and janitor. Terry has $30,000 worth of refrigeration and other equipment invested in the store. Last year, Terry's total sales were $85,000; suppliers and employees were paid $50,000. Terry's revenues exceeded explicit costs by $35,000. Did Terry make a profit last year? The accounting statement for the store will probably show a net profit of $35,000. However, if Terry did not have a $30,000 personal investment in equipment, these funds could be collecting 10 percent interest. Thus, Terry is foregoing $3,000 of interest each year. Similarly, if the building that Terry owns were not being used as a grocery store, it could be rented to someone else for $500 per month. Rental income thus foregone is $6,000 per year. In addition, since Terry is tied up working in the grocery store, a $28,000 managerial position with the local Safeway is foregone. Considering the interest, rental, and salary income that Terry had to forego in order to operate the grocery store last year, Terry's implicit costs were $37,000. The total costs were $87,000. The total revenue of Terry's grocery store was less than the opportunity cost of the resources utilized. Terry incurred an economic loss of $2,000, despite the accounting profit of $35,000.

Total revenue		**$85,000**
Sales (groceries)		
Total (explicit costs)		
Groceries, wholesale	$38,000	
Utilities	2,000	
Taxes	3,000	
Advertising	1,000	
Labor services (employees)	6,000	
Total (explicit) costs	$50,000	
Net (accounting) profit	$35,000	
Additional (implicit) costs		
Interest (personal investment)	$ 3,000	
Rent (Terry's building)	6,000	
Salary (Terry's labor)	28,000	
Total implicit costs	$37,000	
Total explicit and implicit costs		**$87,000**
Economic profit (**total revenue minus explicit and implicit costs**)		**–$2,000**

availability quickly may be very expensive or even impossible. Economists often speak of the **short run** as a time period so short that the firm is unable to alter its present plant size. In the short run, the firm is "stuck" with its existing plant and heavy equipment. They are "fixed" for a given time period. The firm can alter output, however, by applying larger or smaller amounts of variable resources, such as labor and raw materials. Existing plant capacity can thus be used more or less intensively in the short run.

In sum, we can say that the short run is that period of time during which at least one factor of production, usually the size of the firm's plant, cannot be varied. How long is the short run? The length varies from industry to industry. In some industries, substantial changes in plant size can be accomplished in a few months. In other industries, particularly those that use assembly lines and mass production techniques (for example, aircraft and automobiles), the short run might be a year or even several years.

The **long run** is a time period of sufficient length to allow a firm the opportunity to alter its plant size and capacity and all other factors of production. All resources of the firm are variable in the long run. In the long run, from the viewpoint of an entire industry, new firms may be established and enter the industry; other firms may dissolve and leave the industry.

Short run (in production)
A time period so short that a firm is unable to vary some of its factors of production. The firm's plant size typically cannot be altered in the short run.

Long run (in production)
A time period long enough to allow the firm to vary all factors of production.

Perhaps an example will help to clarify the distinction between the short- and long-run time periods. If a battery manufacturer hired 200 additional workers and ordered more raw materials to squeeze a larger output from the existing plant, this would be a short-run adjustment. In contrast, if the manufacturer built an additional plant (or expanded the size of its current facility) and installed additional heavy equipment, this would be a long-run adjustment.

OUTPUT AND COSTS IN SHORT RUN

We have emphasized that in the short run some of a firm's factors of production, such as the size of the plant, will be fixed. Other productive resources will be variable. In the short run, then, we can break the firm's costs into these two categories—fixed and variable. Examining how each category of costs behaves, and seeing that behavior graphically, will illustrate characteristics of the profit-maximizing level of output for a firm.

Fixed costs
Costs that do not vary with output. They will be incurred as long as a firm continues in business and the assets have alternative uses.

Fixed costs will remain unchanged even though output is altered. For example, a firm's insurance premiums, its property taxes, and, most significantly, the opportunity cost of using its fixed assets will be present whether the firm produces a large or small rate of output. These costs will not vary with output. They are "fixed" as long as the firm remains in business. Fixed costs will be present at all levels of output, including zero. They can be avoided only if the firm goes out of business.

Average fixed cost
Fixed cost divided by the number of units produced. It always declines as output increases.

What will happen to **average fixed cost** (*AFC*) as output expands? Remember that the firm's fixed cost will be the same whether output is 1, 100, or 1,000. The *AFC* is simply fixed cost divided by output. As output increases, *AFC* declines since the fixed cost will be spread over more and more units (see part "a" of **Exhibit 18–2**).

Variable costs
Costs that vary with the rate of output. Examples include wages paid to workers and payments for raw materials.

Variable costs are those that vary with output. For example, additional output can usually be produced by hiring more workers and expending additional funds on raw materials. Variable costs involve expenditures on these and other variable inputs. At any given level of output, the firm's **average variable cost** is the total variable cost divided by output.

Average variable cost
The total variable cost divided by the number of units produced.

We have noted that total cost includes explicit and implicit costs. The total cost of producing a good is also the sum of the fixed and variable costs at each output level. At zero output, total cost will equal fixed cost. As output expands from zero, variable cost and fixed cost must be added to obtain total cost. **Average total cost** (*ATC*), sometimes referred to as *unit cost,* can be found by dividing total cost by the total number of units produced. *ATC* cost is also equal to the sum of the average fixed and average variable costs. It indicates the amount per unit of output that must be gained in revenue if total cost is to be covered.

Average total cost
Total cost divided by the number of units produced. It is sometimes called per unit cost.

Marginal cost
The change in total cost required to produce an additional unit of output.

The economic way of thinking emphasizes the importance of what happens "at the margin." How much does it cost to produce an additional unit? **Marginal cost** (*MC*) is the change in total cost that results from the production of one additional unit. The profit-conscious decision maker recognizes *MC* as the addition to cost that must be covered by additional revenue if producing the marginal unit is to be profitable. In the short run, as illustrated by Exhibit 18–2, *MC* will generally decline if output is increased, then eventually reach a minimum, and then increase.

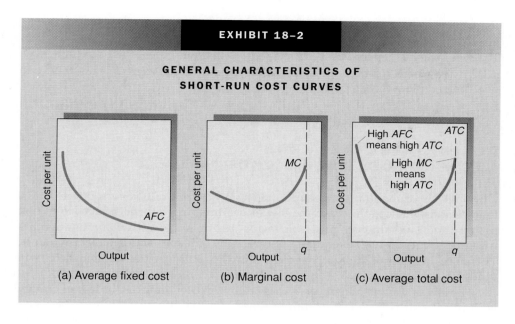

EXHIBIT 18–2

GENERAL CHARACTERISTICS OF SHORT-RUN COST CURVES

(a) Average fixed cost

(b) Marginal cost

(c) Average total cost

Average fixed costs (a) will be high for small rates of output, but they will always decline as output expands. Marginal cost (b) will rise sharply as the plant's production capacity q is approached. As graph (c) illustrates, ATC will be a U-shaped curve, since AFC will be high for small rates of output and MC will be high as the plant's production capacity is approached.

The rising *MC* simply reflects the fact that it becomes increasingly difficult to squeeze additional output from a plant as the facility's maximum capacity (the dotted line of part "b" of Exhibit 18–2) is approached. The accompanying "Thumbnail Sketch" summarizes the interrelationships among a firm's various costs.

As a firm alters its rate of output in the short run, how will unit cost be affected? First, let us look at this question intuitively. In the short run, the firm can vary output by using its fixed plant size more (or less) intensively. As Exhibit 18–2 illustrates, there are two extreme situations that will result in a high unit cost of output. First, when the output rate of a plant is small relative to its capacity, it is obviously being underutilized. Under these circumstances, *AFC* will be high, and therefore *ATC* will also be high. It will be costly and inefficient to operate a large plant substantially below its production capacity. At the other extreme, overutilization can also result in high unit cost. An overutilized plant will mean congestion, time spent by workers waiting for machines, and similar costly delays. As

THUMBNAIL SKETCH

HOW ARE A FIRM'S VARIOUS CATEGORIES OF COSTS RELATED TO ONE ANOTHER?

1. Total cost = explicit cost + implicit cost.
2. Total cost = fixed cost + variable cost.
3. Marginal cost = change in total cost per additional unit of output.
4. Average total cost = total cost/output.

5. Average fixed cost = fixed cost/output.
6. Average variable cost = variable cost/output.
7. Average total cost = average fixed cost + average variable cost.

output approaches the maximum capacity of a plant, overutilization will lead to high *MC* and therefore to high *ATC*.

Thus, the *ATC* curve will be U-shaped, as pictured in part "c" of Exhibit 18–2. *ATC* will be high for both an underutilized plant (because *AFC* is high) and an overutilized plant (because *MC* is high).

DIMINISHING RETURNS AND PRODUCTION IN SHORT RUN

Law of diminishing returns
The postulate that as more and more units of a variable resource are combined with a fixed amount of other resources, employment of additional units of the variable source will eventually increase output only at a decreasing rate. Once diminishing returns are reached, it will take successively larger amounts of the variable factor to expand output by one unit.

Our analysis of the link between unit cost and output rate is corroborated by a long established economic law, the **law of diminishing returns,** which states that as more and more units of a variable factor are applied to a fixed amount of other resources, output will eventually increase by smaller and smaller amounts. Therefore, in terms of their impact on output, the returns to the variable factor will diminish.

The law of diminishing returns is as famous in economics as the law of gravity is in physics. It is based on common sense and real-life observation. Have you ever noticed that as you apply a single resource more intensively, the resource eventually tends to accomplish less and less? Consider a farmer who applies fertilizer (a resource) more and more intensively to an acre of land (a fixed factor). At some point, the application of additional 100-pound units of fertilizer will expand the wheat yield by successively smaller amounts.

Essentially, the law of diminishing returns is a constraint imposed by nature. If it were not valid, it would be possible to raise all the world's foodstuffs on an acre of land, or even in a flowerpot. Logically, then, there would be no point in cultivating any of the less fertile land. We would be able to increase output simply by applying another unit of labor and fertilizer to the world's most fertile flowerpot! In the real world, of course, this is not the case; the law of diminishing returns is valid and it restricts our options.

Total product
The total output of a good that is associated with alternative utilization rates of a variable input.

Marginal product
The increase in the total product resulting from a unit increase in the employment of a variable input. Mathematically, it is the ratio of the change in total product to the change in the quantity of the variable input.

Average product
The total product (output) divided by the number of units of the variable input required to produce that output level.

Exhibit 18–3 illustrates the law of diminishing returns numerically. Column 1 indicates the quantity of the variable resource, labor in this example, that is combined with a specified amount of the fixed resource. Column 2 shows the **total product** that will result as the utilization rate of labor increases. Column 3 provides data on the **marginal product,** the change in total output associated with each additional unit of labor. Without the application of labor, output would be zero. As additional units of labor are applied, total product (output) expands. As the first three units of labor are applied, total product increases by successively larger amounts (8, then 12, then 14). Beginning with the fourth unit, however, diminishing returns are confronted. When the fourth unit is added, marginal product—the change in the total product—declines to 12 (down from 14, when the third unit was applied). As additional units of labor are applied, marginal product continues to decline. It is increasingly difficult to squeeze a larger total product from the fixed resources (for example, plant size and equipment). Eventually, marginal product becomes negative (beginning with the tenth unit).

Column 4 of Exhibit 18–3 provides data for the **average product** of labor, which is simply the total product divided by the units of labor applied. Note the average product increases as long as the marginal product is greater than the average product. Whenever the marginal unit's contribution is greater than the average, it must

EXHIBIT 18-3

LAW OF DIMINISHING RETURNS
(HYPOTHETICAL DATA)

(1) UNITS OF THE VARIABLE RESOURCE, LABOR (PER DAY)	(2) TOTAL PRODUCT (OUTPUT)	(3) MARGINAL PRODUCT	(4) AVERAGE PRODUCT
0	0		—
		8	
1	8		8.0
		12	
2	20		10.0
		14	
3	34		11.3
		12	
4	46		11.5
		10	
5	56		11.2
		8	
6	64		10.7
		6	
7	70		10.0
		4	
8	74		9.3
		1	
9	75		8.3
		-2	
10	73		7.3

cause the average to rise. This is true through the first four units. The marginal product of the fifth unit of labor, though, is 10, less than the average product for the first four units of labor (11.5). Therefore, beginning with the fifth unit, the average product declines as additional labor is applied. When marginal productivity is below the average, it brings down the average product.

Using the data from Exhibit 18–3, **Exhibit 18–4** illustrates the law of diminishing returns graphically. Initially, the total product curve (part "a") increases quite rapidly. As diminishing marginal returns are confronted (beginning with the fourth unit of labor), total product increases more slowly. Eventually, a maximum output (75) is reached with the application of the ninth unit of labor. The marginal product curve (part "b") reflects the total product curve. Geometrically, marginal product is the slope—the rate of increase—of the total product curve. That slope, the marginal product, reaches its maximum with the application of three units of labor. Beyond three units, diminishing returns are present. Eventually, at ten units of labor, the marginal product becomes negative. When marginal product becomes negative, total product is necessarily declining. The average product curve rises as long as the marginal product curve is above it, since each added unit of labor is raising the average. The average product reaches its maximum at four units of labor. Beyond that, each additional unit of labor brings down the average product, and the curve declines.

As units of the variable input (labor) are added to a fixed input, total product will increase, first at an increasing rate and then at a declining rate (a). This will cause both the marginal and average product curves (b) to rise at first and then decline. Note that the marginal product curve intersects the average product curve at its maximum (when 4 units of labor are used) The smooth curves indicate that labor can be increased by amounts of less than a single unit.

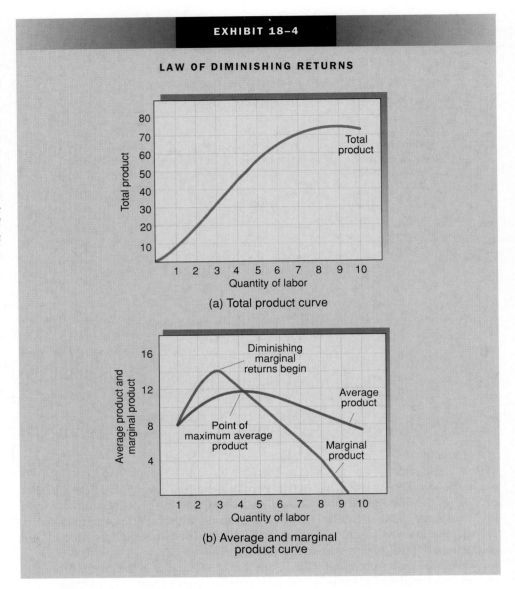

EXHIBIT 18–4

LAW OF DIMINISHING RETURNS

(a) Total product curve

(b) Average and marginal product curve

DIMINISHING RETURNS AND COST CURVES

What impact will diminishing returns have on a firm's costs? Once a firm confronts diminishing returns, larger and larger additions of the variable factor are required to expand output by one unit. Marginal costs (*MC*) rise until, eventually, they exceed average total cost. Until that point, *MC* is below *ATC*, bringing *ATC* down. When *MC* is greater than *ATC*, *ATC* increases. It is easy to see why. What happens when an above average student is added to a class? The class average goes up. What happens if a unit of above average cost is added to output? Average total cost rises. The firm's *MC* curve therefore crosses the *ATC* curve at the *ATC's* lowest point. For output rates beyond the minimum *ATC*, the rising *MC* causes *ATC* to increase. Again, the *ATC* curve is U-shaped.

EXHIBIT 18–5

NUMERICAL SHORT-RUN COST SCHEDULES OF ROYAL ROLLER BLADES, INC.

TOTAL COST DATA (PER DAY)				AVERAGE / MARGINAL COST DATA (PER DAY)			
(1) OUTPUT PER DAY	(2) TFC	(3) TVC	(4) TC (2) + (3)	(5) AFC (2) ÷ (1)	(6) AVC (3) ÷ (1)	(7) ATC (4) ÷ (1)	(8) MC Δ(4) ÷ Δ(1)
0	$50	$ 0	$ 50	—	—	—	—
1	50	15	65	$50.00	$15.00	$65.00	$15
2	50	25	75	25.00	12.50	37.50	10
3	50	34	84	16.67	11.33	28.00	9
4	50	42	92	12.50	10.50	23.00	8
5	50	52	102	10.00	10.40	20.40	10
6	50	64	114	8.33	10.67	19.00	12
7	50	79	129	7.14	11.29	18.43	15
8	50	98	148	6.25	12.25	18.50	19
9	50	122	172	5.56	13.56	19.11	24
10	50	152	202	5.00	15.20	20.20	30
11	50	202	252	4.55	18.36	22.91	50

Exhibit 18–5 numerically illustrates the implications of the law of diminishing returns for a firm's short-run cost curve. Here, we assume that Royal Roller Blades, Inc., combines units of a variable input with a fixed factor to produce units of output (pairs of the popular blades). Columns 2, 3, and 4 indicate how the total cost schedules vary as output is expanded. Total fixed costs (TFC), representing the opportunity cost of the fixed factors of production, are $50 per day. For the first four units of output, total variable costs (TVC) increase at a *decreasing rate.* Why? In this range, there are increasing returns to the variable input. Beginning with the fifth unit of output, however, diminishing marginal returns are present. From this point on, TVC and TC increase by successively larger amounts as output is expanded.

Columns 5 through 8 of Exhibit 18–5 reveal the general pattern of the average and marginal costs schedules. For small output rates, the ATC of producing roller blades is high, primarily because of the high AFC. Initially, MC is less than ATC. When diminishing returns set in for output rates beginning with five units, however, MC rises. Beginning with the sixth unit of output, MC exceeds AVC, causing AVC to rise. Beginning with the eighth unit of output, MC exceeds ATC, causing it also to rise. ATC thus reaches a minimum at seven units of output. Look carefully at the data of Exhibit 18–5 to be sure that you fully understand the relationships among the various cost curves.

Using the numeric data of Exhibit 18–5, **Exhibit 18–6** graphically illustrates both the total and the average (and marginal) cost curves. Note that the MC curve

EXHIBIT 18-6

COSTS IN THE SHORT RUN

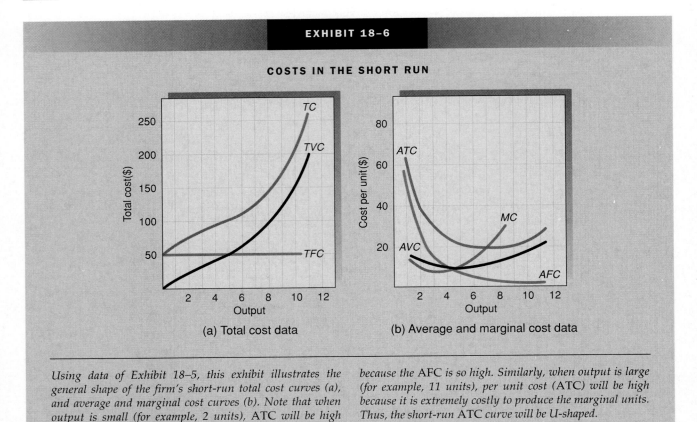

(a) Total cost data

(b) Average and marginal cost data

Using data of Exhibit 18–5, this exhibit illustrates the general shape of the firm's short-run total cost curves (a), and average and marginal cost curves (b). Note that when output is small (for example, 2 units), ATC will be high because the AFC is so high. Similarly, when output is large (for example, 11 units), per unit cost (ATC) will be high because it is extremely costly to produce the marginal units. Thus, the short-run ATC curve will be U-shaped.

intersects both the *AVC* and *ATC* curves at the minimum points (part "b"). As *MC* continues to rise above *ATC*, unit costs rise higher and higher as output increases beyond seven units.

In sum, the firm's short-run cost curves are merely a reflection of the law of diminishing marginal returns. Assuming that the price of the variable resource is constant, *MC* declines so long as the marginal product of the variable input is rising. This results because, in this range, smaller and smaller additions of the variable input are required to produce each extra unit of output. The situation is reversed, however, when diminishing returns are confronted. Once diminishing returns set in, more and more units of the variable factor are required to generate each additional unit of output. *MC* will rise, because the marginal product of the variable resources is declining. Eventually, *MC* exceeds *AVC* and *ATC*, causing these costs also to rise. A U-shaped short-run average total cost curve results.

OUTPUT AND COSTS IN LONG RUN

The short-run analysis relates costs to output *for a specific size of plant.* Firms, though, are not committed forever to their existing plant. In the long run, a firm can alter its plant size and all other factors of production. All resources used by the firm are variable in the long run.

How will the firm's choice of plant size affect production costs? **Exhibit 18–7** illustrates the short-run *ATC* curves for three plant sizes, ranging from small to large. If these three plant sizes were the only possible choices, which one would be best? The answer depends on the rate of output the firm expects to produce. The smallest plant would have the lowest cost if an output rate of less than q_1 were produced. The medium-sized plant would provide the least-cost method of producing output rates between q_1 and q_2. For any output level greater than q_2, the largest plant would be the most cost-efficient.

The long-run *ATC* curve shows the minimum average cost of producing each output level when the firm is free to choose among all possible plant sizes. It can best be thought of as a *planning curve,* because it reflects the expected per unit cost of producing alternative rates of output while plants are still in the blueprint stage.

Exhibit 18–7 illustrates the long-run *ATC* curve when only three plant sizes are possible, and the planning curve *ABCD* is thus mapped out. But, of course, given sufficient time, firms can usually choose among many plants of various sizes. **Exhibit 18–8** presents the long-run planning curve under these circumstances. It is a smooth curve, with each short-run *ATC* curve tangent to it.[6]

It is important to keep in mind that no single plant size could produce the alternative output rates at the costs indicated by the planning curve *LRATC* in Exhibit 18–8. Any of the planning-curve options are available before a plant size is chosen and the plant is built, but while the firm can plan for the long run, choosing among many options, it can *operate* only in the short run. The *LRATC* curve outlines the possibilities available in the planning stage, indicating the expected average total costs of production for each of a large number of plants, which differ in size.

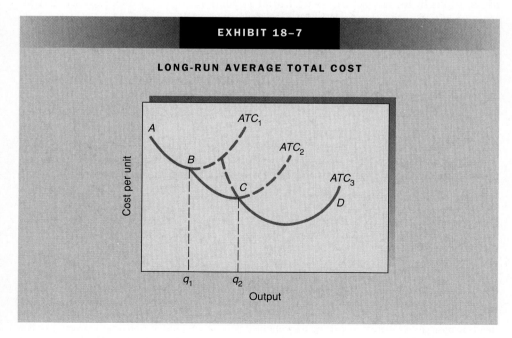

EXHIBIT 18–7

LONG-RUN AVERAGE TOTAL COST

The short-run average total cost curves are shown for three alternative plant sizes. If these three were the only possible plant sizes, the long-run average total cost curve would be ABCD.

---

[6]The tangency, though, will occur at the least-cost output level for the short run only when the long-run curve is parallel to the *x*-axis, as in q_n, Exhibit 18–8.

When many alternative plant sizes are possible, the long-run average total cost curve LRATC is mapped out.

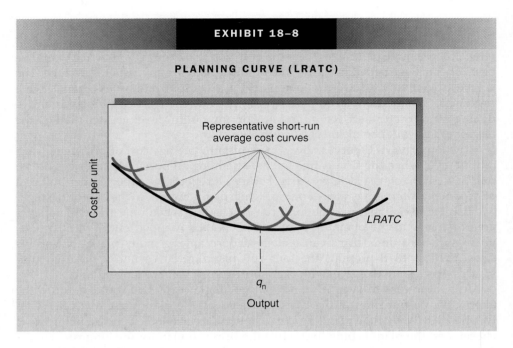

EXHIBIT 18–8

PLANNING CURVE (LRATC)

Representative short-run average cost curves

Cost per unit

LRATC

q_n

Output

SIZE OF FIRM AND UNIT COST IN LONG RUN

Do larger firms have lower minimum unit costs than smaller ones? The answer to this question depends on which industries are being considered. There is a sound basis, though, for expecting some initial reductions in per unit cost from large-scale production methods. Why? Large firms typically produce a large total volume of output.[7] Volume of output denotes the total number of units of a product that the firm expects to produce.[8] There are three major reasons why planning a larger volume generally reduces, at least initially, unit costs: (1) mass production, (2) specialization, and (3) improvements in production as a result of experience, or "learning by doing." Let us consider each of these factors.

Mass-production techniques usually are economical only when large volumes of output are planned, since they tend to involve large development and setup costs. Once the production methods are established, though, marginal costs are low. For example, the use of molds, dies, and assembly-line production methods reduce the per unit cost of automobiles only when the planned volume is in the

---

[7]Throughout this section, we assume that firms with larger plants necessarily plan a larger volume of output than do their smaller counterparts. Reality approximates these conditions. Firms choose large plants because they are planning to produce a large volume.

[8]Note the distinction between rate and volume of output. Rate of output is the number of units produced during a specific period (for example, the next six months). Volume is the total number of units produced during all time periods. For example, Boeing might produce two 767 airplanes per month (rate of output) while planning to produce a volume of two hundred 767s during the expected life of the model. Increasing the rate (reducing the time period during which a given output is produced) tends to raise costs, whereas increasing the volume (total amount produced) tends to lower costs. For additional information on production and costs, see Armen Alchian, "Costs" in *International Encyclopedia of the Social Sciences* (New York: Macmillan, 1968), pp. 404–415; and Jack Hirshleifer, "The Firm's Cost Function: A Successful Reconstruction," *Journal of Business* (July 1962), pp. 235–255.

Ability to adopt mass-production processes and methods often allows large-scale enterprises to achieve lower per unit costs, although such techniques are usually unfeasible for small firms.

millions. High-volume methods, although cheaper to use for high rates of output and high volumes, will typically require high fixed costs, and therefore will cause unit costs to be far higher for low volumes of production.

Large-scale operation also permits specialized use of labor and machines. Adam Smith noted 200 years ago that the output of a pin factory is much greater when one worker draws the wire, another straightens it, a third cuts it, a fourth grinds the point, a fifth makes the head of the pin, and so on.[9] In economics, the whole can sometimes be greater than the sum of the parts. Specialization provides the opportunity for people to become exceptionally proficient at performing small but essential functions. The result is faster production.

---

[9]Smith went on to state, "I have seen a small manufactory of this kind where ten men only were employed, and where some of them consequently performed two or three distinct operations. Those ten persons, therefore, could make among them upwards of forty-eight thousand pins in a day. But if they had all wrought separately and independently, and without any of them having been educated to this peculiar business, they certainly could not each of them have made twenty, perhaps not one pin in a day," (Adam Smith, *An Inquiry into the Nature and Causes of the Wealth of Nations,* 1776 [Cannan's edition, Chicago: University of Chicago Press, 1976], pp. 8–9).

Workers and managers in a firm that has made more units have probably learned more from their experience than their counterparts in smaller firms that have produced less output. Improvements in the production process result. Baseball players improve by playing baseball, and pianists by playing the piano. Similarly, the employees of a firm improve their skills as they "practice" productive techniques. This factor of "learning by doing" has been found to be tremendously important in the aircraft and automobile industries, among others. As managers and workers learn and develop skills producing the first 50 airplanes, for example, they are able to use these resources to produce the next batch of 50 airplanes more economically. Thus, firms that produce a large volume of output are able to achieve lower per unit costs because of their prior production experience.

ECONOMIES AND DISECONOMIES OF SCALE

Economies of scale
Reductions in the firm's per unit costs that are associated with the use of large plants to produce a large volume of output.

Economic theory suggests that, at least initially, larger firms have lower unit costs than comparable smaller firms. When unit costs decline as output expands, **economies of scale** are present over the initial range of outputs. The long-run *ATC* curve is falling.

Are *diseconomies of scale* possible—that is, are there ever situations in which the long-run average total costs are greater for larger firms than they are for smaller ones? The economic justification for diseconomies of scale is less obvious (and less tenable) than that for economies of scale. However, as a firm gets bigger and bigger, bureaucratic inefficiencies *may* result. Code-book procedures tend to replace managerial genius. Motivating the work force and carrying out managerial directives are also more complex when the firm is larger and principal-agent problems grow as there are more employees and more levels of monitoring to be done. Coordinating more people and conveying information to them is more difficult. These factors combine to cause rising long-run average total costs in some, though certainly not all, industries.

Economies and diseconomies of scale stem from different sources than do increasing and diminishing returns, because the former are long-run concepts. They relate to conditions of production when all factors are variable. In contrast, increasing and diminishing returns are short-run concepts, applicable only when the firm has a fixed factor of production.

Exhibit 18–9 outlines three different long-run average total cost (*LRATC*) curves that describe real-world conditions in differing industries. For part "a," both economies and diseconomies of scale are present. Higher per unit costs will result if the firm chooses a plant size other than the one that minimizes the cost of producing output *q*. If each firm in an industry faces the same cost conditions, we can generalize and say that any plants that are larger or smaller than this ideal size will experience higher unit costs. A very narrow range of plant sizes would be possible in industries with the *LRATC* depicted by part "a." Some lines of retail sales and agriculture might approximate these conditions.

Constant returns to scale
Unit costs are constant as the scale of the firm is altered. Neither economies nor diseconomies of scale are present.

Part "b" demonstrates the general shape of the *LRATC* that economists believe is present in most industries. Initially, economies of scale exist, but once a minimum efficient scale is reached, wide variation in firm size is possible. Firms smaller than the minimum efficient size would have higher per unit costs, but firms larger than that would not gain a cost advantage. **Constant returns to scale** are present for broad range of output rates (between q_1 and q_2). This situation is

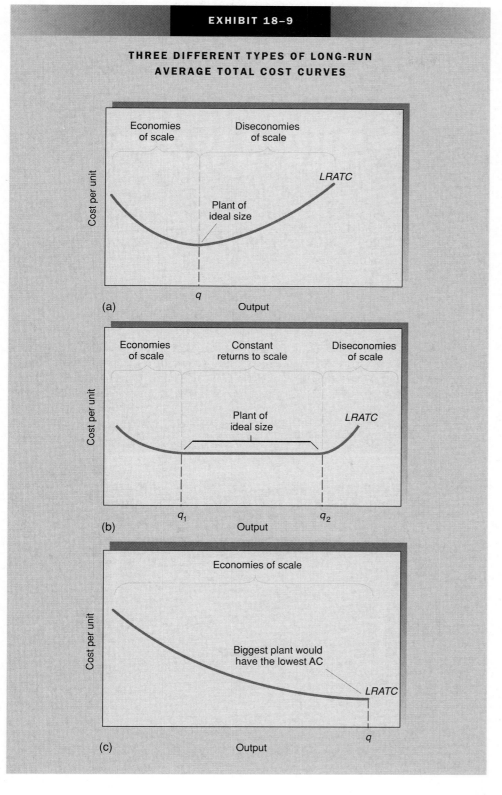

EXHIBIT 18-9

THREE DIFFERENT TYPES OF LONG-RUN AVERAGE TOTAL COST CURVES

(a)

Economies of scale | Diseconomies of scale

Cost per unit

LRATC

Plant of ideal size

q

Output

(b)

Economies of scale | Constant returns to scale | Diseconomies of scale

Cost per unit

Plant of ideal size

LRATC

q_1 | q_2

Output

(c)

Economies of scale

Cost per unit

Biggest plant would have the lowest AC

LRATC

q

Output

For one type of LRATC curve, economies of scale are present for output levels less than q, but immediately beyond q, diseconomies of scale dominate (a). In another instance, economies of scale are important until some minimum output level (q_1) is attained. Once the minimum has been attained, there is a wide range of output levels (q_1 to q_2) that are consistent with the minimum ATC for the industry (b). In a third situation, economies of scale exist for all relevant output levels. As we will see later, this type of LRATC curve has important implications for the structure of the industry.

consistent with real-world conditions in many industries. For example, small firms can be as efficient as larger ones in such industries as apparel, lumber, shoes, publishing, and in many lines of retailing.

In part "c" of Exhibit 18–9, economies of scale exist for all relevant output levels. The larger the firm size, the lower the per unit cost. The *LRATC* in the local telephone service industry may approximate the curve shown here.

WHAT FACTORS CAUSE COST CURVES TO SHIFT?

In outlining the general shapes of a firm's cost curves in both the long run and short run, we assumed that certain other factors—resource prices, taxes, and technology—remained constant as the firm altered its rate of output. Let us now consider how these other factors would affect production costs if they did not remain constant.

PRICES OF RESOURCES

If the price of resources used should rise, the firm's cost curves will shift upward, as **Exhibit 18–10** illustrates. Higher resource prices will increase the cost of producing each alternative output level. For example, what happens to the cost of producing automobiles when the price of steel rises? The cost of producing automobiles also rises. Conversely, lower resource prices will result in cost reductions. Thus, the cost curves for any specific plant size will shift downward.

An increase in resource prices will cause the firm's cost curves to shift upward.

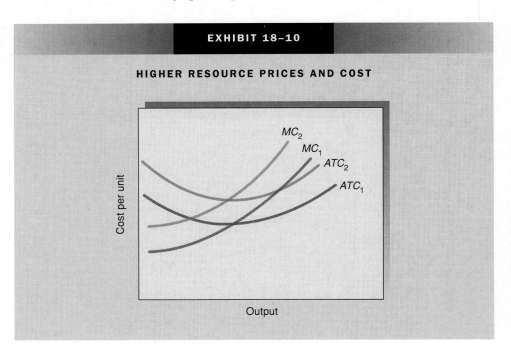

EXHIBIT 18–10

HIGHER RESOURCE PRICES AND COST

MC_2
MC_1
ATC_2
ATC_1

Cost per unit

Output

TAXES

Taxes are a component of a firm's cost. Suppose that an excise tax of 20 cents were levied on each gallon of gasoline sold by a service station. What would happen to the seller's costs? They would increase, just as they did in Exhibit 18–10. The firm's average total and marginal cost curves would shift upward by the amount of the tax. If the tax were an annual business license fee instead, it would raise the average cost, but not the variable cost.

TECHNOLOGY

Technological improvements often make it possible to produce a specific output with fewer resources. For example, the printing press drastically reduced the number of labor-hours required to print newspapers and books. The spinning wheel reduced the labor-hours necessary to weave cotton into cloth. More recently, computers and robots have reduced costs in many industries. As **Exhibit 18–11** shows, a technological improvement will shift the firm's cost curves downward, reflecting the reduction in the amount of resources used to produce alternative levels of output.

ECONOMIC WAY OF THINKING ABOUT COSTS

When analyzing the firm's costs, economists often present a highly mechanical—some would say unrealistic—view. The role of personal choice in uncertain circumstances tends to be glossed over.

It is important to keep in mind that costs are incurred when choices are made. When business decision makers choose to purchase raw materials, hire new employees, or renew the lease on a plant, they incur costs. All these decisions, like other choices, must be made under conditions of uncertainty. Of course, past experience acts as a useful guide, yielding valuable information. Because of this, business decision makers will have a good idea of the costs that will be associated with alternative decisions.

Opportunity costs are usually *expected costs*—they represent the highest valued option that the decision maker expects to give up as the result of a choice. Think for a moment of what the cost curves developed in this chapter really mean. The firm's short-run *MC* curve represents the opportunity cost of expanding output, *given the firm's current plant size*. The firm's long-run *ATC* curve represents the opportunity cost per unit of output associated with varying plant sizes and rates of output, *given that the alternative plants are still on the drawing boards*. Opportunity costs look forward, reflecting expectations—often based on the past record—as to what will be foregone as a result of current decisions. At the time decisions must be made, neither the short-run *MC* nor the long-run *ATC* can be determined from accounting records, since accounting costs look backward. Accounting figures yield valuable information about historical costs, but, as the following discussion will show, they must be interpreted carefully when forecasting future costs.

Suppose that an egg producer discovers (or develops) a "super" mineral water that makes it possible to get more eggs from the same number of chickens. Because of this technological improvement, various output levels of eggs can now be produced with less feed, space, water, and labor. Costs will be reduced. The egg producer's ATC and MC curves will shift downward.

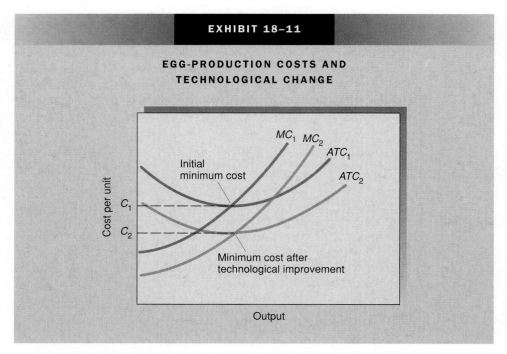

EXHIBIT 18–11

EGG-PRODUCTION COSTS AND TECHNOLOGICAL CHANGE

SUNK COSTS

Sunk costs

Costs that have already been incurred as a result of past decisions. They are sometimes referred to as historical costs.

Historical costs associated with past decisions that cannot be reversed—economists call them **sunk costs**—will provide knowledge relevant to current decisions, but the specific costs themselves are no longer relevant. When past choices cannot be reversed, money that has been spent is gone for good. Current choices must be based on the costs and benefits expected in relation to *current and future* market conditions, if mistakes are to be avoided (see the "Myths of Economics" boxed feature).

If they are to minimize costs, business decision makers must recognize the irrelevance of sunk costs. Let us consider a simple example that emphasizes this point. Suppose that the firm of Exhibit 18–5 pays $100,000 to purchase and install a roller blade–producing machine. The machine is expected to last ten years. The company's books record the cost of the machine as $10,000 each year under the heading of depreciation. The machine can be used only to make roller blades. Since dismantling and reinstallation costs are high, it cannot be leased or sold to another firm. Also, it has no scrap value. In other words, there are no alternative uses for the machine. The machine's annual production of roller blades will generate $50,000 of revenues for the firm when it is employed with raw materials and other factors of production that cost $46,000.

Should the firm continue to use the machine? Its annual depreciation cost suggests that the firm loses $6,000 annually on its output. The depreciation cost, however, is a sunk cost. It was incurred when the machine was installed. The current opportunity cost of the machine is precisely zero. The firm is not giving up anything by continuing to use it. Since operating the machine generates $4,000 of additional net revenue, the firm can gain by continuing the operation of the machine. Of course, if current market conditions are not expected to improve, the firm will not purchase a similar machine or replace the machine when it wears

MYTHS OF ECONOMICS

"A GOOD BUSINESS DECISION MAKER WILL NEVER SELL A PRODUCT FOR LESS THAN ITS PRODUCTION COSTS."

This statement contains a grain of truth. A profit-seeking entrepreneur would not *undertake* a project knowing that the costs could not be covered. However, this view fails to emphasize (1) the time dimension of the production process and (2) the uncertainty associated with business decisions. The production process takes time. Raw materials must be purchased, employees hired, and plants equipped. Retailers must contract with suppliers. As these decisions are made, costs result. Many of the firm's costs of production are incurred long before the product is ready for marketing.

Even a good business decision maker is not always able to predict the future. Market conditions may change in an unexpected manner. At the time the product is ready for sale, buyers may be unwilling to pay a price that will cover the seller's past costs of production. These past costs, however, are now sunk costs and no longer relevant. Current decisions must be made on the basis of current cost and revenue considerations.

Should a grocer refuse to sell oranges that are about to spoil because their wholesale cost cannot be covered? The grocer's current opportunity cost of selling the oranges may be nearly zero. The alternative may be to throw them in the garbage next week. Almost any price, even one far below past costs, would be better than letting the oranges spoil.

Consider another example. Suppose a couple who own a house plan to relocate temporarily. Should they refuse to rent their house for $400 (if this is the best offer available) because their monthly house payment is $600? Of course not. The house payment will go on, regardless of whether they rent the house. If the homeowners can cover their opportunity costs (perhaps wear and tear plus a $60 monthly fee for a property management service), they will gain by renting rather than leaving the house vacant.

Past mistakes provide useful lessons for the future, but they cannot be reversed. Bygones are bygones, even if they resulted in business loss. Only current revenue and cost considerations are relevant to current decisions about prices and profitability. There is no need to fret over spilt milk, burnt toast, or yesterday's business losses.

out, but this should not influence the decision of whether to continue operating the current one. The irrelevance of sunk costs helps explain why it often makes sense to continue operating older equipment (it has a low opportunity cost), even though it may not be wise to purchase similar equipment again.

COST AND SUPPLY

Economists are interested in cost because they seek to explain the supply decisions of firms. A strictly profit-maximizing firm will compare the expected revenues derived from a decision or a course of action with the expected costs. If the expected revenues exceed costs, the course of action will be chosen because it will expand profits (or reduce losses).

In the short run, when making supply decisions, the marginal cost of producing additional units is the relevant cost consideration. A profit-maximizing decision maker will compare the expected marginal costs with the expected additional revenue from larger sales. If the latter exceeds the former, output (the quantity supplied) will be expanded.

Whereas marginal costs are central to the choice of short-run output, the expected average total cost is vital to a firm's long-run supply decision. *Before entry into an industry,* a profit-maximizing decision maker will compare the expected market price with the expected long-run average total cost. Profit-seeking potential entrants will supply the product if, and only if, they expect the market price to exceed their long-run average total cost. Similarly, existing firms will continue to supply a product only if they expect that the market price will enable them at least to cover their long-run average total cost.

LOOKING AHEAD

In this chapter, we outlined several basic principles that affect costs for business firms. We will use these basic principles when we analyze the price and output decisions of firms under alternative market structures in the chapters that follow.

CHAPTER SUMMARY

1. The business firm is used to organize productive resources and transform them into goods and services. There are three major business structures—proprietorships, partnerships, and corporations. Proprietorships are the most numerous, but most of the nation's business activity is conducted through corporations. To solve the principal-agent problem, which tends to reduce worker efficiency in team production, every firm must provide work incentives and monitoring. The business structure chosen can influence the cost of those provisions and ultimately, of course, the cost of the product.

2. The demand for a product indicates the intensity of consumers' desires for the item. The (opportunity) cost of producing the item indicates the desire of consumers for other goods that must be given up because the necessary resources are being used in the production of the item. In a market economy, these two forces—demand and costs of production—balance the desire of consumers for more of a good against the reality of scarce resources, which requires that other goods be foregone in order to supply more of any one specific item.

3. Economists employ the opportunity-cost concept when figuring a firm's costs. Therefore, total cost includes not only explicit payments for resources employed by the firm, but also the implicit costs associated with the use of productive resources owned by the firm.

4. Since accounting procedures generally omit the opportunity cost of the firm's equity capital and sometimes (in the case of owner-operated firms) omit the cost of owner-provided services, accounting costs understate the opportunity cost of producing a good. As a result of these omissions, the accounting profits of a firm are generally larger than the firm's economic profits.

5. Economic profit (loss) results when a firm's sales revenues exceed (are less than) its total costs, both explicit and implicit. Firms that are making the market rate of return on their assets will therefore make zero economic profit. Firms that transform resources into products of greater value than the opportunity cost of the resources used will make an economic profit. On the other hand, if the opportunity cost of the resources used exceeds the value of the product, losses will result.

6. The firm's short-run average total cost (*ATC*) curve will tend to be U-shaped. When output is small (relative to plant size), average fixed cost (*AFC*)—and therefore *ATC*—will be high. As output expands, however, *AFC*—and initially *ATC*—will fall. As the firm attempts to produce a larger and larger rate of output with its fixed plant size, diminishing returns will eventually set in, and marginal cost (*MC*) will rise quite rapidly as the plant's maximum capacity is approached. Thus, the short-run *ATC* will also be high because *MC* is high when the existing size of the plant is over-utilized.

7. The law of diminishing returns explains why a firm's short-run marginal and average total costs will eventually rise. When diminishing marginal returns are present, successively larger amounts of the variable input will be required to increase output by one more unit. Thus, marginal costs will eventually rise as output expands. Eventually, *MC* will exceed *ATC*, causing the latter to rise also.

8. The ability to plan a larger volume of output often leads to cost reductions. These cost reductions associated with the scale of one's operation result from (a) a greater opportunity to employ mass production methods, (b) specialized use of resources, and (c) learning by doing.

9. The long-run *ATC* (*LRATC*) reflects the costs of production for plants of various sizes. When economies of scale are present (that is, when larger plants have lower minimum per unit costs of production), *LRATC* will decline. When constant returns to scale are experienced,

LRATC will be constant. A rising *LRATC* is also possible. Bureaucratic decision making and other diseconomies of scale may in some cases cause *LRATC* to rise.

10. In analyzing the general shapes of a firm's cost curves, we assumed that the following factors were constant: (a) resource prices, (b) technology, and (c) taxes. Changes in any of these factors would cause the cost curves of a firm to shift.

11. In any analysis of business decision making, it is important to keep the opportunity-cost principle in mind. Economists are interested in costs primarily because costs affect the decisions of suppliers. Short-run *MC* represents the supplier's opportunity cost of producing additional units with the existing plant facilities of the firm. The *LRATC* represents the opportunity cost of supplying alternative rates of output, given sufficient time to vary all factors, including plant size.

12. Sunk costs are costs that have already been incurred and cannot be recovered. They should not exert a direct influence on current business choices. However, they may provide information that will be useful in making current decisions.

CRITICAL-ANALYSIS QUESTIONS

*1. What is economic profit? How might it differ from accounting profit? Explain why firms that are making zero economic profit are likely to continue in business.

*2. Which of the following statements do you think reflect sound economic thinking? Explain your answer.
   a. "I paid $200 for this economics course. Therefore, I'm going to attend the lectures even if they are useless and boring."
   b. "Since we own rather than rent, and the house is paid for, housing doesn't cost us anything."
   c. "I own 100 shares of stock that I can't afford to sell until the price goes up enough for me to get back at least my original investment."
   d. "It costs to produce private education, whereas public schooling is free."

3. Suppose a firm produces bicycles. Will the firm's accounting statement reflect the opportunity cost of producing bicycles? Why or why not? What costs would an accounting statement reveal? Should current decisions be based on accounting costs? Explain.

4. What is the principal-agent problem? When will the principal-agent problem be most severe? Why might there be a principal-agent problem between the stockholder-owners and the managers of a large corporation?

5. Suppose that Ajax, Inc., is the target of a takeover attempt by the management of Beta Corporation, which is

offering to buy stock from any Ajax stockholder who wants to sell at 20 percent above its current rate. Explain how the resistance of Ajax management to the takeover attempt might illustrate the principal-agent problem. Is it possible that the Beta Corporation management's action is itself an illustration of the principal-agent problem? Explain.

6. (a) Why might the managers of large corporations have some leeway to follow policies that provide them with utility, even if the policies conflict with the interests (maximum profit) of the stockholder-owners? (b) What conditions will tend to limit the ability of managers of business enterprises to pursue "opportunistic behavior" in a market economy?

7. What are some of the advantages of the corporate business structure of ownership for large business firms? What are some of the disadvantages? Is the corporate form of business ownership cost-efficient? In a market economy, how would you tell whether or not the corporate structural form was efficient?

8. Explain the factors that cause a firm's short-run average total costs to decline initially, but eventually to increase as the rate of output rises.

9. Which of the following are relevant to a firm's decision to increase output: (a) short-run average total cost, (b) short-run marginal cost, (c) long-run average total cost? Justify your answer.

10. Economics students often confuse (a) diminishing returns to the variable factor and (b) diseconomies of scale. Explain the difference between the two, and give one example of each.

11. *What's wrong with this way of thinking?* "The American steel industry cannot compete with Korean and Japanese steel producers. These countries built modern, efficient mills that made use of the latest technology. In contrast, American mills are older and less efficient. Our costs are higher because we are stuck with old facilities."

*12. Is profit maximization consistent with the self-interest of corporate owners? Is it consistent with the self-interest of corporate managers? Is there a conflict between the self-interest of owners and of managers?

*13. What is the opportunity cost of (a) borrowed funds and (b) equity capital? Under current tax law, firms can take the opportunity cost of borrowed funds, but not equity capital, as an expense. How does this tax feature affect the debt/equity ratio of business firms?

*14. "If a firm maximizes profit, it must minimize the cost of producing the profit-maximum output." Is this statement true or false? Explain your answer.

15. Why do economists consider normal returns to capital as a cost? How does economic profit differ from normal returns (or "normal profit")?

---

*Asterisk denotes questions for which answers are given in Appendix C.

*16. Draw a U-shaped short-run *ATC* curve for a firm. Construct the accompanying *MC* and *AVC* curves.

17. (a) Prior to legislation passed in 1986, appreciation in the market value of a stock was taxed at a lower rate than dividends from the stocks. How would this affect the incentive of firms to use internal financing relative to debt? (b) Subsequent to the 1986 legislation, capital gains (appreciation in the stock) and dividends were taxed at identical rates. The 1986 legislation was followed by a rash of takeover moves against firms with low debt/equity ratios. Did the 1986 tax change contribute to these moves? Why or why not?

18. What is shirking? If the managers of a firm are attempting to maximize the profits of the firm, will they have an incentive to limit shirking? How might they go about doing so?

19. What are implicit costs? Do implicit costs contribute to the opportunity cost of production? Should an implicit cost be counted as cost? Give three examples of implicit costs. Does the firm's accounting statement take implicit costs into account? Why or why not?

*20. Consider a machine purchased one year ago for $12,000. The machine is being depreciated $4,000 per year over a three-year period. Its current market value is $5,000, and the expected market value of the machine one year from now is $3,000. If the interest rate is 10 percent, what is the expected cost of holding the machine during the next year?

*21. Investors seeking to take over a firm often bid a positive price for the business even though it is currently experiencing losses. Why would anyone ever bid a positive price for a firm operating at a loss?

22. "A wise business decision maker is on the lookout for diminishing marginal returns and will not operate where diminishing returns have set in." Evaluate this statement.

23. Fill in the blanks in the following table:

Units of Variable Input	Total Product	Marginal Product	Average Product	Price of Input	Total Variable Cost	Average Variable Cost	Total Fixed Cost	Total Cost	Average Total Cost	Marginal Cost
0	0		——	$1	——	——	$2	——	——	
		——								——
1	6		——	$1	——	——	$2	——	——	
		——								——
2	15		——	$1	——	——	$2	——	——	
		——								——
3	27		——	$1	——	——	$2	——	——	
		——								——
4	37		——	$1	——	——	$2	——	——	
		——								——
5	45		——	$1	——	——	$2	——	——	
		——								——
6	50		——	$1	——	——	$2	——	——	
		——								——
7	52		——	$1	——	——	$2	——	——	
		——								——
8	50		——	$1	——	——	$2	——	——	

a. What happens to total product when marginal product is negative?

b. What happens to average product when marginal product is greater than average product?

c. What happens to average product when marginal product is less than average product?

d. At what point does marginal product begin to decrease?

e. At what point does marginal cost begin to increase?

f. Summarize the relationship between marginal product and marginal cost.

g. What happens to marginal costs when total product begins to fall?

h. What is happening to average variable costs when they equal marginal costs?

i. Marginal costs equal average variable costs between what output levels?

j. What is happening to average total costs when they equal marginal costs?

k. Marginal costs equal average total costs between what output levels?

CHAPTER NINETEEN

THE FIRM UNDER PURE COMPETITION

Competition is a rivalry between individuals (or groups or nations), and it arises whenever two or more parties strive for something that all cannot obtain.

GEORGE J. STIGLER[1]

Competition . . . leads some producers to eliminate wastes and cut costs so that they may undersell others. It compels others to adopt similar measures in order that they may survive. It weeds out those whose costs remain high and thus operates to concentrate production in the hands of those whose costs are low.

CLAIR WILCOX[2]

CHAPTER FOCUS

- *What does competition mean in economics?*
- *What is the purely competitive model, and why is it important?*
- *What determines the output and price of a competitive firm?*
- *What is the role of time in determining the elasticity of supply?*
- *How do consumers fare under pure competition?*
- *How is the competitive model related to economic efficiency?*

---

[1]George Stigler, "Competition," in *The New Palgrave: A Dictionary of Economics* edited by John Eatwell, Murray Milgate, Peter Newman (New York: Stockton Press, 1987), p. 531.

[2]Clair Wilcox, *Competition and Monopoly in American Industry*, monograph no. 21, Temporary National Economic Committee, Investigation of Concentration of Economic Power, 76th Congress, 3rd session (Washington, D.C.: U.S. Government Printing Office, 1940).

I n the last chapter, we outlined some basic principles that determine the general relationship between output and costs of production for any firm. Of course, a firm's output decisions will be influenced by its costs and its revenues. In this and the next two chapters, we will illustrate how the structure of an industry affects the revenues and output levels of firms. We will analyze four models of industrial structure: pure competition, monopoly, monopolistic competition, and oligopoly. These models will help us understand the role of competitive forces under various market conditions. This chapter focuses on pure competition.

THE PROCESS OF COMPETITION

Competition as a dynamic process

A term that denotes rivalry or competitiveness between or among parties (for example, producers or input suppliers), each of which seeks to deliver a better deal to buyers when quality, price, and product information are all considered. Competition implies a lack of collusion among sellers.

Before we introduce the model of pure competition, a few comments about the use of the term *competition* are in order. It is important not to lose sight of the function of **competition as a dynamic process** to explain the mechanics of alternative forms of industrial structure. As the quotation from Professor Stigler reminds us, scarcity guarantees competition. Firms compete for the scarce dollars spent by consumers. In a market open to all entrants, the competitive process emphasizes rivalry among firms—the effort on the part of a seller to gain consumer sales by outperforming alternative suppliers. Competing firms may use a variety of methods—quality of product, style, convenience of location, advertising, and price—to attract consumers.

Markets serve consumers well when they are open to rival sellers so that each is under intense competition to cater to consumer preferences, and to sell at low prices as well. For producers, open markets have both rewards and risks. Profits are possible for entrepreneurs who are good at finding and implementing new ways to better satisfy consumer wants. But producers who offer low quality at a high price find that their customers turn to rival sellers.

As the quotation from Professor Wilcox indicates, competition also places pressure on producers to operate efficiently and to avoid waste. Competition weeds out the inefficient—those who are incapable of providing consumers with quality goods at low prices. Competition also keeps producers on their toes in other areas. The production techniques and product offerings that lead to success today will not necessarily pass the competitive market test tomorrow. Producers who survive in a competitive environment cannot be complacent. They must be forward-looking and innovative. They must be willing to experiment and quick to adopt improved methods.

Each competitor is, of course, in business to make a profit. Rival firms struggle for the dollar votes of consumers. Competition, though, is the taskmaster that forces producers to serve the interests of consumers and to do so at the lowest possible level of profit. As Adam Smith noted more than 200 years ago, competition harnesses the profit motive and puts it to work elevating our standard of living and directing our resources toward the production of those goods that we desire most intensely relative to their cost. Smith explained how aggregate output would be vastly expanded if individuals specialized in those things they did best and cooperated with others desirous of their services. He believed that self-interest directed by competitive markets would generate precisely these two ingredients—specialization and cooperation. In Book 1 of *The Wealth of Nations*, he put it this way:

> *It is not from the benevolence of the butcher, the brewer, or the baker, that we expect our dinner, but from their regard to their own self-interest. We address ourselves, not to their humanity but to their self-love, and never talk to them of our own necessities, but of their advantages.*[3]

In Smith's time, as today, many thinkers erred because they did not understand that productive action and voluntary exchange offer the potential for mutual gain. That is, both parties to an economic exchange generally gain, rather than one gaining at the other's expense (see "Myths of Economics" on p. 49). Bridled by competition, self-interest leads to economic cooperation and provides a powerful fuel for the benefit of humankind. Paradoxical as it seems, even though benevolence may be the more admirable attitude, it cannot generate the cooperative effort that is a natural outgrowth of self-interest directed by competition. Unilateral giving does not produce the information and feedback to buyers and sellers inherent in the competitive market process. Thus, the competitive process occupies center stage in economic analysis, as one of the forces directing the economic behavior of human beings in ways favorable to most.

Competition is the disciplining force of a market economy. The presence of alternative sellers more or less forces business firms to cater to the wishes of consumers.

---

[3]Adam Smith, *An Inquiry into the Nature and Causes of the Wealth of Nations*, 1776 (Cannan's edition, Chicago: University of Chicago Press, 1976), p. 18.

Before we move on to more technical material, two additional points should be addressed. First, a dual usage of the term *competition* has evolved through the years. The term is used to describe a rivalry or competitiveness among sellers, as we have already noted, but, in addition, it is used—especially when combined with the adjective *pure*—to describe a hypothetical model of industrial structure characterized by independent firms and a large number of sellers. This dual usage can sometimes be confusing. It is important to recognize that firms can be competitive in the sense of rivalry even though they may not be competitive in the industrial-structure sense. To avoid confusion, we will use the complete expression, *pure competition,* when we discuss the competitive model of industrial structure.

Second, we have emphasized the role of competition as the taskmaster forcing sellers to obey the desires of consumers. Nobody likes a taskmaster, and sellers often try to escape the discipline imposed by competitive forces. The models of industrial structure that we examine are useful because they provide a framework for analyzing both the likelihood of a business firm escaping the directives of competition and the economic implications of its doing so.

PURELY COMPETITIVE MODEL: ITS ASSUMPTIONS AND ITS IMPORTANCE

Pure competition
A model of industrial structure characterized by a large number of small firms producing a homogeneous product in an industry (market area) that permits complete freedom of entry and exit.

Homogeneous product
A product of one firm that is identical to the product of every other firm in the industry. Consumers see no difference in units of the product offered by alternative sellers.

Barriers to entry
Obstacles that limit the freedom of potential rivals to enter an industry.

Pure competition presupposes that the following conditions exist in a market.

1. *All firms in the market are producing a homogeneous product.* The product of Firm A is identical to the product offered by Firm B and the products of all other firms in this market. This presupposition of **homogeneous products** rules out advertising, location preferences, quality differences, and other forms of nonprice competition.

2. *A large number of independent firms produce the product.* The independence of the firms rules out joint actions designed to restrict output and raise prices.

3. *Each buyer and seller is small relative to the total market.* Therefore, no single buyer or seller is able to exert any noticeable influence on the market supply and demand conditions. For example, a wheat farmer selling 5,000 bushels annually would not have a noticeable impact on the U.S. wheat market, in which 2,500,000,000 bushels are traded annually.

4. *There are no artificial barriers to entry into or exit from the market.* Under pure competition, any entrepreneur is free either to produce or fail to produce in the industry. There are no **barriers to entry** limiting this freedom to compete. New entrants need not obtain permission from the government or the existing firms. Nor does control of an essential resource limit market entry.

The purely competitive model, like other theories, is abstract. Keep in mind that the test of a theory is not the realism of its assumptions but its ability to make *predictions* that are consistent with the real world (see Chapter 1). Assumptions are made and ideas are simplified in models for the purpose of helping us better organize our thoughts. Based on these simplifications and assumptions, models can often help us develop the economic way of thinking.

Previously, we discussed how supply and demand jointly determine market price. The model of pure competition is another way of looking at the operation of market forces. It helps us understand the relationship between the decision making of individual firms and market supply. If we familiarize ourselves with the way in which economic incentives influence the supply decisions of firms within the competitive model, we will be better able to understand the behavior of firms in markets, including some that are less than purely competitive.

There are other reasons for the model's importance. Its conditions are approximated in a few important industries, most notably in many parts of agriculture. The model will help us understand these industries. In addition, as we will show later, the equilibrium conditions in the purely competitive model yield results that are identical with the conditions necessary for ideal static efficiency. Many economists thus use it as a standard by which to judge other industrial structures.

THE WORKINGS OF THE PURELY COMPETITIVE MODEL

Since a purely competitive firm by itself produces an output that is small relative to the total market, it cannot influence the market price. Each firm must accept the market price if it is to sell any of its product. Thus, the firms in a purely competitive market are **price takers.**

Exhibit 19–1 illustrates the relationship between market forces (part "b") and the demand curve facing a purely competitive firm (part "a"). If a pure competitor

Price takers
Sellers who must take the market price in order to sell their product. Because each price taker's output is small relative to the total market, price takers can sell all of their output at the market price, but are unable to sell any of their output at a price higher than the market price. Thus, they face a horizontal demand curve.

The market forces of supply and demand determine price (b). Under pure competition, individual firms have no control over price. Thus, the demand for the product of the firm is perfectly elastic (a).

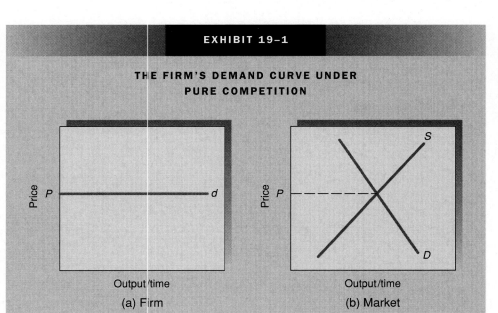

EXHIBIT 19–1

THE FIRM'S DEMAND CURVE UNDER PURE COMPETITION

(a) Firm

(b) Market

sets a price above the market level, consumers will simply buy from other sellers. Why pay the higher price when the identical good is available elsewhere at a lower price? For example, if the price of wheat were $3 per bushel, a farmer would be unable to find buyers for wheat at $3.50 per bushel. A firm could lower its price, but since it is small relative to the total market, it can already sell as much as it wants at the market price. A price reduction would merely reduce revenues. A purely competitive firm thus confronts a perfectly elastic demand curve for its product.

DECIDING HOW MUCH TO PRODUCE— THE SHORT RUN

The firm's output decision is based on comparison of benefits with costs. If a firm produces at all, it will continue expanding output as long as the benefits (additional revenues) from the production of the additional units exceed their marginal costs.

How will changes in output influence the firm's costs? In the last chapter, we discovered that the firm's short-run marginal costs will *eventually* increase as the firm expands its output by working its fixed plant facilities more intensely. The law of diminishing marginal returns assures us that this will be the case. *Eventually,* both the firm's short-run marginal and average total cost curves will turn upward.

Marginal revenue

The incremental change in total revenue derived from the sale of one additional unit of a product.

What about the benefits or additional revenues from output expansion? **Marginal revenue** (*MR*) is the change in the firm's total revenue per unit of output. It is the additional revenue derived from the sale of an additional unit of output. Mathematically,

$$MR = \frac{\text{Change in total revenue}}{\text{Change in output}}$$

Since the purely competitive firm sells all units at the same price, its *MR* will be equal to the market price (*P*).

In the short run, the purely competitive firm will expand output until *MR* (its price) is just equal to marginal cost (*MC*). This decision-making rule will maximize the firm's profits (or minimize its losses).

Exhibit 19–2 helps explain why. Since the firm can sell as many units as it would like at the market price, the sale of one additional unit will increase revenue by the price of the product. As long as *P* exceeds *MC*, revenue will increase more than cost as output is expanded. Since profit is merely the difference between total revenue and total cost, production of units that add more to revenue than to cost will increase profit. This happy state of affairs comes to an end when *MC* has risen enough to make *MC* = *MR* = *P*. For the pure competitor, then, profit will be at a maximum when *P* = *MR* = *MC*. In Exhibit 19–2, this occurs at output level *q*.

Why would the firm not expand output beyond *q*? The cost of producing such units is given by the height of the *MC* curve. The sale of these units would increase revenues only by *P*, the price of the product. Production of units beyond *q* would add more to cost than to revenue. Therefore, production beyond *q*, the *P* = *MC* output level, would reduce the firm's profits.

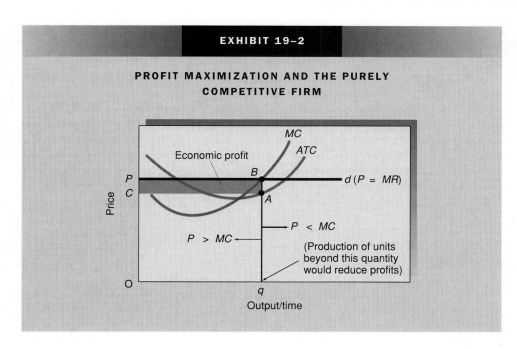

EXHIBIT 19-2

PROFIT MAXIMIZATION AND THE PURELY COMPETITIVE FIRM

The purely competitive firm would maximize profits by producing the output level q, where P = MC.

A profit-maximizing firm with the cost curves indicated by Exhibit 19–2 would produce exactly q. The total revenue of the firm would be the sales price, P, multiplied by output sold, q. Geometrically, the firm's total revenues would be $POqB$. The firm's total cost would be found by multiplying the average total cost by the output level. Geometrically, total costs are represented by $COqA$. The firm's total revenues exceed total costs, and the firm is making short-run economic profit (the shaded area).

In the real world, of course, decisions are not made by entrepreneurs who sit around drawing curves labeled MC and P. Many have not even heard of these concepts. Our model also ignores the problem of uncertainty. Very often, businesspeople must make decisions without complete knowledge of what costs or product price will be. In addition, there may be problems of "lumpiness." The manager may prefer to use 1.7 machines and 2.5 people to carry out a production process. Managers, however, know that machines and people alike come in discrete "lumps," or whole units. They may not be able to approximate what they want even by renting, or changing the machine size they use, or hiring part-time employees.

Despite the inconvenience and uncertain facts of real life, our simple model does make fairly accurate predictions. A business decision maker who has never heard of the $P = MC$ rule for profit maximization probably has another rule that yields approximately the same outcome. For example, the rule might be: Produce those units, and only those units, that add more to revenue than to cost. This ensures maximum profit (or minimum loss). It also takes the firm to the point at which $P = MC$. Why? To stop short of that point would mean not producing some profitable units—units that would add more to revenue than to cost. Similarly, the decision maker would not go beyond that point because production of such units would add more to costs than to revenues. This commonsense rule thus leads to the same outcome as the purely competitive model, even when the decision maker knows none of the technical jargon of economics. No wonder economics is sometimes thought of as "organized common sense."

Just how accurate is the purely competitive model in predicting behavior in real markets? Do other models, which assume that sellers collude to eliminate competition, make better predictions? Direct scientific evidence bearing on such questions is highly desirable. As the "Applications in Economics" boxed feature on the purely competitive model indicates, such evidence has been produced repeatedly in recent decades by the relatively new subdiscipline of experimental economics. The evidence supports the purely competitive model surprisingly well under a variety of circumstances.

PROFIT MAXIMIZING— A NUMERIC EXAMPLE

Exhibit 19–3 uses numeric data to illustrate profit-maximizing decision making for a competitive firm. The firm's short-run total and marginal cost schedules have the general characteristics we discussed in the previous chapter. Since the firm confronts a market price of $5 per unit, its marginal revenue is $5. Total revenue thus *increases* by $5 per additional unit that is produced and sold. The firm maximizes its profit when it supplies an output of 15 units.

There are two ways of viewing this profit-maximizing output rate. First, we could examine the difference between total revenue and total cost, identifying the output rate at which this difference is greatest. Column 6, the profit data, provides this information. For small output rates (less than 11), the firm would actually experience losses. But, at 15 units of output, an $11 profit is earned ($75 total revenue minus $64 total cost). Inspection of the profit column indicates that it is impossible to earn a profit larger than $11 at any other rate of output.

Part "a" of **Exhibit 19–4** (on page 539) presents the total revenue (*TR*) and total cost (*TC*) approach in graph form. (However, the curves are drawn smoothly, as though output could be increased in any amounts, including tiny amounts, not just in whole-unit increments as shown in Exhibit 19–3.) Profits will be maximized when the total revenue line exceeds the total cost curve by the largest vertical amount. That takes place, of course, at 15 units of output.

The marginal approach also can be used to determine the profit-maximizing rate of output for the competitive firm. Remember, as long as price (marginal revenue) exceeds marginal costs, production and sale of additional units will add to the firm's profit (or reduce its losses). Inspection of columns 4 and 5 of Exhibit 19–3 indicates that *MR* is greater than *MC* for the first 15 units of output. Production of these units will expand the firm's profit. In contrast, the production of each unit beyond 15 adds more to cost than to revenue. Profit will therefore decline if output is expanded beyond 15 units. Given the firm's cost and revenue schedule, the profit-maximizing manager will choose to produce 15, and only 15, units per day.

Part "b" of Exhibit 19–4 graphically illustrates the marginal approach. Note here that the output rate (15 units) at which the *MC* and *MR* curves intersect coincides with the output rate in part "a" at which the *TR* curve exceeds the *TC* curve by the largest amount.

APPLICATIONS IN ECONOMICS

EXPERIMENTAL ECONOMICS—TESTING THE PURELY COMPETITIVE MODEL

Do individual decision makers, without any economics training, behave as if they understand marginal costs? Do they act according to the purely competitive model, even though not all of the assumptions of that model are satisfied? Or when there are only a few sellers, do they collude successfully so as to raise price above marginal cost?

Answering such questions is important, but verifying economic principles and comparing alternative economic models by scientific testing is not an easy task. Simply observing people to see whether they behave as economic principles suggest is not completely satisfactory. Since a normal economic event that we can observe is the result of more than one cause, the economist trying to isolate the impact of one causal factor must try to be sure that other factors influencing the outcome do not vary, or else try to take them into account in the analysis. To isolate the impact of a change in the price of a product on consumer behavior, for example, the economist must somehow account for the impact of all other price changes, income changes, and so on, that may have occurred. In other disciplines, scientists use experiments in the laboratory, with all factors controlled, to tackle this problem. They test the principles on which their science is built, using carefully detailed methods, so that other scientists can replicate the experiment.

Beginning about the middle of the twentieth century, economists also began to conduct laboratory experiments. A good many experiments have been conducted to investigate the predictive power of the purely competitive model.

In one of the earliest, conducted in 1956 by leading experimental economist Vernon Smith of the University of Arizona, individual subjects were brought into a laboratory setting and arbitrarily assigned roles as buyers and sellers, in a game-like setting.

Each buyer was given a different "limit price" (that is, a maximum price he or she was allowed to pay) for a paper asset. If the buyer could purchase the paper commodity for less than the limit price, he or she received a cash payment equal to the difference between the limit price and the amount actually paid. Therefore, as in other markets, each buyer gained financially by purchasing at lower prices. The sellers were treated in a parallel fashion. Each had a "limit price" (a minimum selling price) and received in cash any extra revenue above that price.

Buyers and sellers were free to make verbal offers to buy or sell. How did markets develop? Did the outcomes resemble a competitive market, or did sellers collude, controlling the market price for their own benefit, so that a monopoly model would better describe the outcome?

The purely competitive model predicts that trades among buyers and sellers will occur at a market price that will allow every efficient trade to take place. The market price equates the quantity demanded with the quantity willingly supplied. Prior to the work in experimental economics, many economists thought this model was relevant only under highly restrictive conditions. The experimental work indicates that this is not the case. The wide applicability of the purely competitive model surprised many observers. As Vernon Smith points out, "Since 1956, several hundred experiments using different supply and demand conditions, experienced as well as inexperienced subjects, buyers and sellers with multiple unit trading capacity, a great variation in the numbers of buyers and sellers, and different trading institutions have established the replicability and robustness of these results [competitive outcomes]."[1]

The experimental approach allows researchers to test theories under a wide range of conditions. By changing the number of sellers, the type of trading rules, and so on, researchers can find out whether predicted outcomes hold only in special cases or under a wide variety of circumstances. Without the control that is possible in the laboratory, questions about the relevance of a theory might lead only to heated debate, with little light shed on the topic.

Experimental economics, like laboratory work in other sciences, cannot answer all questions about what might happen in nonlaboratory settings. But it has already provided a great deal of precision and certainty to a world of economics needing just those things. The results have also provided reason for optimism about markets. As experimental practitioners Vernon Smith and Arlington Williams have noted,

APPLICATIONS IN ECONOMICS *(continued)*

"Experimental market research has provided an empirical foundation for tenets of economic theory that were already well established, and it has also yielded insight into the details of how particular rules affect the outcome of the trading process. Thirty years of experiments have also brought good news: under most circumstances, markets are extremely efficient in facilitating the movement of goods from the lowest-cost producers to the consumers who place the highest value on them. Organized exchange thus effectively advances human welfare."[2]

[1]Vernon L. Smith, "Experimental Methods in Economics" in *The New Palgrave: A Dictionary of Economics*, edited by John Eatwell et al. (London: Macmillan Press Ltd., 1987), pp. 241–249.

[2]Vernon L. Smith and Arlington W. Williams, "Experimental Market Economics," *Scientific American* (December 1992), pp. 116–121. For additional background, see Charles R. Plott, "Will Economics Become an Experimental Science," *Southern Economic Journal* (April 1991).

LOSSES AND GOING OUT OF BUSINESS

Suppose changes take place in the market that depress the price below a firm's average total cost. How will a profit-maximizing (or loss-minimizing) firm respond to this situation? The answer to this question depends on both the firm's current sales revenues relative to its *variable cost* and its expectations about the future. The firm has three options: it can continue to operate in the short run, shut down temporarily, or go out of business.

If the firm anticipates that the lower market price is temporary, it may want to continue operating in the short run as long as it is able to cover its variable cost.[4] **Exhibit 19–5** illustrates why. The firm shown in this exhibit would minimize its loss at output level q, where $P = MC$. At q, total revenues ($OqBP_1$) are, however, less than total costs ($OqAC$). The firm confronts short-run economic losses. Even if it shuts down completely, it will still incur fixed costs, *unless it goes out of business*. If the firm anticipates that the market price will increase enough that it will be able to cover its average total costs (ATC) in the future, it may not want to sell out. It may choose to produce q units in the short run, even though losses are incurred. At price P_1, production of output q is clearly more advantageous than shutting down, because the firm is able to cover its average variable costs (AVC) and pay some of its fixed costs. If it were to shut down, *but not sell out*, the firm would lose the entire amount of its fixed cost.

---

[4]In thinking about this issue, we must keep in mind the *opportunity-cost concept*. The firm's fixed costs are opportunity costs that do not vary with the level of output. They can be avoided if, and only if, the firm goes out of business. Following this course releases the fixed-cost resources to their best alternative use, and thus eliminates the fixed costs. Fixed costs are *not* (as some economics texts have stated) the depreciated value of the firm's fixed assets. Such accounting measures may have little to do with the firm's opportunity cost of those fixed assets. To specify fixed costs, we need to know (1) how much the firm's fixed assets would bring if they were sold or rented to others and (2) any other costs, such as operating license fees and debts, which could be avoided if the firm declared bankruptcy and/or went out of business. These costs can be avoided if the firm goes out of business. A profit-maximizing firm will not operate, even in the short run, if it cannot cover its fixed costs (unless it expects conditions to improve in the future). See Marshall Colberg and James King, "Theory of Production Abandonment," *Revista Internazionale di Scienze Economiche e Commerciali* 20 (1973), pp. 961–1072.

EXHIBIT 19–3

PROFIT MAXIMIZATION OF A COMPETITIVE FIRM—A NUMERIC ILLUSTRATION

(1) OUTPUT (PER DAY)	(2) TOTAL REVENUE (TR)	(3) TOTAL COST (TC)	(4) MARGINAL REVENUE (MR)	(5) MARGINAL COST (MC)	(6) PROFIT (TR – TC)
0	$ 0.00	$ 25.00	$0.00	$ 0.00	$ –25.00
1	5.00	29.80	5.00	4.80	–24.80
2	10.00	33.75	5.00	3.95	–23.75
3	15.00	37.25	5.00	3.50	–22.25
4	20.00	40.25	5.00	3.00	–20.25
5	25.00	42.75	5.00	2.50	–17.75
6	30.00	44.75	5.00	2.00	–14.75
7	35.00	46.50	5.00	1.75	–11.50
8	40.00	48.00	5.00	1.50	– 8.00
9	45.00	49.25	5.00	1.25	– 4.25
10	50.00	50.25	5.00	1.00	– 0.25
11	55.00	51.50	5.00	1.25	3.50
12	60.00	53.25	5.00	1.75	6.75
13	65.00	55.75	5.00	2.50	9.25
14	70.00	59.25	5.00	3.50	10.75
15	75.00	64.00	5.00	4.75	11.00
16	80.00	70.00	5.00	6.00	10.00
17	85.00	77.25	5.00	7.25	7.75
18	90.00	85.50	5.00	8.25	4.50
19	95.00	95.00	5.00	9.50	0.00
20	100.00	108.00	5.00	13.00	– 8.00
21	105.00	125.00	5.00	17.00	–20.00

What if the market price declines below the firm's AVC (for example, P_2)? Under these circumstances, a temporary **shutdown** is preferable to short-run operation. If the firm continues to operate in the short run, operating losses merely add to losses resulting from the firm's fixed costs. Therefore, even if the firm expects the market price to increase, enabling it to survive and prosper in the future, it will shut down in the short run when the market price falls below its AVC. In the real world, we do observe the temporary shutdown of businesses.

The excess inventories of industrial plants are often sold while the plant is idle, during a period of unexpectedly low demand. Temporary shutdown is actually planned on a regular basis in some markets. For example, restaurants and motels in some areas shut down in slow seasons, operating only when tourists, vacationers, or other seasonal visitors provide enough demand. The purely competitive model predicts that these firms will operate only when they expect to cover their variable costs.

Shutdown

A temporary halt in the operation of a business in which the firm anticipates a return to operation in the future and therefore does not sell its assets. The firm's variable cost is eliminated for the duration of the shutdown, but its fixed costs continue.

Going out of business
The sale of a firm's assets and its permanent exit from the market. By going out of business, a firm is able to avoid fixed costs, which would continue during a shutdown.

The firm's third option when faced with losses, is **going out of business** immediately. After all, even the losses resulting from the firm's fixed costs can be avoided if the firm sells out. (Remember that if they are costs of doing business, they must be avoidable by not doing business.) If market conditions are not expected to change for the better, then going out of business is the preferred option.

THE PURELY COMPETITIVE FIRM'S SHORT-RUN SUPPLY CURVE

The competitive firm that intends to stay in business will maximize profits (or minimize losses) when it produces the output level at which $P = MC$ and variable costs are covered. Therefore, the portion of the firm's short-run MC curve that lies above its AVC is the *short-run supply curve* of the firm.

Exhibit 19–6 illustrates that as the market price increases, the purely competitive firm will expand output along its MC curve. If the market price were less than P_1, the firm would shut down immediately because it would be unable to cover even its variable costs. If the market price is P_1, however, a price equal to the firm's AVC, the firm may supply output q_1—though only in the short run. Economic losses will result, but the firm would incur similar losses if it shut down completely. As the market price increases to P_2, the firm will happily expand output along its MC curve to q_2. At P_2, price is also equal to ATC. The firm is making a

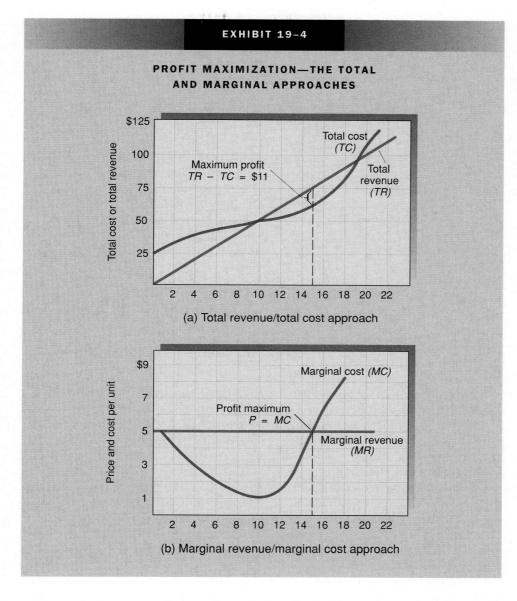

EXHIBIT 19-4

PROFIT MAXIMIZATION—THE TOTAL AND MARGINAL APPROACHES

(a) Total revenue/total cost approach

Maximum profit
$TR - TC = \$11$

Total cost (TC)

Total revenue (TR)

(b) Marginal revenue/marginal cost approach

Marginal cost (MC)

Profit maximum
$P = MC$

Marginal revenue (MR)

Using the data of Exhibit 19–3, here we provide two ways of viewing profit maximization. In the first, the profits of the purely competitive firm are maximized at the output level at which total revenue exceeds total cost by the maximum amount (a). In the second, the maximum-profit output is identified by comparing marginal revenue and marginal cost (b).

"normal rate of return," or zero economic profits. Higher prices will result in a still larger short-run output. The firm will supply q_3 units at market price P_3. At this price, economic profits will result. At still higher prices, output will be expanded even more. As long as price exceeds AVC, the firm will expand supply along its MC curve, which therefore becomes the firm's short-run supply curve.

THE MARKET'S SHORT-RUN SUPPLY CURVE

The *short-run market supply curve* corresponds to the total amount supplied by all of the firms in the industry. For a purely competitive industry, then, it is the horizontal summation of the MC curves (above the level of AVC) for all firms in the

A firm making losses will operate in the short run if it (1) can cover its variable costs now and (2) expects price to be high enough in the future to cover all its costs.

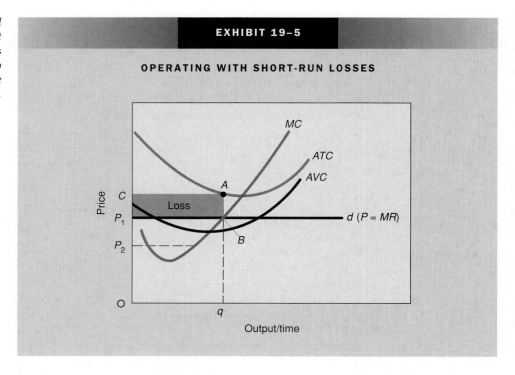

EXHIBIT 19–5

OPERATING WITH SHORT-RUN LOSSES

industry. Since individual firms will supply a larger amount at a higher price, the short-run market supply curve will slope upward to the right.

Exhibit 19–6 illustrates this relationship. As the price of the product rises from P_1 to P_2 to P_3, the individual firms (part "a") expand their output along their MC curves. Since they supply a larger output as the market price increases, the total amount supplied to the market (part "b") also expands.

Our construction of the short-run market supply curve assumes that the prices of the resources used by the industry are constant. But when the entire industry (rather than just a single firm) expands output, resource prices may rise. If so, the short-run market supply curve (reflecting the higher prices of purchased inputs) will be slightly more inelastic (steeper) than the sum of the supply curves of the individual firms.

Together with the demand curve for the industry's products, the short-run market supply curve will determine the market price. At the short-run equilibrium market price, each of the firms will have expanded output until MC has risen to the market price. They will have no desire to change output, *given their current size of plant.*

OUTPUT ADJUSTMENTS IN LONG RUN

In the long run, firms have the opportunity to alter their plant size and enter or exit from an industry. As long-run adjustments are made, output in the whole industry may either expand or contract.

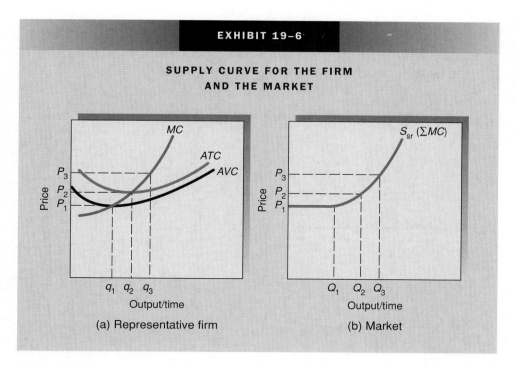

EXHIBIT 19-6

**SUPPLY CURVE FOR THE FIRM
AND THE MARKET**

(a) Representative firm

(b) Market

When resource prices are constant, the short-run market supply of the firm (a) is merely the sum of the supply produced by all the firms in the market area (b).

LONG-RUN EQUILIBRIUM

In addition to the balance between quantity supplied and quantity demanded necessary for short-run equilibrium, the firms in a purely competitive industry must earn the normal rate of return, and only the normal rate, before long-run equilibrium can be attained. If economic profit is present, new firms will enter the industry, and the current producers will have an incentive to expand the scale of their operations. This will lead to an increase in supply, placing downward pressure on prices. In contrast, if firms in the industry are suffering economic losses, they will leave the market. Supply will decline, placing upward pressure on prices.

Therefore, as **Exhibit 19–7** illustrates, when a purely competitive industry is in long-run equilibrium, (1) the quantity supplied and the quantity demanded will be equal at the market price, and (2) the firms in the industry will be earning normal (zero) economic profit (that is, their minimum *ATC* will just equal the market price).

ADJUSTING TO EXPANSION IN DEMAND

Suppose a purely competitive market is in equilibrium. What will happen if there is an increase in demand? **Exhibit 19–8** presents an example. An entrepreneur introduces a fantastic new candy product. Consumers go wild over it. However, since it sticks to one's teeth, the market demand for toothpicks increases from D_1 to D_2. The price of toothpicks rises from P_1 to P_2. What impact will the higher market price have on the output level of toothpick-producing firms? It will increase (from q_1 to q_2 in part "a" of the exhibit) as the firms expand output along their *MC*

The two conditions necessary for equilibrium in a purely competitive market are depicted here. First, quantity supplied and quantity demanded must be equal in the market (b). Second, the firms in the industry must earn zero economic profit, that is, the "normal rate of return," at the established market price (a).

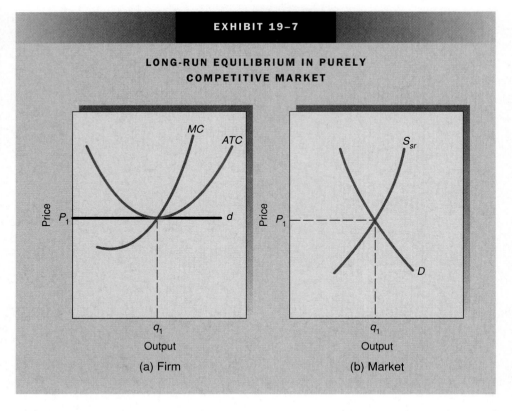

EXHIBIT 19-7

LONG-RUN EQUILIBRIUM IN PURELY COMPETITIVE MARKET

(a) Firm

(b) Market

curves. In the short run, the toothpick producers will make economic profits. The profits will attract new toothpick producers to the industry and cause the existing firms to expand the scale of their plants.[5] Hence, the market supply will increase (shift from S_1 to S_2) and eventually eliminate the short-run profits. If cost conditions are unchanged in the industry, the market price for toothpicks will return to its initial level, even though output has expanded to Q_3.

ADJUSTING TO DECLINE IN DEMAND

Economic profits attract new firms to an industry. In contrast, economic losses (when they are expected to continue) encourage capital and entrepreneurship to move out of the industry and into other areas where the profitability potential is more favorable. Economic losses mean that the owners of capital in the industry are earning less than the market rate of return. The opportunity cost of continuing in the industry exceeds the gain.

---

[5]If the *long-run* average total cost curve results in only one possible minimum-cost output level (see part "a" of Exhibit 18–9 of the previous chapter), the expansion in the long-run supply will be generated entirely by the entry of new firms. However, when the long-run average total cost is such that a wide range of minimum-cost output levels are possible (see part "b" of Exhibit 18–9), both the entry of new firms and expansion by the established firms will contribute to the increase in supply.

EXHIBIT 19-8

MARKET RESPONSE TO INCREASED DEMAND

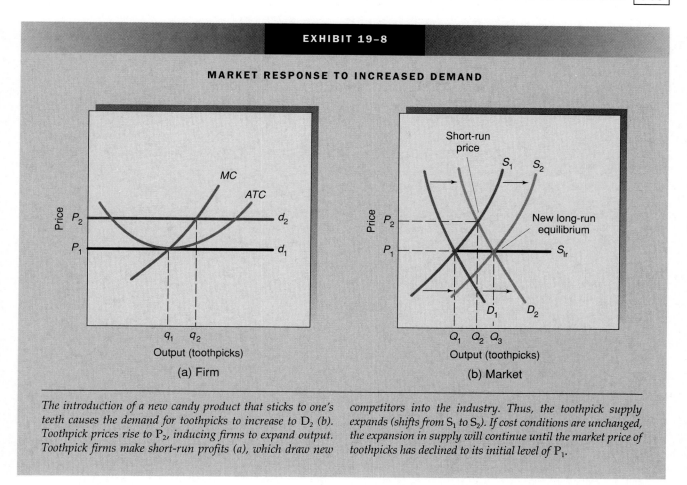

(a) Firm

(b) Market

The introduction of a new candy product that sticks to one's teeth causes the demand for toothpicks to increase to D_2 (b). Toothpick prices rise to P_2, inducing firms to expand output. Toothpick firms make short-run profits (a), which draw new competitors into the industry. Thus, the toothpick supply expands (shifts from S_1 to S_2). If cost conditions are unchanged, the expansion in supply will continue until the market price of toothpicks has declined to its initial level of P_1.

Exhibit 19–9 illustrates how market forces react to economic losses. Initially, an equilibrium price exists in the industry. The firms are able to cover their average costs of production. Now suppose there is a reduction in consumer income, causing the market demand for the product to decrease and the market price to decline. At the new, lower price, firms in the industry will not be able to cover their costs of production. In the short run, they will reduce output along their MC curve. This reduction in output by the individual firms results in a reduction in the quantity supplied in the market. For an illustration of demand reduction from a different source, see the "Applications in Economics" boxed feature on a shift in demand.

In the face of short-run losses, there will be a reduction even in the inflow of capital for the replacement of worn out equipment in this industry. Some firms will leave the industry as their fixed costs become variable when they are no longer able to cover their variable costs at the prevailing price. Others will reduce the scale of their operations. These factors will cause the industry supply to decline, to shift from S_1 to S_2. What impact will this have on price? It will rise. In the long run, the short-run market supply curve will decline until the price rises sufficiently to permit the firms remaining in the industry to once again earn "normal profits."

A SHIFT IN DEMAND—IMPACT OF PAPAL DECREE ON PRICE OF FISH

Sometimes changes in institutions, legal restrictions, or regulatory policies influence the demand for a product. The 1966 papal decree lifting the Roman Catholic Church's ban on the eating of meat on Fridays provides an interesting illustration of this point. Prior to the lifting of the ban, most of the nearly 600 million Roman Catholics consumed fish on Fridays. After the decree, many shifted to substitute goods such as beef, pork, and chicken. The demand for fish therefore declined. As our analysis indicates, a decline in demand will lead to a lower market price in the short run.

Economist Frederick Bell of Florida State University estimated the impact of the reduction in demand on the market price of fish in the Northeastern United States, an area where Catholics comprise a large proportion of the total population.[1] As we discussed earlier, changes in personal income and the price of related commodities (beef, pork, and poultry in this case) will influence the demand for a good. Bell utilized statistical techniques to adjust for these factors. This permitted him to isolate the independent effect of the papal decree on the price of fish.

The prices of seven different species of fish were considered. As the accompanying exhibit illustrates, Bell's analysis showed that the price of each variety fell. In the case of large haddock, it was 21 percent lower after the papal decree than for the previous ten years.

In other instances, the decline in price was smaller. On average, Bell estimated, the price of fish in the Northeastern United States fell by 12.5 percent as a result of the papal decree. Just as economic theory indicates, a reduction in demand for a product leads to a lower price in the short run (see Exhibit 19–9).

THE PAPAL DECREE AND THE PRICE OF FISH

SPECIES	PERCENT CHANGE IN PRICE OF FISH AFTER PAPAL DECREE
Sea scallops	–17
Yellowtail flounder	–14
Large haddock	–21
Small haddock (scrod)	–2
Cod	–16
Ocean perch	–10
Whiting	–20
All species (average)	–12.5

Source: F. W. Bell, "The Pope and the Price of Fish." *American Economic Review* (December 1968).

[1]Frederick W. Bell, "The Pope and The Price of Fish," *American Economic Review* 58 (December 1968), pp. 1346–1350.

LONG-RUN SUPPLY CURVE

The *long-run market supply curve* indicates the minimum price at which firms will supply various market output levels, given sufficient time both to adjust plant size (or other fixed factors) and to enter or exit from the industry. The shape of the curve is dependent on what happens to the cost of production as the output of an industry is altered. Three possibilities emerge, although one is far more likely than the other two.

Constant-cost industry
An industry for which factor prices and costs of production remain constant as market output is expanded. Thus, the long-run market supply curve is horizontal.

CONSTANT-COST INDUSTRIES

If factor prices remain unchanged, the long-run market supply curve will be perfectly elastic. In terms of economics, this describes a **constant-cost industry.** Exhibits 19–8 and 19–9 both picture constant-cost industries. As Exhibit 19–8

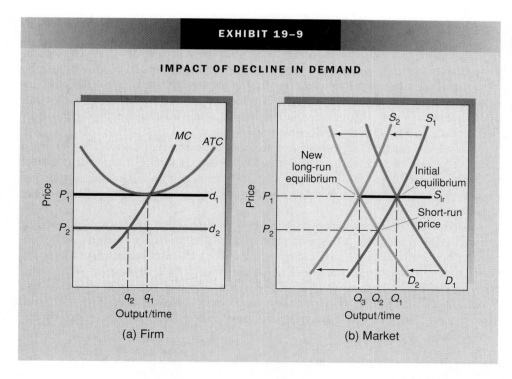

EXHIBIT 19-9

IMPACT OF DECLINE IN DEMAND

(a) Firm

(b) Market

A reduction in market demand will cause price to fall and short-run losses to occur. The losses will cause some firms to go out of business and others to reduce their scale. In the long run, the market supply will fall, causing the market price to rise. The supply will continue to decline and price will continue to rise until the short-run losses have been eliminated (S_2).

illustrates, an expansion in demand causes prices to increase *temporarily*. The high prices and profits stimulate additional production. The short-run market supply continues to expand (the entire schedule shifts to the right) until the market price returns to its initial level and profits return to their normal level. In the long run, the larger supply will not require a permanent price increase. The *long-run supply curve* (S_{lr}) is thus perfectly elastic. Exhibit 19–9 illustrates the impact of a decline in demand in a constant cost industry. Again, the long-run supply curve is perfectly elastic, reflecting the basically unchanged cost at the lower rate of industry output.

A constant-cost industry is most likely to arise when the industry's demand for resource inputs is quite small relative to the total demand for these resources. For example, since demand of the matches industry for wood, chemicals, and labor is so small relative to the total demand for these resources, doubling the output of matches would exert only a negligible impact on the price of the resources used by the industry. Matches therefore approximate a constant-cost industry.

INCREASING-COST INDUSTRIES

For most industries, called **increasing-cost industries** by economists, an expansion in total output causes a firm's production cost to rise. As the output of an industry increases, demand for resources used by the industry expands. This usually results in higher resource prices, which cause the firm's cost curves to shift upward. For example, an increase in demand for housing places upward pressure on the prices of lumber, roofing, window frames, and construction labor, causing the cost of housing to rise. Similarly, an increase in demand (and market output) for beef may cause the prices of feed grains, hay, and grazing land to rise. Thus, the production costs of beef rise as more of it is produced.

Increasing-cost industry
An industry for which costs of production rise as the industry output is expanded. Thus, the long-run quantity supplied to the market is directly related to price.

In some industries, additional demand may lead to industrial congestion, which will reduce the efficiency of the industry and cause costs to rise, even though resource prices are constant. For example, as the demand for lobster increases, additional fishermen are attracted to the industry. However, the increase in the number of fishermen combing lobster beds typically leads to congestion, which reduces the catch per hour of individual fishermen. The lobster beds themselves may be unpriced, but the production cost in the lobster industry rises as output per labor-hour declines.

For an increasing-cost industry, an expansion in market demand will bid up resource prices and/or lead to industrial congestion, causing the per unit cost of the firms to rise. As a result, a larger market output will be forthcoming only at a higher price. The long-run market supply curve for the product will therefore slope upward.

Exhibit 19–10 depicts an increasing-cost industry. An expansion in demand causes higher prices and a larger market output. The presence of short-run profit attracts new competitors to the industry, expanding the market output even more. *As the industry expands,* factor prices rise and congestion costs increase. What happens to the firm's cost curves? Both the average and marginal cost curves rise (shift to ATC_2 and MC_2). This increase in production cost necessitates a higher long-run price (P_2). Hence, the long-run supply curve slopes upward to the right.

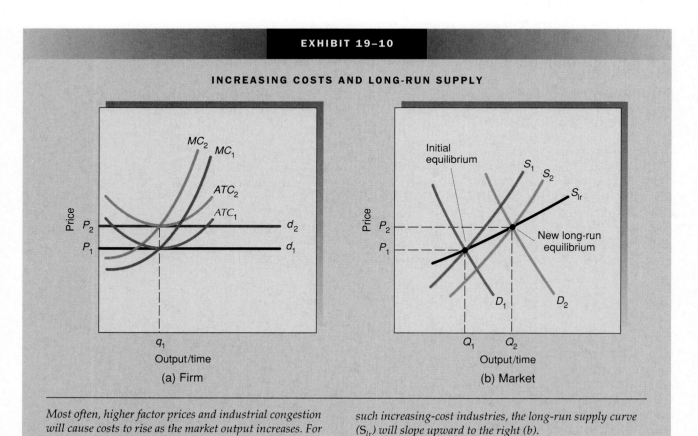

EXHIBIT 19–10

INCREASING COSTS AND LONG-RUN SUPPLY

(a) Firm

(b) Market

Most often, higher factor prices and industrial congestion will cause costs to rise as the market output increases. For such increasing-cost industries, the long-run supply curve (S_{lr}) will slope upward to the right (b).

DECREASING-COST INDUSTRIES

Conceivably, factor prices could decline if the market output of a product were expanded. Since a reduction in factor prices would lead to a lower long-run competitive market price for the product, economists refer to such industries as **decreasing-cost industries.** The long-run (but not the short-run) market supply curve for a decreasing cost industry would slope downward to the right. For example, as the electronics industry expands, suppliers of components may be able to adopt large-scale techniques that will lead to lower component prices. If this occurs, the cost curves of the electronics firms may shift downward, causing the industry supply curve for electronics products to slope downward to the right (at least temporarily). However, since expansion of an industry is far more likely to cause rising rather than falling input prices, decreasing-cost industries are atypical.

Decreasing-cost industries
Industries for which costs of production decline as the industry expands. The market supply is therefore inversely related to price. Such industries are atypical.

SUPPLY ELASTICITY AND THE ROLE OF TIME

The market supply curve is more elastic in the long run than in the short run because the firm's short-run response is limited by the "fixed" nature of some of its factors. The short- and long-run distinction offers a convenient two-stage analysis, but in the real world there are many intermediate production "runs." Some factors that could not be easily varied in a one-week time period can be varied over a two-week period. Expansion of other factors might require a month, and still others, six months. To be more precise, the cost penalty for quicker availability is greater for some production factors than for others. In any case, a faster expansion usually means that greater cost penalties are necessary to provide for an earlier availability of productive factors.

When a firm has a longer time period to plan output and adjust all of its productive inputs to the desired utilization levels, it will be able to produce any specific rate of output at a lower cost. Because it is less costly to expand output slowly in response to a demand increase, the expansion of output by firms will increase with time, as long as price exceeds cost. Therefore, the elasticity of the market supply curve will be greater when more time is allowed for firms to adjust output.

Exhibit 19-11 illustrates the impact of time on the response by producers to an increase in price resulting from an expansion in demand. When the price of a product increases from P_1 to P_2, the *immediate* supply response of the firms is small because it is costly to expand output hastily. After one week, firms are willing to expand output only from Q_1 to Q_2. After one month, due to cost reductions possible because of the longer production-planning period, firms are willing to offer Q_3 units at the price P_2. After three months, the rate of output expands to Q_4. In the long run, when it is possible to adjust all inputs to the desired utilization levels (after a six-month time period, for example), firms are willing to supply Q_5 units of output at the market price of P_2. Thus, the supply curve for products is typically more elastic over a longer time period than for a shorter period. The length of time necessary to bring about large changes in quantity supplied, however, can vary dramatically across industries. The "Applications in Economics" feature on increasing milk supplies, shows that the adjustment process in that particular industry takes many years.

The elasticity of the market supply curve usually increases as more time is allowed for adjustment to a change in price.

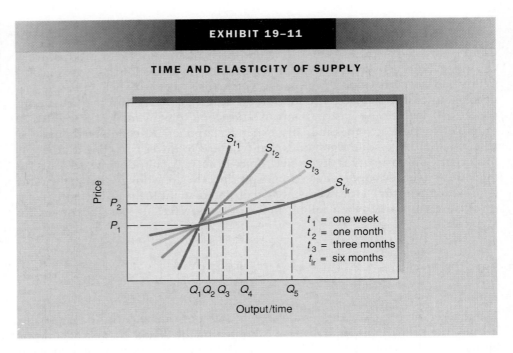

EXHIBIT 19–11

TIME AND ELASTICITY OF SUPPLY

t_1 = one week
t_2 = one month
t_3 = three months
t_{lr} = six months

ROLE OF PROFITS IN PURELY COMPETITIVE MODEL

In the purely competitive model, profits and losses are signals sent to producers by consumers. Economic profits will be largest in those areas in which consumer wants at the margin are greatest *relative to costs of production*. Profit-seeking entrepreneurs will guide additional resources into these areas. Supply will increase, driving prices down and eliminating the profits. Free entry and the competitive process will protect the consumer from arbitrarily high prices. In the long run, competitive prices will reflect costs of production.

Economic profits result because a firm or entrepreneur increases the value of resources by using them to produce something valued more highly (as measured by buyers' willingness to pay for it) than the resources themselves (as measured by the cost of bidding the resources away from all other users). Losses discipline firms that waste resources in producing products that cost more than they are valued by consumers. Losses and bankruptcies are the market mechanism's way of bringing wasteful activities to a halt.

Producers, like other decision makers, of course, confront uncertainty and dynamic change. Entrepreneurs, at the time they must make investment decisions, cannot be sure of either future market prices or costs of production. They must base their decisions on expectations. Within the framework of the purely competitive model, however, the reward-penalty system is clear. Firms that efficiently produce and correctly anticipate the products and services for which future demand will be most urgent (relative to production cost) will make economic profits. Those that are inefficient and incorrectly allocate resources into areas of weak future demand will be penalized with losses.

APPLICATIONS IN ECONOMICS

INCREASING MILK SUPPLIES—SLOWLY

When milk prices rise and are expected to remain higher, other things being equal, dairies will expand their output of milk. They will retain more older cows past their prime—cows that would have been sent to slaughter. New dairy cows will be added to the herd, and more expensive feed rations may be used to boost milk output from each cow in the herd. Research will be conducted to more effectively utilize feed rations, medicines, and other techniques to raise milk output. Genetically advanced cows, capable of producing more milk, will be sought. New firms will enter the dairy business.

Some of these changes will begin immediately. Others, though, especially research efforts and changes in the size and composition of the dairy herd, will take years to complete. Similarly, a decrease in milk production which would be desirable if milk prices fall, will take many years.

Just how slow is the response in the dairy industry? The supply-elasticity numbers in the accompanying table, from a study published in 1985 at the University of Wisconsin, indicate that even after 25 years, some of the long-run effects of a milk price increase are felt. A 10 percent increase in the price of milk will, after one year, lead to only a 1.2 percent increase in the quantity of milk supplied. But, after six years, the same price increase would lead to a 12 percent quantity increase, and after 10 years, the response would be 25 percent. Given 20 years to react, dairies would provide a 50 percent increase in the quantity of milk supplied, in response to the same 10 percent price increase. After 30 years, the response would be greater still. So on the dairy farm, at least, changes can take a great deal of time.

SUPPLY ELASTICITIES FOR MILK

LENGTH OF RUN (YEARS)	PERCENT CHANGE IN THE QUANTITY OF MILK SUPPLIED DUE TO A 10% RISE IN THE PRICE OF MILK
1	1.2
3	2.3
6	11.7
10	24.6
15	39.0
20	50.3
25	59.5
30	67.0

Source: Richard Klemme and Jean-Paul Chavas, "The Effects of Changing Milk Price on Milk Supply and National Dairy Herd Size," *Economic Issues*, University of Wisconsin, June 1985.

A look at the market for the videotape rental business shows how profits are a powerful—but temporary and potentially treacherous—lure for new entrants when entry barriers are low.[6] In 1982 videotape rental stores were new, and there were only an estimated 5,000 stores in the United States. They could charge $5 and more per 24-hour rental. The availability of rentals and the falling prices of home video players meant that profits could at times reach 80 percent of rental revenues. More importantly, *expected* profits were very high. This optimism led to the rapid entry of many new stores, which increased competition and forced prices down. By 1990 there were about 25,000 stores. Prices had fallen dramatically. Even new releases were typically renting for $1.99, and most videos rented for even

---

[6]The facts in this example are taken from Tim Tregarthen, "Supply, Demand, and Videotape," *The Margin* 6 (September–October, 1990), p. 29.

less. At times, video rental supply expanded faster than the demand for rentals, and some of the firms had to leave the business. Even for those who were efficient and stayed in the business, profits were slim. Consumers, however, benefited tremendously from the highly competitive nature of the video rental business.

EFFICIENCY AND THE PURELY COMPETITIVE MODEL

Economists often seem to be enchanted by the purely competitive model, often using it as the standard by which to judge other models. What accounts for the special significance of pure competition? Most economists agree that under rather restrictive assumptions, resource allocation within the purely competitive model is ideal from society's viewpoint. Let us explore the reasons for this consensus.

PRODUCTION EFFICIENCY ($P = ATC$)

In the long run, competition forces firms to minimize their average total cost of production and to charge a price just sufficient to cover production costs. Consequently, competitive firms must use production methods that minimize costs if they are going to survive. In addition, they must choose a scale of operation that minimizes their long-run average total cost of production. Consumers of competitively produced goods will benefit, since they will receive the largest quantity at the lowest possible price, given the prevailing cost conditions. Competitive markets will eliminate waste and production inefficiency. Inefficient, high-cost producers will confront economic losses and be driven from a competitive industry.

ALLOCATIVE EFFICIENCY ($P = MC$)

Allocative efficiency
The allocation of resources to the production of goods and services most desired by consumers. The allocation is "balanced" in such a way that reallocation of resources could not benefit anyone without hurting someone else.

Allocative efficiency refers to the balance achieved by the allocation of available resources to the production of goods and services most desired by consumers, given their incomes. It is present when all markets are in long-run competitive equilibrium. Each good is produced as long as consumers value it more than the alternative goods that might be produced with the same resources. Conversely, no unit of the good is produced if a more valuable alternative must be forgone in order to produce it. Therefore, no reallocation of resources toward production of different goods—or different combinations of goods—could benefit any one person without simultaneously hurting someone else.

The profit-maximization rule ($P = MC$) assures allocative efficiency within the competitive model. The market demand (price) reflects consumers' valuation of an additional unit of a good. The seller's marginal cost indicates the value of the resources (in their alternative uses) necessary to produce an additional unit of the good. When the production of each good is expanded so long as price exceeds marginal cost, each good will be produced if, and only if, consumers value it more than the alternatives that might have been produced. In purely competitive markets, therefore, profit-maximizing producers will be led to produce the combination of goods most desired by consumers.

PURE COMPETITION AND THE REAL WORLD

In the purely competitive model, the "invisible hand" that Adam Smith spoke of does its job very well indeed. Producers who are motivated purely by the desire to make a profit act no differently than they would if they cared only about the efficient satisfaction of consumers' desires. Because of the resulting price structure, even the desire of a very selfish consumer for a consumption item is balanced against the value of the good (and the resources embodied within it) to other people. In other words, prevailing prices provide each person with the information and incentive to heed the wishes of others. An incredibly complex array of consumer desires, production possibilities, and resource availabilities can be optimally coordinated in the model. No central person or group need know or understand all the aspects of the model. Market prices condense the needed information and convey it to each decision maker.

However, remember that pure competition is a hypothetical model. Even though it predicts fairly well in many circumstances, it ignores some important features of real markets. First, in many industries, the production costs of large firms are less than those of small firms, due to economies of scale. Under these circumstances, it may not be economical to have the industry's output divided among a large number of small producers.

Second, the preferences of consumers differ widely with regard to product design, quality, and location of purchase. Real-life consumers want variety rather than the homogeneous products implied by the purely competitive model.

Third, we live in a dynamic world. Frequent changes in knowledge and technology bring about a continual parade of new products that are better, or cheaper, or both. Surprises are normal. Profit-seeking behavior, where firms take those actions for which they expect added revenues to exceed costs, replaces the neat and tidy profit maximization of the economic model. Although the model often accurately predicts the directions of change, adjustments take time, and the expectations of decision makers are frequently disappointed. In the real world we often observe disequilibrium rather than the stable equilibrium of the purely competitive model.

Fourth, competition in the sense of rivalry is multidimensional. Pure competition features only one dimension—price. But product quality, producer reliability, convenience, location of service, and other competitive factors are important in the real world.

LOOKING AHEAD

Pure competition is important because it can help us understand real-world markets characterized by low barriers to entry and a substantial number of independent sellers. At the opposite end of the spectrum lie markets characterized by high barriers to entry and a single seller. The following chapter focuses on the hypothetical model developed by economists to analyze markets of this type—pure monopoly.

CHAPTER SUMMARY

1. Competition as a process should not be confused with pure competition, a model of industrial structure. Competition as a process implies rivalry and entrepreneurial behavior. Rival firms use quality, style, location, advertising, and price to attract consumers. Pure competition, on the other hand, is a model of industrial structure that assumes the presence of a large number of small (relative to the total market) firms, each producing a homogeneous product in a market for which there is complete freedom of entry and exit.

2. The competitive process places producers under strong pressure to operate efficiently and heed the views of consumers. Those who do not offer quality goods at economical prices lose customers to rivals. As Adam Smith recognized long ago, self-interest is a powerful motivator of human beings. If it is bridled by competition, self-interest leads to economic cooperation and productive effort.

3. Under pure competition, firms are price takers—they face a perfectly elastic demand curve. Profit-maximizing (or loss-minimizing) firms will expand output as long as the additional output adds more to revenues than to costs. Therefore, the competitive firm will produce the output level at which marginal revenue (and price) equals marginal cost.

4. The firm's short-run marginal cost (MC) curve—above its average variable cost (AVC)—is its supply curve. Under pure competition, the short-run supply curve for the market is the horizontal sum of the MC curves (when MC is above AVC) for all firms in the industry.

5. If a firm (a) is covering its average variable cost and (b) anticipates that the price is only temporarily below average total cost, it may operate in the short run even though it is experiencing a loss. However, even if it anticipates more favorable market conditions in the future, loss minimization will require the firm to shut down if it is unable to cover its average variable cost. If the firm does not anticipate that it will be able to cover its average total cost even in the long run, loss minimization requires that it immediately go out of business (even if it is covering its average *variable* cost) so that it can at least avoid its fixed cost.

6. When price exceeds average total cost, a firm will make economic profits. Under pure competition, profits will attract new firms into the industry and stimulate the existing firms to expand. The market supply will increase, pushing price down to the level of average total cost. Competitive firms will be unable to make long-run economic profits.

7. Losses exist when the market price is less than the firm's average total cost. Losses will cause firms to leave the industry or reduce the scale of their operations. Market supply will decline until price rises sufficiently for firms to earn normal (that is, zero economic) profits.

8. As the output of an industry expands, marginal costs will increase in the short run, causing the short-run market supply curve to slope upward to the right. If the prices of resources purchased by the industry remain unchanged as the market output is expanded, the long-run supply curve will be perfectly elastic. However, as the output of an industry expands, rising factor prices and industrial congestion will normally cause the firm's costs to increase. The long-run market supply curve for such an increasing cost industry will slope upward to the right.

9. Within the framework of the purely competitive model, firms that efficiently produce and correctly anticipate those goods for which future demand will be most urgent (relative to costs of production) will make profits. Firms that produce inefficiently and incorrectly allocate resources to the production of goods for which future demand turns out to be weak (relative to costs of production) will be penalized with losses. In the short run, firms might make either profits or losses, but in the long run, competitive pressures will eliminate economic profits (and losses).

10. Economists often argue that pure competition leads to ideal economic efficiency because (a) average costs of production are minimized and (b) output is expanded to the level at which the consumer's evaluation of an additional unit of a good is just equal to its marginal cost.

CRITICAL-ANALYSIS QUESTIONS

*1. Farmers are often heard to complain about the high cost of machinery, labor, and fertilizer, suggesting that these costs drive down their profit rate. Does it follow that

---

*Asterisk denotes questions for which answers are given in Appendix C.

if, for example, the price of fertilizer fell by 10 percent, farming (a highly competitive industry with low barriers to entry) would be more profitable? Explain your answer.

*2. If the firms in a competitive industry are making short-run profits, what will happen to the market price in the long run? Explain your answer.

3. What factors will cause the supply curve for a product to slope upward in the long run? Be specific.

4. A sales tax collected from the seller will shift the firm's cost curves upward. Outline the impact of a sales tax within the framework of the competitive model. Use diagrams to indicate both the short-run and long-run impact of the tax. Who will bear the burden of the sales tax?

5. "In the model of perfect competition, there is no room for the entrepreneur." How would you defend this position? Is it always true? Is it true in equilibrium?

*6. "In long-run equilibrium for a competitive industry, the firms in the industry are just able to cover their cost of production. Economic profit is zero. Therefore, if there were a reduction in demand causing prices to go down even a little bit, all of the firms in the industry would be driven out of business." Evaluate this statement.

7. "Under pure competition, the average total cost of production determines the price of each good." Is this statement true or false?

*8. Within the framework of the purely competitive model, how will an unanticipated increase in demand for a product affect each of the following in a market that was initially in long-run equilibrium?
   a. The short-run market price of the product.
   b. Industry output in the short run.
   c. Profitability in the short run.
   d. The long-run market price in the industry.
   e. Industry output in the long run.
   f. Profitability in the long run.

*9. Suppose that the development of a new drought-resistant hybrid seed corn leads to a 50 percent increase in the average yield per acre without increasing the cost to the farmers who use the new technology. If the conditions in the corn-production industry are approximated by the purely competitive model, what will happen to the following?
   a. The price of corn.
   b. The profitability of corn farmers who quickly adopt the new technology.
   c. The profitability of corn farmers who are slow to adopt the new technology.
   d. The price of soybeans, a substitute product for corn.

10. Are the following statements true or false?
   a. "If the demand for a product is inelastic, a technological change that reduces the production cost of the good will lead to a reduction in the expenditures on the good."
   b. "If the demand for a product is inelastic, a reduction in the good's cost of production will reduce the total utility derived from the good."

*11. Explain why the firms in a highly competitive industry are unable to earn long-term economic profit. Since long-run economic profit in a competitive industry is absent, does it follow that profits and losses are unimportant in industries that are competitive? Why or why not?

12. "In a competitive market, if a business operator produces efficiently—that is, if the cost of producing the good is minimized—the operator will be able to make at least a normal profit. Is this statement true or false?

13. During the summer of 1988, drought conditions throughout much of the United States substantially reduced the size of the corn, wheat, and soybean crops, three commodities for which demand is inelastic. Use the purely competitive model to determine how the drought affected (a) grain prices, (b) revenue from the three crops, and (c) the profitability of farming.

*14. Suppose that the government of a large city levies a 5 percent sales tax on hotel rooms. How will the tax affect (a) prices of hotel rooms, (b) the profits of hotel owners, and (c) gross (including the tax) expenditures on hotel rooms.

15. Explain why the market supply curve is slightly less elastic than the summation of the marginal cost curves for the firms in a competitive industry.

*16. "Competition is never between the buyer and the seller. It is always between a seller and other sellers (both actual and potential) and a buyer and other buyers (both actual and potential)." Is this statement true or false?

17. In a market economy, what are the major factors that provide business firms with an incentive to produce goods at a low cost?

*18. The accompanying table presents the expected cost and revenue data for the Tucker Tomato Farm. The Tuckers produce tomatoes in a greenhouse and sell them wholesale in a purely competitive market.
   a. Fill in the firm's marginal cost, average variable cost, average total cost, and profit schedules.
   b. If the Tuckers are profit maximizers, how many tomatoes should they produce when the market price is $500 per ton? Indicate their profits.
   c. Indicate the firm's output level and maximum profit if the market price of tomatoes increases to $550 per ton.
   d. How many units would the Tucker Tomato Farm produce if the price of tomatoes declined to $450? Indicate the firm's profits. Should the firm continue in business? Explain.

---

*Asterisk denotes questions for which answers are given in Appendix C.

COST AND REVENUE SCHEDULES—TUCKER TOMATO FARM, INC.

OUTPUT (TONS PER MONTH)	TOTAL COST	PRICE PER TON	MARGINAL COST	AVERAGE VARIABLE COST	AVERAGE TOTAL COST	PROFITS (MONTHLY)
0	$1000	$500	—	—	—	—
1	1200	500				
2	1350	500				
3	1550	500				
4	1900	500				
5	2300	500				
6	2750	500				
7	3250	500				
8	3800	500				
9	4400	500				
10	5150	500				

19. In the accompanying table, you are given information about two firms in a competitive industry. Assume that fixed costs for each firm are $20.

a. Complete the table.

b. What is the lowest price at which Firm A will produce?

c. How many units of output will it produce at that price? (Assume that it cannot produce fractional units.)

d. What is the lowest price at which Firm B will produce?

e. How many units of output will it produce?

f. How many units will Firm A produce if the market price is $20?

g. How many units will Firm B produce at the $20 price? (Assume it cannot can produce fractional units.)

h. If each firm's total fixed costs are $20 and the price of output is $20, which firm would be receiving a higher net profit or smaller loss?

i. How much would that net profit or loss be?

FIRM A

QUANTITY	TOTAL VARIABLE COST	MARGINAL COST	AVERAGE VARIABLE COST
1	$ 24		
2	30		
3	38		
4	48		
5	62		
6	82		
7	110		

FIRM B

QUANTITY	TOTAL VARIABLE COST	MARGINAL COST	AVERAGE VARIABLE COST
1	$ 8		____
2	10	____	____
3	16	____	____
4	24	____	____
5	36	____	____
6	56	____	____
7	86	____	____

*20. Emma is a landscape architect for a large design firm. She earns a salary of $50,000 per year, but is considering quitting to start her own business. She talks to her accountant, who helps her draw up the accompanying chart with their best predictions about costs and revenues.

PREDICTED ANNUAL COSTS		PREDICTED ANNUAL REVENUES
Basic wage (Emma)	$22,000	Sales $80,000
Rent of space	10,000	
Rent of equipment	6,000	
Plants	14,000	
Utilities	2,000	
Miscellaneous	5,000	

The accountant admits that the basic wage seems low, but she tells Emma to keep in mind that since she will own her business, Emma will get to keep any profit she earns. From an economist's point of view, is the accountant's list of costs complete? From the accountant's perspective, what are Emma's expected profits? From an economist's perspective, what are Emma's expected profits?

---

*Asterisk denotes questions for which answers are given in Appendix C.

CHAPTER TWENTY

MONOPOLY AND HIGH
BARRIERS TO ENTRY

Monopoly affords the consumer little protection against exorbitant prices.

WALTER ADAMS, 1971[1]

CHAPTER FOCUS

- *What, exactly, is a monopoly? What are the barriers that allow monopoly to exist?*
- *What price will a monopolist set?*
- *Why is monopoly a problem?*
- *What problems occur when we regulate monopolies?*
- *In dealing with monopoly, what are the policy alternatives, and what can we expect from each one?*
- *What impact does dynamic change have on the monopoly power of a business?*

---

[1]Walter Adams, *The Structure of American Industry*, 4th ed. (New York: Macmillan Co., 1971), p. 460.

P ure competition, as we saw in the last chapter, is a hypothetical market structure characterized by numerous sellers. At the other extreme of market structure spectrum is pure monopoly, the topic of this chapter. The word *monopoly*, derived from two Greek words, means "single seller." When only a single seller for a product exists, the firm will exert more control over price and output. This does not mean that a monopolist is completely free from competitive pressures, though. Consumers are not forced to buy from any business firm, including those with monopoly power. Even a monopolist must compete to some extent with other sellers of goods and services for the dollar votes of consumers.

However, the presence of substantial entry barriers and the absence of direct rivals producing close substitutes does influence both decision making within the firm and the operation of markets. When barriers to entry are high, what price will a monopolist charge? How does the presence of monopoly influence the efficiency of a market? Can government regulation promote economic efficiency when monopoly is present? This chapter focuses on these questions and related issues.

DEFINING MONOPOLY

Monopoly

A market structure characterized by (a) a single seller of a well-defined product for which there are no good substitutes and (b) high barriers to the entry of other firms into the market for the product.

We will define **monopoly** as a market structure characterized by (1) high barriers to entry and (2) a single seller of a well-defined product for which there are no good substitutes. Even this definition is ambiguous because "high barriers" and "good substitutes" are both relative terms. Are the barriers to entry into the automobile or steel industries high? Many observers would argue that they are. After all, it would take a great deal of financial capital to compete successfully in these industries. However, there are no legal restraints that prevent an entrepreneur from producing automobiles or steel. If price is well above cost, so that substantial profits are being made, it should not be difficult to find the necessary investment capital. After all, even a tiny portion of the investors who make up the capital market would be enough to finance a full-scale steel plant, for example. And profit, it seems, draws investment capital the way honey draws bears. Then again, would the new factory, perhaps one making cars, require a new and extensive marketing network? Or could other sales outlets be enticed into carrying the new competitor? Barriers to entry are like expected profits: in both cases, assessing their size requires subjective judgments.

"Good substitutes" is also a subjective term. There is always some substitutability among products, even those produced by a monopolist. Is a letter a good substitute for telephone communication? For some purposes—legal correspondence, for example—a letter is often a very good substitute. In other cases, when the speed of communication and immediacy of response are important, telephone communication has a tremendous advantage over letter writing. Are there any good substitutes for electricity? Most of the known substitutes for electric lighting (candles, oil lamps, and battery lights, for example) are inferior to electric lights run by power from your electric company. Natural gas, fuel oil, and wood, though, are often excellent substitutes for electric heating.

Monopoly, then, is always a matter of degree. Pure monopoly, like pure competition, is a rare phenomenon. Nevertheless, there are two reasons why it is important to understand how markets work under pure monopoly. First, the monopoly model will help us understand markets in which there are few sellers and little active rivalry. When there are only two or three producers in a market, rather than competing with each other, they may seek to collude and thus together behave like a monopoly. Second, in a few important industries there is usually only a single producer. Local telephone and electricity services are examples. The monopoly model will illuminate the operation of such markets.

BARRIERS TO ENTRY

Four types of barriers can make it difficult for potential competitors to enter a market: economies of scale, government licensing, patents, and control over essential resources.

ECONOMIES OF SCALE

In some industries, firms experience declining average total costs over the full range of output that consumers are willing to buy. When this is true, firms with a larger share of the total market will have lower unit costs. Since small firms have high per unit costs, they will be unable to enter the market, build a reputation, and compete effectively with larger firms. Under these circumstances, a single firm will tend to emerge from the competitive process in the industry, and the cost advantage resulting from its size will provide the firm with protection from potential rivals.

GOVERNMENT LICENSING

Legal barriers are the oldest and most effective method of protecting a business firm from potential competitors. Kings once granted exclusive business rights to favored citizens or groups in return for tax revenues and political support. Today governments continue to establish barriers that restrict the right to buy and sell goods. To compete in the communications industry in the United States (for example, in order to operate a radio or television station), one must obtain a government franchise. The U.S. Postal Service, a corporation formed by government, is granted the exclusive right to deliver first-class mail, although this is sometimes challenged. Potential private competitors are eliminated by law. Local governments generally grant exclusive franchises to public utilities in most areas of the United States.

Licensing, a requirement that potential competitors obtain a certificate of permission from the government, is often used to limit entry in various occupations and business activities. Many states allow only licensed persons to operate a liquor store, barbershop, taxicab, funeral home, or drugstore. Sometimes these licenses cost little and are designed to ensure certain minimum standards. In other cases, they are costly to acquire and are designed primarily to limit competition.

PATENTS

Patent

The grant of an exclusive right to use a specific process or produce a specific product for a period of time (17 years in the United States).

Most countries have established **patent** laws to provide inventors with a property right to their inventions. These laws grant the owner a legal monopoly on the commercial use of a newly invented product or process for a limited period of time, 17 years in the United States. Once a patent is granted, other persons are prohibited from producing the product or using the procedure unless they obtain permission from the patent holder. Costs, as well as benefits, accompany a patent system. As we will soon illustrate, the monopoly created by the grant of a patent generally leads to higher prices for consumers. On the positive side, however, patents encourage scientific research and technological improvements since they help inventors reap the benefits of their inventions. Patent laws increase the incentive of individuals and firms to invest the time and money that is often involved in the discovery and development of improved products and machines. The new discoveries add to producer and consumer choices, as they will find a market only if they provide more output or more consumer satisfaction per unit of cost. If other firms could freely copy new products and techniques, there would be less incentive to develop them. Thus, without patents, the pace of technological development would be slowed.

CONTROL OVER AN ESSENTIAL RESOURCE

If a single firm has sole control over a resource essential for entry into an industry, it can eliminate potential competitors. An example often cited is the Aluminum Company of America, which before the Second World War controlled the known supply of bauxite conveniently available to American firms. Without this critical raw material, potential competitors could not produce aluminum. With time, however, other supplies of bauxite were found, and this source of monopoly was lost to the company.

New technology, mineral exploration, and other ways to exploit profitable situations are always sought. Over time, they are usually found. Nevertheless, let us move on to see what happens when at least a temporary monopoly is gained.

HYPOTHETICAL MODEL OF MONOPOLY

Suppose you invent, patent, and produce a microwave device that locks the hammer of any firearm in the immediate area. This fabulous invention can be used to immobilize potential robbers or hijackers. Since you own the exclusive patent right to the device, you are not concerned about a competitive supplier in the foreseeable future. Although other products are competitive with your invention, they are poor substitutes. In short, you are a monopolist.

What price should you charge for your product? Like the purely competitive firm, you will want to expand output as long as marginal revenue exceeds marginal cost. Unlike the purely competitive firm, however, you will face a downward-sloping demand curve. Since you are the only firm in the industry, the industry demand curve will coincide with your demand curve. Consumers will buy less of your product at a higher price. At high prices, even a monopolist will have few customers.

TOTAL REVENUE, MARGINAL REVENUE, AND ELASTICITY OF DEMAND

Since the demand curve of a monopolist slopes downward, there are two conflicting influences on total revenue when the seller reduces price in order to expand output and sales. As **Exhibit 20–1** illustrates, the resultant increase in sales (from q_1 to q_2) will, by itself, add to the revenue of the monopolist. But since the price reduction also applies to units that *would have been* sold at a higher price (P_1, rather than the lower price P_2) this factor by itself would cause a *reduction* in total revenue for the monopolist. Together, the higher quantity and the lower price produce a change in total revenue (the marginal revenue associated with the added sales) that is smaller than the price at which the added units are sold.

Since marginal revenue derived from additional sales by a monopolist will be less than the sales price, the marginal-revenue curve of the monopolist will lie inside (below) the demand curve of the firm.[2] Exhibit 20–1 illustrates this relationship.

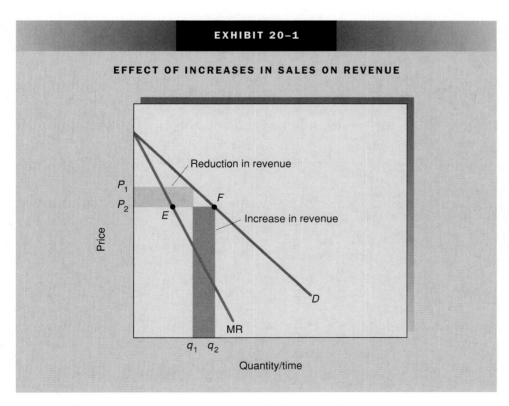

EXHIBIT 20–1

EFFECT OF INCREASES IN SALES ON REVENUE

When a firm faces a downward-sloping demand curve, a price reduction that increases sales will exert two conflicting influences on total revenue. First, total revenue will rise because of an increase in the number of units sold (from q_1 to q_2). However, revenue losses from the lower price (P_2) on units that could have been sold at a higher price (P_1) will at least partially offset the additional revenues due to increased sales. Therefore, the marginal-revenue (MR) curve will lie inside the firm's demand curve.

---

[2]For a straight-line demand curve, the *MR* curve will bisect any line parallel to the *x*-axis. For example, the *MR* curve will divide the line P_2F into two equal parts, P_2E and EF.

The demand curve not only shows the number of units that can be sold at different prices, but also reveals how revenues vary as price and output are altered. Using a straight-line demand curve, **Exhibit 20–2** illustrates how total and marginal revenue are related to elasticity of demand. At very high prices, the sales of the monopolist will be small, and demand will tend to be elastic. As price is reduced and output is expanded on the elastic portion of the monopolist's demand curve, total revenue will rise. Marginal revenue will be positive. Suppose the monopolist charged $15 for a product and sold 25 units, yielding a total revenue of $375. If the monopolist cut the price to $10, sales would expand to 50 units.

For the elastic portion of the monopolist's demand curve (prices greater than $10), a price reduction will be associated with rising total revenue (b) and positive marginal revenue. At unitary elasticity (output of 50 units), total revenue will reach a maximum. When the monopolist's demand curve is inelastic (output beyond 50 units), lower prices will lead to declining total revenue and negative marginal revenue.

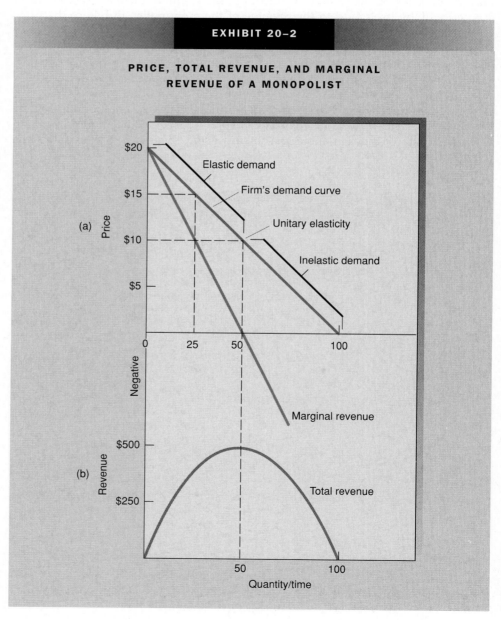

EXHIBIT 20–2

PRICE, TOTAL REVENUE, AND MARGINAL REVENUE OF A MONOPOLIST

Total revenue would rise to $500. A price reduction from $15 to $10 would thus increase the total revenue of the monopolist.

Consider the output rate at which elasticity of demand is equal to unity. At that point, total revenue reaches its maximum. Marginal revenue is equal to zero. As price falls below $10, into the inelastic portion of the monopolist's demand curve, total revenue declines as output is expanded. For this range of price and output, marginal revenue will be negative. Thus, marginal revenue goes from positive to negative as the elasticity of demand changes from elastic to inelastic (at output 50 in Exhibit 20–2).

This analysis has clear implications. For a monopolist operating on the inelastic portion of its demand curve, a price increase would lead to more total revenue as well as less total cost (since fewer units would be produced and sold). Because of this, we would never expect a profit-maximizing monopolist to push the sales of a product into the range in which the product's demand curve becomes inelastic.

PROFIT-MAXIMIZING OUTPUT

Both costs and revenues must be considered when analyzing profit maximization under monopoly. The profit-maximizing monopolist will continue expanding output until marginal revenue equals marginal cost. The price at which that output level can be sold is given by the demand curve of the monopolist.

Exhibit 20–3 provides a graphic illustration of profit maximization. Since the monopolist maximizes profit by expanding output as long as marginal revenue (MR) exceeds marginal cost (MC), output will be expanded to Q, where MR = MC. The monopolist will be able to sell the profit-maximizing output Q for

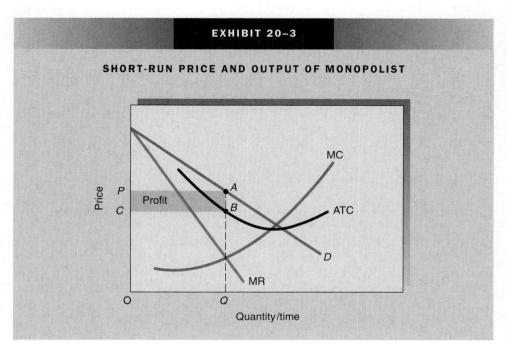

EXHIBIT 20–3

SHORT-RUN PRICE AND OUTPUT OF MONOPOLIST

The monopolist will reduce price and expand output as long as MR *exceeds* MC. *Output* Q *will result. When price exceeds average total cost at any output level, profit will accrue at that output level.*

a price indicated by the height of the demand curve. At any output less than Q, the benefits (marginal revenue) of producing the additional units will exceed their costs. The monopolist will gain by expanding output. For any output greater than Q, the monopolist's costs of producing additional units will be greater than the benefits (marginal revenue). Production of such units will reduce profits.

Exhibit 20–3 also depicts the profits of a monopolist. At output Q, the monopolist would charge price P. Price times the number of units sold yields the firm's total revenue ($PAQO$). The firm's total cost would be $CBQO$, the average per unit cost multiplied by the number of units sold. The firm's profits are merely total revenue less total cost, the shaded area of Exhibit 20–3. Even though competitive and monopolistic firms alike expand output until $MR = MC$, there is one important difference. For the competitive firm, price is always equal to marginal revenue, so that price will also equal marginal cost when profit is maximized. For the monopolist, however, price must be reduced to sell more, so marginal revenue is always less than price. This means that when profit is maximized and $MR = MC$, price will exceed marginal cost. This difference between pure monopoly and pure competition has implications for efficiency in the market, which we will discuss later in this chapter.

Exhibit 20–4 provides a numeric illustration of profit-maximizing decision making. At low output rates, MR exceeds MC. The monopolist will continue to expand output as long as MR is greater than MC. Thus, an output rate of eight units per day will be chosen. Given the demand for the product, the monopolist

EXHIBIT 20–4

PROFIT MAXIMIZATION FOR A MONOPOLIST

Rate of Output (Per Day) (1)	Price (Per Unit) (2)	Total Revenue (1) × (2) (3)	Total Cost (Per Day) (4)	Profit (3) – (4) (5)	Marginal Cost (6)	Marginal Revenue (7)
0	—	—	$ 50.00	$–50.00	—	—
1	$25.00	$ 25.00	60.00	–35.00	$10.00	$25.00
2	24.00	48.00	69.00	–21.00	9.00	23.00
3	23.00	69.00	77.00	–8.00	8.00	21.00
4	22.00	88.00	84.00	4.00	7.00	19.00
5	21.00	105.00	90.50	14.50	6.50	17.00
6	19.75	118.50	96.75	21.75	6.25	13.50
7	18.50	129.50	102.75	26.75	6.00	11.00
8	17.25	138.00	108.50	29.50	5.75	8.50
9	16.00	144.00	114.75	29.25	6.25	6.00
10	14.75	147.50	121.25	26.25	6.50	3.50
11	13.50	148.50	128.00	20.50	6.75	1.00
12	12.25	147.00	135.00	12.00	7.00	–1.50
13	11.00	143.00	142.25	.75	7.25	–4.00

can sell eight units at a price of $17.25 each. Total revenue will be $138, compared to a total cost of $108.50. The monopolist will make a profit of $29.50. The profit rate will be smaller at all other output rates. For example, if the monopolist reduces the price to $16 in order to sell nine units per day, revenue will increase by $6. However, the marginal cost of producing the ninth unit is $6.25. Since the cost of producing the ninth unit is greater than the revenue it brings in, profit will decline.

MARKET FORCES AND THE MONOPOLIST

High barriers to entry insulate monopolists from direct competition with rival firms producing a similar product. In contrast with competitive markets, in a monopolized industry, profits will not attract—at least not quickly—rivals who will expand supply, cut prices, and spoil the market. Protected by high entry barriers, a monopolist may be able to earn profits even in the long run.

Does this mean that monopolists can charge as high a price as they want? Indeed, monopolists are often accused of price gouging. In evaluating this charge, however, it is important to recognize that, like other sellers, monopolists will seek to maximize profit, not price. Since consumers will buy less as price increases, a higher price is not always best for monopolists. Exhibit 20–4 illustrates this point. What would happen to the profit of the monopolist if price were increased from $17.25 to $18.50? At the higher price, only seven units would be sold and total revenue would equal $129.50. The cost of producing seven units would be $102.75. Thus, when price is $18.50 and output seven units, profit is only $26.75, less than could be attained at the lower price ($17.25) and larger output (eight). The highest price is not always the best price for the monopolist. Sometimes a price reduction will increase the firm's total revenue more than its total cost.

Will a monopolist always be able to make economic profit? The profitability of a monopolist is limited by the demand for the product that it produces. In some cases, even a monopolist may be unable to sell for a profit. For example, there are thousands of clever, patented items that are never produced because demand-cost conditions are not favorable. **Exhibit 20–5** illustrates this possibility. When the average total cost curve of a monopolist is always above its demand curve, economic losses will result. Even a monopolist will not want to operate under these conditions. If market conditions are expected to improve, the monopolist will produce output Q (at which $MR = MC$) and charge price P — *operating in the short run* as long as variable cost can be covered. If the loss-producing conditions persist, however, the monopolist will discontinue production.

REALITY VERSUS MONOPOLY MODEL

Thus far, we have proceeded as if monopolists always knew exactly what their revenue and cost curves looked like. Of course, this is not true in the real world. A monopolist cannot be sure of the demand conditions for a product. Demand curves frequently shift, and choices must be made without the benefit of perfect knowledge.

The monopolist is, in fact, a **price searcher**—a seller trying to find the price at which profit will be maximized. How many sales will be lost if the price is raised?

Price searcher
A seller with imperfect information, facing a downward sloping demand curve, who tries to find the price that maximizes profit.

Even a monopolist will incur short-run losses if the average total cost curve lies above the demand curve.

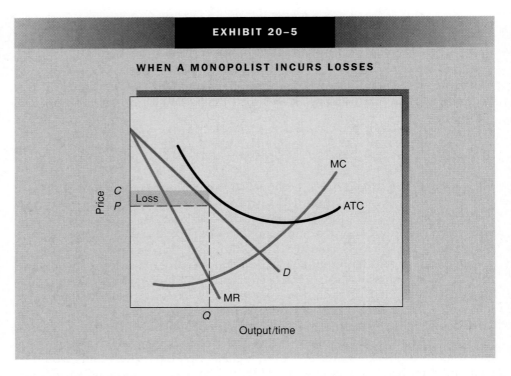

EXHIBIT 20-5

WHEN A MONOPOLIST INCURS LOSSES

How many sales will be added if the price is lowered? Trial-and-error is often necessary to learn the answers. A firm that is a price searcher will price its product on the basis of what it expects to happen if the price is changed.

The revenue and cost data illustrated in Exhibits 20–3, 20–4, and 20–5 might be thought of as representing *expected* revenues and costs associated with various output levels. A monopolist, of course, seldom calculates what we have called demand, marginal revenue, and cost curves. Even so, the monopolist asks the same questions: Would a lower price add more to revenue than to cost? Would a higher price decrease revenue more than cost? The profit-maximizing price is usually just approximated. However, the monopolist who is maximizing profits acts *as if* marginal revenue and marginal cost had been calculated, so our model of monopoly shows what a profit-maximizing monopolist is trying to do.

DEFECTS AND PROBLEMS OF MONOPOLY

Monopolists, by keeping the market constantly understocked, by never fully supplying the effectual demand, sell their commodities much above the natural price, and raise their emoluments, whether they consist of wages or profit, greatly above their natural rate.

ADAM SMITH, 1776[3]

What types of problems arise under monopoly? Can public policy improve resource allocation in markets characterized by monopoly?

_____

[3]Adam Smith, *An Inquiry into the Nature and Causes of the Wealth of Nations*, 1776, Cannan's ed. (Chicago: University of Chicago Press, 1976), p. 69.

FOUR DEFECTS OF MONOPOLY

From Adam Smith's time to the present, economists have generally considered monopoly a necessary evil at best. There are four major reasons for this view.

1. Monopoly severely limits the options available to consumers. If you do not like the food at a local restaurant, you can go to another restaurant. If you do not like the wares of a local department store, you can buy good substitutes somewhere else. The competition of rivals protects the consumer from the arbitrary behavior of a single seller. What, though, are your alternatives if you do not like the local telephone service? Other sellers of local telephone service are not allowed by law. If you are dissatisfied, you can send a letter or deliver your message in person, or you can write to your legislative representative and complain. But these are not always satisfactory alternatives to the service of the monopolist. You often have no feasible alternative but to accept poor service, rude treatment, or high prices if that is what is offered.

In the presence of monopoly, the option is to buy from the monopolist or do without. This reduction in options greatly reduces the consumer's ability to discipline monopolists.

2. Monopoly results in allocative inefficiency. Allocative efficiency requires that an activity be undertaken when it generates additional benefits that exceed its added costs. This means that a firm should expand output as long as price exceeds marginal cost. A profit-maximizing monopolist, however, would expand output only as long as marginal revenue exceeds marginal cost, which is a lesser output rate.

The logic of this criticism is pictured in **Exhibit 20–6.** Demand is a measure of the degree to which consumers value additional units of a product. The marginal-cost curve represents the opportunity cost of the resources used to produce the additional units. Ideal economic efficiency would require output to be expanded as long as the height of the demand curve (the value of added units) exceeded that of the marginal-cost curve (the cost of the added units). From the viewpoint of the entire community, output level Q_i would be best.

The monopolist, however, will produce only Q_m units, the profit-maximizing output rate. If output were expanded beyond Q_m to Q_i, how much would consumers gain? The area under the demand curve, ABQ_iQ_m, reveals the answer. How much would it cost the monopolist to produce these units? CBQ_iQ_m reveals that answer. The benefits of expanding output from Q_m to Q_i exceed the costs by ABC. The monopolist, though, will not produce these additional units because they would add less to the monopoly's revenues (assuming that all consumers are charged the same price) than to its costs. Potential gains represented by ABC, then, are lost under monopoly. As Adam Smith observed 200 years ago, the monopolist understocks the market in order to charge a higher price.

3. Under monopoly, profits and losses do not properly induce firms to enter and to exit from industries. When barriers to entry are low, profits induce firms to produce goods for which consumers are willing (because of the expected benefits) to pay prices sufficient to cover costs of production. Inefficient firms face competition and are unable to cover their costs. They are forced to either improve efficiency or leave the market. Losses also discourage firms from producing goods for which consumers are unwilling to cover the costs of production. Profits and losses therefore direct resources into those activities for which consumer valuation is highest.

For the monopolist, profits play a smaller role because entry barriers are high. The disciplining force of competition from producers offering similar products is

A monopolist will produce only output Q_m, even though Q_i is best for the entire community. If output were expanded from Q_m to Q_i, the benefits to the community would exceed the costs by ABC. However, since the profit of the monopolist is maximized at Q_m, units beyond that level will not be produced. What is best for the monopolist (output Q_m) conflicts with what is best for the community (output Q_i).

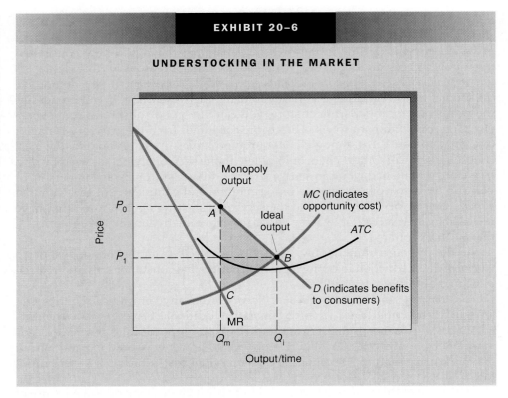

EXHIBIT 20–6

UNDERSTOCKING IN THE MARKET

missing. Even though losses will induce exit from the market, when costs are high relative to demand, the ability of profits and losses to discipline firms under monopoly is weakened. Firms that are earning profits, or that are inefficient, may nonetheless be protected from potential new competitors by barriers to entry. Their benefits are enjoyed at the consumer's expense.

4. *Government grants of monopoly will encourage rent seeking; resources will be wasted by firms attempting to secure and maintain grants of monopoly power.* The inefficiency emanating from government licenses, franchises, and other grants of monopoly power will exceed the welfare losses due to allocative inefficiency. As we discussed in Chapter 4, grants of special favor by the government will lead to rent-seeking activities. Individuals, firms, and organized interest groups will compete for government favors. When government licenses or other grants of monopoly power increase profitability and provide protection from the rigors of market competition, people will expend scarce resources in an attempt to secure and maintain these monopoly grants. From an efficiency standpoint, such rent-seeking activities are wasteful; they consume valuable resources without contributing to output. In aggregate, output is reduced as the result of these wasteful activities.[4]

---

[4]These costs were first discussed in Gordon Tullock, "The Welfare Costs of Tariffs, Monopolies, and Theft," *Western Economic Journal* 5 (June 1967), pp. 224–232.

By way of illustration, suppose the government issues a license providing a seller with the exclusive right to sell liquor in a specific market. If this grant of monopoly power permits the licensee to earn monopoly profit, potential suppliers will expend resources trying to convince government officials that they should be granted the license. The potential monopolists will lobby government officials, make political contributions, hire representatives to do consulting studies, and undertake other action designed to convince politicians and their appointees that they can best "serve the public interest" as a monopoly supplier. Any firm that expects its rent-seeking activities to be successful will be willing to spend up to the present value of the future expected monopoly profits, if necessary, to obtain the monopoly protection. Other suppliers, of course, may also be willing to invest in rent-seeking activities. When several suppliers believe they can win, the total expenditures of all firms on rent-seeking activities may actually consume resources worth more than the economic profit expected from the monopoly enterprise.

How much is spent on rent seeking? Data on spending by individual firms is not available, but spending by groups is publicly recorded. To advance their group interests, firms often form associations. For example, the privately owned electric utilities in the United States, which typically have monopoly grants of rights to service territories, formed the Edison Electric Institute (EEI), headquartered in Washington, D.C. In 1991, EEI spent $63.6 million, primarily to lobby government. The National Electric Rural Cooperative Association, another group of utilities, spent $49.7 million in the same year. Their chief executives received $210,000 and $204,000 respectively. Seeking favors in monopoly markets pays well, but it is also costly and wasteful from the viewpoint of economic efficiency.

PRICE DISCRIMINATION

Thus far, we have assumed that all sellers of a product will charge each customer the same price. Sometimes, though, sellers can increase their revenues (and profits) by charging different prices to different groups of consumers. This practice is called **price discrimination.** As we will see, it can help sellers, but it can also increase market efficiency and lower the price available to buyers whose demands are elastic.

If price discrimination is going to be attractive to a seller, three conditions must be met. First, the firm must confront a downward-sloping demand curve for its product. A monopolist will meet this criterion; a pure competitor will not. Second, there must be at least two identifiable groups of consumers whose price elasticities of demand for the firm's product differ. The seller must be able to identify and separate these consumers at a low cost. Third, the sellers must be able to prevent the customers who are charged a low price from reselling the product to customers who are charged higher prices.

Can you think of any examples of price discrimination? Businesses such as hotels, fast-food restaurants, and drugstores often charge senior citizens less than other customers. Students (and children) are often given discounts at movie theaters and athletic events. Sometimes bars and sports teams charge women lower prices than men.

Price discrimination
A practice whereby a seller charges different consumers different prices for the same product or service.

GAINING FROM PRICE DISCRIMINATION

Why do sellers charge different prices to their customers? When a seller can identify specific groups of customers and distinguish among them at a relatively low cost, profits can be increased if (1) groups with the most inelastic demand are charged high prices and (2) groups with a more elastic demand are charged low prices. Pricing of airline tickets illustrates this point. The airline industry has found that the demand of business fliers is substantially more inelastic than the demand of vacationers, students, and other travelers. Thus, airlines usually charge high fares to persons who are unwilling to stay over a weekend, who spend only a day or two at their destination, and who make reservations a short time before their flight. These high fares fall primarily on business travelers, who are less sensitive to price. In contrast, discount fares are offered to fliers willing to make reservations well in advance, travel during off-peak hours, and stay at their destinations over a weekend before returning home. Such travelers are likely to be vacationers and students, who are highly sensitive to price.

Exhibit 20–7 illustrates the logic of this policy. Part "a" shows what would happen if a single price were charged to all customers. Given demand, the profit-

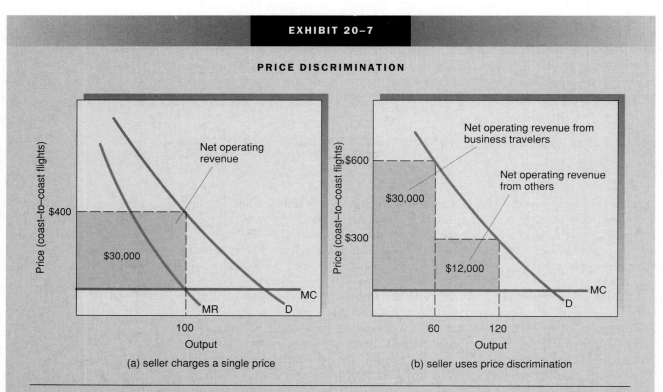

EXHIBIT 20–7

PRICE DISCRIMINATION

(a) seller charges a single price

(b) seller uses price discrimination

A $400 ticket price will maximize profits on coast-to-coast flights if an airline charges a single price (a). However, the airline can do still better if it raises the price to $600 for passengers (business travelers) with a highly inelastic demand and reduces the price to $300 for travelers (for example, students and vacationers) with a more elastic demand (b). When sellers can segment their market, they can gain by (1) charging a higher price to consumers with an inelastic demand and (2) offering discounts to customers whose demand is more elastic.

maximizing firm expands output to 100, where *MR* equals *MC*. The profit-maximizing price on coast-to-coast flights is $400, which generates $40,000 of revenue per flight. Since the marginal cost per passenger is $100, this provides the airline with net operating revenue of $30,000 with which to cover other costs.

However, as part "b" of Exhibit 20–7 shows, even though the market demand schedule is unchanged, the airline can do even better if it uses price discrimination. When it charges business travelers (those who travel on weekdays, do not stay over a weekend, and who make their reservations only a few days in advance) $600, most of these passengers continue to travel, since their demand is highly inelastic. While a *price increase* generates additional revenue from those with an inelastic demand, a $100 price reduction would generate a substantial increase in sales (and revenues) from vacationers, students, and other groups with a more elastic demand. With price discrimination, the airline can sell 60 tickets primarily to business travelers at $600 and 60 additional tickets to others at $300. Total revenue jumps to $54,000 and this leaves the airline with $42,000 ($54,000 − 120 × $100) of revenue in excess of variable cost. Compared to the single-price outcome (part "a"), the price-discrimination strategy expands profit by $12,000 (part "b").

A seller need not be a pure monopolist to gain from price discrimination. Any firm that faces a downward-sloping demand curve for its product may employ the technique. In fact, differential prices accompanying discounts and economy

THE WALL STREET JOURNAL

VISTA AIRLINES

"Folks, we're ready to begin boarding. We'll start with those passengers who paid more than $99 for the trip."

Reprinted by permission of *The Wall Street Journal*. © Cartoon Features Syndicate.

fares are often indicative of intense rivalry among firms. We introduce the concept while discussing monopoly merely to illustrate the general point.

Sometimes price discrimination is quite subtle. Discount coupons, for example, reflect the use of price discrimination as a competitive strategy. Many businesses recognize that shoppers who take the time and effort to cut out and save coupons are more price-sensitive (their demand is more elastic) than other consumers. As our analysis indicates, it makes sense to charge these customers a lower price. Even colleges engage in price discrimination. Many colleges charge a high standard tuition, which allows them to get additional revenue from wealthy families with a more inelastic demand. At the same time, however, they provide low-income students with scholarships based on need (tuition "discounts"). The partial-tuition scholarships given to students whose parents are less wealthy helps the college increase its enrollment by attracting more students among those with a more elastic demand. Poorer students thus are not priced out of their market by the high standard tuition.

WINNERS AND LOSERS FROM PRICE DISCRIMINATION

When a monopolist can price-discriminate, some buyers (those with an inelastic demand) are forced to pay more than they would have if a single intermediate price had been offered. They purchase fewer units, and they are worse off. In contrast, those (with a more elastic demand) for whom the price-discrimination process lowers the price are better off. (Of course, with some products, such as airline transportation, a single buyer might be better off with some purchases and worse off with others.)

On balance, however, we can expect that output will be greater with price discrimination than with a single price; the market is not as understocked. Thus, from an allocative standpoint, price discrimination gets high marks; it reduces the allocative inefficiency due to monopolistic pricing. Some of the gains that would accrue to consumers with an inelastic demand are transferred to the monopolist as increased revenue, but additional gains from trade are created by the increased output of goods—an output that would have been lost if the monopolist did not (or could not) price-discriminate.

In some markets, there is an additional gain emanating from price discrimination: socially beneficial production may occur that would have been lost were it not for the price discrimination. Remember, a monopolist is not guaranteed a profit. Sometimes it is unable to cover cost (see Exhibit 20–5), in which case, of course, it will likely go out of business. With price discrimination, however, some otherwise unprofitable firms may be able to generate enough additional revenue to operate successfully in the marketplace. For example, some small towns in Montana might not provide enough revenue at a single price to enable a local physician to cover his or her opportunity costs. However, if the physician is able to discriminate on the basis of income, charging wealthier people more and poorer people less than normal rates, the resulting revenues from practice in the small town may enable the physician to stay in the community. In this case, all residents of the town may be better off as the result of the price discrimination, since it provides them with access to a local physician. After all, even those being charged the highest prices are not disadvantaged if the price discrimination keeps the physician in town. They are just as able to seek physician services elsewhere as they would have been in the absence of the price-discriminating local doctor.

WHEN CAN A MONOPOLIZED INDUSTRY BE MADE COMPETITIVE?

The most serious problems raised by a monopoly would be avoided if the monopolist faced the threat of rivals producing the same product or even close substitutes. The presence of competitors would prevent independent firms from restricting output and raising prices.

Why not break up the monopoly into several rival units, substituting competition for monopoly? When economies of scale are not important, this can be a very good strategy.

Exhibit 20–8 compares competition and monopoly, assuming that economies of scale are unimportant in the industry. The minimum-cost output conditions for purely competitive firms in this case would not differ from those of monopolists. If the industry were purely competitive, price would be determined by supply and demand. As part "a" of Exhibit 20–8 illustrates, under these conditions, competition would drive price down to P_c in the long run. An industry output of Q_c would result. The market price would just equal the marginal opportunity costs of production.

In contrast, if the industry were monopolized, the profit-maximizing monopolist would equate marginal revenue with marginal cost (part "b"). This would

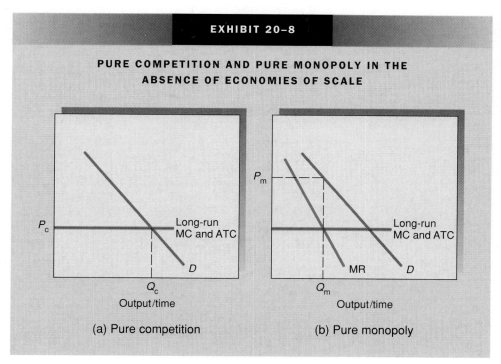

EXHIBIT 20–8

PURE COMPETITION AND PURE MONOPOLY IN THE ABSENCE OF ECONOMIES OF SCALE

(a) Pure competition

(b) Pure monopoly

Here we assume that a product can be produced by either numerous small firms or a monopolist at the same average total and marginal costs. When there are no cost disadvantages of small-scale production, competition serves to reduce price. For a purely competitive industry (a), supply and demand would dictate price P_c. The firms would just be able to cover their cost. If all the firms merged into a monopoly and cost conditions remained the same, the monopolist would restrict output to Q_m (where MC would equal MR). Price would rise to P_m.

lead to an output level of Q_m. The monopolist would charge P_m, a price higher than would exist in a competitive industry. When economies of scale are unimportant, imposition of competitive conditions on a monopolized industry will result in lower prices, a larger output, and improved economic efficiency.

ECONOMIES OF SCALE AND NATURAL MONOPOLY

Unfortunately, it is often unrealistic to expect similar cost conditions for pure competition and monopoly. Economies of scale may be the reason that certain industries tend to be monopolized. If economies of scale are important, larger firms will have lower per unit cost than smaller rivals. Sometimes economies of scale may be so important that per unit cost of production will be lowest when the entire output of the industry is produced by a single firm. In the absence of government intervention, the "natural" tendency will then be toward monopoly, because increases in firm size through merger, or "survival of the fittest," will lead to a lower per unit cost.

Natural monopoly
A market situation in which the average costs of production continually decline with increased output. Therefore, average costs of production will be lowest when a single large firm produces the entire output demanded.

Exhibit 20–9 depicts a **natural monopoly**. The long-run average total cost (*LRATC*) in the industry declines and eventually crosses the demand curve. To take full advantage of the economies of scale, given the demand for the product, the total output of the industry would have to be produced by a single firm. If the firm were an unregulated monopolist, it would produce output Q_m and charge price P_m. The firm would realize economic profits, because average total cost would be less than price at the profit-maximizing output level. It would be very difficult for any firm to begin to compete with the natural monopolist; initially,

When economies of scale are important, efforts to impose a competitive market structure are self-defeating. For an industry with cost (and demand) curves like those indicated here, prices (and costs) would be lower under monopoly than if there were ten competitors of size Q_c.

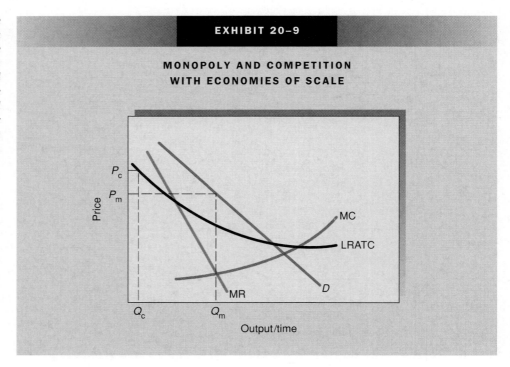

EXHIBIT 20–9

MONOPOLY AND COMPETITION WITH ECONOMIES OF SCALE

while the new competitor was still small, it would have very high costs of production and would be unable to make profits at price P_m. The natural-monopoly conditions of the industry would act as an entry barrier to potential competitors.

Therefore, when a natural monopoly exists, a competitive market structure will be both costly and difficult to maintain. Suppose the output of an industry were divided among ten firms of size Q_c (see Exhibit 20–9). These small firms would have per unit average costs of P_c. Even if they charged a price equal to their average total cost, the price would be higher than the monopolistic price of P_m. In addition, since firms larger than Q_c would always have lower per unit costs, there would be a strong tendency for firms to merge and become larger. Imposition of a competitive structure would be self-defeating in cases where monopoly exists because of the economies of scale.

In what situations are substantial economies of scale present? It is difficult for an observer to know, especially when technology is constantly changing. Existing and potential suppliers sometimes have different opinions as to the importance of scale economies, at a given time and place. However, it is commonly assumed that delivery of local telephone service, water, and electricity exhibit natural-monopoly conditions. If there were several telephone companies operating in the same area, each with its own lines and transmission equipment, the resulting duplication would be costly. In such industries, a large number of firms might not be feasible.

POLICY ALTERNATIVES TO NATURAL MONOPOLY

When monopoly or near monopoly results from economies of scale, there are three policy alternatives. First, monopolists could be permitted to operate freely. We have already pointed out that this option limits consumer choice and results in a higher product price (and smaller output) than is consistent with ideal economic efficiency. Second, government regulation could be imposed on the monopolists. Third, the government could completely take over production in the industry. Government operation is an alternative to private monopoly. Let us take a closer look at the last two alternatives, and compare them with private monopoly.

REGULATING THE MONOPOLIST

Can government regulation improve the allocative efficiency of unregulated monopoly? In theory, the answer to this question is clearly yes. Government regulation can force the monopoly to reduce its price; at the lower government-imposed price ceiling, the monopolist will produce a larger output.

Exhibit 20–10 illustrates why ideal government price regulation would improve resource allocation. The profit-maximizing monopolist sets price at P_0 and produces output Q_0, where $MR = MC$. Consumers, however, would value *additional* units more than the opportunity cost. How can the regulatory agency improve on the situation that would result from unregulated monopoly?

If unregulated, a profit-maximizing monopolist with the costs indicated here would produce Q_0 units and charge P_0. If a regulatory agency forced the monopolist to reduce price to P_1, the monopolist would expand output to Q_1. Ideally, we would like output to be expanded to Q_2, where P = MC, but regulatory agencies usually do not attempt to keep prices as low as P_2. Can you explain why?

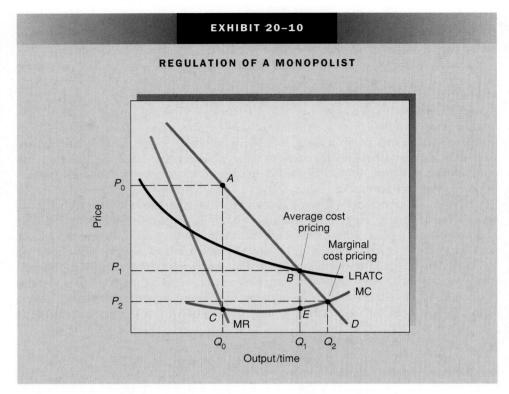

EXHIBIT 20–10

REGULATION OF A MONOPOLIST

AVERAGE COST PRICING.

If a regulatory agency forces the monopolist to reduce price to P_1, where the firm's *ATC* curve intersects with the market (and firm) demand curve, the monopolist will expand output to Q_1. Since the firm cannot charge a price above P_1, it cannot increase revenues by selling a smaller output at a higher price. Once the price ceiling is instituted, the firm can increase revenues by P_1, and by only P_1, for each unit it sells. The regulated firm's *MR* is constant at P_1 for all units sold until output is increased to Q_1. Since the firm's *MC* is less than P_1 (and therefore less than *MR*), the profit-maximizing, regulated monopolist will expand output from Q_0 to Q_1. The benefits from the consumption of these units (ABQ_1Q_0) clearly exceed their costs (CEQ_1Q_0). Social welfare has improved as a result of the regulative action (we will ignore the impact on the distribution of income). At that output level, revenues are sufficient to cover costs. The firm is making zero economic profit (or "normal" accounting profit).

MARGINAL COST PRICING.

Ideally, since even at the Q_1 output level marginal cost is still less than price, additional welfare gains are possible if output is increased to Q_2. However, if a regulatory agency forced the monopolist to reduce price to P_2 (so that price would equal marginal cost at the output level Q_2), economic losses would result. Even a monopolist, unless subsidized, would not undertake production if the regulatory agency set the price at P_2 or any price below P_1. Usually, problems associated with determining and allocating the necessary subsidy would make this option infeasible.

WHY REGULATION MAY GO ASTRAY

It is not easy to regulate an industry well. The cost-plus orientation toward which pricing methods gravitate weakens incentives for efficiency.

F. M. SCHERER[5]

Even though government regulation of monopoly seems capable of improving market results, as in the preceding example of average cost pricing, economic analysis suggests that regulating monopolies will usually not be an ideal solution. Why? As Professor Scherer indicates in the quote, the lack of incentive to produce at a low cost is important. Information is another factor. Together, the lack of incentives and information form a serious principal-agent problem for regulators who would act on behalf of citizens to control monopoly. Let us look at the various factors that make this such a difficult task.

LACK OF INFORMATION.   In discussing ideal regulation, we assumed that we knew what the firm's *ATC, MC,* and demand curves looked like. In reality, of course, regulators do not have this knowledge. The firms themselves have difficulty knowing their costs for the future period covered by a rate currently being set, and even more trouble predicting their demand curves.

Because estimates of demand and marginal costs are difficult to obtain, regulatory agencies usually use profits (or rate of return) as a gauge to determine whether the regulated price is too high or too low. The regulatory agency, guarding the public interest, seeks to impose a "fair" or "normal" rate of return on the firm. If the firm is making economic profits (that is, an abnormally high rate of return), the price must be higher than P_1 and thus it should be lowered. Alternatively, if the firm is incurring economic losses (less than the fair or normal rate of return), the regulated price must be less than P_1, and the firm should be allowed to increase price.

The actual existence of profits, though, is not easily detected. Accounting profit, even allowing for a normal rate of profit, is not the same as economic profit. In addition, regulated firms have a definite incentive to adopt reporting techniques and accounting methods that conceal profits. This will make it difficult for a regulatory agency to identify and impose the price consistent with allocative efficiency.

COST SHIFTING.   When demand is sufficient, the owners of the regulated firm can expect the long-run rate of profit to be essentially fixed, regardless of whether efficient management reduces costs or inefficient management allows costs to increase. If costs decrease, the "fair return" rule imposed by the regulatory agency will force a price reduction; if costs increase, the same rule will allow a price increase. Thus, the owners of the regulated firm have less incentive to be concerned about costs than the owners of unregulated firms. Managers will have a freer hand to pursue personal objectives. They will be less likely to work overtime in searching for ways to cut costs, and more likely to fly first class, entertain lavishly on an expense account, give their relatives and friends good jobs, grant

---

[5]F. M. Scherer, *Industrial Market Structure and Economic Performance,* 2d ed. (Boston: Houghton Mifflin, 1980), p. 485.

unwarranted wage increases, and in general to make decisions that increase costs but yield personal benefits. Since monopoly means that buyers do not have a close substitute to turn to, consumers will bear the burden of managerial inefficiency. Normally, wasteful activities would be policed by the owners, but since the firm's rate of return is set by the regulatory agency, the owners have little incentive to be concerned.

Exhibit 20–11 demonstrates the impact of inefficient management. If the firm's costs were effectively policed by the owners and the forces of competition, average total cost ATC_1 would result. As the result of production inefficiency, however, per unit costs shift to ATC_2. A regulatory agency, granting the firm a fair return, would in this case allow a price increase to P_2. Even though P_2 might be less than the unregulated profit-maximizing monopolist would charge, some of the gains of the regulatory policy would be lost as the result of production inefficiency.

Alternatively, Exhibit 20–11 could represent a very different situation. Suppose that the firm's costs previously were ATC_2, but now ATC_1 has been attained due to the firm's innovative and efficient operation. In this case, ironically, if the rate adjustments by the regulatory agency come only after a delay, permitting the firm temporarily to continue charging P_2 despite the lower costs, then there is a beneficial incentive effect. The temporary ability to profit from increased efficiency is a spur to generating more efficiency. In the short run, consumers may have failed to gain immediately from the lower costs, but when innovation and increased efficiency are rewarded, even temporarily, cost-reducing innovation is encouraged. Regulatory lag is not always beneficial to the regulated firm, however. During inflationary times, the costs of labor, energy resources, and other factors of production rise, pushing up the cost of producing the product or service of

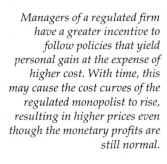

Managers of a regulated firm have a greater incentive to follow policies that yield personal gain at the expense of higher cost. With time, this may cause the cost curves of the regulated monopolist to rise, resulting in higher prices even though the monetary profits are still normal.

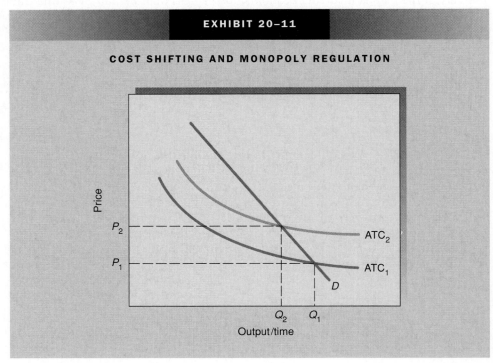

EXHIBIT 20–11

COST SHIFTING AND MONOPOLY REGULATION

the regulated firm. Regulatory lag in this case keeps prices below cost increases, reducing profits during periods of inflation.

QUALITY REGULATION. It is much easier to regulate product price than to regulate quality. Regulated firms desiring to raise the price of their product can often do so by taking cost-reducing steps that result in quality deterioration. Consider the quality dimension of a seemingly uniform good such as telephone service. The speed at which your call goes through, the likelihood that you will have to redial the desired number, how often your phone is out of order, and how quickly it gets repaired are included in the quality of telephone service. Since these factors are hard to control, it is extremely difficult for a regulatory agency to impose a price *per constant quality unit.* During inflationary times, regulated firms caught in a cost-regulated price squeeze may be particularly tempted to lower the quality of their product.

SPECIAL INTEREST EFFECT. The difficulties of government regulation discussed thus far are practical limitations that a regulatory agency, seeking to perform its duties efficiently, would confront. But, the special interest effect suggests that regulatory authorities cannot necessarily be expected to pursue only efficiency. Regulated firms have a strong incentive to see that "friendly," "reasonable" people serve as regulators, and they will invest political and economic resources to this end. Just as rent-seeking activities designed to gain monopoly privileges can be expected, so can activities to influence regulatory decisions.

What about consumer interests? Do you know who serves on the Interstate Commerce Commission or the public utility regulatory boards? Do you know any consumer who voted against a politician because of his or her appointments to a regulatory commission? Chances are that you do not. Consumer interests are widely dispersed and disorganized. Ordinarily, consumers cannot be expected to invest time, resources, votes, and political contributions to ensure that a particular regulatory commission represents their views. The firms that are regulated can, however, be expected to make such investments.[6] Even though the initial stimulus for a regulating agency might come from consumer interests, economic theory suggests that such agencies will eventually reflect the views of the business and labor interests they are supposed to regulate. The general public, then, may not be served well by regulation. In fact there is a good deal of evidence that the flaws of regulation often outweigh its potential benefits. (See the "Applications in Economics" boxed feature on the benefits of deregulation.)

THE GOVERNMENT-OPERATED FIRM

Government-operated firms—socialized firms such as the U.S. Postal Service, the Tennessee Valley Authority, and many local public utilities—present an alternative to both private monopoly and regulation. How do socialized firms operate in the real world? The decision makers of firms owned by the government are influenced by political and economic factors alike. With the rise of public-sector action, economists have recently expressed renewed interest in the socialized firm.

---

[6]The special interest effect will be weaker when regulatory commissions are elected rather than appointed, allowing the voter to separate this issue from other issues of greater importance.

APPLICATIONS IN ECONOMICS

BENEFITS OF DEREGULATION

How important are the flaws in government regulation of private firms that have some degree of monopoly power? Are consumers provided with lower prices and good quality when an industry is regulated, despite the imperfect nature of the regulatory process? One way to get some indication of the best answer to these questions is to see what happens when regulation is removed. How do prices and the quality of output respond? Are consumers helped or hurt?

During the late 1970s, the U.S. government began to lift controls on transportation. Two articles in the recently-published *Fortune Encyclopedia of Economics* describe the results of the deregulation of trucking and airlines.[1]

Before 1980 trucking was regulated by the Interstate Commerce Commission, which discouraged competition. Any trucker who wanted to carry goods on a route that was already served by a trucking firm had to obtain permission from the ICC, and the holder of that route could challenge the request. So, writes economist Thomas Gale Moore, it was almost impossible to enter a territory unless a company bought the rights from an existing carrier. And if it did, the authority might be extremely limited. Moore cites the example of a motor carrier who had the right to carry goods from Cleveland to Buffalo. If the firm bought the right to go from Buffalo to Pittsburgh, it had to carry goods from Cleveland through Buffalo, even though another route was quicker. The ICC also controlled the right to carry specific products, so sometimes a trucker carried a product from one city to another but had to return empty because it didn't have the authority to carry a different product back. Carriers also had to file their rates with the commission, and if the rate changes were challenged by another carrier, they were usually suspended.

In 1980 the Motor Carrier Act plus several deregulation-minded commissioners largely decontrolled trucking. The ICC eliminated most of the restrictions on routes and commodities and allowed truckers to make price changes (of up to 15 percent) without ICC permission.

Many new companies entered the business. By 1990 the number of licensed carriers was twice what it had been in 1980. Prices for truckload hauls fell by 25 percent between 1977 and 1982 (in real terms). Shippers reported that service had improved, and service to small communities increased. Complaints to the ICC went down dramatically.

The savings were larger than the direct price cuts. Today, because truckers offer flexible and reliable service, manufacturers don't have to keep such large inventories of production inputs on hand. Instead, the inputs can be delivered "just in time." A Department of Transportation study estimated that when all the savings from the deregulation of trucking are considered, they amount to between $38 and $56 billion per year.

Airline deregulation has shown similar results. Until 1978 the Civil Aeronautics Board controlled airline ticket prices and routes. This regulation largely kept the airlines from competing on the basis of price or scheduling, although airlines did compete on such things as the frequency of flights at popular times, and lack of crowding (the number of empty seats). Congress deregulated the airlines in 1978. Alfred Kahn (who was chairman of the Civil Aeronautics Board at the time of deregulation) writes that one result is lower passenger fares. He reports that they are between 10 and 18 percent lower (in real terms) than they would have been under regulation. This represents savings of $5 to $10 billion per year.

Most passengers have much greater choice now as well. For example, someone who wanted to travel between Boston and Phoenix in early 1992 had a choice of six airlines, compared with only two in 1977. By 1988 more than 55 percent of all passengers traveled on routes served by three or more competitors, compared with only 27 percent in 1979.

Kahn notes that deregulation brought an increase in congestion and delays, but that was partly because so many people were willing to put up with long lines and congestion to obtain lower prices. Governments continue to control the airports and have not allowed bidding for landing slots, or set landing fees in a way that allocates landing rights efficiently.

Airline deregulation did not reduce safety. Accident rates between 1979 and 1990 were 20 to

---

[1]Thomas Gale Moore, "Trucking Deregulation," and Alfred E. Kahn, "Airline Deregulation," in *The Fortune Encyclopedia of Economics*, edited by David R. Henderson (Warner Books, 1993), pp. 433–437, 379–384, respectively.

45 percent (depending on how they are measured) below their levels in the years before deregulation. This continues a decades-long increase in safety. Kahn points out that low airfares encourage people to travel by air, which is much safer than by car.

In both airlines and trucking, prices went down and service improved after the government stopped regulating. These examples suggest that government regulation does not necessarily serve the interests of the general public very well.

The ideal theoretical solution is straightforward. The socialized firm should (1) operate efficiently and (2) set price equal to marginal cost. When cost conditions are like those illustrated by Exhibit 20–6, the government-operated monopoly firm will ideally expand output to Q_i (where $P = MC$) and charge price P_1. The firm will make profits that can be channeled into the public treasury. On the other hand, marginal cost pricing may sometimes result in economic losses, requiring a subsidy for the government-operated firm. Exhibit 20–10 illustrates this possibility. Output should be expanded to Q_2 if the potential marginal welfare gains are to be fully realized. Price P_2 will be charged. The consumer's valuation of the marginal unit (P_2) will equal its marginal cost. Since losses result at this price and output, it will be necessary to subsidize the public enterprise.

This analysis assumes that the socialized firm will both operate efficiently and set the proper price. How realistic are these assumptions? The same "perverse" managerial incentives—incentives to ignore efficiency and pursue personal or professional objectives at the firm's expense—that regulated firms confront also tend to plague the government-operated firm. Professor John Kenneth Galbraith and others have pointed out that there is a principal-agent problem in private corporations. Poorly informed stockholders may be unable to police management inefficiency. Managers may pursue their own objectives at the expense of "owners."

The socialized firm, however, is the extreme case of this principal-agent problem. The "owners" (voters) are typically uninformed about how well a socialized firm is run, or how it might be run better. This is especially true when the firm has no direct competitors. As we indicated in Chapter 4, voters tend to be *rationally ignorant* about matters on which, as individuals, they have no decisive vote. This contrasts sharply with the position of an individual investor, who can personally "bail out" of ownership in a firm simply by selling stock holdings upon seeing trouble coming for the firm, or who can buy more stock upon seeing promising management initiatives. Each stockholder, having these options, has an incentive to monitor the firm (although some choose not to do so) and to act upon their observations by buying or selling stock. The resulting changes in stock prices instantly signal investor evaluations to managers and other observers.

Unlike investors in the private sector, no small group of voters normally is in a position to gain substantial wealth by taking over the socialized firm and improving its management. Even more than with monopoly in the private sector, customers of the socialized monopoly (voter-taxpayers) cannot easily switch their business or their investments to support other sellers. If the firm is subsidized, even those voter-taxpayers who do not consume the product will have to pay taxes to support the socialized firm. The end result is that when the government operates a business—particularly one with monopoly power—there is typically less consumer and investor scrutiny, less reward for efficiency, and less penalty for inefficiency. Higher costs result.

The ability of special interests to use public sector firms for private purposes also reduces the attractiveness of government-operated firms. The managers, employees, and specialized users of public enterprises often comprise special interest groups, particularly if the employees are well organized (for example, unionized) for political action. Should the wages of public-sector employees be raised and their working conditions improved? Should comfortable offices, lengthy coffee breaks, and lucrative fringe benefits be provided to employees? Should attractive positions in the public enterprise be provided to the politically faithful? Should management resist pressure to lay off unneeded workers (particularly at election time), abandon unprofitable service areas, and charge users low prices (that is, less than the marginal cost) when the opportunity cost of providing the service is high? On all these issues, the interests of special interest groups involved with public-sector production and its consumption will be in conflict with the interests of the disorganized, uninformed taxpayers. Under these circumstances, economic theory suggests that the views of the special interest groups will usually dominate, even when inefficiency and higher costs result.

Public enterprises can thus be expected to use at least some of their monopoly power, not to benefit the wide cross section of disorganized taxpayers and consumers, but as a cloak for inefficient operation and actions that advance the personal and political objectives of those who exercise control over the firm. Government ownership, like unregulated monopoly and government regulation, is a less than ideal solution. It is not especially surprising that those who denounce monopoly in, for instance, the telephone industry seldom point to a government-operated monopoly—such as the U.S. Post Office—as an example of how an industry should be run.[7]

POLICY IMPLICATIONS OF ANALYSIS OF MONOPOLY

The policy implications that can legitimately be drawn from an analysis of monopoly are more limited than they might initially seem to be. We may not like monopolistic power or its effects, but the alternatives are not terribly attractive. Monopoly power based on economies of scale poses a particularly troublesome problem. When average total costs decline with the size of firm, per unit costs will be minimized if a single firm produces the entire market output. However, if a monopolist is permitted to dominate the market, inefficiency will arise because a monopolist will restrict output and charge a price in excess of marginal cost. Since smaller firms have higher per unit costs, restructuring the industry to increase the

---

[7]For an analysis of potential cost savings in the case of the U.S. Postal Service, see *Privatization: Toward More Effective Government,* Report of the President's Commission on Privatization, (March 1988), chapter 7, pp. 101–128.

number of firms is an unappealing option. Neither is regulation an ideal situation. Since regulators do not possess the information necessary to impose an efficient outcome, and since the special interest effect indicates that regulators are susceptible to manipulation by the industrial interests, regulation is unlikely to achieve our hypothetical ideal-efficiency conditions. Finally, since public-sector managers are likely to pursue political objectives at the expense of economic efficiency, public ownership is also a less than ideal solution. Thus, economic theory indicates that there are no ideal solutions when natural monopoly is present. Choices must be made among alternatives, all of which are imperfect.

DYNAMIC CHANGE, MONOPOLY POWER, AND RESOURCE ALLOCATION

We have analyzed monopoly within a static framework and emphasized the lack of competition (sellers of alternative products) *within the industry.* No firm, though, is an island unto itself. Each firm competes with every other firm for the dollar votes of consumers. Dynamic change is present in the real world, and the expectation of monopoly profit may influence its speed. If a monopoly is profitable, rivals will seek to develop substitutes. Actual and potential substitutes exist for almost every product. With the passage of time, dynamic competition in the form of technological change and the development of new substitute products will threaten the position of firms with monopoly power. For example, the development of fax machines has reduced the monopoly power of the postal service.

In fact, high monopoly prices will encourage the development of substitutes. The high price of natural rubber spurred the development of synthetic rubber. High rail-shipping rates accelerated the development of long-distance trucking. The strong exercise of monopoly power by the Organization of Petroleum Exporting Countries (OPEC) subjected oil to vastly intensified competition from coal, solar energy, and other nonpetroleum energy sources, as well as from greatly expanded exploration efforts in non-OPEC nations. The result was a long tumble in the price OPEC could charge for its oil. What seemed to be a secure monopoly position for OPEC in the 1970s turned out to be something very different during the 1980s.

This dynamic competition from substitute products and suppliers, both actual and potential, is important for two reasons. First, a monopolist will sometimes choose to produce a larger output and charge a lower price—lower than the short-run profit-maximizing price—to discourage potential rivals from developing substitutes. When this happens, the allocative inefficiency associated with monopoly will be less than our static model implies. Second, the expectation of monopoly profits may spur product development. In fact, the patent system is based on this premise. (See the "Applications in Economics" boxed feature on product obsolescence.) When a new product or production method is patented, monopoly power is granted to the patent owner for a period of 17 years. Others are prohibited from copying the product or technique. If this "reward" of temporary monopoly power and profit did not exist, businesses would be less inclined to undertake research

APPLICATIONS IN ECONOMICS

PRODUCT OBSOLESCENCE, MONOPOLY POWER, AND THE DYNAMICS OF PRODUCT DEVELOPMENT

Many Americans believe that business firms can gain by producing shoddy merchandise that wears out quickly. It is often charged that business firms, over the objections of consumers, produce goods with a short life expectancy so they can sell replacements. Economists have sometimes been at the forefront of those deploring such planned obsolescence.

Yet, a solid majority of economists believe that price indexes overstate the measured rate of inflation because they fail to make an adequate allowance for actual observed improvements in product quality. Why has the quality of products, on the average, risen, if firms have an incentive to produce shoddy, non-durable goods?

SHOULD A CAR LAST A LIFETIME? When thinking about this question, it is important to keep three points in mind. First, the production of longer-lasting, higher-quality goods will increase costs. There are no free lunches. A car that lasts 15 years will be more expensive than one with a shorter life expectancy. We should expect consumers to trade off lower prices for more durability. At some point, the greater durability will not be worth the price.

Second, durability is only one facet of a product that is attractive to consumers. Product variation and the incorporation of new design features are also preferred by many people. For example, operational reliability aside, many consumers would prefer three differently styled, new-model cars lasting five years each to a single car of equal cost that lasts fifteen years. *Under these conditions,* the production of goods with less than the maximum available life expectancy is perfectly consistent with consumer tastes.

Third, goods engineered to last a relatively short time put their owners in a more adaptable position. For example, buyers of new American cars in 1971–1972 preferred large cars. At the time, this made good sense because gasoline prices were low and had been falling in real terms for many years. The value of large, gas-guzzling cars dropped sharply in 1974, though, as gasoline prices soared and spot shortages developed. Years later, in the mid-1980s, the reverse happened: gasoline prices fell sharply, and buyers found it economical to buy cars with more size, comfort, and safety. If those who bought large cars in 1971–1972 and small cars in the early 1980s had paid for years of extra durability, their losses (and the nation's) would have been greater. In a dynamic world, one decision every ten years is less flexible (and, if wrong, more costly to correct) than a decision every five years.

THE MONOPOLIST AND THE DURABILITY OF PRODUCTS Will a monopolist ever introduce a new, improved longer-lasting product, even if the new product is expected to drive the existing profitable product off the market? Strange as it may seem, a monopolist will introduce the new product if two conditions are met.

1. The product must be a genuine improvement—it must give the consumer more service per dollar of opportunity cost (to the monopolist) than the monopolist's current product.

2. The monopolist must be able to enforce property rights over gains from the new product. A patent preventing others from copying the innovative idea serves this purpose.

If these two conditions are met, the monopolist will be able to price the new product such that it will be profitable to introduce, even though it may eventually replace the monopolist's current product line. Two examples will help to clarify this point.

SUPER SHARP: THE BETTER BLADE Suppose Super Sharp Razor, Inc., has a monopoly on razor blades, which sell for 5 cents and give one week of comfortable shaves. Currently, Super Sharp makes a 3-cent profit (return above opportunity cost) on each blade. Assume the firm discovers (and quickly patents) a blade made with the same machines at the same cost but with a slightly different metal alloy.[1] It gives two

---

[1] If the blade requires new and different machines that render the firm's current machines obsolete, the firm will still introduce the product. It will do so, however, at a slower pace, because the cost associated with new machines is higher than the zero *opportunity cost* (assuming the old machines have no alternative use) of using existing machines. Phasing in the new product so that the existing machines may be more fully used could be a cheaper alternative for Super Sharp. If so, it will also be cheaper for society.

weeks of comfortable shaves instead of one. Will the firm market the new blade, even though it will lose one half of its weekly sales of blades? Yes! Customers will gladly pay up to 10 cents per blade for the new blades, which last twice as long. Instead of making 3 cents net profit per customer per week, the firm now will make up to 8 cents per customer every two weeks. Profits will rise. In fact, a price of 9 cents per blade will benefit the buyer *and* Super Sharp alike.

WOULD MONOPOLY OIL SELL THE MIRACLE CARBURETOR?

For years, it has been rumored that a much more efficient "miracle carburetor" for automobiles has been discovered, but that the big oil companies have plotted to keep it off the market because it would reduce their profits from the sale of gasoline.

Suppose an oil cartel, Monopoly Oil, sells all the oil and gasoline in the world. This hypothetical organization has also obtained the patent on a miracle carburetor. The real improvement is simply a little plastic gizmo that can be inserted into ordinary carburetors. The gizmo can be made in quantity for 1 cent each, and each gizmo lasts just long enough (one year, on average) to save its buyer 1,000 gallons of gas. If Monopoly Oil makes 5 cents per gallon economic profit on each gallon of gasoline, the sales lost *per gizmo* will cost the firm $50 per year. Will Monopoly Oil sell the gizmo? Of course! If gas sells for 95 cents per gallon (but the opportunity cost of crude oil, refining, and so on is only 90 cents), the cartel will *increase* its profit by selling the gizmo (cost 1 cent), which replaces 1,000 gallons of gasoline, as long as the price of the gizmo exceeds $50.01. The consumer would certainly pay far more than $50.01 to save 1,000 gallons of gas. Indeed, any price below $950 per gizmo would help the motorist.[2]

DO PATENTS HELP OR HURT THE CONSUMER?

A patent right is crucial, of course, to both of these examples. If firms could not at least partially capture the gains to be made from introducing a new product, they might prefer to keep it off the market and thereby prevent other firms from cutting into their profits by copying the new idea.

The patent system has a dual impact on the allocation of resources. First, the patent monopoly grants, as any monopoly does, the patent owner the ability (for a limited time) to keep the price of the patented item higher than costs of production warrant. Thus, *for patented inventions that have already been introduced*, consumers would be better off if competition replaced patent monopolies.

There is, however, a second effect. The fact that one can patent a new product or production process encourages the development of improved, lower-cost goods. Public policy in the United States allows temporary patent monopolies, which are costly to consumers in the short-run, in order to provide firms (and individuals) with a strong incentive to undertake the risk and effort involved in the development of technological improvements, which may lead to lower costs and greater efficiency in the long run.

---

[2]If the gizmo were invented by someone other than Monopoly Oil, the inventor would have an even stronger incentive to introduce the product. However, the introduction of the product *by someone else* would detract from the net profit of Monopoly Oil. The latter would have an incentive to suppress the product if possible. The cartel might attempt to use political power or extralegal methods to keep the product off the market. Of course, such actions would conflict with the efficient use of resources.

designed to reduce costs and improve product quality. Thus, even though some of these dynamic competitive forces will operate more slowly than when barriers to entry into an industry are low, the development of substitutes will nonetheless tend with the passage of time to erode the market power of a monopolist.

LOOKING AHEAD

Most markets do not fit neatly into either the pure competition or pure monopoly models. Many markets are characterized by low barriers to entry and competition on the basis of product quality, design, convenience of location, and producer reliability. Other markets involve a small number of rival firms, operating under widely varying entry conditions. In the next chapter, we will investigate market structures that lie between pure competition and monopoly.

CHAPTER SUMMARY

1. Pure monopoly is a market structure characterized by (a) high barriers to entry and (b) a single seller of a well-defined product for which there are no good substitutes. Pure monopoly is at the opposite end of the market-structure spectrum from pure competition.

2. Analysis of pure monopoly is important for two reasons. First, the monopoly model will help us understand the operation of markets dominated by a few firms. Second, in a few important industries, such as local telephone services and utilities, there is often only a single producer in a market area. The monopoly model will enhance our knowledge of these markets.

3. The four major barriers to entry into a market are government licensing, economies of scale, patents, and control of an essential resource.

4. The monopolist's demand curve is the market demand curve. It slopes downward to the right. The marginal revenue curve for a monopolist will lie inside the demand curve because of revenue losses from the lower price for units that could have been sold at a higher price.

5. For the elastic portion of a monopolist's demand curve, a lower price will increase total revenue. For the inelastic portion of the demand curve, a price reduction will cause total revenue to decline. A profit-maximizing monopolist will not operate on the inelastic portion of the demand curve because in that range it is always possible to increase total revenue by raising the price and producing fewer units.

6. A profit-maximizing monopolist will lower price and expand output as long as marginal revenue exceeds marginal cost. At the maximum-profit output, *MR* will equal *MC*. The monopolist will charge the price on its demand curve corresponding to that rate of sales.

7. If losses occur in the long run, a monopolist will go out of business. If profit results, high barriers to entry will shield a monopolist from competitive pressures. Therefore, *long-run* economic profits for a monopoly are sometimes possible.

8. Economists are critical of a monopoly because (a) it severely limits the options of consumers and their ability to discipline sellers; (b) the unregulated monopolist produces too little output and charges a price in excess of the marginal cost; (c) profits are less able to stimulate new entry, which would expand the supply of the product until price declined to the level of average production costs; and (d) legal monopoly encourages rent-seeking activity.

9. Under certain conditions, a monopolist will sell output at more than one price. Price discrimination reduces the degree to which a monopolist understocks the market. This practice allows the seller to convert some of the market's consumer surplus into revenue, and to profit by offering some units at lower prices.

10. Natural monopoly exists when long-run average total costs continue to decline as firm size increases (economies of scale). Thus, a larger firm always has lower costs. When natural monopoly is present, costs of production will be lowest when a single firm generates the entire output of the industry.

11. In the presence of natural monopoly, there are three policy alternatives: (a) private, unregulated monopoly; (b) private, regulated monopoly; and (c) government ownership. Economic theory suggests that each of the three will fail to meet our criteria for ideal efficiency. Private monopoly will result in higher prices and less output than would be ideal. Regulation will often fail to meet our ideal efficiency criteria because (a) the regulators will not have knowledge of the firm's cost curves and market demand conditions; (b) firms have an incentive to conceal their actual cost conditions and take profits in disguised forms; and (c) the regulators often end up being influenced by the firms they are supposed to regulate. Under public ownership, managers often derive personal gain from policies that conflict with cost control and cater to the views of special interest groups (for example, well-organized employees and specialized customers) who will be able to help them further their political objectives.

12. Even a monopolist is not completely free from competitive pressures. All products have some type of substitute. Monopolists who raise the price of their products provide encouragement for other firms to develop substitutes, which may eventually erode the market power of the monopolist. Some monopolists may charge less than the short-run, profit-maximizing price in order to discourage potential competitors from developing substitute products.

13. Monopoly profits derived from patents have two conflicting effects on resource allocation. Once a product or process has been discovered, the monopoly rights permit the firm to restrict output and raise price above the current marginal (and average) cost of production. However, the possibility of future monopoly rights granted by a patent

encourages entrepreneurs to improve products and develop lower-cost methods of production.

CRITICAL-ANALYSIS QUESTIONS

*1. "Barriers to entry are crucial to the existence of long-run profits, but they cannot guarantee the existence of profits." Evaluate this statement.

2. "Monopoly is good for producers but bad for consumers. The gains of the former offset the losses of the latter. On balance, there is no reason to think that monopoly is bad for the economy." Evaluate this statement.

*3. Do monopolists charge the highest prices for which they can sell their products? Do they maximize their average profit per sale? Are monopolistic firms always profitable? Why or why not?

4. The retail liquor industry is potentially a competitive industry. However, the liquor retailers of a southern state organized a trade association that sets prices for all firms. For all practical purposes, the trade association transformed a competitive industry into a monopoly. Compare the price and output policy for a purely competitive industry with the policy that would be established by a profit-maximizing monopolist or trade association. Who benefits and who is hurt by the formation of the monopoly?

5. Does economic theory indicate that a monopoly forced by an ideal regulatory agency to set prices according to either marginal or average cost would be more efficient than an unregulated monopoly? Explain. Does economic theory suggest that a regulatory agency will follow a proper regulation policy? What are some of the factors that complicate the regulatory function?

6. Is a monopolist subject to any competitive pressures? Explain. Would an unregulated monopolist have an incentive to operate and produce efficiently? If so, why?

*7. If a university has some monopoly power, explain why it would allocate more of its financial aid to students from low-income families than to those from richer families if it seeks to maximize revenue.

8. Explain why it is impossible to draw a supply curve for a monopolist.

*9. "The patent system provides a monopoly to the producer and raises consumer prices. It is inefficient." Evaluate this statement, giving economic arguments for and against it.

10. Which of the following are monopolists: (a) your local newspaper, (b) the Boston Celtics, (c) General Motors, (d) the U.S. Postal Service, (e) Michael Jackson, (f) the American Medical Association? Is the definition of an industry or market area important in the determination of a seller's monopoly position? Explain.

11. How can a firm, through rent-seeking activities, hope to "buy" monopoly profits? Is there competition for monopoly-seller positions? How does competition among rent seekers for monopoly profit influence the efficiency of resource allocation?

*12. Suppose that there is an increase in demand for a product such that a monopolist confronting a straight-line demand curve is able to sell a 10-percent-larger quantity at each price. If the product is produced at a constant marginal cost, will the increase in demand cause the monopolist to raise its price? Explain.

*13. In the midst of the sharply higher oil prices of the 1970s, it was often charged that (a) the big oil companies colluded and set prices as if they were a monopolist and (b) the higher prices of petroleum products failed to reduce consumption. Is there a conflict between these two propositions?

14. Once a manuscript is supplied to the publisher, the personal services of the author are a sunk cost. Generally, authors bear none of the production cost and are paid a percentage of total revenue. Given this arrangement, would authors generally prefer a lower sales price for the book than would their publishers? Explain.

*15. Historically, the real cost of transporting both goods and people has declined substantially. What impact does a reduction in transportation cost have on the monopoly power of producers? Do you think the U.S. economy is more or less competitive today than it was 100 years ago? Explain.

16. Is price discrimination harmful to the U.S. economy? How does price discrimination affect the gains from exchange? Why do firms often charge students, the elderly, or people with coupons different prices than others? Explain.

17. Adam Smith, writing before the importance of marginal costs and marginal revenues was discovered by economists, stated, "The price of monopoly is upon every occasion the highest which can be got." Explain why, taken literally, this would seldom be correct. When would it be true for a profit-maximizing seller?

*18. There is only one National Basketball Association team in Seattle—the Seattle Supersonics. Do the Supersonics have a monopoly in Seattle? A monopoly on what? Discuss.

19. When the Alcoa aluminum company was the only large aluminum producer in the United States for several decades prior to the Second World War, it was accused of monopolizing the industry by expanding output in anticipation of demand and by keeping prices so low that competitors had no chance to enter. If the accusation is true, how did Alcoa's monopoly affect the welfare of consumers?

*Asterisk denotes questions for which answers are given in Appendix C.

20. Why do the owners of theaters and sports teams often provide students, senior citizens, and the military with discount admission tickets, but they almost never provide these groups with discounts on food and drinks at the event?

*21. The Montana Stormers are the only professional baseball team within several hundred miles. The marginal cost of admitting a fan to a Stormer game is $2. Fixed costs, which include player salaries, are $200,000. The demand curve for tickets is given here. The quantity column gives this season's expected attendance.

TICKET PRICE	QUANTITY	REVENUES	MARGINAL REVENUE
$16	50,000	———	
			———
$14	75,000	———	
			———
$12	100,000	———	
			———
$10	125,000	———	
			———
$8	150,000	———	
			———
$6	175,000	———	
			———
$4	200,000	———	

a. Compute total and marginal revenues.
b. At what price and level of ticket sales will profits be maximized?
c. Compute the Stormers' cost and profits at this price.
d. Suppose that the players win the right to negotiate with any team, and the increase in salaries raises fixed costs to $300,000. What is the Stormers' profit-maximizing price and quantity, and how much profit does the team earn?

*22. The accompanying table contains data on the demand for snow tires in two towns, Muddville and Sunnyside. Sunnyside does not get much snow, and the demand for snow tires is quite elastic. Muddville is smaller and gets more snow than Sunnyside. Therefore, it is not surprising that the demand for snow tires in Muddville is less elastic than is the demand in Sunnyside. One firm is the only supplier providing snow tires to both towns. Its fixed costs are $2,000,000, and its marginal costs are constant at $10 a tire.

PRICE	QUANTITY DEMANDED SUNNYSIDE	MUDDVILLE	TOTAL DEMAND	TOTAL REVENUE	MARGINAL REVENUE
$45	7,000	37,000	44,000	———	
					———
$42	22,000	40,750	62,750	———	
					———

PRICE	QUANTITY DEMANDED SUNNYSIDE	MUDDVILLE	TOTAL DEMAND	TOTAL REVENUE	MARGINAL REVENUE
$39	37,000	44,500	81,500	———	
					———
$36	52,000	48,250	100,250	———	
					———
$33	67,000	52,000	119,000	———	
					———
$30	82,000	55,750	137,750	———	
					———
$27	97,000	59,500	156,500	———	
					———
$24	112,000	63,250	165,250	———	

a. Assume the tire supplier charges the same price for snow tires in both towns. Complete the table.
b. What is the supplier's profit-maximizing price and output level?
c. How much profit is being earned?
d. Now assume the supplier can charge different prices in the two towns, and thereby become a price discriminator. Complete the accompanying table.

	SUNNYVILLE		MUDDVILLE	
PRICE	TOTAL REVENUE	MARGINAL REVENUE	TOTAL REVENUE	MARGINAL REVENUE
$45	———		———	
		———		———
$42	———		———	
		———		———
$39	———		———	
		———		———
$36	———		———	
		———		———
$33	———		———	
		———		———
$30	———		———	
		———		———
$27	———		———	
		———		———
$24	———		———	

e. What is the profit-maximizing price and quantity of tires sold in Sunnyside?
f. What is the profit-maximizing price and quantity of tires sold in Muddville?
g. How much profit is the supplier earning now?
h. In which town did the supplier raise the price? In which town did it lower the price? Why should a monopolist (our tire supplier) charge a higher price in the town with the lower elasticity of demand? Explain?

CHAPTER TWENTY-ONE

BETWEEN COMPETITION AND MONOPOLY: MODELS OF RIVALRY AND STRATEGY

Differences in tastes, desires, incomes and locations of buyers, and differences in the uses which they wish to make of commodities all indicate the need for variety and the necessity of substituting for the concept of a "competitive ideal," an ideal involving both monopoly and competition.

EDWARD H. CHAMBERLIN[1]

There are many ways that companies can compete while making the market better for themselves and customers.

BARRY NALEBUFF[2]

CHAPTER FOCUS

■ *How do economists account for competitive advertising, price cutting, coupons for shoppers, and other rivalrous behavior by firms?*
■ *What is monopolistic competition, and how does it serve consumers?*
■ *What is oligopoly, and why have economists been unable to construct a general theory of oligopoly?*
■ *What is game theory, and how does it help us to understand decisions made by oligopolists?*
■ *What is the theory of contestable markets? What outcomes does it predict?*
■ *How competitive is the U.S. economy? Has its competitiveness changed in the past several decades?*
■ *How large are accounting profits? Have profit levels changed over the years? What would happen if accounting profits were eliminated?*

---

[1]Edward H. Chamberlin, *The Theory of Monopolistic Competition* (Cambridge: Harvard University Press, 1948), p. 214.

[2]Yale Professor Barry Nalebuff, quoted in "Businessman's Dilemma," interviewed by Rita Koselka, *Forbes*, October 11, 1993, p. 108.

T he models of pure competition and monopoly presented in the two previous chapters are extremely useful in predicting the pricing and output behavior of firms and how they react to changes in costs and changes in demand. But there is no room in those simplified models for the rivalrous behavior that we see every day in markets around us.

Consider the huge sums spent by Ford and Chevrolet, each advertising that its pickup trucks are best. This does not fit the monopoly model: a monopolist has no direct rivals. Although the firms clearly are competing, it also does not fit the model of pure competition: a pure competitor can sell any desired amount at the market price and is unable to raise that price by advertising. Or think about the weekly grocery store fliers and newspaper ads, with their "cents-off" coupons and special sale prices to bring in more customers. Once again, the actions of these competitors do not fit into either the pure competition or pure monopoly model.

Airlines wage "price wars" and use frequent-flier programs to gain customers and earn their loyalty. Producers of breakfast cereal advertise extensively, and some even give away prizes for children in their cereal boxes. Active rivalries among sellers are all around us.

How do economists explain these activities within the context of the economic way of thinking? How are the pricing policies and the profits of rivalrous firms determined in markets with advertising, price wars, and other practices that are costly to the firms? To answer these questions we turn now to some different models of the firm—models in which the firm has rivals and must predict how those rivals will react to alternative pricing, output, and product-quality decisions it is considering.

We will look at models of the firm operating in markets that are competitive, but in which each firm can charge higher prices without losing all its customers and must lower its price if it is to sell a larger quantity. These markets are between competition and monopoly, sharing some of the characteristics of each and having the added factor of active rivalry among the firms.

Before moving on, we pause to note that the models assume that decision makers have perfect knowledge of their costs and demand conditions. Real-world firms do not have such information. Entrepreneurs must rely on past experience, market surveys, experimentation, and other business skills when they make price, output, and production decisions. (See the "Applications in Economics" feature on entrepreneurship.) The models describe the decisions facing these business decision makers once they have exercised their judgment and have made the interrelated decisions regarding product characteristics, cost estimates, and demand conditions associated with those characteristics.

Market structure
The classification of a market with regard to key characteristics, including the number of sellers, entry barriers into the market, the control of firms over price, and type of products (homogeneous or differentiated) in the market.

Monopolistic competition
A situation in which there are a large number of independent sellers, each producing a differentiated product in a market with low barriers to entry. Construction, retail sales, and service stations are good examples of monopolistically competitive industries.

DIFFERENT TYPES OF MARKET STRUCTURE

Differences in **market structure** allow us to classify the degree of competition among sellers in each market. Competitiveness in a market is influenced by the number of sellers, by whether similar products are available from alternative firms, and by the existence of barriers to entry and exit. Competitiveness is also correlated with the firm's degree of control over price.

APPLICATIONS IN ECONOMICS

THE LEFT-OUT VARIABLE: ENTREPRENEURSHIP

To help us understand facts and make predictions, a scientific model must simplify what it describes, and draw attention to the most important relationships. Economic models are no exception. Our model of decision making in business firms is designed to highlight for us the decision-making elements common to all firms, and it performs this job quite well. But it leaves out some important steps in the decision-making process of real-world firms. Typically, a great many judgments are needed before the process we describe can even begin.

Would profits increase if prices were raised, or would lower prices lead to larger profits? Real-world decision makers cannot go into the back room and look at their demand-cost diagram to answer these questions. They must search for clues, experiment with actual price changes, and interpret what they see, often using a great deal of "seat-of-the-pants" judgment. The successful entrepreneur will search and find (or at least approximate) the profit-maximizing price—the $MR = MC$ price and output combination that our model identifies so easily.

For real-world entrepreneurs, the problem of uncertainty goes well beyond setting the profit-maximizing price and output. How can an entrepreneur decide whether demand and cost conditions will make entry into a monopolistically competitive field profitable? How large should the plant be? How should production be organized? How much variety, and what combination of qualities should be built into the firm's product or service? What location will be best? What forms of advertising will be most effective? These questions and many more require entrepreneurial judgment. Entrepreneurial judgment is necessary when there is no decision rule that can be applied using only information that is freely available. For this reason, the entrepreneurial function has not been put into economic

models. There simply is no way to model such judgmental decisions. All we can do is note their importance and recognize that our models are limited by the fact that they are missing this critical element of successful business decision making.

THE ENTREPRENEUR: A JOB DESCRIPTION

If we cannot put entrepreneurship into our models, what can we say about its function? One way to answer this question is to consider a generalized job description for an entrepreneurial position. An investor who lacks the desire, or perhaps the skill, to be an entrepreneur, but nonetheless wants to be in business, may well seek someone to act as the business entrepreneur, while the investor provides some of the capital. A newspaper ad to find such a person (while perhaps not the usual way for the investor to search) might read as follows:

Wanted: Entrepreneur. *Must have many qualities: (1) Alert to new business opportunities and to new problems before they become obvious. (2) Willing to back judgments with investments of hard work and creative effort before others recognize correctness of judgments. (3) Able to make correct decisions and to convince others of their validity so as to attract additional financial backing. (4) Able to recognize own inevitable mistakes and to back away from incorrect decisions without wasting additional resources. Exciting, exhausting, high-risk position. Pay will be very good for success, and very poor for failure.*

Entrepreneurship is not for the fainthearted or the lazy. Entrepreneurs are at the center of the action in the real world, even if they do not have a place in most economic models.

Note: For a more complete overview of entrepreneurship, and references on the topic, see Mark Crosson, "Entrepreneurship" in *The New Palgrave: a Dictionary of Economics,* edited by John Eatwell, et al. (New York: Stockton Press, 1987), pp. 151–153.

Market conditions that approximate the models of pure competition and pure monopoly are the exception rather than the rule in the real world. Most real-world firms are better described by one of the two additional forms of market structure used by economists to describe and analyze the behavior of firms when rivalry is present. The first is called **monopolistic competition.** It pertains to a market with many sellers, in which no small group of firms dominates the market. The second is **oligopoly,** and it applies when the market is dominated by a few sellers.

Oligopoly
A market situation in which a small number of sellers comprise the entire industry. Oligopoly is competition among the few.

The four types of market structure, ranging from pure competition to monopoly, are listed in **Exhibit 21–1,** along with their market structure characteristics. They form a continuum from left to right, from market types that are more competitive to those that are less competitive. In general, the closer a market is to the purely competitive end, the more efficiently it will operate, and the better off consumers will be. Toward that end of the competitive spectrum, more substitutes are available for consumers, firms' demand curves are more elastic, and firms are closer to selling and producing at marginal costs. In addition, profits are more likely to result in the entry of firms and/or an increase in quantity supplied by existing firms, while losses generally lead to the exit of firms and a reduction in production.

The market-structure characteristics listed in Exhibit 21–1 suggest that monopolistically competitive and oligopolistic firms have different degrees of freedom in setting prices, altering quality, and choosing a marketing strategy than do firms in purely competitive or purely monopolistic markets. Most firms, unlike those under purely competitive conditions, will lose some *but not all* of their customers when they increase the price of their product. These firms face a downward-sloping demand curve. Like monopolists, they are price searchers: they must search for the price most consistent with their overall goal—maximum profit, for example. In contrast to the case of pure monopoly, however, the existence

---

EXHIBIT 21–1

MODELS OF MARKET STRUCTURE

MORE COMPETITIVE ⟵———————————————————————————⟶ LESS COMPETITIVE

	PURE COMPETITION	MONOPOLISTIC COMPETITION	OLIGOPOLY	MONOPOLY
NUMBER OF SELLERS	Many	Many	Few	One
PRODUCTS IN MARKET	Identical	Differentiated	Identical or differentiated	No close substitutes
BARRIERS TO ENTRY	None	No legal or scale barriers	Economies of scale	Economies of scale or legal barriers
FIRM'S CONTROL OVER PRICE	None	Some	Considerable	Considerable, if not regulated
EXAMPLES	Wheat, corn	Retail food; clothing; home construction	Automobiles, breakfast cereals	Local phone service; electric and gas utilities

These four market structures form a continuum from most competitive, on the left, to least competitive, on the right. In general, the closer a market is to the competitive end, the better the consumers will be served.

of actual and potential competitors offering similar products substantially limits the ability of most price searchers to raise their prices.

The major difference between the two models of rivalrous competition is the number of firms in the market. Under monopolistic competition, each seller confronts many rivals. In contrast, there are only a few rivals in an oligopolistic market. This variation in the number of rivals results in two important differences between monopolistic competition and oligopoly. First, monopolistic competitors generally are more limited than oligopolists in their ability to raise price. There are lots of firms producing good substitutes for the product or service of a monopolistic competitor. Thus, if the firm increases its price very much, sales will decline sharply. Put another way, the demand curve confronting a monopolistic competitor is generally quite elastic.

Second, since all have many rivals, economists assume that each monopolistic competitor reacts to general conditions in the market rather than to the actions of any specific firm. In contrast, oligopolistic firms face only a few rivals and therefore are expected to think strategically about how those rivals will react to any change in product price, quality, or location. There is little chance that oligopolistic rivals will fail to notice any significant action among their small number attempting to lure customers away from one another.

Both of these models can incorporate the competitive advertising, product differentiation, and other rivalrous behavior that neither pure competition nor monopoly models can explain. We turn now to a discussion of how the models have been developed and how they work.

CHARACTERISTICS OF MONOPOLISTIC COMPETITION

Markets such as retail sales, construction, service businesses, and small manufacturing are generally characterized by numerous firms offering different but closely related products or services. The need for a model that was more descriptive of markets like these led to the theory of monopolistic competition. The theory was developed independently by Joan Robinson, a British economist, and Edward Chamberlin, an American economist. The major works of Robinson and Chamberlin were both published in 1933.[3] These economists outlined three distinguishing characteristics of monopolistic competition: product differentiation, low barriers to entry, and the existence of many independent firms.

PRODUCT DIFFERENTIATION

Monopolistic competitors offer **differentiated products** to consumers. Goods and services of one seller are differentiated from those of another by convenience of

Differentiated products
Products distinguished from similar products by such characteristics as quality, design, location, and method of promotion.

---

[3]See Joan Robinson, *The Economics of Imperfect Competition*, 1933, reprint (New York: St. Martin's, 1969); and Edward H. Chamberlin, *The Theory of Monopolistic Competition* (Cambridge: Harvard University Press, 1933).

location, product quality, reputation of the seller, advertising, and various other product characteristics. How a seller competes with rivals in each of these areas is critical to the success of the firm. Such decisions are among the most important to be made by entrepreneurial rivals.

Since the product of each monopolistic competitor is slightly different from that of its rivals, the individual firm faces a downward-sloping demand curve. A price reduction will enable the firm to attract new customers. Alternatively, the firm will be able to increase its price by a small amount and still retain many of its customers, who prefer the location, style, dependability, or other product characteristics offered by the firm. The demand curve confronted by the monopolistic competitor is highly elastic, however. Even though each firm has some control over price, that control is extremely limited, since the firm faces competition from rivals offering very similar products. The availability of close substitutes and the ease with which consumers can turn to rival firms (including new firms that are free to enter the market) force a monopolistically competitive firm to think twice before raising its price.

LOW BARRIERS TO ENTRY

Under monopolistic competition, firms are free to enter into or exit from the market. There are neither legal barriers nor market obstacles hindering such movement. Monopolistic competition resembles pure competition in this respect, and firms in both these types of markets confront the constant threat of competition from new, innovative rivals.

MANY INDEPENDENT FIRMS

A monopolistic competitor faces not only the potential threat posed by new rivals, but competition from many current sellers as well. Each firm is small relative to the total market. No single firm or small group of firms is able to dominate the market.

Retailing is perhaps the sector of our economy that best typifies monopolistic competition. In most market areas, there is a large number of retail stores offering similar products and services. Rivalry is intense, and stores are constantly trying new combinations of price and quality of service (or merchandise) to win customers. The free entry that typifies most retailing makes for rapid change.

OUTSTANDING ECONOMIST

JOAN ROBINSON (1903–1983)

Along with Edward Chamberlin, Joan Robinson is given credit for developing the theory of monopolistic competition. Her other works in economics include the subjects of capital theory, international trade, Marxian economics, and growth theory.

Yesterday's novelty can quickly become obsolete as new rivals develop still better (or more attractive) products and marketing methods.

PRICE AND OUTPUT UNDER MONOPOLISTIC COMPETITION

How does a monopolistic competitor decide what price to charge and what level of output to produce? Like a pure monopolist, a monopolistic competitor will face a downward-sloping demand curve for its product. Additional units can be sold only at a lower price. Therefore, the marginal-revenue curve of the monopolistic competitor will always lie below the firm's demand curve.

Any firm can increase profits by expanding output as long as marginal revenue exceeds marginal cost. Therefore, a monopolistic competitor will lower its prices and expand its output until marginal revenue is equal to marginal cost.

Exhibit 21–2 illustrates the profit-maximizing price and output under monopolistic competition. A profit-maximizing monopolistic competitor will expand output to q, where marginal revenue is equal to marginal cost and price P can be charged. Beyond q, to sell more output would require a reduction in price so large that profit would be reduced. For any output level less than q (for example, R), a price reduction and sales expansion will add more to total revenues than to total costs. At output R, marginal revenues exceed marginal costs. Thus, profits will be greater if price is reduced so output can be expanded. On the other hand, if output exceeds q (for example, S), sale of additional units beyond q will *add* more to costs

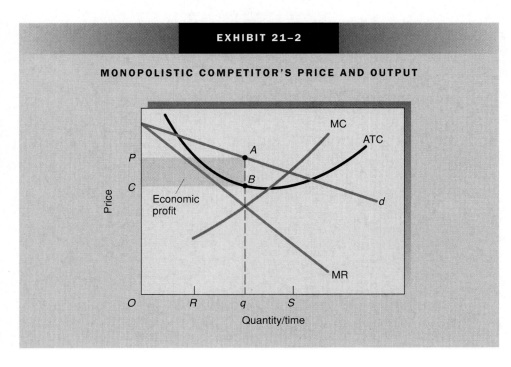

EXHIBIT 21–2

MONOPOLISTIC COMPETITOR'S PRICE AND OUTPUT

A monopolistic competitor maximizes profits by producing output q, for which MR = MC, and charging price P. The firm is making economic profits. What impact will they have if this is a typical firm?

(MC) than to revenues (MR). The firm will therefore gain by raising the price to P, even though the price rise will result in the loss of customers. Profits will be maximized by charging price P and producing the output level q, where MC = MR. At this stage, the analysis resembles that for a monopolist. Under monopolistic competition, however, there are no barriers to entry or exit. Therefore in contrast with monopoly, the number of firms in the market will respond to changes in profitability.

The firm pictured by Exhibit 21–2 is making economic profit. Total revenues, PAqO, exceed the firm's total costs, CBqO, at the profit-maximizing output level. Since barriers to entry in monopolistically competitive markets are low, profits will attract rival competitors. If this is a typical firm, other firms will attempt to duplicate the product (or service) offered by the profit-making firms.

What impact will the entry of new rivals have on the demand for the products of profit-making firms already in the market? These new rivals will draw customers away from existing firms. As long as monopolistically competitive firms can make economic profits, new competitors will be attracted to the market. This pressure will continue until the competition among rivals has shifted the demand curve for monopolistic competitors inward far enough to eliminate economic profits. In the long run, as illustrated by **Exhibit 21–3,** a monopolistically competitive firm will just be able to cover its production costs. It will produce to the MR = MC output level, but for the typical firm, the entry of new competitors will force the price down to the average per unit cost.

If losses exist in a monopolistically competitive industry, some of the existing firms in the industry will go out of business over a period of time. The failure of one firm releases resources for use by others. (See the "Applications in Economics"

Since entry and exit are free, competition will eventually drive prices down to the level of average total cost for the representative monopolistically competitive firm.

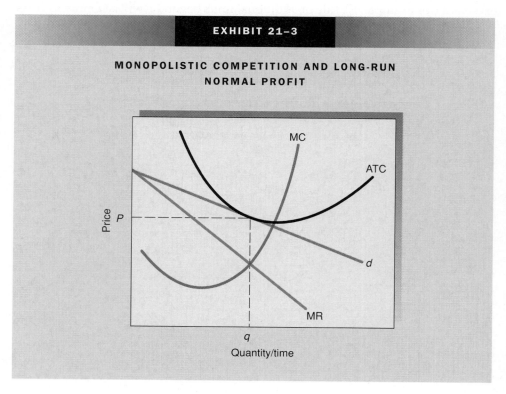

EXHIBIT 21–3

MONOPOLISTIC COMPETITION AND LONG-RUN NORMAL PROFIT

feature on the benefits of failure.) As firms leave the industry, some of their previous customers will buy from other firms. The demand curve facing the remaining firms in the industry will shift outward until the economic losses are eliminated and the long-run, zero-profit equilibrium illustrated by Exhibit 21–3 is again restored.

Under monopolistic competition, profits and losses play basically the same role as they do under pure competition. Economic profits will attract new competitors to the market. The increased availability of the product (and similar products) will drive the price down until the profits are eliminated. Conversely,

APPLICATIONS IN ECONOMICS

BENEFITS OF FAILURE IN THE MARKET

The presence of business failure is the consequence of decisions made under uncertainty, and of innovation. New techniques, new designs, new products, and even new locations are risky because entrepreneurs cannot be sure what consumer reaction will be. Many new businesses fail. But those that succeed bring about the improved quality, the price reductions, and the increased product availability that are the core ingredients of economic progress. Each success, however, means failure elsewhere as buyers switch their purchases and resources are bid away from established businesses. So economic progress brings not only business success, but also business failure.

Economists Dwight Lee and Richard McKenzie[1] point out that in a progressive market economy, business failure is inevitable. More than that, they say, business failure is a blessing in disguise. Losses—and bankruptcy in extreme cases—provide both the information and the incentives to move resources to more highly valued, more productive uses. However, failure, or at least the negative consequences of failure for those involved, can always be delayed or reduced by a government that is willing to take enough income from successful enterprises and their employees and use it to subsidize failed efforts. There is constant political pressure for government to do just that for those facing difficult circumstances when the firm that they own, or work for, has failed to earn enough revenue to cover its costs. It is compassionate, after all, to want to help those in financial trouble.

Lee and McKenzie point out, though, that because it is the new, low-cost and highly productive enterprises that force the failure of less efficient firms, government support for a firm using highly valued resources to produce less highly valued output promotes wasteful activity. The resources have higher alternative uses elsewhere. The failure of an inefficient firm provides its employees and other suppliers with the signal and the incentive to search for the higher-valued uses for their resources, including their talents.

Using tariffs or other laws to prevent buyers from switching to low-cost suppliers, or having government purchase high-cost output (as in the case of some farm commodities purchased for storage or destruction), deadens the market signal, allowing firms and resource owners to ignore it. Resources continue then to be wasted in low-valued uses. Even providing assistance to workers who have become unemployed has its negative consequences. If the assistance is in amounts sufficient to reduce workers' eagerness to seek alternative employment, the result is that they are unavailable to the firms that need them.

Only when inefficient, high-cost businesses are allowed to fail, and workers and other resource owners feel the lack of income (relative to market opportunities) pushing them to seek alternative employment, are the customers, workers, and capital of resource-wasting firms made available to more efficient, low-cost producers. And only when the more efficient enterprises gain the resources and the business, will the economy produce more at a lower cost. Then the economy can conserve resources by using them wisely in production, thus allowing all participants in the economy, rich and poor, to buy the better and cheaper goods and services that are the mark of economic progress.

[1]Dwight R. Lee and Richard B. McKenzie, *Failure and Progress: The Bright Side of the Dismal Science* (Washington: Cato Institute, 1993).

economic losses will induce competitors to exit from the market. The decline in the availability of the product (supply) will allow the price to rise until firms are once again able to cover their average total cost.

In the short run, a monopolistic competitor may make either economic profits or losses, depending on market conditions. In the long run, however, only a normal profit rate (that is, zero economic profits) will be possible because of competitive conditions and freedom of entry.

As we use the model of monopolistic competition, it is important to keep in mind that like all models, it is a simplification of the real world. The market process is more complex. Entrepreneurs in a monopolistically competitive situation recognize that, since each firm is producing a slightly different product, which is sold in a slightly different market, losses for one firm do not necessarily mean losses for another, which might well succeed using a slightly different strategy. Similarly, just because some of the firms in a market have discovered a successful combination of product, service, location, marketing, and operational efficiency, there is no guarantee that others will be able to do so. The restaurant business in most cities illustrates this point. While some restauranteurs are operating successfully and earning economic profit, there are always others closing their doors.

Competition is an ongoing, dynamic process. Entrepreneurs who are good at discovering and producing things consumers value highly relative to their cost will prosper. Those who are not, will fail, releasing resources for use by other producers. Therefore, while we often focus on what is happening to the typical firm under monopolistic competition, it is important to recognize that there is an ongoing competitive process at work. Thus, the experience of a specific market participant may differ from that of the typical firm in the market.

COMPARING PURE AND MONOPOLISTIC COMPETITION

As you can see, determination of price and output under monopolistic competition is in some ways very similar to that under pure competition. Also, since the long-run equilibrium conditions under pure competition are consistent with ideal economic efficiency, it is useful to compare and contrast this market structure with that of monopolistic competition. There are both similarities and differences between the two structures.

SIMILARITIES BETWEEN PURE AND MONOPOLISTIC COMPETITION

Since barriers to entry are low, neither pure nor monopolistic competitors will be able to earn long-run economic profit. In the long run, competition will drive the price of both pure and monopolistic competitors down to the level of average total cost.

In each case, entrepreneurs have a strong incentive to manage and operate their businesses efficiently. Inefficient operation will lead to losses and forced exit from the market. Pure and monopolistic competitors alike will be motivated to develop and adopt new cost-reducing procedures and techniques because lower costs will mean higher short-run profits (or at least smaller losses).

The response of pure and monopolistic competitors to changing demand conditions is very similar. In both cases, an increase in market demand leads to higher prices, short-run profits, and the entry of additional firms. With the entry of new producers, and the concurrent expansion of existing firms, the market supply will increase, lowering the demand facing each firm. The process will continue until the market price falls to the level of average total cost, squeezing out all economic profit. Similarly, a reduction in demand will lead to lower prices and short-run losses, causing output to fall and some firms to exit. With time, this will permit the remaining firms to increase their prices until eventually the short-run losses are eliminated. Profits and losses will direct the activities of firms under both pure and monopolistic competition.

DIFFERENCES BETWEEN PURE AND MONOPOLISTIC COMPETITION

As **Exhibit 21–4** illustrates, the pure competitor confronts a horizontal demand curve, while the demand curve faced by a monopolistic competitor is downward-sloping. This is important because it means that the marginal revenue of the monopolistic competitor will be less than, rather than equal to, price. So when the profit-maximizing monopolistic competitor expands output until $MR = MC$, price will still exceed marginal cost (part "b" of Exhibit 21–4). In contrast, in long-run equilibrium, the price charged by the pure competitor will equal marginal cost (part "a"). In contrast with pure competition, when long-run equilibrium (zero economic profit) is present in a monopolisitcally competitive market, the firms

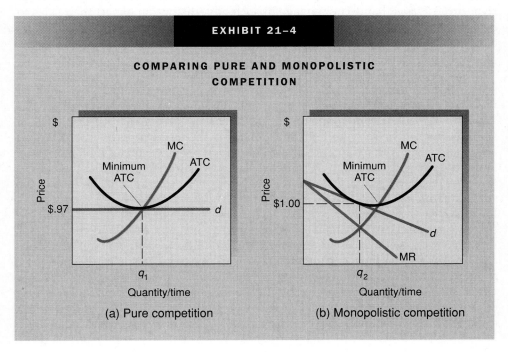

EXHIBIT 21–4

COMPARING PURE AND MONOPOLISTIC COMPETITION

(a) Pure competition

(b) Monopolistic competition

The long-run equilibrium conditions of firms under pure and monopolistic competition are illustrated here. In both cases, price is equal to average total cost, and economic profit is absent. However, since the monopolistically competitive firm confronts a downward-sloping demand curve for its product, its equilibrium price exceeds marginal cost, and equilibrium output is not large enough to minimize average total cost. For identical cost conditions, the price of the monopolistic competitor will be slightly higher than that of the pure competitor. Edward H. Chamberlin referred to this slightly higher price as the premium a society pays for variety and convenience (product differentiation).

will fail to minimize their long-run average total cost. As Exhibit 21–4 illustrates, the monopolistic competitor would have a lower per unit cost (97 cents rather than $1) if a larger output were produced.

ALLOCATIVE EFFICIENCY UNDER MONOPOLISTIC COMPETITION

The efficiency of monopolistic competition has been the subject of debate among economists for many years. At one time, the dominant view seemed to be that allocative inefficiency results because monopolistic competitors fail to operate at an output level that minimizes their long-run average total cost. Due to the proliferation in the number of monopolistic competitors, the sales of each competitor fall short of the firm's least-cost capacity level. The potential social gain associated with the expansion of production to the $P = MC$ output rate is lost. The advocates of this view point out that if there were fewer producers, they would each be able to operate at a minimum-cost output rate. Instead, there is costly duplication—too many producers each operating below their minimum-cost output capacity. According to this traditional view, the location of two or more filling stations, restaurants, grocery stores, or similar establishments side by side is indicative of the economic waste generated by monopolistic competition.

In addition, the critics of monopolistic competition argue that it often leads to self-defeating, wasteful advertising. Firms have an incentive to use advertising to promote artificial distinctions between similar products. Each firm bombards consumers with advertisements proclaiming (or implying) that its own product is fancier, has greater sex appeal, and/or brings quicker relief than the products of rival firms. Firms that do not engage in such advertising can expect their sales to decline. Advertising, though, results in higher prices for consumers and thus is costly from society's point of view.

In recent years, this traditional view has been seriously challenged. Most economists now believe that such a view is mechanistic and fails to take into account the significance of dynamic competition. Most important, the traditional view assumes that consumers place no value on the wider variety of qualities and styles that results from monopolistic competition. Prices might very well be slightly lower if there were fewer gasoline stations, if they were located farther apart, and if they offered a more limited variety of service and credit plan options. Similarly, the prices of groceries might very well be slightly lower if there were fewer supermarkets, each a bit more congested and located less conveniently for some customers. However, since customers value product diversity as well as lower prices, they might be better off under the conditions created by monopolistic competition. Edward Chamberlin, one of the developers of the theory, argues that higher prices (and costs) are simply the premium consumers pay for variety and convenience. When consumers receive utility from product diversity, one cannot conclude that pure competition with a lower price, but less variety from which to select, would be preferable to monopolistic competition. The fact that consumers willingly pay more for a variety of products, rather than all flocking to a single, cheaper version of the product, suggests that many prefer the variety.

The defenders of monopolistic competition also deny that this leads to excessive, wasteful advertising. They point out that advertising often reduces the consumer's search time and provides valuable information on prices. If advertising really raises prices, it must also provide the consumer with something valuable. Otherwise, the consumer would purchase lower-priced, non-advertised goods. When consumers prefer lower prices and less advertising, firms offering that combination do quite well. In fact, proponents argue that real-world monopolistic competitors often use higher quality service and lower prices to compete with rivals who advertise heavily.

The debate among economists has helped clarify this topic's issues. Nevertheless, for some observers the efficiency of monopolistic competition continues to be an unresolved issue.

REAL-WORLD MONOPOLISTIC COMPETITORS

Despite the high hopes of entrepreneurs, many firms go out of business every year. In recent years, among corporate establishments alone, the number of firms going out of business has generally exceeded 250,000 annually. A great many unsuccessful businesses are small, monopolistically competitive firms that are the victims of losses stemming from market competition.

Why do losses occur in the real world? Business decisions must be made under a great deal of uncertainty, and mistakes sometimes result. Losses are the market's method of bringing such activities to a halt. They signal that the resources would be valued more highly if they were put to other uses. The fact that losses reduce the wealth of firms' owners also provides the incentive to correct this allocative inefficiency. As the "Applications in Economics" feature on market failure illustrates, the role played by economic losses in a market economy is extremely valuable.

CHARACTERISTICS OF OLIGOPOLY

"Oligopoly" means "few sellers." So when there are only a few firms in an industry, the industrial structure is called an oligopoly. In the United States, the great majority of output in such industries as automobiles, steel, cigarettes, and aircraft is produced by five or fewer dominant firms. In addition to a small number of producers, there are several other characteristics that oligopolistic industries have in common: interdependence among firms, substantial economies of scale, significant barriers to entry, and existence of both homogeneous and differentiated products.

INTERDEPENDENCE AMONG FIRMS

Since the number of sellers in an oligopolistic industry is small, each firm must take the potential reactions of rivals into account when it makes business

MYTHS OF ECONOMICS

"THE PRICES OF MOST GOODS ARE UNNECESSARILY INFLATED BY AT LEAST 25 PERCENT AS A RESULT OF THE HIGH PROFIT RATE OF PRODUCERS."

Profits are about as popular with consumers as failing grades are with students at the end of a term. When food prices rise, the profits of farmers, meat processors, and food store chains are heavily publicized by the news media. If gasoline prices jump, many people believe that they are being pushed up by greedy profiteering on the part of the major oil companies. The casual observer might easily be left with the impression that large profits are the major source of the high cost of living.

This issue is clouded by the fact that both the size of profits and their function are largely misunderstood by most people. Surveys show that young people believe the after-tax profits of corporations comprise between 25 and 30 percent of sales. A national sample poll of adults conducted by Opinion Research of Princeton found that the average person thought profits comprised 29 cents of every dollar of sales in manufacturing. In reality, as the accompanying exhibit shows, the after-tax accounting profits of manufacturing corporations are about 4 to 5 percent of sales. The public believes that the rate of profit as a percentage of sales is nearly six times as great as the actual figure!

Why are people so misinformed on this issue? The popular media are one source of confusion. They

HOW GREAT ARE PROFITS?

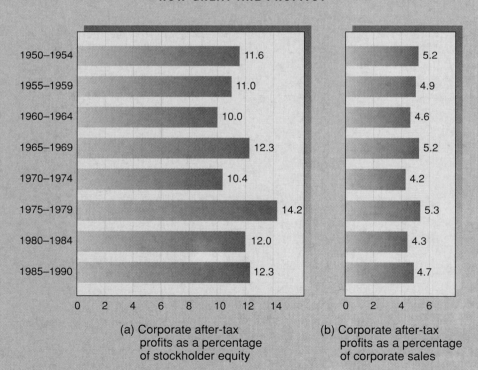

(a) Corporate after-tax profits as a percentage of stockholder equity

(b) Corporate after-tax profits as a percentage of corporate sales

After-tax corporate profits average about 12 percent of stockholder equity and 5 percent of sales in the United States.

Source: *Economic Report of the President, 1991.* As the result of changes in definitions and accounting procedures, the data for one period may not be perfectly comzparable to the figures for other periods. Such changes in 1992 make comparisons with 1991–1993 especially difficult.

nearly always report the accounting profits of firms in dollar terms, instead of comparing them to sales, stockholder equity, or the value of the firms' assets. A favorite device is to report that profits, either annually or quarterly, were up by some astonishing percentage.[1] Unless we know whether profits were high, normal, or low during the previous period, this type of statement tells little or nothing about the firm's earnings rate on its capital assets. For example, suppose a corporation with $100 million of assets earned a profit of $2 million last year, a 2 percent rate of return on its capital assets. Now, suppose the firm's earnings this year are $4 million, generating only a 4 percent rate of return. It would not be unusual for the popular media to report, "The profits of corporation X soared to $4 million, a 100 percent increase over last year." What this statement conceals is that the profits of the firm as a percentage of its capital assets were less than one could earn on a savings account.

Not only is the average person misinformed about the size of profits, but most people do not understand their function. Many believe that if profits were eliminated, our economy would continue to operate as if nothing had happened. This erroneous view indicates a misunderstanding of what accounting profits are. Accounting profits are primarily a monetary return to those who have invested in machines, buildings, and nonhuman productive resources. Investment in physical capital involves both risk and the forgoing of

current consumption. If profits were eliminated, the incentive of persons to invest and provide the tools that make the American worker the most productive in the world would be destroyed. Who would invest in either physical or human capital (for example, education) if such investments did not lead to an increase in future income—that is, if investment did not lead to accounting profit?

Profits play an important role in our economy. People who increase the value of resources—who produce something that is worth more than the resources that went into it—are rewarded with economic profit (and generally an above average accounting profit). Those who allocate resources to a venture producing outputs that consumers value less than the venture's opportunity cost will experience economic losses (below average accounting profits). Without this reward-penalty system, individuals (and firms) would have neither the information nor the incentives to use resources wisely and produce the goods that consumers desire most, relative to their opportunity costs.

---

[1]This is equally true for large wage increases. Apparently, the extreme example rather than the norm helps to sell newspapers. We should note that such reports do not imply an antibusiness bias. *The Wall Street Journal*, not noted for such bias, regularly headlines its stories in the same manner.

decisions. The decisions of one seller often influence the price of products and the profits of rival firms. In an oligopoly, the welfare of each seller is dependent on the policies followed by its major rivals.

SUBSTANTIAL ECONOMIES OF SCALE

In an oligopolistic industry, large-scale production (relative to the total market) is necessary to attain a low per unit cost. Economies of scale are significant. They can enable a small number of large-scale, cost-efficient firms to meet the demand for an industry's product.

Using the automobile industry as an example, **Exhibit 21–5** illustrates the importance of economies of scale as a source of oligopoly. It has been estimated that each firm must produce approximately 1 million automobiles annually before its per unit cost of production is minimized. However, when the selling price of automobiles is barely sufficient for firms to cover their costs, the total quantity demanded from these producers is only 6 million. To minimize costs, then, each

Oligopoly exists in the automobile industry because firms do not fully realize the cost reductions from large-scale output until they produce approximately one-sixth of the total market.

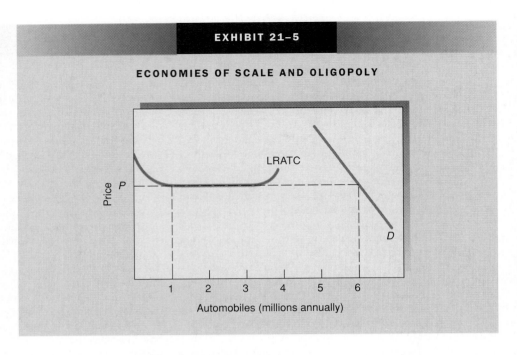

EXHIBIT 21–5

ECONOMIES OF SCALE AND OLIGOPOLY

firm must produce at least one-sixth (1 million of the 6 million) of the output demanded. In other words, the industry can support no more than five or six domestic firms of cost-efficient size.

SIGNIFICANT BARRIERS TO ENTRY

As with monopoly, barriers to entry limit the ability of new firms to compete effectively in oligopolistic industries. Economies of scale are probably the most significant entry barrier. A potential competitor may be unable to start out small and gradually grow to the optimal size, since a firm in an oligopolistic industry must gain a large share of the market before it can minimize per unit cost. The manufacture of refrigerators and diesel engines, as well as automobile production, seems to fall into this category.

Other factors, including patent rights, control over an essential resource, and government-imposed monopoly may also prevent new competitors from entering profitable oligopolistic industries. Without substantial barriers to entry, oligopolistic competition would be similar to monopolistic competition.

PRODUCTS MAY BE EITHER HOMOGENEOUS OR DIFFERENTIATED

The products of sellers in an oligopolistic industry may be either homogeneous or differentiated. When firms produce identical products, such as milk or gasoline, there is less opportunity for nonprice competition. On the other hand, rival firms producing differentiated products are more likely to use style, quality, and advertising as competitive weapons.

PRICE AND OUTPUT UNDER OLIGOPOLY

Unlike a monopolist or a pure competitor, an oligopolist cannot determine the product price that will deliver maximum profit simply by estimating market demand and cost conditions. An oligopolist must also predict how rival firms (that is, the rest of the industry) will react to price (and quality) adjustments. Since each oligopolist confronts such a complex problem, it is impossible to determine the precise price and output policy that will emerge in oligopolistic industries. Economics does, however, indicate a potential range of prices, and the factors that will determine whether prices in the industry will be high or low relative to costs of production.

Consider an oligopolistic industry in which seven or eight rival firms produce the entire market output. Substantial economies of scale are present. The firms produce identical products and have similar costs of production. **Exhibit 21–6** depicts the market demand conditions and long-run costs of production of the individual firms for such an industry.

What price will prevail? We can answer this question for two extreme cases. First, suppose that each firm sets its price independently of the other firms. There is no collusion, and each competitive firm acts independently, seeking to maximize profits by offering consumers a better deal than its rivals. Under these conditions, the market price would be driven down to P_c. Firms would be just able to cover their per unit costs of production. What would happen if a *single firm* raised its price? Its customers would switch to rival firms, which would now expand to

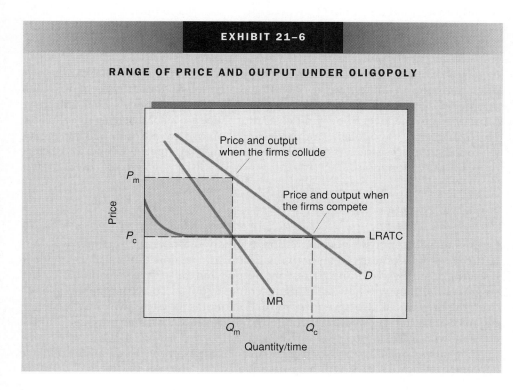

EXHIBIT 21–6

RANGE OF PRICE AND OUTPUT UNDER OLIGOPOLY

If oligopolists competed with one another, price cutting would drive price down to P_c. In contrast, perfect cooperation among firms would lead to a higher price of P_m and a smaller output (Q_m rather than Q_c). The shaded area shows profit if firms collude. Demand here is the market demand.

accommodate the new customers. The firm that raised its price would lose out. It would be self-defeating for any one firm to raise its price if the other firms did not raise theirs.

What would happen if supply conditions were such that the market price was above P_c? Since the demand curve faced by each *individual firm* is relatively elastic, rival sellers would have a strong incentive to reduce their price. Any firm that reduced its price slightly, by 1 percent, for example, would gain numerous customers. The price-cutting firm would attract some new buyers to the market, but more importantly, that firm would also lure many buyers away from rival firms charging higher prices. The price-cutters profit would expand as it gained a larger share of the total market. But, what would happen if all firms attempted to undercut their rivals? Price would be driven down to P_c, and the economic profit of the firms would be eliminated.

When rival oligopolists compete (pricewise) with one another, they drive the market price down to the level of costs of production. They do not always compete, however. There is a strong incentive for oligopolists to collude, raise price, and restrict output.

Cartel
An organization of sellers designed to coordinate supply decisions so that the joint profits of the members will be maximized. A cartel will seek to create a monopoly in the market.

Suppose the oligopolists, recognizing their interdependence, acted cooperatively to maximize their joint profit. They might form a **cartel,** such as OPEC, to accomplish this objective. Alternatively, they might collude without the aid of a formal organization. Under federal antitrust laws, collusive action to raise price and expand the joint profit of the firms would, of course, be illegal. Nevertheless, let us see what would happen if oligopolists followed this course. Exhibit 21–6 shows the marginal revenue curve that would accompany the demand market, D, for the product. Under perfect cooperation, the oligopolists would refuse to produce units for which marginal revenue was less than marginal cost. Thus, they would restrict joint output to Q_m, where $MR = MC$. Market price would rise to P_m. With collusion, substantial joint profits (the shaded area of Exhibit 21–6) could thus be attained. The case of perfect cooperation would be identical with the outcome under monopoly.

In the real world, though, the outcome is likely to fall between the extremes of price competition and perfect cooperation. Oligopolists generally recognize their interdependence and try to avoid vigorous price competition, which will drive price down to the level of per unit costs. But there are also obstacles to collusion. Thus, prices in oligopolistic industries do not rise to the monopolistic level. Oligopolistic prices are typically above the purely competitive level but below those for pure monopoly.

Collusion
Agreement among firms to avoid various competitive practices, particularly price reductions. It may involve either formal agreements or merely tacit recognition that competitive practices will be self-defeating in the long run. Tacit collusion is difficult to detect. The Sherman Act prohibits collusion and conspiracies to restrain interstate trade.

OBSTACLES TO COLLUSION

Collusion is the opposite of competition. It involves cooperative actions by sellers to turn the terms of trade in favor of the group, and against buyers. Since oligopolists can profit by colluding to restrict output and raise price, economic theory suggests that they will have a strong incentive to do so. To accomplish this, however, the firms must also agree on production quotas for each firm or a division of the market so that production is limited to the level that will be purchased at the chosen cartel price.

Each *individual* oligopolist, though, also has an incentive to cheat on collusive agreements. **Exhibit 21–7** will help us understand why. An undetected price cut

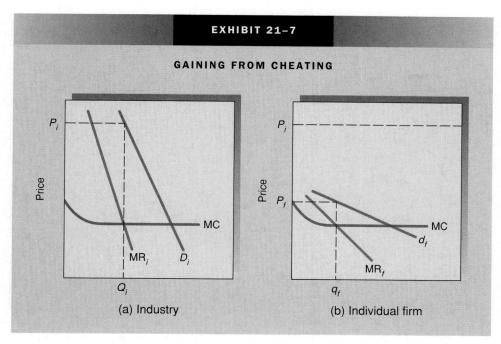

EXHIBIT 21–7

GAINING FROM CHEATING

(a) Industry

(b) Individual firm

The industry demand (D_i) and marginal revenue (MR_i) curves show that the joint profits of oligopolists would be maximized at Q_i, where $MR_i = MC$. Price P_i would be best for the industry as a whole (a). However, the demand curve (d_f) facing each firm (under the assumption that no other firms cheat) would be much more elastic than D_i. Given the greater elasticity of its demand curve, an individual firm (b) would maximize its profit by cutting its price to P_f and expanding output to q_f, where $MR_f = MC$. Thus, individual oligopolists could gain by secretly shaving price and cheating on the collusive agreement.

will enable a firm to attract (1) customers who would not buy from any firm at the higher price *and* (2) those who would normally buy from other firms. The demand facing the oligopolistic firm will thus be considerably more elastic than the industry demand curve. As Exhibit 21–7 shows, the price, P_i, that maximizes the industry's profits will be higher than the price, P_f, that is best for each individual oligopolist. If a firm can find a way to undercut the price set by the collusive agreement while other sellers maintain the higher price, expanded sales—beyond the level agreed upon by the cartel—will more than make up for the reduction in per unit profit margin.

In oligopolistic industries, there are two conflicting tendencies. An oligopolistic firm has a strong incentive to cooperate with its rivals so that joint profit can be maximized. However, it also has a strong incentive to cheat secretly on any collusive agreement in order to increase its share of the joint profit. Oligopolistic agreements therefore tend to be unstable. This instability exists whether the cooperative behavior is formal, as in the case of a cartel, or informal.

There are certain situations in which it is difficult for oligopolists to collude. Five major obstacles can limit collusive behavior.

1. When the number of oligopolists is larger, effective collusion is less likely. Other things constant, as the number of major firms in an industry increases, it becomes more costly for the oligopolists to communicate, negotiate, and enforce agreements among themselves. Developing and maintaining collusive agreements become more difficult. In addition, the greater the number of firms, the more likely it is that the objectives of individual firms will conflict with those of the industry. Each firm will want a bigger slice of the pie. Opinions about the best collusive price arrangement will differ because marginal costs, unused plant capacity, and estimates of market demand elasticity are likely to differ among firms. Aggressive, less mature firms may want to expand their share of total output. These conflicting interests will make it difficult to maintain collusive agreements.

Collusive agreements among oligopolists and cartels like OPEC are difficult to maintain because each country would be better off if it could cheat on the agreement and charge a slightly lower price.

2. When it is difficult to detect and eliminate price cuts, collusion is less attractive. Unless a firm has a way of policing the pricing activities of its rivals, it may be the "sucker" in a collusive agreement. Firms that secretly cut prices may gain a larger share of the market, while others maintain their higher prices and lose customers and profits. Price cutting can sometimes be accomplished in ways that are difficult for the other firms to identify. For example, a firm might provide better credit terms, faster delivery, and other related services "free" to improve slightly the package offered to the consumer.[4]

When firms sell a differentiated product, improvements in quality and style can be used as competitive weapons. "Price cuts" of this variety are particularly attractive to an oligopolist because they cannot be easily and quickly duplicated by rivals. Competitors can quickly match a reduction in money price, but it will take time for them to match an improvement in quality. When firms can freely use improvements in quality to gain a larger share of the market, collusive agreements on price are of limited value. When cheating (secret price cutting) is profitable and difficult for rivals to police, it is a good bet that oligopolistic rivals will be induced to cheat.

3. Low entry barriers are an obstacle to collusion. Unless potential rivals can be excluded, oligopolists will be unable to make unusually large profits. Successful collusion will merely attract competitors into the industry, which will eliminate the profits. Even with collusion, long-run profits will not be possible unless entry into the industry can be blocked.

Local markets are sometimes dominated by a few firms. For example, many communities have only a small number of ready-mix concrete producers, bowling alleys, accounting firms, and furniture stores. In the absence of government

---

[4]See Marshall R. Colberg, Dascomb Forbush, and Gilbert R. Whitaker, *Business Economics,* 5th ed. (Homewood: Irwin, 1975), for an extensive discussion of the alternative methods by which business firms are able to alter price.

restrictions, however, entry barriers into these markets are often low. (See the "Applications in Economics" feature on **contestable markets.**) The threat of potential rivals reduces the gains from collusive behavior under these conditions.

 4. *Unstable demand conditions are an obstacle to collusion.* Demand instability tends to increase the honest differences of opinion among oligopolists about what is best for the industry. One firm may want to expand because it anticipates a sharp increase in future demand, while a more pessimistic rival may want to hold

Contestable market
A market in which costs of entry and exit are low, so that a firm risks little by entering.

APPLICATIONS IN ECONOMICS

CONTESTABLE MARKETS: LOW ENTRY BARRIERS MAY YIELD COMPETITIVE RESULTS

Markets with few sellers are sometimes more competitive than they seem. Consider the case of the airline route between Salt Lake City, Utah, and Albuquerque, New Mexico. Only two airlines serve this route directly, since it has so little traffic. Further, there would seem to be high barriers to entry, since it takes multimillion-dollar airplanes to compete, as well as facilities for reservations, ticketing, baggage handling, and so on. The two airlines are well aware of the rivalry (with or without competition) between them, and they both charge the same price. One might expect that price to be high, perhaps close to the monopoly level. But, there is reason to believe that the two airlines, much as they would like to collude and drive up the price, will not be able to do so, as long as other airlines are free to enter this market.

 What we have just described is a contestable market, a market in which the costs of entry and exit are low, so that a firm risks little by entering. Efficient production and zero economic profits should prevail in a contestable market. And a market can be contestable even if capital requirements are high.

 To compete on an airline route may require millions of dollars in equipment, but the barriers to entry are much lower than that fact suggests. The Salt Lake City–Albuquerque market, for example, can be entered simply by shifting aircraft, personnel, and equipment from other locations. The aircraft can even be rented or leased. By the same token, if a new entrant (or an established firm) wants to leave that market, nearly all the invested capital values can be recovered through shifting the aircraft and other capital equipment to other routes or leasing them to other firms. An airline route then, in the absence of legal barriers, is a classic case of a contestable market.[1] If entry is later judged to be a

mistake, exit is relatively easy because fixed costs are not sunk costs, but are instead recoverable. Entry into a contestable market may require the use of large amounts of capital, but so long as the capital is recoverable, and not a sunk cost, the large capital requirement is not a high barrier to entry.

 In a contestable market, potential competition, as well as actual entry, can discipline firms selling in the market. When entry and exit are not expensive, even a single seller in a market faces the serious prospect of competition. Contestable markets yield two important results: (1) prices will not for long be higher than the level necessary to achieve zero economic profits, and (2) firms will seek to minimize the cost of producing any given output level and quality of product. The reason is that both inefficiency and prices above costs present a profitable opportunity to new entrants. Potential competitors who see an opportunity for economic profit can be expected to enter and move the market toward the perfectly competitive result.

 These results have a policy implication: if policymakers want to correct an oligopoly (or monopoly) situation, they should consider what might be done to make the market in question contestable. Much of the enthusiasm of economists for deregulation can be traced to the fact that regulation often is the primary restraint to entry. Many economists believe that deregulation permitting new entry can make many markets contestable, achieving lower prices and more efficiency than can direct regulation of producers. We will have more to say about this in the next chapter.

[1]The classic article on this topic is William J. Baumol's "Contestable Markets: An Uprising in the Theory of Industry Structure," *American Economic Review* 72 (March 1982), pp. 1–15.

the line on existing industrial capacity. Greater differences in expectations about future demand create greater conflict among oligopolistic firms. Successful collusion is more likely when demand is relatively stable.

5. Vigorous antitrust action increases the cost of collusion. Under existing antitrust laws, collusive behavior is prohibited. Secret agreements are, of course, possible. Simple informal cooperation might be conducted without discussions or collusive agreements. However, like other illegal behavior, such agreements are not legally enforceable. Vigorous antitrust action can discourage firms from making such illegal agreements. As the threat of getting caught increases, participants will be less likely to attempt collusive behavior.

LIMITS OF THE OLIGOPOLY MODEL

Uncertainty and imprecision characterize the theory of oligopoly. Economists can be more specific about predicted strategy choices and outcomes when additional assumptions can be specified about how each competitor expects to be rewarded or penalized by the various alternative strategies. (See the "Applications in Economics" feature on game theory.) In general, we know that firms will gain if they can successfully agree to restrict output and raise price. However, collusion also has its costs. We have outlined some of the conflicts and difficulties (costs) associated with the establishment of perfect cooperation among oligopolistic firms. In some industries, these difficulties are considerable, and the **market power,** or the ability of the firm to profit by maintaining its price above the competitive level, of the oligopolists is therefore relatively small. In other industries, oligopolistic cooperation, although not perfect, may raise prices significantly. Economists would say that such firms have market power, indicating that even though these firms are not pure monopolists, they do possess some monopoly power. Analysis of the costs and benefits of collusive behavior at this general level, while it does not yield precise predictions on oligopoly pricing, at least allows us to determine when discipline by competitive pressures is more likely for an oligopolist.

Market power

The ability of a firm to profit by raising its price significantly above the competitive level for a considerable period of time.

Concentration ratio

The total sales of the four (or sometimes eight) largest firms in an industry as a percentage of the total sales of the industry. The higher the ratio, the greater is the market dominance of a small number of firms. The ratio can be seen as a measure of the potential for oligopolistic power.

Game theory

Analyzes the strategic choices made by competitors in a conflict situation, such as decisions made by members of an oligopoly.

Which industries are dominated by a small number of firms? How important is oligopoly? Economists have traditionally used a tool, the **concentration ratio,** to help answer these questions.

This ratio is the percentage of total industry sales made by the four (or sometimes eight) largest firms of an industry. It can vary from nearly zero to 100, with 100 indicating that the sales of the four largest firms comprise those of the entire industry.

The concentration ratio can be thought of as a broad indicator of competitiveness. In general, the higher (lower) it is, the more (less) likely that the firms of the industry will be able to successfully collude against the interests of the consumers. This ratio, though, is by no means a perfect measure of competitiveness. Since the

THE PRISONER'S DILEMMA AND GAME THEORY

In an oligopoly, a few firms compete by selling into the same market, and the actions of each influence the demand faced by rival sellers. Because they sell similar products and compete for the same customers, the

THE PRISONER'S DILEMMA

		Al's Choice	
		Confess	Not Confess
Bob's Choice	Confess	6 months each	Al: 12 months Bob: 6 months
	Not Confess	Al: 6 months Bob: 12 months	3 months each

Al and Bob must each decide, without communicating with each other, whether to confess. Al knows that if Bob does not confess, then either Al can confess and spend 6 months in jail, or not confess and spend 3 months. But if Bob does confess, then Al's failure to confess would cost him an additional 6 months in jail. Bob is in a similar situation, facing the same options under the same assumptions about whether Al confesses. Each has the incentive to confess if he thinks the other one will, but to not confess if he thinks the other will also remain silent.

interests of each firm are in conflict with the interests of the others. One firm can gain customers, at the expense of the others, by reducing its price or increasing its advertising. But if the other firms react competitively by doing the same, then all the firms may lose. Yet if other firms cut their price or take other steps to offer consumers a better deal, firms that fail to follow suit will lose customers to their more aggressive rivals. Thus, each firm finds itself on the horns of a dilemma—in this case a variant of the classic "prisoner's dilemma."

Economists have increasingly used **game theory,** such as the prisoner's dilemma, to analyze strategic

choices made by competitors in a conflict situation, such as members of an oligopoly. Such choices depend on the anticipated actions of others.

To understand the prisoner's dilemma, consider the hypothetical case of Al and Bob, two touring Americans who just met at a train station in a small foreign country. They are taken prisoner and hauled into the local police station to be questioned separately. They are suspected of being the two men who robbed a local merchant, and each is told that if he makes the job of the police easier by confessing immediately, he will get only a six-month sentence. But each is also told that if he says nothing while the other confesses, then the one who did not confess immediately will get a twelve-month sentence. If neither confesses, both will be held for three months while the investigation continues. Al and Bob will not be allowed to communicate with each other. Will they confess?

To analyze such situations, the game theorist begins by laying out the alternative outcomes and showing how they are related to choices made by the players of the game, as we do in the accompanying illustration. For each man individually, in this version of the dilemma, the box reveals that the best choice depends on what the other does. If Al confesses, then Bob can save six months of jail time by also confessing. The same holds for Al, if he thinks Bob will confess. But if neither confesses, both serve only three months in jail.[1] The proper strategy for each prisoner depends heavily on his estimate of the likelihood that the other will confess. The problem becomes more complex if we consider prisoners who face a series of such decisions over time, each prisoner learning the other's previous choice before the next set of choices must be made.

Firms in an oligopoly must make decisions somewhat like those of the prisoners: Should a firm cut its price, luring more customers, some from competitors, or should it keep its price high and risk losing customers to competitors who cut prices? If all firms keep the price high, then as a group they will reap more profit. If all cut prices, then as a group they will reap less profit. But the firm that fails to cut price when others do will lose many customers to the other competing firms. The decision about whether to spend large amounts on advertising has similar characteristics.

For example, consider the pricing policy or advertising strategy of large automakers such as Ford,

APPLICATIONS IN ECONOMICS (continued)

General Motors, and Chrysler. Suppose the profit rate of each would be 15 percent if all of the major automobile producers raised their prices (or cut their advertising expenditures) by a similar amount. In contrast, each would have only a profit rate of 10 percent if intense competition leads to lower prices and/or larger advertising expenditures. Industry profits are highest when all firms decide to charge high prices. However, if one automaker reduces its price or advertises more heavily, it will be able to win customers away from rivals and increase its profit rate to 20 percent. Thus, if the firm thinks its rivals will continue to charge higher prices (or fail to match its advertising expenditures), it will be able to gain from cutting its prices (and increasing its advertising). If the other firms follow a similar course, however, this strategy will backfire and the profit rate of all of the firms in the industry will be less than the level that would have been achieved had they all charged higher prices (or spent less on advertising).

While our simplified analysis highlights the interdependence among the firms and the importance of probability estimates concerning the strategy of rivals, the real world is much more complex. The choices of the rival firms will be repeated over and over again, although often in modified forms. A prior strategy may be modified in light of previous reactions on the part of rivals. The attractiveness of a strategy will be influenced by the likelihood it will be detected by rivals and the speed with which they might be able to react effectively. In addition, the strategies of oligopolistic firms will be influenced by market conditions and the threat of foreign competition, factors that change with the passage of time. Within the framework of game theory models, additional assumptions must be made in order to account for these and other complex factors—factors that often change in the real world. In turn, if the assumptions incorporated into game theory models are not consistent with real world conditions, the implications of the game theory analysis may well be invalid.

Economists have used game theory extensively to show how results change when the "rules of the game"

change for the firms in an oligopolistic market, as well as for auction-bidding markets and other business decision-making situations. When the rules of the game are carefully defined and enforced, as in the case of economic experiments in laboratories, game theory has yielded interesting and important testable conclusions. But in open markets in the real world, empirical work using game theory has been less successful. The use of complex mathematical models is always difficult when the problem to be solved is complex, and human expectations about the changing strategy choices of other human beings must be taken into account. There is no question, however, that game theory can be useful for scholars and business practitioners alike, in helping them to frame the issues involved in strategic decision making.[2]

---

[1]If the numbers were slightly different than those in the accompanying chart, both Al and Bob would have an incentive to confess regardless of what they thought the other would do. For example, if each were told that they would get only a one month sentence if they confessed and the other party did not, then confession would become the dominant strategy for both Bob and Al. Under these circumstances, if Bob thought Al would remain silent, then Bob would spend only one month in jail if he confessed (compared to 3 months if he also remained silent). Al would also be in a similar situation if he believed Bob would remain silent. On the other hand, if Bob thought Al would confess, then Bob's best option would be to also confess since confession would lead to only a six month sentence while silence would result in a 12 month jail term. The same would also be true for Al if he thought Bob would confess. Thus, in this classic prisoner's dilemma case, both have an incentive to confess even though confession leads to more jail time for both of them—6 months rather than 3 months. What is best for the individual (or firm) does not always lead to the best outcome from the viewpoint of the group (or industry).

[2]For a further explanation of game theory and the prisoner's dilemma, see Avinash Dixit and Barry Nalebuff, "Game Theory" in *The Fortune Encyclopedia of Economics* (New York: Warner Books, 1993), pp. 640–643.

---

sales of foreign producers are excluded, it overstates the degree of concentration in industries where foreign firms compete. Neither does it reveal the elasticity of demand for products, an important piece of information since concentration is not as great a problem if good substitutes for a product are available. For example, the market power of aluminum producers is partially limited by competition from steel, plastics, copper, and similar products. Similarly, the monopoly power of commercial airlines is substantially reduced by the availability of automobiles, buses, chartered private flights, and even conference telephone calls. Concentration ratios tend to conceal such competitiveness among products.

The concentration ratio can also overstate the competitiveness in instances in which the relevant market area is a city or region. For example, consider the case of newspaper publishing companies. In 1987 there were more than 9,000 such companies in the United States. Sales of the four largest companies amounted to only 22 percent of the national market. Most cities, however, were served by only one or two newspapers. Thus, in most market areas, newspaper publishing is a highly concentrated industry, even though this is not true nationally. In this instance, the low national concentration ratio in the newspaper publishing industry probably understates the market power of local newspapers.

CONCENTRATION AND COMPETITIVENESS IN THE U.S. ECONOMY

Economist William G. Shepherd has examined the structure of the U.S. economy in depth, using four categories, based in part on concentration ratios, to classify the structure of various industries. He has also looked at how much of the U.S. national income is produced by firms in each category, and how those percentages have changed over time. As **Exhibit 21–8** shows, he finds that firms in competitive industries have produced a rising share of national income, while monopolies have produced a falling share. The intermediate categories have also declined in importance. Shepherd attributes the sharp increase in competition from 1958 to 1980 to antitrust policy, increased import competition, and deregulation. Other economists also point to reductions in transportation costs as a contributing factor to the increase in competition.

CONCENTRATION AND MERGERS

While William Shepherd has shown that the concentration ratio, carefully utilized, is a useful tool, a newer measure of concentration is the **Herfindahl index,** being used in antitrust policy, which we will describe in the next chapter (See "Measures of Economic Activity" box on this newer index.) At some point in American history, especially when American manufacturing was just developing, mergers had an important influence on the structure of markets in our economy. The desire of oligopolistic firms to merge is not surprising. A **horizontal merger,** the combining of two or more firms' assets under the same ownership, provides the firms with an alternative to both the rigors of competition and the insecurity of collusion.

There have been two great waves of horizontal mergers. The first occurred between 1887 and 1904; the second between 1916 and 1929. Many corporations whose names are now household words—U.S. Steel, General Electric, Standard Oil, General Foods, General Mills, and American Can, for example—are products of mergers formed during these periods. Mergers led to a dominant firm in

Herfindahl index
A measure of industry concentration, calculated by squaring the percentage share of each firm in the industry, then summing the squares. The index can range from zero to 10,000. It is a more sophisticated measure of concentration than the traditional concentration ratio, and is used by the Justice Department in antitrust policy.

Horizontal merger
The combining of the assets of two or more firms engaged in the production of similar products into a single firm.

This chart presents the findings of a study by William Shepherd, an industrial organization economist from the University of Michigan. Shepherd found that the share of national income produced by the competitive sectors of the U.S. economy has been rising for several decades, while the share produced in less competitive markets has been falling. The "single dominant firm" here is one with more than a 50 percent market share in a market with high barriers to entry, and the dominant firm has the ability to control pricing and to influence innovation. A "tight oligopoly" means a four-firm concentration ratio above 60 percent and stable market shares, or government-regulated firms with the ability to strongly influence the regulated prices.

Source: William G. Shepherd, "Causes of Increased Competition in the U.S. Economy, 1939–1980," *Review of Economics and Statistics*, November 1982, p. 618.

Vertical merger
The creation of a single firm from two firms, one of which was a supplier or customer of the other—for example, a merger of a lumber company with a furniture manufacturer.

Conglomerate merger
The combining under one ownership of two or more firms that produce unrelated products.

EXHIBIT 21–8

THE INCREASING COMPETITIVENESS OF U.S. ECONOMY, 1939–1980

MARKET-STRUCTURE CATEGORY	PERCENTAGE SHARES OF NATIONAL INCOME PRODUCED IN EACH CATEGORY		
	1939	1958	1980
1. Pure Monopoly	6.2	3.1	2.5
2. Single Dominant Firm	5.0	5.0	2.8
3. Tight Oligopoly	36.4	35.6	18.0
4. Effectively Competitive	52.4	56.3	76.7
Total	100.0	100.0	100.0

---

manufacturing industries such as steel, sugar refining, agricultural implements, leather, rubber, distilleries, and tin cans. In 1950 the Celler-Kefauver Act made it substantially more difficult to use horizontal mergers as a means of developing oligopolistic power. Today mergers involving large firms seldom involve former competitors.

Another type of merger, the **vertical merger,** joins a supplier and a buyer—for example, an automobile maker and a steel producer. A vertical merger might simplify the long-range planning process for both firms and reduce the need for costly legal contracting between the two. Even though vertical mergers generally do not increase concentration within industries, some economists are concerned that such mergers may reduce competition if either the buyer or the supplier grants a market advantage to the other.

A **conglomerate merger** combines two firms in unrelated industries. The stated intent is usually to introduce new and superior management into the firm being absorbed. This type of merger results in increased size but not necessarily in reduced competition. Since the 1960s, when some very large corporations were formed by conglomerate merger, some observers have expressed concern that the concentration of political power created by such mergers and the enormous financial assets available to the operating units may be potentially dangerous. Others have argued that conglomerate mergers often lead to more efficient management and increased competitiveness within specific industries.

CONCENTRATION AND PROFITS

The model of oligopoly implies that if the firms in concentrated industries cooperate with one another, they can *jointly* exercise monopoly power. Is there a relationship between industrial concentration and profitability in the real world?

MEASURES OF ECONOMIC ACTIVITY

HERFINDAHL INDEX

The Herfindahl index measures market concentration in a way that gives a great deal of weight to the share of the largest one or two firms in the market. It does so by squaring the percentage each firm has in the market and summing the squares. If there are n firms in the market, then H, the Herfindahl index, is:

$$H = S_1^2 + S_2^2 + S_3^2 + ... + S_n^2$$

where S_1 in the formula is the percentage share of the largest firm in the market, S_2 is the percentage share of the second largest firm, and so on. Each S can vary from 100 (a pure monopoly, with only one firm in the market) down to almost zero. For a pure monopoly,

$$H = (100)^2 = 10,000$$

This is the largest possible value for the Herfindahl index. By contrast, if there are 100 firms in a market, each with an equal 1 percent share, then

$$H = (1)^2 + (1)^2 + (1)^2 + ... + (1)^2 = 100$$

The Herfindahl index is a more sophisticated tool for measuring market power than the traditional concentration ratio, which treats a market with four firms of equal size the same as a market with four firms, one of which has 70 percent of the market and three that have 10 percent each. The Herfindahl index would assign the equal-shares market an index of 2,500 (4×25^2) and the unequal-shares market an index of 5,200 ($70^2 + 10^2 + 10^2 + 10^2$), indicating the larger potential for market power when one firm has a 70 percent share of the market. Only the shares of the larger firms are needed to approximate the index, since firms with small shares add little to the Herfindahl index.

Researchers in this area have not been able to arrive at a definite conclusion. An early study by Joe Bain showed a distinctly positive relationship between concentration and profitability. George Stigler, in a detailed study of manufacturing industries, found that from 1947 to 1954 "the average [profit] rate in the concentrated industries was 8.00 percent, while that in the unconcentrated industries was 7.16 percent." Later, both a study by William Shepherd covering the period from 1960 to 1969 and the White House Task Force on Antitrust Policy presented evidence that the rate of profitability is higher in concentrated industries.

More recent research results indicate that greater profits for larger firms are likely to come from greater efficiency, making prices lower. As Sam Peltzman concluded in his 1977 study, "Briefly, more concentration raises profitability not because prices rise, but because they fall less than cost."[5] Other researchers are not fully convinced. In any case, the weight of the evidence is that the profit rate of firms in concentrated industries is only slightly higher than the profit rate of other firms. Demand conditions, efficient management, and superior entrepreneurship are the main determinants of profitability. Thus, the odds are only a little better than fifty-fifty that a more concentrated industry will be more profitable than a less concentrated one.

---

[5]Sam Peltzman, "The Gains and Losses from Industrial Concentration," *Journal of Law and Economics 20* (October 1977): 257. For a detailed analysis of this issue, see Leonard W. Weiss, "The Concentration-Profits Relationship and Antitrust," *Industrial Concentration: the New Learning*, edited by H. J. Goldschmid, et al. (Boston: Little, Brown, 1974), 184–232; and John S. McGee, *Industrial Organization* (Englewood Cliffs, Prentice-Hall 1988), 332–337.

"*And though in 1969, as in previous years, your company had to contend with spiralling labor costs, exorbitant interest rates, and unconscionable government interference, management was able once more, through a combination of deceptive marketing practices, false advertising, and price fixing, to show a profit which, in all modesty, can only be called excessive.*"

Drawing by Lorenz. © 1970 *The New Yorker* Magazine, Inc.

MARKET POWER AND PROFIT— THE EARLY BIRD CATCHES THE WORM

In the last chapter, we saw that under certain conditions an unregulated monopolist can earn economic profit, even in the long run. Similarly, our analysis of oligopoly suggests that if barriers to entry are high, firms might be consistently able to earn above-average profits, even in the long run. Suppose a well-established firm, such as Exxon or IBM, is able to use its market power to earn consistent economic profits. Do its current stockholders gain because of its monopoly power? Surprisingly, the answer is no. The ownership value of a share of corporate stock for such a corporation long ago began to reflect its market power and profitability. Many of the *present* stockholders paid high prices for their stock because they expected the firm to be highly profitable. In other words, they paid for any above-normal economic profits that the firm was expected to earn because of its monopoly power.

Do not expect to get rich buying the stock of monopolistic or oligopolistic firms known to be highly profitable. You are already too late. The early bird catches the worm. Those who owned the stock when these firms initially developed their market position have already captured the gain. The value of their stock increased at that time. After a firm's future prospects are widely recognized, subsequent stockholders fail to gain a higher-than-normal rate of return on their financial investment.

LOOKING AHEAD

The competitiveness of a market economy is influenced not only by the various market structures operating within it but also by public policy. Business activity is often directly regulated by the government. In the next chapter, we will consider the impact of regulatory activities.

CHAPTER SUMMARY

1. Economic models of monopoly and competition, while quite useful, do not account for rivalrous business behavior, such as competitive advertising, "cents-off" coupons, and airline frequent-flier programs. Economists use models of monopolistic competition and oligopoly to illustrate and analyze the behavior of firms when these factors are present, and when firms attempt to collude.

2. Although standard economic models do not include the judgments made under uncertainty by entrepreneurs, economists generally recognize that the world is not so simple as our models indicate, and that entrepreneurial judgments are, in fact, important.

3. The distinguishing characteristics of monopolistic competition are (a) firms that produce differentiated products, (b) low barriers to entry into and exit from the market, and (c) a substantial number of independent, rival firms.

4. Monopolistically competitive firms face a gently downward-sloping demand curve. They often use product quality, style, convenience of location, advertising, and price as competitive weapons. Since all rivals within a monopolistically competitive industry are free to duplicate another's products (or services), the demand for the product of any one firm is highly elastic.

5. A profit-maximizing firm will expand output as long as marginal revenue exceeds marginal cost. Thus, a firm under monopolistic competition will lower its price so that output can be expanded until $MR = MC$. The price charged by the profit-maximizing monopolistic competitor will be greater than its marginal cost.

6. If monopolistic competitors are making economic profits, rival firms will be induced to enter the market. They will expand the supply of the product (and similar products), enticing some customers away from established firms. The demand curve faced by an individual firm will fall (shift inward) until the profits have been eliminated.

7. Economic losses will cause monopolistic competitors to exit from the market. The demand for the products of each remaining firm will rise (shift outward) until the losses have been eliminated.

8. Since barriers to entry are low, firms in a monopolistically competitive industry will make only normal profits in the long run. In the short run, they may make either economic profits or losses, depending on market conditions.

9. Traditional economic theory has emphasized that monopolistic competition is inefficient because (a) price exceeds marginal cost at the long-run equilibrium output level; (b) long-run average total cost is not minimized; and (c) excessive advertising is sometimes encouraged. However, other economists have argued more recently that this criticism is misdirected. According to the newer view, firms under monopolistic competition have an incentive to (a) produce efficiently, (b) undertake production if and only if their actions will increase the value of the resources used, (c) offer a variety of products, and (d) be innovative in offering new product options.

10. Oligopolistic market structure is characterized by (a) an interdependence among firms, (b) substantial economies of scale that result in only a small number of firms in the industry, and (c) significant barriers to entry. Oligopolists may produce either homogeneous or differentiated products.

11. There is no general theory of price, output, and equilibrium for oligopolistic markets. If rival oligopolists acted totally independently of their competitors, they would drive price down to the level of cost production. Alternatively, if they used collusion to obtain perfect cooperation, price would rise to the level that a monopolist would charge. The actual outcome lies between these two extremes. Game theory provides insights into the strategic decisions of the sort that oligopolists must make, under fully specified "rules of the game."

12. Collusion is the opposite of competition. Oligopolists have a strong incentive to collude and raise their prices. However, the interests of individual firms will conflict with those of the industry as a whole. Since the demand curve faced by individual firms is far more elastic than the industry demand curve, each firm could gain by cutting its price (or raising product quality) by a small amount so that it could attract customers from rivals. If several firms tried to do this, however, the collusive agreement would break down.

13. Oligopolistic firms are less likely to collude successfully against the interests of consumers if (a) the number of rival firms is large, (b) it is costly to prohibit competitors from offering secret price cuts (or quality improvements) to customers, (c) entry barriers are low, (d) market demand conditions tend to be unstable, and/or (e) the threat of antitrust action is present.

14. Competition can come from potential, as well as actual rivals. If entry and exit are not expensive, and if there are no legal barriers to entry, the theory of contestable markets indicates that competitive results may occur even if only one or a few firms are actually in the market.

15. Analysis of concentration ratios suggests that, on balance, there has been an increase in the competitiveness of the U.S. economy during the last several decades.

16. Accounting profits as a share of stockholder equity are probably slightly greater in highly concentrated industries than in those that are less concentrated. The relationship between profits and concentration, however, is not a close one. This suggests that several other factors—such as changing market conditions, quality competition, risk, and ability to exclude rivals—are the major determinants of profitability.

17. The after-tax accounting profits of business firms average about 5 cents of each dollar of sales, substantially less than most Americans believe to be the case. Accounting profits average approximately 12 percent of stockholder equity. This rate of return (accounting profit) provides investors with the incentive to sacrifice current consumption, assume the risk of undertaking a business venture, and supply the funds to purchase buildings, machines, and other assets.

CRITICAL-ANALYSIS QUESTIONS

1. Street-corner vendors using pushcarts have sometimes engaged in price wars at popular locations within Washington, D.C. Each vendor would like to drive out the other sellers and have the prime location to himself. Explain why a strategy of cutting price below cost in order to drive out other vendors would not make sense if there are no legal barriers to entry.

*2. Suppose that a group of investors wants to start a business operated out of a popular Utah ski area, and the group is considering either building a new resort or starting a new local airline serving that market. Each new business would require about the same amount of capital and personnel hiring. The group believes each to have the same profit potential. Which is the safer (less likely to result in a substantial capital loss) investment? Why? Is there an offsetting advantage to the other investment?

3. "Monopolistic competition is inefficient. Not only are prices higher than marginal cost, and average cost above the minimum in long-run equilibrium, but the firms do not make long-run profits! Consumers lose, and even the firms don't gain." Evaluate this statement.

4. "The important functions of entrepreneurs cannot be put into an economic model. The models therefore are useless." Evaluate this stateent.

*5. "My uncle just bought stock in Mammoth Insurance, Incorporated. It has long been one of the most profitable firms in the business. He'll make a bundle on that one!" Evaluate this statement.

*6. Why is oligopolistic collusion more difficult when there is product variation than when the products of all firms are identical?

7. "Market conditions in the world oil market are constantly changing. This makes it difficult for the Organization of Petroleum Exporting Countries (OPEC) to collude successfully and hold price far above the marginal cost of oil." Evaluate this statement.

8. "World markets are impossible to control, because you cannot keep out new competitors. Brazil, once a major oil importer, illustrated the problem when it reached a production level of 600,000 barrels a day. OPEC, the oil cartel, will never again be able to raise prices as it did for a time at the beginning, and again at the end of the 1970s." Evaluate this statement.

*9. "A high concentration ratio virtually guarantees monopoly pricing and excess profits." Evaluate this statement.

10. We have a theory to explain the equilibrium price and output for monopoly, but not for oligopoly. Why? What role can game theory play in helping us to understand decisions made by oligopolists?

11. "Successful collusion by a group of oligopolists contains the seeds of its own destruction, generating incentives that will destroy cooperation." Evaluate this statement.

*12. What determines the *variety* of styles, designs, and sizes of different products? Why do you think there are only a few different varieties of toothpicks, but lots of different types of napkins on the market?

*13. How would the imposition of a fixed, per unit tax of $2,000 on new automobiles affect the average *quality of* automobiles if the proceeds of the tax were used to subsidize a government-operated lottery?

14. What is the primary function of the entrepreneur? Some economists have charged that the major market-structure models of economic theory assume away the function of the entrepreneur. In what sense is this true? Is the function of the entrepreneur important? Discuss.

15. Is quality and style competition as important as price competition? Would you like to live in a country where government regulation restricted the use of quality and style competition? Why or why not? Do you think you would get more or less for your consumer dollar if quality and style competition were restricted? Discuss.

16. Suppose that a monopolistic competitor is currently charging a price that maximizes the firm's total revenue. Will this price also maximize the firm's profit? Why or why not? Explain.

*17. The American Honeymakers Association has 1,000 members. Each member firm faces essentially the same cost structure. The demand for honey and the supply curve of

---

*Asterisk denotes questions for which answers are given in Appendix C.

one typical producer can be determined from the data in the accompanying table.

MARKET DEMAND		FIRM'S SUPPLY	
PRICE	QUANTITY (QUARTS)	PRICE	QUANTITY (QUARTS)
$10	10,000	$10	60
9	15,000	9	55
8	20,000	8	50
7	25,000	7	45
6	30,000	6	40
5	35,000	5	35
4	40,000	4	30

a. If all the members of the Honeymakers Association agree to collude to maximize industry profits, what is the profit-maximizing price? How many quarts of honey will be sold at this price? How many quarts of honey will each firm produce to sustain this price?

b. If the cartel charges the price computed in "a," how many quarts would an individual firm like to produce?

c. Suppose all the firms cheat and the market becomes competitive. What is the new market-clearing price and quantity?

*18. Gouge-em Cable Company is the only cable television service company licensed to operate in Backwater County. Most of its costs are access fees and maintenance expenses. These fixed costs total $640,000 monthly. The marginal cost of adding another subscriber to its system is constant at $2 per month. Gouge-em's demand curve can be determined from the data in the accompanying table.

SUBSCRIPTION PRICE (PER MONTH)	NUMBER OF SUBSCRIBERS
$25	20,000
20	40,000
15	60,000
10	80,000
5	100,000
1	150,000

a. What price will Gouge-em charge for its cable services? What are its profits at this price?

b. Now suppose the Backwater County Public Utility Commission feels that cable subscription rates in the county are too expensive and that Gouge-em's profits are unfairly high. What regulated price will it set so that Gouge-em makes only a normal rate of return on its investment?

---

*Asterisk denotes questions for which answers are given in Appendix C.

CHAPTER TWENTY-TWO

BUSINESS STRUCTURE, ANTITRUST, AND REGULATION

People of the same trade seldom meet together, even for merriment and diversion, but the conversation ends in a conspiracy against the public, or in some contrivance to raise prices.

ADAM SMITH (1776)[1]

CHAPTER FOCUS

■ *How is the U.S. economy structured? In particular, what role does big business play? How has public policy toward big business evolved?*
■ *What are the objectives of antitrust policy? What forms does it take?*
■ *How effective has antitrust policy been? What new directions has it taken? What is the effect of mergers on the economy?*
■ *What theories do economists put forth to explain and predict government regulation of business?*
■ *What has been the history of traditional economic regulation?*
■ *What changes have been occurring?*
■ *How does the regulation of health and safety differ from traditional economic regulation? What can we say about its costs and benefits?*

---

[1]See Adam Smith, *An Inquiry into the Nature and Causes of the Wealth of Nations*, 1776, Cannan's edition (Chicago: University of Chicago Press, 1976), p. 144.

Economists today recognize, just as Adam Smith did, that in the presence of competition and rivalry, business firms provide benefits to consumers and workers alike. Competition forces producers to operate efficiently and to supply consumers with goods that have the qualities they most intensely desire (relative to costs). Similarly, competition for resources forces each producer to treat workers and other resource suppliers fairly, offering them pay rates and work environments that are attractive relative to those available elsewhere.

But as Adam Smith was keenly aware, and as we have seen in the previous two chapters, forces are present that sometimes undermine competition. Should government, then, step in to enhance competition? Consumers and workers sometime lack enough information to make good choices. Should government protect them against market choices they might regret? Have the actions of government promoted or retarded the development of competitive markets? Have they helped consumers and workers to avoid dangerous products and jobs? Economists often disagree on the answers to these questions.

Some economists point out that regulatory policy, by limiting various types of noncompetitive behavior, can effectively increase the discipline of the market. Others charge that past regulatory policies have often reduced market competitiveness, contributed to economic inefficiency, and in general, have not served the interests of consumers and workers. In this chapter, we will analyze the structure of the U.S. economy and examine how regulatory policies of various kinds can influence economic behavior in the light of these controversies.

STRUCTURE OF U.S. ECONOMY

The U.S. economy is extremely diverse. About 87 percent of all establishments hire fewer than 20 employees. These workers add up to more than one-quarter of the labor force. In the recent period of 1988 to 1990, this employer category added more than a million jobs. Only one establishment in every 1,000 employs more than 1,000 workers, but they still provide employment for about 13 percent of the labor force. More than 10 million workers, or one worker in 12, were self-employed in 1992.

The structure of our economy has changed significantly over the years. In 1870, 50 percent of all workers were employed in agriculture, 24 percent were in service industries, and 18 percent worked in manufacturing. By 1992, agricultural employment had declined to less than 3 percent, services (including the provision of information and management services) had risen gradually to more than 60 percent, and manufacturing, which had risen to a peak of 35 percent in 1948, totaled 17 percent.

Changes in the occupational composition of the labor force also reveal how our economy has changed. Federal Reserve Bank economist Mack Ott researched changes in the labor force over more than 100 years.[2] (Some of his findings are

---

[2]The evidence cited here is largely from Mack Ott, "The Growing Share of Services in the U.S. Economy—Degeneration or Evolution?" *Review: Federal Reserve Bank of St. Louis* 69, no. 6 (June–July 1987) *The Statistical History of the United States, from Colonial Times to the Present* (New York: Basic Books, 1976), pp. 164, 165; *Economic Report of the President, 1988,* pp. 60–75; and David M. O'Neil, "We're Not Losing Our Industrial Base," *Challenge* May–June 1986, pp. 19–25.

shown in **Exhibit 22–1.**) Dividing workers' occupations into three categories, Ott found a very long and steady trend in the United States away from direct, physical production work—including such occupations as farmers and farm workers, craft workers, factory supervisors, machine operators, and nonfarm laborers—which we usually think of as "blue-collar work."

Blue-collar workers declined from 73 percent of the work force in 1900 to only 34 percent in 1980. Nonetheless, there has been little growth in the number of non-informational service jobs. Thus, the data do not suggest that we are becoming a nation of food service and laundry workers, as some have charged. The shift has been primarily toward "information provision/decision-making" occupations, or "white-collar jobs." This category includes professional and technical workers, managers, clerks, and sales workers. White-collar workers rose from an 18 percent share of the work force in 1900 to a 53 percent share in 1980. As these large, but gradual changes took place, annual earnings per worker rose more than 500 percent! Meanwhile the noninformational service work force rose much less, from 9 percent to 13 percent during the same period. The trend continues. Since 1980 about half of all new jobs in the U.S. economy have been managerial and professional jobs. New employment is shifting toward better paying jobs requiring more skills and education. These labor force shifts have been one key to our sustained growth of output.

COMPETITION IN OUR ECONOMY

Not every firm sells into a market that is competitive. Yet in a very real sense, every firm competes with every other firm for the consumer's additional dollar

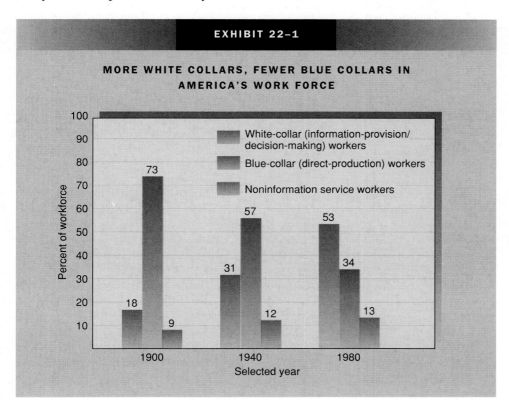

EXHIBIT 22–1

MORE WHITE COLLARS, FEWER BLUE COLLARS IN AMERICA'S WORK FORCE

White-collar (information-provision/decision-making) workers

Blue-collar (direct-production) workers

Noninformation service workers

A dramatic shift has steadily occurred over the past century and more, from direct production, or blue-collar jobs, to white-collar occupations that provide information or decision-making services. At the same time, annual earnings per worker rose more than 500 percent.

Source: Mack Ott, "The Growing Share of Services in the U.S. Economy—Degeneration or Evolution?" *Review,* 69, no. 6 (June–July 1987), Federal Reserve Bank of St. Louis. (Derived from Table 5.)

of spending. Competition is everywhere; the seller of compact discs, for example, competes with the book store and the local restaurant for our entertainment budgets.

Competition, even within a highly concentrated industry, is multidimensional. Available substitutes reduce the monopoly power of firms in some concentrated industries. Other firms are restrained by the threat of entry from potential rivals. Still others face stiff competition from foreign producers.

Product-quality competition may also create strong rivalry even among a limited number of competitors. Moreover, in a firm as big as General Motors, the rivalry among divisions (Buick versus Oldsmobile, for example) may be intense as well. Direct price competition within the firm is presumably controlled, but competition involving quality remains. Leaders in each division compete for recognition and advancement, and each is judged by monthly sales and profit figures. Thus, competitive forces are not entirely absent even in a highly concentrated industry.

The relative importance of competitive and noncompetitive sectors within the economy changes with time. Moreover, it is not even clear where the line should be drawn between competitive and noncompetitive industries. Most economists would probably classify unregulated industries in which the four largest firms produce less than 20 or 25 percent of the market as competitive. (As we noted in the last chapter, the concentration ratio of an industry provides an indication of competitiveness, with high concentration meaning market dominance by a small number of firms.) Industries in which the largest firms produce more than half of the output would generally be classified as oligopolistic, suggesting the presence of noncompetitive elements. These categories, however, are arbitrary.

Although measuring the degree to which an economy is competitive is not easy, meaningful estimates can be made. As we reported in the previous chapter, economist William G. Shepherd's in-depth study of competition in the U.S. economy finds that firms in competitive industries have produced a rising share of national income, while monopolies and intermediate categories have produced falling shares. (See especially Exhibit 21–8 in the previous chapter.) Shepherd attributes the sharp rise in competition to antitrust policy, increased import competition, and deregulation. Other economists also point to reductions in transportation costs as a contributing factor to the increase in competition.

BIG BUSINESS, COMPETITION, AND PROFITS

The stated objective of public policy has been to restrain various aspects of big-business activity, especially when competition seems threatened. Some observers feel that large firms threaten our decentralized economic institutions and our democratic political structure, and that antitrust action can help promote efficiency and keep political power and income more equally distributed. However, we should keep three points in mind as we evaluate this issue.

First, bigness and absence of competition are not necessarily the same thing. A firm can be big and yet function in a highly competitive industry. For example, Sears and Kmart are both large, but they are also part of a highly competitive industry—retail sales.

Second, large size does not ensure greater profitability. The real-world data indicate that profits as a percentage of stockholder equity are unrelated to corporate size.[3] Many corporate giants discovered this when their earnings took a nosedive in the early 1990s.

Third, the firms that comprise the largest 100 or 200 corporations are heterogeneous and constantly changing. As successful management and the vagaries of business fortune exert their influences, some firms are pushed out of the top group and others enter. Following the fate of various firms over time is not easy, since mergers occur and names change, but historical research indicates that of the largest 100 manufacturing corporations in 1909, only 36 remained on the list in 1948. Of the 50 largest in 1947, only 25 remained on the list in 1972, and 5 failed to make even the top 200. Of the firms on the *Fortune* 500 list in 1980, only about half were able to make the list again in 1990. With time, even giants tumble and fall, as technology and preferences change.

ANTITRUST LEGISLATION— THE POLICY OBJECTIVES

Economists generally believe that monopolies and other restraints of trade are bad because they usually have the effect of reducing total output and, therefore, aggregate economic welfare.

FRED S. MCCHESNEY[4]

The development of antitrust laws in the United States followed the rapid industrialization of the 1870s and 1880s. Producers in the oil, railroad, sugar, and tobacco industries, among others, merged or formed trusts with the ability to fix prices and control output. In a **trust,** the assets of several firms are placed in the custody of trustees who manage the trust for the benefit of the owners. Prior to 1890, there was no legal penalty against monopoly. But populist opinion leaders such as writer Ida Tarbell decried the ability of these industrial giants, "the trusts," to control much of their industries' output and, potentially at least, to raise prices.

Economists at the time did not support antitrust laws, recognizing that while a reduction in output was one possible result of the increased concentration in the hands of a few producers, increased efficiency and lower costs were another. Producers who were more efficient would naturally expand at the expense of those who were not. In fact, Standard Oil, Ida Tarbell's main target, grew precisely because John D. Rockefeller expanded the firm's share of the market by lowering

Trust
In American history, an arrangement in which the assets of several firms were placed in the custody of trustees who managed the trust for the benefit of the owners. Trusts were used to form cartels in the United States in the late 1800s.

---

[3]See William G. Shepherd, *The Economics of Industrial Organization* (Englewood Cliffs, NJ: Prentice-Hall, 1979), pp. 270–272, for evidence on this issue. Shepherd found that large corporate size had a mild *negative* impact on the rate of profit of firms.

[4]Fred S. McChesney, "Antitrust" in *The Fortune Encyclopedia of Economics*, edited by David R. Henderson (New York: Warner Books, 1993), p. 385. In this section we utilize the content of McChesney's essay, which provides a fascinating overview of the rationale for, and history of, antitrust policy.

prices and buying out many competitors. The pressure to enact antitrust legislation was probably due as much to a populist dislike of big business as to any economic argument against the results of reduced output and higher prices. Tarbell herself conceded that the trusts might be more efficient producers. As antitrust legislation evolved, however, it was shaped by economists and others who spoke in terms of promoting economic efficiency.

Modern antitrust legislation focuses on restraints to trade (see quote from economist Fred S. McChesney). It seeks to (1) ensure that the economy is structured so that competition exists among firms in the same industry (or market area) and to (2) prohibit business practices that tend to stifle competition. Once these objectives are accomplished, it is assumed that market forces can be relied on to avoid restraints of trade that would allow firms to reduce output in order to seek higher prices and greater profits.

There are numerous tactics business entrepreneurs might use to avoid the rigors of competition. We have already stressed that collusion and price agreements are potential weapons with which to turn trade in favor of the seller. Potential competitors might also decide to divide a market geographically, agreeing not to compete in certain market areas. Large, diversified firms might use **predatory pricing**, a practice by which a firm temporarily reduces its price below cost in certain market areas in order to damage or eliminate weaker rivals. Once the rivals have been eliminated, the firm then uses its monopoly power to raise prices above costs. A competitor might also use **exclusive contracts** and reciprocal agreements to maintain an advantage over rivals. Here the manufacturer of a line of products prohibits retailers from selling any of the products of rival producers. An established firm offering many product lines might use this tactic to limit the entry into retail markets by rivals offering only narrow product lines.

These and other business practices might be used in attempts to increase market power rather than to achieve superior performance. In one form or another, they are illegal under current antitrust legislation.

Predatory pricing
The practice in which a dominant firm in an industry temporarily reduces price to damage or eliminate weaker rivals, so that prices can be raised above the level of costs at a later time.

Exclusive contract
An agreement between manufacturer and retailer that prohibits the retailer from carrying the product lines of firms that are rivals of the manufacturer. Such contracts are illegal under the Clayton Act when they "lessen competition."

MAJOR ANTITRUST LEGISLATION

The United States, to a greater degree than most Western countries, has adopted antitrust legislation designed to promote competitive markets. Three major legislative acts—the Sherman Act, the Clayton Act, and the Federal Trade Commission Act—form the foundation of antitrust policy in the United States.

SHERMAN ACT. Passed in 1890, the Sherman Act was the first response to the populist demands for antitrust measures. Its most important provisions are

Section 1: Every contract, combination in the form of trust or otherwise, or conspiracy, in restraint of trade or commerce among the several states or with foreign nations, is hereby declared illegal.
Section 2: Every person who shall monopolize, or conspire with any other person or persons to monopolize any part of the trade or commerce among the several states, or with foreign nations, shall be guilty of a misdemeanor.

The language of the Sherman Act is vague and subject to interpretation. What does it mean to attempt to "monopolize" or "conspire to monopolize" with another person? Initially, the courts were hesitant to apply the act to manufacturing corporations. In 1911, however, the Supreme Court ruled that Standard Oil and American Tobacco had used "unreasonable" tactics to restrain trade. At the time, the Standard Oil trust controlled 90 percent of the country's refinery capacity. American Tobacco controlled three-fourths of the tobacco manufacturing market. Both firms were broken up into several smaller rival firms.

The Supreme Court, however, did not prohibit monopoly per se. In fact, passage of the Sherman Act was followed by a great wave of mergers, which, between 1898 and 1902 alone, involved perhaps half of the U.S. manufacturing capacity. Firms that could not conspire, could merge. It was "unfair or unethical" business practices that the courts would not condone. Since the Sherman Act did not clearly define unfair or unethical business practices, additional legislation was required. In 1914 Congress passed two other antitrust laws to remedy the situation.

CLAYTON ACT.   The Clayton Act was an effort to spell out and prohibit specific business practices. The following are prohibited by the Clayton Act when they "substantially lessen competition or tend to create a monopoly":

1. *Price discrimination*—charging purchasers in different markets different prices that are unrelated to transportation or other costs.
2. *Tying contracts*—a practice whereby the seller requires the buyer to purchase another item.
3. *Exclusive dealings*—an agreement between a manufacturer and retail distributor that prohibits the distributor from handling the products of firms that are competitors of the manufacturer.
4. *Interlocking stockholding*—one firm purchasing the stock of a competing firm.
5. *Interlocking directorates*—the same individual(s) serving on the boards of directors of competing firms.

Although somewhat more specific than the Sherman Act, the Clayton Act is still vague. At what point do the prohibited actions actually become illegal? Under what circumstances do these actions "substantially lessen competition"? The task of interpreting this ambiguous phrase still remains with the courts.

FEDERAL TRADE COMMISSION ACT.   The Federal Trade Commission Act declared unlawful all "unfair methods of competition in commerce." The Federal Trade Commission (FTC), composed of five members appointed by the president to seven-year terms, was established to determine the exact meaning of "unfair methods." However, a 1919 Supreme Court decision held that the courts, not the FTC, had the ultimate responsibility for interpreting the law. Today the FTC is concerned primarily with (1) enforcing consumer protection legislation, (2) prohibiting deceptive advertising, a power it acquired in 1938, and (c) preventing overt collusion.

When a complaint is filed with the FTC, usually by a third party, the commission investigates. If there is a violation, the FTC initially attempts to settle the dispute by negotiation between the parties. If the attempts to negotiate a settlement fail, a hearing is conducted before one of the commission's examiners. The decision of the hearing examiner may be appealed to the U.S. Court of Appeals. The great majority of cases brought before the FTC are now settled by mutual consent of the parties involved.

MORE RECENT ANTITRUST LEGISLATION

Additional antitrust legislation was passed in the 1930s. The Robinson-Patman Act of 1936 prohibits selling "at unreasonably low prices" when such practices reduce competition. The section of the Clayton Act dealing with price discrimination was aimed at eliminating predatory pricing. The Robinson-Patman Act went beyond this. It was intended to protect competitors not just from stronger rivals who might temporarily sell below cost, but also from more efficient rivals who were actually producing at a lower cost. Chain stores and mass distributors were the initial targets of the legislation. Economists have often been critical of the Robinson-Patman Act, since it has tended to reduce price competition and thereby protect inefficient producers.

In 1938 Congress passed the Wheeler-Lea Act, which was designed to strengthen sectors of the Federal Trade Commission Act that had been weakened by restrictive court decisions. Before the passage of the act, the courts were reluctant to prohibit unfair business practices, such as false and deceptive advertising, unless there was proof of damages to either consumers or rival firms. The Wheeler-Lea Act removed this limitation and gave the FTC extended powers to prosecute and ban false or deceptive advertising.

In 1950 Congress passed the Celler-Kefauver Act (sometimes referred to as the antimerger act), which prohibits a firm from acquiring the assets of a competitor if the transaction substantially lessens competition. The Clayton Act, though it prohibits mergers through stock acquisition, proved unable to prevent business combinations from being formed by sale of assets. The Celler-Kefauver Act closed this loophole, further limiting the ability of firms to combine to escape competitive pressures.

Since the intent of the Celler-Kefauver Act is to maintain industrial competition, its applicability to mergers between large firms in the same industry is obvious. The act also prohibits vertical mergers between large firms if competition is reduced by such mergers. For example, the merger of a publishing company with a paper producer is illegal if the courts find that it lessens competition. However, few vertical merger cases have been brought under this act since the early 1970s, when antitrust policy began to focus more on consumer welfare and less directly on the structure of industries.

CURRENT ANTITRUST POLICY

An important trend over the past two decades has been the increased weight given by antitrust policymakers to consumer welfare. If a proposed merger would increase a firm's market share, but is expected to reduce the prices paid by buyers of the industry's output, then opposition to the merger is less likely than before. This position was particularly emphasized by the Reagan administration in the 1980s. The Justice Department signaled that shift with its 1982 Merger Guidelines, recognizing the potential value of mergers for efficiency purposes. The Merger Guidelines called for challenges only to proposed mergers deemed likely to harm consumers.

The new merger policy uses the relatively new Herfindahl index to measure market concentration. (See the "Measures of Economic Activities" boxed feature in the previous chapter.) The 1982 Merger Guidelines, as clarified and extended in

1984 by the Justice Department—and agreed upon in effect by the Federal Trade Commission—indicate that if a merger results in a Herfindahl index of less than 1,000, then the resulting market is unconcentrated, and the merger generally will not be challenged. If the index would be above 1,000 after the merger, and the merger would add at least 100 points to the index, then a challenge is likely.

Other factors also are considered under the guidelines, especially in border-line cases. A merger is less likely to be challenged if

1. Foreign firms are an important source of competition in the industry.
2. One of the firms might otherwise go out of business.
3. The firms in the industry do not produce a homogeneous product (thus, quality competition is more likely).
4. New competitors are likely to enter the industry if the current producers increase their prices.

In general, the purpose of the new guidelines is to bring a challenge against only those mergers likely to harm consumers by significantly increasing the market power of affected firms.

WHICH ACTIONS ARE ANTICOMPETITIVE?

Unfortunately for the conduct of good antitrust policy, it is often difficult to know when observed behavior is really anticompetitive. The same actions described earlier as ways to reduce competition can also be used to produce and sell more economically, or better satisfy customers.

Consider predatory pricing. Price cutting by a more efficient firm in an industry will tend to drive less efficient firms out of business, but this is not considered

---

THUMBNAIL SKETCH

WHAT DOES ANTITRUST LEGISLATION PROHIBIT?

Antitrust laws prohibit the following practices:

1. Collusion—contracts and conspiracies to restrain trade (Sherman Act, Sec. 1)
2. Monopoly and attempts to monopolize any part of trade or commerce among the several states (Sherman Act, Sec. 2)
3. Persons serving on the board of directors of competing firms with more than $1 million of assets (Clayton Act, Sec. 8)
4. Unfair and deceptive advertising (Federal Trade Commission Act as amended by Wheeler-Lea Act)
5. Price discrimination if the intent is to injure a competitor (Robinson-Patman Act)

Antitrust laws prohibit the following practices when they substantially lessen competition or tend to create a monopoly:

1. Tying contracts (Clayton Act, Sec. 3)
2. Exclusive dealings (Clayton Act, Sec. 3)
3. Interlocking stockholdings and horizontal mergers (Clayton Act, Sec. 7, as amended by Celler-Kefauver Act)
4. Interlocking directorates (Clayton Act, Sec. 8)

"predatory" unless the pricing is below cost. And how can anyone know whether the price is truly below the cost of production and delivery without knowing intimate details about how the firm's costs vary with the season, the territory, with other products produced, and so on? Investigating many cases of alleged predatory pricing over the years, economists have found that the evidence often failed to support the charges. A price cutter's competitors may be unhappy, but that may simply reflect vigorous competition rather than the presence of anticompetitive behavior.

Exclusive contracts, or dealerships, are another tool that can have legitimate uses. If two manufacturers sell competing products, and one advertises heavily to stimulate consumer interest, the other may benefit without bearing the cost. For example, suppose that A-OK and X-tra Good are both manufacturers of lawn mowers. The A-OK company decides to spend $20 million on a massive advertising campaign. Customers, drawn by the campaign, flock to Marty's Mower Mart, where X-tra Good mowers are also sold, and they are able to make price and performance comparisons between the two brands. Obviously, without spending a penny on advertising, X-tra Good will benefit from the expensive campaign of its competitor, and since its advertising costs are lower, it may be able to sell at a lower price. Similarly, if A-OK trains Marty's personnel in service methods that could be used for both products, X-tra Good also gets a free ride on the service offered. A-OK could avoid these undesirable spillover effects of its advertising campaign and its training program if it could require that Marty's Mower Mart carry only the A-OK brand. If it cannot so require, it may forgo these activities, and consumers will forgo the benefits of those activities.

Unfortunately, it is often difficult to identify and separate anticompetitive behavior from competitive actions that cut the costs of marketing and product service. Thus, formulating and administering a set of antitrust laws that consistently promote competition in the marketplace is not an easy task.

ANTITRUST POLICY—DISSENTING VIEWS

For the reasons just given and for others as well, economists have always been somewhat critical of antitrust policy. People in business also are critical, often arguing that current legislation is so vague that it is difficult to determine whether a proposed action is in compliance. In addition to the need for greater clarity, some analysts believe that there is a need for stronger laws and more vigorous enforcement. Another school of thought holds that antitrust policy does more harm than good and actually is unnecessary. Let us look briefly at each of these positions.

ANTITRUST POLICIES SHOULD BE STRONGER AND MORE VIGOROUSLY ENFORCED. The proponents of this position argue that greater effort is required to ensure the existence of competitive markets. They often point out that antitrust policy has functioned primarily as a holding action. That is, it prevents large firms from increasing their market share, but it is ineffective as a means for reducing industrial concentration. Policy can end up working against its own objectives. For example, an established firm controlling 50 or 60 percent of a market is generally left untouched, whereas two smaller firms with a combined market share of as little as 10 percent may be prohibited from merging. Current policy, therefore, often protects strong, established firms while weakening their smaller rivals. Those who view current policy as self-defeating typically favor an antitrust policy that would more thoroughly restructure concentrated industries, dividing large firms into smaller, independent units.

ANTITRUST POLICY IS UNNECESSARY OR HARMFUL. The advocates of this position argue that antitrust legislation places too much emphasis on the number of competitors without recognizing the positive role of dynamic competition. They believe an antitrust policy that limits business concentration will often promote inefficient business organization and will therefore encourage higher prices. They reject the notion that pure competition is a proper standard of economic efficiency.[5] As Joseph Schumpeter, an early proponent of this view of competition and regulation, emphasized more than four decades ago, "It . . . is a mistake to base the theory of government regulation of industry on the principle that big business should be made to work as the respective industry would work in perfect competition."[6]

Like Schumpeter, current advocates of this position believe innovative activity is at the heart of competition. An ingenious innovator may forge ahead of competitors, but competition from other innovators will always be present. The competitor facing such innovation may seek shelter by demanding agency enforcement of antitrust laws against its successful competitors, or it may file suit itself. In fact, for every antitrust case brought by government, 20 are brought by private parties. Competition, according to this view, is a perpetual game of leapfrog, not a process that is dependent on the number of firms in an industry. Bigness is a natural outgrowth of efficiency and successful innovation. One of the leading proponents of this position, John McGee, a long-time Professor of Economics at the University of Washington, argues that concentration is neither inefficient nor indicative of a lack of competition:

> Take an industry of many independent producers, each of which is efficiently using small scale and simple methods to make the same product. . . . Suppose that a revolution in technology or management techniques now occurs, so that there is room in the market for only one firm using the new and most efficient methods. Whether it occurs quickly through merger or gradually through bankruptcy, an atomistic industry is transformed into a "monopoly," albeit one selling the same product at a lower price than before. If expected long-run price should rise, resort can still be had to the old and less efficient ways, which were compatible with . . . small firms. It would be incomplete and misleading to describe that process as a "decline of competition."[7]

Some observers point out that where other forces, such as foreign competition, protect consumers by offering additional options, antitrust measures that may reduce efficiency can harm competitiveness and disadvantage domestic producers. MIT economist Lester Thurow writes that "in markets where international trade exists or could exist, national antitrust laws no longer make sense. If they do anything, they only serve to hinder U.S. competitors who must live by a code that their foreign competitors can ignore."[8]

---

[5]See Dominick T. Armentano, *Antitrust and Monopoly: Anatomy of a Policy Failure* (New York: John Wiley, 1982), for an excellent presentation of this viewpoint.

[6]Joseph Schumpeter, *Capitalism, Socialism and Democracy* (New York: Harper Torchbooks, 1950), p. 106.

[7]John S. McGee, *In Defense of Industrial Concentration* (New York: Praeger, 1971), pp. 21–22.

[8]Lester Thurow, *The Zero Sum Society* (New York: Basic Books, 1980), p. 146.

MERGERS: ARE THEY PRODUCTIVE?

Mergers have periodically swept over the U.S. economy in waves. The first great wave occurred between 1887 and 1904 and the second between 1916 and 1929. The latest began with a surge in the early 1980s, and continued strongly into the second half of the decade. The largest acquisition occurred in 1988 when the investment firm of Kohlberg Kravis Roberts & Company (KKR) bought the RJR Nabisco Company for $24.7 billion.

A new method of financing was used in the KKR takeover, and in many others that received so much attention during the period. These were *leveraged buyouts* (LBOs), in which the acquiring firm borrowed large amounts of money in order to make the purchases. KKR borrowed $18 billion by selling bonds secured by RJR Nabisco's assets and future profits. These were called *junk bonds* because the risk of nonrepayment was considered to be high. They were also called *high-yield bonds* because lenders (the bond buyers) demanded a high rate of return as compensation for the additional risk. The newly formed firms had a large debt to repay, at a high interest rate. KKR did very well, as it sold off some parts of RJR Nabisco at attractive prices and paid off much of the debt. Some of the other acquiring firms did not perform so well, however, and could not fully pay off the junk bonds.

PROS AND CONS OF MERGERS

On balance, were the leveraged buyouts a good thing? Economists are not in total agreement on their evaluations of the costs and benefits of the 1980s' wave of mergers and acquisitions. Their discussions shed light on the current state of economic thinking on the benefits and costs of corporate reorganization via the market for corporate control.[9]

Economists who defend the merger and acquisition wave of the 1980s point to several ways in which the additional corporate reorganizations may have enhanced economic productivity.

LARGER (OR SMALLER) FIRMS MAY BE MORE EFFICIENT.   The merger of Piedmont Airlines and U.S. Air gave the combined firm the ability to provide better service by integrating their routes and schedules. With other reorganizations, such as RJR Nabisco, decentralization (breaking up the parts of the firm) created more market value. As junk bonds allowed broader public participation and reduced the costs of large mergers and acquisitions, the restructuring of large corporations by outsiders as well as by corporate officials became more practical.

COMPLEMENTARY STRENGTHS.   Merging two complementary firms can make both of them more productive and more profitable. For example, if one firm is very good at making textbooks, and another is very good at marketing them, then merging the two may make a new firm that is more productive than the two were separately.

---

[9]The remainder of this section draws heavily on the symposium on takeovers printed in *The Journal of Economic Perspectives* 2, no. 1 (Winter 1988), pp. 3–82.

MANAGEMENT EFFICIENCIES. Suppose that Oil Incorporated, a hypothetical firm, earns a high profit now because of wise choices made years ago, but it is using those profits to support unproductive parts of the firm. As a result of such wasteful activity, it is earning only a normal profit on average. Our imaginary firm is worth less, and its stock price is lower, than it could be if the unproductive components were shut down or sold off to more productive users. Its managers do not want to drop the unproductive activities, however, and stockholders have not been able to elect a board of directors that will force the needed change. In such a situation, another more profit-oriented firm might profit by taking over (buying) Oil Inc. and making the productive changes. The value of the combined firms would be increased.

For these and other reasons, the mergers and takeovers in the 1980s created some benefits in the form of greater economic efficiency. However, some economists are skeptical that increased productivity was always the purpose of the many deals made. As the following list points out, deals might be undertaken for reasons that have little to do with greater efficiency.

1. *Tax benefits.* If Corporation X makes large accounting profits, it will pay high taxes. If Firm Y shows accounting losses, it will pay no tax. If the two firms merge, so that the profits of X are offset by the accounting losses of Y, then the combined firm pays little or no taxes. A merger might be arranged simply to reduce the total taxes paid by the participants.

2. *Gains in market or political power.* If a merger reduces competition between firms in an industry, their combined market power may be enhanced. Product price would increase and output would fall. Even if that is not the case, the combined firms might gain political power, enabling them to influence legislation in their own interest at the expense of other market participants. Either of these changes would probably decrease total productivity even though the firms might become more profitable.

3. *Manager ambitions.* The personal ambitions of managers might lead them to seek mergers to add to the size and visibility of the firms they manage, independent of whether productivity is enhanced. Their personal desire to control a larger firm may cloud their judgment about the profitability of a merger.

These and other factors mean that not every merger or acquisition is likely to increase efficiency in the economy. What can be said, on balance, about the net benefits of mergers, from observing the merger wave of the 1980s? Studies indicate that stock-market participants, at least, believed that on average, the mergers and acquisitions were productive. Buyers and sellers in the stock market clearly were more willing to buy and hold stock in firms targeted for takeover mergers, demonstrating their belief that takeovers are likely to improve the performance of firms being purchased. Takeovers usually caused the value of stock in the "target" firm—the one purchased—to rise. The value of stock in acquiring firms did not do as well, however, especially when other firms had made competing bids for the target firm. The price of stock in acquiring companies went down as often as it went up for the winning firms when there was more than one bid for a target firm. While market results suggest that takeovers were productive on average, they also indicate that most of the productivity gains occurred in target firms. Certainly most of the market benefits flowed to those holding stock in the target firms.

THEORIES OF REGULATION AND REGULATORY POLICY

Antitrust policy seeks to assure that the structure of industry is competitive. Paradoxically, though, modern monopoly is often the result of government policy, as we see in the markets for local telephone service, broadcasting, airports, and taxi service. When government itself has established the monopoly, antitrust policy is not useful to protect market participants from monopoly results. For this reason, to protect consumer and worker health and safety, and for other purposes as well, business regulation is often used.

Regulatory policies are usually direct and specific, often dictating prices or operating procedures of business firms. What results can we expect from regulation? To date, economists have been unable to develop a complete theory of regulation. Given the complex array of political and economic factors involved, this should not be surprising. In regulated markets, predicting what sellers will offer and how much consumers will be willing to buy at various prices is not enough. The regulatory process also must take account of (1) buyers who are unwilling to pay the full cost, (2) sellers who are inefficient producers, (3) politicians who are simultaneously considering thousands of pieces of legislation, and (4) voters who are, for the most part, "rationally uninformed" on regulatory issues. It is not easy to predict how such a complex system will deal with economic problems.

We can, however, facilitate our discussion of regulation by breaking it down into two major types: traditional economic regulation and the newer health and safety regulation. We can also draw some conclusions about the decision making of economic and political participants in the regulatory process. For example, economic analysis indicates that decision makers in the regulatory process, like those in other areas, respond to incentives. There are three incentive-related characteristics of the regulatory process that should be kept in mind:

1. The demand for regulation often stems from special-interest effects and redistribution considerations rather than from the pursuit of economic efficiency. The wealth of an individual (or business firm) can be increased by an improvement in efficiency and an expansion in production. Regulation introduces another possibility. Sellers can gain if competition in their market is restricted. Buyers can gain, at least in the short run, if a legal requirement forcing producers to supply goods below cost is passed. Regulation opens up an additional avenue whereby those most capable of bending the political process to their advantage can increase their wealth.

Our earlier analysis suggested that special-interest groups, such as well-organized, concentrated groups of buyers or sellers, exert a disproportionate influence on the political process. In addition, the regulators themselves often comprise a politically powerful interest group. Bureaucratic entrepreneurs are key figures in the regulatory process. Their cooperation is important to those who are regulated. In exchange for cooperation, politicians and bureaucrats are offered all manner of political support.

These factors suggest that there will be demand for economic regulation even if it contributes to economic inefficiency. The wealth of specific groups of buyers, sellers, and political participants may be enhanced, even though the total size of the economic pie is reduced. This is particularly true if organized opposition is lacking, because then the burden of economic inefficiency is widely dispersed among rationally uninformed taxpayers and consumers.

2. *Regulation is inflexible—it often fails to adjust to changing market conditions.* Dynamic change often makes regulatory procedures obsolete. The introduction of the truck vastly changed the competitiveness of the ground transportation industry (previously dominated by railroad interests). Nevertheless, the regulation of price, entry, and routes continued for years after competitive forces had eliminated the monopoly power of firms in this industry. Similarly, city building codes that may have been appropriate when adopted have become obsolete and now retard the introduction of new, more efficient materials and procedures. In many cities regulatory procedures have prevented builders from introducing such cost-saving materials as plastic pipes, preconstructed septic tanks, and prefabricated housing units.

Why does the process work this way? In contrast with the market process, regulatory procedures generally grant a controlling voice to established producers. The introduction of new, more efficient products would reduce the wealth of the existing producers of protected products. The political (regulatory) process is

8-18

Dunagin

1977 Sentinel Star
Field Newspaper Syndicate

"OF COURSE YOU MAY REGISTER A COMPLAINT ABOUT ALL THE GOVERNMENT PAPERWORK, SIR... BUT IT HAS TO BE IN WRITING."

Dunagin's People by Ralph Dunagin © Field Enterprises, Inc. 1977. Permission of News America Syndicate.

often responsive to these producers' charges that substitute materials (or new producers) would create unfair competition, violate safety codes, or generally be unreliable. Hearings are held. Lawsuits are often filed. Regulatory commissions meet and investigate—again and again. These procedures result in high costs, long delays, and inflexibility.

3. With the passage of time, regulatory agencies often adopt the views of the business interests they are supposed to regulate. Although the initial demand for regulatory action sometimes originates with disorganized groups seeking protection from practices they consider unfair or indicative of monopolistic power, forces are present that will generally dilute or negate the impact of such groups in the long run. Individual consumers (and taxpayers) have little incentive to be greatly concerned with regulatory actions. Often they are lulled into thinking that since there is a regulatory agency, the "public interest" is served. In contrast, firms (and employees) in regulated industries are vitally interested in the structure and composition of regulatory commissions. Favorable actions by the commission could lead to larger profits, higher-paying jobs, and insulation from the uncertainties of competition. Thus, firms and employee groups, recognizing their potential gain, invest both economic and political resources to influence the actions of regulatory agencies.

How do vote-maximizing political entrepreneurs behave under these conditions? The payoffs from supporting the views of an apathetic public are small. Clearly, the special-interest effect is present. When setting policy and making appointments to regulatory agencies, political entrepreneurs have a strong incentive to support the position of well-organized business and labor interests—often the very groups the regulatory practices were originally designed to police.

Regulatory activity in the United States has expanded substantially in the past two decades. As **Exhibit 22–2** shows, federal regulatory spending and staffing levels increased rapidly in the 1970s, dropped in the early 1980s, then resumed their expansion in the late 1980s and early 1990s. Budgeted 1994 federal spending for economic regulation was $2.8 billion, while the figure for health and safety regulation expenditures was $11.5 billion. Compliance costs are much larger. For example, budgeted federal expenditures on environmental regulation for 1991 were $4.6 billion, but the Environmental Protection Agency estimates that annual expenditures by others to meet the objectives of environmental regulation brought the national spending total to $115 billion.

TRADITIONAL ECONOMIC REGULATION

Economic regulation

Regulation of product price or industrial structure, usually imposed on a specific industry. By and large, the production processes used by the regulated firms are unaffected by this type of regulation.

Regulation of business activity is not a new development. In 1887 Congress established the Interstate Commerce Commission (ICC), providing it with the authority to regulate the railroad industry. In 1935 the trucking industry was also brought under the ICC's regulatory jurisdiction. State regulatory commissions began to oversee local delivery of electricity, natural gas, and telephone services as early as 1907. Little was done at the federal level to expand regulation beyond the railroads until the 1930s, when commissions were formed during the Roosevelt administration to regulate interstate telephone service, broadcasting, airlines, natural gas pipelines, and other industries. These activities focus on **economic regulation** and usually control the product price or the structure of a particular industry rather than specifying the production processes used by the regulated firm.

EXHIBIT 22-2

TRENDS IN REGULATORY SPENDING AND STAFFING BY FEDERAL GOVERNMENT, 1970–1994

TRENDS IN REGULATORY SPENDING

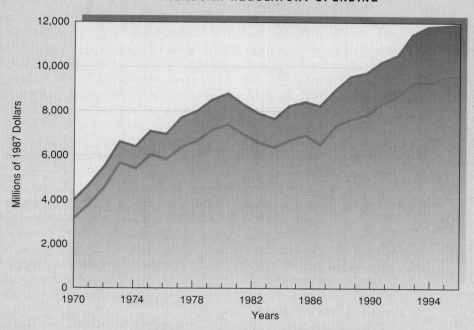

FEDERAL REGULATORY STAFFING TRENDS

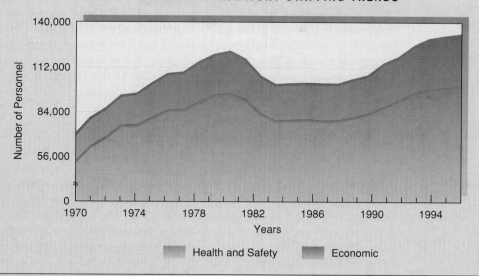

Health and Safety   Economic

Source: Center for the Study of American Business, Washington University. Derived from the *Budget of the United States Government* and related documents, various fiscal years.

Regulation is normally justified as action taken to protect the general public. There are three main purposes given for the economic regulation of firms:

1. To control a natural monopoly. If the delivery of electricity in a local area is thought to be a natural monopoly, then encouraging competition by increasing the numbers of firms in the industry would be an inefficient way to try to keep prices from high monopoly levels; regulation is typically used instead.

2. To prevent "cutthroat" competition. If firms in an industry have low marginal cost, but high fixed cost—airlines might be a current example—then some observers fear that as each firm competes for extra business, the industry price might be driven down to marginal cost. If this happens, and fixed costs are not covered, firms will eventually be driven out of business until survivors can raise the price enough to cover full cost. Instability in the industry may result. Regulators, by fixing prices, might help to provide orderly competition.

3. To cross-subsidize certain services. Some customers, such as rural families wanting electrical service from a utility, can only be served at a high cost. Regulators, however, can require that an average price be charged in order to serve high-cost customers at a low price without government subsidies. Other customers pay more to provide the low price to high-cost users.

Regulation may be established to promote orderly competition and to keep prices more equal across classes of customers, but it will have other effects as well. Rules designed to restrict entry and control competition among members of an industry are not likely to encourage efficient production. Detailed restrictions on what firms can produce, when and where they can sell it, and on other actions may be needed to prevent disputes among potentially competitive firms with many incentives to get around the rules. In a constantly changing economic environment, because they reduce the discipline of competition from new entrants, such regulations often become costly.

High costs and production inefficiencies helped to generate widespread dissatisfaction with the traditional regulation of several industries during the 1970s. Major steps toward deregulation were taken in the ground and air transportation industries as a result. Consumers benefited substantially from that change, confirming many of the criticisms that many economists and others had leveled at the regulatory process. The recent debate over the restructuring of health care is due mainly to rising costs, which are due partly to the effects of regulation on segments of that industry. (See "Applications in Economics" box on health care.)

THE NEW HEALTH AND SAFETY REGULATION

Health and safety regulation

Legislation designed to improve the health, safety, and environmental conditions available to workers and/or consumers. The legislation usually mandates production procedures, minimum standards, and/or product characteristics to be met by producers and employers.

Along with movement toward deregulation of industrial structure and prices, there has been a sharp increase in **health and safety regulation.** In the late 1960s and early 1970s, people had great faith in the ability of government to improve the quality of life. The economy was prospering, and people turned their attention more toward reducing health hazards, preserving environmental quality, and reducing the negative impacts of new technologies and the booming economy. For a wealthier nation, reducing air and water pollution and other externalities became more feasible and more desirable. Added regulation to protect individuals against risks from occupational hazards as well as risks from newly developed drugs and other consumer products was also demanded by activist groups.

The new health and safety regulation resulted from these demands. As Exhibit 22–2 indicates, agencies such as the Occupational Safety and Health

APPLICATIONS IN ECONOMICS

AT&T AND CROSS-SUBSIDIES

Cross-subsidies are a perennial issue in regulation. When a regulated firm serves more than one market, regulators must allocate fixed costs to each market if they are to set prices according to the average (or total) costs of production. In economics, there is no logical way to allocate such joint costs between the two markets. An unregulated firm has no need to do so. Based on marginal costs and marginal revenues, the firm charges a price to maximize profit (or minimize loss) in each market. Any economic profit leads to more entry, until the price is driven down to average cost. When price (and entry) are regulated, however, the arbitrary division of joint costs is necessary, and consumers in one market may be required to subsidize those in the other market. So it was in the case of telephones.

Local telephone lines are a fixed cost of providing both local and long-distance services. Until the AT&T divestiture settlement in 1982, state and federal regulators had agreed to load much of the fixed cost of the local lines onto the long-distance bills, which were charged according to minutes of use by customers. Rather than recognize the fixed nature of these costs (the same wires had to be in place and maintained regardless of how many minutes they were used, and whether any long-distance calls were made) and charge each customer the true fixed cost, fixed charges were kept low. Long-distance rates were set high enough to make up the difference.

The result of this system was to provide large subsidies to local service at the expense of long-distance telephone customers. Those who used more than 50 minutes per month[1] of long-distance service paid more than their share of the combined system's costs, while those using less than 50 minutes (a large majority) paid less than the costs they generated. In general, businesses and a few other users paid far more than their share.

The system was politically very popular at the state and local level, because as telephone customers paid their bills each month, they had detailed information before them. Seldom is there a situation like this in which consumers know just who to blame in case of a rate increase. In large numbers, they complained to their state regulatory commissioners whenever commissioners allowed those bills to rise. The large users were unable to counter the popular pressure on politically selected commissioners. The majority was understandably less upset when others paid the higher bills. This system was very inefficient, however. Long-distance calls costing only 7 to 9 cents a minute at the margin were charged at 30 to 40 cents, so everyone used far less than the optimal amount of long-distance service. The net result was an estimated loss to the economy of $10 to $14 billion. AT&T did not mind the cross-subsidy of local service by long distance, since it provided both, and was assured a fixed rate of return by the regulators.

When technical advances made it possible for new suppliers to enter the industry and serve large customers at a lower rate, the system began to come apart. If the new suppliers could offer a better deal to the biggest customers, the source of the cross-subsidies would disappear. Regulators could keep newcomers out, but now the really huge size of the penalties paid by large users was becoming obvious, and the politics of continuing the system of cross-subsidies to large customers became less attractive.

Following the divestiture agreement, AT&T continued to provide long-distance service at rates regulated by the Federal Communications Commission, but MCI, GTE Sprint, and other competitors were also allowed into the market. State regulators still would like to keep local rates low and load costs onto long-distance users, but now AT&T and the other long-distance suppliers, not owning the local firms, are hurt by such an arrangement and will fight it. Lower long-distance rates and higher fixed charges for local service are observable effects of the competitive forces now in place.

---

[1]This estimate, and the others in this feature, were reported by Professor John T. Wenders in ". . . And Now Learn to Love the Chaos," *The Wall Street Journal*, November 29, 1985.

SHOULD THE U.S. HEALTH-CARE INDUSTRY BE RESTRUCTURED?

Health care in the United States is costly, and the cost has been rising. In real terms, health-care expenditures more than doubled from 1970 to 1990. Much of the cost is paid by employers, including payments for retirees. These costs can be substantial. In 1992 General Motors, for example, was forced by a change in accounting rules to record a $22.2 billion charge on its balance sheet for retiree and future retiree health costs.[1] Rising costs have led to concerns that some consumers will be priced out of the health-care market, that increases in the costs of doing business in the United States harm the nation's ability to compete in world trade, and that higher government health-care program costs will force an increase in taxes or deficit spending. These concerns made a restructuring of the health-care industry a high priority for the Clinton administration.

What sort of restructuring, if any, would help reduce the rate of increase in health-care costs? The economic approach to seeking an answer to this question indicates that we must first understand why costs have risen. If rising health expenditures are due to distortions in demand, then reforming consumer incentives may help to solve the problem. If distortions in supply are the problem, then policies that affect the suppliers would be appropriate. A careful look at the health-care market indicates that costs are raised by several factors.

Consider the following demand-side factors:

1. Patients pay only about 20 percent of their medical bills out-of-pocket, so they use more medical services than they would if they paid all of their bills directly. A rising share of individual health-care costs is paid by government or by private insurers. The cost to individuals is only loosely tied to their expenditures. Consumers purchase more, and are less careful shoppers when someone else picks up all or most of the bill, so there is less incentive for health-care providers to find new ways to cut the cost of their services. The demand for new, higher-quality services rises under these circumstances.

2. Since World War II, payments for medical insurance have been untaxed, encouraging consumers to take a larger share of their income as insurance payments, even though this reduces their take-home pay.

The untaxed good (insurance in this case) is more attractive. A study in 1992 estimated that the "tax subsidy" reduced government revenue by $65 billion and increased private health-insurance spending by roughly one-third. In addition, the Clinton administration and others argue that complex billing procedures add transaction costs when many competing insurance plans pay a large portion of all medical bills. The tax subsidy is larger for individuals in higher-income (and thus higher-income-tax) brackets, so higher-income individuals choose much more medical coverage, while lower-income individuals receive a much smaller subsidy.

3. The increasing affluence of consumers has led to more purchases of most goods, including medical services.

4. Demographics have also played a part. The aging of the U.S. population has substantially increased the demand for medical services. Individuals under 19 years of age, for example, used less than $900 worth of medical care annually in 1987, while those aged 64–84 used $5,000 worth of care.

Supply-side factors also have increased the cost of services delivered:

1. Government restrictions on suppliers of health-care goods and services have raised health costs. For example, one study estimated that in 1982 state restrictions on the use by dentists of dental assistants cost consumers $700 million. Drug reviews by the federal Food and Drug Administration (FDA) delay the introduction of new drugs by an estimated 2.5 years, and add millions of dollars to the development cost of each drug. The benefit of this policy is that fewer ineffective or dangerous drugs are introduced, so some harm is avoided. But many useful drugs are kept off the market for several extra years, harming those who would have been helped, and the cost of all drugs is increased. These and other regulatory costs drive up health-care prices substantially.

2. Information is highly imperfect in the health-care market, even among health-care professionals. For example, a 1992 study by economist Charles Phelps showed that there is substantial disagreement within the medical profession about the usefulness of alternative medical treatments. Costs rise due to the utilization of less useful treatments and due to lawsuits over

alleged medical mistakes. These lawsuits, and defensive medical practice to avoid such liability, add an estimated $36 billion per year to the nation's medical bills. Consumers know even less about medical options than the professionals, and so there is a principal-agent problem. Health-care providers may increase their own incomes by dispensing costlier options than fully informed patients would choose.

In light of these factors, what policy approaches are suggested by the economic way of thinking? First, the factors that distort demand and supply might be removed. Insurance policies could be modified to increase the portion of most medical bills paid out-of-pocket by consumers. Many private insurance schemes are doing just that, as a cost-control measure. Government tax policies that subsidize medical insurance purchases, especially by high-wage employees, could be altered to reduce the subsidy. Record-keeping and billing procedures might be simplified. State and federal government restrictions on entry into health-care provision (often enacted at the request of specific groups of health providers in order to shelter them from competition) could be loosened or removed to increase competition and lower costs.

Currently, Congress is considering a number of proposals which would require all individuals to join health plans providing uniform coverage regardless of income or employment. Most of these plans, including the one advocated by the Clinton administration, would limit total health-care expenditures, with legal penalties imposed on violators. Economists recognize a serious problem with this approach: If the spending limits are low enough to make a difference, quality deterioration and shortages will occur.

Some of the factors contributing to high prices in the health-care market are not amenable to control by policy measures. Demographic factors, such as rising incomes and an aging population, will not be changed if the health-care market is restructured. Together, these two factors accounted for an estimated one-quarter of the increase in expenditures from 1960 to 1990. Also, restructuring the health-care industry would do little to reduce the lack of information within the health community on the causes and the best cures for many human ills.

Unfortunately, economics suggests that there is no easy answer to the problem of rising health-care costs.

---

[1]This dollar figure and many other specifics in this feature are taken from an excellent review of the health-care problem by Beverly Fox, Lori L. Taylor, Mine K. Yucel, "America's Health Care Problem: an Economic Perspective," *Economic Review,* third quarter 1993, Federal Reserve Bank of Dallas, pp. 21–31. They cite many sources for the facts and estimates in their review.

Administration (OSHA), Consumer Product Safety Commission (CPSC), Food and Drug Administration (FDA), and Environmental Protection Agency (EPA) grew rapidly. These new agencies as a group are now far larger, in terms of number of employees and size of budgets, than the older regulatory agencies.

There are several significant differences between the two types of regulation. The older economic regulation focuses on a specific industry, whereas health and safety regulation applies to the entire economy. Also, though more broadly based, health and safety regulation is much more involved than economic regulation in the actual operation of individual firms. Economic regulation confines its attention to price and product quality—the final outcomes of production. The health and safety regulatory agencies, on the other hand, frequently specify in detail the engineering processes to be followed by regulated firms and industries.

The major cost of health and safety regulation is generally felt in the form of higher production costs and thus higher prices. As producers alter production techniques and facilities in accordance with dictated standards—to install more restrooms, to emit less pollution, or to reduce noise levels, for example—costs rise. And, of course, there are costs associated with the process of regulation itself as well: employment and operating costs of regulatory agencies must be met, which

means higher taxes. The primary cost of health and safety regulation, however, comes in the form of higher operating costs of firms striving to meet the new standards. In effect, these higher costs are like a tax. As **Exhibit 22–3** illustrates, the higher cost shifts the supply curve to the left for a good affected by the regulation. Higher prices and a decline in the output of the good result.

Who pays the cost? As with any tax, the burden is shared by buyers and sellers according to the elasticity of supply and demand. When consumers have more options to the taxed good, so that their demand is more elastic, they will pay a small portion of the tax. In Exhibit 22–3, the new price $(P_2 + t)$ will be closer to P_1 when demand is more elastic. On the other hand, sellers will pay a smaller portion when the supply curve is more elastic, meaning that they have other options besides production of this regulated good. In the short run, suppliers of goods may have few options for the use of capital already committed to the production

BUYING FUEL CONSERVATION—EXPENSIVELY

Fear of global warming—which some scientists think could be caused by rising levels of carbon dioxide in the air—has led to louder calls for more fuel-efficient cars, since cars that burn less fuel emit less carbon dioxide. In 1991 U.S. Senator Richard Bryan introduced a bill into Congress that would require auto makers to boost their average mileage per gallon (mpg) from 27.5 mpg to 40 mpg.

Would such a mandatory fuel economy reduce fuel usage significantly? And if so, at what cost? We have some answers to these questions because Congress has been mandating fuel-economy standards since 1975. Experience with these standards reveals some severe problems and indicates that large sacrifices will be required if standards are further tightened. The problems also illustrate the complex effects of government regulations.

Congress mandated Corporate Average Fuel Economy (CAFE) standards in 1975 after the price of oil went up dramatically. Supporters said that the standards would conserve energy and make the United States less dependent on foreign oil. However, if Congress had simply allowed gasoline prices to rise, the higher prices would have encouraged people to adjust their habits in ways that suited them individually and minimized their personal cost. Some consumers would have simply driven less; others would have saved on gasoline by buying smaller cars or having more tune-ups. Some people who lived far from their workplaces might have bought larger cars and car-pooled; others might have chosen to live in places where they could walk to work.

Indeed, before the CAFE standards had an impact, people began to respond to higher gasoline prices by purchasing fuel-efficient cars. According to the *1986 Economic Report of the President*, average fuel economy in the United States increased by 43 percent between 1973 and 1979, as consumers responded to higher fuel prices. By the time the fuel-efficiency standards influenced the design of cars, which probably occurred with model year 1986, much fuel economy had already been achieved and the price of gasoline was going down.

By that time, some consumers wanted larger cars, but the CAFE standards forced auto makers to offer smaller cars. Although they could make some reductions in fuel usage by such steps as redesigning transmissions or fuel-injection systems, car companies had to reduce vehicle weight to meet the standards. Robert W. Crandall of the Brookings Institution and John Graham of the Harvard School of Public Health estimate that model year 1989 cars were on average 500 pounds lighter than they would have been without the CAFE standards.[1]

A serious problem with lighter cars is that they are less safe than larger cars in crashes. Crandall and Graham estimated that 2,200 to 3,900 lives would be lost over a 10-year period as a result of the application of the CAFE standards to the cars of the 1989 model year, with similar numbers of lives likely to be lost with each succeeding model year. These findings led Jerry Ralph Curry, administrator of the National Highway Traffic Safety Administration, to oppose tighter standards in 1991. "The bottom line is drastically smaller cars and more injuries and deaths," he wrote in *The Washington Post*.

The CAFE standards have had other unwanted effects. To sell enough small cars to raise the fuel-economy average, domestic auto makers reduced small-car prices and raised prices for large cars. Buying decisions were distorted, and consumers paid more on balance for their cars.

Because Congress required the car companies to calculate average fuel economy separately for their domestic-manufactured cars and their imports, they cannot use their smaller, more fuel-efficient imports to bring down their domestic fleets' average. This has encouraged small-car production in the United States, even though production might be cheaper overseas, and has led the Ford Motor Company to move some of its large-car production out of the country.

Another outcome of the CAFE regulations was to set in motion a big lobbying effort in Washington D.C.—taking creative skills and energy away from productive activity. General Motors and Ford have lobbied to keep the government from tightening the standards. In contrast, Chrysler Corporation, which specializes in small cars, has a vested interest in keeping the standards tight, because the standards increase the costs of their rivals.

Were the CAFE standards effective in reducing fuel use? Not very. According to the Federal Highway Administration, even though fuel usage per vehicle has

APPLICATIONS IN ECONOMICS *(continued)*

fallen since 1969, total fuel consumption has been rising since 1982. With large cars more expensive as a result of the standards, some people probably kept their old cars longer, increasing gas consumption (and pollution). The lower prices of small cars probably increased the total number of cars purchased. More cars on the road meant greater fuel consumption because the marginal cost of driving in a small car is lower than in a large car, and because smaller car sizes lead people to share fewer rides. Robert A. Leone of Boston University estimates that a 2- or 3-cent tax on gasoline beginning in 1984 would have saved as much fuel as the CAFE standards did, at much less cost to society. In sum, the evidence suggests that the standards did not accomplish what was intended and placed costly burdens on society.

Source: Jane S. Shaw, Senior Associate at the Political Economy Research Center, Bozeman, Montana.

[1]Robert W. Crandall and John D. Graham, "The Effect of Fuel Economy Standards on Automobile Safety," *Journal of Law and Economics* 32, no. 1 (April 1989), 97–118.

process. Therefore, the short-run supply is likely to be inelastic. In the long run, of course, capital is quite mobile among uses, and the supply should be more elastic.

Sometimes the opportunity cost of health and safety regulation is nearly impossible to calculate. For example, the FDA often bans the sale of a new drug until years of tests costing millions of dollars are completed. Two important opportunity costs of this regulation, if the drug finally proves (or would have proven) to be safe, are (1) some drugs are never developed because of the expensive tests and delays, and (2) people who could have been helped by the drug have to forgo it for several years. Deaths may even result from these delays. These opportunity costs may be very large, but they do not show up as expenditures.

Even when the costs of a regulation are measurable largely in cash, it is frequently difficult to assess the costs per unit of results. For example, there is strong disagreement about the costs and benefits of proposed new regulations for automobile safety. A study by the Brookings Institution[10] indicates that the auto safety regulations of the early 1980s probably provided enough benefits to at least offset their costs. The same study, however, concluded that regulations requiring emission controls to reduce air pollution and other changes to increase fuel efficiency for automobiles have been very costly, while yielding few, if any, benefits. An unintended result of the increased regulatory costs of buying and operating new automobiles has been to reduce their sales, keeping older cars on the road longer. The earlier design of these older cars, and the wear they have experienced, increase the pollution they emit, while decreasing the safety and fuel efficiency they provide. Moreover, the study criticizes the lack of coordination among the many regulations on automobiles. Rules requiring greater fuel economy, for example, make cars smaller, lighter, and less safe. Thus, emission controls often reduce fuel economy, while safety requirements increase weight and decrease performance and fuel economy. Yet each regulation is established with little regard to these conflicting impacts on the consumers.

Health and safety regulation is costly, but it can have important benefits. The primary goal of health and safety regulation is the attainment of a cleaner, safer,

---

[10]See Robert W. Crandall, Howard K. Gruenspecht, Theodore E. Keeler, and Lester B. Lave, *Regulating the Automobile* (Washington, DC: The Brookings Institution, 1986).

EXHIBIT 22–3

THE REGULATION "TAX"

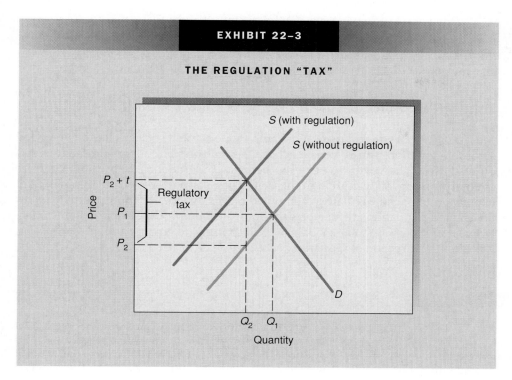

Regulation that requires businesses to adopt more costly production techniques is similar to a tax. If the regulation increases per unit costs by t, the supply curve shifts upward by that amount. Higher prices and a smaller output result.

healthier environment. Nearly everyone agrees that this is a worthy objective. There is, however, considerable disagreement about the procedures that are most likely to accomplish this objective and the price that should be paid to make improvements. Resources are scarce. More health and safety regulation will mean less of other things.

It should not be any more surprising that people disagree on the proper consumption level of environmental amenities than it is that they differ on the proper consumption level of ice cream, for example. If 100 people were asked the best rate of consumption for strawberry ice cream, there would be a wide variety of answers. Similarly, the extent to which we should bear costs to make our air and water cleaner, and drugs safer is a question that each person may answer quite differently. One's preferred consumption rate for these benefits, like the preferred rate for strawberry ice cream, will depend in part on the expected cost and who pays that cost. Those who expect others to foot the bill will naturally prefer more of any valued good, whether it is ice cream or safety.

Differing preferences as to how much of other goods should be given up to attain a safer, cleaner, healthier environment comprise only part of the problem faced by regulators. An important characteristic of most activities covered by health and safety regulations is a lack of information about their effects. This is not a coincidence. In most cases, the lack of information contributes directly to the demand for the regulation. For example, if consumers knew exactly what the effect of a particular drug would be, there would be little need for the FDA to regulate its availability. Many people, though, are unaware of the precise effects of drugs, air pollution, or workplace hazards. Even when the information is available to experts, consumers may never receive it because of the cost of communicating information, particularly highly technical information. A case can be made, therefore, that we should let the experts decide which drugs, how much air pollution, and what forms of workplace safety should be sought. While the lack of information generates much of the demand for health and safety regulation, it also makes it difficult to evaluate the effectiveness of the regulatory activity.

FUTURE DIRECTION FOR REGULATORY POLICY

Most people concede that regulation, both economic and social, is like a two-edged sword. Regulations can be beneficial, but they can also be counter-productive. It is quite difficult, however, to separate beneficial regulations from those that are counterproductive. Even though there is strong support for the continuation and expansion of social regulatory activities, recent experience indicates that forces favoring deregulation are also present. Improved empirical evidence on the effectiveness of specific regulatory policies will continue to emerge and, in some cases, will alter the direction of regulatory activities.

CHAPTER SUMMARY

1. For more than a century, the relative size of the agricultural sector has declined, while the service sector has expanded. Blue-collar occupations have also declined markedly during the past century. The largest increase has been in white-collar jobs, in which employees provide or process information and make decisions.

2. An increasing proportion of the U.S. economy has become competitive over the past several decades, probably due to antitrust policy, rising import competition, and deregulation.

3. Antitrust legislation seeks to (a) maintain a competitive structure in the unregulated private sector and (b) prohibit business practices that are thought to stifle competition.

4. The Sherman, Clayton, and Federal Trade Commission Acts form the foundation of antitrust policy in the United States. The Sherman Act prohibits conspiracies to restrain trade and/or monopolize an industry. The Clayton Act prohibits specific business practices, such as price discrimination, tying contracts, exclusive dealings, and mergers and acquisitions (as amended), when they "substantially lessen competition or tend to create a monopoly." As it has evolved through the years, the Federal Trade Commission is concerned primarily with enforcing consumer protection legislation, prohibiting deceptive advertising, and investigating industrial structure.

5. The merger wave of the 1980s included many hostile takeovers and leveraged buyouts, financed in part by junk bonds. Research to date indicates that such mergers usually increased the efficiency of the target firms, but did not necessarily benefit the acquiring firms.

6. Antitrust policy is made more difficult by the fact that it is not always easy to determine when a business practice is being used to further competition, and when it will have an anticompetitive result. Most economists believe that antitrust policy in the United States has promoted competition and reduced industrial concentration, but not to a dramatic extent.

7. To date, economists have been unable to develop a complete theory of regulation. However, economic analysis does suggest that (a) the demand for regulation often stems from special-interest and redistribution considerations, as when producers are protected against competition, or when one class of customers is cross-subsidized, rather than from the pursuit of economic efficiency; (b) regulation often fails to adjust to changing market conditions; and (c) with the passage of time, regulatory agencies are likely to adopt the views of the interest groups they are supposed to regulate.

10. Traditional economic regulation has generally sought to fix prices and/or influence industrial structure. During the 1970s, changing market conditions and empirical studies generated widespread dissatisfaction with economic regulation. Significant moves toward deregulation were made in the late 1970s, particularly in the trucking and airline industries. New entrants, intense competition, and discount prices have accompanied the deregulation of these industries.

11. In recent years, economic regulation has been relaxed as health and safety regulation has expanded rapidly. Health and safety regulation seeks to provide a cleaner, safer, healthier environment for workers and consumers. Pursuit of this objective is costly, bringing about higher product prices and higher taxes. Since the costs, and

particularly the benefits, are often difficult to measure and evaluate, the efficiency of social regulatory programs is a controversial topic, and the subject of much current research.

CRITICAL-ANALYSIS QUESTIONS

*1. "Manufacturing is dying in the U.S. economy. We are becoming a nation of service workers—hamburger flippers and people who take in each others' laundry—and inevitably a second-rate economy." Evaluate this statement.

2. "Big business is taking over the U.S. economy. Giant firms decide what we can buy, and even what government does." Evaluate this statement.

3. Does the fact that a firm is large indicate that it does not face important competition? Do large firms usually earn a high rate of profit?

*4. "Any merger that reduces competition hurts consumers and clearly should be stopped." Evaluate this statement.

5. "Efficiency requires large-scale production. Yet big businesses mean monopoly power, high prices, and market inefficiency. We must choose between production efficiency and monopoly." Evaluate this statement.

*6. Legislation mandating stronger automobile bumpers has presumably made cars both safer and more expensive, as would legislation requiring air bags for front-seat drivers and passengers. Should these laws be imposed? Why or why not?

7. "Without legal safety requirements, products such as lawn mowers would be unsafe." Evaluate this statement.

*8. Will health and safety legislation mandating workplace and product safety reduce the profitability of the regulated firms? Who bears the cost and who gains the benefits of such legislation?

*9. If tariff and quota barriers for foreign imports are lifted, making imports easier to obtain, does this strengthen or weaken the case for strict antitrust legislation and enforcement?

10. AT&T, which sells long-distance service but no longer is in the local phone service business, now opposes the higher long-distance rates it previously supported. Why?

11. "Voters in our state should insist on state utility regulators who are tough on business. Consumers will benefit if prices are kept from rising above the per unit cost of production." Evaluate this statement.

*12. With rate regulation and control of routes, as the Civil Aeronautics Board imposed on interstate airlines before deregulation, new entry was permitted only when it was shown to be "necessary." What definitions of "necessary" would you expect to hear from (a) existing airlines and (b) customers? Which one would you expect to prevail, and why?

13. "The leveraged buyout craze of the 1980s was an example of capitalism at its worst. Greedy corporate heads were just trying to expand their empires. Huge mountains of debt were generated simply to feed the egos of a few executives." Why might an economist disagree with this statement? Might there be some truth in it, from an economic point of view? Why or why not?

14. "We owe it to our coal miners to see that mines become much safer. Regulations can accomplish this, and the mine owners will pay. Since users of coal have many sources of supply, they will not pay for these regulations. Workers will clearly be better off." Explain the logic here, and show what additional assumptions must be made about mine owners, and about mine workers, before the statement can be true.

*15. "If we force increased safety measures in the workplace by regulation, business may bear the cost in the short run, but capital will receive the market rate of return in the long run." Evaluate this statement, and explain your reasoning.

16. "Regulations on the introduction of new drugs should be strengthened. Fewer people would die if more research were required prior to the introduction of new drugs. Only an economist could possibly disagree. Sure, it would cost more, but saving even one life would surely be worth more than whatever it costs." Evaluate this statement.

*17. "People cannot be expected to make good decisions on their own regarding auto safety. Only experts know enough to make such decisions." Evaluate this statement.

18. "Safety regulation is not an economic question. Where lives and health are at stake, economics has no place." Evaluate this statement.

19. In large cities, taxi fares are often set above the market equilibrium rate. Sometimes the number of licenses is limited in order to maintain the above market price. In other cases, licenses are automatically granted to anyone wanting to operate a taxi. When taxi fares are set above market equilibrium, compare and contrast resource allocation under the restricted license system (assume the licenses are tradable) and the free-entry system. In which case will it be easier for customers to get a taxi? In which case will the amount of capital required to enter the taxi business be greater?

*Asterisk denotes questions for which answers are given in Appendix C.

PART FOUR

FACTOR MARKETS
AND INCOME DISTRIBUTION

CHAPTER TWENTY-THREE

THE SUPPLY OF
AND DEMAND FOR
PRODUCTIVE RESOURCES

It is . . . necessary to attach price tags to the various factors of production . . . in order to guide those who have the day-to-day decisions to make as to what is plentiful and what is scarce.

PROFESSOR JAMES MEADE[1]

CHAPTER FOCUS

■ Why do business firms demand labor, machines, and other resources?
■ Why is the demand for a productive resource inversely related to its price?
■ How do business firms decide how many skilled laborers, unskilled laborers, machines, and other factors of production to employ?
■ How is the quantity supplied of a resource related to its price in the short run? In the long run?
■ What determines the market price in resource markets?

---

[1]James E. Meade, "Economic Efficiency and Distributional Justice" in *Contemporary Issues in Economics*, edited by Robert W. Crandall and Richard S. Eckaus (Boston: Little, Brown, 1972), p. 319.

Resource markets

Markets in which business firms demand factors of production (for example, labor, capital, and natural resources) from household suppliers. The resources are then used to produce goods and services. These markets are sometimes called factor markets.

In previous chapters we focused on the demand and supply conditions in product markets. In these markets, consumers purchase goods and services that are produced by business firms. We now turn to an analysis of **resource markets,** or, as they are sometimes called, *factor markets.* Compensation derived from the sale of the services of productive resources provides the major source of income for most of us. Clearly, conditions in resource markets are vitally important to all of us.

When producing commodities, business firms hire productive resources, which are either directly or indirectly owned by households. The roles of households and business firms in resource markets are reversed from what they were in product markets. In resource markets, households are sellers; they supply resources in exchange for income. Business firms are the purchasers; they demand resources that are used to produce goods and services.

There is a close relationship between resource and product markets. The circular flow diagram of **Exhibit 23–1** illustrates this point. Households earn income by selling factors of production—for example, the services of their labor and capital—to business firms. Their offers to sell form the supply curve in resource markets (bottom loop). In turn, the income households derive from the sale of

Until now, we have focused on product markets, where households demand goods and services which are supplied by firms (upper loop). We now turn to resource markets, where firms demand factors of production—human capital (for example, skills and knowledge of workers) and physical capital (for example, machines, buildings, and land) which are supplied by households in exchange for income (bottom loop). In resource markets, firms are buyers and households are sellers, just the reverse of the case for product markets.

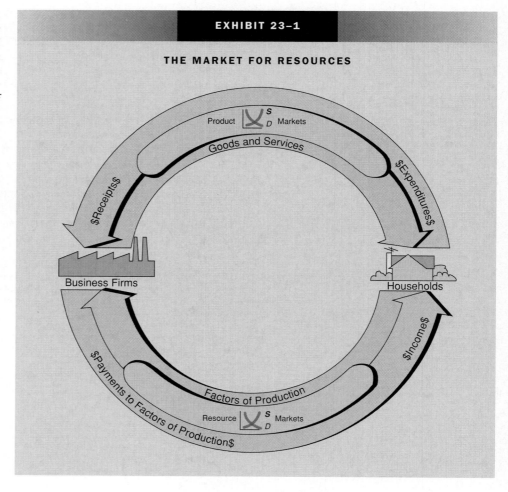

EXHIBIT 23–1

THE MARKET FOR RESOURCES

resources provides them with the buying power required to purchase goods and services in product markets. These household expenditures for products generate revenues that provide business firms with the incentive to produce goods and services (top loop). Finally, the revenues of business firms from product sales underlie their demand for resources.

Business firms demand resources because they contribute to the production of goods and services. Since resources must be bid away from competitive firms seeking to put them to alternative uses, costs are incurred whenever resources are employed. Prices in resource markets coordinate the actions of the firms demanding factors of production and the households supplying them. Resource prices provide both resource suppliers and resource-using producers with information about scarcity. Resource prices (and the accompanying income payments) provide individuals with the incentive to offer their productive services to producers. An increase in the price of a resource will encourage potential suppliers to provide more of the resource. Resource prices also provide profit-seeking firms with an incentive to economize on resource use. Firms will find that it is profitable to hire a resource, if, and only if, the resource adds more to the firm's revenue than to its cost. Thus, an increase in a resource price will encourage firms to cut back on their use of that resource.

HUMAN AND NONHUMAN RESOURCES

Broadly speaking, there are two different types of productive inputs—nonhuman and human. **Nonhuman resources** can be further broken down into the categories of physical capital, land, and natural resources. *Physical capital* consists of man-made goods used to produce other goods, such as tools, machines, and buildings.

Net investment can increase the supply of nonhuman resources—though at the expense of current consumption goods. Resources that are used to produce machines, upgrade the quality of land, or discover natural resources could be used to produce current goods and services directly. Why take the roundabout path? The answer is that sometimes indirect methods of producing goods are less costly in the long run. Robinson Crusoe found he could catch more fish by taking some time off from hand-fishing to build a net. Even though his initial investment in the net reduced his current catch, once the net was completed he was able to more than make up for his earlier loss of output.

Additions to capital stock, then, whether they are fishing nets or complex machines, involve current sacrifices. Capital-intensive methods of production are adopted only when decision makers expect the benefits of a larger future output to more than offset the current reduction in the production of consumption goods.

Just as the supply of machines can be increased, so too can wise land-clearing and soil-conservation practices be used to upgrade both the quantity and quality of land. Similarly, the supply of natural resources can be increased (within limits) by the application of more resources to discovery and development.

Human resources are comprised of the skills and knowledge of workers. Laypersons sometimes act as if these resources are strictly the result of inheritance or happenstance. This is not the case. Investment in such things as education, training, health, and skill-building experience can increase worker productivity

Nonhuman resources
The durable, nonhuman inputs that can be used to produce both current and future output. Machines, buildings, land, and raw materials are examples. Investment can increase the supply of nonhuman resources. Economists often use the term physical capital *when referring to nonhuman resources.*

Human resources
The abilities, skills, and health of human beings that can contribute to the production of both current and future output. Investment in training and education can increase the supply of human resources.

Investment in human capital

Expenditures on training, education, skill development, and health designed to increase the productivity of an individual.

and thereby the availability of human resources. Economists refer to such activities as **investment in human capital.**[2] Like physical capital, human capital also depreciates (as the skills of a person decline with age or lack of use). During any given year, education and training will add to the stock of human capital while depreciation detracts from it.

Decisions to invest in human capital involve all the basic ingredients of other investment decisions. Consider the decision of whether to go to college. As many of you will testify, an investment in a college education requires the sacrifice of current earnings as well as payments for direct expenses such as tuition and books. The investment is expected to lead to a better job (when both monetary and nonmonetary aspects are considered) and other benefits associated with a college education. The rational investor will weigh the current costs against the expected future benefits. College will be chosen only if the latter are greater than the former.

Some may be offended by the term "human capital." Men and women are, of course, far more than a factor of production. However, the term "human capital" has validity in that the effort, skill, ability, and ingenuity of individuals can be applied productively, that is, as a productive resource.

Human resources differ from nonhuman resources in two important respects. First, human capital is embodied in the individual. Individuals cannot be separated from their knowledge, skills, and health conditions in the same way that they can be separated from physical capital like buildings or machines that they might own. As a result, choices concerning the use of human resources are vitally affected by working conditions, location, job prestige, and similar nonpecuniary factors. Although monetary factors influence human-capital decisions, individuals will often choose to trade off some money income for better working conditions.

Second, human resources cannot be bought and sold in nonslave societies. Although the *services* of human resources are bought and sold daily, individuals have the option of quitting, selling their labor services to another employer, or using them in an alternative manner.

In competitive markets, the price of resources, like the price of products, is determined by supply and demand. We will begin our analysis of resource markets by focusing on the demand for resources, both human and nonhuman.

DEMAND FOR RESOURCES

Derived demand

Demand for an item based on the demand for products the item helps to produce. The demand for resources is a derived demand.

Profit-seeking producers employ laborers, machines, raw materials, and other resources because they help produce goods and services. The demand for a resource exists because there is a demand for goods that the resource helps to produce. The demand for each resource is thus a **derived demand;** it is derived from the demand of consumers for products.

For example, a service station hires mechanics because customers demand repair service, not because the service station owner receives benefits simply from having mechanics around. If customers did not demand repair service, mechanics

[2]The contributions of T. W. Schultz and Gary Becker to the literature on human capital have been particularly significant. See Daniel S. Hamermesh and Albert Rees, *The Economics of Work and Pay* (New York: Harper & Row, 1988), chapter 3, for additional detail on human-capital theory.

OUTSTANDING ECONOMIST

GARY BECKER (1930–   )

This 1992 Nobel Prize recipient is best known for his role in the development of human capital theory and his innovative application of that theory to areas as diverse as employment discrimination, family development, and crime. In his widely acclaimed book, *Human Capital*,[1] he developed the theoretical foundation for human investment decisions in education, on-the-job training, migration, and health. Becker is a past president of the American Economic Association and a longtime professor at the University of Chicago.

[1]Gary Becker, *Human Capital* (New York: Columbia University Press, 1964).

would not be employed for long. Similarly, the demand for such inputs as carpenters, plumbers, lumber, and glass windows is derived from the demand of consumers for houses and other consumer products these resources help to make.

Most resources contribute to the production of numerous goods. For example, glass is used to produce windows, ornaments, dishes, light bulbs, and mirrors, among other things. The total demand for a resource is the sum of the derived demand for it in each of its uses. Consequently, when economists study the demand for factors of production, they must consider how firms will respond to a change in the price of a resource and the impact of that price change on the product market.

How will firms respond to an increase in the price of a resource? In the long run, the higher price of a resource will lead to two distinct adjustments, both reflecting an inverse relationship between price and the amount of the resource demanded. First, firms will seek to reduce their use of the now more expensive input by substituting other resources for it. Second, the increase in the price of the resource will lead to both higher costs and higher product prices. Consumers will buy less of the higher-priced product and substitute other goods for it, leading to a decline in the demand for resources used to make it. Therefore, the amount demanded of a factor of production will decline as its price increases. The demand curve for a resource will slope downward.

Let us look a little more closely at both of these adjustments.

SUBSTITUTION IN PRODUCTION

Firms will use the input combination that minimizes their cost. When the price of a resource goes up, cost-conscious firms will turn to lower-cost substitutes and cut back on their use of the more expensive resource. For example, if the price of walnut lumber increases, furniture manufacturers will use other wood varieties, metals, and plastics more intensely. Similarly, if the price of copper tubing increases, construction firms and plumbers will substitute plastic pipe for the more expensive tubing. The methods of substitution may differ. Sometimes producers will alter the style and dimensions of a product in order to conserve on the use of a more expensive resource. In other cases, a shift in location may play a role in the substitution process. For example, if prices of office space and land increase in the downtown area of a large city, firms may move to the suburbs in order to cut back on their use of the more expensive resources. The degree to which firms will be able to reduce their use of a more expensive resource will vary. If good substitutes in production are available, making it relatively easy to conserve on the use of a more expensive resource, then this substitution effect ensures not only that quantity demanded will be inversely related to price, but also that the demand for the resource will be highly elastic.

SUBSTITUTION IN CONSUMPTION

An increase in the price of a resource will lead to higher prices for products that the input helps to produce. The higher product prices will encourage consumers to purchase substitute goods, reducing the consumption of the more expensive product. When less of that product is produced, however, producer demand for resources (including the one that has risen in price) will decline. The experience of the American automobile industry in the early 1980s illustrates the point. Throughout much of the 1970s, wages in that industry increased quite rapidly. The higher wages placed upward pressure on the prices of American-made automobiles. However, as auto prices rose, many consumers switched to substitute products, particularly foreign-produced automobiles. American auto sales declined, causing a reduction in the quantity of labor demanded (and employment) in the automobile industry.

Other things constant, the more elastic the demand for the product, the more elastic the demand for the resource. This relationship stems from the derived nature of resource demand. An increase in the price of a product for which the demand is highly elastic will cause a sharp reduction in the sales of the good. There will thus also be a relatively sharp decline in the demand for the resources used to produce the good.

How important is the factor-pricing mechanism? Some economies use a planning process rather than factor markets to allocate resources. When a resource becomes more scarce, planners in these economies do not have the necessary information to reallocate resources among users. Neither do the users have the incentive to voluntarily cut back on their use of the resource. As a result, resource conservation in response to increased scarcity is weaker in centrally planned economies. See the "Applications in Economics" feature for evidence on this point.

TIME AND THE DEMAND FOR RESOURCES

It takes time for producers to adjust fully to a change in the price of a resource. Typically, a producer will be unable to alter a production process or the design of a product immediately to conserve on the use of a more expensive input or to use more efficiently an input whose price has declined. Consumers, too, may be unable to alter their consumption patterns immediately in response to price changes. Thus, the short-run demand for resources is typically less elastic than the demand in the long run.

Using steel as an example, **Exhibit 23–2** illustrates the relationship between time and the demand for resources. Initially, higher steel prices may lead to only a small reduction in usage. If the high price of steel persists, however, automobile manufacturers will alter their designs, moving toward lighter-weight cars that

APPLICATIONS IN ECONOMICS

THE IMPORTANCE OF FACTOR MARKETS: THE CASE OF ENERGY

Prices in factor markets provide users with information on scarcity and the incentive to economize on resource use when producing output. Of course, these functions might be done in other ways. Central planning replaces factor markets in economies where resources are not privately owned. But will planners be able to recognize all the places where a resource, such as energy, is most valuable and the various methods—including the adoption of alternative technologies—that might be used to conserve on its use when (and where) energy is more costly?

Without a factor market to formulate prices that reflect energy cost and demand information, economic thinking suggests that efficient use of a factor of production such as energy will be more difficult. Is this view supported by what we see in the real world? Economist Mikhail Bernstam, in a book written for London's Institute of Economic Affairs, compares the efficiency of energy use in socialist nations, which use central planning, with energy efficiency in nations where factor markets are used to allocate energy resources such as oil, electricity, and coal. He uses data from the 1980s, before the fall of socialist regimes in Europe, and the results of his research are striking. Socialist economies used nearly three times as much energy per unit of GDP as economies employing factor markets. The comparison holds also for countries that are similar except for their use of markets. Centrally planned North Korea used three times as much energy per unit of GDP as South Korea, where factor markets distributed energy. And centrally planned East Germany consumed 3.5 times as much energy per unit of output as West Germany.[1]

Energy prices rose sharply during the 1973–1980 period. Bernstam found that in North America and Europe, per capita energy consumption (which had been increasing) began to decline during the period following the price increases of the 1970s. Resource markets in these areas directed users toward substitutes and away from the more expensive energy resources during the post-1973 period. In contrast, there was no evidence of a similar response on the part of central planners in the former Soviet Union. Per capita energy consumption continued to rise in the former Soviet Union throughout the 1970s and 1980s.

As our theory indicates, resource markets are able to encourage conservation and direct users away from more expensive resources. In contrast, centrally planned economies often find it difficult to achieve a similar response without the information and incentives generated by prices in markets.

---

[1]Mikhail S. Bernstam, *The Wealth of Nations and the Environment* (London: Institute of Economics Affairs, 1991).

---

require less steel. Architectural firms will design buildings that permit more substitution of plastics, wood, aluminum, glass, and other resources for steel. Products made with steel will increase in price, which will encourage consumers to find more and more ways to cut back on their use. These and numerous similar adjustments will help conserve on the use of the more expensive steel. It will take time, however, for decision makers to carry out many of these adjustments. Therefore, the demand for steel, like that for most other resources, will be more inelastic in the short run (D_{sr}) than in the long run (D_{lr}).

SHIFTS IN THE DEMAND FOR RESOURCES

The entire demand curve for a resource, like that for a product, may shift, for one of three reasons.

1. A change in the demand for a product will cause a similar change in the demand for the resources used to make the product. Anything that increases the demand for a

An increase in the price of steel will lead to a much larger reduction in consumption in the long run than in the short run. Typically, the demand for resources will be more inelastic in the short run.

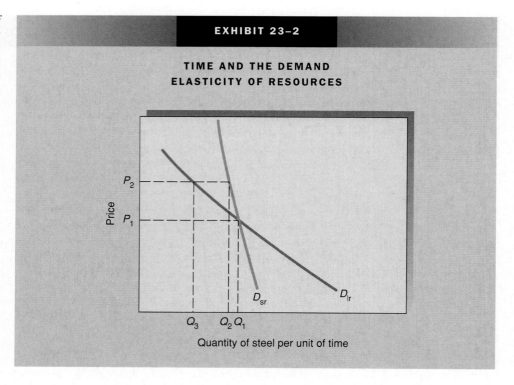

EXHIBIT 23-2

TIME AND THE DEMAND ELASTICITY OF RESOURCES

consumer good simultaneously increases the demand for resources required to make it. Conversely, a decline in product demand will reduce the demand for resources embodied in the product. During the 1970s the demand for small automobiles increased sharply, primarily because of higher gasoline prices. This increase in demand for small cars led to an increase in demand for workers to produce them. Employment at plants producing small cars expanded during the 1970s, even while auto workers were being laid off at plants producing large cars. Falling gasoline prices in the mid-1980s reversed this situation. Propelled by the lower gasoline prices, the demand for larger automobiles increased, while the demand for small cars declined. Reflecting the demand in product markets, employment at automobile plants making full-size cars expanded, while employment at plants producing small cars fell.

2. Changes in the productivity of a resource will alter the demand for the resource. The higher the productivity of a resource, the greater will be the demand for it. Several factors combine to determine the productivity of a resource. First, the **marginal product (MP)** of any resource will depend on the amount of other resources with which it is working. In general, additional capital will tend to increase the productivity of labor. For example, someone with a lawn mower can mow more grass than the same person with a pair of shears. A student working with a textbook, class notes, and tutor can learn more economics during a semester than the same student without these tools. The quantity and quality of the tools with which we work significantly affects our productivity.

Second, technological advances can improve the productivity of resources, including labor. Advances in the computer industry illustrate this point. Working with computer technology, an accountant and a data-entry person can maintain

Marginal product (MP)
The change in total output that results from the employment of one additional unit of a factor of production—one workday of skilled labor, for example.

business records and create bookkeeping reports that previously would have required 10 to 15 workers. Improvements in word-processing equipment have vastly increased the productivity of typists, journalists, lawyers, and writers. Similarly, computers have substantially increased the productivity of typesetters, telephone operators, quality-control technicians, and workers in many other occupations.

Third, improvements in the quality (skill level) of a resource will increase productivity and therefore the demand for the resource. As workers obtain valuable new knowledge and/or upgrade their skills, they enhance their productivity. In essence, such workers move into a different skill category, one where demand is greater.

All these factors help explain why wage rates in the United States, Canada, Western Europe, and Japan are higher than in most other areas of the world. Given the skill level of workers, the technology, and the capital equipment with which they work, individuals in these countries produce more goods and services per hour of labor. The demand for labor (relative to supply) is greater because of the high labor productivity. Essentially, the workers' greater productivity leads to higher wage rates.

3. A change in the price of a related resource will affect the demand for the original resource. An increase in the price of a substitute resource will lead to an increase in demand for the given resource. For example, when the wage rates of unionized workers in a given field or industry increase, demand for nonunion workers who are good substitutes for the union workers will expand. Conversely, an increase in the price of a resource that is a complement to a given resource will decrease the demand for the given resource. Thus, higher prices for computers would most likely cause the demand for computer programmers to fall.

MARGINAL PRODUCTIVITY AND THE FIRM'S HIRING DECISION

How does a producer decide whether to employ additional units of a resource? We noted previously that the marginal product of a resource is the increase in output that results when the employment of that resource is expanded by one unit. The resource's marginal product multiplied by the marginal revenue of the product being produced yields what is known as the **marginal revenue product (MRP).** The MRP is simply the change in the firm's total revenue brought about by the employment of one extra unit of a resource. Thus, the MRP reveals how much is added to the firm's revenue by the employment of the additional unit of the resource.

A profit-maximizing firm will, of course, continue to expand output as long as marginal cost is less than marginal revenue. This rule can be generalized to include the firm's employment of resources. Since firms are usually *price takers* (meaning they are too small to affect the market price) when they buy resources, the price of a resource is its marginal cost. Firms maximize profits by hiring units of a resource so long as the employment of each additional unit adds more to the firm's revenues than it adds to the firm's cost. Thus, additional units of a variable

Marginal revenue product (MRP)

The change in the total revenue of a firm that results from the employment of one additional unit of a factor of production. The marginal-revenue product of an input is equal to its marginal product multiplied by the marginal revenue (price) of the good or service produced.

resource will be hired up to the employment level at which the price of the resource (the firm's marginal cost) is just equal to the MRP of the resource (the firm's additional revenue generated by the employment of the resource). This profit-maximization rule applies to all firms, pure competitors and price searchers alike.

Value marginal product (VMP)

The marginal product of a resource multiplied by the selling price of the product it helps to produce. Under pure competition, a firm's marginal-revenue product (MRP) will be equal to the value-marginal product (VMP).

The marginal product of a resource multiplied by the selling price of the product yields the resource's **value marginal product (VMP).** When a firm sells its product in a purely competitive market, the selling price and the marginal revenue of the product are equal. Under pure competition, therefore, the MRP of a resource is equal to its VMP.

Exhibit 23–3 illustrates how a firm decides how much of a resource to employ. Compute-Accounting, Inc., uses computer equipment and data-entry operators to supply clients with monthly accounting statements. The firm sells its service in a competitive market for $200 per statement. Given the fixed quantity of computer equipment owned by Compute-Accounting, column 2 relates the employment of data-entry operators to the expected total output (quantity of accounting statements). One data-entry operator can process five statements per week. When two operators are employed, nine statements can be completed. Column 2 indicates how total output is expected to change as additional data-entry operators are

---

EXHIBIT 23–3

SHORT-RUN DEMAND SCHEDULE OF A FIRM

UNITS OF VARIABLE FACTOR (DATA-ENTRY OPERATORS) (1)	TOTAL OUTPUT (ACCOUNTING STATEMENTS PROCESSED PER WEEK) (2)	MARGINAL PRODUCT (CHANGE IN COLUMN 2 DIVIDED BY CHANGE IN COLUMN 1) (3)	SALES PRICE PER STATEMENT (4)	TOTAL REVENUE (2) × (4) (5)	MRP (3) × (4) (6)
0	0.0	—	$200	$ 0	—
1	5.0	5.0	200	1,000	1,000
2	9.0	4.0	200	1,800	800
3	12.0	3.0	200	2,400	600
4	14.0	2.0	200	2,800	400
5	15.5	1.5	200	3,100	300
6	16.5	1.0	200	3,300	200
7	17.0	0.5	200	3,400	100

Compute-Accounting, Inc., uses computer technology and data-entry operators to provide accounting services in a competitive market. For each accounting statement processed, the firm receives a $200 fee (column 4). Given the firm's current fixed capital, column 2 shows how total output changes as additional data-entry operators are hired. The marginal revenue product (MRP) schedule (column 6) indicates how hiring an additional operator affects the total revenue of the firm. Since a profit-maximizing firm will hire an additional employee if, and only if, the employee adds more to revenues than to costs, the marginal revenue product curve is the firm's short-run demand curve for the resource (see Exhibit 23–4).

employed. Column 3 presents the marginal product schedule for data-entry operators. Column 6, the MRP schedule, shows how the employment of each additional operator affects total revenue.

Since Compute-Accounting sells its service competitively, both the marginal revenue product and the value marginal product of labor equal the marginal product (column 3) times the sales price of an accounting statement (column 4). What if the firm is not a perfect competitor? The MRP must always equal marginal revenue multiplied by marginal product. When the firm confronts a downward-sloping demand curve for its product, the marginal revenue of the product will be less than its price. When this is the case, the MRP of a resource will be less than its VMP.

How does Compute-Accounting decide how many operators to employ? As additional operators are employed, the output of processed statements (column 2) will increase, which will expand total revenue (column 5). Employment of additional operators, though, will also add to production costs since the operators must be paid. Applying the profit-maximization rule, Compute-Accounting will hire additional operators as long as their employment adds more to revenues than to costs. This will be the case as long as the MRP (Exhibit 23–3, column 6) of the data-entry operators exceeds their wage rate. Thus, as **Exhibit 23–4** illustrates, the MRP curve of operators is also the firm's short-run demand curve for the resource.[3] At a weekly wage of $1,000, Compute-Accounting would hire only one operator. If the weekly wage dropped to $800, two operators would be hired. At still lower wage rates, additional operators would be hired.

The location of the firm's MRP curve depends on (1) the price of the product, (2) the productivity of the resource, and (3) the amount of other resources with which the resource is working. Changes in any one of these three factors will cause the MRP curve to shift. For example, if Compute-Accounting obtained additional computer equipment that made it possible for the operators to complete more statements each week, the MRP curve for labor would increase. This increase in the quantity of the other resources working with labor would increase labor's productivity.

ADDING OTHER FACTORS OF PRODUCTION

Thus far, we have analyzed the firm's hiring decision, assuming that it employed one variable resource (labor) and one fixed resource. Production, though, usually involves the use of many resources. How should these resources be combined to produce the product? We can answer this question by considering either the conditions for profit maximization or the conditions for cost minimization.

PROFIT MAXIMIZATION WHEN MULTIPLE RESOURCES ARE EMPLOYED   The same decision-making considerations apply when the firm employs several factors of production. The profit-maximizing firm will expand its employment of a resource as long as the MRP of the resource exceeds its employment cost. If we assume that resources are perfectly divisible, the profit-maximizing decision rule

---

[3]Strictly speaking, this is true only for a variable resource that is employed with a fixed amount of another factor.

The firm's demand curve for a resource will reflect the marginal revenue product (MRP) of the resource. In the short run, it will slope downward because the marginal product of the resource will fall as more of it is used with a fixed amount of other resources. The location of the MRP curve will depend on (1) the price of the product and (2) the productivity of the resource, which depends on technology and the quantity of other factors working with the resource.

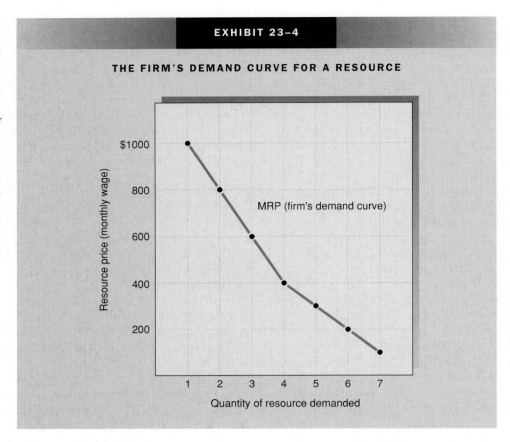

EXHIBIT 23–4

THE FIRM'S DEMAND CURVE FOR A RESOURCE

MRP (firm's demand curve)

Resource price (monthly wage)

Quantity of resource demanded

implies that, in equilibrium, the MRP of each resource will be equal to the price of the resource. Therefore, the following conditions will exist for the profit-maximizing firm:

MRP of skilled labor = P_{SL} (wage rate of skilled labor)
MRP of unskilled labor = P_{UL} (wage rate of unskilled labor)
MRP of machine A = P_M (explicit or implicit rental price of machine A)

and so on, for all other factors.

COST MINIMIZATION WHEN MULTIPLE RESOURCES ARE EMPLOYED   If the firm is maximizing profits, clearly it must produce the profit-maximizing output at the least possible cost. If the firm is minimizing costs, the marginal dollar expenditure for each resource will have the same impact on output as every other marginal resource expenditure. Factors of production will be employed such that the marginal product per last dollar spent on each factor is the same for all factors.

To see why, consider a situation in which a dollar expenditure on labor caused output to rise by ten units, whereas an additional dollar expenditure on machines generated only a five-unit expansion in output. Under these circumstances, five more units of output (at no added cost) would result if the firm spent $1 less on machines and $1 more on labor. The firm's per unit cost would be reduced if it substituted labor for machines.

If the marginal dollar spent on one resource increases output by a larger amount than a dollar expenditure on other resources, costs can always be reduced by substituting resources with a high marginal product per dollar expenditure for those with a low one. This substitution continues to reduce costs (and add profit) until the marginal product per dollar expenditure is equalized—that is, until the resource combination that minimizes cost is attained. When this is true, the proportional relationship between the price of each resource and its marginal product will be equal for all resources.

Therefore, the following condition exists when per unit costs are minimized:

$$\frac{MP \text{ of skilled labor}}{\text{price of skilled labor}} = \frac{MP \text{ of unskilled labor}}{\text{price of unskilled labor}}$$

$$= \frac{MP \text{ of machine A}}{\text{price (rental value) of machine A}}$$

and so on, for the other factors.

This relationship indicates why, with competition, there will be a tendency for wage differences across skill categories to reflect productivity differences. If skilled workers are twice as productive as unskilled workers, their wage rates will tend toward twice the wage rates of unskilled workers. For example, suppose that a construction firm hiring workers to hang doors is choosing among skilled and unskilled workers. If skilled door hangers can complete four doors per hour, while unskilled workers can hang only two doors per hour, a cost-minimizing firm would hire only skilled workers—as long as their wages are less than twice the wages of unskilled workers. On the other hand, only unskilled workers would be hired if the wages of skilled workers are more than twice that of unskilled workers. With competition, wages across skill categories will tend to mirror productivity differences.

In the real world, it is sometimes difficult to measure the marginal product of a factor. Business decision makers may not necessarily think in terms of equating the marginal product/price ratio (MP_i/P_i) for each factor of production. Nevertheless, if they are minimizing cost, this ratio will be equal for all factors of production. Real-world decision makers may use experience, trial and error, and intuitive rules, but the question always is, "Can we reduce costs by using more of one resource and less of another?" Thus, when profits are maximized and the cost-minimization method of production is attained, regardless of the procedures used, the outcome will be as if the employer had followed the profit-maximization and cost-minimization decision-making rules just discussed.

MARGINAL PRODUCTIVITY, DEMAND, AND ECONOMIC JUSTICE

According to the law of diminishing marginal returns, as the employment level of a resource increases, other things constant, the marginal product (and MRP) of the resource will decline. As we have just seen, a profit-maximizing employer will expand the use of a resource until its MRP is equal to the price of the resource. If the price of the resource declines, employers will increase their utilization level of that resource. Therefore, as **Exhibit 23–5** shows, the marginal-productivity approach can be used to illustrate the inverse relationship between quantity demanded and resource price.

Some observers, noting that under pure competition the price of each resource is equal to the value of what it produces (that is, input price equals the marginal product of the input multiplied by the price of the product), have argued that competitive markets are "just" or "equitable" because each resource gets paid exactly what it is worth. There is a major defect in this line of reasoning, however. When a product is produced by a combination of factors, as is almost invariably the case, it is impossible to assign a specific proportion of the total output to each resource. For example, if one uses a tractor, an acre of land, and a pound of seed to produce wheat, one cannot accurately state that labor (or the seed or the land) produced one half or any other proportion of the output. The marginal product can be used as a measure of the change in total output associated with the use of an additional unit of a resource, but this measurement does not directly link one resource with one segment of output.

The marginal-productivity theory is really a theory about the demand for resources. The central proposition of the theory is that profit-maximizing employers will never pay more for a unit of input, whether it is skilled labor, a machine, or an acre of land, than the input is worth to them. The worth of a unit of input to the firm is determined by how much additional revenue (marginal revenue product) is expected when the unit is used. That is, pursuit of profit will induce employers to hire additional units of each resource as long as the units' marginal productivity generates revenues in excess of costs. Resource prices will tend to reflect—though somewhat roughly in the real world—the marginal productivity of the resource.

Other things constant, an increase in the employment level will cause the MRP of a resource to decline. The larger quantity of the resource can be employed only at a lower price.

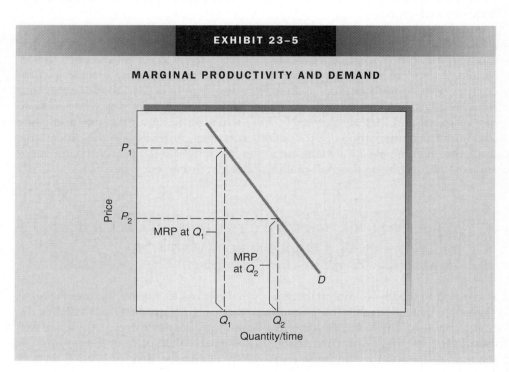

EXHIBIT 23–5

MARGINAL PRODUCTIVITY AND DEMAND

But, the price of each resource is determined by conditions of supply as well as conditions of demand. Even though marginal-productivity theory helps us understand the demand side of the market, it reveals nothing about the share of the total product produced by a resource or the justice of a resource price. We must analyze the supply of resources in order to complete the picture.

SUPPLY OF RESOURCES

In essence, our analysis of resource demand concludes that employers will hire a resource so long as they can gain by doing so. The same basic postulate also applies to resource suppliers. Resource owners will supply their services to an employer only if they perceive that the benefits of doing so exceed their costs (other things they could do with their time or resources). Thus, in order to attract factors of production, employers must offer resource owners at least as good a deal as they can get elsewhere. For example, if an employer does not offer a potential employee a package of income payments and working conditions that is as good or better than the employee can get elsewhere, the employer will be unable to attract the employee. Resource owners will supply their services to those who offer them the best job, all factors considered.

Resource owners will seek to use their factors of production in a manner that leads to their greatest net advantage. Other things constant, as the price of a specific resource (for example, engineering services, craft labor, or wheat farmland) increases, the incentive of potential suppliers to provide the resource increases.

An increase in the price of a resource will attract potential resource suppliers into the market. A decrease will cause them to shift into other activities. Thus, the supply curve for a specific resource will slope upward to the right.

SHORT-RUN SUPPLY

As in the case of demand, the supply response in resource markets may vary between the short run and long run. In the short run, there is insufficient time to alter the availability of a resource through investment in human and physical capital. In contrast, in the long run, resource suppliers have time to fully adjust their investment choices to a change in resource prices. Let us begin by considering the supply response in the short run.

Most resources have alternative uses; they can be used to perform a variety of functions. Those that can be easily transferred from one use to another in response to changing price incentives (in other words, those resources with a great many alternative uses or locations) are said to have high **resource mobility.** The supply of such factors to any specific use will be elastic. Factors that have few alternative uses are said to be immobile and will have an inelastic short-run supply.

Consider the mobility of labor. When labor skills can be transferred easily and quickly, human capital is highly mobile. Within a skill category (for example, plumber, store manager, accountant, or secretary), labor will be highly mobile within the same geographic area. Movements between geographic areas and from one skill category to another are more costly to accomplish. Labor will thus be less mobile for movements of this variety.

Resource mobility
A term that refers to the ease with which factors of production are able to move among alternative uses. Resources that can easily be transferred to a different use or location are said to be highly mobile. In contrast, when a resource has few alternative uses, it is immobile. For example, the skills of a trained rodeo rider would be highly immobile, since they cannot be easily transferred to other lines of work.

What about the mobility of land? Land is highly mobile among uses when location does not matter. For example, the same land can often be used to raise corn, wheat, soybeans, or oats. Thus, the supply of land allocated to production of each of these commodities will be highly responsive to changes in their relative prices. Undeveloped land on the outskirts of cities is particularly mobile among uses. In addition to its value in agriculture, such land might be quickly subdivided and used for a housing development or a shopping center. However, since land is totally immobile physically, supply is unresponsive to changes in price that reflect the desirability of a location.

Machines are typically not very mobile among uses. A machine developed to produce airplane wings is seldom of much use in the production of automobiles, appliances, or other products. Steel mills cannot easily be converted to produce aluminum. There are, of course, some exceptions. Trucks can typically be used to haul a variety of products. Building space can often be converted from one use to another. In the short run, however, immobility and inelasticity of supply characterize much of our physical capital.

LONG-RUN SUPPLY

In the long run, the supply of resources can change substantially. Machines wear out, human skills depreciate, and even the fertility of land declines with use and erosion. These factors reduce the supply of resources. Through investment, though, the supply of productive resources can be expanded. Resources can be invested to maintain and expand the stock of machines, buildings, and durable assets. Alternatively, current resources can be used to train, educate, and develop the skills of future labor-force participants. The supply of both physical and human resources in the long run is determined primarily by investment and depreciation.

Price incentives will, of course, influence the investment decisions of firms and individuals. Considering both monetary and nonmonetary factors, investors will choose those alternatives they believe to be most advantageous. Higher resource prices will induce utility-maximizing individuals to undertake investments that will permit them to supply more of the higher-priced resource. In contrast, other things constant, lower resource prices will reduce the incentive of individuals to invest and expand the future supply of those resources. Thus, there is a direct relationship between the price of a resource and quantity supplied in the long run.

The theory of long-run resource supply is general. The expected payoff from an investment alternative will influence the decisions of investors in human, as well as physical, capital. For example, the higher salaries of physical and space scientists employed in the expanding space program during the early 1960s induced an increasing number of college students to enter these fields. Similarly, attractive earning opportunities in accounting and law led to an increase in investment and quantity supplied in these areas during the period from 1965 to 1975. During the last decade, job opportunities for computer programmers, systems analysts, and computer technicians have been highly attractive as the computer revolution spread throughout our economy. As salaries in these areas rose, the number of students in computer science and technology courses expanded substantially.

Irrespective of nonmonetary factors, investors will not knowingly invest in areas of low return when higher returns are available elsewhere. Of course, since human capital is embodied in the individual, nonpecuniary considerations of employment will typically be more important for human than for physical capital. Workers experience their jobs in ways that the owners of physical capital do not. Nevertheless, expected monetary payoffs will influence investment decisions in both areas.

The long run, of course, is not a specified length of time. Investment can increase the availability of some resources fairly quickly. For example, it does not take very long to train additional over-the-road truck drivers. Thus, in the absence of barriers to entry, the quantity of truck drivers supplied will expand rapidly in response to higher wages. However, the gestation period between expansion in investment and an increase in quantity supplied is substantially longer for some resources. It takes a long time to train physicians, dentists, lawyers, and pharmacists. Higher earnings in these occupations may have only a small impact on their current availability. Additional investment will go into these areas, but it will typically be several years before there is a substantial increase in the quantity supplied in response to higher earnings for these resources.

Because supply can be substantially expanded over time by investment, the supply of a resource will be much more elastic in the long run than in the short run. This is particularly true when there is a lengthy gestation period between an increase in investment and an actual increase in the availability of a resource.

Using engineering services as an example, **Exhibit 23–6** illustrates the relationship between the short- and long-run supply of resources. An increase in the price of engineering services (the wage rate of engineers) will result in some immediate increase in quantity supplied. Persons currently employed as engineers may

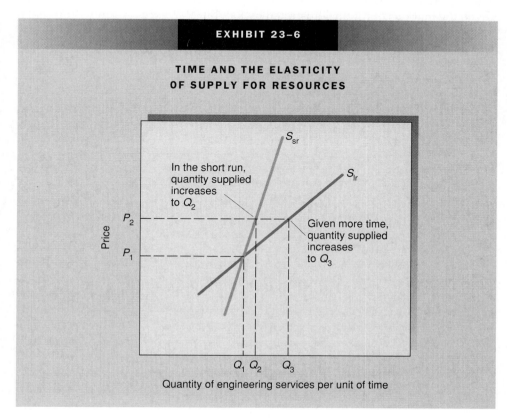

EXHIBIT 23–6

TIME AND THE ELASTICITY OF SUPPLY FOR RESOURCES

The supply of engineering services (and other resources that require a substantial period of time between current investment and expansion in the future quantity supplied) will be far more inelastic in the short run than in the long run.

choose to work more hours. In addition, the higher wage may induce workers with engineering skills currently employed in mathematics, physics, or similar fields to switch to engineering. While these adjustments are important, they may fail to substantially increase the quantity supplied in the short run. With time, however, the more attractive earning opportunities in engineering will raise the level of investment in human capital in this area. More students will enter engineering programs. Since it takes time to acquire an engineering degree, several years may pass before the additional degrees exert a major impact on supply. Nevertheless, the expanded human-capital investments will eventually exert important effects. Thus, in the long run, the supply of engineering services may be quite elastic, even though supply is highly inelastic in the short run.

SUPPLY, DEMAND, AND RESOURCE PRICES

The theories of supply and demand for resources have been analyzed. This is all we need to develop the theory of resource pricing in competitive markets. When factor prices are free to vary, resource prices will bring the choices of buyers and sellers into line with each other. Continuing with our example of engineers, **Exhibit 23–7** illustrates how the forces of supply and demand push the market price toward equilibrium, where quantity demanded and quantity supplied are equal. Equilibrium is achieved when the price (wage) of engineering services is P_1. Given the market conditions illustrated by Exhibit 23–7, excess supply is present if the price of engineering services exceeds P_1. Some resource owners are unable to

The market demand for a resource, such as engineering services, is a downward-sloping curve, reflecting the declining MRP of the resource. The market supply slopes upward since higher resource prices (wage rates) will induce individuals to supply more of the resource. Resource price P_1 brings the choices of buyers and sellers into harmony. At the equilibrium price (P_1), the quantity demanded will just equal the quantity supplied.

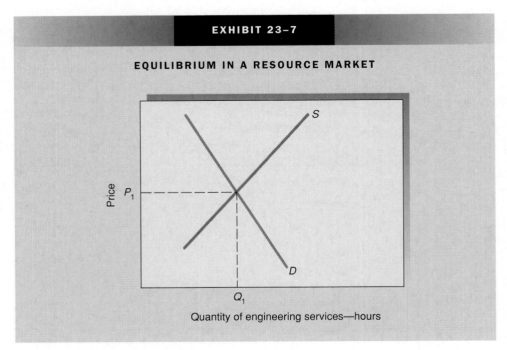

EXHIBIT 23–7

EQUILIBRIUM IN A RESOURCE MARKET

Quantity of engineering services—hours

sell their services at the above-equilibrium price. Responding to this situation, they will cut their price (wage) and thereby push the market toward equilibrium. In contrast, if the resource price is less than P_1, excess demand is present. Employers are unable to obtain the desired amount of engineering services at a below-equilibrium resource price. Rather than doing without the resource, employers will bid the price up to P_1 and thereby eliminate the excess demand.

How will a resource market adjust to an unexpected change in market conditions? As is true for product markets, adjustment to changes do not take place instantaneously in resource markets. Our analysis of short-run and long-run responses makes the nature of the adjustment process clear. Suppose there is an unanticipated increase in demand for a resource. As **Exhibit 23–8** illustrates, an increase in market demand (from D_1 to D_2) initially leads to a sharp rise in the price of the resource (from P_1 to P_2), particularly if the short-run supply is inelastic. However, at the higher price, the quantity of the resource supplied will expand with time. If it is a natural resource, individuals and firms will put forth a greater effort to discover and develop the now more valuable productive factor. If it is physical capital (for example, a type of building or machine), current suppliers will have greater incentive to work intensively to expand production. New suppliers will be drawn into the market. Higher prices for human-capital resources will also lead to an expansion in the quantity supplied. With time, more people will acquire the training, education, and experience necessary to supply the service that now commands a higher price. And the expansion of the supply will eventually moderate the price rise. Because of these forces, as Exhibit 23–8 (the move from b to c) illustrates, the long-run price increase will be less than the short-run increase.

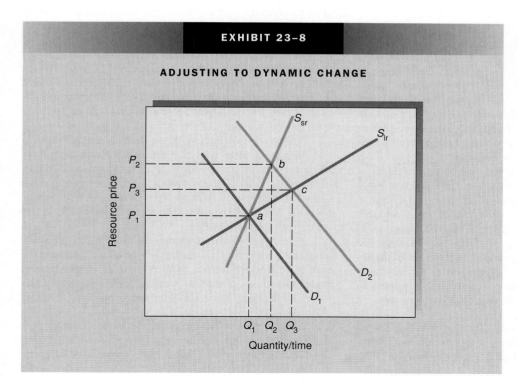

EXHIBIT 23–8

ADJUSTING TO DYNAMIC CHANGE

An increase in demand for a resource will typically cause price to rise more in the short run than in the long run. Can you explain why?

The market adjustment to an unexpected reduction in demand for a resource is the same. The price falls further in the short run than in the long run. At the lower price, some resource suppliers will use their talents in other areas, and the incentive for potential new suppliers to offer the resource will be reduced. Thus, with time, the quantity of the resource supplied will decline, making the decline in price more moderate. Those with the poorest alternatives (that is, lowest opportunity cost) will continue to provide the resource at the lower prices. Those with better alternatives will move to other areas.

LOOKING AHEAD

Now that we have outlined the theoretical underpinnings of factor markets, we can apply the analysis to a broad range of economic issues. The next chapter will focus on the labor market and the determination of wage rates. Later, we will focus on the capital market and the allocation of resources over time. The operation of these two markets plays an important role in determining the distribution of income, a topic that will also be analyzed in detail in a subsequent chapter.

CHAPTER SUMMARY

1. Factor markets, where productive resources and services are bought and sold, help to determine what is produced, how it is produced, and how the distribution of income (output) is accomplished. There are two broad classes of productive resources—nonhuman capital and human capital. Both are durable in the sense that they will last into the future, thereby enhancing future productive capabilities. Both yield income to their owners. Investment can expand the future supply of both.

2. The demand for resources is derived from demand for products that the resources help to produce. The quantity of a resource demanded is inversely related to its price. There are two reasons why, if the price of a resource increases, less of it will be used. First, producers will substitute other resources for the now more expensive input (substitution in production). Second, the higher resource price will lead to higher prices for products that the resource helps to make, inducing consumers to reduce their purchases of those goods (substitution in consumption).

3. The short-run market demand curve will be more inelastic than the long-run curve. It will take time for producers to adjust their production process to use more of the resources that have become cheaper and less of the ones that are more expensive.

4. The demand curve for a resource, like the demand for a product, may shift. The major factors that can increase the demand for a resource are (a) an increase in demand for products that use the resource, (b) an increase in the productivity of the resource, and (c) an increase in the price of substitute resources.

5. Profit-maximizing firms will hire additional units of a resource as long as the marginal revenue product (MRP) of the resource exceeds its hiring cost, usually the price of the resource. If resources are perfectly divisible, firms will expand their usage of each resource until the MRP of each resource is just equal to its price.

6. When a firm is minimizing its costs, it will employ each factor of production up to the point at which the marginal product per last dollar spent on the factor is equal for all factors. This condition implies that the marginal product of labor divided by the price of labor must equal the marginal product of capital (machines) divided by the price of capital, and that this ratio (MP_i/P_i) must be the same for all other inputs used by the firm. When real-world decision makers minimize per unit costs, the outcome will be as if they had followed these mathematical procedures, even though they may not consciously do so.

7. Resource owners will use their factors of production in the manner that they consider most personally advantageous. Many resources will be relatively immobile in the short-run. The less mobile a resource is, the more inelastic its short-run supply. There will be a positive relationship, however, between amount supplied and resource price, even in the short run.

8. In the long run, investment and depreciation will alter the availability of resources. Resource owners will shift factors of production toward areas in which resource prices have risen and away from areas in which resource prices have fallen. Thus, the long-run supply will be more elastic than the short-run supply.

9. The prices of resources will be determined by both supply and demand. The demand for a resource will reflect the demand for products that it helps to produce. The supply of resources will reflect the human and physical capital investment decisions of individuals and firms.

10. Changing resource prices will influence the decisions of users and suppliers alike. Higher resource prices give users a greater incentive to turn to substitutes and suppliers a greater incentive to provide more of the resource. Since these adjustments take time, when the demand for a resource expands, the price will usually rise more in the short run than in the long run. Similarly, when there is a fall in resource demand, price will decline more in the short run than in the long run.

CRITICAL-ANALYSIS QUESTIONS

1. What is the meaning of the expression "invest in human capital"? In what sense is the decision to invest in human capital like the decision to invest in physical capital? Is human capital investment risky? Explain.

2. "The demand for resources is a derived demand." What is meant by that statement? Why is the employment of a resource inversely related to its price?

*3. Use the information of Exhibit 23–3 to answer the following:

a. How many employees (operators) would Compute-Accounting hire at a weekly wage of $250 if it were attempting to maximize profits?

b. What would the firm's maximum profit be if its fixed costs were $1,500 per week?

c. Suppose there was a decline in demand for accounting services, reducing the market price per monthly statement to $150. At this demand level, how many employees would Compute-Accounting hire at $250 per week in the short run? Would Compute-Accounting be able to stay in business at the lower market price? Explain.

*4. Are productivity gains the major source of higher wages? If so, how does one account for the rising real wages of barbers, who by and large have used the same technique for half a century? (Hint: Do not forget opportunity cost and supply.)

5. Are the following statements both correct? Are they inconsistent with each other? Explain.

a. "Firms will hire a resource only if they can make money by doing so."

b. "In a market economy, each resource will tend to be paid according to its marginal product. Highly productive resources will command high prices, whereas less productive resources will command lower prices."

6. "However desirable they might be from an equity viewpoint, programs designed to reduce wage differentials will necessarily reduce the incentive of people to act efficiently and use their productive abilities in those areas where demand is greatest relative to supply." Do you agree or disagree? Why?

7. What's wrong with this way of thinking? "The downward-sloping MRP curve of labor shows that better workers are hired first. The workers hired later are less productive."

*8. A dressmaker uses labor and capital (sewing machines) to produce dresses in a competitive market. Suppose the last unit of labor hired cost $1,000 per month and increased output by 100 dresses. The last unit of capital hired (rented) cost $500 per month and increased output by 80 dresses. Is the dressmaker minimizing cost? If not, what changes need to be made?

9. Suppose that lawn service operators always use one worker with one mower to produce output. The resources are always used in the same proportion; there is no substitutability between labor and capital. Under these circumstances, would a change in wages influence employment? Explain.

*10. "The earnings of engineers, doctors, and lawyers are high because lots of education is necessary to practice in these fields." Evaluate this statement.

11. Other things constant, what impact will a highly elastic demand for a product have on the elasticity of demand for the resources used to produce the product? Explain.

*12. The following chart provides information on a firm that hires labor competitively and sells its product in a competitive market:

UNITS OF LABOR	TOTAL OUTPUT	MARGINAL PRODUCT	PRODUCT PRICE	TOTAL REVENUE	MRP
1	14	___	$5	___	___
2	26	___	$5	___	___
3	37	___	$5	___	___
4	46	___	$5	___	___
5	53	___	$5	___	___
6	58	___	$5	___	___
7	62	___	$5	___	___

a. Fill in the missing columns.

b. How many units of labor would be employed if the market wage rate was $40? Why?

c. What would happen to employment if the wage rate rose to $50? Explain.

13. College professors in subjects such as accounting, engineering, computer science, and even economics generally have more attractive nonteaching employment opportunities

---

*Asterisk denotes questions for answers are given in Appendix C.

than their colleagues in such areas as history, English, physical education, and home economics. Nonetheless, colleges sometimes pay faculty members in the same rank the same salary across all disciplines. How will this strategy influence the unemployment rate and the ability of colleges to hire (and retain) high-quality faculty members across disciplines? How easy will it be for a person in computer science to find an academic job relative to a similarly qualified person in history?

14. Leisure Times, Inc., employs skilled workers and capital to install hot tubs. The capital includes the tools and equipment that the workers use to construct and install the tubs. The i tallation services are sold in a competitive market for $1,200 per hot tub. Leisure Times is able to hire workers for $2,200 per month, including the cost of wages, fringe benefits, and employment taxes. As additional workers are hired, the increase in the number of hot tubs installed is indicated in the table.

No. of Workers Employed	No. of Hot Tubs Installed (per month)
1	5
2	12
3	18
4	23
5	27
6	30
7	32
8	33
9	34

a. Indicate the marginal product and MRP schedules of the workers.
b. What quantity of workers should Leisure Times employ if it is maximizing profit?
c. If a construction boom pushes the wages of skilled workers up to $2,500 per month, how many workers would Leisure Times employ if it is maximizing profit?
d. Suppose that strong demand for hot tubs pushes the price of installation services up to $1,500 per month. How would this affect employment of the skilled workers if the wage rate of the workers remained at $2,500 per month?

CHAPTER TWENTY-FOUR

EARNINGS, PRODUCTIVITY, AND THE JOB MARKET

A fair day's-wages for a fair day's-work; it is as just a demand as governed men ever made of governing. It is the everlasting right of man.

THOMAS CARLYLE

CHAPTER FOCUS

- *Why do some people earn more than others?*
- *Are earnings differences according to race and gender the result of employment discrimination?*
- *Who pays for fringe benefits? Do government-mandated fringe benefits increase employee compensation?*
- *Why are wages higher in the United States than in India or China? Why are the wages of Americans higher today than they were 50 years ago?*
- *Does automation destroy jobs?*
- *Can we legislate higher wages?*

T he major source of income for most people is labor earnings, income derived from current work. The earnings of U.S. workers are among the highest in the world, and they have been increasing. Among individuals, however, earnings vary widely. An unskilled laborer may earn $5 per hour, or even less. Lawyers and physicians often earn $75 per hour. Dentists and even economists might receive $50 per hour. This chapter focuses on the reasons why some groups earn more than others.

WHY DO EARNINGS DIFFER?

The earnings of individuals in the same occupation or with the same amount of education often differ substantially. The earnings of persons with the same family background also vary widely. For example, one researcher found that the average earnings differential between brothers was $23,200, compared with $25,700 (figures are in 1993 dollars) for men paired randomly.[1] In addition, the earnings of persons with the same intelligence quotient, level of training, or amount of experience typically differ. How do economists explain these variations? Several factors combine to determine the earning power of an individual. Some seem to be the result of good or bad fortune. Others are clearly the result of conscious decisions made by individuals. In the previous chapter, we analyzed how the market forces of supply and demand operate to determine resource prices. The subject of earnings differentials can be usefully approached within the framework of this model.

If (1) all individuals were homogeneous, (2) all jobs were equally attractive, and (3) workers were perfectly mobile among jobs, the earnings of all employees in a competitive economy would be equal. If, given these conditions, higher wages existed in any area of the economy, the supply of workers to that area would expand until the wage differential was eliminated. Similarly, low wages in any area would cause workers to exit until wages in that area returned to parity. However, the conditions necessary for earnings equality do not exist in the real world. Thus, earnings differentials are present.

EARNINGS DIFFERENTIALS FROM NONHOMOGENEOUS LABOR

Workers differ in several important respects that influence both the supply of and demand for their services.

WORKER PRODUCTIVITY AND SPECIALIZED SKILLS.   The demand for employees who are highly productive is greater than the demand for those who are less productive. Persons who can operate a machine more skillfully, hit a baseball more consistently, or sell life insurance policies with greater regularity will have a higher MRP than their less skillful counterparts. As a result, their services will command a higher wage from employers.

---

[1]Christopher Jencks, *Inequality* (New York: Basic Books, 1972), p. 220.

Worker productivity is the result of a combination of factors, including native ability, parental training, hard work, and investment in human capital. The link between higher productivity and higher earnings provides individuals with the incentive to invest in themselves and thereby upgrade their knowledge and skills. If additional worker productivity did not lead to higher earnings, individuals would have little incentive to incur the direct and indirect cost of productivity-enhancing educational and training programs.

Exhibit 24–1 illustrates the impact of worker productivity and the cost of investment in human capital on the wages of skilled and unskilled workers. Since the productivity of skilled workers exceeds the productivity of unskilled workers, the demand for skilled workers (D_s) exceeds the demand for unskilled workers (D_u). The vertical distance between the two demand curves reflects the higher marginal product (MP) of skilled workers relative to the unskilled workers (part a). Since investments in human capital (for example, education or training) are costly, the supply of skilled workers (S_s) will be smaller than the supply of unskilled workers (S_u). The vertical distance between the two supply curves indicates the wage differential that is necessary to compensate workers for the costs incurred in the acquisition of their skills (part b). Wages are determined by demand relative to supply (part c). Since the demand for skilled workers is large, while their supply is small, the equilibrium wage of skilled workers will be high ($20 per hour). In contrast, since the supply of unskilled workers is large relative to the demand, the wages of unskilled workers will be substantially lower ($5 per

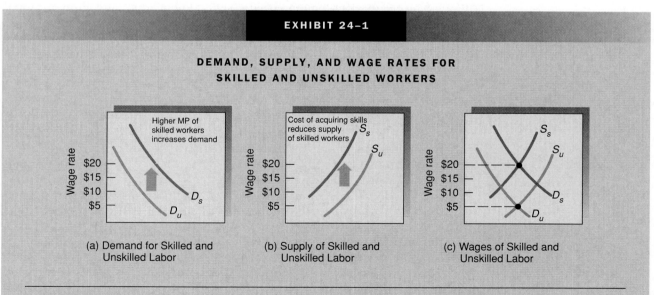

EXHIBIT 24–1

DEMAND, SUPPLY, AND WAGE RATES FOR SKILLED AND UNSKILLED WORKERS

(a) Demand for Skilled and Unskilled Labor

(b) Supply of Skilled and Unskilled Labor

(c) Wages of Skilled and Unskilled Labor

The productivity — and therefore marginal product (MP) — of skilled workers is greater than that of unskilled workers. Therefore, as part a illustrates, the demand for skilled workers (D_s) will exceed the demand for unskilled workers (D_u). Education and training generally enhance skills. Since upgrading skills through investments in human capital is costly, the supply of skilled workers (S_s) is smaller than the supply of unskilled workers (part b). As part c illustrates, the wages of skilled workers are high relative to unskilled workers due to the strong demand and small supply of skilled workers relative to unskilled workers. (Note: The quantity of skilled labor hired may be far smaller, far larger, or by accident equal to the quantity of unskilled labor hired.)

hour). (Note that while economic logic tells us why the wages will differ, it does not tell us about the number of workers hired from each group.)

Of course, native ability and motivation will influence the rate at which an individual can transform educational and training experience into greater productivity. Individuals differ in the amount of valuable skills they develop from a year of education, vocational school, or on-the-job training. We should not expect, therefore, a rigid relationship to exist between years of training (or education) and skill level.

Nevertheless, detailed empirical studies indicate that investment in human capital leads to higher earnings once the person enters the labor force full-time. For example, in 1992 the median annual income of males, working full time, year-round, aged 25 to 34 was $34,648 for those with a college degree, compared to $22,638 for high school graduates. The parallel figure for female college graduates was $27,097 compared to $17,559 for high school graduates. Some of the additional earnings of college graduates may reflect native ability, intelligence, and motivation. Research, however, indicates that a large proportion of the additional earnings also reflects knowledge and skills acquired as the result of investment in additional education. Similarly, economic research has shown that on-the-job training enhances the earnings of workers.

Investment in human capital and development of specialized skills can protect high-wage workers from the competition of others willing to offer their services at a lower price. Few persons could develop the specialized skills of a Whitney Houston or a Tom Hanks. Similarly, the supply of heart surgeons, trial lawyers, engineers, business entrepreneurs, and many other specialized workers is limited in occupations where specific skills, knowledge, and human-capital investments contribute to job performance.

Other things constant, a skilled specialist will command a higher wage than one with less skill, but high skill will not guarantee high wages in the absence of demand. For example, expert harness makers and blacksmiths typically command low wages today.

WORKER PREFERENCES. An important source of earnings differentials that is sometimes overlooked is worker preferences. People have different objectives in life. Some want to make a great deal of money. Many are willing to work long hours, undergo agonizing training and many years of education, and sacrifice social and family life to make money. Others may be "workaholics" because they enjoy their jobs. Still others may be satisfied with enough money to get by on, preferring to spend more time with their family, the Boy Scouts, television, or the local tavern keeper.

Employment discrimination

Unequal treatment of persons on the basis of their race, sex, or religion, restricting their employment and earnings opportunities compared to others of similar productivity. Employment discrimination may stem from the prejudices of employers, consumers, and/or fellow employees.

Economics does not indicate that one set of worker preferences is more desirable than another, any more than it suggests that people should eat more spinach and less pastrami. Economics does indicate, however, that these factors contribute to differences in wages and earnings. Other things constant, persons who are more highly motivated by monetary objectives will be more likely to do the things necessary to command higher wage rates.

RACE AND GENDER. Discrimination on the basis of race or gender contributes to earnings differences among individuals. Employment discrimination may directly limit the earnings opportunities of minorities and women. **Employment discrimination** exists when minorities or women employees are treated in a manner different from similarly productive whites or men. Of course, the earnings of minorities or women may differ from those of whites or men, respectively, for reasons other than employment discrimination. Nonemployment discrimination may limit the opportunity of minority groups and women to acquire human capital (for example, access to high-quality education or specialized training) that would enhance both productivity and earnings. Limited opportunities as the result of growing up in a low-income or a single-parent family may also influence skill development and educational achievement. Thus, factors other than employment discrimination will influence earnings differences among individuals according to race or ethnic status. The following section will analyze the impact of employment discrimination in some detail.

EARNINGS DIFFERENTIALS FROM NONHOMOGENEOUS JOBS

When individuals evaluate employment alternatives, they consider working conditions as well as wage rates. Is a job dangerous? Does it offer the opportunity to acquire the experience and training that will enhance future earnings? Is the work strenuous and nerve-racking? Are the working hours, job location, and means of transportation convenient? These factors are what economists call **nonpecuniary job characteristics.** People will accept jobs with unpleasant working conditions if the wages are high enough (compared to jobs with better working conditions for which the workers are qualified) to compensate for the undesirable nonpecuniary job characteristics. Since the higher wages, in essence, compensate workers for the unpleasant nonpecuniary attributes of a job, economists refer to wage differences stemming from this source as **compensating wage differentials.** There are numerous examples of compensating wage differences. Because of the dangers involved, aerial window washers (those who hang from windows 20 stories up) earn higher wages than other window washers. Sales jobs involving a great deal of out-of-town travel typically pay more than similar jobs without such inconvenience. Coal miners and sewer workers accept these jobs because they generally pay more than the alternatives available to low-skill workers. Compensating factors even influence the earnings of economists. When economists work for colleges or universities, they generally enjoy a more independent work environment and stimulating intellectual climate than when they are employed in the business sector. Unsurprisingly, the earnings of economists in academia are typically lower than those of economists in business.

Nonpecuniary job characteristics
Working conditions, prestige, variety, location, employee freedom and responsibilities, and other nonwage characteristics of a job that influence how employees evaluate the job.

Compensating wage differentials
Wage differences that compensate workers for risk, unpleasant working conditions, and other undesirable nonpecuniary aspects of a job.

EARNINGS DIFFERENTIALS FROM IMMOBILITY OF LABOR

It is costly to move to a new location or train for a new occupation in order to obtain a job. Such movements do not take place instantaneously. In the real world, labor, like other resources, does not possess perfect mobility. Some wage differentials thus result from an incomplete adjustment to change.

Since the demand for labor resources is a derived demand, it is affected by changes in product markets. An expansion in the demand for a product causes a rise in the demand for specialized labor to produce the product. Since resources are often highly immobile (that is, the supply is inelastic) in the short run, the expansion in demand may cause the wages of the specialized laborers to rise sharply. This is what happened in the oil-drilling industry in the late 1970s. An expansion in demand triggered a rapid increase in the earnings of petroleum engineers, oil rig operators, and other specialized personnel. Falling oil prices triggered the opposite effect in the mid-1980s. The demand for and employment opportunities of specialized resources declined substantially as output in the oil industry fell during 1985–1986. Demand shifts in the product market favor those in expanding industries but work against those in contracting industries.

Institutional barriers may also limit the mobility of labor. Licensing requirements, for example, limit the mobility of labor into many occupations—medicine, taxicab driving, architecture, and mortuary science among them. Unions may also follow policies that limit labor mobility and alter the free-market forces of supply and demand. Minimum wage rates may retard the ability of low-skill workers to obtain employment in certain sectors of the economy. These restrictions on labor mobility will influence the size of wage differentials among workers.

SUMMARY OF WAGE DIFFERENTIALS

As the "Thumbnail Sketch" shows, wage differentials stem from many sources, which can be categorized in three main ways: differences in workers, differences in jobs, and immobility of resources. Many of these factors play an important allocative role, compensating people for (1) human-capital investments that increase their productivity or (2) unfavorable working conditions. Other wage differentials reflect, at least partially, locational preferences or the desires of individuals for higher money income rather than nonmonetary benefits. Still other

---

THUMBNAIL SKETCH

WHAT ARE THE SOURCES OF EARNINGS DIFFERENTIALS?

DIFFERENCES IN WORKERS:
1. Productivity and specialized skills (reflects native ability, parental training, and investment in human capital).
2. Worker preferences (trade-off between money earnings and other things).
3. Race and sex discrimination.

DIFFERENCES IN JOBS:
1. Location of job.
2. Working conditions (for example, job safety, likelihood of temporary layoffs, and comfort of work environment).
3. Opportunity for training and skill-enhancement work experience.

IMMOBILITY OF RESOURCES:
1. Temporary disequilibrium resulting from dynamic change.
2. Institutional restrictions (for example, occupational licensing and union-imposed restraints).

differentials, such as those related to discrimination and occupational restrictions, are unrelated to worker preferences and are not required to promote efficient production.

THE ECONOMICS OF EMPLOYMENT DISCRIMINATION

How does employment discrimination affect the job opportunities available to women and minorities? Do employers gain from discrimination? Economics sheds light on both of these questions. There are two outlets for labor-market discrimination: wage rates and employment restrictions. **Exhibit 24–2** illustrates the impact of wage discrimination. When majority employees are preferred to minority workers (or male to female workers), the demand for the latter groups is reduced. Consequently, the wages of minorities and women decline relative to those of white men.

Essentially, there is a dual labor market—one market for the favored group and another for the group against which the discrimination is directed. The favored group, such as whites, is preferred, but the less expensive labor of minority workers is a substitute productive resource. Both white and minority employees are employed, but the whites are paid a higher wage rate.

Exclusionary practices may also be an outlet for employment discrimination. Either in response to outside pressure or because of their own views, employers may primarily hire whites and males for certain types of jobs. When minority and female workers are excluded from a large number of occupations, they are

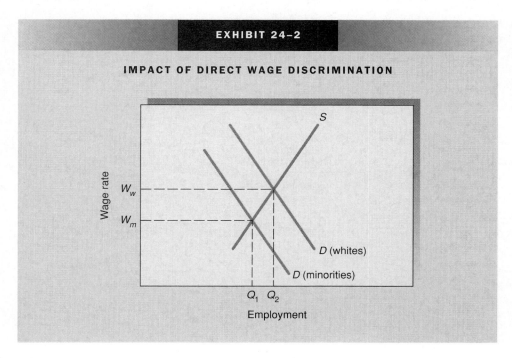

EXHIBIT 24–2

IMPACT OF DIRECT WAGE DISCRIMINATION

If there is employment discrimination against minorities or women, the demand for their services will decline, and their wage rate will fall from W_w to W_m.

APPLICATIONS IN ECONOMICS

EMPLOYMENT DISCRIMINATION AND THE EARNINGS OF WOMEN

Since the Second World War, there has been a dramatic shift in the household/work-force role of women, particularly married women. In 1992, 58.4 percent of women were in the labor force, compared with 33.2 percent in 1949, and 37.6 percent in 1960 (see **Exhibit 1**). Married women accounted for most of this dramatic increase; their labor-force participation rate soared from 32 percent in 1960 to 59 percent in 1992. While more women were working, prior to 1980 their earnings changed little relative to men. In fact, the female-male, (F/M), earnings ratio for full-time workers was approximately 60 percent throughout the 1950–1980 period. As the exhibit shows, the earnings of women have improved relative to men during the last decade.

Nevertheless, women working full-time earned only 70.6 percent as much as their male counterparts in 1992. (Note: Women employed full-time still work approximately 10 percent fewer hours than men who are employed full-time. Therefore, the hourly earnings of full-time working women were approximately 77 percent as high as their male counterparts in 1992.)

EMPLOYMENT DISCRIMINATION AND FAMILY SPECIALIZATION Why are the earnings of women so low compared to men? Most people blame employment discrimination. A Presidential Task Force in the 1970s concluded that widespread and pervasive discrimination accounted for the lower earnings of women relative to men. There is substantial evidence supportive of this view. In contrast with minorities relative to

EXHIBIT 1

LABOR-FORCE EXPERIENCE OF FEMALES, 1960–1992

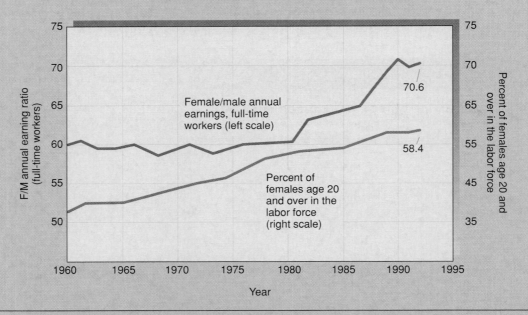

Between 1960 and 1992, the labor-force participation of females rose from 37.6 to 58.4 percent. However, the F/M earning ratio fluctuated around 60 percent during the 1960–1980 period, before climbing throughout the 1980s. By 1992, the F/M earnings ratio had risen to 70.6 percent.

whites, the age, education, marital status, language, and regional locational characteristics of men and women are similar. Thus, correcting for these factors does little to reduce the earnings differential between men and women. Occupational data are consistent with the view that women are crowded into a few low-paying jobs. Until recently, more than half of all women were employed in just four occupations—clerical workers, teachers, nurses, and food-service workers. High-paying professional, managerial, and craft occupations, particularly occupations where on-the-job experience leads to upward mobility, appear to be reserved primarily for men.

Despite this evidence, the case that employment discrimination is the sole or even the major source of the earnings differential between men and women is less than airtight. First, the size of even the adjusted differential should cause one to pause. If an employer could really hire women who are willing and able to do the same work as men for 30 percent less, the profit motive would provide the employer with a strong incentive to do so. Remember, the average business earns a profit of about 5 percent on total sales (or total cost). If an employer could really cut labor costs 30 percent merely by hiring women (primarily) rather than men, surely many less "sexist" employers (both men and women), would jump at the chance. Of course, as more and more employers substituted women for men workers, the earnings ratio of women to men would move toward parity.[1]

Second, it is important to recognize that married men and women have different areas of traditional specialization within the family. Married men typically pursue paid employment aggressively because they are expected to be the family's primary breadwinner. Since men envision continuous labor-force participation, they are more likely to make a geographic move to improve their earnings and choose jobs for which employment experience leads to higher earnings. Given their traditional responsibility for monetary earnings, men are also more likely to accept jobs with long hours, uncertain schedules, and out-of-town travel.

In contrast, married women have traditionally had the primary responsibility for operating the household and caring for children. Given these areas of specialization, historically many women anticipated intermittent labor-force participation. Thus, women sought different sorts of jobs than men. They sought jobs with less travel time, flexible hours, and other characteristics comple-

mentary with household responsibilities. Similarly, many women sought jobs that would allow them to reenter the labor force with only a small reduction in earning power.[2] Viewed in this light, it is not particularly surprising that women found nursing, teaching, secretarial, and other jobs with easily transportable skills and credentials highly attractive.

How important are gender differences in specialization within the family? Since preferences cannot be directly observed, the family specialization theory is difficult to test. However, **Exhibit 2** sheds some light on its importance. Here we illustrate the median annual earnings of women relative to men, according to marital status. Clearly, married women earn substantially less than married men. Even when working full-time, year-round, married women earn only 64 percent as much as men. However, the earnings gap between men and women is substantially less for singles, the group least influenced by actual and potential differences in specialization within the traditional family. In fact, in 1992 the female-male annual earnings ratio for full-time, full-year workers was 100 percent for singles. Thus, the earnings of single women were essentially the same as those of single men. This pattern of earnings differences according to marital status implies that, although employment discrimination may well be a contributing factor, family specialization is also an important determinant of the overall earnings differential between men and women.

---

[1] The employment and earnings data of self-employed workers are also inconsistent with the employment-discrimination hypothesis. One would expect that many women would shift to self-employment in order to escape the effects of discrimination, resulting in an overrepresentation of women and a higher female-male earnings ratio in self-employment occupations. In fact, the opposite results occur. See Robert L. Moore, "Employer Discrimination: Evidence from Self-Employed Workers," *Review of Economics and Statistics* LXV (August 1983).

[2] For an analysis of how family specialization influences the employment and earnings of women, see Solomon Polachek, "Discontinuous Labor Force Participation and Its Effect on Women's Market Earnings" in Cynthia B. Lloyd (ed.), *Sex Discrimination and the Division of Labor* (New York: Columbia University Press, 1975); and James Gwartney and Richard Stroup, "Measurement of Employment Discrimination According to Sex," *Southern Economic Journal* (April 1973).

EXHIBIT 2

FEMALE-MALE EARNINGS ACCORDING TO MARITAL STATUS, 1992

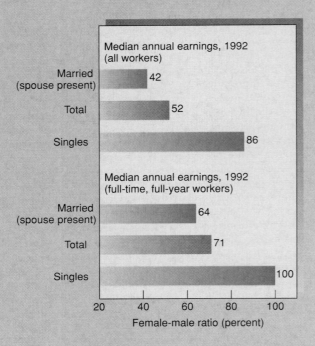

Although the female-male earning ratio varies considerably according to marital status and time worked, the earnings of single women relative to the earnings of single men are much higher than the earnings of women in other marital status groupings.

Source: U.S. Department of Commerce, "Money Income of Households, Families and Persons in the United States: 1992," *Current Population Reports*, Series P-60–184.

THE FUTURE   What can we say about the future direction of earnings according to gender? In the past, the career objectives of men and women have often differed substantially. There is evidence that these differences are beginning to narrow. In 1968 a national sample of women 14 to 24 years of age found that only 27 percent expected to be working at age 35. In contrast, a similar sample of young women in 1979 found that 72 percent would be working at that age.[3] These figures indicate that

EXHIBIT 3

WOMEN AS A PROPORTION OF PERSONS EARNING SELECTED PROFESSIONAL DEGREES, 1970–1971 AND 1990–1991

Field of Study	1970–1971	1990–1991
Engineering	0.8	15.4
Dentistry	1.2	32.1
Optometry	2.4	43.9
Law	7.3	43.0
Veterinary Medicine	7.8	57.2
Medicine	9.2	36.0
Accounting	10.1	53.8
Economics	11.2	30.3
Architecture	12.0	38.7
Pharmacy	25.2	61.8

Source: Commission of Professionals in Science and Technology, *Professional Women and Minority* (Washington, DC: CPST, 1987); and U.S. Department of Education, *Digest of Educational Statistics, 1993* (Washington, DC: U.S. Government Printing Office, 1994).

there has been a dramatic increase in the proportion of young women who are preparing for a career and planning for a lifetime of labor-force participation.

The dramatic change in the career plans of women is also reflected in their educational choices. In the past, women were less likely than men to study mathematics, engineering, medicine, law, and similar fields leading to high-paying professional jobs. As **Exhibit 3** illustrates, more and more women are now preparing for the professions rather than for the office. For example, women earned 53.8 percent of the accounting degrees in 1990–1991, up from only 10.1 percent in 1970–1971. In 1990–1991, more than half of the persons earning a degree in veterinary medicine were women, compared with only 7.8 percent in 1970–1971. During the last 20 years, there has also been a dramatic increase in the number of women earning degrees in medicine, law, architecture, pharmacy, economics, and several other professional areas.

[3]See Chapter 7 of the *Economic Report of the President: 1987*. The numbers presented here are from Table 7–3 of the report.

During the last two decades there has been a dramatic change in the attachment of women to the labor force. An increasing number of women are committed to continuous, full-time market work. In contrast with the past, many women now only take a short period of time off when they have children. Thus, the continuous labor for experience, education plans, and career objectives of women and men are becoming more and more similar.[4] This factor was the moving force underlying the growth of the F/M earnings ratio in the 1980s and it will almost surely continue to erode earnings differences according to gender during the 1990s.

---

[4]For additional details on this topic, see James P. Smith and Michael P. Ward, "Women in the Labor Market and in the Family," *Journal of Economic Perspectives* (Winter 1989), pp. 9–23; and Claudia Goldin, "Gender Gap," *Fortune Encyclopedia of Economics*, edited by David R. Henderson (New York; Warner Books, 1993).

---

crowded into a smaller number of remaining jobs and occupations. (See the "Applications in Economics" feature.) If entry restraints prevent people from becoming supervisors, plumbers, electricians, and truck drivers, they will be forced to accept alternatives. When the supply of labor in the unrestricted occupations increases, wage rates fall. The exclusionary practices thus result in higher wages for white males holding jobs from which minorities and females are excluded. The outcome is an overrepresentation of white males in the higher-paying occupations, while a disproportionate number of minorities and women will occupy the lower-paying, nonrestricted positions. The result will be a reduction in the earnings of minorities and women relative to white males.

While employment discrimination undoubtedly influences earning opportunities available to minorities and women, economic theory indicates that discrimination is costly to employers when they are merely reflecting their own prejudices. If employers can hire equally productive minority employees (or women) at a lower wage than whites (or men), the profit motive gives them a strong incentive to do so. Hiring the higher-wage whites when similar minority employees are available will increase the costs of firms that discriminate. Employers who hire employees regardless of their race or gender will have lower costs and higher profits than rival firms who try to fill positions with (mostly) white males. Thus, competitive forces tend to reduce the profitability of firms that discriminate.[2]

EMPLOYMENT DISCRIMINATION AND THE EARNINGS OF MINORITIES

Earnings may differ among groups for reasons other than employment discrimination. (See "Applications in Economics" for an analysis of earnings differences according to gender.) If we want to isolate the impact of employment discrimination, we must (1) adjust for differences between groups in education, experience,

---

[2]For empirical evidence that competition reduces the effects of employer discrimination, see James Gwartney and Charles Haworth, "Employer Cost and Discrimination: The Case of Baseball," *Journal of Political Economy* (June 1974).

Source: Leonard A. Carlson and Caroline Swartz, "The Earnings of Women and Ethnic Minorities, 1959–1979," *Industrial and Labor Relations Review,* 41 (July 1988). The estimates are based on 1980 census data.

EXHIBIT 24–3

ACTUAL AND PRODUCTIVITY-CORRECTED WAGES OF MINORITY MALES COMPARED WITH WHITE MALES

	THE WAGE OF MINORITY MEN RELATIVE TO WHITE MEN, 1979	
	ACTUAL	CORRECTED
White	100	100
African American	67	83
Mexican American	66	98
Japanese American	105	101
Chinese American	89	88
Puerto Rican American	63	95
American Indian	74	90
Cuban American	79	96
Vietnamese American	64	98

and other productivity-related factors and (2) then make comparisons between *similarly qualified* groups of employees who differ only with regard to race (or gender). This is precisely the methodology followed by Leonard Carlson and Caroline Swartz of Emory University in their detailed study of earnings differences among minority groups.[3] In essence, Carlson and Swartz calculated what the earnings of white men would be if they had the same average education, age, language (English), marital status, native birth, annual hours worked, and regional location as minority men. The actual earnings of minority men were then compared to the "corrected" (productivity-adjusted) earnings of white men.

Exhibit 24–3 summarizes the findings of Carlson and Swartz. The actual earnings of black men were only 67 percent of the earnings of white men in 1979. However, when the work-force characteristics (education, age, language, marital status, and so on) of black men were taken into account, the corrected earnings of black men rose to 83 percent of the white male earnings. Productivity-related factors accounted for almost half of the earnings differential between white and black men. Nonetheless, the 17 percent earnings difference between similarly qualified

---

[3]Leonard A. Carlson and Caroline Swartz, "The Earnings of Women and Ethnic Minorities, 1959–1979," *Industrial and Labor Relations Review* 41 (July 1988). Also see Barry R. Chiswick, "Differences in Education and Earnings Across Racial and Ethnic Groups: Tastes, Discrimination, and Investments in Child Quality," *Quarterly Journal of Economics* (August 1988), pp. 571–599; and June O'Neill, "The Role of Human Capital in Earnings Differences Between Black and White Men," *Journal of Economic Perspectives* (Fall 1990), pp. 25–45.

whites and blacks indicates that the earnings of blacks are substantially reduced as the result of employment discrimination.

Mexican-Americans constitute the second-largest minority group in the United States. Even though the actual earnings of Mexican-American men were only 66 percent of the earnings of white men, their "corrected" earnings were almost equal (98 percent) to the white earnings. This implies that if Mexican men possessed the same worker characteristics as white men, their earnings would be very close to parity with their white counterparts.

The actual and corrected earnings for other minority groups are also presented in Exhibit 24–3. Interestingly, both the actual and corrected earnings of Japanese-American men were slightly greater than for their white counterparts. The two most recent arrivals among the minority groups—Cubans and Vietnamese—appear to be doing quite well, given their worker characteristics. The corrected relative wage of both groups was only a little less than the white wage. The corrected earnings of both Chinese Americans and American Indians (Native Americans) were approximately 10 percent less than those of similar whites. Except for Japanese Americans and Chinese Americans, the corrected earnings of each minority group were significantly higher relative to whites than their actual earnings figure. This indicates that differences in worker characteristics as well as employment discrimination contribute to earnings differences between white and minority men.

THE ECONOMICS OF FRINGE AND MANDATED BENEFITS

When referring to wages or compensation, we have proceeded as if employees were compensated only with money payments. Of course, this is an oversimplification. There are generally two components of employee compensation: (1) money wages and (2) **fringe benefits,** which include items such as health-care insurance, layoff benefits, pension benefits, on-the-job training, on-the-premises child-care services, severance benefits, use of an automobile, discounts on life and auto insurance, parental-leave benefits, and paid time off for sickness, personal business, vacation, jury duty, and holidays. In 1992 fringe benefits comprised approximately 28 percent of the total compensation of employees in the United States. In the manufacturing sector, fringe benefits accounted for one-third of the total compensation of employees.

Like money wages, provision of fringe benefits is costly to employers. When deciding whether to employ a worker, the employer must consider the total cost of the compensation package. Employment will be expanded as long as the employee's MRP exceeds the cost of the employee's total compensation package, including the cost of the fringe benefits. Conversely, workers will not be hired if their employment adds more to cost than to revenue.

In any specific skill category, the compensation package of employees will reflect market conditions. Employers will have to pay a compensation package equal to the market wage, or they will lose employees to rival firms. And employees

Fringe benefits
Benefits other than normal money wages that are supplied to employees in exchange for their labor services.

who demand a compensation package in excess of the market wage will be unable to find employment. Fringe benefits are nothing more than a component of the market-determined compensation package. Employers who offer more attractive fringe benefits will be able to attract workers with a lower money wage. Those who offer little in the way of fringe benefits will have to pay higher wages. In essence, employees pay for fringe benefits in the form of lower money wages. Contrary to the view of some, fringe benefits are not a "gift" from the employer. Rather, they are earned by the employees as a component of their total compensation package.

Why might employers and employees find a compensation package that included fringe benefits mutually advantageous? There are two major reasons. First, it may be cheaper for the employees of a firm to purchase certain benefits as a group rather than separately as individuals. When this is the case, employees may prefer the group-purchased benefit rather than additional money wages of equal cost. Health-care insurance is an example. It is often cheaper for an insurance company to provide a single policy covering 100 employees (and their families) than it would be for workers to buy 100 separate policies. Therefore, group-purchase provides the employees of a firm with a more economical insurance coverage than they could achieve if they were paid a higher wage (equal to the cost of the insurance) and bought the insurance separately.

Second, compensation in the form of fringe benefits may lead to a tax savings. For example, employer-provided child-care services or use of company-purchased football tickets generate "income" to the employee, but such in-kind benefits are usually not taxable. Therefore, compensation in this form may increase the employee's after-tax compensation more than an equivalent amount of money earnings.

The cost of providing fringe benefits will vary among employers. Large firms may be able to provide some fringe benefits—health-care insurance and child-care services, for example—much more cheaply than small firms. Moreover, employees will vary in their personal valuation of various fringe benefits. For example, parental-leave benefits or child-care services may be a highly valued benefit to one employee while yielding little or no utility to another.

In the absence of legislation, agreements between employers and employees (and their representatives) determine the proportion of money wages and fringe benefits in the total compensation package. Employers and employees have an incentive to structure the compensation package so that it will transfer the maximum amount of value to employees for any given cost to the employer. Compensation packages of this type will attract employees and thereby minimize the employer's labor costs.

The extent to which any given fringe benefit will be included in a compensation package depends upon both the cost of the employer's provision and the employee's personal valuation of the benefit. It will cost an employer the same to pay an employee $1,000 per month as it will to pay $800 per month plus a fringe-benefit package that costs $200 per month. In both cases, the employer's monthly cost is $1,000. When the employer's cost of providing a fringe benefit is low (relative to its cost if purchased directly by the employee) and the employee's valuation of the benefit is high, employers and employees will find it mutually advantageous to substitute the fringe benefits for higher money wages. Conversely, when there is little or no advantage derived from employer-coordinated group provision, or when employees value a fringe benefit less than its cost, employees will prefer higher money wages rather than the fringe benefit. In fact, failure to include a fringe benefit in a wage package is strong evidence that it costs more than the value it provides to employees.

IMPACT OF MANDATED BENEFITS

In recent years several states, and in some cases the federal government, have mandated that employers supply their employees with various fringe benefits, including health-care insurance, parental leave, and child-care services. Proponents of **mandated benefits** argue that they provide protection for employees who work for employers who are unwilling to provide various fringe benefits. Critics charge that mandated benefits are not worth their price—by pushing up labor costs, they reduce employment.

Mandated benefits
Fringe benefits that the government forces employers to include in their total compensation package paid to employees.

In analyzing the full impact of mandated benefits, there are three key points to keep in mind. First, a mandated benefit is only one component of the total compensation package. Increasing a single component of the package will not necessarily increase the size of the overall package. The parties will adjust. As they adjust, money wages and other fringe benefits will be reduced below what they would have been in the absence of the mandated benefits. Legislation mandating benefits thus reduces flexibility. It forces employers and employees to include a specific item in the total compensation package even when the parties would have preferred to structure the compensation package differently. In many cases, employer-provision of a benefit—particularly provision by small firms—will cost more than the benefit is valued by employees. When this is the case, mandated benefits will increase labor costs without providing a proportional increase in value to employees.

Second, employees earn and ultimately pay for all components of their compensation package—including any benefits mandated by government. Workers will not be hired if their employment adds more to costs than to revenues. The view that fringe benefits are a gift from the employer, and that the size of the benefits package can be increased by requiring employers to include various government-mandated benefits, is purely and simply wrong.

Third, fringe benefits are often an inefficient form of compensating employees. When there are neither savings from group purchase nor tax advantages, employees will prefer money wages to in-kind benefits. When in-kind compensation is efficient—when employees value a fringe benefit more than the additional money that it costs—an employer has a strong incentive to adopt (and employees have a strong incentive to bargain for) this form of compensation. When efficient, substitution of a fringe benefit for wages can increase the value of the compensation package of employees without increasing the employer's cost. However, failure of a fringe benefit to emerge in a given employment setting is strong evidence that it is inefficient—that employees would prefer additional money wages rather than the fringe benefit (given its cost of provision).

How do mandated benefits affect the welfare of workers? Our analysis indicates that adjustments in other dimensions of employment contracts will erode much of their impact. Even when they alter the structure of compensation, mandated benefits are unlikely to increase the overall level of employee compensation. In cases where employees would prefer additional money wages rather than the benefits, forcing the mandated benefits into the compensation package will reduce the welfare of employees because, as labor markets adjust, losses from reductions in other components of the compensation package will more than off-set the gains derived from the mandated benefits. Even if employees value the benefits more than their costs, lower money wages will partially offset the positive effects of the mandated benefits. Thus, any positive impact of mandated benefits on the total compensation of employees will generally be substantially less than the proponents believe. Similarly, the negative impact on labor costs and employment will generally be substantially less than the critics charge.

PRODUCTIVITY AND WAGES

Productivity and real wages are closely linked. Real earnings are vastly greater in the United States than they are in India or China, because the output per hour of U.S. workers is much greater than the output of their counterparts in those countries. In other words, U.S. workers earn more because they produce more. Similarly, the *growth* of productivity and real earnings are closely linked. Average real earnings (total compensation) per hour in the United States in 1992 were approximately double the earnings of U.S. workers 40 years earlier. Growth of productivity per hour explains this increase in earnings. The output of goods and services per hour of U.S. workers in 1992 was approximately twice the level of the early 1950s.

Differences in labor productivity—output produced per worker-hour—are the major source of variations in real wages between nations and between time periods. When the amount produced per worker-hour is high, real wages will be high.

In the last chapter, we showed that the productivity of a resource, including labor, is dependent on the amount of other resources with which it works. Contrary to what many believe, the physical capital represented by **automation**—any production technique that reduces the amount of labor required to produce a good or service—is not the enemy of high real wages (see the "Myths of Economics" feature). In fact, just the opposite is true. Machines make it possible for labor to produce more per worker-hour. Are jobs destroyed in the process? Specific jobs are sometimes eliminated, but this merely releases human resources so that they can be used to expand output in other areas. Output and productivity, not jobs, are the source of high real wages.

Investment in both human and nonhuman capital is vital to the growth of productivity. For several decades, the educational level of members of the work force in the United States (representing investment in human capital) has steadily increased. The median number of years of schooling of persons in the labor force in 1992 was 13, compared with 10.6 years in 1949. Simultaneously, the nonhuman capital per worker has expanded (although the growth rate of capital investment per worker has slowed considerably in recent years). Both the development and innovative application of improved technological methods are important to productivity, making it possible to obtain a larger output from the same resource base. Of course, modern technological advancements are often linked to investments in both physical and human capital.

Automation

A production technique that reduces the amount of labor required to produce a good or service. It is beneficial to adopt the new labor-saving technology only if it reduces the cost of production.

Production of goods and services that people value is the source of income. Since improved machinery and technology increase productivity, they also are a source of higher incomes.

MYTHS OF ECONOMICS

"AUTOMATION IS THE MAJOR CAUSE OF UNEMPLOYMENT. IF WE KEEP ALLOWING MACHINES TO REPLACE PEOPLE, WE ARE GOING TO RUN OUT OF JOBS."

Machines are substituted for people if, and only if, the machines reduce costs of production. Why has the automatic elevator replaced the operator, the tractor replaced the horse, and the power shovel replaced the ditch digger? Because each is a cheaper method of accomplishing a task.

The fallacy that automation causes unemployment stems from a failure to recognize the secondary effects. Employment may decline in a specific industry as the result of automation. However, lower per unit costs in that industry will lead to either (1) additional spending and jobs in other industries or (2) additional output and employment in the specific industry as consumers buy more of the now cheaper good.

Perhaps an example will help illustrate the secondary effects of automation. Suppose someone develops a new toothpaste that actually prevents cavities and sells it for half the current price of Colgate. Think of the impact the invention will have on dentists, producers of the old toothpaste and their employees, and even the advertising agencies that give us those marvelous toothpaste commercials. What are these people to do? Haven't their jobs been destroyed?

These are the obvious effects; they are seen to be the direct result of the toothpaste invention. What most people do not see are the additional jobs that will indirectly be created by the invention. Assuming an inelastic demand, consumers will now spend less on toothpaste, dental bills, and pain relievers. Their real incomes will be higher. They will thus be able to spend more on other products they would have forgone had it not been for the new invention. Spending on clothes, recreation, vacations, swimming pools, education, and many other items will increase. This additional spending, which would not have taken place if dental costs had not been reduced by the technological advancement, will generate additional demand and employment in other sectors.

When the demand for a product is elastic, a cost-saving invention can even generate an increase in employment in the industry affected by the invention.

This was essentially what happened in the automobile industry when Henry Ford's mass-production techniques reduced the cost (and price) of cars. When the price of automobiles fell 50 percent, consumers bought three times as many cars. Even though the worker-hours per car decreased by 25 percent between 1920 and 1930, employment in the industry increased from 250,000 to 380,000 during the period, an increase of approximately 50 percent.

Of course, technological advances that release labor resources may well diminish the earnings of specific individuals or groups. Home appliances such as automatic washers and dryers, dishwashers, and microwave ovens reduced the job opportunities of maids. Computer technology has reduced the demand for telephone operators. In the future, videotaped lectures may even reduce the job opportunities available to college professors. It is understandable why those groups directly affected this way by automation fear and oppose it.

Focusing on jobs alone, though, can lead to a fundamental misunderstanding about the importance of machines, automation, and technological improvements. The real impact of cost-reducing machines and technological improvements is an increase in production. Technological advances make it possible for us to produce as much with fewer resources, thereby releasing valuable resources so that production (and consumption) can be expanded in other areas. Other tasks can be accomplished with the newly available resources.

Since there is a direct link between improved technology and rising output, automation exerts a positive influence on economic welfare from the viewpoint of society as a whole. In aggregate, running out of jobs is not a problem. Jobs represent obstacles, tasks that must be accomplished if we desire to loosen the bonds of scarcity. As long as our ability to produce goods and services falls short of our consumption desires, there will be jobs. A society running out of jobs would be in an enviable position: It would be nearing the impossible goal—victory over scarcity.

THE GREAT PRODUCTIVITY SLOWDOWN

What has happened to productivity in recent decades? **Exhibit 24–4** sheds light on this question. For two decades following the Second World War, the output per worker in the United States increased at an annual rate of 3 percent or more. As would be expected, the real compensation per hour grew at a similar rate. However, since 1968 productivity growth has sagged badly. During the 1969–1980 period, the annual growth rate of output per hour of U.S. workers fell to 1.2 percent. Real compensation per hour grew by only 1.0 percent during that period. And this low growth rate of both productivity and real compensation has continued during the 1981–1992 period.

Productivity growth has lagged in other countries as well. **Exhibit 24–5** presents data on the growth of per capita GNP during 1955–1973 and 1974–1993 for seven major industrial economies. In every case, growth declined substantially subsequent to 1973. For the seven countries in aggregate, per capita real GNP declined from more than 4 percent during the 1955–1973 period to approximately 2 percent subsequent to 1973.

What accounts for the decline in the growth rate of productivity and real earnings during the last two decades? Researchers in this area believe that at least four major factors contributed to the slowdown in productivity. First, there was a slowdown in net capital formation per worker during the 1970s and 1980s. Workers are generally able to produce more when they are working with more equipment and better tools. Thus, when the supply of productivity-enhancing capital assets grows more slowly, the growth of labor productivity also tends to slow. This is precisely what happened during the last two decades. During the 1950–1970 period, the net annual growth rate of the fixed capital stock increased 2.5 percent faster than the number of persons in the labor force. During the 1970s

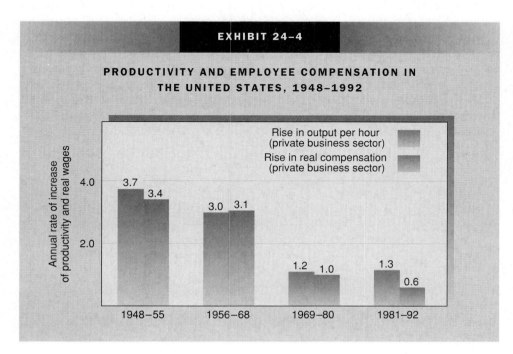

EXHIBIT 24–4

PRODUCTIVITY AND EMPLOYEE COMPENSATION IN THE UNITED STATES, 1948–1992

Rise in output per hour (private business sector)

Rise in real compensation (private business sector)

Annual rate of increase of productivity and real wages

4.0

2.0

	1948–55	1956–68	1969–80	1981–92
Output per hour	3.7	3.0	1.2	1.3
Real compensation	3.4	3.1	1.0	0.6

As illustrated in the graph, worker productivity and employee compensation per hour are closely linked. During the last two decades, the growth rate of worker productivity in the United States has been sagging.

Source: *The Economic Report of the President, 1994.*

Source: Stanley Fischer, "Symposium on the Slowdown in Productivity Growth," *Journal of Economic Perspectives* 2 (Fall 1988), Table 1. Data from the *Economic Report of the President, 1994*, were used to update the figures.

EXHIBIT 24–5

POST-1973 DECLINE IN GROWTH RATES OF MAJOR INDUSTRIAL ECONOMIES

	ANNUAL GROWTH RATE OF PER CAPITA GNP	
	1955–1973	1974–1993
United States	2.0	1.3
Japan	8.8	3.2
Germany	4.2	2.1
United Kingdom	2.5	1.1
Italy	4.9	2.0
France	4.6	1.8
Canada	3.0	1.9

and 1980s, however, the growth of the capital stock per worker slowed to only 1.0 percent. Both a decline in the rate of net capital formation and an acceleration in the growth rate of the labor force contributed to the slowdown in the growth of the capital stock per worker.

Second, both sharply higher energy prices and an increase in government regulation of business activities also reduced the productivity of capital during the last two decades. The sharply higher oil prices of the 1973–1981 period substantially reduced the efficiency of vast amounts of capital. Machines and structures designed for cost effectiveness at pre-1973 energy prices were suddenly rendered obsolete. They were too costly to operate at the higher level of energy prices. At the same time, regulations designed to improve the environment and reduce the level of pollution also reduced the effectiveness of capital. Many firms were forced either to terminate their use of various equipment or to undertake costly modifications in order to meet the more rigid regulatory standards of the 1970s and 1980s.[4] As Robert Solow, the 1987 recipient of the Nobel Prize in Economics, notes,

> Since the 1970s a substantial fraction of all investment has gone into pollution control and environmental improvement. That may be very valuable, but it doesn't contribute to the output we measure for the economy.[5]

Third, changing demographic factors in the United States also adversely affected productivity. Beginning in the latter half of the 1960s, there was a sharp

---

[4]See Edward F. Denison, *Trends in American Economic Growth, 1929–1982* (Washington, DC: Brookings Institution, 1985); and the articles in *The Journal of Economic Perspectives* (Fall 1988) for additional details on this topic.

[5]Robert Solow, quoted in Timothy Tregarthen, "Explaining the Great Slowdown," *The Margin* (November–December 1988).

influx of less experienced workers into the work force as the labor-force participation of women increased and the children of the post–Second World War "baby boom" came of working age. Economics indicates that a rapid growth of the labor force—particularly the growth of inexperienced and less skilled workers—will reduce productivity.

Finally, recent evidence indicates that a decline in the average achievement level of the new labor-force entrants has also retarded the growth rate of productivity.[6] The SAT scores of high school graduates and other measures of basic skills have been declining in the United States since the late 1960s. Prior to that time, these basic-skills test scores had been improving for at least 50 years. Thus, compared with the 1950s and 1960s, the new labor-force entrants during the last two decades have been less well-qualified, thus reducing the overall quality of the labor force and retarding the growth of productivity.

Clearly, the lagging growth rate of productivity is a serious matter. Unless it is reversed, the future growth of income will be quite slow compared with previous historical rates. For example, a 3 percent annual growth rate means that annual earnings expand by 35 percent during a decade, while a 1 percent growth rate increases earnings only by approximately 10 percent during the same period. Some of the unfavorable trends—for example, the oil price increases and the rapid growth of inexperienced workers—have reversed. Perhaps these positive developments will lead to more productivity improvements in the near future. However, most researchers are pessimistic. Few are predicting a return to the 3 percent growth rate of productivity experienced during the two decades subsequent to the Second World War.

DIVIDING THE ECONOMIC PIE

We have emphasized that wage rates generally reflect the availability of tools (physical capital) and the skills and abilities of individual workers (human capital). Wages tend to be high when physical capital is plentiful, technology is advanced, and the work force is highly skilled. When the equipment available to the typical worker is primitive and most workers lack education and skills, wages are low. Human capital and physical capital alike contribute to the productive process.

How is the pie divided between these two broad factors of production in the United States? **Exhibit 24–6** provides an answer. In 1950, 81 percent of the national income was earned by employees and self-employed proprietors, the major categories reflecting the earnings of human capital. In 1992 the share of national income allocated to human capital was 82.6 percent. Income earned by nonhuman capital—rents, interests, and corporate profits—accounted for between 17 and 19 percent of the national income during both years. These earnings shares of labor and capital have been relatively constant for several decades.

---

[6]See John H. Bishop, "Is the Test Score Decline Responsible for the Productivity Decline?" *American Economic Review* (March 1989), pp. 178–197.

Including self-employment income, approximately four-fifths of the national income is earned by owners of human capital.

Source: *Economic Report of the President, 1994,* Table B–25.

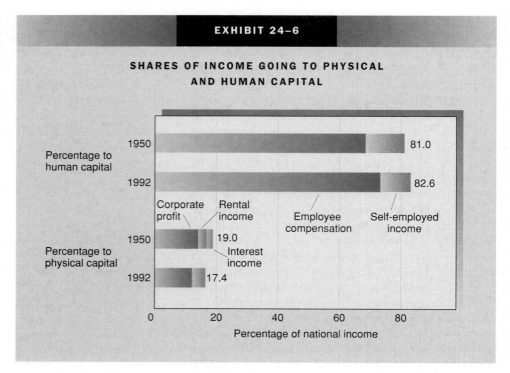

EXHIBIT 24–6

SHARES OF INCOME GOING TO PHYSICAL AND HUMAN CAPITAL

Percentage to human capital

1950 — 81.0

1992 — 82.6

Corporate profit — Rental income — Employee compensation — Self-employed income

Percentage to physical capital

1950 — 19.0 — Interest income

1992 — 17.4

Percentage of national income

CAN HIGHER WAGES BE LEGISLATED?

Minimum wage legislation
Legislation requiring that all workers in specified industries be paid at least the stated minimum hourly rate of pay.

In 1938 Congress passed the Fair Labor Standards Act, which provided for a national **minimum wage** of 25 cents per hour. During the last 50 years, the minimum wage has been increased several times. Currently, federal legislation requires most employers to pay wage rates of at least $4.25 per hour. Minimum wage legislation is intended to help the working poor. There is good reason to question, however, whether it actually does so.

Economic theory indicates that the quantity demanded of labor, particularly a specific skill category of labor, will be inversely related to its wage rate. If a higher minimum wage increases the wage rates of unskilled workers above the level that would be established by market forces, the quantity of unskilled workers employed will fall. The minimum wage will price the services of the least productive (and therefore lowest-wage) workers out of the market.

Exhibit 24–7 provides a graphic illustration of the direct effect of a $4.25 minimum wage on the employment opportunities of a group of low-skill workers. Without a minimum wage, the supply of and demand for these low-skill workers would be in balance at a wage rate of $3.50. Since the minimum wage makes low-skill labor service more expensive, employers will substitute machines and highly skilled workers (whose wages have not been raised by the minimum) for the now more expensive low-productivity employees. Jobs in which low-skill employees are unable to produce a marginal-revenue product equal to or greater than the minimum wage will be eliminated. In addition, as the cost (and price) of goods

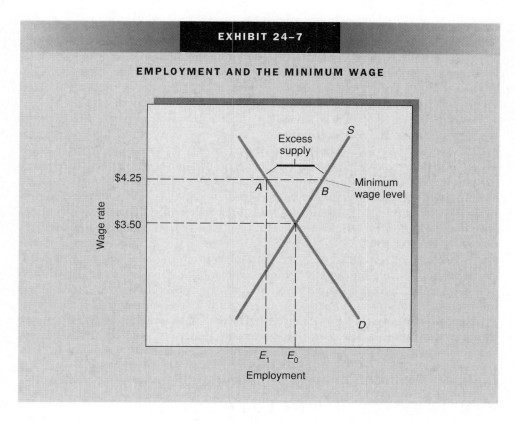

EXHIBIT 24–7

EMPLOYMENT AND THE MINIMUM WAGE

If the market wage of a group of employees were $3.50 per hour, a $4.25-per-hour minimum wage would increase the earnings of persons who were able to maintain employment but would reduce the employment of others (E_0 to E_1), pushing them onto the unemployment rolls or into less-preferred jobs.

and services produced by low-skill employees rises, consumers will rely more heavily on substitute goods produced by highly skilled labor or in foreign markets. The net effect of these substitutions will be a reduction in the quantity demanded of low-skill labor.

Of course, some low-skill workers—most likely the better qualified among those whose previous wages were near the minimum—will be able to maintain their jobs at the higher wage rate. Workers who retain their jobs will gain. Others, particularly those with the lowest pre-legislation wage rates and skill levels, will be unable to find work.[7] They will be pushed into the ranks of the unemployed or out of the labor force and onto welfare rolls.

INDIRECT EFFECTS OF THE MINIMUM WAGE

When analyzing the effects of the minimum wage, we must not forget that money wages are only one dimension of the exchange. Other aspects of the labor-service exchange will be affected by the imposition of the minimum wage. When a minimum wage rate pushes wages of low-skill workers above the market level, employers will have no trouble hiring workers. Therefore, they have little incentive to offer

---

[7]The impact of minimum wage legislation could differ from the theoretical results we have outlined if labor markets were dominated by a single buyer. Economists refer to this situation as *monopsony*. We choose not to present the monopsony model here because (1) in a modern society, where labor is highly mobile, the major assumptions of the model are seldom met, and (2) the bulk of the empirical evidence in this area is consistent with the competitive model.

workers training, convenient working hours, continuous employment, fringe benefits, and other nonwage components of the total compensation package. Predictably, a higher minimum wage will lead to an erosion in the quality of the nonwage components of minimum wage jobs.[8] As we discussed previously, higher mandated benefits do not necessarily increase total compensation. Neither does a higher mandated money wage—at least not by the amount of the increase in the money wage.

Of the nonwage elements adversely affected by minimum wage legislation, the decline in training opportunities is particularly important. Many inexperienced workers face a dilemma: they cannot find a job without experience (or skills), but they cannot obtain experience without a job. This is particularly true for younger workers. Employment experience obtained at an early age, even on seemingly menial tasks, can help one acquire work habits (for example, promptness and self-confidence), skills, and attitudes that will enhance one's value to employers in the future. Since minimum wage legislation prohibits the payment of even a temporarily low wage, it is often too costly for employers to offer low-skill workers jobs with training. In effect, the minimum wage acts as an institutional barrier limiting on-the-job training opportunities. In a comprehensive study of this issue, Masanori Hashimoto estimated that a 28 percent increase in the minimum wage reduced the value of on-the-job training available to the affected low-skill workers by 2.7 percent to 15 percent.[9] As a result, opportunities for on-the-job training are limited and low-skill workers are generally pushed into dead-end jobs—positions with little opportunity for future advancement.

MINIMUM WAGE AND TEENAGE UNEMPLOYMENT

Most empirical studies linking the minimum wage to employment have focused on teenagers, since there is a higher proportion of low-wage workers (reflecting their lack of skill-building experience) in this age group. Most of the studies in this area indicate that a 10 percent increase in the minimum wage reduces teenage employment by 1 to 3 percent.[10] Given the expected adverse impact of the minimum wage on other forms of compensation, this relatively small decline in employment is not surprising.

---

[8]Our treatment here is parallel to that for rent controls in Chapter 3. There we noted that in response to a below-market price and accompanying excess demand, the quality of rental housing deteriorates because sellers (landlords) have little incentive to maintain quality in order to attract buyers (renters). Correspondingly, in response to an above-equilibrium price and accompanying excess supply, the nonwage characteristics of jobs deteriorate because buyers (employers) have little incentive to maintain the quality of working conditions and fringe benefits in order to attract sellers (workers). It is hard to repeal the laws of supply and demand.

[9]Masanori Hashimoto, "Minimum Wage Effects on Training on the Job," *American Economic Review*, 72 (December 1982), pp. 1070–1087; and Charles Brown, "Minimum Wage Laws: Are They Overrated?" *Journal of Economic Perspectives* (Summer 1988), pp. 133–145.

[10]See Jacob Mincer, "Unemployment Effects of Minimum Wages," *Journal of Political Economy* 84 (August 1976); James Ragan, "Minimum Wages and the Youth Labor Market," *Review of Economics and Statistics* 59 (May 1977); Finis Welch, *Minimum Wages: Issues and Evidence* (Washington, DC: American Enterprise Institute, 1978); Charles L. Betsey and Bruce H. Dunson, "Federal Minimum Wage Laws and the Employment of Minority Youth," *American Economic Review* 71 (May 1981); and Charles Brown, Curtis Gilroy, and Andrew Kohen, "The Effect of the Minimum Wage on Employment and Unemployment," *Journal of Economic Literature* 20 (June 1982).

The minimum wage exerts its greatest impact on the employment opportunities of youthful African and Latin Americans. When a minimum wage pushes earnings into a skill category above the market level, an excess supply of labor will result. Employers will be in a position to choose among a surplus of applicants for each position. They will generally choose those workers within the low-productivity group who have the most skill, experience, and education. These are generally not younger African and Latin Americans. In addition, since all workers must be paid the minimum, the employer's incentive to hire less skilled and less favored groups is destroyed.

Black economists such as Walter Williams of George Mason University and Andrew Brimmer, a former member of the Federal Reserve Board, have been among the leading critics of the minimum wage. Brimmer argues,

> A growing body of statistical and other evidence accumulated by economists shows that increases in the statutory minimum wage dampen the expansion of employment and lengthen the lineup of those seeking jobs. Advances in the minimum wage have a noticeably adverse impact on young people—with the effects on black teenagers being considerably more severe.[11]

WOULD A HIGHER MINIMUM WAGE HELP THE POOR?

The proponents of a higher minimum wage argue that the current minimum wage will not provide the head of a family with enough income to keep the family out of poverty. This is true. When considering the relevance of this fact, however, it is important to keep two points in mind. First, the minimum wage does not assure one a job. A minimum wage high enough for a worker to support a family of three or four at an above-poverty income level will reduce the employment of low-skill workers, including some who are supporting families. Presumably, these workers would be better off working at a low wage than they would be unemployed. Second, and perhaps more important, most minimum wage workers are not supporting a family. In 1992 less than 10 percent of the workers earning the minimum wage were heads of families with incomes below the poverty level. Perhaps surprising to some, more than half of all the minimum wage workers were members of a family with an income above the median. Most (62 percent) of the minimum wage workers were employed only part-time. More than one-third were teenagers.

The typical minimum wage worker is a spouse or a teenage member of a household with an income well above the poverty level. Therefore, even if the adverse impact of a higher minimum wage on both employment and nonwage forms of compensation is ignored, a higher minimum wage would exert little impact on the income of the poor. This is precisely the conclusion reached in a recent study by William R. Johnson and Edgar K. Browning. Johnson and Browning estimated that a 22 percent increase in the minimum wage would add less than one-half of one percent to the income of households in the bottom 30 percent of the income distribution even if there were no reductions in employment.[12] The view that a higher minimum wage is an effective device with which to assist the poor is, purely and simply, incorrect.

---

[11]Andrew Brimmer, quoted in Louis Rukeyser, "Jobs Are Eliminated," Naught News Service (August 1978).

[12]William R. Johnson and Edgar K. Browning, "The Distributional and Efficiency Effects of Increasing the Minimum Wage: A Simulation," *American Economic Review* 73 (March 1983), pp. 204–211.

LOOKING AHEAD

While this chapter focused on the labor market, the following chapter will analyze the capital market. The real income and output of a nation is strongly influenced by the amount of both the physical and human capital with which people work. The next chapter analyzes the factors that underlie the availability of capital and the investment choices of decision makers.

CHAPTER SUMMARY

1. There are three major sources of wage differentials among individuals: differences in workers, differences in jobs, and degree of labor mobility. Individual workers differ with respect to productivity (skills, human capital, motivation, native ability, and so on), specialized skills, employment preferences, race, and gender. These factors influence either the demand for or the supply of labor. In addition, differences in nonpecuniary job characteristics, changes in product markets, and institutional restrictions that limit labor mobility contribute to variations in wages among workers.

2. Both employment discrimination and differences in employability characteristics (the quality and quantity of schooling, skill level, prior job experience, and other human-capital factors) contribute to earning differentials among groups. Economic research indicates that more than half of the earnings disparity between whites and blacks is due to differences in employability (productivity) characteristics rather than employment discrimination.

3. In the early 1990s women working full-time, year-round earned only about 70 percent as much as men. Some of this differential may emanate from discrimination in the labor market. However, differences between men and women in other areas that influence earnings—particularly differences in their attachment to the labor force and historical roles within the family—also contribute to earnings differences between men and women. Differences between men and women in these areas have changed substantially during the last two decades. Increasingly, women are continuously in the labor force and acquiring education suitable for professional careers. These developments pushed the female-male earnings ratio upward during the 1980s and will almost surely continue to do so during the 1990s.

4. Fringe benefits are a component of employee compensation. When the employer's cost of providing a fringe benefit is low, and the employee's personal valuation of the benefit is high, employers and employees will find it mutually advantageous to substitute fringe benefits for money wages in the total compensation package. Conversely, when these conditions are absent, money wages are the more efficient form of compensation.

5. Other forms of compensation will be scaled back as markets adjust to legislation mandating various fringe benefits. These adjustments will largely erode both the positive effects of the mandated benefits on employee compensation and the adverse effects of the benefits on labor costs and employment.

6. Productivity is the ultimate source of high wages. Workers in the United States, Canada, Japan, and other industrial countries earn high wages because their output per hour is high as the result of (a) worker knowledge and skills (human capital) and (b) the use of modern machinery (physical capital).

7. During the last 25 years, the growth of productivity in the United States and other major industrial nations has lagged well below the growth rate achieved during the two decades following the Second World War. A slowdown in the growth of capital per worker, higher energy prices, environmental regulations, an influx of inexperienced younger workers, and a decline in the basic skill levels of new labor-force entrants contributed to the slowdown in productivity in the United States. If the slowdown in productivity continues, future improvements in our standard of living will come about more slowly.

8. Approximately 80 percent of national income in the United States is allocated to human capital (labor), and 20 percent is allocated to owners of physical (nonhuman) capital.

9. Automated methods of production will be adopted only if they reduce costs. Although automation might reduce revenues and employment in a specific industry, the lower cost of production will increase real income, causing demand in other industries to expand. These secondary effects will cause employment to rise in other industries. Improved technology expands our ability to produce. It is expanded production, not the number of jobs, that determines our economic well-being.

10. Minimum wage legislation increases the earnings of some low-skill workers, but others are forced to accept inferior employment opportunities, join the ranks of the unemployed, or drop out of the labor force. The direct effects, however, will be moderated by an erosion in the quality of the nonwage components in response to the minimum rate. These adjustments will moderate both (a) the increase in total compensation and (b) the adverse employment effects emanating from the minimum wage. The minimum wage exerts its most adverse effects on the employment and training opportunities available to inexperienced workers with few skills, particularly youthful workers and minorities.

CRITICAL-ANALYSIS QUESTIONS

1. What are the major reasons for the differences in earnings among individuals? Why are wages in some occupations higher than in others? How do wage differentials influence the allocation of resources? Explain.

*2. Why are real wages in the United States higher than in other countries? Is the labor force itself responsible for the higher wages of American workers? Explain.

3. What are the major factors that would normally explain earnings differences between (a) a lawyer and a minister, (b) an accountant and an elementary school teacher, (c) a business executive and a social worker, (d) a country lawyer and a Wall Street lawyer, (e) an experienced, skilled craftsperson and a 20-year-old high school dropout, and (f) an upper-story and a ground-floor window washer?

4. Is employment discrimination the only important cause of earnings differences between whites and blacks? Carefully justify your answer.

5. "Higher wages help everybody. Workers are helped because they can now purchase more of the things they need. Business is helped because the increase in the worker's purchasing power will increase the demand for products. Taxpayers are helped because workers will now pay more taxes. Union activities and legislation mandating higher wages for workers will promote economic progress." Evaluate this view.

*6. "Jobs are the key to economic progress. Unless we create more jobs, our standard of living will fall." Is this statement true or false? Explain.

7. If Jones has a skill that is highly valued, she will be able to achieve high market earnings. In contrast, Smith may work just as hard or even harder, and still earn only a low income.
   a. Does hard work necessarily lead to a high income?
   b. Why are the incomes of some workers high and others low?
   c. Do you think the market system of wage determination is fair? Why or why not?
   d. Can you think of a more equitable system? If so, explain why it is more equitable.

*8. People who have invested heavily in human capital (for example, lawyers, doctors, and even college professors) generally have higher wages, but they also generally work more hours than other workers. Can you explain why?

*9. Analyze the impact of an increase in the minimum wage from the current level to $7.00 per hour. How would the following be affected:

a. Employment in skill categories previously earning less than $7 per hour.
b. The unemployment rate of teenagers.
c. The availability of on-the-job training for low-skill workers.
d. The demand for high-skill workers who provide good substitutes for the labor services offered by low-skill workers, assuming the low-skill workers are paid higher wage rates due to the increase in the minimum wage.

*10. "If individuals had identical abilities and opportunities, earnings would be equal." Is this statement true or false?

11. "If it were not for employment discrimination against women, the average earnings of men and women would be equal." Is this statement true or false?

*12. Other things being constant, how will the following factors influence hourly earnings?
   a. The employee must work the midnight to 8:00 A.M. shift.
   b. The job involves broken intervals (work 3 hours, off 2 hours, work 3 additional hours, and so on) of employment during the day.
   c. The employer provides low-cost child-care services on the premises.
   d. The job is widely viewed as prestigious.
   e. The job requires employees to move often from city to city.
   f. The job requires substantial amounts of out-of-town travel.

*13. In addition to money-wage compensation, some employers provide employees with health-care benefits, paid time off for sickness, vacation, and jury duty, on-the-premises child-care services, and severance benefits in case of termination.
   a. How do these benefits affect the employer's cost of employment? Do you think employers offering the benefits would be willing to pay higher wages if the benefits were not offered?
   b. Would you be willing to work for an employer who did not offer any of these benefits if the money-wage payments were high enough?
   c. Are these benefits "gifts" from employers offering them? Who really pays for the benefits?

14. Does it sometimes make sense for employers to pay workers with in-kind benefits (health-care insurance, child-care services, termination payments, and the like) rather than higher money wages? Why? Discuss.

15. A recent national poll of Americans found that 60 percent of the respondents thought that an increase in the

---

*Asterisk denotes questions for which answers are given in Appendix C.

"employer's share" of the payroll tax should be used to finance the additional cost of a universal health-care plan.

   a. Would this method of finance really impose the cost of the plan on employers? Why or why not?

   b. Analyze the impact of this method of financing health-care benefits (for nonemployees) on the real wages of employees and the level of employment. What factors would determine the incidence of this tax?

*16. Consider two occupations (A and B) that employ persons with the same skill and ability. When employed, workers in the two occupations work the same number of hours per day. In occupation A, employment is stable throughout the year, while employment in B is characterized by seasonal layoffs. In which occupation will the hourly wage rate be highest? Why? In which occupation will the annual wage be highest? Why?

*17. Recognizing that one cannot support a large family at the current minimum wage, suppose that Congress passes legislation requiring that businesses employing workers with three or more children pay these employees at least $7.50 per hour. How would this legislation affect the employment level of low-skill workers with three or more children? Do you think some workers with large families might attempt to conceal the fact? Why?

18. Top officials of large firms already offering health-care insurance, parental leave, and child-care benefits are often at the forefront of those favoring legislation mandating that all firms provide these benefits. They usually argue that "good corporate citizens" should provide the benefits to their employees. Can you think of a less altruistic reason why the officials may favor the mandated benefits?

*19. In 1992 the median earnings of single men working full-time, year-round were only 64 percent of their married counterparts. Does this indicate that there was employment discrimination against single men and in favor of married men?

20. During the last three decades, the labor-force participation of married females approximately doubled. How would this influx of married workers into the labor force influence (a) the average years of work experience of women relative to men, (b) the mean hours of work time of women relative to men, and (c) the female-male earnings ratio.

---

*Asterisk denotes questions for which answers are given in Appendix C.

CHAPTER TWENTY-FIVE

INVESTMENT, CAPITAL FORMATION, AND THE WEALTH OF NATIONS

To produce capital, people must forgo the opportunity to produce goods for current consumption. People can choose whether to spend their time picking apples or planting apple trees. In the first case there are more apples today; in the second, more apples tomorrow.

STEVEN LANDSBURG[1]

CHAPTER FOCUS

■ *Why do people invest? Why are capital resources often used to produce consumer goods?*

■ *Why are investors willing to pay interest to acquire loanable funds? Why are lenders willing to loan funds?*

■ *What is the interest rate? How is the nominal interest rate influenced by the inflation rate and the riskiness of a loan?*

■ *Why is the interest rate so important when evaluating costs and revenues across time periods?*

■ *When is an investment profitable? How do profitable and unprofitable investments influence the wealth of nations?*

■ *How important are investment and the efficient use of capital to the wealth of a nation?*

---

[1]Steven E. Landsburg, *Price Theory and Applications* (Fort Worth: The Dryden Press, 1992), p. 581.

I n the previous chapter we noted that the income of both individuals and nations is closely related to their productivity—their ability to supply goods and services that are highly valued by others. In turn, productivity is influenced by investment choices. Consider choices such as whether to construct an office building, purchase a harvesting machine, or go to law school. The returns derived from investments such as these are generally spread over several years (or even decades). In some cases, the costs of investments may also be incurred over a lengthy time period. How can people compare the benefits and costs of an activity when they are spread across lengthy periods of time? What factors determine whether an investment project should be undertaken? How can investment funds be channeled toward projects that will increase the wealth of people and nations? This chapter will address these questions and related issues.

WHY PEOPLE INVEST

Capital

Resources that enhance our ability to produce output in the future.

Investment

The purchase, construction, or development of capital resources, including both nonhuman capital and human capital. Investments increase the supply of capital.

Saving

Current income that is not spent on consumption goods.

Capital is a term used by economists to describe long-lasting resources that are valued because they can help us produce goods and services in the future. As we previously discussed, there are two broad categories of capital: (1) nonhuman resources such as buildings, machines, tools, and natural resources, and (2) human resources, that is, the knowledge and skills of people. **Investment** is the purchase, construction, or development of a capital resource. Thus, investments expand the availability of capital resources. For example, when a road construction firm purchases a grader, it is making an investment that will expand the firm's future output.

Saving is income not spent on current consumption. Investment and saving are closely linked. In fact, the two words describe different aspects of the capital-formation process. Saving applies to the nonconsumption of income, while investment applies to the use of the unconsumed income to produce a capital resource. Sometimes saving and investment are conducted by the same person, as when a farmer saves current income (refrains from spending it on consumption goods) in order to purchase a new tractor (an investment good).

It is important to recognize that saving is required for investment. Someone must save—refrain from consumption—in order to provide the resources for investment. When investors finance a project with their own funds, they are also saving (refraining from current consumption). Investors, however, do not always use their own funds to finance investments. Sometimes they will borrow funds from others. When this is the case, it is the lender rather than the investor that is doing the saving.

The alternative use of resources also highlights the linkage between investment and saving. Resources used to produce capital will be unavailable for the direct production of consumption goods. If we invest more—if we use more of our resources to produce capital resources today, fewer current resources will be available to produce consumption goods. Thus, if we invest more, we will have to reduce our current consumption.

Why would anyone want to delay consumption in order to undertake an investment? Consumption is the ultimate objective of all production. However, we can sometimes magnify our production of consumption goods by first using resources to produce capital resources and then applying these resources to the production of the desired consumer goods. The use of capital to produce consumption goods makes sense only when the capital enhances our total production of consumption goods.

Perhaps a simple illustration will help clarify the major considerations involved in the use of capital to produce consumption goods. Suppose that Robinson Crusoe could catch fish by either (1) combining his labor with natural resources (direct production) or (2) constructing a net and eventually combining his labor with this capital resource (indirect production). Let us assume that Crusoe could catch 2 fish per day by hand-fishing, but could catch 3 fish per day if he constructed and used a net that would last for 310 days. Suppose it would take Crusoe 55 days to build the net. The opportunity cost of constructing the net would be 110 fish (2 per day for each of the 55 days Crusoe spent building the net). As the accompanying chart indicates, if Crusoe invested in the capital resource (the net), his output during the next year (including the 55 days required to build the net) would be 930 fish (3 per day for 310 days). Alternatively, hand-fishing during the year would lead to an output of only 730 (2 fish per day for 365 days).

NUMBER OF FISH CAUGHT

	WITHOUT NET	WITH NET
Per day	2	3
Annual	730	930

Crusoe's investment in the net will enhance his productivity. With the net, his total output during the year will increase by 200 fish. In the short term, however, investing in the net will impose a sacrifice. During the 55 days it takes to construct the net, Crusoe's production of consumption goods will decline.

How can Crusoe or any other investor know if the value of the larger future output is worth the short-term cost? Most of us have a preference for goods now rather than later. For example, if you are typical, you would prefer a sleek new sports car now rather than the same car 10 years from now. On average, individuals possess a **positive rate of time preference.** By this we mean that people subjectively value goods obtained in the immediate or near future (including the present) more highly than goods obtained in the distant future.

When only Crusoe is involved, the attractiveness of the investment in the fishing net is dependent upon his time preference. If he places a high value on a couple of fish per day during the next 55 days, as indeed he may if he is on the verge of starvation, the cost of the investment may well exceed the value of the larger future output. If Crusoe could find someone who would loan him fish while he built the net, however, this would open up an additional option. In this case, the attractiveness of the investment would be influenced by the price of borrowing fish, or more broadly, by the interest rate.

Positive rate of time preference
The desire of consumers for goods now rather than in the future.

INTEREST RATES

In making decisions across time periods, the interest rate is of central importance because it links the future to the present. The interest rate allows individuals to place a current evaluation on future income and costs. In essence, it is the price of earlier availability; it is the premium that must be paid if you want to acquire goods now rather than later. From the lender's viewpoint, interest is a reward for waiting—a return received if you are willing to delay possible expenditures into the future.

In a modern economy, people often borrow funds in order to finance current investments and consumption. Because of this, the interest rate is often defined as the price of loanable funds. This definition is proper. But we should remember that it is the earlier availability of goods and services purchased, not the money itself, that is desired by the borrower.

DETERMINATION OF INTEREST RATES

Interest rates are determined by the demand for and supply of loanable funds. Investors demand funds in order to finance capital assets that they believe will increase output and generate profit. Simultaneously, consumers demand loanable funds because they have a positive rate of time preference; they prefer earlier availability.

The demand of investors for loanable funds stems from the productivity of capital. Investors are willing to borrow in order to finance the use of capital in production because they expect that an expansion in future output will provide them with the resources to repay both the principal and interest on the loan. Our prior example of Robinson Crusoe illustrates this point. Remember, Crusoe could increase his output by 200 fish this year if he could take off 55 days to build a net. Crusoe's fish production, however, would decline (by 2 fish per day) while he was constructing the net. Suppose a fishing crew from a neighboring island visited Crusoe and offered to lend him 110 fish so that he could undertake the capital investment project (building the net). If Crusoe could borrow the 110 fish (the principal) in exchange for, say, 165 fish a year later (110 to repay the principal and 55 as interest on the loan), the investment project would be highly profitable. Crusoe could repay the funds borrowed, plus the 50 percent interest rate, and still have 145 additional fish (the 200 additional fish caught minus the 55 fish paid in interest).

Crusoe's demand for loanable fish—and more generally, the demand of investors for loanable funds—stems directly from the productivity of the capital investment. Crusoe can gain by borrowing to finance the construction of a fishing net only because the net enables him to expand his total output during the year. Similarly, investors can gain by borrowing funds to undertake investment projects only when the capital assets purchased permit them to expand output (or reduce costs).

As **Exhibit 25–1** illustrates, the interest rate brings the choices of investors and consumers wanting to borrow funds into harmony with the choices of lenders willing to supply funds. Higher interest rates make it more costly for investors to undertake capital spending projects and for consumers to buy now rather than later. Both investors and consumers will therefore curtail their borrowing as the interest rate rises. Investors will borrow less because some investment projects that would be profitable at a low interest rate will be unprofitable at higher rates. Some consumers, rather than pay the high interest premium, will reduce their current consumption when the interest rate increases. Therefore, the amount of funds demanded by borrowers is inversely related to the interest rate.

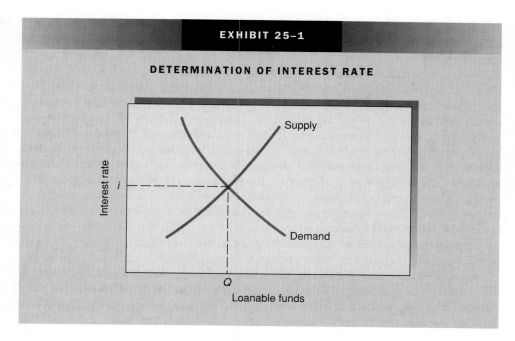

EXHIBIT 25–1

DETERMINATION OF INTEREST RATE

The demand for loanable funds stems from the consumer's desire for earlier availability and the productivity of capital. As the interest rate rises, current goods become more expensive in comparison with future goods. Therefore, borrowers will demand less loanable funds. On the other hand, higher interest rates will stimulate lenders to supply additional funds to the market.

The interest rate also provides a reward to persons (lenders) willing to reduce their current consumption in order to provide loanable funds to others. If some individuals are going to borrow in order to undertake an investment project (or consume more than their current income), others must curtail their current consumption by an equal amount. In essence, the interest rate provides lenders with the incentive to reduce their current consumption so that borrowers can either invest or consume beyond their current income. Higher interest rates provide persons willing to save (willing to supply loanable funds) with more future goods in exchange for the sacrifice of current consumption. Even though people have a positive rate of time preference, they will give up current consumption to supply funds to the loanable funds market if the price is right—that is, if the interest rate is attractive enough. Therefore, as the interest rate rises, the quantity of funds supplied to the loanable funds market expands.

As Exhibit 25–1 illustrates, the interest rate will bring the quantity of funds demanded into balance with the quantity supplied. At the equilibrium interest rate, the quantity of funds borrowers demand for investment and consumption now (rather than later) will just equal the quantity of funds lenders save. So the interest rate brings the choices of borrowers and lenders into harmony.

MONEY RATE VERSUS REAL RATE OF INTEREST

We have emphasized that the interest rate is a premium paid by borrowers for earlier availability and a reward received by lenders compensating them for delaying consumption. However, during a period of inflation—a general increase in prices—the nominal, or **money rate of interest** is a misleading indicator of how much borrowers are paying and lenders are receiving. Inflation reduces the

Money rate of interest
The rate of interest in monetary terms that borrowers pay for borrowed funds. During periods when borrowers and lenders expect inflation, the money rate of interest exceeds the real rate of interest.

purchasing power of a loan's principal. When the principal is repaid in the future, it will not purchase as much as it would have when the funds were initially loaned.

Recognizing the decline in the purchasing power of the dollars with which they will be repaid, lenders reduce the amount of loanable funds supplied unless they are compensated for the anticipated rate of inflation. When borrowers are aware that they will be paying back their loans with dollars of less purchasing power, they are, of course, willing to pay this **inflationary premium,** an additional amount that reflects the expected rate of future price increases. If borrowers and lenders fully anticipate a 5 percent rate of inflation, for example, they will be just as willing to agree on a 10 percent interest rate as they were to agree on a 5 percent interest rate when both anticipated stable prices. The advantage to borrowers is that they can purchase goods and services before they become even more expensive in the future.

Compared to the situation when the general price level is stable, the supply of loanable funds will decline (the curve will shift to the left) and the demand will increase (the curve will shift to the right) once decision makers anticipate future inflation. The money interest rate thus rises, overstating the "true" cost of borrowing and yield from lending. This true cost is the **real rate of interest,** which is equal to the money rate of interest minus the inflationary premium. It reflects the real burden to borrowers and payoff to lenders in terms of command over goods and services.

Our analysis indicates that high rates of inflation will push up the money rate of interest. The real world is consistent with this view. Money interest rates rose to historical highs in the United States as inflation soared to double-digit rates during the 1970s. Cross-country comparisons also illustrate the linkage between inflation and high interest rates. The lowest money interest rates in the world are found in Germany and Switzerland, and in recent years Japan. All are countries with low rates of inflation. In contrast, the highest money interest rates are observed in Brazil, Argentina, Israel, and other countries with high rates of inflation.

INTEREST RATES AND RISK

We have proceeded as though there were only a single interest rate present in the loanable funds market. In the real world, of course, there are many interest rates. There is the mortgage rate, the prime interest rate (the rate charged to business firms with strong credit ratings), the consumer loan rate, and the credit card rate, to name only a few.

Interest rates in the loanable funds market will differ primarily as the result of differences in the risk associated with the loan. It is riskier to loan funds to an unemployed worker than to a well-established business with substantial assets. Similarly, extending an unsecured loan like that accompanying purchases on a credit card is riskier than extending a loan that is secured by an asset, such as a mortgage loan on a house. The risk also increases with the duration of the loan. The longer the time period, the more likely that the financial standing of the borrower will deteriorate or that market conditions will change unfavorably.

As **Exhibit 25–2** illustrates, the money rate of interest on a loan has three components. The pure-interest component is the real price one must pay for earlier availability. The inflationary-premium component reflects the expectation that the loan will be repaid with dollars of less purchasing power as the result of inflation.

Inflationary premium
A component of the money interest rate that reflects compensation to the lender for the expected decrease, due to inflation, in the purchasing power of the principal and interest during the course of the loan. It is determined by the expected rate of future inflation.

Real rate of interest
The money rate of interest minus the expected rate of inflation. The real rate of interest indicates the interest premium, in terms of real goods and services, that one must pay for earlier availability.

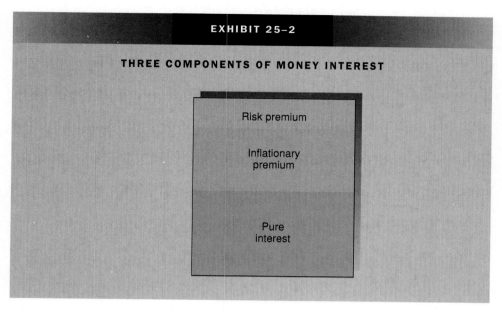

EXHIBIT 25–2

THREE COMPONENTS OF MONEY INTEREST

Risk premium

Inflationary premium

Pure interest

The money interest rate reflects three components: pure interest, inflationary premium, and risk premium. When decision makers expect a high rate of inflation during the period in which the loan is outstanding, the inflationary premium will be substantial. Similarly, the risk premium will be large when the probability of default by the borrower is substantial.

The risk-premium component reflects the probability of default—the risk imposed on the lender by the possibility that the borrower may be unable to repay the loan.

PRESENT VALUE OF FUTURE INCOME AND COSTS

If you deposited $100 today in a savings account earning 6 percent interest, you would have $106 one year from now. Therefore, the present value of $100 one year from now is equal to the amount that you would have to invest today in order to have that amount at that time. The interest rate allows us to make this calculation. The interest rate connects the value of dollars (and capital assets) today with the value of dollars (and expected receipts) in the future. It is used to discount the value of a dollar in the future so that its present worth can be determined today.

The **present value (PV)** of a payment received one year from now can be expressed as follows:

$$PV = \frac{\text{receipts one year from now}}{1 + \text{interest rate}}$$

If the interest rate is 6 percent, the current value of the $100 to be received one year from now is

$$PV = \frac{\$100}{1.06} = \$94.34$$

If you placed $94.34 in a savings account yielding 6 percent interest, during the year the account would earn $5.66 interest (6 percent of $94.34) and therefore grow to $100 one year from now. Thus, the present value of $100 a year from now is $94.34.

Present value (PV)
The current worth of future income after it is discounted to reflect the fact that revenues in the future are valued less highly than revenues now.

Discounting

The procedure used to calculate the present value of future income, which is inversely related to both the interest rate and the amount of time that passes before the funds are received.

Economists use the term **discounting** to describe this procedure of reducing the value of a dollar to be received in the future to its present worth. Clearly, the value of a dollar in the future is inversely related to the interest rate. For example, if the interest rate is 10 percent, the present value of $100 received one year from now would be only $90.91 ($100 divided by 1.10).

The present value of $100 received two years from now is

$$PV = \frac{\$100}{(1 + \text{interest rate})^2}$$

If the interest rate is 6 percent, $100 received two years from now would be equal to $89 today ($100 divided by 1.06^2). In other words, $89 invested today would yield $100 two years from now.

The present-value procedure can be used to determine the current value of any future income (or cost) stream. If R represents receipts received at the end of various years in the future (indicated by the subscripts) and i represents the interest rate, the present value of the future income stream[2] is

$$PV = \frac{R_1}{(1 + i)} + \frac{R_2}{(1 + i)^2} + \cdots + \frac{R_n}{(1 + i)^n}$$

Exhibit 25–3 shows the present value of $100 received at various times in the future at several different discount rates. The chart clearly illustrates two points. First, the present value of income received at a date in the future declines with the interest rate. The present value of the $100 received one year from now, when discounted at a 4 percent interest rate, is $96.15, compared to $98.04 when a 2 percent discount rate is applied. Second, the present value of the $100 also declines as the date of its receipt is set farther into the future. If the applicable discount rate is 6 percent, the present value of $100 received one year from now is $94.34, compared to $89 if the $100 is received two years from now. If the $100 is received five years from now, its current worth is only $74.73. So the present value of a future dollar payment is inversely related to both the interest rate and to how far in the future the payment will be received.

PRESENT VALUE, PROFITABILITY, AND INVESTMENT

Investment decisions involve an up-front cost of acquiring a machine, skill, or other asset that is expected to generate additional output and revenue in the future. How can an investor know if the expected future revenues will be sufficient to cover the costs? The discounting procedure helps provide the answer, since it permits the investor to place both the costs and the expected future revenues of an investment project into present-value terms. If the present value of the revenue derived from the investment exceeds the present value of the cost, it

---

[2]For a specific annual income stream in perpetuity, the present value is equal simply to R/i, where R is the annual revenue stream and i the interest rate. For example, if the interest rate is 10 percent, the *PV* of a $100 annual income stream in perpetuity is equal to $100/.10 or $1,000.

EXHIBIT 25–3

PRESENT VALUE OF $100
TO BE RECEIVED IN THE FUTURE

PRESENT VALUE OF $100 TO BE RECEIVED
A DESIGNATED NUMBER OF YEARS
IN THE FUTURE FOR ALTERNATIVE INTEREST RATES

YEARS IN THE FUTURE	2 PERCENT	4 PERCENT	6 PERCENT	8 PERCENT	12 PERCENT	20 PERCENT
1	98.04	96.15	94.34	92.59	89.29	83.33
2	96.12	92.46	89.00	85.73	79.72	69.44
3	94.23	88.90	83.96	79.38	71.18	57.87
4	92.39	85.48	79.21	73.50	63.55	48.23
5	90.57	82.19	74.73	68.06	56.74	40.19
6	88.80	79.03	70.50	63.02	50.66	33.49
7	87.06	75.99	66.51	58.35	45.23	27.08
8	85.35	73.07	62.74	54.03	40.39	23.26
9	83.68	70.26	59.19	50.02	36.06	19.38
10	82.03	67.56	55.84	46.32	32.20	16.15
15	74.30	55.53	41.73	31.52	18.27	6.49
20	67.30	45.64	31.18	21.45	10.37	2.61
30	55.21	30.83	17.41	9.94	3.34	0.42
50	37.15	14.07	5.43	2.13	0.35	0.01

The columns indicate the present value of $100 to be received a designated number of years in the future for alternative interest rates. For example, at a discount rate of 2 percent, the present value of $100 to be received five years from now is $90.57. Note that the present value of the $100 declines as either the interest rate or the number of years in the future increases.

makes sense to undertake the investment. If revenues and costs of such an investment turn out as expected, the investor will reap economic profit. In turn, profitable investments will increase the value of resources, and thereby create wealth.

On the other hand, if the cost of the project exceeds the discounted value of the future receipts, losses will result. The losses indicate the resources used to undertake the investment were more valuable than the future revenues generated by the investment. Thus, investments that result in losses reduce the value of resources and thereby diminish wealth. Such investments are counterproductive.

Suppose a truck rental firm is contemplating the purchase of a new $40,000 truck. Past experience indicates that after making allowances for operational and maintenance expenses, the firm can rent out the truck for net revenues of $12,000 per year (received at the end of each year) for the next four years, the expected life of the vehicle.[3] Since the firm can borrow and lend funds at an interest rate of 8 percent, we will discount the future expected income at an 8 percent rate. **Exhibit 25–4** illustrates the calculation. Column 4 shows how much $12,000, available at year-end for each of the next four years, is worth today. In total, the present value of the expected rental receipts is $39,744—less than the purchase price of the truck. Therefore, the project should not be undertaken.

---

[3]For the sake of simplicity, we assume that the truck has no scrap value at the end of four years.

EXHIBIT 25–4

**DISCOUNTED PRESENT VALUE OF $12,000
OF TRUCK RENTAL FOR FOUR YEARS
(INTEREST RATE = 8 PERCENT)**

YEAR (1)	EXPECTED FUTURE INCOME RECEIVED AT YEAR-END (2)	DISCOUNTED VALUE (8 PERCENT RATE) (3)	PRESENT VALUE OF INCOME (4)
1	$12,000	0.926	$11,112
2	12,000	0.857	10,284
3	12,000	0.794	9,528
4	12,000	0.735	8,820
			$39,744

If the interest rate in our example had been 6 percent, the present value of the future rental income would have been $41,580.[4] Since it pays to purchase a capital good whenever the present value of the income generated exceeds the purchase price of the capital good, the project would have been profitable at the lower interest rate.

EXPECTED FUTURE EARNINGS AND ASSET VALUES

The present value of the expected revenue minus cost of an investment reveals whether the project should be undertaken. However, *once an investment project has been completed,* the present value of the expected future net earnings will determine the market value of the asset. If the present value of the expected net earnings rises (falls), so too will the value of the asset.

The value of an asset is equal to the present value of the expected net revenues that can be earned by the asset. If the asset is expected to generate a constant annual net income each year in the future, its value would be equal to

---

[4]The derivation of this figure is shown in the following tabulation:

Year	Expected Future Income (dollars)	Discounted Value per Dollar (6% rate)	Present Value of Income (dollars)
1	12,000	0.943	11,316
2	12,000	0.890	10,680
3	12,000	0.840	10,080
4	12,000	0.792	9,504
			41,580

$$\text{Asset value} = \frac{\text{Annual net income from the asset}}{\text{Interest rate}}$$

How much would a tract of land that was expected to generate $1,000 of rental income net of costs each year indefinitely in the future be worth? If the market interest rate is 10 percent, investors would be willing to pay $10,000 for the land. When purchased at this price, the land would provide an investor with the 10 percent market rate of return. Correspondingly, if an asset generates $2,500 of net earnings annually and the market interest rate is 10 percent, the asset would be worth $25,000. There is a direct relationship between the expected future earnings of an asset and the asset's market value.

This linkage between expected future earnings and the price of an asset provides a strong incentive for the owners of business assets to make sure that the assets are being used wisely. Some entrepreneurial investors are particularly good at (1) identifying a business that is poorly operated, (2) purchasing the business at a depressed price, (3) improving the operational efficiency of the firm, and (4) then reselling the business at a handsome profit. Suppose that a poorly run business currently has net earnings of $1 million per year. What is the market value of the business? If the firm is expected to continue earning $1 million per year, the market value of the firm would be $10 million if the interest rate is 10 percent. Suppose that an alert entrepreneur buys the business for $10 million, hires new management, and improves the operational efficiency of the firm. As the result of these changes, the annual net earnings of the firm increase to $2 million per year. Now how much is the firm worth? If the $2 million annual earnings are expected to continue into the future, the net present value of the firm would rise to $20 million. Thus, the entrepreneur who improved the performance of the firm would be able to sell the firm for a very substantial profit.

In a competitive environment, there is a strong incentive for business managers and asset owners to use the resources under their control efficiently. If they do not, the value of the assets will decline, and the business will be vulnerable to a takeover by alert entrepreneurs capable of operating the firm more efficiently and using the assets more profitably.

INVESTORS AND CORPORATE INVESTMENTS

In modern market economies, investors typically are not entrepreneurs who personally decide which factories to expand, which machine tools to build, and which research investments to undertake. Instead corporate officers, under the scrutiny of corporate boards of directors, make the entrepreneurial capital investment choices. Nevertheless, individual investors (buyers and sellers of stock) influence that process through the stock market itself. Stock-market investors who believe that a corporation is making sound investment decisions that are likely to yield future profits will buy more of the corporation's stock, driving up its price. Similarly, stockholders who believe that the corporation's current investment decisions will not prove to be profitable have an incentive to "bail out" by selling their stock holdings. Either way, the stock-market price of a

Changes in stock values provide immediate feedback on what investors think about business strategy and management decisions.

corporation's stock gives corporate officers very fast feedback on how market investors evaluate their investment decisions. The choices of individual buyers (and nonbuyers) of the firm's product provide the ultimate judgments on business performance. However, the choices of investors provide early returns on the expected success of business ventures.

INVESTING IN HUMAN CAPITAL

In principle, investments in human capital—a choice about continuing in school, for example—involve all of the ingredients of other investment decisions. And since the returns and some of the costs normally accrue in the future, the discounting procedure is as helpful here as in decisions about physical capital.

Exhibit 25–5 is a simplified illustration of the human-capital decision confronting Susan, an 18-year-old high school graduate contemplating the pursuit of a bachelor's degree in business administration. Just as an investment in a truck involves a cost in order to generate a future income, so too does a degree in business administration. If Susan does not go to college, she will be able to begin work immediately at annual earnings of E_1. Alternatively, if she goes to college, she will incur direct costs (C_d) in the form of tuition, books, transportation, and related expenses. She will also bear the opportunity cost (C_o) of lower earnings while in college. However, the study of business will expand Susan's knowledge and skills, and thereby enable her to earn a higher future income (E_2 rather than E_1).

Will the higher future income be worth the cost? To answer this question, Susan must discount each year's additional income stemming from completion of the business degree and compare that with the discounted value of the cost, including the opportunity cost of earnings lost during the period of study. If the

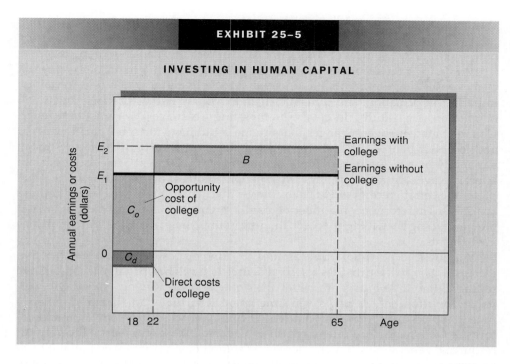

EXHIBIT 25–5

INVESTING IN HUMAN CAPITAL

Annual earnings or costs (dollars)

E_2

E_1

B — Earnings with college

Earnings without college

C_o — Opportunity cost of college

0

C_d — Direct costs of college

18 22   65   Age

Here we provide a simplified illustration of the human-capital investment decision confronting Susan, an 18-year-old who just finished high school. If Susan goes to college and majors in business administration, she will incur the direct cost (C_d) of the college education (tuition, books, transportation, and so on) plus the opportunity cost (C_o) of earnings forgone while in college. However, with a business degree, she can expect higher future earnings (B) during her career. If the discounted present value of the additional future earnings exceeds the discounted value of the direct and indirect cost of a college education, the business degree will be a profitable investment for Susan.

discounted present value of the additional future income exceeds the discounted present value of the cost, acquiring the degree is a worthwhile human-capital investment.

Of course, nonmonetary considerations may also be important, particularly for human-capital investment decisions, since human capital is embodied in the individual. For example, Susan's preferences might be such that she would really prefer working as a college graduate in the business world (rather than in the jobs available to high school graduates) even if she did not make more money. Thus, the nonmonetary attractiveness of business may induce her to pursue the business degree even if the monetary rate of return is low (or even negative).

Although nonmonetary factors are more important in human capital decision making, opportunity cost and the pursuit of profit influence human-capital investors just as they do physical-capital investors. As with choosing to purchase a new machine, choosing a human-capital investment project such as Susan's degree involves cost, the possibility of profit, and uncertainty. The same principles apply to both types of decisions. Giving due consideration to nonmonetary factors as a potential "benefit," human-capital investors, like physical-capital investors, seek to undertake only those projects that they anticipate will yield benefits in excess of costs.

PROFIT AND PROSPERITY

As we previously discussed, firms and individual investors are often able to earn economic profit—a return in excess of the opportunity cost of funds—if they are able to restrict entry into various industries and occupations. Economic profit, however, may also be present in competitive markets. In a competitive market economy, there are two sources of economic profit: uncertainty and entrepreneurship.

While investment places people in a position to earn a handsome return, it also exposes them to additional uncertainty. We live in a world of uncertainty, imperfect information, and dynamic change. No one knows precisely what will happen in the future. In a sense, investing resembles a game of chance. Unanticipated changes, changes that no one could have foreseen, create winners and losers. If people did not care whether their income experienced substantial variability or not, the uncertainty accompanying investment projects would not affect the average rate of return. Most people, though, dislike uncertainty. They prefer the certain receipt of $1,000 to a fifty-fifty chance of receiving either nothing or $2,000. Therefore, people must be paid a premium—and economic profit—if they are going to willingly accept the uncertainty that necessarily accompanies investments.

Alertness to potential opportunities to combine resources in a manner that increases their value provides a second source of economic profit in a competitive setting. Some individuals are better than others at identifying potentially profitable opportunities. At any given time, there is virtually an infinite number of potential investment projects. Some will increase the value of resources and therefore lead to a handsome rate of return on capital. Others will reduce the value of resources, generating economic losses. Entrepreneurship involves the ability to recognize and undertake economically beneficial projects that have gone unnoticed by others. Originality, quickness to act, and imagination are important aspects of entrepreneurship. Successful entrepreneurship involves leadership; most profits will be gone by the time the imitators arrive on the scene. But, of course, there is usually risk involved. Frequently, the entrepreneur's vision turns out to have been a mirage. What appeared to be a profitable opportunity turns out to have been an expensive illusion.

The great Harvard economist Joseph Schumpeter believed that entrepreneurship and innovative behavior were the moving forces behind capitalism. According to Schumpeter, this entrepreneurial discovery of new, improved ways of doing things is a central element of economic progress and improvements in living standards. As Schumpeter put it:

OUTSTANDING ECONOMIST

JOSEPH SCHUMPETER (1883–1950)

Born in Austria, Schumpeter was a long-time professor of economics at Harvard University. Generally recognized as one of the top five economists of this century, he is perhaps best known for his views on entrepreneurship and the future of capitalism. He believed that the creative and innovative behavior of business entrepreneurs was the primary fuel of economic progress under capitalism.

The fundamental impulse that sets the capitalist engine in motion comes from the new consumer's goods, the new methods of production or transportation, and new markets, and the new forms of industrial organization that capitalist enterprise creates.[5]

Potential entrepreneurs are confined to using their own wealth and that of co-venturers, in addition to whatever can be borrowed. Entrepreneurs with a past record of success will be able to attract funds more readily for investment projects. Therefore, in a market economy, previously successful entrepreneurs will exert a disproportionate influence over decisions as to which projects will be undertaken and which will not.

THE CAPITAL MARKET AND THE WEALTH OF NATIONS

Both interest and profit perform important allocative functions.[6] Interest induces people to give up current consumption, a sacrifice that is a necessary ingredient for capital formation. Economic profit provides both human and physical capital decision makers with the incentive to (1) undertake investments yielding an uncertain return and (2) discover and develop beneficial and productive investment opportunities.

If a nation is going to realize its potential, it must have a mechanism capable of attracting savings and channeling them into investment projects that create wealth. In a market economy, the capital market performs this function. This highly diverse market includes markets for stocks, real estate, and businesses, as well as the loanable funds market.

The capital market brings together people who are willing to save with those willing to invest. Some people save and supply funds to the capital market in exchange for a fixed rate of return. People who purchase bonds and maintain savings deposits are examples. Other people supply funds in exchange for an uncertain return linked to the success or failure of a business or investment project. Stockholders and partnership investors fall into this category. Still others supply funds to the capital market when they use their own funds to purchase a business or acquire additional schooling.

---

[5]Joseph A. Schumpeter, *Capitalism, Socialism, and Democracy* (New York: Harper Torchbooks, 1950), p. 83.

[6]In addition to wages, interest, and profits, economists often discuss *rent* as a return to a factor of production, the supply of which is perfectly inelastic. We have not included this discussion for two reasons. First, one can legitimately argue that the supply of all factors of production has some elasticity. After all, even the supply of usable land can be expanded through drainage, clearing, and conservation. Therefore, rent is always a matter of degree. Second, the term *rent* is used in a variety of ways, even by economists. The macroeconomic usage differs substantially from the usage in microeconomics. The term is sometimes used to define the returns to a specialized resource, such as an actor's talent, even though training plays an integral part in the supply of the resource. Rent is also sometimes applied to a factor the supply of which is temporarily fixed, even though it can clearly be expanded in the future. Since the returns to capital can be adequately discussed without introducing rent, we concluded that the cost of the ambiguity of the term exceeded the benefits of an extended discussion.

The key attribute of the capital market is its ability to direct funds toward wealth-creating projects. When investment in a capital asset generates additional output (and revenue) that is valued more highly than the value of the resources required for its production, the investment will create wealth. When property rights are securely defined and enforced, wealth-creating investments will also be profitable.

Private ownership and a competitive capital market provide investors with a strong incentive to evaluate potential projects carefully and search for profitable projects. In an uncertain world, however, private investors will sometimes make mistakes, undertaking projects that prove unprofitable. If investors were unwilling to take such chances, many new ideas would go untested and many worthwhile but risky projects would not be undertaken. Thus, mistaken investments are a necessary price paid for fruitful innovations in new technologies and products. The capital market will at least assure that the mistakes are self-correcting. Losses will signal investors to terminate unprofitable and unproductive projects.

Without a private capital market, it is virtually impossible to attract funds and consistently channel them into wealth-creating projects. When investment funds are allocated by the government rather than the market, an entirely different set of criteria comes into play. Political clout replaces market return as the basis for allocating the funds. As a result, investment projects that reduce wealth rather than enhance it become more likely.

The experience of Eastern Europe and the former Soviet Union illustrates this point. The investment rates of these countries were among the highest in the world. The central planners of these countries channeled approximately one-third of the national output into investment. But even these high rates of investment did little to improve the standard of living. Political rather than economic considerations determined which investment projects would be undertaken. Therefore, investment funds were often wasted on political boondoggles and high-visibility projects favored by important political leaders.

EMPIRICAL EVIDENCE ON THE LINKAGE BETWEEN INVESTMENT AND GROWTH

Economic analysis indicates that investment in both physical and human capital is an important source of productivity and income growth. A secretary working with word-processing equipment (physical capital) can type more letters than an equally skilled secretary working with a traditional typewriter. Likewise, training, education, and other investments in human capital that improve the skills of workers will enhance productivity. Other things constant, countries that invest more and channel more of their investments into productive projects today will tend to have a higher income tomorrow.

Exhibit 25–6 compares the growth rates for 1980 through 1991 of the 10 countries that invested the largest share of their total output during the 1980s against the 10 countries with the lowest investment rates. A diverse set of countries are included in the group with a high investment rate. Some (Singapore, Hong Kong, Switzerland, and Norway) are small countries. Others (Japan and Indonesia) are quite large. Seven Asian and three European nations are included in the group. Several in the high-investment group are high-income industrial nations (Japan,

Source: Derived from the
World Bank, *World Development
Report* (annual).

EXHIBIT 25-6

ANNUAL GROWTH RATE OF DOMESTIC OUTPUT FOR COUNTRIES WITH HIGHEST AND LOWEST INVESTMENT RATES

COUNTRY	INVESTMENT AS SHARE OF ECONOMY, 1980–1990	AVERAGE ANNUAL GROWTH RATE OF OUTPUT PER CAPITA, 1980–1991
Highest Investment Rates		
Singapore	41.5	4.9
Japan	30.2	3.7
South Korea	29.9	8.5
Malaysia	29.6	3.1
Switzerland	26.8	1.6
Hong Kong	26.5	5.7
Portugal	26.4	2.8
Thailand	26.4	6.0
Norway	26.0	2.3
Indonesia	26.0	3.8
Average Growth Rate		**4.2**
Lowest Investment Rates		
Ghana	8.6	0.0
Uganda	10.0	0.3
Central Africa Repub.	10.8	−1.3
Uruguay	11.3	0.0
Bolivia	12.2	−2.2
Sierra Leone	12.7	−1.3
Haiti	13.2	−2.6
Guatemala	13.3	−1.8
Argentina	13.5	−1.7
Niger	13.8	−4.3
Average Growth Rate		**−1.5**

Switzerland, and Norway), while several others are relatively poor (South Korea, Malaysia, Thailand, and Indonesia). All of the high-investment countries experienced an average annual growth rate of per capita output of at least 1.6 percent during the 1980-1991 period. The average annual growth rate of per capita output for the 10 high-investment countries was 4.2 percent.

Now look at the economic record of the 10 low-investment countries. Only one (Uganda) of the 10 low-investment countries experienced an increase in per capita output during the 1980–1991 period. On average, annual output in the 10 low-investment countries *declined* by 1.6 percent. None was able to achieve a growth rate even close to that of a high-investment country.

Just as economic theory predicts, the countries with a high investment rate tended to grow rapidly, while those with a low investment rate stagnated and often regressed.

THE DESTRUCTIVENESS OF INTEREST-RATE CONTROLS

Many countries impose a ceiling on the nominal interest rate in the loanable funds market and couple this policy with an inflationary monetary policy. Suppose that a country is following a monetary policy that has resulted in a 20 percent rate of inflation. In a market setting, the nominal interest rate would rise to reflect the high rate of inflation. If the money interest rate was 22 percent, for example, lenders would earn a modest 2 percent real return on their savings. **Exhibit 25–7** illustrates what happens when an inflationary policy is coupled with a ceiling on the nominal interest rate. When the government fixes the nominal interest rate below equilibrium, 10 percent in our example, people who save are stuck with a negative real return. When such a policy is present, there is little or no incentive for people to supply funds to the domestic loanable funds market. The quantity of loanable funds supplied to the domestic market will decline sharply (from Q_1 to Q_2). Domestic financial investors will seek positive returns abroad. Foreign investors will completely shun the country. Such policies destroy the domestic capital market.

Predictably, the savings and investment rate will be low in countries that follow policies that lead to negative real interest rates! The level of investment in such countries may not even be sufficient to replace the machines and structures that wear out during the period. Under these circumstances, the growth of income will stagnate or even regress.

Here we illustrate the impact of a 10 percent interest-rate ceiling in a country that is experiencing a 20 percent rate of inflation. If it were not for the interest-rate ceiling, the nominal interest rate would be 22 percent and lenders would earn a modest 2 percent real return. With the interest-rate ceiling, however, the real interest rate is minus 10 percent! Lenders lose purchasing power if they supply funds to the loanable funds market. Such policies remove the incentive to save and virtually destroy the financial capital market.

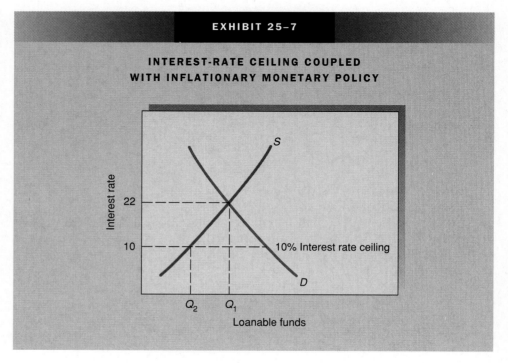

EXHIBIT 25–7

INTEREST-RATE CEILING COUPLED WITH INFLATIONARY MONETARY POLICY

Exhibit 25–8 provides data on real interest rates, investment, and the growth of output for 10 countries that followed such policies throughout much of the 1980s. The real interest rate in each of these countries was at least 10 percent negative during both 1983–1985 and 1988–1990. With a couple of exceptions, the investment rate of these countries was quite low. In fact, 5 of these countries (Ghana, Uganda, Bolivia, Sierra Leone, and Argentina) rank among the 10 countries with the lowest investment rates in the world (see Exhibit 25–6).

All of these countries fixed the nominal interest rate while following an inflationary monetary policy. Thus, they destroyed the mechanism that would normally provide potential private investors with loanable funds and channel those funds toward wealth-creating projects. Lacking a mechanism to perform this vitally important function, these countries regressed. On average, the output per capita of the 10 countries declined during the 1980–1991 period at a 1.2 percent annual rate. Only one (Uganda) of the 10 was able to achieve any positive growth in per capita output. Capital formation and its efficient allocation are important sources of economic growth. Countries that destroy their capital markets will pay a severe price for their folly.

The agricultural price support program illustrates the importance of many of the concepts incorporated into this chapter (for example, the relationship between the expected future income and the present value of an asset). For an analysis of this issue, see the accompanying "Application in Economics" box.

EXHIBIT 25–8

CHANGES IN OUTPUT FOR COUNTRIES WITH PERSISTENT NEGATIVE REAL INTEREST RATES

COUNTRY	AVERAGE REAL INTEREST RATE[a] 1983–1985	1988–1990	INVESTMENT AS SHARE OF ECONOMY 1980–1990	AVERAGE ANNUAL GROWTH RATE OF OUTPUT PER CAPITA 1980–1991
Argentina	−163	−1179	13.5	−1.7
Bolivia	−4240	n/a	12.2	−2.2
Peru	−101	n/a	19.6	−2.6
Uganda	−74	−65	10.0	0.3
Zambia	−16	−77	15.3	−2.8
Ghana	−46	−15	8.6	0.0
Somalia	−35	−69	25.3	−0.7
Sierra Leone	−37	−41	12.7	−1.3
Ecuador	−19	−21	21.3	−0.5
Tanzania	−21	−12	19.1	−0.1
Average Growth Rate				**−1.2**

[a]The real interest rate for each country is equal to the country's nominal deposit interest rate minus the inflation rate of the country.

Source: The data on the change in per capita income are from the World Bank, *World Development Report 1992*, Tables 2 and 26. The deposit interest rate data are from the International Monetary Fund, *International Financial Statistics Yearbook* (various issues).

APPLICATIONS IN ECONOMICS

AGRICULTURAL PRICE SUPPORTS

Since the 1930s the U.S. government has instituted various types of price-support programs for agricultural products. The programs establish a minimum price for various agriculture products, including wheat, cotton, tobacco, peanuts, rice, and feed grains. This minimum price is generally set above the market equilibrium. The price support program is designed to increase the profitability of farming. However, there is reason to question its effectiveness.

Using wheat as an example, **Exhibit 1** illustrates the nature of the early price-support programs. These programs established a price floor (support) for wheat above the market equilibrium level and pledged that any wheat that could not be sold at the support price would be purchased by the government. Of course, the above-equilibrium price led to an excess supply of wheat. As part "a" of Exhibit 1 illustrates, the excess supply was initially relatively small (A_1, B_1), since both the demand for and the supply of wheat were highly inelastic in the short run. With the passage of time, however, both the demand and supply curves became more elastic. Given sufficient time to adjust, farmers cultivated wheat land more intensively and also increased the amount of land allotted to wheat. Therefore, the excess supply the government had pledged to purchase increased substantially with the passage of time. (Compare the size of the excess supply in parts "a" and "b" of the Exhibit.)

The costs of storing the excess supply expanded rapidly. In fact, during the 1950s, these storage costs became a national scandal. The public outcry over the huge costs, economic waste, spoilage, and fraud eventually led to an alteration of the program.

EXHIBIT 1

IMPACT OF AGRICULTURAL PRICE SUPPORTS

a.

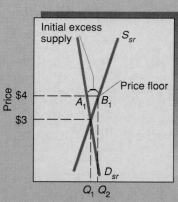

(a) Impact in Short Run

b.

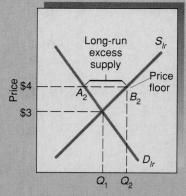

(b) Impact in Long Run

When a price-support program pushes the price of an agricultural product, such as wheat, above the market equilibrium, an excess supply of the product results. Initially, the excess supply may be small (A_1B_1 of frame a). However, as farmers adjust their planting and cultivation, the long-run supply of wheat becomes increasingly elastic, causing the excess supply to expand (A_2B_2, frame b).

In an effort to maintain a policy of support for farmers without creating surplus crops and the attendant problems, Congress adopted an acreage restriction program designed to reduce the output of agricultural products. Under this plan, price is still fixed above the market equilibrium, but the number of acres that farmers are allowed to plant is limited in an effort to reduce supply and bring it into balance with demand at the above-equilibrium support price. Each farm is granted an acreage allotment of wheat (and other supported products), based on the acres planted during a base year. The allotments are attached to the farm. Owners of farms are prohibited from planting more than the specified number of acres for each product.

Exhibit 2 illustrates the economics of the acreage-restriction program. Restricting the number of acres planted causes the supply of the product to be reduced until the price of the product rises to the support level. If the government has to purchase the product at the support price, it can reduce the acreage allotments of farmers during the next period. In contrast, if the market price rises above the support level, the government can relax the allotment a little during the next period. In this manner, the government is able to bring the amount demanded and amount supplied into balance at the supported price level (for example, as Exhibit 2 illustrates, at the $4 price floor for wheat).

The acreage restrictions make it more costly to grow any given amount of a product. Normally, farmers would minimize their cost of growing more wheat (or any other product) by using a little more of each of the factors of production (land, labor, fertilizer, machinery, and so on). The acreage-restriction program prohibits them from using more land. The support price provides farmers with an incentive to produce more wheat, for example, but they must do so by using factors of production other than land—such as fertilizer—more intensively. Higher costs result, shifting the supply curve of Exhibit 2 to the left (to S_2). Supply curve S_1 is unattainable once the acreage restrictions are imposed, since it would require a larger amount of land than is permissible under the allotment program.

Acreage-restriction programs also exert an impact on the environment. As heavier and heavier dosages of fertilizer and chemicals are used to expand output on the limited number of acres, these chemicals often affect the quality of groundwater, rivers, and lakes. Environmental degradation from this source has been particularly significant in the European Economic Community, where agricultural price supports are even higher than in the United States and where, as a result, farmers generally use more than twice as much fertilizer per acre as U.S. farmers.

Is farming more profitable in the long run after the imposition of the acreage restrictions and price-support programs? Surprisingly, the answer is no. To the extent that price supports make farming more profitable in the short run, the demand for land with acreage allotments increases (see **Exhibit 3**). Competition bids up the price of land with acreage allotments until the investors receive only the normal rate of return. Just as one cannot earn an abnormally high rate of return by purchasing stock ownership rights of a firm already earning monopoly profit,

EXHIBIT 2

ACREAGE RESTRICTIONS AND LIMITING OUTPUT

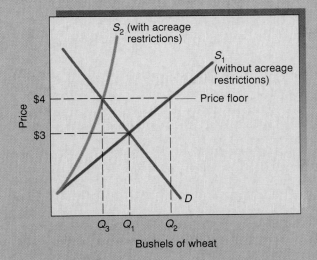

Rather than permit farmers to raise an amount of wheat that would generate an excess supply at the support price, under the acreage-restriction program the government restricts the number of acres allocated to the growing of wheat, causing the supply of wheat to decline to S_2. With the acreage restrictions, the excess supply is eliminated, and the $4 support price is maintained.

APPLICATIONS IN ECONOMICS *(continued)*

EXHIBIT 3

RISING LAND VALUES AND CAPITALIZING PROFIT

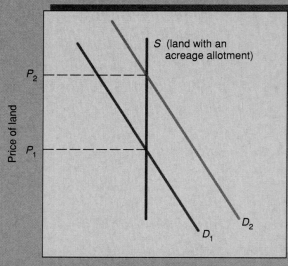

Quantity of land

"My ambition is to get so good at growing things, that the government will pay me not to."

Grin and Bear It by Fred Wagner © by and Permission of News America Syndicate.

Since land with an acreage allotment permits one to plant wheat and sell it at an above market-equilibrium price, the price-support program makes such land more valuable. Competition drives the price of land *with an allotment* upward until the higher land values fully capture the larger profits resulting from the program. But once land values have risen, the farmer's rate of return on investment is no higher with the program than it was prior to the program's establishment. The major beneficiaries of price-support programs have been those who owned land with acreage allotments *at the time the programs were established.*

neither can a farmer earn an abnormally high rate of return by purchasing the ownership rights of farms with acreage allotments.

Suppose the price-support program permitted wheat growers to earn an additional $100 each year from an acre of land planted in wheat. If that were true,

the present value (PV) of the land with a wheat allotment would rise by $100, divided by the interest rate. At a 10 percent rate of interest, the value of the additional $100 per year would equal $1,000 (PV = R/i = $100/.10 = $1,000). The value of an acre of land with a wheat allotment would rise by $1,000. Essentially, the value of the monopoly-profit income stream derived from the price-support program would be capitalized into the value of land with a wheat allotment.

The major beneficiaries of the price-support and acreage-restriction programs have been the owners of land with an allotment at the time the programs were established. Competition for land with acreage allotments has driven the price of such land up until the rate of return on agricultural land with allotments is equal to the market rate of return. Thus, the profit rate of the current owners of the land is no higher than it would have been had Congress never adopted any kind of price support system in the first place.[1]

---

[1]For additional details on specific agricultural price support programs, see E. C. Pasour Jr., *Agriculture and the State:*

Bureaucracy and the Market Process (San Francisco: The Independent Institute, 1989). For a brief, highly readable analysis of the programs, see Robert L. Thompson, "Agricultural Price Supports" in *The Fortune Encyclopedia of Economics*, edited by David R. Henderson (New York: Warner Books, 1993).

LOOKING AHEAD

As the last two chapters have stressed, investment in physical and human capital will influence the wealth and income of both individuals and nations. Differences among individuals in these factors will also contribute to income inequality. After analyzing the importance of unions in the labor market, we will consider the issue of income inequality in some detail.

CHAPTER SUMMARY

1. We can often produce more consumption goods by first using our resources to produce physical- and human-capital resources and then using those capital resources to produce the desired consumption goods. Resources used to produce capital goods will be unavailable for the direct production of consumption goods. Therefore, someone must save—refrain from current consumption—in order to release the resources required for investment.

2. People have a positive rate of time preference; they generally value present consumption more highly than future consumption.

3. In decisions made across time periods, the interest rate is of central importance because it allows individuals to place a current evaluation on future revenues and costs. The demand for loanable funds stems from the productivity of capital resources and the positive rate of time preference of consumers.

4. The interest rate is the price of earlier availability. Interest provides lenders with an incentive to curtail current consumption and to supply loanable funds to others. The market interest rate will bring the quantity of funds demanded by borrowers (to undertake current investments and to consume beyond their current income) into balance with the supply of funds provided by lenders

willing to forgo current consumption in exchange for the interest premium.

5. During inflationary times, the money rate of interest incorporates an inflationary premium reflecting the expected future increase in the price level. Under these circumstances, the money rate of interest exceeds the real rate of interest.

6. The money rate of interest on a specific loan reflects three basic factors—the pure interest rate, an inflationary premium, and a risk premium that is directly related to the probability of default by the borrower.

7. Since a dollar in the future is valued less than a dollar today, the value of future receipts must be discounted to calculate their current worth. The discounting procedure can be used to calculate the present value of an expected net income stream from a potential investment project. If the present value of the expected revenues exceeds the present value of the expected costs, the project will be profitable when things turn out as expected.

8. The present value of expected future net earnings will determine the market value of existing assets. An increase (decline) in the expected future earnings derived from an asset will increase (reduce) the market value of the asset.

9. If a nation is to grow and prosper, it must have a mechanism that will attract savings and channel them into investment projects that create wealth. The capital market performs this function in a market economy. When the value of the output (and revenue) derived from an investment exceeds its costs (the value of the resources required for the production of the capital good), the investment will be productive. When property rights are defined and securely enforced, productive investments will also be profitable. Then the profit motive will prompt private investors to search for and undertake productive investments.

10. Investment in both physical and human capital is an important source of productivity growth. The

economies of countries that invest more and channel their investment funds into more productive projects generally grow more rapidly.

11. The empirical evidence confirms the importance of investment. Per capita output has grown rapidly in countries like Singapore, Japan, and South Korea that have high rates of investment. In contrast, per capita output has usually declined in countries with low investment rates.

CRITICAL-ANALYSIS QUESTIONS

*1. How would the following changes influence the rate of interest in the United States?
   a. An increase in the positive time preference of lenders.
   b. An increase in the positive time preference of borrowers.
   c. An increase in domestic inflation.
   d. Increased uncertainty about a nuclear war.
   e. Improved investment opportunities in Europe.

2. "Any return to capital above the pure-interest yield is unnecessary. The pure-interest yield is sufficient to provide capitalists with the earnings necessary to replace their assets and to compensate for their sacrifice of current consumption. Any return above that is pure gravy; it is excess profit." Do you agree with this view? Why or why not?

3. How are human- and physical-capital investment decisions similar? How do they differ? What determines the profitability of a physical-capital investment? Do human-capital investors make profits? If so, what is the source of the profit? Explain.

*4. A lender made the following statement to a borrower, "You are borrowing $1,000, which is to be repaid in 12 monthly installments of $100 each. Your total interest charge is $200, which means your interest rate is 20 percent." Is the effective interest rate on the loan really 20 percent? Explain.

5. Suppose U.S. investors are considering the construction of bicycle factories in two different countries, one in Europe and the other in Africa. Projected costs and revenues are at first identical, but the chance of guerrilla warfare (and possible destruction of the factory) is suddenly perceived in the African nation. In which country will the price of bicycles (and the current rate of return to bicycle factories) probably rise? Will the investors be better off in the country with the higher rate of return? Why or why not?

6. In a market economy, investors have a strong incentive to undertake profitable investments. What makes an investment profitable? Do profitable investments create wealth? Why or why not? Do all investments create wealth? Discuss.

*7. Over long periods of time, the rate of return of an average investment in the stock market has exceeded the return on high-quality bonds. Is the higher return on stocks surprising? Why or why not?

8. The interest rates charged on outstanding credit card balances are generally higher than the interest rate that banks charge customers with a good credit rating. Why do you think the credit card rate is so high? Should the government impose an interest rate ceiling of, say, 4 percent, above the prime lending rate (the rate banks charge customers with a good credit rating) on credit card loans? If it did, who would be hurt and who would be helped? Discuss.

*9. If the money rate of interest on a low-risk government bond is 10 percent and the inflation rate for the last several years has been steady at 4 percent, what is the estimated real rate of interest?

10. Will low interest rates encourage investment? If the current interest rate in a country is 15 percent, would the investment rate be higher if the government imposed a ceiling reducing the rate of interest in the loanable funds market to 8 percent? Why or why not?

11. The data presented in Exhibit 25–6 indicate that countries investing more of their total output grow more rapidly. Explain in your own words why this is true. Do you think the government should adopt policies designed to increase the saving and investment rates of citizens? Why or why not? Discuss.

*12. Alicia's philosophy of life is summed up by the proverb "A penny saved is a penny earned." She plans and saves for the future. In contrast, Mike's view is "Life is uncertain; eat dessert first." Mike wants as much as possible now.
   a. Who has the highest rate of time preference?
   b. Do people like Alicia benefit from the presence of people like Mike?
   c. Do people like Mike benefit from the presence of people like Alicia? Explain.

*13. Some countries with very low incomes per capita are unable to save very much. Are people in these countries helped or hurt by people in high-income countries with much higher rates of saving?

14. Suppose you are contemplating the purchase of a minicomputer at a cost of $1,000. The expected lifetime of the asset is three years. You expect to lease the asset to a business for $400 annually (payable at the end of each year) for three years. If you can borrow (and lend) money at an interest rate of 8 percent, will the investment be a profitable undertaking? Is the project profitable at an interest rate of 12 percent? Provide calculations in support of your answer.

---

*Asterisk denotes questions for which answers are given in Appendix C.

*15. According to a news item, the owner of a lottery ticket paying $3 million over 20 years is offering to sell the ticket for $1.2 million cash now. "Who knows?" the ticket owner explained, "We might not even be here in 20 years, and I do not want to leave it to the dinosaurs."

    a. Assuming that the ticket pays $150,000 per year at the end of each year for the next 20 years, what is the present value of the ticket if the appropriate rate for discounting the future income is thought to be 10 percent?

    b. Assuming the discount rate is in the 10 percent range, is the offer price of $1.2 million reasonable?

    c. Can you think of any disadvantages of buying the lottery earnings rather than a bond?

16. Suppose you decide to rent an apartment for five years. Further suppose that the owner offers to provide you with a used refrigerator for free and promises to maintain and repair the refrigerator during the next five years.

You also have the option of buying a new energy-efficient refrigerator (with a five-year free maintenance agreement) for $700. The new refrigerator will reduce your electric bill by $150 per year and will have a market value of $200 after five years. If necessary, you can borrow money from the bank at an 8 percent rate of interest. Which option should you choose?

*17. Suppose that you are considering whether or not to enroll in a summer computer training program that costs $2,500. If you take the program, you will have to give up $1,500 of earnings from your summer job. You figure that the program will increase your earnings by $500 per year for each of the next 10 years. Beyond that, it is not expected to affect your earnings. If you take the program, you will have to borrow the funds at an 8 percent rate of interest. From strictly a monetary viewpoint, should you enroll in the program?

*Asterisk denotes questions for which answers are given in Appendix C.

CHAPTER TWENTY-SIX

LABOR UNIONS AND
COLLECTIVE BARGAINING

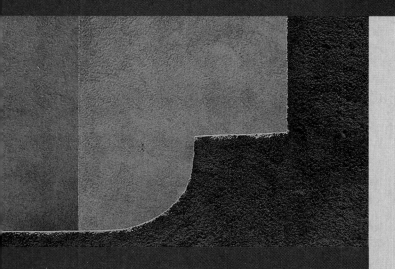

Analysts who have attributed national economic problems ranging from unemployment to wage inflation to low productivity to unions will have to find a new culprit to blame: unless there is a remarkable renaissance in unionism, critics won't have unions to kick around any more.

RICHARD B. FREEMAN[1]

CHAPTER FOCUS

■ *How much of the U.S. work force is unionized?*
■ *How does the collective-bargaining process work?*
■ *How important is the strike in the bargaining process?*
■ *Can unions increase the wages of their members? What makes a union strong? What factors limit the power of a union?*
■ *Can unions increase the share of income going to labor?*
■ *Do unions cause inflation?*
■ *What impact have unions had on the legal structure of worker-management relations?*

[1]Richard B. Freeman, "Contraction and Expansion: The Divergence of Private Sector and Public Sector Unionism in the United States," *Journal of Economic Perspectives* 2 (Spring 1988), p. 86.

Labor union
A collective organization of employees who bargain as a unit with employers.

In an earlier chapter, we mentioned that labor unions may be able to establish institutional arrangements that will affect supply and demand and therefore alter wage rates. We are now prepared to examine the labor-market effects of unions. A **labor union** is an organization of employees, usually working either in the same occupation or industry, who have consented to joint bargaining with employers concerning wages, working conditions, grievance procedures, and other elements of employment. The primary objective of a labor union is to improve the welfare of its members.

Unions have historically been controversial. Some see them as a necessary shield protecting workers from employer greed. Others charge that unions are monopolies seeking to provide their members with benefits at the expense of economic efficiency, consumers, and other workers. Still others argue that the economic influence of unions—both for good and for bad—is vastly overrated. This chapter will enhance our understanding of labor unions and the economic factors that influence their ability to achieve desired objectives.

UNION MEMBERSHIP AS SHARE OF WORK FORCE

Historically, the proportion of the U.S. labor force belonging to a labor union has fluctuated substantially. In 1910 approximately 10 percent of the nonfarm employees belonged to a union. As **Exhibit 26–1** shows, this figure rose to 18 percent in 1920. In the aftermath of the First World War, union membership declined, falling to 12 percent of the nonfarm work force by 1929. Favorable legislation adopted during the Great Depression of the 1930s encouraged unions and union membership as a share of the nonfarm labor force rose from 13.5 percent in 1935 to 30.4 percent by 1945. By 1954 one-third of the nonfarm work force in the United States was unionized.

Since the mid-1950s, however, union membership has waned. As Exhibit 26–1 illustrates, it declined as a share of the labor force slowly during 1955–1975, and then quite sharply since 1975. By 1992 union workers accounted for only 16 percent of nonfarm employment, down from 32 percent in 1954 (and 28 percent as recently as 1975).

Several factors have contributed to this decline. First, most of the recent growth in employment has been with relatively small firms (less than 100 employees) in service and high-tech industries. Small firms are costly for unions to organize, and unions have traditionally been weak in service and high-tech industries. Second, competition has eroded union strength in several important industries. Foreign producers have increased their market share in steel, mining, automobiles, and other heavy-manufacturing industries. Employment has thus been shrinking in these areas of traditional union strength. Deregulation in transportation and communication industries has further reduced the effectiveness of unions. As these industries have become more competitive, unionized firms have faced increased competition from nonunion producers. Finally, even regional growth patterns have adversely affected union strength. During the 1960s and 1970s, population and employment grew rapidly in the Sunbelt, while stagnating

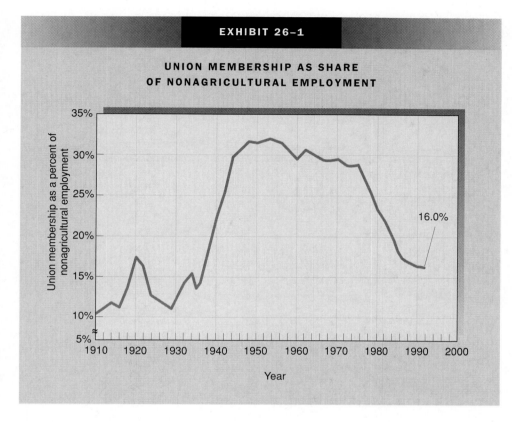

EXHIBIT 26–1

**UNION MEMBERSHIP AS SHARE
OF NONAGRICULTURAL EMPLOYMENT**

Union membership as a percent of nonagricultural employment

16.0%

Year

Between 1910 and 1935, union membership fluctuated between 12 percent and 18 percent of nonagricultural employment. During the 1935–1945 period, union membership increased sharply to approximately one-third of the nonfarm work force. Since the mid-1950s, union membership has declined as a percent of nonfarm employment, and the decline has been particularly sharp since 1975.

Source: Leo Troy and Neil Sheflin, *Union Source Book: Membership, Structure, Finance, Directory* (West Orange, NJ: Industrial Relations and Information Services, 1985); and U.S. Department of Labor, *Employment and Earnings* (various issues).

in the Northeast and upper Middle West. Since the former is an area of union weakness and the latter an area of strength, this pattern also retarded the growth of union membership.

All of these factors, of course, have to some extent been caused by union success in raising union wages. Wages that increase more than productivity act to retard the growth of employment in the geographic areas, the industries, and the classes of firms employing the high-wage workers. In contrast, where wages are low relative to productivity, business investment and the growth of employment are encouraged.

As **Exhibit 26–2** shows, there is substantial variation in the incidence of union membership across gender, racial, and occupational groups. Men are more likely than women to belong to a union. In 1992, 18.7 percent of employed men were union members compared with only 12.7 percent of employed women. The incidence of unionization among African Americans (21.3 percent) was a little higher than for whites (15.1 percent) and Hispanics (14.9 percent). There is substantial variation in unionization according to occupation. Only about 10 percent of the workers in technical, sales, clerical, and service occupations were unionized in 1992. In contrast, more than a quarter of the workers in craft, operative, and laborer occupations belonged to a union.

The biggest difference in unionization is found when comparing the private and public sectors. While only 11.5 percent of the private wage and salary workers are unionized, 36.7 percent of the government employees belong to a union. And while the share of the private work force belonging to a union has been shrinking, ᵃExcluding protective service workers.

Source: U.S. Department of Labor, *Employment and Earnings* (January 1993).

EXHIBIT 26–2

INCIDENCE OF UNION MEMBERSHIP ACCORDING TO SEX, RACE, OCCUPATION, AND SECTOR

	UNION MEMBERS AS A PERCENT OF GROUP, 1992
By Sex	
Men	18.7
Women	12.7
By Race	
Whites	15.1
Blacks	21.3
Hispanics	14.9
By Occupation	
Technical, sales, and clerical	10.4
Serviceᵃ	9.9
Precision production, craft, and repair	25.1
Operators, fabricators, and laborers	25.8
By Sector	
Private wage and salary	11.5
Government	36.7

unionization has been increasing in the public sector. During the last three decades, the proportion of government employees belonging to a union has more than tripled, rising from 11 percent in 1960 to 36.7 percent in 1992.

COLLECTIVE-BARGAINING PROCESS

Collective-bargaining contract
A detailed contract between a group of employees (a labor union) and their employer. It covers wage rates and conditions of employment.

Each year, **collective-bargaining contracts** covering wages and working conditions for 6 to 9 million workers are negotiated. These are union-management agreements prescribing the conditions of employment. Union negotiators, acting as agents for a group of employees, bargain with management about the provisions of a labor contract. If the union representatives are able to obtain a contract they consider acceptable, they will typically submit it to a vote of the union members. If approved by the members, the contract establishes in detail wage rates, fringe benefits, and working conditions for a future time interval, usually the next two or three years. During that time interval, union and management alike must abide by the conditions of the contract. While the labor contract is between management and union, it also applies to the nonunion bargaining unit members who are employed by the firm in positions covered by the agreement.

Some labor-management contracts contain a **union-shop provision** requiring all workers to join the union after a specified length of employment, usually 30 days. Proponents of this provision argue that since all workers in the bargaining unit enjoy the benefits of collective bargaining, all should be required to join and pay dues.

Opponents of the union shop argue that all employees are not helped by a union. Some unions lack the necessary power to obtain wage increases. Some employees may feel that they would be better off if they could bargain for themselves. In addition, unions often engage in political activities that may run counter to the views of individual employees. Why should an employee be forced, as a condition of employment, to support activities he or she does not approve? In 1947 Congress passed the Taft-Hartley Act; Section 14-B allows states to enact **right-to-work laws** prohibiting union-shop contracts. Thus, when a state has a right-to-work statute, a union-management contract cannot require a worker to join a union as a condition of employment. Right-to-work legislation is currently present in 21 states, most of them in the Sunbelt.

THE STRIKE AND COLLECTIVE BARGAINING

Typically, management and labor negotiators begin the bargaining process for a new labor contract several months, or even a year, before the termination of the current agreement. The new contract is usually approved before the old contract is terminated. However, at the termination of the old labor-management agreement, if the bargaining process has broken down and there is no agreement on a new contract, either side may use its economic power to try to bring the other to terms.

Employers can withhold employment from workers at the expiration of the old contract. However, since employers can unilaterally announce their terms for continued employment, they seldom discontinue operations.

The major source of work stoppage is the **strike,** which consists of two major actions by a union: (1) employees, particularly union employees, refuse to work, and (2) steps are taken to prevent other employees from working for the employer. Both conditions are essential to a strike. Unless other employees, often referred to as *scabs* or strike-breakers, are prevented from accepting jobs with the employer, the strike becomes merely a mass resignation. A strike also involves picketing to restrict and discourage the hiring of other workers, actions to prevent free entry and exit from a plant, and perhaps even violence or the threat of violence against workers willing to cross the picket lines.

The purpose of a strike is to impose economic costs on an employer so that the terms proposed by the union will be accepted. When the strike can be used to disrupt the production process and interfere with the employer's ability to sell goods and services to customers, it is a very powerful weapon. Under such conditions, the employer may submit to the wage demands of the union as a means of avoiding the costs of the strike.

Given the nature of the strike, it is not surprising that the "right to strike" has had an uneven history. At times, striking was prohibited because it was thought to interfere with the rights of nonunion workers. Before the passage of legislation in the early 1900s clearly establishing the right to strike, courts were sometimes willing to intervene and limit certain types of strikes. The role of law enforcement in strikes also has had a mixed history. In some areas, the police have given

Union-shop provision
The requirement that all employees join the recognized union and pay dues to it within a specified length of time (usually 30 days) after their employment with the firm begins.

Right-to-work laws
Laws that prohibit the union shop — the requirement that employees must join a union (after 30 days) as a condition of employment. Each state has the option to adopt (or reject) right-to-work legislation.

Strike
An action of unionized employees in which they (1) discontinue working for the employer and (2) take steps to prevent other potential workers from offering their services to the employer.

nonstrikers, employees who desire to continue working, protection to and from their jobs. In other cases, they have permitted pickets to block entry and have turned their backs on violence between strikers and nonstrikers. Even today, the protection a nonstriker can expect from the police varies from location to location.

The United States has established some limitations on the right to strike. The use of the strike by government employees—the single area of union growth—is substantially restricted. Most states limit the right of public employees to strike. Prohibitions against strikes by police officers and firefighters are particularly commonplace. Strikes by federal employees are also prohibited by law. When the federally-employed air-traffic controllers called a strike during the summer of 1981, striking workers who refused to return to work were fired and eventually replaced. The Taft-Hartley Act allows the president to seek a court injunction prohibiting a private sector strike for 80 days when it is believed that the strike would create a "national emergency." During the 80-day period, work continues under the conditions of the old contract. If a settlement has not been reached during this "cooling-off" period, however, employees again have the option of using the strike as a weapon.

COST OF A STRIKE

A strike can be costly to both union and management. From the firm's viewpoint, a work stoppage may mean that it will be unable to meet the current demand for its product. It may lose customers, and they may be difficult to win back once they have turned to competitors during the strike. A strike will be more costly to the firm when (1) demand for its product is strong, (2) it is unable to stockpile its product, and (3) its fixed costs are high even during the strike. If the firm can stockpile its product in anticipation of a strike, a work stoppage may not have much impact on current sales. For example, automobile producers, particularly during slack times, often have an inventory of new cars that allows them to meet current demand during a 60- or even 90-day strike. In contrast, the shipping revenues of a trucking firm may be completely eliminated by a truckers' strike. The firm is unable to deliver its service because of the strike, and potential customers therefore turn to rail, air, postal, and other forms of shipping. The firm suffers a permanent loss of sales.

Careful timing can also magnify the cost of a strike. Agricultural unions can threaten farmers with the loss of an entire year's income by striking at harvesttime. Similarly, baseball players and umpires can strengthen their position by threatening a strike shortly before or during the playoffs and World Series.

The nature of the product, the level of current demand, and the ability of the firm to continue to meet the requests of its customers during a strike all influence the effectiveness of the strike as a weapon. The more costly a work stoppage would be to a firm, the greater the pressure on it to yield to the demands of the union.

Strikes, particularly if they are long, are also quite costly to employees. Although a carnival attitude often prevails during the early days of a strike, a few weeks without a paycheck imposes an extreme hardship on most families. Strike funds are usually inadequate to deal with a prolonged strike. Some workers may be able to arrange for a temporary job to help pay the bills, but such employment will generally be much less attractive than their regular jobs. Therefore, as a strike continues, pressures build on the union to arrive at a settlement.

Strikes sometimes exert a substantial impact on secondary parties who are unable to influence union-management relations. For example, a prolonged strike in the steel industry might cause a loss of work time in automobile, construction, and other industries. A teachers' strike might force a working parent to quit his or her job to care for the children. A public transit strike in New York can paralyze Fun City. Should third parties be protected when strikes involve the public interest? Many would answer this question in the affirmative. But how can the public be protected without interfering with the bargaining process? These questions have not yet been fully answered.

KEEPING WORK STOPPAGES IN PERSPECTIVE

Since a strike is news, work stoppages receive considerable media exposure. Nevertheless, work stoppages due to strikes must be placed in proper perspective. The strike, or the threat of it, forces both management and labor to bargain seriously. Both have a strong incentive to settle without a work stoppage. This is usually what happens. Each year an estimated 120,000 labor-and-management bargaining teams sit across the bargaining table from each other. They deal with the important issues of wages, fringe benefits, grievance procedures, and conditions of employment. More than 99 percent of the time, labor-management contracts are agreed to without the use of strikes. One seldom hears about these contracts because peaceful settlements are back-page news at best. It is the strikes that rate the headlines.

As **Exhibit 26–3** illustrates, very little work time is lost as the result of strikes. During the last three decades, the number of worker-hours lost because of strikes was approximately one-tenth of 1 percent of the total working time—and the

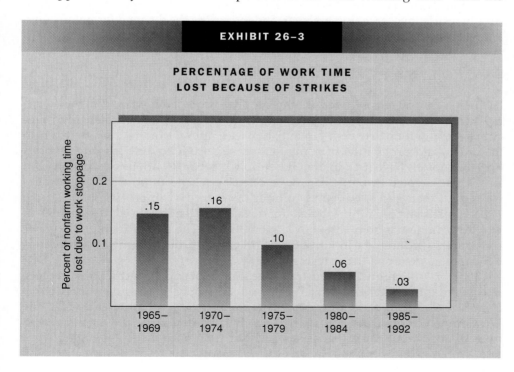

EXHIBIT 26–3

PERCENTAGE OF WORK TIME LOST BECAUSE OF STRIKES

Percent of nonfarm working time lost due to work stoppage

- 0.2
- 0.1

| 1965–1969 | 1970–1974 | 1975–1979 | 1980–1984 | 1985–1992 |
| .15 | .16 | .10 | .06 | .03 |

Since 1965, only one-tenth of 1 percent of nonfarm working time has been lost due to labor disputes, and the annual figure has been declining. These data are for work stoppages involving 1,000 or more workers.

Source: *Statistical Abstract of the United States* (annual) and *Monthly Labor Review* (various issues).

proportion has been falling. The amount of work time lost due to strikes is substantially less than the work time lost because of absenteeism.

HOW CAN UNIONS INFLUENCE WAGES?

The collective-bargaining process often gives one the impression that wages are established primarily by the talents of the union-management representatives who sit at the bargaining table. It might appear that market forces play a relatively minor role. However, as both union and management are well aware, market forces provide the setting in which the bargaining process is conducted. They often tip the balance of power one way or the other.

High wages increase the firm's costs. When union employers face stiff competition from nonunion producers or foreign competitors, they will be less able to pass along higher wage costs to their customers. Competition in the product market thus limits the bargaining power of a union. Changing market conditions also influence the balance of power between union and management. When the demand for a product is strong, the demand for labor will be high, and the firm will be much more willing to consent to a significant wage increase. When demand is weak, however, the product inventory level of the firm (or industry) is more likely to be high. The firm's current demand for labor will be weakened. It will be much less vulnerable to a union work stoppage. Under such conditions, wage increases will be much more difficult to obtain. (Note: When we speak of wage rates, we are referring to the total compensation package, including both fringe benefits and money wages.)

A union can use three basic strategies to increase the wages of its members: supply restrictions, bargaining power, and increasing the demand for union labor. We will examine each of these in turn.

SUPPLY RESTRICTIONS

If a union can successfully reduce the supply of competitive labor, higher wage rates will automatically result. Licensing requirements, long apprenticeship programs, immigration barriers, high initiation fees, refusal to admit new members to the union, and prohibition of nonunion workers from holding jobs are all practices that unions have used to limit the supply of labor to various occupations and jobs. Craft unions, in particular, have often been able to obtain higher wages because of their successful effort to limit the entry of competitive labor. In the 1920s unions successfully lobbied for legislation that reduced the torrent of worker-immigrants from abroad to a mere trickle. The tighter immigration laws considerably reduced the influx of new workers, reducing the growth of supply in U.S. labor markets and thus causing higher wages to prevail.

Part "a" of **Exhibit 26–4** illustrates the impact of supply restrictions on wage rates. Successful exclusionary tactics will reduce supply, shifting the supply curve from S_0 to S_1. Facing the supply curve S_1, employers will consent to the wage rate W_1. Compared to a free-entry market equilibrium, the wage rate has increased from W_0 to W_1, but employment has declined from E_0 to E_1. At the higher wage rate, W_1, an excess supply of labor, AB, will result. The restrictive practices will

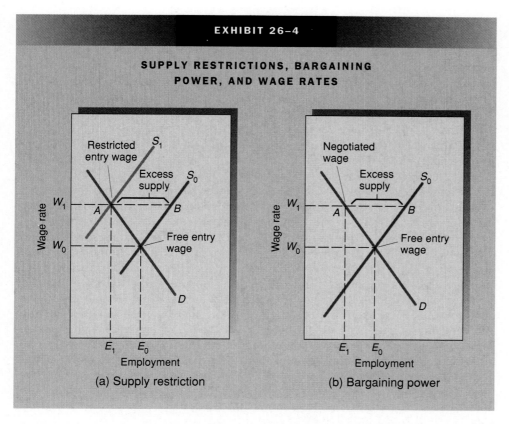

EXHIBIT 26–4

SUPPLY RESTRICTIONS, BARGAINING POWER, AND WAGE RATES

(a) Supply restriction

(b) Bargaining power

The impact of higher wages obtained by restricting supply is very similar to that obtained through bargaining power. As illustrated by part a, when union policies reduce the supply of one type of labor, higher wages result. Similarly, when bargaining power is used in order to obtain higher wages (part b), employment declines and an excess supply of labor results.

prevent this excess supply from undercutting the above-equilibrium wage rate. Because of the exclusionary practices, the union will be able to obtain higher wages for E_1 employees. Other employees who would be willing to accept work even at wage rate W_0 will now be forced into other areas of employment.

BARGAINING POWER

Must unions restrict entry? Why can they not simply use their bargaining power, enhanced by the strike threat, as a vehicle for raising wages? If they have enough economic power, this will be possible. A strike by even a small percentage of vital employees can sometimes halt the flow of production. For example, a work stoppage by airline mechanics can force major airlines to cancel their flights. Because the mechanics perform an essential function, an airline cannot operate without their services, even though they constitute only 10 percent of all airline employees.

If the union is able to obtain an above-free-entry wage rate, the impact on employment will be similar to a reduction in supply. As part "b" of Exhibit 26–4 illustrates, employers will hire fewer workers at the higher wage rate obtained through bargaining power. Employment will decline below the free-entry level (from E_0 to E_1) as a result of the rise in wages. An excess supply of labor, AB, will exist, at least temporarily. More employees will seek the high-wage union jobs than employers will choose to hire. Nonwage methods of rationing jobs will become more important.

INCREASE THE DEMAND

Unions may attempt to increase the demand for union labor by appealing to consumers to buy only union-produced goods. Union-sponsored promotional campaigns instructing consumers to "look for the union label" or "buy American" are generally designed to increase the demand for union-made products.

Most people, however, are primarily interested in getting the most for their consumer dollar. Thus, the demand for union labor is usually determined primarily by factors outside of the union's direct control, such as the availability of substitute inputs and the demand for the product. Unions, though, can sometimes use their political power to increase the demand for their services. They may be able to induce legislators to pass laws requiring the employment of certain types or amounts of labor for a task (for example, unneeded firemen on trains, allegedly for safety reasons, or a certain number of stage engineers). Unions often seek import restrictions as a means of increasing the demand for domestic labor. For example, automobile workers generally support high tariffs and other restrictions limiting the sale of foreign-made automobiles in the United States. Garment workers have used their political muscle to raise tariffs and reduce import quotas for clothing goods produced abroad. Such practices increase the demand for domestic automobiles and clothing, thereby increasing the demand for domestic auto and garment workers. It is not surprising that the management and union representatives of a specific industry often join hands in support of trade restrictions limiting foreign competition. As **Exhibit 26–5** illustrates, successful union actions

If a union can follow policies that will lead to an increase in the demand for its services, wages will rise automatically.

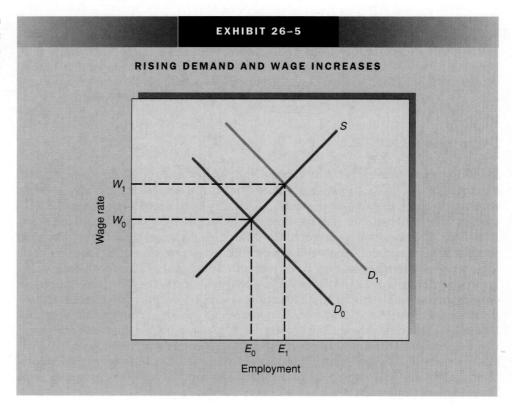

EXHIBIT 26–5

RISING DEMAND AND WAGE INCREASES

to increase demand for the services of union members result in both higher wages and an expansion in employment, usually at the expense of consumers.

A union in a strong bargaining position may shift the firm off its demand curve. This can happen if the union offers an "all-or-none" settlement in which the union specifies both wage and the quantity of labor (or restrictive work rules). To get any labor at all in this case, the firm must hire more labor at the union wage than it wants. For example, the International Typographical Union sometimes stipulated that advertisements printed from molded mats supplied by advertisers must be set, proofread, and corrected in the newspaper's composing room. This "bogus type" was then discarded. But the newspaper was nevertheless required to either pay its typesetters to produce the unneeded "bogus" work or make other bargaining concessions to induce the union to withdraw the rule. This type of "make-work rule" is another way in which a union may be able to loosen the connection between higher wages and lower levels of employment.

UNION POWER, EMPLOYMENT, AND MONOPSONY

Is unionization necessary to protect employees from the power of employers? The answer may be yes or no depending on the circumstances. When there are a large number of employers in a market, the interests of employees will be protected by competition among employers. Under these circumstances, each employer must pay the market wage to employees to keep them from shifting to higher-paying alternative employers. In a modern society, labor is highly mobile. Most employees work in a labor market in which there are many employers. However, a few workers may confront a situation in which there is only a single employer, at least for the specific skill category of labor supplied by the workers. For example, if a single large employer—perhaps a textile manufacturer or lumber mill—dominates the labor market of a small town, local workers may have few alternative employment opportunities.

Monopsony refers to this type of market situation where there is a single buyer for a specific resource—for example, a specific skill category of labor. As we previously discussed, when the seller has a monopoly, the seller can profit by restricting output and charging a price above the marginal cost of production. Under monopsony, the buyer has a monopoly. Since the alternatives available to sellers are limited, the monopsonist-buyer will be able to profit by restricting the purchase of the resource and paying a price (wage rate) that is less than the marginal revenue generated by the resource.

Exhibit 26–6 illustrates the impact of monopsony in the labor market. Since the monopsonist is the only employer (purchaser of labor), its supply curve for the resource in question will coincide with the market supply curve for that resource. The supply curve for the resource will slope upward to the right because higher wages are necessary to attract the additional workers desired. For now, we will assume that both the old and new employees will be paid the higher wage rates if employment is expanded. The **marginal factor cost (MFC)** curve indicates the marginal cost of labor to the monopsonist. This cost of labor will exceed the wage

Monopsony
A market in which there is only one buyer. The monopsonist confronts the market supply curve for the resource (or product) bought.

Marginal factor cost (MFC)
The cost of employing an additional unit of a resource. When the employer is small relative to the total market, the marginal factor cost is simply the price of the resource. In contrast, under monopsony, marginal factor cost will exceed the price of the resource, since the monopsonist faces an upward-sloping supply curve for the resource because wages must be raised for all workers.

As part a illustrates, the monopsonist's supply curve for labor will slope upward to the right. The marginal factor cost (MFC) curve for labor will be steeper than the labor supply curve (S). The monopsonist will hire E_1 units of labor and pay a wage rate W_1, along its labor supply curve. If a union establishes a wage floor, W_2 of part b, for example, the monopsonist may hire additional workers (E_2 rather than E_1) at the higher wage rate.

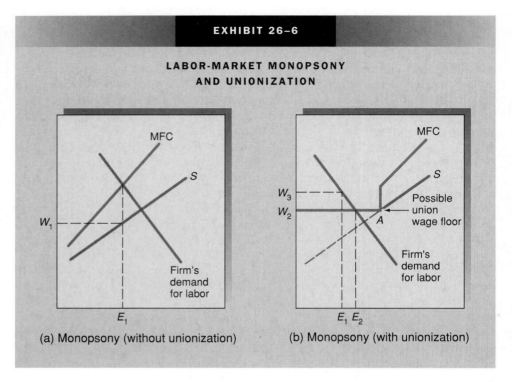

EXHIBIT 26-6

LABOR-MARKET MONOPSONY AND UNIONIZATION

(a) Monopsony (without unionization)

(b) Monopsony (with unionization)

rate because the higher wages necessary to attract each additional worker must be paid to all employees. As illustrated by Exhibit 26–6, the monopsonist's MFC curve will therefore be steeper than the labor supply curve.

How many workers should a profit-maximizing monopsony employ? The monopsonist's demand curve for labor indicates how much each additional worker adds to the firm's total revenue. The monopsonist will continue to expand employment as long as hiring additional workers adds more to total revenues than to total costs. This means that the monopsonist will choose employment level E_1 in the exhibit, where the firm's demand curve, reflecting the marginal revenue product of labor, is just equal to the marginal factor cost of labor. A wage rate of W_1 will be sufficient to attract E_1 employees. For employment levels beyond E_1, it would cost the monopsonist more to hire an additional worker (MFC) than that worker would add to total revenue. As the result of this cost, the monopsonist firm will hire fewer employees than it would if it were not the only buyer in the labor market.

Part "b" of Exhibit 26–6 illustrates what would happen if a union established a wage floor—W_2, for example—for a monopsonist. The wage floor would prohibit the monopsonist from paying low wages even if employment dropped. The union would confront the employer with the supply curve W_2AS. In essence, the wage floor would become the firm's MFC curve until the wage floor intersected the labor supply curve at A. As long as the MFC of additional units of labor was less than the firm's demand curve, additional workers would continue to be employed. Thus, if a union imposed wage rate W_2, the monopsonist would expand employment to E_2. In this case unionization would result in both higher wages and an expansion in employment. If the union expanded the wage rate above W_3, employment would fall below E_1, the level employed by a nonunion monopsonist. But for any wage floor less than W_3, the monopsonist would expand employment beyond E_1.

While this analysis is sound as far as it goes, there are three additional factors that should be considered.[2] First, a higher wage rate will obviously increase the firm's total costs of production. In the long run, when the firm sells its product in a competitive market, higher per unit costs will almost certainly force the firm to raise its price. A decline in the firm's market share and output is a likely result. As the firm's market share declines, employment of all factors of production, including labor, will fall.

Second, a monopsonist will often be able to confine the higher wage rates to new employees only. When this is the case, the MFC curve of the monopsonist will not differ from its labor supply curve. Rather than restricting employment to keep wages low, the firm may simply expand employment along its supply curve, offering new employees (but not old ones) higher job classifications and more attractive employment conditions to obtain their services.

Third, given the speed of transportation, employers often draw workers from 30 to 50 miles away. In addition, many employees (particularly skilled workers, professionals, and managers) compete in a much broader labor market, a national labor market in some cases. Over a period of time, such workers will flow into and away from local labor markets. Given the mobility of labor, then, most employers will be small relative to their labor market, and their decisions to expand or contract their work force will not exert much impact on the market wage rate. Under these circumstances, MFC is nearly the same as the wage rate in the competitive-market model. A rise in the wage rate will therefore almost certainly reduce employment.

All of these factors reduce the relevance of the monopsony model in most labor markets. When economic researchers have compared the predictive power of the monopsony model with the competitive model, unsurprisingly, the latter has generally performed better. Empirical evidence indicates that unions normally operate in labor markets characterized by competition rather than monopsony.

WHAT GIVES A UNION STRENGTH?

Not all unions are able to raise the wages of their workers. What are the factors that make a union strong? Simply stated, if a union is to be strong, the demand for its labor must be inelastic. This will enable the union to obtain large wage increases while suffering only modest reductions in employment. In contrast, with an elastic demand for union labor, a substantial rise in wages will mean a large loss in jobs.

There are four major determinants of the demand elasticity for a factor of production: (1) the availability of substitutes, (2) the elasticity of product demand, (3) the share of the input as a proportion of total cost, and (4) the supply elasticity

---

[2]See Armen Alchian and William Allen, *Exchange and Production: Competition, Coordination, and Control* (Belmont: Wadsworth, 1983), pp. 334–339, for additional theoretical analysis of monopsony.

of substitute inputs.[3] We now turn to the importance of each of these conditions as a determinant of union strength.

AVAILABILITY OF GOOD SUBSTITUTE INPUTS

When it is difficult to substitute other inputs for unionized labor when producing a good, the union is strengthened. The demand for union labor is then more inelastic, and reductions in employment tend to be small if the union is able to use its bargaining power and the threat of a strike to push wages up. In contrast, when there are good substitutes for union labor, employers will turn to the substitutes and cut back on their use of union labor as it becomes more expensive. Under these circumstances, higher union wages will price the union workers out of the market and lead to a sharp reduction in their employment.

Some employers may be able to automate various production operations—in effect, substituting machines for union workers if their wages increase. When machines are a good substitute for union labor, the demand for union labor will be fairly elastic. An elastic demand for union labor will substantially reduce the ability of the union to gain above-market wages.

The best substitute for union labor is generally nonunion labor. Thus, the power of unions to gain more for their members will be directly related to their ability to insulate themselves from competition with nonunion labor. When employers are in a position to substitute nonunion labor for unionized workers, it will be difficult for a union to push wages above the market level.

Within a given plant, a union will negotiate the wages and employment conditions for all workers, both union and nonunion. However, as union wages rise, it may be economical for unionized firms to contract with nonunion firms to handle specific operations or supply various components used in production. Thus, contracting out often permits employers to indirectly substitute nonunion for union workers. In addition, many large firms in automobile, textile, and other manufacturing industries operate both union and nonunion plants. They may be able to substitute nonunion for union labor by shifting more and more of their production to their nonunion plants, including those located overseas or in right-to-work states where unions are generally weaker.

ELASTICITY OF DEMAND FOR PRODUCTS OF UNIONIZED FIRMS

Wages are a component of costs. An increase in the wages of union members will almost surely lead to higher prices for goods produced with union labor. Unless the demand for the good produced by union labor is inelastic, the output and employment of unionized firms will decline if the union pushes up wages (and costs). If a union is going to have a significant impact on wages (without undermining employment opportunities), its workers must produce a good for which the demand is inelastic.

Our analysis implies that a union will be unable to significantly increase wages above the free market rate when producing a good that competes with

---

[3]Alfred Marshall, *Principles of Economics,* 8th ed. (New York: Macmillan, 1920).

similar (or identical) goods produced by nonunion labor or foreign producers. The demand for the good produced by union labor will almost surely be highly elastic when the same product is available from nonunion and foreign producers. Thus, if the union pushes up wages and costs, the market share of unionized firms will shrink and their employment will fall substantially.

Both past history and recent events are consistent with this view. In the 1920s the United Mine Workers obtained big wage gains in unionized coal fields. The union, however, was unable to halt the growth of nonunion mining, particularly in the strip mines of the West. The unionized mines soon lost the major share of their market to nonunionized fields, leading to a sharp reduction in the employment of unionized miners.

More recently, the strength of the Teamsters' union was substantially eroded when deregulation subjected the unionized segment of the trucking industry to much more intense competition from nonunion firms in the early 1980s. With deregulation, nonunion firms with lower labor costs entered the industry. Given their labor-cost advantage, many of the new entrants cut prices to gain a larger share of the market. The market share of the unionized firms declined. More than 100,000 Teamsters lost their jobs. Given the sharp reduction in the employment of their members, the Teamsters eventually agreed to wage concessions and a reduction in their fringe-benefit package.[4]

Unions sometimes negotiate substantial wage increases, even though they may eventually result in significant reductions in employment. This appears to be the case in both the steel and automobile industries. The hourly earnings of production workers in these two industries rose sharply compared with other workers in the private sector during the 1970s. By 1982 the average hourly earnings of steel workers were 74 percent greater than for all private-sector workers, up from a 19 percent premium in 1969. The parallel wage premium in the automobile industry was 51 percent in 1982, up from 21 percent in 1969. These substantial wage increases during the 1970s pushed up the costs of American steel and automobile producers relative to their foreign competitors. Foreign producers were able to capture a larger share of the U.S. market and, as a result, the employment of unionized labor in both the steel and automobile industries declined sharply. Between 1978 and 1982, membership in the United Steel Workers Union fell by 45 percent. The United Automobile Workers (UAW) lost 142,000 members, approximately 16 percent of their total, in the late 1970s and early 1980s. The experience of workers in both the steel and automobile industries provides vivid evidence that higher wages at unionized firms will mean less employment when the unionized firms compete with nonunion and foreign competitors.

UNION LABOR AS SHARE OF COST OF PRODUCTION

If the unionized labor input comprises only a small share of total production cost, demand for that labor will tend to be relatively inelastic. For example, since the

---

[4]A recent study found that after the deregulation of the trucking industry, the wage premium of unionized truckers fell between 30 percent and 48 percent in the regulated sector of the industry. See Barry Hirsch, "Trucking Regulation, Unionization, and Labor Earnings," *The Journal of Human Resources* 23 (Summer 1988), pp. 296–319.

wages of plumbers and pilots comprise only a small share of the total cost of production in the housing and air travel industries, respectively, a doubling or even tripling of their wages would result in only a 1 or 2 percent increase in the cost of housing or air travel. A large increase in the price of such inputs would have little impact on product price, output, and employment. This factor has sometimes been called "the importance of being unimportant," because it is important to the strength of the union.

SUPPLY ELASTICITY OF SUBSTITUTE INPUTS

We have just explained that if wage rates in the unionized sector are pushed upward, firms will look for substitute inputs, and the demand for these substitutes will increase. If the supply of these substitutes (such as nonunion labor) is inelastic, however, their price will rise sharply in response to an increase in demand. The higher price will reduce the attractiveness of the substitutes. An inelastic supply of substitutes will thus strengthen the union by making the demand for union labor more inelastic.

WAGES OF UNION AND NONUNION EMPLOYEES

The precise impact of unions on the wages of their members is not easy to determine. In order to isolate the union effect, differences in other factors must be eliminated. Comparisons must be made between union and nonunion workers who have similar productivity (skills) and who are working on similar jobs.

Numerous studies have examined the effect of unions on wages. The pioneering work in this area was a 1963 study by H. Gregg Lewis of the University of Chicago.[5] Lewis estimated that, on average, union workers during the 1950s received wages between 10 and 15 percent higher than those of nonunion workers with similar productivity characteristics. The findings of other researchers using data from the 1950s and 1960s are generally consistent with the early work of Lewis.[6]

In a 1986 work, Lewis reviewed the evidence from nearly 200 studies on this topic and used more recent data to develop estimates of the union wage premium for the 1960s and 1970s.[7] **Exhibit 26–7** summarizes the findings of Lewis's work and projects his estimates up to 1988–1992. Research in this area indicates that the

---

[5]H. Gregg Lewis, *Unionism and Relative Wages in the United State*s (Chicago: University of Chicago Press, 1963).

[6]See Albert Rees, *The Economics of Trade Unions* (Chicago: University of Chicago Press, 1967); and Michael J. Boskin, "Unions and Relative Wages," *American Economic Review* LXII (June 1972), pp. 466–472.

[7]H. Gregg Lewis, *Union Relative Wage Effects: A Survey* (Chicago: University of Chicago Press, 1986).

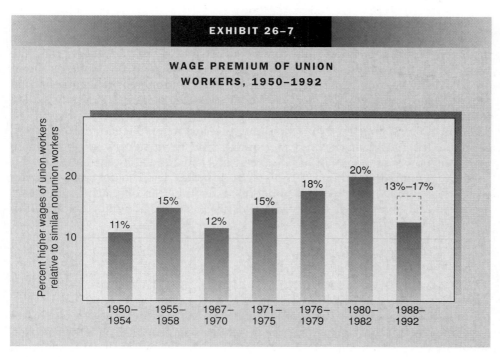

EXHIBIT 26-7

WAGE PREMIUM OF UNION WORKERS, 1950–1992

Most studies indicate that the wages of union workers have been between 10 percent and 20 percent higher than similar nonunion workers during the last several decades. The union-nonunion wage differential widened during the 1970s, but it has declined since 1982. On average, union workers earned between 13 percent and 17 percent more than similar nonunion workers in the late 1980s and early 1990s.

Source: H. Gregg Lewis, *Unionism and Relative Wages in the United States: An Empirical Inquiry* (Chicago: University of Chicago Press, 1963), p. 222; and H. Gregg Lewis, *Union Relative Wage Effects: A Survey* (Chicago: University of Chicago Press, 1986), p. 9. The 1980–1982 and 1988–1992 data are estimates by the authors based on the annual change in the Employment Cost Index of union and nonunion labor since 1979, as reported by the U.S. Department of Labor.

union-nonunion wage differential widened during the 1970s.[8] Lewis estimates that union workers received an 18 percent premium compared with similar nonunion workers during the 1976–1979 period, up from a 12 percent premium during 1967–1970. During the early 1980s, the wages of union workers continued to grow more rapidly than their nonunion counterparts, leading to an estimated 20 percent differential during 1980–1982. Since 1983, however, the trend has reversed—the wages of nonunion workers have increased more rapidly than those of unionized workers. As of 1992, most researchers in this area estimate that the premium of union members is in the 13 percent to 17 percent range, approximately the same as the estimated union-nonunion differential during the 1950–1975 period.[9]

Our theory indicates that some unions will be much stronger than others, that is, better able to achieve higher wages for their members. In some occupations, the size of the union-nonunion differential will be well above the average, while in other occupations, unions will exert little impact on wages.

---

[8]See William J. Moore and John Raision, "The Level and Growth of Union/Nonunion Relative Wage Effects, 1967–1977," *Journal of Labor Research* 4 (Winter 1983), pp. 65–79; Richard B. Freeman and James L. Medoff, *What Do Unions Do?* (New York: Basic Books, 1984); and Barry T. Hirsch and John T. Addison, *The Economic Analysis of Unions: New Approaches and Evidence* (Boston: Allen & Unwin, 1986), for evidence on this point.

[9]The studies referred to in the text compared the wages of similarly productive union and nonunion workers at a point in time. Another approach would be to compare the change in the wages of the same worker in cases where the worker moves from a union to a nonunion job and vice versa. Research using this approach has generally placed the union wage premium in the 10 percent range, somewhat smaller than the estimates derived from cross-section studies. For evidence provided by studies using this methodology, see Wesley Mellow, "Unionism and Wages: A Longitudinal Analysis," *Review of Economics and Statistics* 63 (February 1981), pp. 43–52; and Richard B. Freeman, "Longitudinal Analysis and Trade Union Effects," *Journal of Labor Economics* 2 (January 1984), pp. 1–26.

Lewis estimated that strong unions, such as those of the electricians, plumbers, tool and die makers, metal craft workers, truckers (this was prior to the moves toward deregulation), and commercial airline pilots were able to raise the wages of their members substantially more than the average for all unions. Other economists have found that the earnings of unionized merchant seamen, postal workers, and rail, auto, and steel workers exceed the wages of similarly skilled nonunion workers by 25 percent or more.

Unionization appears to have had the least impact on the earnings of cotton-textile, footwear, furniture, hosiery, clothing, and retail sales workers. In these areas, the power of the union has been considerably limited by the existence of a substantial number of nonunion firms in these industries. The demands of union workers in these industries are moderated by the fear of placing unionized employers at a competitive disadvantage in relation to the nonunion employers of the industry.

UNIONS, PROFITABILITY, AND EMPLOYMENT IN UNIONIZED SECTOR

If unions increase the wages of unionized firms above the competitive market level, the costs of those firms will rise unless (as seems unlikely) there is a corresponding increase in productivity. The higher costs will reduce the profitability of the unionized firm. Recent research indicates that this was true during the 1970s. Barry Hirsch of Florida State University found that as the union-nonunion wage premium increased during the 1970s, the profitability of unionized firms lagged behind the profitability of other firms.[10]

If unions are able to transfer profits from unionized firms to union workers, clearly this is a two-edged sword. In the short run, workers enjoy higher wages. In the long run, investment will move away from areas of low profitability. Like other mobile resources, capital may be exploited in the short run, but this will not be the case in the long run. Therefore, to the extent that the profits of unionized firms are lower, investment expenditures on fixed structures, research, and development will flow into the nonunion sector and away from unionized firms. As a result, the growth of both productivity and employment will tend to lag in the unionized sector. Investment, production, and employment will all shift away from unionized operations and toward nonunion firms.

The larger the wage premium of unionized firms, the greater the incentive will be to shift production toward nonunion operations. The recent findings of Linneman, Wachter, and Carter are highly supportive of this view.[11] They found that industries with the largest union wage premiums were precisely the industries with the largest declines in the employment of unionized workers. On the

---

[10]Barry Hirsch, *Labor Unions and the Economic Performance of Firms* (Kalamazoo, Mich.: Upjohn Institute for Employment Research, 1991). Also see Richard B. Freeman and James L. Medoff, *What Do Unions Do?* (New York: Basic Books, 1984), chapter 12, for evidence that unions exert a negative impact on the profits of unionized firms.

[11]Peter D. Linneman, Michael L. Wachter, and William Carter, "Evaluating the Evidence on Union Employment and Wages," *Industrial and Labor Relations Review* 44, (October 1990). Linneman, Wachter, and Carter estimate that increases in the union wage premium were responsible for up to 64 percent of the decline in the union share of employment during the last two decades.

other hand, union employment tended to be either constant or increasing in those industries with only a small union wage premium. Viewed from this perspective, the sharp decline in union membership during recent years (see Exhibit 26–1) is at least partially the result of the union wage premium—and the increase in the size of that premium in important industries during the 1970s (see Exhibit 26–7).

IMPACT OF UNIONS ON WAGES OF ALL WORKERS

While unions have increased the average wages of their members, there is no reason to believe that they have increased the average overall compensation of workers—both union and nonunion. At first glance, this may seem paradoxical. However, the economic way of thinking enhances our understanding of this issue. As unions push wages up in the unionized sector, employers in this sector will hire fewer workers. Unable to find jobs in the high-wage union sector, some employees will shift to the nonunion sector. This increase in labor supply will depress the wages of nonunion workers. Thus, higher wages for union members do not necessarily mean higher wages for all workers. (See the accompanying "Myths of Economics" feature for additional detail on this subject.)

With regard to the impact of unions on the overall level of wages, it is important to keep one other key point in mind. The general level of wages is dependent upon productivity—output of goods and services that people value. Income is simply the flip side of output. Increases in the general level of wages are dependent upon increases in productivity per hour. Of course, improvements in (1) technology, (2) the machines and tools available to workers (physical capital), (3) worker skills (human capital), and (4) the efficiency of economic organization provide the essential ingredients for higher levels of productivity. Higher real wages can be achieved only if the production of goods and services is expanded. Although unions can increase the wages of union workers, they cannot increase the wages of all workers unless their activities increase the total productivity of labor.

DO UNIONS CAUSE INFLATION?

Labor unions are often accused of pushing up wages and thereby triggering price increases that cause inflation. Inspection of this view, however, indicates that it suffers from a major defect; it fails to incorporate the secondary effects of higher union wages. Let us consider this issue in more detail.

Suppose an economy were initially experiencing stable prices and the normal (natural) rate of unemployment. What would happen if a major union, that of the automobile workers, for example, used its economic power and the threat of a strike to obtain a very substantial increase in wages? The higher wages would trigger both direct and secondary effects. The increased labor costs would push up the prices of automobiles, trucks, and buses, particularly if imports could also be restrained. The direct effect of the higher automobile prices would be an increase in the consumer price index.

"UNIONS HAVE INCREASED THE WAGES OF WORKERS AND THEREBY EXPANDED THE SHARE OF INCOME GOING TO LABOR."

It is one thing for unions to increase the wages of union members. It is quite another for them to increase the wages of all workers, both nonunion and union. Neither economic theory nor empirical evidence indicates unions are able to increase the general level of wages. If unions were the primary source of high wages, the real wages of workers would be higher in highly unionized countries such as Australia, Italy, and the United Kingdom than they are in the United States. But this is not what we observe. For example, real wages are at least 40 percent lower in the United Kingdom than they are in the United States, even though more than 40 percent of the work force is unionized in the United Kingdom compared to 16 percent in the United States (see **Exhibit 1**).

The real source of high wages is high productivity, not labor unions. In turn, high productivity depends on abundant physical capital, the knowledge and skill of the work force, and institutional arrangements that encourage the creation of wealth.

To the extent unions increase the wages of union members, there is good reason to believe they do so primarily at the expense of nonunion workers. Higher union wages (and costs) will lead to a reduction in the output of products that intensively use union labor. This factor will cause employment in the unionized sectors to fall. What will happen to employees who are unable to find jobs in the unionized sector? They will compete for nonunion jobs, increasing supply and depressing nonunion wages. Labor economist Gregg Lewis has estimated that the real wages of nonunion workers are 3 to 4 percent lower than they would be in the absence of unionism.[1]

If labor unions increased the wages of all workers and therefore the share of income going to labor, we

EXHIBIT 1

UNION MEMBERSHIP: AN INTERNATIONAL COMPARISON

COUNTRY	UNION MEMBERSHIP AS A PERCENT OF TOTAL CIVILIAN WAGE AND SALARY EMPLOYEES[a]	
	1970	1989
Italy	36	47
United Kingdom	45	41
Australia	42	34
Germany	33	33
Canada	—	33
Japan	35	26
United States	27	16
France	22	11

[a]Data are adjusted to cover wage and salary union members only. Pensioners, the unemployed and self-employed union members are excluded.

Source: Clara Chang and Constance Sorrentino, "Union Membership Statistics in 12 Countries," *Monthly Labor Review*, December 1991.

would expect labor's share of income to be directly related to union membership. Again, the evidence is inconsistent with this view. **Exhibit 2** presents data on labor's share of income since 1930. Total employee

However, there would also be important secondary effects that are often overlooked. Confronting the higher automobile prices, consumers must either (1) purchase significantly fewer automobiles (quality-constant units) or (2) increase their expenditures on automobiles. To the extent that consumers purchased fewer (or less expensive) automobiles, the amount of labor services required by the automobile industry would decline. Automotive employment would fall (or at least expand by an abnormally small amount). Some workers who would have been able to find jobs in the automobile industry will now be forced into other

EXHIBIT 2

LABOR'S SHARE OF NATIONAL INCOME, 1930–1993

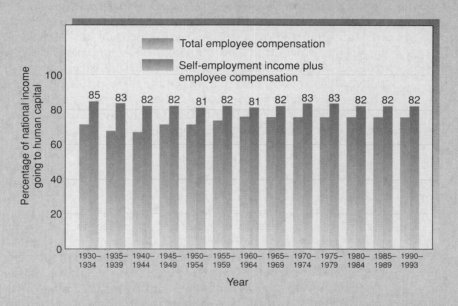

As a share of the nonfarm work force, union membership increased from 12 percent in the early 1930s to nearly 35 percent in the mid-1950s. Since 1960, union membership has declined substantially as a proportion of the U.S. labor force (see Exhibit 26–1). Despite these fluctuations, the share of national income allocated to labor (employee compensation and self-employment income) has been virtually constant throughout the 1930–1993 period.

Source: Derived from the national estimates of the U.S. Department of Commerce published in *Survey of Current Business.*

compensation (including the social security contribution of the employer) has increased slightly since the Second World War. However, this is primarily a reflection of the decline in the number of self-employed persons in agriculture and the corresponding increase in the proportion of employed workers. Since the earnings of self-employed proprietors such as farmers, sales personnel, accountants, and small-business operators emanate primarily from their labor services, a clearer picture of the labor-physical capital components of income emerges when self-employment income is added to employee compensation. As Exhibit 2 shows, this measure of labor's share has been amazingly constant. Between 81 and 83 percent of national income in the United States has gone to labor during each five-year period since 1935. The share of national income going to labor did not rise as union membership grew as a proportion of the labor force during the 1935–1955 period. Neither has it fallen as union membership has declined since 1955.

In conclusion, while there is evidence that unions often increase the wages of their members, there is no evidence that they are able to increase the general level of real wages or the share of income earned by labor relative to physical capital.

[1]H. Gregg Lewis, *Unionism and Relative Wages in the United States* (Chicago: University of Chicago Press, 1963).

lines of employment. The labor supply in these alternative employment areas would increase, placing downward pressure on wages and costs in these sectors.

On the other hand, if the high auto prices cause consumers to spend more on automobiles, they would have less income to spend on other things. Consumers would be forced to cut back their spending in other areas. The demand for other products, the consumption of which must now be forgone as a result of the increase in expenditures on automobiles, would decline. Market adjustments would place downward pressure on prices in these areas.

Clearly, neither of these secondary effects would trigger an inflationary spiral. In fact, quite the opposite is true. Both (purchasing fewer automobiles and increasing expenditures on automobiles) would place downward pressure on costs and prices outside of the automobile industry, which would, at least partially, offset the impact of higher automobile prices on the general price level. Once we consider the secondary effects, there is no reason to expect that an increase in the wages of automobile or other unionized workers would trigger a sustained increase in the general price level.[12]

UNIONISM IN OTHER COUNTRIES

Exhibit 1 in the "Myths of Economics" feature presented data on the level of unionism for several Western industrial economies. The data illustrate that union workers comprise a larger share of the labor force in other major industrial countries than they do in the United States. In 1989, nearly half of the wage and salary workers in Italy and slightly more than two-fifths in the United Kingdom were union members. Approximately one-third of the work force of Australia, Canada, and Germany was unionized. Except for France, the degree of unionization in the late 1980s was substantially greater in other major industrial countries than in the United States.

We must be cautious, however, in our interpretation of the international data on unionism. The role of unions varies substantially among countries. In Europe, unions are often more closely tied to a political party and are more heavily involved in political activities than unions in the United States. In contrast, unions are less political and more directly involved with the firm's personnel policies in Japan. Approximately 90 percent of the union members in Japan belong to an enterprise or "company union," a type of organization that has been illegal in the United States since the passage of the Wagner Act in 1935. These variations in the role of unions contribute to the substantial differences in union membership among countries.

UNIONS AND THE NATURE OF THE WORKPLACE

If one talks to any worker long enough, and candidly enough, one discovers that his loyalty to the union is not simply economic. One may even be able to show him that, on a

---

[12]For an in-depth analysis of the impact of unions on inflation, see Daniel J. Mitchell, *Unions, Wages, and Inflation* (Washington, DC: Brookings Institution, 1980).

strictly cost-benefit analysis, measuring income lost from strikes and jobs lost as a result of contract terms, the cumulative economic benefits are delusions. It won't matter. In the end, he will tell you, the union is the only institution that ensures and protects his "dignity" as a worker.

IRVING KRISTOL[13]

Economists generally focus on wages and employment when discussing the impact of unions. However, unions also exert important effects on the operation of the workplace and the structure of compensation. When evaluating the overall contribution and significance of unions, the following points should also be considered.

1. Unions have played a central role in the development of contractual or formal rules and procedures that govern promotions, raises, layoffs, terminations, and other aspects of the relationship between employers and employees. In essence, unions have established a system of "industrial jurisprudence" that protects workers against arbitrary actions by a supervisor or management representative. Labor contracts define a worker's rights and provide the worker with a series of industrial appeal courts. Specifically, a worker cannot be fired without good cause, which must be proved to the satisfaction of his or her union representative. Actions the worker considers arbitrary or unfair can be taken to a shop steward, appealed through labor-management channels, and eventually brought to an objective arbitrator. Production at multimillion-dollar plants has been brought to a halt because a single worker's rights, as specified by the collective-bargaining agreement, were violated. In addition, these contractual procedures provide employers with a strong incentive to pay attention to the complaints of workers and to treat them with dignity.

The contribution of unions in this area may also enhance employer-employee relations in a nonunion setting. Many employers are anxious to avoid the time-consuming procedures and inflexible rules that often accompany collective-bargaining agreements. One of the best ways of doing that is to establish a positive work environment and open lines of communication with employees. Put another way, positive personnel relations deter union organizing. Thus, concern about possible unionization provides nonunion employers with a strong incentive to treat their employees right.

2. Unions tend to elevate the importance of seniority. In a union setting, employees with more seniority generally have more job security and protection than similar employees in a nonunion setting. Senior employees are also more likely to receive favorable treatment with regard to promotion. As a result of this emphasis on seniority, the managers of unionized firms generally have less opportunity for the subjective evaluation of employees than their nonunion counterparts. The greater weight given to seniority in the determination of wages in a union environment tends to reduce wage variation among workers. Consequently, the dispersion of wages among workers in union plants is generally less than the dispersion in nonunion plants.

3. In unionized firms, fringe benefits usually comprise a larger component of the total compensation package than is true for nonunion firms. Studies indicate that the fringe benefits of union employees—particularly deferred benefits for pensions and life, accident, and health insurance—exceed the benefits of nonunion employees with similar pay rates. Senior union members are often more active and in positions of

---

[13]Irving Kristol, "Understanding Trade Unionism," *The Wall Street Journal* (October 23, 1978). Reprinted with permission of *The Wall Street Journal.*

greater influence within the union than their younger counterparts. The higher pension and health benefits and greater protection against layoffs will also be particularly attractive to union members with substantial amounts of seniority.

4. Unions tend to reduce the turnover rate of employees. Union employees are less likely to quit than their nonunion counterparts. This may partially reflect the union wage premium. But it may also reflect other factors. Freeman and Medoff argue that unions provide employees with a "collective voice" through which they can communicate their problems and grievances to management.[14] This collective voice provides employees an alternative to quitting as a way of sending a message to management. The closer relationship between seniority and employee benefits (for example, pension benefits and job protection) in the unionized sector also reduces the incentive of employees to quit. These factors increase the workforce stability of unionized firms relative to their nonunion counterpart. In turn, the greater stability reduces the firm's recruitment, hiring, and training costs. However, the more rigid system may also reduce the firm's ability to establish a close relationship between employee productivity and wage rates. Therefore, on balance, it is difficult to determine the impact of the unionized wage structure on the firm's costs.

Unions have played a central role in the shaping of the current work environment in both the union and nonunion sectors. Their role in the establishment of the governance system between employers and employees has been particularly important. In fact, many would argue that these nonwage effects of unions are even more important than their role in the determination of wage rates.

LOOKING AHEAD

In the last four chapters we have analyzed markets for human and physical resources. Wages, prices, and employment levels in these markets determine our personal incomes. The next chapter will focus on the distribution of income among individuals.

CHAPTER SUMMARY

1. Union membership as a share of the nonagricultural labor force has fluctuated substantially during the last 80 years. During the 1910–1935 period, union workers comprised between 12 percent and 18 percent of the nonfarm labor force. Unionization increased rapidly during the 1935–1945 period, soaring to one-third of the nonfarm work force. Since the mid-1950s, union membership has waned. In 1992 only one in six nonfarm workers was a union member.

2. The strike is a major source of union power. A strike can cause the employer to lose sales while incurring continuing fixed costs. The threat of a strike, particularly when inventories are low, is an inducement for the employer to consent to the union's terms.

3. A strike is also costly to employees. Strike funds are usually inadequate to deal with a prolonged strike. The loss of just a few paychecks can impose extreme hardship on most families. The potential cost o a strike to both union and management provides each with an incentive to bargain seriously to avoid a work stoppage.

4. Agreement on most collective-bargaining contracts is reached without a work stoppage. During the last three decades, the number of hours lost due to strikes is approximately one-tenth of one percent of the total work time—and the proportion of work time lost due to strikes has been declining.

5. There are three basic methods a union can use to increase the wages of its members: (a) restrict the supply of competitive inputs, including nonunion workers; (b) apply bargaining power enforced by a strike or threat of one; and (c) increase the demand for the labor service of union members.

---

[14]Richard B. Freeman and James L. Medoff, *What Do Unions Do?* (New York: Basic Books, 1984).

6. When a large number of employers compete in the market for labor services, each employer will have to pay the market wage rate to keep employees from shifting to higher-wage alternatives. However, when monopsony is present, the single purchaser of labor may be able to profit by restricting employment and paying a wage rate that is less than the marginal revenue generated by the labor. Under these circumstances, a wage floor established by a union can result in both higher wages and increased employment.

7. If a union is going to increase the wages of its members without experiencing a significant reduction in employment, the demand for union labor must be inelastic. The strength of a union is enhanced if (a) there is an absence of good substitutes for the services of union employees, (b) the demand for the product produced by the union labor is highly inelastic, (c) the union labor input is a small share of the total cost of production, and/or (d) the supply of available substitutes is highly inelastic. An absence of these conditions weakens the power of the union.

8. Studies suggest that the wage premium of union members relative to similar nonunion workers increased during the 1970s, but declined during the 1980s. Most researchers placed the union-nonunion wage differential in the 13 percent to 17 percent range in the early 1990s, down from approximately 20 percent in 1980.

9. Recent research indicates that the profitability of unionized firms is lower than the profitability of nonunion firms. Responding to the lower profitability rates, investment expenditures for fixed structures, research, and development have tended to flow into the nonunion sector and away from the unionized sector. As a result, employment in the unionized sector has declined, particularly in industries where the union wage premium is large.

10. Union workers are a substantially larger proportion of the work force in other industrial countries than they are in the United States. Since the role of unions varies among countries, this factor may contribute to the variation in the level of unionism among countries.

11. Even though unions have increased the average wage of their members, there is no indication that they have either increased the average wage of all workers or increased the share of national income going to labor (human capital rather than physical capital). Even though union membership rose sharply during the 1935–1955 period and declined sharply between 1975 and 1992, the share of national income going to labor (human capital) was virtually constant throughout the entire period. The real wages of workers are a reflection of their productivity rather than the share of the work force that is unionized.

Thus, there is no relationship between the unionization of the labor force and real wages across countries.

12. An increase in the wages of union members will either reduce expenditures on goods produced by nonunion labor or increase the supply of nonunion labor. In either case, the secondary effects of higher union wages will tend to reduce prices in the nonunion sector. Thus, there is no reason to believe that unions cause sustained increases in the general price level (inflation).

13. Unions have played a central role in the development of the current system of industrial jurisprudence which governs the relationship between employers and employees. Many think that the positive role of unions in this area is as important, if not more important, than their role in the determination of wage rates.

CRITICAL-ANALYSIS QUESTIONS

1. Assume that the primary objective of a union is to raise wages.
   a. Discuss the conditions that will help the union achieve this objective.
   b. Why might a union be unable to meet its goal?

*2. Suppose that Florida migrant workers are effectively unionized. What will the impact be of the unionization on (a) the price of Florida oranges, (b) the profits of Florida fruit growers in the short run and in the long run, (c) the mechanization of the fruit-picking industry, and (d) the employment of migrant farm workers?

*3. Unions in the North have been vigorously involved in efforts to organize lower-wage workers in the South. Union leaders often express their compassion for the low-money-wage Southern workers. Can you think of a reason, other than compassion, for Northern union leaders' (and workers') interest in having the higher union scale extended to the South? Explain.

4. "Unions cannot repeal the law of demand; they cannot have both high wages and high employment. The more successful they are at raising wages above competitive levels, the smaller the number of unionized employees."
   a. Evaluate this view.
   b. Does the success of unions at enlarging their wage premium tend to undermine their growth? Why or why not?

5. Evaluate the following statements.
   a. "An increase in the price of steel will be passed along to consumers in the form of higher prices for automobiles, homes, appliances, and other products made with steel." Do you agree or disagree?

---

*Asterisk denotes questions for which answers are given in Appendix C.

b. "An increase in the price of craft-union labor will be passed along to consumers in the form of higher prices of homes, repair and installation services, appliances, and other products that require craft-union labor." Do you agree or disagree?

c. Are the interests of labor unions in conflict primarily with the interests of union employers? Explain.

6. "The purpose of unions is to push the wage rate above the competitive level. By their very nature, they are monopolists. Therefore, they will necessarily cause resources to be misallocated." Do you agree or disagree? Explain.

*7. "If a union is unable to organize all the major firms in an industry, it is unlikely to exert a major impact on the wages of union members." Indicate why you either agree or disagree.

8. The Retail Clerks Union has organized approximately one-third of the department stores in a large metropolitan area. Do you think the union will be able to significantly increase the wages of its members? Explain.

*9. "When an industry is highly unionized, higher labor costs will reduce industry profitability. Unions benefit workers at the expense of capitalists." True or false?

*10. "Unions provide the only protection available to working men and women. Without unions, employers would be able to pay workers whatever they wanted." True or false?

11. Suppose that the United Automobile Workers (UAW) is able to substantially increase wages in the auto industry. What impact will the higher wages in the auto industry have on the following:

a. Wages of nonunion workers outside of the automobile industry.

b. Price of automobiles made by the UAW.

c. Demand for foreign-produced automobiles.

d. Profitability of U.S. automobile manufacturers.

*12. Even though the wage scale of union members is substantially greater than the minimum wage, unions have generally been at the forefront of those lobbying for higher minimum rates. Why do you think unions fight so hard for a higher minimum wage?

*13. Suppose that Congress was considering the following revenue measures: (1) a 10-cent-per-gallon increase in the gasoline tax or (b) an increase in the tariff (tax) on imported automobiles that would raise an equivalent amount of revenue. Which of the two options would the United Auto Workers be most likely to favor? Which would American automobile manufacturers be most likely to favor? Explain.

14. "Unions provide workers with protection against the greed of employers." Evaluate this statement. Be sure to consider the following questions:

a. With whom do union workers compete?

b. When union workers restrict entry into a market, whom are they trying to keep out?

*15. A survey of firms in your local labor market reveals that the average hourly wage rate of unionized production workers is $1.50 higher than the average wage rate of nonunion production workers. Does this indicate that unionization increases the wage rates of workers in your area by $1.50? Why or why not?

16. Are the wages of union members determined by the bargaining skill of union officials? Do market conditions influence the wages of unionized employees? Discuss.

17. What are the major forces that influence the ability of a union to increase the wages of the employees it represents? Why are some unions able to attain higher wages for members than others? Explain.

---

*Asterisk denotes questions for which answers are given in Appendix C.

CHAPTER TWENTY-SEVEN

INCOME INEQUALITY
AND POVERTY

*All animals are equal, but some animals are more equal
than others.*

GEORGE ORWELL[1]

CHAPTER FOCUS

■ *How much income inequality is there in the United
States?*
■ *What are the major factors that influence the
distribution of income?*
■ *Why has income inequality increased in recent years
in the United States?*
■ *How does the degree of income inequality in the
United States compare with that of other countries?*
■ *How much income mobility is there in the United
States—do the rich remain rich while the poor remain
poor?*
■ *What are the characteristics of the poor? Have they
changed in recent decades?*
■ *Have income transfers reduced the poverty rate?*

[1]George Orwell, *Animal Farm* (New York: Harcourt Brace and
Company, 1946), p. 112.

I n a market economy, people have a strong incentive to produce goods and generate income. As we have explained, the personal income of market participants is determined by their productivity: those who use their human and physical resources to produce a lot of things that are highly valued by others will therefore have very high incomes. The close link between personal prosperity and productivity provides market participants with a strong incentive to work, use their resources productively, and find better ways to do things.

With markets, there is no central distributing agency that carves up the economic pie and allocates slices to various individuals. Rather, the income of each individual is received from others in exchange for productive services or as a gift. In a market economy, returns to work effort are by far the largest contributor to income—more than 80 percent of national income in the United States, for example, comes in return for work performed. But people differ with regard to their productive abilities, opportunities, preferences, and intestinal fortitude. Some will be able to hit a baseball, perform a rock concert, design a computer, or operate a restaurant so effectively that people will pay millions to consume the product or service that they supply. There will be others with disabilities and/or few skills who may be unable even to support themselves. Income from physical capital is less than 20 percent of total income. Like the capability for work, however, ownership of physical capital and income derived from it are unequally distributed. When markets are used to allocate resources, income inequality will result.

There is substantial income variation in all societies. Substituting politics and central planning for markets does not eliminate economic inequality. Efforts to reduce income differences also reduce the productive incentives provided by those differences. Nonetheless, most of us are troubled by the extremes of inequality—extravagant luxury on the one hand and grinding poverty on the other. How much inequality is there in a market economy such as the United States? Do the same families continually enjoy high incomes, while those in poverty are unable to escape that condition? How have income-transfer programs designed to reduce poverty influenced the distribution of income and the welfare of the poor? This chapter focuses on these questions and related issues.

INCOME INEQUALITY IN UNITED STATES

Money income is only one component of economic well-being. Such factors as leisure, noncash transfer benefits, the nonpecuniary advantages and disadvantages of a job, and the expected stability of future income are also determinants of economic welfare. Nevertheless, since money income represents command over market goods and services, it is highly significant. Moreover, it is readily observable. Consequently, it is the most widely used measure of economic well-being and the degree of inequality prevailing in society.

Exhibit 27–1 indicates the share of *before-tax* annual money income received by quintile—that is, each fifth of families, ranked from the lowest to the highest. If there were total equality of annual income, each quintile of the population would have received 20 percent of the aggregate income. Clearly, that is not the case. In 1992 the bottom 20 percent of family income recipients received 4.4 percent of the

EXHIBIT 27-1

INEQUALITY IN MONEY INCOME OF FAMILIES
DURING SELECTED YEARS, 1935–1992

	PERCENTAGE OF AGGREGATE MONEY INCOME RECEIVED BY:				
BEFORE TAXES	LOWEST 20 PERCENT OF RECIPIENTS	SECOND QUINTILE	THIRD QUINTILE	FOURTH QUINTILE	TOP 20 PERCENT OF RECIPIENTS
1935–1936	4.1	9.2	14.1	20.9	51.7
1950	4.5	12.0	17.4	23.4	42.7
1960	4.8	12.2	17.8	24.0	41.3
1970	5.4	12.2	17.6	23.8	40.9
1980	5.2	11.5	17.5	24.3	41.5
1985	4.7	10.9	16.8	24.1	43.5
1990	4.6	10.8	16.6	23.8	44.3
1992	4.4	10.5	16.5	24.0	44.6
AFTER TAXES AND TRANSFERS					
1990	6.5	11.2	16.1	23.2	43.0

Source: Bureau of the Census, *Current Population Reports*, Series P-60, No. 167, Table 10; No. 168, Table 6; No. 180, Table B-7; and *Economic Report of the President, 1992* (Washington DC: U.S. Government Printing Office, 1992), Table 4–2.

total before-tax money income. At the other end of the spectrum, the 20 percent of families with the highest annual incomes received 44.6 percent of the total money income in 1992. The top quintile of income recipients thus received ten times as much of the before-tax money income as the bottom quintile.

As Exhibit 27–1 illustrates, there was a substantial reduction in income inequality between the mid-1930s and 1950. In 1950 the top quintile of recipients received 42.7 percent of the aggregate money income, down from 51.7 percent in the mid-1930s. Simultaneously, the income shares of the other quintile groupings increased during the 1935–1950 period. The trend toward less income inequality among families continued, albeit at a slower pace, during the 1950s and 1960s. By 1970, the income share earned by the bottom 20 percent of recipients had risen to 5.4 percent, up from 4.5 percent in 1950. For the top quintile, the income share declined from 42.7 percent in 1950 to 40.9 percent in 1970.

Since 1970 the trend toward income equality has reversed. The income share of the lowest quintile of income recipients fell to 4.4 percent in 1992, well below the 1970 figure. Simultaneously, the income share received by the top quintile of earners rose from 40.9 percent in 1970 to 44.6 percent in 1992. Because of this trend reversal during the 1970s and 1980s, the income shares received by each quintile grouping were approximately the same in 1992 as they were in 1950.

Two points emerge from Exhibit 27–1. First, there is a great deal of inequality in annual income in the United States. Second, after four decades of movement toward greater equality in family income, the trend reversed, and inequality has increased since 1970.

A CLOSER LOOK AT FACTORS INFLUENCING INCOME DISTRIBUTION

How meaningful are the data of Exhibit 27–1? If all families were similar except in the amount of income received, the use of annual income data as an index of inequality would be more defensible. However, the fact is that the aggregate data lump together (1) small and large families, (2) prime-age earners and elderly retirees, (3) multi-earner families and families without any current earners, and (4) husband-wife families and single-parent families.

Consider just one factor: the impact of age and the pattern of lifetime income. Typically, the annual income of young people is low, particularly if they are going to school or acquiring training. Many persons under 25 years of age studying to be lawyers, doctors, engineers, and economists will have a low annual income during this phase of their life. But this does not mean they are poor, at least not in the usual sense. After completing their formal education and acquiring work experience, such individuals move into their prime working years, when annual income is generally quite high, particularly for families in which both husband and wife work. Remember, though, that this is also a time period when families are purchasing houses and providing for children. Consequently, all things considered, annual income during the prime working years may overstate the economic well-being of most households. Finally, there is the retirement phase, characterized by less work, more leisure, and smaller family size. Even families who are quite well off tend to experience income well below the average for the entire population during the retirement phase. Given the life cycle of income, lumping together families of different ages (phases of their life cycle earnings) would result in substantial inequality in the *annual income* figures even if incomes over a lifetime were approximately equal.

Exhibit 27–2 highlights major differences between high- and low-income families that underlie the distributional data of Exhibit 27–1. The typical high-income family (top 20 percent) is headed by a well-educated person in the prime working-age phase of life whose income is supplemented with the earnings of other family members, particularly working spouses. In contrast, persons with little education, nonworking retirees, younger workers (under age 35), and single-parent families are substantially overrepresented among low-income families (bottom 20 percent of income recipients). The mean number of years of schooling in 1992 for the household heads of high-income families was 14.7 years, compared with only 10.5 years for heads of families with low annual incomes. Seventy-nine percent of the high-income families had household heads in the prime working-age category (age 35 to 64), compared with only 41 percent of the low-income families. Only one parent was present in 50 percent of the low-income families, whereas 94 percent of the high-income group were husband-wife families. Contrary to the views of some, high-income families are larger than low-income families. In 1992 there were 3.39 persons per family in the top income quintile, compared to only 2.90 family members among the bottom quintile of income recipients.

Source: U.S. Department of
Commerce, *Money Income of
Households, Families, and Persons in
the United States: 1992* (Washington,
DC: U.S. Government Printing
Office, 1993).

EXHIBIT 27–2

DIFFERING CHARACTERISTICS OF HIGH- AND LOW-INCOME FAMILIES, 1992

	BOTTOM 20 PERCENT OF INCOME RECIPIENTS	TOP 20 PERCENT OF INCOME RECIPIENTS
Mean years of schooling (household head)	10.5	14.7
Age of household head (percent distribution)		
Under 35	36	13
35–64	41	79
65 and over	23	8
Family status		
Married-couple family (percent of total)	50	94
Single-parent family (percent of total)	50	6
Persons per family	2.90	3.39
Earners per family	.79	2.25
Percent of married-couple families in which wife works	28	79
Percent of total weeks worked supplied by group	7	32

There was a striking difference in the work time between low- and high-income families. No doubt, much of this difference reflected factors such as family size, age, working spouses, and the incidence of husband-wife families. In high-income families, the average number of workers per family was 2.25, compared with .79 for low-income families. In 79 percent of the high-income families both spouses were working, compared with only 28 percent for low-income married families.

The top 20 percent of income recipients contributed 32 percent of the total number of weeks worked, while the low-income group contributed only 7 percent of the total work time. Thus, high-income families worked 4.6 times as many weeks as low-income families and earned almost 10 times as much income. This implies that the earnings per week worked of the top income recipients were only slightly greater than twice the earnings per week worked of the low-income recipients. Clearly, differences in the amount of time worked were a major factor contributing to the income inequality of Exhibit 27–1.

In summary, Exhibit 27–2 sheds substantial light on the distributional data of Exhibit 27–1. The high-income recipients were better educated, more likely to be in their prime working years, and they worked approximately 4.6 times as many weeks as low-income families in 1992. Given these factors, it is not surprising that the top 20 percent of recipients had substantially higher annual incomes than the bottom quintile.

Except for the last row, the income data of Exhibit 27–1 are for money income before taxes and noncash transfers. Low-income households are the primary beneficiaries of noncash transfer programs that provide people with food (food stamps), health care, and housing. Correspondingly, under a system of progressive taxation, taxes take a larger share of income as one's income increases. After taxes and transfers, the bottom quintile of income recipients received 6.5 percent of the aggregate income in 1990, compared to 43 percent for the top quintile of earners. Thus, the top quintile received approximately 6.6 times the annual income of the bottom 20 percent of recipients after taxes and transfers (including noncash transfers), compared with almost 10 times the amount of their income prior to taxes and noncash transfers.

WHY HAS INCOME INEQUALITY INCREASED?

Exhibit 27–1 indicates that there has been an increase in income inequality in the United States during the last couple of decades. Why has the gap between the rich and the poor been growing? The answer to this question is a point of controversy among social scientists. No single factor can be isolated. Research in this area, however, indicates that at least three factors contributed substantially to the recent shift toward greater inequality.

1. The increasing proportion of single-parent and dual-earner families has contributed to the increase in the inequality of family income. The nature of the family and the allocation of work responsibilities within the family have changed dramatically in recent decades. In 1992 slightly more than one-fifth (22 percent) of all families were headed by a single parent, double the figure of the mid-1960s. At the same time, the labor-force participation rate of married women increased from 40 percent in 1970 to nearly 60 percent in 1992.

By way of comparison with the late 1960s and early 1970s, we now have both more single-parent families and more dual-earner families. Both of these changes tend to promote income inequality. Perhaps an example will illustrate why. Consider two hypothetical families, the Smiths and the Browns. In 1970 both were middle-income families with two children and one market worker earning $30,000 (in 1994 dollars). Now consider their 1994 counterparts. The Smiths of 1994 are divorced and one of them, probably Mrs. Smith, is trying to work part-time and take care of the two children. The probability is very high that the single-parent Smith family of 1994 will be in the low-, rather than the middle-, income category. They may well be in the bottom quintile of the income distribution. In contrast, the Browns of 1994 both work outside the home, and each earns $30,000 annually. Given their dual incomes, the Browns are now a high-, rather than a middle-, income family. Along with many other dual-income families (see Exhibit 27–2), the Browns' 1994 family income will probably place them in the top quintile of income recipients.

Even if there were no changes in earnings between skilled and less-skilled workers, the recent changes within the family would enhance income inequality among families and households. More single-parent families like the Smiths increase the number of families with low incomes, while more dual-earner families like the Browns increase the number of high-income families. Both will promote income inequality.

2. *Earnings differentials between skilled and less-skilled workers have increased in recent years, further magnifying income inequality.* In 1970 workers with little education who were willing to work hard, often in a hot and sweaty environment, were able to command high wages. This is less true today. Throughout the 1950s and 1960s, guidance counselors told high school students that a college education was essential for economic success. For a long time, it appeared that they were wrong. As **Exhibit 27–3** shows, in 1974 the annual earnings of men who graduated from college were only 27 percent higher than the earnings of male high school graduates, hardly a huge payoff for the time and cost of a college degree. Since 1974, however, things have changed dramatically. By the mid-1980s, the earnings premium of male college graduates relative to male high school grads had risen to the 50 to 60 percent range, approximately twice the premium of 1974. By 1992, the income premium of male college graduates relative to high school graduates had risen to 70 percent. Similarly, the earnings of women college graduates increased sharply relative to women with only a high school education during the 1974–1992 period. In 1992 women college graduates earned more than twice as much as their counterparts with only a high school education.

Changes in the income of high school dropouts (persons with 9 to 11 years of schooling) relative to high school graduates provide further proof that income differences across skill categories have increased in recent years. While the earnings of high school graduates *declined relative to college graduates* in the late 1970s and

Source: U.S. Commerce Department, *Current Population Reports*, Series P-60, No. 167; *Trends in Income by Selected Characteristics: 1947 to 1988*, Table 50; and *Money Income of Households, Families, and Persons in the United States: 1992*, No. 184, Table 24.

EXHIBIT 27–3

INCREASING EARNINGS DIFFERENCES ACCORDING TO EDUCATIONAL ATTAINMENT

	PERCENT THAT MEDIAN INCOME OF COLLEGE GRADUATES EXCEEDS MEDIAN INCOME OF HIGH SCHOOL GRADUATES		PERCENT THAT MEDIAN INCOME OF HIGH SCHOOL GRADUATES EXCEEDS MEDIAN INCOME OF PERSONS WITH 9 TO 11 YEARS OF SCHOOLING	
YEAR	MALES	FEMALES	MALES	FEMALES
1974	27	54	27	34
1980	35	63	40	39
1984	49	74	50	41
1986	60	93	48	43
1988	53	89	51	55
1990	62	91	44	51
1992	70	105	52	50

early 1980s, they *increased (for both men and women) relative to persons with only 9 to 11 years of schooling* during the same time period (see Exhibit 27–3).

Why have the earnings of persons with more education (and skill) risen relative to those with less education (and skill)? Deregulation of the transport industry and the waning power of unions may have reduced the number of high-wage, blue-collar jobs available to workers with little education. No doubt, international competition has also played an important role here. Increasingly, American workers compete in a global economy. Recent innovations and cost reductions in both communications and transportation provide firms with greater flexibility with regard to location. Firms producing goods that require substantial amounts of low-skill labor are now better able to move to places such as Korea, Taiwan, and Mexico, where low-skill labor is cheaper. As firms using lots of low-skill labor move overseas, both the demand for and earnings of Americans with few skills and little education will decline. In an international setting, the United States will be far more attractive to firms requiring substantial amounts of high-skill, well-educated workers. Thus, the globalization of our economy tends to expand the earnings differences across skill categories in the United States. (Note: Globalization also reduces income inequality worldwide.)

3. As marginal tax rates were reduced during the 1980s, the observed incomes of high-income Americans increased sharply because they had more incentive to earn and less incentive to engage in tax shelter activities. Prior to 1981, high-income Americans confronted top marginal tax rates of up to 70 percent (50 percent on earnings). Such high marginal tax rates encouraged high-income earners to undertake investments and structure their business affairs in a manner that sheltered much of their income from the Internal Revenue Service. As we indicated in Chapter 5 (see Exhibit 5–9), the taxable incomes of the top 10 percent of earners expanded sharply when the top marginal tax rates were reduced to the 30 percent range during the 1980s. Some of this increase in income reflected greater work effort due to the increased incentive to earn. Much of it, however, merely reflected a reduction in tax-shelter activities in response to the lower marginal tax rates. The flip side of the reduction in tax-shelter activities accompanying the lower marginal tax rates of the 1980s was an increase in the visible income of the rich. In essence, after the rate cuts, the earnings of the rich were more readily observable. To the extent this factor contributed to the increase in the measured income of wealthy Americans, the increase in income inequality was more imaginary than real.

INCOME INEQUALITY IN OTHER COUNTRIES

How does income inequality in the United States compare with that in other nations? **Exhibit 27–4** presents a summary of household income data compiled by the World Bank. These data indicate that the degree of income inequality in the United States exceeds that of most other large industrial economies. Among the developed nations, income appears to be most equally distributed in Japan, Sweden, Italy, and Germany (prior to unification). In light of their relatively homogeneous populations—that is, uniformity with respect to race and ethnicity—and welfare-state policies (except for Japan), the lesser degree of inequality in

Source: The World Bank, *World Development Report 1993*, Table 30; and Peter Saunders, Helen Stott, and Garry Hobbes, "Income Inequality in Australia and New Zealand: International Comparisons and Recent Trends," *Review of Income and Wealth*, March 1991, pp. 63–79.

EXHIBIT 27–4

INCOME INEQUALITY AROUND THE WORLD

COUNTRY	YEAR	PERCENTAGE SHARE OF HOUSEHOLD INCOME RECEIVED BY:		
DEVELOPING NATIONS		BOTTOM 20 PERCENT	MIDDLE THREE QUINTILES	TOP 20 PERCENT
Indonesia	1990	8.7	49.0	42.3
India	1989–1990	8.8	49.9	41.3
Ghana	1988–1989	7.0	49.7	44.1
Jamaica	1990	6.0	45.6	49.4
Venezuela	1989	4.8	45.7	49.5
Malaysia	1989	4.6	41.7	53.7
Colombia	1988	4.0	43.0	53.0
Costa Rica	1989	4.0	45.2	50.8
Mexico	1984	4.1	40.0	55.9
Chile	1989	3.7	33.4	62.9
Botswana	1985–1986	1.4	32.2	66.4
Brazil	1989	2.1	30.4	67.5
DEVELOPED NATIONS				
Japan	1979	8.7	53.8	37.5
Sweden	1981	8.0	55.1	36.9
Italy	1986	6.8	52.2	41.0
Germany	1984	6.8	54.5	38.7
New Zealand	1985–1986	5.7	53.5	40.8
Canada	1987	5.7	54.1	40.2
United States	1985	4.7	53.4	41.9
Australia	1985	4.4	53.4	42.2

these countries is not surprising. Among the developed countries for which data are available, only Australia has a similar amount of income inequality as the United States.

The share of income going to the wealthy is usually greater in less developed countries. According to the World Bank study, the top 20 percent of income recipients received 67.5 percent of the aggregate income in Brazil, 66.4 percent in Botswana, 62.9 percent in Chile, 55.9 percent in Mexico, 53.7 percent in Malaysia, and 53 percent in Colombia. Among the developing nations of Exhibit 27–4, only Indonesia, India, and Ghana were marked by a degree of inequality similar to that of developed countries.[2]

---

[2]See Gir S. Gupta and Ram D. Singh, "Income Inequality Across Nations Over Time: How Much and Why," *Southern Economic Journal* 51 (July 1984), pp. 250–257, for an analysis of factors that influence income inequality among countries.

The data of Exhibit 27–4 are not adjusted for either differences across countries in size of households or the demographic composition of the population. In addition, procedures used to make the estimates and the reliability of the data vary across countries. Thus, these data should be interpreted with a degree of caution.

INCOME MOBILITY—DO THE POOR STAY POOR AND THE RICH STAY RICH?

Income mobility

Movement of individuals and families either up or down income-distribution rankings when comparisons are made at two different points in time. When substantial income mobility is present, one's current position will not be a very good indicator as to what one's position will be a few years in the future.

Statistics on the distribution of annual income fail to reveal **income mobility**—the degree of movement across income groupings—and thus they may be misleading. Consider two countries with identical distributions of annual income.[3] In both cases, the annual income of the top quintile of income recipients is eight times greater than the bottom quintile. Now, suppose that in the first country—we will refer to it as Static—the same people are at the top of the income distribution, year after year. Similarly, the poor people of Static remain poor year after year. Static is characterized by an absence of income mobility. In contrast, earners in the second country, which we will call Dynamic, are constantly changing places. Indeed, during every five-year period, each family spends one year in the upper-income quintile, one year in each of the three middle-income quintiles, and one year in the bottom-income quintile. In Dynamic, no one is rich for more than one year (out of each five), and no one is poor for more than a year. Obviously, the degree of economic inequality in Static is vastly different from that in Dynamic. You would not know it, though, by looking at their identical annual income distributions.

The contrast between Static and Dynamic indicates why it is important to consider income mobility when addressing the issue of economic inequality. Until recently, detailed data on income mobility were sparse. Fortunately, this situation is changing, primarily as the result of a group of researchers at the University of Michigan's Survey Research Center. Under the direction of James Morgan and Greg Duncan, the center collects detailed socioeconomic data on a representative sample of the U.S. population and tracks the same individuals and their families each year.[4] With these data, researchers are now able to see how income and other indicators of economic status change with time.

Isabel V. Sawhill and Mark Condon of the Urban Institute used the Michigan panel data to study the income mobility between 1977 and 1986 for families headed by a person 25 to 54 years old.[5] **Exhibit 27–5** summarizes their major

---

[3]The authors are indebted to Mark Lilla, from whom this illustrative method was drawn. See Mark Lilla, "Why the 'Income Distribution' Is So Misleading," *The Public Interest* 77 (Fall 1984), pp. 63–76.

[4]Greg J. Duncan et al., *Years of Poverty, Years of Plenty: The Changing Fortunes of American Workers and Families* (Ann Arbor: Institute for Social Research, University of Michigan, 1984). Also see Bradley R. Schiller, "Relative Earnings Mobility in the United States, " *American Economic Review* 67, no 5 (1977), pp. 926–939, for an earlier pioneer study of income mobility.

[5]Isabel Sawhill and Mark Condon, "Is U.S. Income Inequality Really Growing," *Policy Bites* (Washington DC: Urban Institute, June 1992). Also see Richard B. McKenzie, *The "Fortunate Fifth Fallacy,"* (St. Louis: Center for the Study of American Business, May 1992); and Joseph H. Haslag and Lori L. Taylor, "A Look at Long-Term Developments in the Distribution of Income," *Economic Review: Federal Reserve Bank of Dallas*, First Quarter 1993, for additional research on the topic of income mobility.

EXHIBIT 27–5

INCOME MOBILITY—FAMILY INCOME RANKING, 1977 AND 1986

	INCOME STATUS IN 1986				
INCOME STATUS IN 1977	TOP-PAID QUINTILE	NEXT-HIGHEST PAID QUINTILE	MIDDLE QUINTILE	NEXT-LOWEST PAID QUINTILE	LOWEST-PAID QUINTILE
Top-Paid Quintile	50.0	20.5	12.5	11.0	6.0
Next-Highest-Paid Quintile	25.0	34.0	21.5	14.5	5.0
Middle Quintile	13.0	24.0	29.5	19.0	14.5
Next-Lowest-Paid Quintile	8.5	14.5	25.5	30.0	21.5
Lowest-Paid Quintile	4.0	7.0	11.0	25.0	53.0

Note: Sample limited to adults, ages 25–54 in 1977.

Source: Isabel V. Sawhill and Mark Condon, "Is U.S. Income Inequality Really Growing?" *Policy Bites* (Washington, DC: Urban Institute, June 1992).

findings. After grouping families by their income in 1977, the table then shows the relative income position of the families nine years later. For example, the first row indicates the relative income position in 1986 of families who were in the top quintile of income recipients in 1977. Surprisingly, only 50 percent of the Americans who were best off (the top quintile) in 1977 were able to retain the same position nine years later. Almost 30 percent of the top earners in 1977 fell to the bottom three quintiles of the 1986 income distribution. The bottom row of Exhibit 27–5 tracks the experience of families in the lowest-income quintile in 1977. A little more than half (53 percent) of these families remained in the bottom quintile in 1986, while 22 percent were able to move into one of the top three income quintiles.

Apparently, then, many of the families in the top quintile were there because they had a particularly good year. Similarly, many of those in the bottom quintile were there only temporarily, because things went poorly during the year—perhaps a family member lost a job or suffered a business setback. The degree of income inequality among families and individuals over a longer time period—a decade, for example—was less than the income inequality during any given year.

Sawhill and Condon were also able to calculate the changes in the income of the families that started out in each quintile. As **Exhibit 27–6** shows, the average real income (that is, income adjusted for inflation) of families in every quintile increased between 1977 and 1986. Those starting in the bottom quintile, however, had much greater income increases than those starting in any of the higher income brackets. In nine years, their incomes, corrected for inflation, rose by 77 percent. By contrast, the real income of those starting in the highest income quintile rose by

Note: Sample limited to adults, ages 25–54 in 1977.

Source: Isabel V. Sawhill and Mark Condon, "Is U.S. Income Inequality Really Growing?" *Policy Bites* (Washington, DC: Urban Institute, June 1992).

EXHIBIT 27–6

INCOME MOBILITY: HOW 1977 QUINTILES FARED IN 1986

INCOME STATUS IN 1977	AVERAGE FAMILY INCOME (IN 1991 DOLLARS)		
	1977 QUINTILE MEMBERS IN 1977	1977 QUINTILE MEMBERS IN 1986	PERCENT GAIN
Top-Paid Quintile	$92,531	$97,140	5%
Next-Highest-Paid Quintile	57,486	63,314	10
Middle Quintile	43,297	51,796	20
Next-Lowest-Paid Quintile	31,340	43,041	37
Lowest-Paid Quintile	15,873	27,998	77
All Families	$48,101	$56,658	18

only 5 percent. On average, families who were in any quintile in 1977 other than the top quintile had larger percentage income increases than families of any quintile above them.

We noted earlier that since 1970, income inequality has slowly increased in the United States. Those in the highest quintile have received a gradually larger share of national income, and those in the lowest quintile gradually less. These "static" income data suggest, erroneously, that "the rich are getting richer while the poor are getting (relatively) poorer." They conceal the dynamics of the situation. As Exhibit 27–6 illustrates, low-income families have experienced substantial real income gains—more rapid than those of the rich—in recent years. Many of those with incomes in the lowest quintiles have moved up the income ladder into middle and upper income quintiles. As they exit from lower brackets, however, they are replaced by a new group of youthful, inexperienced families with low incomes. Thus, the income inequality during any given year does not change very much, even though the income gains of the poor, on average, are substantially greater than those of the rich.

The data of Exhibits 27–5 and 27–6 focus on changes in the income of families. What can we say about income mobility across generations? If your parents are poor (or wealthy), does it mean you will be poor (or wealthy)? The Michigan panel's data are just now starting to yield information related to this issue. Nearly 1,500 young adults in the study have now left their parents and formed families of their own. Among those who came from families with incomes in the top quintile, 36 percent were able to attain this lofty ranking relative to the other newly formed families. In contrast, 41 percent of the offspring of families in the highest-income quintile fell to the bottom three income quintiles among the newly formed families. Among the offspring of poor families, less than half (44 percent) remained in the bottom quintile among the newly formed families. For middle-income families (the three middle quintiles), offspring were spread almost evenly among the five quintiles of the income distribution for newly formed families.

The data thus indicate that while high-income families are able to influence the economic status of their offspring, they are unable to pass along their lofty income position to most of their children. Similarly, the children of low-income families face disadvantages, but they frequently achieve income levels well above those of their parents. For the three middle-income quintiles, parents fail to exert a systematic impact on the success or failure of their children. Thus, the intergenerational distribution of income approaches perfect mobility among the middle-income groupings.

The findings of the Michigan panel are highly consistent with the findings of Christopher Jencks, based on a less detailed, but much earlier study by the Center for Educational Policy Research at Harvard. Writing in 1972, Jencks stated,

> *Among men born into the most affluent fifth of the population. . . we estimate that less than half will be part of the same elite when they grow up. Of course, it is also true that very few will be in the bottom fifth. Rich parents can at least guarantee their children that much. Yet, if we follow families over several generations, even this will not hold true. Affluent families often have at least one relatively indigent grandparent in their background, and poor families, unless they are black or relatively recent immigrants, have often had at least one prosperous grandparent.*[6]

Our analysis indicates that conclusions based on annual income data must be made with care. The annual data camouflage the fact that many high-income earners had much lower incomes just a few years before, and that many with low current incomes have attained significantly higher incomes previously (and can be expected to do so again in the future). The panel's income data (data that track the income of the same individuals and families over time) indicate that the inequalities observed at a point in time are substantially reduced over time as individuals and families exchange relative economic positions. This income mobility is particularly important across generations. The ability of American parents to pass along their economic status to their children is limited.

POVERTY IN THE UNITED STATES

In an affluent society such as the United States, income inequality and poverty are related issues. Poverty could be defined in strictly relative terms—the bottom one-fifth of all income recipients, for example. However, this definition would not be very helpful, since it would mean that poverty could never decline.

The official definition of poverty in the United States is based on the perceived minimum income necessary to provide food, clothing, shelter, and basic necessities economically for a family. This **poverty threshold income level** varies with family size and composition, and it is adjusted annually for changes in prices. For purposes of determining whether or not income is above the poverty threshold, the official poverty rate considers only money income. (See the "Measures of Economic Activity" feature for additional details on how the poverty rate is measured.)

Poverty threshold income level
The level of money income below which a family is considered to be poor. It differs according to family characteristics (for example, number of family members) and is adjusted when consumer prices change.

---

[6]Excerpt from Christopher Jencks et al., *Inequality: Reassessment of the Effect of Family and Schooling in America* (New York: Basic Books, 1972), p. 216.

How many people are poor? According to the official definition of poverty, there were 37 million poor people and 8 million poor families in 1992. As **Exhibit 27–7** indicates, 14.5 percent of the population and 11.7 percent of the families were officially classified as poor in 1992. During the 1950s and 1960s, the poverty rate declined substantially. By 1970 the official poverty rate for families had fallen to 10.1 percent, down from 18.1 percent in 1960 and 32.0 percent in 1947. During the 1970s this rate changed little. In fact, it was slightly higher in 1980 than it was in 1970. During the early 1980s, the poverty rate rose. Most commentators point to the stagnating economy during 1979–1982 and to cutbacks in transfer programs during the early years of the Reagan administration as the source of the rising poverty rates in the 1980s. As we proceed, we will investigate the link between poverty and income transfers in more detail.

In recent years, the composition of the poverty population has changed substantially. As **Exhibit 27–8** indicates, elderly persons and the working poor formed the core of the poverty population in 1959. Twenty-two percent of the poor families were headed by an elderly person in 1959. Most poor people (70 percent) worked at least some hours during the year. By 1992 the picture had changed dramatically: only 11 percent of the poor families were headed by an elderly person. In recent years, there has been a substantial growth in the proportion of female-headed families and an accompanying decline in the proportion of husband-wife families. Since the poverty rate of female-headed families is several times higher than the rate for husband-wife families (34.9 percent compared with 6.2 percent in 1992), an increase in family instability tends to push the poverty rate upward. In 1992 more than half (53 percent) of the poor families were headed by a female, compared with only 23 percent in 1959. Many of these women were not in the work force. As a result, only 49 percent of the heads of poor households worked at all during 1992, compared with 70 percent who worked in 1959.

The poverty rate of blacks in 1992 was 30.9 percent, compared to 8.9 percent for whites. Nonetheless, 69 percent of the poor people in the United States were

Source: Bureau of the Census, *Current Population Reports,* Series P60–185; Table 7. *Poverty in the United States: 1992,* Table B and *Economic Report of the President 1964,* Table 7.

EXHIBIT 27–7

POVERTY RATE OF PERSONS AND FAMILIES IN THE UNITED STATES, 1947–1992

	POVERTY RATE (PERCENT)	
YEAR	PERSONS	FAMILIES
1947	n.a.	32.0
1960	22.2	18.1
1970	12.6	10.1
1980	13.0	10.3
1985	14.0	11.4
1990	13.5	10.7
1991	14.2	11.5
1992	14.5	11.7

MEASURES OF ECONOMIC ACTIVITY

DETERMINING THE POVERTY RATE

Families and individuals are classified as poor or nonpoor based on the *poverty threshold income level* originally developed by the Social Security Administration (SSA) in 1964. Since consumption survey data indicated that low- and median-income families of three or more persons spent approximately one-third of their income on food, the SSA established the poverty threshold income level at three times the cost of an economical, nutritionally adequate, food plan. A slightly larger multiple was used for smaller families and individuals living alone. The poverty threshold figure varies according to family size, because the food costs vary by family size and composition. It is adjusted annually to account for rising prices. The following chart illustrates how the poverty threshold for a family of four has increased as prices have risen from 1959 to 1993:

1959	$ 2,973
1970	3,968
1980	8,414
1990	13,359
1992	14,343
1993	14,773

Even though the poverty threshold income level is adjusted for prices, it is actually an absolute measure of economic status. As real income increases, the poverty threshold declines relative to the income of the general populace.

The official poverty rate is the number of persons or families living in households with a money income below the poverty threshold as a proportion of the total. When determining a person's or family's income, the official poverty rate considers only money income. Income received in the form of noncash benefits such as food stamps, medical care, and housing subsidies, is completely ignored in the calculation of the official poverty rate.

Since noncash benefits targeted for low-income households have grown rapidly since the late 1960s, the failure of the official poverty rate to count this "income" reduces its accuracy as a measurement tool. To remedy this deficiency, the Bureau of Census has also developed three alternative measures of poverty that include noncash benefits as income. In addition to the official poverty rate, the bureau now publishes annual data for three "adjusted" poverty rates based on alternative methods of accounting for noncash benefits. Economists generally favor the use of the recipient value-adjusted poverty rate. This method values noncash benefits at the equivalent amount of cash income a recipient would be willing to exchange for the noncash benefits. It thus takes into account the possibility that recipients might rather have cash than in-kind benefits.

When the value of noncash benefits is added to money income, the adjusted poverty rate for all age groups is reduced. For example, while the official poverty rate for families was 11.7 percent in 1992, the adjusted poverty rate based on the recipient value method of evaluating food, housing, and medical benefits was only 9.2 percent.

The poverty rate is calculated each year based on a current population survey of nearly 60,000 households designed to reflect the population of the United States. The most comprehensive source for detailed data on this topic is the Bureau of Census annual publication, *Poverty Status in the United States.*

white. Perhaps the most tragic consequence of poverty is its impact on children. During the last two decades, the poverty rate among children has increased substantially. In 1992, 21.1 percent of the children in the United States lived in poverty, up from 14.9 percent in 1976.

TRANSFER PAYMENTS AND POVERTY RATE

In the mid-1960s, it was widely believed that an increase in income transfers directed toward the poor would substantially reduce, if not eliminate, the incidence of poverty. The *1964 Economic Report of the President* (page 77) presented the dominant view:

Source: U.S. Department of Commerce, *Characteristics of the Population Below the Poverty Level: 1982*, Table 5; and *Money Income and Poverty Status in the United States: 1991*, Tables 1, 18, and 19.

EXHIBIT 27-8

CHANGING COMPOSITION OF POOR AND POVERTY RATE OF SELECTED GROUPS: 1959, 1976, AND 1992

	1959	1976	1992
Number of Poor Families (in millions)	8.3	5.3	8.0
Percent of Poor Families Headed by a:			
Female	23	48	53
Black	26	30	31
Elderly person (age 65 and over)	22	14	11
Prime working-age (25–64) person	57	72	76
Person who worked at least some during the year	70	55	49
Poverty Rate			
All families	18.5	10.1	11.7
Married-couple families	15.8	7.2	6.2
Female-headed families	42.6	32.5	34.9
Whites	16.5	8.1	8.9
Blacks	54.9	32.2	30.9
Children (under age 18)	26.9	14.9	21.1

Conquest of poverty is well within our power. About $11 billion [approximately $47 billion measured in 1992 dollars] a year would bring all poor families up to the $3,000 income level [the equivalent of $14,343 in 1992] we have taken to be the minimum for a decent life. The majority of the nation could simply tax themselves enough to provide the necessary income supplements to their less fortunate citizens. The burden—one fifth of the annual defense budget, less than 2 percent of GNP—would certainly not be intolerable.

Following the declaration of "War on Poverty" by the Johnson administration, expenditures on transfer programs increased rapidly. Overall transfers, including those directed toward the elderly, approximately doubled as a proportion of personal income between 1965 and 1975. Including both cash and noncash benefits, the transfers directed toward the poor also grew rapidly. Measured in 1982–1984 dollars, **means-tested income transfers**—those limited to people with incomes below a certain cutoff point—tripled, expanding from $24 billion in 1965 to $70 billion in 1975. *As a proportion of personal income,* means-tested transfers jumped from 1.5 percent in 1965 to 3.0 percent in 1975. During the 1975–1990 period both total transfers and means-tested transfers continued to increase as a percent of personal income, although at a much slower rate than during the

Means-tested income transfers

Transfers that are limited to persons or families with an income below a certain cutoff point. Eligibility is thus dependent on low-income status.

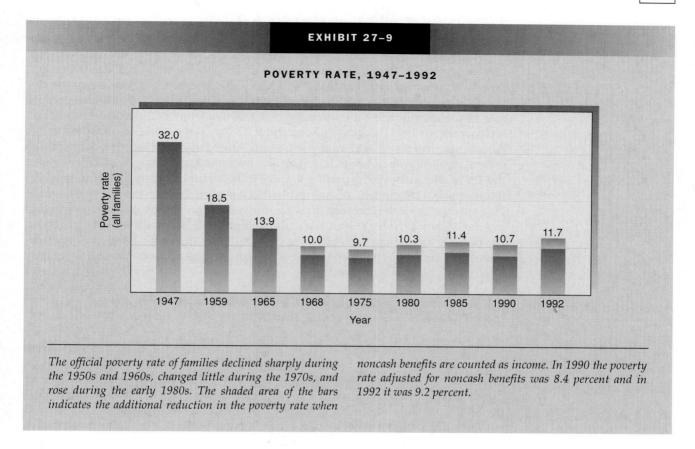

EXHIBIT 27–9

POVERTY RATE, 1947–1992

The official poverty rate of families declined sharply during the 1950s and 1960s, changed little during the 1970s, and rose during the early 1980s. The shaded area of the bars indicates the additional reduction in the poverty rate when noncash benefits are counted as income. In 1990 the poverty rate adjusted for noncash benefits was 8.4 percent and in 1992 it was 9.2 percent.

decade following the 1964 declaration of the War on Poverty. By 1990, means-tested transfers had risen to 3.7 percent of personal income.[7]

Did the expansion in government income transfers reduce the poverty rate as the *1964 Economic Report of the President* anticipated? Antipoverty programs provide both cash and noncash benefits. **Exhibit 27–9** shows the poverty rate with and without the benefits of noncash transfer programs counted as income. Continuing the trend of the post–Second World War era, the official poverty rate fell throughout the 1960s. During the 1970s, however, the rate leveled off. By 1980

---

[7]The following chart indicates the expenditures on both total income transfers and means-tested transfers as a percent of personal income for 1965, 1975, 1985, and 1990. Both cash and in-kind benefits are included in the figures.

	PERCENT OF PERSONAL INCOME	
YEAR	TOTAL TRANSFER PAYMENTS	MEANS-TESTED TRANSFER PAYMENTS
1965	8.5	1.5
1975	17.4	3.0
1985	18.8	3.4
1990	19.6	3.7

The means-tested noncash transfers included food (food stamps, school lunch subsidies, and WIC program), housing, and energy assistance benefits, plus medicaid payments. In addition to these benefits, medicare payments were also included in the total transfer figures. Expenditures on job training and educational subsidies are not included. See *Statistical Abstract of the United States: 1993*, Table 583.

it was 10.3 percent, virtually unchanged from the 1968 rate. By 1992, as we reported earlier, the rate had drifted up to 11.7 percent.

Aggregate poverty-rate data as presented in Exhibit 27–9 conceal an important difference between the experience of the elderly and nonelderly that has largely gone unnoticed. **Exhibit 27–10** highlights this point. The poverty rate for the elderly continued to decline throughout the 1970s. By 1990, the official poverty rate of the elderly had fallen to 6.3 percent, down from 17.0 percent in 1968 and 30.0 percent in 1959 (see part "a" of Exhibit 27–10). The experience of working-age Americans, however, was vastly different. After falling for several decades, the official poverty rate of nonelderly families bottomed in 1968 and rose throughout the 1970s and early 1980s (part "b"). In 1992 the official poverty rate of nonelderly families was 12.4 percent, compared with 9.0 percent in 1968 (and 10.9 percent in 1965, just prior to the increase in expenditures on transfer programs accompanying the War on Poverty). Even after adjustment for the noncash benefits (part "c"), the poverty rate of the nonelderly in the late 1980s and early 1990s was approximately the same as it had been in the 1960s prior to the War on Poverty programs.

FACTORS LIMITING EFFECTIVENESS OF TRANSFER PROGRAMS

Why weren't the income-transfer programs more effective? Clearly, a slowdown in economic growth has retarded progress against poverty. While the employment rate has increased during the last 15 years, real wages have stagnated. As we previously indicated, the real wages of workers with few skills and little education have actually declined in recent years. Social changes have also slowed progress against poverty. The divorce rate, proportion of births to unwed mothers, and the incidence of female-headed households have all increased significantly in recent years, pushing the poverty rate upward.[8]

Nonetheless, the results achieved have been disappointing. After all, per capita income adjusted for inflation in the United States was more than 50 percent greater in 1992 than 1965. Why didn't this growth of income significantly reduce the poverty rate? Many economists believe that the secondary effects accompanying transfer programs provide part of the answer. While government transfers improve the living standards of many poor people, the programs also severely penalize self-improvement efforts by low-income Americans. Some individuals are in poverty because they are victims of debilitating disease, or physical, mental, or emotional disability. For others, however, periods of poverty reflect factors such as loss of job, change in family status, premature termination of schooling (or training), or choice of a high-risk lifestyle. For them, personal choices exert an impact on the incidence and duration of poverty. Transfer programs, in turn, can influence those decisions.

There are three major secondary effects that reduce the ability of transfer programs to uplift the living standards of the poor, particularly the marginally poor.[9]

---

[8]For additional analysis of why antipoverty income transfers have not been more effective, see Lawrence M. Mead, *The New Politics of Poverty: The Nonworking Poor in America* (New York: Basic Books, 1990); and Robert Rector, "Requiem for the War on Poverty," *Policy Review,* Summer 1992.

[9]See James Gwartney and Thomas S. McCaleb, "Have Antipoverty Programs Increased Poverty?" *The Cato Journal* (Spring–Summer 1985), for additional details on this topic.

Source: Derived from Department of Commerce, *Money Income and Poverty Status of Families and Persons in the United States: 1984; Poverty in The United States, 1990 and 1992,* and *Measuring the Effects of Benefits and Taxes on Income and Poverty, 1990 and 1992.* See also James Gwartney and Thomas S. McCaleb, "Have Antipoverty Programs Increased Poverty?" *The Cato Journal* (Spring/Summer, 1985).

EXHIBIT 27–10

CHANGING POVERTY RATES FOR ELDERLY VERSUS NONELDERLY, 1959–1992

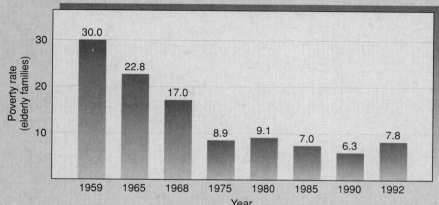

(a) The official poverty rate for elderly families has declined sharply since 1959.

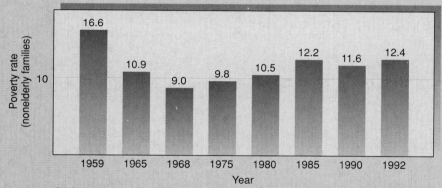

(b) In contrast, the official poverty rate for nonelderly families has been rising since the late 1960s.

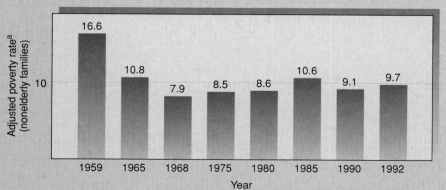

(c) Adjusting for noncash transfers reduces the poverty rate of the nonelderly but it does not alter the basic pattern.

Marginal tax rate

The amount of additional (marginal) earnings that must be paid explicitly in taxes or implicitly in the form of a reduction in income supplements. Since it establishes the fraction of an additional dollar earned that an individual is permitted to keep, it is an important determinant of the incentive to work.

First, high implicit marginal tax rates reduce the incentive of the poor to earn. When the size of the transfer payment is linked to income, an increase in transfers tends to increase the implicit **marginal tax rate** of the poor—the percentage of additional earnings that must be paid explicitly in taxes or implicitly in the form of a reduction in income supplements. As the poor's incomes rise, they qualify for fewer programs, and the size of their transfer income is reduced. Higher earnings, then, mean less transfer income. For example, food-stamp benefits are reduced by $30 for each $100 of monthly earnings up to monthly earnings of $800 for a family of four. The implicit marginal tax rates for some programs are even higher.

The problem is much greater, of course, when the potential benefits from multiple programs are considered. For a family that is eligible for several antipoverty transfer programs, an increase in earned income will reduce benefits and thereby substantially reduce the net increase in income derived from work. In extreme cases, higher earnings may even reduce the individual's net income once the accompanying loss of transfer benefits is considered. These high implicit marginal tax rates reduce the incentive of low-income recipients to earn income. As a result, some portion of the transfer benefits is merely replacement income; that is, it simply replaces income the recipient would have earned in the absence of the transfer. Thus, the net income of recipients increases by less than the amount of the transfer.

Second, when the poor opt out of the labor force because of the high implicit marginal tax rates, declining skills further limit their ability to escape poverty. This is another secondary negative effect. Individuals who do not use their skills for extended periods of time will find it difficult to compete with otherwise similar individuals with continuous labor-force participation. The long-term consequences of an incentive structure that encourages nonwork is even more destructive than the short-term effects. As marginally poor people opt for nonwork, their work record deteriorates. With the passage of time, they become less and less able to support themselves.

Finally, some economists believe that transfer programs may encourage individuals to engage in behavior that can lead to poverty. By partially ensuring against various adversities that often accompany certain choices, the transfer programs reduce the opportunity cost of births by single mothers, marital dissolution, abandonment of children by fathers, dependence on drugs or alcohol, and dropping out of school or the labor force. Indirectly, antipoverty transfer programs, as currently structured, subsidize and thereby encourage choices that often lead to low-income status. This is not the intent of the transfers, but it is nonetheless a secondary effect. In the short run, this secondary effect is probably not very important. Over the longer term, however, the unintended negative consequences may be substantial.

In addition, government antipoverty transfers crowd out private charitable efforts by families, individuals, churches, and civic organizations. When taxes are levied to do more, private individuals and groups will predictably adjust and do less. This, too, erodes the effectiveness of the programs.

Consideration of all these secondary effects makes it easier to understand why increased spending on transfer programs has failed to reduce the poverty rate as much as most people expected.

MECHANICS OF SIMPLE NEGATIVE INCOME TAX

Would it be possible to devise an income transfer system that would avoid the disincentive effects associated with the current system? Some economists, most notably Milton Friedman, believe that the cost of redistribution would be substantially reduced if a simple **negative income tax** were substituted for the current jungle of complex and sometimes conflicting welfare programs.

How would the negative income tax work? To begin with, a base income level would be established. This guaranteed income level would reflect family size, with larger families receiving greater income supplements. As income was earned, the base income supplement would be reduced by a fraction of the family's outside income. This fraction would be the *marginal tax rate*. A family would always face a marginal tax rate of substantially less than 100 percent. (Most plans suggest a 33 or 50 percent rate.) Recipients would always get to keep a significant amount of any additional earnings.

Exhibit 27–11 illustrates the mechanics of a negative income tax. Under this plan, a family of four would be guaranteed an income of $6,000 and a marginal tax rate of 33 percent. As outside income rose, the family's disposable income would increase by two-thirds of the amount earned. For example, initial earnings of $1,500 would increase their disposable income by $1,000, from $6,000 to $7,000. The family would receive more in supplementary income than it would pay in taxes until income reached $18,000, the **break-even point**. At the break-even point, the family's tax bill would equal the income supplement; beyond the break-even point, the family would face a positive tax bill.

Would a negative income tax help the poor without generating major counterproductive side effects? During the 1968–1982 period, the U.S. government funded a number of negative income tax experiments in New Jersey, rural Iowa, Gary (Indiana), Seattle, and Denver. The data generated by these experiments have been extensively analyzed by economists. The results indicate that even a negative income tax transfer program would result in a significant reduction in work effort by the poor. Philip Robins, of the University of Miami, summarizes the findings in the following manner:

Negative income tax
A system of transferring income to the poor whereby a minimum level of income is guaranteed by the provision of income supplements. The supplement is reduced by some fraction (less than 1) of the additional income earned by the family. An increase in earnings, thus, would always cause the disposable income available to the family to rise.

Break-even point
Under a negative income tax plan, the income level at which one neither pays taxes nor receives supplementary income transfers.

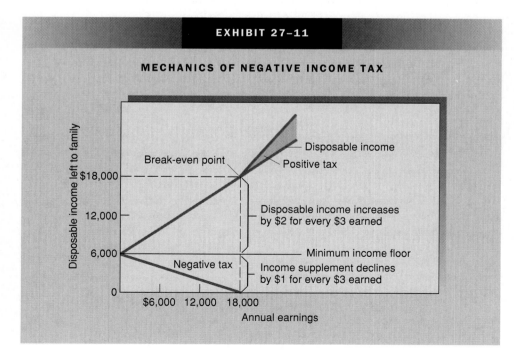

EXHIBIT 27–11

MECHANICS OF NEGATIVE INCOME TAX

Disposable income left to family

Break-even point

$18,000

Disposable income

Positive tax

12,000

Disposable income increases by $2 for every $3 earned

6,000

Minimum income floor

Negative tax

Income supplement declines by $1 for every $3 earned

0

$6,000   12,000   18,000

Annual earnings

The graph illustrates how a negative income tax with a 33 percent marginal tax rate and a minimum income of $6,000 for a family of four would work. If the family had zero earnings during the year, it would receive a $6,000 annual subsidy. As earnings rose, the family's after-tax income would increase by 67 cents (and the subsidy would decline by 33 cents) for every dollar of income earned, until the break-even income level of $18,000 was attained.

The labor supply responses from the four NIT [negative income tax] experiments are remarkably consistent. On average, husbands reduced labor supply by about the equivalent of two weeks of full-time employment. Wives and single female heads reduced labor supply by about the equivalent of three weeks of full-time employment. Youth reduced labor supply by about the equivalent of four weeks of full-time employment. Because women and youth work fewer hours per year than do husbands, their effects are correspondingly much larger in percentage terms. All of these responses may be viewed as those forthcoming from a fairly generous NIT program—one having a guarantee level equal to the poverty level and a tax rate equal to 50 percent.[10]

Once again, the NIT experiments indicate that in economics there are no solutions, only trade-offs.

ESTIMATING COSTS OF REDISTRIBUTION

Estimating the loss of output emanating from redistributive activities is a highly complex issue. Income transfers from the rich to the poor will increase the marginal tax rates (either explicit or implicit) of both. High marginal tax rates reduce the effectiveness of markets to allocate resources efficiently. They also tend to reduce labor supply.

A recent study by Edgar Browning and William Johnson sought to measure the loss of output due to the reduction in the supply of labor associated with the rise in marginal tax rates accompanying income transfers.[11] Browning and Johnson estimated that it would cost $3.49 in terms of lost output to transfer an additional $1 from the top 60 percent to the bottom 40 percent of recipients under a negative income tax plan.

So transferring income from producers to nonproducers is an expensive undertaking. Perhaps a negative income tax might be able to reduce the loss of output compared to the current system. However, both the NIT experiments and the work of Browning and Johnson indicate that it is not a cure-all.

Are redistribution programs worth the cost? Economics cannot answer that question. It can only help identify and quantify the possibilities for redistributing income in relation to the total amount of income available to be distributed—the size of the economic pie. Since social security is the largest single income-redistribution program, the accompanying "Applications in Economics" feature focuses on this important subject.

FAIRNESS—CONCLUDING THOUGHTS

Throughout this chapter, we have presented descriptive data on income inequality and poverty. These data focus our attention on outcomes. When considering the significance of these data, two additional points should be kept in mind. First,

---

[10]Philip K. Robins, "A Comparison of the Labor Supply Findings from Four Negative Income Tax Experiments," *Journal of Human Resources* (Fall 1985), p. 580.

[11]See Edgar K. Browning and William Johnson, "The Trade-off between Equality and Efficiency," *Journal of Political Economy* (April 1984).

SOCIAL SECURITY AND THE INTERGENERATIONAL REDISTRIBUTION OF INCOME

Social security—officially known as Old Age, Survivors, Disability and Health Insurance (OASDHI)—is by far, the largest income-transfer program. It offers protection against the loss of income that usually accompanies old age or death or dismemberment of a breadwinner. Its medicare provisions are designed to offset the heavier health-care expenses often incurred by the elderly and the disabled. In 1991 more than $391 billion was paid out to 41 million recipients under the various provisions of OASDHI.

THE FINANCING OF SOCIAL SECURITY Private pension and insurance programs invest the current premiums of customers in stocks and bonds, which finance the development of real assets. In turn, the assets generate income, which increases the value of the pension funds and provides the resources with which the pension fund (or insurance company) fulfills the future obligations made to its customers. Social security does not follow this saving-and-investment model. Most of the funds flowing into the system are paid out to current retirees and other beneficiaries of the program. In essence, the social security system is an intergenerational income-transfer program. Taxes are collected from the present generation of workers and, for the most part, paid out to current beneficiaries.

The social security system is financed by a payroll tax of 7.65 percent levied on both the employee and the employer. Therefore, the total tax is equal to 15.3 percent of employee earnings. In 1993 the tax applied to all employee earnings up to $57,600. Thus, employees earning $57,600 or more paid $8,813 (counting both employee and employer payments) in social security taxes in 1993.

When the program was initiated in 1935, there were lots of workers and few eligible retirees. As recently as 1950, there were 16 taxpaying workers to finance the benefits of each social security recipient. As the accompanying illustration shows, by 1970 there were only 4 workers per social security recipient, and the present ratio has fallen to 2.9. By the year 2025, the ratio of workers to beneficiaries is expected to drop to just 2. As the number of workers per social security recipient has declined through the years, higher and higher taxes per worker have been required to maintain

EXHIBIT 1

THE DECLINING NUMBER OF WORKERS PER SOCIAL SECURITY RECIPIENT

In 1950, there were 16 workers for each social security beneficiary.

In 1970, there were 4 workers for each social security beneficiary.

In 1993, there were 2.9 workers for each social security beneficiary.

By 2025, there will be just 2 workers for each social security beneficiary.

Result: an increasing burden on each worker whose social security taxes support the program.

a constant level of benefits. Measured in real dollars, the maximum social security tax in 1993 was approximately 6.5 times the amount of 1960.

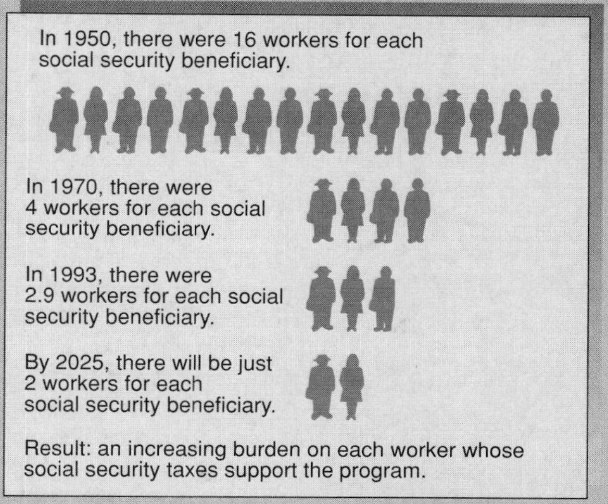

WINNERS AND LOSERS UNDER SOCIAL SECURITY The primary beneficiaries of social security have been persons close to retirement during periods when benefits were increased substantially. These workers paid lower tax rates (or higher rates for only brief periods of time). Yet they received the higher benefits. Today's social security retirees are receiving real benefits of four or five times the amount they paid into the system. The return on the social security taxes they paid generally exceeds 25 percent, much better than they could have done had they invested the funds privately.

In contrast, studies indicate the workers paying for these large benefits will not do nearly as well. For example, those now at age 35 can expect to earn a real rate of return of only 2 or 3 percent on their social security tax dollars, less than what they could earn from personal investments. For two-earner couples just entering the labor force, the expected return from social security taxes is negative.

In summary, social security has been a good deal for current and past retirees. But, it is not a very good deal for younger workers. Workers now entering the labor force would probably be better off if they could invest their tax dollars elsewhere.

FAIRNESS AND SOCIAL SECURITY Fairness is not an economic concept. Nevertheless, economics does reveal information about benefits and costs that allow individuals to make more informed, subjective judgments. Three characteristics of the current social security system are important in this regard:

1. The elderly are no longer the least well-off age group. In the 1950s the income status and poverty rate of the elderly indicated that they were significantly less well-off than the rest of the population. This is no longer the case. Adjusted for family size, the income of the elderly is now higher than for any other age grouping. The wealth holdings (ownership of houses, stocks, bonds, and so on) of the elderly are much higher than for the rest of the population. The official poverty rate of the elderly in 1992 was 7.8 percent, compared to 12.4 percent for nonelderly families and 21.1 percent rate for children (Exhibits 27–8 and 27–10). In contrast with the situation two decades ago, the social security system today transfers income from persons who are, on average, less well-off (current workers) to people who are better off (current retirees).

2. The social security retirement system transfers income from African Americans to whites. This is not the intent of the program. Nevertheless, it is a result. Since African Americans generally begin working earlier and have a lower life expectancy, their tax payments relative to retirement benefits will be substantially greater than for whites. Consider the case of two 20-year-old men, one white and the other black. Given his life expectancy, the average 20-year-old black male who works and pays social security taxes can expect to receive only 1.7 years of retirement benefits before his death. The white male of the same age can expect to draw benefits for 9.0 years, nearly five times longer than his black coworker. Similarly, an African-American woman at age 20 can expect to draw social security retirement benefits for 10.3 years, compared to 15.3 years for her white counterpart.[1] Given the expected low or negative rate of return of youthful

workers in general, the program clearly imposes a major net cost on African Americans in general, and youthful workers in particular.

3. The social security system taxes working wives while providing them little or no additional benefits. The social security system was designed in the 1930s when few wives were in the labor force. Women are thus permitted to draw benefits based on either the earnings of their husband or their personal earnings. Generally, the benefits based on the work history of the husband are greater. When this is the case, the working wife pays taxes into the system and receives no additional retirement benefits in return.

PLANNING FOR THE RETIREMENT OF THE BABY BOOMERS During the 15 years following the Second World War, the birthrate in the United States was very high. Demographers refer to this large group of people born during 1946–1960 as the "baby boom" generation. When these people retire between 2010 and 2025, they will place enormous strain on the social security system. The number of workers per beneficiary is expected to decline to only two by 2025 (refer again to Exhibit 1). With so few workers per beneficiary, the social security system is projected to run a huge deficit during the 2025–2050 period.

Recognizing that the retirement of the baby boom generation will present a serious problem for the social security system, Congress increased social security taxes in 1983 and planned large surpluses for the system during the 1990–2010 period. During the 1990s the system is expected to run $50 to $100 billion surpluses each year. According to plan, these funds would then be used to help finance the deficit of the 2025–2050 period and cushion the tax burden during the latter period when there are so few workers per social security recipient. However, there is a major problem with this strategy: the surplus of the social security system is currently mixed with other government revenues and is being used to finance current government expenditures. There is no mechanism forcing politicians to keep their hands off the social security surplus. And even with the surplus, the federal government

---

[1]These figures are based on 1990 life-expectancy data. See National Center for Policy Analysis, *Social Security and Race* (Dallas: National Center for Policy Analysis, 1987) for additional information on the differential impact of social security on racial groups.

continues to run huge unified budget deficits. No funds are being set aside or invested to cover future benefit payments to social security recipients. Neither is the surplus being used to reduce government borrowing, or lower interest rates and thereby encourage private capital formation.

When the social security system reduces its holdings of government bonds during the system's deficit years (beginning in approximately 2015), other federal taxes will have to be raised (or additional funds borrowed) to finance the redemption of the bonds held by the social security trust fund. The current financing method will not reduce the overall tax burden required to finance the social security deficit during the 2020s and 2030s. It will merely shift some of that tax burden to income and other taxes which will have to be raised in order to finance the redemption of the government bonds held by the social security system.

If the current real social security benefit levels are going to be maintained, staggering increases in taxes will be required. Fifty years from now, projections indicate that it will take 15 percent of national income just to finance this one program, up from 8 percent in the early 1990s.

What might be done to reduce the burden accompanying the retirement of the baby boom generation? Several alternatives have been suggested. First, some advocate that the normal eligibility age for social security retirement be raised with life expectancy. The retirement age is already scheduled to increase to age 67 after the turn of the century. Linking it to life expectancy would provide for additional increases in the eligibility age and thereby reduce the number of retirees per worker.

Second, Senator Patrick Moynihan of New York has introduced legislation that would reduce current social security taxes and eliminate the planned surpluses during the next 15 years. The proponents of this view believe that the lower taxes and the elimination of the social security surplus would leave people with more funds to plan for their own retirement and, once the cover of the social security surplus was removed, force Congress and the president to reduce the size of the current budget deficit.

Finally, some have suggested that individuals be allowed to substitute, at least partially, individual retirement accounts (IRAs) and/or the purchase of government bonds for social security taxes. Essentially, this plan would permit individuals to use their social security tax dollars to acquire a property right to either a private investment fund or a government bond. Should the individual die prior to retirement, the property could be passed on to his or her heirs. As more people opted for this alternative plan over time, the provision of retirement benefits would shift away from social security and toward private investments and government bonds. This plan would also alleviate the adverse impact of the current system on African Americans and working women. Interestingly, the United Kingdom has recently modified its social retirement system in this direction.[2]

---

[2]See Michael D. Hurd, "Research on the Elderly: Economic Status, Retirement, and Consumption and Savings," *Journal of Economic Literature*, June 1990, for an excellent review article on issues related to the social security system.

---

economics does not indicate that one pattern of outcomes (distribution of income) is superior to another. Such a conclusion would involve interpersonal comparisons among individuals—the value judgment that some people (or groups) are more deserving than others. Modern economists are unwilling to make such comparisons.

Second, some would argue that the pattern of economic outcomes is not nearly so important as the process that generates the outcomes. According to this view, the fairness of the outcome should be judged by the fairness of the process, rather than its results—the pattern of the income distribution. Most people who have high income generate those incomes by supplying goods and services that others value more highly than what they have to pay them. If this were not the case, the purchasers of these services would not buy them.

People who earn large incomes almost always provide services that improve the well-being of numerous other people. For example, the entertainers and athletes who earn huge incomes do so because millions of people are willing to pay to see them perform. Business entrepreneurs who succeed in a big way do so by making their products affordable to millions of consumers. The late Sam Walton (founder of Wal-Mart Stores) became the richest man in the United States because he figured out how to manage large inventories more effectively and bring discount prices on brand-name merchandise to small-town America. Later, Bill Gates, the founder and president of Microsoft, rose to the top of the *Forbes* magazine "Wealthiest Four Hundred" list by developing a product that dramatically improved the efficiency and compatibility of desktop computers. Millions of consumers who never heard of either Walton or Gates nonetheless benefited from their entrepreneurial talents and low-priced products. In other words, Walton and Gates made a lot of money because they helped a lot of people.

When income inequality merely reflects voluntary and mutually advantageous exchanges between responsible individuals, what is unfair about this situation? Those who stress the importance of the process would generally conclude that since the process was fair, so, too, was the outcome, even though it resulted in substantial inequality.

CHAPTER SUMMARY

1. In the early 1990s the annual income data, before taxes and transfers, indicated that the bottom 20 percent of families received 4.5 percent of the aggregate income, while the top 20 percent received almost 45 percent.

2. During the 1940s there was a substantial reduction in income inequality in the United States, and the trend toward less inequality continued at a slower rate throughout the 1950s and 1960s. Since 1970, the earlier trend has reversed; there has been an increase in income inequality in the United States during the last two decades.

3. A substantial percentage of the inequality in the annual income distribution reflects differences in age, education, family status, number of earners in the family, and time worked. Young, inexperienced workers, students, and retirees are overrepresented among those with low incomes. Persons in their prime working years are overrepresented among high-income recipients. Persons with high incomes have substantially more years of schooling. Married-couple families with multi-earners are overrepresented among the high-income recipients, while single-parent families with few earners make up a large share of the low-income recipients.

4. Differences in time worked contributed substantially to the inequality of annual income. The income of families in the top earnings quintile was almost 10 times the income of families in the bottom quintile in 1992; the number of weeks worked by members of the top quintile of families was 4.6 times the weeks worked by families in the bottom quintile of income recipients. Thus, the before-tax income *per week worked* of the top earners was only about twice (not 10 times) the income *per week worked* of the low-income families.

5. No single factor can explain the shift toward greater measured income inequality during the 1970s and 1980s in the United States. However, the following three factors contributed to this shift: (a) the increasing number of single-parent and dual-earner families, (b) an increase in earnings differentials between high- and low-skill (and high- and low-education) groups, and (c) reduced tax-shelter activities due to the sharp reduction in marginal tax rates during the 1980s.

6. Among the advanced industrial nations, there is less income inequality in Japan, Sweden, Italy, Germany, and Canada than in the United States. In general, income is distributed more equally in the advanced industrial countries than in less developed nations.

7. In interpreting the significance of the annual income distribution, it is important to recognize that the data camouflage the movement of persons up and down the distribution over time. Many persons with middle and high current income had substantially lower incomes just a few years ago. Similarly, many low-income recipients have attained significantly higher incomes in the past (and many will do so again in the future).

8. There is substantial intergenerational income mobility in the United States. Of the children born to parents who are in the top 20 percent of all income recipients, studies indicate that only 36 percent are able to attain this high-income status themselves. Similarly, more than half of the children of families in the bottom quintile of the income distribution attain a higher relative position when they form their own families.

9. According to the official data, 11.7 percent of the families in the United States were poor in 1992. Those living in poverty were generally younger, less educated, less likely to be working, and more likely to be living in families headed by a single parent than those who were not poor.

10. During the 1965–1975 period, transfer payments—including means-tested transfers—increased quite rapidly in both real dollars and as a share of personal income. As income transfers expanded, the poverty rate of the elderly continued to decline. However, beginning in the late 1960s, the poverty rate for working-age Americans began to rise. Even after adjustment for in-kind food, housing, and medical benefits, the poverty rate of working-age Americans has been rising gradually since the late 1960s.

11. When considering the impact of current income-transfer programs on the poverty status of working-age persons, it is important to recognize the following points:

a. When the transfer benefits of low-income families decline with income, the incentive of the poor to earn a personal income is reduced. Thus, means-tested transfers tend to increase the net income of the poor by less than the amount of the transfer.

b. When high marginal tax rates accompanying transfers induce the poor to opt out of the labor force, their skills depreciate, further limiting their ability to escape poverty.

c. The effectiveness of transfers may also be limited as the result of the tendency of programs designed to protect against adversity to encourage choices that actually increase the occurrence of the adversity.

12. Some economists believe that the cost of redistribution could be substantially lowered if the negative income tax were substituted for current social welfare programs. The major advantages of the negative income tax (relative to present programs) are (a) its simplicity and (b) its provision for the transfer of income to people because they are poor, rather than on the basis of other selective characteristics. However, the results of the negative income tax experiments indicate that it is no cure-all. Even transfers based on a negative income tax would reduce work effort and real output.

13. The social security program is primarily an intergenerational transfer program. At current levels of benefits and taxes, the program is expected to run a substantial surplus during the 1995–2015 period and a huge deficit during the 2025–2050 period as individuals in the post–Second World War baby boom generation go through their "prime working years" and then their "retirement phase." Currently, the program surplus is being used to finance the budget deficit.

CRITICAL-ANALYSIS QUESTIONS

1. Do you think the current distribution of income in the United States is too unequal? Why or why not? What criteria do you think should be used to judge the fairness of the distribution of income?

*2. Is annual money income a good measure of economic status? Is a family with a $50,000 annual income able to purchase twice the quantity of goods and services as a family with $25,000 of annual income? Is the standard of living of the $50,000 family twice as high as the $25,000 family? Discuss.

3. What is income mobility? If there is substantial income mobility in a society, how does this influence the importance of income distribution data?

*4. Consider a table such as Exhibit 27–5 in which the family income of parents is grouped by quintiles down the rows, and that of their offspring is grouped by quintiles across the columns. If there were no intergenerational mobility in this country, what pattern of numbers would be present in the table? If the nation had attained complete equality of opportunity, what pattern of numbers would emerge? Explain.

5. Do individuals have a property right to income they acquire from market transactions? Is it a proper function of government to tax some people in order to provide benefits to others? Why or why not? Should there be any constitutional limitations on the use of the political process to take income from some in order to provide benefits to others? Discuss.

*6. Since income transfers to the poor typically increase the marginal tax rate confronted by the poor, does a $1,000 additional transfer payment necessarily cause the income of poor recipients to rise by $1,000? Why or why not?

*7. Sue is a single parent with two children. She is considering a job that pays $800 per month ($5 per hour). She is currently drawing monthly cash benefits of $300, plus food-stamp benefits of $100, and medicaid benefits valued at $80. If she accepts the job, she will be liable for employment taxes of $56 per month and lose all transfer benefits. What is Sue's implicit marginal tax rate for this job?

8. Between 1965 and 1975, there was a substantial increase in transfer payments, both in real dollars and as a

*Asterisk denotes questions for which answers are given in Appendix C.

share of total income. What impact did the government's expanded tax-transfer role have on the distribution of income and the poverty rate? Discuss.

9. Some argue that taxes exert little effect on people's incentive to earn income. In considering this issue, suppose you were required to pay a tax rate of 50 percent on all money income you earn while in school. Would this affect your employment? How might you minimize the personal effects of this tax?

*10. Transfer payments targeted at the poor make up only a small portion of the total government income transfers. Large income transfers are targeted toward the elderly, farmers, and the unemployed, regardless of their economic condition. Why do you think this is so? Does an expansion in the size of tax-transfer activities reduce income inequality?

11. "Welfare is a classic case of conflicting goals. Low welfare payments continue to leave people in poverty, but high welfare payments attract people to welfare rolls, reduce work incentives, and cause higher rates of unemployment" (quoted from the *There Is No Free Lunch* newsletter).
   a. Evaluate this statement. (Hint: apply the opportunity cost concept.)
   b. Can you think of a plan to resolve the dilemma? Is the dilemma resolvable? Why or why not?

12. Suppose the government decides to increase taxes in order to provide a $2,000 per year real-income supplement to persons aged 65 years and over. Will the real income of the elderly be $2,000 greater in the future than it would have been in the absence of this program? Why or why not?

13. "Means-tested transfer payments reduce the current poverty rate. However, they also create an incentive

structure that discourages self-provision and self-improvement. Thus, they tend to increase the future poverty rate. Welfare programs essentially purchase a lower poverty rate today in exchange for a higher poverty rate in the future." Evaluate this statement.

*14. Under legislation passed in 1983, after-tax social security benefits are reduced as income increases for recipients with incomes above $25,000. Recently, some have advocated that social security benefits be completely eliminated for elderly persons with high incomes. Do you think this is a good idea? Why or why not? If social security benefits are reduced (and perhaps eliminated in some cases) as income increases, how will this influence the incentive of the elderly to save and provide income support for their own retirement? How will the number of low-income elderly be affected?

*15. From the viewpoint of the entire economy, can the benefits of a "pay-as-you-go" social security system be called wealth? Might future retirees treat the benefits as wealth? If so, what will happen to the rate of private saving relative to the saving rate if there were no social security program? (Assume that people consume a fixed fraction of their wealth each year.)

16. Why do you think the social security system is operated by the government? Could a private insurance company establish the same type of plan? Why or why not?

17. "The social security system ensures a minimum income for the elderly, but the system also transfers income from the young to the old, from blacks to whites, and from the relatively poor to the relatively well-to-do." Evaluate this statement.

---

*Asterisk denotes questions for which answers are given in Appendix C.

CHAPTER TWENTY-EIGHT

THE ENVIRONMENT, NATURAL RESOURCES, AND THE FUTURE

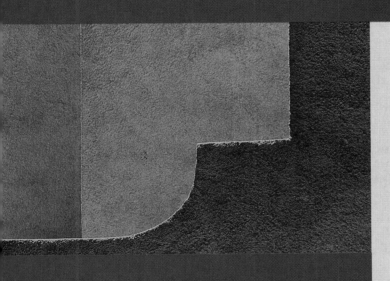

In nearly every case, environmental problems stem from insecure, unenforceable, or nonexistent property rights.

JANE S. SHAW[1]

CHAPTER FOCUS

■ *What does the economic way of thinking have to say about resource markets and environmental decision making?*
■ *Are we in danger of running out of vital natural resources in the future?*
■ *Is economic growth harmful to the environment?*
■ *How do private ownership and competitive markets affect the quality of the environment?*
■ *Can government regulation help protect the quality of the environment?*

---

[1]Jane S. Shaw, "Private Property Rights: Hope for the Environment," *Liberty* 2, no. 2, November 1988, p. 55.

N atural-resource and environmental issues have become increasingly important, especially over the past 30 years. Will there be enough minerals, water, and other natural resources for future generations? Will pollution increase as capital formation and technological improvements lead to greater production of goods and services? What does economics have to say about protecting the environment and using natural resources wisely? This chapter will focus on these questions and related topics.

RESOURCE MARKETS AND THE ENVIRONMENT

For most goods and services, as we saw in earlier chapters, both suppliers and demanders are influenced by the price they pay or receive and by the availability of substitutes. A higher price for one good makes others more attractive as substitutes. If, for example, movie tickets rise in price, then a host of substitutes, such as cable television subscriptions, books, and live concerts become more attractive options for entertainment. The price increase causes fewer movie tickets to be purchased. Similar forces are at work on the supply side, since investors and workers have options as well. For example, if the price of television sets increases, those manufacturers will be able to bid more capital and labor away from other uses, and will supply more televisions at the higher price.

THE CASE OF RESOURCE MARKETS

Are the demand and supply of natural resources shaped by similar influences? For something so basic as water, for example, are good substitutes readily available? The use of water by industry, as illustrated in **Exhibit 28–1,** provides a good example of the extent to which capital, or different production processes, can provide substitution possibilities. When auto makers, steel producers, or oil refineries need water for their production processes, the amount they use will depend on the price they must pay. A higher water price will justify more efficient radiators, or perhaps filtration devices providing for the reuse of water. Some processes use much more water than others, so when water costs are high, producers will tend to avoid using these processes in favor of others requiring less water.

When economists examine markets for water, petroleum products, access to wilderness recreation, and other natural resources, they find that the sensitivity of decision makers to price and cost is similar to that found for other goods and services. Substitutes, it seems, are everywhere. For example, when the price of gasoline rises, users find many ways to use less of it: smaller cars, less distant vacation destinations, fewer shopping trips, and the use of public transportation or carpooling, to name just a few. Users always seem to find ways to achieve their goals while using less of a resource whose price has risen.

Higher prices will also induce resource suppliers to search for more of the commodity resource and recover more of the known deposits. For example, when oil prices increase, wildcatters will search new territories, drillers will dig deeper, and water flooding and other techniques will be used to recover more oil from existing wells. Thus, the quantity supplied of oil—or any other resource—is

EXHIBIT 28–1

HOW WATER "REQUIREMENTS" CAN VARY

PRODUCT OR USER AND UNIT	DRAFT (IN GALLONS)		
	MAXIMUM	TYPICAL	MINIMUM
Steam-electric power (kw-h)	170	80	1.32
Petroleum refining (gallon of crude oil)	44.5	18.3	1.73
Steel (finished ton)	65,000	40,000	1,400
Soaps, edible oils (pound)	7.5	—	1.57
Carbon black (pound)	14	4	0.25
Natural rubber (pound)	6	—	2.54
Butadiene (pound)	305	160	13
Glass containers (ton)	667	—	118
Automobiles (per car)	16,000	—	12,000
Trucks, buses (per unit)	20,000	—	15,000

When the use of water is expensive, people find ways to use less of it. These numbers, all from actual industrial plants, demonstrate the wide variations possible, even within specific industrial use. How much water is needed to generate a unit of electricity? That depends very much on how costly water is, as the table shows. The "need" can vary from 1.32 gallons to 170 gallons. With time, technology can further expand this range of options.

Source: H.E. Hudson and Janet Abu-Lughod, "Water Requirements," *Water for Industry*, Publication No. 45 edited by Jack B. Graham and Meredith F. Burrill, (Washington, DC: American Association for the Advancement of Science, 1956), pp. 19-21.

positively related to price. Similarly, as incomes grow and the demand for access to fly fishing, attractive wooded homesites, and hiking trails in relatively undisturbed natural areas grows too, owners of such land will work to preserve those characteristics that make the land more valuable. When lands are owned or controlled by government, political pressures will tend to move in the same *directions* as market pressures, although the decision process is different.

As in other markets, the responsiveness of producers and users will vary with time. The longer a sharp rise or fall in price persists, the stronger the response will be to the price change. It takes time for both users and suppliers to adjust fully to new market prices by changing the equipment they use, their consumption patterns, and the capital and labor used to produce items whose prices have changed. Product innovation and technological change are among the additional factors that have greater impact over time, both on quantities demanded and on those supplied, in response to a price change.

Resource markets, then, are quite similar to other markets. The quantity of a natural resource demanded will fall and the quantity supplied will rise when its price increases (other things constant). Higher resource prices will increase the incentive of users to conserve on their use of a resource and find substitutes for it. The higher price also brings forth extra production, providing additional supplies. Lower prices have the opposite effects, reducing the quantity supplied of the resource and increasing the quantity demanded.

ECONOMIC PRINCIPLES AND ENVIRONMENTAL DECISIONS

Markets coordinate the choices of people with regard to natural-resource use. But what about environmental decisions, which often are made outside the markets,

APPLICATIONS IN ECONOMICS

PRICES AND QUANTITIES: HOW ENERGY BUYERS RESPOND

Economic theory tells us that the demand for a commodity depends on the price of the commodity, the income of buyers, and the price of both substitutes and complements. The theory is demonstrated clearly in energy markets.

Consumers determine how much electricity, gas, or other energy form is used. For example, in the case of electricity, they choose whether or not to use electric heat and how high to set the thermostat. But they also decide how much aluminum (made with large quantities of electricity) to buy and which producers (those using more electricity per ton of aluminum, or less per ton) to buy from. Higher electricity prices raise aluminum prices relative to the prices of substitute metals and increase costs more significantly for producers using more electricity per ton. Producers using techniques and equipment that conserve more fully on the use of materials that are increasing in price will enjoy a competitive advantage. Thus, even with very little knowledge of how or why electricity prices are rising throughout the economy, consumers make choices that move sales away from the energy form rising fastest in cost, and toward conservation, other energy sources, and other means of satisfying their wants.

How much less will be consumed when the price of an energy form rises? The accompanying table, summarizing the results of several statistical studies, provides some answers in the form of estimated price elasticities. For residential electricity, a 10 percent rise in price would lead to a 2 percent short-run reduction in quantity demanded. The short run here means one year. When buyers have up to 10 years to respond, the long-run elasticity indicates that the same 10 percent price rise would cause a 7 percent decline in residential use of electricity, other factors held constant.

Price elasticities are useful in predicting fuel usage as fuel prices change. However, other factors, such as income and the price of substitutes, will also influence consumption. In addition, we cannot expect the same reaction to a price change from people in different situations. Once auto manufacturers have spent years in researching and developing techniques to save fuel, for example, even a return to the much lower gasoline prices of years past would not bring back the previous level of gas guzzling. Measured elasticities reflect history, but history can never be retraced exactly, even if the path of prices is somehow repeated. Estimated price elasticities are a rough but often useful guide to buyer behavior when prices of an important commodity such as energy change.

PRICE RESPONSIVENESS OF ENERGY FORMS: ESTIMATED PRICE ELASTICITIES OF DEMAND

| | ESTIMATED ELASTICITY[a] | |
FUEL	SHORT RUN	LONG RUN
Residential electricity	0.2	0.7
Residential natural gas	0.1	0.5
Gasoline	0.2	0.7

[a]When income and other factors such as other fuel prices are held constant, the elasticities indicate the ratio of percent change in quantity to the percent change in price causing the quantity change. Each elasticity is actually a negative number, since price and quantity demanded move in opposite directions.

Source: Douglas R. Bohi, *Analyzing Demand Behavior* (Baltimore: Johns Hopkins University Press, 1981), p. 159.

and thus without the benefit of fully priced goods and services? There are relatively few markets for clean air, water purity, and endangered species. As we have previously discussed, the absence of clearly defined and securely enforced property rights and the resulting lack of markets and decision-maker accountability are at the heart of pollution and other externality problems. Can we nevertheless use the economic way of thinking to enhance our understanding of decisions that affect the environment? Let us illustrate the usefulness of some basic economic principles from Chapter 1, in the context of environmental decisions.

1. Incentives matter. One economics professor demonstrated the importance of incentives in environmental decisions by walking into class with a lighted cigarette, taking a puff, then dropping the cigarette on the floor, and grinding it out with his shoe. Then he pointed out that he would never do such a thing in his own living room, where he personally would bear the cost of having to clean up the mess. In fact, he said, he probably would not do it if the building's janitor were watching and likely to voice strong disapproval of the behavior. Further, he said that he would be less likely to grind out the cigarette on a classroom floor if an ashtray were handy—in other words, if he were not required to go to the trouble of finding one. The professor's actions regarding the environment around him thus depended on the incentives given him.

Do incentives matter in the preservation of wildlife? Consider the case of African elephants, which are valuable for their meat and ivory, among other factors. Poachers like to kill the wild elephants illegally, to take the most valuable parts. Poaching is illegal, but the animals in central African nations are not owned by the local residents, who might most easily help prevent poaching. The local residents gain nothing from the presence of the elephants, yet they must endure the loss of crops and water, and even the danger to their children that elephants bring. Many local residents would therefore prefer fewer of them. The control of poaching is consequently weak, and the herds in Central Africa have been declining—almost to the point of extinction.[2]

In southern African nations, however, many elephants are owned privately. Even when the elephants are not owned privately, the residents of the villages near each herd are allowed to share the gains from the human use of elephants, whether from hunting or tourism. These partial private-ownership rights provide local residents with an incentive to help control poaching, and they have been quite effective in doing so. As a result, elephant herds thrive in southern African nations.

As these simple examples demonstrate, when people make decisions affecting the environment, their actions will be guided by expected benefits and opportunity costs, just as they are for other decisions.

2. The value of a good or service is subjective. The fact that values are subjective also bears on environmental decisions. How valuable is a tract of unroaded wilderness land, relative to the same land with roads and campgrounds added to enhance recreation, or the same land developed for high-quality residential use? Individuals will differ dramatically in their evaluations of those alternatives. Some believe that wilderness is the highest and best use for such a tract of land. Others view more intensive recreational use or tastefully planned residential development, where people can be in close contact with the beauty of nature, to be a better use of such land.

Consider another, similar question: Will persons living near a river be willing to vote for sewage plant improvements to help clean up a half-mile stretch of the river, even though that will add an extra $12 per month to their water bill? Again, we can expect people to differ in how much value they place on making a stretch of river a little cleaner. Some will be quite happy to pay the fee, while others will probably object.

Environmental values, like all others, are subjective. Individuals will differ substantially in the value they place on various options for environmental management.

---

[2]See Randy Simmons and Urs Kreuter, "Herd Mentality: Banning Ivory Sales Is No Way to Save the Elephant," *Policy Review* (Fall 1989), pp. 46–49.

3. *Remember secondary effects.* As in other areas of human action, the secondary effects of environmental actions must be considered. For example, when citrus growers use chemical pesticides to protect their fruit against certain insects, the pesticides may impose some danger to consumers if they are not washed completely from the fruit. To avoid such danger to consumers, government agencies control the use of most pesticides and have banned the use of certain compounds. That was the case for DDT, which was banned by the U.S. Environmental Protection Agency in 1972 because it was believed to be a source of human health risk and damage to wild birds. Unfortunately, the ban had unwanted secondary effects. In place of DDT, some other pesticides were used that were more risky to the workers who applied them in the fields.

In other nations, the results were even more tragic when DDT was stopped. In Sri Lanka, for example, where mosquitoes had been controlled by DDT, the incidence of malaria had declined from 2.8 million cases in 1946 to only 110 cases in 1961. After the government of Sri Lanka stopped the use of DDT in the early 1960s, however, the number of malaria cases jumped back up to 2.5 million in 1968–1969.

It is important that environmental decision makers, like those in other policy areas, be alert for secondary effects. This basic economic principle is just as important for environmental decision making as it is in other areas of human action.

We have seen that economic principles apply to decisions people make regarding natural resources and the environment just as they do to other areas of human action. But since markets and easily defended property rights are not always present, especially for air and water quality and other environmental services, observers often worry that as an economy grows, more resources will be used and additional waste will be imposed on the environment. Clearly, this is an extremely important concern. What can economists say about the effects of economic growth on environmental quality? We turn now to examine this important question.

IS ECONOMIC GROWTH HARMFUL TO THE ENVIRONMENT?

The need to choose between economic growth and environmental quality may seem obvious when economic activities affect the quality of our air or water. In the United States, the federal government has been asked to constrain polluters, and, historically, courts have protected the rights of those harmed by pollution, requiring polluters to pay damages, clean up their emissions, and sometimes ordering them to stop the polluting activities. As a result, certain economic activities are made more costly and specific economic outputs are reduced in order to maintain environmental quality. It is not surprising, then, that many people believe a choice must be made between economic growth on the one hand and environmental protection on the other. Yet data from around the world support a more optimistic view.

As we will see, many of the same forces that encourage economic growth, such as market institutions and the acceptance of technological advance, also help to reduce pressures on the environment. In addition, rising incomes foster the willingness and ability to pay for a cleaner, more pleasant environment. While environmental protection often imposes some cost on economic activities, growth can still proceed when the controls are intelligently applied. And growth itself, properly controlled to avoid environmental harms, has important beneficial effects on the environment.

Once people have enough income so that they are not struggling to put food on the table, they become more willing and able to take actions to reduce (or avoid) environmental damage and improve the quality of environment. For example, as incomes have risen in North America, Europe, and other parts of the world, private actions to maintain nature preserves have proliferated. Individuals, firms, and nonprofit groups have established areas for the protection of plant and animal habitats.[3] Profit-seeking firms such as Big Sky of Montana, find it profitable to buy large tracts of mountainous land, far more than they plan to develop, then sell some of the tracts with environmentally protective restrictions. By guaranteeing the pristine quality of the resort with legal restrictions on what every owner can do, they increase the value of the property they sell.

Economic growth generally leads to environmental improvements because people with higher incomes are willing to pay more for environmental quality. Economist Donald Coursey has studied this topic extensively. He finds that in the United States and in other industrial nations, citizens' support for measures to improve environmental quality is highly sensitive to income changes.[4] In economic terms, willingness to pay for environmental measures, such as costly environmental regulations, is highly elastic with respect to income. He estimates that in industrial nations the income elasticity of demand for environmental quality is 2.5. Thus, a 10 percent increase in income leads to a 25 percent increase in citizens' willingness to pay for environmental measures. Similarly, a 10 percent decline in a community's income leads to a 25 percent decline in that community's support for costly environmental measures. According to Coursey, the demand for environmental quality has approximately the same income elasticity as the demand for luxury automobiles like the BMW and Mercedes-Benz.

Technological change is another factor that generally improves the environment. Economic growth and technological change generally accompany each other. The same market processes that encourage growth also encourage technological advances. In the United States, advancing technology was itself cleaning the environment well before major environmental laws were passed.

In a market system, producers using advanced technology can profit by getting a given performance from a smaller amount of a costly resource. **Exhibit 28–2** illustrates this process for producers and users of soft-drink and beer cans. As they sought greater profits, producers found ways to reduce the amount of metal used per can, and also switched to lightweight, recyclable aluminum. As a result, less ore was dug and processed, and less energy was needed to transport both the raw materials and the filled cans, reducing pollution from the use of the cans. Because this search for lower-cost means of producing each marketed service is

---

[3]Chapter 9 of *Environmental Quality, 1984,* the annual report of the President's Council on Environmental Quality, describes a representative sample of these private projects, some of which date back to the last century, to benefit the environment.

[4]Donald Coursey discussed this topic in "The Demand for Environmental Quality," a paper presented January 1993 at the annual meeting of the American Economic Association in Anaheim, California.

By improving their engineering techniques and switching to a thinner can made of lightweight aluminum, producers reduced their use of metal per can by almost 80 percent between 1965 and 1990.

Source: Lynn Scarlett, "Make Your Environment Dirtier—Recycle," *The Wall Street Journal,* January 14, 1991.

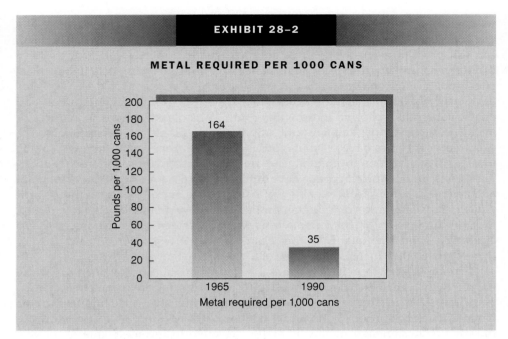

EXHIBIT 28-2

METAL REQUIRED PER 1000 CANS

going on constantly in a market economy, the result is a continuing series of reductions in the emissions of polluting wastes. Partially offsetting this, of course, is the increased quantity of goods and services produced, which, in turn, can also mean more resource use and more pollution, depending on the amount of resource-saving technical progress that accompanies income growth.

Exhibit 28–3 illustrates the general relationship between three types of environmental problems and per capita income, showing that some problems are ameliorated with higher income, others are worsened, and still others are worsened only up to a point, and then improve with still higher levels of economic development. Problems, such as a lack of safe drinking water (part "a") are steadily reduced as income rises. As people become richer, they are more able to reduce waterborne diseases by installing sewers to handle human waste, and by reducing water contamination by animals. Certain pollutants, however, such as particulates in the air (part "b") tend initially to become worse as incomes rise from extremely low levels. But as income levels rise further, heavily used roads are paved and industrial processes become more efficient, emitting smaller amounts of waste. As a result, particulate pollution in the air declines with additional income increases. Especially among developed countries, economic growth most often brings cleaner air and water, along with improvements in several other aspects of environmental quality.

Unfortunately, the amount of solid waste generated normally increases steadily with economic development (part "c"). But proper disposal facilities can minimize the negative effects of that problem also. On balance, richer seems to be environmentally better.[5] One reason lies in the fact that markets and property

---

[5]The *World Development Report, 1992* (New York: World Bank), especially chapters 2 and 3, provides a detailed look at the connection between economic development and environmental quality.

Note: Estimates are based on cross-country regression analysis of data from the 1980s.

Source: World Bank, *World Development Report, 1992*, p. 11.

EXHIBIT 28–3

POLLUTION PROBLEMS AS NATIONAL INCOME RISES

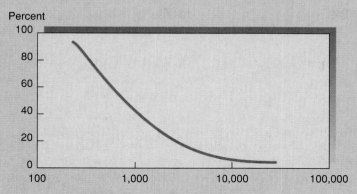

(a) Population without safe water

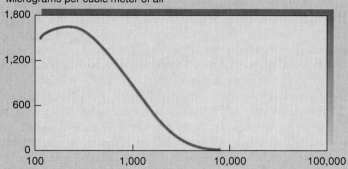

(b) Urban concentration of particulate matter

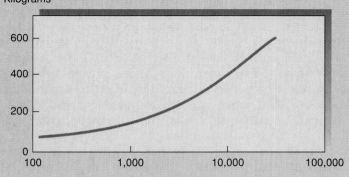

(c) Municipal wastes per capita

rights allow citizens to achieve both growth and environmental protection from identifiable polluters. Without enforceable rights to resources, both goals are more difficult to reach. We turn now to a discussion of how property rights have helped the environment in several nations around the world.

PROPERTY RIGHTS AND THE ENVIRONMENT

When people have open access to forests, pastureland, or fishing grounds, they tend to overuse them. Providing land titles to farmers in Thailand has helped reduce damage to forests. The assignment of property titles to slum dwellers in Bandung, Indonesia, has tripled household investment in sanitation facilities. Providing security of tenure to hill farmers in Kenya has reduced soil erosion. Formalizing community rights to land in Burkina Faso is sharply improving land management. And allocating transferable rights to fishery resources has checked the tendency to overfish in New Zealand.

WORLD BANK[6]

Income growth helps to increase the demand for environmental quality, while technological advances help to lower the cost of reducing resource use. Yet incomes above the poverty level and an understanding of technology are not enough to protect the environment. The recent opening up of Eastern European nations and the Soviet Union exposed widespread environmental disasters. These occurred despite good technical capabilities in those nations and per capita incomes that were well above the world average.

Why did these relatively advanced nations not take better care of their environments? The answer appears to lie in the fact that property rights and market exchange were largely missing. As indicated in the preceding quote from a World Bank report on economic development and the environment, property rights are an important factor influencing environmental quality. The former Soviet Union and the Eastern European nations, in the decades during which they were controlled by socialist governments, refused to allow most resources to be privately owned and declared that most market exchanges were criminal acts. Entrepreneurship of most kinds was declared to be criminal behavior. Production instead was centrally planned. Land and other resources were owned by the state, rather than by individuals.

In a competitive market, the profit motive provides clear incentives to reduce resource usage and waste products. When a firm is privately owned, the personal wealth of the owners is enhanced by effective economizing behavior. For government-operated enterprises, this is much less true. There is no owner (or group of owners) whose wealth is directly affected by economizing behavior (or the lack of it) on the part of the managers of government enterprises. Thus, government-owned firms are less likely than their market counterparts to minimize cost and resource use.

One index of resource conservation is energy use per unit of output. In modern economies, energy constitutes more than half of all the resources utilized.

---

[6]The quoted passage is from *World Development Report, 1992* (New York: World Bank), p. 12.

PROPERTY RIGHTS AND WATER QUALITY

Can property rights protect water quality in rivers and streams that are not privately owned? Just as downwind victims of air pollution damage have successfully sued copper and lead smelter operators in the United States, people whose property is damaged by water pollution can protect their rights against polluters in court. Private ownership of fishing rights in England shows one way that this can happen.

In England the adjacent landowner has title to fishing rights out to the middle of the stream. The fishing right can be rented, leased, or sold. Fishing clubs and owners of country inns are among those who have purchased those rights. Club members and guests of the inns may then have access to fishing there.

Some clubs are exclusive and expensive. The Houghton Club, with fewer than 25 members, owns fishing rights on 17 miles of the Test River, estimated in 1988 to be worth more than $35 million. But fishing rights on an adjacent stretch of the same river, a few hundred yards long, is owned by the Greyhound Inn bed and breakfast. The owner allows two guests (at about $55 each, in 1988), to fish each day. "Rough fishing" (non-trout fishing) is available from clubs organized at local pubs, for perhaps $50 per year. In all cases, access is strictly controlled to eliminate crowding, and the stream banks are generally kept cleared of brush and are well-protected against cattle and other potential sources of pollution and disturbance to the fish.

Historically, as trout fishing became more popular and the rights became more valuable over the years, fishing-rights owners became more serious about protecting them, and more willing to go to court to do so. In 1948, long before the first Earth Day in 1970 and 20 years before the government established authorities to control water pollution, the Anglers' Cooperative Association (ACA) was formed to help clubs and anglers obtain damage awards or court orders to cease polluting activities. The ACA won its first major case in 1951 against two chemical companies and the city of Derby for pumping untreated sewage, hot water, and tar products into the River Derwent. It won several other cases in the 1950s, and has lost only one case since. In fact, in 1987 it won a case against the Thames Water Authority for fouling the Thames River. It has established enough court precedents that it seldom has to go to court now.

In the United States, fishing rights on most streams are owned by state governments, which might in principle sue to protect its rights just as the ACA does in England. However, without their own wealth at stake, bureaucratic decision makers seem less inclined to aggressively protect the fish or the water quality. Instead, control of water pollution in streams is typically left up to environmental regulators. England, however, has demonstrated what seems to be a more sure and far less expensive way—private ownership of fishing rights—to protect waters that are valuable for fishing.

Source: This feature is based on Jane S. Shaw and Richard L. Stroup, "Gone Fishin'," *Reason* 20, no. 4 (August 1988), pp. 34–37.

Mikhail Bernstam has compiled data to compare the energy use in the largest 12 industrialized market economies with its use in the Eastern European socialist countries (plus North Korea). The market-based economies used only 37 percent as much energy per $1,000 worth of output as the socialist nations in 1986. The figure had fallen from 44 percent in 1980.

The same sort of comparison applies to the use of steel. Socialist economies used more than three times as much steel per unit of output as market economies did.[7] The data gathered by Bernstam show that across a variety of socialist economies, resource use is far greater per unit of output than across a variety of market-oriented economies. All of these nations have the capability of using

---

[7]The facts in this paragraph are from Mikhail Bernstam, *The Wealth of Nations and the Environment* (London: Institute of Economic Affairs, 1991), pp. 1–28.

advanced technologies, but without a market process in which producers and consumers individually choose among competing options, and individually pay for what they choose, there is a failure to conserve resources effectively. And a less efficient economy tends to be a less clean economy.

After the fall of rigidly socialist regimes in the Soviet Union and Eastern Europe, leaders in several of these countries are now seeking ways to increase private ownership and the role of markets. What, exactly, is important about private ownership of resources? Four functions of property rights are especially important to the economy and to the environment:

1. Private property rights provide owners with the incentive to share (sell to others) resource access, while resource prices provide users with the incentive to conserve. As we learned in earlier chapters, markets cannot function unless sellers own rights that they can, if they wish, sell to buyers in the marketplace. If a resource is utilized in highly productive ways, its owner can receive high levels of payment from the resource users. Lower valued uses will pay less in competitive markets. When resources are privately owned, producers will have a strong incentive to conserve on their use of the costly resources. In essence, private ownership encourages less resource usage per unit of output. In addition, pursuit of profits provides business firms with a strong incentive to implement new technologies that conserve on the use of resources. Thus, it should not be surprising that resource-saving changes tend to occur earlier in a market setting than under socialism. The experience of Eastern Europe and the former Soviet Union under socialism is consistent with this view.

2. A resource owner has a strong incentive to exercise good stewardship. Private ownership of property provides an incentive for good care that is lacking under government control. If the resource is well cared for, it will be more valuable and add more to the wealth of its owner. If the owner allows the resource to deteriorate, he or she personally bears the cost of that negligence in the form of a decline in the value of the resource. The value of the property right to the resource is, in a very real sense, a hostage to good care of that resource.

3. A resource owner has legal rights against anyone seeking to harm the resource. A private owner of a resource has more than just the incentive to preserve the value of that resource. Private property rights also provide the owner with legal rights against anyone (usually including a government agency) who invades—physically or by pollution—and harms the resource. Much environmental damage is prevented this way. The private owner of a forest or a farm will not sit idly by if someone is cutting down trees or invading the property with hazardous pollutants. Lawsuits can be used to protect those rights. For example, owners of copper and lead smelters in the United States have been forced to compensate owners of land and homes for damage from sulfur dioxide emissions. Once such a company has been successfully sued, the decision sets a legal precedent that effectively discourages further such action.

Before they closed it down, the owners of a smelter near Tacoma, Washington, had been sued in such a manner. After they were found to be liable, they took measures to reduce pollution damages. Moreover, whenever unusual weather conditions nonetheless caused sulfur dioxide from its smokestack to damage the foliage or the homes of downwind households, the company routinely made payments of compensation to avoid further lawsuits.

When resources are not privately owned, no individual will receive large personal rewards for bringing suit against polluters, even when the source of the pollution is clear. In the United States, fish in a river might be damaged by pollution, but they are not owned by anyone whose personal wealth depends on their safety. Political and bureaucratic authorities must be counted on to protect the resource. In England, by contrast, where fishing rights on a stream are privately owned, the owners guard jealously the quality of the water. (See the "Application in Economics" feature on property rights and water quality.)

4. *Changes in the value of a privately owned resource bring all of the anticipated future benefits and costs of today's resource decisions immediately to bear on the resource owner.* An additional benefit of private property rights is their ability to bring expected future effects of current decisions to bear now. Property rights provide long-term incentives for maximizing the value of a resource, even for owners whose personal outlook is short term. If using a tract of land for the construction of a toxic waste dump reduces its future productivity, its value *today* falls, and the decline in the land's value reduces the owner's wealth. That happens because land's current worth reflects the net present value of its future services—the revenue from production or services received directly from the land, minus the costs (including amounts that must be paid to anyone harmed by escaping wastes) required to generate the revenues, both discounted to present value terms.

Thus, fewer services from a privately owned resource, or greater costs associated with it in the future, mean lower value (and less wealth for the owner) now. In fact, as soon as an appraiser or potential buyer can see future problems, the wealth of the owner declines by the amount of the reduction in potential buyers' willingness to pay for the resource. Not only does using land to store hazardous waste reduce future options for the land's productivity, but the value also may be reduced by the risk of future lawsuits if the wastes leak and cause damage to other people or property.

This is true even if the owner of the resource is a corporation, and the corporate officers, rather than the owner-stockholders, are in control. Corporate officers may be concerned mainly about the short term, not expecting to be present when future problems arise. However, property rights hold such decision makers accountable. If a current action causes the expectation of future problems, or if current expenditures are seen to promise future benefits, those who buy and sell stock will push the stock price up or down accordingly, capturing the reduction or the increase in future net benefits. Corporate officers are concerned with current profits, but must be equally concerned with changes in the value of the corporation's stock.

Of course, the average owner of stock is not a pollution expert, but anyone can gain the necessary knowledge by reading the published reports of business journalists or stock analysts who are tuned in to all phases of the industry they cover. Watchdog environmental groups also spread the word about suspected problems. It is in the stockholder's interest to keep an "ear to the ground" because correctly anticipating how the market will react can allow the discerning investor to buy before good news is fully captured in the stock price, or to sell before bad news is fully reflected in a falling stock price. Such self-interested scrutiny and the resultant decisions of investors provide a continual assessment of corporate strategies, and thus an influence on them as stock prices rise or fall accordingly.

Property rights are an important factor in preserving and enhancing environmental quality. Another, alternative way to seek environmental quality is through government regulation. It, too, has important effects on both the economy and the environment.

GOVERNMENT REGULATION AND THE ENVIRONMENT

Environmental quality is an economic good. People are willing to pay for it, and as their incomes rise, they demand more of it. Substantial contributions to environmental quality are made through the normal operation of property rights and a market system. However, certain kinds of environmental problems cannot be solved merely by the enforcement of individual property rights. Only when pollution is local, affecting strongly a few people who can enforce their rights in court, can property rights deal effectively with the problem. Most pollutants capable of doing proven and serious damage are of this sort. But others of potentially great harm are not. If the effects of an emitted substance are both serious and very widespread, or if the substance has many sources, making it impossible to assign individual responsibility, then the protective role of government may require it to step in with regulation. (Chapter 29, Problem Areas for the Market, explains in more detail why regulation may be called for, and how regulators might best reduce environmental problems with the use of a variety of policy tools.)

Regulation, however, is seldom efficient and can be enormously expensive. The Environmental Protection Agency has estimated that in 1994 environmental regulation in the United States cost about $150 billion. Regulation is seldom based on market signals, and so it is subject to all the problems caused by lack of information and lack of incentives that have plagued the socialist nations. It can by very wasteful.[8] Scientific uncertainty is often great in cases where regulation is demanded, and the stakes can be very high.

Consider the issue of global warming. Emissions of carbon dioxide from the efficient burning of all fuels cause no harm where they are emitted. No one's rights are being violated by the invasion of a harmful pollutant. Yet these emissions have been building up in the atmosphere and may in the future require regulation if the buildup acts as an invisible blanket and causes the earth to warm, as some scientists claim that it will. Such warming could change weather patterns, making hurricanes and other storms more intense, and might even result in rising sea levels around the globe. If the "worst-case scenarios" suggested by scientists were to materialize, some communities would face the flooding of their lands, serious ecological disruptions, and other problems.

Some scientists and many environmental groups argue that the threat of global warming is so serious that despite high costs, the nations of the world must impose strong regulations quickly. Government limits of some sort, they point out, are the only way that carbon dioxide emissions can be controlled. Other scientists, and many policy analysts, believe that imposing strong regulation at this time would be a mistake. They point out that the science of global warming is filled with uncertainties. For example:

---

[8]For a more thorough explanation of why environmental regulation is often inefficient, and some quantitative estimates of how costly it is, see Robert Crandall, *Why Is the Cost of Environmental Regulation So High?* Policy Study No. 110 (St Louis: Center for the Study of American Business, February 1992).

1. We do not know whether changes in the Earth's cloud cover will enhance the warming effects of carbon dioxide or offset them. Water vapor and clouds in the atmosphere account for more than 98 percent of the total warming we now experience, so even small changes in where that water is in the atmosphere, and the form it takes, could easily overcome the impact of the buildup in carbon dioxide. All scientists agree that the atmospheric models used to predict global warming do not accurately incorporate the effects of atmospheric water vapor.

2. It is true that in the past, over thousands of years, added carbon dioxide has been associated with warming, but the warming seems to have come first. Did carbon dioxide buildups cause the warming, or did warming cause the buildups?

3. If warming does occur, will sea levels rise or fall? Warming would cause the polar ice caps to melt and shrink at the edges, but warmer air carries more moisture, and the added precipitation would build up snow and ice in their still-frigid centers, increasing their thickness. Whether the net effect on the sea level would be positive or negative is unknown.

These questions and many more are in dispute. We cannot even be sure whether the buildup and a warmer world would, on balance, be better or worse. Some people would gain from a warmer, wetter world. Also, the direct effects of carbon dioxide are helpful to plants. Owners of greenhouses routinely purchase carbon dioxide to enrich the enclosed atmosphere and enhance plant growth. These facts and the many scientific uncertainties combine to make many economists unwilling to endorse strong regulations to force reductions in the emissions of carbon dioxide.

The cost of such policies is another consideration. One large study estimates that in the United States alone, the cost of merely stabilizing emissions at their current levels, with no net reduction, would be $95 billion in the first year, with larger costs after that. Economist William Nordhaus, in an article about global warming, suggests, "The best investment today may be in learning about climatic change, rather than in preventing it."[9]

In sum, environmental regulation is a powerful tool, capable of providing important improvements in environmental quality, but it tends to be very costly, and its unintended consequences can be serious also. The results of regulations banning DDT proved that point, as we described earlier, especially in the tragic case of Sri Lanka.

Policy-makers and analysts considering environmental regulations should recognize that environmental quality is an economic good. Like food, clothing, and shelter, it is something that people are willing to pay for, though not in unlimited amounts. In addition, policy-makers should recognize that the linkage between environmental quality and economic prosperity is important. Environmental regulations can exert a powerful influence on both, for good or for ill. Finally, they should not forget that enforceable property rights were for many years our main form of regulating environmental pollution and allowing far-sighted individuals and groups to exercise their visions of natural areas preservation. Overall, property rights continue to play a positive role in the preservation of a quality environment.

---

[9]William Nordhaus, "Global Warming: Slowing the Greenhouse Express," in Henry J. Aaron, ed., *Setting National Priorities: Policies for the Nineties* (Washington, DC: The Brookings Institution, 1990), p. 207.

MYTHS OF ECONOMICS

"WE ARE RUNNING OUT OF ENERGY, MINERALS, TIMBER, AND OTHER NATURAL RESOURCES. DOOMSDAY IS JUST AROUND THE CORNER."

For centuries, various social commentators have argued that the world is about to run out of trees, vital minerals, or various sources of energy. In sixteenth-century England, fear arose that the supply of wood would soon be exhausted as that resource was widely used as a source of energy. As Clayburn LaForce notes, however, the price of wood "gradually rose as forests around urban centers receded. In response to higher prices, people gradually began to substitute coal for charcoal, a wood derivative, in both personal and commercial uses. England entered its greatest period of economic growth and that 'sceptered isle' still has forests."[1]

In the middle of the nineteenth century, dire predictions arose that the United States was about to run out of whale oil, at that time the primary fuel for artificial lighting. As the demand for whale oil increased, many predicted that all of the whales would soon be gone and that Americans would face long nights without light. Whale-oil prices rose sharply from 23 cents per gallon in 1820 to $1.42 per gallon in 1850. As LaForce explains, higher prices again motivated consumers and entrepreneurs to seek alternatives, including distilled vegetable oils, lard oil, and coal gas. By the early 1850s, coal oil (kerosene) had won out. And very soon thereafter, a new substitute for whale oil appeared: Petroleum replaced coal oil as the source of kerosene. As for whale oil, by 1896 its price had fallen to 40 cents per gallon, and even at that price few people used it. The whale-oil crisis had passed.

As people switched to petroleum, doomsday predictions about its exhaustion arose almost as soon as the resource was developed. In 1914 the Bureau of Mines reported that the total U.S. supply of oil was 6 million barrels, an amount less than the United States now produces approximately every 20 months. In 1926 the Federal Oil Conservation Board informed people that the U.S. supply of oil would last only seven years. A couple of decades later the secretary of interior forecast that the United States would run out of oil in just a few more years.

Dire predictions about our natural-resource future became a fad during the 1970s. The "year of exhaustion" of important natural resources, especially crude oil, was a popular news item. The arithmetic of the doomsday calculations was unassailable. One simply found the current annual consumption rate (averaged over, say, the last two decades) and divided that number into the quantity of proved reserves of the resource. That provided the years of the resource remaining. Add that number to the current date, and you had the "year of exhaustion."

So why have such projections proved to be so wrong? There are two major reasons for their inaccuracy. First, "proved reserves" of a mineral resource are the verified quantity of the resource that producers have discovered that they believe can be produced *at current prices and levels of technology.* Contrary to popular belief, they reveal little or nothing about the sufficiency of a mineral reserve for the future. Proved reserves are quite similar to inventories in manufacturing industries. Just as it is costly to produce and hold inventories of a manufactured good—for example, automobiles—so, too, it is costly to find and verify reserves of a mineral resource. Just as automobile dealers choose to hold only a two- or three-month inventory of cars, mineral producers commonly hold only a 10- to 15-year supply of mineral resources. And just as the current inventory of automobiles reveals little about their future availability, the size of current proved reserves reveals little about the absolute quantity of a mineral resource that can be supplied in the future.

Second, doomsday predictions have generally failed to consider the role of price changes. When a resource becomes more scarce, its price rises. This provides additional incentive for (1) resource users to cut back on their consumption, (2) suppliers to develop new methods of discovering and recovering larger quantities of the resource, and (3) both users and producers to search for and develop substitutes. To date, these forces have pushed "doomsday" farther and farther into the future.

In fact, the empirical evidence indicates that the relative scarcity of most resources is declining, and as a result, the relative price of most resources is falling. The classic study of Harold Barnett and Chandler Morse illustrates this point.[2] Using data from 1870 to 1963, Barnett and Morse found that the real price of resources declined during that long period. Updates and extensions of this work indicate that resource prices are continuing to decline. In 1980 economist Julian Simon bet doomsday environmentalist Paul Ehrlich that the inflation-adjusted price of any five natural resources of Ehrlich's choosing would decline during the 1980s. In fact, the prices of all five of the resources chosen by Ehrlich declined, and Simon won the highly publicized bet. A recent study found that of 38 major natural resources, only two (manganese and zinc) increased in price (after adjustment for inflation) during the 1980s.[3]

Far from suggesting that doomsday is just around the corner, the price data paint a rather optimistic picture. Historical data on relative prices of key resources indicate that technology and the ever-increasing availability of substitutes tend to outrun our use of scarce natural resources. When price changes are allowed to reflect changing scarcities, constructive human responses to specific scarcities are a predictable occurrence. Just as they have been wrong in the past, future doomsday

forecasts that fail to incorporate human response to relative price changes will likely prove to be wrong in the future.

[1]J. Clayburn LaForce, "The Energy Crisis: The Moral Equivalent of Bamboozle," International Institute for Economic Research, Original Paper 11 (Los Angeles, April 1978).

[2]Harold Barnett and Chandler Morse, *Scarcity of Growth: The Economics of Natural Resource Availability* (Baltimore: The Johns Hopkins University Press for Resources for the Future, 1963). For an update of this study, see Manuel H. Johnson, Fredrick W. Bell, and J.T. Bennett, "Natural Resource Scarcity: Empirical Evidence and Public Policy," *Journal of Environmental Economics and Management* 7 (September 1980), pp. 258–269.

[3]Stephen Moore, "So Much for 'Scarce Resources,'" *The Public Interest* (Winter 1992).

PULLING IT ALL TOGETHER

We have seen that in matters of natural resources and the environment, as in other matters, economic principles can help us to understand and predict the actions that individuals will take. Providing for resource conservation and the prevention of harmful pollution can often be accomplished by the use of property rights, market exchange, and the resulting signals and incentives that emanate from market prices. The market for capital assets even provides a voice for future resource users. As Jane S. Shaw pointed out in the opening quote, it is when property rights are not properly applied, or cannot be, that problems occur. Property rights and market prices are not a panacea, because property rights cannot always be specified and enforced. As in other economic issues, government regulation may provide improvements when markets fail. But here, as elsewhere, government is not an automatic corrective device. The section on public choice analyzes more fully the factors that indicate when political (government) action might be needed, and the problems that these actions themselves can bring.

CHAPTER SUMMARY

1. In resource markets, as in other markets, incentives matter. Both the quantity demanded of a resource and the quantity supplied depend on the resource price. Substitutes can be found everywhere. Both the demand and the supply curves will be more elastic when buyers and sellers have more time in which to respond to a price change.

2. Even though environmental decisions are often made outside a market context, the basic principles of economics still apply. Purposeful choices, influenced by prices and other incentives, are made without full knowledge. Values are subjective, and the secondary effects of decisions are often important.

3. Environmental quality and economic growth tend to go together. People living in poverty are hard on the environment. Technological improvements enhance economic growth and reduce resource waste. The demand for environmental quality is positively and strongly linked to income levels.

4. Resources are better protected and more efficiently allocated, producing less waste and pollution, when property rights are protected and markets are utilized to allocate resources. The stronger economic and environmental performance of market economies relative to socialist economies confirms this point.

5. Private resource ownership is important to environmental quality and resource conservation because it (a) is necessary for the wide, but controlled, access encouraged by the market process, (b) provides an incentive for resource stewardship, (c) gives owners legal standing against those who would overuse or harm the resource, and (d) through asset value, gives future users a voice in today's markets.

6. Environmental policy is implicit in property rights and a market system. Enforceable property rights cannot always be put into place, therefore, government regulation may be required. Since regulatory choices are not based on information and incentives from market prices, however, regulation has the same potential for inefficiency and ineffectiveness faced by the socialist governments whose citizens have suffered many environmental harms. Environmental regulations cost the U.S. economy about $150 billion per year. Benefits are mostly unmeasured, but potentially large.

7. Neither economic analysis nor empirical evidence is supportive of the view that the world is about to run out of key natural resources. When private property rights are present, increased scarcity (relative to demand) of a natural resource will increase the price of the resource and thereby encourage (a) conservation, (b) the use of substitutes, and (c) the development of new technologies capable of both enhancing the supply of the resource and reducing our reliance on it. The fact that the real prices of most natural resources have declined during the last century is inconsistent with the doomsday view of resource scarcity.

CRITICAL-ANALYSIS QUESTIONS

*1. Does a resource that is not owned, and therefore is not priced, have a zero opportunity cost? Might it be treated as if it did? Explain.

2. Why is the price elasticity of demand for resources, such as water and natural gas, greater in the long run than the short run? What examples of responses to price changes can you think of that are more complete after one year than after one week?

*3. "Steel production typically requires 40,000 gallons of water per finished ton of steel. Steel is important to U.S. industry and our national defense. As water becomes more scarce in the nation, it is imperative that the required amounts of water be reserved for the steel industry." Evaluate this statement.

4. "The federal government should do a complete survey of mineral availability in the nation. It is inexcusable that we do not know how much oil, for example, the country can ultimately produce." Evaluate this statement.

*5. Why will more oil in total be produced from an oil well when the price of crude oil is higher?

6. "Unlike in a marketplace, where pollution is profitable, government control of resources and pollution can take into account the desires of all the people." What does economic thinking have to say about this statement?

*7. "Private ownership of a natural resource, such as a lake in the woods, is tantamount to setting aside that resource for the personal, selfish enjoyment of one owner. Society will be better off if it is recognized that such a resource was provided by nature, for all to enjoy." Evaluate this statement.

8. Will the world ever run out of any mineral resource? In your answer, be sure to consider the role played by rising extraction costs and by the existence of property rights to minerals. Does a negative answer to the question imply that increasing resource scarcity will never be a problem?

*9. "Corporations should not be allowed to own forests. Corporate managers are just too shortsighted. Their philosophy is to make a profit now, regardless of the future consequences. For example, trees may be cut after growing 30 years to get revenue now, even though another 20 years' growth would yield a very high rate of return. The long-run health of our forests is too important to entrust them to this sort of management." Evaluate this statement.

10. "Since our national forests are owned by all the people, their resources will be conserved for the benefit of all, rather than exploited in a shortsighted way, to produce benefits only for the owners." Evaluate this statement.

---

*Asterisk denotes questions for which answers are given in Appendix C.

PART FIVE

PUBLIC CHOICE

CHAPTER TWENTY-NINE

PROBLEM AREAS FOR
THE MARKET

The principal justification for public policy intervention lies in the frequent and numerous shortcomings of market outcomes.

CHARLES WOLF[1]

CHAPTER FOCUS

■ *Why do market decision makers face inappropriate incentives when an externality is present?*
■ *What role do imperfect information and imperfect property rights play in causing externalities?*
■ *What can we learn from the theory of external effects about pollution problems and alternative solutions? Why are some solutions to pollution problems less effective than others?*
■ *What is the "free rider" problem? What kinds of goods are likely to be susceptible to this problem?*
■ *What can we say about buyers' and sellers' lack of knowledge in the market, and when is this problem likely to be most serious? What market innovations have entrepreneurs used to reduce this problem?*

[1]Charles Wolf, Jr., *Markets or Government* (Cambridge: MIT Press, 1988), p. 17.

W e have emphasized that a properly functioning market system uses prices to coordinate the decisions of buyers and sellers. Market prices give each decision maker the information needed to make intelligent production and consumption decisions, weighing the relative desires of others. Each individual has the incentive to use that information to reduce the costs to others (reflected in market costs) and to increase the value of goods made available to others (reflected in prices of goods that could be sold). Even when they think only of themselves, decision makers facing appropriate prices have the incentive to act *as if* they care about others. For example, resource owners are rewarded for moving their resources to uses which others value more highly. Owning the right to use or let others use a resource provides one with an incentive to think creatively about how others might benefit from using that resource.

Efficiency in production is encouraged by properly working markets, which reward producers for getting the most highly valued production from the bundle of resources they use, and for minimizing the cost (the value to others) of those resource inputs. Buyers are rewarded if they economize on their consumption of each good and service in order to get as much satisfaction as possible from their limited budgets.

In short, the "invisible hand" of Adam Smith provides each decision maker in the market economy with the information and incentive to act efficiently, and to consider the needs of others. Individuals will spend their income on the goods and services they value most. Therefore, those who are providing the goods and services must consider the needs—and wants—of buyers if they wish to stay in business. This arrangement is efficient in that no production will pay for itself if the buyer does not expect to value its benefits more than competing uses of the valuable resources needed for the production of the good. Similarly, owners will put the resources at their command to uses valued the most by buyers, unless they themselves value the resource enough to "outbid" all others by rejecting the highest market offer. This arrangement assures that projects that would produce higher value, in the judgment of buyers, are not neglected.

Even when the market is working with ideal efficiency, however, some observers may object to its results. They may argue that income is not distributed to those who most deserve it, and therefore they may prefer that even ideal market results be rejected or modified in order to redistribute income. Economics has little to say about which income distribution is best, but does indicate that (1) replacing a well-functioning market with other arrangements will normally reduce economic efficiency, and that (2) impediments to trade, such as restrictions, taxes, and subsidies, which are intended to redistribute income will often, after individuals have adjusted to them, not have their intended distributional results in any case. Even when these factors are recognized, economics cannot tell us whether a well-functioning market should be replaced or modified in order to change income distribution. This is a question of values and priorities, not just economics.

Does economics tell us that markets always function well? To the contrary, economic thinking gives us reason to expect that markets will consistently fail to achieve ideal efficiency. As we pointed out in Chapter 4, the invisible hand can slip. (At this point, the reader might wish to review Chapter 4.) Market prices will not always reflect the full range of costs and benefits produced by an action. There are several potential causes of such **market failure,** that is, economic activity that results in allocative inefficiency relative to the hypothetical ideal of economists.

Market failure

The failure of the market system to attain hypothetically ideal *allocative efficiency. This means that potential gain exists that has not been captured. However, the cost of establishing a mechanism that* could *potentially capture the gain may exceed the benefits. Therefore, it is not always possible to improve the situation.*

These causes can be grouped into four general classes: externalities, public goods, poorly informed buyers or sellers, and monopoly. Since the impact of monopoly on the product and factor markets has already been investigated, this chapter will emphasize the other three categories of market failure. We will also explore possible responses, especially government responses.

Keep in mind that market failure is merely a failure to attain conditions of *ideal* efficiency. Alternative forms of economic organization may also have defects. Even though the government can sometimes improve the situation, this will not always be the case; sometimes it may even be counterproductive. After analyzing market failure in this chapter, we will focus on the operation of the public sector and its problems in the next.

MARKET FAILURE AND PROPERTY RIGHTS

Most economic arguments for government intervention are based on the idea that the marketplace cannot provide public goods or handle externalities.

TYLER COWAN[2]

Tyler Cowan points out that critics claiming market failure on economic grounds most often point either to external effects such as pollution, or to the market's inability to provide the optimal amount of a public good. Both of these problems can be serious; and both occur only when secure property rights are not privately held. Resources that are not under the effective protection of a private owner are likely to be wasted or abused. **Private-property rights** give owners the exclusive right to control and benefit from their resources as long as their actions do not harm others. It is important to notice the last part of that definition. For example, private-property rights do not grant the owners of rocks the right to throw them at automobiles.

Private-property rights
A set of usage and exchange rights held exclusively by the owner(s).

An important function of property rights is to provide legal protection against damage, abuse, or theft. Property rights are often associated with selfishness on the part of owners, since owners have the option of doing as they wish with what they own. But selfishness requires that an owner reject even the most attractive offers to buy or rent. Private ownership permits owners (including corporate owners) to protect their property against unauthorized use or harm by others. However, owners will, if adequately compensated, often allow others to use their assets, even though it is costly for them to do so. Rental car firms sell individuals the right to use their automobiles despite the reduction in the resale value of the car. Housing is often rented, even though normal use by the renter imposes a maintenance and upkeep cost on the homeowner. Since property rights are clearly defined and enforceable in these cases, the market exchange system induces people who use the property

[2]Tyler Cowen, "Public Goods and Externalities," *Fortune Encyclopedia of Economics* (Ithaca, NY: Warner, 1993), p. 74.

(including the owner, whose wealth is tied up in the value of the property) to fully consider the costs of their actions. This will not be the case, however, when property rights are not clearly defined, or are not fully enforceable. Problems will arise under these circumstances.

ENFORCEABLE PROPERTY RIGHTS AND INFORMATION

To legally enforce property rights, the owner must be able to show in court that those rights have in fact been violated. If John runs into Mary's car, the case is often fairly simple, and the parties may not even have to go to court. When John knows that Mary can prove him at fault and quantify the damages, he (or his insurance company) will simply compensate Mary for the damage done. (If John was insured, his rates will likely rise.) Such actions may also be brought to protect the rights of individuals against polluters. In the United States, many lawsuits have been successfully filed against smelters and other polluting sources. In England, where rights to fish for trout and salmon are privately owned, (but not the water or the fish themselves) fishing-rights owners have successfully sued polluters of streams on the basis of pollution interfering with the value of fishing. All of these legal actions to protect the rights of individuals have been brought under the traditional English *common law*, sometimes called *private law*, since individuals have the rights, and they individually can bring actions to protect themselves. Government, however, provides the courts and the enforcement of court orders.

Enforcement of property rights under private law is not automatic. To collect damages from pollution, or to stop polluting activities before serious damage occurs, the court must be convinced that the weight of the evidence is that pollution in fact has done (or would do) the damage claimed. That is, the court will take action against the polluter only if it is convinced that the claim of damage, whether past or expected, is more likely true than false.

The burden of proof on whoever is asking the court to act against a polluter, for example, requires evidence that connects pollution with suspected damage. But the important facts are not always easy to know or to demonstrate. Consider the case of Mr. Steel, the factory owner whose smoke fouls the air at Mary's home. Mary may have a right to clean air, which is violated by Mr. Steel's smoke. To receive compensation, however, she must be able to demonstrate in court: (1) significant damage inflicted by the pollution, (2) that the pollutant in question actually caused the damage, and (3) that the pollutant came from Mr. Steel's plant. Such lawsuits are not uncommon, and have been successful. But if any of the three elements is in serious doubt, then Mary's property rights, although defined, may not be enforceable. If damage is done but cannot be shown, then Mary's property rights are unenforced, and **external cost** is the result, defined as the harmful effects of an individual or group's action on the welfare of a nonconsenting secondary party, not accounted for in market prices. We will discuss external costs at greater length later in this chapter. Courts take the position in such cases that mere suspicion is not enough to justify its siding with one citizen against another. Cases of this type, especially when they involve a large number of parties and uncertainty of information about violators and magnitude of damages, are particularly troublesome ones for a system of private law to handle efficiently. As a result, government often steps in to protect individuals against possible damage, using, for example, pollution-control regulation.

External costs
Harmful effects of an individual's or a group's action on the welfare of nonconsenting secondary parties, not accounted for in market prices. Litterbugs, drunk drivers, and polluters, for example, create external costs.

It is the high cost (or the unavailability) of information that can make property rights unenforceable, and bring about market failure. Unfortunately, turning the problem over to government regulators does not produce the information needed for efficient resource allocation. Whoever is in charge of controlling pollution needs the same information that courts need to enforce property rights. If the consequences of emitting a specified amount of a pollutant at a specified time and place cannot be reasonably estimated, then no rational evaluation of the problem is possible. When claimed pollution damages cannot be shown to be more likely true than false, courts will refuse to act. Regulators may be more willing to act on the basis of suspicion than the courts, but when information is missing, mistakes are likely whether a property-rights (market) approach or government regulation is utilized.

COMMON-PROPERTY RESOURCES AND EFFICIENCY

Property rights sometimes are not enforced in a market setting because they are held in common. A **common-property resource** is one for which rights are held in common by a group of individuals, none of whom has a transferable ownership interest. Access to a common-property resource may be unrestricted, as in the case of air, or may be controlled politically, as wildlife is controlled by state governments in the United States.

If access to the resource is unrestricted, it is an **open-access resource.** When there is more of it than people wish to use, then the open-access resource is not scarce and there is no problem. However, trouble arises when such a resource becomes scarce. (See the "Applications in Economics" boxed feature on common and private property rights.) Without some form of political control to replace the ownership functions of controlling access and of caring for or maintaining the resource, external costs are almost guaranteed. For example, when water users are harmed by pollution but cannot sue for damages, then external costs due to pollution are likely to occur. The polluter (who does not own the water) has no incentive to curtail the activities that are causing the pollution. Streams, like other resources, are much more likely to be abused when they are treated as open-access resources. We have established environmental control agencies in order to deal with the problems that arise when there is open access to a resource.

As we will see in more detail in the next chapter, political control of a common-property resource, such as the air or a river, has its own problems. Typically, no one person or small, easily organized group has a large stake in seeing to it that decision makers protect the resource and allocate its use efficiently. Would private ownership, then, be more efficient? Not necessarily. It is costly to establish and defend the property rights of certain resources.[3] Exclusive ownership can easily be defined and defended for such commodities as apples, cabbages, waterbeds, cars, and airline tickets, but how would one establish and defend property rights to an oil pool that is located on the property of hundreds of different landowners?

Common-property resource
A resource for which rights are held in common by a group of individuals, none of whom has a transferable ownership interest. Access to the resource may be open (unrestricted), or may be controlled politically.

Open-access resource
A resource to which access is unrestricted. No one has the right to exclude others from using the resource. Overuse and abuse of such a resource is typical.

---

[3]The problems entailed in defining and enforcing private, transferable property rights are discussed in Terry L. Anderson and P. J. Hill, "Privatizing the Commons: An Improvement?" *Southern Economic Journal* 50, no. 2 (October 1983).

APPLICATIONS IN ECONOMICS

IMPORTANCE OF COMMON AND PRIVATE PROPERTY RIGHTS

What is common to many is taken least care of, for all men have greater regard for what is their own than for what they possess in common with others.

ARISTOTLE[1]

The point made by Aristotle more than 2,000 years ago is as true now as it was then. It is as important in primitive cultures as it is in developed ones. When resources are held in common and access is unrestricted, the resource typically is abused and endangered. In contrast, when the rights are held by an individual (or family), conservation and wise utilization generally result. The following examples from sixteenth-century England, nineteenth-century Native-American culture, present-day Africa, and ocean fisheries illustrate the point.

CATTLE GRAZING ON THE ENGLISH COMMONS   Many English villages in the sixteenth century had *commons*, or commonly held pastures, that were available to any villagers who wanted to graze their animals. Since the benefits of grazing an additional animal accrued fully to the individual, whereas the cost of overgrazing was an external one, the pastures were grazed extensively. Since the pastures were communal property, there was little incentive for any individual person to conserve grass in the present so that it would be more abundant in the future. When everyone used the pasture extensively, there was not enough grass at the end of the grazing season to provide a good base for next year's growth. What was good for the individual was bad for the village as a whole. In order to preserve the grass, pastures were fenced in the Enclosure Movement. After the Enclosure Movement established private-property rights, owners and managers saw to it that overgrazing no longer occurred.

PROPERTY RIGHTS OF NATIVE AMERICANS   Among Native-American tribes, common ownership of the hunting grounds was the general rule. Because the number of Native Americans was small and their hunting technology was not highly developed, hunted animals seldom faced extinction. However, there were at least two exceptions.

One was the beaver hunted by the Montagnais Indians of the Labrador Peninsula. When the French fur traders came to the area in the early 1600s, the beaver increased in value and therefore became increasingly scarce. Recognizing the depletion of the beaver population and the animal's possible extinction, the Montagnais began to institute private-property rights. Each beaver-trapping area on a stream was assigned to a family, and conservation practices were adopted. The last remaining pair of beavers was never trapped, since the taker would only be hurting his own family the following year. For a time, the supply of beavers was no longer in jeopardy. However, when a new wave of European trappers invaded the area, the Native Americans, because they were unable to enforce their property rights, abandoned conservation to take the pelts while they could.[2] Individual ownership was destroyed, and conservation disappeared with it.

PROPERTY RIGHTS AND AFRICAN ELEPHANTS   The excessive exploitation of wildlife can be linked to an absence of property rights. Because herds of Great Plains buffalo were available for everyone to use, allowing individuals to kill animals without facing the costs of herd depletion, the buffalo suffered near-extinction during the nineteenth century.[3] Today we see contrasting approaches to such a problem with the African elephant. In Kenya, elephants roam unowned on unfenced terrain. The Kenyan government tries to protect them from poachers seeking valuable ivory by banning all commercial use of the elephant except tourism. In the decade that this policy has been in effect, the Kenyan elephant population has fallen from 65,000 to 19,000. In other East and Central African countries that have followed the Kenyan approach, the collective elephant populations have dropped from 1,044,050 to 429,520 between 1979 and 1989.[4]

In Zimbabwe, by contrast, shops openly sell ivory and hides, and legislation was passed giving the local people on whose land the elephant roam the right to hunt the elephants. This encourages them to preserve elephants and to permit only controlled hunting. Since assigning property rights in elephants, Zimbabwe has seen its elephant population grow from 30,000 to 43,000. Elephant populations in the countries adopting a similar approach—Botswana, South Africa, Malawi, and Namibia—are increasing at a rate of 5 percent a year.

PROPERTY RIGHTS AND OCEAN FISHERIES   Once, the waters off the northeastern United States teemed with Atlantic cod, haddock, flounder, and pollock—fish that many people love to eat, and many fishermen love to catch. But fish populations have fallen sharply in recent years due to overfishing, a problem for wild fisheries all over the world.[5] Wild fisheries of the oceans are open-access resources. The only way to claim ownership of fish is to catch them. In addition, there is no individual incentive to leave some fish for next year's catch; other fishermen will probably catch them. Without an authority, such as an owner, in place to control access, the fish population faces possible extinction.

When demand for the fish is high, and new people enter the fishing occupation as a result, overfishing occurs. As the population of fish falls, costs rise because the sparser population of fish requires that a more intensive effort be made to find them. The smaller catch may reduce supply enough to raise the price of fish, but entry of new fishermen will occur until there is no profit; and if the population is falling, profit is likely to turn negative. Yet, in the short run, fishermen will continue to fish so long as they can cover their variable costs, keep the fishing pressure intense, and further reduce the number of fish and the available breeding stock.

Compare this open-access fishery with one where the fish population or its territory is owned by a person or group who can control the rate of take, practicing conservation to protect next year's profits, which, after all, belong to the owner. We would expect that more conservation would be practiced, and overfishing would not occur. As a result, the income of fishermen would be higher. Richard J. Agnello and Lawrence P. Donnelley found just such results when they compared open-access and private-property oyster beds.[6] Using data from Maryland, Virginia, Louisiana, and Mississippi, they found that from 1945 to 1970 the ratio of harvest in the earlier part of the season to the later part was 1.35 for open-access oyster beds and 1.01 for the private-property beds. In the open-access beds, each fisherman tried to catch as many fish as possible, as quickly as possible, just as our logic predicts. Too much fishing effort was expended all season, relative to the more efficient allocation of fishing effort under the private-property regime. Fishermen in the private-property state of Louisiana earned $3,207, while their counterparts in the open-access state of Mississippi earned $807. Such a finding supports the expectation of higher incomes and larger harvests over the years under the private-property regime. By solving the open-access problem, private-property rights help conserve a fishery resource and encourage more efficient management of it.

Could property rights be established for fisheries on the high seas? Such a scheme is not costless, and both federal and state governments have held that private rights there would violate antitrust laws. Informal unions of fishermen have tried to limit entry, but they have had limited success, since any agreement is difficult to maintain without an authority to enforce it.[7] Although private ownership of fishing grounds appears to be the solution to overfishing, this solution also appears unlikely to be instituted without further innovations in technology.

---

[1] Aristotle, as quoted by Will Durant in *The Life of Greece* (New York: Simon and Schuster, 1939), p. 536.

[2] For an economic analysis of the Montagnais management of the beaver, together with historical references, see Harold Demsetz, "Toward a Theory of Property Rights," *American Economic Review* (May 1967), pp. 347–359.

[3] See Francis Haines, *The Buffalo* (New York: Crowell, 1970).

[4] The facts used in this section were provided by Randy Simmons and Urs Kreuter, "Herd Mentality: Banning Ivory Sales Is No Way to Save the Elephant," *Policy Review* (Fall 1989), pp. 46–49.

[5] See Jennifer A. Kingston, "Northeast Fishermen Catch Everything, and That's a Problem," *The New York Times*, November 13, 1988.

[6] Richard J. Agnello and Lawrence P. Donnelley, "Prices and Property Rights in the Fisheries," *Southern Economic Journal* XLII (October 1979), pp. 253–262.

[7] Ronald N. Johnson and Gary D. Libecap, "Contracting Problems and Regulation: The Case of the Fishery," *American Economic Review* (December 1982), pp. 1005–1022.

Source: Don Leal, Senior Research Associate, Political Economy Research Center, Bozeman, Montana.

Similarly, who owns salmon or whales, which travel thousands of miles each year? In the absence of clearly assigned property rights, spillover costs and over-utilization are inevitable.

Certain whales have been on the verge of extinction because no single individual (or small group) has the ability to protect the whales, nor even an incentive to reduce its own current catch so that the future catch will be larger. Each tries to catch as many whales as possible now; someone else will catch those whales, the argument goes, if the first person (or group) does not. The same principle applies to oil-pool rights when many well owners can draw from the pool and no single owner can control the rate of withdrawal. In the absence of regulation, each oil-well operator has an incentive to draw the oil *from a common pool* as rapidly as possible. When all operators do so, though, the commonly owned oil is drawn out too rapidly, and the total amount that can be withdrawn falls.

We shall not be too quick to despair about such property rights problems, however. The common-pool problem in oil and similar areas has been addressed by government creation of joint operating rights, and other such solutions, so the creation of a new property-rights arrangement may also be possible. (See the "Application in Economics" box on creating property rights.)

EXTERNAL EFFECTS AND THE MARKET

The genius of a market exchange system lies in its ability to bring personal and social welfare into harmony. When two parties trade, and only they are affected, production and voluntary exchange also promote the social welfare. As we explained in Chapter 4, though, when externalities are present, production and exchange can impose costs or confer benefits on nonconsenting parties. Externalities are likely when property rights are not assigned, as in the case of open-access resources, or are not readily enforceable.

If nonconsenting parties are harmed by actions not accounted for in market prices, the spillover effects are called *external costs,* as mentioned earlier. The steel mill pouring pollution into the air imposes an external cost on surrounding residents who prefer clear air. A junkyard creates an eyesore, making an area less pleasant for passersby. Similarly, litterbugs, drunk drivers, muggers, and robbers impose unwanted costs on others. If the spillover effects enhance the welfare of secondary parties, they are called **external benefits.** A beautiful rose garden provides external benefits for the neighbors of the gardener. A golf course often provides spillover benefits to owners of surrounding property since it raises the market value of that property. Scientific research often produces knowledge that benefits others in addition to those who financed the research. The broadcast of a television program over the air is typically available to all in the area, including those who have not contributed to the cost of its production. When external costs and external benefits are present, market prices will not send the proper signals to producers and consumers. This situation results in market failure.

EXTERNAL COSTS

From the viewpoint of economic efficiency, an action should be undertaken only if it generates benefits in excess of its **social costs,** which are (1) the private cost

External benefits
Beneficial effects of group or individual action on the welfare of non-paying secondary parties.

Social costs
The sum of (1) the private costs incurred by a decision maker and (2) any external costs imposed on nonconsenting secondary parties. If there are no external costs, private and social costs will be equal.

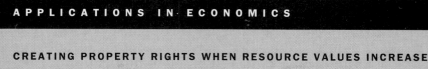

APPLICATIONS IN ECONOMICS

CREATING PROPERTY RIGHTS WHEN RESOURCE VALUES INCREASE

The creation and protection of property rights is not always easy, and is never free. When there is a payoff for better protection and more careful management of a resource, however, the incentive to protect and manage it well rises. Economic historians Terry Anderson and P. J. Hill have shown how, as a resource becomes more valuable, entrepreneurs, using technological inventions or legal innovations, often have been able to come up with new ways to create wealth by establishing property rights and defending them.[1] Technology enabled the establishment of property rights in the case of the grazing lands in the Great Plains of the United States as entrepreneurial individuals used various kinds of newly invented barbed wire to fence and thus effectively privatize grazing areas. In England, polluters of trout and salmon streams found themselves the targets of legal actions by owners of the fishing rights, forcing them to "clean up their act" on the grounds that their polluting actions were damaging the fishing rights, even though damage to the water itself was not grounds for action as no one had property rights to the actual water. Once legal precedents were set, future trips to court were seldom needed. Potential polluters got the message.[2]

Texas state government found a property-rights solution to the problem of too many wells drilled into common oil pools by multiple-surface landowners. This tends to reduce the total amount of oil obtained. By "unitizing" the oil field, the state government forced surface owners (potential drillers for the oil in a pool) to join an owners' association authorized to regulate oil production from that pool.

Other common-pool problems have yet to be solved, and salmon and whales in the ocean are more difficult cases for the establishment of private rights since they move from one ocean area to another, but the preceding examples give reason for optimism. Technical and institutional entrepreneurship may again find solutions, as the value of certain resources continues to rise.

[1]See Terry L. Anderson and Donald R. Leal, with Timothy Iijima, *Free Market Environmentalism* (San Francisco: Pacific Research Institute, 1991), pp. 37–50.
[2]On this topic, see Jane S. Shaw and Richard L. Stroup, "Gone Fishin'," *Reason* (August–September 1988), pp. 34–37.

borne by the consenting parties and (2) an external cost imposed on nonconsenting secondary parties. When external costs are present, market prices understate the social cost generated by the use of resources or consumption of products. Decision makers are not forced to fully bear the cost to others generated by their actions. Motivated by self-interest, they may undertake actions that generate a net loss to the community. The harm done to nonconsenting parties may exceed the net private gain. When this happens, private interest and economic efficiency are in conflict.

EXTERNAL BENEFITS

Sometimes the actions of an individual (or firm) generate external benefits: gains that accrue to nonparticipating (and nonpaying) secondary parties. As in the case of external costs, external benefits occur when property rights are undefined or unenforceable. Because of this, it is costly—or impossible—to withhold these benefits from nonconsenting parties and retain them for oneself at the same time. The producer of a motion picture has rights to the film and can collect a fee from anyone who sees or rents it. In contrast, the production of rose gardens, golf courses, scientific research, and television broadcasts, as mentioned above, will often produce benefits for individuals who do not pay for them. Of course, when those

The problem of pollution emanates from external costs that arise when property rights are ambiguously defined or poorly enforced.

WIZARD OF ID   **BY BRANT PARKER & JOHNNY HART**

Reprinted by permission of Johnny Hart and Creators Syndicate, Inc.

benefits are large, entrepreneurs will seek ways to capture the benefits. Rose gardens are often planted by landlords who can then charge higher rents in their apartments, or planted at community expense in condominium communities, for example. Developers of golf courses in recent years typically purchase the land around the planned course before it is built, in order to resell it at a higher price reflecting the benefits produced when the golf course is completed. Television broadcasters sometimes scramble their signals, so they will be accessible only to those who pay a fee for a descrambler. But ingenious as their efforts may be, entrepreneurs cannot always capture all the benefits of their output; some benefits remain external to the producer.

When external benefits are present, the market demand understates the social gains of conducting the beneficial activity. Social gains from potentially valuable projects may go unrealized because no potential producer can fully appropriate or capture the projects' gains.

PUBLIC-SECTOR RESPONSES TO EXTERNALITIES

What can the government do to improve the efficiency of resource allocation when externalities are present? Sometimes private-property rights can be more clearly defined and more strictly enforced. The granting by government of property rights to ranchers and homesteaders minimized the threat of overgrazing and improved the efficiency of land use in the Old West, once barbed wire made enforcement of land rights economical. More recently, the establishment of enforceable property rights to the oyster beds of the Chesapeake Bay improved the efficiency of oyster farming in the area. The granting to inventors of government-enforced patents, or sole rights to use (or license the use of) their new inventions, encourages productive research and development of technology. Thus, government action can sometimes bring market incentives more in line with society's interests. In many instances, however, it is difficult to delineate boundaries for a resource, determine who owns what portion, and enforce those rights. In those cases, externalities result.

Why not simply prohibit activities that result in external cost? After all, why should we allow nonconsenting parties to be harmed? This idea has an initial appeal, but closer inspection reveals its flaw. The activities that impose costs also usually provide benefits, too. Buses that pour out exhaust fumes that impose external costs on pedestrians and bicyclists also provide public transportation. Dogs that are notorious for using neighborhood lawns for bone burying and relief purposes also are often someone's beloved pets. Motorboats are noisy and frighten fish, much to the disgust of fishermen, but also provide enjoyment to boaters. Few people would argue that we should do away with buses, dogs, and motorboats. From a social viewpoint, prohibition is often a less desirable alternative than tolerating some external costs. Tolerance has its limits, however, so activities that generate external costs are often regulated in an attempt to keep the costs within those limits. The gains from the activity must be weighed against the costs imposed on those who are harmed, as well as against practical problems associated with controlling the activity.

Apart from establishing and enforcing property rights, there are four general approaches that government might take in controlling resources such as air and water:

1. A government agency might act as a resource manager, charging the users of the resource a fee.
2. A regulatory agency might establish a maximum pollution-emission standard and require that polluters attain at least that standard.
3. The agency might establish a maximum level of total emissions, assign each polluter a certain share of those emissions, and then allow the polluters to trade emission quotas.
4. The agency might specify exactly what pollution-control steps each polluter must take.

POLLUTION-TAX APPROACH

Some economists favor a user's charge, which we will call a pollution tax. **Exhibit 29–1** uses actual cost estimates from a copper smelter (which subsequently was dismantled) to illustrate the economics of this approach. The copper-producing firm has minimum costs of production when it spends nothing on pollution control. The marginal control-cost curve reveals the cost savings (control costs avoided) that accrue to the firm when it pollutes. The marginal damage-cost curve shows the estimated cost ($32.50 per ton) imposed on parties downwind from the smelter. Without any tax or legal restraints, the smelter would emit 190,000 tons of sulfur dioxide into the air per year, causing $6.2 million in damage. A tax equal to the marginal damage cost of $32.50 per ton emitted would cause the firm to reduce its emissions of 17,100 tons per year and thus would reduce pollution damage from $6.2 million to about $0.6 million per year. The control cost of reducing emissions to this level would be about $2.9 million per year. Total social costs each year would fall from $6.2 million (all borne by those suffering pollution damage) to $3.5 million (combined costs of pollution damage and control, paid entirely by the firm and its customers). The net social gain would be $2.7 million.

The tax approach would promote efficient resource allocation by altering several economic incentives in a highly desirable way. First, the pollution tax would increase the cost of producing pollution-intensive goods, causing the supply in these industries to decline. A properly set tax would approximate the true cost of emissions, internalizing the cost of pollution. The revenues generated by the tax

The marginal control-cost curve shows that the firm, if it pays no damage costs itself, will emit 190,000 tons per year while spending nothing on control costs. However, if taxed according to the marginal damages it imposes ($32.50 per ton), it will voluntarily cut back its emissions to 17,100 tons per year, which is the socially efficient level. Further control would cost more than its social benefit.

Source: Richard L. Stroup, "The Economics of Air Pollution Control" (Ph.D. diss., University of Washington, 1970).

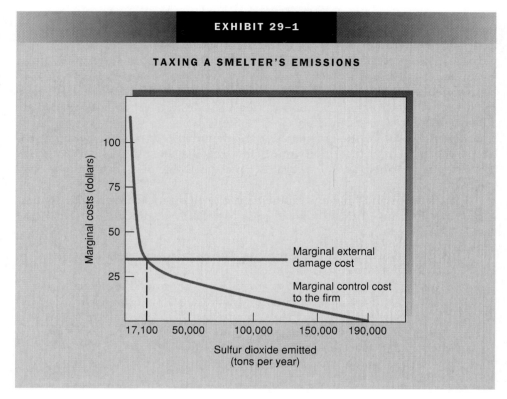

EXHIBIT 29–1

TAXING A SMELTER'S EMISSIONS

could be used to compensate secondary parties harmed by the pollutants; the pollution authority would in effect be acting as a court, recognizing the rights of those harmed by pollution, and awarding them compensation for damages suffered. Alternatively, the revenues could be used to finance a wide range of projects, including applied research on alternative methods of improving air quality.

Second, a pollution tax would give firms an economic incentive to use methods of production (and control technology) that would create less pollution. As long as it was cheaper for the firm to control harmful emissions than to pay the emission fee (tax), the firm would opt for control. Third, since firms would be able to lower their tax bills by controlling pollution, the market for innovative emission-control devices would be strengthened. Entrepreneurs would be induced to develop low-cost control devices and market them to firms that would now have a strong and continuing incentive to reduce their levels of emissions.

The pollution tax has several advantages, but observers often cite four problems with the tax approach:

1. It allows some pollution harms to continue. Even if those who suffer the harms are compensated, some would object that polluters should have no right to knowingly cause harm and then "buy their way out."
2. To be efficient, it must be based on damage costs of the emissions, and it is difficult to estimate these costs (which is why property rights are difficult to enforce). Of course, this same lack of knowledge hinders any strategy which might be intended to be efficient.

3. Emissions would have to be monitored, since, again, any efficient approach would require knowledge of who is polluting, and how much.
4. Very large tax payments required of polluters would mean that whole industries could be shaken up, and some firms put out of business. Lobbyists for polluters have successfully prevented such taxes up to this point.

Given the damage and control costs estimates of Exhibit 29–1, the pollution-tax approach does not fully eliminate damages from pollution emissions. Should it? For a person to whom only zero harm is morally acceptable, the answer is yes. But if the goal is to minimize the total costs of pollution, including the cost of controlling it, the answer clearly is no. At pollution-emission levels of less than 17,100 tons per year, the marginal costs of pollution control would exceed the marginal benefits of the control. In cases such as that illustrated by the exhibit, substantial improvement can be made at a modest cost. At some point, however, it will become extremely costly to make additional improvements. As in the case of noise abatement, airplane and highway safety measures, and other health and safety matters, most of us are willing to tolerate small harms and risks to gain freedoms and benefits, including reasonably priced goods and services.

The pollution-tax approach recognizes that cleaning up the environment is like squeezing water from a wet towel. Initially, a great deal of water can be squeezed from the towel with very little effort, but it becomes increasingly difficult to squeeze out still more. So it is with reducing environmental pollution. At some point, the marginal benefit of a cleaner environment declines to the level where the additional clean-up efforts (or reductions in emissions) are simply not worth the cost. Thus, the optimal level of pollution is seldom zero.

People want clean air and water. However, since they want other things as well, those entrusted with the authority to control pollution should ask themselves two critical questions: How many other goods and services are we willing to give up to fight each battle against pollution? And how much would the public like us to spend, from its own pockets, to achieve additional freedom from pollution? Since we all want to obtain the maximum benefit from expenditures on pollution control, it is important that these questions be answered carefully, no matter which control strategy we adopt.

MAXIMUM-EMISSION-STANDARD APPROACH

Although economics suggests that the pollution-tax approach would be much more efficient, a **maximum emission standard** is more often imposed. In this case, the regulatory agency forces all producers to reduce their emissions to a designated level. The level may be chosen to produce a tolerable level of total pollution. Producers who are unable to meet the standard are required to pay a fine or even to terminate production.

One problem with this approach is that the costs of eliminating pollution emissions generally vary widely among polluters. Some can control pollution much more cheaply than others, but the maximum emission standard fails to use this fact to get more control per dollar of expenditure in control costs, or to

Maximum emission standard
The maximum amount of pollution that a polluter is permitted to emit, established by the government or a regulatory authority. Fines are generally imposed on those who are unwilling or unable to comply.

minimize the costs of achieving a given level of total pollution. It thus results in less pollution control per dollar than, for example, the pollution-tax strategy.

Exhibit 29–2 illustrates why the maximum emission standard is an inefficient method of reducing the pollution level. Estimated minimum costs of added control by three particulate pollution emitters are listed. Suppose the regulatory agency wants to reduce the total particulate emissions from the three firms by 3 tons. The emission-standards approach might accomplish this simply by requiring each firm to reduce its particulate emissions by 1 ton. The cost of these equal reductions will differ substantially among the firms; it will cost the electric utility $80, the steel plant $990, and the petroleum refiner $573. If this method is adopted, it will cost society $1,643 in control costs to meet the new maximum pollution standard, which is 3 tons below the previous level of emissions.

Alternatively, the regulatory agency might levy a pollution tax and eliminate the same amount of pollution for much less. If we assume that a 3 ton reduction is small for each producer, so that each additional ton of pollution reduction raises control costs only by one dollar, then a tax of just $82.50 per ton would cause the electric utility to reduce particulate emissions by 3 tons, at a total cost of $243 ($80 + $81 + $82 = $243). That would allow the utility to escape 3 × $82.50 = $247.50 in added tax. The other polluters would not cut back emissions, but would choose to pay the tax, which is cheaper for them than the control costs. With the tax approach, which causes the cheapest control to take place, society buys the 3 ton reduction in pollution for $243, about one-seventh the cost incurred in the elimination of the same amount of pollution under the maximum-emission control strategy.

TRANSFERABLE EMISSION RIGHTS

A much more efficient form of the maximum-emission strategy is to require the same 1 ton reduction of each firm, but allow the remaining rights to pollute (their original pollution rate, minus 1 ton each) to be traded among the three. In this case, the electric utility would sell 2 tons of its rights-to-pollute, one to each of the other two firms. Why? It can profit by reducing its pollution by 3 tons for $243, then selling its "excess" pollution rights to the other two firms, saving the steel firm $990 and the refinery $573. The amount paid by the two firms to the utility for its service (added pollution control, beyond its own requirement) would be more than $80 per ton, but no higher than the $990 plus $573 saved by the other two. The net savings to society in getting the full 3 ton reduction in pollution is again the same as in the pollution-tax case. The emission-rights-trading strategy also has an important political advantage: no large payments (or small ones either) have to be made by the firms to the tax collector.

Since each polluter has a different control-cost schedule, either the pollution-tax strategy or the emission-rights trading strategy would result in the most pollution control per control dollar spent, and reach any desired pollution level at the lowest possible price. Some people object to the emissions-trading strategy because pollution emitted at one location may cause more damage or less damage than the same pollution at another place. This is true, but any efficient strategy would have to make adjustments to recognize this fact. The emissions-trading strategy might allow polluters in densely populated areas to exchange their pollu-

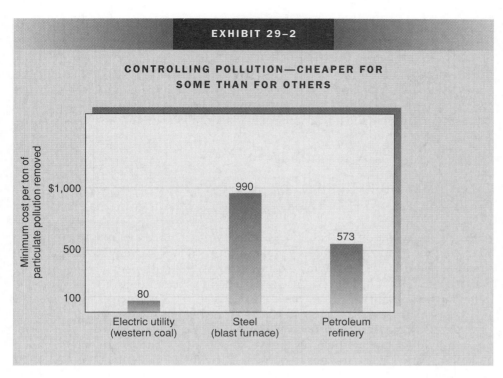

EXHIBIT 29–2

CONTROLLING POLLUTION—CHEAPER FOR SOME THAN FOR OTHERS

Some polluters face much higher control costs than others. If the authorities' control strategy does not properly take this into account, control may be needlessly expensive and opposition to control needlessly strong. If each polluter were required to reduce particulate pollution by one ton, total control costs for that change would be $80 + $990 + $573 = $1,643. But, if a pollution tax of $82.50 were levied, the steel and petroleum plants would pay it, while the electric utility would find it cheaper to control some of its particulate pollution, and a reduction of 3 tons of emissions would cost roughly $240 instead of more than $1,640.

Source: EPA reports, summarized by Robert Crandall in *Controlling Industrial Pollution* (The Brookings Institution, Washington, D.C., 1983), page 36.

tion rights with polluters in a sparsely populated area with a bonus. Two tons of pollution rights in Manhattan might trade for 3 tons on a sparsely populated part of the coast, where the winds usually blow the particulates out to sea with much less damage.

The emissions-trading strategy was incorporated, in a limited way, into the Clean Air Act amendments of 1990. Beginning in 1995, power plants fueled by coal are required to scale back their emissions of sulfur dioxide by more than half from 1980 levels. Those who control more than required, however, will be able to sell their "allowances" (the amount they are allowed by the new law to emit) to other power plants. Other forms of pollution are not affected, but if this project is judged to be a success, additional uses of this strategy can be expected.

SPECIFIC-PRESCRIPTION APPROACH

We have shown how the emissions-standard approach (without emissions trading) is less efficient than the pollution tax. Even less efficient is the approach taken earlier by Congress requiring the Environmental Protection Agency (EPA) to implement the Clean Air Act of 1970 for coal-burning electric-power plants. Instead of setting emission standards, Congress ordered the EPA to require that new plants use a specific kind of pollution-control apparatus—giant "scrubbers" to clean exhaust gases from new coal-burning electric-power plants. Even though cheaper and more reliable means are frequently available to produce electricity with the same or less pollution, especially the use of clean coal, the far more expensive scrubbers were mandated. This rule favored certain regions of the country over others, and delayed the construction of newer, cleaner power plants, so that the air was dirtier than it would have been with the cheaper control methods. As ironic and as well known as this situation was,[4] more efficient approaches were not politically feasible until 1990, when the Clean Air Act amendments began to focus on emission standards. For reasons that we will explore more fully in the next chapter, the government solution to market failure is often inefficient.

SHOULD GOVERNMENT ALWAYS TRY TO CONTROL EXTERNALITIES?

When an externality is present, ideal efficiency of resource allocation may not be attained. It does not follow, though, that the government can always improve the situation and bring the economy closer to its ideal allocation level. In evaluating the case for a public-sector response to externalities, one should keep in mind the following three points:

1. Sometimes the economic inefficiency resulting from externalities is small; therefore, given the cost of public-sector action, net gain from intervention is unlikely. The behavior of individuals often influences the welfare of others. The length of hair, choice of clothing, and personal hygiene of some individuals may affect the welfare of secondary parties. Should an agency in charge of personal appearance and hygiene be established to deal with externalities in these areas? Persons who value personal freedom would answer with a resounding no. And from the standpoint of economic efficiency, their view is correct. The effects of externalities in these and similar areas are small. The costs of correcting externalities of this type would often be greater than the benefit.

Government intervention requires the use of scarce resources. Regulatory agencies must be established; suits and countersuits are typically filed. These actions require the use of scarce and costly legal resources. Most public-sector decision makers lack the information necessary to determine which activities should be taxed and which should be subsidized. Administrative problems such as these greatly reduce the attractiveness of public-sector action. When the external effects are small, the cost of government intervention is likely to exceed the loss due to market inefficiency, *relative to the hypothetical ideal.* Under these circumstances, the best approach is usually to do nothing.

2. The market often finds reasonably efficient means of dealing with externalities. The existence of externalities implies the presence of *potential* gain. When external effects are significant, market participants have an incentive to organize economic activity in a manner that will enable them to capture the potential gain. If the

---

[4]See Robert Crandall, *Controlling Industrial Pollution: The Economics and Politics of Clean Air* (Washington: The Brookings Institution, 1983); and Bruce Yandle, *The Political Limits of Environmental Regulation: Tracking the Unicorn* (New York: Quorum Books, 1989), for fascinating accounts of the politics and economics of this situation. Eastern coal-mine owners, and the United Mine Workers Union who wanted less mining of the cleaner western coal, joined forces with environmental interests in the West to push through the requirement that costly scrubbers be used instead of allowing power plants to switch to cleaner western coal.

number of parties affected by the externality is small, they may be able to arrive at a multi-party bargain that will at least partially negate the inefficiency and loss resulting from the externality.

Some entrepreneurs have devised ingenious schemes to capture benefits that were previously external to private parties. We mentioned earlier that private developers of country clubs and golf courses often capture the benefits of these amenities by placing them on large tracts of land. The purchasers of lots and houses will benefit from trees, gardens, manicured lawns, and so on. When consumers are willing to pay for these amenities, tract developers who provide them benefit in the form of higher prices on the sale of surrounding lots.[5] The greater the potential gains, the greater the incentive to find answers to these kinds of problems. Thus, market participants will often devise efficient arrangements for dealing with external effects when those effects become sufficiently large.

3. Government action may also impose an external cost on secondary parties. Government intervention designed to correct the inefficiencies created by externalities is costly. When the costs of public-sector intervention exceed the benefits, efficiency requires that intervention should be rejected. In addition, we should recognize that even democratic public-sector action results in the imposition of an externality—political winners impose an external cost on those opposed to the action. Just as an individual may carry an activity too far when some of the costs are borne by others, a winning political coalition may also carry an action beyond the point of ideal efficiency. The gains that accrue to the political winners may be less than the costs imposed on others. (Limits to the effectiveness of government action will be discussed more fully in the next chapter.)

MARKET FAILURE: PUBLIC GOODS

Public goods comprise the extreme case of external benefits. They are nonexcludable, so producers cannot exclude those who do not pay. In addition, they are nonrival in consumption, meaning that consumption by one person does not reduce the good's availability to others. It is important to note that only goods with these two characteristics qualify as public goods in an economic sense. Goods provided in the public sector, ranging from medical services and education

---

[5]The development of Walt Disney World in Florida is an interesting case of how entrepreneurial ingenuity made it possible to capture external benefits more fully. When Walt Disney developed Disneyland in California, the market value of the land in the immediate area soared as a result of the increase in demand for services (food, lodging, gasoline, and so on). Since the land in the area was owned by others, the developers of Disneyland were unable to capture these external benefits. However, when Walt Disney World was developed near Orlando, Florida, the owners purchased an enormous plot of land, far more than was needed for the amusement park. As was the case with Disneyland in California, the operation of Walt Disney World caused land values in the immediate area to rise sharply. Since the developers of Walt Disney World had initially purchased that land, they were able to capture the external benefits by selling it to hotels, restaurants, and other businesses desiring a nearby location.

to trash collection, are not necessarily public goods. Examples of pure public goods are rare. National defense is one. The defense system that protects you provides similar protection to all other citizens. The quality of the atmosphere might also be classified as a public good.

THE FREE-RIDER PROBLEM

Free rider

One who receives the benefit of a good without contributing to its costs. Public goods and commodities that generate external benefits offer people the opportunity to become free riders.

Since nonpaying consumers cannot be excluded (at a reasonable cost), the market mechanism may not provide a sufficient amount of public goods. This result is likely because each of us has an incentive to become a **free rider,** one who receives the benefits of a good without paying toward its costs. Why contribute to the cost of supplying clean air, pure water, national defense, or legal justice when your contribution will have a negligible impact? The sensible path will lead you to do nothing. As long as you travel that path alone, or in minimal company, you will ride along, free and easy. If enough others join you, however, the aggregate lack of action will lead to an insufficient quantity of public goods.

Suppose national defense were provided entirely through the market. Would you voluntarily help to pay for it? Your contribution would have a negligible impact on the total supply of defense available to each of us, even if you made a large personal contribution. Many citizens, even though they might value defense highly, would become free riders, and few funds would be available to finance the necessary supply. If the military-industrial complex were dependent on market forces alone, it would be small indeed!

The harmony between private and social interests tends to break down for public goods. The amount of a public good available to an individual (and others) will be virtually unaltered by whether or not the individual pays for it. Each individual thus has an incentive to become a free rider. When numerous individuals become free riders, however, less than the ideal amount of the public good is likely to be produced. (It should be noted that markets will sometimes supply public goods. See the "Applications in Economics" box on private provision of public goods.)

NEAR PUBLIC GOODS

Few commodities are pure public goods, but a much larger set of goods are jointly consumed even though nonpaying customers can be excluded. For example, such goods as radio and television broadcasts, national parks, interstate highways, movies, and football games may be jointly consumed. Until congestion sets in, additional consumption of these "near public goods," *once they are produced,* is costless to society.

Should nonpaying customers be excluded when the marginal cost of providing the good to them is zero? Many economists argue that such near public goods as highways, national parks, and television programming should be provided free to consumers, at the expense of the taxpayers. Why exclude people from the consumption of these near public goods when their use of the goods does not add to the costs? The argument has a certain appeal.

We must be careful, however. Television programs, highways, parks, and other public goods are scarce. The consumption of other products must be sacrificed to

APPLICATIONS IN ECONOMICS

PRIVATE PROVISION OF PUBLIC GOODS

An excellent example of a public good is the preservation of a locally or nationally significant form of wildlife. Hawks, sea lions, and wild geese belong to no one, but their survival keeps ecosystems in balance and intact. We all benefit when habitats are kept available to ensure that such species do not become extinct. The fact is that each of us can be a free rider if others make the effort and sacrifice needed to bring about such preservation, and successful voluntary efforts in the private sector have done just that: thousands of organizations, each defying the free-rider problem, have for many decades led the conservation movement, privately establishing successful conservation projects.

Some of these groups are very large. The Nature Conservancy owns and manages a national system of nearly 800 sanctuaries and has preserved some 2.4 million acres since 1951. The National Audubon Society has a sanctuary system of over 63 units totaling over 250,000 acres. Others are small—a local garden club might own and manage two acres to preserve a particular wildflower.

Private groups have often been leaders in educating the public, and have been well ahead of government in providing their particular public good. Two examples involve hawks and sea lions.

EXAMPLE 1: THE HAWK MOUNTAIN SANCTUARY   In the 1930s hawks were considered a nuisance or worse, since they killed certain other birds, including domestic chickens. There was often a bounty on them—the government would pay people who killed hawks. Conservationists, however, had begun to worry about the declining numbers of hawks, pointing out that among other things, hawks ate rodents, keeping down the grain losses experienced by farmers. The environmental movement was still very weak, however, and the slaughter of hawks continued.

In one area in particular, Hawk Mountain of eastern Pennsylvania, thousands of hawks were killed on certain days each year. So upset was Rosalie Edge, an early conservationist (and leading suffragist), that when reasoning with government authorities failed, she organized a small group of conservationists who simply bought Hawk Mountain for $3,500. They prevented further shooting from that critical spot and established a nonprofit educational and conservation group—the Hawk Mountain Sanctuary Association. Seven thousand members from all over the nation, in addition to admission fees paid by 50,000 visitors per year, support a visitor and education center at the mountain where previously the hawks were slaughtered by the thousands each year.

EXAMPLE 2: SEA LION CAVES, INC.   Like hawks, sea lions on the Oregon coast were formerly hunted, and bounties were paid to those who killed them. Sea lions feed on fish, and during the 1920s the state of Oregon paid $5 per sea lion killed. Several bounty hunters made their living in this fashion. The intent was to reduce sea lion consumption of coastal salmon. Earlier, commercial fishing interests had hired professional hunters to exterminate the sea lion. However, one important area of the sea lion's Oregon habitat was privately owned and used as a tourist attraction—Sea Lion Caves, where the animals could be viewed up close, in a natural setting. The owners of the caves had to spend a good deal of time driving off bounty hunters. By 1931 conservation legislation was passed to protect sea lions in most areas of the Oregon coast. Nevertheless, while the extermination pressure was on, the profit-seeking Sea Lion Cave operation played an important part in the survival of the sea-going mammals. The sea lions themselves are not owned, and their survival is largely a public good. But private ownership of the habitat had concentrated enough of the benefits in the hands of a tourist-based business to help guarantee the survival of the endangered animals at a critical time.

Can private clubs and businesses eliminate the public goods problem? Not necessarily, since there is no guarantee that the optimal amount of public goods will be provided. However, these private-sector philanthropic and entrepreneurial solutions to certain public-goods problems remind us that whenever the will exists to solve such problems, government action is not the only possible way. The same sort of informed and determined efforts needed to convince government to do the right thing can frequently find private solutions even more quickly and cheaply.

produce such goods. If a zero price is charged, how does one determine whether or not consumers value additional units enough to cover their opportunity cost? How can an intensely concerned minority communicate its views as to the types of near public goods that should be produced? If some users become dissatisfied, will the government-funded producer have an incentive to consider change, as happens when users reduce their patronage of market establishments? Taxes will be necessary to cover the costs of making near public goods freely available. Will such taxes lead to inefficiency? These factors reduce the attractiveness of public-sector provision of jointly consumed commodities, especially when exclusion of nonpaying consumers is possible.

MARKET FAILURE: POOR INFORMATION

In the real world, market choices, like other decisions, are made with incomplete information. Consumers do not have perfect knowledge about the quality of a product, the price of alternative products, or side effects that may result from a product. They may make incorrect decisions, decisions they will later regret, because they do not possess good information.

The reality of imperfect knowledge is not, of course, the fault of the market. In fact, the market provides consumers with a strong incentive to acquire information. Because consumers must bear the consequences of their mistakes, they certainly will seek to avoid the deliberate purchase of "lemon" products.

GETTING YOUR MONEY'S WORTH

The consumer's information problem is minimal if the item is purchased regularly. Consider the purchase of soap. There is little cost associated with trying alternative brands. Since soap is a regularly purchased product, trial and error is an economical means of determining which brand is most suitable to one's needs. Soap, like toothpaste, most food products, lawn service, and gasoline, is a **repeat-purchase item.** The consumer can use past experience to good advantage when buying such items.

Repeat-purchase item
An item purchased often by the same buyer.

What incentive does the producer have to supply accurate information that will help the consumer make a satisfying long-run choice? Is there a conflict between consumer and producer interests? The answers to these questions are critically affected by the seller's dependence on return customers.

If dissatisfaction on the part of *current* customers is expected to have a strong adverse effect on *future* sales, a business entrepreneur will attempt to provide accurate information to help customers make wise choices. The future success of business entrepreneurs who sell repeat-purchase products is highly dependent on the future purchases of currently satisfied customers. There is a harmony of interest because buyer and seller alike will be better off if the customer is satisfied with the product purchased.

LET THE BUYER BEWARE

Major problems of conflicting interests, inadequate information, and unhappy customers arise when goods either (1) are difficult to evaluate on inspection and are seldom repeatedly purchased from the same producer or (2) are potentially capable of serious and lasting harmful side effects that cannot be predicted by a layperson. Under these conditions, human nature being what it is, we would expect some unscrupulous producers to sell low-quality, defective, and even harmful goods.

When customers are unable to distinguish between high-quality and low-quality goods, their ability to police quality and price is weakened. When this is the case, business entrepreneurs have a strong incentive to cut costs by reducing quality. Consumers get less for their dollars. Since sellers in this situation are not dependent on repeat customers, those who cut cost by cutting quality may survive and even prosper in the marketplace. The probability of customer dissatisfaction is thus increased because of inadequate information and poor quality. Accordingly, the case for an unhampered market mechanism is weakened.

Consider the consumer's information problem when an automobile is purchased. Are most consumers capable of properly evaluating the safety equipment? Except for a handful of experts, most people are not. Some consumers might individually seek expert advice. It may be more efficient, though, to prevent market failure by having the government regulate automobile safety and require certain safety equipment.

As another example of the problem of inadequate consumer information, consider the case of a drug manufacturer's exaggerated claims for a new product. Until consumers have had experience with the drug or have listened to others' experiences, they might make wasteful purchases. Government regulation might benefit consumers by forcing the manufacturer to modify its claims.

ENTREPRENEURS AND INFORMATION

Consumers have the incentive to seek good information, even though it is costly. Entrepreneurial publishers and other providers of information help consumers find what they seek by providing expert evaluations of the special characteristics built into complex products. For car buyers and computer buyers, for example, publishers market dozens of specialized magazines containing expert analyses and opinions from almost any point of view. Laboratory test results and detailed product evaluations are provided by *Consumer Reports*, *Consumer Research*, and other publications on a wide variety of goods.

Entrepreneurial sellers, when they are in fact providing good value, have an incentive to bridge the information gap, and to let consumers know it. Comparative advertising is utilized to illustrate for potential buyers the advantage of one product or service relative to rivals. Consumers who will soon have to choose among the products being compared, and will be required to pay for their choice, will tend to be especially receptive to comparative advertising.

Franchises are another way that entrepreneurs have responded to the consumer need for more information, as we pointed out in Chapter 2. The tourist traveling through an area for the first time—and very possibly the last—may find that eating at a franchised food outlet and sleeping at a franchised motel is the

Brand names and franchises provide consumers with valuable information that helps them make more informed choices.

cheapest way to avoid annoying and costly mistakes. The franchiser sets the standards for all firms in the chain and establishes procedures, including continuous inspection, designed to maintain the standards. Franchisers have a strong incentive to maintain their reputation for quality, because if it declines, their ability to sell new franchises is hurt. Even though the tourist may visit a particular establishment only once, the franchise turns that visit into a "repeat purchase," since the reputation of the entire national franchise operation is at stake.

Similarly, the advertising of a brand name nationally develops a reputation that is at stake when purchases are made. How much would the Coca-Cola Company pay to avoid a dangerous bottle of Coke being sold? Surely, it would be a large sum. The company's brand name is worth an estimated $24 billion, and that good name is a hostage to quality control. Because it is a household name worldwide, any serious quality-control problem would be broadcast worldwide, and do enormous financial damage to the firm. Advertising investments act as a signal that the firm is serious about its future business and guarantees that it has something important to lose if it cheats customers.

Source Perrier's experience with its Perrier mineral water is a concrete example of how far a company is willing to go to protect a brand name. On February 2, 1990, Source Perrier learned that tiny traces of benzene, a cancer-causing chemical, had been discovered in a few bottles of Perrier mineral water. The U.S. Food and Drug Administration announced that the amounts of benzene were so small—less than 20 parts per billion—that there was no danger even to steady drinkers of the water, unless the contamination problem persisted for many years. Nevertheless, the company announced on February 8 that it was not only shutting down until it found and corrected the problem, but that it was also recalling all 100 million bottles from store shelves in 120 countries. To protect its reputation for product purity, the company set aside 835 million French francs, or about $152 million, to finance the dramatic recall. In the end, Source Perrier spent an estimated $80 million to assure consumers that its product was safe and pure.

Enterprising entrepreneurs have found ways to assure buyers that products meet high standards of quality, even when the producer is small and not so well known. Consider the case of Best Western Motels.[6] Best Western owns no motels, but it publishes rules and standards that motel owners must comply with if they are to use the Best Western brand name and the reservation service that the company also operates. In order to protect its brand name, Best Western sends out inspectors to see that each Best Western motel in fact meets the standards. Every disappointed customer reduces the value of the Best Western name, and reduces the willingness of motel owners to pay for use of the name. The standards are designed to keep customers satisfied. Even though each motel owner has only a relatively small operation, renting the Best Western name provides the small operator with the kind of international reputation formerly available only to large firms. In effect, Best Western acts as a regulator of all motels bearing its name. It does so to the benefit of consumers and producers, and the entire operation is a voluntary, market solution to the information problem.

Another kind of private regulator is Underwriters Laboratories, or UL. It establishes its own standards for safety in electrical equipment. Manufacturers voluntarily submit their equipment to UL and pay the firm to test the product. They do so because if UL certifies that the product meets UL standards, that fact can be advertised, and consumers, knowing the UL reputation, will be more willing to buy the product. Again, the certifying firm, UL in this case, has a strong incentive to certify only those electrical products that do indeed meet their safety standards, because the value of the UL name is at stake. That value depends entirely on the effectiveness of its claims that UL-certified products are safe to use.

As these examples indicate, entrepreneurial measures such as assuring the quality of a firm, a franchise, or otherwise protecting a brand name can be both expensive and effective. They cannot, however, guarantee that customers will never be cheated or disappointed after a transaction. Despite the best efforts of entrepreneurs, the lack of consumer information will continue to assure that the market will remain imperfect relative to the economists' ideal, and that government will have a potential role to play in improving on the market's results.

ONE-SIDED INFORMATION

As useful and important as the published evaluations of experts, franchise operations, advertising, brand-name reputations and private regulatory firms are, they cannot solve a kind of information problem that has little to do with product design or manufacture. This is called the **asymmetric-information problem,** and

Asymmetric-information problem
A problem arising when either buyers or sellers have important information about the product that is not possessed by the other side in potential transactions.

---

[6]This section draws from Randall G. Holcombe and Lora P. Helcombe, "The Market for Regulation," *Journal of Institutional and Theoretical Economics* 142, no. 4, (1986), pp. 684–696.

it can make markets themselves, for some products, difficult to operate effectively. The problem arises when either the potential buyer or potential seller has important information that the other side does not have.

Think for a moment about buyers trying to avoid "lemons" in the used car market. Sellers know which cars are above average quality and which are below average. Buyers on the other hand, cannot tell which is which simply by looking at and test-driving them. Thus buyers will be willing to pay no more than what they believe is the average value of all cars on the market. But if better-than-average cars cannot bring better-than-average prices, then fewer of them will be sold in the market, and if below-average cars bring average prices, then more of the below-average cars will be offered. Buyers understand this, so they expect the average car in such a market to be below the average of all existing cars of that age and type. Owners of better cars are reluctant to sell at the low market price and it is hard to make a market for cars of above average quality when buyers cannot be convinced that they actually are better than average.

Can anything be done to reduce this kind of asymmetric-information problem? Sellers of the better cars have an incentive to provide additional information in order to get a higher price for their superior goods. But how is this done? How can they support their claims about their product being better? The answers differ according to whether the seller is a private owner or a dealership. Car owners can present their records of oil changes and lubrications to show that these services, important to the long-run durability of a car, have been performed on schedule. Dealers, whose mechanics inspect the cars before they are offered for sale, may offer money-back guarantees, or warranties that promise free repairs if needed within a specified time, on the most reliable cars they sell. The other cars they sell will be sold "as is" with no warranty. Sellers of products can even give price guarantees, as some stores do when they advertise that if the buyer finds a lower price for the same product within a specified period of time, the seller will refund the difference. By offering to bear such risks, sellers provide credibility to their claims about better products and prices. In other words, they improve the quality of the information offered and reduce the problem of asymmetric information.

The problem of asymmetric information also arises when buyers know more than sellers. Consider the market for health insurance. Buyers know their own health problems better than insurance companies. Those whose health history and life-styles threaten greater potential health costs may pay the same as others but later collect more from the insurance company. In contrast, the same insurance at the same price is less attractive to the healthiest people, and fewer of them will buy it. When the company is unable to identify those with the greatest potential health costs and charge them more, it will have to charge its healthier customers a rate that exceeds their expected future insurance claims. But this would drive away even more of the healthier potential buyers, making the situation even worse. As in the case of used cars, asymmetric information reduces the effectiveness of the market. Just as the best used cars may be hard to sell, so, too, may the healthiest individuals be hard to insure when asymmetric information is present.

What can be done about asymmetric information when buyers have information but sellers do not? Buyers, like sellers, are willing to provide information when it is to their advantage to do so. In the case of insurance buyers, those buyers with the best health record, who are therefore least likely to have future insurance claims, can often get lower insurance rates by opening their private medical records to the insurance company. Sellers who otherwise have no right to see that information may find it gladly offered by the healthiest buyers when buyers know they will be offered lower insurance prices in return.

Another strategy sellers use to deal with the insurance problem is to offer "bundle purchases." Knowing that some employees in any sizable firm are likely to have good health and some bad health, insurance companies find it economical to offer a "group rate" policy covering all the employees of the firm. By screening out only the easily identified bad risks, so that they can save the cost of carefully screening every employee's medical history, they can offer moderate rates.

We have discussed many ways in which market participants can reduce the problems they face due to the scarcity and cost of information. These are not totally effective, however, and poor information remains a problem that keeps markets from reaching their hypothetical ideal.

LOOKING AHEAD

In this chapter we focused on the failures of the market. In the next chapter, we will use economic analysis to come to a better understanding of the workings of the public sector. We will also discuss some of the expected shortcomings of public-sector action. Awareness of both the strengths and weaknesses of alternative forms of economic organization will help us to make more intelligent choices in this important area.

CHAPTER SUMMARY

1. The sources of market failure can be grouped into four major categories: externalities, public goods, poor information, and monopoly. Externality and public-goods problems are present when property rights are undefined or poorly enforced.

2. When externalities are present, the market may fail to confront decision makers with the proper incentives. When decision makers are not forced to consider external cost, they may find it personally advantageous to undertake an economic activity even though it generates a net loss to the community. In contrast, when external benefits are present, decision makers may fail to undertake economic action that would generate a net social gain.

3. When external costs originate from the activities of a business firm, the firm's costs will understate the social cost of producing the good. If production of the good generates external costs, the price of the product under competitive conditions will be too low and the output too large to meet the *ideal requirements* of economic efficiency.

4. Clearly established private-property rights enable owners to prohibit others from using or abusing their property. In contrast, common-property rights with open access

normally result in overutilization, since most of the cost of overutilization (and misuse) is imposed on others.

5. When external benefits are present, market demand will understate the social gains of conducting the activity. The consumption and production of goods that generate external benefits will tend to be lower than the socially ideal levels.

6. The efficient use of air and water resources is particularly troublesome for the market because the resources themselves are usually not owned, and it is often difficult to know what damages are done when pollution is released into them at a particular time and place. That means that the property rights of those harmed may not be protected. Government regulation will not produce the needed information, but may improve the situation. A system of emission charges or of transferable emission rights might induce individuals to make wiser use of these resources. Either strategy will (a) increase the cost of releasing pollution, (b) grant firms an incentive to use methods of production that create less pollution, and (c) provide producers with an incentive to seek effective and innovative control devices.

7. When the control costs of firms vary, the emission-charge (pollution-tax) approach will permit society to reduce pollution by a given amount at a lower cost than will the maximum-emission-standard method that is currently widely used. The marginal cost of attaining a cleaner environment will rise as the pollution level is reduced. At some point, the economic benefits of a still cleaner environment will be less than the costs.

8. When the marginal benefits (for example, cleaner air) derived from ending pollution are less than the social gains associated with a pollution-generating activity, prohibition of the activity that results in pollution (or other external cost) is not an ideal solution.

9. In evaluating the case for government intervention in situations involving externalities, one must consider the

following factors: (a) the magnitude of the external effects relative to the cost of government action; (b) the ability of the market to devise means of dealing with the problem without intervention; and (c) the possibility that the political majority may carry the government intervention too far if the external costs imposed on the minority are not fully considered.

10. When it is costly or impossible to withhold a public good from persons who do not or will not help pay for it, the market system breaks down because everyone has an incentive to become a free rider. When this happens, production of the public good will be lower than the socially ideal level.

11. The market provides an incentive for buyers and sellers to acquire information. When a business is dependent on repeat customers, it has a strong incentive to promote customer satisfaction. However, when goods are either (a) difficult to evaluate on inspection and seldom purchased repeatedly from the same producer or (b) have potentially serious and lasting harmful effects, consumer trial and error may be an unsatisfactory means of determining quality. Franchising, brand names, and voluntary regulatory schemes often communicate reliable information on product quality to consumers and thereby reduce the likelihood that consumers will be cheated or misled, even in cases when the specific item is not purchased regularly. Asymmetric information provides an additional challenge to market participants.

CRITICAL-ANALYSIS QUESTIONS

*1. When cattle grazed on the English commons—open-access pastures—overgrazing took place. Eventually, many of the pastures became private property. What other option might have solved the open-access problem?

2. Why might businesses that are causing pollution problems prefer transferable emission rights to the pollution-tax approach? When might they not?

3. "Elementary education is obviously a public good. After all, it is provided by government." Evaluate this statement.

*4. Why is it difficult to determine the proper output of a pure public good?

5. "Since free riders can enjoy public goods, there is no way that they will be provided privately." Evaluate this statement.

*6. Are people more likely to take better care of an item they own jointly (communally) or one they own privately? Why? Does the presence of private-property rights affect the behavior of persons in noncapitalist nations? Why or why not?

*7. *What's wrong with this way of thinking?* "Corporations are the major beneficiaries of our lax pollution control policy. Their costs are reduced because we permit them free use of valuable resources—clean water and air—in order to produce goods. These lower costs are simply added to the profits of the polluting firms."

8. *What's wrong with this way of thinking?* "Private-property rights are a gamble. What if the owner doesn't take good care of what he owns? Communal property rights are better because there are more people to take care of what they own. Surely someone will exercise the needed care." (Hint: What was Aristotle's position on the issue?)

*9. Can you think of any public goods, or near public goods, that are supplied privately? Do such examples show that there is no such thing as a free-rider problem?

*10. What factor limits the private supply of public goods?

*11. "Corporations in America are being persecuted unfairly by environmental legislation such as air-pollution-control laws. Corporate leadership is responsible and would work for cleaner air without all this legal hassle." Evaluate this statement using the economic way of thinking.

*12. In a small town located next to an interstate highway are two prospering family restaurants. Both are locally owned, but one is franchised, a part of a nationally advertised chain of such restaurants. The other does not advertise. Assuming that highway travelers and local residents have seen equal amounts of advertising from the chain, in which restaurant would you expect to find more highway travelers? Why?

13. Many consumers are willing to pay more for brand-name products (for example, Bayer aspirin or Minute Maid orange juice) than for generic versions of the same products. Is this irrational? Do consumers get anything for their additional expense? Explain.

14. It is reported that prior to the overthrow of the Bulgarian communist regime in 1989, industrial pollution damaged 70 percent of Bulgaria's farmland. If the farmland had been privately owned, do you think the same damages would have occurred? Explain your answer.

15. "Restaurants that offer consumers low-quality food at relatively high prices are more likey to be present in an area where most customers are tourists than in an area where most customers are local residents." Is this true? Explain your answer.

---

*Asterisk denotes questions for which answers are given in Appendix C.

CHAPTER THIRTY

PUBLIC CHOICE:
UNDERSTANDING GOVERNMENT
AND GOVERNMENT FAILURE

It does not follow that whenever laissez faire falls short government interference is expedient; since the inevitable drawbacks of the latter may, in any particular case, be worse than the shortcomings of private enterprise.

HARRY SIDGWICK, 1887[1]

CHAPTER FOCUS

- *What is government? Which of its functions provide its most important benefits?*
- *What are the major forces that determine outcomes under representative democracy?*
- *Can government action be mutually advantageous to all citizens? Does it sometimes reduce the economic welfare of citizens?*
- *Will government action sometimes be more efficient than market exchange? When is it likely to be less efficient?*
- *Why does representative democracy often tax some people in order to provide benefits to others? What types of income transfers are attractive to politicians?*
- *Can constitutional rules influence political outcomes? What types of constitutional rules and restraints make sense?*

---

[1]Quoted in Charles Wolf, Jr., *Markets or Government* (Cambridge: MIT Press, 1988), p. 17.

About two-fifths of U.S. national income is channeled through various government departments and agencies. As we pointed out in Chapter 5, that figure has been growing for several decades. In addition, about two-fifths of the nation's land is owned by the government, and the legal framework set by the government establishes many of the "rules of the game" for the market sector. Government regulation of prices, of the use of land, water, and air, along with labor relations and business practices, exert a major impact on the operation of the economy. Given the size and influence of government, understanding how it works is a crucial issue. In this chapter, building on materials presented in Chapter 4 and the previous chapter, we will examine further the workings of government.

WHAT IS GOVERNMENT?

At the most basic level, the distinguishing characteristic of government is its monopoly on the use of coercive force to modify the actions of adults. Most societies allow parents to use force to influence the actions of their children. But with regard to adults, governments possess the exclusive right to use force. No individual has a right to use violence in order to take your wealth. Neither can a business firm, no matter how large or powerful, levy a "tax" on your income or force you to buy its product. The legitimate use of force to tax and control the behavior of adults is reserved for government.

How large should the scope of government action be? From an economic viewpoint, what are the proper functions of government? Philosophers, economists, and other scholars have disputed these issues for centuries. General agreement exists, however, that there are two legitimate economic functions of government: (1) protection against invasions by others and (2) provision of goods that cannot easily be provided through markets. These two functions correspond to what Nobel laureate James Buchanan conceptualizes as the protective and productive functions of government.

PROTECTIVE FUNCTION

People can gain from the assignment of the exclusive use of violence to the government for the purpose of protecting citizens and their property from other citizens and from outsiders. As philosopher John Locke wrote more than three centuries ago, individuals are constantly threatened by "the invasions of others." Therefore, each individual "is willing to join in society with others, who are already united, or have a mind to unite, for the mutual preservation of their lives, liberties, and estates."[2]

---

[2]John Locke, *Treatise of Civil Government*, 1690, edited by Charles Sherman (New York: Appleton-Century-Crofts, 1937), p. 82.

The protective function encompasses the government's maintenance of a framework of security and order, an infrastructure of rules within which people can interact peacefully with one another. It entails the enforcement of rules against theft, fraud, and the like. It also involves provision of national defense designed to protect domestic residents against invasions from a foreign power.

It is easy to see the economic importance of this function. Without the assurance that the wealth they create will not be taken from them by others, individuals will have little incentive to produce. Simply put, this protection provides citizens with assurance that if they sow (produce), they will be permitted to reap. When individuals are protected in this way, their resources will be directed toward productive activities that benefit the society as a whole. When they are not, so that property rights are not secure, problems of external costs and benefits are the result, as we discussed in the previous chapter.

PRODUCTIVE FUNCTION

Governments may also enhance the wealth of people by undertaking productive activities that cannot easily be organized through market transactions. The production of public goods such as national defense, a monetary system that provides price stability, a system of legal justice, flood-control projects, and insect-abatement programs in some parts of the country, are examples of productive activities that markets are likely to undersupply, increasing the likelihood that government might provide them to the advantage of its citizens. It is easy to see why markets have difficulty supplying the services. In each case, there are strong elements of nonexcludability and nonrival consumption—the two conditions that define public goods.

While pure public goods are rare, several goods generate spillover benefits that accrue to persons other than the primary consumer. Consider the example of education. Clearly education is not a pure public good. As the presence of private schools illustrates, consumption of schooling can be linked to payment by the consumer. Nonetheless, many believe that consumption of schooling promotes better citizenship, reduces crime, and in many other ways generates spillover benefits for persons other than the students going to school. When such spillover benefits are present, market allocation is expected to produce less than the ideal quantity of such goods. Some government provision or subsidy of private provision may be productive.

For still other near public goods, it may be costly to administer a market collection system linking consumption and payment. Consider the case of streets and highways. It would be costly to set up a tollbooth to charge for the use of streets in heavily congested urban areas. New technology shows some promise of lowering these costs dramatically. Up to now however, given the resources required to establish the payment-consumption link, it has been generally more efficient to have the government supply highways and streets for the use of all. When these roads are financed with gasoline taxes, the system may even approximate the outcome that would result if people were required to pay directly for their use of the roads.

Finally, a productive government will also promote competitive markets. In this area, the first guideline should be borrowed from the medical profession: make sure that you do no harm. A productive government will refrain from the imposition of licenses, discriminatory taxes, price controls, tariffs, quotas, and other entry and trade restraints that lessen the intensity of competition. When there are only a few firms in an industry, and competition from new firms (including rival foreign firms) can be restricted, market participants may collude in an effort to rig the market. Government rejection of the inevitable political demands for trade restraints, together with legislation prohibiting collusion and price-fixing agreements, can help promote competition in such markets.

ECONOMICS OF REPRESENTATIVE DEMOCRACY

Government is controlled by the political process. During the last three decades, public-choice economists have studied democratic politics, greatly enhancing our knowledge of that topic and providing us with insight on how we might better design the rules of politics. As we proceed in this chapter, we will consider this issue. Most political decisions in Western countries are made legislatively. Therefore, we will focus our analysis on a democratic system of representative government. Let us see what the tools of economics reveal about the political process.

DEMAND FOR GOVERNMENT

Public-choice theory indicates that there are two general forces underlying political action: (1) the correction of market failure and (2) *rent seeking*, which is the pursuit of private gain at public expense. Citizens can reap gains from government action that reduces market inefficiency emanating from externalities, public goods, an absence of competition, and poor information. However, the political process is merely an alternative form of economic organization, not an automatic corrective device. It is not a pinch-hitter we can count on to supply a base hit whenever we fear the market might strike out. (See "Myths of Economics.")

As with markets, there are categories of activity that economic theory indicates even democratic governments will do poorly. As we discussed briefly in previous chapters, there is government failure, as well as market failure. **Government failure** is present when the political process leads to economic inefficiency and the waste of scarce resources.

Government failure
Failure of government action to meet the criteria of ideal economic efficiency.

In modern representative democracies, voters elect representatives to direct the actions of governments. In turn, the representatives establish agencies and hire bureaucrats to conduct the day-to-day government affairs. Voters, politicians, and bureaucrats are the major players in the democratic political process. Under representative democracy, government action is the result of a complex set of interrelationships among the members of these three groups. Like consumers in the market, voters use their electoral support, money, and other political resources to express their demand for legislation. Like business entrepreneurs, politicians are suppliers: they design and shape legislation. Finally, just as managers and

MYTHS OF ECONOMICS

"WHENEVER MARKETS FAIL TO ALLOCATE RESOURCES EFFICIENTLY, GOVERNMENT ACTION WILL IMPROVE THE SITUATION."

Sometimes there is a tendency to think of government, particularly democratically elected government, as a tool that can be used to solve all types of problems ranging from inadequate health care to the high cost of housing. Even some economists act as if government were a corrective device available to cure the economic ills of the world. If there is a problem of monopoly, government regulation can set the "optimal price." In the case of externalities, government can levy the "optimal tax." Some even argue that government can use income transfers to achieve the "optimal distribution of income."

It is, of course, important to understand alternative actions that might *potentially* lead to outcomes that are more consistent with economic efficiency and prosperity. But it is also important to recognize that government is merely an alternative method of social organization—an institutional process through which individuals collectively make choices and carry out activities. It is in no way an entity that can always be counted on to correct the deficiencies of the market or make decisions in the "public interest," however that nebulous expression might be defined.

Collective outcomes, including those that are determined by democratic political procedures, reflect the choices of the participants and the incentive structure that influences those choices. No matter how lofty the rhetoric of political officials, the people (for example, voters, legislators, lobbyists, and bureau managers) who make the choices that determine political outcomes are ordinary mortals, persons with ethical standards and personal motivations very much like those present in the market sector.

Since the incentive structure emanating from the political process generally differs from that of the market, collective outcomes will often differ from market outcomes. For some categories of economic activity, there are reasons to believe that democratic political procedures will generate outcomes consistent with economic efficiency. But this will not always be the case. Furthermore, in certain cases (for example, when a policy generates substantial benefits for well-organized interest groups at the expense of a disorganized majority), there is good reason to expect that democratic-representative government will lead to the adoption of policies that conflict with economic efficiency. There is "government failure" just as there is "market failure." Recognition of this point is important because it challenges us to think more seriously about both how the political process works and how procedures and constitutional rules might be designed to make it work better.

employees are assigned the details of the production process in the market, bureaucrats perform this task in the public sector.[3]

Economists use the self-interest postulate to enhance our understanding of consumer behavior, business decision making, and resource-supply decisions. Likewise, public-choice economists apply the self-interest postulate to political decision making. They assume that, just as people are motivated by personal wealth, power, and prestige in the market sector, so, too, will these factors influence them when they make decisions in the political arena.

Closely related to self-interest as a motivator for politicians and bureaucrats are the concepts of survival and expansion. In the private sector, even if there are some managers not primarily seeking profits, it will be the profit-making firms that are most likely to survive, prosper, and expand; and they are the firms that will be imitated. Similarly, in the public sector, politicians and the bureaucrats they hire must often act in the narrow self-interest of their constituents (and thus

---

[3]For a more comprehensive view of public-choice theory and the operation of democratic governments, see James Gwartney and Richard Wagner, eds., *Public Choice and Constitutional Economics* (Greenwich : JAI Press, 1988). Our analysis borrows from this work.

in their own career self-interests) if they hope to survive. Those who cooperate most closely with powerful constituency groups will obtain more political clout and have the opportunity to lead larger government agencies.

THE VOTER-CONSUMER

How do voters decide whom to support? No doubt, many factors influence their decisions. Which candidate is the most persuasive, and which presents the best television image? Who appears to be honest, sincere, and competent? However, the self-interest postulate indicates that voters, like market consumers, will also ask, "What can you do for me, and how much will it cost me?" The greater the voter's perceived net personal gain from a particular candidate's platform, the more likely it is that the voter will favor that candidate. In contrast, the greater the perceived net economic cost imposed on the voter by the positions of a candidate, the less inclined the voter will be to support the candidate. Other things equal, voters will tend to support those candidates whom they believe will provide them the most political goods, services, and transfer benefits, net of personal costs. Unfortunately, rational voters frequently lack the detailed information needed to cast their ballots in a truly knowledgeable fashion.

As we discussed in Chapter 4, when decisions are made collectively, the direct link between the individual voter's choice and the outcome of the issue is broken. The choice of a single voter is seldom decisive when the decision-making group is large. Recognizing that the outcome will not depend on one vote, the individual voter has little incentive to seek information (which is costly) on issues and candidates in order to cast a more informed vote. Economists refer to this phenomenon as the *rational-ignorance effect* (see Chapter 4, pages 106–107).[4] The rational-ignorance effect explains why few voters are able to accurately identify their congressional representatives, much less identify and understand their position on issues such as minimum wage legislation, tariffs, and agricultural price supports. The fact that voters acquire scanty information merely indicates that they are responding rationally to economic incentives.

It is interesting to compare the incentives of consumers versus voters to choose wisely. The consumer who makes a poor choice—for example, by purchasing a product that does not work well—will personally bear the consequences. Thus, each consumer has a strong incentive to acquire information, choose wisely, and search for quality goods that are attractively priced. In contrast, there is little direct incentive for voters to be concerned about the quality of their choices of candidates. Even if informed about the candidates, the individual voter will exert little impact on the outcome of any congressional election. Whether mistaken or not, there is only a miniscule chance that an individual voter's decision will decide the election. Therefore, it makes no sense for the voter to "waste" time and effort making a careful choices. Given this incentive structure, there is reason to believe that the choices of consumers will be better informed and more carefully made than those of voters.

---

[4]The concept of rational ignorance among voters was initially developed by Anthony Downs. See Downs, *An Economic Theory of Democracy* (New York: Harper & Row, 1957).

To see in a more personal way why citizens are likely to make better informed decisions as consumers than as voters, imagine that you are planning to buy a car next week and also to vote for one of two Senate candidates. You have narrowed your car choice to either a Ford or a Honda. In the voting booth, you will choose between candidates Smith and Jones. Both the car purchase and the Senate vote involve complex trade-offs for you. The two cars come with many options, and you must choose among dozens of different combinations; the winning Senate candidate will represent you on hundreds of issues, although you are limited to voting for one of the two choices.

Which decision will command more of your scarce time for research and thinking about the best choice? Since your car choice is decisive, and you must pay for what you choose, an uninformed car purchase could be very costly for you. But if you mistakenly vote for the wrong candidate out of ignorance, the probability is virtually zero that your vote will be decisive. Since your vote will not swing the election, a mistake or poorly informed choice is of little consequence. It would not be surprising, then, if you spent substantial time considering the car purchase and very little time becoming informed about either the candidates or the political issues at election time.

Car choices are not perfectly informed decisions, but the buyer is certain to benefit from giving careful consideration to the alternatives. As a result, car companies may well be guided by better-informed votes (dollar votes) than the U.S. Senate, even though Senate activities are far more important than cars to the voters as a group.

The fact that one's vote is unlikely to be decisive explains more than lack of information on the part of voters. It also helps to explain why many citizens fail to vote. Even when there is a presidential election, only about half of all voting-age Americans take the time to register and vote. Given the low probability that one's vote will be decisive, this low voter turnout should not be surprising. The rationality of voters is further indicated by the fact that when voters perceive that the election is close, voter turnout is larger.[5] A vote in a close election has a greater chance of actually making a difference.

THE POLITICIAN-SUPPLIER

Public-choice theory postulates that pursuit of votes is the primary stimulus shaping the behavior of political suppliers. In varying degrees, such factors as pursuit of the public interest, compassion for the poor, and the achievement of fame, wealth, and power may influence the behavior of politicians. But regardless of ultimate motivation, the ability of politicians to achieve their objectives is sorely dependent upon their ability to get elected and reelected.

Rationally uninformed voters often must be convinced to "want" a candidate. Voter perceptions may be based on realities, but it is always perceptions, not the realities themselves, that influence decisions. This is true regardless of whether the decisions are private or political. As a result, a candidate's positive attributes

---

[5]This and other results consistent with the rational actions of voters have long been observed by economists. An early exposition can be found in Yoram Barzel and Eugene Silberberg, "Is the Act of Voting Rational?" *Public Choice* XVI (Fall 1973), pp. 51–58.

must be brought to the attention of the rationally ignorant voter, who may well be more interested in the local sports teams (which are probably more entertaining) than in seeking out detailed knowledge about the attributes of the various candidates. An expert staff, polls to ferret out which issues and which positions will be favored by voters, high-quality advertising to present the candidate's image and favored positions, and other forms of political resources are of great value in politics. Thus, political campaigns are costly. Senate campaign expenditures for the 1992 election cycle, when there were 34 contested seats, were $271.6 million. Senator Alfonse D'Amato alone spent $11.6 million in his successful bid for reelection in New York. Candidates for the House of Representatives in the same two years spent $406.7 million.[6]

Are we implying that politicians are selfish, caring only for their pocketbooks and reelection chances? The answer is no. When people act in the political sphere, they may genuinely want to help their fellow citizens. Factors other than personal political gain, narrowly defined, influence the actions of many political suppliers. On certain issues, one may feel strongly that one's position is best for the nation, even though it may not be currently popular. The national interest as perceived by the political supplier may conflict with the position that would be most favorable to reelection prospects. Some politicians may opt for the national interest even when it means political defeat. None of this is inconsistent with an economic view of political choice.

However, the existence of political suicide does not change the fact that most politicians who win elections are those who prefer political survival. There is a strong incentive for political suppliers to stake out positions that will increase their vote total in the next election. In fact, competition more or less forces politicians to make decisions in light of political considerations. *Regardless of ultimate motivation, the ability of politicians to achieve their objectives is dependent upon their ability to get elected and reelected. Just as profits are the lifeblood of the market entrepreneur, votes are the lifeblood of the politician.* Many factors undoubtedly influence political suppliers. Political competition, however, limits their options. In the same way that neglect of economic profit is the route to market oblivion, neglect of potential votes is the route to political oblivion.

WHEN VOTING WORKS WELL

We have shown how the theory of market failure highlights the potential for protective and productive governmental action—action that generates benefits in excess of costs. Will voting and representative government provide support for productive projects while rejecting unproductive projects? People have a tendency to believe that support by a majority makes a political action productive or legitimate. Perhaps surprising to some, if a government project is really productive, it will always be possible to allocate the project's cost so that *all* voters will gain. **Exhibit 30–1** illustrates this point. Column 1 presents hypothetical data on

---

[6]Data are from Michael Barone and Grant Ujifusa, *The Almanac of American Politics—1994*, (Washington: National Journal, 1993), pp. 1496–97.

EXHIBIT 30–1

BENEFITS DERIVED BY VOTERS FROM HYPOTHETICAL ROAD CONSTRUCTION PROJECT

		TAX PAYMENT	
VOTER	BENEFITS RECEIVED (1)	PLAN A (2)	PLAN B (3)
Adams	$20	$5	$12.50
Brown	12	5	7.50
Green	4	5	2.50
Jones	2	5	1.25
Smith	2	5	1.25
Total	$40	$25	$25.00

There are two methods of calculating GDP. It can be calculated either by summing the expenditures on the "final-user" goods and services purchased in each sector of the economy (left, below) or by summing the income payments and indirect cost items that accompany the production of goods and services.

the distribution of benefits from a government road-construction project. These benefits sum to $40, which exceeds the $25 cost of the road. Since voter benefits exceed costs, the project is indeed productive. If the project's $25 cost were allocated equally among the voters (Plan A), Adam and Brown gain substantially, but Green, Jones, and Smith will lose. The value of the project to the latter three voters is less than their $5 cost. If the fate of the project were decided by majority vote, the project would be defeated by the "no" votes of Green, Jones, and Smith.

In contrast, look what happens if the cost of the project is allocated among voters in proportion to the benefits that they receive (Plan B). Under this arrangement, Adams would pay half ($12.50) of the $25 cost, since he receives half ($20) of the total benefits ($40). The other voters would all pay in proportion to their benefits received. Under this finance plan, all voters would gain from the proposal. Even though the proposal could not muster a majority when the costs were allocated equally among voters, it would be favored by all five voters when they are taxed in proportion to the benefits that they receive (Plan B).

This simple illustration highlights an extremely important point about voting and productive projects. *When voters pay in proportion to benefits received,* all voters will gain if the government action is productive (and all will lose if it is unproductive).[7] When the benefits and costs of voters are directly related, productive government actions will be favored by almost all voters. Correspondingly, if a project is counterproductive—if the costs exceed the benefits generated for voters—

---

[7]The principle that productive projects generate the potential for political unanimity was initially articulated by Swedish economist Knut Wicksell in 1896. See Wicksell, "A New Principle of Just Taxation" in *Public Choice and Constitutional Economics,* edited by James Gwartney and Richard Wagner (Greenwich: JAI Press, Inc., 1988). Nobel laureate James Buchanan has stated that Wicksell's work provided him with the insights that led to his large role in the development of modern public-choice theory.

it will be opposed by almost all voters. Therefore, when voters pay in proportion to benefits received, there is a harmony between good politics and sound economics.

With public-sector action, however, the link between receipt of and payment for a good can be broken in that the beneficiaries of a proposal may not bear its cost. Public-choice theory indicates that the pattern of benefits and costs among voters will influence the workings of the political process. The benefits derived from a government action may be either widespread among the general populace or concentrated among a small subgroup (for example, farmers, students, business interests, or members of a labor union). Similarly, the costs may be either widespread or highly concentrated among voters. As **Exhibit 30–2** illustrates, there are four possible patterns of voter benefits and costs: (1) widespread benefits and widespread costs, (2) concentrated benefits and widespread costs, (3) concentrated benefits and concentrated costs, and (4) widespread benefits and concentrated costs.

When both the benefits and costs are widespread among voters (Type 1), essentially everyone benefits and everyone pays. While the costs of Type 1 measures may not be precisely proportional to benefits, there will be a rough relationship. When Type 1 measures are productive, almost everyone gains more than they pay. There will be little opposition, and political representatives have a strong incentive to support such proposals. In contrast, when Type 1 proposals generate costs in excess of benefits, almost everyone loses, and representatives will confront

It is useful to visualize four possible combinations for the distribution of benefits and costs among voters and to consider how the alternative distributions affect the operation of representative government. When the distribution of benefits and costs are both widespread among voters (1) or both concentrated among voters (3), representative government will tend to undertake projects that are productive and reject those that are unproductive. In contrast, when the benefits are concentrated and the costs are widespread (2), representative government is biased toward adoption of counterproductive activity. Finally, when benefits are widespread but the costs concentrated (4), the political process may reject projects that are productive.

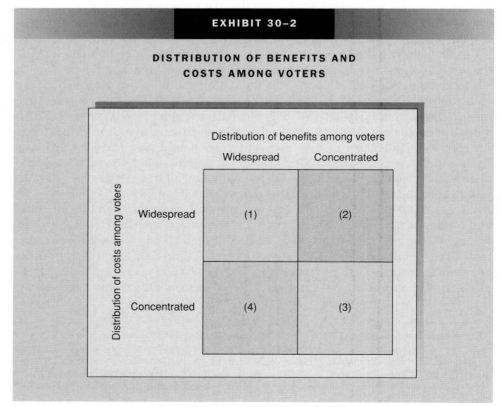

EXHIBIT 30–2

DISTRIBUTION OF BENEFITS AND COSTS AMONG VOTERS

pressure to oppose such issues. Thus, for Type 1 projects, the political process tends to be consistent with economic efficiency.

Interestingly, the provision of traditional public goods—like provision of national defense, a legal system for the protection of persons and property and enforcement of contracts, and a monetary system to oil the wheels of exchange—best fits Type 1. Nearly everyone pays and nearly everyone benefits from public-sector action of this type.

Similarly, there is reason to believe that the political process will work pretty well for Type 3 measures—those for which both benefits and costs are concentrated on one or more small subgroups. In some cases, the concentrated beneficiaries may pay for the government to provide services. This would be the case when user charges finance public services (for example, air safety or garbage collection) benefiting subgroups of the populace. Under these circumstances, voter support will provide politicians with an incentive to provide public services that generate value in excess of cost.

Of course, the subgroup of beneficiaries might differ from the subgroup footing the bill. But even in this case, if the benefits exceed the costs, the concentrated group of beneficiaries will have an incentive to expend more resources supportive of the measure than those harmed by it will expend opposing it. Thus, productive measures will tend to be adopted. Similarly, unproductive measures will tend to be rejected when both the benefits and costs are concentrated.

WHEN VOTING CONFLICTS WITH ECONOMIC EFFICIENCY

While the political process works well when there is close relationship between receipt of benefits and payment of cost, the harmony between good politics and sound economics sometimes breaks down. There are four major reasons why unrestrained majority-rule voting may conflict with economic prosperity. (Note: several of the concepts analyzed here were briefly introduced in Chapter 4.)

SPECIAL-INTEREST EFFECT

Public-choice analysis indicates that problems will arise when an issue generates substantial personal benefits for a small number of constituents while imposing a small individual cost on a large number of other voters (Type 2 in Exhibit 30–2). Measures of this type are special interest issues. A number of factors combine to make special-interest groups far more powerful in a representative democracy than their numbers would indicate.

It is easy to see how politicians can improve their election prospects by catering to the views of special interests. Since their personal stake is large, members of the interest group (and lobbyists representing their interests) have a strong incentive to inform themselves and their allies and to let legislators know how strongly they feel about an issue of special importance. Many of them will vote for or against candidates strictly on the basis of whether they support their interests. In addition, such interest groups are generally an attractive source of campaign resources, including financial contributions. In contrast, most other voters will care little about a special-interest issue. For the non-special-interest voter, opportunity cost of the time and energy necessary to examine the issue will generally exceed any possible personal gain from a preferred resolution. Thus, most non-special-interest voters will simply ignore such issues.

If you were a vote-seeking politician, what would you do? Clearly, little gain would be derived from supporting the interest of the largely uninformed and uninterested majority. In contrast, support for the interests of easily identifiable, well-organized groups would generate vocal supporters, campaign workers, and most importantly, campaign contributors. Predictably, politicians will be led as if by an invisible hand to support legislation that provides concentrated benefits to interest groups at the expense of disorganized groups (such as taxpayers and consumers), even if such policies waste resources.

The "rational ignorance" of voters strengthens the power of special interests. Since the cost imposed on individual voters is small, and since the individual is unable to avoid the cost even by becoming informed, voters bearing the cost of special-interest legislation tend to be uninformed on the issue. This will be particularly true if the complexity of the issue makes it difficult for voters to think through how an issue affects their personal welfare. Thus, politicians often make special-interest legislation complex in order to hide the cost imposed on the typical voter.

The ability of the voter to punish politicians for supporting special-interest legislation is further hindered by the fact that many issues are bundled together when the voter chooses between one candidate and another. Even if the voter knows and dislikes the politician's stand on one or a few issues, the bundling of hundreds of future issues into one candidate choice severely limits the voter's ability to take a stand at the ballot box for or against any particular issue.

Bureaucratic interests can be an additional factor favoring special-interest programs. The interests of bureaucrats are often complementary with those of interest groups. The bureaucrats who staff an agency usually want to see their department's goals furthered, whether the goals are to protect more wilderness, build more roads, or provide additional subsidized irrigation projects. To accomplish these things requires larger budgets, which—not so incidentally—are likely to provide the bureaucrats with expanded career opportunities while helping to satisfy their professional aspirations as well. Bureaus, therefore, are usually happy to work to expand their programs to deliver benefits to special-interest groups, who, in turn, work with politicians to expand their bureau budgets and programs.

Logrolling
The exchange between politicians of political support on one issue for political support on another issue.

Pork-barrel legislation
A package of spending projects benefiting local areas at federal expense. The projects typically have costs that exceed benefits, but are intensely desired by the residents of the district getting the benefits without having to pay much of the costs.

Yet another force that strengthens the political clout of special-interest groups is **logrolling,** the practice of trading votes by a representative (and his or her constituents) in order to pass intensely desired legislation. Representative A promises to vote for measures favored by other representatives in exchange for their support of a measure that A strongly favors. With logrolling, legislative bodies often pass a bundle of proposals, each of which would be rejected if voted on separately.

Pork-barrel legislation is a variant of logrolling. This type of legislation bundles together a set of projects to benefit regional interests (for example, water projects, dredging of harbors, or expenditures on military bases) at the expense of the general taxpayer. As in the case of logrolling, the bundle of pork-barrel projects can often gain approval even if the items by themselves would be seen as counterproductive and would individually be rejected by the legislative assembly.

Exhibit 30–3 provides a numeric illustration of the forces underlying logrolling and pork-barrel legislation. Here we consider the operation of a five-member legislative assembly considering three projects: construction of a post office in District A, dredging of a harbor in District B, and expenditures on a military base in District C. In each case, the project is inefficient—the net cost of the project exceeds the net benefit (by a 12-to-10 ratio). If the projects were voted on separately, and the representatives reflected the views of their constituents, each project would lose by a 4-to-1 vote. However, when the projects are bundled together through either logrolling or pork-barrel legislation, Representatives A, B, and C will vote yes. The legislative bundle will pass 3 to 2 even though it is counterproductive (on average, the projects, as a bundle, reduce the wealth of constituents by $6).[8]

Legislation providing subsidies to electricity consumers in California, Nevada, and Arizona illustrates the relevance of logrolling and pork-barrel legislation. Under legislation passed in 1937, electricity generated by Hoover Dam has been sold to residents in the three surrounding states at rates ranging between 10 percent and 25 percent of the market price. The law providing for the subsidized rates was scheduled to expire in 1987. However, before it did, Congress extended the subsidies for another 30 years. The residents of many western states are the recipients of federally subsidized electricity. Every senator west of Missouri voted to continue the subsidized rates for electricity generated by Hoover Dam. In turn, they can expect senators and representatives from California, Arizona, and Nevada to support subsidized electricity rates in their states. In contrast, residents of other states will pay higher taxes so that many residents in western states can enjoy cheap electricity.

[a]We assume the districts are of equal size.

EXHIBIT 30-3

VOTE TRADING AND PASSING COUNTERPRODUCTIVE LEGISLATION

	NET BENEFITS (+) OR COSTS (−) TO EACH VOTER IN DISTRICT			
VOTERS OF DISTRICT[a]	CONSTRUCTION OF POST OFFICE IN A	DREDGING HARBOR IN B	CONSTRUCTION OF MILITARY BASE IN C	TOTAL
A	+ $10	− $ 3	− $ 3	+ $4
B	− $ 3	+ $10	− $ 3	+ $4
C	− $ 3	− $ 3	+ $10	+ $4
D	− $ 3	− $ 3	− $ 3	−$9
E	− $ 3	− $ 3	− $ 3	−$9
Total	− $ 2	− $ 2	− $ 2	−$6

---

[8]Logrolling and pork-barrel policies can lead to the adoption of productive measures. However, if a project is productive, there would always be a pattern of finance that would lead to its adoption even if logrolling were absent. Thus, the tendency for logrolling and pork-barrel policies to result in the adoption of inefficient projects is the more significant point.

Why don't representatives oppose measures that force their constituents to pay for projects that benefit others? There is some incentive to do so, but the constituents of any one representative can capture only a small portion of the benefits of tax savings from improved efficiency, since they would be spread nationwide among all taxpayers. Just as we do not expect a corporation's president to devote the firm's resources to projects not primarily benefiting stockholders, we should not expect an elected representative to devote political resources to projects such as defeating pork-barrel programs, when the benefits of greater efficiency would not go primarily to that representative's constituents. Instead, each representative has a strong incentive to work for programs whose benefits are concentrated among his or her constituents—especially the organized interest groups who can help the representative be reelected. Heeding such incentives is a survival (reelection) characteristic.

The bottom line is clear: public-choice analysis indicates that majority voting and representative democracy does not work so well when concentrated interests benefit at the expense of widely dispersed interests. This special-interest bias of the political process helps to explain the presence of many programs that reduce the size of the economic pie. For example, the agricultural price-support programs of the United States and Western Europe promote inefficient methods of production (such as the use of too much fertilizer relative to land), protect high-cost producers, and result in higher food prices. Approximately 1 percent of the populace (primarily large farmers) individually gain a lot at the expense of consumers and taxpayers, each of whom pay somewhat higher food prices and taxes than they otherwise would. Given their substantial personal gain, the agricultural interests feel strongly about the price-support programs, while most others are uninformed and largely uninterested in the issue. Therefore, politicians find it advantageous to support the programs even though they waste resources and reduce the general standard of living. (An example of an agricultural price-support program is given in the "Applications in Economics" box.)

Examples of special-interest programs abound. Tariffs and quotas retard the gains from specialization and trade. But they also benefit concentrated industrial interests (manufacturers and workers in steel, automobiles, and textiles, for example) at the expense of consumers. Economic studies have shown that government support for subsidized water and irrigation projects in the western United States, for example, generate substantially smaller benefits than costs. Legislation mandating that Alaskan oil be transported by the high-cost American maritime industry promotes inefficiency. These programs and numerous others like them demonstrate the conflict between economic efficiency and good politics when the benefits are highly concentrated and the costs widely dispersed.

The analysis is symmetrical. When the benefits of a government action are widespread and the costs highly concentrated (Type 4 of Exhibit 30–2), the concentrated interests will strongly oppose the proposal. Most others will be largely uninterested. Once again, politicians will have an incentive to respond to the views of the concentrated interests. Projects of this type will tend to be rejected even when they are productive—that is, when they would generate larger benefits than costs.

SHORTSIGHTEDNESS EFFECT

It is difficult for voters to identify the effects of complex issues over time. Thus, voters will tend to rely primarily on current economic conditions when evaluating

APPLICATIONS IN ECONOMICS

THE POWER OF SPECIAL INTERESTS: THE CASE OF RICE FARMERS

There are roughly 33,000 rice farmers in the United States. In essence, the government guarantees them an above-market price for rice by paying them to grow less rice so the artificially high price can be maintained. The program reduces output, pushes up the price of rice, and requires higher taxes. As a nation, we are worse off as a result.

Nonetheless, Congress continues to support the program. The rice farmers gain more than $800 million in gross income, approximately $25,000 per rice farm. More than 60 percent of these subsidies go to rice farmers receiving payments of $50,000 or more. Given the sizable impact on their personal wealth, it is perfectly sensible for rice farmers to inform themselves and use their votes, contributions, and political influence to help politicians who support their interests. In contrast, it makes no sense for the average voter to investigate this issue or give it any significant weight when deciding for whom to vote. In fact, most Americans are unaware that they pay approximately $4 more per year to help rice growers, most of which goes to wealthy farmers. As a result, politicians can generally gain more by continuing to support the rice farmers, even though the subsidy program wastes resources and reduces the wealth of the nation.

the performance of political incumbents. Unfortunately, policies that look good around election day may have substantial negative side effects after the election. On the other hand, policies that generate preelection costs in order to provide long-term gains that emerge only after the next election reduce the reelection prospects of incumbents. As a result, the political process is biased toward the adoption of shortsighted policies and against the selection of sound long-range policies that involve observable costs prior to the next election. As we noted in Chapter 4, this bias is called the *shortsightedness effect*.

This bias, inherent in the collective decision-making process, is another problem made worse by the rational ignorance of voters. It is also compounded by the lack of tradeable property rights—the lack of a capital market—in government enterprises. For comparison, consider the problem of choosing programs and strategies for a large corporation such as General Motors. Its stockholders elect a board of directors, which sets policy and selects professional management leadership. The corporation, like a government, faces complex choices of programs that are difficult for the individual stockholder to fully understand and evaluate. However, when evaluating the business programs and strategy of the corporation, the stockholder has an incentive, very different than that of a voter. Why? Any stockholder who senses trouble before others do can sell out before the stock price falls. Similarly, the stockholder (or other observer) can profit individually by buying more stock if a good new program choice is sensed early. These choices of stockholders will be registered and passed on almost instantly. Individual decisions to buy or sell stock causes the stock price to rise or fall, signaling whether trouble or a winning program is forecast by attentive stock buyers and sellers. A strategy choice, or a new program that investors like, will quickly be signaled by a rising share price that rewards management choices well ahead of actual changes in profits and losses. No such incentives, and no such advanced market signals, exist in the collective decision-making processes of government. The result is the restriction of the planning horizon of elected officials.

The result of the shortsightedness effect is that a government program that benefits all citizens, rather than concentrating its benefits on organized special-interest groups, must have observable benefits by the next election in order to generate voter support for the program's political supporters. The politician who fails to heed this unfortunate fact will be vulnerable to replacement by someone willing to promise more rapid results. The shortsighted nature of the political process, even when decisions are made democratically, will tend to result in economic inefficiency.

It is easy to think of instances where positive short-term effects have increased the political attractiveness of policies that exert a long-term detrimental impact. For example, budget deficits allow politicians to finance current projects with future taxes. This strategy has political attractiveness even though it will probably result in higher interest rates and less capital formation. Rent controls that reduce the current price of rental housing provide another example. The short-term results will be far more positive than the effects in the long run (housing shortages, black markets, and deterioration in the quality of housing).

RENT SEEKING

There are two ways individuals can acquire wealth: production and plunder. When they produce things (or services) and exchange them for income, they not only enrich themselves but they also enhance the wealth of the society. Sometimes the rules also allow people to get ahead by plundering what others have produced, a method that enriches one at the expense of another, consumes additional resources, and thereby reduces the wealth of the society.

Rent seeking is the term describing actions taken by individuals and groups seeking to use the political process to plunder the wealth of others. The incentive to engage in rent-seeking activities is directly proportional to the ease with which the political process can be used for personal (or interest group) gain at the expense of others. When the effective law of the land makes it difficult to take the property of others or force others to pay for projects favored by you and your interest group, rent seeking is unattractive. Under such circumstances, its benefits are relatively low, and few resources flow into rent-seeking activities. In contrast, when government fails to levy user fees or similar forms of financing to allocate the cost of its projects to the primary beneficiaries, or when it becomes heavily involved in tax-transfer activities, the payoff for rent seeking expands.

Rent seeking will also increase when governments, including democratic governments, become more heavily involved in erecting trade barriers, mandating employment benefits, prohibiting various types of agreements, providing subsidies, fixing prices, and levying discriminatory taxes (taxes unrelated to the provision of public services to the taxpayer).

When a government, rather than acting as a neutral force protecting property rights and enforcing contracts, attempts to favor some at the expense of others, counterproductive activities will expand while positive-sum productive activities will shrink. People will spend more time organizing and lobbying politicians and less time producing goods and services. Since fewer resources will be utilized to create wealth (and more utilized in rent-seeking activities), economic progress will be retarded.

INEFFICIENCY OF GOVERNMENT OPERATIONS

Until now in this chapter, we have dealt primarily with the problems faced by citizens in causing government to produce an efficient set of outputs. But there is an additional question, once the outputs are chosen: Will government goods and services be produced efficiently? Professional pride, and pride in doing a job well, are likely to be present as they are in the private sector, and these will help. However, the incentive for managers to operate government bureaus efficiently is weak. In the private sector, there is a strong incentive to produce efficiently because lower costs mean higher profits. Public-sector enterprises confront an incentive structure that is less conducive to operational efficiency. Direct competition in the form of other firms trying to take an agency's customers is rare in the public sector. Since there is no easily identifiable index of performance analogous to profit rate in the private sector (often easily compared to other firms in the same industry), public-sector managers may hardly be aware of economic inefficiency. Without good data and the need to reconsider their operations, it is easy to gloss over inefficiency. While bankruptcy weeds out inefficiency in the private sector, there is no parallel mechanism to eliminate inefficiency in the public sector. In fact, poor performance and failure to achieve objectives are often used as an argument for *increased* funding in the public sector. Furthermore, public-sector managers are seldom in a position to gain personally from measures that reduce costs. The opposite is often true. If an agency fails to spend this year's allocation, its case for a larger budget next year is weakened. Agencies typically go on a spending spree at the end of the budget period if they discover that they have failed to spend all of this year's appropriation.

It is important to note that the argument of internal inefficiency is not based on the assumption that employees of a bureaucratic government are necessarily lazy or incapable. Rather, the emphasis is on the structure of information and incentives under which managers and other workers toil. No individual or relatively small group of individuals has much incentive to ensure efficiency. Their performances cannot readily be judged, and without private ownership, their personal wealth cannot be significantly altered by changes in the level of efficiency. Since public officials and bureau managers spend other people's money, they are likely to be less conscious of cost than they would be with their own resources. Without a need to compare sales revenues to costs, there is no test with which to define economic inefficiency or measure it accurately, much less eliminate it. The perverse incentive structure of a bureaucracy is bound to have an impact on its internal efficiency.

The empirical evidence is consistent with this view. Economies dominated by government control, like those of Eastern Europe, the former Soviet Union, and Latin America, have fashioned a poor economic record. The level of output per unit of resource input in those economies is low.[9] Similarly, when private firms are compared with government agencies providing the same goods or services, the private firms generally have been shown to provide them more economically.

---

[9]For an overall comparison of the efficiency of resource utilization in socialist nations compared to market economies, see Mikhail Bernstam, *The Wealth of Nations and the Environment* (London: Institute of Economic Affairs, 1991).

PUBLIC SECTOR VERSUS THE MARKET: A SUMMARY

Throughout this text, we have argued that theory can explain why both market forces and public-sector action sometimes break down—that is, why they sometimes fail to meet the criteria for ideal efficiency. The deficiencies of one or the other sector will often be more or less decisive depending on the type of economic activity. Nobel laureate Paul Samuelson has stated, "There are not rules concerning the proper role of government that can be established by a priori reasoning."[10] This does not mean, however, that economics has nothing to say about the *strength* of the case for either the market or the public sector in terms of specific classes of activities. Nor does it mean that social scientists have nothing to say about institutional arrangements for conducting economic activity. It merely indicates that each issue and type of activity must be considered individually.

The case for government intervention is obviously stronger for some activities than for others. For example, if an activity involves substantial external effects, market arrangements often result in economic inefficiency, and public-sector action may allow for greater efficiency. Similarly, when competitive pressures are weak and when there is reason to expect consumers to be poorly informed, market failure may result, and again government action may be called for. (See the "Thumbnail Sketch" for a summary of factors that influence the case for market or for public-sector action.)

The identical analysis holds for the public sector. When there is a good reason to believe that special-interest influence will be strong, the case for government action to correct market failures is weakened. Similarly, the lack of a means to identify and weed out public-sector inefficiency weakens the case for government action. More often than not, the choice of proper institutions may be a choice among evils. For example, we might expect private-sector monopoly if an activity is left to the market, or perverse regulation due to the special-interest effect if we turn to the public sector. Understanding the shortcomings of both the market and the public sectors is important if we are to improve our current economic institutions.

ECONOMICS, POLITICS, AND THE TRANSFER SOCIETY

As **Exhibit 30–4** illustrates, direct income transfers through the public sector have increased sharply during the last six decades. In 1929 cash income transfers accounted for only 1.8 percent of national income; by 1992 the figure had risen to

---

[10]Paul A. Samuelson, "The Economic Role of Private Activity" in *The Collected Scientific Papers of Paul A. Samuelson*, vol. 2, edited by J. E. Stiglitz (Cambridge: MIT Press, 1966), p. 1423.

THUMBNAIL SKETCH

WHAT WEAKENS THE CASE FOR MARKET-SECTOR ALLOCATION VERSUS PUBLIC-SECTOR INTERVENTION, AND VICE VERSA?

These factors weaken the case for market-sector allocation:

1. External costs and benefits
2. Public goods
3. Monopoly
4. Uninformed consumers

These factors weaken the case for public-sector intervention:

1. The power of special interests
2. The shortsightedness effect
3. Rent seeking
4. Little incentive for operational efficiency

17.3 percent. If in-kind benefits such as food stamps, medical care, and housing were included, the size of the transfer sector would have constituted well over 20 percent of national income.

As in other areas, both the market failure and rent-seeking models of government underlie public-sector income transfers. As we discussed in Chapter 4, sometimes income transfers reflect the public-good characteristics of antipoverty efforts. Since the number of poor people, like the strength of our national defense, is largely independent of one's personal contribution, individuals motivated by the desire to reduce poverty in general may simply become *free riders*. When a large number of people become free riders, though, less than the desired amount of antipoverty effort will be voluntarily supplied. If everyone is required to contribute through the

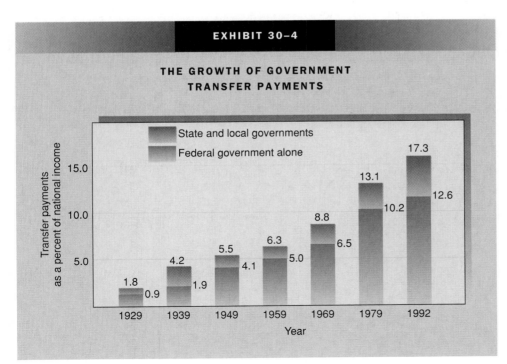

EXHIBIT 30–4

THE GROWTH OF GOVERNMENT TRANSFER PAYMENTS

The government now taxes approximately 17 percent of national income away from some people and transfers it to others. Means-tested income transfers—those directed toward the poor—account for only about one-sixth of all income transfers.

Source: *Economic Report of the President, 1994.* Tables B-25, B-82, B-83.

tax system, then the free-rider problem can be overcome. Under these circumstances, transfers directed to the poor may be consistent with economic efficiency.

However, in the United States, *means-tested transfers,* those directed toward the poor, constitute only about one-sixth of all income transfers. No income test is applied to the other five-sixths, and they are generally directed toward groups that are either well organized or easily identifiable. The recipients of these transfers often have incomes well above the average. This suggests that the rent-seeking model of government also plays an important role in the allocation of income transfers.

Within the framework of public-choice analysis, the relatively small portion of income transfers directed toward the poor is not surprising. There is little reason to believe that transfers to the poor will be particularly attractive to vote-seeking politicians. After all, in the United States, the poor are less likely to vote than middle- and upper-income recipients. They are less likely than others to be well-informed on political issues and candidates. They are not united. Neither are they a significant source of financial resources that exert a powerful influence on the political process.

Farm subsidies provide an excellent example of an income-transfer program. The subsidies clearly reflect the rent-seeking model of government. In 1989 the federal government paid about $15 billion in direct crop subsidies to farmers. The subsidy programs distort resource use and generate market surpluses of agriculture products. As **Exhibit 30–5** illustrates, the primary recipients of these income transfers are high-income farmers. Only one-sixth of the farms in the United States had annual sales of $100,000 or more in 1989. Yet this small group of large farmers received more than two-thirds of the direct crop payments in 1989. More than $6 out of $7 of the transfer payments went to farmers with annual sales in excess of $40,000. The complex array of income transfers to farmers cost the average

Source: Economic Research Services USDA (unpublished data).

EXHIBIT 30–5

DISTRIBUTION OF GOVERNMENT INCOME TRANSFERS TO FARMERS BY FARM SIZE, 1989

Farm Size (Annual Sales in Dollars)	Percent of Farms	Direct Government Payments	
		Payments per Farm ($)	Percent of Payments Received
500,000 and over	2.0	48,400	13.0
250,000 to 500,000	3.9	28,100	19.6
100,000 to 250,000	11.1	16,100	34.4
40,000 to 100,000	13.7	8,900	19.3
10,000 to 40,000	22.7	4,500	11.0
10,000 or Less	46.6	1,700	2.7
All Farms	100.0	10,700	100.0

taxpayer-consumer about $100 per year, while generating an average gain in gross income of about $10,000 per participating farmer. The persistence of these programs indicates that the prospect of a $10,000 gain for a small subgroup is much more effective at generating political support than the prospect of a $100 savings is in generating political opposition. The result is highly consistent with the rent-seeking, special-interest view of how government programs are formulated.

Before leaving the topic of transfers, one final point should be stressed. Market adjustments and competition for the transfers will erode much of the long-run gain of the intended beneficiaries. This point follows from a standard proposition of economic theory: Competitors will be attracted to activities that yield abnormally high rates of return until the abnormally high profit is eroded. Application of this proposition to politics indicates that whenever the government establishes a criteria (as it must in a world of scarce resources) that must be met in order to qualify for transfers or other political favors, competition to meet the standard will erode the opportunity for profit. Unanticipated changes in public policy will impose temporary gains and losses on various groups. However, paradoxical as it may appear, it is extremely difficult to bestow favors upon a class of recipients in a manner that will *permanently* improve their well-being.

As people and markets adjust to the transfers, any abnormally high returns derived by recipients of government subsidies will be dissipated. Generally, government transfer programs require recipients to either own something (for example, land with an acreage allotment), do something, or be something in order to qualify for the transfer. When one considers all that is required to qualify as a beneficiary, it is clear that the net gain of the recipients is substantially less than the size of the transfers. In the case of the poor, high implicit marginal tax rates accompanying income-tested transfers severely retard the incentive of the poor to earn. Thus, the net increase in income of the poor is much less than the dollars transferred. To a large extent, the transfers merely replace income that would have been earned in their absence. The high implicit tax rates often induce the poor to drop out of the work force. When this happens, the skills of the poor depreciate, further reducing their ability to support themselves and escape poverty. Government involvement in antipoverty transfers crowds out private charitable efforts by families, individuals, churches, and civic organizations. When taxes are levied to do more, predictably, private individuals and groups will adjust and do less. When the affects of these adjustments are considered, it is not at all clear that the poor benefit very much from transfers, particularly in the long run.

If transfer programs fail to provide significant benefits to recipients beyond the windfall gains at the time the programs are instituted or unexpectedly expanded, what accounts for the continued political support for such programs? Gordon Tullock's work on the transitional gains trap provides the answer.[11] Elimination of the programs would be costly for recipients who have adjusted to or "bought into" the programs. Even though the programs do little to improve their welfare, the current beneficiaries would be harmed by the elimination or unexpected reduction in the programs. Thus, they form a vocal lobby supportive of the programs.

---

[11]Gordon Tullock, "The Transitional Gains Trap," *Bell Journal of Economics* 6 (Autumn 1975).

CONSTITUTIONAL ORGANIZATION AND GETTING MORE FROM GOVERNMENT

The role of government is central to the achievement of economic progress. When government performs its protective function well, it will improve the efficiency of markets. Similarly, government's production of public goods can create wealth and help promote prosperity. Public-choice analysis, however, indicates that unconstrained democratic governments will often enact programs that waste resources and impair the general standard of living of citizens. How can we reap the benefits available from government while minimizing its unwanted, counterproductive activities?

An efficient political organization does not emerge naturally. It must be shaped by the legal environment. The Founding Fathers of the United States recognized this point. They sought to establish a constitutional order that would limit the misuse of the ordinary political process, while allowing government to undertake activities important to the welfare of citizens. With time, many of the safeguards embodied in the U.S. Constitution have either eroded or been modified. Nonetheless, the general idea was a sound one.

What would a constitutional structure consistent with economic efficiency look like? Interestingly, public-choice analysis indicates that it would include a number of the ideas incorporated into the U. S. Constitution. First, it would seek to constrain government from taking rights and wealth from some in order to bestow them on others. The U.S. Constitution contains provisions designed to prevent such takings. The Fifth Amendment states "nor shall private property be taken for public use without just compensation."[12] Article I, Section 10, mandates, "No state shall . . . pass any . . . law impairing the obligations of contracts." These provisions might be strengthened and supplemented with prohibitions against the use of government to fix prices and to bar entry into the production of otherwise legal goods, both of which restrain trade and are indirect forms of taking property without compensation. With regard to income-transfer programs, federal transfer activities might be restricted to those directed toward the poor (means-tested programs).

Second, the efficiency of the political process would be enhanced if the primary beneficiaries of government activities were required to foot the bill for their cost. Again, there is evidence that this is what the Founding Fathers had in mind. The U.S. Constitution, Article I, Section 8, states, "The Congress shall have power to lay and collect taxes, duties, imports and excises to . . . provide for the common defense and general welfare of the United States, but all duties, imports and excises shall be uniform throughout the United States." This constitutional provision indicates that it was the intent of the Founders that, at the federal level, uniformly levied taxes would be used only for the finance of expenditures yielding general benefits—the common defense and general welfare (Type I issues in

---

[12]For a detailed analysis of the importance of this clause from a law and economics viewpoint, see Richard A. Epstein, *Takings: Private Property and the Power of Eminent Domain* (Cambridge: Harvard University Press, 1985).

Exhibit 30–2). In order to strengthen this substantive provision, tax and spending proposals at the federal level could be required to secure the approval of a supramajority (for example, three-fourths) of the legislative members. Such a provision would reduce the power of interest groups and the viability of pork-barrel spending projects.

Finally, if we want efficiency in government, the constitutional structure could strengthen independent state and local governments. One reason to expand the role of lower levels of government, is that higher levels, such as the federal government, have a greater ability to spread costs for projects that provide benefits to only a few. Another reason is to promote competition. In *The Federalist Papers*, James Madison argues that competition among state and local governments will help check abusive and counterproductive government action.[13] Public-choice analysis indicates that Madison's perception was correct.

How might the constitutional order promote competition among governments? One way would be to require more inclusive majorities in the higher levels of government. For example, local legislative bodies (city commissions, county commissions, regional authorities, and so on) might continue to act with the approval of only a simple majority, while a three-fifths majority might be required for legislative action at the state level, and a three-fourths majority at the federal level. The increasing majorities required for legislative action at higher levels of government would help remedy a deficiency of the current system—the tendency of federal and state governments to get involved with issues that are best dealt with at lower levels of governments. Decentralization in government would permit states and localities to adopt different government environments. Those that people like best—the ones that supply public-sector goods highly valued relative to their tax cost—would grow and prosper relative to those that people appreciate less. This structure would allow individuals and businesses to "vote with their feet" as well as with their ballots.

Of course, public-choice theorists are continuing to investigate the operation of alternative forms of political organization. The challenge is to develop political institutions capable of bringing, to the fullest extent possible, the self-interest of politicians, bureaucrats, and voters into harmony with the general welfare of a society.

LOOKING AHEAD

Democratic governments are a creation of the interactions of human beings. Public-choice analysis helps us better understand these interactions and the constitutional rules capable of improving the results achieved from government. As we consider trade among nations, how economies develop, and alternative forms of economic organization, public-choice analysis will again prove helpful to our understanding.

[13]See Charles Tiebout, "A Pure Theory of Local Expenditures," *Journal of Political Economy* (October 1956); Vincent Ostrom, *The Political Theory of a Compound Republic* (Fairfax: Center for Study of Public Choice, George Mason University, 1971); and Robert Bish, "Federalism: A Market-Economics Perspective" in *Public Choice and Constitutional Economics*, edited by James Gwartney and Richard Wagner (Greenwich: JAI Press, 1988) for additional information on the importance of competition among government units.

CHAPTER SUMMARY

1. It is fruitful to analyze the public sector in the same way we analyze the private sector. The public sector is an alternative to the market—it provides an alternative means of organizing production and/or distributing output.

2. Voters cast ballots, make political contributions, lobby, and adopt other political strategies to demand public-sector action. Other things constant, voters have a strong incentive to support the candidate who offers them the greatest gain relative to personal costs. Obtaining information is costly. Since group decision-making breaks the link between the choice of the individual and the outcome of the issue, it is rational for voters to remain uninformed on many issues. Candidates are generally evaluated on the basis of a small subset of issues that are of the greatest personal importance to individual voters.

3. Under a democratic system, politicians have a strong incentive to follow a strategy that will enhance their chances of getting elected (and reelected). Political competition more or less forces politicians to focus on how their actions influence their support among voters.

4. Market failure presents government with an opportunity to undertake action that will result in additional benefits relative to costs. Other things constant, the greater the social loss resulting from the market failure, the stronger is the incentive for public-sector action. Ultimately, though, it is votes, not efficiency, that will determine political outcomes.

5. The distribution of the benefits and costs among voters influences how the political process works. When voters pay in proportion to the benefits they receive from a public-sector project, democratic decision making works quite well. Productive projects tend to be approved and counterproductive ones rejected. However, problems arise when the pattern of benefits among voters differs from the pattern of costs.

6. There is a strong incentive for political entrepreneurs to support special-interest issues and to make the issues difficult for the unorganized, largely uninformed majority to understand. Special-interest groups supply both financial and direct elective support to the politician. Constitutional rules are one way to limit the power of special interests to use the political process to achieve their interests at the expense of the group as a whole.

7. In government, where decision makers normally do not hold private property rights to the resources they control, the shortsightedness effect is another potential source of conflict between good politics and sound economics. Both voters and politicians tend to support projects that promise substantial current benefits at the

expense of difficult-to-identify future costs. There is also a bias against legislation that involves immediate and easily identifiable costs but complex future benefits.

8. The economic incentive for operational efficiency is small for public-sector action. No individual or relatively small group of individuals can capture the gains derived from improved operational efficiency. There is no force analogous to the threat of bankruptcy in the private sector that will bring inefficient behavior to a halt. Since public-sector resources, including tax funds, are communally owned, their users are less likely than private resource owners to be cost-conscious.

9. A growing portion of public-sector activity involves income redistribution. Economic analysis indicates two potential sources of pressure for income redistribution: (a) the public-good nature of antipoverty efforts and (b) rent seeking. From the viewpoint of a vote-maximizing politician, there is incentive to support redistribution from unorganized to well-organized groups. Considerable income redistribution in the United States is of this type.

10. Keeping government from engaging in counterproductive activities while encouraging it to undertake things that it does well is difficult. Properly designed constitutional rules and restraints can help us achieve that objective.

CRITICAL-ANALYSIS QUESTIONS

*1. "Voters should simply ignore political candidates who play ball with special-interest groups, and vote instead for candidates who will represent all the people when they are elected. Government will work far better when this happens." Evaluate this view.

*2. "Government can afford to take a long view when it needs to, while a private firm has a short-term outlook. Corporate officers, for example, typically care about the next three to six months, not the next 50 to 100 years. Government, not private firms, should own things like forests, that take decades to develop." Evaluate this view.

3. Suppose that you are part of a group of nature enthusiasts that has discovered a bog it would like to preserve, although the site might soon be transferred to another use. Your group has some cash and could spend it several ways: it could buy the land and lease it, obtaining the right to manage it as it wishes. Alternatively, it could lobby the local authorities to regulate the land's use, preventing the current owner from changing the bog's condition or use. Using economic thinking, what analysis of the options could you provide to the group? The group wants to get the most for its money in the long run, and it prefers cooperation to conflict.

---

*Asterisk denotes questions for which answers are given in Appendix C.

4. Do you think that advertising exerts more influence on the type of car chosen by a consumer than on the type of politician chosen by the same person? Explain your answer.

5. Do you think that the political process works to the advantage of the poor? Explain your answer. Are the poor well organized? Do they make substantial campaign contributions to candidates? Are they likely to be well informed? Is it surprising that only about one-sixth of the approximately $900 billion of cash income-transfer payments in the United States is directed toward the poor? Explain.

6. Which of the following public-sector actions are designed primarily to correct "market failure": (a) laws against fraud, (b) truth-in-lending legislation, (c) rate regulation in the telephone industry, (d) legislation setting emission-control standards, (e) subsidization of pure research, and (f) operation of the post office? Explain your answer.

*7. "When an economic function is turned over to the government, social cooperation replaces personal self-interest." Is this statement true? Why or why not?

*8. The liquor industry contributes a large share of the political funds to political contests on the state level. Yet its contributions to candidates for national office are minimal. Why do you think this is true? (Hint: Who regulates the liquor industry?)

9. One explanation for the shortsightedness effect in the public sector is that future voters cannot vote now to represent their future interests. Are the interests of future generations represented in market decisions? For example, if the price of chromium were expected to rise rapidly over the next 30 years due to increased scarcity, how could speculators grow rich while providing the next generation with more chromium at the expense of current consumers?

*10. *What's wrong with this way of thinking?* "Public policy is necessary to protect the average citizen from the power of vested interest groups. In the absence of government intervention, regulated industries, such as airlines, railroads, and trucking, would charge excessive prices, products would be unsafe, and the rich would oppress the poor. Government curbs the power of special interest groups."

11. Are shoppers making decisions in the local supermarket likely to make better informed choices than voters making choices in political races? Why or why not?

12. Economics indicates that "principals" in both the private and public sector cannot be sure that their "agents" will act in their interests. Compare this principal-agent problem between (a) stockholders and managers in the private sector and (b) voters and politicians (and bureaucrats) in the public sector. Do you think inefficiencies arising from the principal-agent problem will be more or less severe in the public sector than in the private sector? Why?

13. Why might members of Congress who work for special-interest and pork-barrel legislation under an unconstrained system of representative democracy nonetheless favor constitutional restraints limiting such spending?

14. "Since government-operated firms do not have to make a profit, they can usually produce at a lower cost and charge a lower price than privately owned enterprises." Evaluate this view.

15. "Governments can promote economic growth by using taxes and subsidies to direct investment funds toward high-tech, heavy manufacturing, and other growth industries that will enhance the future income of the nation." Evaluate this view.

16. Several countries in Latin America, Eastern Europe, and the former Soviet Union have recently adopted more democratic political decision-making procedures. Many people in these countries, perhaps encouraged by Western political leaders, associate democracy (voting by the citizenry and competitive elections) with economic prosperity. Is this association valid? Why or why not? Discuss.

---

*Asterisk denotes questions for which answers are given in Appendix C.

PART SIX

INTERNATIONAL ECONOMICS AND COMPARATIVE SYSTEMS

CHAPTER THIRTY-ONE

GAINING FROM INTERNATIONAL TRADE

Free trade consists simply in letting people buy and sell as they want to buy and sell. It is protection [trade restrictions] that requires force, for it consists in preventing people from doing what they want to do. Protective tariffs are as much applications of force as are blockading squadrons, and their objective is the same—to prevent trade. The difference between the two is that blockading squadrons are a means whereby nations seek to prevent their enemies from trading; protective tariffs are a means whereby nations attempt to prevent their own people from trading.

HENRY GEORGE, 1886[1]

CHAPTER FOCUS

■ *How does the size of the international trade sector vary across countries?*
■ *What are the major import and export products of the United States? Which countries are the major trading partners of the United States?*
■ *Under what conditions can a nation gain from international trade?*
■ *What impact do trade restrictions have on an economy?*
■ *Do trade restrictions create jobs? Does trade with low-wage countries depress wage rates in high-wage countries like the United States?*
■ *Why do nations adopt trade restrictions?*
■ *How does the economic record of countries that impose trade restrictions compare with that of countries following free-trade policies?*

---

[1]Henry George, *Protection or Free Trade*, 1886, reprint (New York: Robert Schalkenbach Foundation, 1980), p. 47.

We live in a shrinking world. The breakfast of many Americans includes bananas from Honduras, coffee from Brazil, or hot chocolate made from Nigerian cocoa beans. Americans often drive a car produced by a Japanese or European manufacturer that consumes gasoline refined from petroleum extracted in Saudi Arabia or Venezuela. Similarly, many work for companies that sell a substantial amount of the goods produced to foreigners. Trade statistics reflect these factors. The volume of international trade, enhanced by improved transportation and communications, has grown rapidly in recent years. Approximately 21 percent of the world's total output is now sold in a country other than that in which it was produced—double the figure of three decades ago.

Perhaps surprising to some, most international trade is not between the governments of the nations involved but between individuals (or business firms) that happen to be located in those countries. International trade, like other voluntary exchange, results because both the buyer and the seller gain from it. If both parties did not expect to gain, there would be no trade.

SIZE OF TRADE SECTOR

The size of the trade sector varies substantially among nations. Some of the difference is due to size of country. For industries in which economies of scale are important, the domestic market of a less-populated country may not be large enough to support cost-efficient firms. Therefore, in small countries, firms in such industries will tend to export a larger share of their output, and consumers will be more likely to purchase goods produced abroad. As a result, the size of the trade sector as a share of the economy tends to be inversely related to the population of the country.

Exhibit 31–1 illustrates the variation in the size of the trade sector (as measured by exports) as a share of total output for countries of similar size. Among the countries with a large population, the trade sector is largest in Indonesia and smallest in India. The United States, Japan, and Brazil are between these two extremes. The trade sectors of these three countries constitute approximately 10 percent of their total output. Among the mid-size countries of Exhibit 31–1, the size of the trade sectors of Thailand, Germany, Egypt, and South Korea are larger than those of Iran, Turkey, Italy, France, and the United Kingdom.

As a share of domestic output, Singapore and Hong Kong have the largest international trade sectors in the world. Both of these countries import large quantities of raw materials and unfinished goods and manufacture them into products that are often exported abroad. Therefore, the gross exports of these two vibrant trade centers actually exceed their gross domestic product. In contrast, the exports of Haiti, Guatemala, and Bolivia are quite small, given the size of these countries.

The data of Exhibit 31–1 illustrate the growth of trade in recent decades. Note that in almost every case, exports comprised a larger share of the aggregate economy in 1991 than in 1970.

[a]Population more than 120 million.
[b]Population between 40 and
 65 million.
[c]Population less than 10 million.

Source: World Bank, *World Development Report*, 1993 Table 9.

EXHIBIT 31-1

SIZE OF TRADE SECTOR OF SELECTED COUNTRIES

	EXPORTS AS PERCENT OF TOTAL OUTPUT	
	1970	1991
Large countries[a]		
Indonesia	13%	27%
Japan	11	10
United States	6	11
Brazil	7	10
India	4	9
Mid-size[b]		
Thailand	15	38
Germany	21	34
Egypt	14	30
South Korea	14	29
United Kingdom	23	24
France	16	23
Italy	16	20
Turkey	6	20
Iran	24	20
Small Countries[c]		
Singapore	102	185
Hong Kong	92	141
Belgium	52	73
Norway	42	45
Switzerland	33	35
Costa Rica	22	28
Israel	25	28
Sweden	24	25
Bolivia	22	18
Guatemala	19	18
Haiti	14	12

THE TRADE SECTOR OF THE UNITED STATES

Exhibit 31–2 summarizes the leading products that the U.S. imports and exports. The United States both imports and exports a substantial quantity of food and agricultural products. The major imported products, however, are generally quite

EXHIBIT 31–2

**MAJOR EXPORT AND IMPORT PRODUCTS OF
UNITED STATES BY CATEGORIES, 1992**

EXPORTS	VALUE (IN BILLIONS)	PERCENT OF TOTAL EXPORTS	IMPORTS	VALUE (IN BILLIONS)	PERCENT OF TOTAL IMPORTS
Food and Agriculture Products			*Food and Agriculture Products*		
Vegetables & fruits	$ 5.7	1.3	Fish	$ 5.7	1.1
Corn	4.9	1.1	Fruits/Vegetables	5.7	1.1
Soybeans	4.4	1.0	Coffee	1.6	0.3
Wheat	4.5	1.0	Alcoholic beverages	1.8	0.3
Minerals and Raw Materials			*Minerals and Raw Materials*		
Plastics	13.0	2.9	Petroleum	49.8	9.4
Coal	4.3	1.0	Aluminum	2.5	0.5
Manufactured Goods			*Manufactured Goods*		
Aircraft	35.7	8.0	Automobiles	72.0	13.5
Electrical machinery	32.0	7.1	Office machines	36.4	6.8
Automobiles	32.3	7.2	Clothing	31.2	5.9
Power-generating machinery	18.0	4.0	Telecommunications equipment (incl. TV sets)	25.8	4.8
Scientific instruments	14.4	3.2	Paper	8.0	1.5
Telecommunications equipment	11.2	2.5	Footwear (shoes)	10.2	1.9
			Toys	10.7	2.0
Total	$448.2	—	Total	$532.5	—

Source: *Statistical Abstract of the United States, 1993*, pp. 817–18.

different from primary products that are exported. Reflecting the temperate climate and fertile agricultural lands of the United States, vegetables and fruits, corn, soybeans, and wheat are the primary food and agricultural exports. In contrast, the primary imported products in this category are fish, fruits and vegetables, coffee, and alcoholic beverages. The mineral and raw material products exported are also quite different from those that are imported. In this category, coal and plastics comprise the primary export goods, while petroleum (particularly crude oil) and aluminum are major imports. In the manufacturing area, automobiles and telecommunications equipment are major items among both imports and exports. The markets for automobiles, computer equipment, televisions, and telephone equipment are worldwide markets. Therefore, in these markets U.S. producers sell substantial quantities abroad, while at the same time, many U.S. consumers purchase these goods from foreign manufacturers.

Clearly, international trade exerts a different impact on some industries than on others. In some industries, domestic producers find it very difficult to compete with their rivals abroad. For example, approximately 90 percent of the shoes purchased by Americans and nearly two-thirds of the radio and television sets, watches, and motorcycles are produced abroad. Imports also supply a high percentage of the clothing and textile products, paper, and toys consumed in the United States. On the other hand, a large proportion of the aircraft, power-generating equipment, scientific instruments, construction equipment, and fertilizers produced in the United States is exported to purchasers abroad.

With which countries does the United States trade the most? As **Exhibit 31–3** illustrates, Canada and Japan head the list. In 1992 approximately one-third of U.S. exports were sold to purchasers in Canada and Japan. Almost 40 percent of U.S. imports were produced in those two countries. Mexico, and the nations of the European Economic Community (particularly Germany, the United Kingdom, France, and Italy), China, and the four "Asian tigers" (Taiwan, South Korea, Hong Kong, and Singapore) were also among the leading trading partners of the United States. During the 1970s, U.S. trade with petroleum-exporting countries such as Saudi Arabia and Venezuela grew rapidly. However, the volume of trade with these nations declined as the price of crude oil fell in the 1980s.

GAINS FROM SPECIALIZATION AND TRADE

If a foreign country can supply us with a commodity cheaper than we ourselves can make it, [we had] better buy it of them with some part of our own industry, employed in a way in which we have some advantage.

ADAM SMITH[2]

As we discussed in Chapter 2, the law of **comparative advantage** explains why a group of individuals, regions, or nations can gain from specialization and exchange. Trading partners are better off if each specializes in the production of goods for which it is a low-opportunity-cost producer and trades for those goods for which it is a high-opportunity-cost producer. Specialization in the area of one's comparative advantage minimizes the cost of production and leads to maximum joint output.

International trade leads to mutual gain because it allows each country to specialize more fully in the production of those things that it does best. Labor-force skills and resource endowments differ substantially across countries. These differences influence costs. Therefore, a good that is quite costly to produce in one country may be economically produced in another country. For example, the warm, moist climate of Brazil and Colombia enhance the economical production of coffee. Countries like Saudi Arabia and Venezuela with rich oil fields can produce petroleum cheaply. Countries with an abundance of fertile land, like Canada and Australia, are able to produce products like wheat, feed grains, and beef at a

Comparative advantage
The ability to produce a good at a lower opportunity cost than others can produce it. Relative costs determine comparative advantage. A nation will have a comparative advantage in the production of a good when its production costs (other goods forgone) for the good are low relative to the production cost of other nations for the same good.

---

[2]Adam Smith, *An Inquiry into the Nature and Causes of the Wealth of Nations*, 1776, Cannan's ed. (Chicago: University of Chicago Press, 1976), pp. 478–479.

EXHIBIT 31–3

THE LEADING TRADING PARTNERS OF THE UNITED STATES, 1992

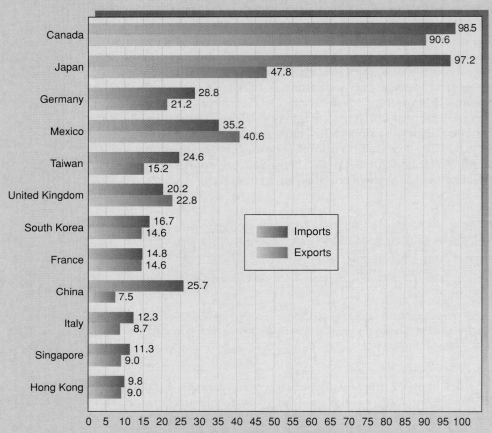

Value of U.S. exports and imports with selected countries, 1992
(billions of dollars)

Canada, Japan, Mexico, and Western European countries are the leading trading partners of the United States. In recent years, Taiwan, South Korea, China, Hong Kong, and Singapore have also emerged as important trading partners of the United States.

Source: *Statistical Abstract of the United States: 1993,* Table 1351.

low cost. In contrast, land is scarce in Japan, a nation with a highly skilled labor force. The Japanese therefore specialize in manufacturing, using their comparative advantage to produce cameras, automobiles, and electronic products for export. With international trade, each country can gain by specializing in the production of goods that it can produce economically and using the proceeds to import goods that would be expensive to produce domestically.

It is easy to see why trade and specialization expand joint output and lead to mutual gain when the resource bases of regions differ substantially. However, even when resource differences among nations are less dramatic, mutual gain is possible. Since failure to comprehend the principle of mutual gains from trade is often a source of "fuzzy thinking," we will take the time to illustrate the principle in detail.

In order to keep things simple, we will consider a case involving only two countries, the United States and Japan, and two products, food and clothing. Furthermore, we will assume that labor is the only resource used to produce these products. In addition, since we want to illustrate that gains from trade are nearly always possible, we are going to assume that Japan has an **absolute advantage**— that the Japanese workers are more efficient than the Americans—in the production of both commodities. **Exhibit 31–4** illustrates this situation. Perhaps due to their prior experience or higher skill level, Japanese workers can produce three units of food per day, compared with only two units per day for U.S. workers. Similarly, Japanese workers are able to produce nine units of clothing per day, compared to one unit of clothing per day for U.S. workers.

Let us consider the following question: Can two countries gain from trade if one of them can produce both goods with fewer resources? Perhaps surprising to some, the answer is yes. As long as *relative* production costs of the two goods differ between Japan and the United States, gains from trade will be possible. Consider what would happen if the United States shifted three workers from the clothing industry to the food industry. This reallocation of labor would allow the United States to expand its food output by six units (two units per worker), while clothing output would decline by three units (one unit per worker). Suppose Japan reallocates labor in the opposite direction. When Japan moves one worker from the food industry to the clothing industry, Japanese clothing production expands by nine units while food output declines by three units. The exhibit shows that this reallocation of labor *within* the two countries has increased their joint output by three units of food and six units of clothing.

Absolute advantage
A situation in which a nation, as the result of its previous experience and/or natural endowments, can produce more of a good (with the same amount of resources) than another nation.

Columns 1 and 2 indicate the daily output of either food or clothing of each worker in the United States and Japan. If the United States moves 3 workers from the clothing industry to the food industry, it can produce 6 more units of food and 3 fewer units of clothing. Similarly, if Japan moves 1 worker from food to clothing, clothing output will increase by 9 units while food output will decline by 3 units. With this reallocation of labor, the United States and Japan are able to increase their aggregate output of both food (3 additional units) and clothing (6 additional units).

^aChange in output if the United States shifts three workers from the clothing to the food industry and if Japan shifts one worker from the food to the clothing industry.

EXHIBIT 31–4

GAINS FROM SPECIALIZATION AND TRADE

COUNTRY	OUTPUT PER WORKER DAY		POTENTIAL CHANGE IN OUTPUT^a	
	FOOD (1)	CLOTHING (2)	FOOD (3)	CLOTHING (4)
United States	2	1	+6	−3
Japan	3	9	−3	+9
Change in Total Output			+3	+6

The source of this increase in output is straightforward: aggregate output is expanded when each country uses more of its resources to produce those goods that it can produce at a *relatively* low cost. Our old friend, the opportunity-cost concept, reveals the low-cost producer of each good. If Japanese workers produce one additional unit of food, they sacrifice the production of three units of clothing. Therefore, in Japan the opportunity cost of one unit of food is three units of clothing. On the other hand, one unit of food in the United States can be produced at an opportunity cost of only one-half unit of clothing. U.S. workers are therefore the low-opportunity-cost producers of food, even though they cannot produce as much food per day as the Japanese workers. Simultaneously, Japan is the low-opportunity-cost producer of clothing. The opportunity cost of producing a unit of clothing in Japan is only one-third unit of food, compared to two units of food in the United States. The reallocation of labor illustrated in Exhibit 31–4 expanded joint output because it moved resources in both countries toward areas where they had a comparative advantage.

As long as the relative costs of producing the two goods differ in the two countries, gains from specialization and trade will be possible. When this is the case, each country will find it cheaper to trade for goods that can be produced only at a high opportunity cost. For example, both countries can gain if the United States trades food to Japan for clothing at a trading ratio greater than one unit of food equals one-half unit of clothing (the U.S. opportunity cost of food) but less than one unit of food equals three units of clothing (the Japanese opportunity cost of food). Any trading ratio between these two extremes will permit the United States to acquire clothing more cheaply than it can be produced within the country and simultaneously permit Japan to acquire food more cheaply than it could be produced domestically.

HOW TRADE EXPANDS CONSUMPTION POSSIBILITIES

Since trade permits nations to expand their joint output, it also allows each nation to expand its consumption possibilities. The production-possibilities concept can be used to illustrate this point. Suppose that there were 200 million workers in the United States and 50 million in Japan. Given these figures and the productivity of workers indicated in Exhibit 31–4, the production-possibilities curves for the two countries are presented in **Exhibit 31–5.** If the United States used all of its 200 million workers in the food industry, it could produce 400 million units of food per day (two units per worker) and zero units of clothing. Alternatively, if the United States used all of its workers to produce clothing, daily output would be 200 million units of clothing and no food. Intermediate output combinations along the production-possibilities line (*MN*) intersecting these two extreme points also could be achievable. For example, the United States could produce 150 units of clothing and 100 units of food (point US_1).

Part "b" of Exhibit 31–5 illustrates the production possibilities of the 50 million Japanese workers. Japan could produce 450 million units of clothing and no food (*R*), 150 million units of food and no clothing (*S*), or various intermediate combinations, like 225 million units of clothing and 75 million units of food (J_1). The slope of the production-possibilities constraint reflects the opportunity cost of

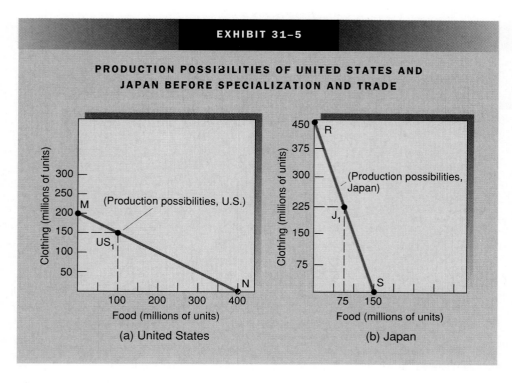

EXHIBIT 31–5

PRODUCTION POSSIBILITIES OF UNITED STATES AND JAPAN BEFORE SPECIALIZATION AND TRADE

(a) United States

(b) Japan

Here we illustrate the daily production possibilities of a U.S. labor force of 200 million workers and a Japanese labor force of 50 million workers, given the cost of producing food and clothing presented in Exhibit 31–4. In the absence of trade, consumption possibilities will be restricted to points such as US_1 in the United States and J_1 in Japan along the production possibilities curve of each country.

food relative to clothing. Since Japan is the high-opportunity-cost producer of food, its production-possibilities constraint is steeper than the constraint for the United States.

In the absence of trade, the consumption of each country is constrained by the country's production possibilities. Trade, however, expands the consumption possibilities of both. As we previously indicated, both countries can gain from specialization if the United States trades food to Japan at a price greater than one unit of food equals one-half unit of clothing but less than one unit of food equals three units of clothing. Suppose that they agree on an intermediate price of one unit of food equals one unit of clothing. As part "a" of **Exhibit 31–6** illustrates, when the United States specializes in the production of food (where it has a comparative advantage) and trades food for clothing (at the price ratio where one unit of food equals one unit of clothing), it can consume along the line ON. If the United States insisted on self-sufficiency, it would be restricted to consumption possibilities like US_1 (100 million units of food and 150 million units of clothing) along its production-possibilities constraint of MN. With trade, however, the United States can achieve combinations such as US_2 (200 million units of food and 200 million units of clothing) along the line ON. Trade permits the United States to expand its consumption of both goods.

Simultaneously, Japan is also able to expand its consumption of both goods when it is able to trade clothing for food at the one-to-one price ratio. As part "b" of Exhibit 31–6 illustrates, Japan can specialize in the production of clothing and consume along the constraint RT when it can trade one unit of clothing for one unit of food. Without trade, consumption in Japan would be limited to points like J_1 (75 million units of food and 225 million units of clothing) along the line RS.

EXHIBIT 31–6

CONSUMPTION POSSIBILITIES WITH TRADE

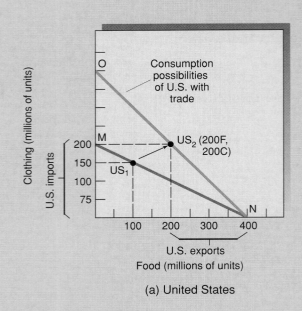

(a) United States

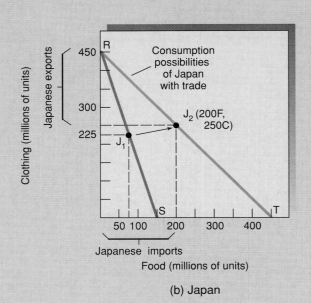

(b) Japan

With specialization and trade, the consumption possibilities of a country can be expanded. If the United States can trade one unit of clothing for one unit of food, it can specialize in the production of food and consume along the ON line (rather than its original production-possibilities constraint, MN). Similarly, when Japan is able to trade one unit of clothing for one unit of food, it can specialize in the production of clothing and consume any combination along the line RT. For example, with specialization and trade, the United States could increase its consumption from US₁ to US₂, gaining 50 million units of clothing and 100 million units of food. Simultaneously, Japan could increase consumption from J₁ to J₂, a gain of 125 million units of food and 25 million units of clothing.

With trade, however, it is able to consume combinations like J_2 (200 million units of food and 250 million units of clothing) along the constraint *RT*.

Look what happens when Japan specializes in clothing and the United States specializes in food. Japan can produce 450 million units of clothing, export 200 million to the United States (for 200 million units of food), and still have 250 million units of clothing remaining for domestic consumption. Simultaneously, the United States can produce 400 million units of food, export 200 million to Japan (for 200 million units of clothing), and still have 200 million units of food left for domestic consumption. After specialization and trade, the United States is able to consume at the point of US_2 and Japan at point J_2, consumption levels that would otherwise be unattainable. Specialization and exchange permit the two countries to expand their joint output, and as a result, both countries can increase their consumption of both commodities.

The implications of the law of comparative advantage are clear: trade between nations will lead to an expansion in total output and mutual gain for each trading partner when each country specializes in the production of goods it can produce at a relatively low cost and uses the proceeds to buy goods that it could produce only at a high cost. It is comparative advantage that matters. As long as there is some variation in the relative opportunity cost of goods across countries, each country will always have a comparative advantage in the production of some goods.

ADDITIONAL CONSIDERATIONS ON INTERNATIONAL TRADE

In order to keep things simple, we ignored the potential importance of transportation costs, which, of course, reduce the potential gains from trade. Sometimes transportation costs, both real and artificially imposed, even exceed the mutual gain. In this case, exchange does not occur.

While our hypothetical example illustrates the case of complete specialization, a country need not specialize in the production of just a few products in order to realize gains from trade. The example of complete specialization was used for illustrative purposes only.

We also assumed that the cost of producing each good was constant in each country. This is seldom the case. Beyond some level of production, the opportunity cost of producing a good will often increase as a country produces more and more of it. Rising marginal costs as the output of a good expands will limit the degree to which a country will specialize in the production of a good.

Sometimes, however, an expansion in the size of the market will permit firms to realize economies that accompany large-scale production, marketing, and distribution. Under these circumstances, international trade will allow domestic firms to produce larger outputs and achieve lower costs than would be possible if they were unable to sell abroad. This point is particularly important for small countries. For example, textile manufacturers in Hong Kong, Taiwan, and South Korea would have much higher costs if they could not sell abroad. The domestic textile markets of these countries are too small to support large, low-cost firms in this industry. With international trade, however, textile firms in these countries operate at a large scale and compete quite effectively in the world market.

Simultaneously, international trade benefits domestic consumers, particularly those in small countries, because it permits them to purchase from large-scale producers abroad. The aircraft industry provides a vivid illustration of this point. Given the huge designing and engineering costs, the domestic market of almost all countries would be substantially less than the quantity required for the efficient production of jet planes. With international trade, however, consumers around the world are able to purchase planes economically from large-scale producers such as Boeing or McDonnell Douglas.

Finally, international trade promotes competition in domestic markets and allows consumers to purchase a wide diversity of goods at economical prices. Competition from abroad helps keep domestic producers on their toes. Domestic producers that otherwise might have few rivals will have to constantly be seeking ways to improve quality and keep costs low. Simultaneously, the diversity of goods that is available from abroad provides consumers with a broader array of choices than would be available in the absence of international trade.

EXPORT-IMPORT LINK

Doubts about the merits of international trade often result from a failure to consider all the consequences. Why are other nations willing to export their goods to the United States? So they can obtain dollars. Yes, but why do they want dollars? Would foreigners be willing to continue exporting oil, radios, watches, cameras, automobiles, and thousands of other valuable products to Americans in exchange for pieces of paper? If so, Americans could all be semiretired, spending only an occasional workday at the dollar printing-press office! Of course, foreigners are not so naive. They trade goods for dollars so they can use the dollars to import goods and purchase ownership rights to U.S. assets.

Exports, broadly perceived to include goods, services, and assets, provide the buying power that makes it possible for a nation to import. If a nation did not export goods, it would not have the foreign currency that is required for the purchase of imports. Similarly, if a nation did not import goods from foreigners, foreigners would not have the purchasing power to buy that nation's export products. Therefore, if imports decline, so will the demand for the nation's exports. Exports and imports are closely linked.

SUPPLY, DEMAND, AND INTERNATIONAL TRADE

How does international trade affect prices and output levels in domestic markets? Supply-and-demand analysis will help us answer this question. Given our modern transportation and communication networks, the market for many commodities is worldwide. When a product can be transported long distances at a low cost (relative to its value) the domestic price of the product is in effect determined by the forces of supply and demand in the worldwide market.

Using soybeans as an example, **Exhibit 31–7** illustrates this relationship between the domestic and world markets for an internationally traded commodity. Worldwide market conditions determine the price of soybeans. In an open economy, domestic producers are free to sell and domestic consumers are free to buy the product at the world market price (P_W). At this price, U.S. producers will supply Q_p, while U.S. consumers will purchase Q_c. Reflecting their comparative advantage, U.S. soybean producers will export $Q_p - Q_c$ units at the world market price.

Let us compare the open-economy outcome with the situation in the absence of trade. If U.S. producers were not allowed to export soybeans, the domestic price would be determined by the domestic supply (S_d) and demand (D_d) only. A lower "no-trade" price (P_n) would emerge. Who are the winners and losers as the result of free trade in soybeans? Clearly, soybean producers gain. Free trade allows domestic producers to sell a larger quantity (Q_p rather than Q_n). As a result, the net revenues of soybean producers will rise by $P_W bcP_n$. On the other hand, domestic consumers of soybeans will have to pay a higher price under free trade. Consumers will lose both (1) because they have to pay P_W rather than P_n for the Q_c

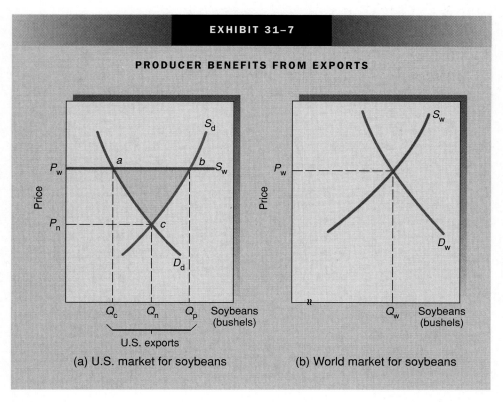

EXHIBIT 31–7

PRODUCER BENEFITS FROM EXPORTS

(a) U.S. market for soybeans

(b) World market for soybeans

The price of soybeans and other internationally traded commodities is determined by the forces of supply and demand in the world market (b). If U.S. soybean producers were prohibited from selling to foreigners, the domestic price would be P_n (a). Free trade permits the U.S. soybean producers to sell Q_p units at the higher world price (P_w). The quantity $Q_p - Q_c$ is exported abroad. Compared to the no-trade situation, the producers' gain from the higher price ($P_w bcP_n$) exceeds the cost imposed on domestic consumers ($P_w acP_n$) by the triangle abc.

units they purchase, and (2) because they lose the consumer surplus on the $Q_n - Q_c$ units now purchased at the higher price. Thus, free trade imposes a net cost of $P_W acP_n$ on consumers. As can be seen in Exhibit 31–7, however, the gains of producers outweigh the losses to consumers by the triangle *abc*. Free trade leads to a net welfare gain.

When one focuses only on an export product, it appears that free trade benefits producers relative to consumers—but this ignores the secondary effects. How will foreigners generate the dollars they need to purchase the export products of the United States? If foreigners do not sell goods to us, they will not have the purchasing power necessary to purchase goods from us. U.S. imports—that is, the purchase of goods from low-cost foreign producers—provide foreigners with the dollar purchasing power necessary to buy U.S. exports. In turn, the lower prices in the import-competitive markets will benefit the U.S. consumers who appeared at first glance to be harmed by the higher prices (compared to the no-trade situation) in export markets.

Exhibit 31–8 illustrates the impact of imports, using shoes as an example. In the absence of trade, the price of shoes in the domestic market would be P_n, the intersection of the domestic supply and demand curves. However, the world price of shoes is P_W. In an open economy, many U.S. consumers would take advantage of the low shoe prices available from foreign producers. At the lower world price, U.S. consumers would purchase Q_c units of shoes, importing $Q_c - Q_p$ from foreign producers.

Compared to the no-trade situation, free trade in shoes results in lower prices and an expansion in domestic consumption. The lower prices lead to a net consumer

In the absence of trade, the domestic price of shoes would be P_n. Since many foreign producers have a comparative advantage in the production of shoes, international trade leads to lower prices. At the world price P_W, U.S. consumers will demand Q_c units, of which $Q_c - Q_P$ are imported. Compared to the no-trade situation, consumers gain P_nabP_w, while domestic producers lose P_nacP_w. A net gain of abc results.

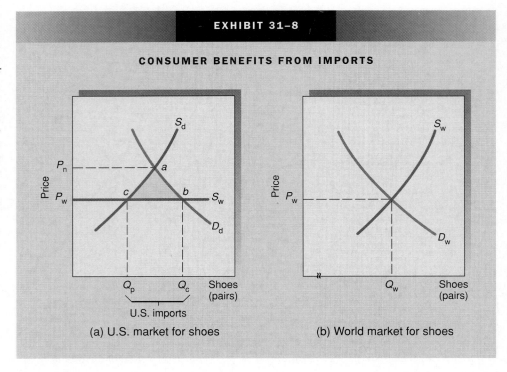

EXHIBIT 31–8

CONSUMER BENEFITS FROM IMPORTS

(a) U.S. market for shoes

(b) World market for shoes

gain of P_nabP_W. Domestic producers lose P_nacP_W in the form of lower sales prices and reductions in output. However, the net gain of consumers exceeds the net loss of producers by *abc*.

For an open economy, international competition directs the resources of a nation toward the areas of their competitive advantage. When domestic producers have a comparative advantage in the production of a good, they will be able to compete effectively in the world market and profit from the export of goods to foreigners. In turn, the exports will generate the purchasing power necessary to buy goods that foreigners can supply more economically. Relative to the no-trade alternative, international trade and specialization result in lower prices (and higher domestic consumption) for imported products and higher prices (and lower domestic consumption) for exported products. More importantly, trade permits the producers of each nation to concentrate on the things they do best (produce at a low cost), while trading for those they do least well. The result is an expansion in both output and consumption compared to what could be achieved in the absence of trade.

The pattern of U.S. exports and imports is consistent with this view. The United States is a nation with a technically skilled labor force, fertile farmland, and substantial capital formation. Thus, we export computers, aircraft, power-generated equipment, scientific instruments, and land-intensive agricultural products—items we are able to produce at a comparatively low cost. Simultaneously, we import substantial amounts of petroleum, textile (clothing) products, shoes, coffee, and diamonds—goods costly for us to produce. Clearly, trade permits us to gain by specializing in those areas in which our comparative advantage is greatest.

ECONOMICS OF TRADE RESTRICTIONS

Despite the potential benefits from free trade, almost all nations have erected trade barriers. Tariffs, quotas, and exchange-rate controls are the most commonly used trade-restricting devices. Let us consider the impact of each.

ECONOMICS OF TARIFFS

A **tariff** is nothing more than a tax on foreign imports. As **Exhibit 31–9** shows, tariffs of between 30 and 50 percent of product value were often levied prior to the 1940s. During the last 50 years, however, the tariff rates of the United States have declined substantially. In 1991 the average tariff rate on imported goods was only 3.3 percent.

    Exhibit 31–10 illustrates the impact of a tariff on automobiles. In the absence of a tariff, the world market price of P_W would prevail in the domestic market. At that price, U.S. consumers purchase Q_1 units. Domestic producers supply Q_{d1}, while foreigners supply $Q_1 - Q_{d1}$ units to the U.S. market. When the United States levies a tariff, t, on automobiles, Americans can no longer buy cars at the world price. U.S. consumers have to pay $P_W + t$ to purchase an automobile from foreigners. The domestic market price thus rises to $P_W + t$. At that price, domestic consumers demand Q_2 units (Q_{d2} supplied by domestic producers and $Q_2 - Q_{d2}$ supplied by foreigners). The tariff results in a higher price and lower level of domestic consumption.

Tariff
A tax levied on goods imported into a country.

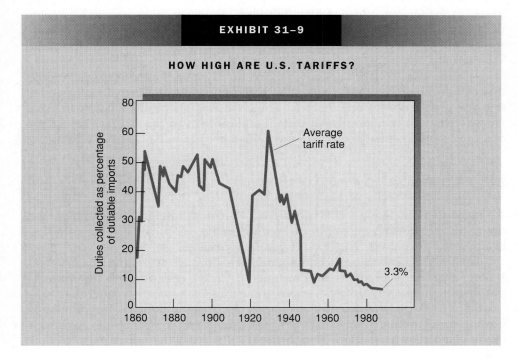

EXHIBIT 31–9

HOW HIGH ARE U.S. TARIFFS?

Tariff rates in the United States fell sharply during the period from 1930 to 1950. Subsequently, after rising slightly during the 1950s, they have trended downward since 1960. In 1991, the average tariff rate on merchandise imports was 3.3 percent.

Here we illustrate the impact of a tariff on automobiles. In the absence of the tariff, the world price of automobiles is P_w: U.S. consumers purchase Q_1 units (Q_{d1} from domestic producers plus $Q_1 - Q_{d1}$ from foreign producers). The tariff makes it more costly for Americans to purchase automobiles from foreigners. Imports decline and the domestic price increases. Consumers lose the sum of the areas S + U + T + V in the form of higher prices and a reduction in consumer surplus. Producers gain the area S and the tariff generates T tax revenues for the government. The areas U and V are deadweight losses due to a reduction in allocative efficiency.

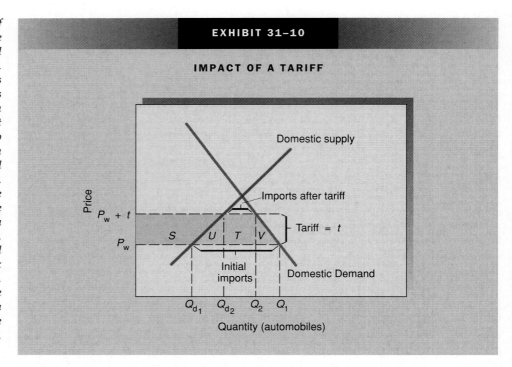

EXHIBIT 31–10

IMPACT OF A TARIFF

The tariff benefits domestic producers and the government at the expense of consumers. Since they do not pay the tariff, domestic producers will expand their output in response to the higher (protected) market price. In effect, the tariff acts as a subsidy to domestic producers. Domestic producers gain the area S (Exhibit 31–10) in the form of additional net revenues. The tariff raises revenues equal to the area T for the government. The areas U and V represent costs imposed on consumers that do not benefit either producers or the government. Simply put, U and V represent a *deadweight loss* (loss of efficiency).

As a result of the tariff, resources that could have been used to produce goods that U.S. firms produce efficiently (compared to producers abroad) are diverted into the production of automobiles. Thus, we end up producing less in areas where we have a comparative advantage and more in areas where we are a high-cost producer. Potential gains from specialization and trade go unrealized.

ECONOMICS OF QUOTAS

Import quota
A specific quantity (or value) of a good permitted to be imported into a country during a given year.

An **import quota**, like a tariff, is designed to restrict foreign goods and protect domestic industries. A quota places a ceiling on the amount of a product that can be imported during a given period (typically a year).

The United States imposes quotas on several products including brooms, steel, shoes, sugar, dairy products, and peanuts. As in the case of tariffs, the primary purpose of quotas is to protect domestic industries from foreign competition.

Since 1953 the United States has imposed a quota to limit the importation of peanuts to 1.7 million pounds per year, approximately two peanuts per American. Using peanuts as an example, **Exhibit 31–11** illustrates the impact of a quota. If

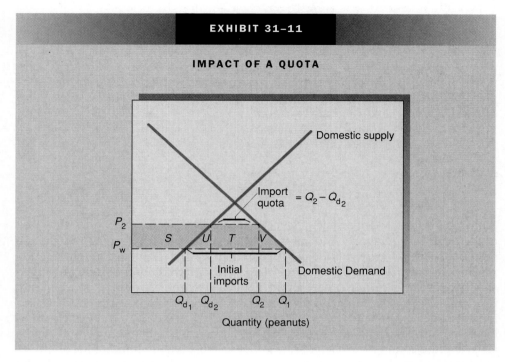

EXHIBIT 31–11

IMPACT OF A QUOTA

Domestic supply

Import quota $= Q_2 - Q_{d2}$

P_2

P_w

S U T V

Initial imports

Domestic Demand

Q_{d1} Q_{d2} Q_2 Q_1

Quantity (peanuts)

Here we illustrate the impact of a quota such as the one the United States imposes on peanuts. The world market price of peanuts is P_w. If there were no trade restraints, the domestic price would also be P_w, and the domestic consumption would be Q_1. Domestic producers would supply Q_{d1} units, while $Q_1 - Q_{d1}$ would be imported. A quota limiting imports to $Q_2 - Q_{d2}$ would push up the domestic price to P_2. At the higher price, the amount supplied by domestic producers increases to Q_{d2}. Consumers lose the sum of the areas $S + U + T + V$, while domestic producers gain the area S. In contrast with tariffs, quotas generate no revenue for the government. The area T goes to foreign producers who are granted permission to sell in the U.S. market.

there were no trade restraints, the domestic price of peanuts would be equal to the world market price (P_W). Under those circumstances, Americans would purchase Q_1 units. At the price P_W, domestic producers would supply Q_{d1}, and the amount $Q_1 - Q_{d1}$ would be imported from foreign producers.

Now consider what happens when a quota limits imports to $Q_2 - Q_{d2}$, a quantity well below the free trade level of imports. Since the quota reduces the foreign supply of peanuts to the domestic market, the price of the quota-protected product increases (to P_2). At the higher price, U.S. consumers will reduce their purchases to Q_2, and domestic producers will happily expand their production to Q_{d2}. With regard to the welfare of consumers, the impact of a quota is similar to that of a tariff. Consumers lose the area $S + U + T + V$ in the form of higher prices and the loss of consumer surplus. Similarly, domestic producers gain the area S, while the areas U and V represent deadweight losses from allocative inefficiency. However, there is a big difference between tariffs and quotas with regard to the area T. Under a tariff, the U.S. government would collect revenues equal to T, representing the tariff rate multiplied by the number of units imported. With a quota, however, these revenues will go to the foreign producers, who are granted import permits to sell in the U.S. market. Clearly, this right to sell at a premium price (since the domestic price exceeds the world market price) is extremely valuable. Thus, foreign producers will compete for the permits. They will hire lobbyists, make political contributions, and engage in other rent-seeking activities in an effort to secure the right to sell at a premium price in the U.S. market.

In many ways, quotas are more harmful than tariffs. With a quota, foreign producers are prohibited from selling additional units regardless of how much lower their costs are relative to domestic producers. In contrast with a tariff, a quota brings in no revenue for the government. While a tariff transfers revenue from U.S. consumers to the Treasury, quotas transfer these revenues to foreign producers. Obviously, this politically granted privilege creates a strong incentive for foreign producers to engage in wasteful rent-seeking activities. Thus, by rewarding both domestic producers with higher prices and foreign producers with valuable import permits, quotas generate two strong interest groups supportive of their continuation. As a result, removal of a quota is often even more difficult to achieve than a tariff reduction.

EXCHANGE-RATE CONTROLS AS A TRADE RESTRICTION

Many countries, particularly less developed countries, fix the exchange-rate value of their currency above the market rate. At the official (artificially high) exchange rate, the country's export goods will be extremely expensive to foreigners. As a result, foreigners will purchase goods elsewhere, and the country's exports will be small. In turn, the low level of exports will make it extremely difficult for domestic residents to get their hands on the foreign currency required for the purchase of imports. Such exchange-rate controls both reduce the volume of trade and lead to black-market currency exchanges. Indeed, a large black-market premium indicates that the country's exchange-rate policy is substantially limiting the ability of its citizens to trade with foreigners. The greater the black-market premium, the larger the expected decline in the size of the country's international trade sector as the result of the exchange rate controls.

WHY DO NATIONS ADOPT TRADE RESTRICTIONS?

Physical obstacles, like bad roads and stormy weather, that increase transaction costs will retard the gains from trade. Tariffs, quotas, exchange-rate controls, and other man-made trade restrictions have similar effects. Henry George compared trade restrictions to a blockade (see the chapter's opening quote). Both the blockade imposed by an enemy and a self-imposed blockade in the form of trade restrictions will retard the gains from specialization and exchange.

If trade restrictions promote inefficiency and reduce the potential gains from exchange, why do nations adopt them? Several factors play a role. First, there are some partially valid arguments for the protection of specific industries under certain circumstances. Second, economic illiteracy plays a role. Failing to comprehend the implications of the law of comparative advantage and the linkage between imports and exports, many people fallaciously believe that trade restrictions increase employment and help keep the wages of Americans high. (See the accompanying "Myths of Economics" box on these topics.) Finally, and most importantly, trade restrictions reflect the political power of concentrated interests. We will now take a look at each of these factors.

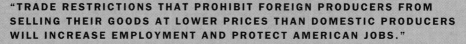

MYTHS OF ECONOMICS

"TRADE RESTRICTIONS THAT PROHIBIT FOREIGN PRODUCERS FROM SELLING THEIR GOODS AT LOWER PRICES THAN DOMESTIC PRODUCERS WILL INCREASE EMPLOYMENT AND PROTECT AMERICAN JOBS."

Many people sincerely believe that trade restrictions increase employment and "save American jobs." This fallacious belief stems from a failure to consider the secondary effects of import restrictions on export industries. Tariffs, quotas, exchange-rate controls, and other trade restrictions may result in more employment *in industries shielded by the restraints,* but they will *destroy jobs in other industries.*

Remember, the sales from foreigners to us (our imports) provide them with the purchasing power required to buy from us (our exports). If foreigners are unable to sell as much to Americans, then they will have fewer dollars with which to buy from Americans. Therefore, there is a secondary effect that accompanies trade restrictions: the demand for American export goods declines. As a result, output and employment in export industries will be smaller, offsetting any jobs saved in protected industries. Since most noneconomists fail to recognize the link between a decline in imports due to trade restrictions and a decline in exports because foreigners have acquired fewer dollars, it is easy to see why this myth is so widely believed.

In addition, import restrictions push up the price of resources such as machine tools, steel, raw materials, and delivery trucks that are often imported and used by American businesses to produce goods and services. These higher resource prices both make it more costly to produce all domestic output and reduce the competitiveness of American exporters—factors that also tend to reduce employment.

When trade restraints are lowered (or there is discussion about lowering them), predictably many workers and business officials in import competitive industries will charge that jobs will be lost to foreign competitors. In contrast, the additional jobs in the export industries do not yet exist. There will not be anyone saying, "I will not be employed next year if the trade restraints are not lowered." Since the jobs (and employees) in the import-competitive industries are highly visible, while the future jobs in the exporting industries are invisible, this also helps explain why it is so difficult to reduce trade restraints.

Actually, the focus on jobs is misleading. After all, it is income and high productivity, not jobs, that are the source of prosperity. The real issue is not jobs, but rather what we are going to produce with our resources. In essence, import restraints direct resources away from areas where domestic producers have a comparative advantage and into areas where domestic producers are relatively inefficient. Since fewer of our resources are used to produce things that we are good at (as indicated by our ability to compete effectively) and more resources are squandered attempting to produce things that we do poorly (as evidenced by our inability to compete in the world market), the per capita output and income of Americans is lower than would be the case in the absence of the restraints.

Consider the following: If import restrictions are a good idea, why don't we use them to restrict trade among the 50 states? After all, think of all of the jobs that are lost when, for example, Michigan "imports" oranges from Florida, apples from Washington, wheat from Kansas, and cotton from Georgia. All of these products could be produced in Michigan. However, the residents of Michigan generally find it cheaper to "import" these commodities rather than produce them domestically. Michigan gains by using its resources to produce and "export" automobiles (and other goods it can produce economically) and then using the sales revenue to "import" goods that would be expensive to produce in Michigan.

Most people recognize that free trade among the 50 states is a major source of prosperity for each of the states. Similarly, most recognize that "imports" from other states do not destroy jobs—at least not for long. Instead, the "imports" release workers for employment in "export" industries, where they will be able to produce more value and therefore generate more income. The source of gains from trade among nations is exactly the same as for trade among people in different states. Free trade among the 50 states promotes prosperity; so, too, does free trade among nations.

Of course, sudden removal of trade barriers might harm producers and workers in protected industries. It may be costly to quickly transfer the protected resources to other more productive activities. Gradual removal of the barriers would minimize this shock effect and the accompanying cost of relocation.

More than one-fifth of the world's output is produced in one country and sold in another. The gains from specialization, division of labor, and adoption of mass production methods that accompany international trade allow the trading partners to achieve a larger output and higher living standards than would otherwise be the case.

PARTIALLY VALID ARGUMENTS FOR RESTRICTIONS

There are three major, at least partially valid, arguments for protecting certain domestic industries from foreign competitors: the national-defense, infant-industry, and anti-dumping arguments.

NATIONAL-DEFENSE ARGUMENT.   According to the national-defense argument, certain industries—aircraft, petroleum, and weapons, for example—are vital to national defense and therefore should be protected from foreign competitors so that a domestic supply of necessary materials would be available in case of an international conflict. Would we want to be entirely dependent on Arabian or Russian petroleum? Would complete dependence on French aircraft be wise? Many Americans would answer no, even if trade restrictions were required to prevent such dependence by preserving domestic industries.

While the national-defense argument has some validity, it is often abused. Relatively few industries are truly vital to our national defense. In cases where a resource is important for national defense, often it would make more sense to stockpile the resource during peacetime rather than follow protectionist policies to preserve a domestic industry. Since the national-defense argument is often used by special interests to justify protection for their industry, the merits of each specific case must be carefully evaluated.

THE INFANT-INDUSTRY ARGUMENT.   Advocates of the infant-industry argument hold that new domestic industries should be protected from older, established foreign competitors. As the new industry matures, it will be able to stand on its own feet and compete effectively with foreign producers, at which time protection can be removed.

The infant-industry argument has a long and often notorious history. Alexander Hamilton used it to argue for the protection of early U.S. manufacturing. While it is an argument for only *temporary* protection, the protection, once granted, is generally difficult to remove. For example, a century ago, this argument was used to gain tariff protection for the newly emerging steel industry in the United States. With time, the steel industry developed and became very powerful, both politically and economically. Despite this maturity, the tariffs remained. To this day, legislation continues to provide the industry with various protections that limit competition from abroad.

ANTI-DUMPING ARGUMENT.   In some cases, **dumping,** the sale of goods abroad at a price below their cost (and below their price in the domestic market of the exporting nation), merely reflects the exporter's desire to penetrate a foreign market. In other instances, dumping may be prompted by export subsidies of foreign governments. At various times in the past, it has been alleged that Argentina has dumped textiles, Korea has dumped steel, and Canada has dumped radial tires into the U.S. market. Dumping is illegal. The Trade Agreements Act of 1979 provides for special anti-dumping *duties* (tariffs) when a good is sold in the United States at a price lower than that found in the domestic market of the exporting nation.

As in the case of imports, dumping generally benefits domestic consumers and imposes costs on domestic producers of goods for which the imports are good substitutes. The lower prices of the "dumped" goods permit consumers to obtain the goods more economically than they are available from domestic producers. Simultaneously, the lower prices make it more difficult for domestic producers of the goods to compete. Predictably, domestic producers (and their employees) are the major source of the charges that dumping is unfair.

Economists generally emphasize two points with regard to dumping. First, dumping can, in a few instances, be used as a weapon to gain monopoly power. For example, if the foreign firm temporarily cuts its price below cost, it might eliminate domestic competition and later raise its price to a higher level after the domestic competitors have been driven from the market. However, this is usually not a feasible strategy. After all, domestic producers might reenter the market if the price rises in the future. In addition, alternative foreign suppliers limit the monopoly power of a producer attempting this strategy.

Second, the law of comparative advantage indicates that a country (as a whole) can gain from the purchase of foreign-produced goods when they are cheaper than domestic goods. This is true regardless of whether the low price of foreign goods reflects comparative advantage, subsidies by foreign governments, or poor business practices. Unless the foreign supplier is likely to monopolize the domestic market, there is little reason to believe that dumping harms the economy receiving the goods.

Dumping
The sale of a good by a foreign supplier in another country at a price lower than the supplier sells it in its home market.

SPECIAL INTERESTS AND THE POLITICS OF TRADE RESTRICTIONS

Protectionism is a politician's delight because it delivers visible benefits to the protected parties while imposing the costs as a hidden tax on the public.

MURRAY L. WEIDENBAUM[3]

---

[3]Former chairman of the President's Council of Economic Advisers.

While the support for trade restrictions arises from multiple sources, as Professor Weidenbaum points out, there is no question as to the primary reason for their adoption. Trade restrictions provide highly invisible, concentrated benefits for a small group of people, while imposing widely dispersed costs that are often difficult to identify on the general citizenry. As we discussed in Chapter 4, politicians have a strong incentive to favor issues of this type, even if they conflict with economic efficiency.

Trade restrictions almost always benefit producers (and resource suppliers) at the expense of consumers. In general, the former group—investors and workers in a specific industry—are well organized, and the "jobs saved" and "high wages protected" in these industries are often highly visible (refer again to the "Myths of Economics" box on trade restrictions). Thus, organized interest groups that benefit from trade restrictions frequently provide contributions and other resources to politicians willing to support trade restrictions favorable to their industry. In contrast, consumers, who will pay higher prices for the products of a protected industry, are an unorganized group. Most of them will not associate the higher product prices with the trade restrictions. Similarly, potential workers and investors in export industries harmed by the restrictions are often unaware of their impact. Thus, most of the people harmed by trade restrictions are likely to be uninformed and unconcerned about trade policy.

Predictably, well-organized special interests favoring trade restrictions will generally have more political clout than those harmed by the restrictions. As a result, politicians will often be able to gain more votes by supporting trade restrictions that benefit organized interest groups than they could gain from the support of consumers and exporters. In the case of trade restrictions, sound economics often conflicts with a winning political strategy.

EMPIRICAL EVIDENCE ON THE IMPACT OF TRADE RESTRICTIONS

Our analysis indicates that countries imposing trade barriers will fail to realize their full economic potential. There are various ways—tariffs, quotas, exchange-rate controls, and licensing requirements, for example—that countries can restrain international trade. It is not easy to determine the extent to which various countries are restricting trade.

Taxes on international trade are generally substantially lower in high-income industrial countries than the less developed countries (LDCs) of Latin America, Africa, and parts of Asia. Similarly, while exchange-rate controls are a negligible restrictive factor in developed countries, they are a major factor restricting trade in several less developed countries. Therefore, adjusted for size of country, the size of the trade sector tends to be larger in the high-income industrial countries. This is not surprising, since the gains from specialization and international exchange also contribute to the prosperity of these countries.

Among LDCs, there is considerable variation in the height of trade barriers. Some LDCs impose exceedingly high tariffs. Others impose exchange-rate controls. When a country both imposes high tariffs and fixes the value of its currency at unrealistic rates (relative to convertible currencies like the dollar and yen), its international trade will be retarded substantially.

Exhibit 31–12 presents data for ten LDCs with relatively low trade barriers.[4] Given the size of their population, the trade sectors of these ten countries are large. Their tariff rates are low, and the exchange-rate value of their currencies is pretty much in line with market forces (a low black-market exchange-rate premium provides evidence on this point). Data are also provided for ten countries that impose substantial restrictions on trade. For this latter group, the size of the trade sector is small (given the size of the country), tariffs are high, and the black-market exchange-rate premium for the conversion of the domestic currency is high. As we previously discussed, a high black-market premium indicates that the country has imposed tight exchange-rate controls. Compared to the low-restriction countries, on average, the tax (tariff) rates imposed on international trade were approximately four times higher for the high-restriction countries. Similarly, the black-market exchange-rate premium for the domestic currency was much higher in the high-restriction countries.

Look at the growth of per capita GDP during the 1980–1991 period for the two groups. Singapore and Hong Kong, the two countries that most closely follow free-trade policies—their tariffs are negligible and their currencies are fully convertible—both achieved impressive growth rates during the period. The average annual growth of per capita GDP in the low-restriction countries was 4.7 percent during 1980–1991. In contrast, the growth rate of the ten countries with high trade restrictions was minus 0.7 percent. Per capita GDP declined during 1980–1991 in six of the ten countries that imposed substantial restrictions on international trade. None of the countries with high trade restrictions were able to achieve even half of the average growth rate of the countries following policies more consistent with free trade. Just as our theory implies, these data indicate that trade barriers are harmful to the economic health of a country.[5]

RECENT REDUCTIONS IN TRADE RESTRICTIONS

ROLE OF GATT

Despite their vulnerability to special-interest politics, the potential gains from reductions in trade restrictions have not been ignored. Reacting to a wave of trade

---

[4]The empirical data presented in this section is part of a larger study undertaken by one of the authors. See James Gwartney, Walter Block, and Robert Lawson, *Rating the Economic Freedom of 100 Countries: 1975–1990,* chapter 5, paper presented at Fraser Institute conference, "Rating Economic Freedom VI," November 18–21, 1993, Sonoma, California. Also see Gwartney, Block, and Lawson, "Measuring Economic Freedom" in *Rating Global Economic Freedom,* edited by Steven T. Easton and Michael A. Walker (Vancouver, British Columbia: The Fraser Institute, 1992).

[5]For additional evidence that trade restrictions retard economic growth, see Robert Barro, "Economic Growth in a Cross-Section of Countries," *Quarterly Journal of Economics,* May 1991, pp. 407–443; David M. Gould, Roy J. Ruffin, and Graeme L. Woodbridge, "The Theory and Practice of Free Trade", *Economic Review—Federal Reserve Bank of Dallas,* Fourth Quarter 1993, pp. 1–16; and Michael Michaely, Demetris Papageorgiou, and Armeane M. Choksi, eds. *Liberalizing Foreign Trade: Lessons of Experience in the Developing World* (Cambridge, MA: Basil Blackwell, 1991).

EXHIBIT 31–12

ECONOMIC GROWTH OF LESS DEVELOPED COUNTRIES WITH LOW AND HIGH TRADE RESTRICTIONS

	SIZE OF TRADE SECTOR AS PERCENT OF GDP, 1990[a]	AVERAGE TAX RATE ON INTERNATIONAL TRADE		BLACK MARKET EXCHANGE-RATE PREMIUM[b]		GROWTH OF PER CAPITA GDP, 1980–1991
		1980	1990	1980	1990	
Low Trade Restrictions[a]						
Singapore	183.4	0.5	0.2	0	0	4.9
Hong Kong	134.1	0.0	0.0	0	0	5.7
Malaysia	81.6	7.7	3.1	0	0	3.1
Ireland	65.0	3.0	2.7	0	1	3.3
Taiwan	45.3	3.6	2.1	1	0	6.5
Portugal	41.1	2.1	1.1	2	3	2.8
Thailand	39.6	6.8	5.6	5	0	6.0
Chile	37.6	2.8	3.9	6	0	1.9
South Korea	31.8	4.1	3.3	11	1	8.5
Indonesia	26.7	2.9	2.5	2	0	3.8
Average	68.6	3.4	2.5	3	1	**4.7**
High Trade Restrictions[a]						
Somalia	7.5	10.5	n.a.*	41	200	−2.2
Peru	11.0	10.6	6.7	18	16	−2.6
Nepal	13.1	8.6	12.9	0	16	0.7
Uganda	13.3	3.1	11.6	360	40	−0.5
Bangladesh	13.3	13.4	12.1	111	165	2.1
Rwanda	13.7	13.3	n.a.*	67	28	−2.4
Iran	15.6	8.5	27.7	164	2197	−1.4
Burundi	17.1	18.1	17.0	45	6	1.1
Ghana	21.3	17.3	11.4	304	7	0.0
Sierra Leone	22.7	13.3	6.2	62	165	−1.3
Average	14.9	11.7	13.3	117	284	**−0.7**

[a]The size of the trade sector is equal to one-half of exports plus imports as a percent of GDP. As Exhibit 31–1 shows, the size of the trade sector tends to be inversely related to the population of a country. Given population, the size of the trade sector is generally large in countries with low trade restrictions and small in countries with high trade restrictions.

[b]A sizable black-market exchange-rate premium indicates that the country has imposed exchange-rate controls that substantially limit the ability of domestic citizens to convert the national currency to other currencies.

*Data not available.

Source: Derived from World Bank, *World Tables, 1991* and *World Development Report, 1992;* International Money Fund, *Government Finance Yearbook, 1991;* and International Currency Analysis, *The World Currency Yearbook, 1989–90.* Also see James Gwartney, Robert Lawson, and Walter Block, "Rating the Economic Freedom of 100 Countries: 1975–1990" (Chapter 5), a paper presented at the conference, "Rating Economic Freedom VI" sponsored by The Fraser Institute of Vancouver, British Columbia. The conference was held in Sonoma, California on November 18–21, 1993.

restrictions adopted during the 1930s, the major industrial nations established a multi-nation organization called **General Agreement on Tariffs and Trade (GATT)** shortly following the Second World War. GATT has grown from 22 members to an international organization of 115 members representing nations that conduct approximately 85 percent of the world trade. This organization spells out the rules for international trade and oversees bargaining designed to reduce trade barriers among nations.

GATT has played a central role in the multi-lateral tariff reductions and the relaxation (or elimination) of quotas. Since its inception almost five decades ago, the average tariff rates of GATT members have fallen from approximately 40 percent to their current level of less than 5 percent. The most recent GATT session—the Uruguay Round—was finally completed at year-end 1993, after seven years of intense negotiations. This round primarily focused on nontariff issues such as quotas and agricultural subsidies. As the result of the recent GATT proceedings, members agreed to (1) eliminate quotas (however, countries are permitted to maintain tariffs) on textile products, (2) accept uniform standards of evidence that will make it more difficult to take unilateral action against alleged dumping, (3) reduce tariffs on wood, paper, nonferrous metals, and some electronic products, (4) adopt standards that will make it easier to prosecute parties that violate intellectual property rights (copyrights, patents, and software and movie rights), and (5) reduce agricultural subsidies gradually during the next decade.

General Agreement on Tariffs and Trade (GATT)
An organization composed of 115 countries designed to set the rules for the conduct of international trade and reduce barriers to trade among nations.

NORTH AMERICAN FREE TRADE AGREEMENT (NAFTA)

The United States, Canada, and Mexico also adopted a North American Free Trade Agreement (NAFTA) in 1993. As the result of the NAFTA agreement, tariffs on the shipment of most products between the three countries will be eliminated during the next ten years. The agreement will also remove limits on financial investments, liberalize trade in services such as banking, and establish uniform legal requirements for the protection of intellectual property.

Coming on the heels of the 1988 trade agreement between the United States and Canada, NAFTA will further expand the free movement of goods and investments among the countries of North America. Domestic producers in all three countries will have free access to a larger market. Many products will now be produced at a lower per unit cost because producers will be able to plan for and produce a larger volume of output. The economies of scale are likely to be particularly important for producers in Canada and Mexico. Elimination of trade barriers will also provide consumers with greater variety and an expanded choice among suppliers.

Compared with the Canadian-American trade agreement, the free trade agreement with Mexico was—and continues to be—much more controversial. As we have discussed, trade flows among nations are determined by comparative advantage, not relative wage rates. Nonetheless, many Americans and Canadians fear that competition from low-wage workers will adversely affect their earnings (see the "Myths of Economics" box on free trade with low-wage countries). As in the case of the U.S.–Canada agreement, economics indicates that NAFTA will help

MYTHS OF ECONOMICS

"FREE TRADE WITH LOW-WAGE COUNTRIES SUCH AS CHINA AND INDIA WOULD CAUSE THE WAGES OF U.S. WORKERS TO FALL."

Many Americans believe that if it were not for trade restrictions, the wages of American workers would fall to the level of workers in less-developed countries. How can U.S. labor compete with Indian and Chinese workers that are willing to work for $1 per hour or less? The fallacy of this argument stems from a misunderstanding of the source of high wages and ignorance of the law of comparative advantage.

High hourly wages do not necessarily mean high per unit labor cost. Labor productivity must also be considered. For example, suppose a U.S. steel worker receives an hourly wage rate of $20 and a steel worker in India receives only $2 per hour. Given the skill level of the workers and the capital and production methods used in the two countries, however, the U.S. worker produces 20 times as many tons of steel per worker-hour as the Indian worker. Because of the higher productivity per worker-hour, labor cost per unit of output is actually lower in the United States than in India!

Labor in the United States possesses a high skill level and works with large amounts of capital equipment. These factors contribute to the high productivity per worker, which is the source of the high wages. Similarly, low productivity per worker-hour is the foundation of the low wages in such countries as India and China.

When analyzing the significance of wage and productivity differentials across countries, one must remember that gains from trade emanate from comparative advantage, not absolute advantage (see Exhibits 31–4, 31–5, and 31–6). The United States cannot produce everything cheaper than China or India merely because U.S. workers are more productive and work with more capital than workers in China and India. Neither can the Chinese and Indians produce every-

thing cheaper merely because their wage rates are low compared to the U.S. workers. When resources are directed by relative prices and the principle of comparative advantage, both high-wage and low-wage countries gain from the opportunity to specialize in those activities that, relatively speaking, they do best.

The comparative advantage of low-wage countries is likely to be in the production of labor-intensive goods such as wigs, rugs, toys, textiles, and assembled manufactured products. On the other hand, the comparative advantage of the United States lies in the production of high-technology manufacturing products (computers, aircraft, and scientific instruments, for example) and land-intensive agricultural products (wheat, corn, and soybeans). (See Exhibit 31–2).

Trade permits both high- and low-wage countries to reallocate their resources away from productive activities in which they are inefficient (relative to foreign producers) to activities in which they are highly efficient. The net result is an increase in output and consumption opportunities for both trading partners.

If foreigners, even low-wage foreigners, will sell us a product cheaper than we ourselves could produce it, we can gain by using our resources to produce other things. Perhaps an extreme example will illustrate the point. Suppose a foreign producer, perhaps a Santa Claus who pays workers little or nothing, were willing to supply us with free winter coats. Would it make sense to enact a tariff barrier to keep out the free coats? Of course not. Resources that were previously used to produce coats could now be freed to produce other goods. Output and the availability of goods would expand. The real wage of U.S. workers would rise. It makes no more sense to erect trade barriers to keep out cheap foreign goods than to keep out the free coats of a friendly, foreign Santa Claus.

all trading partners. It will tend to reduce the cost of labor-intensive goods to U.S. and Canadian consumers while simultaneously increasing the availability of high-tech manufactured goods for Mexican consumers. Adjustment will be required by suppliers and workers, leading to temporary unemployment for some. The benefit, however, is that all three countries can expect to gain by using their resources more fully in those areas where they have the greatest comparative advantage.

FALLING TRADE BARRIERS IN OTHER COUNTRIES

In many ways the recent GATT and NAFTA agreements were merely a reflection of changes that were already taking place worldwide—particularly among LDCs. No doubt influenced by the economic success of relatively open economies like those of Hong Kong and Singapore, many LDCs unilaterally reduced their trade barriers during the late 1980s and early 1990s. Among Latin American countries, Chile began moving toward freer trade policies in the early 1980s. Spurred by the rapid economic growth of Chile during the latter half of the 1980s, other Latin American countries also reduced their trade barriers. Mexico cut its tariff rates by more than 50 percent during the late 1980s. In 1991 Argentina cut its average tariff level from 18 percent to 11 percent. Brazil, Bolivia, Columbia, Ecuador, Peru, and Venezuela have also made substantial cuts in their tariff rates and reduced other trade barriers in the 1990s.[6] Exchange-rate controls have also been relaxed or eliminated throughout much of Latin America during the last five years.

In other parts of the world, even some of the most "protectionist" countries—including Bangladesh, Pakistan, Philippines, and Turkey—cut their tariffs and/or relaxed restrictive quotas during the early 1990s. Perhaps the stage is now set for many of these countries to follow the path of Chile and the trade-oriented countries of Southeast Asia toward a more prosperous future.

LOOKING AHEAD

There are many similarities between trade within national borders and trade across national boundaries. However, there is also a major difference. In addition to the exchange of goods for money, trade across national borders generally involves the exchange of national currencies. The next chapter deals with the financial arrangements under which international trade is conducted.

CHAPTER SUMMARY

1. The volume of international trade has grown rapidly in recent decades. In the early 1990s approximately 21 percent of the world's output was sold in a different country than it was produced. The size of the trade sector as a share of the economy varies substantially among countries. It is generally larger in countries with a smaller population.

2. The trade sector is approximately 11 percent of the U.S. GDP. More than half of all U.S. trade is with Canada, Japan, and the developed nations of Western Europe.

3. Comparative advantage rather than absolute advantage is the source of gains from trade. As long as the relative production costs of goods differ among nations, the nations will be able to gain from trade.

4. Mutual gains from trade accrue when each nation produces goods for which it is a low-opportunity-cost producer and trades for goods for which it is a high-opportunity-cost producer. This pattern of specialization and trade allows trading partners to maximize their joint output and expand their consumption possibilities.

5. Exports and imports are closely linked. The exports of a nation are the primary source of purchasing power used to import goods. When a nation restricts imports, it simultaneously limits the ability of foreigners to acquire the purchasing power necessary to buy the nation's exports.

6. International competition directs the resources of a nation toward its areas of comparative advantage. In an open economy, when domestic producers have a comparative advantage in the production of a good, they will be able to export their product and compete effectively in the world market. On the other hand, for commodities in which foreign producers have the comparative advantage,

---

[6]See Susan Hickok, "Recent Trade Liberalization in Developing Countries: The Effects of Global Trade and Output," *Quarterly Review: Federal Reserve Bank of New York*, Autumn 1993, pp. 6–19.

a nation could import the goods more economically (at a lower opportunity cost) than they could be produced domestically.

7. Relative to the no-trade alternative, international exchange and specialization result in lower prices for products that are imported and higher domestic prices for products that are exported. However, the net effect is an expansion in the aggregate output and consumption possibilities available to a nation.

8. The application of a tariff, quota, or other import restriction to a product reduces the amount that foreigners supply to the domestic market. As a result of diminished supply, consumers face higher prices for the protected product. Essentially, import restrictions are subsidies to producers (and workers) in protected industries at the expense of (a) consumers and (b) producers (and workers) in export industries. Restrictions reduce the ability of domestic producers to specialize in those areas for which their comparative advantage is greatest.

9. National-defense, infant-industry, and anti-dumping arguments can be used to justify trade restrictions for specific industries under certain conditions. It is clear, though, that the power of special-interest groups and voter ignorance about the harmful effects of trade restrictions offer the major explanations for real-world protectionist public policies.

10. Trade restrictions are often attractive to politicians because they generate visible benefits to special interests—particularly business and labor interests in protected industries—while imposing costs on consumers and taxpayers that are individually small and largely invisible.

11. Trade restrictions do not create jobs. Jobs protected by import restrictions are offset by jobs destroyed in export industries. Since this result of restrictions often goes unnoticed, their political popularity is understandable. Nevertheless, trade restrictions are inefficient, since they lead to the loss of potential gains from specialization and exchange.

12. Both high-wage and low-wage countries gain from the opportunity to specialize in the production of goods that they produce at a low opportunity cost. If a low-wage country can supply a good to the United States cheaper than the United States can produce it, the United States can gain by purchasing the good from the low-wage country and using U.S. resources to produce other goods for which the United States has a comparative advantage.

13. There is substantial variation among LDCs with regard to the imposition of trade restrictions. LDCs that have low tariff rates, a freely convertible currency, and large trade sectors (relative to the size of their population) grew rapidly during the 1980–1991 period, while the per capita GDP of countries following the most restrictive trade policies generally declined.

CRITICAL-ANALYSIS QUESTIONS

*1 "Trade restrictions limiting the sale of cheap foreign goods in the United States are necessary to protect the prosperity of Americans." Evaluate this statement made by an American politician.

2. Suppose at the time of the Civil War the United States had been divided into two countries, and that through the years no trade existed between the two. How might the standard of living in the "divided" United States have been affected? Explain.

*3. Can both of the following statements be true? Why or why not?

    a. "Tariffs and import quotas promote economic inefficiency and reduce the real income of a nation. Economic analysis suggests that nations can gain by eliminating trade restrictions."

    b. "Economic analysis suggests that there is good reason to expect trade restrictions to exist in the real world."

4. "Tariffs and quotas are necessary to protect the high wages of the American worker." Do you agree or disagree with this statement? Why or why not?

*5. "An increased scarcity of a product benefits producers and harms consumers. In effect, tariffs and other trade restrictions increase the domestic scarcity of products by reducing the supply from abroad. Such policies benefit domestic producers of the restricted product at the expense of domestic consumers." Evaluate this statement.

*6. The United States uses an import quota to maintain the domestic price of sugar well above the world price. Analyze the impact of the quota. Use supply-and-demand analysis to illustrate your answer. To whom do the gains and losses of this policy accrue? How does the quota affect the efficiency of resource allocation in the United States? Why do you think Congress is supportive of this policy?

7. Suppose that it costs American textile manufacturers $20 to produce a shirt, while foreign producers can supply the same shirt for $15.

    a. Would a tariff of $6 per shirt help American manufacturers compete with foreigners?

    b. Would a subsidy of $6 per shirt to domestic manufacturers help them compete?

    c. Is there any difference between the tariff and a direct subsidy to the domestic manufacturer?

*8. "Getting more Americans to realize that it pays to make things in the United States is the heart of the competitiveness issue." (This is a quote from an American business magazine.)

    a. Would Americans be better off if more of them paid higher prices in order to "buy American" rather

---

*Asterisk denotes questions for which answers are given in Appendix C.

than purchase from foreigners? Would U.S. employment be higher? Explain.

b. Would Californians be better off if they bought only goods produced in California? Would the employment in California be higher? Explain.

*9. It is often alleged that Japanese producers receive subsidies from their government that permit them to sell their products at a low price in the U.S. market. Do you think we should erect trade barriers to keep out cheap Japanese goods if the source of their low price is governmental subsidies? Why or why not?

10. How do tariffs and quotas differ? Can you think of any reason why foreign producers might prefer a quota rather than a tariff? Explain your answer.

11. *What's wrong with this economic experiment?* A researcher hypothesizes that higher tariffs on imported automobiles would cause total employment in the United States to increase. Automobile tariffs are raised, and the following year employment in the U.S. auto industry increases by 50,000. The researcher concludes that the higher tariffs created 50,000 jobs.

*12. Does international trade cost American jobs? Does interstate trade cost your state jobs? What is the major effect of international and interstate trade?

13. "The United States is suffering from a huge excess of imports. Cheap foreign products are driving American firms out of business and leaving our economy in shambles." Evaluate this statement from an American politician.

14. Do you think the United States will benefit as trade barriers with Mexico are reduced? Will Mexico benefit? Will trade with a low-wage country like Mexico push wages down in a high-wage country like the United States? Why or why not?

*15. Tariffs not only reduce the volume of imports, they also reduce the volume of exports. Is this statement true or false? Explain your answer.

16. If the workers in one country are substantially more productive because they are more skilled and work with more capital than the workers of another country, trade between the two countries will drive wages of the less productive workers even lower than is currently the case. Is this statement true, false, or are you uncertain? Explain your answer.

17. (a) Would the people of Europe be better off if there were dangerous rivers with no bridges that ran along the borders between countries? Why or why not? (b) Would the people of Europe be better off if there were sizable tariffs (taxes on imports), import quotas, and other regulations that limited foreigners from selling goods cheaply in the domestic market of another country? Why or why not? (c) If foreigners were "dumping" their goods—if they were selling below their production costs in another country—would your answer to part b have been different?

*18. When you travel abroad, you are permitted to bring a limited amount of goods into the United States duty-free. Will the presence of a U.S. tariff on a certain good affect the likelihood that you will find a bargain on the good while abroad?

19. *Special problem on the economics of trade:* Suppose that farmers in Ukraine can produce either 125 bushels of wheat or 50 bushels of corn on an acre of land. Farmers in the Czech Republic can produce either 50 bushels of wheat or 40 bushels of corn.

a. Measured in terms of corn, what is the opportunity cost of producing a bushel of wheat in Ukraine? What is the opportunity cost of raising a bushel of wheat in the Czech Republic?

b. Which country has a comparative advantage in the production of wheat?

c. Which has a comparative advantage in the production of corn?

d. Suppose the residents of the two countries are each currently consuming 10 million bushels of wheat and 6 million bushels of corn. If there is no trade between the two countries (or with any other country), how many acres of farm land will the two countries have to devote to the production of wheat and corn?

e. Suppose the people in the two countries begin trading with each other. Indicate the range of wheat prices (measured in terms of corn) that would permit the people in both countries to gain. (In order to simplify matters, assume that the transport cost of the grains is zero.)

f. Suppose that the midpoint of the range of potentially advantageous prices emerges as the market price. What is that midpoint? If the Czech Republic reallocates all of the land it previously used to produce wheat and corn to the production of the grain for which it has a comparative advantage, how much will it produce? If it trades half of that crop to Ukraine for the other grain at the market price, how much of the two grains will the Czech Republic be able to consume?

g. If Ukraine devotes all of the land it previously used to produce both wheat and corn to the crop for which it has a comparative advantage, how much of the two grains will Ukraine be able to consume after the trade for half the Czech output (of the grain that the Czechs are best at producing) at the market price?

h. Who gains and who loses from the trade?

*Asterisk denotes questions for which answers are given in Appendix C.

CHAPTER THIRTY-TWO

INTERNATIONAL FINANCE AND THE FOREIGN EXCHANGE MARKET

Currencies, like tomatoes and football tickets, have a price at which they are bought and sold. An exchange rate is the price of one currency in terms of another, such as the price of a French franc in U.S. dollars or German marks.

GARY SMITH[1]

CHAPTER FOCUS

■ *What determines the exchange-rate value of the dollar relative to other currencies?*
■ *What are the major factors that would cause the exchange-rate value of a currency to change?*
■ *What information is included in the balance-of-payments accounts of a nation? Why are these accounts important?*
■ *Will the balance-of-payments accounts of a country always be in balance? Will the balance of trade always be in balance?*
■ *How do monetary and fiscal policies influence the exchange-rate value of a nation's currency?*
■ *Will a healthy economy run a balance-of-trade surplus? Does a balance-of-trade deficit indicate that a nation is in financial trouble?*
■ *What impact do restrictions on the convertibility of a currency have on people in the countries that impose them?*

---

[1]Gary Smith, *Macroeconomics* (New York: W. H. Freeman and Company, 1985), p. 514.

A s we discussed in the last chapter, the volume of international trade has grown in recent decades. Trade across national boundaries is complicated by the fact that nations generally use different currencies to buy and sell goods in their respective domestic markets. Germans use marks, the British pounds, the Japanese yen, the Mexicans pesos, and so on.

When exchange is between people in different countries, it generally involves the conversion of one currency to another. For example, farmers in the United States want dollars, not some foreign currency, when they sell their wheat. Therefore, foreign purchasers must exchange their currency for dollars before they buy U.S. wheat. Similarly, French winemakers will prefer payment in francs, not dollars. Thus, U.S. importers will have to exchange dollars for francs (or, if they are paid in dollars, the French winemakers will want to change dollars for francs) when Americans purchase French wines.

In this chapter, we analyze how international currencies are linked and how the rates for their exchange are determined. We will also analyze the balance-of-payments accounting that is utilized to keep track of international transactions.

FOREIGN EXCHANGE MARKET

Foreign exchange market
The market in which the currencies of different countries are bought and sold.

The **foreign exchange market** is a widely dispersed, highly organized market in which the currencies of different countries are bought and sold. Commercial banks and currency brokers around the world are the primary organizers of the market.

Let's assume you own a shoe store in the United States and are preparing to place an order for sandals from a manufacturer. You can purchase the sandals from a domestic manufacturer and pay for them with dollars. Or you can buy them from a British manufacturer and pay for them in pounds. If you buy from the British firm, either you will have to change dollars into pounds at a bank and send them to the British producer, or the British manufacturer will have to go to a bank and change your dollar check into pounds. In either case, purchasing the British sandals will involve an exchange of dollars for pounds.

If the British producer sells sandals for 10 pounds per pair, how can you determine whether the price is high or low? To compare the price of the sandals produced by the British firm with the price of domestically produced sandals, you

Exchange rate
The domestic price of one unit of foreign currency. For example, if it takes $1.50 to purchase one English pound, the dollar-pound exchange rate is 1.50.

must know the **exchange rate** between the dollar and the pound. This is simply the price of one national currency (the pound, for example) in terms of another national currency (such as the U.S. dollar). Exchange rates enable consumers in one country to translate the prices of foreign goods into units of their own currency. For example, if it takes $1.50 to obtain 1 pound, then the British sandals priced at 10 pounds would cost $15.00 (ten times the $1.50 price of the pound).

Suppose the dollar-pound exchange rate is $1.50 = 1 pound and that you decide to buy 200 pairs of sandals from the British manufacturer at 10 pounds ($15) per pair. You will need 2,000 pounds in order to pay the British manufacturer. If you contact an American bank that handles exchange-rate transactions and write the bank a check for $3,000 (the $1.50 exchange rate multiplied by 2,000), it will supply the 2,000 pounds. The bank will typically charge a small fee for handling the transaction.

Where does the American bank get the pounds? The bank obtains the pounds from British importers who want dollars to buy things from Americans. Note that the U.S. demand for foreign currencies (such as the pound) comes from the demand of Americans for things purchased from foreigners. On the other hand, the U.S. supply of foreign exchange comes from the demand of foreigners for things bought from Americans.

Exhibit 32–1 presents data on the exchange rate between the dollar and selected foreign currencies during the 1973–1993 period, as well as an index of the exchange-rate value of the dollar against ten major currencies. Under the flexible-rate system (discussed in detail later in this chapter) present in most industrial countries, the exchange rate between currencies changes from day to day and even from hour to hour. Thus, the annual exchange rate data given in Exhibit 32–1 are really averages for each year.

Between 1980 and 1985, the exchange-rate value of the dollar appreciated against the major foreign currencies. An **appreciation** in the value of a nation's currency means that fewer units of the currency are now required to purchase one unit of a foreign currency. For example, in 1985 only 34 cents were required to purchase a German mark, down from 55 cents in 1980.[2] As the result of this appreciation in the value of the dollar relative to the mark, West German goods became less expensive to Americans. The direction of change in the prices that West Germans paid for American goods was just the opposite. An appreciation of the U.S. dollar in terms of the mark is the same thing as a depreciation in the mark relative to the dollar.

A **depreciation** makes foreign goods more expensive, since it decreases the number of units of the foreign currency that can be purchased with a unit of domestic currency. As Exhibit 32–1 shows, the number of cents required to purchase a French franc, German mark, Japanese yen, British pound, or Canadian dollar rose substantially between 1985 and 1990. Thus, during this period the dollar depreciated against these currencies, increasing the price of goods purchased by Americans from producers in these countries.

The ten-currency index of the dollar's exchange-rate value presented in Exhibit 32–1 provides evidence on what is happening to the dollar's general exchange-rate value.[3] An increase in the index implies an appreciation in the dollar, while a decline is indicative of a depreciation in the dollar. During the 1970s, the ten-currency index changed by only small amounts from year to year. However, between 1980 and 1985, the index indicates that the exchange-rate value of the dollar increased sharply each year. The dollar appreciated by more than 60 percent during the five-year period. In contrast, it depreciated by a similar amount during 1986–1990.

Appreciation
An increase in the value of a domestic currency relative to foreign currencies. An appreciation increases the purchasing power of the domestic currency over foreign goods.

Depreciation
A reduction in the value of a domestic currency relative to foreign currencies. A depreciation reduces the purchasing power of the domestic currency over foreign goods.

---

[2]Since an appreciation means a lower price of foreign currencies, some may think it looks like a depreciation. Just remember that a lower price of the foreign currency means that one's domestic currency will buy more units of the foreign currency and thus more goods and services from foreigners. For example, if the dollar price of the pound falls, this means that a dollar will buy more pounds and thus more goods and services from the British. Therefore, a lower dollar price of the pound means the dollar has appreciated relative to the pound.

[3]In the construction of this index, the exchange rate of each currency relative to the dollar is weighted according to the proportion of U.S. trade with the country. For example, the index weights the U.S. dollar–Japanese yen exchange rate more heavily than the U.S. dollar–Swiss franc exchange rate because the volume of U.S. trade with Japan exceeds the volume of trade with Switzerland.

EXHIBIT 32–1

FOREIGN EXCHANGE RATES, 1973–1993: U.S. CENTS PER UNIT OF FOREIGN CURRENCY

YEAR	FRENCH FRANC	GERMAN MARK	JAPANESE YEN	BRITISH POUND	CANADIAN DOLLAR	INDEX OF EXCHANGE-RATE VALUE OF THE DOLLAR (TEN CURRENCIES)[a]
1973	22.5	37.8	0.369	245.10	99.9	99.1
1975	23.4	40.7	0.337	222.16	98.3	98.5
1977	20.3	43.1	0.373	174.49	94.1	103.4
1979	23.5	54.6	0.458	212.24	85.3	88.1
1980	23.7	55.1	0.443	227.74	85.5	87.4
1981	18.4	44.4	0.453	202.43	83.4	103.4
1982	15.2	41.2	0.402	174.80	81.0	116.6
1983	13.1	39.2	0.421	151.59	81.1	125.3
1984	11.4	35.1	0.421	133.68	77.1	138.2
1985	11.1	34.0	0.419	129.74	73.2	143.0
1986	14.4	46.1	0.594	146.77	72.0	112.2
1987	16.6	55.6	0.691	163.98	75.4	96.9
1988	16.8	56.9	0.780	178.13	81.3	92.7
1989	15.7	53.2	0.724	163.82	84.4	98.6
1990	18.4	61.9	0.690	178.41	85.7	89.1
1991	17.7	60.2	0.743	176.74	87.3	89.3
1992	18.9	64.0	0.789	176.63	82.7	86.6
1993	17.6	60.4	0.900	150.16	77.5	93.2

[a]March 1973 = 100. In addition to the five currencies listed above, the index includes the Belgian franc, Italian lira, Netherlands guilder, Swedish krona, and Swiss franc.

Source: Council of Economic Advisers, *Economic Report of the President* (Washington, D.C.: U.S. Government Printing Office, 1993), and *Federal Reserve Bulletin*, April 1994.

DETERMINANTS OF EXCHANGE RATE

Flexible exchange rates
Exchange rates that are determined by the market forces of supply and demand. They are sometimes called floating *exchange rates.*

What determines the exchange rate between two currencies? Under a system of **flexible exchange rates,** also called *floating exchange rates,* the value of currencies in the exchange-rate market is determined by market forces. Just as the forces of supply and demand determine other prices, so, too, they determine the exchange-rate value of currencies in the absence of government intervention.

The exchange-rate system in effect since 1973 might best be described as a *managed* flexible-rate system. It is flexible because all of the major industrial countries allow the exchange-rate value of their currencies to float. Several small countries maintain **fixed exchange rates** against the dollar, the English pound, or some other major currency. Therefore, the exchange-rate value of these currencies rises and falls with the major currency to which they are tied. The system is "managed" because the major industrial nations have from time to time attempted to alter supply and demand in the exchange-rate market by buying and selling various currencies. Compared to the size of the exchange-rate market, however, these transactions have been relatively small. Thus, the exchange-rate value of major currencies like the U.S. dollar, British pound, German mark, Japanese yen, and French franc is determined primarily by market forces.

Fixed exchange rates
Exchange rates for each country's currency set at a fixed rate relative to all other currencies; government policies are used to maintain the fixed rate.

EQUILIBRIUM EXCHANGE RATE

To simplify our explanation of how the exchange-rate market works, let us assume that the United States and Great Britain are the only two countries in the world. When Americans buy and sell with each other, they use dollars. Therefore, American sellers will want to be paid in dollars. Similarly, when the British buy and sell with each other, they use pounds. As a result, British sellers will want to be paid in pounds.

If Americans want to buy from British sellers, they will need to acquire pounds. In our two-country world, the demand for pounds in the exchange-rate market originates from the demand of Americans for British goods, services, and assets (either real or financial). For example, when U.S. residents purchase men's suits from a British manufacturer, travel in the United Kingdom, or purchase the stocks, bonds, or physical assets of British business firms, they demand pounds from (and supply dollars to) the foreign exchange-rate market to pay for these items.

Similarly, when the British buy from American sellers, they will need to exchange pounds for dollars. The supply of pounds (and demand for dollars) in the exchange-rate market comes from the demand of the British for items supplied by Americans. When the British purchase goods, services, or assets from Americans, they supply pounds to (and demand dollars from) the foreign exchange market.

Exhibit 32–2 illustrates the demand and supply curves of Americans for foreign exchange—British pounds in our two-country case. The demand for pounds is downward sloping because a lower dollar price of the pound—meaning a dollar will buy more pounds—makes British goods cheaper for American importers. The goods produced by one country are generally good substitutes for the goods of another country. This means that when foreign (British) goods become cheaper, Americans will increase their expenditures on imports (and therefore the quantity of pounds demanded will increase). Thus, Americans will increase their expenditures on the lower-priced (in dollars) British goods and therefore they will demand more pounds as the pound's dollar price declines.

Similarly, the supply curve for pounds is dependent on the purchases of American goods by the British. An increase in the dollar price of the pound means that a pound will purchase more dollars and more goods priced in terms of dollars. The price (in terms of pounds) of American goods, services, and assets to British consumers declines as the dollar price of the pound increases. The British will purchase more from Americans and therefore supply more pounds to the exchange-rate market as the dollar price of the pound rises. Because of this, the supply curve for pounds tends to slope upward to the right.

The dollar price of the pound is measured on the vertical axis. The horizontal axis indicates the flow of pounds to the foreign exchange market. The equilibrium exchange rate is $1.50 = 1 pound. At the equilibrium price, the quantity demanded of pounds just equals the quantity supplied. A higher price of pounds such as $1.80 = 1 pound would lead to an excess supply of pounds, causing the dollar price of the pound to fall. On the other hand, a lower price, for example, $1.20 = 1 pound, would result in an excess demand for pounds, causing the pound to appreciate.

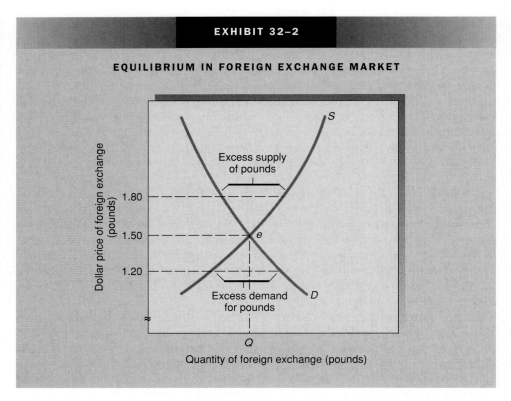

EXHIBIT 32–2

EQUILIBRIUM IN FOREIGN EXCHANGE MARKET

As Exhibit 32–2 shows, equilibrium is present at the dollar price of the pound that brings the quantity demanded and quantity supplied of pounds into balance, $1.50 = 1 pound in this case. The market-clearing price of $1.50 per pound not only equates demand and supply in the foreign exchange market, it also equates (1) the value of U.S. purchases on items supplied by the British with (2) the value of items sold by U.S. residents to the British. Demand and supply in the currency market are merely the mirror images of these two factors.

What would happen if the price of the pound were above equilibrium—$1.80 = 1 pound, for example? At the higher dollar price of the pound, British goods would be more expensive for Americans. Americans would cut back on their purchases of English shoes, glassware, textile products, financial assets, and other items supplied by the British. Reflecting this reduction, the quantity of pounds demanded by Americans would decline. Simultaneously, the higher dollar price of the pound would make U.S. exports cheaper for the British. For example, an $18,000 American automobile would cost British consumers 12,000 pounds when 1 pound trades for $1.50, but it would cost only 10,000 pounds when 1 pound exchanges for $1.80. If the price of the pound were $1.80, the British would tend to supply more pounds to the exchange-rate market to purchase the cheaper American goods. Thus, at the $1.80 = 1 pound price, the quantity of pounds demanded by Americans falls, and the quantity supplied by the British increases. As can be seen in Exhibit 32–2, an excess supply of pounds results, causing the dollar price of the pound to decline until equilibrium is restored at the $1.50 = 1 pound price.

At a below-equilibrium price such as $1.20 = 1 pound, an opposite set of forces would be present. The lower dollar price of the pound would make English goods cheaper for Americans and American goods more expensive for the British. The quantity demanded of British goods and pounds by Americans would increase. Simultaneously, the quantity of American goods demanded and pounds supplied by the British would decline. An excess demand for pounds would result at the $1.20 = 1 pound price. The excess demand would tend to cause the dollar price of the pound to rise until equilibrium was restored at $1.50 = 1 pound.

CHANGES IN EXCHANGE RATES

When exchange rates are free to fluctuate, the market value of a nation's currency will appreciate and depreciate in response to changing market conditions. Any change that alters the quantity of goods, services, or assets bought from foreigners relative to the quantity sold to foreigners will also alter the exchange rate. What types of change will alter the exchange-rate value of a currency?

CHANGES IN INCOME.   An increase in domestic income will encourage the nation's residents to spend a portion of their additional income on imports. When the income of a nation grows rapidly, the nation's imports tend to rise rapidly as well. As **Exhibit 32–3** illustrates, an increase in imports also increases the demand for foreign exchange, the pound in our two-country case. As the demand for pounds increases, the dollar price of the pound rises (from $1.50 to $1.80). This depreciation of the dollar reduces the incentive of Americans to import British goods and services, while increasing the incentive of the British to purchase U.S.

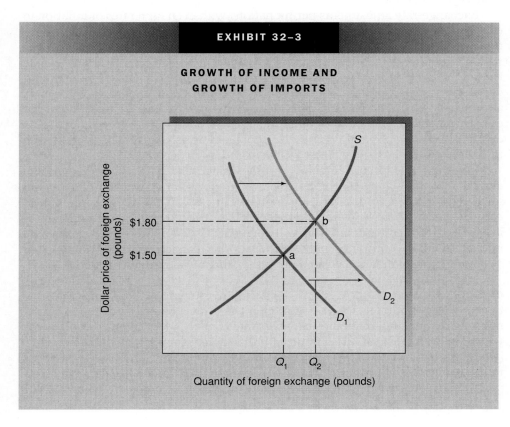

EXHIBIT 32–3

GROWTH OF INCOME AND GROWTH OF IMPORTS

Other things constant, if incomes grow in the United States, U.S. imports will grow. The increase in the imports will increase the demand for pounds, causing the dollar-price of the pound to rise (from $1.50 to $1.80).

exports. These two forces will restore equilibrium in the foreign exchange market at a new, higher dollar price of the pound.

Just the opposite takes place when the income of a trading partner (Great Britain in our example) increases. Rapid growth of income abroad will lead to an increase in U.S. exports, causing the demand for the dollar to rise. This will result in dollar appreciation—equilibrium at a new, lower dollar price of the pound.

What happens to the exchange rate if income increases in both countries? The key here is to identify the nation that is growing the fastest. For countries that are similar in size and propensity to import, the country that is growing the fastest will increase its demand for imports relatively more than its trading partner, resulting in a decrease in the value of the more rapidly growing nation's currency. Thus, as paradoxical as it may seem, sluggish growth of income relative to one's trading partners tends to cause the slow-growth nation's currency to appreciate, since the nation's imports decline relative to exports.

DIFFERENCES IN RATES OF INFLATION.   Other things constant, domestic inflation will cause the nation's currency to depreciate on the exchange market, whereas deflation will result in appreciation. Suppose prices in the United States rise by 50 percent while our trading partners are experiencing stable prices. The domestic inflation will cause U.S. consumers to increase their demand for imported goods (and foreign currency). In turn, the inflated domestic prices will cause foreigners to reduce their purchases of U.S. goods, thereby reducing the supply of foreign currency to the exchange market. As **Exhibit 32–4** illustrates, the exchange rate will adjust to this set of circumstances. The dollar will depreciate relative to the pound.

Exchange-rate adjustments permit nations with even high rates of inflation to engage in trade with countries experiencing relatively stable prices. A depreciation in a nation's currency in the foreign exchange market compensates for the nation's inflation rate. For example, if inflation increases the price level in the United States by 50 percent, and the value of the dollar in exchange for the pound depreciates 50 percent, then the prices of American goods measured in pounds are unchanged to British consumers. Thus, when the exchange-rate value of the dollar changes from $1.50 = 1 pound to $2.25 = 1 pound, the depreciation in the dollar restores the original prices of U.S. goods to British consumers even though the price level in the United States has increased by 50 percent.

What if prices in both England and the United States are rising at the same annual rate, say 10 percent? The prices of imports (and exports) will remain unchanged relative to domestically produced goods. Equal rates of inflation in each of the countries will not cause the value of exports to change relative to imports. Identical rates of inflation will not disturb an equilibrium in the exchange market. Inflation contributes to the depreciation of a nation's currency only when a country's rate of inflation is more rapid than that of its trading partners.

CHANGES IN INTEREST RATES.   Financial investments will be quite sensitive to changes in real interest rates—that is, interest rates adjusted for the expected rate of inflation. International loanable funds will tend to move toward areas where the expected real rate of return (after compensation for differences in risk) is highest. If real interest rates increase in the United States relative to Western Europe, investors in Britain, France, and Germany will demand dollars (and supply their currencies) in the exchange-rate market to purchase the high-yield

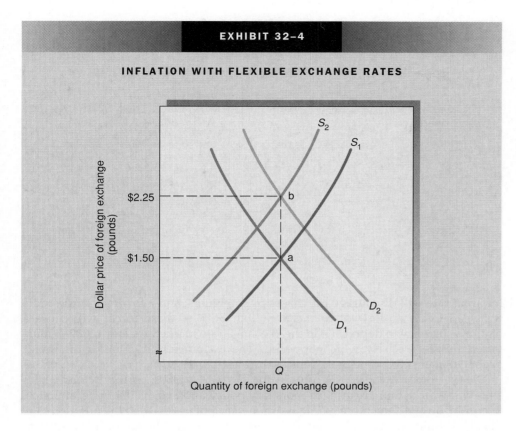

EXHIBIT 32-4

INFLATION WITH FLEXIBLE EXCHANGE RATES

Dollar price of foreign exchange (pounds)

$2.25 ---- b

$1.50 ---- a

S_2 S_1 D_2 D_1 Q

Quantity of foreign exchange (pounds)

If prices were stable in England while the price level increased 50 percent in the United States, the U.S. demand for British products (and pounds) would increase, whereas U.S. exports to Britain would decline, causing the supply of pounds to fall. These forces would cause the dollar to depreciate relative to the pound.

American assets. The increase in demand for the dollar and supply of European currencies will cause the dollar to appreciate relative to the British pound, French franc, and German mark.

In contrast, when real interest rates in other countries are high relative to the United States, short-term financial investors will move to take advantage of the improved earnings opportunities abroad. As investment funds move from the United States to other countries, there will be an increase in the demand for foreign currencies and an increase in the supply of dollars in the foreign exchange market. A depreciation in the dollar relative to the currencies of countries experiencing the high real interest rates will be the result. The accompanying "Thumbnail Sketch" summarizes the major forces that cause a nation's currency to appreciate or depreciate when exchange rates are determined by market forces.

EXCHANGE-RATE VALUE OF DOLLAR, 1973–1993

During the late 1970s, the United States was in the midst of double-digit inflation. Compared to most of its major trading partners, the inflation rate was higher and real interest rates were lower in the United States. As our analysis indicates, a high

THUMBNAIL SKETCH

WHAT FACTORS CAUSE A NATION'S CURRENCY TO APPRECIATE OR DEPRECIATE?

These factors will cause a nation's currency to appreciate:

1. A slow rate of growth in income that causes imports to lag behind exports.
2. A rate of inflation that is lower than one's trading partners.
3. Domestic real interest rates that are greater than real interest rates abroad.

These factors will cause a nation's currency to depreciate:

1. A rapid rate of growth in income that stimulates imports relative to exports.
2. A rate of inflation that is higher than one's trading partners.
3. Domestic real interest rates that are lower than real interest rates abroad.

inflation rate will discourage purchases by foreigners, and a low real interest rate will lead to an outflow of financial capital. Both of these forces will cause a nation's currency to depreciate in the exchange rate market. As **Exhibit 32–5** illustrates, this is precisely what happened. The exchange-rate value of the dollar declined against most major currencies during 1977–1979.

These forces reversed sharply during the early 1980s, as the United States shifted toward a more restrictive monetary policy and expansionary fiscal policy. Beginning in 1981, the more restrictive monetary policy retarded the inflation rate. The U.S. inflation rate plunged from the double-digit levels of 1979–1980 to 3.2 percent in 1983. Simultaneously, pushed along by both the restrictive monetary policy and large budget deficits, real interest rates in the United States rose to historic highs. As Exhibit 32–5 shows, during 1981–1984 real interest rates in the United States were between 2 percent and 4 percent higher than real rates in Europe and Japan. Attracted by the high real return, financial capital flowed into the United States. This combination of forces—a low inflation rate and capital inflow attracted by high real interest rates—sharply increased the demand for the dollar. The dollar appreciated by approximately 60 percent against an index of ten major currencies during 1980–1984.

However, beginning in early 1985, the situation again changed abruptly. As the low rate of inflation persisted, real interest rates declined in the United States. The inflow of foreign capital slowed. Simultaneously, the U.S. economy rebounded strongly from the 1982 recession. Responding to both the rapid economic growth and the strong dollar, U.S. imports surged relative to exports during 1983–1985. Then, during 1985–1986, declining U.S. interest rates relative to other countries, and fears arising from the large excess of imports compared to exports, resulted in a sharp reduction in the exchange-rate value of the dollar (see Exhibit 32–5).

During 1989–1990, real interest rates in the United States declined further, relative to the real rates of our trading partners. As a result, the demand for dollars to undertake financial investments in the United States weakened further, and the exchange-rate value of the dollar declined. Finally, a modest reduction in the

EXHIBIT 32-5

REAL INTEREST RATES AND EXCHANGE-RATE VALUE OF DOLLAR, 1974-1993

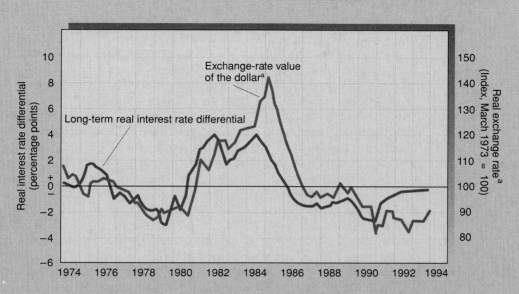

Our model indicates that a reduction in real U.S. interest rates compared with the rates in other countries will, other things constant, cause the dollar to depreciate. As illustrated, this is precisely what happened in the late 1970s, 1985–1987, and again in 1990. In contrast, when real interest rates are higher in the United States than in other countries, strong demand for dollars in order to make financial investments in the United States will cause the dollar to appreciate. The 1980–1984 period illustrates the potency of high real interest rates as a factor pushing the exchange-rate value of the dollar upward.

[a]Weighted average of the ten countries referred to in Exhibit 32–1.

Source: Charles P. Thomas, "U.S. International Transactions in 1986," *Federal Reserve Bulletin*, May 1987; and Federal Reserve Bank of St. Louis, *International Economic Conditions* (monthly).

differential between real interest rates in the United States and the rates of other industrial countries in 1991–1993 led to a slight appreciation in the exchange-rate value of the dollar.

FIXED EXCHANGE RATES

Between 1944 and 1971, most of the world operated under a system of fixed exchange rates, where each nation "pegs" the price of its currency to another currency, such as the dollar (or gold), for long periods of time. Governments intervene in the foreign exchange market or alter their economic policies in an effort to maintain the fixed value of their currency.

Fixing the price of a currency in the exchange market, like fixing other prices, results in surpluses and shortages. As market conditions change, the exchange rate that equates the quantity supplied of each currency with the quantity demanded of that currency also changes. What happens when the fixed rate differs from the equilibrium rate? Building on the analysis of Exhibit 32–2, suppose the equilibrium exchange rate were $1.50 = 1 pound. If the price of the pound is fixed at $1.80 = 1 pound, an excess supply of pounds will result. At the $1.80 = 1 pound rate, the pound is overvalued (and the dollar undervalued). At the $1.80 per pound exchange rate, the United States will persistently export more goods, services, and assets to the British than it will import from the British. The central bank in the United States will have to continually increase its holdings of pounds—that is, buy the excess supply of pounds, to maintain the above-equilibrium price of the pound. In essence, this situation leads to a surplus of exports over imports for the United States in its trade with England.

What would happen if the dollar price of the pound were set below equilibrium, such as $1.20 = 1 pound (Exhibit 32–2)? The below-equilibrium price of the pound would lead to an excess demand for pounds. Since the pound is undervalued (and the dollar overvalued) at the $1.20-per-pound price, British imports are cheap to Americans (and U.S. exports expensive for the British). In its trade with the British, the United States would persistently buy (import) more than it sells (exports). To defend the $1.20-per-pound fixed rate, the U.S. central bank would have to draw down its holdings of pounds, balances that were perhaps built up during periods when the dollar-price of the pound was above equilibrium.

To make a fixed-rate system work, each country must maintain a reserve balance of other currencies that will permit it to weather temporary periods of excess demand relative to supply. When the fixed-rate system was put in place at the end of the Second World War, the **International Monetary Fund (IMF)** was established to perform this function. The IMF required each of its more than 100 member countries to deposit a specified amount of its currency into a reserve fund held by the IMF. Thus, it possessed substantial holdings of dollars, francs, pounds, marks, and other currencies of the participating nations. As the need arose, these reserves were loaned to nations experiencing difficulties with their balance of payments.

The premise of a fixed-rate system is that a nation ordinarily pays for its imports with exports. Of course, countries may temporarily experience periods where imports exceed exports. During such periods, nations can draw down their reserve balance. However, chronic debtor nations—nations persistently importing more than they export—must take corrective action designed to bring exports and imports into balance. During the 1944–1971 period, the IMF provided discipline to the system by encouraging—and in some cases requiring member nations as a condition for the receipt of loans—to adopt policies that would bring their exports and imports into balance.

What steps can a nation experiencing an excess of imports over exports take to remedy this situation under a fixed-rate system? Basically, there are three alternatives.

1. A nation can devalue its currency. **Devaluation** is a one-step reduction in the value of a nation's currency under a fixed-rate system. When a currency is overvalued, a devaluation can restore equilibrium between the demand and supply of the currency in the exchange market. For example, if there is an excess supply of dollars (excess demand for pounds) in the exchange market when the fixed exchange rate is $1.20 = 1 pound, a devaluation of the dollar (perhaps to $1.50 = 1

International Monetary Fund (IMF)
An international banking organization, with more than 100 member nations, designed to oversee the operation of the international monetary system. Although it does not control the world supply of money, it does hold currency reserves for member nations and makes currency loans to national central banks.

Devaluation
An official act that changes the level of the fixed exchange rate downward in terms of other currencies. In essence, it is a one-step depreciation of a currency under a fixed-exchange-rate system.

pound) could restore balance. A devaluation makes imports more expensive to domestic consumers, while encouraging exports. It thus tends to correct an excess of imports relative to exports.

2. A nation can heighten trade barriers, adopting tariffs and quotas in an effort to reduce imports and bring the value of its currency on the foreign exchange market into equilibrium. This strategy is in conflict with economic efficiency and the promotion of the free flow of trade between nations. Nevertheless, it was often adopted during the period of 1944–1971. Once a nation's exchange rate was established, it tended to become sacred. Politicians during that period, including many in the United States, frequently argued that even though they did not like to impose trade restrictions, the barriers were necessary to avoid devaluation. The balance-of-payments issue was an excellent excuse to promote trade restrictions—which were advocated by special interests—against low-cost foreign goods.

3. A nation can follow restrictive macroeconomic policy designed to promote deflation (or at least retard inflation) and high interest rates. Policy-makers might use restrictive monetary and fiscal policy to retard inflation and increase interest rates. A slower rate of inflation relative to one's trading partners would encourage exports and discourage imports. Higher domestic real interest rates would attract foreign investment and thereby increase the nation's supply of foreign exchange.

When a nation uses macroeconomic policy to restore balance in the exchange market, an important point emerges. This method of bringing about equilibrium in the exchange market attempts to manipulate the level of all other prices to maintain one price—the fixed exchange rate. In contrast, a flexible exchange-rate system changes one price, the foreign exchange rate, to restore balance between what is bought from and what is sold to foreigners.

BALANCE OF PAYMENTS

Just as countries calculate their gross domestic product (GDP) so that they have a general idea of their domestic level of production, most countries also calculate their balance of international payments in order to keep track of their transactions with other nations. The **balance of payments** summarizes the transactions of the country's citizens, businesses, and governments with foreigners. It provides information on the nation's exports, imports, earnings of domestic residents on assets located abroad, earnings on domestic assets owned by foreigners, international capital movements, and official transactions by central banks and governments.

Balance-of-payments accounts are kept according to the principles of basic bookkeeping. Any transaction that supplies the nation's domestic currency (or creates a demand for foreign currency) in the foreign exchange market is recorded as a debit, or minus, item. Imports are an example of a debit item. Transactions that create a demand for the nation's currency (or a supply of foreign currency) on the foreign exchange market are recorded as a credit, or plus, item. Exports are an example of a credit item. Since the quantity demanded will equal the quantity supplied in the foreign exchange market, the total debits will equal the total credits.

Balance-of-payments transactions can be grouped into three basic categories: current account, capital account, and official reserve account. Let us take a look at each of these.

Balance of payments
A summary of all economic transactions between a country and all other countries for a specific time period—usually a year. The balance-of-payments account reflects all payments and liabilities to foreigners (debits) and all payments and obligations (credits) received from foreigners.

CURRENT-ACCOUNT TRANSACTIONS

Current account

The record of all transactions with foreign nations that involve the exchange of merchandise goods and services, current income derived from investments, and unilateral gifts.

Balance of merchandise trade

The difference between the value of merchandise exports and the value of merchandise imports for a nation. The balance of merchandise trade is only one component of a nation's total balance of payments. Also called simply balance of trade *or net exports.*

All payments (and gifts) related to the purchase or sale of goods and services and income flows during the designated period are included in the **current account.** In general, there are four major types of current-account transactions: the exchange of merchandise goods, the exchange of services, income from investments, and unilateral transfers.

MERCHANDISE-TRADE TRANSACTIONS.   The export and import of merchandise goods comprise by far the largest portion of a nation's balance-of-payments account. When U.S. producers export their products, foreigners will supply their currency in exchange for dollars in order to pay for the U.S.-produced goods. Since U.S. exports generate a demand for dollars in the foreign exchange market, they are a credit (plus) item. In contrast, when Americans import goods, they will supply dollars and demand a foreign currency in the exchange-rate market. Thus, imports are a debit (minus) item.

As **Exhibit 32–6** shows, the United States exported $440 billion of merchandise goods in 1992, compared to imports of $536 billion. The difference between the value of a country's merchandise exports and the value of its merchandise imports is known as the **balance of merchandise trade** (or *balance of trade*). If the value of a country's merchandise exports falls short of (exceeds) the value of its

Source: *Survey of Current Business,* October 1993; and *Federal Reserve Bulletin,* November 1993.

EXHIBIT 32–6

U.S. BALANCE OF PAYMENTS, 1992

	BILLIONS OF DOLLARS	
	AMOUNT	DEFICIT (-) OR SURPLUS (+)
Current Account		
1a. U.S. merchandise exports	+440	
1b. U.S. merchandise imports	−536	
Balance of merchandise trade		−96
2a. U.S. service exports	+192	
2b. U.S. service imports	−126	
Balance on goods and services		−30
3. Net investment income	+6	
4. Net transfers	−42	
Balance on current account		−66
Capital Account		
5. Capital inflow to U.S.	+89	
6. Outflow of U.S. capital	−53	
Balance on capital account		+36
Current and capital account balance		−30
Official reserve-account transactions		+30

merchandise imports, it is said to have a balance-of-trade deficit (surplus). In 1992 the United States ran a balance-of-trade deficit of $96 billion.

Other things constant, a U.S. merchandise-trade deficit implies that Americans are supplying more dollars to the exchange market in order to purchase foreign-made goods than foreigners are demanding for the purchase of American goods. If the merchandise-trade deficit were the only factor influencing the value of the dollar on the exchange market, one could anticipate a decline in the foreign exchange value of the U.S. currency. However, several other factors also affect the supply of and demand for the dollar on the exchange market.

SERVICE EXPORTS AND IMPORTS. The export and import of *invisible services*, as they are sometimes called, also exert an important influence on the foreign exchange market. The export of insurance, transportation, and banking services generates a demand for dollars by foreigners just as the export of merchandise does. A French business that is insured with an American company will demand dollars with which to pay its premiums. When foreigners travel in the United States or transport cargo on American ships, they will demand dollars with which to pay for these services. These service exports are thus entered as credits on the current account.

On the other hand, the import of services from foreigners expands the supply of dollars to the exchange market. Therefore, service imports are entered on the balance-of-payments accounts as debit items. Travel abroad by U.S. citizens, the shipment of goods on foreign carriers, and the purchase of other services from foreigners are all debit items, since they supply dollars to the exchange market.

These service transactions are substantial. As Exhibit 32–6 illustrates, in 1992 the U.S. service exports were $192 billion, compared with service imports of $126 billion. Thus, the U.S. ran a $66 billion surplus on its service trade transactions.

When we add the balance of service exports and imports to the balance of merchandise trade we obtain the **balance on goods and services.** In 1992 the United States ran a $30 billion deficit (the sum of the $96 billion trade deficit minus the $66 billion service surplus) in the goods and services account.

INCOME FROM INVESTMENTS. In the past, Americans have made substantial investments in stocks, bonds, and real assets in other countries. As these investments abroad generate income, dollars will flow from foreigners to Americans. Since the income of Americans from their investments abroad supplies foreign currency (and creates a demand for dollars) in the foreign exchange market, it enters as a credit item on the current account.

Correspondingly, foreigners hold substantial investments in the United States. As these investments earn dividends, interest, and rents, they earn income for foreigners. This income of foreigners leads to an outflow of dollars. As foreigners convert their dollar earnings to their domestic currency, the supply of dollars (and demand for foreign currency) increases on the foreign exchange market. Thus, the income of foreigners from their investments in the United States is a debit item in the balance-of-payments accounts.

As Exhibit 32–6 shows, in 1992 Americans earned $6 billion more on their investments abroad than foreigners earned on their investments in the United States. Since these items resulted in a net flow of income to the United States, the result is recorded as a credit.

UNILATERAL TRANSFERS. Monetary gifts to foreigners, such as U.S. aid to a foreign government or private gifts from U.S. residents to their relatives abroad, supply dollars to the exchange market. Thus, these gifts are debit items in the

Balance on goods and services
The exports of goods (merchandise) and services of a nation minus its imports of goods and services.

balance-of-payments accounts. Monetary gifts to Americans from foreigners are credit items. Gifts in kind are more complex. When products are given to foreigners, goods flow abroad, but there is no offsetting influx of foreign currency—that is, a demand for dollars. Balance-of-payments accountants handle such transactions as though the United States had supplied the dollars with which to purchase the direct grants made to foreigners. So these items are also entered as debits. Because the U.S. government and private U.S. citizens made grants of $42 billion more to foreigners than we received from them, this net unilateral transfer was entered as a debit item on the current account in 1992.

BALANCE ON CURRENT ACCOUNT. The difference between (1) the value of a country's current exports and earnings from investments abroad and (2) the value of its current imports and the earnings of foreigners on their domestic assets (plus net unilateral transfers to foreigners) is known as the **balance on current account.** Current-account transactions involve only current exchanges of goods and services and current income flows (and gifts). They do not involve changes in the ownership of either real or financial assets. The current-account balance provides a summary of all current-account transactions. As with the balance of trade, when the value of the current-account debit items (import-type transactions) exceeds the value of the credit items (export-type transactions), we say that the country is running a current-account deficit. Alternatively, if the credit items are greater than the debit items, the country is running a current-account surplus. In 1992 the United States ran a current-account deficit of $66 billion.

CAPITAL-ACCOUNT TRANSACTIONS

In contrast with current-account transactions, **capital-account** transactions focus on changes in the ownership of real and financial assets. These transactions are composed of (1) direct investments by Americans in real assets abroad (or by foreigners in the United States) and (2) loans to and from foreigners. When foreigners make investments in the United States—for example, by purchasing stocks, bonds, or real assets from Americans—their actions will supply foreign currency and generate a demand for dollars in the foreign exchange market. Thus, these capital-inflow transactions are a credit.

On the other hand, capital-outflow transactions are recorded as debits. For example, if a U.S. investor purchases a shoe factory in Mexico, the Mexican seller will want to be paid in pesos. The U.S. investor will supply dollars (and demand pesos) on the foreign exchange market. Since U.S. citizens will supply dollars and demand foreign currency when they invest in stocks, bonds, and real assets abroad, these transactions enter into the balance-of-payments accounts as a debit.

In 1992 foreign investments in the United States (capital inflow) summed to $89 billion while U.S. investments abroad (capital outflow) totaled $53 billion. Since the capital inflow exceeded the outflow, the United States ran a $36 billion capital-account surplus in 1992.

OFFICIAL RESERVE ACCOUNT

Governments maintain official reserve balances in the form of foreign currencies, gold, and **special drawing rights (SDRs)** with the International Monetary Fund

Balance on current account
The import-export balance of goods and services, plus net investment income earned abroad, plus net private and government transfers. If the value of the nation's export-type items exceeds (is less than) the value of the nation's import-type items (plus net unilateral transfers to foreigners), a current-account surplus (deficit) is present.

Capital account
Transactions with foreigners that involve either (1) the exchange of ownership rights to real or financial assets or (2) the extension of loans.

Special drawing rights (SDRs)
Supplementary reserves, in the form of accounting entries, established by the International Monetary Fund (also called paper gold). Like gold and foreign currency reserves, they can be used to make payments on international accounts.

(IMF), which is, as explained earlier, a type of international central bank. Countries running a deficit on their current- and capital-account balances can draw on their reserves. Similarly, countries running a surplus can build up their reserves of foreign currencies and reserve balances with the IMF. Under the fixed-rate exchange system present during 1944–1971, these reserve transactions were highly significant. Countries experiencing balance-of-payments difficulties were forced to draw on their reserves to maintain their fixed exchange rate. Countries that were selling more to foreigners than foreigners were buying from them accumulated the currencies of other nations.

Under the current (primarily) flexible-rate system, changes in the official reserve account of nations are generally quite small. Changes in the exchange rate are generally relied on to balance the amount of goods, services, and assets purchased from foreigners and the amount sold to foreigners. However, sometimes nations have their central banks buy and sell currencies in an attempt to reduce sharp swings in the exchange rate. During some years, a nation might build up its holdings of foreign currencies, while in other years it might permit them to be drawn out.

Under the current system, these official reserve transactions are generally quite modest relative to the total of all international transactions. In 1992 the U.S. official reserve holdings of foreign currencies declined by $30 billion (compared to trade and capital flows of more than $700 billion). When a country reduces its official reserve holdings, it supplies foreign currency to the exchange-rate market. Therefore, such transactions are a credit item. Similarly, when a country increases its official reserve holdings, the action is a debit, since it increases the demand for foreign currency in the foreign exchange market.

BALANCE OF PAYMENTS MUST BALANCE

The aggregated balance-of-payments accounts must balance. The following identity must hold:

$$\text{Current-account balance} + \text{Capital-account balance}$$
$$+ \text{Official-reserve-account balance} = 0$$

However, the specific components of the accounts need not balance. For example, the debit and credit items of the current account need not be equal. Specific components may run either a surplus or a deficit. Nevertheless, since the balance of payments as a whole must balance, a deficit in one area implies a surplus in another.

If a nation is experiencing a deficit on its current-account balance, it must experience an offsetting surplus on the sum of its capital-account and official-reserve-account balances. Under a pure flexible-rate system, official reserve transactions are zero; therefore, a current-account deficit implies a capital-account surplus. Similarly, a current-account surplus implies a capital-account deficit.

A current-account deficit means that, in aggregate, the citizens of a nation are buying more goods and services from foreigners than they are selling to foreigners. Under a pure flexible-rate system, this excess of expenditures relative to receipts is paid for by borrowing from and selling assets to foreigners.

Since countries, to some extent, engage in official reserve transactions, the current system is not a pure flexible-rate system. If it were, there would be no official reserve transactions. In 1992 the United States ran a $66 billion deficit on its current account and a $36 billion surplus on its capital account. This $30 billion combined deficit was exactly offset by a $30 billion surplus on the official-reserve-account transactions. Thus, the deficits and surpluses on current-account, capital-account, and official-reserve-account transactions summed to zero.

MACROECONOMIC POLICY IN OPEN ECONOMY

During the post–Second World War period, there has been a dramatic increase in international trade and in the flow of investment capital across national boundaries. This increasing mobility of both goods and capital influences the effects of macroeconomic policy, even in a country such as the United States with a relatively small trade sector. We now live in a global economy. No country can conduct its macroeconomic policy in isolation.

Throughout this text, we have focused on the impact of macroeconomic policy within the framework of an open economy. To date, however, we have paid little attention to the impact of macroeconomic policy on exchange rates and on the components of a nation's balance-of-payment accounts. We now turn to these issues.

MACROECONOMIC POLICY AND EXCHANGE RATE

Since monetary and fiscal policies exert an impact on income growth, inflation, and real interest rates, they will also influence exchange rates. Because these two major macropolicy tools differ with regard to their impact on the foreign exchange market, we will consider them separately.

MONETARY POLICY AND EXCHANGE RATE   Suppose the United States began to follow a more expansionary monetary policy. How would this policy influence the exchange-rate market? When the effects are not fully anticipated, expansionary monetary policy will lead to more rapid economic growth, an acceleration in the inflation rate, and lower real interest rates.[4] As we previously discussed, each of these factors will increase the demand for foreign exchange, causing the dollar to depreciate. The rapid growth of income will stimulate imports. Similarly, the acceleration in the U.S. inflation rate (relative to our trading partners) will make U.S. goods less competitive abroad, causing a decline in exports. Simultaneously, the lower real interest rate will encourage the flow of capital abroad. The expected short-run effect of an unanticipated shift to a more expansionary monetary policy is a depreciation in the exchange-rate value of the dollar.

---

[4]A complete analysis would show that neither growth nor the real interest rate will change if people fully anticipate the effects of the change in monetary policy on the price level. In this chapter, we assume for simplicity that the price-level effects of monetary policy are unanticipated. This clearly is more relevant in the short run rather than in the long run.

The expected outcome of an unanticipated switch to a more restrictive monetary policy will be just the opposite. The restrictive monetary policy will retard economic growth, decelerate the inflation rate, and push real interest rates upward. Exports will grow relative to imports. Investment funds from abroad will be drawn by the high real interest rates in the United States. Foreigners will demand more dollars with which to purchase goods, services, and real assets in the United States. The strong demand for the dollar will cause it to appreciate.

FISCAL POLICY AND EXCHANGE RATE.   Fiscal policy tends to generate conflicting influences on the foreign exchange market. Suppose the United States unexpectedly shifts toward a more restrictive fiscal policy, planning a budget surplus or at least a smaller deficit. Just as with restrictive monetary policy, the restrictive fiscal policy will tend to cause a reduction in aggregate demand, an economic slowdown, and a decline in the rate of inflation. These factors will discourage imports and stimulate exports, placing upward pressure on the exchange-rate value of the dollar. However, restrictive fiscal policy will also mean less government borrowing, which will reduce real interest rates in the United States. The lower real interest rates will cause financial capital to flow from the United States. This will increase the supply of dollars in the foreign exchange market, and thereby place downward pressure on the exchange-rate value of the U.S. dollar.

Which of these two effects is likely to dominate? When answering this question, it is important to consider the mobility of capital relative to trade flows. Financial capital is highly mobile. Investors can and do quickly shift their funds from one country to another in response to changes in interest rates. In contrast, importers and exporters often enter into long-term contracts when buying and selling goods. Thus, they are likely to respond more slowly to changing market conditions. Consequently, to the extent that a more restrictive fiscal policy places downward pressure on interest rates, the outflow of capital is likely to dominate in the short run. At least a temporary depreciation in the nation's currency is the most likely outcome.

The analysis of expansionary fiscal policy is symmetrical. To the extent that larger budget deficits stimulate aggregate demand and domestic inflation, they will encourage imports, which will place downward pressure on the exchange-rate value of a nation's currency. However, the increased borrowing to finance larger budget deficits will push real interest rates up and draw foreign investment to the United States, causing the dollar to appreciate. In the short run, the latter outcome is more likely.

MACROECONOMIC POLICY AND CURRENT ACCOUNT

How does macroeconomic policy affect a nation's balance on current account? When considering this question, it is important to remember that the current- and capital-account balances must sum to zero under a pure flexible-rate system. Thus, any deficit on current (capital) account must be exactly offset by a capital (current) account surplus of equal size. Since unanticipated shifts in macroeconomic policy influence both the demand for imports and real interest rates, then, clearly, they will exert an impact on both current account and capital account balances.

MONETARY POLICY AND CURRENT ACCOUNT. Suppose that the Federal Reserve suddenly increases the growth rate of the money supply. How will this shift to a more expansionary monetary policy influence the U.S. balance on current account? As we just indicated, the more rapid money growth will stimulate income, place upward pressure on the inflation rate, and reduce real interest rates. Think how this combination of factors will affect the current and capital accounts. The growth of income and higher domestic prices will stimulate imports, retard exports, and thus cause the current account to shift toward a larger deficit (or smaller surplus). At the same time, the lower domestic interest rates will encourage investors, both domestic and foreign, to shift funds from the United States to other countries where they can earn a higher rate of return. Predictably, this outflow of capital will cause a capital-account deficit and depreciation in the exchange-rate value of the dollar. In turn, the dollar depreciation will encourage exports, discourage imports, and act as a partial offset to the direct effects of the more rapid income growth. Since capital is far more mobile than goods in international markets, the outflow of capital effect will generally dominate in the short run. For a time, therefore, the shift to the expansionary monetary policy will tend to cause a capital-account deficit (reflecting the outflow of capital) and a current-account surplus.

Now consider the impact of an unanticipated shift to a more restrictive monetary policy on a nation's current-account balance. The restrictive policy will tend to slow growth and inflation, which will reduce the demand for imports. However, it will also increase real interest rates, leading to an inflow of capital and appreciation in the nation's currency. In the short run, the inflow of capital will generally dominate. The expected result is a capital-account surplus (reflecting the inflow of capital), currency appreciation, and at least a short-term current-account deficit.

FISCAL POLICY AND CURRENT ACCOUNT. What impact will large budget deficits have on a nation's current account? Expansionary fiscal policy will tend to stimulate aggregate demand and push domestic interest rates upward (the *crowding-out effect*). The increase in aggregate demand will encourage the purchase of imports, and thereby shift the current account toward a deficit (or smaller surplus). Simultaneously, the higher real interest rates will both attract foreign capital and help keep domestic capital at home. Predictably, there will be a net capital inflow, which will shift the capital account toward a surplus.

When fiscal policy is expansionary, both the increase in imports due to the demand stimulus and the increase in the net capital inflow as the result of the higher interest rates will shift the current account toward a deficit and the capital account toward a surplus. In this way, large budget deficits will also tend to result in large current-account deficits.

Once again, the analysis is symmetrical. A shift to a more restrictive fiscal policy—for example, a reduction in the size of a budget deficit—will retard demand and reduce interest rates. As the result of the decline in aggregate demand, imports will tend to fall, shifting a nation's current account toward a surplus (or smaller deficit). Simultaneously, the low interest rates will lead to a net capital outflow, which will shift the capital account toward a deficit. Thus, restrictive fiscal policy will tend to cause a current-account surplus and a capital-account deficit. The accompanying "Thumbnail Sketch" summarizes the expected impacts of unanticipated shifts in monetary and fiscal policy.

MACROECONOMIC POLICY AND CURRENT ACCOUNT DEFICITS OF 1980s AND 1990s

We are now in a position to analyze the impact of recent macroeconomic policy on the foreign exchange value of the dollar and the current account of the United States. Responding to the double-digit inflation rates of 1979–1980, the Federal Reserve shifted toward a more restrictive monetary policy in the early 1980s. In addition, legislation passed in 1981 substantially reduced tax rates. Thus, in the early 1980s, monetary policy was more restrictive and fiscal policy was more expansionary. How will this macroeconomic policy combination affect exchange rates and a nation's current account? Look at the accompanying "Thumbnail Sketch." Both a more restrictive monetary policy and a more expansionary fiscal policy will tend to cause higher real interest rates, an inflow of capital, currency appreciation, and a current-account deficit.

This is precisely what occurred. As part "a" of **Exhibit 32–7** illustrates, the dollar appreciated sharply beginning in 1981 (see also Exhibit 32–1). Shortly thereafter, as part "b" of Exhibit 32–7 shows, the current account began to shift dramatically

THUMBNAIL SKETCH

WHY IS THE AGGREGATE QUANTITY DEMANDED INVERSELY RELATED TO THE PRICE LEVEL?

A. IMPACT OF UNANTICIPATED SHIFT IN MONETARY POLICY:

	EXPANSIONARY MONETARY POLICY	RESTRICTIVE MONETARY POLICY
Exchange rate[a]	Depreciates.	Appreciates.
Real interest rates	Decline.	Increase.
Flow of capital	Capital outflow.	Capital inflow.
Current account	Shifts toward a surplus.	Shifts toward a deficit.

B. IMPACT OF UNANTICIPATED SHIFT IN FISCAL POLICY:

	EXPANSIONARY FISCAL POLICY	RESTRICTIVE FISCAL POLICY
Exchange rate[a]	Uncertain, but the interest rate effect is likely to cause appreciation.	Uncertain, but the interest rate effect is likely to cause depreciation.
Real interest rates	Increase.	Decline.
Flow of capital	Capital Inflow.	Capital Outflow.
Current account	Shifts toward a deficit.	Shifts toward a surplus.

[a]Value of domestic currency.

EXHIBIT 32–7

**EXCHANGE-RATE VALUE OF DOLLAR AND THE CURRENT-ACCOUNT DEFICIT,
1973–1993**

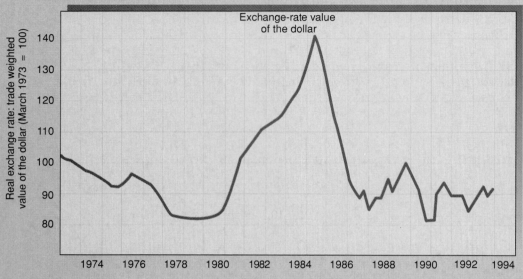

(a) Exchange-rate value of the dollar
(Compared with ten currencies)

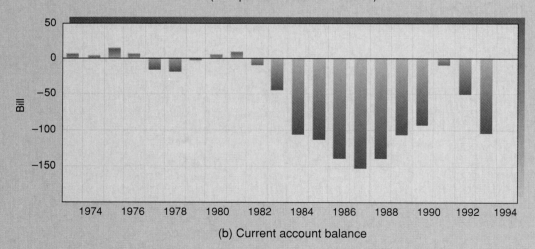

(b) Current account balance

As the dollar appreciated during the early 1980s, the current-account deficit of the United States soared. In early 1985 the dollar reversed course and began to depreciate. The current-account deficit (b), however, continued to expand throughout 1986 and 1987. It was not until 1988, approximately three years after the dollar began to depreciate, that the current-account deficit began to shrink. Just as the J-curve analysis (discussed later in this chapter) indicates, there will be a substantial lag between a change in the exchange-rate value of a currency and the ultimate change in a nation's current-account balance.

toward a deficit position. The annual current account of the United States turned from a $6.9 billion surplus in 1981 to a $46 billion deficit in 1983 and continued upward, reaching a deficit of $154 billion in 1987. As the dollar appreciated throughout 1981–1985, capital continued to flow into the United States and the current-account deficit continued to widen.

J-CURVE EFFECT

Beginning in 1985, the rise in the exchange rate value of the dollar reversed itself. The dollar depreciated sharply during 1986–1987. Why didn't the decline in the exchange-rate value of the dollar reverse the current-account deficit? It takes time for a depreciation in a nation's currency to turn around a current-account deficit, and, initially, the depreciation generally enlarges rather than shrinks it.

The impact of a currency depreciation on a current-account deficit can be broken down into a *price effect* and a *quantity effect*. A 10 percent depreciation in the dollar means that import prices increase by 10 percent in terms of dollars. Of course, this increase in the dollar price of imports will discourage purchases. However, the 10 percent depreciation also means that *for a given quantity sold*, foreigners will earn 10 percent more dollars. Therefore, unless Americans reduce the *quantity* of their imports by more than 10 percent, their *expenditures* on imports will increase in response to a depreciation in the dollar. Similarly, the depreciation will make U.S. exports 10 percent cheaper to foreigners. Unless foreigners increase their *quantity* purchased by more than 10 percent, their demand for dollars in the exchange market will *decrease* as the result of the depreciation.

Since American and foreign-produced goods are excellent substitutes for one another, there is good reason to expect that both the U.S. demand for imports and foreign demand for U.S. exports will be highly elastic in the long run. However, this may not be true in the short run. When the dollar depreciates, it will take time for American consumers to substitute for the more expensive imports and for foreign consumers to adjust their consumption, purchasing more of the now cheaper American exports. The new suppliers (or new customers) must be contacted. New agreements must be completed. In some cases, these developments must await the expiration of prior contracts. Therefore, initially, the increase in the quantity of exports may be less than the 10 percent reduction in price. If this is the case, for a time the depreciation will actually cause the current account deficit to worsen—the dollar expenditures on imports will rise while the dollar sales of exports will decline. Eventually, this situation will reverse. With the passage of time, the U.S. demand for imports and foreign demand for U.S. exports will become more elastic. The quantity effects will dominate, and a depreciation will reduce the current account deficit.

Economists refer to this time path of adjustment as the **J-curve effect.** A nation's current-account deficit will initially widen (slide down the hook of the "J") before it shrinks (moves up the stem of the "J") as the result of a currency depreciation. This occurs because the short-run elasticity of domestic demand for imports and foreign demand for exports is inelastic. Thus, the depreciation initially increases import expenditures and export sales. However, in the long run,

J-curve effect
The tendency of a nation's current-account deficit to widen initially before it shrinks in response to an exchange-rate depreciation. This tendency results because the short-run demand for both imports and exports is often inelastic, even though the long-run demand is almost always elastic.

the demand for both imports and exports is elastic. Therefore, the depreciation of a nation's currency will eventually shrink the nation's current-account deficit.[5]

Empirical studies are consistent with the J-curve analysis. There is often a lag of two or three years before a change in the exchange-rate value of a nation's currency will exert a major impact on current-account transactions. This lagged effect can be observed from the data of Exhibit 32–7. As part "a" illustrates, the exchange value of the dollar appreciated substantially (approximately 30 percent) during 1981 and 1982. Initially, however, there was only a small impact on current-account transactions. The size of the current-account deficit in 1981 and 1982 was not much different from the levels of 1978–1980. Beginning in 1983, two years after the dollar began to appreciate, the current-account deficit began to widen considerably. Clearly, the appreciation in the dollar during 1981–1985 reduced the price of imports (and increased the price of U.S. exports) and, with approximately a two-year lag, contributed to the sizable increase in the current-account deficit.

Beginning in mid-year 1985, the exchange-rate value of the dollar took a sharp plunge, and it declined by 40 percent during 1986 and 1987. Nonetheless, the current-account deficit continued to widen during that time. It was not until 1988, approximately two and a half years after the dollar began to depreciate, that the current-account deficit began to shrink. Just as the J-curve analysis implies, there was a lengthy lag between the depreciation of the dollar and the reversal in the direction of the nation's current-account deficit.

TRADE DEFICITS AND SURPLUSES

There is a tendency to think that a balance-of-trade surplus is good and a deficit bad. This is certainly understandable. In other contexts, the implications associated with a surplus are generally preferable to those of a deficit. In the area of trade, however, there are often two ways of viewing transactions.

When the service sector is included, a balance-of-trade deficit means that, in aggregate, the citizens of a nation are buying more goods and services from foreigners than they are receiving from them. A surplus implies that the sales to foreigners (exports) exceed purchases from them (imports). It is not obvious that a surplus is preferable to a deficit. After all, a nation that is running a deficit is getting more goods and services from others than it is supplying to them. What is so bad about that? Similarly, a trade surplus implies that a nation is producing more goods and services for foreigners to consume than it is receiving from foreigners. Is this something that people will want to continue to do?

A nation's trade deficit or surplus is an aggregation of the voluntary choices of businesses and individuals. In contrast with a budget deficit of an individual, business, or government, there is no legal entity that is responsible for the trade deficit. As Herbert Stein, a former Chairman of the President's Council of Economic Advisers, states,

---

[5]See Jeffrey A. Rosensweig and Paul D. Koch, "The U.S. Dollar and the 'Delayed J-Curve,'" Federal Reserve Bank of Atlanta, *Economic Review,* July–August 1988, pp. 2–15, for an interesting article on the J-curve effect as it applies to the trade imbalances of the United States during the 1980s.

The fact is that a certain (unknown) number of Americans bought more abroad than they sold abroad and a certain other (unknown) number of Americans sold more than they bought abroad. The trade deficit is the excess of the net foreign purchases of the first group over the net foreign sales of the second group. The trade deficit does not belong to any individual or institution. It is a pure statistical aggregate, like the number of eggs laid in the U.S. or the number of bald-headed men living here.[6]

Whether a nation runs a trade deficit—or more broadly, a current-account deficit—or surplus depends upon the investment opportunities in the country relative to the nation's saving rate. Under a flexible-rate exchange system, countries with more attractive investment opportunities and a lower saving rate than their trading partners will run current-account deficits. Correspondingly, countries with less attractive investment opportunities and a higher saving rate will run current-account surpluses.

Of course, a current-account deficit must be financed with a capital-account surplus under a flexible-rate exchange system. A capital-account surplus indicates that foreigners are investing more in the United States than Americans are investing abroad. Is this inflow of real and financial capital bad? The answer to this question depends on why Americans are investing so little abroad and foreigners are investing so much in the United States. If it is because large budget deficits have induced Americans to reduce their saving and consume beyond their means, and as a result pushed interest rates up, then there is cause for concern. However, if this is the case, it is important to note that the problem is not the current-account deficit, but rather the large budget deficits that are encouraging current consumption and diverting the savings of Americans away from capital formation. To the extent that Americans save and invest less as the result of budget deficits, the growth of their future income will be slower.

On the other hand, if the capital-account surplus merely reflects that investment opportunities in a country are attractive relative to investment opportunities elsewhere, the inflow of capital reflects positively on the economic health of that country.

How long can a nation continue to run a current-account deficit? Perhaps surprising to some, the answer is a long time. A current-account deficit is not like business losses or an excess of household spending relative to income—conditions that eventually force decision makers to change their ways. The United States ran a current (trade) account deficit almost every year from 1800 to 1875. On the other hand, it consistently ran current-account surpluses from 1946 to 1976. The trade accounts of other countries have followed similar lengthy periods of both deficits and surpluses.

Currently, the United States has a rapidly growing labor force (compared with Europe and Japan), a system of secure property rights, and political stability. This makes it an attractive country in which to invest. On the other hand, the saving rate of the United States, perhaps as the result of budget deficits, cultural factors, or less favorable tax treatment of saving, is low compared to our major trading partners. A continuation of this combination of factors—attractive investment opportunities and a low saving rate—will result in the long-term inflow of foreign capital and a corresponding current-account deficit.

---

[6]Herbert Stein, "Leave the Trade Deficit Alone," *The Wall Street Journal,* March 11, 1987.

The forces underpinning the U.S. current-account deficit may change in the near future. The growth rate of the U.S. labor force may slow, reducing the return on investment and the inflow of capital. Or a period of slow growth in the income of Americans may motivate them to save a larger proportion of their income. Correspondingly, as the income of foreigners increases, they may decide to consume more and save less. Perhaps the federal government will reduce the size of its deficit and thereby push U.S. interest rates lower. Changes of this type will close the current-account deficit. But such changes need not take place. And if they do not, the current-account deficit will continue, and there is little reason to believe that it is exerting a harmful impact on the U.S. economy.

IMPORTANCE OF CURRENCY CONVERTIBILITY

If the people of one country are going to trade with buyers and sellers in other countries, they must be able to convert their domestic currency into foreign currencies. For example, American sellers will not want to be paid in Iranian rials because the Iranian currency cannot be used to buy things in the United States. Neither is it freely convertible to U.S. dollars. Nonconvertibility of one's domestic currency is a major obstacle that will reduce the ability of people to realize gains from trade and specialization in areas where they have a comparative advantage.

Of course, if a country has a flexible exchange rate—if it permits its currency to be freely and legally converted to other currencies in foreign exchange markets—currency convertibility is no problem. Many governments, however, fix the price of their currency and prohibit currency exchanges at other prices. Both a fixed exchange rate and free convertibility of a currency can be maintained *if a country is willing to use its monetary policy to maintain the fixed exchange rate.* Put another way, a country can either (1) follow an independent monetary policy and allow its exchange rate to fluctuate or (2) tie its monetary policy to the maintenance of the fixed exchange rate. It cannot, however, maintain convertibility if it is going to both fix the exchange-rate value of its currency and follow an independent monetary policy. It must either give up its monetary independence or allow its exchange rate to fluctuate if its currency is going to be fully convertible with other currencies.

Some countries, particularly small countries, have chosen to forgo monetary independence and tie the exchange-rate value of their domestic currency to a widely accepted currency like the U.S. dollar, the German mark, or the French franc. This is not a bad strategy. Worldwide, people already have confidence in currencies like the dollar, mark, and franc. Thus, tying one's currency to those currencies increases its acceptability.

Hong Kong has followed this strategy. It does not have a central bank that conducts monetary policy. Instead it has a currency board that issues Hong Kong dollars in exchange for U.S. dollars at an exchange rate of 7.7 Hong Kong dollars = 1 U.S. dollar. When U.S. dollars are received in exchange for newly issued Hong Kong dollars, the U.S. dollars are invested in U.S. government bonds. Thus, the Hong Kong dollar is fully backed by the U.S. dollar (or U.S. bonds). If prices were to rise in Hong Kong relative to the United States, fewer people would want to use Hong Kong dollars and more would want to use U.S.

dollars. Thus, people would ask the currency board to exchange Hong Kong dollars for U.S. dollars, which would have more purchasing power. In response, however, the supply of Hong Kong dollars would shrink, which would put a brake on inflation in Hong Kong.

In contrast, if inflation in the United States were greater than in Hong Kong, just the opposite would happen. People would exchange U.S. dollars (which would have less purchasing power) for Hong Kong dollars. In turn, the supply of Hong Kong dollars would increase and bring prices in Hong Kong back into line with prices in the United States. Thus, the purchasing power of the Hong Kong dollar is closely tied to the U.S. dollar (7.7 Hong Kong dollars is essentially the same thing as a U.S. dollar), and recognition of this fact increases its acceptability around the world.

In contrast with countries like Hong Kong that give up their monetary independence in order to tie the exchange-rate value of their currency to another that is widely accepted, several countries try to both fix the exchange-rate value of their currency and maintain monetary independence, which is often used to follow a highly inflationary monetary policy. This strategy generally results in the exchange-rate value of the country's currency being fixed above the market level.

When a country fixes the exchange-rate value of its currency above the market level, however, it is simultaneously fixing the price of foreign currencies below market level. This policy will make it extremely difficult for domestic residents to convert their domestic currency to foreign exchange. Since domestic citizens are less able to acquire foreign currencies, they will be less able to trade with foreigners. As a result, the volume of the country's international trade will decline.

Using the Dominican Republic as an example, **Exhibit 32–8** illustrates the impact of exchange-rate controls. When the Dominican Republic fixes the price

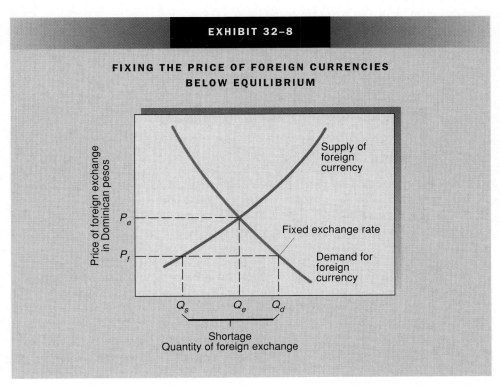

EXHIBIT 32–8

FIXING THE PRICE OF FOREIGN CURRENCIES BELOW EQUILIBRIUM

When the price of foreign currency in terms of a country's domestic currency is fixed below equilibrium, a shortage of foreign currency will emerge. Illegal black markets will develop as the citizens of the country seek more foreign currency so they can trade with people in other countries.

EXHIBIT 32-9

GROWTH RECORD OF COUNTRIES WITH SIGNIFICANT BLACK-MARKET EXCHANGE-RATE PREMIUM, 1980–1991

COUNTRY/REGION	BLACK-MARKET EXCHANGE-RATE PREMIUM			ANNUAL GROWTH RATE OF PER CAPITA GDP
	1980	1985	1990	1980–1991
North and South America				
Dominican Republic	37	14	66	−0.5
Jamaica	61	19	27	0.6
Paraguay	7	213	26	−0.4
Trinidad/Tobago	49	39	40	−5.7
Middle East, Europe, Asia				
Czechoslovakia	387	423	61	0.3
Egypt	9	146	56	2.3
Iran	164	533	2197	−1.4
Syria	35	251	301	−0.7
Bangladesh	111	168	165	2.1
Africa				
Algeria	263	335	140	0.0
Ethiopia	39	122	202	−1.5
Mauritania	41	136	170	−1.0
Mozambique	142	4107	117	−2.7
Rwanda	67	49	28	−2.4
Sierra Leone	62	206	165	−1.3
Somalia	41	147	200	−2.2
Tanzania	224	259	78	−0.1
Uganda	360	25	40	0.5
Zambia	70	38	212	−2.8
Average growth rate				**−0.9**

Source: The black-market exchange-rate data are from International Currency Analysis, *World Currency Yearbook* (various issues). The data on growth of per capita GDP are from the World Bank, *World Development Report, 1993.* All countries with a population of more than 1 million and a black-market exchange-rate premium of more than 25 percent in 1990, for which the data were available, are included.

of foreign exchange (in terms of the Dominican peso) below equilibrium, the quantity of foreign exchange demanded by Dominicans (so they can buy from foreigners) will exceed the quantity generated by Dominican exports. Under a flexible-rate system, this excess demand for foreign currency would be eliminated by a depreciation of the Dominican peso in the exchange-rate market. The price of foreign exchange would rise from P_f to P_e. With a fixed rate, however, this cannot happen. Instead, Dominican citizens will confront a shortage ($Q_d − Q_s$) of foreign exchange. Since they are able to obtain only Q_s units of foreign exchange, the volume of their trade with foreigners will decline (from Q_e to Q_s). In other words, since Dominicans cannot, at least not legally, convert as much of their currency to foreign exchange as they would like, they will not be able to buy as much from foreigners as they would like.

Of course, when price controls—exchange-rate controls are a type of price control—lead to shortages, as they inevitably do, black markets develop. Currency markets are not an exception to this rule. If you have ever traveled in a country that imposes exchange-rate controls and been approached by someone offering to trade local currency at a premium for your foreign currency, you have observed the black market in foreign exchange. The greater the black-market premium, the more the fixed price of the country's currency is out of line with market conditions, thereby restricting the volume of trade with foreigners.

Our analysis illustrates that fixing exchange rates and limiting the convertibility of one's currency will retard international trade and reduce the ability of people to realize gains from specialization and adoption of mass-production methods. Like other trade restrictions, this limitation on exchange will reduce both productivity and living standards.

Exhibit 32–9 presents data on the average annual growth rate of per capita GDP during 1980–1991 in countries where the black-market exchange rate differed from the official rate by more than 25 percent in 1990. These countries imposed tight exchange-rate controls throughout most all of the 1980s. Thirteen of the 19 countries experienced declines in per capita GDP during the 1980–1991 period. Only two (Egypt and Bangladesh) of the 19 were able to achieve an annual growth rate in excess of 0.6 percent during the 11-year period. On average, the per capita GDP of these 19 countries declined at an annual rate of 0.9 percent during 1980–1991. Given the negative impact of exchange-rate controls on trade and prosperity, the poor economic performance of these countries is not surprising.

CONCLUDING REMARKS

The current international monetary system is the product of an evolutionary process. Future changes are likely. However, a return to a system of fixed exchange rates such as existed for nearly three decades following the Second World War seems unlikely. The major industrial nations are simply unwilling to subject their monetary and fiscal policies to the constraints that a system of fixed rates would require. Currently, there is widespread recognition that the economic health of nations is influenced by the flow of international trade. Perhaps this recognition will lead to a greater coordination of monetary and fiscal policies among the major industrial nations and future policies that are consistent with currency convertibility among more countries of the developing world.

CHAPTER SUMMARY

1. The foreign exchange market is a highly organized market in which currencies of different countries are bought and sold. The exchange rate is the price of one national currency in terms of another. The exchange rate permits consumers in one country to translate the prices of foreign goods into units of their own currency.

2. When international trade takes place, it is usually necessary for one party to convert its currency to the currency of its trading partner. Imports of goods, services, and assets (both real and financial) by the United States generate a demand for foreign currency with which to pay for these items. On the other hand, exports of goods, services, and assets supply foreign currency to the exchange market because foreigners exchange their currency for the dollars needed to purchase the export items.

3. The value of a nation's currency on the exchange market is in equilibrium when the supply of the currency generated by imports (that is, the sale of goods, services, and assets to foreigners) is just equal to the demand for the currency generated by exports (the purchases of goods, services, and assets from foreigners).

4. Under a flexible-rate system, if there is an excess supply of dollars (excess demand for foreign currencies) on

the foreign exchange market, the value of the dollar will depreciate relative to other currencies. A depreciation will make foreign goods and assets more expensive to U.S. buyers and U.S. goods and assets cheaper for foreign purchasers, reducing the value of U.S. imports and increasing the value of its exports until equilibrium is restored. On the other hand, an excess demand for dollars (excess supply of foreign currencies) will cause the dollar to appreciate, stimulating imports and discouraging exports until equilibrium is restored.

5. With flexible exchange rates, a nation's currency tends to appreciate when (a) rapid economic growth abroad (relative to growth at home) stimulates exports relative to imports, (b) the rate of domestic inflation is below that of the nation's trading partners, and (c) domestic real interest rates increase relative to one's trading partners. The reverse of these conditions will cause a nation's currency to depreciate.

6. During the period of 1944–1971, most nations operated under a system of fixed exchange rates. Under this system, if the value of the goods, services, and capital assets exported to foreigners is less than the value of the items imported, there is an excess supply of the country's currency on the foreign exchange market. When this happens, the country must (a) devalue its currency, (b) take action to reduce imports (for example, heighten its trade barriers), or (c) pursue a restrictive macropolicy designed to increase interest rates and retard inflation. During the period when the fixed rates were in effect, corrective action taken to maintain the rates was often in conflict with free trade in international markets and the macropolicy objective of full employment.

7. The balance-of-payments accounts record the flow of payments between a country and other countries. Transactions that supply a nation's currency to the foreign exchange market (for example, imports) are recorded as debit items. Transactions that generate a demand for the nation's currency on the foreign exchange market (for example, exports) are recorded as credit items.

8. In aggregate, the balance-of-payments accounts must balance. Thus, (a) the current-account balance plus (b) the capital-account balance plus (c) the official-reserve-account balance must equal zero. However, the individual components of the accounts need not be in balance. A deficit in one area implies an offsetting surplus in other areas.

9. Under a pure flexible-rate system, there will not be any official-reserve-account transactions. Under these circumstances, a current-account deficit implies a capital-account surplus (and vice versa).

10. An unanticipated shift to a more restrictive monetary policy will raise the real interest rate, reduce the rate of

inflation, and, at least temporarily, reduce aggregate demand and the growth of income. These factors will in turn cause the nation's currency to appreciate on the foreign exchange market. In turn, the currency appreciation along with the inflow of capital will result in a current-account deficit. In contrast, the effects of a more expansionary monetary policy will be just the opposite: lower interest rates, an outflow of capital, currency depreciation, and a shift toward a current-account surplus.

11. An unanticipated shift to a more expansionary fiscal policy will tend to increase real interest rates, lead to an inflow of capital, and cause the nation's current account to shift toward a deficit. The effects of a shift to a more restrictive fiscal policy will be just the opposite: lower interest rates, an outflow of capital, and movement toward a current-account surplus.

12. Under a flexible-rate exchange system, a nation's current-account position is an aggregation of the voluntary choices of individuals and businesses. Some will have bought more abroad than they sold, while others will have sold more than they bought. The current-account deficit simply indicates that the net foreign purchases (and unilateral gifts) of the first group exceed the net foreign sales of the latter group.

13. While flexible exchange rates bring the sum of the current and capital accounts into balance, they do not bring either component into balance. Thus, it is possible for a country to experience a long-term current-account deficit or surplus. Whether a country runs a current-account deficit or surplus is dependent upon the attractiveness of domestic investment opportunities relative to the nation's saving rate. Countries with more attractive investment opportunities and a low saving rate will tend to run capital-account surpluses and current-account deficits. On the other hand, countries with less attractive investment opportunities and a high saving rate will tend to experience capital outflow and current-account surpluses under a flexible-rate system.

14. When a country fixes the exchange-rate value of its currency above the market level (and that of foreign currencies below the market level), a shortage of foreign exchange will result. Since residents of the country are less able to acquire foreign exchange, they are less able to engage in international trade. The decline in the volume of trade accompanying such exchange-rate controls will tend to reduce the productivity and income level of the country.

CRITICAL-ANALYSIS QUESTIONS

*1. If the dollar depreciates relative to the German mark, how will your ability to purchase the BMW you

---

*Asterisk denotes questions for which answers are given in Appendix C.

have longed for be affected? How will this change influence the quantity of BMWs purchased by Americans? How will it affect the dollar expenditures of Americans on BMWs?

2. How do flexible exchange rates bring about balance in the exchange-rate market? Do they lead to a balance between merchandise exports and imports? Do you think the United States should continue to follow a policy of flexible exchange rates? Why or why not?

3. "If a current-account deficit means that we are getting more items from abroad than we are sending to foreigners, why is it considered a bad thing?" Answer this question.

*4. The accompanying chart indicates the actual newspaper quotation of the exchange rate of various currencies. On February 2, did the dollar appreciate or depreciate against the British pound? How did it fare against the French franc?

U.S. DOLLAR EQUIVALENT

	FEB. 1	FEB. 2
British pound	1.755	1.746
French franc	.1565	.1575

*5. Suppose the exchange rate between the United States and Mexico freely fluctuated in the open market. Indicate which of the following would cause the dollar to appreciate (or depreciate) relative to the peso.

a. An increase in the quantity of drilling equipment purchased in the United States by Pemex, the Mexican oil company, as a result of a Mexican oil discovery.

b. An increase in the U.S. purchase of crude oil from Mexico as a result of the development of Mexican oil fields.

c. Higher real interest rates in Mexico, inducing U.S. citizens to move their financial investments from U.S. to Mexican banks.

d. Lower real interest rates in the United States, inducing Mexican investors to borrow dollars and then exchange them for pesos.

e. Inflation in the United States and stable prices in Mexico.

f. An increase in the inflation rate from 2 percent to 10 percent in both the United States and Mexico.

g. An economic boom in Mexico, inducing Mexicans to buy more U.S.–made automobiles, trucks, electric appliances, and television sets.

h. Attractive investment opportunities, inducing U.S. investors to buy stock in Mexican firms.

6. Explain why a current-account balance and a capital-account balance must sum to zero under a pure flexible-rate system.

7. "A nation cannot continue to run a deficit on current account. A healthy growing economy will not persistently expand its indebtedness to foreigners. Eventually, the trade deficits will lead to national bankruptcy." Evaluate this view.

8. In recent years, a substantial share of the domestic capital formation in the United States has been financed by foreign investors. Is this inflow of capital from abroad indicative that the U.S. economy is in poor health? If not, what does it indicate?

*9. Suppose that the United States were running a current account deficit. How would each of the following changes influence the size of the current account deficit?

a. A recession in the United States.

b. A decline in the attractiveness of investment opportunities in the United States.

c. An improvement in investment opportunities abroad.

10. "Foreigners are flooding our markets with goods and using the proceeds to buy up America. Unless we do something to protect ourselves, the Japanese, Europeans, and Arabs are going to own America." Evaluate this recent statement by an American political figure.

*11. If foreigners have confidence in the U.S. economy and therefore move to expand their investments in the United States, how will the U.S. current-account balance be affected? How will the exchange-rate value of the dollar be affected?

12. Is a trade surplus indicative of a strong, healthy economy? Why or why not?

13. During the early 1980s, the United States shifted toward a more restrictive monetary policy that sharply decelerated the domestic inflation rate. Simultaneously, the federal government was running a large budget deficit. Explain how this policy mix influenced the value of the dollar in the exchange-rate market.

14. What is the J-curve effect? According to the J-curve effect, how will a depreciation in a nation's currency affect its current-account balance?

*15. Changes in exchange rates will automatically direct a country to a current-account balance under a flexible-rate exchange system. Is this statement true or false?

16. Suppose that a country fixes the rate that its currency can legally be converted to foreign exchange (other currencies) above the market level. As a result, a black-market exchange rate emerges, and domestic citizens are willing to pay more than the legally fixed rate for foreign exchange.

a. Measured in terms of the domestic currency, will imports be cheaper or more expensive at the legally fixed exchange rate?

---

*Asterisk denotes questions for which answers are given in Appendix C.

b. Will export goods be cheaper or more expensive at the legally fixed rate?

c. How will this fixed-exchange-rate policy influence the country's volume of trade and level of investment?

d. Do you think this policy will help promote economic growth and prosperity? Why or why not?

e. Can you think of any reasons why people in politically powerful positions might favor the fixed-exchange-rate policy?

17. The newly independent country of Estonia recently tied the exchange-rate value of its currency to the German mark and pledged to conduct its monetary policy in a manner that would maintain the fixed exchange rate with the mark. Do you think this is a sound strategy? Why or why not? How will the policy affect the ability of the Estonian government to finance government programs with money creation? What impact do you think the policy will have on the level of investment and the operation of its capital market in Estonia?

*18. In recent years many American political figures have been highly critical of the fact that U.S. imports from Japan have consistently exceeded U.S. exports to Japan.

a. Under a flexible exchange-rate system, is there any reason to expect that the imports from a given country will tend to equal the exports to that country?

b. Can you think of any reason why the U.S. might persistently run a trade deficit with a country such as Japan?

---

*Asterisk denotes questions for which answers are given in Appendix C.

CHAPTER THIRTY-THREE

ECONOMIC DEVELOPMENT AND GROWTH OF INCOME

Certain fundamental principles—formulating sound monetary and fiscal policies, removing domestic price controls, opening the economy to international market forces, ensuring property rights and private property, creating competition, and reforming and limiting the role of government—are essential for a healthy market economy.

ECONOMIC REPORT OF THE PRESIDENT, 1991, P. 211.

CHAPTER FOCUS

- *How is income measured across countries?*
- *How does per capita income vary among nations?*
- *How long does it take for sustained economic growth to change the income level of a country by a substantial amount?*
- *What are the major sources of economic growth?*
- *What policies will help promote economic growth?*
- *How do the policies of prosperous growing economies differ from those of countries that are stagnating?*
- *Are the rich countries getting richer while the poor countries are getting poorer?*

T hroughout history, economic growth and income levels substantially greater than those required for survival have been rare. As recently as 250 years ago, people around the world struggled 50, 60, and 70 hours per week just to obtain the basic necessities of life—food, clothing, and shelter. During the last two centuries, sustained economic growth has changed that situation for most people in North America, Europe, Oceania, Japan, and a few other countries. Subsistence levels of food, shelter, and clothing are now taken for granted, and the typical family in high-income industrial countries worries instead about financing summer vacations, purchasing new cars and nicer homes, and providing for the children's college educations.

Rising incomes and improvements in the standard of living have not always been present in Western countries. According to Phelps Brown, the real income of English building trade workers was virtually unchanged between 1215 and 1798, a period of nearly six centuries. In other parts of Europe, workers experienced a similar stagnation of real earnings throughout much of this period.

Low incomes and widespread poverty are still the norm in most countries—particularly those of South and Central America, Africa, and Southern Asia. Are these low-income countries showing any growth? Why have some countries that were poor just a few decades ago prospered in recent decades, while others have continued to stagnate? What can governments do to promote economic prosperity? At various points throughout this book, we have addressed these questions and related issues. We are now prepared to pull together the lessons of basic economics and consider the topic of economic growth and prosperity in a more comprehensive manner.

MEASURING INCOME ACROSS COUNTRIES

The gross domestic product (GDP) of a country is a measurement of how much output (and income) is generated domestically by the residents of the nation. Per capita GDP is a measure of output per person, and therefore a broad indicator of the standard of living. However, when we use GDP to compare output and income across countries, there is an obvious problem. The GDP of each country is measured in units of the country's domestic currency. Mexico's GDP is measured in pesos, Japan's in yen, Germany's in marks, and so on. How, then, can these various measures of GDP be compared?

The simplest way is to convert the income figures to a common currency by the **exchange-rate conversion method.** Here the value of each nation's currency in the foreign exchange market is used to convert the nation's GDP (or GNP) to a common currency, such as the U.S. dollar. For example, if the British pound is worth 1.5 times as much as the U.S. dollar in the foreign exchange market, then the GDP of the United Kingdom is converted to dollars by multiplying the British GDP in pounds by 1.5.

While income comparisons based on the exchange-rate conversion method are widely reported, they are sometimes highly misleading. The foreign exchange value of a currency is influenced by only a limited number of goods and services

Exchange-rate conversion method

Method that uses the foreign exchange-rate value of a nation's currency to convert that nation's GDP (or GNP) to another monetary unit, such as the U.S. dollar.

that are traded internationally and by the purchase and sale of assets—particularly financial assets—across countries. In addition, some countries fix their exchange rates at a level that may differ substantially from the equilibrium rate. Thus, the exchange-rate value of a currency may not be a reliable indicator of the currency's purchasing power over the typical bundle of goods and services purchased by households in the domestic market. For example, merely because a British pound purchases 1.5 dollars in the foreign exchange market, it does not follow that it will purchase 1.5 times as much housing, recreation, child-care service, and similar items in the United Kingdom as a dollar will purchase in the United States. For this reason, income comparisons based on the exchange-rate conversion method are not highly regarded among economists.

Rather, economists favor the use of the **purchasing-power parity method** to make income comparisons across nations. This method compares the cost of purchasing the typical bundle of goods and services consumed by households in the domestic market of various nations. Each category in the bundle is weighted according to its contribution to GDP. The cost of purchasing the typical bundle in each nation is then compared to the dollar cost of purchasing the same bundle in the United States. Once the purchasing power of each nation's currency (in terms of the typical bundle) is determined, this information can be used to convert the GDP of each country to a common monetary unit (for example, the U.S. dollar).

Purchasing-power parity method
Method for determining the relative purchasing power of different currencies by comparing the amount of each currency required to purchase a typical bundle of goods and services in domestic markets. This information is then used to convert the GDP (or GNP) of each nation to a common monetary unit.

INCOME DIFFERENCES AMONG COUNTRIES

In recent years, Robert Summers and Alan Heston of the University of Pennsylvania have spearheaded a project of the United Nations Statistical Office that has used the purchasing-power parity method to develop measures of output for approximately 150 countries.[1] **Exhibit 33–1** presents the 1991 per capita GDP data (measured in 1991 U.S. dollars) from this project for the 83 largest countries for which data were available. These data illustrate that there is wide variation in per capita GDP among countries. In 1991 there were 21 countries with a population of 5 million or more with a per capita GDP of less than $1,200. In Chad, the poorest of these countries, the estimated annual per capita GDP was only $447. At the other end of the spectrum, there were also 21 countries with a population of 5 million or more that had per capita incomes of more than $7,500. The estimated per capita annual GDP of the United States in 1991 was $21,866, the highest in the world. The U.S. figure was approximately $400 more than Switzerland, the country with the next highest level of annual output in 1991.

Most of the poorest countries (annual GDP less than $1,200) were in Africa. On the other hand, with the exception of Saudi Arabia, Australia, Japan, and Hong Kong, the high-income countries were either European or North American. South and Central American countries and the other nations of Asia generally fell into the middle categories with annual per capita incomes in the $1,200 to $7,500 range.

Does it really make much difference whether income comparisons are based on purchasing-power parity or the more widely cited exchange-rate conversion method? **Exhibit 33–2** presents the World Bank estimates for 1991 per capita GNP

---

[1]Robert Summers and Alan Heston, "The Penn World Table (Mark 5): An Expanded Set of International Comparisons, 1950–1988," *Quarterly Journal of Economics*, May 1991, pp. 327–368.

EXHIBIT 33-1

ANNUAL PER CAPITA OUTPUT OF NATIONS BY PURCHASING-POWER PARITY METHOD, 1991

POOREST COUNTRIES (ANNUAL OUTPUT LESS THAN $1,200)		LOW-INCOME COUNTRIES (ANNUAL OUTPUT $1,200 TO $3,000)		MIDDLE-INCOME COUNTRIES (ANNUAL OUTPUT $3,000 TO $7,500)		HIGH-INCOME COUNTRIES (ANNUAL OUTPUT MORE THAN $7,500)	
COUNTRY	PER CAPITA GDP, 1991	COUNTRY	PER CAPITA GDP, 1991	COUNTRY	PER CAPITA GDP, 1991	COUNTRY	PER CAPITA GDP, 1991
Chad	$ 447	Senegal	$1,297	Uzbekistan	$3,226	Saudi Arabia	$ 7,963
Zaire	469	Cameroon	1,344	Tunisia	3,416	Greece	8,001
Niger	542	Yemen	1,374	Ecuador	3,466	Russia	8,115
Tanzania	573	India	1,458	Iran	3,569	Portugal	8,208
Mali	599	Bangladesh	1,546	So. Africa	3,855	Spain	12,291
Malawi	613	Honduras	1,571	Colombia	3,978	Unit. Kingdom	15,494
Burundi	640	Zimbabwe	1,592	Turkey	4,531	Italy	15,779
Burkina Faso	666	Pakistan	1,702	Poland	4,569	Finland	16,236
Madagascar	733	Bolivia	1,940	Thailand	4,600	Austria	16,316
Rwanda	738	El Salvador	2,077	Argentina	4,603	Netherlands	16,585
Guinea	747	Egypt	2,102	Brazil	4,787	France	17,402
Somalia	759	Philippines	2,104	Kazakhstan	4,807	Sweden	17,550
Mozambique	921	Dominican Rep.	2,397	Bulgaria	4,813	Australia	17,761
Haiti	925	Indonesia	2,454	Syria	5,225	Denmark	17,821
Nigeria	929	Peru	2,484	Chile	5,342	Belgium	17,849
Ghana	930	Morocco	2,554	Ukraine	5,601	Japan	19,290
Zambia	983	Guatemala	2,562	Hungary	6,055	Hong Kong	19,397
Uganda	1,036	Sri Lanka	2,658	Malaysia	6,256	Germany	19,646
Kenya	1,100	Algeria	2,870	Mexico	6,776	Canada	20,571
Sudan	1,162	China	2,946	Venezuela	7,453	Switzerland	21,448
Ivory Coast	1,185			South Korea	7,485	United States	21,866

Source: Data were supplied to the authors by Robert Summers and Alan Heston. See Summers and Heston "The Penn World Table (Mark 5): An Expanded Set of International Comparisons, 1950–1988," *Quarterly Journal of Economics*, May 1991. All countries with a 1991 population of 5 million or more for which the data were available are included.

based on the exchange-rate conversion method as well as the Summers-Heston per capita GDP estimates derived by the purchasing-power parity method.[2] These

---

[2]The World Bank per capita income estimates are for GNP, while the Summers and Heston data are for GDP. In most cases, the difference between the GNP and GDP of a country is very small—only 1 or 2 percent. Thus, the differences in the cross-country estimates are mostly due to the method used to convert the figures to a common currency, rather than the differences between the GNP and GDP data.

EXHIBIT 33-2

COMPARISON OF PER CAPITA OUTPUT OF VARIOUS COUNTRIES BY EXCHANGE-RATE CONVERSION VERSUS PURCHASING-POWER PARITY METHODS

COUNTRY	1991 PER CAPITA GNP BY EXCHANGE-RATE CONVERSION	1991 PER CAPITA GDP BY PURCHASING-POWER PARITY
China	$ 370	$ 2,946
India	330	1,458
Thailand	1,570	4,600
Brazil	2,940	4,787
Argentina	2,790	4,603
Mexico	3,030	6,776
Hong Kong	13,430[a]	19,397
United Kingdom	16,550	15,494
France	20,380	17,402
United States	22,240	21,866
Germany	23,650	19,646
Japan	26,930	19,290
Switzerland	33,610	21,448

[a]Data are for GDP per capita.

Source: The exchange-rate conversion estimates are from the World Bank, *World Development Report, 1993,* Table 1. The purchasing-power parity estimates were supplied to the authors by Robert Summers and Alan Heston. See Summers and Heston, "The Penn World Table (Mark 5): An Expanded Set of International Comparisons, 1950–1988," *Quarterly Journal of Economics,* May 1991. While the World Bank data are for GNP and the Summers-Heston estimates are for GDP, as we have previously discussed, the two are generally quite similar. Thus, the primary source of the differences in these estimates is due to the different methods (exchang-rate conversion versus purchasing-power parity) used to convert the data to a common currency.

comparisons illustrate that the distortions produced by the exchange-rate method are often substantial. For example, the per capita income (GNP) of Switzerland is estimated to be more than 50 percent greater than the United States by this method. In contrast, the purchasing-power parity method indicates that the per capita income (GDP) of the United States is slightly greater than the figure for Switzerland. Similarly, the exchange-rate conversion method shows the income of Japan as 21 percent greater than that of the United States, while the purchasing-power parity method indicates that of the United States to be approximately 13 percent greater than Japan.

The differences are particularly large when comparisons are made between **less developed countries (LDCs)** and industrial countries. In general, the exchange-rate conversion method understates the per capita income figure for LDCs. For example, the per capita income estimate for India derived by the exchange-rate conversion method is less than one-fourth of the income figure derived by the purchasing-power parity method ($330 compared with $1,458).

Less developed countries (LDCs)

Low-income countries generally characterized by rapid population growth and an agriculture-household sector that dominates the economy. Sometimes these countries are referred to as developing countries.

The exchange-rate conversion method indicates that the per capita income of the United States is 67 times that of India; more realistically, the purchasing-power parity data estimates that the U.S. figure is 15 times that of India. In the case of China, the distortions are even greater. The per capita income of China derived by the exchange-rate conversion method is only one-eighth of the estimate ($370 compared with $2,946) based on purchasing-power parity! The exchange-rate conversion method places the per capita income of the United States at 60 times the figure for China; the purchasing-power parity method, at only 7.4 times.

For almost all LDCs, including Thailand, Brazil, Mexico, and Argentina, the per capita income estimates based on the purchasing-power parity method are substantially greater than the parallel estimates derived by exchange-rate conversion. Since the informal economy—including production in the household sector—is undoubtedly a larger share of the total output in LDCs, even the purchasing-power parity method probably understates the standard of living in these countries relative to more highly developed market economies. At least, however, the purchasing-power parity figures reflect the prices of a broader set of commodities than just the items traded in international markets. Consequently, most economists judge them a more accurate indicator of per capita income than the more widely circulated estimates based on exchange-rate conversions. This is particularly true with regard to comparisons of income and living standards in developed countries against those in LDCs.[3]

ARE GROWTH AND DEVELOPMENT THE SAME THING?

Most economists draw a distinction between economic growth and development. Economic growth is defined in strictly positive terms—the rate of change in GDP. Since economists are interested primarily in the well-being of individuals, they generally focus on a nation's per capita real output (or income). When a nation's GDP is increasing more rapidly than its population, per capita GDP will also expand. An economist would say that the country was experiencing **intensive economic growth.** Conversely, if the population of the nation is expanding more rapidly than GDP, per capita real income (GDP) will decline.

Intensive economic growth
An increase in output per person. When intensive economic growth is present, output is growing more rapidly than population.

Specialists in the area consider economic development to be a broader concept than economic growth. Development encompasses not only growth, but also distributional and structural changes that imply an improvement in the standard of living for most of the populace. Development requires not only growth in output per person but also an improvement in the availability of consumption goods for a wide spectrum of the populace, including those people in the bottom half of the income distribution.

Obviously, economic growth and development are closely related. Growth is necessary for development. Without sustained economic growth, continuous

[3]For additional data on income differences across nations, see Stephen L. Parente and Edward C. Prescott, "Changes in the Wealth of Nations" *Quarterly Review: Federal Reserve Bank of Minneapolis,* Spring 1993, pp. 3–16.

improvement in the economic opportunities and status of a nation's populace, including those at the bottom of the economic spectrum, will be impossible.

Since increases in per capita GDP, on average, increase the availability of goods and services per person, they are generally associated with economic development—that is, an improvement in the standard of living broadly throughout the populace. There are exceptions, however. For example, during the 1965–1980 period, Brazil achieved substantial economic growth. The distribution of income in Brazil, however, was highly skewed. More than 60 percent of the aggregate income was allocated to the wealthiest 20 percent of the population. By way of comparison, the wealthiest one-fifth of the population earn between 40 and 45 percent of the aggregate income in the developed countries of Europe and North America. The economic growth of Brazil during the 1965–1980 period did little to alter the economic status of the overwhelming majority of its citizens. Thus, Brazil experienced growth but was unable to achieve economic development.

IMPACT OF SUSTAINED ECONOMIC GROWTH

With the passage of time, economic growth—increases in per capita GDP—can exert a substantial impact on incomes. When the income per person of a country grows at an annual rate of 3.5 percent, per capita income will double every 20 years. (Note: In order to approximate how many years it will take for income to double, you can simply divide 70 by the country's growth rate. In this case, 70 divided by 3.5 equals 20. This approximation method is sometimes called the *simple 70 rule.*) In contrast, if a country's growth rate of income per person is 1.75 percent, it would take 40 years for per capita income to double. Consider the case where two countries initially have the same level of income, but the annual growth rate of Country A is 3.5 percent while that of Country B is 1.75 percent. Even though the two started with the same income level, after 40 years the income of Country A would be twice that of Country B.

Differences in sustained growth rates over two or three decades will substantially alter relative income positions of countries. Nations that experience sustained periods of rapid economic growth will move up the income ladder and eventually achieve high-income status. On the other hand, nations that grow slowly or experience declines in real GDP per capita will slide down the economic ladder.

A comparison of the income status of Hong Kong and Japan relative to Argentina and Venezuela during the last three decades vividly illustrates how sustained growth influences the relative incomes of nations. Measured in 1991 dollars, the per capita GDP of Hong Kong was $2,880 in 1960, compared to $4,293 for Argentina and $4,892 for Venezuela. The per capita income of Japan in 1960 was $3,260, well below the comparable figure for the two Latin American countries. During the 1960–1991 period, the per capita GDP of both Hong Kong and Japan expanded at an annual rate of more than 5 per cent. In contrast, both Argentina and Venezuela experienced annual growth rates of less than 1 percent.

As a result, by 1991 the per capita incomes of both Hong Kong and Japan were more than 2.5 times the figure for Venezuela and more than 4 times the per capita GDP of Argentina.

SOURCES OF ECONOMIC GROWTH

Why have some countries like Hong Kong and Japan prospered, while others like Argentina and Venezuela experienced economic stagnation? Laypersons often argue that natural resources are the key ingredient of economic growth. Of course, other things constant, countries with abundant natural resources do have an advantage. It is clear, though, that natural resources are neither a necessary nor sufficient condition for economic growth. Hong Kong has practically no natural resources (other than its harbor), very little fertile soil, and no domestic sources of energy. Japan likewise has few natural resources, and it imports almost all of its industrial energy supply. Nonetheless, both Hong Kong and Japan have grown rapidly and are prosperous. In contrast, Argentina has a great deal of fertile land and several other natural resources and Venezuela is one of the most oil-rich countries in the world. Yet these countries, along with other resource-rich countries like Ghana, Kenya, and Bolivia, are poor, and they have been growing slowly, if at all. Natural resources can help promote economic prosperity, but clearly they are not the primary determinant of growth.

Economic growth is a complex process. Several factors contribute to it, and they are often interrelated. Much as the performance of an athletic team reflects the joint output of the team members, economic growth is jointly determined by several factors. And just as one or two weak players can substantially reduce overall team performance, a counterproductive policy in one or two key areas can substantially harm the overall performance of an economy.

Although economics cannot provide us with a precise recipe for economic growth, it does reveal the important sources of such growth: investment in physical and human capital, technological advances, and improvement in economic organization.

INVESTMENT IN PHYSICAL AND HUMAN CAPITAL

Machines can have a substantial impact on a person's ability to produce. Even Robinson Crusoe on an uninhabited island can catch far more fish with a net than he can with his hands. Farmers working with modern tractors and plows can cultivate many more acres than their great-grandparents, who probably worked with hoes. Similarly, education and training that improve the knowledge and skills of workers can vastly improve their productivity. For example, a cabinetmaker, skilled after years of training and experience, can build cabinets far more rapidly and efficiently than a neophyte.

Investment in both physical capital (machines) and human capital (knowledge and skills) can expand the productive capacity of a worker. In turn, people that produce more goods and services valued by others will tend to have higher incomes. Economics suggests that, other things constant, countries using a larger share of their resources to produce tools, machines, and factories will tend to grow more rapidly. Allocation of more resources to education and training will also tend to enhance economic growth.

Of course, investment is not a free lunch; an opportunity cost is involved. When more resources are used to produce machines and factories and develop skills, fewer resources are available for production of current-consumption goods. Economics is about trade-offs. It does, however, indicate that people who save and invest more will be able to produce more in the future.

TECHNOLOGICAL PROGRESS

Technological advancement—the adoption of new improved techniques or methods of production—enables workers to generate additional output with the same amount of resources. Such improvements reduce the cost of producing goods and services. Less human and physical capital per unit of output is required.

Clearly, improved technology—the result of using brainpower to discover economical new products and/or less costly methods of production—has substantially enhanced our production possibilities. During the last 250 years, the substitution of power-driven machines for human labor, the development of miracle grains, fertilizer, new sources of energy, and improvements in transportation and communication have vastly improved living standards around the world. Technological improvements continue to change our lives. Consider the impact of compact disk players, microcomputers, word processors, microwave ovens, video cameras and cassette players, fax machines, and automobile air conditioners. Development and improvement of these products during just the last couple of decades has vastly changed the way many people work and play.

Obviously, technological progress encompasses **invention,** the discovery of new products or processes. But, it also includes **innovation,** the practical and effective adoption of new techniques. In comparison to invention, it is sometimes easy to overlook the significance of innovation, but it is crucial to economic development. Many innovators were not even involved in the invention of the products for which they are now famous. Henry Ford played a minor role in the discovery and development of the automobile. His contribution was an innovative one—the adoption of mass-production techniques that enabled the low-cost production of reliable automobiles. Ray Kroc, the developer of the McDonald's fast-food chain, did not invent anything. In fact, he was not even involved in the operation of the first McDonald's restaurant. But he recognized a good idea when he saw it. Kroc was an innovator. He franchised the business, trained operators of McDonald's, and in the process changed the eating habits of a nation. Inventions are important, but without innovators, inventions are merely ideas waiting to be exploited.

As in the case of natural resources, it is important to keep the contribution of technology in perspective. Modern technology is available to all nations—rich and poor alike. Poor nations do not have to invest in research and development—they can emulate or import the proven technologies of the developed countries. Thus, the opportunity to grow by adopting improved technology is greater for poor developing countries than it is in high-income developed nations.

Technological advancement
The introduction of new techniques or methods of production that enable a greater output per unit of input.

Invention
The discovery of a new product or process, often facilitated by the knowledge of engineering and scientific relationships.

Innovation
The successful introduction and adoption of a new product or process; the economic application of inventions.

If technology were the primary factor limiting the creation of wealth, most all low-income countries would be growing more rapidly than developed nations. This is sometimes the case. As we will see in a moment, most of the countries with the highest growth rates were relatively poor just a few years ago. But rapid growth is not a general characteristic of low-income countries. Many poor countries continue to stagnate even though the proven technologies of high-income industrial countries are freely (or at a low cost) available to them.

EFFICIENT ECONOMIC ORGANIZATION

The efficiency with which the economic activity of a country is organized will influence the country's output and growth rate. If the economic organization of a nation encourages waste and fails to reward the creation of wealth, economic growth will be stunted.

Regardless of the form of economic organization present, certain basic conditions must be met if waste and inefficiency are to be avoided. The incentive structure must encourage production of the goods and services that are most desired by people (relative to their costs). **Allocative inefficiency** results when a nation's resources are used to produce the wrong products. For example, in a nation whose people need (intensely desire) more food and better housing, valuable resources might be used to produce unwanted national monuments and luxurious vacations for political leaders. In the same way, waste results when a nation ill-equipped to manufacture steel and automobiles insists on using resources that could be productive in other areas (for example, agriculture) to produce these prestige goods.

Efficient economic organization must also encourage producers to choose low-opportunity-cost methods of production. Regardless of whether an economy is centrally planned or market-directed, efficient production requires that the marginal productive contribution of each resource reflect its opportunity cost. Waste results when producers are discouraged from the adoption of the least-cost resource combination. For example, if unfavorable tax treatment or price controls distort prices and cause producers to choose higher-cost methods of production, the nation's production possibilities will be reduced.

The supply of public goods and goods that generate substantial external benefits is also an important ingredient of efficient economic organization. Broadly speaking, this issue relates to the provision of an economic **infrastructure,** a term used by economists to describe the economy's legal, monetary, educational, transportation, and communication structure. The provision of an adequate infrastructure involves several things. Foremost among these items would be: a legal system that clearly defines property rights, an educational system that encourages children of all social classes to develop their skills and abilities, and the development of highways, telephones, and power sources necessary for the realization of gains from specialization, division of labor, and mass-production methods. These networks often are provided by government, but each has also been provided privately since users can be made to pay for the benefits they receive through tolls and user charges. However they are provided, a sound infrastructure is an integral part of efficient economic organization.

Allocative inefficiency
The use of an uneconomical combination of resources to produce goods and services, or the use of resources to produce goods that are not intensely desired relative to their opportunity cost.

Infrastructure
The provision of a legal, monetary, educational, transportation, and communication structure necessary for the efficient operation of an exchange economy.

POLICIES THAT IMPROVE EFFICIENCY OF ECONOMIC ORGANIZATION

The efficiency of economic organization is not the result of happenstance or the forces of nature. It results from certain institutional arrangements and economic policies. Both economic theory and real-world experience suggest that six factors are beneficial:

1. Private ownership.
2. Competitive markets.
3. Stable money and prices.
4. International trade and an open economy.
5. An open capital market.
6. Avoidance of high marginal tax rates.

PRIVATE OWNERSHIP

So long as they do not invade or infringe upon the property rights of another, private owners have the legal right to use their property as they see fit. But this does not begin to tell the whole story. The important thing about private ownership is the incentive structure that emanates from it. Perhaps surprisingly to some, private ownership provides individuals with a strong incentive to consider the views of others—what it is that others value. Development and provision of goods and services that others value highly (relative to cost) will increase one's earnings potential. Moreover, private owners have an incentive to practice wise maintenance and conservation. If owners fail to maintain their assets properly, the value of those assets will fall and, so too, will the owner's wealth. Whenever the expected future value of a resource exceeds its current value, private owners can gain by conserving the resource for future users.

When the property rights of all citizens—including the vitally important property right to their labor—are clearly defined and securely enforced, trade replaces plunder as the means through which wealth is acquired. When this is true, people get ahead by helping and cooperating with others. Employers, for example, have to provide prospective employees and other resource suppliers with at least as good a deal as they can get elsewhere. Similarly, business owners have to provide potential customers with at least as much value for their consumer dollar as they could obtain from other businesses.

Throughout history, people have searched for and established other forms of ownership that they thought would be more humanitarian or more productive. These experiences have ranged from unsuccessful to disastrous. To date, we do not know of any alternative institutional arrangement that provides individuals with as much incentive to use resources productively and efficiently as private ownership.

COMPETITIVE MARKETS

Competition is a disciplining force for both buyers and sellers. In a competitive environment, producers must provide goods at a low cost and serve the interests of consumers since they will have to woo them away from other suppliers. Firms that develop improved products and figure out how to produce them at a low cost will succeed. Sellers that are unable to provide consumers with quality goods at competitive prices will be driven from the market. This process leads to improvement in both products and production methods, while directing resources toward projects where they are able to produce more value. It is a powerful stimulus for economic progress.

As Adam Smith stressed long ago, when competition is present, even self-interested individuals will tend to promote the general welfare. Conversely, when competition is weakened, business firms have more leeway to raise prices and pursue their own objectives and less incentive to innovate and develop better ways of doing things. Policies like free entry into businesses and occupations, and freedom of exchange with foreigners, will enhance competition and thereby help to promote economic progress. In contrast, policies like business subsidies, price controls, entry restraints, and trade restrictions stifle competition and conflict with economic progress.

STABLE MONEY AND PRICES

A stable monetary environment provides the foundation for the efficient operation of a market economy. In contrast, monetary and price instability make both the price level and relative prices unpredictable, generate uncertainty, and undermine the security of contractual exchanges. When prices increase 20 percent this year, 50 percent the next year, 15 percent the year after that, and so on, individuals and businesses are unable to develop sensible long-term plans. The uncertainty will reduce the attractiveness of time-dimension exchanges, particularly investment decisions. Rather than dealing with the uncertainties that accompany double- and triple-digit inflation rates, citizens will save less, while many investors and business decision makers will move their activities to countries with a more stable environment. Foreigners will invest elsewhere, and citizens will often go to great lengths to get their savings (potential funds for investment) out of the country. As a result, potential gains from capital formation and business activities will be lost.

INTERNATIONAL TRADE AND AN OPEN ECONOMY

In the absence of trade barriers, producers in various countries will be directed toward those areas where they have a comparative advantage, and the competition from abroad will help keep domestic producers on their toes. International trade allows the residents of each country to use more of their resources to produce and sell things that they do well and use the proceeds to purchase goods that could be produced domestically only at a high cost. As a result, the trading partners are each able to produce a larger output and purchase a wider variety of products at more economical prices than would otherwise be possible.

Policies that retard international trade stifle this process and thereby retard economic progress. Obviously, tariffs and quotas fall into this category since they limit the ability of domestic citizens to trade with people in other countries. So, too, do exchange-rate controls. When a nation fixes the exchange-rate value of its currency above the market level, the country's export products will be unattractive to foreigners. But if domestic citizens sell less to foreigners, they will have less foreign currency with which to buy from foreigners. Thus, exchange-rate controls will reduce the volume of both exports and imports. Like other policies that stifle trade, exchange-rate controls will retard economic progress.

OPEN CAPITAL MARKET

If investment is going to increase the wealth of a nation, capital must be channeled into productive projects. When the value of the additional output derived from an investment exceeds the cost of the investment, the project will increase wealth. In contrast, if the value of the additional output is worth less than the cost of the investment, undertaking the project will reduce the wealth of the nation. If a nation is going to realize its potential, it must have a mechanism capable of attracting savings and channeling them into wealth-creating projects. A competitive capital market performs this function.

When a nation's capital market is integrated with the world capital market, it will be able to attract savings (financial capital) from throughout the world at the cheapest possible price (interest rate). Similarly, its citizens will have access to the most attractive investment opportunities regardless of where they are located.

In a competitive capital market, private investors have a strong incentive to evaluate projects carefully and allocate their funds toward those projects expected to yield the highest rates of return. In turn, profitable projects will tend to increase the wealth of not only the investor, but also that of the nation. Without a capital market, it will be virtually impossible to attract funds and consistently allocate them into wealth-creating projects. If investment funds are allocated by governments rather than the capital market, political clout rather than the expected rate of return will determine which investment projects are undertaken. And when politics replaces economic considerations, more unprofitable and counterproductive investment projects will predictably be undertaken.

The experience of Eastern Europe and the former Soviet Union highlights the importance of a capital market. For four decades (1950–1990), the investment rates (as a share of GDP) of these countries were among the highest in the world. The central planners of these countries channeled approximately one-third of GDP into investment. Even these high rates of investment, however, did little to improve living standards. Without the direction of a capital market, the investment funds were often directed toward political and military projects favored by the planners rather than projects that would increase the future availability of consumer goods.

Similarly, when governments fix interest rates, they hamper the ability of the capital market to bring savers and investors together and channel funds into wealth-creating projects. Worse still, when the fixed interest rates are combined with inflationary monetary policy in a manner that leads to negative interest rates, the incentive to supply funds to the domestic capital market will be eliminated. The result is "capital flight" as domestic investors seek positive returns abroad and foreign investors completely shun the country's potential investment projects. Lacking both financial capital and a mechanism to direct funds toward wealth-creating projects, productive investments in such countries will come to a standstill. Clearly, such policies reduce the efficiency of economic organization.

AVOIDANCE OF HIGH MARGINAL TAX RATES

When high marginal tax rates take a large share of the fruits generated by productive activities, the incentive of individuals to work and undertake business projects is reduced. High tax rates may also drive a nation's most productive citizens to other countries where taxes are lower and discourage foreigners from financing domestic investment projects. In short, economic theory indicates that high marginal tax rates will retard productive activity, capital formation, and economic growth.

The most detailed study of the impact of high marginal tax rates on the economic growth of LDCs has been conducted by Alvin Rabushka of Stanford University.[4] Rabushka undertook the tedious task of reconstructing the 1960–1982 tax structure for 54 LDCs for which data could be obtained. He found that some countries levied very high marginal tax rates, which took effect only at very high income thresholds. Others levied high marginal rates on even modest levels of income. A few countries imposed only low or medium tax rates.

Rabushka found that the countries that kept marginal tax rates low generally experienced more rapid economic growth. He summarized his findings as follows:

> Good economic policy, including tax policy, fosters economic growth and rising prosperity. In particular, low marginal income tax rates, or high thresholds for medium- and high-rate tax schedules, appear consistent with higher growth rates. The key in any system of direct taxation is to maintain low tax rates or high (income) thresholds.[5]

Exhibit 33–3 presents data similar to that used by Rabushka in his study. The developing countries with the highest and lowest top marginal rates during the 1980s are included in the table. Several developing countries imposed exceedingly high marginal tax rates and applied them at a very low income level. For example, Zambia, Tanzania, Zaire, Ghana, and Uganda levied marginal tax rates of 50 percent or more beginning at an equivalent income level of less than $10,000 (1982–1984 dollars). Among the ten high-tax countries, only one (Morocco) was able to achieve a positive growth rate of per capita GDP during the 1980–1991 period. The average annual change in GDP of the high-tax countries was −0.6 percent.

---

[4]See Alvin Rabushka, "Taxation, Economic Growth, and Liberty," *Cato Journal,* Spring–Summer, 1987, pp. 121–148.

[5]Alvin Rabushka, "Taxation and Liberty in the Third World," paper presented at conference on "Taxation and Liberty," Santa Fe, New Mexico, September 26–27, 1985.

EXHIBIT 33–3

GROWTH RATE OF DEVELOPING COUNTRIES WITH HIGHEST AND LOWEST MARGINAL TAX RATES

	TOP MARGINAL RATE		ANNUAL GROWTH RATE OF PER CAPITA GDP,
	1984	1989	1980–1991
High-Tax Countries			
Iran	90	75	−1.4
Morocco	87	87	1.6
Zambia	80	75[a]	−2.8
Dominican Republic	73	73	−0.5
Tanzania	95	50[a]	−0.1
Zimbabwe	63	60	−0.3
Zaire	60[a]	60[a]	−2.3
Cameroon	60	60	−1.4
Ghana	60[a]	55[a]	0.0
Uganda	70[a]	50[a]	−0.5
Average Growth Rate			**−0.8**
Low-Tax Countries			
Uruguay	0	0	0.0
Hong Kong	25	25	5.7
Paraguay	30	30	−0.4
Mauritius	30	35	5.7
Indonesia	35	35	3.8
Singapore	40	33	4.9
Colombia	49	30	1.7
Guatemala	48	34	−1.8
Malaysia	45	45	3.1
Honduras	46	46	−0.6
Average Growth Rate			**2.2**

[a]Indicates that the top rate applied at an equivalent income level of less than $10,000.

Source: The marginal tax rate data are from Price Waterhouse, *Individual Tax Rates, 1984 and 1989* (New York: Price Waterhouse, 1991). The growth-rate data are from the World Bank, *World Development Report*, (Oxford: Oxford University Press, 1993).

Among the low-tax countries, the average growth of per capita GDP was 2.3 percent. Five of the nine low-tax countries experienced a growth rate of 3 percent or more, while three (Paraguay, Honduras, and Guatemala) experienced declines in per capita GDP. The data in Exhibit 33–3 indicate that low taxes alone will not guarantee economic growth. As we have stressed throughout, sustained economic growth reflects the joint contribution of several factors. However, the rapid growth of a majority of the low-tax countries, along with the extremely poor performance of the high-tax countries does suggest that marginal tax rates—particularly when they are quite high—influence the magnitude of economic growth.

POLICIES OF HIGH-GROWTH VERSUS STAGNATING ECONOMIES

Policy can influence growth, either for good or ill, in many ways. The task is thus to try to exploit as many as possible of these avenues for good.

ARNOLD C. HARBERGER[6]

The accompanying "Thumbnail Sketch" summarizes the three major sources of economic growth and six key elements that influence the efficiency of resource use. Other factors may also be important—remember, we do not have a complete theory of economic growth. Some countries may be able to grow while following policies that conflict with some of the key elements we present. In other cases, perhaps even sound policies will fail. There is no single recipe that will work in all instances.

Nonetheless, as Professor Harberger points out, policies do matter—they influence the growth and prosperity of nations. Countries that consistently follow policies that harmonize with the key elements of economic growth and efficient resource use greatly enhance the likelihood that they will prosper. Conversely, nations adopting policies that conflict with several of these key ingredients will tend to experience stagnation and poverty.

Exhibit 33–4 and **Exhibit 33–5** present data on the population and per capita GDP in 1991 for the high- and low-growth countries of the 1980–1990 period. Both the World Bank and the estimates developed for the United Nations by Summers

THUMBNAIL SKETCH

WHAT ARE THE SOURCES OF ECONOMIC GROWTH AND THE POLICIES THAT ENHANCE ECONOMIC EFFICIENCY?

Sources of Economic Growth

1. Investment in physical and human capital.
2. Advancements in technology.
3. Improvements in the efficiency of economic organization.

Key Policies Enhancing Efficiency of Economic Organization

1. Private ownership.
2. Competitive markets.
3. Stable money and prices.
4. Free trade.
5. Open capital markets.
6. Avoidance of high marginal tax rates.

---

[6]Arnold C. Harberger, *Economic Policy and Economic Growth* (San Francisco: International Center for Economic Growth, 1985), p. 8.

EXHIBIT 33-4

COUNTRIES WITH BEST GROWTH RECORD, 1980–1990

COUNTRY	POPULATION (IN MILLIONS)	PER CAPITA GDP, 1991	ANNUAL GROWTH OF PER CAPITA GDP, 1980–1990	
			WORLD BANK	SUMMERS-HESTON
Asia				
China	1133.7	2,946	8.1	6.8
Hong Kong	5.8	19,397	5.7	5.1
Japan	123.5	19,290	3.5	3.2
Pakistan	112.4	1,702	3.2	3.6
Singapore	3.0	14,734	4.2	5.4
S. Korea	42.8	7,485	8.6	6.9
Thailand	55.8	4,600	5.8	4.9
Taiwan	20.0	7,550	—	5.4
Africa				
Botswana	1.3	3,662	8.0	4.1
Mauritius	1.1	2,178	5.0	3.8
Europe				
Malta	0.4	7,575	3.7	4.5
Average Growth Rate			**5.6**	**4.9**

Source: The population and World Bank growth-rate data are from the World Bank, *World Development Report, 1992.* The per capita GDP data were supplied to the authors by Robert Summers and Alan Heston. The growth-rate data of Summers and Heston are from Summers and Heston, "The Penn World Table (Mark 5): An Expanded Set of International Comparisons, 1950–1988," *Quarterly Journal of Economics,* May 1991. The growth-rate data were updated by the authors. Growth-rate data from both sources are presented. All countries with an annual growth rate of per capita GDP of 3 percent or more as measured by both sources are included.

and Heston indicate that the per capita GDP of the 11 countries of Exhibit 33–4 grew at an annual rate of 3 percent or more during the 1980s. In many ways these countries are quite diverse. Only three (Hong Kong, Japan, and Singapore) are high-income countries. The per capita income in China, Pakistan, and Botswana is still less than $3,000 despite rapid economic growth. In terms of population, several (Hong Kong, Singapore, Botswana, Mauritius, and Malta) of the high-growth countries are quite small. Others (China, Japan, and Pakistan) are large. Eight are Asian countries, while only one—the small island nation of Malta—is European.

Exhibit 33–5 presents similar data for the 17 countries with the poorest growth record during 1980–1990. Both the World Bank and Summers-Heston estimate that the per capita GDP of these countries *declined* by 1 percent or more annually during 1980–1990. While none are high-income countries at this point, several had relatively high incomes at one time. Even after a decade of declining income, the per capita GDP of two—Mexico and Venezuela—exceeded $6,500 in 1991. As in

EXHIBIT 33–5

COUNTRIES WITH POOREST GROWTH RECORD, 1980–1990

COUNTRY	POPULATION (IN MILLIONS)	PER CAPITA GDP, 1991	ANNUAL GROWTH OF PER CAPITA GDP, 1980–1990	
			WORLD BANK	SUMMERS-HESTON
Africa				
Ivory Coast	11.9	1,185	–3.3	–4.4
Ethiopia	51.2	365	–1.3	–1.3
Madagascar	1.7	733	–1.9	–3.4
Mozambique	15.7	921	–3.3	–4.9
Niger	7.7	541	–4.6	–3.3
Nigeria	115.5	929	–1.8	–3.8
Rwanda	7.1	738	–2.3	–1.8
Zaire	37.3	469	–1.4	–1.1
Zambia	8.1	983	–2.9	–3.2
Latin America				
Argentina	32.3	4,603	–1.7	–2.0
Bolivia	7.2	1,940	–2.6	–2.9
Guatemala	9.2	2,562	–2.1	–1.6
Haiti	6.5	925	–2.5	–2.2
Mexico	86.2	6,776	–1.0	–1.2
Peru	21.7	2,484	–2.6	–3.0
Venezuela	19.7	7,452	–1.7	–3.0
Other				
Syria	12.4	5,225	–1.5	–2.2
Average Growth Rate			**–2.3**	**–2.7**

Source: The population and World Bank growth-rate data are from the World Bank, *World Development Report, 1992*. The per capita GDP data were supplied to the authors by Robert Summers and Alan Heston. The growth-rate data of Summers and Heston are from Summers and Heston, "The Penn World Table (Mark 5): An Expanded Set of International Comparisons, 1950–1988," *Quarterly Journal of Economics,* May 1991. The data were updated to 1990 by the authors. Growth-rate data from both sources are presented. All countries for which both sources indicate a negative annual growth rate of per capita GDP of 1 percent or more during the period are included.

the case of the high-growth countries, both large countries (such as Nigeria and Mexico) and small countries are included among the stagnating economies.

On average, the per capita income of the high-income economies increased at an annual rate of almost 5 percent, while that of the stagnating economies declined by more than 2 percent annually during the 1980–1990 period. Over the entire 11 years, the per capita income of the high-growth economies rose by approximately 70 percent while that of the stagnating economies fell by more than 30 percent.

If the factors presented in the "Thumbnail Sketch" are really important, we should find that the high-growth countries followed policies that harmonized

ARE RICH COUNTRIES GETTING RICHER AND POOR COUNTRIES POORER?

Three centuries ago, most people in every country of the world spent their entire lives trying to eke out a living that was barely above the subsistence level. Sustained economic growth has changed this situation dramatically throughout most of Europe, North America, Oceania, Japan, and a few other spots around the world.

Observing the income differences between the wealthy industrial nations and LDCs, some have argued that the rich are consistently getting richer while the poor are getting poorer. As the growth-rate data of Exhibits 33–4 and 33–5 illustrate, this view is, at best, an oversimplification. The LDCs are not a monolithic block of low-income, slow-growth countries. Except for Japan, all of the rapid-growth countries of Exhibit 33–4 are LDCs, or at least they were a couple of decades ago. The growth of per capita income during the last decade (and in most cases during the last two decades) in China, South Korea, Singapore, Hong Kong, Thailand, Taiwan, Pakistan, Botswana, Mauritius, and Malta has exceeded the growth rates of the wealthy developed countries of Europe and North America. The growth rate of other LDCs, including Indonesia, Egypt, and India, have also generally exceeded the growth of per capita income of the industrial countries. In varying degrees, the economic status of people in these countries is improving.

Unfortunately, as Exhibit 33–5 illustrates, there is another group of LDCs that are not growing. All 17 of the countries that experienced negative growth rates of 1 percent or more during the 1980s were LDCs. Per capita incomes in Ethiopia, Zaire, Uganda, Ghana,

Nicaragua, and Bolivia were actually lower in 1991 than in 1965. The twentieth century has passed by the people of these countries. Like their ancestors for centuries, they spend their lives struggling for the necessities.

The picture that emerges is one of diversity. Some LDCs are growing rapidly and closing the gap relative to their counterparts in wealthier countries. At the same time, others are doing very poorly and falling farther and farther behind. These views are reflected in the findings of a recent study covering a more lengthy time period by Stephen Parente of Northeastern University and Edward Prescott of the University of Minnesota.[1] Summarizing their study of changes in the wealth of nations during the 1960–1985 period, Parente and Prescott concluded:

- *Wealth disparity has not increased or decreased. The distance between the richest and poorest countries remained essentially the same throughout the 1960–1985 period.*
- *The wealth distribution shifted up: the richer got richer, but the poor did, too. Therefore, no absolute poverty trap exists.*
- *There have been development miracles and disasters. During the 1960–1985 period, 10 countries increased their wealth relative to the wealthy leaders by a factor of 2 or more. These miracles were matched by an equal number of development disasters: during the same period, the relative wealth of another 10 countries decreased by a factor of about 2.*

[1]Stephen L. Parente and Edward C. Prescott, "Changes in the Wealth of Nations" *Quarterly Review: Federal Reserve Bank of Minneapolis*, Spring 1993, pp. 3–16.

with growth and prosperity more consistently than the low-growth countries. Unfortunately, some of the factors are difficult to quantify. For example, we do not have a precise measure of how the security of property rights or the competitiveness of markets varies across countries.

In some cases, however, it is possible to quantify important policy variables and determine their consistency with economic prosperity. **Exhibit 33–6** provides data on several policy indicators for both the high-growth and low-growth countries during the 1980s. First, look at the inflation-rate data. As we have previously shown, inflation is closely linked with monetary expansion. Countries experience high inflation rates because they finance government expenditures with

EXHIBIT 33-6

INFLATION, TARIFFS, EXCHANGE RATES, INTEREST RATES, AND INVESTMENT
IN HIGH- VERSUS LOW-GROWTH COUNTRIES, 1980s

	AVERAGE ANNUAL INFLATION RATE	AVERAGE TARIFF RATE[a]		BLACK-MARKET EXCHANGE-RATE PREMIUM		AVERAGE REAL INTEREST RATE		INVESTMENT AS A SHARE OF GDP
	1980–1990	1985	1989	1985	1988	1983–1985	1988–1990	1980–1990
High-Growth Countries								
China	5.8	—	—	9	168	—	—	35.5
Hong Kong	7.2	0.00	0.00	0	0	2.2	–1.3	26.5
Japan	1.5	0.72	0.71	0	0	2.5	1.1	30.2
Pakistan	6.9	15.11	16.07	4	10	1.9	–1.6	18.7
Singapore	1.7	0.36	0.18	0	0	4.1	0.1	41.5
S. Korea	5.3	3.55	2.96	11	10	4.9	3.4	29.9
Thailand	4.2	6.48	5.24	3	1	11.5	4.8	26.4
Taiwan	3.1	2.80	2.16	3	1	5.5	4.2	21.0
Botswana	12.1	7.60	6.21	22	53	0.9	–14.0	27.1
Mauritius	8.8	9.64	8.18	1	3	2.5	1.5	24.2
Malta	6.2	4.46	5.30	7	3	4.6	1.7	28.2
Median	5.3	4.00	4.13	3	3	3.3	1.3	27.1
Low-Growth Countries								
Ivory Coast	2.7	9.70	9.70	1	2	0.2	4.6	16.5
Ethiopia	2.1	13.27	13.72	122	226	—	2.2	12.0
Madagascar	17.1	8.50	12.46	9	16	—	—	11.2
Mozambique	36.5	—	—	4108	104	—	—	20.5
Niger	3.3	8.40	—	1	2	0.2	4.0	13.8
Nigeria	18.2	5.09	4.00	270	87	–3.1	–15.0	17.1
Rwanda	3.8	13.30	—	49	30	–1.8	3.4	15.4
Zaire	60.9	8.51	9.81	6	15	—	—	15.7
Zambia	42.3	6.69	4.20	38	900	–16.2	–77.2	15.3
Argentina	395.1	12.46	7.00	40	50	–163.6	–1178.9	13.5
Bolivia	318.4	5.24	2.74	9	6	–4240.6	—	12.2
Guatemala	14.6	7.47	8.01	89	28	–0.8	–5.9	13.3
Haiti	7.2	8.03	6.70	60	151	—	—	13.2
Mexico	70.4	2.56	3.03	25	15	–14.6	–6.5	21.8
Peru	233.7	8.82	4.95	51	240	–101.1	—	21.0
Venezuela	19.3	8.97	2.75	25	0	–2.6	–28.3	19.6
Syria	14.7	5.63	3.40	251	354	—	—	20.7
Median	18.2	8.45	5.83	40	30	–3.1	–1.8	15.4

[a]Taxes on international trade as a percent of exports plus imports.

Source: Derived from World Bank, *World Development Report: 1992* (and various earlier issues); *World Tables, 1992;* The International Monetary Fund, *Government Finance Statistics Yearbook, 1992;* and International Currency Analysis, *The World Currency Yearbook, 1989–90.*

"printing-press" money. Except for Botswana, which had an inflation rate of 12.1 percent, the average annual inflation rate during the 1980s was less than 10 percent in each of the high-growth countries. The *median* (meaning the middle, the point where 50 percent are higher and 50 percent are lower) annual inflation rate of the high-growth countries was 5.3 percent, compared to 18.2 percent for the low-growth countries. Five of the 17 low-growth countries (Ivory Coast, Ethiopia, Niger, Rwanda, and Haiti) also experienced single-digit inflation rates during the 1980s. The other 12 low-growth countries, however, followed policies of monetary expansion that led to inflation. In seven of the low-growth countries, excessive monetary expansion caused severe inflation during the 1980s. The annual inflation rates of Mozambique, Zaire, Zambia, and Mexico ranged from 36.5 percent to 70.4 percent. Three of the low-growth countries (Argentina, Bolivia, and Peru) experienced triple-digit average annual rates of inflation during the 1980s. Clearly, inflation rates at this level generate enormous uncertainty and undermine the usefulness of information provided by the pricing system.

How open were the economies of the high- and low-growth countries during the 1980s? Exhibit 33–6 also presents data on tariff rates and exchange-rate controls (the black-market exchange-rate premium) that shed light on this question. Of course, high tariffs tend to discriminate against foreign producers and reduce the volume of international trade. Similarly, exchange-rate controls restrict trade because they make it more difficult for domestic citizens to get their hands on the foreign currencies. In turn, the controls lead to black markets. The more restrictive the exchange-rate controls, the larger the black-market premium that must be paid to obtain foreign currencies, and the greater the negative impact on the volume of international trade.

Compared to the low-growth countries, both the tariff rates and the black-market exchange-rate premiums were substantially lower in the high-growth countries. The tariff rates of Hong Kong, Japan, and Singapore were exceedingly small, less than 1 percent of the volume of their international trade during the 1980s. Among the high-growth countries, only Pakistan had an average tax rate on international trade of more than 10 percent. In contrast, only Mexico among the 17 low-growth countries, had an average tariff rate that was less than the median for the high-growth countries during both 1985 and 1989. On average, the tariff rates of the low-growth countries were approximately 50 percent higher than the rates for the high-growth countries.

The differences in the black-market exchange-rate premiums are even more dramatic. Six of the low-growth countries (Ethiopia, Mozambique, Zambia, Haiti, Peru, and Syria) had a black-market exchange-rate premium that exceeded 100 percent in 1988; it was between 15 percent and 87 percent in 7 other low-growth countries (Madagascar, Nigeria, Rwanda, Zaire, Argentina, Guatemala, and Mexico). Among the high-growth countries, only China and Botswana imposed exchange controls resulting in black-market premiums in this range. The premium was consistently less than 10 percent in 7 of the 11 high-growth countries, but only 3 (Ivory Coast, Niger, and Bolivia) of the 17 low-growth countries.

Taken together, the data on tariffs and black-market exchange rates indicate that the economies of the high-growth countries were considerably more open than those of the low-growth countries. Only one (Bolivia) of the 17 low-growth countries had *both* an average tariff rate of less than 8 percent and a black-market exchange rate premium of less than 12 percent. In contrast, 7 of the 11 high-growth countries followed policies that achieved these results.

Finally, Exhibit 33–6 also presents data on capital markets—interest rates and investment as a share of GDP—for each country. If a country's capital market is well integrated with the world capital market, its real interest rate will be near the world rate—approximately 1 percent to 5 percent throughout most of the 1980s. On the other hand, if the country imposes interest-rate controls and follows inflationary policies, its real interest rate may differ substantially from the world rate. With the exception of Botswana during 1988–1990, the real interest rate of the high-growth countries did not differ much from the world rate. In contrast, 7 of the 12 low-growth countries (Nigeria, Zambia, Argentina, Bolivia, Mexico, Peru, and Venezuela) for which the data were available, had double-digit *negative* real interest rates at various times throughout the 1980s. This indicates that these countries were following policies that disrupted their capital markets and restricted the flow of funds between savers and investors.

Perhaps the most dramatic difference between the high- and low-growth countries involves the rate of investment.[7] The median investment rate as a share of GDP in the high-growth countries was 27.1 percent, compared to 15.4 percent in the low-growth countries. Only two (Pakistan and Taiwan) of the 11 high-growth countries had an average investment rate of less than 24 percent of their GDP during the 1980–1990 period. In contrast, none of the 17 low-growth countries invested as much as 22 percent of their GDP during the same period. Only four of the low-growth countries were able even to match the investment rate (18.7 percent of GDP) of Pakistan, the lowest investment rate among the high-growth countries.

With regard to capital markets and investment, the data of Exhibit 33–6 are clear. Countries that grow rapidly tend to (1) utilize capital markets to allocate saving and investment and (2) invest a large share of their GDP. Conversely, the low-growth countries generally invest a much smaller portion of their GDP and they often follow monetary and capital market policies that result in negative real interest rates.

The data of Exhibit 33–6 shed light on the process of economic growth. The high-growth countries have not done everything right. Neither have the low-growth countries—at least not all of them—done everything wrong. A pattern, however, emerges. Compared to the low-growth countries, the high-growth countries have tended to follow monetary policies more consistent with price stability, and they have imposed lower tariff rates, maintained the convertibility of their currency, and allowed capital markets to attract savings and allocate investment. Economic analysis indicates that these are key elements of growth and prosperity. Political decision makers seeking to promote prosperity should take heed.

We previously noted that the growth rates of Hong Kong and Japan during the last three decades were quite rapid, while the income per capita grew much more slowly in Argentina and Venezuela. Exhibit 33–6 helps to explain why this was the case. Hong Kong and Japan have generally followed policies consistent

---

[7]While our data have focused on investments in physical capital, a recent study by the World Bank found that the high-growth countries of East Asia also invested heavily in elementary and secondary education. For example, Indonesia, South Korea, and Thailand allocated more than 80 percent of their educational spending to elementary and secondary education in the mid-1980s. By way of comparison, Argentina devoted less than 50 percent of its educational spending to basic education during the same time period. See World Bank, *The East Asian Miracle* (Washington, DC, The World Bank, 1993).

with prosperity and growth. In contrast, throughout the 1980s Argentina and Venezuela (1) followed policies of monetary expansion that fueled inflation, (2) imposed high tariffs and exchange controls that have restricted trade, and (3) fixed interest rates at levels that have resulted in negative real interest rates and low rates of capital investment. In contrast with the policies of Japan and Hong Kong, those of Argentina and Venezuela often conflicted with growth and prosperity.

LESSONS FOR DEVELOPING COUNTRIES

As Adam Smith noted more than two centuries ago, the wealth of nations is crucially dependent upon gains from (1) specialization and trade, (2) expansion in the size of the market, and (3) the discovery of better ways of doing things. Governments that respect property rights and freedom of exchange while following monetary (and fiscal) policies consistent with relatively stable prices establish the foundation for economic growth. This is the strategy that resulted in the "economic miracles" of West Germany and Japan following World War II. It is also the strategy followed by the growth economies of the 1980s.

In contrast with this approach, governments around the world have often used price controls, trade restraints, regulations, industrial subsidies, and government planning in an effort to promote growth. In addition, governments have often followed expansionary monetary policies that have generated double- and even triple-digit inflation rates. Many governments have also levied high marginal tax rates, which in turn discourage production and drive both capital and productive citizens elsewhere. In varying degrees, these types of policies plague almost all poor countries. They constitute a strategy that doesn't work. And countries that follow this course will continue to experience poverty and economic stagnation.

Increasingly, there is evidence that several developing countries are beginning to take note of the differences between the policies followed by the high-growth and low-growth countries. Several LDCs have adopted major policy changes in recent years. Among Latin American countries, Chile began shifting away from policies of monetary expansion, price controls, and trade restrictions in the 1980s. The annual inflation rate in Chile during the 1980s was approximately 20 percent, down from 130 percent during the 1970s. Tariff rates were cut; the top marginal tax rate was reduced from 80 percent to 50 percent; interest rates and exchange rate controls were eliminated; and several state enterprises were privatized during the 1980s. The result? In recent years, Chile has become the growth economy of Latin America. While most Latin American economies stagnated, the real GDP of Chile expanded at an average annual rate of 6.5 percent during the 1984–1992 period.

Beginning in the late 1980s, both Mexico and Argentina began emulating the course followed by Chile. Both shifted toward substantially more restrictive monetary policies that decelerated their inflation rates. Both reduced tariffs sharply, relaxed exchange rate controls, sliced high marginal tax rates, and began privatizing various government enterprises. While it is too early to fully assess the results

GROWTH RATE OF CHINA

Some may be surprised to find China among the high-growth countries of Exhibit 33–4. After all, isn't China a centrally planned socialist economy that has generally followed policies inconsistent with growth and prosperity?

When considering the recent growth of China, it is important to keep two points in mind. First, China has taken several important steps toward economic liberalization in recent years. The initial reforms adopted in the late 1970s focused on agriculture, a sector of the economy encompassing nearly three-fourths of the Chinese work force. The collective farms were dismantled and replaced with what the Chinese refer to as a "contract responsibility system." Under this organizational form, individual families are permitted to lease land for up to 15 years in exchange for supplying the state with a fixed amount of production at a designated price (which is generally below the market price). Amounts produced over and above the required quota belong to the individual farmers, and they may either be directly consumed or sold at a free market price. Even though the legal ownership remains with the state, this system of long-term land leases provides farmers with something akin to a private property right and low marginal rates of taxation. Over and above the fixed quota, the farmers get to keep everything that they produce. Thus, at high rates of productivity the farmer's marginal tax rate is zero. Clearly, this system provides farmers with a strong incentive to increase output.

Other reforms were adopted that enhanced the development of markets in agricultural products. Restrictions on individual stock breeding, household sideline occupations, transport of agricultural goods, and trade fairs (marketplaces) were removed. Farmers were permitted to own tractors and trucks, and even hire laborers to work in their "leased" fields. By the late 1980s, less than 15 percent of the grain (rice, wheat, and barley) produced in China was turned over to the state. The rest was marketed privately.

The success in agriculture encouraged reforms in other sectors. Restrictions on the operation of small-scale service and retail businesses were relaxed. Private restaurants, stores, and repair shops sprang up and began to compete with state-operated enterprises.

Restraints on both trade and joint ventures with foreigners have also been relaxed. By the mid-1980s, Chinese cities were teeming with sidewalk vendors, restaurants, small retail businesses, and hundreds of thousands of individuals providing personal services. After losing their monopoly position, even state enterprises began to stay open longer and pay more attention to serving their customers. In the late 1980s China began to take steps toward greater reliance on markets in the production and distribution of industrial products and allow far greater freedom for private firms to compete in these areas. No doubt, these moves toward liberalization have contributed substantially to the recent growth of the Chinese economy.

However, there may be a second factor at work here: the growth-rate data of China may be significantly overstated. Clearly, this was the case for the former Soviet Union and the countries of Eastern Europe during the 1970s and 1980s. Since centrally planned economies do not rely on product prices to allocate goods and services, output is measured by the physical quantities of goods produced and inputs used. These factors may be a highly unreliable indicator of the value of what is actually being produced. As China has moved away from a command/barter economy in recent years toward greater reliance on prices, some productive activities that were not counted (or were counted only at a depressed level) are now being counted as part of GDP. Similarly, as the monetary exchange sector of the economy grows relative to the household sector, the growth of GDP will be exaggerated.

Finally, some suspect that the GDP estimates may be overstated because, to a degree, they involve an extrapolation of the more reliable and readily available output data from the coastal provinces across from Hong Kong. Certainly, this part of China has achieved extraordinary growth during the last 15 years. But China is a huge, diverse country, and these coastal provinces contain only about 15 percent of its population. Thus, projections for the entire country based on this area may be highly distorted. As the result of all of these factors, most economists believe that the income estimates for China should be interpreted with caution.

of these changes, the early returns are encouraging. In contrast with the 1980s, the economies of both Mexico and Argentina were growing in the early 1990s.

Several LDCs now appear more receptive to sound policies than at any other time in the recent past. In addition, the formerly communist countries of Eastern Europe and Asia are instituting changes and searching for forms of economic organization more consistent with growth and prosperity. The dynamic forces of economic change will make the 1990s an exciting time to study economics and apply its basic principles.

LOOKING AHEAD

For more than four decades the economies of most countries in Eastern Europe were centrally planned. In the case of the countries of the former Soviet Union, central economic planning has an even longer history. In the next chapter, we will use economic tools to analyze centrally planned economies and consider the problems that arise when a socialist country attempts to move toward a market-directed economy.

CHAPTER SUMMARY

1. Most income comparisons across countries are derived by the exchange-rate conversion method. Since this method reflects the exchange-rate value of a currency rather than its purchasing power over a broad range of goods and services, income comparisons derived by it are often unreliable.

2. The purchasing-power parity method uses data on the cost of purchasing a typical bundle of consumer goods and services to determine the relative purchasing power of each currency and estimate the GDP of each nation in terms of a common currency. Most economists believe that income comparisons derived by this method provide a more accurate measure of income levels and living standards across countries.

3. Most of the poorest countries—those with a per capita annual GDP of less than $1,200—are located in Africa. Most of the high-income countries are located in North America, Europe, Oceania, and East Asia (Japan and Hong Kong).

4. Income comparisons based on the exchange-rate conversion method generally understate the income of less developed countries relative to the income of industrial countries. As the cases of India and China indicate, oftentimes this understatement is substantial.

5. The availability of domestic natural resources is not the major determinant of growth. Countries such as Japan and Hong Kong have impressive growth rates without such resources, while many resource-rich nations continue to stagnate.

6. Economic growth is a complex process. While economists have been unable to develop a general theory of economic growth and development, three major sources of economic progress have been pinpointed: (a) investment in physical and human capital, (b) development and dissemination of technologically improved production methods and products, and (c) efficient economic organization.

7. Economic policies influence the efficiency of economic organization. In general, private ownership, competitive markets, monetary stability, international trade, integration into the world capital market, and avoidance of high taxes will enhance the efficiency of economic organization.

8. Countries that have grown rapidly during the 1980s generally followed a stable monetary policy, imposed few restrictions on international trade, relied on markets to determine exchange and interest rates, and invested a large portion of their GDP. In contrast, stagnating economies were characterized by rapid monetary expansion, high inflation rates, high tariffs, exchange and interest rate controls, and low rates of investment.

9. As Adam Smith noted more than 200 years ago, the wealth of nations is dependent upon gains from (a) specialization and trade, (b) expansion in the size of the market, and (c) the discovery of better (more productive) ways of doing things. Governments that respect property rights, protect the freedom of exchange, and follow monetary and fiscal policies consistent with a stable price level help provide the framework for the creation of wealth. In contrast, governments retard economic progress when policies are adopted that restrict trade, generate uncertainty, undermine property rights, and reduce competition.

10. There is substantial diversity among LDCs. Most of the countries with the highest growth rates in recent decades were low-income LDCs in the 1960s. On the other hand, the nations that have experienced negative growth rates in recent decades are also LDCs.

CRITICAL-ANALYSIS QUESTIONS

1. How do the exchange-rate conversion and purchasing-power parity methods differ as tools for comparing relative incomes among countries? Which is the most widely cited in the popular news media? Why? Which is the most reliable? Why?

*2. If is often argued that the rich nations are getting richer and the poor are getting poorer. Is this view correct? Is it an oversimplification? Explain.

*3. "Without aid from the industrial nations, poor countries are caught in the poverty trap. Because they are poor, they are unable to save and invest; and lacking investment, they remain poor." Evaluate this view.

4. Imagine you are an economic adviser to the president of Mexico. You have been asked to suggest policies to promote economic growth and a higher standard of living for the citizens of Mexico. Outline your suggestions, and discuss their rationale.

5. Evaluate each of the following policies in terms of its impact on the growth and prosperity of a nation.
   a. Adoption of a regulation that would limit foreign ownership of domestic businesses.
   b. Imposition of a surtax on the corporate profits of foreign firms operating in the country.
   c. A 50 percent increase in tariff rates.
   d. Adoption of a minimum wage equal to 50 percent of the country's average hourly wage.
   e. Legislation requiring employers to provide health care for all of their employees.
   f. Legislation requiring employers to provide one year of severance pay to any employee who is dismissed from employment.

6. Discuss the importance of the following as determinants of economic growth: (a) natural resources; (b) physical capital; (c) human capital; (d) technical knowledge; (e) attitudes of the work force; (f) size of the domestic market; and (g) economic policy.

*7. Do you think that the absence of international trade barriers would be more important for a small country like Costa Rica than for a larger country like Mexico? Explain.

8. "Since government-operated firms do not have to make a profit, they can usually produce at a lower cost and charge a lower price than privately-owned enterprises." Evaluate this view.

9. "Governments can promote economic growth by using taxes and subsidies to direct investment funds toward high-tech, heavy manufacturing, and other growth industries that will enhance the future income of the nation." Evaluate this view.

10. If the investment funds of a country are going to promote prosperity, they must be directed toward the production of goods that are valued more highly than the resources used in their production. Why is this important? Will additional investment always increase the wealth of a nation? Explain.

---

*Asterisk denotes questions for which answers are given in Appendix C.

CHAPTER THIRTY-FOUR

ECONOMIES IN TRANSITION

We know what doesn't work; now we are trying to figure out what will work.

<small>RUSSIAN TOURIST GUIDE[1]</small>

CHAPTER FOCUS

■ *What are the characteristics of a socialist economy?*
■ *Why did the centrally planned economies of Eastern Europe and the former Soviet Union fail?*
■ *What are the key elements of a successful transition plan?*
■ *What are some of the major problems that arise when a country attempts to move from central planning to a market economy?*
■ *How are the transitional economies doing?*
■ *Why might the official output statistics during the transition period be misleading?*

---

[1]This statement was made by a Russian tourist guide to one of the authors during a visit to St. Petersburg in August 1992.

M ore than 400 million people live in formerly communist countries that were either part of or under the domination of the former Soviet Union. Until recently, these economies were characterized by central planning and government ownership of productive physical assets. Currently, they are in a transitional state. The central-planning process has broken down, and these countries are now searching for an alternative form of economic organization more conducive to prosperity. In varying degrees, they have attempted to shift to a private-property, market-directed economy. This chapter focuses on why the central-planning process broke down and analyzes a number of the issues confronting these transitional economies.

Exhibit 34–1 provides data on the population and estimated per capita income in 1991 for the former Soviet bloc countries. The per capita incomes of these countries are well below the comparable figures for the United States and the other major industrial countries. Compared to the rest of the world, however, these countries are not particularly poor. In most instances, their per capita incomes are between $5,000 and $8,000, well above the world average. Just a few decades ago several of these countries were quite wealthy. For example, just prior to the Second World War, the average income level of Czechoslovakia (now the Czech and Slovak republics) was about the same as that of Germany, France, and Austria. In general, the skill level and literacy rate of the people living in these countries is quite high. Thus, their potential for achievement of higher income levels should be quite good.

CHARACTERISTICS OF A SOCIALIST ECONOMY

Two central factors underlie the differences between capitalism and socialism: (1) ownership of physical capital and (2) the mechanism used to allocate resources.

Capitalism is characterized by private ownership of physical assets and the use of market forces to coordinate the actions of buyers and sellers and thereby determine the allocation of goods and resources. This is not to say that everything is privately owned in a capitalist, or market, economy. Even in market economies, governments often operate public utilities, transportation systems, and other business enterprises. However, most things, including houses, farms, land, businesses, and even large manufacturing plants, are generally owned privately in market economies. Even more importantly, the legal structure is one that respects and enforces the ownership rights of the private parties. Thus, we might say that a market economy is characterized by a private-ownership regime.

In contrast, under **socialism** most physical assets—particularly those that are used to produce goods and services—are owned by the state. Private parties are not permitted to own various classes of physical assets or operate most types of businesses. Thus, everyone (or almost everyone) in the labor force is employed by the government. Government ownership of physical assets and conduct of business activity is a dominant characteristic of a socialist economy.

With regard to resource allocation, market economies rely on the choices of consumers, private owners of the resources, and business entrepreneurs to direct

Capitalism
An economic system based on private ownership of productive resources and allocation of goods according to the price signals provided by free markets.

Socialism
A system of economic organization where (1) the ownership and control of the basic means of production rest with the state and (2) the allocation of resources and products is determined by centralized planning rather than by market forces.

EXHIBIT 34-1

POPULATION AND ESTIMATED PER CAPITA GDP IN 1991 EASTERN EUROPE AND SOVIET UNION

COUNTRY	POPULATION (IN MILLIONS, MID-1991)	PER CAPITA GDP SUMMERS-HESTON	PER CAPITA GDP WORLD BANK
EASTERN EUROPE			
Albania	3.3	–	–
Bulgaria	9.0	$4,813	$4,980
Croatia	4.8	–	–
Czech Republic	10.3	6,570[a]	6,280[a]
Hungary	10.3	6,055	6,080
Poland	38.2	4,569	4,840
Romania	23.0	–	6,900
Slovak Republic	5.3	6,570[a]	6,280[a]
Slovenia	2.0	–	–
FORMER SOVIET UNION			
Armenia	3.4	4,438	4,610
Azerbaijan	7.1	3,658	3,670
Belarus	10.3	–	6,850
Estonia	1.6	6,170	8,090
Georgia	5.5	4,384	3,670
Kazakhstan	16.8	4,507	4,490
Kyrgyzstan	4.5	3,289	3,289
Latvia	2.6	6,721	7,540
Lithuania	3.7	4,901	5,410
Moldova	4.4	3,984	4,640
Russia	148.7	8,115	6,930
Tajikistan	5.5	–	2,180
Turkmenistan	3.8	–	3,540
Ukraine	52.0	5,603	5,180
Uzbekistan	20.9	3,226	2,790
BENCHMARK			
United States		21,866	22,130

[a]Indicates data are for the former Czechoslovakia.

Source: World Bank, *World Development Report: 1993* (Oxford: Oxford University Press, 1993) tables 1 and 30. The Summers and Heston per capita GDP data were supplied directly to the authors. See Robert Summers and Alan Heston, "The Penn World Table (Mark 5): An Expanded Set of International Comparisons, 1950–1988," *Quarterly Journal of Economics*, May 1991, for earlier data and a description of how their estimates were derived. Both the Summers and Heston and World Bank estimates were derived by the purchasing-power parity method.

activities. Their choices are coordinated by prices reflecting the forces of supply and demand, which determine what is going to be produced, how goods will be produced, and who will consume them. In contrast, under socialism resources are used and allocated in accordance with the priorities of a centrally determined and administered plan. Economic decisions, such as what and how much will be produced, how resources will be used in production, and to whom the product will

---

THUMBNAIL SKETCH

WHAT ECONOMIC CHARACTERISTICS DISTINGUISH CAPITALISM FROM SOCIALISM?

	Capitalism	Socialism
Property rights	Nonhuman resources are owned by private parties (that is, individuals or corporations).	Nonhuman resources are owned by the government.
Allocation of goods and resources	Determined by market forces.	Determined by central planning.
Employment	Workers are self-employed or employed by private firms.	Workers are employed by the government or government-controlled cooperatives.
Investment	Undertaken by private parties seeking profits and higher future incomes.	Undertaken by the government in accordance with the objectives of the planners.

---

be distributed are made by a central-planning authority (and the political officials that it represents). The central plan may also include decisions on quantities of raw materials and inputs, techniques of production, prices, wages, locations of firms and industries, and the employment of labor. Thus, socialist economic objectives generally reflect the preferences and value judgments of central planners and political authorities.

In a market economy, the interaction between savers and investors will determine the share of current income allocated to investment, and pursuit of profit will tend to direct funds toward those projects yielding the highest rate of return. Under central planning, the political process will determine both the share of current output allocated to investment and which projects will be undertaken. To the extent that the planners (and the political officials they represent) give priority to future income relative to current consumption, centrally planned economies will be able to achieve high rates of capital formation. The accompanying "Thumbnail Sketch" summarizes the distinctive characteristics of capitalist and socialist economic organization.

CENTRAL PLANNING: AN OVERVIEW

As we have stressed throughout this text, scarcity constrains all of us. No economic system, regardless of how it is organized, is able to produce as much as its citizens would like to consume. Therefore, choices must be made. The decision to satisfy one desire leaves many other desires unsatisfied. Economies may differ with regard to how they decide which demands to satisfy, but all must nonetheless operate within the constraints imposed by scarcity.

Organizationally, a centrally planned economy is similar to a huge vertically and horizontally integrated corporation. Government central planners establish economic policy objectives, allocate resources to business firms (enterprises), and provide the enterprises with directives that they are supposed to implement.

Since centrally planned economies use directives rather than prices to allocate resources, they are sometimes referred to as **command economies.** Detailed directives send commands (instructions) to agents controlling productive resources concerning what they are to do and how they are to do it.

The government's central-planning agency acquires various types of information from the enterprises and drafts the basic plan for the entire economy. It is charged with the responsibility of making sure that the plan is internally consistent—that for example, the sum of the inputs promised to the various enterprises does not exceed their aggregate availability. The planning agency tells each enterprise what quantity of each commodity it is required to produce, the amounts of labor and raw materials that it will be allocated, what new machinery should be installed, what the timing of available credit will be, and other operational details. The task of the enterprise is to transform its allotted inputs into the target output. The operational targets of the annual plan are used to evaluate the performance of firms and reward them accordingly.

The central planners decide how much of each good will be produced and the quantity of resources, including intermediate goods, that will be supplied to the enterprises. Accordingly, the planners prepare a balance sheet of all available resource supplies and sources of resource demand. Labor, raw materials, minerals, imports, and so on, are all allocated this way—in the quantities believed necessary to produce each enterprise's target output. Obviously, central planning presents an enormous coordination problem. Since the output of one enterprise (steel, for example) is often the input of another enterprise (a tractor-producing firm, for example), each enterprise must be supplied with just the right amount of labor and materials at just the right time in order to keep things moving smoothly. If one firm fails to meet its output quota, perhaps as the result of equipment failure or bad weather, other firms will lack the resources required for the achievement of their production targets. Literally millions of output objectives must be both properly interfaced and achieved in a timely fashion for the system to work.

Consider the problems that arise if the target output for, say, trucks is increased by 20 percent. The planners must take steps to ensure that the truck-producing enterprises receive the additional required labor, capital equipment, component parts manufactured by other enterprises, and raw materials such as steel, aluminum, glass, and copper. Suppliers of these inputs must either increase their output or cut back on the quantity provided to other producers so more can be supplied to the truck producers. If any of the input suppliers fail to meet their increased quotas to the truck-manufacturing enterprises, the truck producers will be unable to produce the additional output.

Prices play a secondary role in this entire process. The supply of goods is determined by the objectives of planners, rather than prices relative to opportunity costs. When a good is in short supply, there is no assurance that more of it

Command economy
An authoritarian socialist economy characterized by centralized planning and detailed directives to productive units. Individual enterprises have little discretionary decision-making power.

will be produced in the future. Prices are used as one means of rationing goods among consumers, but they reflect the preferences of planners rather than market forces.

Exhibit 34–2 and **Exhibit 34–3** illustrate how the planning process works within the framework of supply and demand. Since the aggregate supply of each good is determined by the priorities of the central plan, the supply curve for each good is vertical. Of course, the planners are constrained by resource scarcity, and if they choose to produce more of one good, they will have to reduce the output of other goods. This trade-off, however, reflects the choices of the planners rather than the prices of the goods. The law of demand—the inverse relation between the price and amount purchased of a good—is just as relevant in socialist countries as it is in market economies. If the planners reduce the price of a good, consumers in centrally planned economies will buy a larger quantity. Thus, the demand curve for each good is the usual downward-sloping curve.

EXHIBIT 34–2

ALLOCATION UNDER CENTRAL PLANNING WHEN PRICE IS LESS THAN COST AND ENTERPRISES ARE SUBSIDIZED

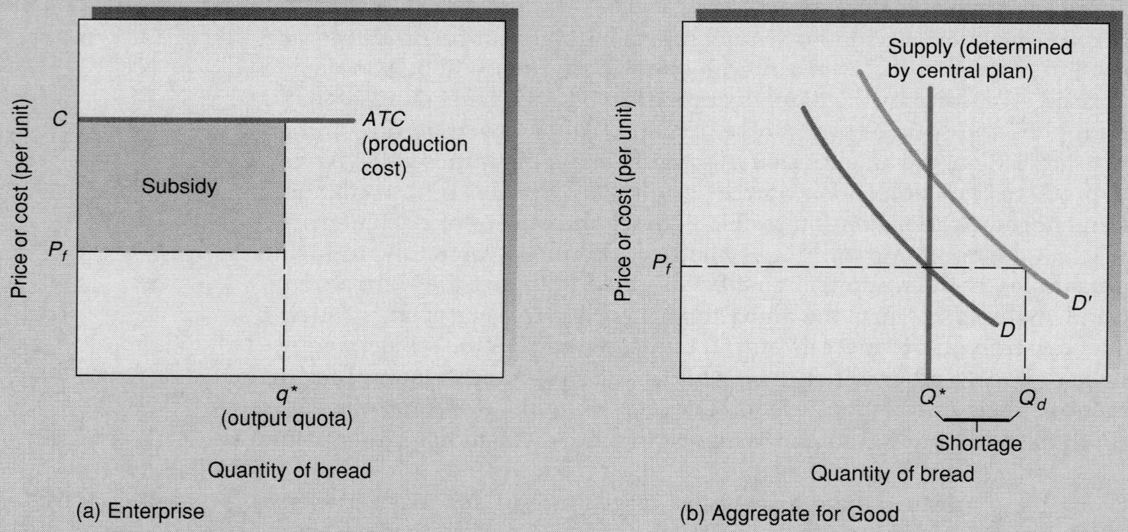

(a) Enterprise

(b) Aggregate for Good

The central planners set both the quantity supplied and price for each good. Each enterprise producing the good, bread for example, will be given an output quota such as q* (part a). The aggregate quantity produced (Q* of part b) is the sum of the quantity produced by the bread-producing enterprises. This quantity reflects the priorities of the central planners. When the price set by the planners (P_f) is less than the per unit production cost, enterprises producing the good will have to be granted a subsidy by the state (shaded area of part a). If the demand for the good is D, the amount supplied and demanded will be in balance. On the other hand, if the demand is D', a shortage of the good will result. In reality, the planners often set prices such that an excess demand is present in the market. Shortages and waiting lines are the visible results.

Since central planning rather than prices determines the amount of each good supplied, the prices of goods do not have to reflect per unit production cost. Often the planners will set prices substantially below cost of production. Exhibit 34–2 illustrates this case. Each enterprise producing a good, bread for example, will be given a production quota (q^*). The sum of the amount produced by all of the bread producers will equal Q^*, the supply of bread called for by the central plan. Since the planners have set the price at P_f, which is below the cost of the labor and other inputs required to produce a unit of bread, the enterprises producing bread will have to be subsidized (the shaded area of Exhibit 34–2).

Sometimes the planners will attempt to set the product price such that the amount demanded by consumers is approximately equal to the amount supplied under the central plan. If the demand schedule for bread was D (part "b" of

---

EXHIBIT 34–3

ALLOCATION UNDER CENTRAL PLANNING WHEN PRICE IS GREATER THAN COST AND ENTERPRISES GENERATE GOVERNMENT REVENUE

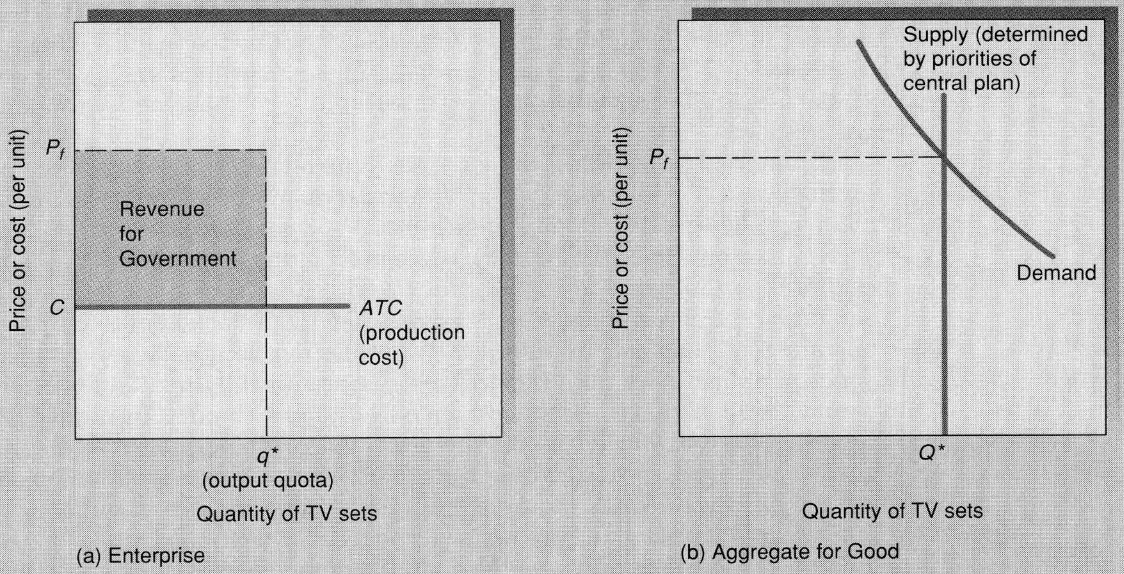

(a) Enterprise

(b) Aggregate for Good

Here we illustrate the case where the planners set the price for a good (television sets, for example) above the per unit cost of producing it. Once again, the enterprises producing the good are given a target output (q* in part a) and the aggregate amount produced by all suppliers is Q* (part b), the amount called for by the central plan. Since the price (P_f) set by the planners is above the per unit cost, production and sale of this good generates net revenue for the government

(shaded area of part a). The revenue derived from selling above cost need not equal the subsidies to firms selling below cost (the situation illustrated by Exhibit 34–2). When the subsidies exceed the state revenues, the people of the planned economy will have more income than will be required to purchase the output produced, given the prices and quantities of the goods that are available.

Exhibit 34–2), the P_f price would bring the amount demanded into balance with the amount supplied. But this may not be the case. The demand for bread might be greater, for example, schedule D'. When this is true, the planners will often choose to maintain the price at a low level, presumably so the good will be affordable to more people. When the price set by the planners is below equilibrium, consumers will want to buy a larger quantity than the amount available. Shortages and waiting lines will result. Given the supply, if the demand for bread was D', a shortage of Q_d minus Q^* would be present at the price P_f.

The pricing of housing in Russia and other centrally planned economies generally reflected this below-equilibrium (and below-cost) pricing structure. Under socialism, almost all housing was (and generally still is) owned by the state and rented to households at very low prices. But the availability of housing in these countries is substantially less than the quantity demanded. Thus, families wait for years before an apartment is available.

Sometimes the central planners will set the price of a good substantially higher than its production cost. When this is the case, the government reaps a "profit"—an excess of revenues relative to cost—from the production and supply of the good. Using television sets as an example, Exhibit 34–3 illustrates the case where the planners fix price above per unit production cost. Once again, they provide each of the enterprises producing television sets with a quota (q^* of part "a"), and the sum of the output of the enterprises is equal to the quantity called for by the central plan (Q^* of part "b"). At the price P_f set by the planners, the revenues from the sales of the television sets are greater than their costs of production. Thus, the production and sale of televisions generates net revenue for the government.

Under central planning, there is often little relationship between the prices of products and the opportunity cost of their production. In some cases, the government supplies goods at a substantial "loss" (and therefore enterprises producing such goods have to be subsidized), while in other instances the government reaps a "profit."

With central planning, there is no reason why the subsidies to the enterprises operating at a loss cannot exceed the revenues derived by the government from goods supplied at a profit. If prices were determined by market forces, inflation would result if the government created additional money in order to finance spending in excess of revenues. Under central planning, however, the prices of goods and services are fixed by the planners. Thus, the excess of the subsidies relative to the revenues derived from "profitable" state enterprises will simply mean that, *at current prices,* the resource suppliers will have more than the required amount of income to purchase the quantity of goods produced. If this is the case, the demand for goods will persistently exceed the limited supply. As a result, non-price factors such as queuing, favors, and bribes will play a greater role in the allocation of goods and services among consumers. These factors are a secondary effect of a central-planning process where prices are set such that the subsidies to the state enterprises operated at a "loss" exceed the net revenues generated by enterprises operated at a "profit."

Enterprise subsidies that exceed revenues also result in what is referred to as **monetary overhang,** the building up of monetary reserves because the income of individuals exceeds the amount required to purchase the current output, *given the availability and prices of goods.* As we will see later, this monetary overhang complicates matters when prices are decontrolled during the transitional period.

Monetary overhang
The accumulation of money balances that results when the aggregate money-income payments to employees exceed the amount required to purchase the aggregate quantity of goods and services produced at the prices set by the central plan.

WHY DID SOCIALIST CENTRAL PLANNING FAIL?

The man of system . . . is apt to be very wise in his own conceit. . . . [H]e seems to imagine that he can arrange the different members of a great society with as much ease as the hand arranges the different pieces upon a chess-board; he does not consider that the pieces upon the chess-board have not another principle of motion besides that which the hand impresses upon them; but that, in the great chess-board of human society, every single piece has a principle of motion of its own, although different from that which the legislature might choose to impress upon it. If those two principles coincide and act in the same direction, the game of human society will go on easily and harmoniously, and is very likely to be happy and successful. If they are opposite or different, the game will go on miserably, and the society must be at all times in the highest degree of disorder.

ADAM SMITH[2]

Several factors contributed to the failure of the centrally planned economies of Eastern Europe and the former Soviet Union. Most all of them, however, are a reflection of a single factor: the personal interests of various individuals—for example, regional planners, local enterprise managers, group leaders, and workers—often conflicted with the objectives of the central plan. As Adam Smith noted in a book that he wrote prior to *The Wealth of Nations*, when this happens problems are sure to arise. More specifically, centrally planned economies suffer from four major weaknesses that tend to undermine their effectiveness. Let us consider each of them.

1. The central planners will be unable to attain the vast amount of information required to develop a sensible central plan and induce local decision makers to carry it out. The diversity of wants and desires among consumers is both highly fragmented and incredibly complex. Similarly, the production process is highly complex and influenced by prior experience, learning by doing, and circumstances that are unique to the enterprise. There is no way that a central-planning agency can even begin to command the required knowledge of local circumstances and elements of timing that affect both costs of production and the consumer evaluation of goods. Furthermore, we live in a dynamic world. Changing demands and weather conditions, technological advances, development of new products and superior production processes, and the discovery of new resources are constantly altering the relative scarcity of both goods and resources.

Put simply, the widely dispersed but highly relevant information along with the constantly changing conditions make central planning infeasible. It is unrealistic to expect that a central-planning authority will be able to acquire the necessary information, process and communicate it through the chain of command quickly, and provide local enterprise managers and workers with both the instructions and motivation to carry out the plan sensibly. The required information is too vast, the coordination problem is too complicated, and the central-planning process is too slow for the planners to keep up with a modern dynamic economy.

---

[2]Adam Smith, *The Theory of Moral Sentiments*, 1959 (New York: A. M. Kelley, 1966).

2. Under socialism, there is little incentive for enterprises to produce quality products that are highly valued by consumers, and to produce them in an economical manner. In a market economy, business owners have a property right to the residual income of the firm. This provides them with a strong incentive to produce goods and services that are highly valued by consumers—and to produce them at a low cost. Doing so will increase their income. In a centrally planned socialist economy, neither plant managers nor the central planners have a property right to the net income of the enterprise. Thus, there is little incentive for them to keep cost down and quality up.

Predictably, enterprise managers will confront the central planners with the image of overworked managers and employees squeezing the maximum output from an unrealistically small quantity of resources. They will seek more resources in order to maintain or expand the quantity of output and provide benefits (for example, vacation houses in the countryside, better recreation and health facilities, and less work effort) for themselves. From the viewpoint of an enterprise manager, the ideal plan is one that provides a quantity of resources such that the firm's output target can be easily achieved. Thus, enterprise officials have an incentive to provide the central planners with misleading and even false information with regard to the actual productive capability of the firm. Since high-level central planners have limited knowledge of the real output that an efficiently operated firm can achieve in its particular circumstances, they are in a weak position to contradict the enterprise managers.

In addition, the problem is complicated by the fact that without market prices as a guide to value per unit, central-planning systems have to measure the output of enterprises in terms of quantity (rather than value). Enterprises are rewarded on the basis of the weight, surface area, or number of units produced (relative to the target). Whether consumers actually value the output has little impact on the income of producers. Variety and quality of products are, at best, secondary considerations. This focus on gross output leads to numerous anomalies and the wasteful use of resources. Consider the case of an enterprise that produces nails. If output is measured in terms of weight, the enterprise will produce mostly large nails. On the other hand, if output is measured in terms of number of nails, the enterprise will produce small nails (since they can be produced with a smaller quantity of inputs). When output is measured in physical units rather than value, predictably suppliers will be less responsive to the preferences of consumers.

3. Under central planning, the incentive to innovate and invest resources wisely is weak. Under the gross-output planning system, enterprise managers have little incentive to improve quality, to innovate, or to experiment with alternative production techniques. The potential gains to the managers associated with the discovery of better ways of doing things are small, while the risks are great if an innovative method proves to be a failure. In addition, resource combinations supplied by the central-planning authority often limit the adoption of innovative production methods. As long as enterprise managers can get goods past the inspector, there is little incentive to try to improve the quality, reliability, or durability of the product.[3]

---

[3]Under the openness of the Gorbachev era, the problem of shoddy product quality became well publicized. The Soviet magazine *Ogonek* reported that exploding TV sets caused 18,000 fires, 512 serious injuries, and 929 deaths between 1980 and 1986. The Soviet press reported that when independent quality-inspector groups were established at plants manufacturing consumer goods and machine tools, up to 30 percent of the output in these plants was initially rejected. Seventy percent of the shoes at a factory in Volgograd were rejected, and 40 percent of all products from plants in Ukraine were rejected.

Similarly, there is little reason to expect that investment funds will be allocated efficiently under central planning. The link between the selection of profitable projects and the personal wealth of the central planners will be weak. Even if a project is productive—if it increases wealth—the personal gain of planners, including those directing the project, is likely to be modest. Neither will an unproductive project exert any significant negative impact on the personal wealth of planners. In fact, the planner may be in a stronger position to reap personal gain from wasteful projects that channel subsidies and other benefits toward politically powerful groups.

It is interesting to compare the incentive structure confronting market investors with that facing the central planner. If a market investor is going to earn economic profit, he or she must discover and invest in projects that increase the value of resources. If the market investor makes a mistake—if the project turns out to be a loser—the private investor will bear the consequences directly. Given this incentive structure, there is strong justification for the belief that individuals risking their own money will make better investment choices than central planners using the funds of the general citizenry.

4. *The priorities of the central plan will reflect the preferences of those with political power rather than those of consumers.* Real-world central planners are not a group of altruistic saints seeking to serve the general interests. They are people with their own personal objectives and political ambitions. In some cases, their self-interest might be promoted by an expansion in the employment level of a firm or the regional development of a favored area. In other instances, catering to those willing to offer political and economic favors that enhance the power or wealth of planners in key positions may be personally advantageous. In still other cases, military expenditures that strengthen one's political hold or provide the resources for foreign expansionism may be a priority. All of these factors will influence how those in charge of the planning process will dole out subsidies and allocate investment funds. Neither theory nor experience suggests that this politicized process will result in operational efficiency and lead to the production of goods and services that are highly valued by the general citizenry.

THE NATURE OF THE TRANSITION PROBLEM

The general nature of the transition problem is straightforward: how can resources be used more efficiently and be directed more consistently toward the production of goods and services that people value more highly relative to their costs?

Under socialism, the incentive to minimize cost was weak and, from the viewpoint of consumers, the planners often directed the enterprises to produce the wrong things. If markets can provide an incentive structure that will (1) encourage worker and management efficiency and (2) reallocate resources toward goods that are valued more highly, the living standards of people can be improved.

This will not be an easy task. In many of the formerly communist countries, the production bundle produced under central planning was way out of line with the bundle that would have been chosen by consumers. Conversion of enterprises designed to produce military weapons or goods that are now technologically obsolete to plants producing useful consumer goods is likely to be a painful process. Furthermore, many of the state-owned enterprises are grossly over-staffed. The amount of labor used by many of them is three or four times the quantity used by firms in market economies producing similar commodities.

Markets use losses and bankruptcies to bring high-cost, inefficient business activities to a halt. Obviously, this is an unpleasant experience for the workers and owners of the firms involved. A normal, healthy economy will minimize these costs by providing workers in declining industries and inefficient firms with options—employment with firms in expanding industries, for example. But the situation of transitional economies is not that of a healthy economy. Since a huge proportion of the enterprises of these economies may be unable to compete effectively, the options available to the workers of inefficient and bankrupt enterprises are likely to be extremely limited—particularly if they are employed by a dominant enterprise in an obscure location.

KEY ELEMENTS OF SUCCESSFUL TRANSITION

Four key elements are required for a successful transition from socialist central planning to a market economy: (1) decontrol of prices, (2) competition among suppliers, (3) establishment of a monetary policy that will keep inflation under control, and (4) privatization. The precise sequencing of these elements and the speed with which they should be instituted are matters of considerable controversy. We will amplify on this topic as we proceed. For now, we want to focus on why these ingredients are important.

DECONTROL OF PRICES

The easiest step of a transition plan to institute is decontrol of prices. To a large degree, all of the economies in transition have adopted this element. If resources are going to be allocated by markets rather than central planning, people must be allowed to exchange goods and services at mutually agreeable prices.

COMPETITION AMONG SUPPLIERS

If decontrol is going to bring prices into line with opportunity costs, competition is essential. Remember, competition is the disciplining force of a market economy. Several steps can be taken that will help promote competitive markets in a formerly socialist economy. First and foremost, new firms must be allowed to enter markets. Licensing requirements, discriminatory taxation, restraints on the establishment of new businesses, and other forms of preserving privilege through bureaucratic control must be removed (or reduced to a simple formality). Laws protecting private property against those who would use violence as a competitive weapon must be adopted and strictly enforced. Foreigners must be allowed to establish new businesses and compete on a level playing field with domestic producers. Enterprises that continue to be operated by the state must not be allowed to discriminate against the newly established private firms.

Second, removal of barriers limiting international trade is also vitally important for the development of competitive markets. This will be particularly true for sectors of the economy dominated by a single producer or small number of firms. It may not be feasible or even desirable to quickly privatize large state-owned firms. Reflecting the prior socialist organization, many of these firms will have substantial monopoly power. Often, they will be in a position to impose bottlenecks limiting the production of other firms. These factors will permit such firms to charge exorbitant prices. In an open economy, however, competition from foreign suppliers will limit the power of monopolistic domestic firms and force them to charge prices more in line with lowest achievable costs.

MONETARY AND PRICE STABILITY

Inflation creates uncertainty, distorts price signals, and retards both domestic and foreign investment. High rates of inflation will undermine the development of a market economy. Therefore, monetary and price stability are critical to the success of economies in transition.

For transitional economies, control of inflation means a balanced government budget. Until credibility is established, the governments of transitional economies will be unable to borrow funds in credit markets. Therefore, if the government does not balance its budget, the only alternative means of financing government is printing money.

PRIVATIZATION

Privatization involves more than the mere shift of legal title to an entity other than the state. When firms are really private—when a regime of private ownership is present, the firms will derive their revenues from sales to consumers rather than

In some cases, state enterprises in Eastern Europe were privatized through the sale of assets to foreign firms with an established record in the industry. A state-owned detergent manufacturing plant in Rakona, Czech Republic that was sold to Proctor & Gamble in 1991 is pictured. Proctor & Gamble invested in the modernization of equipment and productivity at this plant has increased substantially since it was privatized.

Hard budget constraint
Situation where the enterprise is fully dependent on revenues from sales to cover its costs. The constraint is "hard" because, if losses are present, they will have to be covered by enterprise owners; continuing losses will result in bankruptcy since government subsidies and special grants are unavailable.

subsidies from the government. Owners will both confront a **hard budget constraint** and be in a position to assert their property right to the firm's residual income. Furthermore, private firms will have to raise their investment funds in the capital market rather than seeking the favor and approval of government planners. These three elements—derivation of revenues from sales, owners that are in a position to control the enterprises, and derivation of investment funds from the capital market—are the central elements of private ownership. Unless they are present, depoliticalization of enterprises is unlikely.

PRIVATIZATION, OUTPUT, AND EMPLOYMENT

How has the transition process from socialism to a market-based economy fared thus far? The next three exhibits will shed light on this issue. Let us begin by considering how rapidly various countries have moved toward the development of a private sector.

CHANGES IN SIZE OF PRIVATE SECTOR

Even under communism, the size of the private sector varied among the countries of Eastern Europe. For example, in Poland small private farmers, who were given land that was confiscated from large landowners when the communists came to power in the late 1940s, were the legal owners of most of the Polish farmland prior to the fall of communism in 1989. In contrast, the agricultural sectors of Russia, Ukraine, and the former Czechoslovakia were dominated by state-operated farms and government-organized cooperatives.

As **Exhibit 34–4** illustrates, the private sector in Poland and Romania was somewhat larger in 1989 than was the case in other Eastern European countries. During 1989–1992, some countries moved toward private ownership more rapidly than others. In Czechoslovakia (the Czech and Slovak republics) the share of GDP generated by the private sector rose from 4 percent in 1989 to 20 percent in 1992. As a share of GDP, the size of the private sector also increased substantially in Hungary, Poland, Bulgaria, Romania, Estonia, and Lithuania. Both privatization of state enterprises and the establishment and growth of new private firms contributed to the private-sector growth. By 1992 private-sector output accounted for approximately one-third of the GDP of Hungary and nearly one-half (counting the output of cooperatives) in the case of Poland.

In contrast, the growth of the private sector was much more modest in Russia, Belarus, Ukraine, and Latvia. In 1992 it accounted for 10 percent or less of the GDP of those countries.

CHANGES IN GDP

Given the way that it is calculated, an initial decline in measured GDP during the transition period would not be surprising. Remember, when GDP is derived, government expenditures on goods and services—including the spending on

Source: European Bank for Reconstruction and Development, *Annual Economic Outlook,* September 1993, p. 97. These estimates are based on both output and employment data.

EXHIBIT 34-4

ESTIMATED SHARE OF GDP PRODUCED IN PRIVATE SECTOR FOR SELECTED COUNTRIES OF EASTERN EUROPE AND SOVIET UNION, 1989–1992

COUNTRY	1989	1990	1991	1992
Czechoslovakia	4	5	9–10	20
Hungary	–	10–19	27–28	33–35
Poland (includes co-ops)	28–29	30–31	42–43	45–50
Bulgaria	7	9–10	12	16
Romania	13	16–17	21	25–26
Russia	2–6	2–6	5–10	–
Belarus	1–5	1–6	2–7	3–8
Ukraine	9	10	10–12	–
Estonia	–	–	10–18	15–22
Latvia	1–2	2–3	2–3	5–6
Lithuania	2–10	4–12	15–16	34–26

resources used by government-operated enterprises—enter the GDP accounts at cost. Thus, the full production cost of goods supplied by government enterprises is added to GDP even if the ultimate consumers of these goods do not value them very much. When socialism collapsed, many of the state enterprises were producing goods for which there was little or no demand. When such enterprises are forced to sell their products at something approximating per unit costs, they will simply not be viable. The closing of such enterprises, however, will reduce measured GDP by the cost of their operation. Of course, with the passage of time, these resources will be reallocated toward activities that are both productive and profitable. But this transformation process will take time. In the meantime, the official statistics are likely to show a decline in output.

The official statistics, however, indicate that output has declined substantially more than was anticipated. **Exhibit 34–5** indicates the path of GDP for various transitional economies. According to the official data, all of the transitional economies of Eastern Europe and the former Soviet Union have experienced sharp reductions in output since 1989. The estimated reduction in output for Hungary and Poland, the two countries with the largest private sectors in 1992, is approximately 20 percent. A similar decline in output is estimated for the Czech Republic, a country that has moved rapidly toward privatization and done a reasonably good job of controlling inflation. Among the transitional economies, only Poland managed to achieve a positive growth rate in 1992–1993.

Other countries—most of which have moved more slowly toward privatization and liberalization—have experienced catastrophic reductions in output. The official GDP figures for Bulgaria, Romania, Russia, Ukraine, and the three Baltic Republics (Estonia, Latvia, and Lithuania) indicate that their 1993 output was between 30 and 60 percent lower than the comparable figure for 1989. These output

Source: European Bank for Reconstruction and Development, *Annual Economic Outlook,* September 1993. The 1992 and 1993 data for the Czech Republic, Hungary, Poland, Romania, Slovak Republic, and Ukraine are from "Facts and Figures," *Business Central Europe,* February 1994, p. 64.

EXHIBIT 34–5

GROWTH RATE OF REAL GDP FOR SELECTED COUNTRIES OF EASTERN EUROPE AND SOVIET UNION, 1990–1993

COUNTRY	1990	1991	1992	1993
Czech Republic	0	−14	−6.9	0
Slovak Republic	0	−16	−8.3	−6.0
Hungary	−4	−12	−4.0	−1.5
Poland	−12	−7	+1.5	+4.5
Bulgaria	−9	−12	−8	−5
Romania	−7	−14	−15	−9
Russia	−4	−11	−19	−15
Belarus	−3	−3	−11	−3
Ukraine	–	−14	−14	−20
Estonia	−4	−13	−26	−10
Latvia	+3	−8	−44	−19
Lithuania	−5	−13	−35	−10

reductions are even greater than the declines experienced by the United States and other industrial countries during the Great Depression.

Can the official figures really be correct? There is no question that several countries, including Russia, Ukraine, Romania, and Bulgaria, have experienced very substantial declines in output. However, there are three reasons to suspect that the official figures overstate the actual reductions in output, particularly for countries like the Czech Republic, Poland, and Hungary where the private sector has grown rapidly. First, the income generated by small-business activities such as construction renovation and the operation of retail shops and restaurants is difficult for the authorities to measure accurately. This is particularly true when the income, if it is fully reported, is heavily taxed. Tax rates throughout Eastern Europe are exceedingly high. In most of these countries, payroll taxes are between 40 percent and 60 percent. The top marginal tax rates on personal income are generally 40 percent and up, and they take effect at modest levels of income. In addition, most of these countries have a *valued-added tax* that is generally between 20 percent and 30 percent. Given tax rates of this magnitude, unreported income is almost certainly quite high. Weak tax administration and the fact that almost all transactions in this part of the world are conducted in cash rather than by check make enforcement of tax laws more difficult. Given these conditions, it is a virtual certainty that a sizable portion of the income generated in the newly emerging private sectors of these economies is undetected by both the taxing authorities and the national-income accountants.

Second, there is a strong tendency for price indexes to overstate the magnitude of price increases during the transition phase. In turn, the use of these overstated indexes to adjust the nominal income figures results in an understatement of GDP. The problem here is one of failure to adjust fully to changes in availability and product quality. Prior to decontrol, the prices of many products were fixed below equilibrium, but the quality was poor and the availability uncertain. In the transitional economies that have managed to bring inflation under control, the queues have disappeared, the quality of goods has improved rapidly, and the diversity of products available has expanded by leaps and bounds. Many goods that were simply unavailable under central planning are now taken for granted. Price indexes do not pick up these qualitative factors. This measurement error leads to both an overstatement of the inflation rate and an understatement of output and its growth.

Finally, the official figures understate the growth of GDP because the earlier figures under central planning were grossly overstated. There are several reasons why this was the case. When goods are produced in the government sector, their production costs add to GDP. It makes no difference whether consumers actually value the good. For example, if it cost the equivalent of $500 to produce a 1950s style and quality refrigerator, production of that good adds $500 to GDP. In addition, under socialist planning, the enterprises had a strong incentive to overstate their output figures and ignore poor quality. Following the fall of communism, this prior overstatement of output became more obvious. For example, the best estimates now indicate that the per capita income level of East Germany was only about 40 percent of the figure for West Germany prior to 1989. Based on the accounting data available under central planning, it was previously thought that the average income of East Germans was between 60 percent and 70 percent of the comparable figure for West Germans. Similarly, the output figures for Russia were previously thought to be significantly higher than is now believed to be the case. Since the earlier output figures are systematically overstated, the growth figures following the transition are systematically understated.

UNEMPLOYMENT IN TRANSITIONAL ECONOMIES

Given the declines in the official GDP figures, substantial increases in the rate of unemployment would be expected. As **Exhibit 34–6** illustrates, the unemployment rates of the Slovak Republic, Hungary, Poland, Bulgaria, and Romania have increased sharply. At year-end 1993, double-digit levels of unemployment were present in all of these countries. In contrast, the unemployment rates of the Czech Republic, Estonia, and Lithuania—three countries that have moved rather rapidly toward privatization—remain at relatively low levels.

Perhaps most interestingly, the unemployment rates of Russia and Belarus are estimated to be approximately 1 percent—essentially unchanged from the levels under communism. Thus, even though output in both Russia and Belarus has declined substantially, employment remains at a high level. As we previously indicated, privatization has been exceedingly modest in these two countries. To date, the industrial structure of these two countries is virtually unchanged. The government enterprises of these two countries continue to operate, albeit at a lower level, regardless of whether there is demand for the goods that they are producing.

Source: European Bank for Reconstruction and Development, *Annual Economic Outlook*, September 1993, p. 97. The 1993 data for Estonia, Latvia, and Lithuania are from *The Baltic Observer*, January 34–26, 1994, p. 8. The 1993 data for the Czech Republic, Slovak Republic, Hungary, Poland, Bulgaria, Romania, and Russia are from "Facts and Figures," *Business Central Europe*, May 1994.

EXHIBIT 34-6

UNEMPLOYMENT RATE FOR SELECTED COUNTRIES OF EASTERN EUROPE AND SOVIET UNION, 1990–1993

COUNTRY	1990	1991	1992	1993 (YEAR END)
Czech Republic	1	4	3	3.7
Slovak Republic	2	12	10	14.4
Hungary	2.5	8	12	12.1
Poland	6	12	14	15.7
Bulgaria	1.5	10	15	16.2
Romania	–	3	9	9.9
Russia	0	0	1	1.0
Belarus	–	–	–	1
Ukraine	–	–	–	–
Estonia	–	–	1	1.7
Latvia	–	–	2	5.3
Lithuania	–	–	1	1.4

WHY IS THE TRANSITION FROM SOCIALISM TO MARKETS SO DIFFICULT?

The transition from socialism to markets has proven to be substantially more difficult than many people, including a good number of economists, thought would be the case. It is now abundantly clear that the initial conditions of the centrally planned economies complicated the process. In addition, political factors have proven to be a major stumbling block. Let us consider the major factors that have slowed the transition process and, in a number of countries, led to policies that are undermining the development of a market economy.

1. The central-planning process left behind an aftermath of oversized enterprises and industry-wide monopolies. Under socialism, the planning agency's control over and direction of the enterprises was easier when the number of firms in each industry was small. Therefore, the industrial structure of these economies is now characterized by a small number of very large enterprises in each industry. Sometimes a single huge firm is the sole supplier of the domestic market. Many of these enterprises are substantially larger than the optimal size—that is, the size that would be consistent with minimum per unit cost of production. Furthermore, since there are only a few producers in each industry, initially the existing industrial capital structure is one of monopoly and oligopoly. This makes it more difficult to privatize the enterprises and existing industrial capital in a manner that will result in competitive markets.

2. Absence of a legal framework for the protection of private property and enforcement of contracts. Secure property rights and enforceable contracts are essential for the smooth operation of markets. Widely recognized legal codes—common law practices—and a system of courts to assist in the development and enforcement of these codes provide this infrastructure in market economies. Since the state owned all, or virtually all, physical capital under socialism, there was no need for institutions that would protect property rights and enforce contracts. In fact, since the official ideology of the state was hostile toward private ownership, the existing legal codes often limited and undermined the security of privately owned property. It takes time to develop this institutional structure that is vitally important for a market economy.[4] (See boxed feature on the following page.)

At the same time, the local, regional, and national planning institutions that were central to the government planning process are no longer needed in a market economy. Thus, the institutional infrastructure required for a market economy differs from that present under central planning. The development of market institutions and withering of the planning apparatus takes time, and it is costly.

3. Monetary overhang made price decontrol more difficult. As we previously mentioned, since the subsidies generally exceeded the "profits" of the state firms, the income of households in centrally planned economies was greater than the amount required to purchase the available goods. Since ownership of physical assets was prohibited, households had little choice but to hold these funds as savings deposits. When prices were decontrolled during the transition period, predictably this monetary overhang led to a sharp jump in the price level. For example, when prices were decontrolled in Poland at the beginning of 1990, the price level increased by 500 percent in three months. In Russia, a partial decontrol of prices led to a 250 percent increase in prices in one day. Other countries went through a similar experience. Understandably, as these sharp price increases wiped out the savings of many people, the enthusiasm and political support for markets dissipated.

4. Both the industrial structure of centrally planned economies and political considerations make it extremely difficult to reduce enterprise subsidies. If prices of goods are going to reflect their per unit opportunity cost, the subsidies granted to enterprises under the old socialist regime must be reduced. However, the structure of industries often makes this strategy very costly. In many cases, the central planners located a dominant manufacturing enterprise and constructed high-rise apartment complexes in sparsely populated areas. Often small and medium-sized cities were developed around such firms. Since the dominant enterprise employs almost everyone in these cities, unemployment in such areas will skyrocket if removal of the subsidies causes the firm to go bankrupt. In other instances, a firm may be a key supplier or purchaser for most of the output of another firm. Under these circumstances, the failure of one enterprise may cause several other enterprises to fail

---

[4]Some of the problems accompanying privatization in Poland illustrate the importance of this factor. Since Poland did not have a registry or any common record of either bankruptcies or mortgages, borrowers were able to obtain large business loans from state-operated banks even though they had recently taken bankruptcy. Sometimes this was done several times, and each time the "business operator" would then use the funds for private purposes (for example, payment of a large personal salary or the purchase of expensive automobiles). In other instances, the same property was used several times to arrange for mortgages from different lenders. Admittedly, arrangement of such "scam loans" also generally involved bribes to state banking officials and other corrupt practices. However, if there had been an easy way to check for recent bankruptcies and prior mortgages, practices of this type would have been both more risky and less widespread.

LEGAL INSTITUTIONS AND THE DEVELOPMENT
OF ECONOMIES IN TRANSITION

The following condensed version of the *USA Today* cover story (May 13, 1994) "Eastern Europe Hung in Red Tape" by James Cox illustrates how the uncertainties emanating from the legal structure of Poland adversely affect both private investment and the growth of the private sector.

"Polish women deserve a better brassiere," said Elizabeth Coleman, who'd like to be the one to give it to them.

If only it were that easy.

Coleman, chairman of Maidenform, and dozens of other executives came to Warsaw last week to meet with trade ministers from former Eastern Bloc countries and Soviet republics. It was an exercise in masochism for the ministers, who wanted to know why their 10 countries have drawn 23 percent less in foreign investment dollars the past five years than China attracted last year alone. The executives' blunt answer to the ministers: Look in the mirror—bureaucratic dithering and inertia are stifling economic reform in Eastern Europe and Central Asia.

Maidenform, for instance, would love to peddle bras to Poland's 20 million female consumers. Up against Polish-made bras and a lone imported German brand, Maidenform could offer greater size selection, plus better design and fabric quality. Yet nearly five years after the fall of communism, the New York-based company, which does business in 55 countries, has not ventured into any of the former Soviet satellites.

Before it will go to Poland, Maidenform needs answers. Is it required to import through a Polish company? Do fabric-content and care labels have to be written in Polish? What are the import duties?

"I sense a real desire on the part of the Polish government to have people like us come here," Coleman said. "But nothing is written down like it is in the United States There's no commercial code. There are secret laws, hidden rules, and they change constantly."

It's a familiar lament. "In this part of the world, there's so much focus on doing things right—getting all 16 stamps on a piece of paper—instead of doing the right things," says Edward Bush, who heads Hungarian operations for insurance giant AIG. Bush, president of the American Chamber of Commerce in Hungary, says

even the most well-intentioned governments in the region continually issue decrees and pass laws without informing the businesses affected by them.

In the countries known as the E-10—Poland, Hungary, the Czech Republic, Slovakia, Romania, Bulgaria, Russia, Belarus, Ukraine, and Kazakhstan—business can be unpredictable. Companies say it's impossible to calculate what they will owe in taxes because new tax laws go on the books every day. They gripe that they can't get clear title to land or convert profits from local currency to dollars, marks, or other "hard" currencies they can spend anywhere in the world.

In addition to a dire shortage of modern banking services, there is nowhere for companies to turn for impartial legal remedies when they have contract disputes, particularly battles involving government partners in joint ventures.

The E-10 countries hope to pull in $200 billion in foreign investment in the next six years—10 times what they've attracted since 1989. There are signs the flow of Western capital to Eastern Europe may be about to increase dramatically:

- PepsiCo and its partners say they will spend $100 million on new bottling operations in Poland, part of an overall $500 million PepsiCo investment here.
- Coca-Cola said Wednesday that it will spend $150 million to add three new bottling and distribution plants to the four it already has in Poland.

The problem is that for every Pepsi in Poland, there is a Chevron in Kazakhstan. By year's end, the oil company was to have spent nearly $1 billion to develop Kazakhstan's massive Tengiz oil field. But this week, Chevron announced it would scale back work there. The reason: an impasse over who will pay for the $1.4 billion pipeline needed to transport the oil to a Russian port.

Indeed, more companies appear willing to walk away from their investments in the region. Amoco recently let lapse its contract for gas exploration south of Warsaw. The U.S. oil company wanted to use losses from exploration in the early years to offset taxes on revenue from production later on. After two years of talks, the tax issue remained unresolved.

as well. Cascading unemployment throughout the economy as the result of these complex networks and interrelationships among monopoly and monopsony suppliers might well lead to sharp reductions in output, unacceptably high rates of unemployment, and social unrest.

Even if such circumstances are not present, the nature of the issue indicates that from a political viewpoint, significant reductions in enterprise subsidies will be difficult to achieve. The subsidies are a special-interest issue and, at least in the short run, the managers and workers of the enterprises are dependent upon them. They comprise a concentrated interest group that can be expected to fight the subsidy reductions with all of their might. In contrast, the benefits derived from a subsidy reduction to any given enterprise will be spread thinly throughout the economy. Given the special-interest nature of this issue, reduction of such subsidies would be difficult to achieve even in a well-developed, diversified market economy. Predictably, it will be doubly difficult in a tenuous democracy.

Furthermore, the network of enterprise managers and economic planners under socialism—for example, organizations like the Civic Union in Russia—will generally be better organized than the elements of the economy interested in economic reform. Predictably, this will also make it more difficult to reduce the subsidies and balance the government's budget.

THE TRANSITIONAL TRAP: BUDGET DEFICITS, MONEY CREATION, AND INFLATION

Our experience shows that reform must start with a heavy dose of restrictive macroeconomic policy. This prepares the ground for price and foreign trade liberalization and, by cutting subsidies, announces the dramatic change of the whole economic climate. A reforming country that does not implement this crucial measure at an early moment inevitably falls into what I call the "reform trap." This is a vicious circle of high inflation or even hyperinflation, repeated devaluations, growing foreign indebtedness, budget deficits, and the like.

VACLAV KLAUS, PRIME MINISTER OF THE CZECH REPUBLIC[5]

Several of the formerly communist countries have fallen into what Prime Minister Vaclav Klaus of the Czech Republic refers to as the "reform trap." After liberalizing prices, they sought to reduce the subsidies available to state enterprises. If this could be accomplished, the enterprises would face a hardened budget constraint that would increase their incentive to reduce costs and produce things that consumers value. As the firms increasingly confronted competition from both other domestic firms and foreign suppliers, prices of goods would begin to reflect the opportunity cost of their production.

Obviously, the weak link in this scenario is whether the subsidies to the enterprises can, in fact, be cut. If they cannot, the cost of the subsidies will have to be covered by higher taxes, borrowing, or the creation of money. Given the number of state-owned enterprises and the small size of the private sector, raising taxes on

---

[5]Vaclav Klaus, *The Ten Commandments of Systematic Reform* (Washington, DC: Group of Thirty, 1993), p. 3.

private firms to subsidize the state-operated firms is not a viable option. Borrowing to finance a budget deficit will generally be impossible as the result of the political insecurity of the governments and their recent record of high inflation (when prices were decontrolled). Lacking credibility in the financial credit market, the only way that the state can continue to subsidize the government enterprises is through money creation. When this happens on a large scale, budget deficits, rapid growth of the money supply, and hyperinflation are the result. In turn, the hyperinflation leads to capital flight. Prices lose much of their meaning, the reform process comes to a halt, and the economy continues to decline.

Several of the countries of the former Eastern bloc, including Russia, Ukraine, Belarus, and Romania, fell into this trap in the early 1990s. As the result of their inability or unwillingness to reduce enterprise subsidies and confront state-operated firms with a hard budget constraint, the reform process slowed, and they were plagued with hyperinflation.

CONTRASTING POLICIES—THE CZECH REPUBLIC AND RUSSIA

There is sometimes a tendency to think that the countries of Eastern Europe and the former Soviet Union confront similar problems and have followed similar transition strategies. This is not the case. Comparing and contrasting the conditions and policies of the Czech Republic and Russia illustrates this point. The Czech Republic, which comprised approximately two-thirds of Czechoslovakia prior to the peaceful split of that country into the Czech and Slovak republics at year-end 1992, was under communism for a little more than 40 years. Russia was under communism for more than 70 years. The Czech Republic is a relatively small country—its population is 10.3 million—in the center of Europe. In contrast, Russia is a huge country spanning 11 time zones and boasting a population of almost 150 million. More significantly, the transition policies of these two countries have differed substantially. We now turn to an explanation of these differences.

TRANSITION POLICIES OF CZECH REPUBLIC

Following the fall of communism in late 1989, the newly elected government of Czechoslovakia began laying the groundwork for the transition from socialism to a market economy. Monetary policy prior to and during the period of price decontrol was very tight. During 1990 and 1991 the supply of money grew very slowly. It was only slightly higher—about 4 percent—in 1991 than at year-end 1989 (see **Exhibit 34–7**). Therefore, when prices were decontrolled on approximately 85 percent of the goods in January of 1991, the restrictive monetary policy helped reduce the magnitude of the jump in prices. Following price decontrol, there was a sharp increase in prices. Consumer prices rose 47 percent during the first six months of 1991. The inflation rate, however, soon became moderate. The annual rate of inflation in 1992 was 11 percent.

Fiscal policy also played an important role in the stabilization policy of Czechoslovakia and the newly established Czech Republic. The government balanced its budget in 1990 and again in 1993. During 1991 and 1992, the budget deficit was approximately 2.5 percent of GDP, relatively low for a transitional economy. Reductions in subsidies to enterprises contributed substantially to the tight budgetary policies of the Czech Republic (and the former Czechoslovakia). Of course, these enterprise subsidies were a central element of the prior socialist regime. In 1989, 37 percent of the government budget was channeled into enterprise subsidies. This figure was reduced to 27 percent (this figure is for Czechoslovakia) in 1990 and was subsequently pared to 11 percent (this figure is for the Czech Republic) in 1993. Clearly, the monetary and fiscal policies of the Czech

EXHIBIT 34-7

ANNUAL RATE OF CHANGE IN MONEY SUPPLY AND INFLATION RATE FOR THE CZECH REPUBLIC, POLAND, HUNGARY, ROMANIA, BULGARIA, AND RUSSIA, 1989–1993

COUNTRY	1989	1990	1991	1992	1993
Czech Republic					
Budget deficit[a]	–2.4	+0.1	–2.0	–3.3	0.0
Money supply	5	0	4	26	24
Inflation rate	1	10	58	11	21
Poland					
Budget deficit[a]	–7.4	+3.5	–6.2	–7.0	–4.8
Money supply	137	556	66	31	20
Inflation rate	251	566	70	43	35
Hungary					
Budget deficit[a]	–1.3	+0.4	–4.6	–8.3	–6.0
Money supply	11	21	17	27	20
Inflation rate	17	29	34	23	23
Romania					
Budget deficit[a]	+8.4	+1.2	+0.6	–6.1	–6.0
Money supply	14	8	60	153	100
Inflation rate	1	4	231	210	316
Bulgaria					
Budget deficit[a]	–1.4	–12.7	–15.1	–14.0	na
Money supply	11	15	125	41	na
Inflation rate	6	26	334	83	90
Russia					
Budget deficit[a]	na	na	–21.2	–4.3	–10 to 15
Money supply	14	18	99	610	665
Inflation rate	2	6	93	1354	900

[a]The budget-deficit data are presented as a percent of GDP.

Source: The money-supply data are from the International Monetary Fund, *International Financial Statistics*. The inflation-rate data are from the prior publication and the European Bank for Reconstruction and Development, *Annual Economic Outlook*, September 1993; *Central European Economic Review*, Winter 1994, p. 6; and "Facts and Figures," *Business Central Europe*, various issues. The budget-deficit data are from "Statistical Tables," *The Economics of Transition* 1, 4 (1993).

Republic steered the country away from the transition trap of continual enterprise subsidies, budget deficits, rapid monetary growth, and inflation.

The tight macropolicy was coupled with privatization and liberalization of trade. Both the establishment of new enterprises and the sale of enterprises previously owned by the state contributed to the growth of the private sector in the Czech Republic. By 1993 there were more than 1 million unregistered private enterprises there. A large proportion of these enterprises were new small businesses that had sprung up since the fall of communism. (See the feature on the following page for information on the impact of the growing private retail sector in the Czech Republic and other Eastern European countries.)

Following the passage of legislation in 1990, privatization of small state-owned enterprises began in earnest in 1991. Restitution and sales at public auctions were the two primary methods used to privatize restaurants, shops, small buildings, and other small enterprises. In the case of restitution, assets were returned to previous owners (or their heirs) from whom the property was taken during the nationalization of the late 1940s and the 1950s under the communist regime. Since proof of the restitution claims was often complex, this method of privatization is generally a slow and tenuous process. Nonetheless, restitution was used to privatize approximately 30,000 industrial and administrative buildings and nearly half of the agriculture and forest land previously owned by the state. In addition, more than 20,000 small state enterprises—mostly stores and companies providing services—were sold at public auctions during 1991 and 1992.

The centerpiece of the Czech privatization strategy was the use of a voucher plan to transfer the ownership of medium and large-scale enterprises to the market sector. Under this plan, each Czech citizen was eligible to purchase voucher points for a nominal price (the equivalent of approximately $30). These points were then used to purchase shares in large-scale state-owned enterprises that were thought to be suitable for operation in the private sector. Individuals could either use their voucher points to bid directly for enterprise shares, or they could invest them in mutual funds that would use them to purchase shares. During the first wave of privatization in 1992, approximately 1,500 state enterprises, with an estimated value of between $5 and $10 billion, were privatized by the voucher method.

A second-wave voucher privatization plan of a slightly smaller size is currently (in 1994) in progress. When the second wave is completed, it is estimated that approximately 40 percent of the GDP of the Czech Republic will be generated by the private sector, up from less than 4 percent in 1989.[6]

Finally, trade liberalization has also been an important component of the overall transition strategy of the Czech Republic. The average tariff rates are about 5 percent, and there are few quota restrictions limiting the entry of foreign produced goods. Adjusted for inflation, both exports and imports declined in 1991,

---

[6]For additional details on the privatization of state enterprises in the Czech Republic, Russia, and other countries of Eastern Europe, see John S. Earle, Roman Frydman, and Andrzej Rapaczynski, "Transition Policies and the Establishment of a Private Property Regime in Eastern Europe" a paper delivered at a meeting of Economic Policy: A European Forum hosted by the National Bank of Belgium in Brussels on October 22–23, 1993; Roman Frydman and Andrzej Rapaczynski, "Privatization in Eastern Europe: Is the State Withering Away?" *Finance and Development* (June 1993), pp. 10–13; Maxim Boycko, Andrei Shleifer, and Robert W. Vishny, "Privatizing Russia", a paper delivered to the Brookings Panel on Economic Activity in Washington, DC on September 9–10, 1993; and Czech Republic Ministry for the Administration of the National Property and Its Privatization, *Report on the Privatization Process for the Years 1989 to 1992*, published by the Czech Republic Ministry in 1993.

APPLICATIONS IN ECONOMICS

MARKET COMPETITION AND THE CHANGING RETAIL SECTOR OF EASTERN EUROPE

Under communism, shopping for Eastern Europeans was an ordeal. The state-operated stores were typically dark and dingy. Shopping hours were limited—almost all stores closed at 6:00 P.M. on weekdays and at 1:00 on Saturday afternoons. At grocery stores, as well as the various sections of a retail store, it was required that you have a basket or cart in order to enter. Usually there was a line to obtain the obligatory basket. Once inside a retail area the customer would be faced with a line waiting to inspect the low-quality merchandise being tightly controlled by an unsmiling, unhelpful clerk. Having made a selection, it would then be necessary to take an order form to a cashier and then return to collect the purchase, being careful to maintain one's position in each queue. Of course, the chances were always high that once inside the store you would find the desired item was not even available.

As restrictions on private-sector business activities were relaxed in Poland, the former nation of Czechoslovakia, and other Eastern European countries, market competition began to change this situation. Since entry into retailing is relatively easy, privatization has moved forward rapidly in this sector. For example, in the Czech Republic private-sector retail sales have increased as a proportion of the total from 20 percent in 1991 to 68 percent in 1992 to 83 percent at year-end 1993.[1]

Initially, most of the new private retail firms were small shops, owned and operated by an adventurous entrepreneur. More recently, major retailers like Kmart and Hit, a German supermarket chain, have entered the market. Kmart purchased 13 formerly government-operated stores that were privatized by the Czechoslovakian government prior to the split into the Czech and Slovak republics. After spending millions of dollars on remodeling, several of the stores began operation under the Kmart logo in 1993–1994. Bright lighting and the colorful Kmart decor replaced the dingy gray, and clerks were retrained to be helpful and courteous and to smile. The initial advertising campaign emphasized that at Kmart you could enter without a basket. Goods were located conveniently for the customers' inspection. Evening and late Saturday afternoon shopping became commonplace. Bar-code pricing made the checkout process faster and more convenient.

Hit has exerted a similar impact in Warsaw. After renovating a 10,000-square-meter factory, Hit opened a giant one-stop shopping mart complete with parking for 600 cars, a wide variety of products, and economical prices kept low by purchasing in bulk directly from producers. Approximately 80 percent of the products offered in its Polish stores are produced in Poland. The nature of shopping in Prague, Bratislava, Warsaw, and other cities throughout Eastern Europe is rapidly changing thanks to competition from both small entrepreneurs and larger established firms.

---

[1]Czech Statistical Office, *Monthly Statistics of the Czech Republic*, February 1994, table 18.

but they rebounded sharply in 1992. In 1992 exports summed to slightly more than half of the Czechoslovakian GDP, up from less than 40 percent in 1990.[7] The liberal trade policies and the strong trade sector have helped to bring the relative prices of goods produced by both private and public sector enterprises into line with their opportunity cost.

Perhaps the most serious problem currently confronting the Czech Republic is the high rate of taxation. The payroll tax is 59 percent, one of the highest in the region. Personal income is taxed at marginal rates ranging from 15 percent to 47 percent. The top 47 percent rate begins taking effect at an equivalent income of approximately $30,000. In addition, there is a flat rate corporate tax of 45 percent and a value-added tax of 23 percent. Given these tax rates and the current

---

[7]Andreas Worgotter et al., *The Czech Republic, More Than Prague* (Vienna: Bank of Austria, 1994).

The development of both small businesses and large-scale established firms, like this Kmart store in Prague (Czech Republic), are playing a role in the transformation of the retail sector throughout much of Eastern Europe.

enforcement policies, tax evasion is thought to be widespread in the Czech Republic. To the extent this is true, the official figures almost surely underestimate both the size of the private sector and the growth of real output during the transition period. But this is not a healthy situation. Imposing high tax rates on honest citizens while driving large numbers of people into the underground economy is not a solid foundation for prosperity. The Czech Republic needs to couple substantial reductions in tax rates with the development of a system that will improve tax compliance.

The Czech Republic has not done everything right during the transition period. Nonetheless, the transition record is a good one. Privatization is continuing at a rapid rate, large budget deficits have been avoided, and the inflation rate is low by the standards of Eastern Europe. If it continues to follow the current policy path, most economists and investors are optimistic about the future growth potential of this transitional economy.

TRANSITION POLICIES OF RUSSIA

As Boris Yeltsin assumed the presidency of Russia in 1991, both the Soviet Union and the Russian economy were in a state of collapse. There had been a lot of talk about reform and restructuring, but very little had in fact taken place. Output declined by 4 percent in 1990 and another 11 percent in 1991 (see Exhibit 34–5). In 1991 Russia's budget deficit was 21 percent of its GDP, and the money supply doubled during the year (see Exhibit 34–7). Even though price controls remained in place on most goods, the annual rate of inflation in 1991 was 93 percent.

It was against this background that the team assembled by President Yeltsin moved to decontrol prices in January of 1992. In contrast with the situation a year earlier in Czechoslovakia, the monetary and fiscal policies of Russia prior to decontrol were highly expansionary. Clearly, these policies aggravated the problems arising from the decontrol of below-equilibrium prices and the monetary overhang. The results were predictable. Price controls were lifted on 90 percent of the tradeable goods on January 2, 1992, and by the next day prices rose by an average of 250 percent.

During the next six months, the new government tried valiantly to get the budget under control. To a degree it was successful; the budget deficit was reduced to 4 percent of GDP in 1992, down from more than 20 percent during the previous year. These efforts, however, were eventually undermined by the issuing of credits by the state enterprises that dominated the economy. Rather than restructure or lay off workers in order to cut costs, the state enterprises in Russia continued with operations as usual. Workers were paid with company credits—coupons or vouchers, or even ruble-like notes with the picture of the company manager—which could be used to purchase things supplied by the company. Given the major role of enterprises in the provision of health care, education, housing, and the operation of stores, these credits had some value.

The inter-company debt of state enterprises rose from 39 billion rubles in January of 1992 to 3.200 trillion rubles by the end of June 1992, an amount greater than the quantity of money in circulation in Russia.[8] Of course, this pyramid scheme could not be maintained without the assistance of the central government (and the central monetary authorities). Recognizing this point, a powerful coalition of state-enterprise managers and employees lobbied the Parliament and convinced it to supply the enterprises with the rubles to pay for the credits. By mid-year 1992, the Parliament had arranged the appointment of Viktor Gerashchenko, the former head of the old Soviet Central planning agency (the Gosplan), as the head of the Russian central bank. Under Gerashchenko's supervision, the supply of rubles began to increase at a *monthly* rate of greater than 20 percent. During the next 12 months (from mid-year 1992 until mid-year 1993) the domestic money supply of Russia increased by approximately tenfold. Unsurprisingly, prices followed suit, and Russia moved into hyperinflation. It was against this background that Yeltsin dismissed the Parliament and called for a new election. Various national parties and parties dominated by old-line Communists did quite well in the December 1993 parliamentary elections. Thus, prospects for a quick reversal of the policies feeding Russia's hyperinflation are dim.

Obviously, the political climate for privatization of Russian state enterprises was exceedingly poor in 1992–1993. Nonetheless, the Yeltsin administration perceived that moving forward with privatization was crucially important. In order to make privatization more palatable to enterprise workers and managers, substantial accommodations were required. While a citizen-wide voucher privatization plan was instituted, workers and managers of the privatized enterprises were allowed to choose whether they wanted to receive 25 percent of the enterprise shares free, or whether they would prefer to pay 1.7 times the nominal book value and purchase 51 percent of the shares. Since the latter option assured workers that

[8]"Reforming Russia's Economy," *The Economist,* December 11, 1993. For additional background on the macro policies of Russia, see Michael Ellman, "Shock Therapy in Russia: Failure or Partial Success," *RFE RL Research Report,* August 28, 1992.

they would retain control of the enterprise, and inflation was rapidly reducing this nominal payment, more than three-fourths of the enterprises opted for this second option. Therefore, even after the privatization, workers will generally retain control of the enterprises, and the minority owners who purchased stock with vouchers will receive only what the majority employee shareholders want to pay out in dividends. If the employee shareholders simply pay higher wages, they will not have to share the residual income with the other shareholders. Therefore, substantial wage payments and low (if any) dividends are the expected result under the ownership structure that emerged from the Russian voucher plan. (See the boxed feature below for an analysis of why owner control of enterprise is important.)

Equally important, it is unclear whether the privatization in Russia will lead to any change in the relationship between the enterprises and the central government. To date, subsidies to the enterprises have continued to flow, and therefore there is little reason for the enterprises to undertake genuine restructuring, develop alternative product lines, or search for alternative markets. To the extent that the subsidies continue, the enterprises will continue to spend a substantial amount of their time and resources seeking political favors, while failing to undertake steps that will reduce costs, improve products, and shift resources toward the

---

APPLICATIONS IN ECONOMICS

WHY PRIVATIZATION AND OWNER CONTROL OF ENTERPRISES ARE IMPORTANT

In a market economy, firms are dependent on sales to consumers for their revenues and are disciplined by the forces of competition. Owners of private firms have a strong incentive to produce efficiently—to keep costs per unit low and quality high—because lower costs and higher quality will increase the size of the owner's residual income.

For this process to work well, however, two conditions are vitally important. First, the enterprises must confront a hard budget constraint—that is, they must be dependent on sales to customers rather than subsidies and favorable tax treatment for their revenues. It is this dependence on sales revenues that provides enterprises with the incentive to produce efficiently and cater to the preferences of consumers. In contrast, government enterprises (and subsidized private firms) confront what Hungarian economist Janos Kornai calls a "soft budget constraint."[1] When the costs of public sector enterprises rise or their sales revenues fall, governments have a tendency to bail them out—to provide them with larger subsidies rather than forcing them to either operate more efficiently or go out of business. This soft budget constraint reduces operational efficiency and encourages the managers of the firm to engage in wasteful rent-seeking activities.

Second, the owners must be in a position to capture the residual income. Their property right to this residual income is what provides them with the incentive to monitor the firm's managers and keep them on their toes. When there is a small group of owners who can benefit substantially from an improvement in the operational efficiency of the firm, predictably this vitally important monitoring function will be conducted well. On the other hand, if the ownership of the firm is widely dispersed, control of the managers (and employees) is likely to be lax and the operational efficiency of the firm will tend to suffer. Predictably, this will be a major problem with privatization as it has unfolded in Russia. In most cases, the employees and managers hold the majority ownership shares while the minority shareholders (who acquired their shares through the voucher method) are widely dispersed. Both of these factors will tend to promote continued "insider control" of the enterprises and weaken the incentive to improve the firm's operational efficiency.

[1]Janos Kornai, "The Soft Budget Constraint" in *The Road to Capitalism* edited by David Kennett and Marc Lieberman (Fort Worth: The Dryden Press, 1992).

production of goods that are highly valued by consumers. Since the "outside owners" are minority stockholders, the likelihood that they will be able to play a constructive role in future direction of the firm is extremely low. Under these circumstances, the Russian privatization is mostly decorative.

In addition, the current legal environment in Russia and throughout most of the former Soviet Union is extremely hostile to the development and enforcement of secure private property rights. The activities of the so-called "Russian Mafia"— an underground network generally comprised of criminals, former communist party officials, and local government officials—are a major factor in this area. Essentially the Russian mafia uses violence (car bombings, kidnapping of family members, and even murder) and the threat of violence as a means of extorting "payments" from private businesses in exchange for "protection." In some cases, the mafia is organized along industrial lines and protection of existing state enterprises from competition from newly established private firms appears to be an objective. In other instances, mafia members are apparently only interested in the raising of funds through extortion. Regardless of the objectives, the atmosphere is undermining the development of the private sector in Russia and the legitimate government authorities are currently either too weak, or unwilling to do much about it.

Given (a) the insider control of state enterprises, (b) the vicious cycle of subsidies, budget deficits, money creation, inflation, and (c) the insecurity of private property rights, the prospects for the development of business activity and a market economy in Russia and most of the former Soviet Union in the near future are bleak.

LESSONS FROM THE EXPERIENCE OF CHINA

In contrast with the turmoil, inflation, and falling output of transitional economies in Europe and the former Soviet Union, more modest moves toward liberalization in China have resulted in rapid economic growth. Why has the Chinese experience been so different, and what lessons can be drawn from it? It should be recognized that the structural characteristics of the Chinese economy differ substantially from those of the former Soviet bloc countries. China is a predominately agricultural economy. When the Chinese liberalization program began in 1978, three-fourths of the population lived and worked in rural areas. By way of comparison, less than 20 percent of the employment and output of Russia and the Eastern European countries is derived from agriculture.

The Chinese liberalization began with the dismantling of collective farms and providing of long-term land leases to peasant farmers in exchange for a fixed production quota. Since the farmers were permitted to either keep or sell everything over and above the state quota, they had a strong incentive to expand output. In effect, the farmers confronted a marginal tax rate of zero.

Later, the liberalization focus shifted to the small-business and industrial sectors. In these areas, the Chinese have moved more slowly than the former Soviet bloc countries. While private firms were allowed to develop and compete with the existing state enterprises, there was virtually no privatization of existing state firms. The state enterprises continued to operate and, in large degree, their subsidies continued to flow. Nonetheless, the private sector of China has grown rapidly. This growth has been particularly strong in sectors where small and medium-sized businesses can compete effectively with large state enterprises.

The China experiment would appear to contain two important lessons for Eastern Europe and the former Soviet Union. First, the agricultural sector is easier to divide up and privatize than the industrial sector. Since the former Soviet bloc countries specialize in wheat and feed grain rather than the rice and vegetables that tend to dominate Chinese agriculture, privatization will be a bit more complicated than it was in China. However, the productivity on the small private plots in the former Soviet Union has long been substantially higher than that of the collective farms.[9] Increases in the size of the private plots and the use of shares to divide up ownership of both larger land plots and equipment is a promising way for the Russia and other Soviet bloc countries to proceed.

Second, if political obstacles retard industrial privatization, providing an attractive environment for the development of new private firms probably offers the surest path for private-sector growth. This would mean removal of all registration and permits required to form new businesses, keeping taxes on the private sector low, and providing for a stable monetary environment. While "bottom-up" privatization will take longer, the Chinese experience indicates that it can work.[10]

---

[9]In the 1970s, even though these small private plots constituted only a little more than 1 percent of the agriculture land under cultivation, they accounted for approximately 25 percent of the total value of the Soviet agricultural output. The number of households working these garden plots has increased in recent years, and their share of the aggregate output is now thought to be even higher. See Zhores Medvedev, *Soviet Agriculture* (New York: W. W. Norton, 1987), for additional information on this topic.

[10]For additional information on the relevance of China to the problems of transition economies, see Marshall I. Goldman, "The Chinese Model: the Solution to Russia's Economics Ills?" *Current History*, October 1993; and Jeffrey Sachs and Wing Thya Woo, "Structural Factors in the Economic Reforms of China, Eastern Europe, and the Former Soviet Union," a paper presented to the Economic Policy Panel in Brussels, Belgium, October 22–23, 1993.

CONCLUDING THOUGHTS

The landscape of economics is constantly changing. Who would have predicted a few years ago that in the 1990s economists would be addressing the problems of how countries make the transition from socialism to an organizational structure capable of providing more opportunity and prosperity. This issue is sure to continue enlivening the study and research of economists in the decade ahead. What will be the next major issue? We cannot be sure, but whatever it is, the tools of economics will enhance our ability to understand and deal with it.

CHAPTER SUMMARY

1. Capitalist economies are characterized by private ownership of productive assets and the use of markets to allocate goods and resources. The distinguishing characteristics of socialist economies are government ownership of physical capital and resource allocation by central planning.

2. Under socialism, the central planners set the prices of all goods and provide the enterprises with directives concerning the resources that will be provided to them, new machines that are to be installed, the firm's target output, and other aspects of production. The task of the firm is to transform the resources into the output quota.

3. Under central planning, the supply of each good reflects the priorities of the planners and price plays a secondary role. Sometimes the planners attempt to set the price of a good such that the amount demanded will balance the amount supplied. But this is not generally the case. When the price of a good produced by an enterprise is set below the good's production cost, the enterprise has to be subsidized. On the other hand, when price exceeds

opportunity cost, the state reaps a "profit."

4. When the subsidies to firms selling at prices below cost exceed the revenues derived from goods sold at prices above cost, the income payments to the resource suppliers will be greater than the amount required to purchase the available goods, *at the prices fixed by the planners.* This process leads to both queuing (and other non-price forms of rationing) and a monetary overhang—the accumulation of money deposits by households.

5. Several factors contributed to the poor performance and eventual breakup of the central-planning regimes of Eastern Europe and the former Soviet Union., The most important of these were the

   a. Inability of a central-planning agency to acquire and react to widely dispersed but highly relevant information concerning local circumstances, elements of timing, and changing conditions.

   b. Weak incentive of enterprises to maintain quality, produce efficiently, and provide products highly valued by consumers.

   c. Weak incentive for central planners and enterprises to innovate and invest resources wisely.

   d. Misallocation of resources that results because the priorities of the plan inevitably reflect political factors and the views of the planners rather than economic considerations and the preferences of consumers.

6. The nature of the transition problem is straightforward: the efficiency of enterprises needs to be improved, and resources need to be moved away from uses that provide consumers with little value (relative to their cost). This is likely to be a painful process when so many enterprises are operated inefficiently and are producing goods for which demand is weak.

7. Successful transition plans will almost certainly involve the following four elements: market determination of prices, competition among suppliers, monetary (and price) stability, and privatization.

8. Since 1989 the size of the private sector has increased substantially in several countries—most notably the Czech Republic, Poland, and Hungary. In contrast, other countries, including Russia, Belarus, and Ukraine, have moved slowly toward privatization and have failed to develop a comprehensive transition strategy.

9. The GDP data indicate that all transitional economies have experienced sharp declines in output. These official GDP figures probably overstate the reductions in output because (a) they do not fully measure the new private-sector activities, (b) they fail to consider adequately the rapid changes in product quality and availability that have occurred during the transition period, and (c) the prior output figures under central planning were overstated.

10. The transition from socialism to a market-based economy is more difficult than was initially perceived because (a) socialism left behind an aftermath of oversized firms and industry-wide monopolies; (b) the legal framework for the protection of private property, enforcement of contracts, and operation of financial markets was almost totally absent in formerly socialist countries, and the development of these institutions takes time; (c) the monetary overhang made price decontrol more complicated; and (d) political considerations continue to make it extremely difficult to reduce enterprise subsidies.

11. Several countries, including Russia and Ukraine, have fallen into the transition trap of budget deficits, money creation, and inflation. Decontrol of prices without reducing enterprise subsidies leads to large budget deficits that can be financed only through money creation. In turn, the money creation and high rates of inflation that it causes lead to capital flight, a plunging investment rate, and falling incomes.

CRITICAL-ANALYSIS QUESTIONS

1. Compare and contrast the role of firm managers under socialism versus those in a market economy. In which case would a manager have the greatest incentive to (a) operate the firm efficiently, (b) maximize the profits of a firm, and (c) adopt a new innovative production method or introduce a new product?

2. Are there economic functions that you think a centrally planned economy can accomplish more effectively than a market economy? Why or why not? What are the major disadvantages of a centrally planned economy? Do you believe that market allocation is superior or inferior to centralized planning? Explain your answer.

3. Under central planning, managers of state enterprises were generally told what resources to use, what price to charge, and how many units to produce. Why aren't instructions of this type given to owners and managers of firms in a market setting? Who controls the actions of firms in a market economy?

4. "Socialism means production for use, not for profit. Workers contribute according to their qualifications, and they are rewarded according to egalitarian principles. Socialism takes power from the business elite and grants it to the workers, who, after all, produce the goods." Analyze this point of view.

*5. When an economy is centrally planned, the subsidies paid to enterprises selling below cost may exceed the revenues the government derives from enterprises selling above cost. Why doesn't this lead to inflation? What are two major side effects of this strategy?

---

*Asterisk denotes questions for which answers are given in Appendix C.

*6. When the prices of a centrally planned economy are decontrolled, there is generally a major jump in the price level. What is the cause of this sharp increase in the level of prices. Is this the same thing as inflation? Why or why not?

7. How did the voucher plan used by the former Czechoslovakia (and later by the Czech Republic) differ from the voucher plan implemented in Russia? What are the advantages and disadvantages of the alternative plans? Which is most likely to result in an effective regime of private ownership? Explain.

8. Compare and contrast the transition policies and experiences of Russia and the Czech Republic. How did the policies of these two countries differ? How have these differences influenced the rate of inflation, growth of the private sector, and future economic prospects of the two countries.

9. The text indicates that there are four key elements of a successful transition plan. What are these four elements? Which do you think could be implemented most rapidly? Are the four elements interrelated—that is, will the failure to implement one of the elements reduce the effectiveness of other elements? Which of the elements do you think should be introduced first? Why?

*10. Socialists often claim that under capitalism resources are wasted producing luxury goods for the rich. Evaluate this charge.

11. If the investment funds of a country are going to promote prosperity, they must be directed toward the production of goods that are valued more highly than the resources used in their production. Why is this important? Will additional investment always increase the wealth of a nation? Explain.

12. Suppose you were hired as a consultant to develop a comprehensive economic reform plan for Russia. What specific reforms would you suggest? Indicate why you think they would be effective.

*13. "Capitalism is better at producing wealth; socialism is better at distributing it fairly." Evaluate this statement.

---

*Asterisk denotes questions for which answers are given in Appendix C.

PRODUCTION THEORY AND ISOQUANT ANALYSIS

When analyzing production theory and input utilization, economists often rely on isoquant analysis. Since the technique is widely used at the intermediate level, some instructors explain the concept in their introductory course.

WHAT ARE ISOQUANTS?

Generally, several alternative input combinations can be used to produce a good. For example, 100 bushels of wheat might be produced with 2 acres of land, 5 bushels of seed, and 100 pounds of fertilizer. Alternatively, the wheat could be produced with more land and less fertilizer, or more seed and less land, or more fertilizer and less seed. Many input combinations could be used to produce 100 bushels of wheat.

Isoquant
A curve representing the technically efficient combinations of two inputs that can be used to produce a given level of output.

The word "isoquant" means "equal quantity." An **isoquant** is a curve that indicates the various combinations of two inputs that could be used to produce an equal quantity of output. **Exhibit 1** provides an illustration. The isoquant labeled "100 units of cloth" shows the various combinations of capital and labor that a technically efficient producer could use to produce 100 units of cloth. Every point on an isoquant is technically efficient. By that we mean that it would not be possible, given the current level of technology, to produce a larger output with the input combination. If a producer wanted to produce a larger output, 140 units of cloth, for example, it would be necessary to use more of at least one of the resources. Since larger output levels require additional resources, isoquants representing larger levels of output always lie to the northeast, in an isoquant diagram.

An isoquant represents all input combinations that, if used efficiently, will generate a specific level of output. As illustrated here, 100 units of cloth could be produced with the input combinations L_1K_1 or L_2K_2 or any other combination of labor and capital that lies on the isoquant representing 100 units of cloth.

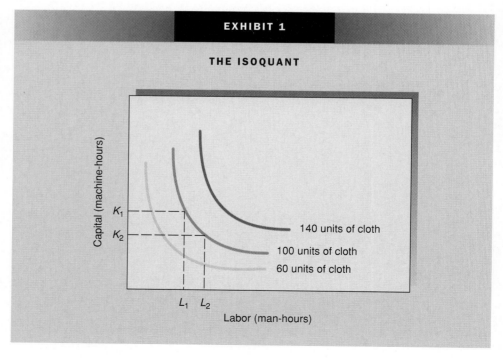

EXHIBIT 1

THE ISOQUANT

CHARACTERISTICS OF ISOQUANTS

Isoquant analysis must be consistent with the laws of production. What do the laws of production imply about the characteristics of isoquants?

1. Isoquants Slope Downward to the Right.   Within the relevant range of utilization, an increase in the usage level of an input makes it possible to expand output. If, for example, the use of the labor input is expanded, it is possible to produce the same output level (stay on the same isoquant) with a smaller quantity of capital. Since both labor and capital can be used to increase production, they can be substituted for each other. Constant output can be maintained either by (a) using more labor and less capital or (b) by using more capital and less labor. Thus, every isoquant runs from the northwest to the southeast, as illustrated by Exhibit 1.

2. Isoquants Are Convex When Viewed from the Origin.   The convexity of isoquants stems from the fact that as one continues to substitute labor for capital, larger and larger amounts of labor are required to maintain output at a constant level. As labor is used more intensively, it becomes increasingly difficult to substitute labor for each additional unit of capital. Since larger and larger amounts of labor are required to compensate for the loss of each additional unit of capital (and thus maintain the constant level of output), the isoquant becomes flatter as labor is used more intensively (see **Exhibit 2,** point *B*).

   On the other hand, when capital is used more and more intensively, larger and larger amounts of capital are required to compensate for the loss of a unit of labor. Thus, an isoquant becomes steeper as capital (the *y* factor) is used more intensively (see Exhibit 2, point *A*). It is convex when viewed from the origin.

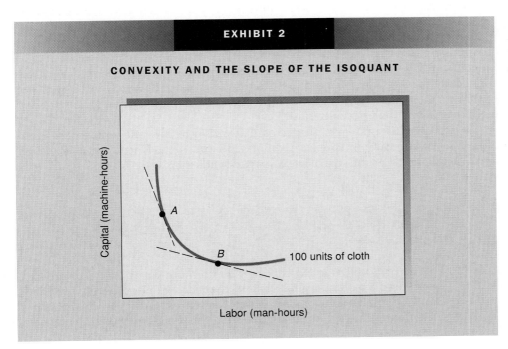

EXHIBIT 2

CONVEXITY AND THE SLOPE OF THE ISOQUANT

Capital (machine-hours)

A

B   100 units of cloth

Labor (man-hours)

When labor is used intensively relative to capital (point B), the slope of the isoquant is much flatter than it is when capital is used more intensively (point A). The slope of an isoquant is the ratio of the marginal products of the two factors (MP$_L$ divided by MP$_K$). When labor is used more intensively relative to capital, its marginal product falls (and that of capital increases). Since the marginal product of labor is low (and the marginal product of capital is high) when labor is used intensively (as at point B), the isoquant is relatively flat.

3. The Slope of the Isoquant Is the Marginal Product of Labor Divided by the Marginal Product of Capital. The slope of the isoquant is determined by the amount of labor that must be added to maintain a constant level of output when one less unit of capital is used. This slope is dependent on the marginal productivity of labor relative to capital. When labor is used intensively relative to capital, its marginal product is low, relative to capital. Under these circumstances, as Exhibit 2 (point *B*) illustrates, the slope of the isoquant is small (the isoquant is relatively flat). In contrast, when capital is used intensively (Exhibit 2, point *A*), the marginal product of labor is high, relative to capital. The steepness of the isoquant reflects this fact. At any point on the isoquant, the slope of the isoquant is equal to MP_L / MP_K.

THE ISOCOST LINE

A set of isoquants outlines the technically efficient input combinations that could be used to produce alternative levels of output. Before we can determine the economically efficient input combinations for producing a level of output, we must also incorporate information about cost and resource prices.

Isocost Line

A line representing the various combinations of two factors that can be purchased with a given money budget (cost).

Firms generally can purchase inputs at a fixed price per unit. The **isocost line** shows the alternative combinations of inputs that can be purchased with a given outlay of funds. As the term implies, the cost of purchasing an input combination on the isocost line is equal to the cost of purchasing any other input combination on the same line. To construct an isocost line, two pieces of information are required: (a) the prices of the resources and (b) the specific outlay of funds. **Exhibit 3** illustrates the construction of three different isocost lines, assuming that the price of labor is $5 per unit and that the price of capital is $10 per unit. Consider the $500 isocost line. If all funds were spent on labor, 100 units of labor could be purchased. Alternatively, if the entire $500 were expended on capital, 50 units of capital could be purchased. It would be possible to purchase any input combination between these two extremes—for example, 80 units of labor and 10 units of capital—with the $500. The input combinations are represented by a line connecting the two extreme points, 100 units of labor on the *x*-axis and 50 units of capital on the *y*-axis. Note that the slope of the isocost line is merely the price of labor divided by the price of capital (P_L / P_K).

If the outlay of funds were to increase, it would be possible to purchase more of both labor and capital. Thus, as Exhibit 3 illustrates, the isocost lines move in a northeast direction as the size of the outlay of funds increases.

MINIMIZING THE COST OF PRODUCTION

A profit-seeking firm will want to choose the minimum-cost method of production. We can combine isoquant analysis and the isocost line to derive the minimum-cost input combination for producing a given output level. As **Exhibit 4** illustrates, the minimum-cost input combination for producing 100 units of cloth

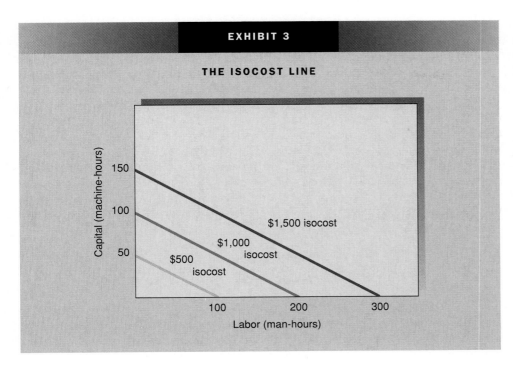

EXHIBIT 3

THE ISOCOST LINE

The isocost line indicates the alternative combinations of the resources that can be purchased with a given outlay of funds. When the price of a unit of labor is $5 and that of a unit of capital is $10, the three isocost lines shown here represent the alternative combinations of labor and capital that could be purchased at costs of $500, $1,000 and $1,500. The slope of the isocost line is equal to P_L/P_K ($5/$10 = $^1/_2$ in this case).

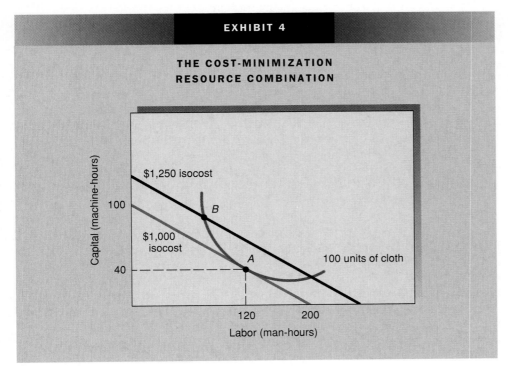

EXHIBIT 4

THE COST-MINIMIZATION
RESOURCE COMBINATION

When the cost of producing an output level (for example, 100 units of cloth) is minimized, the isoquant is tangent to the isocost line. At that point (A), $MP_L/MP_K = P_L/P_K$.

is represented by the point at which the lowest isocost line just touches (is tangent to) the isoquant for 100 units of cloth. At that point (*A* of Exhibit 4), the producer will be able to combine 120 units of labor purchased at a cost of $600 ($5 per unit) with 40 units of capital purchased at a cost of $400 ($10 per unit) to produce 100 units of cloth. The total cost of the 100 units is $1,000 ($10 per unit).

Of course, other input combinations could be used to produce the 100 units of cloth. However, they would be more costly, given the current prices of labor and capital. For example, if the input combination *B* were used to produce the 100 units, the total cost would be $1,250 ($12.50 per unit).

When costs are at a minimum, the isoquant is tangent to the isocost line. The slopes of the two are equal at that point. In other words, when the cost of producing a specific output is at a minimum, the MP_L/MP_K (the slope of the isoquant) will be equal to P_L/P_K (the slope of the isocost line). Since:

$$\frac{MP_L}{MP_K} = \frac{P_L}{P_K}$$

then:

$$\frac{MP_L}{P_L} = \frac{MP_K}{P_K}$$

The latter equation represents precisely the condition that our earlier analysis, in the chapter devoted to supply of and demand for productive resources, indicated would be present if the cost of production were at a minimum.

The isoquant analysis indicates that when a firm chooses the minimum-cost method of production, the ratio of the price of labor to the price of capital will equal the ratio of the marginal productivities of the factors. This makes good economic sense. It implies, for example, that if capital is twice as expensive per unit as labor, the firm will want to substitute the cheaper labor for capital until the marginal product of capital is twice that of labor.

COST MINIMIZATION AND CHANGES IN RESOURCE PRICES

The minimum-cost input combination is dependent on both (a) the technical relationship between the productive inputs and output, as illustrated by the isoquant, and (b) the price of the factors, represented by the isocost line. If the ratio of the price of labor to the price of capital changes, the minimum-cost input combination will be altered.

Exhibit 5 illustrates this point. Exhibit 4 shows that if the price of labor were $5 and the price of capital were $10, the minimum-cost input combination to produce 100 units of cloth would be 120 units of labor and 40 units of capital. The total cost of the 100 units would be $1,000. Exhibit 5 indicates what would happen if the price of labor increased from $5 to $10. At the higher price of labor, a $1,000 outlay of funds would now purchase only 100 units of labor, (rather than 200). As a result of the increase in the price of labor, the isocost line would become steeper, as indicated by the change in isocost lines from *MN* to *OP*. The lowest isocost line that is tangent to the isoquant for 100 units would now be *OP*. The new minimum-cost input combination would be 90 units of labor and 60 units of capital. Cost-minimizing producers would substitute capital for labor. The cost of producing the 100 units would rise (from $1,000 to $1,500).

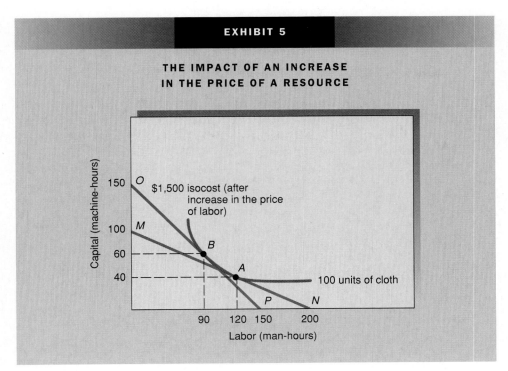

EXHIBIT 5

**THE IMPACT OF AN INCREASE
IN THE PRICE OF A RESOURCE**

The slope of the isocost line increases as the price of a unit of labor rises from $5 to $10. As a result of the increase in the price of labor, (a) cost-minimizing producers substitute capital for the more expensive labor, and (b) the minimum cost of producing 100 units of cloth rises.

THE SIGNIFICANCE OF ISOQUANT-ISOCOST ANALYSIS

Isoquant-isocost analysis is most applicable in the long run, when all factors are variable and the possibilities for substitution are greatest. It is a conceptual tool, more suitable for illustrating principles than for solving management problems. Few firms would try to design their production activities by drawing isoquants, although some managers might make mental use of the model when analyzing and developing alternative manufacturing processes designed to minimize costs. In any case, firms that do maximize profits behave as though they were using the analysis.

Isoquant-isocost analysis helps clarify the production conditions that must be met if a firm is to minimize its production cost and get the largest possible output from a specific outlay of funds.

GENERAL BUSINESS
AND ECONOMIC INDICATORS

Source: *Economic Report of the President*, (1970 and 1994)

SECTION 1:

NATIONAL INCOME AND PRODUCT ACCOUNTS

YEAR	PERSONAL CONSUMPTION EXPENDITURES	GROSS PRIVATE DOMESTIC INVESTMENT	GOVERNMENT PURCHASES OF GOODS & SERVICES	NET EXPORT OF GOODS & SERVICES	GROSS DOMESTIC PRODUCT (GDP)
1929	77.3	16.7	8.9	0.3	103.1
1930	69.9	10.3	9.2	1.0	90.4
1931	60.5	5.6	9.2	0.5	75.8
1932	48.6	1.0	8.1	0.4	58.0
1933	45.8	1.6	8.3	0.4	55.6
1934	51.3	3.3	9.8	0.6	65.1
1935	55.7	6.4	10.0	0.1	72.2
1936	61.9	8.5	12.0	0.1	82.7
1937	66.5	11.8	11.9	0.3	90.4
1938	63.9	6.5	13.0	1.3	84.9
1939	67.0	9.5	13.6	0.8	90.8
1940	71.0	13.4	14.2	1.5	100.0
1941	80.8	18.3	25.0	0.9	125.0
1942	88.6	10.3	59.9	−0.3	158.5
1943	99.5	6.2	88.9	−1.9	192.4
1944	108.2	7.7	97.1	−1.7	211.0
1945	119.6	11.3	83.0	−0.5	213.1
1946	143.9	31.5	29.1	7.4	211.9
1947	161.9	35.0	26.4	11.0	234.3
1948	174.9	47.1	32.6	7.0	260.3
1949	178.3	36.5	39.0	5.5	259.3
1950	192.1	55.1	38.8	1.0	287.0
1951	208.1	60.5	60.4	2.6	331.6
1952	219.1	53.5	75.8	1.3	349.7
1953	232.6	54.9	82.8	−0.3	370.0
1954	239.8	54.1	76.0	−1.0	370.9
1955	257.9	69.7	75.3	1.4	404.3
1956	270.6	72.7	79.7	3.2	426.2
1957	285.3	71.1	87.3	4.9	448.6
1958	294.6	63.6	95.4	1.1	454.7
1959	318.1	78.8	99.0	−1.7	494.2
1960	332.4	78.7	99.8	2.4	513.3
1961	343.5	77.9	107.0	3.4	531.8

NATIONAL INCOME AND PRODUCT ACCOUNTS

Year	Personal Consumption Expenditures	Gross Private Domestic Investment	Government Purchases of Goods & Services	Net Export of Goods & Services	Gross Domestic Product (GDP)
1962	364.4	87.9	116.8	2.4	571.6
1963	384.2	93.4	122.3	3.3	603.1
1964	412.5	101.7	128.3	5.5	648.0
1965	444.6	118.0	136.3	3.9	702.7
1966	481.6	130.4	155.9	1.9	769.8
1967	509.3	128.0	175.6	1.4	814.3
1968	559.1	139.9	191.5	–1.3	889.3
1969	603.7	155.2	201.8	–1.2	959.5
1970	646.5	150.3	212.7	1.2	1,010.7
1971	700.3	175.5	224.3	–3.0	1,097.2
1972	767.8	205.6	241.5	–8.0	1,207.0
1973	848.1	243.1	257.7	0.6	1,349.6
1974	927.7	245.8	288.3	–3.1	1,458.6
1975	1,024.9	226.0	321.4	13.6	1,585.9
1976	1,143.1	286.4	341.3	–2.3	1,768.4
1977	1,271.5	358.3	368.0	–23.7	1,974.1
1978	1,421.2	434.0	403.6	–26.1	2,232.7
1979	1,583.7	480.2	448.5	–23.8	2,488.6
1980	1,748.1	467.6	507.1	–14.7	2,708.0
1981	1,926.2	558.0	561.1	–14.7	3,030.6
1982	2,059.2	503.4	607.6	–20.6	3,149.6
1983	2,257.5	546.7	652.3	–51.4	3,405.0
1984	2,460.3	718.9	700.8	–102.7	3,777.2
1985	2,667.4	714.5	772.3	–115.6	4,038.7
1986	2,850.6	717.6	833.0	–132.5	4,268.6
1987	3,052.2	749.3	881.5	–143.1	4,539.9
1988	3,296.1	793.6	918.7	–108.0	4,900.4
1989	3,523.1	832.3	975.2	–79.7	5,250.8
1990	3,761.2	808.9	1,047.4	–71.4	5,546.1
1991	3,906.4	736.9	1,099.3	–19.6	5,722.9
1992	4,139.9	796.5	1,131.8	–29.6	6,038.5
1993	4,390.6	892.0	1,157.1	–65.7	6,374.0

SECTION 1: *(cont.)*

NATIONAL INCOME AND PRODUCT ACCOUNTS

Year	Gross National Product (GNP)	Less Capital Consumption Allowance	Equals Net National Product (NNP)	Less Indirect Business Taxes	Equals National Income
1929	103.9	9.9	94.0	7.1	84.7
1930	90.4	8.0	82.4	7.2	75.4
1931	76.4	8.4	68.0	8.3	59.7
1932	58.0	7.4	50.7	6.8	42.8
1933	56.0	7.6	48.4	7.1	39.4
1934	65.1	6.8	58.2	7.8	49.5
1935	72.8	7.4	65.4	8.2	57.2
1936	82.5	7.0	75.4	8.7	65.0
1937	91.3	8.0	83.3	9.6	73.7
1938	84.7	7.3	77.4	9.2	67.4
1939	91.3	9.0	82.3	9.4	71.2
1940	100.4	9.4	91.1	10.1	79.6
1941	125.5	10.3	115.3	11.3	102.8
1942	159.0	11.3	147.7	11.8	136.2
1943	192.7	11.6	181.1	12.8	169.7
1944	211.4	12.0	199.4	14.2	182.6
1945	213.4	12.4	201.0	15.5	181.6
1946	212.4	14.2	198.2	17.1	180.7
1947	235.2	17.6	217.6	18.4	196.6
1948	261.6	20.4	241.2	20.1	221.1
1949	260.4	22.0	238.4	21.3	215.2
1950	288.3	23.6	264.6	23.4	239.8
1951	333.4	27.2	306.2	25.3	277.3
1952	351.6	29.2	322.5	27.7	291.6
1953	371.6	30.9	340.7	29.7	306.6
1954	372.5	32.5	340.0	29.6	306.3
1955	405.9	34.4	371.5	32.2	336.3
1956	428.2	38.1	390.1	35.0	356.3
1957	451.0	41.1	409.9	37.4	372.8
1958	456.8	42.8	414.0	38.6	375.0
1959	497.0	44.6	452.5	41.9	410.1
1960	516.6	46.3	470.2	45.5	425.7
1961	535.4	47.7	487.7	48.1	440.5

NATIONAL INCOME AND PRODUCT ACCOUNTS

Year	Gross National Product (GNP)	Less Capital Consumption Allowance	Equals Net National Product (NNP)	Less Indirect Business Taxes	Equals National Income
1962	575.7	49.3	526.5	51.7	474.5
1963	607.7	51.3	556.4	54.7	501.5
1964	653.0	53.9	599.2	58.8	539.1
1965	708.1	57.3	650.7	62.7	586.9
1966	774.9	62.1	712.8	65.4	643.7
1967	819.8	67.4	752.4	70.4	679.9
1968	895.5	73.9	821.5	79.0	741.0
1969	965.6	81.5	884.2	86.6	798.6
1970	1,017.1	88.8	928.3	94.3	833.5
1971	1,104.9	97.6	1,007.3	103.6	899.5
1972	1,215.7	109.9	1,105.7	111.4	992.9
1973	1,362.3	120.4	1,241.9	121.0	1,119.5
1974	1,474.3	140.2	1,334.1	129.3	1,198.8
1975	1,599.1	165.2	1,433.9	140.0	1,285.3
1976	1,785.5	182.8	1,602.7	151.6	1,435.5
1977	1,994.6	205.2	1,789.4	165.5	1,609.1
1978	2,254.5	234.8	2,019.8	177.8	1,829.8
1979	2,520.8	272.4	2,248.4	188.7	2,038.9
1980	2,742.1	311.9	2,430.2	212.0	2,198.2
1981	3,063.8	362.4	2,701.4	249.3	2,432.5
1982	3,179.8	399.1	2,780.8	256.4	2,522.5
1983	3,434.4	418.4	3,016.0	280.1	2,720.8
1984	3,801.5	433.2	3,368.3	309.5	3,058.3
1985	4,053.6	454.5	3,599.1	329.9	3,268.4
1986	4,277.7	478.6	3,799.2	345.5	3,437.9
1987	4,544.5	502.2	4,042.4	365.0	3,692.3
1988	4,908.2	534.0	4,374.2	385.3	4,002.6
1989	5,266.8	580.4	4,686.4	414.7	4,249.5
1990	5,567.8	602.7	4,965.1	444.0	4,491.0
1991	5,737.1	626.1	5,111.0	476.6	4,598.3
1992	6,045.8	657.9	5,387.9	502.8	4,836.6
1993	6,378.1	671.2	5,706.9	530.5	5,176.4

Source: *Economic Report of the President,* (1970 and 1994)

SECTION 2:

REAL OUTPUT AND PRICES

GROSS DOMESTIC PRODUCT 1929–1993

YEAR	1987 PRICES (BILLIONS OF DOLLARS)	ANNUAL REAL RATE OF GROWTH	REAL GDP PER CAPITA (1987 DOLLARS)
1929	821.8	—	6,743
1930	748.9	−8.9	6,079
1931	691.3	−7.7	5,568
1932	599.7	−13.3	4,800
1933	587.1	−2.1	4,671
1934	632.6	7.7	5,001
1935	681.3	7.7	5,349
1936	777.9	14.2	6,069
1937	811.4	4.3	6,292
1938	778.9	−4.0	5,993
1939	840.7	7.9	6,416
1940	906.0	7.8	6,857
1941	1,070.6	18.2	8,025
1942	1,284.9	20.0	9,528
1943	1,540.5	19.9	11,266
1944	1,670.9	8.4	12,067
1945	1,602.6	−4.0	11,453
1946	1,272.1	−20.6	8,997
1947	1,252.8	−1.5	8,692
1948	1,300.0	3.8	8,866
1949	1,305.5	0.4	8,751
1950	1,418.5	8.7	9,352
1951	1,558.4	9.9	10,101
1952	1,624.9	4.3	10,353
1953	1,685.5	3.7	10,563
1954	1,673.8	−0.7	10,307
1955	1,768.3	5.6	10,699
1956	1,803.6	2.0	10,722
1957	1,838.2	1.9	10,733
1958	1,829.1	−0.5	10,504
1959	1,928.8	5.5	10,892
1960	1,970.8	2.2	10,903

REAL OUTPUT AND PRICES

GROSS DOMESTIC PRODUCT 1929–1993

YEAR	1987 PRICES (BILLIONS OF DOLLARS)	ANNUAL REAL RATE OF GROWTH	REAL GDP PER CAPITA (1987 DOLLARS)
1961	2,023.8	2.7	11,014
1962	2,128.1	5.2	11,405
1963	2,215.6	4.1	11,704
1964	2,340.6	5.6	12,195
1965	2,470.5	5.5	12,712
1966	2,616.2	5.9	13,307
1967	2,685.2	2.6	13,510
1968	2,796.9	4.2	13,932
1969	2,873.0	2.7	14,171
1970	2,873.9	0.0	14,013
1971	2,955.9	2.9	14,232
1972	3,107.1	5.1	14,801
1973	3,268.6	5.2	15,422
1974	3,248.1	−0.6	15,185
1975	3,221.7	−0.8	14,917
1976	3,380.8	4.9	15,502
1977	3,533.3	4.5	16,039
1978	3,703.5	4.8	16,635
1979	3,796.8	2.5	16,867
1980	3,776.3	−0.5	16,584
1981	3,843.1	1.8	16,710
1982	3,760.3	−2.2	16,194
1983	3,906.6	3.9	16,672
1984	4,148.5	6.2	17,549
1985	4,279.8	3.2	17,944
1986	4,404.5	2.9	18,299
1987	4,539.9	3.1	18,694
1988	4,718.6	3.9	19,252
1989	4,838.0	2.5	19,556
1990	4,897.3	1.2	19,593
1991	4,861.4	−0.7	19,238
1992	4,986.3	2.6	19,518
1993	5,132.7	2.9	19,874

SECTION 2: *(cont.)*

REAL OUTPUT AND PRICES

PRICE INDEXES: 1929–1993

YEAR	GDP DEFLATOR INDEX (1987 = 100)	GDP DEFLATOR ANNUAL PERCENTAGE CHANGE	CONSUMER PRICE INDEX INDEX (1982–84 = 100)	CONSUMER PRICE INDEX PERCENTAGE CHANGE (DEC. TO DEC.)
1929	12.5	—	17.1	0.0
1930	12.1	–9.1	16.7	–2.5
1931	11.0	–9.1	15.2	–8.8
1932	9.7	–11.8	13.6	–10.3
1933	9.5	–2.1	12.9	–5.1
1934	10.3	8.4	13.4	3.4
1935	10.6	2.9	13.7	2.5
1936	10.7	0.0	13.8	1.0
1937	11.2	5.7	14.3	3.4
1938	10.9	–2.7	14.1	-1.9
1939	10.8	–0.9	13.9	1.4
1940	11.0	1.9	14.0	1.0
1941	11.7	6.4	14.7	5.0
1942	12.3	5.1	16.3	10.7
1943	12.5	1.6	17.3	6.1
1944	12.6	0.8	17.6	1.7
1945	13.3	5.6	18.0	2.3
1946	16.7	25.6	19.5	8.7
1947	18.7	12.0	22.3	14.4
1948	20.0	7.0	24.1	2.7
1949	19.9	–0.5	23.8	–1.8
1950	20.2	1.5	24.1	5.8
1951	21.3	5.4	26.0	5.9
1952	21.5	0.9	26.5	0.9
1953	22.0	2.3	26.7	0.6
1954	22.2	0.9	26.9	–0.5
1955	22.9	3.2	26.8	0.4
1956	23.6	3.1	27.2	2.9
1957	24.4	3.4	28.1	3.0
1958	24.9	2.0	28.9	1.8
1959	25.6	2.8	29.1	1.7
1960	26.0	1.6	29.6	1.4

REAL OUTPUT AND PRICES

PRICE INDEXES: 1929–1993

YEAR	GDP DEFLATOR		CONSUMER PRICE INDEX	
	INDEX (1987 = 100)	ANNUAL PERCENTAGE CHANGE	INDEX (1982–84 = 100)	PERCENTAGE CHANGE (DEC. TO DEC.)
1961	26.3	1.2	29.9	0.7
1962	26.9	2.3	30.2	1.3
1963	27.2	1.1	30.6	1.6
1964	27.7	1.8	31.0	1.0
1965	28.4	2.5	31.5	1.9
1966	29.4	3.5	32.4	3.5
1967	30.3	3.1	33.4	3.0
1968	31.8	5.0	34.8	4.7
1969	33.4	5.0	36.7	6.2
1970	35.2	5.4	38.8	5.6
1971	37.1	5.4	40.5	3.3
1972	38.8	4.6	41.8	3.4
1973	41.3	6.4	44.4	8.7
1974	44.9	8.7	49.3	12.3
1975	49.2	9.6	53.8	6.9
1976	52.3	6.3	56.9	4.9
1977	55.9	6.9	60.6	6.7
1978	60.3	7.9	65.2	9.0
1979	65.5	8.6	72.6	13.3
1980	71.7	9.5	82.4	12.5
1981	78.9	10.0	90.9	8.9
1982	83.8	6.2	96.5	3.8
1983	87.2	4.1	99.6	3.8
1984	91.0	4.4	103.9	3.9
1985	94.4	3.7	107.6	3.8
1986	96.9	2.6	109.6	1.1
1987	100.0	3.2	113.6	4.4
1988	103.9	3.9	118.3	4.4
1989	108.5	4.4	124.0	4.6
1990	113.3	4.4	130.7	6.1
1991	117.7	3.9	136.2	3.1
1992	121.1	2.9	140.3	2.9
1993	124.2	2.5	144.5	2.7

Source: *Economic Report of the President,* (1970 and 1994)

SECTION 3:

POPULATION AND EMPLOYMENT

POPULATION AND LABOR FORCE

YEAR	CIVILIAN NONINSTITUTIONAL POPULATION AGE 16 AND OVER (MILLIONS)	CIVILIAN LABOR FORCE (MILLIONS)	CIVILIAN LABOR FORCE PARTICIPATION RATE	EMPLOYMENT/ POPULATION RATIO (INCLUDING ARMED FORCES)
1929	85.6	49.2	57.5	55.9
1930	87.1	49.8	57.2	52.5
1931	88.2	50.4	57.1	48.4
1932	89.3	51.0	57.1	43.8
1933	90.5	51.6	57.0	43.1
1934	91.7	52.2	56.9	44.9
1935	92.9	52.9	56.9	45.8
1936	94.1	53.4	56.7	47.5
1937	95.2	54.0	56.7	49.0
1938	96.5	54.6	56.6	46.2
1939	97.8	55.2	56.4	47.2
1940	100.4	55.6	55.4	47.8
1941	101.5	55.9	55.0	51.2
1942	102.6	56.4	55.0	56.3
1943	103.7	55.5	53.5	61.2
1944	104.6	54.6	52.2	62.5
1945	105.6	53.9	51.0	60.9
1946	106.5	57.5	54.0	55.1
1947	101.8	59.4	58.3	56.7
1948	103.1	60.6	58.8	57.2
1949	104.0	61.3	58.9	56.1
1950	105.0	62.2	59.2	57.2
1951	104.6	62.0	59.3	59.4
1952	105.2	62.1	59.0	59.5
1953	107.1	63.0	58.8	59.2
1954	108.3	63.6	58.7	57.5
1955	109.7	65.0	59.3	58.6
1956	111.0	66.6	60.0	59.3
1957	112.3	66.9	59.6	58.8
1958	113.7	67.6	59.5	57.1
1959	115.3	68.4	59.3	57.6
1960	117.2	69.6	59.4	57.7

SECTION 3: *(cont.)*

POPULATION AND EMPLOYMENT

	POPULATION AND LABOR FORCE			
YEAR	CIVILIAN NONINSTITUTIONAL POPULATION AGE 16 AND OVER (MILLIONS)	CIVILIAN LABOR FORCE (MILLIONS)	CIVILIAN LABOR FORCE PARTICIPATION RATE	EMPLOYMENT/ POPULATION RATIO (INCLUDING ARMED FORCES)
1961	118.8	70.5	59.3	57.0
1962	120.1	70.6	58.8	57.2
1963	122.4	71.8	58.7	57.0
1964	124.5	73.0	58.6	57.3
1965	126.5	74.5	58.9	57.7
1966	128.1	75.8	59.2	58.6
1967	130.0	77.3	59.5	59.0
1968	132.0	78.7	59.6	59.2
1969	134.3	80.7	60.1	59.7
1970	137.1	82.8	60.4	58.9
1971	140.2	84.4	60.2	58.0
1972	144.1	87.0	60.4	58.3
1973	147.1	89.4	60.8	59.0
1974	150.1	91.9	61.2	59.0
1975	153.2	93.8	61.2	57.1
1976	156.2	96.2	61.6	57.9
1977	159.0	99.0	62.3	58.9
1978	161.9	102.3	63.2	60.3
1979	164.9	105.0	63.7	60.9
1980	167.7	106.9	63.8	60.1
1981	170.1	108.7	63.9	60.0
1982	172.3	110.2	64.0	58.7
1983	174.2	111.6	64.0	58.8
1984	176.4	113.5	64.4	60.5
1985	178.2	115.5	64.8	61.1
1986	180.6	117.8	65.3	61.6
1987	182.8	120.0	65.6	62.5
1988	184.6	121.7	65.9	63.2
1989	186.4	123.9	66.5	63.9
1990	188.0	124.8	66.4	63.6
1991	189.8	125.3	66.0	62.4
1992	191.6	127.0	66.3	62.2
1993	193.6	128.0	66.2	62.4

SECTION 3: *(cont.)*

POPULATION AND EMPLOYMENT

		UNEMPLOYMENT RATES		
YEAR	ALL WORKERS	BOTH SEXES AGE 16–19 YEARS	MEN AGE 20+	WOMEN AGE 20+
1929	3.2	—	—	—
1930	8.7	—	—	—
1931	15.9	—	—	—
1932	23.6	—	—	—
1933	24.9	—	—	—
1934	21.7	—	—	—
1935	20.1	—	—	—
1936	16.9	—	—	—
1937	14.3	—	—	—
1938	19.0	—	—	—
1939	17.2	—	—	—
1940	14.6	—	—	—
1941	9.9	—	—	—
1942	4.7	—	—	—
1943	1.9	—	—	—
1944	1.2	—	—	—
1945	1.9	—	—	—
1946	3.8	—	—	—
1947	3.9	—	—	—
1948	3.8	9.2	3.2	3.6
1949	5.9	13.4	5.4	5.3
1950	5.2	12.2	4.7	5.1
1951	3.2	8.2	2.5	4.0
1952	2.9	8.5	2.4	3.2
1953	2.8	7.6	2.5	2.9
1954	5.4	12.6	4.9	5.5
1955	4.3	11.0	3.8	4.4
1956	4.0	11.1	3.4	4.2
1957	4.2	11.6	3.6	4.1
1958	6.6	15.9	6.2	6.1
1959	5.3	14.6	4.7	5.2
1960	5.4	14.7	4.7	5.1

POPULATION AND EMPLOYMENT

UNEMPLOYMENT RATES

YEAR	ALL WORKERS	BOTH SEXES AGE 16–19 YEARS	MEN AGE 20+	WOMEN AGE 20+
1961	6.5	16.8	5.7	6.3
1962	5.4	14.7	4.6	5.4
1963	5.5	17.2	4.5	5.4
1964	5.0	16.2	3.9	5.2
1965	4.4	14.8	3.2	4.5
1966	3.7	12.8	2.5	3.8
1967	3.7	12.9	2.3	4.2
1968	3.5	12.7	2.2	3.8
1969	3.4	12.2	2.1	3.7
1970	4.8	15.3	3.5	4.8
1971	5.8	16.9	4.4	5.7
1972	5.5	16.2	4.0	5.4
1973	4.8	14.5	3.3	4.9
1974	5.5	16.0	3.8	5.5
1975	8.3	19.9	6.8	8.0
1976	7.6	19.0	5.9	7.4
1977	6.9	17.8	5.2	7.0
1978	6.0	16.4	4.3	6.0
1979	5.8	16.1	4.2	5.7
1980	7.0	17.8	5.9	6.4
1981	7.5	19.6	6.3	6.8
1982	9.5	23.2	8.8	8.3
1983	9.5	22.4	8.9	8.1
1984	7.4	18.9	6.6	6.8
1985	7.1	18.6	6.2	6.6
1986	6.9	18.3	6.1	6.2
1987	6.1	16.9	5.4	5.4
1988	5.4	15.3	4.8	4.9
1989	5.2	15.0	4.5	4.7
1990	5.4	15.5	4.9	4.8
1991	6.6	18.6	6.3	5.7
1992	7.3	20.0	7.0	6.3
1993	6.7	19.0	6.4	5.9

Source: *Economic Report of the President,* (1970 and 1994)

SECTION 4:

MONEY SUPPLY, INTEREST RATES, AND FEDERAL FINANCES

	MONEY SUPPLY DATA				INTEREST RATE
YEAR	MONEY SUPPLY M1 (BILLIONS)	ANNUAL CHANGE IN M1	MONEY SUPPLY M2 (BILLIONS)	ANNUAL CHANGE IN M2	AAA CORPORATE BONDS
1929	26.5	—	(Data not available		4.73
1930	25.4	−4.2	prior to 1958)		4.56
1931	23.6	−7.1			4.58
1932	20.7	−12.3			5.01
1933	19.5	−5.8			4.49
1934	21.5	0.3			4.60
1935	25.6	19.1			3.60
1936	29.1	13.7			3.24
1937	30.3	4.1			3.26
1938	30.1	−0.7			3.19
1939	33.6	11.6			3.01
1940	39.0	16.1			2.84
1941	45.4	16.4			2.77
1942	55.2	21.6			2.83
1943	72.3	31.0			2.73
1944	86.0	18.9			2.72
1945	99.2	15.3			2.62
1946	106.0	6.9			2.53
1947	113.1	6.7			2.61
1948	111.5	−1.4			2.82
1949	111.2	−0.3			2.66
1950	116.2	4.5			2.62
1951	122.7	5.6			2.86
1952	127.4	3.8			2.96
1953	128.8	1.1			3.20
1954	132.3	2.7			2.90
1955	135.2	2.2			3.06
1956	136.9	1.3			3.36
1957	135.9	−0.7			3.89
1958	141.1	3.8			3.79
1959	140.0	0.1	297.8	—	4.38
1960	140.7	0.5	312.3	4.9	4.41

SECTION 4: (cont.)

MONEY SUPPLY, INTEREST RATES, AND FEDERAL FINANCES

| Year | Money Supply Data | | | | Interest Rate |
	Money Supply M1 (billions)	Annual Change in M1	Money Supply M2 (billions)	Annual Change in M2	AAA Corporate Bonds
1961	145.2	3.2	335.5	7.4	4.35
1962	147.8	1.8	362.7	8.1	4.33
1963	153.3	3.7	393.2	8.4	4.26
1964	160.3	4.6	424.8	8.0	4.40
1965	167.9	4.7	459.3	8.1	4.49
1966	172.0	2.4	480.0	4.5	5.13
1967	183.3	6.6	524.3	9.2	5.51
1968	197.4	7.7	566.3	8.0	6.18
1969	203.9	3.3	589.5	4.1	7.03
1970	214.4	5.1	628.0	6.5	8.04
1971	228.3	6.5	712.6	13.5	7.39
1972	249.2	9.2	805.1	13.0	7.21
1973	262.8	5.5	860.9	6.9	7.44
1974	274.3	4.4	908.4	5.5	8.57
1975	287.5	4.8	1,023.1	12.6	8.83
1976	306.3	6.5	1,163.5	13.7	8.43
1977	331.1	8.1	1,286.4	10.6	8.02
1978	358.2	8.2	1,388.5	7.9	8.73
1979	382.5	6.8	1,496.4	7.8	9.63
1980	408.5	6.8	1,629.2	8.9	11.94
1981	436.3	6.8	1,792.6	10.0	14.17
1982	474.4	8.7	1,952.7	8.9	13.79
1983	521.2	9.9	2,186.5	12.0	12.04
1984	552.4	6.0	2,376.0	8.7	12.71
1985	620.1	12.3	2,572.4	8.3	11.37
1986	724.5	16.8	2,816.1	9.5	9.02
1987	750.0	3.5	2,917.2	3.6	9.38
1988	787.1	4.9	3,078.2	5.5	9.71
1989	794.6	1.0	3,233.3	5.0	9.26
1990	827.2	4.1	3,345.5	3.5	9.32
1991	899.3	8.7	3,445.8	3.0	8.77
1992	1,026.6	14.2	3,494.8	1.4	8.14
1993	1,131.2	10.2	3,551.7	1.6	7.22

SECTION 4: *(cont.)*

MONEY SUPPLY, INTEREST RATES, AND FEDERAL FINANCES

Year	FEDERAL BUDGET TOTALS (BILLIONS OF DOLLARS)			NATIONAL DEBT	
	Fiscal Year Outlays	Fiscal Year Receipts	Surplus or Deficit (−)	Billions of Dollars	As a Percent of GDP
1929	3.1	3.9	0.7	16.9	16.4
1930	3.3	4.1	0.8	16.1	17.8
1931	3.6	3.1	−0.5	16.8	22.2
1932	4.7	1.9	−2.7	19.5	33.6
1933	4.6	2.0	−2.6	22.5	40.5
1934	6.6	3.0	−3.6	27.7	42.5
1935	6.5	3.7	−2.8	28.7	39.8
1936	8.4	4.0	−4.4	38.5	46.6
1937	7.7	5.0	−2.8	41.3	45.7
1938	6.8	5.6	−1.2	42.0	49.5
1939	9.1	6.3	−3.9	45.0	49.6
1940	9.5	6.5	−2.9	48.5	48.5
1941	13.7	8.7	−4.9	55.3	44.2
1942	35.1	14.6	−20.5	77.0	48.6
1943	78.6	24.0	−54.6	140.8	73.2
1944	91.3	43.7	−47.6	202.6	96.0
1945	92.7	45.2	−47.6	259.1	121.6
1946	55.2	39.3	−15.9	269.9	127.4
1947	34.5	38.5	4.0	258.4	110.3
1948	29.8	41.6	11.8	252.4	97.0
1949	38.8	39.4	0.6	252.8	97.5
1950	42.6	39.4	−3.1	257.4	90.0
1951	45.5	51.6	6.1	255.3	77.0
1952	67.7	66.2	−1.5	259.2	74.1
1953	76.1	69.6	−6.5	266.1	71.9
1954	70.9	69.7	−1.2	271.3	73.1
1955	68.4	65.5	−3.0	247.4	67.9
1956	70.6	74.6	3.9	272.8	64.0
1957	76.6	80.0	3.4	270.6	60.3
1958	82.4	79.6	−2.8	276.4	60.8
1959	92.1	79.2	−12.8	284.8	57.6
1960	92.2	92.5	−0.3	286.5	55.8

MONEY SUPPLY, INTEREST RATES, AND FEDERAL FINANCES

Year	FEDERAL BUDGET TOTALS (BILLIONS OF DOLLARS)			NATIONAL DEBT	
	FISCAL YEAR OUTLAYS	FISCAL YEAR RECEIPTS	SURPLUS OR DEFICIT (–)	BILLIONS OF DOLLARS	AS A PERCENT OF GDP
1961	97.7	94.4	–3.3	289.2	54.4
1962	106.8	99.7	–7.1	298.6	52.2
1963	111.3	106.6	–4.8	306.5	50.8
1964	118.5	112.6	–5.9	312.5	48.2
1965	118.2	116.9	–1.4	317.9	45.2
1966	134.5	130.8	–3.7	320.0	41.6
1967	157.5	148.8	–8.6	322.3	39.6
1968	178.1	153.0	–25.2	344.4	38.7
1969	183.6	186.9	3.2	351.7	36.7
1970	195.6	192.8	–2.8	369.0	36.5
1971	210.2	187.1	–23.0	396.3	36.1
1972	230.7	207.3	–23.4	425.4	35.2
1973	245.7	230.8	–14.9	456.4	33.8
1974	269.4	263.2	–6.1	473.2	32.4
1975	332.3	279.1	–53.2	532.1	33.6
1976	371.8	298.1	–73.7	619.2	35.0
1977	409.2	355.6	–53.7	697.6	35.3
1978	458.7	399.7	–59.2	767.0	34.3
1979	503.5	463.3	–40.2	819.0	32.9
1980	590.9	517.1	–73.8	906.4	33.5
1981	678.2	599.3	–79.0	996.5	32.9
1982	745.8	617.8	–128.0	1,140.9	36.2
1983	808.4	600.6	–207.8	1,375.8	40.4
1984	851.8	666.5	–185.4	1,559.6	41.3
1985	946.4	734.1	–212.3	1,821.0	45.1
1986	990.3	769.1	–221.2	2,122.7	49.7
1987	1,003.9	854.1	–149.8	2,347.8	51.7
1988	1,064.1	909.0	–155.2	2,599.9	53.1
1989	1,143.2	990.7	–152.5	2,836.3	54.0
1990	1,252.7	1,031.3	–221.4	3,210.9	58.1
1991	1,323.8	1,054.3	–269.5	3,662.8	64.5
1992	1,380.9	1,090.5	–290.4	4,061.8	68.3
1993	1,408.2	1,153.5	–254.7	4,408.6	69.2

Source: *Economic Report of the President,* (1970 and 1994)

SECTION 5:

SIZE OF GOVERNMENT AS A SHARE OF GDP, 1929–1993

	FEDERAL, STATE, AND LOCAL GOVERNMENT				
YEAR	EXPENDITURES (PERCENT OF GDP)	REVENUES (PERCENT OF GDP)	PURCHASES OF GOODS & SERVICES (PERCENT OF GDP)	NON-DEFENSE PURCHASES OF GOODS & SERVICES (PERCENT OF GDP)	TRANSFER PAYMENTS TO PERSONS (PERCENT OF GDP)
1929	10.1	12.0	8.3	—	0.9
1933	22.3	19.4	16.7	—	3.8
1937	19.9	20.4	15.9	—	2.7
1939	33.6	29.4	25.9	23.2	2.8
1940	35.3	34.0	27.1	22.6	2.7
1941	38.6	33.5	33.5	14.8	2.1
1942	54.1	27.6	50.5	8.7	1.7
1943	53.3	28.1	50.8	5.1	1.2
1944	54.3	26.9	51.1	4.8	1.4
1945	53.3	30.6	47.7	5.1	2.8
1946	27.2	30.4	16.8	7.2	6.2
1947	22.7	30.2	13.7	8.6	5.6
1948	24.9	29.1	15.9	10.3	5.5
1949	31.1	29.3	20.3	13.0	6.5
1950	27.5	31.1	17.4	10.8	6.2
1951	26.6	28.7	20.2	8.7	4.4
1952	30.9	29.7	24.9	9.6	4.1
1953	31.6	29.5	25.7	10.5	4.1
1954	31.7	29.4	24.7	11.1	4.6
1955	29.8	28.1	20.9	10.0	4.6
1956	28.4	29.8	21.5	10.5	4.3
1957	29.4	29.6	22.2	10.9	4.9
1958	28.2	25.4	21.0	10.9	5.8
1959	25.8	25.5	19.1	10.2	5.5
1960	25.8	26.4	18.9	10.6	5.6
1961	26.3	25.6	19.0	9.1	6.2
1962	26.8	26.3	19.7	11.2	6.0
1963	26.2	26.3	19.1	11.3	6.0
1964	25.5	25.1	18.6	11.3	5.8
1965	24.7	24.8	18.1	11.4	5.8

SIZE OF GOVERNMENT AS A SHARE OF GDP, 1929–1993

	FEDERAL, STATE, AND LOCAL GOVERNMENT				
YEAR	EXPENDITURES (PERCENT OF GDP)	REVENUES (PERCENT OF GDP)	PURCHASES OF GOODS & SERVICES (PERCENT OF GDP)	NON-DEFENSE PURCHASES OF GOODS & SERVICES (PERCENT OF GDP)	TRANSFER PAYMENTS TO PERSONS (PERCENT OF GDP)
1966	26.6	26.5	19.5	11.9	5.9
1967	27.7	26.1	20.3	12.0	6.7
1968	28.5	27.8	20.6	12.4	7.1
1969	28.8	29.7	20.5	12.7	7.3
1970	29.0	28.0	19.9	12.9	8.4
1971	28.8	27.2	19.3	13.2	9.1
1972	28.0	27.7	18.6	12.8	9.3
1973	28.3	28.9	18.3	13.0	9.5
1974	29.5	29.2	18.9	13.7	10.4
1975	30.8	27.1	19.0	13.9	12.0
1976	30.8	27.9	18.1	13.4	11.8
1977	28.5	27.7	17.4	12.9	11.3
1978	28.0	28.0	17.1	12.8	10.8
1979	28.5	29.0	17.4	12.8	10.9
1980	29.5	28.3	17.6	12.8	11.9
1981	32.1	31.1	18.8	13.4	12.1
1982	32.8	29.5	19.0	13.2	13.0
1983	31.8	28.4	18.1	12.3	12.9
1984	31.9	29.2	18.4	12.4	12.0
1985	33.3	30.0	19.4	13.1	12.0
1986	33.1	29.9	19.4	13.3	12.1
1987	32.3	30.1	18.9	13.0	11.9
1988	31.7	29.9	18.4	12.9	11.8
1989	32.5	30.9	18.8	13.3	11.9
1990	34.1	31.8	19.6	14.1	12.4
1991	34.0	30.7	19.2	13.5	13.5
1992	35.1	30.6	18.7	13.5	14.2
1993	34.4	30.9	18.2	13.4	14.3

Source: The Real Per Capita GDP data were supplied to the authors by Robert Summers and Alan Heston. They were derived by the purchasing power parity method. The other data in this table are from the World Bank, *World Development Report 1993*.

SECTION 6:

BASIC ECONOMIC DATA FOR 63 COUNTRIES

	REAL GDP PER CAPITA	AVERAGE ANNUAL GROWTH RATE OF REAL GDP		POPULATION (MILLIONS)
HIGH INCOME COUNTRIES	1991	1970–1980	1980–1991	1991
United States	21,866	2.8	2.6	252.7
Switzerland	21,448	0.5	2.2	6.8
Canada	20,571	4.6	3.1	27.3
Hong Kong	19,397	9.2	6.9	5.8
Germany	19,646	2.6	2.3	80.1
Japan	19,290	4.3	4.2	123.9
Australia	17,761	3.0	3.1	17.3
Sweden	17,550	1.9	2.0	8.6
Finland	16,236	3.1	3.0	5.0
France	17,402	3.2	2.3	57.0
Denmark	17,821	2.2	2.3	5.2
Belgium	17,849	3.0	2.1	10.0
United Kingdom	15,494	2.0	2.9	57.6
Netherlands	16,585	2.9	2.1	15.1
Italy	15,779	3.8	2.4	57.8
Austria	16,316	3.4	2.3	7.8
Singapore	14,734	8.3	6.6	2.8
Spain	12,291	3.5	3.2	38.0
AFRICA				
Botswana	3,362	14.5	9.8	1.3
Cameroon	1,344	7.2	1.4	11.9
Côte d'Ivoire	1,185	6.6	−0.5	12.4
Ethiopia	—	1.9	1.6	52.8
Ghana	930	−0.1	3.2	15.3
Kenya	1,100	6.4	4.2	25.0
Mauritius	7,178	6.8	6.7	1.1
Mozambique	921	—	−0.1	16.1
Nigeria	929	4.6	1.9	99.0
South Africa	3,855	3.0	1.3	38.9
Tanzania	574	3.0	2.9	25.2
Uganda	1,036	—	—	16.9
Zambia	983	1.4	0.8	8.3
ASIA AND PACIFIC				
Bangladesh	1,546	2.3	4.3	110.6
China	2,946	5.2	9.4	1,149.5
India	1,458	3.4	5.4	866.5
Indonesia	2,454	7.2	5.6	181.3
Korea (South)	7,185	9.6	9.6	43.3
Malaysia	6,256	7.9	5.7	18.2

BASIC ECONOMIC DATA FOR 63 COUNTRIES

	ANNUAL GROWTH RATE OF MONEY SUPPLY	AVG. ANNUAL INFLATION RATE	GROSS INVESTMENT AS SHARE OF GDP
HIGH INCOME COUNTRIES	1980–1991	1980–1991	1991
United States	8.0	4.2	15
Switzerland	6.8	3.8	27
Canada	8.4	4.3	20
Hong Kong	—	7.5	29
Germany	6.4	2.8	21
Japan	8.9	1.5	32
Australia	12.2	7.0	19
Sweden	9.2	7.4	17
Finland	12.9	6.6	21
France	9.9	5.7	21
Denmark	11.1	10.8	17
Belgium	7.0	4.2	20
United Kingdom	—	5.8	16
Netherlands	—	1.8	21
Italy	12.0	9.5	20
Austria	7.4	3.6	26
Singapore	13.5	1.9	37
Spain	10.8	8.9	25
AFRICA			
Botswana	25.8	13.3	—
Cameroon	7.0	4.5	15
Côte d'Ivoire	3.7	3.9	10
Ethiopia	12.5	2.4	10
Ghana	42.9	40.2	16
Kenya	15.1	9.3	21
Mauritius	22.0	8.1	28
Mozambique	—	37.6	42
Nigeria	15.7	18.2	16
South Africa	16.6	14.4	16
Tanzania	—	25.7	22
Uganda	—	—	12
Zambia	—	—	13
ASIA AND PACIFIC			
Bangladesh	21.0	9.3	10
China	25.4	5.8	36
India	16.8	8.2	20
Indonesia	26.2	8.5	35
Korea (South)	21.3	5.7	39
Malaysia	12.6	1.7	36

SECTION 6: *(cont.)*

BASIC ECONOMIC DATA FOR 63 COUNTRIES

	Real GDP per Capita	Average Annual Growth Rate of Real GDP		Population (millions)
High Income Countries	1991	1970–1980	1980–1991	1991
Pakistan	1,702	4.9	6.1	115.8
Philippines	2,104	6.0	1.1	62.9
Taiwan	—	6.5	5.4	20.5
Thailand	4,600	7.1	7.9	57.2
South/Central America				
Argentina	4,603	2.5	−0.4	32.7
Brazil	4,787	8.1	2.5	151.4
Chile	5,342	1.4	3.6	13.4
Colombia	3,978	5.4	3.7	32.8
Dominican Republic	2,397	6.5	1.7	7.2
Guatemala	2,562	5.8	1.1	9.5
Haiti	925	3.7	−0.7	6.6
Mexico	6,776	6.3	1.2	83.3
Peru	2,484	3.5	−0.4	21.9
Venezuela	7,454	3.5	1.5	19.8
Middle East/Mediterranean				
Egypt	2,102	9.5	4.8	53.6
Greece	8,001	4.7	1.8	10.3
Iran	3,569	2.2	2.2	57.7
Israel	10,575	4.8	3.7	4.9
Saudi Arabia	7,963	10.1	−0.2	15.4
Syria	5,225	9.9	2.6	12.5
Turkey	4,531	5.9	5.0	57.3
Eastern Europe				
Bulgaria	4,813	—	1.9	9.0
Hungary	6,055	—	0.6	10.3
Poland	4,569	—	1.1	38.2
Romania	—	—	0.1	23.0
Russia	8,115	—	—	148.7

BASIC ECONOMIC DATA FOR 63 COUNTRIES

	ANNUAL GROWTH RATE OF MONEY SUPPLY	AVG. ANNUAL INFLATION RATE	GROSS INVESTMENT AS SHARE OF GDP
HIGH INCOME COUNTRIES	1980–1991	1980–1991	1991
Pakistan	13.3	7.0	19
Philippines	16.8	14.6	20
Taiwan	8.8	3.1	—
Thailand	18.9	3.7	39
SOUTH / CENTRAL AMERICA			
Argentina	368.5	416.8	12
Brazil	—	327.7	20
Chile	29.8	20.5	19
Colombia	—	25.0	15
Dominican Republic	28.0	24.5	17
Guatemala	17.2	15.9	14
Haiti	8.6	7.1	—
Mexico	62.0	66.5	23
Peru	224.0	287.4	16
Venezuela	20.2	21.2	19
MIDDLE EAST / MEDITERRANEAN			
Egypt	21.8	12.6	20
Greece	22.3	17.7	17
Iran	16.7	14.1	20
Israel	99.2	89.0	23
Saudi Arabia	7.8	–3.1	—
Syria	19.2	14.4	—
Turkey	52.7	44.7	20
EASTERN EUROPE			
Bulgaria	—	7.9	13
Hungary	—	10.3	19
Poland	58.6	63.1	21
Romania	10.3	6.2	34
Russia	—	—	39

ANSWERS TO
SELECTED QUESTIONS

CHAPTER 1

2. Production of scarce goods always involves a cost; there are no free lunches. When the government provides goods without charge to consumers, other citizens (taxpayers) will bear the cost of their provision. Thus, provision by the government affects *how* the costs will be covered, not whether they are incurred.

4. The legislation would increase the cost of traveling by air with a small child. Given the higher cost, some parents may choose to drive rather than fly. Since auto travel is more dangerous than air travel, an increase in injuries and fatalities due to the additional automobile travel—a secondary effect—must also be considered.

6. For most taxpayers, the change will reduce the *after-tax* cost of raising children. Other things constant, one would predict an increase in the birth rate.

7. False. The key to sound policy is not the intentions of the advocate, but rather the ability of the policy to bring individual self-interest and the general welfare into harmony. People are not like pieces on a chess board. They have self-will and personal interests. As Adam Smith pointed out in *The Theory of Moral Sentiments* (1759), "In the great chess board of human society, every single piece [individual] has a principle of motion of its own, altogether different from that which the legislature might choose to impress on it. If the two coincide [the self-interest of individuals and the objectives of a policy], the game of human society will go on easily and harmoniously, and is very likely to be happy and successful. If they are opposite or different, the game will go on miserably, and the society must be at all times in the highest degree of disorder."

9. Raising the price of new cars by requiring safety devices, which customers would not have purchased if given the choice, slows the rate of sales for new cars. Thus the older, less safe cars are driven longer, partially offsetting the safety advantage provided by the newer, safer cars. Also, drivers act a bit differently when they are told that the new cars have the safety devices. They count on them for help in the event of an unexpected accident. In fact, economist Gordon Tullock says that the greatest safety device of all might be a dagger built into the center of the steering wheel, pointed directly at the driver's chest!

10. Money has nothing to do with whether an individual is economizing. Any time a person chooses, in an attempt to achieve a goal, he or she is economizing.

CHAPTER 2

2. Even though the productivity of painters has changed only slightly, rising productivity in *other areas* has led to higher wages in *other occupations*, thereby increasing the opportunity cost of being a house painter.

Since people would not supply house painting services unless they were able to meet their opportunity costs, higher wages are necessary to attract house painters from competitive (alternative) lines of work.

6. The statement reflects the "exchange is a zero sum game" view. The view is false. No private business can force customers to buy. Neither can a customer force a business to sell. Unless both buyer and seller believe the exchange is in their interest, they will not enter into the exchange. Mutual gain provides the foundation for voluntary exchange.

9. Yes. The market value of the land will increase in anticipation of the future harvest, as the trees grow and the expected day of harvest moves closer. Thus, with transferable private property, the tree farmer will be able to capture the value added by his planting and holding the trees for a few years even if the actual harvest does not take place until well after his death.

10. In general, it sanctions all forms of competition except for the use of violence (or the threat of violence), theft, or fraud.

14. If the food from land, now and in the future, is worth more than the housing services from the same land, then developers will not be able to bid the land away from farmers. However, since it is comparative advantage that determines the efficient use of a resource, even the best farm land, if situated in the right location, may be far more valuable for buildings. Other, poorer land can always be made more productive by the use of different (and more costly) farming techniques, irrigation, fertilizer, and so on. Physical characteristics alone do not determine the value or the most valuable use of a resource.

16. A large number of people feel that safety is priceless—that no price is too high to pay for something that saves lives. However, there is a problem with this view: It ignores opportunity costs. If we want more safety we will have to give up other things. Sometimes the opportunity cost of the additional safety will exceed its value. Consider travel safety. We could save lives if we cut our current speed limits in half, doubled the width of every road, and allowed only tank-like automobiles on the roads. But we would have to give up other things—things that are valued more highly than the lives saved—if we did. You could reduce your likelihood of accidental death by refusing to travel by automobile, train, or airplane. However, most people do not choose to do this, because they value the travel more than the additional safety. Remember, economics is about trade-offs, not absolutes.

CHAPTER 3

1. a. and b. would increase the demand for beef; c. and d. would affect primarily the supply of beef, rather than the

demand; e. leads to a change in quantity demanded, not a change in demand.

4. a. Reductions in the supply of feed grains and hay led to sharply higher prices; b. The higher feed grain and hay prices increased the cost of maintaining a cattle herd and thereby caused many producers to sell (an increase in current supply), depressing cattle prices in 1988; c. The reduction in the size of cattle herds led to a smaller future supply and higher cattle prices in 1989.

6. Agreement of both buyer and seller is required for an exchange. Price ceilings push prices below equilibrium and thereby reduce the quantity sellers are willing to offer. Price floors push prices above equilibrium and thereby reduce the quantity consumers wish to buy. Both decrease the actual quantity traded in the market.

8. True. "Somebody" must decide who will be the business winners and losers. Neither markets nor the political process leave the determination of winners and losers to chance. Under market organization, business winners and losers are determined by the decentralized choices of millions of consumers who use their dollar votes to reward firms that provide preferred goods at a low cost and penalize others who fail to do so. Under political decision-making, the winners and losers are determined by political figures and planning boards who use taxes, subsidies, regulations, and mandates to favor some businesses and penalize others.

10. a. Profitable production increases the value of resources owned by people and leads to mutual gain; to resource suppliers, consumers, and entrepreneurs. b. Losses reduce the value of resources which reduces the well-being of at least some people; c. No.

12. In the absence of trade restrictions, modest price increases in France will attract wheat from other regions, minimizing the effects in the drought region and resulting in slightly higher prices worldwide.

14. Rationing by price encourages future output; waiting in a line does not. Like a higher price, a longer wait in line rations the current supply by increasing the consumer's opportunity cost. However, the consumer's cost of waiting in line is wasted. It generates nothing for suppliers. In contrast, while a higher price also increases the consumer's opportunity cost, this cost transfers resources to suppliers, increases their returns, and thereby encourages them to expand the future availability of the good.

16. a. Demand would increase, rising vertically by $3 per meal—the added per-meal cost previously paid separately. b. Both price and quantity will rise in response to the rise in demand.

18. a. The $2,000 is a cost, because it is the forgone opportunity (and pay) required for her to work at this business; b. Total monthly cost (the sum of listed costs) is $14,200; c. Monthly sales revenue is $20 x 800 = $16,000; d. Trina is making a profit of $1,800 = $16,000 – $14,200.

CHAPTER 4

2. When payment is not demanded for services, potential customers have a strong incentive to attempt a "free ride." However, when the number of nonpaying customers becomes such that the sales revenues of sellers are diminished (and in some cases eliminated), the sellers' incentive to supply the good is thereby reduced (or eliminated).

5. Disagree. As long as changes in personal costs and benefits influence choices predictably, theories for both market and public-sector action can be developed and tested against real-world events. Theory building and testing are the essential ingredients of a positive science.

6. The antimissile system is a public good for the residents of Washington, D.C. Strictly speaking, none of the other items are public goods since each could be provided to some consumers (paying customers, for example) without being provided to others.

9. In both markets and government, mutual consent is the only conclusive test of whether an action is productive. If all parties affected by an activity agree to it, then it is productive. Projects favored by a majority are not necessarily productive because the cost imposed on the nonconsenting minority may exceed the net gain to the majority.

11. The invisible hand principle is present only when the self-interest of individuals is consistent with the general welfare. Both the special interest effect and the shortsightedness effect indicate that this will not always be the case, even when political choices are made democratically.

12. True. Since individual computer customers both decide the issue (what computer, if any, will be purchased) and bear the consequences of a mistaken choice, they have a strong incentive to acquire information that will help them make a wise choice. In contrast, voters recognize that their choice, even if mistaken, will not decide the congressional election. Thus, they have little incentive to search for information that will help them make a better choice.

14. When Jack sells his stock, its price will reflect the value of future profits from the investment being undertaken now in lieu of dividends paid. The GM investment reduces Jack's income now, but increases the value of his stock by enough to make up for the loss. But there is no way for him to recapture the value of the tax payments without continuing to live in Los Angeles. (But if he owned a home, the sale price of the home would reflect the value of better city services, such as better streets serving his neighborhood.)

CHAPTER 5

2. Local and state governments operate in a more competitive setting than does the federal government. The competition reduces their ability to exploit taxpayers.

Taxpayers who feel they are paying high taxes and getting little in return can vote with their feet; they can move to another local (or state) governmental unit that offers them more value for their tax dollars.

3. User charges differ from general taxation in that they impose the cost of a government activity on users in proportion to their consumption of the good. If you do not use the good, you do not have to pay for it. Taxes earmarked to finance specific activities may approximate user charges, but general taxation does not. The use of general taxes to finance a government activity breaks the link between consumption and payment and thereby forces nonusers to pay for things enjoyed by others. Like market prices, user charges provide valuable information about value relative to cost. If the revenue from a user charge is sufficient to cover opportunity cost, this is strong evidence that consumers value the good more than the alternatives forgone. Conversely, if user charges are insufficient to cover cost, this is evidence that consumers place a higher value on other things that might be produced.

6. True. In addition to the outlay cost of the project, the collection cost of the taxes and the deadweight losses emanating from the taxes implied by the project must also be covered if the project is going to enhance economic welfare.

7. High marginal tax rates make tax-deductible expenditures (for example, business entertainment, elegant offices, or luxury automobiles for business use) cheap *to the purchaser* (but not to society). A reduction in marginal tax rates will increase the purchaser's cost of deductible expenditures, since the lower rates reduce the tax savings accompanying deductible expenditures. Thus, lower marginal rates will tend to reduce expenditures on deductible items and other forms of tax avoidance.

10. False. Just as businesses do not pay taxes, neither do inanimate objects such as trucks. Only people pay taxes. In this case, the increased costs accompanying the tax translates into higher freight rates. These costs will be paid by consumers of the products transported (in the form of higher prices), by truck owners (in the form of lower profits), and by trucking employees (in the form of lower earnings).

CHAPTER 6

1. a., c., f., g., and h. will exert no impact on GDP; b. and d. will increase GDP by the amount of the expenditure; and e. will increase GDP by $250 (the commission on the transaction).

3. Since the furniture was produced last year, the sale does not affect GDP this year. It reduces inventory investment by $100,000 and increases consumption by $100,000, leaving GDP unchanged.

5. The reliability of GDP comparisons over long periods of time is reduced because the leisure and human costs may change substantially between the two years, and because the types of goods available for consumption during the two years may be vastly different. Likewise, GDP may not be a good index of output differences between countries (for example, the United States and Mexico) for the same reasons. In addition, there may be substantial differences between countries in the production of (a) economic "bads," (b) goods in the household sector, and (c) the size of the underground economy.

7. 250.75

9. a. $1,000; b. $600; c. $200; d. 0; e. $10,000

11. a. False. Inventory investment indicates whether the holdings of unsold goods are *rising* or *falling*. A negative inventory investment (economists refer to this as disinvestment) means that inventories were drawn down during the period; b. False. If gross investment is less than the depreciation of capital goods during the period, net investment would be negative. Net investment in the United States was negative for several years during the Great Depression of the 1930s; c. Not necessarily. Rather, it may be the result of an increase in prices, population, or hours worked.

12. Neither the receipts nor the expenditures on payouts would count toward GDP since they are merely transfers—they do not involve production. However, expenditures on operations, administration, and government-provided goods and services from lottery proceeds would add to GDP.

14. a. 0; b. 0; c. $500; d. $300; e. $300; f. 0; g. 0; h. 0

17. Consideration of this question illustrates some of the problems accompanying income comparisons across widely separated time periods when the bundle of goods available differs substantially. Of course, the price level has risen approximately sevenfold since 1929, so that $40,000 of income in 1929 would be comparable to $280,000 in 1989. However, even with $280,000 of income in 1929, you could not have purchased a C.D. player, color television, personal computer or an airplane ticket for New York to Los Angeles. Neither could you have purchased an automobile that would deliver the service and dependability of even today's economy model. The number of people you could have contacted via telephone would have been limited. Modern household appliances that most people take for granted would have been unavailable. Of course, you could have purchased a lot of other goods, including clothing, land, and wood for heating. Even so, we suspect that many would prefer the choices available today at the lower level of real income.

CHAPTER 7

2. Job seekers do not know which employers will offer them the more attractive jobs. They find out by searching.

Job search is "profitable" and consistent with economic efficiency as long as the marginal gain from search exceeds the marginal cost of searching.

6. One of the most harmful side effects of inflation is the uncertainty it creates with regard to time dimension contracts. As the statement indicates, it tends to undermine the ability of markets to allocate goods and resources to those who value them the most. In effect, it encourages speculation rather than production. The well known economist who made the statement referred to in the question was John Maynard Keynes. See *The Economic Consequences of Peace* (New York: Harcourt Brace, 1920, pages 235–36).

7. When the *actual* unemployment rate is equal to the *natural* rate of unemployment, cyclical unemployment is absent and potential GDP is at its sustainable rate. When the *actual* unemployment rate is greater (less) than the *natural* rate of unemployment, cyclical unemployment is positive (negative) and potential GDP is less (greater) than its sustainable rate.

8. a. 60 percent; b. 8.3 percent; c. 55 percent

9. No. No. It means that there were no jobs available at wage rates acceptable to the potential workers who were unemployed. Thus, they continued to search for more attractive opportunities.

10. The inflation will tend to increase the wealth of a. and e. because it will increase the nominal value of their assets and reduce their real liabilities. It will hurt b., c., and f. because their income will rise less rapidly than prices. With regard to d., it depends on whether his indebtedness is at a fixed or variable interest rate. If it is fixed, the inflation will reduce his real indebtedness, but if it is variable (tied to an interest rate that can be expected to increase with the inflation rate), his interest cost will rise with inflation.

13. Each will encourage additional search.

14. The wages people earn are also prices (prices for labor services) and like other prices they usually rise as the general level of prices increases. The statement ignores this factor. It implicitly assumes that money wages are unaffected by inflation; that they would have increased by the same amount (6 percent) even if prices would have been stable. Generally, this will not be the case.

CHAPTER 8

4. If the inflation rate unexpectedly falls from 3 percent to zero, the real wages of union members will rise. If other unions have similar contracts, the unemployment rate will increase because employment costs have risen relative to product prices. Profit margins will be cut and producers will respond by reducing output and laying off workers. In contrast, if the inflation rate rises to 8 percent, profit margins

will improve, producers will expand their output, and the unemployment rate will decline.

7. The key things held constant when constructing the demand and supply schedules for a specific good are: demand (consumer income, prices of related goods, consumer preferences, expected future price of the good, and number of consumers) and supply (resource prices, technology, and expected future price of the good). Changes in these factors shift the relevant schedule.

The key things held constant when constructing the *aggregate* schedules are: AD (money supply, the government's tax and spending policies, real wealth, real income of one's trading partners, consumer preferences, and the expected future price level); LRAS (size of resource base, technology, and institutional structure of the economy); and SRAS (factors held constant in the LR plus resource prices and the expected price level). Again, change in these factors will shift the schedules indicated.

10. They are all equal.

11. Negative real interest rates are realized when the money interest rate is less than the inflation rate. This generally occurs when decision makers (particularly lenders) underestimate the future rate of inflation and therefore agree to an inflationary premium that proves to be insufficient to compensate for the effects of inflation. This was the case for many loans in the United States during the sharp acceleration in inflation in the mid-1970s. Negative real interest rates are unlikely to persist because lenders losing real purchasing power will alter their expectations of the inflation rate upward and therefore demand a larger inflationary premium.

12. $10,000; $20,000

13. Inversely; an increase in interest rates is the same thing as a reduction in bond prices.

CHAPTER 9

1. a. would decrease AD; b., c., and d. would increase it; and e. would leave it unchanged. For the "why" part of the question, see the section "Factors That Shift Aggregate Demand," at the beginning of the chapter.

2. a., b., c., and d. will reduce SRAS; e. will increase it.

4. When an economy is operating at less than full employment, weak demand in resource markets will tend to reduce (a) the real rate of interest and (b) resource prices *relative to product prices* and thereby restore normal profit and the incentive of firms to produce the long-run potential output level. If resource prices and the real interest rate were inflexible downward, the self-correcting mechanism would not work.

6. At the lower than expected inflation rate, real wages (and costs) will increase *relative* to product prices. This will squeeze profit margins and lead to reductions in output and employment, causing the unemployment rate to rise.

8. Tightness in resource markets will result in rising resource prices *relative to product prices,* causing the *SRAS* to shift to the left. Profit margins will decline, output rate will fall, and long-run equilibrium will be restored at a higher price level. The above normal output cannot be maintained because it reflects input prices that people would not have agreed to and output decisions they would not have chosen if they had anticipated the current price level (and rate of inflation). Once they have a chance to correct these mistakes, they do so; and output returns to the economy's long-run potential.

9. Real wages will tend to increase more rapidly when the unemployment rate is low because a tight labor market (strong demand) will place upward pressure on wages.

12. In the short run, the unanticipated expansion in demand will tend to increase output and employment, while exerting modest upward pressure on the price level. In the long run, the primary impact will be a higher price level, with no change in output and employment.

CHAPTER 10

2. a. Increase current consumption, as the expectation of rising future prices will induce consumers to buy now; b. Decrease current consumption, as people will attempt to save more for hard times; c. Increase current consumption, as the result of an expansion in disposable income; d. May have little effect. However, the tendency will be toward a reduction in consumption, since households have an incentive to save more at the higher interest rate; e. Decrease consumption, as falling stock prices will reduce the wealth of consumers; f. and g. Increase consumption, as the young and the poor typically have a higher marginal propensity to consume than the elderly and wealthy.

4. It is the concept that a change in one of the components of aggregate demand, investment, for example, will lead to a far greater change in the equilibrium level of income. Since the multiplier equals 1/1 – MPC, its size is determined by the marginal propensity to consume. The multiplier makes stabilizing the economy more difficult, since relatively small changes in aggregate demand have a much greater impact on equilibrium income.

7. The funds for the additional spending must come from either a decline in saving or an increase in borrowing. The model implicitly assumes one of the following: either (a) the changes in saving and borrowing exert no impact on the real interest rate or (b) the level of current investment, consumption, and government expenditure is insensitive to changes in the real rate of interest. In essence, the model ignores the interrelation between the goods and services market and the loanable funds market.

9. The statement fails to recognize that association does not imply a direction of causation. The investment

demand conditions differ during periods of boom and recession. During an expansionary boom, investment demand is strong. In turn, the strong investment demand pushes interest rates up, not vice versa. Similarly, during a recession, weak investment demand leads to lower interest rates. Thus, it is the fluctuations in investment demand (shifts of the schedule) that explain the pattern of interest rates over the business cycle.

11. When the change is unanticipated and when it is expected to persist for a substantial period of time. In contrast, changes in expenditures that are anticipated and expected to be temporary will exert little impact on the rate of production. For example, even though expenditures on goods such as lawn mowers, swim suits, toys, and skiing equipment are much higher at certain times of the year, the production and employment of firms producing these goods is relatively stable since the changes in expenditures are both anticipated and expected to be temporary.

13. None. The Keynesian model assumes that wages and prices are inflexible downward. It will take an increase in aggregate expenditures to restore full employment.

15. Recession is an expected impact. The Keynesian model suggests that a stock market crash will tend to adversely affect business and consumer optimism, resulting in a reduction in planned aggregate demand, which in turn is magnified by the multiplier.

In the *AD/AS* model, the impact of the decline in stock prices is less predictable. If businesses and consumers become more pessimistic and therefore reduce their spending, a reduction in business borrowing and an increase in household saving is implied. These forces will place downward pressure on the real interest rate, which will stimulate demand and thereby help cushion any reduction in *AD* emanating from declining stock prices. Thus, the *AD/AS* model indicates that the stability characteristics of a market economy are not nearly so fragile as the Keynesian model implies.

CHAPTER 11

2. The crowding-out effect is the theory that budget deficits will lead to higher real interest rates, which retard private spending. The crowding-out effect indicates that fiscal policy would not be nearly so potent as the simple Keynesian model implies. The new classical theory indicates that anticipation of higher future taxes (rather than higher interest rates) will crowd out private spending when government expenditures are financed by debt.

4. Automatic stabilizers are built-in features (unemployment compensation, corporate profit tax, progressive income tax) that tend automatically to promote a budget deficit during a recession and a budget surplus (or smaller deficit) during an inflationary boom. Automatic stabilizers have the major advantage of providing needed restraint, or

stimuli, without congressional approval which, in turn, minimizes the problem of proper timing.

8. This statement depicts the views of many economists two decades ago. Today, most economists recognize that it is naive. Given our limited ability to accurately forecast future economic conditions, timing of fiscal policy is more difficult than it was previously thought. Political considerations—remember, the government is merely an alternative form of social organization, not a corrective device—reduce the likelihood that fiscal policy will be used as a stabilization tool. Changes in interest rates and private spending may offset fiscal actions and thereby reduce the potency of fiscal policy. All factors considered, it is clear that the use of fiscal policy to stabilize the economy is both difficult and complex.

10. There is a major defect in this view. If the budget deficits stimulated demand and thereby output and employment, we would have expected the inflation rate to accelerate. This was not the case; in fact, the inflation rate declined. The failure of the inflation rate to accelerate during the expansion of the 1980s strongly suggests that factors other than demand stimulus were at work.

13. This is an accurate statement of what economists refer to as the balanced budget multiplier. It is correct under very restrictive assumptions. However, it ignores the secondary effects in the loanable funds market. If the taxes of consumers rise by $10 billion and consumers reduce their spending by only $7.5 billion, then a $2.5 billion reduction in the supply of loanable funds is implied. This will place upward pressure on the real interest rate, which under normal circumstances will crowd out $2.5 billion dollars of private spending. Thus, when the secondary effects are considered, the validity of the statement is highly questionable.

14. Yes. Only the lower rates would increase the incentive to earn marginal income and thereby stimulate aggregate supply.

CHAPTER 12

1. A liquid asset is one that can easily and quickly be transformed into money without experiencing a loss of its market value. Assets such as high-grade bonds and stocks are highly liquid. Assets such as real estate, a family-owned business, business equipment, and artistic works are generally illiquid.

3. Money is valuable because of its scarcity relative to the availability of goods and services. The use of money facilitates (reduces the cost of) exchange transactions. Money also serves as a store of value and a unit of account. Doubling the supply of money, holding output constant, would simply cause its purchasing power to fall without enhancing the services that it performs. In fact, *fluctuations* in the money supply would create uncertainty as to its future value and reduce the ability of money to serve as a

store of value, accurate unit of account, and medium of exchange for time-dimension contracting.

6. a. No change; currency held by the public increases, but checking deposits decrease by an equal amount; b. Bank reserves decrease by $100; c. Excess reserves decrease by $100 minus the required reserve ratio multiplied by $100.

8. Answers b., e., and f. will reduce the money supply; a. and c. will increase it; if the Treasury's deposits (or the deposits of persons who receive portions of the Treasury's spending) are considered part of the money supply, then d. will leave the money supply unchanged.

10. While the transformation of deposits into currency does not *directly* affect the money supply, it does reduce the excess reserves of banks. The reduction in excess reserves will cause banks to reduce their outstanding loans and thereby shrink the money supply. Therefore, an increase in the holding of currency relative to deposits will tend to reduce the supply of money.

12. There are two major reasons. First, the money supply can be altered quietly via open market operations, while a reserve requirement change focuses attention on Fed policy. Second, open market operations are a fine tuning method, while a reserve requirement change is a blunt instrument. Generally, the Fed prefers quiet, marginal changes to headline-grabbing, blunt changes which are more likely to disrupt markets.

13. a. False; statements of this type often use money when they are really speaking about wealth (or income); b. False; the checking deposit also counts as money. In addition, the deposit increases the reserves of the receiving bank, and thereby places it in a position to extend additional loans which would increase the money supply; c. False; only an increase in the availability of goods and services valued by people will improve our standard of living. Without an additional supply of goods and services, more money will simply lead to a higher price level.

17. a. Money supply increases by $100,000; b. $80,000; c. $500,000; d. No; there will be some leakage in the form of additional currency holdings by the public and additional excess reserve holdings by banks.

19. a. Money supply will increase by $2 billion; b. $1.8 billion; c. $20 billion; d. Approximately $10.5 billion; e. Approximately $8.51 billion; the potential money multiplier was 10, but the actual multiplier was only 4.255; f. The leakages in the form of currency held by the public and additions to bank reserves cause the actual money multiplier to be less than the potential multiplier.

CHAPTER 13

2. a. and c. would increase your incentive to hold money deposits; b. and d. would reduce your incentive to hold money.

3. a. The cost of *obtaining* the house is $100,000, but the cost of *holding* it is the interest forgone on the $100,000 sales value of the house; b. The cost of *obtaining* $1,000 is the amount of goods one must give up in order to acquire the $1,000. For example, if a pound of sugar sells for 50 cents, the cost of obtaining $1,000 in terms of sugar is 2,000 pounds. As in the case of the house, the cost of *holding* $1,000 is the interest forgone.

10. If the time lag is long and variable (rather than short and highly predictable), it is less likely that policy-makers will be able to time monetary policy so that it will exert a countercyclical impact on the economy. They will be more likely to make mistakes and thereby exert a destabilizing influence. Such destabilizing effects would be reduced if the policy-makers followed the monetary rule of expanding the money supply at a constant rate. Thus, if the effectiveness lag is long and variable, the case for discretionary monetary policy is weakened and the case for a monetary rule is strengthened.

11. It strengthens the case for discretion and weakens the case for a rule. Discretionary changes in monetary policy could be used to offset fluctuations in the velocity of money. For example, if velocity fell, the money supply could be expanded more rapidly in order to prevent a reduction in aggregate demand and income. Correspondingly, if velocity fluctuates, it means that steady growth in the money supply would fail to stabilize the growth of demand, output, and employment.

12. Association does not reveal causation. Decision makers—including borrowers and lenders—will eventually anticipate a high rate of inflation and adjust their choices accordingly. As the expected rate of inflation increases, the demand for loanable funds will increase and the supply will decrease. This will lead to higher nominal interest rates. Thus, economic theory indicates that the causation tends to run the opposite direction from that indicated by the statement.

13. Aggregate demand will decline as individuals and businesses reduce spending in an effort to build up their money balances (demand more money).

15. The change in the money supply (M) plus the change in velocity (V) must equal the change in real output (Y) plus the change in the price level. Historically, the growth rate of real output (Y) in the United States has averaged approximately 3 percent. During the 1990s, if real output and velocity both grow at a 3 percent annual rate, then the money supply will have to remain constant (zero growth rate) for price stability to be achieved.

CHAPTER 14

4. Traditional monetary and fiscal policy are designed to maintain a high level of aggregate demand to combat the unemployment problem in the short run. The microapproach, on the other hand, is not such a quick-fix strategy. It emphasizes the relative price effects, the microstructure of the economy, and long-run policy prescriptions. If monetary and fiscal policies cannot permanently reduce the long-run natural rate of unemployment, then the microapproach is a viable substitute for traditional macropolicies.

6. Economists in the mid-1970s thought inflation would reduce unemployment; they failed to recognize that decision makers would eventually come to anticipate the inflation. The modern view of the Phillips curve incorporates expectations into the analysis.

9. Compared to the early views of the Phillips curve, modern theory indicates that inflationary policies will be less attractive. Acceptance of the modern view by policy-makers will reduce the likelihood of inflationary policies.

12. A study by Bruce Meyer, *Unemployment Insurance and Unemployment Spells* (Cambridge: National Bureau of Economic Research, 1988) found that the chances of an unemployed person getting a job quadrupled between the sixth week before the end of benefits and one week before the benefits expire. Meyer estimates that a ten percent increase in the share of after-tax earnings replaced by unemployment benefits lengthens the average unemployment spell by one and one-half weeks. Lowering the benefits after a couple of months of job searching reduces both the employment disincentive effects of the benefits and the natural rate of unemployment.

14. With unanticipated inflation, real wages fall because many workers, who did not anticipate the inflation, accepted explicit and implicit contracts at wage rates they would have found unacceptable had they correctly anticipated the magnitude of the price increase. Job search time will decline because many workers will accept jobs at money wage rates they would have rejected if they had been fully aware of how much inflation had increased money wages. Both of these factors will temporarily reduce the unemployment rate. When the inflation is anticipated, it will be fully reflected in long-term wage agreements. Thus, the inflation will fail to reduce real wage rates. Similarly, job search time will be normal because workers will recognize how much inflation has increased the money wages of potential jobs. Thus, anticipated inflation fails to reduce the unemployment rate.

16. a. A change in the expected rate of inflation; b. Changes in factors that influence the natural rate of unemployment.

17. It will reduce the incentive to accept available jobs. Payment for nonwork is a substitute for work, particularly employment at a low wage rate. It is not easy to differentiate between unemployed workers and workers out of the labor force. The payments provide persons out of or marginally attached to the labor force with an incentive to indicate that

they are available for work in order to receive the benefits. This would increase *measured* unemployment.

CHAPTER 15

4. Compared with earlier periods, the United States has experienced less economic instability during the last four decades. There is reason to believe that a more stable monetary policy has contributed to the increase in stability. See text Exhibits 15-1 and 15-3.

5. Nonactivists think that a monetary rule would result in less instability from monetary sources. The changing nature of money may reduce the stabilizing effects of a monetary rule.

9. Activists argue that it has been during only the last four decades that policy-makers have attempted to adjust macroeconomic policy in light of economic conditions. According to the activist view, the improved stability reflects the use of discretionary policy. Nonactivists point out that fluctuations in policy, particularly monetary policy (see Exhibit 15-3), have declined in recent years, and that the increased economic stability merely reflects the more stable policies. According to nonactivists, this linkage indicates that still more stable policies, such as would result from a monetary rule, would lead to a still more stable economy.

11. An unexpected shift to more expansionary monetary policy might temporarily reduce real interest rates. However, persistent use of expansionary policy in an attempt to push real interest rates below market levels will result in inflation (and high nominal interest rates). Once decision makers anticipate an inflation rate, even high rates of inflation will fail to reduce real interest rates.

14. It implies that Americans tend to vote their pocket-books, and as a result, the latter set of factors are much less important than is generally believed.

CHAPTER 16

1. No. Both private corporations and governments can, and often do, have continual debt outstanding. Borrowers can continue to finance and refinance debt as long as lenders have confidence in their ability to pay. This will generally be the case as long as the interest liability is small relative to income (or the potential tax base).

4. No. Remember, trade is a positive-sum game. Bonds are sold to foreigners because they are offering a better deal (acceptance of a lower interest rate) than is available elsewhere. Prohibiting the sale of bonds to foreigners would result in higher real interest rates and less investment, both of which would adversely affect Americans.

5. A failure to anticipate fully the future taxes accompanying debt implies an underestimation of the true cost of government. Since politicians will want to exaggerate the benefits and conceal the cost of their actions, the ability of debt to hide the true cost of government increases its attractiveness with vote-seeking politicians.

6. Rather than defaulting, the federal government could, as a last resort, meet its debt obligations by borrowing from the Fed. In essence, this means the government is paying its debts with printing-press money. It would lead to inflation.

8. It increases. Yes, if inflation reduced the real outstanding national debt by a larger amount than the budget deficit. See the next question for an illustration of this point.

10. No. Yes.

14. In responding to this question, reflect on the following: Will Congressional representatives, subject to political pressures, be more or less likely to adopt an anti-inflationary policy than relatively anonymous central banking policy-makers (for example, the Board of Governors of the Fed)? The empirical evidence indicates that the politicians will be more likely to adopt inflation-generating policies. The central banks of many countries, particularly those in South America, are under the direct control of the political authorities. The inflation rates in these countries are generally quite high.

15. Lower; voters do not enjoy paying taxes and therefore, voter dissatisfaction places a restraint on higher taxes, which would also restrain expenditures if the budget had to be balanced. More efficient; the restraint of tax increases would tighten the budget constraint and make the reality of opportunity cost more visible to both voters and politicians.

CHAPTER 17

1. a. Increase demand; b. Decrease demand; c. Decrease incentive to develop nongasoline powered car; d. Leave demand unchanged, quantity demanded declined; e. Increase demand.

3. a. 0.21; 1.2. b. Substitutes; higher fuel oil prices lead to an increase in demand (and consumption) for insulation.

8. Water is usually cheaper than oil because its marginal utility at current consumption levels is less than that of oil. Since water is so abundant relative to oil, the benefit derived from an additional quart of water is less than the benefit from an additional quart of oil, even though the total utility from all units of water is far greater than the total utility from all units of oil. However, the price of a product will reflect marginal utility, not total utility.

9. Both income and time constrain our ability to consume. Since, in a wealthier society, time becomes more binding and income less binding, time-saving actions will be more common in a wealthier society. As we engage in time-saving actions (fast food, automatic appliances, air travel, and so on) in order to shift the time restraint outward, our lives become more hectic.

12. All three statements are true.

13. a. No. Even for things we like, we will experience diminishing returns. Eventually, the cost of additional units of pizza will exceed their benefits. b. Perfection in any activity is generally not worth the cost. For example, reading every page of this text 3, 4, or 5 times may improve your grade, but it may not be worth it. One function of a text is to structure the material (highlighted points, layout of graphs, and so on) so that the reader will be able to learn quickly (at a lower cost).

14. Carole.

15. False. Since the demand for agricultural products is generally inelastic, farm incomes may well increase. But the total utility of farm output reflects not only the sales revenues but also the consumer surplus. For the units produced, the utility is unchanged as the loss of consumer surplus by consumers is exactly offset by higher payments to farmers. However, both the payments to farmers and consumer surplus are lost for those units not produced. Therefore, the decline in production will reduce the total utility of farm output and the nation will be worse off as a result.

18. Deceit and dishonesty will be encouraged by methods of organization that increase the returns to such behavior. The returns to deceitful and dishonest claims will be inversely related to the ease with which they can be countered by rivals. Other things constant, the presence of rivals will tend to reduce deceitful behavior. Is a politician more or less likely to tell the truth when he or she regularly confronts rivals? Is the news media more or less likely to be balanced and trustworthy when it faces rivals in the news business? Is a court witness more or less likely to tell the truth when there are other witnesses and cross-examination can be expected? Is a firm selling automobiles, cough drops, or hamburgers more or less likely to be honest when it faces competitors? Answers to such questions are obvious.

19. The deadweight loss is the loss of the potential gains of buyers and sellers emanating from trades that are squeezed out by the tax. It is an excess burden because even though the exchanges that are squeezed out by the tax impose a cost on buyers and sellers, they do not generate tax revenue (since the trades do not take place).

CHAPTER 18

1. The economic profit of a firm is its total revenues minus the opportunity cost of all resources used in the production process. Accounting profit often excludes the opportunity cost of certain resources—particularly the equity capital of the firm and any labor services provided by an owner-manager. Zero economic profit means that the resources owned by the firm are earning their opportunity cost—that is, the rate of return is as high as the highest valued alternative forgone. Thus, the firm would not gain by pursuing other lines of business.

2. a. Sunk costs are irrelevant; b. There is an opportunity cost of one's house; c. Sunk costs should not affect one's current decision; d. There is an opportunity cost of public education even if it is provided free to the consumer.

12. Since owners receive profits, clearly profit maximization is in their interest. Managers, if they are not owners, have no property right to profit and therefore no direct interest in profit maximization. Since a solid record of profitability tends to increase the market value (salary) of corporate managers, they do have an indirect incentive to pursue profits. However, corporate managers may also be interested in power, nice offices, hiring friends, expansion of sales and other activities, which may conflict with profitability. Thus, the potential for conflict between the interests of owners and managers is present.

13. a. The interest payments; b. The interest income forgone. The tax structure encourages debt rather than equity financing since the firm's tax liability is inversely related to its debt/equity ratio.

14. True. If it could produce the output at a lower cost, its profit would be greater.

16. Did your marginal cost curve cross the ATC and AVC curves at their low points? Does the vertical distance between the ATC and AVC curves get smaller and smaller as output increases? If not, redraw the three curves correctly. See Exhibit 18–6b.

20. $2,500; the $2,000 decline in market value during the year plus $500 of potential interest on funds that could be obtained if the machine were sold new. Costs associated with the decline in the value of the machine last year are sunk costs.

21. Because they believe they will be able to restructure the firm and provide better management so that the firm will have positive net earnings in the future. If the firm is purchased at a low enough price, this will allow the new owners to cover the opportunity cost of their investment and still earn an economic profit. Alternatively, they may expect to sell off the firm's assets, receiving more net revenue than the cost of purchasing the firm.

CHAPTER 19

1. In a highly competitive industry such as agriculture, lower resource prices might improve the rate of profit in the short run, but in the long run, competition will drive prices down until economic profit is eliminated. Thus, lower resource prices will do little to improve the long-run profitability in such industries.

2. New firms will enter the industry and the existing firms will expand output; market supply will expand, causing the market price to fall until economic profit is eliminated.

6. The statement is nonsense. If a reduction in demand leads to losses and exits from the industry, this reduction in

supply will lead to a higher price and the restoration of normal returns.

8. a. Increase; b. Increase; c. Increase. Firms will earn economic profit; d. Rise (compared with its initial level) for an increasing cost industry, but return to initial price for a constant cost industry; e. Increase even more than it did in the short run; f. Economic profit will return to zero.

9. a. Decline; b. Increase; c. Decline; d. Decline.

11. The firms are unable to earn long-term economic profit because the barriers to entry into a competitive industry are low. Thus, profit attracts rival firms who "spoil the market." Even though competitive firms earn only normal returns in the long run, profits and losses direct entrepreneurs into the production of those goods that are in short supply relative to their cost in the short run. This is a vitally important function.

14. a. Room prices (including the tax) will increase; b. Decline in the short run. In the long run, supply will fall and profit will return to normal; c. Increase when the demand for rooms in the city is inelastic, but decline when demand is elastic.

16. True. Sellers undercut other sellers in order to gain business. Buyers outbid other buyers in order to obtain a good.

18. b. Six or seven tons; $250 profit. c. Seven or eight tons; $600 profit. d. Five or six tons; $50 loss. Since the firm can cover its variable cost, it should stay in business if it believes that the low ($450) price is temporary.

CHAPTER 20

1. Profits cannot exist in the long run without barriers to entry because without them new entrants seeking the profits would increase supply, drive down price, and eliminate the profits. But as the chapter shows, barriers to entry are no guarantee of profits. Sufficient demand is also a necessary condition.

3. No; No; No.

7. With a single tuition for all, it can nevertheless price-discriminate by giving financial aid to effectively lower the cost for students from lower-income families. These students presumably are more sensitive to higher tuition, so that their elasticity demand for the university's services is greater.

9. Once an item has been invented and patented, short-run efficiency is indeed reduced by the monopoly given by the patent. The market will probably be understocked, with a price set higher than the marginal cost. Patents are inefficient in this sense. Over time, however, consumers benefit by the efforts of innovators and the investors who support them. These efforts would be smaller if there were no patents to provide some monopoly power to successful innovators.

12. No. The firm's new profit-maximizing output rate will be 10 percent larger, but the profit-maximizing price

will be unchanged. Construct a graph that illustrates this point.

13. Yes; b. Implies that in the observed price range, the demand for petroleum products was inelastic. But a monopolist would never set price in this range—the inelastic portion of the demand curve—because a higher price would both increase revenues and reduce cost (since fewer units are produced and sold).

15. Reductions in the cost of transportation generally increase competition because they force firms to compete with distant rivals and permit consumers to choose among a wider range of suppliers. As a result, the U.S. economy today is generally more competitive, in the rivalry sense, than it was 100 years ago.

18. The Sonics do have a monopoly on NBA basketball in Seattle. But there are many other college and high school teams, and there are other professional sports to watch in Seattle, such as football. In addition there are numerous other forms of entertainment available in Seattle. All of these options (and more) compete for the entertaining dollars of fans.

21. b. $10, 125,000 tickets are sold; c. Total costs = $450,000, profits = $800,000; d. Profit-maximizing price and quantity remain the same, but profits fall to $700,000.

22. b. $30, 137,750 tires; c. Profits = $755,000; e. Sunnyside: $27 and 97,000 tires; f. Muddville: $42 and 40,750 tires; g. Profits: $953,000; h. Muddville, Sunnyside, the inelastic demand curve means that total revenue will increase when price increases.

CHAPTER 21

2. Building the new resort is more risky (and less attractive) because if the market analysis is incorrect, and demand is insufficient, it probably will be difficult to find other uses for the newly built resort. If the airline proves unprofitable, however, the capital (airplanes) should be extremely mobile. However, the resort would have one off-setting advantage: If demand were stronger than expected, and profits larger, it would take competitors longer to enter the market (build a new resort), and they would be more reluctant to make the more permanent investment.

5. The stock price, when the uncle bought the stock, no doubt reflected the well-known profits of Mammoth. The previous owners of the stock surely would not have sold it at a low price that failed to reflect the future dividends. In the language of the text, the uncle was not an "early bird." It is unlikely that he will profit, in the economic sense, from the purchase.

6. Product variation provides each firm in the oligopoly a chance to "cheat" by raising the quality of its products in order to entice customers from rivals. This raises cost and helps to defeat the purpose, for the oligopolistic group, of controlling price. But if collusion has raised price much

above marginal cost, there will be a powerful incentive for each firm to compete in a hidden way to get more customers.

9. The concentration ratio of an industry depends very much on how the industry is defined by the analyst calculating the ratio. It can overstate or understate the market power of the firms in question. Even potential entrants may influence price decisions by market producers. But sellers in local markets may have much more market power than the concentration ratio indicates. And finally, even a monopoly does not guarantee the ability to cover costs, much less a large profit. The firm's costs, as compared to willingness of consumers to pay, and number of such consumers, also must be considered.

12. The amount of variety is determined by the willingness of consumers to pay for variety relative to the cost of providing it. If consumers value variety highly and the added costs of producing different styles, designs, and sizes is low, there will be a lot of variety. Alternatively, if consumers desire similar products or if variation can be produced only at a high cost, little variety will be present. Apparently, consumers place a substantial value (relative to cost) on variety in napkins, but not in toothpicks.

13. The tax would increase the price of lower quality (and lower priced) automobiles by a larger percentage than higher quality automobiles. Consumers would substitute away from the lower quality autos since their relative price has increased. This substitution would increase the average quality of automobiles sold. Since the funds from the tax are rebated back to citizens through the lottery, one would expect this substitution effect to dominate any possible income effect.

17. a. 25,000 quarts, $7, each firm produces 25 quarts; b. At $7, each firm wants to produce 45 quarts; c. If all firms cheat, the market becomes competitive. The market-clearing price is $5, 35,000 quarts of honey are produced, and each firm produces 35 quarts.

18 a. $15, profits = $110,000; b. $10.

CHAPTER 22

1. Employment in manufacturing is declining, but output is not. Manufacturing productivity is rising, and the sector is holding its own as a share of the economy. The trend for more than a century (see Exhibits 22–1 and 22–2), has been away from blue-collar occupations and toward information-related service occupations, including managers, professional and technical workers, and sales personnel. Noninformation service jobs have risen only a little. Incomes per worker have been rising—not an indication of a second-rate economy.

4. Reduced competition is a potential danger for consumers. But if a merger makes a firm more efficient and better able to undercut the prices of other competitors, it

may in effect increase the degree of competition, even as the firm increases its share of the market.

6. Making cars more safe is good, but if the cost has previously kept consumers from demanding the safety measures, it is possible that they are not worth the cost to many consumers. Some very expensive cars, such as Mercedes-Benz, had airbags when there was no requirement, but Volkswagen did not. Should only the more costly cars be sold? If so, then some people, probably the less affluent, will drive older, even less safe cars. This is not a clearcut issue.

8. Profitability may be adversely affected in the short run, but in the long run prices will rise enough for the firms to cover their opportunity cost of production. Consumers bear the cost of such legislation and get the association benefits, large or small.

9. Since this would increase competition from foreign sources, the effect should be to reduce the fears of market power being held by domestic firms. The need for antitrust action should decline.

12. Existing airlines could be expected to define "necessary" in such a way that no new service would be allowed. Service by existing firms would always, in their view, be sufficient. Customers would be expected to favor (and thus define as necessary) any new service that would reduce prices and/or increase service with a sufficiently small price increase. Since the airlines are far fewer in number and better organized politically than customers, we would expect the airline view of "necessary" to prevail, as it did until the regulatory system grew so that it stifled competition, and prices became so demonstrably high that deregulation occurred and the CAB was abolished.

15. The statement is essentially true. In the short run, capital may be invested in an industry such that it cannot easily be moved elsewhere. If customer demand is elastic, the industry may bear a large part of the cost burden in the short run. In the long run, however, capital is mobile. Factories don't have to be replaced, for example. If costs in the industry are high, relative to the revenues, then capital will migrate over time to other industries, and supply in the regulated industry will fall until the price buyers will pay is again high enough to provide the market rate of return to capital.

17. Experts often do know far more about the technical options than do consumers, although consumers can and do read the advice of experts. Suppliers of safer products also make it a point to advertise data and expert opinion indicating their products are indeed safer. Nevertheless, experts usually do understand the technologies better. On the other hand, experts cannot know about how products will be used. A consumer may prefer to pay for a high degree of safety for the family car, which will carry the whole family at high speeds over long distances, while preferring a much cheaper, less reliable car for running

errands near home. Such choices are hard to allow if all vehicles are strictly regulated for safety. Decision-maker knowledge (and incentives) is, in some cases, better with consumer choice than with thorough and strict regulation.

CHAPTER 23

3. a. Five; b. $350; c. Four. The firm will operate in the short run but it will go out of business in the long run unless the market prices rise.

4. Yes. General increases in the productivity of the labor force will cause a general increase in wages. The higher general wage rates will increase the opportunity cost of barbering and cause the supply of barbers to decline. The reduction in the supply of barbers will place upward pressure on the wages of barbers, even if technological change and worker productivity have changed little in barbering.

8. No. The dressmaker needs to employ more capital and less labor because the marginal dollar expenditures on the former are currently increasing output by a larger amount than the latter.

10. Other things constant, a lengthy training requirement to perform in an occupation reduces supply and places upward pressure on the earnings level. However, resource prices, including those for labor services, are determined by *both* demand and supply. When demand is weak, earnings will be low even though a considerable amount of education may be necessary to perform in the occupation. For example, the earnings of people with degrees in English literature and world history are generally low, even though most people in these fields have a great deal of education.

12. b. 4 c. Employment would decline to 3.

CHAPTER 24

2. U.S. workers are more productive. By investing in human capital, the laborers are somewhat responsible, but the superior tools and physical capital that are available to U.S. workers also contribute to their higher wages.

6. While this statement often made by politicians sounds true, in fact, it is false. Output of goods and services valued by consumers, not jobs, is the key to economic progress and a high standard of living. Real income cannot be high unless real output is high. If job creation was the key to economic progress it would be easy to create millions of jobs. For example, we could prohibit the use of farm machinery. Such a prohibition would create millions of jobs in agriculture. However, it would also reduce output and our standard of living.

8. The opportunity cost of leisure (nonwork) for higher wage workers is greater than for lower wage workers.

9. a. Decreases; b. Increases; c. Decreases; d. Increases.

10. False. Several additional factors including differences in preferences (which would influence time worked, the trade-off between money wage and working conditions, and evaluation of alternative jobs), differences in jobs, and imperfect labor mobility would result in variations in earnings.

12. a., b., e., and f. will generally increase hourly earnings; c. and d. will generally reduce hourly earnings.

13. a. The increase; the cost of employment. Yes. b. Sure, if the higher wages are sufficient to compensate for the absence of the fringe benefits. c. No. Employees pay for them in the form of lower money wages than could be earned on comparable jobs that do not provide the fringe benefits.

16. Hourly wages will be highest in B because the higher wages will be necessary to compensate workers in B for the uncertainty and loss of income during layoffs. Annual earnings will be higher in A in order to compensate workers in A for the additional hours they will work during the year.

17. The employment level of low-skill workers with large families would decline. Some would attempt to conceal the presence of their large family in order to get a job.

19. Not necessarily. Compared with married men, single men tend to be younger, have fewer dependents, are more likely to drop out of the labor force, and less likely to receive earnings-enhancing assistance from another person. All of these factors will reduce their earnings relative to married men.

CHAPTER 25

1. All of the changes would increase interest rates in the United States.

4. No. The *average* outstanding balance during the year is only about half of $1,000. Therefore, the $200 interest charge translates to almost a 40 percent annual rate of interest.

7. *Hints:* Which is more risky? Purchasing a bond or a stock? How does risk influence the expected rate of return?

9. 6 percent.

12. a. Mike; b. Yes, people who save a lot are able to get a higher interest rate on their savings as the result of people with a high rate of time preference. c. Yes, people who want to borrow money will be able to do so at a lower rate when there are more people (like Alicia) who want to save a lot.

13. Helped. This question is a lot like prior questions involving Alicia and Mike. Potential gains from trade are present. If obstacles do not restrain trade, the low-income countries will be able to attract savings (from country's with a high saving rate) at a lower interest rate than would exist in the absence of trade. Similarly, people in the high-income

countries will be able to earn a higher return than would otherwise be possible. Both can gain because of the existence of the other.

15. a. Approximately $1.277 million; b. Yes; c. The lottery earnings are less liquid. Since there is not a well-organized market transforming lottery earnings into present income, the transaction costs of finding a "buyer" (at a price equal to the present value of the earnings) for the lottery earnings "rights' may be higher than for the bond, if one wants to sell in the future.

17. No. The present value of the $500 annual additions to earnings during the next ten years is less than the cost of the schooling.

CHAPTER 26

2. If the union is able to raise the wages of the farm workers: (1) The cost of Florida oranges will rise, causing supply to decline and their price to rise in the long run; (b) profits of the Florida orange growers will decline in the short run, but in the long run they will return to the normal rate; (c) mechanization will be encouraged; and (d) the employment of fruit pickers will decline—particularly in the long run.

3. The higher wages in the South would increase the costs of the southern firms and thereby make them less competitive with their northern rivals.

7. If only part of an industry is unionized, the costs of nonunion firms in the industry will be lower than the costs of unionized firms, if the unionized firms have higher wage rates. If the union wages are much higher than nonunion wages, then the unionized firms will be unable to compete successfully.

9. It may be true in the short run but this will not be the case in the long run. Investors do not have to supply capital to an industry. If the expected profit rate of a highly unionized industry is low, then investment funds will flow elsewhere. An *unanticipated* increase in union wages might reduce profitability in the short run, but it will not be able to do so in the long run. The primary effects of the higher wages will be higher prices. Consumers, rather than investors, will bear the primary cost of high union wages.

10. False. Competition constrains both employers and employees. Employers must compete with *other employers* for labor services. In order to gain the labor services of an employee, an employer must offer a compensation package superior to what the employee can get elsewhere. If the employer does not offer a superior package, the employee will work for a rival employer or choose self-employment. Similarly, employees must compete with *other employees*. Therefore, their ability to demand whatever wage they would like is also restrained. Thus, competition prevents both the payment of low (below market) wages by employ-

ers and the imposition of high (above market) wages by employees.

12. Remember, union members compete with *other workers*, including less skilled workers. An increase in the minimum wage makes unskilled, low-wage workers more expensive. A higher minimum wage increases the demand for high-skill employees who are good substitutes for the low-skill workers. Union members are over-represented among the high-skill group helped by an increase in the minimum wage. Therefore, while union leaders will generally pitch their support for a higher minimum wage in terms of a desire that all workers be paid a "decent wage," the impact of the legislation on union members suggests that self-interest rather than altruism underlies their support for the legislation.

13. The union and the manufacturer would be most likely to favor the tariff because it would make foreign-produced automobiles more expensive and thereby increase the demand for American-made automobiles and the labor with which they are made. In contrast, the higher gasoline tax makes driving more expensive. In response, the demand for higher-gasoline-consumption automobiles will fall, which will adversely affect both American automobile manufacturers and workers.

15. Not necessarily. Adjustment must be made for differences in (a) the productivity characteristics of the union and nonunion workers and (b) the types of jobs they occupy (for example, work environment, job security, likelihood of layoff, and so on). Adjustment for these factors may either increase or reduce the $1.50 differential.

CHAPTER 27

2. Differences in family size, age of potential workers, nonmoney "income," taxes, and cost-of-living among areas reduce the effectiveness of annual money income as a measure of economic status. In general, high-income families are larger, more likely to be headed by a prime-age worker, have less nonmoney income (including leisure), pay more taxes, and reside in higher cost-of-living areas (particularly large cities). Thus, money income comparison between high-and low-income groups often overstates the economic status of the former relative to the latter.

4. If there were no intergenerational mobility, the diagonal numbers would all be 100 percent. If there were complete equality of opportunity and outcomes, the numbers in each column and row would be 20 percent.

6. No. The increase in marginal tax rates will reduce the incentive of the poor to *earn* income. Therefore, their income will rise by $1,000 minus the reduction in their personal earnings due to the disincentive effects of the higher marginal tax rates.

7. 67 percent.

10. Here, as in other areas, it is important to remember that government is merely an alternative form of social organization, rather than a corrective device. The structure of income transfers reflects political clout. The elderly, farmers, and business and labor interests are easily identifiable, politically potent interest groups. In contrast, the poor have a low voter participation rate and offer little in the way of financial support to politicians. Given these factors, it is not surprising that most income transfers go to the nonpoor.

14. Adjustment of individuals to redistributive programs often leads to unintended side effects. If a higher income from private saving means a lower level of social security benefits, people will save less for retirement. Other things constant, the number of low-income (and therefore high-benefit) elderly will grow. Stated another way, programs that subsidize low-income status (and penalize high-income status) during retirement will expand the number of people in the former category and reduce the number in the latter category with the passage of time.

15. Under a pay-as-you-go system, social security benefits do not constitute societal wealth because the benefits imply a liability of equal size. However, *individuals* may treat the expected future benefits as wealth and reduce their saving accordingly. If they do, a society with a pay-as-you-go social security system will have a lower rate of saving and capital formation than a society without such a program.

CHAPTER 28

1. Crude oil, for example, is a gift of nature in the sense that it was put in place without the help of human beings. But as a resource, it is not simply a gift of nature, because human ingenuity and effort are required to make the naturally occurring substance valuable.

3. The "requirement" of water for the steel industry depends on the value placed on water, as well as on the value placed on steel. The same amount of steel can be produced with vastly differing amounts of water, as illustrated in Exhibit 8–1 of this chapter. Also, steel itself is not indispensable in all its uses, including national defense uses. There are many substitutes, not only for water in the making of steel, but also for steel in the making of tanks, and for tanks in providing national defense. So a given amount of water for steel is not really a requirement.

5. Remember the marginal principle. There are a limited number of rich people, and they have a limited amount of time to spend on recreation. It is unlikely that the rich will be willing or able to "buy up all the recreation opportunities." Remember also that if the price of the best fly fishing access, for example, rises because rich people

like it, then more such areas will be provided by profit-seeking entrepreneurs who can improve existing streams and create additional habitat, when it is profitable to do so.

6. Wells are abandoned by producers when the cost of extracting and delivering additional oil exceeds its value. When the value of crude oil rises, additional oil can be produced since water flooding, steam and chemical measures—all of which are costly—can be paid for by the higher prices gained from the extra oil.

7. Total reserves of a mineral include all the resources that are in place, and which might become available in the future, given sufficiently high prices or technological advances. Proved reserves are the resources which producers believe they can produce with current technology, at today's prices. Proved reserves are what count in the short term, but if we are concerned with the long-run prospect of much greater scarcity, with higher prices and incentives for technological advances in mineral exploration and production, then total reserves might also become important.

9. The use of an unowned, unpriced resource might have a high opportunity cost. Yet if there is no owner to protect it, or to allocate it to its highest-valued use, then it might indeed be treated as if it had no opportunity cost. If it is valuable, however, then it might pay an entrepreneur to find a way to establish ownership. That, if fact, is the history of many natural resources in the United States. Ownership of land, for example, was often not established until it became economically attractive enough to reward the initial claimants who established ownership.

11. If an investment, such as leaving the trees to grown another 20 years, yields a higher return than other investments, then the stock price will fall if the trees are cut too soon, or will go higher if a new, more profitable investment path (leaving the trees to grow) is announced. Either way, the stock price immediately rewards good long-term decisions and penalizes bad ones.

12. A lower interest rate would increase the present value of benefits, which occur farther in the future, relative to a high interest rate. (See our earlier chapter on Capital, Interest, and Profit, if this is confusing to you.) Since the project's costs occur sooner, the interest rate chosen has less impact on the present value of costs than on the present value of benefits. As a result, a lower interest rate would make this project look more attractive. A person trying to get the project approved by Congress would want a low interest rate used in the benefit-cost analysis.

CHAPTER 29

1. The commons could have been managed politically, without any private ownership. The open access problem is the absence of both private property and of political control of access to the resource.

4. By definition, a public good cannot be marketed, because free riders (nonpayers) can consume it. There is little incentive for the consumer to state his or her true preference, even if asked. So a producer, including government, has a difficult time knowing how much an extra unit of the public good is worth.

6. We expect that private ownership, which concentrates both the costs and the benefits of stewardship on the owner(s), will result in better care than will joint ownership, at least if the joint owners are many. In the latter case, the benefits are spread among the joint owners, while the costs of care fall on the person doing the care—unless, of course, the group arranges to assign and enforce duties, or to jointly pay for care.

7. Permitting all firms to use air and water resources for "free garbage disposal" services would reduce the producer's costs of supplying pollution-intensive goods. However, as long as free entry is present, the lower cost would lead to lower prices not higher profits. Except for unanticipated changes in pollution control policy, competition will drive the profit rate of all firms, including those in industries that pollute, toward the normal rate of return.

9. Many goods with pubic-good aspects are provided privately. Free museum admission, free concerts, wildlife preservation, and so on defy the free-rider problem. But the public good problem is still with us, and we cannot know whether the right amounts are produced when goods have public good aspects.

10. An inability to exclude nonpaying consumers. Since consumers cannot be prevented (at least not at a low cost) from consuming a pubic good if they fail to pay, each has an incentive to "free ride," which undermines the private supplier's ability to cover the cost of production.

11. Economics doesn't say what is fair, but corporations—like all firms—want to minimize their costs in order to maximize profits. If they can reduce costs by emitting more pollution into the air and by avoiding costly abatement measures, then they are likely to do so. And those who do will gain a competitive advantage over those who do not, so long as the legal system does not hold polluters responsible for downwind damages. Without effective court procedures or bureaucratic action on behalf of those harmed by the pollution it would be folly to expect even public-spirited corporate executives to sacrifice profits to gain a public good—air quality—if their competitors were allowed to pollute.

12. Knowing that the firm's national reputation is at stake at every franchise, travelers would probably find the nationally advertised restaurant more appealing. Also, if they had seen the advertising, they would have a better idea of what sort of food is available. Their relative lack of knowledge about the unadvertised place probably deters their using it. In contrast, the local people would know more than the travelers about the local restaurant, as the result of personal experience or by talking with friends who had tried it.

CHAPTER 30

1. It is difficult for the voter to know what a candidate will do once elected, and the rationally ignorant voter is usually not willing to spend the time and effort required to understand issues, since his or her vote will not be the decisive one anyway. Special interest voters, on the other hand, will know which candidate has promised them the most on their issue. Also, the candidate who is both competent and prepared to ignore special interests will have a hard time getting these facts to voters without financial support from special interest groups. Each voter has an incentive to be a "free rider" on the "good government" issue. Controlling government on behalf of society as a whole is a public good, requiring much private activity. Like other public goods, it tends to be underproduced.

2. Corporate officers, while they surely care about the next few months and the profits during that time, care also about the value of the firm and its stock price. If the stock price rises sufficiently in the next few months—as it will if investors believe that current investments in future-oriented projects (planting new trees, for example) are sound—then the officers will find their jobs secure even if current profits do not look good. Rights to the profits from those (future) trees are saleable now in the form of the corporation's stock. There is no such mechanism to make the distant fruits of today's investments available to the political entrepreneurs who might otherwise fight for the future-oriented project. Only if the project appeals to today's voters, and they are willing to pay today for tomorrow's benefits, will the program be a political success. In any case, the wealth of the political entrepreneur is not directly enhanced by his or her successful fight for the project.

7. No. The government is merely an alternative form of organization. Government organization does not permit us to escape either scarcity or competition. It merely affects the nature of the competition. Political competition (voting, lobbying, political contributions, taxes, and politically determined budgets) replac.es market competition. Neither is there any reason to believe that government organization modifies the importance of personal self-interest.

8. The regulatory and taxation policy toward the liquor industry is usually conducted at the state, rather than at the federal level. Thus, liquor industry interests will be more likely to use lobbying and campaign contributions to influence the action of state-level politicians.

10. When the welfare of a special interest group conflicts with that of a widely dispersed, unorganized majority, the legislative political process can reasonably be expected to work to the benefit of the special interest.

CHAPTER 31

1. Availability of goods and services, not jobs, is the source of economic prosperity. When a good can be purchased cheaper abroad than it can be produced at home, a nation can expand the quantity of goods and services available for consumption by specializing in the production of those goods for which it is a low-cost producer and trading them for the cheap (relative to domestic costs) foreign goods. Trade restrictions limiting the ability of Americans to purchase low-cost goods from foreigners stifle this process and thereby *reduce* the living standard of Americans.

3. Answers a. and b. are not in conflict. Since trade restrictions are typically a special interest issue, political entrepreneurs can often gain by supporting them even when they promote economic inefficiency.

5. True. The primary effect of trade restrictions is an increase in domestic scarcity. This has distributional consequences, but it is clear that as a whole, a nation will be harmed by the increased domestic scarcity accompanying the trade restraints.

6. The quota reduces the supply of sugar to the domestic market and drives up the domestic price of sugar. Domestic producers benefit from the higher prices at the expense of domestic consumers (see Exhibit 31–11). Studies indicate that the quota expanded the gross income of the 11,000 domestic sugar farmers by approximately $130,000 per farm in the mid-1980s, at the expense (in the form of higher prices of sugar and sugar products) of approximately $6 per year to the average domestic consumer. Since the program channels resources away from products for which the U.S. has a comparative advantage, it reduces the productive capacity of the United States. Both the special interest nature of the issue and rent-seeking theory explain the political attractiveness of the program.

8. a. No. Americans would be poorer if we used more of our resources to produce things for which we are a high opportunity-cost producer and less of our resources to produce things for which we are low opportunity-cost producer. Employment might either increase or decrease, but the key point is that it is the value of goods produced, not employment, which generates income and provides for the wealth of a nation; The answer to b. is the same as a.

9. In thinking about this issue, consider the following points. Suppose the Japanese were willing to give products such as automobiles, electronic goods, and clothing to us free of charge. Would we be worse off if we accepted the gifts? Should we try to keep the free goods out? What is the source of real income—jobs or goods and services? If the gifts make us better off, doesn't it follow that partial gifts would also make us better off?

12. While trade reduces employment in import-competing industries, it expands employment in export industries. On balance, there is no reason to believe that trade either promotes or destroys jobs. The major effect of trade is to permit individuals, states, regions, and nations to generate a larger output by specializing in the things they do well and trading for those things that they would produce only at a high cost. A higher real income is the result.

15. True. If country A imposes a tariff, other countries will sell less to A and therefore acquire less purchasing power in terms of A's currency. Thus, they will have to reduce their purchases of A's export goods.

18. Yes. The price equalization theorem indicates that goods will tend to sell for similar prices in all markets except for differences due to taxes and transport costs. Therefore, except in cases where there is a high tariff (or some other U.S. tax) on a good, it is unlikely that the good will be much cheaper abroad than it is in the United States.

CHAPTER 32

1. The depreciation will make the dollar price of BMWs more expensive which will reduce the *quantity purchased* by Americans. If the American demand for BMWs is inelastic (elastic), then the dollar expenditures on BMWs will rise (fall).

4. On February 2, the dollar appreciated against the pound and depreciated against the franc.

5. Answers a. and g. would cause the dollar to appreciate; b., c., d., e., and h. would cause the dollar to depreciate; f. would leave the exchange rate unchanged.

9. Each of the changes would reduce the size of the current account deficit.

11. The current account balance will move toward a larger deficit (or smaller surplus) and the dollar will appreciate.

15. False. Flexible exchange rates bring the *sum* of the current and capital accounts into balance, but they do not necessarily lead to balance for either component.

CHAPTER 33

2. There is considerable diversity among the poor nations. The real GDP of several poor countries has declined during the last two decades (see Exhibit 33–5). Others have stagnated or experienced only slow growth. Still others have experienced rapid growth (see Exhibit 33–4). On the encouraging side, the average growth rates of per capita GDP in China and India (the two most populous less developed countries) were 5.7 percent and 2.2 percent during the 1970–1991 period. These rates—particularly the rate for China—compare quite favorably with the growth rates of industrial developed economies. If these two giants are able to follow the path of Japan, and more recently Hong Kong, South Korea, Singapore, and Indonesia, perhaps two-thirds

of the world's population will have incomes well above subsistence levels early in the next century.

3. Many economists believe that this view is essentially true. However, there are reasons for doubt. Foreign aid has not played a significant role in the progress of most of the high growth, less developed countries. Often, financial aid disrupts markets and retards the incentive of producers in less developed countries. Finally, attractive investment alternatives will draw investment from abroad even if domestic saving is inadequate. Thus, the efficacy of aid as a tool to promote economic growth is highly questionable.

7. Yes. Trade barriers limit the ability of both businesses and consumers to benefit from economies associated with an expansion in the size of the market. This limitation will be more restrictive for small countries (like Costa Rica) than for larger countries (like Mexico) because the latter will often have sizable domestic markets.

CHAPTER 34

5. Because the prices of goods are also fixed by the planners. Thus, an increase in the supply of money cannot be used to bid up prices. The two major side effects are waiting lines (since prices are fixed below equilibrium) and a monetary overhang.

6. The initial monetary overhang. No, inflation is a continuous increase in prices, not a once-and-for-all jump in prices.

10. Under capitalism, mass production and market penetration lead to wealth. But you cannot have large scale production without pricing the product so that it will be affordable to the mass consumer market. Thus, a market system rewards producers who figure out how to make products affordable to lots of consumers rather than just the rich. The careers of Henry Ford and Sir Henry Royce illustrate this point. Ford became a multimillionaire by bringing a low-cost automobile within the budget of mass consumers. In contrast, Royce died a man of modest wealth. He engineered the Rolls Royce, a car far superior to the Ford, but he designed it for the rich. The market rewarded him accordingly.

13. Points to consider in your answer: What kinds of wealth do the two systems produce? Is there more personal security under socialism? If wealth is acquired from production and exchange that does not involve the use of theft, violence, or fraud, is it fair for the wealth to be taken and given to someone else?

GLOSSARY

A

Ability-to-pay principle
The equity concept that people with larger incomes (or more consumption or more wealth) should be taxed at a higher rate because their ability to pay is presumably greater. The concept is subjective and fails to reveal how much higher the rate of taxation should be as income increases.

Absolute advantage
A situation in which a nation, as the result of its previous experience and/or natural endowments, can produce more of a good (with the same amount of resources) than another nation.

Accounting profits
The sales revenues minus the expenses of a firm over a designated time period, usually one year. Accounting profits typically make allowances for changes in the firm's inventories and depreciation of its assets. No allowance is made, however, for the opportunity cost of the equity capital of the firm's owners, or other implicit costs.

Active budget deficits
Deficits that reflect planned increases in government spending or reductions in taxes designed purposely to generate a budget deficit.

Activist strategy
Deliberate changes in monetary and fiscal policy in order to inject demand stimulus during a recession and apply restraint during an inflationary boom and thereby, it is hoped, minimize economic instability.

Adaptive-expectations hypothesis
The hypothesis that economic decision makers base their future expectations on actual outcomes observed during recent periods. For example, according to this view, the rate of inflation actually experienced during the last two or three years would be the major determinant of the rate of inflation expected for next year.

Administrative lag
The time period between when the need for a policy change is recognized and when the policy is actually implemented.

Aggregate-demand curve
A downward-sloping curve indicating an inverse relationship between the price level and the quantity of domestically produced goods and services that households, business firms, governments, and foreigners (net exports) are willing to purchase during a period.

Aggregate-supply curve
A curve indicating the relationship between the nation's price level and quantity of goods supplied by its producers. In the short run, it is probably an upward-sloping curve, but in the long run most economists believe the aggregate-supply curve is vertical (or nearly so).

Allocative efficiency
The allocation of resources to the production of goods and services most desired by consumers. The allocation is "balanced" in such a way that reallocation of resources could not benefit anyone without hurting someone else.

Allocative inefficiency
The use of an uneconomical combination of resources to produce goods and services, or the use of resources to produce goods that are not intensely desired relative to their opportunity cost.

Anticipated change
A change that is foreseen by decision makers in time for them to adjust.

Anticipated inflation
An increase in the general level of prices that is expected by economic decision makers based on their evaluation of past experience and current conditions.

Appreciation of a currency
An increase in the value of a domestic currency relative to foreign currencies. An appreciation increases the purchasing power of the domestic currency over foreign goods.

Asymmetric-information problem
A problem arising when either buyers or sellers have important information about the product that is not possessed by the other side in potential transactions.

Automatic stabilizers
Built-in features that tend automatically to promote a budget deficit during a recession and a budget surplus during an inflationary boom, even without a change in policy.

Automation
A production technique that reduces the amount of labor required to produce a good or service. It is beneficial to adopt the new labor-saving technology only if it reduces the cost of production.

Autonomous expenditures
Expenditures that do not vary with the level of income. They are determined by factors (such as business expectations and economic policy) that are outside the basic income-expenditure model.

Average fixed cost
Fixed cost divided by the number of

units produced. It always declines as output increases.

Average product
The total product (output) divided by the number of units of the variable input required to produce that output level.

Average tax rate (ATR)
One's tax liability divided by one's taxable income.

Average total cost
Total cost divided by the number of units produced. It is sometimes called per unit cost.

Average variable cost
The total variable cost divided by the number of units produced.

B

Balance of merchandise trade
The difference between the value of merchandise exports and the value of merchandise imports for a nation. The balance of merchandise trade is only one component of a nation's total balance of payments. Also called simply balance of trade *or* net exports.

Balance of payments
A summary of all economic transactions between a country and all other countries for a specific time period—usually a year. The balance-of-payments account reflects all payments and liabilities to foreigners (debits) and all payments and obligations (credits) received from foreigners.

Balance on current account
The import-export balance of goods and services, plus net investment income earned abroad, plus net private and government transfers. If the value of the nation's export-type items exceeds (is less than) the value of the nation's import-type items (plus net unilateral transfers to foreigners), a current-account surplus (deficit) is present.

Balance on goods and services
The exports of goods (merchandise) and services of a nation minus its imports of goods and services.

Balanced budget
A situation in which current government revenue from taxes, fees, and other sources is just equal to current expenditures.

Bank reserves
Vault cash plus deposits of the bank with Federal Reserve Banks.

Barriers to entry
Obstacles that limit the freedom of potential rivals to enter an industry.

Benefit principle
The principle that those who receive government services should pay taxes or user charges for their provision according to the amount of the service or benefit derived from the government activity.

Break-even point
Under a negative income tax plan, the income level at which one neither pays taxes nor receives supplementary income transfers.

Budget constraint
The constraint that separates the bundles of goods that the consumer can purchase from those that cannot be purchased, given a limited income and the prices of products.

Budget deficit
A situation in which total government spending exceeds total government revenue during a specific time period, usually one year.

Budget surplus
A situation in which total government spending is less than total government revenue during a time period, usually a year.

Business cycle
Characterized by fluctuations in the general level of economic activity as measured by such variables as the rate of unemployment and changes in real GDP.

C

Capital account
Transactions with foreigners that involve either (1) the exchange of ownership rights to real or financial assets or (2) the extension of loans.

Capital formation
The production of buildings, machinery, tools, and other equipment that will enhance the ability of future economic participants to produce. The term can also be applied to efforts to upgrade the knowledge and skill of workers and thereby increase their ability to produce in the future.

Capital
Resources that enhance our ability to produce output in the future.

Capitalism
An economic system based on private ownership of productive resources and allocation of goods according to the price signals provided by free markets.

Cartel
An organization of sellers designed to coordinate supply decisions so that the joint profits of the members will be maximized. A cartel will seek to create a monopoly in the market.

Checkable deposits
Interest-earning deposits that are also available for checking.

Choice
The act of selecting among alternatives.

Classical economists
Economists from Adam Smith to the time of Keynes who focused their analyses on economic efficiency and production. With regard to business instability, they thought market prices and wages would decline during a recession quickly enough to bring the economy back to full employment within a short period of time.

Collective decision making
The method of organization that relies on public-sector decision making (voting, political bargaining, lobbying, and so on). It can be used to resolve the basic economic problems of an economy.

Collective-bargaining contract
A detailed contract between a group of employees (a labor union) and their employer. It covers wage rates and conditions of employment.

Collusion
Agreement among firms to avoid various competitive practices, particularly price reductions. It may involve either formal agreements or merely tacit recognition

that competitive practices will be self-defeating in the long run. Tacit collusion is difficult to detect. The Sherman Act prohibits collusion and conspiracies to restrain interstate trade.

Command economy
An authoritarian socialist economy characterized by centralized planning and detailed directives to productive units. Individual enterprises have little discretionary decision-making power.

Commercial banks
Financial institutions that offer a wide range of services (for example, checking accounts, savings accounts, and extension of loans) to their customers. Commercial banks are owned by stockholders and seek to operate at a profit.

Common-property resource
A resource for which rights are held in common by a group of individuals, none of whom has a transferable ownership interest. Access to the resource may be open (unrestricted), or may be controlled politically.

Comparative advantage
The ability to produce a good at a lower opportunity cost than others can produce it. Relative costs determine comparative advantage. A nation will have a comparative advantage in the production of a good when its production costs (other goods forgone) for the good are low relative to the production cost of other nations for the same good.

Compensating wage differentials
Wage differences that compensate workers for risk, unpleasant working conditions, and other undesirable nonpecuniary aspects of a job.

Competition as a dynamic process
A term that denotes rivalry or competitiveness between or among parties (for example, producers or input suppliers), each of which seeks to deliver a better deal to buyers when quality, price, and product information are all considered. Competition implies a lack of collusion among sellers.

Complements
Products that are usually consumed jointly (for example, coffee and nondairy creamer). An increase in the price of one will cause the demand for the other to fall.

Concentration ratio
The total sales of the four (or sometimes eight) largest firms in an industry as a percentage of the total sales of the industry. The higher the ratio, the greater is the market dominance of a small number of firms. The ratio can be seen as a measure of the potential for oligopolistic power.

Conglomerate merger
The combining under one ownership of two or mroe firms that produce unrelated products.

Constant returns to scale
Unit costs are constant as the scale of the firm is altered. Neither economies nor diseconomies of scale are present.

Constant-cost industry
An industry for which factor prices and costs of production remain constant as market output is expanded. Thus, the long-run market supply curve is horizontal.

Consumer price index CPI
An indicator of the general level of prices. It attempts to compare the cost of purchasing the market basket bought by a typical consumer during a specific period with the cost of purchasing the same market basket during an earlier period.

Consumer surplus
The difference between the maximum amount a consumer would be willing to pay for a unit of a good and the payment that is actually made.

Consumption
Household spending on consumer goods and services during the current period. Consumption is a flow concept.

Consumption function
A fundamental relationship between disposable income and consumption, in which as disposable income increases, current consumption expenditures rise, but by a smaller amount than the increase in income.

Consumption-opportunity constraint
The constraint that separates the consumption bundles that are attainable from those that are unattainable. In a money-income economy, this is usually a budget constraint.

Contestable market
A market in which costs of entry and exit are low, so that a firm risks little by entering.

Corporation
A business firm owned by shareholders who possess ownership rights to the firm's profits, but whose liability is limited to the amount of their investment in the firm.

Countercyclical policy
A policy that tends to move the economy in an opposite direction from the forces of the business cycle. Such a policy would stimulate demand during the contraction phase of the business cycle and restrain demand during the expansionary phase.

Credit unions
Financial cooperative organizations of individuals with a common affiliation (such as an employer or labor union). They accept deposits, including checkable deposits, pay interest (or dividends) on them out of earnings, and channel funds primarily into loans to members.

Credit
Funds acquired by borrowing.

Crowding-out effect
A reduction in private spending as a result of higher interest rates generated by budget deficits that are financed by borrowing in the private loanable funds market.

Current account
The record of all transactions with foreign nations that involve the exchange of merchandise goods and services, current income derived from investments, and unilateral gifts.

Cyclical unemployment
Unemployment due to recessionary business conditions and inadequate aggregate demand for labor.

D

Deadweight loss
A net loss associated with the forgoing of an economic action. The loss does not lead to an offsetting gain for other participants. It thus reflects economic inefficiency.

Decreasing-cost industries
Industries for which costs of production decline as the industry expands. The market supply is therefore inversely related to price. Such industries are atypical.

Demand deposits
Non-interest-earning deposits in a bank that either can be withdrawn or made payable on demand to a third party via check. In essence, they are "checkbook money" because they permit transactions to be paid for by check rather than by currency.

Demand for money
At any given interest rate, the amount of wealth that people desire to hold in the form of money balances—that is, cash and checking-account deposits. The quantity demanded is inversely related to the interest rate.

Deposit expansion multiplier
The multiple by which an increase (decrease) in reserves will increase (decrease) the money supply. It is inversely related to the required reserve ratio.

Depository institutions
Businesses that accept checking and saving deposits and use a portion of them to extend loans and make investments. Banks, savings and loan associations, and credit unions are examples.

Depreciation (of a currency)
A reduction in the value of a domestic currency relative to foreign currencies. A depreciation reduces the purchasing power of the domestic currency over foreign goods.

Depreciation (of assets)
The estimated amount of physical capital (for example, machines and buildings) that is worn out or used up producing goods during the period.

Depression
A prolonged and very severe recession.

Derived demand
Demand for an item based on the demand for products the item helps to produce. The demand for resources is a derived demand.

Devaluation
An official act that changes the level of the fixed exchange rate downward in

terms of other currencies. In essence, it is a one-step depreciation of a currency under a fixed-exchange-rate system.

Differentiated products
Products distinguished from similar products by such characteristics as quality, design, location, and method of promotion.

Discount rate
The interest rate the Federal Reserve charges banking institutions for borrowing funds.

Discounting
The procedure used to calculate the present value of future income, which is inversely related to both the interest rate and the amount of time that passes before the funds are received.

Discouraged workers
Persons who have given up searching for employment because they believe additional job search would be fruitless. Since they are not currently searching for work, they are not counted among the unemployed.

Discretionary fiscal policy
A change in laws or appropriation levels that alters government revenues and/or expenditures.

Discretionary monetary policy
Changes in monetary policy instituted at the discretion of policy-makers. The policy is not predetermined by rules or formulas.

Disposable income
The income available to individuals after personal taxes. It can either be spent on consumption or saved.

Division of labor
A method that breaks down the production of a commodity into a series of specific tasks, each performed by a different worker.

Dumping
The sale of a good by a foreign supplier in another country at a price lower than the supplier sells it in its home market.

E

Economic efficiency
Economizing behavior. When applied to a community, it implies that (1) an activity

should be undertaken if the sum of the benefits to the individuals exceeds the sum of their costs and (2) no activity should be undertaken if the costs borne by the individuals exceed the benefits.

Economic good
A good that is scarce. The desire for economic goods exceeds the amount that is freely available from nature.

Economic profit
The difference between the firm's total revenues and total costs.

Economic regulation
Regulation of product price or industrial structure, usually imposed on a specific industry. By and large, the production processes used by the regulated firms are unaffected by this type of regulation.

Economic theory
A set of definitions, postulates, and principles assembled in a manner that makes clear the "cause-and-effect" relationships of economic data.

Economies of scale
Reductions in the firm's per unit costs that are associated with the use of large plants to produce a large volume of output.

Economizing behavior
Choosing with the objective of gaining a specific benefit at the least possible cost. A corollary of economizing behavior implies that when choosing among items of equal cost, individuals will choose the option that yields the greatest benefit.

Elasticity of supply
The percent change in quantity supplied, divided by the percent change in the price causing that change in quantity supplied.

Employment discrimination
Unequal treatment of persons on the basis of their race, sex, or religion, restricting their employment and earnings opportunities compared to others of similar productivity. Employment discrimination may stem from the prejudices of employers, consumers, and/or fellow employees.

Entrepreneur
A profit-seeking decision maker who decides which projects to undertake and how they should be undertaken. A

successful entrepreneur's actions will increase the value of resources.

Equation of exchange
$MV = PY$, *where M is the money supply, V is the velocity of money, P is the price level, and Y is the output of goods and services produced.*

Equilibrium
A balance of forces permitting the simultaneous fulfillment of plans by buyers and sellers. A state of balance between conflicting forces, such as supply and demand.

Escalator clause
A contractural agreement that periodically and automatically adjusts the wage rates of a collective-bargaining agreement upward by an amount determined by the rate of inflation. They are sometimes referred to as cost-of-living adjustments or COLAs.

Eurodollar deposits
Deposits of U.S. residents denominated in U.S. dollars at banks and other financial institutions outside the United States. Although this name originated because of the large amounts of such deposits held at banks in Western Europe, similar deposits in other parts of the world are also called Eurodollars.

Excess burden of taxation
A burden of taxation over and above the burden associated with the transfer of revenues to the government. An excess burden usually reflects losses that occur when beneficial activities are forgone because they are taxed.

Excess reserves
Actual reserves that exceed the legal requirement.

Excess supply of money
Situation in which the actual money balances of individuals and business firms are in excess of their desired level. Thus, decision makers will increase their spending on other assets and goods until they reduce their actual balances to the desired level.

Exchange rate
The domestic price of one unit of foreign currency. For example, if it takes $1.50 to

purchase one English pound, the dollar-pound exchange rate is 1.50.

Exchange-rate conversion method
Method that uses the foreign exchange-rate value of a nation's currency to convert that nation's GDP (or GNP) to another monetary unit, such as the U.S. dollar.

Exclusive contract
An agreement between manufacturer and retailer that prohibits the retailer from carrying the product lines of firms that are rivals of the manufacturer. Such contracts are illegal under the Clayton Act when they "lessen competition."

Expansionary fiscal policy
An increase in government expenditures and/or a reduction in tax rates such that the expected size of the budget deficit expands.

Expansionary monetary policy
An acceleration in the growth rate of the money supply.

Expenditure multiplier
The ratio of the change in equilibrium output to the independent change in investment, consumption, or government spending that brings about the change. Numerically, the multiplier is equal to $1/(1 - MPC)$ when the price level is constant.

Explicit costs
Payments by a firm to purchase the services of productive resources.

Exports
Goods and services produced domestically but sold to foreigners.

External benefits
Beneficial effects of group or individual action on the welfare of non-paying secondary parties.

External costs
Harmful effects of an individual's or a group's action on the welfare of nonconsenting secondary parties, not accounted for in market prices. Litterbugs, drunk drivers, and polluters, for example, create external costs.

External debt
The portion of the national debt owed to foreign investors.

Externalities
The side effects, or spillover effects, of an action that influence the well-being of nonconsenting parties. The nonconsenting parties may be either helped (by external benefits) or harmed (by external costs).

F

Fallacy of composition
Erroneous view that what is true for the individual (or the part) will also be true for the group (or the whole).

Federal Deposit Insurance Corporation (FDIC)
A federally chartered corporation that insures the deposits held by commercial banks and thrift institutions.

Federal funds market
A loanable funds market in which banks seeking additional reserves borrow short-term (generally for seven days or less) funds from banks with excess reserves. The interest rate in this market is called the federal funds rate.

Federal reserve system
The central bank of the United States; it carries out banking regulatory policies and is responsible for the conduct of monetary policy.

Fiat money
Money that has neither intrinsic value nor the backing of a commodity with intrinsic value; paper currency is an example.

Final goods and services
Goods and services purchased by their ultimate user.

Fiscal policy
The use of government taxation and expenditure policies for the purpose of achieving macroeconomic goals.

Fixed costs
Costs that do not vary with output. They will be incurred as long as a firm continues in business and the assets have alternative uses.

Fixed exchange rates
Exchange rates for each country's currency set at a fixed rate relative to all other currencies; government policies are used to maintain the fixed rate.

Flexible exchange rates
Exchange rates that are determined by the market forces of supply and demand. They are sometimes called floating exchange rates.

Foreign exchange market
A highly organized market where the currencies of different countries are bought and sold.

Fractional reserve banking
A system that permits banks to hold reserves of less than 100 percent against their deposits.

Free rider
One who receives the benefit of a good without contributing to its costs. Public goods and commodities that generate external benefits offer people the opportunity to become free riders.

Frictional unemployment:
Unemployment due to constant changes in the economy that prevent qualified unemployed workers from being immediately matched up with existing job openings. It results from lack of complete information on the part of both job seekers and employers and from the amount of unemployed time spent by job seekers in job searches (pursuit of costly information).

Fringe benefits
Benefits other than normal money wages that are supplied to employees in exchange for their labor services.

Full employment
The level of employment that results from the efficient use of the labor force after allowance is made for the normal (natural) rate of unemployment due to information cost, dynamic changes, and the structural conditions of the economy. For the United States, full employment is thought to exist when between 94 and 95 percent of the labor force is employed.

G

Game theory
Analyzes the strategic choices made by competitors in a conflict situation, such as decisions made by members of an oligopoly.

GDP deflator
A price index that reveals the cost of purchasing the items included in GDP during the period relative to the cost of purchasing these same items during a base year (currently, 1987). Since the base year is assigned a value of 100, as the GDP deflator takes on values greater than 100, it indicates that prices have risen.

General Agreement on Tariffs and Trade (GATT)
An organization composed of 115 countries designed to set the rules for the conduct of international trade and reduce barriers to trade among nations.

Going out of business
The sale of a firm's assets and its permanent exit from the market. By going out of business, a firm is able to avoid fixed costs, which would continue during a shutdown.

Goods and services market
A highly aggregate market encompassing all final-user goods and services during a period. The market counts all items that enter into GDP. Thus, real output in this market is equal to real GDP.

Government failure
Failure of government action to meet the criteria of ideal economic efficiency.

Government purchases
Current expenditures on goods and services provided by federal, state, and local governments; they exclude transfer payments.

Gross domestic product (GDP)
The total market value of all final goods and services produced domestically during a specific period, usually a year.

Gross national product (GNP)
The total market value of all final goods and services produced by the citizens of a country. It is equal to GDP plus the income the nationals earned abroad minus the income foreigners earned domestically.

H

Hard budget constraint
Situation where the enterprise is fully

dependent on revenues from sales to cover its costs. The constraint is "hard" because, if losses are present, they will have to be covered by enterprise owners; continuing losses will result in bankruptcy since government subsidies and special grants are unavailable.

Head tax
A lump-sum tax levied on all individuals, regardless of their income, consumption, wealth, or other indicators of economic well-being.

Health and safety regulation
Legislation designed to improve the health, safety, and environmental conditions available to workers and/or consumers. The legislation usually mandates production procedures, minimum standards, and/or product characteristics to be met by producers and employers.

Herfindahl index
A measure of industry concentration, calculated by squaring the percentage share of each firm in the industry, then summing the squares. The index can range from zero to 10,000. It is a more sophisticated measure of concentration than the traditional concentration ratio, and is used by the Justice Department in antitrust policy.

Homogeneous product
A product of one firm that is identical to the product of every other firm in the industry. Consumers see no difference in units of the product offered by alternative sellers.

Horizontal merger
The combining of the assets of two or more firms engaged in the production of similar products into a single firm.

Human resources
The abilities, skills, and health of human beings that can contribute to the production of both current and future output. Investment in training and education can increase the supply of human resources.

I

Impact lag
The time period between when a policy

change is implemented and when the change begins to exert its primary effects.

Implicit costs
The opportunity costs associated with a firm's use of resources that it owns. These costs do not involve a direct money payment. Examples include wage income and interest foregone by the owner of a firm who also provides labor services and equity capital to the firm.

Import quota
A specific quantity (or value) of a good permitted to be imported into a country during a given year.

Imports
Goods and services produced by foreigners but purchased by domestic consumers, investors, and governments.

Income effect
That part of an increase (decrease) in amount consumed that is the result of the consumer's real income (the consumption possibilities available to the consumer) being expanded (contracted) by a reduction (rise) in the price of a good.

Income elasticity
The percent change in the quantity of a product demanded divided by the percent change in consumer income causing the change in quantity demanded. It measures the responsiveness of the demand for a good to a change in income.

Income mobility
Movement of individuals and families either up or down income-distribution rankings when comparisons are made at two different points in time. When substantial income mobility is present, one's current position will not be a very good indicator as to what one's position will be a few years in the future.

Increasing-cost industry
An industry for which costs of production rise as the industry output is expanded. Thus, the long-run quantity supplied to the market is directly related to price.

Index of leading indicators
An index of economic variables that historically has tended to turn down prior to the beginning of a recession and turn up prior to the beginning of a business expansion.

Indexing
The automatic increasing of money values as the general level of prices increases. Economic variables that are often indexed include wage rates and tax brackets.

Indifference curve
A curve, convex from below, that separates the consumption bundles that are more preferred by an individual from those that are less preferred. The points on the curve represent combinations of goods that are equally preferred by the individual.

Indirect business taxes
Taxes that increase the business firm's costs of production and therefore the prices charged to consumers. Examples would be sales, excise, and property taxes.

Industrial capacity-utilization rate
An index designed to measure the extent to which the economy's existing plant and equipment capacity is being used.

Inferior goods
Goods for which the income elasticity is negative. An increase in consumer income causes the demand for such a good to decline.

Inflation
A continuing rise in the general level of prices of goods and services. The purchasing power of the monetary unit, such as the dollar, declines when inflation is present.

Inflation premium
A component of the money interest rate that reflects compensation to the lender for the expected decrease, due to inflation, in the purchasing power of the principal and interest during the course of the loan. It is determined by the expected rate of future inflation.

Infrastructure
The provision of a legal, monetary, educational, transportation, and communication structure necessary for the efficient operation of an exchange economy.

Innovation
The successful introduction and adoption of a new product or process; the economic

application of inventions and marketing techniques.

Intensive economic growth
An increase in output per person. When intensive economic growth is present, output is growing more rapidly than population.

Intermediate goods
Goods purchased for resale or for use in producing another good or service.

International Monetary Fund (IMF)
An international banking organization, with more than 100 member nations, designed to oversee the operation of the international monetary system. Although it does not control the world supply of money, it does hold currency reserves for member nations and makes currency loans to national central banks.

Invention
The creation or discovery of a new product or process, often facilitated by the knowledge of engineering and scientific relationships.

Inventory investment
Changes in the stock of unsold goods and raw materials held during a period.

Investment
The flow of expenditures on durable assets (fixed investment) plus the addition to inventories (inventory investment) during a period. These expenditures enhance our ability to provide consumer benefits in the future. The purchase, construction, or development of capital resources, including both nonhuman capital and human capital. Investments increase the supply of capital.

Investment in human capital
Expenditures on training, education, skill development, and health designed to increase the productivity of an individual.

Invisible hand principle
The tendency of market prices to direct individuals pursuing their own interests into productive activities that also promote the economic well-being of the society.

Isocost Line
A line representing the various combinations of two factors that can be

purchased with a given money budget (cost).

Isoquant
A curve representing the technically efficient combinations of two inputs that can be used to produce a given level of output.

J

J-curve effect
The tendency of a nation's current-account deficit to widen initially before it shrinks in response to an exchange-rate depreciation. This tendency results because the short-run demand for both imports and exports is often inelastic, even though the long-run demand is almost always elastic.

L

Labor force
The portion of the population 16 years of age and over who are either employed or unemployed, according to the official definition of "unemployed."

Labor union
A collective organization of employees who bargain as a unit with employers.

Laffer curve
A curve illustrating the relationship between tax rates and tax revenues. The curve reflects the fact that tax revenues are low for both very high and very low tax rates.

Law of comparative advantage
A principle that states that individuals, firms, regions, or nations can gain by specializing in the production of goods that they produce cheaply (that is, at a low-opportunity-cost) and exchanging those goods for other desired goods for which they are a high-opportunity-cost producer.

Law of demand
A principle that states there is an inverse relationship between the price of a good and the amount of it buyers are willing to purchase.

Law of diminishing marginal utility
The basic economic principle that as the consumption of a commodity increases, the marginal utility derived from

consuming more of the commodity (per unit of time) will eventually decline. Marginal utility may decline even though total utility continues to increase, albeit at a reduced rate.

Law of diminishing returns
The postulate that as more and more units of a variable resource are combined with a fixed amount of other resources, employment of additional units of the variable source will eventually increase output only at a decreasing rate. Once diminishing returns are reached, it will take successively larger amounts of the variable factor to expand output by one unit.

Law of supply
A principle that states there is a direct relationship between the price of a good and the amount of it offered for sale.

Less developed countries (LDCs)
Low-income countries generally characterized by rapid population growth and an agriculture-household sector that dominates the economy. Sometimes these countries are referred to as developing countries.

Liquid asset
An asset that can be easily and quickly converted to purchasing power without loss of value.

Loanable funds market
A general term used to describe the market arrangements that coordinate the borrowing and lending decisions of business firms and households. Commercial banks, savings and loan associations, the stock and bond markets, and insurance companies are important financial institutions in this market.

Logrolling
The exchange between politicians of political support on one issue for political support on another issue.

Long run (in production)
A time period long enough to allow the firm to vary all factors of production.

Long run
A time period of sufficient length to enable decision makers to adjust fully to a market change.

Loss
Deficit of sales revenue relative to the cost of production, once all the resources used have received their opportunity cost. Losses are a penalty imposed on those who use resources in lower, rather than higher, valued uses as judged by buyers in the market.

M

M1 (money supply)
The sum of (1) currency in circulation (including coins), (2) demand deposits, (3) other checkable deposits of depository institutions, and (4) traveler's checks.

M2 (money supply)
Equal to M1, plus (1) savings and time deposits (accounts of less than $100,000) of all depository institutions, (2) money market mutual fund shares, (3) money market deposit accounts, (4) overnight loans from customers to commercial banks, and (5) overnight Eurodollar deposits held by U.S. residents.

M3 (money supply)
Equal to M2, plus (1) time deposits (accounts of more than $100,000) at all depository institutions and (2) longer-term (more than overnight) loans of customers to commercial banks and savings and loan associations.

Macroeconomics
The branch of economics that focuses on how human behavior affects outcomes in highly aggregated markets, such as the markets for labor or consumer products.

Mandated benefits
Fringe benefits that the government forces employers to include in their total compensation package paid to employees.

Marginal
Term used to describe the effects of a change in the current situation. For example, the marginal cost is the cost of producing an additional unit of a product, given the producer's current facility and production rate.

Marginal cost
The change in total cost required to produce an additional unit of output.

Marginal factor cost (MFC)
The cost of employing an additional unit of a resource. When the employer is small relative to the total market, the marginal factor cost is simply the price of the resource. In contrast, under monopsony, marginal factor cost will exceed the price of the resource, since the monopsonist faces an upward-sloping supply curve for the resource because wages must be raised for all workers.

Marginal product (MP)
The change in total output that results from the employment of one additional unit of a factor of production—one workday of skilled labor, for example. The increase in the total product resulting from a unit increase in the employment of a variable input. Mathematically, it is the ratio of the change in total product to the change in the quantity of the variable input.

Marginal propensity to consume (MPC)
Additional current consumption divided by additional current disposable income.

Marginal rate of substitution
The change in the consumption level of one good that is just sufficient to offset a unit change in the consumption of another good without causing a shift to another indifference curve. At any point on an indifference curve, it will be equal to the slope of the curve at that point.

Marginal revenue
The incremental change in total revenue derived from the sale of one additional unit of a product.

Marginal tax rate (MTR)
Additional tax liability divided by additional income. Thus, if $100 of additional earnings increases one's tax liability by $30, the marginal tax rate would be 30 percent. The amount of additional (marginal) earnings that must be paid explicitly in taxes or implicitly in the form of a reduction in income supplement. Since it establishes the fraction of an additional dollar earned that an individual is permitted to keep, it is an important determinant of the incentive to work.

Marginal utility
The additional utility received by a person from the consumption of an additional unit of a good within a given time period.

Marginal revenue product (MRP)
The change in the total revenue of a firm that results from the employment of one additional unit of a factor of production. The marginal-revenue product of an input is equal to its marginal product multiplied by the marginal revenue (price) of the good or service produced.

Market
An abstract concept that encompasses the trading arrangements of buyers and sellers that underlie the forces of supply and demand.

Market failure
The failure of the market system to attain hypothetically ideal allocative efficiency. This means that potential gain exists that has not been captured. However, the cost of establishing a mechanism that could potentially capture the gain may exceed the benefits. Therefore, it is not always possible to improve the situation.

Market power
The ability of a firm to profit by raising its rice significantly above the competitive level for a considerable period of time.

Market structure
The classification of a market with regard to key characteristics, including the number of sellers, entry barriers into the market, the control of firms over price, and type of products (homogeneous or differentiated) in the market.

Maximum emission standard
The maximum amount of pollution that a polluter is permitted to emit, established by the government or a regulatory authority. Fines are generally imposed on those who are unwilling or unable to comply.

Means-tested income transfers
Transfers that are limited to persons or families with an income below a certain cutoff point. Eligibility is thus dependent on low-income status.

Medium of exchange
An asset that is used to buy and sell goods or services.

Microeconomics
The branch of economics that focuses on how human behavior affects the conduct of affairs within narrowly defined units, such as individual households or business firms.

Middleman
A person who buys and sells, or who arranges trades. A middleman reduces transaction costs, usually for a fee or a markup in price.

Minimum wage legislation
Legislation requiring that all workers in specified industries be paid at least the stated minimum hourly rate of pay.

Monetarists
A group of economists who believe that (1) monetary instability is the major cause of fluctuations in real GDP and (2) rapid growth of the money supply is the major cause of inflation.

Monetary base
The sum of currency in circulation plus bank reserves (vault cash and reserves with the Fed). It reflects the stock of U.S. securities held by the Fed.

Monetary overhang
The accumulation of money balances that results when the aggregate money-income payments to employees exceed the amount required to purchase the aggregate quantity of goods and services produced at the prices set by the central plan.

Monetary policy
The deliberate control of the money supply, and, in some cases, credit conditions, for the purpose of achieving macroeconomic goals.

Money interest rate
The interest rate measured in monetary units. It overstates the real cost of borrowing during an inflationary period. When inflation is anticipated, an inflationary premium will be incorporated into the nominal value of this rate. The money interest rate is often referred to as the nominal interest rate.

Money market mutual funds
Interest-earning accounts offered by brokerage firms that pool depositors' funds and invest them in highly liquid short-term securities. Since these

securities can be quickly converted to cash, depositors are permitted to write checks (which reduce their share holdings) against their accounts.

Money rate of interest
The rate of interest in monetary terms that borrowers pay for borrowed funds. During periods when borrowers and lenders expect inflation, the money rate of interest exceeds the real rate of interest.

Money supply
The supply of currency, checking account funds, and traveler's checks. These items are counted as money since they are used as the means of payment for purchases.

Monopolistic competition
A situation in which there are a large number of independent sellers, each producing a differentiated product in a market with low barriers to entry. Construction, retail sales, and service stations are good examples of monopolistically competitive industries.

Monopoly
A market structure characterized by a (a) single seller of a well-defined product for which there are no good substitutes and (b) high barriers to the entry of other firms into the market for the product.

Monopsony
A market in which there is only one buyer. The monopsonist confronts the market supply curve for the resource (or product) bought.

N

National debt
The sum of the indebtedness of the federal government in the form of outstanding interest-earning bonds. It reflects the cumulative impact of budget deficits and surpluses.

National income
The total income payments to owners of human (labor) and physical capital during a period. It is also equal to NDP minus indirect business taxes plus net income earned abroad by the citizens of the country.

Natural monopoly
A market situation in which the average

costs of production continually decline with increased output. Therefore, average costs of production will be lowest when a single large firm produces the entire output demanded.

Natural rate of unemployment
The long-run average unemployment rate due to frictional and structural conditions of labor markets. This rate is affected both by dynamic change and by public policy. It is sustainable into the future.

Negative income tax
A system of transferring income to the poor whereby a minimum level of income is guaranteed by the provision of income supplements. The supplement is reduced by some fraction (less than 1) of the additional income earned by the family. An increase in earnings, thus, would always cause the disposable income available to the family to rise.

Net domestic product (NDP)
Gross domestic product minus a depreciation allowance for the wearing out of machines and buildings during the period.

Net exports
Exports minus imports.

Net federal debt
The portion of the national debt owed to domestic and foreign investors. It does not include bonds held by agencies of the federal government or the Federal Reserve.

Neutral tax
A tax that does not (1) distort consumer buying patterns or producer production methods or (2) induce individuals to engage in tax-avoidance activities. There will be no excess burden if a tax is neutral.

New classical economists
Modern economists who believe there are strong forces pushing a market economy toward full-employment equilibrium and that macroeconomic policy is an ineffective tool with which to reduce economic instability.

Nominal GDP
GDP expressed at current prices. It is often called money GDP.

Nominal values
Values expressed in current dollars.

Nonactivist strategy
The maintenance of the same monetary and fiscal policy—that is, no change in money growth, tax rates, or expenditures—during all phases of the business cycle.

Nonhuman resources
The durable, nonhuman inputs that can be used to produce both current and future output. Machines, buildings, land, and raw materials are examples. Investment can increase the supply of nonhuman resources. Economists often use the term physical capital when referring to nonhuman resources.

Nonpecuniary job characteristics
Working conditions, prestige, variety, location, employee freedom and responsibilities, and other nonwage characteristics of a job that influence how employees evaluate the job.

Normative economics
Judgments about "what ought to be" in economic matters. Normative economic views cannot be proved false, because they are based on value judgments.

O

Oligopoly
A market situation in which a small number of sellers comprise the entire industry. Oligopoly is competition among the few.

Open market operations
The buying and selling of U.S. government securities (national debt) by the Federal Reserve.

Open-access resource
A resource to which access is unrestricted. No one has the right to exclude others from using the resource. Overuse and abuse of such a resource is typical.

Opportunity cost of equity capital
The implicit rate of return that must be earned by investors to induce them to continue to supply financial capital to the firm.

Opportunity cost
The highest valued alternative that must be sacrificed as a result of choosing among alternatives.

Other checkable deposits
Interest-earning deposits that are also available for checking.

P

Partnership
A business firm owned by two or more individuals who possess ownership rights to the firm's profits and are personally liable for the debts of the firm.

Passive budget deficits
Deficits that merely reflect reduced tax revenues or increased spending due to a decline in economic activity during a recession.

Patent
The grant of an exclusive right to use a specific process or produce a specific product for a period of time (17 years in the United States).

Permanent income hypothesis
The hypothesis that consumption depends on some measure of long-run expected (permanent) income rather than on current income.

Personal income
The total income received by individuals that is available for consumption, saving, and payment of personal taxes.

Phillips curve
A curve that illustrates the relationship between the rate of change in prices (or money wages) and the rate of unemployment.

Policy-ineffectiveness theorem
The proposition that any systematic policy will be rendered ineffective once decision makers figure out the policy pattern and adjust their decision making in light of its expected effects. The theorem is a corollary of the theory of rational expectations.

Political good
Any good (or policy), whether a public good or a private good, supplied through the political process.

Pork-barrel legislation
A package of spending projects benefiting local areas at federal expense. The projects typically have costs that exceed benefits, but are intensely desired by the residents of the district getting the benefits without having to pay much of the costs.

Positive economics
The scientific study of "what is" among economic relationships.

Positive rate of time preference
The desire of consumers for goods now rather than in the future.

Potential output
The level of output that can be achieved and sustained into the future, given the size of the labor force, expected productivity of labor, and natural rate of unemployment consistent with the efficient operation of the labor market. For periods of time, the actual output may differ from the economy's potential.

Poverty threshold income level
The level of money income below which a family is considered to be poor. It differs according to family characteristics (for example, number of family members) and is adjusted when consumer prices change.

Predatory pricing
The practice in which a dominant firm in an industry temporarily reduces price to damage or eliminate weaker rivals, so that prices can be raised above the level of costs at a later time.

Present value (PV)
The current worth of future income after it is discounted to reflect the fact that revenues in the future are valued less highly than revenues now.

Price ceiling
A legally established maximum price that sellers may charge.

Price discrimination
A practice whereby a seller charges different consumers different prices for the same product or service.

Price elasticity of demand
The percent change in the quantity of a product demanded divided by the percent change in the price causing the change in quantity. Price elasticity of demand indicates the degree of consumer response to variation in price.

Price equalization principle
The tendency for markets, when trade restrictions are absent, to establish a uniform price for each good throughout the world (except for price differences due to transport costs and differential tax treatment of the good).

Price floor
A legally established minimum price that buyers must pay for a good or resource.

Price searcher
A seller with imperfect information, facing a downward sloping demand curve, who tries to find the price that maximizes profit.

Price takers
Sellers who must take the market price in order to sell their product. Because each price taker's output is small relative to the total market, price takers can sell all of their output at the market price, but are unable to sell any of their output at a price higher than the market price. Thus, they face a horizontal demand curve.

Principal-agent problem
The incentive problem arising when the purchaser of services (the principal) lacks full information about the circumstances faced by the seller (the agent) and thus cannot know how well the agent performs the purchased services. The agent may to some extent work toward objectives other than those sought by the principal paying for the service.

Private-property rights
A set of usage and exchange rights held exclusively by the owner(s) and that can be transferred to others at the owner's discretion.

Production-possibilities curve
A curve that outlines all possible combinations of total output that could be produced, assuming (1) the utilization of a fixed amount of productive resources, (2) full and efficient use of those resources, and (3) a specific state of technical knowledge. The slope of the curve indicates the rate at which one product can be traded off to produce more of the other.

Productivity
The average output produced per worker during a specific time period. It is usually measured in terms of output per hour worked.

Profit
An excess of sales revenue relative to the cost of production. The cost component includes the opportunity cost of all resources, including those owned by the firm. Therefore, profit accrues only when the value of the good produced is greater than the sum of the values of the individual resources utilized.

Progressive tax
A tax that requires those with higher taxable incomes to pay a larger percentage of their incomes to the government than those with lower taxable incomes.

Property rights
The right to use, control, and obtain the benefits from a good or service.

Proportional tax
A tax for which individuals pay the same percentage of their income (or other tax base) in taxes, regardless of income level.

Proprietorship
A business firm owned by an individual who possesses the ownership right to the firm's profits and is personally liable for the firm's debts.

Public goods
Jointly consumed goods. When consumed by one person, they are also made available to others. National defense, poetry, and scientific theories are all public goods.

Public-choice analysis
The study of decision making as it affects the formation and operation of collective organizations, such as governments. The discipline bridges the gap between economics and political science. In general, the principles and methodology of economics are applied to political science topics.

Purchasing-power parity method
Method for determining the relative purchasing power of different currencies by comparing the amount of each currency required to purchase a typical bundle of goods and services in domestic markets. This information is then used to convert the GDP (or GNP) of each nation to a common monetary unit.

Pure competition
A model of industrial structure characterized by a large number of small firms producing a homogeneous product in an industry (market area) that permits complete freedom of entry and exit.

Q

Quantity theory of money
A theory that hypothesizes that a change in the money supply will cause a proportional change in the price level because velocity and real output are unaffected by the quantity of money.

R

Rate of employment
The number of persons 16 years of age and over who are employed as a percentage of the total noninstitutional population 16 years of age and over. One can calculate either (1) a civilian rate of employment, in which only civilian employees are included in the numerator, or (2) a total rate of employment, in which both civilian and military employees are included in the numerator.

Rate of labor-force participation
The number of persons 16 years of age or over who are either employed or actively seeking employment as a percentage of the total noninstitutional population 16 years of age and over.

Rate of unemployment
The percent of persons in the labor force who are unemployed, according to the official definition of "unemployed." Mathematically, it is equal to

$$\frac{\text{Number of persons unemployed}}{\text{Number in the labor force}} \times 100$$

Rate-of-return equalization principle
The tendency for capital investment in each market to move toward a uniform, or normal, rate of return. An abnormally high return in a market will attract additional investment, which will drive returns down. Conversely, an abnormally low return will result in investment flight from the market, which will eventually lead to the restoration of normal returns.

Rational ignorance effect
Voter ignorance resulting from the fact that people perceive their individual votes as unlikely to be decisive. Therefore, they rationally have little incentive to seek the information needed to cast an informed vote.

Rational-expectations hypothesis
The hypothesis that economic decision makers weigh all available evidence, including information concerning the probable effects of current and future economic policy, when they form their expectations about future economic events (such as the probable future inflation rate).

Rationing
An allocation of a limited supply of a good or resource to users who would like to have more of it. Various criteria, including charging a price, can be utilized to allocate the limited supply. When price performs the rationing function, the good or resource is allocated to those willing to give up the most "other things" in order to obtain ownership rights.

Real GDP
Gross domestic product adjusted for changes in the price level. Mathematically, real GDP_2 is equal to nominal GDP_2 multiplied by (GDP $Deflator_1$/GDP $Deflator_2$). Thus, if prices have risen between Periods 1 and 2, the ratio of the GDP deflator in Period 1 to the deflator in Period 2 will be less than 1. This ratio will therefore deflate the nominal GDP for the rising prices.

Real interest rate
The interest rate adjusted for expected inflation; it indicates the real cost to the borrower (and yield to the lender) in terms of goods and services.

Real rate of interest
The money rate of interest minus the expected rate of inflation. The real rate of interest indicates the interest premium, in terms of real goods and services, that one must pay for earlier availability.

Real values
Values that have been adjusted for the effects of inflation.

Real-balance effect
The increase in wealth emanating from an increase in the purchasing power of a constant money supply as the price level decreases. This wealth effect leads to an inverse relationship between price (level) and quantity demanded in the goods and services market.

Recession
A downturn in economic activity characterized by declining real GDP and rising unemployment. In an effort to be more precise, many economists define a recession as two consecutive quarters in which there is a decline in real GDP.

Recognition lag
The time period between when a policy change is needed from a stabilization standpoint and when the need is recognized by policy-makers.

Regressive tax
A tax that takes a smaller percentage of one's income as one's income level increases. Thus, the proportion of income allocated to the tax would be greater for the poor than for the rich.

Rent seeking
Actions by individuals and interest groups designed to restructure public policy in a manner that will either directly or indirectly redistribute more income to themselves.

Repeat-purchase item
An item purchased often by the same buyer.

Required reserve ratio
A percentage of a specified liability category (for example, transaction accounts) that banking institutions are required to hold as reserves against that type of liability.

Required reserves
The minimum amount of reserves that a bank is required by law to keep on hand to back up its deposits. Thus, if reserve requirements were 15 percent, banks would be required to keep $150,000 in reserves against each $1 million of deposits.

Residual claimant(s)
Individuals who personally receive the excess, if any, of revenues over costs. Residual claimants gain if the firm's costs are reduced and lose if revenues are increased.

Resource
An input used to produce economic goods. Land, labor, skills, natural resources, and capital are examples.

Resource market
A highly aggregate market encompassing all resources (labor, physical capital, land, and entrepreneurship) that contribute to the production of current output. The labor market forms the largest component of this market.

Resource mobility
A term that refers to the ease with which factors of production are able to move among alternative uses. Resources that can easily be transferred to a different use or location are said to be highly mobile. In contrast, when a resource has few alternative uses, it is immobile. For example, the skills of a trained rodeo rider would be highly immobile, since they cannot be easily transferred to other lines of work.

Restrictive fiscal policy
A reduction in government expenditures and/or an increase in tax rates such that the expected size of the budget deficit declines (or the budget surplus increases).

Restrictive monetary policy
A deceleration in the growth rate of the money supply.

Right-to-work laws
Laws that prohibit the union shop — the requirement that employees must join a union (after 30 days) as a condition of employment. Each state has the option to adopt (or reject) right-to-work legislation.

S

Saving
Disposable income that is not spent on consumption. Saving is a "flow" concept. Thus, it is generally measured in terms of an annual rate.

Savings and loan associations
Financial institutions that accept deposits in exchange for shares that pay dividends. Historically, these funds have been channeled into residential mortgage loans. Under banking legislation adopted in 1980, S&Ls are now permitted to offer a broad range of services similar to those of commercial banks.

Say's Law
The view that production creates its own demand. Thus, there cannot be a general oversupply, because the total value of goods and services produced (income) will always be available for purchasing them.

Scarcity
Fundamental concept of economics which indicates that less of a good is freely available than consumers would like.

Scientific thinking
Development of theory from basic postulates and the testing of the implications of that theory as to their consistency with events in the real world. Good theories are consistent with and help explain real-world events. Theories that are inconsistent with the real world are invalid and must be rejected.

Secondary effects
Economic consequences of an economic change that are not immediately identifiable but are felt only with the passage of time.

Shirking
Working at less than a normal rate of productivity, thus reducing output. Shirking is more likely when workers are not monitored, so that the cost of lower output falls on others than themselves.

Short run (in production)
A time period so short that a firm is unable to vary some of its factors of production. The firm's plant size typically cannot be altered in the short run.

Short run
A time period of insufficient length to permit decision makers to adjust fully to a change in market conditions. For example, in the short run, producers will have time to increase output by using more labor and raw materials, but they will not have time to expand the size of their plants or to install additional heavy equipment.

Shortage
A condition in which the amount of a good offered by sellers is less than the amount demanded by buyers at the existing price. An increase in price would eliminate the shortage.

Shortsightedness effect
Misallocation of resources that results because public-sector action is biased (1) in favor of proposals yielding clearly defined current benefits in exchange for difficult-to-identify future costs and (2) against proposals with clearly identifiable current costs but yielding less concrete and less obvious future benefits.

Shutdown
A temporary halt in the operation of a business in which the firm anticipates a return to operation in the future and therefore does not sell its assets. The firm's variable cost is eliminated for the duration of the shutdown, but its fixed costs continue.

Social costs
The sum of (1) the private costs incurred by a decision maker and (2) any external costs imposed on nonconsenting secondary parties. If there are no external costs, private and social costs will be equal.

Socialism
A system of economic organization in which (1) the ownership and control of the basic means of production rest with the state and (2) resource allocation is determined by centralized planning rather than by market forces.

Special drawing rights (SDRs)
Supplementary reserves, in the form of accounting entries, established by the International Monetary Fund (also called paper gold). Like gold and foreign currency reserves, they can be used to make payments on international accounts.

Special interest issue
An issue that generates substantial individual benefits to a small minority while imposing a small individual cost on many other voters. In total, the net cost to the majority might either exceed or fall short of the net benefits to the special interest group.

Stagflation
A period during which an economy is experiencing both substantial inflation and a slow growth in output.

Strike
An action of unionized employees in which they (1) discontinue working for the employer and (2) take steps to prevent other potential workers from offering their services to the employer.

Structural unemployment
Unemployment due to structural changes in the economy that eliminate some jobs while generating job openings for which the unemployed workers are not well suited.

Substitutes
Products that are related such that an increase in the price of one will cause an increase in demand for the other (for example, butter and margarine, Chevrolets and Fords).

Substitution effect
That part of an increase (decrease) in amount consumed that is the result of a good being cheaper (more expensive) in relation to other goods because of a reduction (increase) in price.

Sunk costs
Costs that have already been incurred as a result of past decisions. They are sometimes referred to as historical costs.

Supply shock
An unexpected event that temporarily either increases or decreases aggregate supply.

Supply-side economists
Modern economists who believe that changes in marginal tax rates exert important effects on aggregate supply.

Surplus
A condition in which the amount of a good that sellers are willing to offer is greater than the amount that buyers will purchase at the existing price. A decline in price would eliminate the surplus.

T

Tariff
A tax levied on goods imported into a country.

Tax base
The level of the activity that is taxed. For example, if an excise tax is levied on each gallon of gasoline, the tax base is the number of gallons of gasoline sold. Since higher tax rates generally make the taxed activity less attractive, the size of the tax base is inversely related to the rate at which the activity is taxed.

Tax incidence
The manner in which the burden of the tax is distributed among economic units (consumers, employees, employers, and so on). The tax burden does not always fall on those who pay the tax.

Tax rate
The per unit or percentage rate at which an economic activity is taxed.

Team production
A process of production wherein employees work together under the supervision of the owner or the owner's representative.

Technological advancement
The introduction of new techniques or methods of production that enable a greater output per unit of input.

Technology
The body of skills and technological knowledge available at any given time. The level of technology establishes the relationship between inputs and the maximum output they can generate.

Total cost
The costs, both explicit and implicit, of all the resources used by the firm. Total cost includes an imputed normal rate of return for the firm's equity capital.

Total product
The total output of a good that is associated with alternative utilization rates of a variable input.

Transaction accounts
Accounts including demand deposits, NOW accounts, and other checkable deposits against which the account holder is permitted to transfer funds for the purpose of making payment to a third party.

Transaction costs
The time, effort, and other resources needed to search out, negotiate, and consummate an exchange.

Transfer payments
Payments to individuals or institutions that are not linked to the current supply of a good or service by the recipient.

Trust
In American history, an arrangement in which the assets of several firms were placed in the custody of trustees who managed the trust for the benefit of the owners. Trusts were used to form cartels in the United States in the late 1800s.

U

Unanticipated change
A change that decision makers could not reasonably foresee. Thus, choices made prior to the event did not take the event into account.

Unanticipated inflation
Increase in the general level of prices that was not expected by most decision makers.

Underground economy
Unreported barter and cash transactions that take place outside recorded market channels. Some are otherwise legal activities undertaken to evade taxes. Others involve illegal activities such as trafficking in drugs and prostitution.

Unemployed
The term used to describe a person not currently employed who is either (1) actively seeking employment or (2) waiting to begin or return to a job.

Union-shop provision
The requirement that all employees join the recognized union and pay dues to it within a specified length of time (usually 30 days) after their employment with the firm begins.

User charge
A payment that users (consumers) are required to make if they want to receive certain services provided by the government.

Utility
The benefit or satisfaction expected from a choice or course of action.

V

Value-marginal product (VMP)
The marginal product of a resource multiplied by the selling price of the product it helps to produce. Under pure competition, a firm's marginal-revenue product (MRP) will be equal to the value-marginal product (VMP).

Variable costs
Costs that vary with the rate of output. Examples include wages paid to workers and payments for raw materials.

Velocity of money
The average number of times a dollar is used to purchase final goods and services during a year. It is equal to GDP divided by the stock of money.

Vertical merger
The creation of a single firm from two firms, one of which was a supplier or customer of the other—for example, a merger of a lumber company with a furniture manufacturer.

CREDITS

CHAPTER 22

Page 635 Reprinted by special permission of North America Syndicate.

Page 642 ZIGGY copyright 1983 ZIGGY AND FRIENDS, INC. distributed by UNIVERSAL PRESS SYNDICATE. Reprinted by permission. All rights reserved.

CHAPTER 23

Page 655 © Reuters/Bettmann.

CHAPTER 24

Page 689 © Grant Hielman Photography.

Page 689 © Grant Hielman Photography.

Page 689 © Grant Hielman Photography.

CHAPTER 25

Page 712 Photo courtesy of the American Stock Exchange.

Page 714 Courtesy of Joseph Schumpeter.

Page 722 Reprinted by special permission of North America Syndicate.

CHAPTER 29

Page 810 by permission of Johnny Hart and Creators Syndicate, Inc.

Page 822 © Butch Gemin.

CHAPTER 31

Page 875 © 1992 Lisa Quinones/Black Star.

CHAPTER 34

Page 955 photo courtesy of Professor James Gwartney.

Page 968 photo courtesy of Professor James Gwartney.

NAME INDEX

COMPANY INDEX

SUBJECT INDEX

POPULATION AND LABOR FORCE

Year	Civilian Noninstitutional Population Age 16 and Over (Millions)	Civilian Labor Force (Millions)	Civilian Labor Force Participation Rate	Employment/ Population Ratio (Including Armed Forces)	Money Supply (M2)* Money Supply M2 (Billions)	Money Supply (M2)* Annual Change in M2
1929	85.6	49.2	57.5	55.9	—	—
1939	97.8	55.2	56.4	47.2	—	—
1949	104.0	61.3	58.9	56.1	—	—
1956	111.0	66.6	60.0	59.3	—	—
1957	112.3	66.9	59.6	58.8	—	—
1958	113.7	67.6	59.5	57.1	—	—
1959	115.3	68.4	59.3	57.6	297.8	—
1960	117.2	69.6	59.4	57.7	312.3	4.9
1961	118.8	70.5	59.3	57.0	335.5	7.4
1962	120.1	70.6	58.8	57.2	362.7	8.1
1963	122.4	71.8	58.7	57.0	393.2	8.4
1964	124.5	73.0	58.6	57.3	424.8	8.0
1965	126.5	74.5	58.9	57.7	459.3	8.1
1966	128.1	75.8	59.2	58.6	480.0	4.5
1967	130.0	77.3	59.5	59.0	524.3	9.2
1968	132.0	78.7	59.6	59.2	566.3	8.0
1969	134.3	80.7	60.1	59.7	589.5	4.1
1970	137.1	82.8	60.4	58.9	628.0	6.5
1971	140.2	84.4	60.2	58.0	712.6	13.5
1972	144.1	87.0	60.4	58.3	805.1	13.0
1973	147.1	89.4	60.8	59.0	860.9	6.9
1974	150.1	91.9	61.2	59.0	908.4	5.5
1975	153.2	93.8	61.2	57.1	1,023.1	12.6
1976	156.2	96.2	61.6	57.9	1,163.5	13.7
1977	159.0	99.0	62.3	58.9	1,286.4	10.6
1978	161.9	102.3	63.2	60.3	1,388.5	7.9
1979	164.9	105.0	63.7	60.9	1,496.4	7.8
1980	167.7	106.9	63.8	60.1	1,629.2	8.9
1981	170.1	108.7	63.9	60.0	1,792.6	10.0
1982	172.3	110.2	64.0	58.7	1,952.7	8.9
1983	174.2	111.6	64.0	58.8	2,186.5	12.0
1984	176.4	113.5	64.4	60.5	2,376.0	8.7
1985	178.2	115.5	64.8	61.1	2,572.4	8.3
1986	180.6	117.8	65.3	61.6	2,816.1	9.5
1987	182.8	120.0	65.6	62.5	2,917.2	3.6
1988	184.6	121.7	65.9	63.2	3,078.2	5.5
1989	186.4	123.9	66.5	63.9	3,233.3	5.0
1990	188.0	124.8	66.4	63.6	3,345.5	3.5
1991	189.8	125.3	66.0	62.4	3,445.8	3.0
1992	191.6	127.0	66.3	62.2	3,494.8	1.4
1993	193.6	128.0	66.2	62.4	3,551.7	1.6

*Data not available for the years 1929 through 1958.

Source: *Economic Report of the President*, (1970 and 1994).